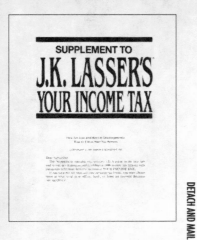

J.K. LASSER'S™
YOUR INCOME TAX
1993

PREPARED BY THE

J. K. LASSER INSTITUTE™

PRENTICE HALL
New York • London • Toronto
Sydney • Tokyo • Singapore

Staff for This Book

J.K. Lasser Editorial

Elliott Eiss, Member of the New York Bar,
   Editorial Director of the J.K. Lasser Institute™
Bernard Greisman, Member of the New York Bar,
   Senior Consultant to the J.K. Lasser Institute™
Bari Fenster, Associate Editor
Charles A. Wall, Vice President and Editor-in-Chief
Nina Hoffman, President and Publisher
Kay Torak, Editorial Assistant

J.K. Lasser Production

Lisa Wolff, Managing Editor
Maria Cianflone, Senior Production Editor
Robin Besofsky, Senior Production Manager
Laurie Barnett, Publishing Manager
Claudine Curry, Editorial Production Assistant

Outside Contributors

Gerry Burstein, Jeanne Borczuk,
   and Richard Tsao of G&H Soho
Darlene Wesemann and Sandy Reinhard of Black Dot Graphics
Maro Riofrancos, Indexing
Walter Allweil, Proofreading

We also wish to acknowledge the contribution and support of
Mark E. Bloom, CPA, spokesperson for the J.K. Lasser Institute™.

Prentice Hall General Reference
15 Columbus Circle
New York, NY 10023

J.K. Lasser, the J.K. Lasser Institute, Prentice Hall and colophons are
registered trademarks of Simon & Schuster, Inc.

Publisher's Note: *Your Income Tax* is published in recognition of the
great need for clarifications of the income tax laws, for the millions of
men and women who must make out returns. We believe the research
and interpretation by the J.K. Lasser Institute™ of the nation's tax laws
to be authoritative and of help to taxpayers. Every care has been taken
in the preparation of the text to ensure its clarity and accuracy.
Taxpayers are cautioned, however, that this book is sold with the
understanding that the Publisher is *not* engaged in rendering legal,
accounting, or other professional service. Taxpayers with specific tax
problems are urged to seek the professional advice of a tax accountant,
lawyer, or preparer.

ISBN 0-13-513896-5

Manufactured in the United States of America

1 2 3 4 5 6 7 8 9 10

Fifty-sixth Edition

NEW TAX DEVELOPMENTS

Item—	Tax Pointer*—
Tax brackets adjusted for inflation	New 1992 tax brackets are at ¶22.2.
Tax Table range increased	Taxable income ceiling has been increased from $50,000 to $100,000; see pages 477-488.
Personal exemption increased	Deductions for personal exemptions are increased from $2,150 to $2,300 for 1992, subject to the phaseout rules for high income taxpayers at ¶1.32.
Higher 1992 standard deduction	Increased standard deduction amounts are listed at ¶13.1.
Higher filing requirements	Higher income thresholds are shown on page 2.
Estimated tax restrictions for high income earners	If your 1992 adjusted gross income increased by more than $40,000 ($20,000 if married filing separately), you may not use the 100% prior-year exception to avoid a 1992 underpayment penalty; see ¶27.2. However, see the Supplement for the status of proposed rules that would allow for purposes of figuring a 1992 penalty a percentage that would apply to estimates in 1993 and later years.
Sex discrimination damages	The Supreme Court has held that back pay damages are taxable if received in a Title VII case filed before November 21, 1991. The Court did not specifically decide whether damages received in cases brought after November 21, 1991, qualify for tax-free treatment, but, tax-free treatment was implied; see ¶12.10.
Tax advice fees paid by self-employed individuals	Self-employed individuals may claim a business deduction on Schedule C for tax preparation fees; see ¶19.25 and ¶40.6.
Schedule C-EZ	New simplified Schedule C-EZ may be used by individuals on the cash basis who did not have a net business loss provided certain other tests discussed at ¶40.5 are met.
Form 2555-EZ	The foreign earned income exclusion may be claimed on a new simplified Form 2555-EZ, if your 1992 foreign wages are less than $70,000, you do not have self-employment income, and do not claim the foreign housing exclusion, moving expenses, or the foreign tax credit. Taxpayers who do not meet these tests must file Form 2555; see ¶36.1.
Increased reimbursement allowance for employee travel	For 1992, the allowance has been increased to $147 in "high" cost areas and to $93 in all other areas. For business trips in January and February of 1992, the prior year rates and localities apply; see ¶20.35.
Automobile depreciation limits increased	The first-year depreciation limit for business automobiles placed in service during 1992 is $2,760, up from $2,660 in 1991. See ¶43.4 for the second and succeeding year annual ceilings.
IRS mileage allowance increased	The allowance has been increased to 28 cents per mile for all 1992 business mileage; see ¶43.1.
Reporting transactions of business cash equivalents	Retailers are required to report receipt of money orders, cashiers' checks, and bank drafts with a face value of $10,000 or less from business sales of consumer durables, such as cars and jewelry. Such payments are reported to the IRS on Form 8300; see ¶40.4.
Imputed interest on continuing care facility fees	For 1992, interest will not be imputed by the IRS on certain refundable fees of $114,100 or less; see ¶34.12.
Points	Points withheld from a loan used to buy or improve a principal residence are deductible, provided the fees paid over at closing, such as attorney fees, abstract fees, and appraisal fees, are at least equal to the amount of points withheld; see ¶15.7.
VA and FHA loan origination fees	Starting in 1992, loan origination fees paid to the Veterans Affairs' (VA) or Federal Housing Administration (FHA) on loans used to purchase or improve a principal residence are deductible as points on Schedule A; see ¶15.7.
Home day-care operators	Day care operators are no longer required to allocate business use for the hours each room was actually used for day care, provided the room is available for day care during regular business hours; see ¶40.11.
3% itemized deduction reduction	If your adjusted gross income exceeds $105,250 ($52,625 if married filing separately), certain itemized deductions such as mortgage interest, taxes, and miscellaneous expenses are reduced by 3% of the excess; see ¶13.8.
20% withholding on retirement distributions	Starting in 1993, a 20% withholding tax will be imposed on nonperiodic payments from qualified employer plans, such as lump-sum distributions, made directly to employees. To avoid the 20% tax, the funds must be directly transferred from the employer's plan to an IRA or defined contribution plan of a new employer; see ¶26.11. The tax may be repealed or modified by Congress before it becomes effective in 1993.
Expanded rollovers	In 1993 and later years, all nonperiodic distributions may be rolled over; see ¶7.8. However, see above for 20% withholding rules.
Pension plans	For 1992, the maximum limitation for the annual pension benefit under defined benefit plans is $112,221, up from $108,963 in 1991; see ¶41.2.
Salary deferral limit for 401(k) and simplified employee pension plans	For 1992 the maximum tax-free salary deferral is $8,728, up from $8,475 in 1991; see ¶7.18 and ¶8.11.
FICA and self-employment tax increased	FICA and self-employment tax applies to income of up to $130,200. Rates vary; see Chapter 46 for self-employment tax, ¶26.10 for FICA taxes.

*Send for the Supplement for further tax developments.

CONTENTS

CONTENTS

PART III CLAIMING DEDUCTIONS

PART IV PERSONAL TAX COMPUTATIONS

CHAPTER CONTENTS

FORM 1040 WITH REFERENCES TO *YOUR INCOME TAX*

					See ¶
Tax Computation (See page 22.)	32	Amount from line 31 (adjusted gross income)	32		¶13.7
	33a	Check if: ☐ **You** were 65 or older, ☐ Blind; ☐ **Spouse** was 65 or older, ☐ Blind. Add the number of boxes checked above and enter the total here . . . . ▶ 33a			¶13.4
	b	If your parent (or someone else) can claim you as a dependent, check here . ▶ 33b ☐			¶13.5
	c	If you are married filing separately and your spouse itemizes deductions or you are a dual-status alien, see page 22 and check here . . . . ▶ 33c ☐			¶13.3
	34	Enter the larger of your: **Itemized deductions** from Schedule A, line 26, **OR** **Standard deduction** shown below for your filing status. **But if you checked any box on line 33a or b,** go to page 22 to find your standard deduction. **If you checked box 33c,** your standard deduction is zero. • Single—$3,600 • Head of household—$5,250 • Married filing jointly or Qualifying widow(er)—$6,000 • Married filing separately—$3,000	34		¶13.1 ¶13.2 & ¶13.4
	35	Subtract line 34 from line 32	35		
If you want the IRS to figure your tax, see page 23.	36	If line 32 is $78,950 or less, multiply $2,300 by the total number of exemptions claimed on line 6e. If line 32 is over $78,950 (see the worksheet on page 23) for the amount to enter	36		¶1.32 Part VIII
	37	**Taxable Income.** Subtract line 36 from line 35. If line 36 is more than line 35, enter -0-	37		¶22.2
	38	Enter tax. Check if from a ☐ Tax Table, b ☐ Tax Rate Schedules, c ☐ Schedule D, or d ☐ Form 8615 (see page 23). Amount, if any, from Form(s) 8814 ▶ e ___	38		¶24.3 ¶24.5
	39	Additional taxes (see page 23). Check if from a ☐ Form 4970 b ☐ Form 4972	39		¶11.3 & 7.4
	40	Add lines 38 and 39	40		
Credits (See page 23.)	41	Credit for child and dependent care expenses. Attach Form 2441	41		¶25.1
	42	Credit for the elderly or the disabled. Attach Schedule R	42		¶34.6
	43	Foreign tax credit. Attach Form 1116	43		¶36.14
	44	Other credits (see page 24). Check if from a ☐ Form 3800 b ☐ Form 8396 c ☐ Form 8801 d ☐ Form (specify) ___	44		¶40.22 ¶23.7
	45	Add lines 41 through 44	45		
	46	Subtract line 45 from line 40. If line 45 is more than line 40, enter -0-	46		
Other Taxes	47	Self-employment tax. Attach Schedule SE. Also, see line 25	47		Chapter 46
	48	Alternative minimum tax. Attach Form 6251	48		¶23.1
	49	Recapture taxes (see page 25). Check if from a ☐ Form 4255 b ☐ Form 8611 c ☐ Form 8828	49		¶40.22
	50	Social security and Medicare tax on tip income not reported to employer. Attach Form 4137 . .	50		¶26.8
	51	Tax on qualified retirement plans, including IRAs. Attach Form 5329	51		¶8.8
	52	Advance earned income credit payments from Form W-2	52		¶25.11
	53	Add lines 46 through 52. This is your **total tax** . . . . ▶	53		
Payments Attach Forms W-2, W-2G, and 1099-R on the front.	54	Federal income tax withheld. If any is from Form(s) 1099, check ▶ ☐	54		¶26.1
	55	1992 estimated tax payments and amount applied from 1991 return .	55		¶27.1
	56	**Earned income credit.** Attach Schedule EIC	56		¶25.8
	57	Amount paid with Form 4868 (extension request)	57		page 444
	58	Excess social security, Medicare, and RRTA tax withheld (see page 26) .	58		¶26.10
	59	Other payments (see page 26). Check if from a ☐ Form 2439 b ☐ Form 4136	59		¶40.22
	60	Add lines 54 through 59. These are your **total payments** . . . . ▶	60		
Refund or Amount You Owe Attach check or money order on top of Form(s) W-2, etc., on the front.	61	If line 60 is more than line 53, subtract line 53 from line 60. This is the amount you **OVERPAID.** ▶	61		
	62	Amount of line 61 you want **REFUNDED TO YOU.** . . . . ▶	62		page 446
	63	Amount of line 61 you want **APPLIED TO YOUR 1993 ESTIMATED TAX** ▶ 63			¶27.1
	64	If line 53 is more than line 60, subtract line 60 from line 53. This is the **AMOUNT YOU OWE.** Attach check or money order for full amount payable to "Internal Revenue Service." Write your name, address, social security number, daytime phone number, and "1992 Form 1040" on it	64		
	65	Estimated tax penalty (see page 27). Also include on line 64 65			¶27.2

Sign Here
Keep a copy of this return for your records.

Under penalties of perjury, I declare that I have examined this return and accompanying schedules and statements, and to the best of my knowledge and belief, they are true, correct, and complete. Declaration of preparer (other than taxpayer) is based on all information of which preparer has any knowledge.

Your signature	Date	Your occupation	
Spouse's signature. If a joint return, BOTH must sign.	Date	Spouse's occupation	¶1.3

Paid Preparer's Use Only

Preparer's signature	Date	Check if self-employed ☐	Preparer's social security no.
Firm's name (or yours if self-employed) and address		E.I. No. ZIP code	

This form is an advance proof. Use the final IRS version for filing

Form **1040** Department of the Treasury—Internal Revenue Service
U.S. Individual Income Tax Return 19**92** | IRS use only—Do not write or staple in this space.

For the year Jan. 1–Dec. 31, 1992, or other tax year beginning , 1992, ending , 19 OMB No. 1545-0074

Label

(See instructions on page 10.)

Use the IRS label. Otherwise, please print or type.

L A B E L H E R E

Your first name and initial | Last name | Your social security number

If a joint return, spouse's first name and initial | Last name | Spouse's social security number

Home address (number and street). If you have a P.O. box, see page 10. | Apt. no.

City, town or post office, state, and ZIP code. If you have a foreign address, see page 10.

For Privacy Act and Paperwork Reduction Act Notice, see page 4.

Presidential Election Campaign
(See page 10.)

Do you want $1 to go to this fund? . . . . | Yes | No
If a joint return, does your spouse want $1 to go to this fund? . | Yes | No

Note: *Checking "Yes" will not change your tax or reduce your refund.*

See ¶

Filing Status

(See page 10.)

Check only one box.

1 ☐ Single — ¶1.1
2 ☐ Married filing joint return (even if only one had income) — ¶1.3
3 ☐ Married filing separate return. Enter spouse's social security no. above and full name here. ▶ — ¶1.2
4 ☐ Head of household (with qualifying person). (See page 11.) If the qualifying person is a child but not your dependent, enter this child's name here ▶ _____ — ¶1.10
5 ☐ Qualifying widow(er) with dependent child (year spouse died ▶19). (See page 11.) — ¶1.6

Exemptions

(See page 11.)

6a ☐ **Yourself.** If your parent (or someone else) can claim you as a dependent on his or her tax return, **do not** check box 6a. But be sure to check the box on line 33b on page 2.

b ☐ **Spouse** . . . .

No. of boxes checked on 6a and 6b — ¶1.18

— ¶1.19

c **Dependents:**

(1) Name (first, initial, and last name)	(2) Check if under age 1	(3) If age 1 or older, dependent's social security number	(4) Dependent's relationship to you	(5) No. of months lived in your home in 1992

No. of your children on 6c who:
• lived with you ____
• didn't live with you due to divorce or separation (see page 13) ____
No. of other dependents on 6c ____

— ¶1.18

— ¶1.28

If more than six dependents, see page 12.

d If your child didn't live with you but is claimed as your dependent under a pre-1985 agreement, check here ▶ ☐
e Total number of exemptions claimed . . . .

Add numbers entered on lines above ▶ ☐ — ¶1.18

Income

Attach Copy B of your Forms W-2, W-2G, and 1099-R here.

If you did not get a W-2, see page 9.

Attach check or money order on top of any Forms W-2, W-2G, or 1099-R.

7 Wages, salaries, tips, etc. Attach Form(s) W-2 . . . . . | 7 | — ¶2.1
8a **Taxable** interest income. Attach Schedule B if over $400 . | 8a | — ¶4.12
b **Tax-exempt** interest income (see page 15). DON'T include on line 8a | 8b | — ¶4.24 & 4.26
9 Dividend income. Attach Schedule B if over $400 . | 9 | — ¶4.1
10 Taxable refunds, credits, or offsets of state and local income taxes from worksheet on page 15 | 10 | — ¶12.7
11 Alimony received . . . . | 11 | — ¶37.1
12 Business income or (loss). Attach Schedule C (or C-EZ) . . . . | 12 | — ¶40.1
13 Capital gain or (loss). Attach Schedule D . . . . . | 13 | — ¶5.4
14 Capital gain distributions not reported on line 13 (see page 16) . . . | 14 | — ¶4.3
15 Other gains or (losses). Attach Form 4797 . . . . . | 15 | — ¶44.1
16a Total IRA distributions . | 16a | b Taxable amount (see page 16) | 16b | — ¶8.8
17a Total pensions and annuities | 17a | b Taxable amount (see page 16) | 17b | — ¶7.22 & 7.25
18 Rents, royalties, partnerships, estates, trusts, etc. Attach Schedule E | 18 | — ¶9.1
19 Farm income or (loss). Attach Schedule F . . . . . | 19 | — ¶45.15
20 Unemployment compensation (see page 17) . . . . | 20 | — ¶2.6
21a Social security benefits | 21a | b Taxable amount (see page 17) | 21b | — ¶34.3
22 Other income. List type and amount—see page 18 .... | 22 | — Chapter 12
23 Add the amounts in the far right column for lines 7 through 22. This is your **total income** . ▶ | 23 |

Adjustments to Income

(See page 18.)

24a Your IRA deduction from applicable worksheet on page 19 or 20 | 24a | — ¶8.3
b Spouse's IRA deduction from applicable worksheet on page 19 or 20 | 24b | — ¶8.3 & 8.7
25 One-half of self-employment tax (see page 20) . . . | 25 | — ¶46.3
26 Self-employed health insurance deduction (see page 20) | 26 | — page 377
27 Keogh retirement plan and self-employed SEP deduction | 27 | — ¶41.5 & 8.11
28 Penalty on early withdrawal of savings . . . . | 28 | — ¶4.16
29 Alimony paid. Recipient's SSN ▶ | 29 | — ¶37.1
30 Add lines 24a through 29. These are your **total adjustments** . . . . . ▶ | 30 |

Adjusted Gross Income

31 Subtract line 30 from line 23. This is your **adjusted gross income.** *If this amount is less than $22,370 and a child lived with you, see page EIC-1 to find out if you can claim the "Earned Income Credit" on line 56* . . . . ▶ | 31 | — ¶13.7

This form is an advance proof. Use the final IRS version for filing

Form **1040** (1992)

HOW TO USE YOUR INCOME TAX 1993

The federal income tax law, despite efforts of simplification, remains a maze of statutes, regulations, rulings, and court decisions written in technical language covering thousands and thousands of pages. For over 55 years, J.K. Lasser's™ *Your Income Tax* has aided and guided millions of taxpayers through this complex law. Every effort has been made to provide a direct and easy-to-understand explanation that shows how to comply with the law and at the same time take advantage of tax-saving options and plans.

The 1993 edition of *Your Income Tax*—our 56th edition—continues this tradition.

To make maximum use of this tax guide, we suggest that you use these aids:

Form 1040 REFERENCE GUIDE—This guide, on pages iv and v, directs you from any line on Form 1040 that you are interested in to the section in *Your Income Tax* that covers the topic.

CHAPTER CONTENTS—The contents, on pages vi–ix, list the chapters in *Your Income Tax.* You will use two types of references: Section references within each chapter and page references. The first number of a section reference identifies the chapter, and the number following the decimal point identifies the section within the chapter. For example, exemptions are discussed in Chapter 1. Thus a reference to ¶1.18 directs you to Chapter 1 and then to section 18 within that chapter. Section and page references are provided in the major index at the back of the book.

NEW TAX DEVELOPMENTS AND PENDING LEGISLATION—Pages x–xii alert you to new developments during 1992 such as new legislation, rulings, court decisions, or changes to the tax forms. References to the text are provided for further details. Also highlighted are proposed law changes pending before Congress.

OUTLINE OF PARTS—Color-coded page xiii shows the nine major parts of the book and directly leads you to each part through the color-coded index tab.

INCOME TAX BASICS—Pages 1–4 alert you to filing requirements, filing addresses shown on a map of IRS service centers, and a calendar with 1992 filing deadlines.

TAX ORGANIZER—This section, starting on page 443, is designed to help you get your data in order and to prepare your tax return. Sample 1992 tax forms are also provided.

TREASURY OF TAX TERMS—The tax law is a technical subject with its own particular terminology. All of the major tax terms are defined in this special glossary in Part IX.

TAX ALERT SYMBOLS—Throughout the text of *Your Income Tax,* these special symbols alert you to advisory tips about filing your return and tax planning opportunities:

A **FILING POINTER** or **FILING INSTRUCTION** helps you prepare your 1992 return.

A **PLANNING POINTER** or **PLANNING STRATEGY** highlights year-end tax strategies for 1992 or planning opportunities for 1993 and later years.

A **CAUTION** alert points out potential pitfalls to avoid and areas where IRS opposition may be expected.

A **LAW ALERT** indicates changes in the tax law and pending legislation before Congress.

A **COURT DECISION** alert highlights key rulings from the Tax Court and other federal courts.

GUIDE TO PENDING LEGISLATION

When this book went to press, Congress was preparing a major tax bill, which if passed, would generally be effective for 1993 (*see* page xii), except for the following provisions that could affect 1992 returns.

A complete legislative update will be in the free Supplement, which you can obtain by mailing in the card at the front of the book.

Pending Legislation for 1992

Provision—	Would*—
Passive losses (¶10.1, ¶10.8)	Allow investors with a net passive activity loss of $200 or less to deduct the loss from nonpassive income, such as salary and portfolio investment income. Other proposals would allow full or partial deductions for rental losses of taxpayers who materially participate in real estate development, construction, rental, management, or brokerage operations.
Depreciation for nonresidential buildings (¶42.13)	Increase the recovery period for nonresidential realty from 31.5 years to 40 years for buildings places in service after a 1992 date to be fixed by Congress.
Tax credit for homebuyers (¶29.1)	Allow "first-time" homebuyers to claim a tax credit of up to $2,500 for purchasing a principal residence after the 1992 effective date of the law and before 1993. Individuals who did not own a home in the prior three years would qualify.
Estimated tax penalty (¶27.2)	Allow individuals who could not use the 100% prior-year penalty exception because their 1992 adjusted gross income exceeded $75,000 to avoid an underpayment penalty if their 1992 payments equaled the percentage of their 1991 tax liability that will be fixed for 1993 estimates.
Home sale rollovers (¶29.8, ¶29.9)	Allow tax deferral on more than one home sale within a two-year period; a second sale would not have to be related to a job relocation. Another provision would allow spouses in a marital breakup situation to treat as their principal residence a residence sold pursuant to a divorce or separation if it was lived in at any time in the two years before the sale.
25% self-employed health insurance deduction (¶17.6)	Extend the deduction at least through the end of 1992. Another proposal would allow the deduction through the end of 1993.
Low-income housing credit (¶9.8, ¶40.22)	Extend the credit through 1993, or permanently under an alternative proposal.
Tax-free employer educational assistance (¶3.5) and legal services (¶3.1)	Extend the $5,250 exclusion for undergraduate and graduate courses at least through the end of 1992. The $70 exclusion for group legal services coverage would also be extended.
Business credit (¶40.22)	Extend the targeted jobs credit and research tax credit until the end of 1993.
Club dues (¶20.24)	Repeal the deduction for club dues paid after the effective date of the new law.
Kiddie tax (¶24.5)	Provide a $1,200 floor for parents who elect on their 1992 return to report their child's investment income.
Donations of appreciated property (¶14.6, ¶23.3)	Extend beyond June 30, 1992, the AMT exception for appreciation on donations of long-term works of art and other tangible personal property, and also extend the AMT break to all other appreciated donations. The extension would be at least through the end of 1993.
Earned income credit (¶25.8)	Increase the basic credit for families with two or more children and repeal the supplemental health insurance and new-born child components of the credit. Another proposal would keep the supplemental credits and permit a medical expense deduction or dependent care credit to be based on expenses that qualify for the credits.
Amortization of intangibles (¶44.9, ¶44.10)	Allow an amortization deduction over a 14-year or 16-year period for the cost of certain intangible property such as goodwill, covenants not to compete, consumer or supplier lists, franchises, trademarks or trade names. The deduction would apply to property acquired after the effective date of the new law.
Attorney fee recoveries (¶48.7)	Allow prevailing taxpayers to recover from the IRS attorney fees of up to $110 per hour, effective for proceedings commenced after the effective date of the new law. The $110 limit would be subject to inflation adjustments after 1992.

*Send for the Supplement for an update on the status of these proposals.

Pending Legislation for 1993 and Later Years

Provision—	Would*—
New estimated tax percentages (¶27.4)	Raise the required payout percentage based on the prior year's tax from 100% to at least 115% and maybe as high as 120%. The Supplement will have the percentage set by Congress for 1993 estimates. The restrictive 1992 rule barring higher income earners from using the prior year safe harbor would be repealed. Such individuals (*See* ¶ 27.2) could use the higher percentage set for 1993 to figure any penalty for 1992 underpayments.
20% withholding on retirement distributions (¶26.11)	Modify or repeal the 20% withholding rule for nonperiodic distributions from employer plans; *see* ¶26.11.
Broader IRA deduction base (¶8.8)	Start the deduction phaseout for active participants in employer retirement plans at adjusted gross income of $80,000 for single persons and $120,000 for married couples filing jointly. The deduction would be completely phased out at $90,000 and $130,000 respectively. As proposed, these rules would not apply until 1994.
Five-year averaging (¶7.4)	Repeal five-year averaging opportunities for those who did not reach age 50 before 1986.
Death benefit exclusion (¶7.28)	Repeal the $5,000 death benefit exclusion for distributions received by beneficiaries after 1992.
Loss on sale of principal residence (¶29.11)	Allow a homeowner to add an otherwise nondeductible loss to the cost basis of another residence purchased within the two-year replacement period.
Enterprise zone tax incentives (¶5.1, ¶42.3)	Create enterprise investment zones and provide tax incentives for investors. A deduction of up to $25,000 would be allowed for stock in qualifying enterprise zone businesses and capital gain on the sale of such stock would be deferred if proceeds were reinvested in other enterprise zone investments. Ordinary loss treatment would be allowed after a two-year holding period for losses on the sale of tangible property used in an enterprise zone business or sales of stock or partnership interests in such businesses. Real estate would qualify for an ordinary business loss if held at least five years. The first-year expensing limit would be increased to $20,000 for depreciable equipment use in an enterprise zone business. Employers could claim the targeted jobs credit for hiring workers who reside in the enterprise zone.
Casualty deduction floor (¶18.11)	Increase the floor for personal use casualty losses to $500 from $100.
Receipts of charitable donations (¶14.1, ¶14.2)	Require taxpayers to obtain written receipts for all donations over $100. Cancelled checks would not be sufficient proof.
Charitable AMT break (¶14.6, ¶23.3)	Extend permanently the AMT break for tangible personal property, such as works of art, and also apply the AMT exception to all donations of appreciated property, including intangibles, such as securities.
Home rentals of less than 15 days (¶29.20)	Impose tax on the income from renting a residence for less than 15 days.
Travel expenses of non-employee family members (¶20.14)	Bar a travel expense deduction for an accompanying spouse, dependent or other companion on business trips after 1992.
Switch from separate to joint return (¶1.2)	Allow the change any time within three years without the need to pay the entire tax due on the joint return.
Top estate and gift tax rates (¶39.5)	Defer for five years the scheduled reduction of the top 55% rate to 50%.
Mutual fund reporting (¶30.4)	Require brokers and mutual funds to give new investors an annual report of their average share costs.
Employment taxes for household employees (¶25.7)	Increase the filing FICA threshold to $300 a year and require employers of household employees to report FICA and FUTA taxes on his or her own income tax return.
U.S. Savings Bond tuition plans (¶33.3)	Repeal the income phaseout for the interest exclusion and the age 24 requirement for bond purchases.
Moving expenses (¶21.1, ¶21.5)	Impose restrictions on the moving expense deduction: The mileage test would increase from 35 to 55 miles; there would either be an overall cap on eligible expenses, or a disallowance of expenses relating to the sale and purchase of the old and new residences; the deduction for unreimbursed costs would be subject to the 2% floor for miscellaneous itemized deductions. Income from reimbursed moving expenses would be offset by an above-the-line deduction from gross income.
Luxury excise tax	Repeal the tax imposed on boats, airplanes, jewelry, and fur sales. The tax would be retained for cars costing over an inflation adjusted floor of $30,000, with an exception for parts or accessories installed to enable or assist an individual with a disability to operate the vehicle. Car dealers would be exempt from paying the luxury tax on demonstrator vehicles used for purposes other than test drives.

*Send for the Supplement for an update on the status of these proposals.

OUTLINE OF PARTS

PART I

INCOME TAX BASICS

In this part, you will learn these income tax basics:

- Whether you must file a return.
- When and where to file your return.
- What filing status you qualify for.
- How to claim exemptions for your dependents.

1

FILING TESTS

If You Are—	You Must File If Gross Income Is At Least—
Single	
Under age 65	$ 5,900
Age 65 or older on or before January 1, 1993	6,600
Married, living together at the end of 1992	
Filing a joint return—both spouses under age 65	10,600
Filing a joint return—one spouse age 65 or older	11,300
Filing a joint return—both spouses age 65 or older	12,000
Filing a separate return—	2,300
Married, living apart at the end of 1992	
Filing a joint or separate return	2,300
Head of household maintained for a child or other relative (see ¶1.1)	
Under age 65	7,550
Age 65 or older	8,450
Widowed in 1991 or 1990 and have a dependent child (see ¶1.6)	
Under age 65	8,300
Age 65 or older	9,000

You have to file a federal tax return if your gross income exceeds an amount specified for your personal tax status and age. In the above chart, find your personal tax status in the first column and then gross income filing threshold in the second column. Marital status is generally determined as of December 31, 1992. Thus, if you were divorced or legally separated during 1992, use the filing threshold for single persons unless you qualify as a head of household (¶1.10). If your spouse died in 1992 and you were living together on the date of death, use the filing threshold shown for married persons living together at the end of 1992. Otherwise, the $2,300 threshold applies. If your 65th birthday is on January 1, 1993, you are treated as age 65 or older for 1992 tax purposes.

Gross income is generally all income you received in 1992, except for items that are specificaly exempt from tax, such as tax-exempt interest (Chapter 4), Social Security (provided adjusted gross income is below the floor specified in Chapter 34), tax-free fringe benefits (Chapter 3), qualifying scholarships (Chapter 12), and life insurance (Chapter 11).

Warning: Even if you are not required to file under the gross income tests, you must file a return if:
Your net self-employment earnings are $400 or more (Chapter 46), *or*
You are entitled to a refund of taxes withheld from your wages or a refund based on the earned income credit for low-income working families (Chapter 25), *or*
You received any earned income credit payments in advance from your employer (Chapter 25), *or*
You owe any tax such as alternative minimum tax (Chapter 23); IRA penalty (Chapter 8); FICA on tips (Chapter 26), *or*
You are a nonresident alien with a U.S. business or tax liability not covered by withholding; *see* Form 1040NR.

FILING TESTS FOR DEPENDENTS

If you can be claimed as a dependent by your parent, or by any other taxpayer, use the Gross Income Organizer below to determine if you must file a return. If your 1992 gross income was less than $2,300, you may be claimed as a dependent if the other dependency tests on page 19 are met. If your 1992 gross income exceeded $2,300, you may be claimed as a dependent only by your parent, and only if at the end of 1992, you were either under age 19 or were a full-time student under age 24 (¶1.23), and the other dependency tests on page 19 are met. A return does not have to be filed for a child who was under age 14 at the end of 1992, and who had only investment income if the child's parents elects to report that income on the parents own return; see ¶24.5.

Gross Income Organizer. First enter the dollar amounts for income earned during 1992 on Lines 1–3. Then proceed to Test 1, 2, 3, or 4, whichever applies. For married dependents, the filing requirements assume that the dependent is not filing a joint return but a separate return. Generally, a married person who files a joint return may not be claimed as a dependent by a third party who provides support; *see* ¶1.30.

1. Enter unearned income* $_____
2. Enter earned income**   _____
3. Total gross income (1 and 2)*** $_____

Test 1: Single, under age 65, and not blind. You must file a 1992 return *if either*: you had any unearned income on Line 1 and your gross income on Line 3 exceeds $600; *or* you did not have any unearned income on Line 1 and your earned income on Line 2 exceeds $3,600.

Test 2: Single, and either age 65 or over, or blind. You must file a 1992 return *if either*: Line 2 exceeds $4,500 ($5,400 if age 65 or over and also blind); *or* Line 1 exceeds $1,500 ($2,400 if age 65 or over and also blind); *or* Line 3 exceeds the greater of Line 2 up to $3,600, or $600, *plus* $900 ($1,800 if age 65 or over and also blind).

Test 3: Married, and under age 65, and not blind. You must file a 1992 return *if either*: Line 2 exceeds $3,000; *or* you had any unearned income on Line 1 and Line 3 exceeds $600; *or* Line 3 is at least $5, and your spouse itemizes deductions on a separate return.

Test 4: Married, and either age 65 or over, or blind. You must file a 1992 return *if either*: Line 2 exceeds $3,700 ($4,400 if age 65 or older and also blind); *or* Line 1 exceeds $1,300 ($2,000 if age 65 or over and also blind); *or* Line 3 exceeds the greater of Line 2 up to $3,000, or $600, *plus* $700 ($1,400 if age 65 or over and also blind); *or* Line 3 is at least $5, and your spouse itemizes deductions on a separate return.

*Include taxable interest, dividends, capital gains, pensions, annuities, and distributions of unearned income from a trust.

**Include wages, tips, self-employment income, and similar earnings for personal services. Also include taxable scholarships or fellowships; *see* Chapter 12.

***If Lines 1 and 2 total $2,300 or more and at the end of 1992, you are over age 18 and not a full-time student under age 24, you may not be claimed as another tax-payer's dependent. Follow the general filing tests in the chart on this page.

WHERE TO FILE

If you are filing—	File with the Service Center—
A personal return	For your place of legal residence. Use the envelope included in the IRS packet of forms if the envelope address is the same as the Center shown below for your residence.
A business return	For the location of your principal place of business.
As a U.S. citizen working abroad	At Philadelphia, PA 19255.
As a service member in the Armed Forces	For the place you are stationed. If you have an APO or FPO address, file with the Service Center at Philadelphia, PA 19255.

KEY TO SERVICE CENTER MAP

Key   Mailing Address
1. Internal Revenue Center, Andover, Maine 05501. *New York residents* file here if they reside *outside* of New York City or counties of Nassau, Rockland, Suffolk or Westchester.
2. Internal Revenue Center, Holtsville, New York, 00501. *New York residents* in New York City or counties of Nassau, Rockland, Suffolk, or Westchester, file here.
3. Internal Revenue Center, Philadelphia, Pennsylvania 19255. *Residents of District of Columbia* file here.
4. Internal Revenue Center, Memphis, Tennessee 37501.
5. Internal Revenue Center, Atlanta, Georgia 39901.
6. Internal Revenue Center, Cincinnati, Ohio 45999.

7. Internal Revenue Center, Kansas City, Missouri 64999.
8. Internal Revenue Center, Austin, Texas 73301.
9. Internal Revenue Center, Ogden, Utah 84201. *California residents* file here if in: counties of Alpine, Amador, Butte, Calaveras, Colusa, Contra Costa, Del Norte, El Dorado, Glenn, Humboldt, Lake, Lassen, Marin, Mendocino, Modoc, Napa, Nevada, Placer, Plumas, Sacramento, San Joaquin, Shasta, Sierra, Siskiyou, Solano, Sonoma, Sutter, Tehama, Trinity, Yolo, and Yuba.
10. Internal Revenue Center, Fresno, California 93888. *California residents* file here if not listed under *Key* 9 above.

FILING DEADLINES

On or Before—

January 15, 1993

Pay the balance of your 1992 estimated tax. If you do not meet this date, you may avoid an estimated tax penalty for the last quarter by filing a final return for 1992 and paying the balance of your 1992 tax by February 1, 1993.

Farmers and fishermen: file your single 1992 estimated tax payment by this date. If you do not, you may still avoid an estimated tax penalty by filing a final tax return and paying the full tax by March 1, 1993.

February 1, 1993

Make sure you have received a Form W-2 from each employer for whom you worked in 1992.

April 15, 1993

File your 1992 tax return and pay the balance of your tax. You may obtain an automatic four-month extension if you cannot meet the April 15 deadline by filing Form 4868 and paying the full amount of tax you estimate that you owe.

If on this date you are a U.S. citizen or resident living and working abroad, or in the military service, outside the U.S. and Puerto Rico, you have an automatic two-month filing extension until June 15, 1993.

Pay the first installment of your 1993 estimated tax.

June 15, 1993

Pay the second installment of your 1993 estimated tax. You may amend your estimate at this time.

If on April 15 you were a U.S. citizen or resident living and working abroad or in the military service outside the U.S. and Puerto Rico, file your 1993 return and pay the balance due. You may obtain an additional two-month filing extension until August 16, 1993 by filing Form 4868 and paying the estimated taxes owed.

If you are a nonresident alien who did not have taxes withheld from your wages, file Form 1040NR by this date and pay the balance due.

August 16, 1993

File your 1992 return if by April 15 you qualified for an automatic four-month filing extension using Form 4868. Also file your 1992 return and pay the balance due if on April 15 you were a U.S. citizen or resident living and working abroad or in the military service outside the U.S. and Puerto Rico, and by June 15 you qualified for an additional two-month extension by filing Form 4868.

September 15, 1993

Pay the third installment of your 1993 estimated tax. You may amend your estimate at this time.

December 31, 1993

If self-employed, this is the last day to set up a Keogh plan for 1993.

January 18, 1994

Pay the balance of your 1993 estimated tax.

April 15, 1994

File your 1993 return and pay the balance of your tax. Pay the first installment of your 1994 estimated tax by this date.

15th day of the 4th month after fiscal year ends

File your fiscal year return and pay the balance of the tax due. If you cannot meet the filing deadline, apply for an automatic four-month extension by filing Form 4868 and paying the full amount of tax that you estimate you owe.

1993

JANUARY
S	M	T	W	T	F	S
					1	2
3	4	5	6	7	8	9
10	11	12	13	14	15	16
17	18	19	20	21	22	23
24	25	26	27	28	29	30
31						

FEBRUARY
S	M	T	W	T	F	S
	1	2	3	4	5	6
7	8	9	10	11	12	13
14	15	16	17	18	19	20
21	22	23	24	25	26	27
28						

MARCH
S	M	T	W	T	F	S
	1	2	3	4	5	6
7	8	9	10	11	12	13
14	15	16	17	18	19	20
21	22	23	24	25	26	27
28	29	30	31			

APRIL
S	M	T	W	T	F	S
				1	2	3
4	5	6	7	8	9	10
11	12	13	14	15	16	17
18	19	20	21	22	23	24
25	26	27	28	29	30	

MAY
S	M	T	W	T	F	S
						1
2	3	4	5	6	7	8
9	10	11	12	13	14	15
16	17	18	19	20	21	22
23	24	25	26	27	28	29
30	31					

JUNE
S	M	T	W	T	F	S
		1	2	3	4	5
6	7	8	9	10	11	12
13	14	15	16	17	18	19
20	21	22	23	24	25	26
27	28	29	30			

JULY
S	M	T	W	T	F	S
				1	2	3
4	5	6	7	8	9	10
11	12	13	14	15	16	17
18	19	20	21	22	23	24
25	26	27	28	29	30	31

AUGUST
S	M	T	W	T	F	S
1	2	3	4	5	6	7
8	9	10	11	12	13	14
15	16	17	18	19	20	21
22	23	24	25	26	27	28
29	30	31				

SEPTEMBER
S	M	T	W	T	F	S
			1	2	3	4
5	6	7	8	9	10	11
12	13	14	15	16	17	18
19	20	21	22	23	24	25
26	27	28	29	30		

OCTOBER
S	M	T	W	T	F	S
					1	2
3	4	5	6	7	8	9
10	11	12	13	14	15	16
17	18	19	20	21	22	23
24	25	26	27	28	29	30
31						

NOVEMBER
S	M	T	W	T	F	S
	1	2	3	4	5	6
7	8	9	10	11	12	13
14	15	16	17	18	19	20
21	22	23	24	25	26	27
28	29	30				

DECEMBER
S	M	T	W	T	F	S
			1	2	3	4
5	6	7	8	9	10	11
12	13	14	15	16	17	18
19	20	21	22	23	24	25
26	27	28	29	30	31	

1994

JANUARY
S	M	T	W	T	F	S
						1
2	3	4	5	6	7	8
9	10	11	12	13	14	15
16	17	18	19	20	21	22
23	24	25	26	27	28	29
30	31					

FEBRUARY
S	M	T	W	T	F	S
		1	2	3	4	5
6	7	8	9	10	11	12
13	14	15	16	17	18	19
20	21	22	23	24	25	26
27	28					

MARCH
S	M	T	W	T	F	S
		1	2	3	4	5
6	7	8	9	10	11	12
13	14	15	16	17	18	19
20	21	22	23	24	25	26
27	28	29	30	31		

APRIL
S	M	T	W	T	F	S
					1	2
3	4	5	6	7	8	9
10	11	12	13	14	15	16
17	18	19	20	21	22	23
24	25	26	27	28	29	30

MAY
S	M	T	W	T	F	S
1	2	3	4	5	6	7
8	9	10	11	12	13	14
15	16	17	18	19	20	21
22	23	24	25	26	27	28
29	30	31				

JUNE
S	M	T	W	T	F	S
			1	2	3	4
5	6	7	8	9	10	11
12	13	14	15	16	17	18
19	20	21	22	23	24	25
26	27	28	29	30		

JULY
S	M	T	W	T	F	S
					1	2
3	4	5	6	7	8	9
10	11	12	13	14	15	16
17	18	19	20	21	22	23
24	25	26	27	28	29	30
31						

AUGUST
S	M	T	W	T	F	S
	1	2	3	4	5	6
7	8	9	10	11	12	13
14	15	16	17	18	19	20
21	22	23	24	25	26	27
28	29	30	31			

SEPTEMBER
S	M	T	W	T	F	S
				1	2	3
4	5	6	7	8	9	10
11	12	13	14	15	16	17
18	19	20	21	22	23	24
25	26	27	28	29	30	

OCTOBER
S	M	T	W	T	F	S
						1
2	3	4	5	6	7	8
9	10	11	12	13	14	15
16	17	18	19	20	21	22
23	24	25	26	27	28	29
30	31					

NOVEMBER
S	M	T	W	T	F	S
		1	2	3	4	5
6	7	8	9	10	11	12
13	14	15	16	17	18	19
20	21	22	23	24	25	26
27	28	29	30			

DECEMBER
S	M	T	W	T	F	S
				1	2	3
4	5	6	7	8	9	10
11	12	13	14	15	16	17
18	19	20	21	22	23	24
25	26	27	28	29	30	31

PERSONAL FILING STATUS AND EXEMPTIONS

Your family and personal status directly affects the tax you pay as follow. It determines the:

• Threshold amount for filing a tax return; *see* page 2.
• Tax rates applied to your taxable income; *see* ¶1.1.
• Dependency exemptions that you may claim; *see* ¶1.18.
• Right to claim the dependent care credit and the earned income credit; *see* Chapter 25.

GUIDE FOR MARRIED PERSONS

Filing Jointly

Married couples may pay less tax by filing jointly. Filing jointly allows the use of joint return rates.

You may file a joint return if you are legally married on the last day of 1992.

You need not live together provided you are legally married. A couple legally separated under a final decree of divorce or separate maintenance as of the end of 1992 may *not* file a joint return.

You may file jointly if your spouse died during 1992; *see* ¶1.5.

If one spouse is a nonresident alien, you may file jointly *only* if you make a special election to be taxed on your worldwide income; *see* ¶1.8.

You *must* file jointly to make an IRA deduction on behalf of a nonworking spouse (¶8.7). To claim the credit for the elderly (Chapter 34), you must file jointly unless you lived apart for the entire year. You must file jointly to claim the dependent care credit or the earned income credit (Chapter 25), unless you live apart and qualify as a head of household as explained in this chart.

On a joint return, each spouse is liable for the entire tax. If one spouse does not pay, the other spouse may be liable even though all of the income was earned by the spouse who failed to pay the tax. An "innocent" spouse who files a joint return may be relieved of fraud penalties and tax liability in certain circumstances; *see* ¶1.2.

For community property rules, *see* ¶1.9.

Filing Separately

Filing separately may be advisable where both spouses earn taxable income and have separate deductions, as explained at ¶1.3. You may not file a joint return and must use tax rates for married persons filing separately in these cases:

1. You and your spouse have different tax reporting years. If you report on the calendar year but your spouse reports on a fiscal year, you must file separately unless you get permission from the IRS to change your reporting year (Form 1128). This bar to joint filing does not apply when your tax year begins on the same day, but ends because of the death of either or both spouses. A spouse who has never filed a tax return may elect to use the other spouse's tax year as his or her first tax year; then they can file a joint return. That a husband and wife had different tax years before their marriage is no bar to a joint return.
2. You or your spouse is a nonresident alien and you do not make an election to be taxed on your worldwide income; *see* ¶1.8.
3. Your spouse files a separate return. If you are experiencing marital discord, you may be forced to file separately unless your spouse consents to a joint return.
4. You or your spouse is claimed by someone else as a dependent; *see* ¶1.30.

Living Apart from Spouse: Filing as Unmarried Head of Household

If you lived apart from your spouse during the last half of 1992, and your child lived with you for most of the year, you may qualify for tax purposes as "unmarried" and use head of household rates, which are lower than rates for married persons filing separately.

The following four tests must be met for you to file separately from your spouse as a head of household:

1. Your spouse was not a member of your household during the last six months of 1992.
2. You maintain your home as a household which was the principal place of abode for your child, adopted child, or stepchild for more than half of 1992. However, a foster child must be a member of your household for the entire year.
3   You are entitled to claim the child as a dependent. Ignore this test if the noncustodial spouse claims the exemption for the child under the rules of ¶1.28.
4. You provide over half of the cost of supporting the household.

GUIDE FOR SINGLE PERSONS

Single Person

If you are not married at the end of 1992, use the rate for single individuals, unless you qualify as a surviving spouse or a head of household.

If you are widowed, you are "unmarried" and use rates for single individuals regardless of the number of years you were married. There is an exception for recent widows or widowers supporting children, as explained in the "qualifying widow(er)" column.

Tax rate schedules for single persons are in Chapter 22.

Head of Household

If at the end of the year you are not married, you may use special head of household rates if you meet these tests:

1. You are not married at the end of the year.
2. You maintain a household for more than half of 1992 for your child or a dependent relative. The household must be your home and the main residence of your dependent relative except that a dependent parent need not live with you. However, you must maintain a dependent parent's separate household for the entire year to claim head of household status based on that support.
3. You pay more than one-half the cost of the household.
4. You are a U.S. citizen or resident alien during the entire tax year.

These rules are explained in detail in ¶1.10. If you qualify as a head of household, you may claim a larger standard deduction if you do not itemize deductions than if you file as a single person; *see* ¶13.1.

Head of household tax rate schedules are in Chapter 22.

Qualifying Widow(er)

If you are a widow or widower and your spouse died in 1990 or 1991, you may use 1992 joint return tax rates if you meet these four tests:

1. You maintain your home as the main home of your child for the entire year and you furnish over half the cost of maintaining the household.
2. You are entitled to claim the child as a dependent; *see* ¶1.18.
3. In the year your spouse died, you could have filed a joint return.
4. You did not remarry before January 1, 1993.

If you meet these tests, your filing status is qualifying widow or widower; *see* ¶1.6.

FAMILY STATUS DETERMINES FILING STATUS

TAX RATES BASED ON FILING STATUS

¶1.1 Your tax rate depends on your personal or family status as of the last day of 1992. There are five filing statuses:

- Single
- Married filing jointly
- Married filing separately
- Head of household
- Qualifying widow(er)

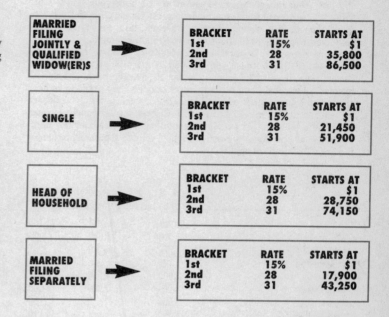

MARRIED FILING JOINTLY & QUALIFIED WIDOW(ER)S	BRACKET	RATE	STARTS AT
	1st	15%	$1
	2nd	28	35,800
	3rd	31	86,500

SINGLE	BRACKET	RATE	STARTS AT
	1st	15%	$1
	2nd	28	21,450
	3rd	31	51,900

HEAD OF HOUSEHOLD	BRACKET	RATE	STARTS AT
	1st	15%	$1
	2nd	28	28,750
	3rd	31	74,150

MARRIED FILING SEPARATELY	BRACKET	RATE	STARTS AT
	1st	15%	$1
	2nd	28	17,900
	3rd	31	43,250

As shown in the next column, each filing status has a separate tax rate schedule except for qualifying widow(er), which uses the schedule for married persons filing jointly. All of the schedules have three rates: 15%, 28%, and 31%, but the amount of income subject to each rate varies from schedule to schedule.

The most favorable brackets apply to married persons filing jointly and qualifying widows(ers). Qualifying widow(er) status generally applies to persons widowed in 1991 or 1990 who have a dependent child; *see* ¶1.6. The least favorable brackets are those for married persons filing separately, but filing separately may still be advisable in certain situations, as discussed in the Guide for Married Persons on page 6 and in ¶1.2.

If an unmarried person maintains a home for a child or other relative, he or she may qualify to use the schedule for head of household (¶1.10), which is more advantageous than using the single person rate schedule. In certain cases, a married person who is living apart from his or her spouse can also use the head of household schedule, instead of the less favorable tax brackets for married persons filing separately; see the Guide for Married Persons on page 6 and also ¶1.10.

Marital status determined at end of year. If by the last day of the year you are divorced under a final decree or you are legally separated under a decree of divorce or separate maintenance, you are not treated as married. However, if at the end of the year you are living apart from your spouse or separated under an "interlocutory" (not final) divorce decree, you are still considered married.

If, at the end of the year, you live together in a common law marriage that is recognized by the law of the state in which you live or the state where the marriage began, you are treated as married.

Tax computations. How to compute your tax using the tax tables or tax rate schedules is discussed in Chapter 22.

JOINT OR SEPARATE RETURNS FOR MARRIED PERSONS

WHEN FILING SEPARATELY MAY BE ADVANTAGEOUS

¶1.2 Filing a joint return will save taxes where you or your spouse earns all, or substantially all, of the taxable income. Where both of you earn taxable income, you should figure your tax on joint or separate returns to determine which method provides the lower overall tax. Separate returns may save taxes where filing separately allows you to claim more deductions. On separate returns, larger amounts of medical expenses may be deductible because lower adjusted gross income floors apply; *see* example on the next page. Moreover, as the range of graduated tax rates is limited to three (15%, 28%, 31%), separate and joint tax rates may be the same, regardless of the type of returns filed. To figure your tax on separate and joint returns, follow the steps of the example worksheet on the next page.

Standard deduction restriction. Keep in mind that if you and your spouse file separately, *both* must either itemize or claim the standard deduction, which is $3,000 in 1992 for married persons filing separately. Thus, if one spouse itemizes, the other spouse must also itemize even if he or she would get a larger deduction from the $3,000 standard deduction.

Joint return required for certain benefits. Also be aware that certain tax benefits may be claimed by married persons only if they file jointly. If you want to take advantage of the $25,000 rental loss allowance (¶10.4) or the credit for the elderly (Chapter 34), you must file jointly unless you live apart for the whole year. You must file jointly to claim an IRA deduction for a nonworking spouse (¶8.7). A joint return is also required to claim the dependent care credit or the earned income credit (Chapter 25), unless you live apart for the last six months of the year. Furthermore, if you receive Social Security benefits, one half of your benefits are generally subject to tax on a separate return, because on a separate return you are not allowed a base amount exemption; *see* Chapter 34.

Switching from Separate to Joint Return

If you and your spouse file separate returns, you have three years from the due date (without extensions) to change to a joint return. If a joint return is filed and the due date has passed, you may not elect to file separate returns. The choice of filing a joint return is irrevocable once the due date is passed. The filing of a separate or joint estimated tax does not commit you to a similar tax return.

EXAMPLE Your 1992 adjusted gross income (AGI) is $65,000 and your spouse's is $56,000. You have medical expenses of $7,000; your spouse has $1,000. You have an $8,000 casualty loss. Your miscellaneous expenses are $2,600; your spouse's are $500. You have deductible mortgage interest expenses of $5,000; your spouse has $2,000. Your deductible state and local taxes are $2,000; your spouse's are $1,000. Neither of you claims exemptions for dependents. As the example worksheet below shows, filing separate returns saves you $1,316 because you can deduct more on separate returns. Furthermore, if you filed jointly you would have received no deduction for medical expenses and casualty losses because they would have been eliminated by the higher adjusted gross income floors. The 3% reduction of itemized deductions (¶13.8) applies whether you file jointly or separately. The phaseout of personal exemptions (¶1.32) does not apply regardless of how you file. Finally, whether you file separately or jointly, the same 31% bracket applies.

Item	You (separately)	Your spouse (separately)	Joint
AGI	**$65,000**	**$56,000**	**$121,000**
Medical expenses	7,000	1,000	8,000
Less 7½% of AGI	4,875	4,200	9,075
*Allowable medical	2,125 *	0	0
*Taxes	2,000	1,000	3,000
*Mortgage interest	5,000	2,000	7,000
Casualty loss	8,000	0	8,000
Less 10% of AGI	6,500		12,100
*Allowable casualty	1,500 *	0	0
Miscellaneous expenses	2,600	500	3,100
Less 2% of AGI	1,300	1,120	2,420
*Net miscellaneous	1,300	0	680
*Total itemized	11,925	3,000	10,680
Less 3% reduction	371	101	473
Net itemized	**11,554**	**2,899**	**10,207**
Personal exemptions	2,300	2,300	4,600
Taxable income	51,146	50,801	106,193
Tax liability	**$12,224**	**$12,131**	**$25,671**
Total tax filing separately			$24,355
Savings from filing separately			*1,316*

Alternative Minimum Tax (AMT). If you are subject to AMT, filing separately may allow a full AMT exemption on one of the separate returns if your spouse's income does not come within the phaseout range for the exemption; see ¶23.1.

Suspicious of your spouse? If you suspect that your spouse may be evading taxes and may not meet tax liabilities due on a joint return, you may want to file a separate return. By filing separately, you avoid liability for unpaid taxes due on a joint return, plus interest and penalties. Although the innocent spouse rules may protect a spouse filing a joint return, this protection will not apply if you have knowledge of your spouse's financial and tax situation; see ¶1.3.

Phaseout of personal exemptions. If you file a 1992 joint return, the 2% phaseout of exemptions starts to apply when adjusted gross income (AGI) exceeds $157,900. On a separate return, the exemption phaseout starts to apply if the AGI on *that* return exceeds $78,950. See ¶1.32 for phaseout rule details.

1040 — Can Filing Separately Avoid Exemption Phaseout?

Where total AGI for both of you exceeds $157,900, filing separately may avoid part of the phaseout if AGI on one of the separate returns is $78,950 or less. On the other hand, where the joint AGI is $157,900 or less, it is possible that filing separately may subject one return to the exemption phaseout if the AGI on that return exceeds $78,950. The exemption phaseout is fully discussed at ¶1.32.

Reduction to certain itemized deductions. If you file jointly and report adjusted gross income (AGI) of over $105,250, your itemized deductions for charitable contributions, miscellaneous deductions, taxes, and mortgage interest will be reduced by 3% of the AGI over $105,250. The reduction does *not* apply to medical deductions, casualty losses, gambling losses, and investment interest.

1040 — Can Filing Separately Avoid 3% Reduction?

If you file separately, part of the itemized deduction reduction may be avoided in a separate return reporting AGI of $52,625 or less. The reduction applies to separate returns showing AGI of $52,626 or more. On the other hand, where joint AGI is $105,250 or less, it is possible that filing separately may subject one return to the itemized deduction reduction if AGI on that return exceeds $52,625. For further details on the 3% reduction; see ¶13.8.

FILING A JOINT RETURN

SIGNING THE JOINT RETURN

¶1.3 Both you and your spouse must sign the joint return. Under the following rules, if your spouse is unable to sign, you may sign for him or her.

If, because of illness, your spouse is physically unable to sign the joint return, you may, with the oral consent of your spouse, sign his or her name on the return followed by the words "By_____, Husband (or Wife)." You then sign the return again in your own right and attach a signed and dated statement with the following information: (1) the return being filed, (2) the tax year, (3) the reason for the inability of the sick spouse to sign, and (4) that the sick spouse has consented to your signing.

To sign for your spouse in other situations, you need authorization in the form of a power-of-attorney, which must be attached to the return. IRS Form 2848 may be used.

If your spouse does not file, you might be able to prove you filed a joint return even if your spouse did *not* sign and you did not sign as your spouse's agent where:

   You intended it to be a joint return—your spouse's income was included (or the spouse had no income).
   Your spouse agreed to have you handle tax matters and you filed a joint return.
   Your answers to the questions on the tax return indicate you intend to file a joint return.
   Your spouse's failure to sign can be explained.

EXAMPLE The Hills generally filed joint returns. In one year, Mr. Hill claimed joint return filing status and reported his wife's income as well as his own; in place of her signature on the return, he indicated that she was out of town caring for her sick mother. She did not file a separate return. The IRS refused to treat the return as joint. The Tax Court disagreed. Since Mrs. Hill testified that she would have signed had she been available, her failure to do so does not bar joint return status. The couple intended to make a joint return at the time of filing.

Joint Liability

When you sign a joint return, you and your spouse may be held individually liable for the entire tax due, plus interest and any penalties. You may be held liable for the entire tax even if your spouse earned all the income.

If you divorce, you remain jointly liable for joint returns filed before the divorce. You remain liable even if your divorce agreement provides that your ex-spouse is responsible for taxes on the prior joint returns; the IRS is not bound by your agreement.

In one case, the Tax Court held that a settlement between the IRS and a bankrupt husband did not extend to the wife. The wife was not involved in the bankruptcy proceeding and the IRS could get a separate assessment against her for the balance of the joint return deficiency.

In limited cases, an innocent spouse may avoid liability, as discussed in ¶1.4.

INNOCENT SPOUSE RULES

¶1.4 To a limited extent, a spouse who files a joint return may be relieved of tax liability based on omitted income or invalid tax deductions or credits. These conditions must be met:

1. There is a tax underpayment exceeding $500 due to the omission of gross income attributable to the other spouse. Alternatively, there is a tax underpayment exceeding $500 due to inflated deductions or credits claimed by the other spouse, provided the "innocent" spouse's tax liability exceeds certain limits discussed below. In determining gross income, community property rules are disregarded, except for income earned from property.
2. In signing the joint return, the innocent spouse did not know of and had no reason to know of the omission of income or inflated deductions or credits; *see* below.
3. Taking into account all the circumstances, it would be inequitable to hold the innocent spouse liable for the tax. The IRS will consider the extent to which the "innocent" spouse benefited from the tax underpayment in deciding the "equity" issue.

Innocent spouse's tax liability must exceed percentage of income. Where relief is based on the other spouse's claiming of invalid deductions or credits, the innocent spouse's tax liability must exceed $500 and also exceed a specific percentage of adjusted gross income for the taxable year preceding the year in which the IRS mails a deficiency notice. If the innocent spouse's adjusted gross income in the year preceding the mailing of a deficiency notice was $20,000 or less, the tax liability attributable to the other spouse's improper deductions must exceed 10% of the preceding year's adjusted gross income. If adjusted gross income was more than $20,000, the tax liability for which relief is sought must exceed 25% of the preceding year's adjusted gross income. If the innocent spouse has remarried as of the end of the preceding year, the new spouse's income must be included to determine the innocent spouse's adjusted gross income for purposes of applying the 10% and 25% tests.

How much "knowledge" on the part of a spouse will defeat a claim for "innocent spouse" status? Where relief from tax liability is based on the other spouse's omission of income, mere knowledge of the underlying transaction that produced the omitted income (such as a tax-sheltered investment) has been held to be enough to defeat innocent spouse status. According to the Tax Court, knowledge of the underlying transaction can also defeat innocent spouse relief based on improper deductions or credits claimed by the other spouse. However, in improper deduction cases, several appeals courts have held that knowledge of the underlying transaction will not block relief for a spouse who shows that at the time the joint return was signed, he or she could not be reasonably expected to know that the improper deduction would substantially lower the tax due. In applying this test, the innocent spouse's level of education and involvement in the couple's financial affairs should be taken into account.

DEATH OF SPOUSE DURING THE YEAR

¶1.5 You do not lose the right to file a joint return when your spouse dies during the year. Generally, a joint return is filed by you and the executor or administrator. But you alone may file a joint return if you are otherwise entitled to file jointly and:

1. The deceased has not filed a separate return, and
2. No executor or administrator has been appointed before the due date for filing the return.

If you do file jointly, you include on the return all of your income and deductions for the full year and your deceased spouse's income and deductions *up to the date of death (see ¶1.12).*

As a surviving spouse, you may *not* file a joint return if:

1. You remarry before the end of the year of your spouse's death (but you may file jointly with new spouse).
2. You or your deceased spouse has a short year because of a change in annual accounting period.
3. Either spouse was a nonresident alien at any time during the tax year; but *see* ¶1.8.
4. The executor or administrator revokes the return. When the executor or administrator is later appointed, he or she may revoke the joint return by filing a separate return for the decedent. Even if you have properly filed a joint return for you and the deceased spouse (as just discussed), the executor or administrator is given the right to revoke the joint return. But, a state court held that a co-executrix could not refuse to sign a joint return where it would save the estate money.

To revoke the joint return, the executor must file a separate return within one year of the due date (including extensions). The executor's separate return is treated as a late return. Interest and a penalty for a late filing must be paid. The joint return filed by the surviving spouse is deemed to be his or her separate return. Tax on that return is recalculated by excluding all items belonging to the deceased spouse.

Signing the return. A joint return reporting a decedent's income should list the names of the surviving spouse and the deceased. Where there is an executor or administrator, the return is signed by the surviving spouse and the executor or administrator in his or her official capacity. If the surviving spouse is the executor or administrator, he or she signs once as surviving spouse and again as the executor or administrator. Where there is no executor or administrator, the surviving spouse signs, followed by the words, "Taxpayer and surviving spouse."

Surviving spouse's liability. If a joint return is filed and the estate cannot pay its share of the joint income tax liability, the surviving spouse may be liable for the full amount. Once the return is filed and the time for filing passes, the survivor can no longer change the joint return election and file a separate return unless an administrator or executor is appointed after the due date of the return. In that case, as previously discussed, the executor may disaffirm the joint return.

If a surviving spouse who will be appointed executor or administrator is concerned about estate insolvency, it may be advisable to hedge as follows: (1) File separate returns. If it is later seen that a joint return is preferable, the surviving spouse has three years to change to a joint return. (2) File jointly but postpone being appointed executor or administrator until after the due date of the joint return. In this way, the joint return may be disaffirmed if the estate cannot cover its share of the taxes.

DEATH OF SPOUSE IN 1990 OR 1991

¶1.6 If your spouse died in either 1990 or 1991 and you meet the following three requirements, your 1992 filing status is *qualifying widow or widower*, which allows you to use joint return rates.

1. You did not remarry before 1993 (if you did remarry you may file a joint return with your new spouse).
2. A dependent child, stepchild, adopted child, or foster child lived with you during 1992 (except for temporary absences) and you paid over half the cost of maintaining your home.
3. You were able to file jointly in the year of your spouse's death, even if you did not actually do so.

If you meet all these tests, use the 1992 tax table or rate schedule for qualifying widows or widowers. *See* Chapter 22 for rate schedules.

Spouse's death before 1990. If your spouse died before 1990 and you did not remarry before 1993, you may be able to use head of household rates if you qualify under the rules of ¶1.10.

DIVORCE OR SEPARATION DECREE

¶1.7 A final decree of divorce or separate maintenance entered into before the end of 1992 prevents you from filing a joint return. Unless you qualify as head of household (¶1.10), you must use the rates for single individuals. You may not claim an exemption for a divorced or legally separated spouse, even if you contribute all of his or her support, but *see* ¶1.19 if the divorce or separation is not final.

If you are married but live apart from your spouse and care for a child, you may be able to qualify as a head of household; *see* ¶1.10.

If before a final decree of divorce has been made, you are separated under an "interlocutory" (not final) decree, you are still considered married and may file a joint return. Once the decree is made final, the privilege to file jointly ends. Alimony paid during the period covered by the interlocutory decree is deducted by one spouse and reported by the other spouse as income if separate returns are filed.

If a divorce decree is interlocutory but another state waives the waiting period and permits a spouse to remarry, the IRS will recognize the new marriage and allow the filing of joint returns by the newly married couple. But a court has refused to allow a joint return where a new marriage took place in Mexico during the interlocutory period in violation of California law.

Invalidated Prior Divorce

The IRS and Tax Court do not allow a joint return with a new spouse if a prior divorce decree has been declared invalid by a state court. The federal appeals court for the Second Circuit allows the joint return; the Ninth Circuit does not.

NONRESIDENT ALIEN SPOUSE

¶1.8 If either you or your spouse was a nonresident alien (¶1.14) during *any part* of the year, a joint return may be filed only if the special election discussed below is made. Thus, if you are a U.S. citizen and your spouse is a nonresident alien at the beginning of the year who becomes a resident (¶1.14) during the year, the special election to file jointly must be made.

If the election is not made, you may be able to claim your nonresident alien spouse as an exemption on a return filed as married filing separately, if the spouse had no income and could not be claimed as a dependent by another taxpayer; *see* ¶1.19. If the alien spouse becomes a resident before the beginning of the next tax year, you may file jointly for that year.

If one spouse is a nonresident alien and the couple does not make the election to file jointly, certain community property rules do not apply; *see* ¶1.9.

Election to file a joint return. Where a U.S. citizen or resident is married to a nonresident alien, the couple may file a joint return if both elect to be taxed on their *worldwide income*. The requirement that one spouse be a U.S. citizen or resident need be met only at the close of the year. Joint returns may be filed in the year of the election and all later years until the election is terminated.

A couple that makes the election must keep books and records of their worldwide income and give the IRS access to such books and records. If either spouse does not provide the necessary information to the IRS, the election is terminated. Furthermore, the election is terminated if either spouse revokes it or dies; revocation before the due date of the return is effective for that return. The election automatically terminates for the year of death of either spouse. However, if the survivor is a U.S. citizen or resident, he or she may claim the benefits of being a qualifying widow(er); *see* ¶1.5. The election to file jointly also terminates if the couple is legally separated under a decree of divorce or separate maintenance. Termination is effective as of the beginning of the taxable year of the legal separation. If neither spouse is a citizen or resident for any part of the taxable year, an election may not be made and an existing election is revoked. Once the election is terminated, neither spouse may ever again make the election.

Electing to file a joint return does not terminate the special withholding on the nonresident alien's income.

Nonresident Alien Becomes Resident

Where one spouse is a U.S. citizen or resident and the other is a nonresident alien who becomes a resident during the tax year, the couple may make a special election to file a joint return for that year and be taxed on their worldwide income. This election will also apply to future returns unless revoked, or the couple legally separates. Thereafter, neither spouse may make the election again even if married to a new spouse. Tests for determining status as a resident or nonresident alien are at ¶1.16.

COMMUNITY PROPERTY RULES

¶1.9 If you live in Arizona, California, Idaho, Louisiana, Nevada, New Mexico, Texas, Washington, or Wisconsin, the income and property you and your spouse acquire during the marriage is generally regarded as community property. But note that there are some instances in which community property rules are disregarded for tax purposes; these instances are clearly highlighted in the pertinent sections of this book.

Community property means that each of you owns half of the community income and community property, even if legal title is held by only one spouse.

Separate property may still be owned. Property owned before marriage generally remains separate property; it does not become community property when you marry. Property received during the marriage by one spouse as a gift or an inheritance from a third party is generally separate property. In some states, if the nature of ownership cannot be fixed, the property is presumed to be community property.

In some states, income from separate property may be treated as community property income. In other states, income from separate property remains the separate property of the individual owner.

Divorce or separation. If you and your spouse divorce, your community property automatically becomes separate property. A wife, while separated from her husband, does not generally report temporary alimony payments. She reports her share of community income until the date of the interlocutory divorce decree.

When community income rules do not apply to separated couples. If a husband and wife in a community property state file separate returns, each spouse must generally report one-half of the community income. However, a spouse may be able to avoid reporting income earned by his or her spouse if they live apart during the entire calendar year and do not file a joint return. To qualify, one or both spouses must have earned income for the year and none of that earned income may be transferred, directly or indirectly, between the spouses during the year. One spouse's payment to the other spouse solely to support the couple's dependent children is not a disqualifying transfer. If the separated couple qualifies under these tests, community income is allocated as follows:

Earned income (excluding business or partnership income) is taxed to the spouse who performed the personal services.

Business income (other than partnership income) is treated as the husband's income, unless the wife exercises substantially all of the management and control of the business. However, a similar rule for self-employment income was held unconstitutional on the basis of sex, and the IRS agreed to follow the court rule that the spouse actually carrying on the business is the spouse subject to self-employment tax.

Partnership income is taxed to the spouse entitled to a distributive share of partnership profits.

Innocent spouse rules applied to community property. As discussed above, community property rules may not apply to earned income where spouses live apart for the entire year and file separate returns. In addition, a spouse who files a separate return may be relieved of tax liability on community income which is attributable to the other spouse if he or she does not know (or have reason to know) about the income and if it would be inequitable under the circumstances for him or her to be taxed on such income. This rule applies to all tax years not closed by the statute of limitations.

The IRS may disregard community property rules and tax income to a spouse who treats such income as if it were solely his or hers and who fails to notify the other spouse of the income before the due date of the return (including extensions).

Death of spouse. The death of a spouse dissolves the community property relationship, but income earned and accrued from community property before death is community income.

Moving from a community property to a common law (separate property) state. Most common law states (those which do not have community property laws) recognize that both spouses have an interest in property accumulated while resident in a community property state. If the property is not sold or reinvested, it may continue to be treated as community property. If you and your spouse sell community property after moving to a common law state and reinvest the proceeds, the reinvested proceeds are generally separate property, which may be held as joint tenants, or in another form of ownership recognized by common law states.

Moving from a common law to a community property state. Separate property brought into a community property state generally retains its character as separately owned property. However, property acquired by a couple *after* moving to a community property state is generally owned as community property. In at least one state (California), personal property which qualifies as community property is treated as such, even though it was acquired when the couple lived in a common law state.

 Claiming Dependents on Separate Returns

Married parents in community property states who plan to file separate returns should be aware that neither parent may be able to claim an exemption for a dependent child. Where all of the couple's income is considered community income, each parent on a separate return is treated as having provided exactly one-half of the child's support, regardless of who actually paid the support. Since neither parent has provided more than one-half of the support, neither can claim the child as a dependent.

To avoid this result, parents whose sole income is community income and who want to file separately should consider signing a multiple support agreement, Form 2120, designating which parent may claim the exemption.

Supporting a dependent with separate income. Filing a Form 2120 multiple support agreement is not necessary where either parent can prove that he or she has income which is considered separate income rather than community income; that parent may be able to satisfy the more than 50% support test. In certain community property states, the law may provide that income of a husband and wife living apart is considered separate income rather than community income.

FILING AS HEAD OF HOUSEHOLD

QUALIFYING AS HEAD OF HOUSEHOLD

¶1.10 If you are unmarried at the end of 1992 and you maintain a household for a child, parent, or other relative under the rules below, you can file as "head of household." Tax rates are lower for a head of household than for a person filing as single (Chapter 22) and the standard deduction is higher (Chapter 13). If you are married but for the last half of 1992 you lived apart from your spouse, you may also be able to qualify for head of household rates that are more favorable than the rates for married persons filing separately; *see* Test 1.

You have to meet the following four tests to qualify as head of household:

Test 1. You are not married at the end of the year.

Test 2. You maintain a household for your child, parent, or other dependent relative.

Test 3. The household you maintain must be your main home as well as the main home of the dependent relative, except in the case of your parent.

Test 4. You are a U.S. citizen or resident alien during the entire tax year. If you are a nonresident alien (¶1.16) for any part of the year, you are not eligible to file as head of household.

MEETING THE HEAD OF HOUSEHOLD TESTS

Test 1. You are "unmarried" for head of household purposes if you are any one of the following:

Single.
A widow or widower and your spouse died before 1992. If a dependent child lives with you, *see* ¶1.6 to determine if you may use the even more advantageous filing status of qualifying widow(er). If your spouse died in 1992, you are treated as married and cannot qualify as a 1992 head of household, but a joint return may be filed; *see* ¶1.5.
Legally separated or divorced under a final court decree. A custody and support order does not qualify as a legal separation. An interlocutory decree (not final), such as a support order *pendente lite* (while action is pending), has no effect for tax purposes until the decree is made final.
Married but living apart from your spouse. You are considered unmarried for 1992 if your spouse was not a member of your household during the last six months of 1992, you file separate returns, and you maintain a household for more than half the year for a dependent child, stepchild, or adopted child. A foster child qualifies if he or she is a member of your household for the whole year. You must be able to claim the child as a dependent unless your spouse (the noncustodial parent) has the right to the exemption under rules of ¶1.28.
Your spouse was a nonresident alien during any part of 1992 and you do not elect to file a joint return reporting your joint worldwide income (¶1.8).

Test 2. You must pay more than half of the costs of maintaining a household for your child, parent, or other dependent relative. A child or relative other than your parent must live with you in that same home, as discussed under Test 3.

Dependent relatives, other than children or parents, who may qualify you for head of household status are:

Sons- or daughters-in-law; fathers- or mothers-in-law; brothers- or sisters-in-law; brothers, sisters, grandparents, step-parents, step-brothers or sisters; half-brothers or sisters; and uncles, aunts, nieces or nephews by blood.

A parent or other relative listed above must qualify as a dependent on your return; *see* page 19.

Your unmarried child, stepchild, adopted child, or grandchild does not have to be your dependent; a foster child does have to be your dependent. If the child is married, he or she must qualify as a dependent for you to claim head of household status unless you are divorced or separated and you have waived the exemption for your married child, or the child's other parent may claim the exemption under a pre-1985 agreement; *see* ¶1.28. A person married on the last day of the year is considered married for the whole year.

If you are married and living apart from your spouse, you must be able to claim your child, married or unmarried, as an exemption unless you waive the exemption or your spouse (the noncustodial parent) may claim the exemption under a pre-1985 agreement, as explained at ¶1.28.

If a child or other relative qualifies as your dependent on the basis of a multiple support agreement (¶1.27), you do not qualify as head of household.

A spouse who is a nonresident alien during any part of the year is not a dependent who can qualify you for head of household status, even though you maintain a home for him or her.

You do not qualify as a head of household if you support an unrelated family unit, such as a mother and her children. This is true even if you are entitled to claim them as exemptions under ¶1.18.

Costs of maintaining the household. You must pay more than half of the property taxes, mortgage interest, rent, utility charges, upkeep and repairs, domestic help, property insurance, and food eaten in the household. Do not consider the rental value of the lodgings provided the dependent or clothing, education costs, medical expenses, vacation costs, life insurance premiums, transportation costs, and the value of your work around the house. However, these expenses may be considered in figuring your support contribution in determining whether you may claim the child or other relative as a dependent; *see* ¶1.24.

HOUSEHOLD COSTS FOR THE YEAR

1. Property taxes	$	_____
2. Mortgage interest		_____
3. Rent paid		_____
4. Insurance		_____
5. Utilities		_____
6. Domestic help		_____
7. Repairs and upkeep		_____
8. Food eaten in the home		_____
9. Total of Lines 1-8		_____
10. 50% of Line 9	$	_____

If you paid more than the amount on Line 10, you "maintain" the household for purposes of Test 2.

EXAMPLE Your mother lived with your sister in your sister's apartment, which cost $4,000 to maintain. Of this amount, you contributed $2,500, your sister $1,500. Your mother has no income and did not contribute any funds to the household. You qualify as head of household: For 1992, you paid over half the cost of maintaining the home for your mother, who also qualifies as an exemption on your return. A child or dependent relative other than your parent would have to live with you (Test 3 below) to enable you to file as head of household.

Two-family house. A mother was allowed head of household status by the Tax Court in the following case. She and her unmarried daughter rented one floor of a multilevel home. A married daughter lived on a different floor with her family. Parts of the home were shared. According to the court, the mother was a head of household, based on support of her unmarried daughter. Although she did not pay more than half of the total household expenses, she paid more than half the expenses attributable to her and her unmarried daughter.

Test 3. The home that you maintain (Test 2) for your dependent relative must be his or her principal residence for more than half of 1992, or for all of 1992 in the case of a dependent parent's separate household. According to the IRS, that same home must also be *your* principal residence for more than half the year, unless you are maintaining a separate household for your parent. The Tax Court has upheld the IRS position; *see* the example below. Other courts have held that the taxpayer must live for a "substantial" period of time in the same house as the dependent. However, an appeals court disagreed in one case; it allowed a mother to claim head of household status where she maintained a home for a child in one state and had her principal residence in another state.

EXAMPLE Doctors advised McDonald that her mentally ill son might become self-sufficient if he lived in a separate residence, but one nearby enough for her to provide supervision. She took the advice and kept up a separate home for her son that was about a mile from her own home. She frequently spent nights at his home and he at hers. The Tax Court agreed with the IRS that McDonald could not file as head of household since her principal place of abode was not the same as her son's.

Temporary absences disregarded. The household relationship is not disqualified by your or your dependent's temporary absences such as for illness, education, business, vacation, military service, or fulfilling a child custody agreement. The IRS also requires that it be reasonable to expect your qualifying dependent to return to your household after such a temporary absence, and that you continue to maintain the household during the temporary absence. Under this rule, you would lose the right to file as head of household if your dependent moved into his or her own permanent residence before the end of the year.

You may claim head of household status when your dependent is confined to a hospital or a sanitarium and his or her absence is temporary and you continue to maintain a household in expectation of his or her return.

In the year a qualifying dependent is born or dies, meeting the residence test for the portion of the year the dependent is alive allows you to claim head of household status.

Child May Be Head of Household

You may be head of household for filing purposes although not head of the family. For example, a son who earns more than his father and contributes more than half of the cost of maintaining the family may qualify as a head of a household. That the father, not the son, exercises family control does not matter. The important factor is a dollar test—whether the head of household for tax purposes contributed more than half the cost of maintaining the household that is his or her home and the principal home of the qualifying dependents.

TAX RETURNS FOR CHILDREN

FILING FOR YOUR CHILD

¶1.11 The income of your minor child is *not* included in your return unless you make a special election to report a child's investment income under the rules of ¶24.5. A minor is considered a taxpayer in his or her own right. If the child is required to file a return, but is unable to do so because of age or for any other reason, the parent or guardian is responsible for filing the return.

A 1992 tax return must be filed for a dependent child who had more than $600 of gross income, where any of it was from investments. If your child had only earned income (for personal services) and no investment income, a 1992 tax return must be filed if the earned income exceeded $3,600.

If the child is unable to sign the return, the parent or guardian should sign the child's name in the proper place, followed by the words "By (signature), Parent (or guardian) for minor child." A parent is liable for tax due on pay earned by the child for services, but not on investment income.

A child who is not required to file a return should still do so for a refund of taxes withheld, if any.

Social Security numbers. A parent or guardian must obtain a Social Security number for a child before filing the child's first income tax return. The child's Social Security number must also be provided to banks, brokers, and other payers of interest and dividends to avoid penalties and backup withholding; *see* ¶26.12. To obtain a Social Security number, file Form SS-5 with your local Social Security office. If you have applied for a Social Security number but not yet received it by the filing due date, write "Applied for" on the tax return in the space provided for the number.

Kiddie Tax

Children who are under age 14 at the end of 1992 generally must use Form 8615 to figure their 1992 tax if they had more than $1,200 of investment income; *see* ¶24.4. On Form 8615, the investment earnings over $1,200 are taxed at the parent's top tax rate. However, in certain cases under the rules of ¶24.5, parents may elect to report their children's investment income on their own return.

Important: Whether or not you are filing a return for a child, you must obtain a Social Security number for a dependent child who reaches age one before 1993 and report the number on your return. Otherwise, you may be subject to a $50 penalty; *see* ¶1.31.

Wages You Pay Your Children

You may deduct wages paid to your children in your business. Keep records showing that their activities are of a business rather than household nature.

Withholding for children. Children with wages are generally subject to withholding and should file Form W-4 with their employer. An exemption from withholding may be claimed only in limited cases. If the child can be claimed as a dependent by a parent or other taxpayer, and has any investment income, the exemption from withholding is allowed only if the expected amount of investment income plus wages is $600 or less. Furthermore, the child must certify on Form W-4 that he or she had no federal tax liability in the prior year and expects to have no liability in the current year.

FILING FOR DECEASED OR INCOMPETENT PERSON

RETURN FOR DECEASED

¶1.12 When a person dies, another taxpaying entity is created—the decedent's estate. Until the estate is fully distributed, it will generally earn income for which a return must be filed. For example, a decedent had a savings account. Decedent died on June 30. Income earned on the account through June 30 is reported on decedent's final income tax return, Form 1040. Income earned on the account from July 1 is reported on the estate's income tax return, fiduciary Form 1041. Form 1041 must be filed if the estate has gross income of $600 or more.

What income tax returns must be filed? If the decedent died after the close of the taxable year, but before the income tax return was filed, the following must be filed:

1. Income tax return for prior year;
2. Final income tax return, covering earnings in period from beginning of taxable year to date of death; and
3. Estate income tax return, covering earnings in period after decedent's death.

If decedent died after filing a return for prior tax year, then only 2 and 3 are filed.

EXAMPLE Jones died on March 31, 1993, before he could file his 1992 tax return due April 15, 1993. A regular income tax return must be filed by April 15, 1993. A final income tax return to report earnings from January 1, 1993, through March 31, 1993, will have to be filed on April 15, 1994. Jones's estate will have to file an income tax return on Form 1041 to report earnings and other income that were not paid to Jones before April 1, 1992.

For purposes of determining whether a final income tax return for the decedent is due, the annual gross income test at page 2 is considered in full. You do not prorate it to the part of the year decedent lived.

Who is responsible for filing? The executor, administrator, or other legal representative is responsible for filing all returns. A surviving spouse may assume responsibility for filing a joint return for the year of death if no executor or administrator has been appointed and other tests are met (¶1.5). However, if a legal representative has been appointed, he or she must consent to the filing of a joint return for the year of decedent's death.

How do you report the decedent's income and deductions? You follow the method used by the decedent during his or her life to account for the income up to death. The income does *not* have to be put on an annual basis. Each item is taxed in the same manner as it would have been taxed had the decedent lived for the entire year.

If the deceased owned U.S. Savings Bonds, *see* ¶4.29.

When one spouse dies in a community property state (¶1.9), how should the income from the community property be reported during the administration of the estate? The IRS says that half the income is the estate's and the other half belongs to the surviving spouse.

Decedent's Final Return

Do not report on the decedent's final return income that is received after his death, or accrues after or because of his death. It is taxed to the estate or beneficiary receiving the income in the year of the receipt. On the decedent's final return, only deductible expenses paid up to and including the date of death may be claimed. If the decedent reported on the accrual basis, those deductions accruable up to and including the date of death are deductible. If a check for payment of a deductible item was delivered or mailed before the date of the decedent's death, a deduction is allowable on the decedent's last return, even though the check was not cashed or deposited until after the decedent's death. If the check was not honored by the bank, the item is not deductible.

Medical expenses of the decedent. The payment of medical expenses of the decedent by his estate within one year after his or her death is treated as having been paid by the decedent when incurred. Consequently, the expenses are deductible on the decedent's last return. However, the expenses are not deductible for income tax purposes if they are deducted for estate tax purposes. To deduct such medical expenses on the decedent's last return, a statement must be filed affirming that no estate tax deduction has been taken and that the rights to the deduction have been waived.

Partnership income. The final return includes partnership income or loss only from a partnership year that ends within the decedent's tax year. Thus, if a partner dies in July 1992 and the partnership's taxable year ends December 31, 1992, no partnership income or loss is included on the partner's final 1992 return. It is reported by the partner's executor or other successor in interest on the estate's income tax return.

Which exemptions are allowed on a final return? Generally, the same exemptions the decedent would have had if he or she had not died. You do not reduce the exemptions because of the shorter taxable year. If the deceased had contributed more than one-half of a dependent's annual support, a dependency exemption is claimed on his or her final return.

Estimated taxes. No estimated tax need be paid by the executor after the death of an unmarried individual; the entire tax is paid when filing the final tax return. But where the deceased and a surviving spouse paid estimated tax jointly, the rule is different. The surviving spouse is still liable for the balance of the estimated tax unless an amended estimated tax voucher is filed. Further, if the surviving spouse plans to file a joint return (¶1.5) which includes the decedent's income, estimated tax payments may be required; *see* Chapter 27.

Where the estate has gross income, estimated tax installments are not required on Form 1041-ES for the first two years after the decedent's death.

Signing the return. An executor or administrator of the estate signs the return. If it is a joint return, *see* ¶1.5.

Promptly Closing the Estate

To expedite the closing of the decedent's estate, an executor or other personal representative of the decedent may file Form 4810 for a prompt assessment. Once filed, the IRS has 18 months to assess additional taxes. Without making the request, the IRS has three years from the due date of the return to make assessments. Form 4810 must be filed separately from the final return, but should be sent to the District Director for the IRS district in which the return is filed.

What if a refund is due? The decedent's return may also be used as a claim for a refund of an overpayment of withheld or estimated taxes. Form 1310 may be used to get the refund, but the form is not required if you are a surviving spouse filing a joint return for the year your spouse died. If you are executor or administrator of the estate and you are filing Form 1040, 1040A, or 1040 EZ for the decedent, you do not need Form 1310, but you must attach to the return a copy of the court certificate showing your appointment as personal representative.

RETURN FOR AN INCOMPETENT PERSON

¶1.13 A legal guardian of an incompetent person files Form 1040 for an incompetent whose gross income meets the filing tests on page 2. Where a spouse becomes incompetent, the IRS says the other spouse may file a return for the incompetent without a power of attorney, if no legal guardian has been appointed. For example, during the period an individual was in a mental hospital, and before he was adjudged legally incompetent, his wife continued to operate his business. She filed an income tax return for him and signed it for him although she had no power of attorney. The IRS accepted the return as properly filed. Until a legal guardian was appointed, she was charged with the care of her husband and his property.

The IRS had accepted a joint return filed by a wife in her capacity as legal guardian for her missing husband. However, the Tax Court has held that where one spouse is mentally incompetent, a joint return may not be filed because the incompetent spouse was unable to consent to a joint return; an appeals court agreed.

HOW NONRESIDENT ALIENS FILE

RESIDENT OR NONRESIDENT?

¶1.14 A resident alien, like a United States citizen, is taxed on income from all sources. A nonresident alien is generally taxed only on income from U.S. sources. Income that is effectively connected with a U.S. business and capital gains from the sale of U.S. real estate are subject to tax at regular U.S. rates. Other capital gains are not taxed unless a nonresident alien has a U.S. business or is in the U.S. for 183 days during the year. Generally, investment income that is not effectively connected with a U.S. business is subject to a 30% tax rate (or lower rate if provided by treaty). Nonresident aliens must file Form 1040NR. If you are a nonresident alien, get a copy of IRS Publication 519, *U.S. Tax Guide for Aliens*. It explains the way nonresident aliens pay tax, if any, to the U.S.

An alien's mere presence in the U.S. does not make him or her a "resident."

An alien is generally treated as a "resident" only if he or she is a lawful permanent resident who has a "green card" or meets a substantial presence test; *see* ¶1.16.

Dual status. An alien may be both a resident and nonresident in the same year, especially in the year of arrival in or departure from the U.S.

EXAMPLE On June 1, 1992, you arrive on a nonimmigrant visa and are present in the U.S. for the rest of the year. From January 1 to May 31, 1992, you are a nonresident; from June 1 to the end of the year, you are a resident. Despite "dual status," you do not file two returns. You file one return, reporting income on the basis of your status for each part of the year.

Certain restrictions apply to dual status taxpayers. For example, a joint return may not be filed, unless you and your spouse agree to be taxed as U.S. residents for the entire year.

For details on filing a return for a dual status year, *see* IRS Publication 519 and the instructions to Form 1040NR.

HOW A RESIDENT ALIEN IS TAXED

¶1.15 A resident alien is taxed on worldwide income like a U.S. citizen. Income earned abroad may be excluded if the foreign physical presence test is satisfied; *see* ¶36.5. A resident alien may generally claim a foreign tax credit; *see* ¶36.14. He or she is taxed on a pension from a foreign government. An alien working in the United States for a foreign government is not taxed on the wages if the foreign government allows a similar exemption to American citizens.

WHO IS A RESIDENT ALIEN?

¶1.16 The following tests determine whether an alien is taxed as a U.S. resident. Intent to remain in the U.S. is not considered.

You are treated as a resident alien and taxed as a U.S. resident if you meet either of the following tests for 1992:

1. You are a lawful permanent resident of the U.S. *at any time* during the calendar year. If you hold a "green card," you meet this test and are considered a U.S. resident. If you were outside the U.S. for part of 1992 and then become a lawful permanent resident, *see* next page for first year of residency.
2. You meet a substantial presence test. Under this test, you are treated as a U.S. resident if you were in the U.S. for at least 31 days during the calendar year and have been in the U.S. for 183 days within the last three years (the current year and the two preceding calendar years). The 183-day test is complicated and there are several exceptions.

183-day test. To determine if you meet the 183-day test, the following cumulative times are totaled. Each day in the U.S. during 1992 is counted as a full day. Each day in 1991 counts as ¹/₃ of a day; each day in 1990 counts as ¹/₆ of a day.

Note that you must be physically present in the U.S. for at least 31 days in the current year. If you are not, the 183-day test does not apply.

Other exceptions to the substantial presence test are: commuting from Canada or Mexico; keeping a tax home and close contacts or connections in a foreign country; having a diplomatic, teacher, trainee, or student status; being a professional athlete temporarily in the U.S. to compete in a charitable sports event; or being confined in the U.S. for certain medical reasons. These are explained in the following paragraphs.

Commute from Mexico or Canada. If you regularly commute to work in the U.S. from Mexico or Canada, commuting days do not count as days of physical presence for the 183-day test.

Tax home/closer connection exception. If you are in the United States for less than 183 days during 1991, show that you had a closer connection with a foreign country than with the U.S., and keep a tax home there for the year, you generally will not be subject to tax as a resident under the substantial presence test. Under this exception, it is possible to have a U.S. abode and a tax home in a foreign country. A tax home is usually where a person has his or her principal place of business; if there is no principal place of business, it is the place of regular abode. Proving a tax home alone is not sufficient; the closer connection relationship must also be shown.

The tax home/closer connection test does not apply to an alien who is present for 183 days or more during a year or who has applied for a "green card." A relative's application is not considered as the alien's application.

Exempt-person exception. Days of presence in the U.S. are not counted if you are considered an exempt person such as a teacher, trainee, student, foreign government-related person, or professional athlete temporarily in the U.S. to compete in a charitable sports event.

A foreign government-related person is any individual temporarily present in the U.S. who (1) has diplomatic status or a visa which the Secretary of the Treasury (after consultation with the Secretary of State) determined represents full-time diplomatic or consular status; (2) is a full-time employee of an international organization; or (3) is a member of the immediate family of a diplomat or international organization employee.

A teacher or trainee is any individual other than a student who is temporarily present in the U.S. under a "J" visa and who substantially complies with the requirements for being so present.

A student is any individual who is temporarily present in the U.S. under either an "F," "J," or "M" visa and who substantially complies with the requirements for being so present.

The exception generally does not apply to a teacher or trainee who has been exempt as a teacher, trainee, or student for any part of two of the six preceding calendar years. However, if during the period you are temporarily present in the U.S. under an "F," "J," or "M" visa all of your compensation is received from outside the U.S., you may qualify for the exception if you were exempt as a teacher, trainee, or student for less than four years in the six preceding calendar years. The exception also does not apply to a student who has been exempt as a teacher, trainee, or student for more than five calendar years, unless you show that you do not intend to reside permanently in the U.S. and that you have substantially complied with the requirements of the student visa providing for temporary presence in the U.S.

Medical exception. An alien who cannot physically leave the U.S. because of a medical condition that arose in the U.S. may be treated as a nonresident, even if present here for more than 183 days during the year.

Tax Treaty Exceptions

The lawful permanent residence test and the substantial physical presence test do not override tax treaty definitions of residence. Thus, you may be protected by a tax treaty from being treated as a U.S. resident even if you would be treated as a resident under either test.

Dual tax status in first year of residency. If you first became a lawful permanent resident of the U.S. (received a green card) during 1992 and were not a U.S. resident during 1991, your period of U.S. residency begins with the first day in 1992 that you are present in the U.S. with the status of lawful permanent resident. Before that date, you are a nonresident alien. This means that if you become a lawful permanent resident after January 1, 1992, you have a *dual status tax year*. On Form 1040, you attach a separate schedule showing the income for the part of the year you are a nonresident.

To figure tax for a dual status year, *see* IRS Publication 519 and the instructions to Form 1040NR.

You also may have a dual status year if you were not a U.S. resident in 1991, and in 1992 you are a U.S. resident under the 183-day presence test. Your period of U.S. residency starts on the first day in 1992 for which you were physically present; before that date you are treated as a nonresident alien. However, if you meet the 183-day presence test (but not the green card test) and also spent 10 days or less in the U.S. during a period in which you had a closer connection to a foreign country than to the U.S., you may disregard the 10-day period. The purpose of this exception is to allow a brief presence in the U.S. for business trips or house hunting before the U.S. residency period starts.

EXAMPLES 1. An alien who has never before been a U.S. resident lives in Spain until May 15, 1992. He moves to the U.S. and remains in the U.S. through the end of the year, thereby satisfying the physical presence test. On May 15, he is a U.S. resident. For the period before May 15, he is taxed as a nonresident.

2. Same facts as in Example 1, but he attends a meeting in the U.S. on February 2 through 8. On May 15, he moves to the U.S.; May 15, not February 2, is the starting date of the residency. During February, he had closer connection to Spain than to the U.S. Thus, his short stay in February is an exempt period.

If you were not a resident during 1991 but in 1992 you satisfy both the lawful resident (green card) test and the 183-day presence test, your residence begins on the earlier of either the first day you are present in the U.S. while a lawful permanent resident of the U.S. or the first day of physical presence.

First-year choice. If you *do not* meet either the green card test or the substantial presence test for the year of your arrival in the United States or for the immediately preceding year, but you do meet the substantial presence test for the year immediately following the year of your arrival, you may elect to be treated as a U.S. resident for part of the year of your arrival. To do this, you must (1) be present in the United States for at least 31 consecutive days in the year of your arrival; and (2) be present in the United States for at least 75% of the number of days beginning with the first day of the 31-consecutive-day period and ending with the last day of the year of arrival. For purposes of this 75% requirement, you may treat up to five days of absence from the United States as days of presence within the United States.

Do not count as days of presence in the United States days for which you are an *exempt individual* as discussed earlier.

You make the first-year election to be treated as a U.S. resident by attaching a statement to your tax return for the year of your arrival. A first-year election, once made, may not be revoked without the consent of the Internal Revenue Service.

If you make the election, your residence starting date for the year of your arrival is the first day of the earliest 31-consecutive-day period of presence that you use to qualify for the choice. You are treated as a U.S. resident for the remainder of the year.

Last year of residence. If you do not hold a green card, you are not treated as a resident after the last day you are present in the U.S., provided (1) that you are not treated as a resident during the next calendar year; and (2) if after leaving the U.S., you had a closer connection to a foreign country than to the U.S. Presence of up to 10 days in the U.S. may be disregarded. If an alien who holds a green card gives up his or her permanent resident status in the current year and meets Rules 1 and 2 on page 16, residency status ends after the day he or she was no longer a permanent resident.

In the last year of residence, the rules for dual status taxpayers apply; *see* ¶1.14.

Interrupted period of residence. If you qualified as a U.S. resident during at least three consecutive calendar years after 1984 and cease to be a U.S. resident, but later return to become a U.S. resident within three calendar years after the end of the initial residency period, you are taxable during the intervening period of nonresidence in the same way as a former U.S. citizen who became expatriated to avoid tax. This treatment applies only if the amount of tax under this rule exceeds the tax that would otherwise apply to you as a nonresident alien. The tax under this special rule is the regular graduated income tax, alternative minimum tax, and tax on lump-sum distributions from an employees' trust, applied only to your gross income effectively connected with a U.S. trade or business and your U.S. source noneffectively connected gross income. For this purpose, U.S. source gross income includes gains from the sale or exchange of (1) property (other than stock or debt obligations) located in the United States, and (2) stock issued by a U.S. domestic corporation or debt obligations of U.S. persons or of the United States, a state or political subdivision thereof, or the District of Columbia.

This rule is designed to prevent a long-time U.S. resident from disposing of assets free of U.S. tax by leaving the United States for a short period and then resuming U.S. residence. The rule applies regardless of a resident's intention to avoid tax.

WHEN AN ALIEN LEAVES THE UNITED STATES

¶1.17 You must obtain a "sailing permit," technically known as a "certificate of compliance," which states that you have fulfilled your income tax obligations to the U.S. Without it, unless you are excused from obtaining one, you will be required at your point of departure to file a tax return and pay any tax due.

You should apply for a sailing permit from your local District Director of Internal Revenue about two weeks, but no earlier than 30 days, before your departure. You submit all information pertaining to your income and stay in the U.S. such as passport and alien registration form, copies of U.S. tax returns for the past two years, bank records, and any profit and loss statements. You also file a Form 1040C, on which you report income received and expected to be received through the date of departure. Form 2063 is a short form that may be used *only* in limited cases.

You may avoid paying tax if you satisfactorily convince the District Director that you are returning to the United States. In other cases, you may avoid paying tax on the current year (or previous year if the filing date has not yet passed) by posting a bond for the amount of tax due.

Aliens in the following categories are not required to obtain a sailing permit—those traveling under a diplomatic passport, members of their households, and servants accompanying them; employees of foreign governments and international organizations, and members of their households whose official compensation is tax exempt and who receive no other income subject to U.S. tax; certain students without taxable income admitted solely on an "F" visa; certain industrial trainees admitted solely on an "H-3" visa; certain aliens temporarily in the U.S. who have received no U.S. taxable income such as visitors on a "B-2" visa, a "C-1" visa, or similar arrangement; aliens admitted to the United States on a border-crossing identification card or for whom passports, visas, and border-crossing identification cards are not required; certain alien military trainees; and an alien resident of Canada or Mexico who frequently commutes between his country and the United States for employment purposes and whose wages are subject to withholding tax.

See IRS Publication 519 for further details.

EXEMPTIONS AND DEPENDENTS

HOW MANY EXEMPTIONS MAY YOU CLAIM?

¶1.18 Each exemption you claim on your 1992 return is the equivalent of a $2,300 deduction. However, if you have a high adjusted gross income, you may lose the benefit of your deduction under a phaseout rule, as discussed in ¶1.32.

You may claim an exemption for:

Yourself. Every taxpayer is allowed one exemption unless he or she is the dependent of another taxpayer. If someone else is entitled to claim you as a dependent (all the dependent tests are satisfied) for 1992, you may not claim a personal exemption for yourself on your own return; this is true even if the other person does not actually claim you as a dependent. This rule prevents your child or other dependent from claiming an exemption on his or her return if you may claim an exemption for the child or other dependent.

Your spouse. You claim your spouse as an exemption when you file a joint return. If you file a separate return, you claim your spouse as an exemption if he or she has no income and is not a dependent of another person; see ¶1.19.

Children, parents, and other dependents. There is no limit to the number of dependents you may claim, provided you satisfy five tests for each dependent—a relationship test; a support test; an income test; a citizenship or residency test; and for married dependents, a joint return test. These tests are discussed in the chart on page 19.

You must obtain and report on your 1992 return the Social Security number of each dependent who is at least a year old before 1993; see ¶1.31.

Phaseout of Personal Exemptions

LAW ALERT Your 1992 deduction for exemptions is phased out if your adjusted gross income exceeds these thresholds: $157,900 if married filing jointly; $131,550 if filing as head of household; $105,250 if filing as single; and $78,950 if married and filing separately. See ¶1.32 for full details and tables providing the exact amount you may deduct.

YOUR SPOUSE AS AN EXEMPTION

¶1.19 Your spouse is not your dependent for tax purposes. An exemption for a wife or husband is based on the marital relationship, not support.

On a joint return, each spouse receives an exemption as a taxpayer.

On a separate return, you may claim your spouse as an exemption if he or she has no gross income and is not the dependent of another taxpayer. You may not claim an exemption for your spouse who has income, *unless you file a joint return which includes that income.* For example, if a wife files a separate return, her husband may not claim her as an exemption, even if she filed the return merely for a refund of taxes withheld on her wages.

If your spouse is a nonresident alien, *see* ¶1.18.

If divorced or legally separated during the year. You may not claim your former spouse as an exemption if you are divorced or legally separated under a *final* decree of divorce or separate maintenance, even if you provided his or her entire support. However, an interlocutory (not final) decree does not bar you from claiming your spouse as an exemption.

EXAMPLE An interlocutory (not final) decree of divorce is entered in 1992; a final decree in 1993. For 1992, the couple may file a joint return on which exemptions for both are claimed. A marriage is not dissolved until a final decree is entered, which in this case is in 1993.

Your spouse died during the year. If you did not remarry and your deceased spouse had gross income, you may claim an exemption for your spouse only if you file a joint return that includes his or her income. You may claim the exemption on a separate return only if your spouse had no gross income and was not a dependent of another taxpayer.

EXAMPLE Mrs. Smith dies on June 27. Mr. Smith files a joint return and claims her as an exemption. They were married as of the date of Mrs. Smith's death. The joint return includes all of Mr. Smith's income for the year, but only that part of Mrs. Smith's income earned up to June 27; see ¶1.5.

If you remarry before the end of the year in which your spouse died, you may not claim an exemption for your deceased spouse. If you file a joint return with your new spouse, you may be claimed as an exemption on that return. If you had *no* income for the year, you may be claimed as an exemption on both your deceased spouse's separate return and on a separate return filed by your new spouse, provided no one else may claim you as a dependent.

BARRON'S

National Business and Financial Weekly
P.O. Box 7018
Chicopee, MA 01021-7018

Six *FREE* Weeks Without Cost or Obligation!

☐ Please send me a *FREE* six week trial subscription to
BARRON'S.

If I decide it's not for me, I'll write "cancel" on your invoice, return it and owe nothing.
Otherwise, I will receive 26 additional weeks—making 32 in all—for only $55. That's the
regular price of a 26-week subscription, so my first six weeks cost me nothing.

Validate by initialing here _____

Name _____

Address _____ Suite/Apt. # _____

City _____ State _____ Zip _____

Note: Offer good for new subscribers only. Limit: Only six free weeks of Barron's per household.
Offer good till 12/31/93 only in the continental U.S.

2WNH

TESTS FOR CLAIMING SOMEONE AS YOUR DEPENDENT

TEST 1. RELATIONSHIP OR MEMBER OF HOUSEHOLD TEST

The person must be either:

Your relative—child, stepchild, adopted child, grandchild, great-grandchild, son- or daughter-in-law, father- or mother-in-law, brother- or sister-in-law, parent, brother, sister, grandparent, stepparent, stepbrother or sister, half-brother or sister, and if related by blood, an uncle, aunt, niece, or nephew. These relatives do not have to live with you. However, a foster child qualifies only if he or she is a member of your household for the entire year, apart from temporary absences; *see* ¶1.20.

Or—any person, whether related or not, who is a member of your household for the entire year, except for temporary absences. The exemption is not allowed if the person was your spouse at any time during the year, or if your relationship with such person is in violation of state law; *see* ¶1.21.

TEST 2. GROSS INCOME TEST

Your child—If at the end of 1992 your child was under age 19, *or* was a full-time student under age 24, (¶1.23), his or her income does not matter. You can claim the child as your dependent if Tests 3, 4, and 5 are met. However, a child who was age 19-23 and not a full-time student at the end of the year, *or* who was age 24 or older, may be claimed as your dependent only if his or her gross income was less that $2,300 in 1992.

Other relatives or household members—must have gross income of less than $2,300 in 1992.

The $2,300 income limit will be adjusted for inflation in 1993.

TEST 3. SUPPORT TEST

You either contribute more than half the dependent's support, or contribute more than 10% and together with others contribute more than half; *see* ¶1.24 and ¶1.27.

Total the dollar amount of support spent on a dependent by you, by others, and by the dependent. If your contribution is:

More than 50% of the total spent—you claim the exemption.

More than 10% of the total spent and together with what you and the other contributors gave is more than 50% of the total spent—you or one of the others who also contributed more than 10% may claim the exemption. You and the others must decide who is to claim the exemption. If you take it, you must attach to your return a Form 2120, "Multiple Support Declaration," signed by each person who contributed more than 10%.

Less than 50%, either alone or with the contribution of others—neither you nor the other contributors may claim the exemption for the dependent.

Special support rules apply to divorced or separated parents; *see* ¶1.28.

TEST 4. CITIZENSHIP OR RESIDENT TEST

Your dependent is a United States citizen or national, or a resident of the United States, Canada, or Mexico; *see* ¶1.29.

TEST 5. JOINT RETURN TEST

Your married dependent does not file a joint return with his or her spouse; *see* ¶1.30 for an exception.

TEST 1. RELATIONSHIP TEST

¶1.20 If the other tests are met, you may claim an exemption for a dependent relative listed in this section, even if he or she is an adult, healthy, and capable of self-support. An unrelated person or distantly related person not listed may still qualify as an exemption under ¶1.21.

Your children:

Stepchildren. Your stepchild is considered your child.

Infants. A child born during the year is a dependent. For example, you may claim an exemption for the year for a child born on December 31.

A stillborn child may not be claimed as an exemption. The exemption is allowed for a child who was born alive even if the infant lived for only a moment.

Adopted children. A legally adopted child is considered your child. A child is legally adopted when a court decree is entered. In states allowing interlocutory (not final) decrees, you may claim the exemption in the year the interlocutory decree is entered. If a court decree has not been entered, a child may be your dependent provided he or she was placed with you for adoption by an authorized adoption agency and was a member of your household for the rest of the year. If the child has not been placed with you for adoption by an agency, you may claim the child as a dependent *only if* he or she was a member of your household for the entire tax year; *see* ¶1.21.

Foster child. A foster child is considered to be your child if he or she is a member of your household for the entire year except for temporary absences.

Other qualifying relatives. The following individuals also meet the relationship test: Your parent, grandparent, stepparent, grandchild, great-grandchild, brother, sister, half-brother, half-sister, stepbrother, stepsister, son- or daughter-in-law, father- or mother-in-law, brother- or sister-in-law. If related by blood, aunts, uncles, nieces and nephews also qualify.

Stepchild's husband or wife or child. Your stepchild's spouse does not meet the relationship test. Nor may you claim an exemption for a stepgrandchild if you file a separate return. They are not on the list of relatives qualifying. But you may claim them as exemptions on a joint return. On a joint return, it is not necessary that the close relationship exist between the dependent and the spouse who furnishes the chief support. It is sufficient that the relationship exists with either spouse.

Nephew, Niece, Uncle, and Aunt

Nephews, nieces, uncles, and aunts must be your blood relatives to qualify under the relationship test. For example, the brother or sister of your father or mother qualifies as your relative; their spouses do not. You may not claim your spouse's nephews, nieces, uncles, or aunts unless you file a joint return; see the following example.

EXAMPLE You contribute more than half of the support of the sister of your wife's mother (your wife's aunt). If you and your wife file a joint return, her aunt is allowed as an exemption on your joint return. But your wife's aunt's husband is not related by blood to you or your wife. You cannot claim an exemption for him, even on a joint return, unless he is a member of your household under ¶1.21.

In-laws. Brother-in-law, sister-in-law, father-in-law, mother-in-law, son-in-law, and daughter-in-law are relatives by marriage. You may claim them as exemptions if you meet the other tests in this chapter.

You may claim an exemption for a dependent who was related to you by marriage and whom you continue to support after divorce or death of your spouse.

EXAMPLE Allen has contributed all the support of his father-in-law since he was married. Allen's wife died in 1991. He continued sole support of his wife's father in 1992. Allen may claim him as an exemption in 1992.

Death during the year. If a relative died during 1992 but was supported by you while alive, and you meet the other tests listed in this chapter, you may claim an exemption.

EXAMPLE On January 21, 1992, your father died. Until that date, you contributed all of his support. You may claim him as an exemption for 1992. The full deduction is taken. Exemptions are not prorated.

UNRELATED OR DISTANTLY RELATED DEPENDENTS LIVING WITH YOU

¶1.21 A friend or a relative not listed in ¶1.20—such as a cousin who lives with you—can be your dependent. You may claim an unrelated or distantly related person as a dependent if the other dependent tests (see chart on page 19) are met and:

1. The person is a member of your household; and
2. Your home is his or her principal home for the entire year, except for absences when attending school, vacationing, or being confined to a hospital. You may not claim a friend as an exemption when you live in his or her house even though you provide support. You are living in his or her household—not your own. Also, you cannot claim an exemption for a friend who lives in your house and renders you services in return for your care.

EXAMPLES 1. You support a friend who lives in your house all year. You can claim him as a dependent member of your household if the gross income and citizenship tests are met.

2. You provide a home for an orphan for seven months. You cannot claim the child as a dependent. He or she did not live in your home for the entire year. However, if the child had been placed in your home for adoption by an authorized adoption agency, he or she may be claimed as your dependent although not a member of your household for the entire year; see adopted children rule at ¶1.20.

3. You support a cousin who lives in a house you own. However, you live elsewhere. You may not claim your cousin as a dependent. You two do not live in the same house.

Your spouse or former spouse. Under the tax law, one spouse is not considered a dependent of the other; see ¶1.19. If you are divorced or legally separated during the year, your former spouse cannot qualify as your dependent even if he or she is a member of your household for the whole year.

Exemption for Unmarried Mate

An exemption for an unmarried mate depends on local law. Where the relationship violates local law, no exemption may be claimed. As the following example indicates, local law prevails in disputes with the IRS about claiming an exemption in such cases.

EXAMPLE Ensminger lived in North Carolina with a woman whom he supported. When he claimed an exemption for her, the IRS disallowed the exemption, claiming that under North Carolina law, it is a misdemeanor for an unmarried man and woman to live together. When the Tax Court supported the IRS position, Ensminger appealed, arguing that the North Carolina law was an unconstitutional invasion of his right to privacy. The appeals court held that constitutionality was not an issue for the IRS and Tax Court to decide. The states are responsible for regulating domestic affairs. Federal tax law merely follows the direction of state law. If Ensminger lived in a state that did not hold his relationship illegal, he could claim the exemption.

In a similar case, a dependency exemption was allowed where the court ruled cohabitation did not violate Missouri law.

TEST 2. GROSS INCOME EARNED BY YOUR DEPENDENT

¶1.22 There is no gross income test for your dependent child who at the end of the year is (1) under age 19; or (2) a full-time student under age 24. He or she may earn any amount, and be claimed as an exemption, provided you meet the support test of ¶1.24 and the tests at ¶1.29 and ¶1.30.

The gross income test applies only to—

Dependents who are not your children—such as parents, in-laws, sisters, brothers, uncles, aunts, and members of your household; *and*
Children who at the end of year are age 19 or over and not full-time students, *or* children who are full-time students age 24 or older at the end of the year; see ¶1.23.

Dependents' 1992 gross income must be less than $2,300. The gross income test requires your dependent to have a gross income of less than $2,300 in 1992. If a dependent earns $2,300 or more, he or she may not be claimed as an exemption, even if all of their support is provided by you. As noted above, the only exception is for your children who are under age 19 or who are full-time students under age 24; see ¶1.23.

Gross income here means income items included in the dependent's tax return. It does not include non-taxed items such as gifts and tax-exempt bond interest. Gross income for a service-type business is gross receipts without deductions of expenses and for a manufacturing or merchandising business is total sales less cost of goods sold. A partner's share of partnership gross income, not the share of net income, is treated as gross income.

Social Security benefits are treated as gross income only to the extent they are taxable under the rules of ¶34.3.

Gross income does not include income earned by a totally and permanently disabled individual at a school operated by a government agency or tax-exempt organization, if the school provides special instruction for alleviating the disability and the income is incidental to medical care received.

EXAMPLES 1. Jones gives $4,000 a year for his father's support. The father owns a two-family house. He lives in one apartment and rents the other for $200 a month, giving him a gross annual income of $2,400. After deducting interest and taxes, his net income is $1,200. Jones may not take his father as a dependent as his gross income is not under $2,300.

2. Your son, age 21 and *not* a full-time student (¶1.23) in 1992, received $10,000 in damages for personal injuries suffered in an accident. His only other income was bank interest of $450. Since the damages are excluded from gross income (¶12.10), the gross income test is satisfied. However, if your son used part of the damages to support himself, you may claim him as a dependent for 1992 only if your support contributions were larger; *see* the checklist of support items in ¶1.24.

3. Your widowed father received $5,000 in Social Security benefits which he used to support himself (¶1.24). He also received $1,200 in bank interest. Under ¶34.3, the benefits are not subject to tax and therefore not treated as gross income. His gross income of $1,200 is below the $2,300 limit. If you contributed more than $5,000 to his support, you meet the support test (¶1.24) and may claim your father as a dependent.

CHILDREN UNDER AGE 19 OR FULL-TIME STUDENTS UNDER AGE 24

¶1.23 The tax law provides the following tax break for dependent children. There is no gross income test for—

1. Your children who are under age 24 as of the end of the year if they are full-time students; *and*
2. Your children under age 19 as of the end of the year.

This rule applies to your child, stepchild, and adopted child. It also applies to a foster child who, for the entire year, is a member of your household. It does not apply to a grandchild, a son- or daughter-in-law, or a brother or sister who is a full-time student; they must have gross income of less than $2,300 to qualify as your dependent.

 Students Age 24 or Older

The favorable rule that disregards income of full-time students applies only to students who are under age 24 as of the end of the year. If your child was age 24 or older at the end of 1992 and had gross income of $2,300 or more, you may not claim him or her as your dependent.

Qualifying as a full-time student. A full-time student is one who attends school full time during at least five calendar months in the tax year. For example: attendance from February through some part of June—or from February through May and then at least one month from September through December—qualifies. The five months do not have to run consecutively. Attendance at a vocational, trade, or technical school for the five-month period qualifies, but not correspondence schools or on-the-job training courses.

EXAMPLES 1. Your unmarried daughter who is age 22 attended college full time until she graduated in June. The gross income test does not apply to her earnings in 1992. However, you must meet the support test (¶1.24) to claim her as your dependent.

2. Your son who is age 19 worked during the first half of the year and then starts college in September. You may not claim him as an exemption if he earned $2,300 or more. Although he is a full-time student, he did not attend school for at least five months during the year.

Night school. Your child who attends night school is considered a full-time student *only if* he or she is enrolled for the number of hours or classes that is considered full-time attendance at a similar daytime school.

 Support of Children Earning Income

Although there is no gross income test for your children who are under age 19 or who are full-time students under age 24, you must still meet the support test of ¶1.24 to claim them as your dependents. If your child has income, be prepared to show either that the income was not used for his or her support, or that your support contributions were larger. Use the checklists at ¶1.24 for determining what must be treated as "support."

TEST 3. 50% SUPPORT TEST

¶1.24 If your dependent has no financial means and you are the only person contributing to his or her support during the year, you can skip the following discussion on support. You meet the support test. You contribute 100% of the dependent's support. If, however, the dependent or other persons or organizations contribute to his or her support, you have to determine whether your contribution exceeds 50% of the dependent's total support.

Meeting the support test. Follow these steps to figure support: (1) Total the value of the support contributed by you, by the dependent and by others for the dependent. Use the checklists below for determining what to include in total support and what to exclude. (2) Determine your share of the total. If your share is more than 50% of the dependent's total support, you meet the support test. It does not matter how many months or days you provided the support; only the total cost of the support is considered. If the dependent or some other person or organization contributed 50% or more of the dependent's support, you may not take the exemption. If the dependent or someone else did not contribute 50% or more of the support, and you contributed more than 10% of the total support, you may be able to claim the exemption under the multiple support agreement rule of ¶1.27.

CHECKLIST OF SUPPORT ITEMS:

- Food and lodging; *see* ¶1.25.
- Clothing.
- Medical and dental expenses, including premiums paid for health insurance policies and supplementary Medicare.
- Education expenses such as tuition, books and supplies. If your child receives a student loan and is the primary obligor, the loan proceeds are considered his or her own support contribution. This is true even if you are a guarantor of the loan. Scholarships received by full-time students are *not* treated as support; *see* the following checklist of non-support items.
- Cars and transportation expenses. Include the cost of a car bought for a dependent as support. If you buy a car but register it in your own name, the cost of the car is *not* support provided by you, but any out-of-pocket expenses you make for car operating expenses are part of your support contribution.
- Recreation and entertainment. A TV set bought for your child or other dependent is support. Also include costs of summer camp, singing and dancing lessons, and musical instruments, as well as wedding expenses.

Divorced or separated parents contributing to support of their children should follow the special support rules at ¶1.28.

Personal savings, Social Security and tax-free income may be support. In figuring a person's total support, include his or her tax-exempt income, personal savings, and Social Security benefits if actually used for support items such as food, lodging or clothing; *see* the checklist on page 21. Also include support items that are financed by loans. Income that is invested and not actually spent for support is not included in the earner's total support.

Where husband and wife are paid Social Security benefits in one check made out in their joint names, 50% is considered to be used by each spouse unless shown otherwise.

Government benefits. In figuring whether you have provided more than 50% of the dependent's support, you have to consider certain government benefits as support provided by a third party. For example, welfare, including AFDC (Aid to Families With Dependent Children), food stamps or housing payments based on need are support payments from the state, assuming they are used for support items. G.I. Bill education assistance is support provided by the government. Foster care payments by a child placement agency to parents are support provided by the agency and not by the parents.

When a person joins the Armed Forces, the value of board, lodging and clothing they receive are treated as the government's support contribution. However, if *you* are in the Armed Forces, dependency allotments withheld from your pay and used to support your dependents are included in *your* support contributions for them. Also included in your support contribution is a military quarters allowance covering a dependent.

CHECKLIST OF ITEMS NOT COUNTED AS SUPPORT:

- Federal, state, local income taxes and Social Security taxes paid by the dependent from his or her own income.
- Funeral expenses.
- Life insurance premiums.
- Medicare Part A (basic Medicare) and Part B (Supplementary Medicare benefits). In one case the IRS argued that Medicaid benefits were includable in total support but the Tax Court disagreed, holding that Medicaid is similar to excludable Medicare benefits.
- Medical insurance benefits received by the dependent.
- Scholarships received by your child, stepchild, or legally adopted child who is a full-time student for at least five calendar months during the year. Scholarship aid is counted as support contributed by the child if he or she is not a full-time student for at least five months. Naval R.O.T.C. payments and payments made under the War Orphans Educational Assistance Act are scholarships that are not counted as support. State aid to a handicapped child for education or training, including room and board, is a scholarship.

EXAMPLES 1. Your son invests half of his earnings from a part-time job and spends the other half on recreation. The invested earnings are not treated as support. If your support payments exceed the amount he spent for recreation, and no one else contributes to his support, you meet the support test.

2. Your father receives his Social Security benefits of $4,400, which he spends on food, clothes, transportation, and recreation. He also receives $300 in bank interest. The $4,400 spent is his contribution to his own support. You pay his rent, utilities, medical expenses, and other necessities. If your payments exceed $4,400 and no one else contributes to his support, you may claim your father as a dependent.

3. Social Security benefits paid to children of deceased workers *which are used for their support* are treated as the children's contribution to their own support. Follow this rule even though benefits are paid to you as the child's parent or custodian. If the Social Security benefits used for a child's support are more than half of the child's total support, no one may claim the child as a dependent.

LODGING AND FOOD AS SUPPORT

¶1.25 You count as support *the fair rental value* of a room, apartment, or house in which the dependent lives. In your estimate, you include a reasonable allowance for the rental value of furnishing and for heat and other utilities. You do *not* add payments of rent, taxes, interest, depreciation, paint, insurance, and utilities. These are presumed to be accounted for in the fair rental estimate. The fair rental value of lodging you furnish a dependent is the amount you could reasonably expect to receive from a stranger for the lodging.

Does dependent live in own home? If the dependent lives in his or her own home, treat the total fair rental value as his or her own contribution to support. However, if you help maintain his or her home by giving cash, or you directly pay such expenses as the mortgage, real estate taxes, fire insurance premiums, and repairs, you reduce the total fair rental value of the home by the amount you contributed.

EXAMPLE You contribute $7,000 as support to your father who lives in his own home, which has a fair rental value of $6,000 a year. He uses $2,600 of the money you give him to pay real estate taxes on the property. He spends $3,000 of his Social Security for recreation and invests the rest. He has no gross income (¶1.22) and receives no other support. His total support is computed as follows:

Cash contributed by you	$7,000
Fair rental value of house ($6,000 less	
$2,600 for taxes)	3,400
Social Security spent	3,000
Father's total support	$13,400

You may claim your father as a dependent because your contribution of $7,000 exceeds half of his total support.

If you lived with your dependent rent-free in his or her home, the fair rental value of lodging furnished to you must be offset against the amounts you spent for your dependent in determining the net amount of your contribution to his or her support.

Do you pay for a relative's care in a health facility? If you pay part of a relative's expenses for care in a state-supported hospital or nursing home, your payment is a support contribution. If you make a lump-sum contribution covering a relative's stay in an old-age home or other care facility, you prorate your payment over the relative's life expectancy to determine the current support contribution.

EXAMPLES 1. A son secures his father's placement in a religious home for a lump-sum payment of $89,600. The payment was determined on the basis of $11,200 a year over the father's life expectancy of eight years. The home makes no refund if the father dies within eight years. The son counts $11,200 as an annual contribution to his father's support. If this is more than half of his father's yearly support costs, the son may claim the exemption. If the father fails to reach his life expectancy, the son may *not* deduct any unused part of the $89,600 as a charitable deduction.

2. In 1992, your father was a patient in a state hospital. The state required you to pay part of his expenses and you paid the state $6,200. In the state budget report for 1992, the average cost of maintaining an individual in the hospital was listed as $12,000. As you contributed over half of your father's support, you may claim him as a dependent. If he required special care, such as private nursing or a major operation, the actual cost to the state agency for maintaining him during the year, rather than the average cost, would be used to measure your father's total support.

Food and other similar household expenses. If the dependent lives with you, you divide your total food expenses equally among all the members of your household, unless you have records showing the exact amount spent on the dependent; *see* the examples in ¶1.26. If he or she does not live with you, you count the actual amount of food expenses spent by or for that dependent.

EXAMPLES OF ALLOCATING SUPPORT

¶1.26

The following examples illustrate how you allocate various items of support.

EXAMPLES

1. Your father lives in your home with you, your spouse, and your three children. He receives Social Security benefits of $9,800; half of which ($4,900) he spends for his own clothing, travel and recreation. You spend $6,600 for food during the year. You also paid his dental bill of $500. You estimate the annual fair rental value of the room furnished him is $3,600. Your father's total support is:

Social Security used for support	$4,900
Share of food costs (⅙ of $6,600)	1,100
Dental bill paid by you	500
Rental value of room	3,600
	$10,100

You can claim him as a dependent. You contributed more than half his total support, or $5,200 ($3,600 lodging, $500 dental, $1,100 food).

2. Your parents live with you, your spouse, and your two children in a house you rent. The fair rental value of their room is $3,000. Your father receives a non-taxable government pension of $5,200, all of which he spent equally for your mother and himself for clothing and recreation. Your parents' only other income was $3,000 of tax-exempt interest. They did not make any other contributions towards their own support. Your total expense in providing food for the household is $6,000. You pay heat and utility bills of $1,200. You paid your mother's medical expenses of $600. You figure the total support of your parents as follows:

	Father	Mother
Fair rental value of room	$1,500	$1,500
Pension used for their support	2,600	2,600
Share of food costs (⅙ of $6,000)	1,000	1000
Medical expenses for mother		600
	$5,100	$5,700

The support you furnish your father, $2,500 (lodging, $1,500; food, $1,000), is *not* over half of his total support of $5,100. The support you furnish your mother, $3,100 (lodging, $1,500; food, $1,000; medical, $600), *is* over half of her total support of $5,700. You do not consider the cost of heat and utilities. It is presumed to be in the rental value estimate. You can claim your mother as a dependent but not your father. Since she did not have taxable income, the gross income test (¶1.22) is satisfied.

Earmarking Support to One Dependent

If you are contributing funds to a household consisting of several persons and the amount you contribute does not exceed 50% of the total support cost of the household, you may be able to claim an exemption for at least one dependent by earmarking your support to his or her use, if your contribution will exceed 50% of this dependent's support costs. You may do this by marking your checks for the benefit of the dependent, or by having a statement of your support arrangement at the time you start your payments. The IRS says its agents will generally accept such evidence of your arrangement. If you do not designate for whom you are providing support, your contribution is allocated equally among all members of a household (*see* Example 1 below).

EXAMPLES

1. A husband who lives apart from his family without a divorce or legal separation sends his wife $3,240 to meet household expenses. A son and daughter live with her. The wife contributes from her own funds $6,480; an uncle sends her $1,080. The total amount going to meet household expenses from all sources is $10,800. On a separate return, the husband may not claim any exemptions for his children; his contributions are less than 50% of their total support. As he has not earmarked who is to get his contributions, his payments are allocated equally among the three members of the household. Each is considered to have received $1,080 from him. His contribution of $1,080 is less than half of the total support of $3,600 allocated to each child.

Contributed by:		Allocated to:		
	Wife	Son	Daughter	Total
Wife	$2,160	$2,160	$2,160	$6,480
Husband	1,080	1,080	1,080	3,240
Uncle	360	360	360	1,080
Total	$3,600	$3,600	$3,600	$10,800

2. Same facts as Example 1 except that the husband notes on his monthly checks of $270 that $180 is for his son; $90 for his daughter. He may claim his son as an exemption on a separate return; he has contributed more than half of the son's support. As total household costs of $10,800 are allocated equally among the three household members, the wife's contribution is reallocated to make up for the difference created by the husband's increased support to the son. Here, the wife is considered to have contributed $3,240 to her own support.

Contributed by:		Allocated to:		
	Wife	Son	Daughter	Total
Wife	$3,240	$1,080	$2,160	$6,480
Husband		2,160	1,080	3,240
Uncle	360	360	360	1,080
Total	$3,600	$3,600	$3,600	$10,800

3. Assume in the above example the mother contributed only $6,240 and her son contributed $240. There would be no change in tax consequences; however, the allocation of support contributions would differ. The son's contribution is added to the total household costs, which are allocated equally among the family members to find how much applies to each person's support. However, in determining support contributions, the son is treated as contributing $240 to his own support.

Contributed by:		Allocated to:		
	Wife	Son	Daughter	Total
Wife	$3,240	$ 840	$2,160	$6,240
Son		240		240
Husband		2,160	1,080	3,240
Uncle	360	360	360	1,080
Total	$3,600	$3,600	$3,600	$10,800

MULTIPLE SUPPORT AGREEMENTS

¶1.27 Are you and others sharing the support of one person, but with no one individual providing more than half of his or her total support? You may claim the dependent as an exemption if:

1. You gave more than 10% of the support;
2. The amount contributed by you and others to the dependent's support equals more than half the support;
3. Each contributor could have claimed the exemption—except that he or she gave less than half the support; *and*
4. Each contributor who gave more than 10% agrees to let you take the exemption. Each signs a Form 2120, "Multiple Support Agreement." You then attach the forms to your return.

EXAMPLES 1. You and your two brothers contribute $2,000 each toward the support of your mother. She contributes $1,000 of her own to support herself. Your two sisters contribute $500 each. Thus, the total support comes to $8,000. Of this, each brother gave 25% ($2,000 ÷ $8,000) for a total of 75%. Each sister gave 6¼% ($500 ÷ $8,000). You or one of your brothers may claim the exemption. The total of your contributions is more than half of your mother's support. Each of you contributed more than 10%. Among yourselves, you must decide who is to claim the exemption. If you claim the exemption, your brothers must sign Forms 2120, which you attach to your return. If one of your brothers claims the exemption, you sign a Form 2120, which is attached to the return of the brother who claims the exemption. Since neither of your sisters furnished more than 10%, neither can claim the exemption; they need not sign Forms 2120.

2. You and your sister each furnished $1,000 to your mother's support. Her two cousins who did not live with her each contributed $1,500. No one may claim her as an exemption. Half of her support of $5,000 was not furnished by persons such as you and your sister, who but for the support test could claim an exemption for her. A cousin does not meet the relationship or member of household test.

3. Your mother's support totals $6,000; you contribute $1,800; your brother, $1,200; your father, $600; and your mother from her savings contributes $2,400. Assume your father does not file a tax return claiming your mother as an exemption. You and your brother cannot use your father's contribution to meet the more than 50% test required by rule 2 above. Your father may not join in a multiple support agreement because your mother is not his dependent for tax purposes although an exemption may be claimed for a wife on the basis of the marital relationship; *see* ¶1.19.

4. Same facts as in Example 3, but another brother contributed $200. Then you and your brothers may join in a multiple support agreement; your contributions exceeded 50% of the support.

DIVORCED OR SEPARATED PARENTS

¶1.28 Divorced or separated parents who together provide more than half of their child's support apply special custodial rules to determine which parent has met the support test for a dependent child. If the following tests are met, the support test is considered to have been met by the "custodial parent"—the parent who had custody for a greater portion of the year than did the other parent. This generally allows the custodial parent to claim the exemption for the child, although the right to the exemption may be waived in favor of the noncustodial parent, or the noncustodial parent may be able to claim it under a divorce decree or separation agreement.

These rules for parents apply only if all of the following tests are met:

1. *Marital status:* You are divorced or legally separated under a decree of divorce or separate maintenance, or separated under a written agreement, or live apart at all times during the last six months of 1992.

2. *Support:* In 1992, over half of the child's total support is from you and the other parent. Neither parent may claim the exemption, unless the parents together give more than 50% of the child's support. If a parent remarries, support contributions made by the new spouse are treated as contributions of the parent. They are not treated as contributions of a third person. If the parties contributing support enter into a multiple support agreement, under which one of them claims the exemption under the rules at ¶1.27, follow those rules; these special rules for parents do not apply.

Form **2120** (Rev. May 1991) Department of the Treasury Internal Revenue Service	**Multiple Support Declaration** ▶ Attach to Form 1040 or Form 1040A.	OMB No. 1545-0071 Expires 5-31-94 Attachment Sequence No. **50**

Name of taxpayer claiming person as a dependent

Richard Adams

Social security number

X10 0X X11X

During the calendar year 19 **92**, I paid over 10% of the support of

Dorothy Adams
(Name of person)

I could have claimed this person as a dependent except that I did not pay over 50% of his or her support. I understand that this person is being claimed as a dependent on the income tax return of

Richard Adams
(Name)

10 Maple Avenue, City State 10XXX
(Address)

I agree not to claim this person as a dependent on my Federal income tax return for any tax year that began in this calendar year.

Elaine Stevens
(Your signature)

0XX 0X 1X10
(Your social security number)

2/5/93
(Date)

2500 Elm Street City State 1X000
(Address)

Avoiding the Exemption Phaseout Rule

Under the exemption phaseout applied to higher-income taxpayers (¶1.32), it might be advisable for the lower-earning spouse to claim the exemptions for the children. The higher income spouse may get no benefit from the exemptions if the phaseout applies.

3. *Custody:* The child is in the custody of one or both parents for more than half of 1992. If the children are not in the custody of either or both parents for more than half of 1992, the exemption is claimed by the person who contributed more than 50% of the child's support, or if there is no such person, by the person designated in a multiple support agreement under the rules at ¶1.27.

Custodial parent. If the previously discussed three tests are met and you had custody for a greater portion of the year than the other parent, you are treated as meeting the support test regardless of your actual support contribution. Thus you may claim the exemption unless barred under the rules of ¶1.22, ¶1.29, ¶1.30 or ¶1.32. However, you may allow the noncustodial parent to claim the exemption by waiving your right to it. The noncustodial parent may also be able to claim it under a divorce decree or separation agreement discussed in the next column.

Custody is determined by the terms of a decree of divorce or separate maintenance or a written separation agreement. If a decree or agreement does not determine custody, the parent with physical custody for most of the year is the custodial parent.

If you were divorced or separated during 1992, and before that time you had joint custody of the child, the custodial parent is the parent who has custody for the greater period of time after the separation.

Custodial parent's waiver on Form 8332. As the custodial parent, you may waive the exemption by signing a written declaration on Form 8332. When you use the form for the first time, you indicate whether you are waiving the exemption for that year only or for future years as well. The noncustodial parent attaches Form 8332 to his or her return and claims the exemption for the child. If the exemption has been waived for future years as well, a copy of Form 8332 must be attached to the noncustodial parent's returns for the later years.

Noncustodial parent granted exemption under agreement after 1984. If you are the noncustodial parent and have been given the unconditional right to the exemption by a divorce decree or separation agreement that went into effect after 1984, you may attach to your return instead of Form 8332 copies of: The page of the agreement allowing you the exemption, the cover page, on which you should write the custodial parent's Social Security number, and the signature page showing the date of the agreement.

Non custodial parent's exemption under pre-1985 agreement. If a pre-1985 agreement gives you, as noncustodial parent, the exemption, you must provide at least $600 for the support of the child in 1992. The exemption must be specifically allocated to you in a decree of divorce or separate maintenance or a written agreement executed before January 1, 1985. On your return, check the box for pre-1985 agreements.

TEST 4. THE DEPENDENT IS A CITIZEN OR RESIDENT

¶1.29 To claim an exemption for a dependent, the dependent must have at some time during 1992 qualified as:

Citizen or resident of the United States;
United States national (one who owes permanent allegiance to the U.S.; principally, a person born in American Samoa who has not become a naturalized American citizen); *or*
Resident of Canada or Mexico. Resident status is discussed at ¶1.14.

Form **8332** (Rev. September 1990) Department of the Treasury Internal Revenue Service	**Release of Claim to Exemption for Child of Divorced or Separated Parents** ▶ **Attach to Tax Return of Parent Claiming Exemption.**	OMB No. 1545-0915 Expires 6-30-93 Attachment Sequence No. **51**

Name(s) of parent claiming exemption   John Jones
Social security number   XX0 10 10XX

Part I   Release of Claim to Exemption for Current Year

I agree not to claim an exemption for   Lisa Jones
Name(s) of child (or children)

for the tax year 19 **92** .

Karen Jones
Signature of parent releasing claim to exemption

XX0 X0-X0XX
Social security number

1/25/93
Date

If you choose not to claim an exemption for this child (or children) for future tax years, complete Part II, as explained in the instructions below.

Part II   Release of Claim to Exemption for Future Years

I agree not to claim an exemption for   Lisa Jones
Name(s) of child (or children)

for tax year(s) "all future years"
(Specify. See instructions.)

Karen Jones
Signature of parent releasing claim to exemption

XX0 X0X0XX
Social security number

1/25/93
Date

Dependents in Puerto Rico. A U.S. citizen or resident may take a dependent who is living in Puerto Rico and is a citizen of Puerto Rico as an exemption, provided he is not a citizen of a foreign country. Most citizens of Puerto Rico are also citizens of the United States.

Child born abroad. A child born in a foreign country whose one parent is a nonresident alien and whose other parent is a U.S. citizen qualifies as a U.S. citizen and thus as a dependent if the other tests are met.

If you are a U.S. citizen living abroad, you may claim as a dependent a legally adopted child who is not a U.S. citizen or resident if for the entire year your home was the child's principal residence and he or she is a member of your household.

TEST 5. THE DEPENDENT DOES NOT FILE A JOINT RETURN

¶1.30 You may not claim an exemption for a dependent who files a joint return with another. For example, you meet all of the four tests entitling you to an exemption for your married daughter as your dependent. She files a joint return with her husband. You may not claim her as your dependent on your tax return.

Exception. Even if your dependent files a joint return, you may claim the exemption where the income of each spouse is under the income limit required for filing a return and the couple files a joint return merely to obtain a refund of withheld taxes. Under these circumstances, their return is considered a refund claim, and a dependency exemption may be claimed.

Should Dependent File Separately?

When a married dependent files a joint return, the parent cannot claim an exemption. The loss of the exemption may cost a parent more than the joint return saves the couple. In such a case, it may be advisable for the couple to file separate returns so that the parent may benefit from the larger tax saving.

If the couple decides to revoke their election to file jointly and then file separately in order to preserve the exemption for a parent, they must do so before the filing date for the return. Once a joint return is filed, the couple may not, after the filing deadline, file separate returns for the same year.

REPORTING SOCIAL SECURITY NUMBERS OF DEPENDENTS

¶1.31 On your 1992 return, you must list the Social Security number of each dependent who is at least a year old. You must include the Social Security number of each child who reaches age one before 1993. Also include the number of parents or other adults you claim as dependents. A Social Security number also must be shown for a dependent living in Mexico or Canada; you may apply for the number at the U.S. embassy or consulate office. Failure to list the number may result in a $50 penalty.

To obtain a Social Security number for a dependent child, contact your local Social Security Administration office. Parents of newborn children may request a number when filling out hospital birth-registration records. If the number is applied for but not yet received by the filing due date, write "applied for" on your return.

PHASEOUT OF PERSONAL EXEMPTIONS FOR HIGHER INCOME TAXPAYERS

¶1.32 You will lose part or all of the $2,300 deduction for each 1992 personal exemption if your adjusted gross income (AGI) exceeds the threshold amount for your filing status. *Adjusted gross income* is explained at ¶13.7. On your 1992 Form 1040, adjusted gross income is the amount shown on line 32.

If your filing status is	Phaseout applies if AGI exceeds*	Exemptions completely phased out if AGI exceeds
Married filing jointly or qualified widow(er)	$157,900	$280,400
Head of household	131,550	254,050
Single	105,250	227,750
Married filing separately	78,950	140,200

*These thresholds will be adjusted for inflation after 1992.

How the phaseout increases your marginal tax rate. The phaseout *increases* 1992 marginal rates according to the number of exemptions claimed. For earnings within the $122,500 phaseout range ($61,250 for married filing separately), the effective marginal tax rate increases by about 0.54% for each exemption. Thus, taxpayers who support many dependents are hurt more by the phaseout than taxpayers who support few dependents; see the example in Chapter 28.

TABLES SHOWING THE PERSONAL EXEMPTION PHASEOUT

Use the tables on pages 27–28 to find the phaseout amount for your AGI and filing status. Use Table 1 if you are single, Table 2 if you are married filing jointly, Table 3 if head of household, or Table 4 if married filing separately. The tables show the percentage reduction for your adjusted gross income and also the amount you may deduct for *each* personal exemption. After finding the deductible amount for each exemption, multiply that amount by the number of exemptions you claim; this is your deduction on Form 1040.

The tables incorporate the phaseout formula specified in the law: 2% of each personal exemption is phased out for every $2,500 of AGI, or part of $2,500, above the $105,250 threshold for singles, $131,550 for heads of households, and $157,900 for married filing jointly and qualified widow(er)s; *see* Example 2. For married persons filing separately, the 2% phaseout applies to every $1,250 of AGI, or part of $1,250, above the $78,950 threshold.

EXAMPLES 1. You are single and claim two exemptions—one for yourself and one for your dependent parent. Your 1992 AGI is $158,000. Table 1 shows that for AGI of $158,000, each exemption is reduced by 44% and that $1,288 (56% of $2,300) is deductible for each exemption. As you claim two exemptions, your allowable deduction is $2,576 (2 × $1,288).

2. You and your spouse file a 1992 joint return with AGI of $173,486. You claim three personal exemptions—one for each of you and one for your son. Table 2 shows that for AGI of $173,486, the phaseout reduction is 14%, and that $1,978 is deductible for each exemption. You deduct $5,934 (3 × $1,978). Using Table 2 saves you the trouble of applying the 2% phaseout formula that is set out in the law to get the phaseout reduction of 14%:

1. Excess of AGI over threshold ($173,486 − $157,900)	$15,586
2. Divide Step 1 by $2,500, rounded to next highest whole number ($15,586 / $2,500 = 6.2 rounded to 7)	7
3. Multiply Step 2 by 2% for phaseout percentage	14%

EXEMPTION PHASEOUT
Table 1: Single

Adjusted gross income over	Up to	Each exemption is reduced by	Deduct for each exemption	Adjusted gross income over	Up to	Each exemption is reduced by	Deduct for each exemption
$105,250	$107,750	2%	$2,254	$167,750	$170,250	52%	$1,104
107,750	110,250	4	2,208	170,250	172,750	54	1,058
110,250	112,750	6	2,162	172,750	175,250	56	1,012
112,750	115,250	8	2,116	175,250	177,750	58	966
115,250	117,750	10	2,070	177,750	180,250	60	920
117,750	120,250	12	2,024	180,250	182,750	62	874
120,250	122,750	14	1,978	182,750	185,250	64	828
122,750	125,250	16	1,932	185,250	187,750	66	782
125,250	127,750	18	1,886	187,750	190,250	68	736
127,750	130,250	20	1,840	190,250	192,750	70	690
130,250	132,750	22	1,794	192,750	195,250	72	644
132,750	135,250	24	1,748	195,250	197,750	74	598
135,250	137,750	26	1,702	197,750	200,250	76	552
137,750	140,250	28	1,656	200,250	202,750	78	506
140,250	142,750	30	1,610	202,750	205,250	80	460
142,750	145,250	32	1,564	205,250	207,750	82	414
145,250	147,750	34	1,518	207,750	210,250	84	368
147,750	150,250	36	1,472	210,250	212,750	86	322
150,250	152,750	38	1,426	212,750	215,250	88	276
152,750	155,250	40	1,380	215,250	217,750	90	230
155,250	157,750	42	1,334	217,750	220,250	92	184
157,750	160,250	44	1,288	220,250	222,750	94	138
160,250	162,750	46	1,242	222,750	225,250	96	92
162,750	165,250	48	1,196	225,250	227,750	98	46
165,250	167,750	50	1,150	227,750		100	0

Table 2: Married Filing Jointly

Adjusted gross income over	Up to	Each exemption is reduced by	Deduct for each exemption	Adjusted gross income over	Up to	Each exemption is reduced by	Deduct for each exemption
$157,900	$160,400	2%	$2,254	$220,400	$222,900	52%	$1,104
160,400	162,900	4	2,208	222,900	225,400	54	1,058
162,900	165,400	6	2,162	225,400	227,900	56	1,012
165,400	167,900	8	2,116	227,900	230,400	58	966
167,900	170,400	10	2,070	230,400	232,900	60	920
170,400	172,900	12	2,024	232,900	235,400	62	874
172,900	175,400	14	1,978	235,400	237,900	64	828
175,400	177,900	16	1,932	237,900	240,400	66	782
177,900	180,400	18	1,886	240,400	242,900	68	736
180,400	182,900	20	1,840	242,900	245,400	70	690
182,900	185,400	22	1,794	245,400	247,900	72	644
185,400	187,900	24	1,748	247,900	250,400	74	598
187,900	190,400	26	1,702	250,400	252,900	76	552
190,400	192,900	28	1,656	252,900	255,400	78	506
192,900	195,400	30	1,610	255,400	257,900	80	460
195,400	197,900	32	1,564	257,900	260,400	82	414
197,900	200,400	34	1,518	260,400	262,900	84	368
200,400	202,900	36	1,472	262,900	265,400	86	322
202,900	205,400	38	1,426	265,400	267,900	88	276
205,400	207,900	40	1,380	267,900	270,400	90	230
207,900	210,400	42	1,334	270,400	272,900	92	184
210,400	212,900	44	1,288	272,900	275,400	94	138
212,900	215,400	46	1,242	275,400	277,900	96	92
215,400	217,900	48	1,196	277,900	280,400	98	46
217,900	220,400	50	1,150	280,400		100	0

EXEMPTION PHASEOUT
Table 3: Head of Household

Adjusted gross income over	Up to	Each exemption is reduced by	Deduct for each exemption	Adjusted gross income over	Up to	Each exemption is reduced by	Deduct for each exemption
$131,550	$134,050	2%	$2,254	$194,050	$196,550	52%	$1,104
134,050	136,550	4	2,208	196,550	199,050	54	1,058
136,550	139,050	6	2,162	199,050	201,550	56	1,012
139,050	141,550	8	2,116	201,550	204,050	58	966
141,550	144,050	10	2,070	204,050	206,550	60	920
144,050	146,550	12	2,024	206,550	209,050	62	874
146,550	149,050	14	1,978	209,050	211,550	64	828
149,050	151,550	16	1,932	211,550	214,050	66	782
151,550	154,050	18	1,886	214,050	216,550	68	736
154,050	156,550	20	1,840	216,550	219,050	70	690
156,550	159,050	22	1,794	219,050	221,550	72	644
159,050	161,550	24	1,748	221,550	224,050	74	598
161,550	164,050	26	1,702	224,050	226,550	76	552
164,050	166,550	28	1,656	226,550	229,050	78	506
166,550	169,050	30	1,610	229,050	231,550	80	460
169,050	171,550	32	1,564	231,550	234,050	82	414
171,550	174,050	34	1,518	234,050	236,550	84	368
174,050	176,550	36	1,472	236,550	239,050	86	322
176,550	179,050	38	1,426	239,050	241,550	88	276
179,050	181,550	40	1,380	241,550	244,050	90	230
181,550	184,050	42	1,334	244,050	246,550	92	184
184,050	186,550	44	1,288	246,550	249,050	94	138
186,550	189,050	46	1,242	249,050	251,550	96	92
189,050	191,550	48	1,196	251,550	254,050	98	46
191,550	194,050	50	1,150	254,050		100	0

Table 4: Married Filing Separately

Adjusted gross income over	Up to	Each exemption is reduced by	Deduct for each exemption	Adjusted gross income over	Up to	Each exemption is reduced by	Deduct for each exemption
$78,950	$80,200	2%	$2,254	$110,200	$111,450	52%	$1,104
80,200	81,450	4	2,208	111,450	112,700	54	1,058
81,450	82,700	6	2,162	112,700	113,950	56	1,012
82,700	83,950	8	2,116	113,950	115,200	58	966
83,950	85,200	10	2,070	115,200	116,450	60	920
85,200	86,450	12	2,024	116,450	117,700	62	874
86,450	87,700	14	1,978	117,700	118,950	64	828
87,700	88,950	16	1,932	118,950	120,200	66	782
88,950	90,200	18	1,886	120,200	121,450	68	736
90,200	91,450	20	1,840	121,450	122,700	70	690
91,450	92,700	22	1,794	122,700	123,950	72	644
92,700	93,950	24	1,748	123,950	125,200	74	598
93,950	95,200	26	1,702	125,200	126,450	76	552
95,200	96,450	28	1,656	126,450	127,700	78	506
96,450	97,700	30	1,610	127,700	128,950	80	460
97,700	98,950	32	1,564	128,950	130,200	82	414
98,950	100,200	34	1,518	130,200	131,450	84	368
100,200	101,450	36	1,472	131,450	132,700	86	322
101,450	102,700	38	1,426	132,700	133,950	88	276
102,700	103,450	40	1,380	133,950	135,200	90	230
103,450	105,200	42	1,334	135,200	136,450	92	184
105,200	106,450	44	1,288	136,450	137,700	94	138
106,450	107,700	46	1,242	137,700	138,950	96	92
107,700	108,950	48	1,196	138,950	140,200	98	46
108,950	110,200	50	1,150	140,200		100	0

PART II

REPORTING YOUR INCOME

In this part, you will learn what income is taxable and what income is tax-free, and how to report income on your tax return.

Pay special attention to—

- Form W-2, which shows your taxable wages and provides other important information on fringe benefits received.
- Tax-free fringe benefit plans.
- Reporting rules for interest and dividend income.
- Reporting gains and losses from sales of property. The 28% maximum rate on long-term capital gains may provide you with a benefit.
- Rules for tax-free exchanges of like-kind property.
- Planning for retirement distributions. Lump-sum distributions from employer plans may qualify for special averaging or tax-free rollover.
- IRA restrictions on contributions and distributions. Penalties for distributions before age $59\frac{1}{2}$ and after age $70\frac{1}{2}$ may be avoided by advance planning.
- Passive activity restrictions. Losses from rentals or passive business operations are generally not allowed, but a special $25,000 loss allowance may be available.
- Reporting refunds of state and local taxes. A refund of previously deducted taxes is generally taxable unless you had no benefit from the deduction.
- Cancellation of debts. When your creditor cancels debts you owe, you generally have taxable income, but there are exceptions for debts discharged while you are bankrupt or insolvent.
- Damages received in court proceedings. Learn when these are tax free and when taxable.

TAXABLE WAGES, SALARY AND OTHER COMPENSATION

Except for tax-free fringe benefits, practically everything you receive for your work or services is taxed, whether paid in cash, property, or services. Your employer will generally report your taxable compensation on Form W-2 and other information returns, such as Form 1099 for certain retirement payments and compensatory distributions of securities. Do not reduce the amount you report on your return by withholdings for income taxes, Social Security taxes, union dues, or U.S. Savings Bond purchases. Your Form W-2 does not include in taxable pay your qualifying salary-reduction contributions to a retirement plan, although the amount may be shown on the form.

Attach Copy B of Form W-2 to your return; do not attach Form 1099.

Unemployment benefits are fully taxable. The benefits are reported to the IRS on Form 1099-G. You do not have to attach your copy of Form 1099-G to your return.

REPORTING SALARY AND WAGE INCOME

¶2.1 The key to reporting your pay is Form W-2, sent to you by your employer. It lists your taxable wages, which may include not only your regular pay, but also other taxable items such as taxable fringe benefits. A guide to the important information listed on Form W-2 is on page 32.

Your employer reports your taxable pay under a simple rule. Unless the item is specifically exempt from tax, you are taxed on practically everything you receive for your work whether paid in cash, property, or services. Taxed pay includes:

Back pay	Honoraria
Bonuses	Jury fees
Commissions	Salaries
Director's fees	Severance pay
Dismissal pay	Sick pay
Employee prizes or awards	Tip
Expense allowances or reimbursements under nonaccountable plans	Vacation pay
	Wages

The items that the law specifically excludes from tax are discussed in Chapter 3. The most common tax-free benefits are employer-paid premiums for health and accident plans and certain group-term life insurance plans for coverage up to $50,000.

Withholdings for retirement plans. Amounts withheld as your contribution to your pension or profit-sharing account are generally taxable unless they are tax-deferred under the limits allowed for Section 401(k) plans (¶7.18), simplified employee pension plans

(¶8.11), or tax-sheltered annuity plans (¶7.20). Tax-deferred amounts are reported in Box 17 of Form W-2. Courts have held that amounts withheld from the pay of both U.S. Civil Service employees and city and county civil service employees are taxable to the employees.

Wages withheld for compulsory forfeitable contributions to a nonqualified pension plan are not taxable if these conditions exist:

1. The contribution is forfeited if employment is terminated prior to death or retirement.
2. The plan does not provide for a refund of employee contributions and, in the administration of the plan, no refund will be made. Where only part of the contribution is subject to forfeiture, the amount of withheld contribution not subject to forfeiture is taxable income.

Check with your employer to determine the status of your contributions.

Assigning your pay. You may not avoid tax on income you earned by assigning the right to payment to another person. For example, you report earnings donated by you but paid directly by your employer to a charity. You may claim a contribution deduction for the donation; *see* Chapter 14. The IRS allowed an exception for doctors working in a clinic. They were required to assign to a foundation all fees derived from treating patients with limited income (teaching cases). The fees were not taxable.

Salary advances. Salary paid in advance for services to be rendered in the future is generally taxable in the year received if it is subject to your free and unrestricted use.

Child's wages. A parent is not taxed on wages paid for a child's services even if payment is made to the parent. However, a parent is taxed on income from work contracted for by the parent even if the child assists in the labor. For example, a parent whose children helped her with part-time work at home claimed that the children should be taxed on 70% of the income since they did 70% of the work. The IRS claimed that the parent was taxable on all the income because she, not the children, was the true earner, and the Tax Court agreed. Although the company knew that the children were doing part of the work, it had no agreement with them.

Employee leave-sharing plan. Some companies allow employees to contribute their unused leave into a "leave fund" for use by other employees who have suffered medical emergencies. If you use up your regular leave and benefit from additional leave that has been donated to the plan, the benefit is taxable and will be reported as wages on Form W-2.

YEAR-END PAYCHECKS

¶2.2 As an employee, you use the cash basis method of accounting. This means that you report all income items in the year they are actually received and deduct expenses in the year you pay them. You are also subject to the "constructive receipt rule," which requires you to report income not actually received but which has been credited to your account, subject to your control, or put aside for you. Thus, if you received a paycheck on December 31, 1992, you must report the pay on your 1992 return, even though you do not cash or deposit it to your account until 1993. This is true even if you receive the check after banking hours and cannot cash or deposit it until the next year. If your employer does not have funds in the bank and asks you to hold the check before depositing it, you do not have taxable income until the check is cashed. If pay for services rendered in 1992 is paid by check dated for 1993, the pay is taxable in 1993.

The IRS has ruled that an employee who is not at home on December 31 to take delivery of a check sent by certified mail must still report the check in that year. However, where an employee was not at home to take certified mail delivery of a year-end check that she did not expect to receive until the next year, the Tax Court held the funds were taxable when received in the following year.

1 Control number			OMB No. 1545-0008					
2 Employer's name, address, and ZIP code National Computer, Inc. 100 Cambridge Avenue City, State 11XXX			6 Statutory employee ☐ Deceased ☐ Pension plan ☑ Legal rep ☐ 942 emp ☐ Subtotal ☐ Deferred compensation ☐ Void ☐					
			7 Allocated tips		8 Advance EIC payment			
			9 Federal income tax withheld 5,800		10 Wages, tips, other compensation 32,000			
3 Employer's identification number 11-X1XOX1X		4 Employer's state I.D. number 11-X1XOX1X	11 Social security tax withheld 2,046		12 Social security wages 33,000			
5 Employee's social security number OXX-11-X10X			13 Social security tips		14 Medicare wages and tips 33,000			
19 Employee's name, address, and ZIP code Charles V. Zahn 355 Joy Lane City, State 1XXX1			15 Medicare tax withheld 478.50		16 Nonqualified plans			
			17 See Instrs. for Box 17 D 1000.00		18 Other			
20		21	22 Dependent care benefits 1,500		23 Benefits included in Box 10			
24 State income tax 1,580	25 State wages, tips, etc. 32,000	26 Name of state State	27 Local income tax 765		28 Local wages, tips, etc. 32,000		29 Name of locality City	

Copy B To Be Filed With Employee's FEDERAL Tax Return   Department of the Treasury—Internal Revenue Service

Form **W-2 Wage and Tax Statement 1992**

This information is being furnished to the Internal Revenue Service.

Key to Your Form W-2

What You Should Know—

Amount In—	
Box 6	In Box 6 your employer identifies the following important tax information: ***Statutory employee.*** If this box is checked you get a tax break. You report your wage income and deductible job expenses on Schedule C. This treatment allows job expenses to avoid the 2% adjusted income (AGI) floor on Schedule A. *See* ¶40.5 for further details. ***Pension plan.*** If the box "Pension plan" is checked, this indicates that you were an active participant in an employer plan during the year. As an active participant, you may be unable to make deductible IRA contributions; IRA deductions start to phaseout if your AGI exceeds $25,000 and you are single, or $40,000 and you are married filing jointly; *see* Chapter 8. ***942 employee.*** This box will be checked if you worked in the employer's home as a babysitter, housekeeper, cook or butler, or you did similar household work. ***Deferred compensation.*** The box "Deferred compensation" is checked if you made salary deferrals to a 401(k) plan (¶7.18), tax-sheltered annuity (¶7.20), or simplified employee pension plan(¶8.11). In Box 17, the employer lists the total elective deferrals to these plans.
Box 7	***Allocated tips.*** If you worked in a restaurant employing at least 10 people, your employer will report in Box 7 your share of 8% of gross receipts unless you reported tips at least equal to that share (¶26.8). The amount shown here is not included in Box 10 wages, but you must add it to wages on Line 7 of Form 1040; you cannot file Form 1040A or 1040EZ.
Box 8	***Advance earned income payment.*** If you filed a Form W-5 asking for a part of the credit to be added to your wages, the amount of the advance is shown in Box 8. You report the advance as a tax liability when you file Form 1040 or 1040A. *See* Chapter 25 for details on claiming the increased earned income credit for 1992, and for advanced earned income payments.
Box 9	***Federal tax withholdings.*** This is the amount of federal income tax withheld from your pay. Enter the amount on Line 54, Form 1040, Line 28a, Form 1040A, or on Line 6, Form 1040EZ. If the amount plus estimated tax exceeds your tax liability, you are entitled to a refund for the excess payments.
Box 10	***Taxable wages and tips.*** Your taxable wages and tips are listed in Box 10. In Box 23, your employer lists the amount of taxable fringe benefits that have been included in Box 10. The value of tax-free fringe benefits is not shown on Form W-2. Mileage or per diem travel allowances will not be reported in Box 10 as taxable wages unless they exceed the IRS rate. *See* Box 17 below. Do not decrease the amount shown in Box 10 by the amount your employer withholds for income taxes, Social Security taxes, disability insurance payments, hospitalization insurance premiums, U.S. Savings Bonds, union dues, or payments to a creditor who has attached your salary. Box 10 does not include salary reduction contributions to a retirement plan. Compensation shown in Box 10 must be reported on Line 7 of Form 1040 or 1040A, or Line 1 of Form 1040EZ.
Boxes 11-13	***Social Security withholdings.*** Withholdings for Social Security coverage are at a rate of 6.20% on up to $55,500 of 1992 wages and tips. If your wages were $55,500 or more, Box 11 should show the maximum tax of $3,441. If you worked for more than one employer, and a total of more than $3,441 was withheld for Social Security taxes, you claim the excess as a tax payment on your tax return; *see* ¶26.2. Wages subject to Social Security withholdings are shown in Box 12. Elective deferrals to a 401(k) plan are included; Social Security withholding applies, although the deferrals are not subject to income tax and are not included in Box 10. Tips you reported to your employer are shown separately in Box 13. The total of Boxes 12 and 13 should not exceed $55,500.
Boxes 14-15	***Medicare tax withholdings.*** Wages and tips subject to Social Security tax (Boxes 12 and 13) are also subject to a 1.45% Medicare tax, except that the 1992 wage base is up to $130,200, rather than $55,500. Wages and tips up to $130,200 will be reported in Box 14. Medicare tax withholdings are shown in Box 15. This amount should not exceed $1,887.90 (1.45% × $130,200).
Box 16	***Nonqualified plans distributions.*** Distributions shown in Box 16 are from a nonqualified deferred compensation plan, or a Section 457 plan (¶7.21). Do not report these distributions separately since they have already been included as taxable wages in Box 10.
Box 17	In Box 17, your employer identifies various fringe benefits you received and certain other items by using IRS codes to label each item. No more than three codes should be entered. If you have more than three Box 17 items, the additional items should be shown on a separate Form W-2. ***Elective deferrals to retirement plans.*** If you made elective salary deferrals to an employer retirement plan, Box 6 will be checked and your contribution (including any excess over the annual deferral limit) is shown in Box 17. Deferrals to a 401(k) plan (¶7.18) should be labeled with Code D. For example, if you made contributions of $4,500 to a 401(k) plan, your employer would enter D 4500 in Box 17. Code E is used for deferrals to a 403(b) tax-sheltered annuity plan (¶7.20), Code F for deferrals to a simplified employee pension (¶8.11), Code G for deferrals to a Section 457 plan (¶7.21), and Code H for contributions to a pension plan created before June 25, 1959 and funded only by employee contributions. If you participated in more than one plan, the total tax-free deferral for 1992 is generally $8,728. However, for 403(b) plans, the limit may be $9,500 or sometimes even higher (¶7.20). Deferrals in excess of the limit must be reported as wages on Line 7 of Form 1040 or Form 1040A. ***Travel allowance reimbursements.*** If you received a flat mileage allowance from your employer for business trips (¶20.36); or a *per diem* travel allowance to cover meals, lodging, and incidentals (¶20.35); and the allowance *exceeded* the IRS rate, the amount up to the IRS rate (the nontaxable portion) is shown in Box 17 using Code L. Do not report this amount as income. If you did *not* substantiate the excess over the IRS rates, that excess is included as taxable wages in Box 10.

Amount In—	What You Should Know—
Box 17 (continued)	**Group-term life insurance over $50,000.** The cost of coverage over $50,000 is taxable. It is shown in Box 17 using Code C. It is also included in Box 10 wages, Box 12 Social Security wages, and Box 14 Medicare tax wages and tips. If you are a retiree or other former employee who received group-term coverage over $50,000, any uncollected Social Security tax is shown using Code M; uncollected Medicare tax, using Code N. The uncollected amount must be reported on Form 1040 in the section for "Other Taxes"; include it on the line for your "total tax" and write "Uncollected Tax" next to it. **Nontaxable sick pay.** If you contributed to a sick pay plan, an allocable portion of benefits received is tax free and is shown using Code J. **Uncollected Social Security and Medicare taxes on tips.** If your employer could not withhold sufficient Social Security on tips, the uncollected amount is shown using Code A. For uncollected Medicare tax, Code B is used. This amount must be reported on Form 1040 in the section for "Other Taxes;" include the amount on the line for your "total tax" and write "Uncollected Tax" next to it.
Box 18	**Miscellaneous payments.** Your employer may use Box 18 to report payments such as union dues, educational assistance, moving expenses, or health insurance premiums.
Box 22	**Dependent care benefits.** Reimbursements from your employer for dependent care expenses and the value of employer-provided care services under a qualifying plan (¶3.6) are included in Box 22. Amounts in excess of $5,000 are also included as taxable wages in Box 10. Generally, amounts up to $5,000 are tax free, but you must determine the amount of the exclusion on Form 2441 if you file Form 1040, or on Schedule 2 if you file Form 1040A. The tax-free amount reduces expenses eligible for the dependent care credit; *see* Chapter 25.
Box 23	**Taxable fringe benefits.** If you received taxable benefits such as for personal use of a company car (¶3.4) or for educational assistance exceeding tax-free limits (¶3.5), your employer shows the amount in Box 23. Do not separately report it as income, since it has already been included in Box 10 as taxable wages.
Box 24 and 27	**State and local taxes.** If you itemize deductions on Schedule A, do not forget to deduct the state and local tax withholdings shown in Boxes 24 and 27. These amounts offset tax liability on your state and local tax returns.

PAY RECEIVED IN PROPERTY IS TAXED

¶2.3 Your employer may pay you with property instead of cash. You report the fair market value of the property as wages.

EXAMPLE For services rendered, you receive a check for $10,000 and property having a fair market value of $5,000. You report $15,000 as wages.

If you receive your company's stock as payment for your services, you include the value of the stock as pay in the year you receive it. However, if the stock is nontransferable or subject to substantial risk of forfeiture, you do not have to include its value as pay until the restrictions no longer apply; see ¶32.6. You must report dividends on the restricted stock in the year you receive the income.

If you receive your employer's note which has a fair market value, you are taxed on the value of the note less what it would cost you to discount it. If the note bears interest, report the full face value. But do not report income if the note has no fair market value. Report income on the note only when payments are made on it.

A debt cancelled by an employer is taxable income.

A salesman employed by a dealer has taxable income on receipt of "prize points" redeemable for merchandise from a distributor.

GIFTS FROM EMPLOYERS

¶2.4 A payment may be called a gift but still be taxable income. Any payment made in recognition of past services or in anticipation of future services or benefits is taxable even if the employer is not obligated to make the payment. Exceptions for employee achievement awards are discussed at ¶3.9.

To prove a gift is tax free, you must show that the employer acted with pure and unselfish motives of affection, admiration, or charity. This is difficult to do, given the employer-employee relationship.

A gift of stock by majority stockholders to key employees has been held to be taxable income.

WHEN COMMISSIONS ARE TAXED

¶2.5 Earned commissions are taxable in the year they are credited to your account and subject to your drawing, whether or not you actually draw them.

On your 1992 tax return, you do not report commissions which were earned in 1992 but which cannot be computed or collected until a later year.

EXAMPLE You earn commissions based on a percentage of the profits. In 1992 you draw $10,000 from your account. However, at the end of 1992 the full amount of your commissions is not known because profits for the year have not been figured. In January 1993, your 1992 commissions are computed to be $15,000, and the $5,000 balance is paid to you. The $5,000 is taxable in 1993 even though earned in 1992.

You may not postpone tax on earned commissions credited to your account in 1992 by not drawing them until 1993 or a later year. However, where a portion of earned commissions is not withdrawn because your employer is holding it to cover future expenses, you are not taxed on the amount withheld.

Advances against unearned commissions. Under standard insurance industry practice, an agent who sells a policy does not earn commissions until premiums are received by the insurance company. However, the company may issue a cash advance on the commissions before the premiums are received. Agents have claimed that they may defer reporting the income until the year the premiums are earned. The IRS, recognizing that in practice companies rarely demand repayment, requires that advances be included in income in the year received if the agent has full control over the advanced funds. A repayment of unearned commissions in a later year is deducted on Schedule A; *see* ¶2.9.

Salesmen have been taxed on commissions received on property bought for their personal use. In one case, an insurance agent was taxed on commissions paid to him on his purchase of an insurance policy. In another case, a real estate agent was taxed on commissions he received on his purchase of land. A salesman was also taxed for commissions waived on policies he sold to friends, relatives, and employees.

An insurance agent's kickback of his commission is taxable where agents may not under local law give rebates or kickbacks of premiums to their clients.

UNEMPLOYMENT BENEFITS ARE TAXABLE

¶2.6 All unemployment benefits you receive in 1992 from a state agency or the federal government are taxable. You should receive Form 1099-G, showing the amount of the payments. Report the payments separately from wages on Line 20 of Form 1040 or Line 12 of Form 1040A.

Supplemental unemployment benefits paid from company financed funds are taxable as wages and not reported as unemployment compensation. Such benefits are usually paid under guaranteed annual wage plans made between unions and employers.

Unemployment benefits from a private or union fund to which you voluntarily contribute dues are taxable as "other" income on Form 1040, but only to the extent the benefits exceed your contributions to the fund. Your contributions to the fund are not deductible.

Worker's compensation payments are not taxable; *see* ¶2.12.

Taxable unemployment benefits include federal trade readjustment allowances (1974 Trade Act), airline deregulation benefits (1978 Airline Deregulation Act), and disaster unemployment assistance (1974 Disaster Relief Act).

If you had to repay supplemental unemployment benefits because of receipt of trade readjustment allowances (1974 Trade Act), taxable unemployment benefits are reduced by repayments made in the same year. If you repay the benefits in a later year, the benefits are taxed in the year of receipt and a deduction may be claimed in the later year. If the repayment is $3,000 or less, the deduction is claimed on the line for "total adjustments" on page 1 of Form 1040. If the repayment exceeds $3,000, a deduction or a credit may be claimed under the rules of ¶2.9.

STRIKE PAY BENEFITS AND PENALTIES

¶2.7 Strike and lockout benefits paid out of regular union dues are taxable as wages unless the payment qualifies as a gift, as discussed in the next column. However, if you have made *voluntary* contributions to a strike fund, benefits you receive from the fund are tax free up to the amount of your contributions and taxable to the extent they exceed your contributions.

Strike benefits as tax-free gifts. Here are factors indicating that benefits are gifts: Payments are based on individual need; they are paid to both union and nonunion members; and no conditions are imposed on the strikers who receive benefits.

If you receive benefits under conditions by which you are to participate in the strike and the payments are tied to your scale of wages, the benefits are taxable.

CAUTION   ## Strike and Lockout Benefits

Strike benefits paid by a union out of regular dues are taxable wages unless you can show they are in the nature of "gifts."

Strike pay penalties. Pay penalties charged striking teachers are not deductible. State law may prohibit public school teachers from striking and charge a penalty equal to one day's pay for each day on strike if they do strike. For example, when striking teachers returned to work after a one-week strike, a penalty of one week's salary was deducted from their pay. Although they did not actually receive pay for the week they worked after the strike, they earned taxable wages. Furthermore, the penalty is not deductible. No deduction is allowed for a fine or penalty paid to a government for the violation of a law.

DEFERRING TAX ON PAY

¶2.8 If you want to avoid current tax on pay, you may contract with your employer to defer pay to future years. To reduce possible IRS opposition, it is advisable to enter into a deferral compensation arrangement before the year in which the services are to be performed; for example, agree in 1992 to defer pay for 1993 services to 1994 or later years. Furthermore, to defer pay to a future period, you must take some risk. You cannot have any control over your deferred pay account. If you are not confident of your employer's ability to pay in the future, you should not enter into a deferred pay plan.

If IRS tests are met, a trust arrangement, commonly nicknamed a "rabbi trust," can be used by an employer to hold deferred pay contributions. Employees (or their beneficiaries) are not taxed until payments are received from the trust, provided that trust assets are available to the employer's general creditors in case of insolvency or bankruptcy, and the employees may not assign their trust interests to their own creditors.

An employee is not taxed on employer contributions to a qualified cash or deferred arrangement (401(k) plan) even though the employee had the option to take the cash; *see* ¶7.17. Qualified salary reductions under a simplified employee pension plan (SEP) (¶8.11) or tax-sheltered annuity plan (¶7.20) are also not taxed, even though you could have received cash currently.

DID YOU RETURN INCOME RECEIVED IN A PRIOR YEAR?

¶2.9 Did you return income in 1992 such as salary or commissions which you reported in a prior taxable year because it appeared you had an unrestricted right to it in the earlier year? If so, you may deduct the repayment as a miscellaneous itemized deduction. If the repayment exceeds $3,000, the deduction is claimed on Line 25 of Schedule A and is *not* subject to the 2% adjusted gross income (AGI) floor (¶19.1). However, the law is not clear on the issue of whether a deduction of

$3,000 or less is subject to the 2% floor; the IRS takes the position that the 2% floor applies.

Repayments Exceeding $3,000

If the repayment exceeds $3,000, a special law (Section 1341) gives this alternative: Instead of claiming an itemized deduction from 1992 income, you may recompute your tax for the prior year as if the income had not been reported. The difference between the actual tax paid in the prior year and the recomputed tax may be claimed as a credit on your 1992 return. The credit is claimed on Line 59 of Form 1040: write to the left of the line "IRC 1341." If you claim the repayment as a miscellaneous itemized deduction, enter it on Line 25 of Schedule A, where it is *not* subject to the 2% floor. Choose either the credit or the itemized deduction, whichever gives you the larger tax reduction.

The Section 1341 credit does not apply to the refund of income arising from the sale of inventory items.

Repayment of supplemental unemployment benefits. Where repayment is required to qualify for trade readjustment allowances, you may deduct the repayment from gross income. Claim the deduction on Line 30 of Form 1040, the line for "total adjustments," and to the left of the line write "subpay TRA." The deduction is allowed even if you do not itemize. If repayment is $3,000 or more, you have the choice of a deduction or claiming a credit based on a recomputation of your tax for the year supplemental unemployment benefits were received, as previously explained.

Repayment of Disallowed T & E Expenses

If a "hedge" agreement between you and your company requires you to repay salary or T & E expenses if they are disallowed to the company by the IRS, you may claim a deduction in the year of repayment. According to the IRS, you may not recalculate your tax for the prior year and claim a tax credit under the rules of Section 1341. An appeals court has rejected the IRS position and allowed a tax recomputation under Section 1341 to an executive who returned part of a disallowed salary under the terms of a corporate by-law.

WAIVER OF EXECUTOR'S AND TRUSTEE'S COMMISSIONS

¶2.10 Commissions received by an executor are taxable as compensation. An executor may waive commissions without income or gift tax consequences by giving a principal legatee or devisee a formal waiver of his or her right to commissions within six months after his or her initial appointment or by not claiming commissions at the time of filing the usual accountings.

The waiver may not be recognized if he or she takes any action that is inconsistent with the waiver. An example of an inconsistent action would be the claiming of an executor's fee as a deduction on an estate, inheritance, or income tax return.

A bequest to an executor is tax free.

DISABILITY AND WORKER'S COMPENSATION

	See ¶		See ¶
Sick pay is taxable	2.11	Employer and federal government disability pensions	2.13
Worker's compensation is tax free	2.12		

SICK PAY IS TAXABLE

¶2.11 Sick pay is generally taxable as wages unless it qualifies as worker's compensation under the rules of ¶2.12. Payments received under accident or health plans are tax free if you paid the premiums. Payments from your employer's plan for certain serious permanent injuries are tax free; see ¶3.1.

Disability pensions are discussed at ¶2.13.

Sick pay received from your employer is subject to withholding as if it were wages. Sick pay from a third party such as an insurance company is not subject to withholdings unless you request it on Form W-4S.

WORKER'S COMPENSATION IS TAX FREE

¶2.12 You do not pay tax on worker's compensation payments for job-related injuries or illness. However, your employer might continue paying your regular salary but require you to turn over your worker's compensation payments. Then you are taxed on the difference between what was paid to you and what you returned.

EXAMPLE You are injured while at work and are out of work for two months. Your company continues your weekly salary of $475. You also receive worker's compensation of $100 a week, which you give to your employer. The $100 is tax free. The balance of $375 a week is considered taxable wages.

To qualify as tax-free worker's compensation, the payments must be made under the authority of a *law* that provides compensation for on-the-job injury or illness. Payments made under a labor agreement do not qualify; *see* the examples on page 36.

Job-Related Injury or Illness

Not all payments for job-related illness or injury qualify as tax-free worker's compensation. For example, payments to a government employee under the Civil Service Retirement Act are not in the nature of worker's compensation because the payments are made regardless of whether disability is caused by on-the-job injuries. Unless payments are restricted to on-the-job injury or illness, payments are taxable even if a particular employee's payments are in fact based on job-related injuries.

Effect of worker's compensation on Social Security. For purposes of figuring whether Social Security benefits are taxable

(¶34.2), worker's compensation that reduces Social Security or equivalent Railroad Retirement benefits is treated as a Social Security (or Railroad Retirement) benefit received during the year. Thus, the worker's compensation may be indirectly subject to tax under ¶34.3.

Is Sick Leave Tax Free Worker's Compensation?

According to the Tax Court, sick leave may qualify as tax-free worker's compensation if it is paid under a specific worker's compensation statute or similar government regulation that authorizes the sick leave payment for job-related injuries or illness. *See* examples 1, 3, and 4 below.

EXAMPLES 1. A teacher, injured while working, received full salary during a two-year sick leave. She argued that the payments, made under board of education regulations, were similar to worker's compensation and thus tax free. The IRS disagreed; the regulations were not the same as a worker's compensation statute. The Tax Court supported the teacher. Although not made under a worker's compensation statute, the payments were made because of job-related injuries and were authorized by regulations having the force of law.

2. A disabled New York City policeman argued that sick leave payments in 1978 under a union labor contract were tax-free worker's compensation because his disability was work related. However, the IRS, Tax Court, and an appeals court disagreed. The payments were made under a labor contract and not a worker's compensation statute or pursuant to government regulations. Furthermore, even if authorized by a statute or regulations, the officer's sick leave would be taxable since under the labor contract, officers received sick pay whether or not their injury or illness was work related. That this officer's injuries were in fact job related does not make his benefits tax free when he could have received benefits in any event.

Note: Under a New York City law effective for line-of-duty injuries after 1987, a police officer's sick leave qualifies as tax-free worker's compensation.

3. The IRS, relying on the court decision in Case 2, claimed that a police officer in Lynbrook, N.Y., was subject to tax on line-of-duty disability pay because the payment was under a labor agreement with the Police Benevolent Association (PBA). The Tax Court supported the police officer's claim that the payments were authorized by a specific state law requiring full salary for job-related police injuries. The PBA agreement did not affect the officer's rights to those state law payments. Furthermore, Lynbrook treated the case as a worker's compensation claim and in fact received reimbursement for the payments made to the officer from the state worker's compensation board.

4. A Los Angeles sheriff injured on the job retired on disability and, under the Los Angeles worker's compensation law, was allowed to elect sick pay in lieu of the regular worker's compensation amount because the sick pay was larger. The IRS argued that the sheriff had merely received taxable sick pay because he would have received the same amount as sick pay if his injuries had been suffered in a personal accident. However, the Tax Court allowed tax-free treatment. The sick leave was paid under a worker's compensation law that applied solely to work-related injuries. The fact that sick leave may also have been available to other employees under other laws does not mean that it may not be included as an option under a worker's compensation statute. The policeman in Case 2 was distinguished by the Tax Court on the grounds that the labor contract in that case did not distinguish between personal and work-related injuries; here, the Los Angeles law which authorized the payment made that distinction.

The IRS announced that it does not agree with the Tax Court's decision allowing full tax-free treatment. According to the IRS, benefits up to the regular worker's compensation amount should be tax free but excess amounts should be taxed.

EMPLOYER AND FEDERAL GOVERNMENT DISABILITY PENSIONS

¶2.13 Disability pensions financed by your employer are reported as wage income unless they are for severe permanent physical injuries that qualify for tax-free treatment under the rules of ¶3.1 or they are tax-free government payments as discussed below. Turn to ¶34.7 to see if you may claim a tax credit for the receipt of a disability pension. A credit, subject to income limitations, is allowed for disability payments received while you are under the age of 65 and permanently and totally disabled.

Taxable disability pensions are reported as wages until you reach the minimum retirement age under the employer's plan. After reaching minimum retirement age, payments are reported as a pension under the rules of ¶7.25.

Federal government services. Certain disability pensions from the military or federal government agencies are tax free. Military disability benefits from the Veterans Administration are tax free, as are payments for combat and terrorist attack-related injuries. Other disability pensions for personal injuries or sickness resulting from active service in the armed forces are *taxable* if you joined the service after September 24, 1975.

Military disability payments are tax free if on September 24, 1975, you were entitled to military disability benefits or if on that date you were a member of the armed forces (or reserve unit) of the U.S. or any other country or were under a binding written commitment to become a member. A similar tax-free rule applies to disability pensions from the following government agencies if you were entitled to the payments on September 24, 1975, or were a member of the service (or committed to joining) on that date: The Foreign Service, Public Health Service, or National Oceanic and Atmospheric Administration. The exclusion for pre-September 25, 1975, service applies to disability pensions based upon percentage of disability. However, if a disability pension was based upon years of service, you do not pay tax on the amount that would be received based upon percentage of disability.

Veterans Administration benefits. Disability pensions from the Veterans Administration (now called the Department of Veterans Affairs) are not taxed. Military retirees who receive disability benefits from other government sources are not taxed on amounts equal to the benefits they would be entitled to receive from the VA. If you retire from the military and are later given a retroactive award of VA disability benefits, retirement pay during the retroactive period is tax free (other than a lump-sum readjustment payment upon retirement) to the extent of the VA benefit.

Pension based on combat-related injuries. Tax-free treatment applies to payments for combat-related injury or sickness which is incurred as a result of any one of the following activities: (1) as a direct result of armed conflict; (2) while engaged in extra-hazardous service, even if not directly engaged in combat; (3) under conditions simulating war, including maneuvers or training; or (4) which is caused by an instrumentality of war, such as weapons.

Terrorist attacks. Tax-free treatment applies to a disability pension paid to a civilian U.S. employee for injuries incurred as a direct result of a violent attack which the Secretary of State determines to be a terrorist attack and which occurred while the employee was working for the United States in the performance of official duties outside the United States.

3

FRINGE BENEFITS

The tax law specifically exempts from tax certain types of employer-furnished fringe benefits if they meet tests discussed in this chapter. The most common tax-free benefits are accident and health plans, group-term life insurance plans, dependent care plans, education assistance plans, tuition reduction plans, cafeteria plans, and plans providing employees with discounts, no-additional-cost services, or employer-subsidized meal facilities.

Highly compensated individuals may be taxed on certain benefits from such plans if nondiscrimination rules are not met.

HEALTH, ACCIDENT, GROUP INSURANCE, AND DEATH BENEFITS

TAX-FREE EMPLOYER ACCIDENT AND HEALTH PLANS

¶**3.1** You are not taxed on *contributions* your employer makes to a health or accident plan to cover you, your spouse, or your dependents. If you are temporarily laid off and continue to receive health coverage, the employer's contributions during this layoff period are tax free. If you are retired, you do not pay tax on insurance paid by your former employer. Medical coverage provided to the family of a deceased employee is tax free since it is treated as a continuation of the employee's fringe-benefit package.

Coverage provided to a live-in companion is taxable where the relationship violates local law; the person is not a qualifying "dependent."

Tax-free premiums include group hospitalization premiums paid by an employer or former employer if you are retired. Medicare premiums paid by your employer are not taxed. If you retire and have the option of receiving continued coverage under the medical plan or a lump-sum payment covering unused accumulated sick leave instead of coverage, the lump sum amount is reported as income at the time you have the option to receive it. If you elect continued coverage, the amount reported as income may be deductible as medical insurance if you itemize deductions; *see* ¶17.6.

Tax-free health benefits from employer plans. You are not taxed on benefits received from your employer's plan if they are a reimbursement of medical expenses or payment for permanent physical injury, as detailed on page 38. However, the tax-free exclusion for reimbursements does not apply to amounts received by certain highly compensated employees from a *self-insured* plan that fails discrimination tests; *see* page 39.

Key to Fringe Benefits

Fringe Benefit—	Tax Pointer—
Athletic facilities	The fair market value of athletic facilities, such as gyms, swimming pools, golf courses, and tennis courts, is tax free if the facilities are on property owned or leased by the employer (not necessarily the main business premises) and substantially all of the use of the facilities is by employees, their spouses, and dependent children. Such facilities must be open to all employees on a nondiscriminatory basis in order for the company to deduct related expenses.
Child or dependent care plans	The value of day care services provided or reimbursed by an employer under a written, nondiscriminatory plan is tax free up to a limit of $5,000, or $2,500 for married persons filing separately. Expenses are excludable if they would qualify for the dependent care credit; see Chapter 25. On your tax return, you must report employer-provided benefits to figure the tax-free exclusion. Tax-free employer benefits reduce eligibility for the dependent care tax credit. See ¶3.6 for details.
De minimis (minor) fringe benefits	These are small benefits that are administratively impractical to tax, such as occasional supper money and taxi fares for overtime work, company parties or picnics, occasional theater or sporting event tickets, and discount transit passes for commuting by public transportation; see ¶3.8.
Discounts on company products and services	Services from your employer that are usually sold to customers are tax free if your employer does not incur additional costs in providing them to you; see ¶3.14. Merchandise discounts and other discounted services are also eligible for a tax-free exclusion; see ¶3.15.
Education plans	Tax-free treatment is allowed for employer-paid undergraduate and graduate expenses up to $5,250 under nondiscriminatory plans, but this benefit ends June 30, 1992, unless Congress extends the law. Expenses over $5,250 in 1992 may also be tax free if the courses are job related; see ¶3.5. See the Supplement for an update on a proposal to extend the exclusion.
Employee achievement awards	Achievement awards are taxable unless they qualify under special rules for length of service or safety achievement; see ¶3.9.
Group-term life insurance	Premiums paid by employers are not taxed if policy coverage is $50,000 or less; see ¶3.2.
Health and accident plan benefits	Premiums paid by an employer are tax free. Benefits under an employer plan are also generally tax free; see ¶3.1.
Interest-free or low-interest loans	Interest-free loans received from your employer may be taxed; see ¶4.30.
Legal services plans	An exclusion of up to $70 is allowed for employer payments to a nondiscriminatory group legal services plan before July 1, 1992. See the Supplement for an update on a proposal to extend the exclusion.
Tuition reductions	Tuition reductions for courses below the graduate level are generally tax free. Graduate students who are teaching or research assistants are not taxed on tuition reduction unless the reduction is compensation for teaching services; see ¶3.5.
Working condition benefits	Benefits provided by your employer that would be deductible if you paid the expenses yourself are a tax-free working condition fringe benefit. Company cars are discussed at ¶3.4, other working condition benefits at ¶3.7.

Reimbursed medical expenses. Tax-free payments include specific reimbursements of medical expenses for yourself, your spouse, or any dependent. Payment does not have to come directly to you; it may go directly to those to whom you owe money for medical expenses. Tax-free treatment does not apply to amounts you would have received anyway, such as sick leave that is not dependent on actual medical expenses. Reimbursements for cosmetic surgery do not qualify for tax-free treatment, unless the surgery is for disfigurement related to congenital deformity, disease, or injury from an accident.

Reimbursements for your dependents' medical expenses are tax free, even if you may not claim them as personal exemptions because they had more than $2,300 of income or filed a joint return. Furthermore, if you are divorced and your children have health coverage under your plan, reimbursements of their expenses are not taxable to you, even if your ex-spouse claims them as dependents; *see* ¶1.28.

A qualifying dependent does *not* include a live-in mate where the relationship violates local law.

If the reimbursement is for medical expenses you deducted in a previous year, the reimbursement may be taxable income to you. *See* ¶17.5 for the rules on how reimbursements affect the medical deduction.

If you receive payments from more than one policy in excess of your actual medical expenses, the excess is taxable if your employer paid the entire premium; *see* examples in ¶17.5.

Special nondiscrimination rules for *self-insured* reimbursement plans are discussed at the end of this section.

Permanent physical injuries. Payments from an employer-plan are tax free if they are for the permanent loss of part of the body, permanent loss of use of part of the body, or for permanent disfig-

urement of yourself, your spouse, or a dependent. To be tax free, the payments must be based on the kind of injury and have no relation to the length of time you are out of work or prior years of service. If the employer's plan does not specifically allocate benefits according to the nature of the injury, the benefits are taxable even if an employee is in fact permanently disabled.

EXAMPLE After he loses a foot in an accident, Jones receives $5,000 as specified in his employer's plan. The payment is tax free because it does not depend on how long Jones is out from work.

An appeals court held that severe hypertension does not involve loss of a bodily part or function and thus does not qualify for the exclusion.

Apart from the exclusion, you may deduct as an itemized deduction any unreimbursed medical expense you have in connection with these injuries subject to the 7.5% adjusted gross income floor; *see* ¶17.4 for details.

Taxable benefits. Benefits not coming within the reimbursement or permanent injury categories are fully taxable if: (1) your employer paid all the premiums; and (2) you were not required to report the premiums as taxable income. If you and your employer each paid part of the premiums and you were not taxed on your employer's payment, the portion of the benefits allocable to the employer's contribution is taxed to you.

Disability payments from profit-sharing plan. The Tax Court has held that a profit-sharing plan may provide benefits that qualify for the exclusion for permanent disfigurement or permanent loss of bodily function. The plan must clearly state that its purpose is to provide qualifying tax-free benefits, and a specific payment schedule must be provided for different types of injuries. Without such provisions, payments from the plan are treated as taxable retirement distributions.

Continuing coverage for group health plans. Employers are subject to daily penalties unless they offer continuing group health and accident coverage to employees who leave the company and to spouses and dependent children who would lose coverage in the case of divorce or the death of the employee. The cost of the continuing coverage is paid by the employee or beneficiary. The employer must wait at least 45 days after continuing coverage is elected to require payment of premiums. Continuing coverage rules do not apply to small employers who in the previous calendar year had fewer than 20 employees on a typical day, or government agencies and churches. For other employers, continuing coverage must be offered in these situations:

1. An employee with coverage voluntarily or involuntarily leaves the company–unless termination is for gross misconduct. Employees who would lose coverage because of a reduction in hours must also be offered continuing coverage. If accepted, the coverage must last for at least 18 months. Within this period, an employee who elects continuing coverage is protected against the possibility of a coverage gap if he or she joins a new company that limits group health coverage for pre-existing conditions; the old employer's continuing coverage must remain available.

   Extended coverage may apply to disabled individuals. The coverage period is extended from 18 months to 29 months for individuals who notify the plan administrator within 60 days of a determination under Title II or XVI of the Social Security Act that they were disabled at the time of the termination of employment or reduction in hours.
2. On the death of a covered employee, continuing coverage must be offered to the surviving spouse and dependent children who are beneficiaries under the plan on the day before the death. Coverage must be for at least 36 months.
3. If a covered employee is divorced or legally separated, continuing coverage must be offered to the spouse and dependent children for at least 36 months.
4. If a covered employee becomes eligible for Medicare benefits, continuing coverage under the employer's plan must be offered to the employee's spouse and dependent children for at least 36 months.
5. If a dependent child becomes ineligible under the plan upon reaching a certain age, continuing coverage must be offered for at least 36 months.

60-Day Election Period

Employers must provide written notice of the continuing coverage option. If one of the above qualifying events occurs, eligible employees, spouses, and/or dependent children generally have 60 days to elect continuing coverage.

Discriminatory self-insured medical reimbursement plans. Reimbursements from an employer plan for medical expenses of an employee and his or her spouse and dependents are generally tax free. However, the exclusion does not apply to certain highly compensated employees and stockholders if the plan is self-insured and it discriminates on their behalf. A plan is self-insured if reimbursement is not provided by an unrelated insurance company. If coverage is provided by an unrelated insurer, these discrimination rules do not apply. If a self-insured plan is deemed discriminatory, rank-and-file employees are not affected; only highly compensated employees are subject to tax.

Highly compensated participants subject to these rules include employees owning more than 10% of the employer's stock, the highest paid 25% of all employees (other than employees who do not have to be covered under the law), and the five highest paid officers.

If highly compensated employees are entitled to reimbursement for expenses not available to other plan participants, any such reimbursements are taxable to them. For example, if only the five highest paid officers are entitled to dental benefits, any dental reimbursements they receive are taxable. However, routine physical exams may be provided to highly compensated employees (but not their dependents) on a discriminatory basis. This exception does not apply to testing for, or treatment of, a specific complaint.

If highly compensated participants are entitled to a higher reimbursement limit than other participants, any excess reimbursement over the lower limit is taxable to the highly compensated participant. For example, if highly compensated employees are entitled to reimbursements up to $5,000, while all others have a $1,000 limit, a highly compensated employee who receives a $4,000 reimbursement must report $3,000 ($4,000 received minus $1,000 lower limit) as income.

A separate nondiscrimination test applies to plan *eligibility*. The eligibility test requires that the plan benefit: (1) 70% or more of all employees, or (2) 80% or more of employees eligible to participate, provided that at least 70% of all employees are eligible. A plan not meeting either test is considered discriminatory unless proven otherwise. In applying these tests, employees may be excluded if they have less than three years of service, are under age 25, do part-time or seasonal work, or are covered by a union collective bargaining agreement. A fraction of the benefits received by a highly compensated individual from a nonqualifying plan is taxable. The fraction equals the total reimbursements to highly compensated participants divided by total plan reimbursements; benefits available only to highly compensated employees are disregarded. For example, assume that a plan failing the eligibility tests pays total reimbursements of $50,000, of which $30,000 are to highly compensated participants. A highly compensated executive who is reimbursed $4,500 for medical expenses must include in income $2,700:

$$\$4,500 \times \frac{\$30,000}{\$50,000}$$

Taxable reimbursements are reported in the year during which the applicable plan year ends. For example, in early 1993 you are reimbursed for a 1992 expense from a calendar-year plan. If under plan provisions the expenses are allocated to the 1992 plan year, the taxable amount should be reported as 1992 income. If the plan does not specify the plan year to which the reimbursement relates, the reimbursement is attributed to the plan year in which payment is made.

GROUP-TERM LIFE INSURANCE PREMIUMS

¶3.2 You are not taxed on your employer's payments of premiums on a policy of up to $50,000 on your life. You are taxed only on the cost of premiums for coverage of over $50,000 as determined by the IRS rates shown in the table on the next page. On Form W-2 your employer should include the taxable amount as wages in Box 10 and separately label the amount in Box 17. You may not avoid tax by assigning the policy to another person.

If two or more employers provide you with group-term insurance coverage, you get only one $50,000 exclusion. You must figure the taxable cost for coverage over $50,000 by using the IRS rates on the next page.

Regardless of the amount of the policy, you are not taxed if for your entire tax year the beneficiary of the policy is a tax-exempt charitable organization or your employer.

Your payments reduce taxable amount. If you pay part of the cost of the insurance, your payment reduces dollar-for-dollar the amount includable as pay on Form W-2.

Retirees. If you retired before 1984 at normal retirement age or on disability and are still covered by a company group-term life insurance policy, you are not taxed on premium payments made by your employer even if coverage is over $50,000. If you retired after 1983 because of disability and remain covered by your company's plan, you are not taxed even if coverage exceeds $50,000. Furthermore, if you retired after 1983 and are not disabled, you may qualify for tax-free coverage over $50,000 if the following tests are met:

1. The insurance is provided under a plan existing on January 1, 1984, or under a comparable successor plan;
2. You were employed during 1983 by the company having the plan, or a predecessor employer; and
3. You were age 55 or over on January 1, 1984.

However, even if the three tests are met, you may be taxed under the rule below for discriminatory plans if you retired after 1986 and were a key employee.

Key employees taxed under discriminatory plans. The $50,000 exclusion is not available to key employees unless the group plan meets nondiscrimination tests for eligibility and benefits. Key employees include: (1) more than 5% owners; (2) more than 1% owners earning over $150,000; (3) one of the 10 largest owners with compensation over $30,000; and (4) officers with 1992 pay over $56,111 (this amount is adjusted annually for inflation). If the plan discriminates, a key employee's taxable benefit is based on the larger of (1) the actual cost of coverage, or (2) the amount for coverage using the IRS rate table.

The nondiscrimination rules also apply to former employees who were "key" employees when they separated from service. The discrimination tests are applied separately with respect to active and former employees.

Group-term life insurance for dependents. Employer-paid coverage for your spouse or dependents is a tax-free *de minimis* fringe benefit (¶3.8) if the policy is $2,000 or less. For coverage over $2,000, you are taxed on the excess of the cost (determined under the IRS table below) over your after-tax payments for the insurance, if any.

Permanent life insurance. If your employer pays premiums on your behalf for permanent nonforfeitable life insurance, you report as taxable wages the cost of the benefit, less any amount you paid. A permanent benefit is an economic value that extends beyond one year and includes paid-up insurance or cash surrender value, but does not include, for example, the right to convert or continue life insurance coverage after group coverage is terminated. Where permanent benefits are combined with term insurance, the permanent benefits are taxed under formulas found in IRS regulations.

Taxable Rates for Insurance Coverage over $50,000

Age*—	Monthly premium per $1,000 of coverage above $50,000—
Under 30	$0.08
30–34	0.09
35–39	0.11
40–44	0.17
45–49	0.29
50–54	0.48
55–59	0.75
60–64	1.17
65–69	2.10
70 and over	3.76

*Age is determined at end of year.

EXAMPLE You are a 52-year-old executive provided with $200,000 of group-term coverage. The taxable amount is $864, based on $150,000 of excess coverage. For every $1,000 of coverage over $50,000, the taxable amount is $0.48 (premium) × 12 (months), or $5.76. Thus, for excess coverage of $150,000, the taxable amount is $864 ($5.76 × 150).

If you paid $120 towards the coverage, the taxable amount would be reduced to $744.

EMPLOYEES' DEATH BENEFITS MAY BE TAX FREE UP TO $5,000

¶3.3 An employer's payment to a deceased employee's beneficiary is tax free up to $5,000 if: (1) it is paid solely because of the employee's death; *and* (2) the employee did not have a nonforfeitable right to the payment while he or she was alive. An employee had a nonforfeitable right if he or she could have received the amount on demand or when he or she left the job. Where benefits were payable under an annuity contract, ask the company paying the benefits what part of the payments, if any, qualify for the $5,000 exclusion. Regardless of whether the employee had a nonforfeitable right, the exclusion applies to a qualified lump-sum distribution from a qualified pension or profit-sharing plan (¶7.7) or qualified annuity plan for employees of tax-exempt schools and charities; *see* ¶7.20.

Beneficiaries of retired employees who retired on disability before reaching mandatory retirement age under Federal Civil Service laws or the Retired Servicemen's Family Protection Plan may claim the $5,000 exclusion.

Payments received from a qualified Keogh plan by beneficiaries of self-employed individuals also qualify; *see* ¶7.7.

EXAMPLES 1. Products Co. pays Brown's widow a $5,000 bonus due Brown. The bonus is fully taxable. Brown had a right to the payment while he was alive. Similarly, payments for unused leave and uncollected salary are not tax free up to $5,000.

2. When an employee dies, Grand Co. pays the deceased's widow or other family beneficiary a death benefit of $1,000; the amount is tax free because the employee had no right to the amount while alive.

The death benefit exclusion per employee may not exceed $5,000 regardless of the number of employers making payments or beneficiaries receiving payments. The $5,000 exclusion is divided among all the beneficiaries. Each claims a part of the exclusion in the same ratio as his share bears to the total benefit paid. Interest paid on tax-free death benefits is taxed.

Where benefits are paid over several years, the $5,000 exclusion must be applied to the first payments.

Death benefits over $5,000. The IRS holds that if a death benefit exceeds $5,000, the excess is taxable even if the payment was made voluntarily by the employer. Some federal courts have allowed tax-free gift treatment for amounts over $5,000. The Tax Court has supported the IRS position.

Possible Repeal of Exclusion

CAUTION When this book went to press, Congress was considering legislation to repeal the $5,000 death benefit exclusion for years after 1992; *see* the Tax Legislation Guide at the front of this book and the Supplement for legislative developments.

COMPANY CARS, EDUCATION ASSISTANCE, DEPENDENT CARE, AND OTHER BENEFITS

COMPANY CARS AS FRINGE BENEFITS

¶3.4 The use of a company car is tax free under the working condition fringe benefit rule (¶3.7), provided you use the car for business. If you use the car for personal driving, you may be taxed on the value of such personal use. Your company has the responsibility of calculating taxable income based on IRS tables that specify the value of various priced cars. For certain cars, a flat mileage allowance may be used to measure personal use. You are also required to keep for your employer a mileage log or similar record to substantiate your business use. Your employer should tell you what type of records are required. Similarly, employees who use a company airplane for personal trips are taxable on the value of the flights, as determined by the employer using IRS tables.

Regardless of personal use, you are not subject to tax for a company vehicle that the IRS considers to be of limited personal value. These are ambulances or hearses; flatbed trucks; dump, garbage, or refrigerated trucks; one-passenger delivery trucks (including trucks with folding jump seats); tractors, combines, and other farm equipment; or forklifts. Also not taxable is personal use of school buses, passenger buses (seating at least 20), and moving vans where such personal use is restricted; police or fire vehicles, or an unmarked law enforcement vehicle, where personal use is authorized by a government agency.

Demonstration cars. The value of a demonstration car used by a full-time auto salesperson is tax free as a working condition fringe benefit if the use of the car facilitates job performance and if there are substantial personal use restrictions, including a prohibition on use by family members and for vacation trips. Furthermore, total mileage outside of normal working hours must be limited and personal driving must generally be restricted to a 75-mile radius around the dealer's sales office.

Chauffeur services. If chauffeur services are provided for both business and personal purposes, you must report as income the value of the personal services. For example, if the full value of the chauffeur services is $30,000 and 30% of the chauffeur's workday is spent driving on personal trips, then $9,000 is taxable (30% of $30,000), and $21,000 is tax free.

If an employer provides a bodyguard-chauffeur for business security reasons, the entire value of the chauffeur services is considered a tax-free working condition fringe benefit if: (1) the automobile is specially equipped for security; and (2) the bodyguard is trained in evasive driving techniques and is provided as part of an overall 24-hour-a-day security program. If the value of the bodyguard-chauffeur services is tax free, the employee is still taxable on the value of using the vehicle for commuting or other personal travel.

Reporting taxable automobile benefits. Social Security tax must be withheld. Income tax withholding is not required, but your employer may choose to withhold income tax. You must be notified by your employer that he or she is not withholding income tax so that you may consider the taxable benefits when determining your estimated tax; *see* Chapter 27. Whether or not withholdings are taken, the taxable value of the benefits is entered on your Form W-2 in Box 23, or on a separate Form W-2 for fringe benefits.

A special IRS rule allows your employer to include on Form W-2, 100% of the value of using the car, even if you used the car primarily for business. In this case, you should claim 100% of the value as a vehicle expense on Form 2106 and claim unreimbursed amounts as miscellaneous itemized deductions subject to the 2% AGI floor

(¶19.1). On Form 2106, you must claim actual expenses; the flat IRS mileage allowance may not be used since you are not the owner.

Your employer may also decide to treat fringe benefits provided during the last two months of the calendar year as if they were paid during the following year. For example, if this election is made for a company car in 1992, only the value of personal use from January through October is taxable in 1992; personal use in November and December is taxable in 1993. If your employer has elected this special year-end rule, you should be notified near the end of the year or when you receive Form W-2.

EDUCATION ASSISTANCE PLANS

¶3.5 If before July 1, 1992, your employer paid for your undergraduate or graduate school costs (tuition, other fees, books, and supplies) under a written, nondiscriminatory plan, the first $5,250 is tax free. Courses generally do not have to be job related; the only exception is for courses involving sports, games, or hobbies that are not part of a degree program.

Employer payments *exceeding* $5,250 also may be tax free. They qualify as a tax-free working condition fringe benefit (¶3.7) if the courses are job-related, do not satisfy the employer's minimum education standards, and do not qualify you for a new profession. If the courses do not meet these tests, the excess over $5,250 will be reported as taxable wages on your Form W-2.

When this book went to press, Congress was considering an extension of the up-to-$5,250 exclusion beyond June 30, 1992. If it is not extended, all employer-provided education will be taxable after June 30, 1992 unless qualifying as a tax-free working-condition fringe benefit (¶3.7). See the Tax Legislation Guide at the front of this book and the Supplement for legislative developments.

Tuition reductions. Employees and retired employees of educational institutions, their spouses, and their dependent children are not taxed on tuition reductions for courses below the graduate level. Widows or widowers of deceased employees or of former employees also qualify. Officers and highly paid employees may claim the exclusion only if the employer plan does not discriminate on their behalf. The exclusion applies to tuition for education at any educational institution, not only the employer's school.

Graduate students who are teaching or research assistants at educational organizations are not taxed on tuition reductions from the school if the tuition reduction is in addition to regular pay for the teaching or research services.

DEPENDENT CARE ASSISTANCE

¶3.6 The value of qualifying day-care services provided by your employer under a written, nondiscriminatory plan is generally not taxable up to a limit of $5,000, or $2,500 if you are filing separately. The same tax-free limits apply if you make pre-tax salary deferrals to a flexible spending account for reimbursing dependent care expenses (¶3.13). However, you may not exclude from income more than your earned income. If you are married and your spouse earns less than you do, your tax-free benefit is limited to his or her earned income. If your spouse does not work, all of your benefits are taxable unless he or she is a full-time student or is disabled. If a full-time student or disabled, your spouse is treated as earning $200 a month if your dependent care expenses are for one dependent, or $400 a month if the expenses are for two or more dependents.

Expenses are excludable only if they would qualify for the dependent care credit; *see* Chapter 25. If you are being reimbursed by your employer, the exclusion is not allowed if dependent care is provided by a relative who is your dependent (or your spouse's dependent) or by your child under the age of 19. You must give your employer a record of the care provider's name, address, and tax identification number. The identifying information also must be listed on your return.

Reporting employer benefits on your return. Your employer will show the total amount of your dependent care benefits in Box 22 of your Form W-2. Any benefits over $5,000 will also be included as taxable wages in Box 10 of Form W-2. If you file Form 1040, you must report the benefits on Part III of Form 2441. If you file Form 1040A, you report the employer benefits on Schedule 2. On these forms, you determine both the tax-free and taxable (if any) portions of the employer-provided benefits. If any part is taxable, that amount must be included on Line 7 of your return as wages and labeled "DCB." Follow IRS instructions for identifying the care provider (employer, babysitter, etc.) on Form 2441 or on Schedule 2 of Form 1040A.

The tax-free portion of employer benefits reduces eligibility for the dependent care credit; see Chapter 25.

Figuring Tax-Free Exclusion

You cannot assume that your employer-provided dependent care benefit is completely tax free merely because your employer has not included any part of it as taxable wages in Box 10 of Form W-2. Although up to $5,000 of benefits are generally tax free, the tax-free amount is reduced where you or your spouse earns less than $5,000 or where you file separately from your spouse. You must show the amount of your qualifying dependent care expenses and figure the tax-free exclusion on Form 2441 if you file Form 1040, or on Schedule 2 of Form 1040A.

WORKING CONDITION FRINGE BENEFITS

¶3.7 An employer-provided benefit that would be deductible by you if you paid for it yourself (¶19.3) is a tax-free working condition fringe benefit. Under IRS regulations, such benefits include:

Company car or plane. The value of a company car or plane is tax free to the extent that you use it for business; *see* ¶3.4 for more on company cars.

Employer-paid business subscriptions or reimbursed membership dues in professional associations.

Free or reduced rate parking on or near the employer's business premises. A parking allowance is also tax free if you substantiate your parking costs. If you do not substantiate parking expenses, the allowance is taxable.

When this book went to press, Congress was considering a limit on the value of parking benefits that may be excluded from income; see the Tax Legislation Guide at the front of this book.

Product testing. This is a limited exclusion for employees who test and evaluate company manufactured goods away from company premises.

Employer-education assistance. Employer-paid undergraduate and graduate courses over the $5,250 exclusion may be a tax-free working condition fringe benefit if the courses are job related; *see* ¶3.5.

Does job-placement assistance qualify? The IRS has not yet decided. It first held in a 1989 private ruling that job placement assistance for discharged employees would not qualify as a tax-free working condition fringe benefit because the assistance relates to finding a new job. This ruling was criticized and in 1990 the IRS withdrew it, announcing that it was reconsidering the issue. Although the IRS has not announced an official position, there are indications that placement assistance will generally be treated as a tax-free working condition benefit if offered to employees on a nondiscriminatory basis. However, even if this position is taken, the IRS says that an employee who elects placement services instead of taking cash will be taxed on the cash that could have been received.

DE MINIMIS FRINGE BENEFITS

¶3.8 Small benefits that would be administratively impractical to tax are considered tax-free *de minimis* (minor) fringe benefits. Examples are personal use of company copying machines, company parties, or tickets for the theater or sporting events. Other *de minimis* benefits include:

Occasional overtime meal money or cab fare. If you work overtime and occasionally receive meal money or cab fare home, the amount is tax free. The IRS has not provided a numerical standard for determining when payments are "occasional."

Company eating facility. The operation of an eating facility for employees is a tax-free *de minimis* fringe benefit if it is located on or near the business premises, and the cost of the meals to employees equals or exceeds the company's operating costs. Do not confuse this type of meal benefit with employer-supplied meals for employees who must be on call on an employer's premises; these are tax free under ¶3.10.

Highly compensated employees or owners with special access to executive dining rooms may not exclude the value of their meals as a *de minimis* fringe benefit; however, the meals may be tax free under rules of ¶3.10 if meals must be taken on company premises.

Transit passes and reimbursements. Public transit passes are tax free up to $21 per month. If a $30 monthly pass is provided, the entire $30 is taxable—not just the $9 excess over $21.

Employer reimbursements are also taxfree if the employer reviews employee costs.

The $21 cap may be increased by Congress for 1993; see the Tax Legislation Guide at the front of this book.

Commuting under unsafe circumstances. If you are asked to work outside of your normal working hours and due to unsafe conditions your employer provides transportation such as taxi fare, the first $1.50 per one-way commute is taxable but the excess over $1.50 is tax free. This exclusion is not available to certain highly-compensated employees and officers, corporate directors, or owners of 1% or more of the company.

Even when working their regular shift, hourly employees who are not considered highly compensated ($62,345 in 1992) are taxed on only $1.50 per one-way commute if their employer pays for car service or taxi fare because walking or taking public transportation to or from work would be unsafe. The excess value of the transportation over $1.50 is tax free. These rules can apply to day-shift employees who work overtime as well as night-shift employees working regular hours so long as transportation is provided because of unsafe conditions.

EMPLOYEE ACHIEVEMENT AWARDS

¶3.9 Achievement awards are taxable unless they meet special rules for awards of tangible personal property (such as a watch, television or golf clubs) given to you in recognition of length of service or safety achievement. As a general rule, if your employer is allowed to deduct the cost of the award, you are not taxed. The deduction limit, and therefore the excludable limit, is $400 for awards from nonqualified plans and $1,600 for awards from qualified plans or from both qualified and nonqualified plans. If your employer's deduction is less than the item's cost, you are taxed on the greater of: (1) the difference between the cost and your employer's deduction, but no more than the award's fair market value; or (2) the excess of the item's fair market value over your employer's deduction. Deduction tests for achievement awards are discussed at ¶20.28. It is up to your employer to tell you if the award qualifies for full or partial tax-free treatment.

An award will not be treated as a tax-free safety achievement award if employee safety achievement awards (other than those of *de minimis* value) were granted during the year to more than 10% of employees (not counting managers, administrators, clerical employees, or other professional employees). An award made to a manager, administrator, clerical employee, or other professional employee for safety achievement does not qualify for tax-free treatment.

Tax-free treatment also does not apply when you receive an award for length of service during the first five years of employment or when you previously received such awards during the last five years, unless the prior award qualified as a *de minimis* fringe benefit.

Underpriced Items

CAUTION

If the value of the item is disproportionately high compared to the employer's cost, the IRS may conclude that the award is disguised compensation, in which case the entire value would be taxable.

MEALS AND LODGING

EMPLOYER-FURNISHED MEALS OR LODGING

¶3.10 The value of employer-furnished food is not taxable if furnished on your employer's business premises for his or her convenience. The value of lodgings is not taxable if as a condition of your employment you must accept the lodging on the employer's business premises for the employer's convenience. The key words here are: business premises, convenience of the employer, and condition of employment. For *meals,* you must satisfy the business premises and convenience of the employer tests. For *lodging,* you must satisfy these two tests plus the condition of employment test.

Business premises test. The IRS generally defines business premises as the place of employment such as a company cafeteria in a factory for a cook or an employer's home for a domestic. The Tax Court has a more liberal view, extending the area of business premises beyond the actual place of business in such cases as these:

A house provided a hotel manager, although located across the street from the hotel. The IRS has agreed to the decision.

A house provided a motel manager, two blocks from the motel. However, a court of appeals reversed the decision and held in the IRS's favor.

A rented hotel suite used daily by executives for a luncheon conference.

House One Block Away

COURT DECISION

Two federal courts held that a school superintendent received tax-free lodging where the home was one block away from the school and separated by a row of other houses. This met the business premises test. The IRS disagrees with the result and says that it will continue to litigate similar cases arising outside of the Eighth Circuit in which the case arose. The Eighth Circuit includes the states of Arkansas, Iowa, Minnesota, Missouri, Nebraska and North and South Dakota.

Convenience of employer. This requires proof that an employer provides the free meals or lodging for a business purpose other than

providing extra pay. However, that the board and lodging are described in a contract or state statute as extra pay does not bar tax-free treatment provided they are *also* furnished for other substantial, noncompensatory business reasons; for example, you are required to be on call 24 hours a day.

Generally, the value of meals furnished before or after working hours or on nonworking days is taxable, but there are exceptions; *see* Examples 1 and 3 below.

EXAMPLES 1. A waitress who works from 7 A.M. to 4 P.M. is furnished two meals a day without charge. Her employer encourages her to have her breakfast at the restaurant before working, but she is required to have her lunch there. The value of her breakfast and lunch is not income because it is furnished during her work period or immediately before or after the period. But say she is also allowed to have free meals on her days off and a free supper on the days she works. The value of these meals is taxable income because they are not furnished during or immediately before or after her work period.

2. A hospital maintains a cafeteria on its premises where all of its employees may eat during their working hours. No charge is made for these meals. The hospital furnishes meals to have the employees available for emergencies. The employees are not required to eat there. Since the hospital furnishes the meals in order to have employees available for emergency call during meal periods, the meals are not income to any of the hospital employees who obtain their meals at the hospital cafeteria.

3. You are required to occupy living quarters on your employer's business premises as a condition of employment. The value of *any* meal furnished to you without charge on your employer's premises is excluded from taxable income.

4. In order to assure adequate bank teller service during the busy lunch period, a bank limits tellers to 30 minutes for lunch and provides them with free meals in a cafeteria on the premises. The value of the meals is tax free.

Meal charges. Your company may charge for meals on company premises and give you an option to accept or decline the meals. The IRS will point to this option as evidence that the meals are not furnished for the convenience of your employer.

Where your employer provides meals on business premises at a fixed charge which is subtracted from your pay whether you accept the meals or not, the amount of the charge is excluded from your taxable pay. If the meal is provided for the employer's convenience, as in Example 2 or 4 on page 43, the value of the meals received is also tax free. If not for the employer's convenience, the value is taxable whether it exceeds or is less than the amount charged.

Partners Are Not Employees

The IRS does not consider partners or self-employed persons as employees and so does not allow them an exclusion under the rules of this section. The IRS also does not allow a partnership to deduct the cost of meals and lodging provided a partner-manager of a hotel. Courts are split on this issue.

Lodging must be condition of employment. This test requires evidence that the lodging is necessary for you to perform your job properly, as where you are required to be available for duty at all times. If housing is not provided to all employees with the same job, the IRS may hold that the lodging is not a condition of employment. For example, the IRS taxed medical residents on the value of hospital lodging where other residents lived in their own apartments. If you are given the choice of free lodging at your place of employment or a cash allowance, the lodging is not considered as a condition of employment, and its value is taxable.

Lodging includes heat, electricity, gas, water, sewerage, and other utilities. Where these services are furnished by the employer and their value is deducted from your salary, the amount deducted is also not included as part of your wage income. But if you pay for the utilities yourself, you may not exclude their cost from your income.

Are Your Board and Lodging Tax Free?

Yes—	No—
A state civil service employee working at a state institution is required to live at the institution and eat there so he or she may be available for duty at any time. Hotel executives, managers, housekeepers, and auditors who are required to live at the hotel. Domestics, farm laborers, fishermen, canners, seamen, servicemen, building superintendents, hospital and sanitarium employees who are required to have meals and lodging on employer premises. Restaurant and other food service employees for meals furnished during or immediately before or after working hours. Employees who must be available during meal periods for emergencies. Employees who, because of the nature of the business, are given short meal periods. Workers who have no alternative but to use company-supplied facilities in remote areas. Park employees who voluntarily live in rent-free apartments provided by a park department in order to protect the park from vandalism.	Your employer gives you a cash allowance for your meals or lodgings. You have a choice of accepting cash or getting the meals or lodgings. For example, under a union contract you get meals, but you may refuse to take them and get an automatic pay increase. A state hospital employee is given a choice: He or she may live at the institution rent free or live elsewhere and get an extra $30 a month. Whether he or she stays at the institution or lives outside, the $30 a month is included in his or her income. A waitress, on her days off, is allowed to eat free meals at the restaurant where she works. You may buy lunch in the company's cafeteria or bring your own.

EXAMPLE Jones is employed at a construction project at a remote job site. His pay is $600 a week. Because there are no accessible places near the site for food and lodging, the employer furnishes meals and lodging for which it charges $120 a week, which is taken out of Jones's pay. Jones reports only the net amount he receives—$480. The value of the meals and lodging is a tax-free benefit.

Groceries. An employer may furnish unprepared food, such as groceries, rather than prepared meals. Courts are divided on whether the value of the groceries is excludable from income. One court allowed an exclusion for the value of nonfood items, such as napkins and soap—as well as for groceries—furnished to a doctor who ate at his home on hospital grounds so he would be available for emergencies.

Cash allowances. A cash allowance for meals and lodging is taxable. Only meals furnished in kind are permitted tax-free treatment.

EXAMPLE A hotel manager's wife bought groceries, the cost of which was reimbursed by the hotel. Milk was delivered to their apartment and paid for by the hotel. The reimbursement of the grocery bills was taxable because the groceries were not furnished in kind by the hotel. However, the cost of the milk was not taxable because the delivery to the apartment and the payment of the bill by the hotel was considered food furnished in kind.

Faculty lodging. Teachers and other employees (or spouses and dependents) do not have to pay tax on the value of school-provided lodging if they pay a minimal rent. The minimal required rent is the smaller of: (1) 5% of the appraised value of the lodging; or (2) the average rental paid for comparable school housing by persons who are neither employees nor students. Appraised value must be determined by an independent appraiser and the appraisal must be reviewed annually.

EXAMPLE A professor pays annual rent of $6,000 for university housing appraised at $100,000. The average rent for comparable university housing paid by non-employees and non-students is $7,000. The professor does not have to pay any tax on the housing since his rental payments exceed 5% of the appraised housing value (5% of $100,000, or $5,000). If the professor's rent was $4,000, he would have to report income of $1,000 ($5,000 required rent − $4,000).

Peace Corps and VISTA volunteers. Peace Corps volunteers working overseas may exclude subsistence allowances from income under a specific Code provision. The law does not provide a similar exclusion for the small living expense allowances received by VISTA volunteers.

MINISTER'S RENTAL ALLOWANCE

¶3.11 A duly ordained minister pays no tax on the rental value of a home provided as part of his pay. If he is not provided a home but is paid a rental allowance, he pays no tax on the allowance if he uses the entire amount to pay his rent (including the rent of a furnished or unfurnished apartment or house, garage, and utilities).

Where a minister buys or owns his own home, he pays no tax on an allowance used as a down payment on the house for mortgage installments, or for utilities, interest, tax, and repair expenses of the house. Any part of the allowance not used for these housing purposes is taxed. For example, that part of an allowance used to pay rent on business or farm property or for food or the services of a maid is taxed.

A minister who rents his home while abroad on church business may exclude his rental allowance only up to amounts used for capital improvements. These amounts are treated as expenses of keeping up his regular home. The balance of his rental allowance is taxable compensation even though he had expenses for maintenance, interest, taxes, repairs, and utilities during the rental period. The expenses may be deducted from rental income.

Allowance Must Be Authorized

The church or local congregation must officially designate the part of the minister's compensation that is a rental allowance. To qualify for tax-free treatment, the designation must be made in advance of the payments. Official action may be shown by an employment contract, minutes, a resolution, or a budget allowance.

Who qualifies for tax-free allowance? Tax-free treatment is allowed to ordained ministers, rabbis, and cantors who receive housing allowances as part of their compensation for ministerial duties. Retired ministers qualify if their allowance is furnished in recognition of past services.

The IRS has allowed the tax-free exclusion to ministers working as teachers or administrators for a parochial school, college, or theological seminary which is an integral part of a church organization. A traveling evangelist was allowed to exclude rental allowances from out-of-town churches to maintain his permanent home. Church officers who are not ordained, such as a "minister" of music (music director) or "minister" of education (Sunday School director), do not qualify.

The IRS has generally barred an exclusion to ordained ministers working as executives of nonreligious organizations even where services or religious functions are performed as part of the job. The Tax Court has focused on the duties performed. A minister employed as a chaplain by a municipal police department under church supervision was allowed a housing exclusion, but the exclusion was denied to a minister-administrator of an old-age home that was not under the authority of a church and a rabbi who worked for a religious organization as director of inter-religious affairs.

Allowance subject to self-employment tax. Although parsonage allowances are not taxable income, they are reported as self-employment income for Social Security purposes; *see* Chapter 46. If you do not receive a cash allowance, report the rental value of the parsonage as self-employment income. Rental value is usually equal to what you would pay for similar quarters in your locality. Also include as self-employment income the value of house furnishings, utilities, appurtenances supplied—such as a garage—and the value of meals furnished that meet the rules at ¶3.10.

CAFETERIA PLANS AND FLEXIBLE SPENDING ARRANGEMENTS

CAFETERIA PLANS PROVIDE CHOICE OF BENEFITS

¶3.12 "Cafeteria plans" is a nickname for plans that give an employee a choice of selecting tax-free fringe benefits or cash. You are not taxed when you elect qualifying non-taxable benefits, although cash could have been chosen instead. A cafeteria plan may offer benefits such as group health insurance or life insurance coverage, long-term disability coverage, dependent care assistance, or medical expense reimbursements.

Under a flexible spending arrangement (FSA), employees may be allowed to make tax-free salary-reduction contributions to a medical or dependent care reimbursement plan; *see* ¶3.13. Salary-reductions also may be used to purchase group health insurance or life insurance coverage on a pre-tax basis.

A qualified cafeteria plan must be written and not discriminate in favor of highly compensated employees and stockholders. If the plan provides for health benefits, a special rule applies to determine whether the plan is discriminatory. If a plan is held discriminatory, the highly compensated participants are taxed to the extent they could have elected cash. Furthermore, if key employees (¶3.2) receive more than 25% of the "tax-free" benefits under the plan, they are taxed on the benefits.

FLEXIBLE SPENDING ARRANGEMENTS

¶3.13 A flexible spending arrangement (FSA) allows employees to pay for enhanced medical coverage or dependent care expenses on a tax-free basis. Under a typical FSA, you agree to a salary reduction which is deducted from each paycheck and deposited in a separate account. As expenses are incurred, you are reimbursed from the account. Funds from a health FSA may be used to reimburse you for the annual deductible under your employer's regular health plan, co-payments you must make to physicians, and any other expenses that your health plan does not cover. These may include eye examinations, eyeglasses, routine physicals, and orthodontia work for you and your dependents.

The tax advantage of an FSA is that the salary deferral avoids federal income tax and Social Security taxes while allowing personal expenses to be paid with pre-tax rather than after-tax income. The salary deferrals are also exempt from most state and local taxes; check your state tax instructions. In the case of a health FSA, paying medical expenses with pre-tax dollars allows you to avoid the 7.5% adjusted gross income (AGI) floor (¶17.1) that limits itemized deductions for medical costs. However, there are severe restrictions on FSAs, as discussed below.

FSA restrictions. The IRS has imposed restrictions on FSAs that make them unattractive for many employees. An election to set up an FSA for a given year must be made before the start of that year. You elect how much you want to contribute during the coming year and that amount will be withheld from your pay in monthly installments. Once the election takes effect, you may not discontinue contributions to your account and elect to receive the amounts as compensation unless there is a change in family status. In addition, only expenses incurred during the plan year may be reimbursed, and a *"use it or lose it"* rule applies: any unused balance at the end of the plan year is forfeited. Unused amounts may not be refunded to you or carried over to the next year. There is a grace period, generally until April 15 of the following year, to submit reimbursement claims for expenses incurred during the previous year.

There are different reimbursement rules for health care and dependent care FSAs, as discussed below.

Health care FSA. At all times during the year, you may receive reimbursements up to your designated limit, even if your payments to the FSA are less. For example, if you elect to make salary-reduction contributions of $100 per month to a health FSA, and you incur $500 of qualifying medical expenses in January, you may get the full $500 reimbursement even though you have paid only $100 into the plan. Your employer may not require you to accelerate contributions to match reimbursement claims.

You may *not* receive tax-free reimbursements for cosmetic surgery expenses unless the surgery is necessary to correct a deformity existing since birth or resulting from a disease or from injury caused by an accident. Nonqualifying reimbursements are taxable.

Estimating FSA Contributions

Because of the "use it or lose it" rule for FSA contributions, make a conservative estimate of your expenses when you make your election. This is particularly true for medical expenses which are generally difficult to project in advance.

Dependent care FSA. You may contribute to a dependent care FSA if you expect to have dependent care expenses qualifying for the tax credit discussed in Chapter 25, but if you contribute to a dependent care FSA, any tax-free reimbursement from the account reduces the expenses eligible for the credit. If you are married, both you and your spouse must work in order for you to receive tax-free reimbursements from an FSA, unless your spouse is disabled or a full-time student; *see* ¶3.6. The maximum tax-free reimbursement under the FSA is $5,000, but if either you or your spouse earns less than $5,000, the tax-free limit is the lesser earnings. If your spouse's employer offers a dependent care FSA, total tax-free reimbursements for both of you are limited to $5,000. Furthermore, if you are considered highly compensated, your employer may have to lower your contribution ceiling below $5,000 to comply with nondiscrimination rules.

Unlike health FSAs, an employer may limit reimbursements from a dependent care FSA to your account balance. For example, if you contribute $400 a month to the FSA, and in January you pay $1,500 to a day care center for your child, your employer may reimburse you $400 a month as contributions are made to your account.

Tax-free Dependent Care Reimbursements

Whether all or only part of your dependent care FSA reimbursements are tax free is figured on Part III of Form 2441 if you file Form 1040. If you file Form 1040A, the calculation is made on Part III of Schedule 2.

FREE OR LOW-COST COMPANY SERVICES OR PRODUCTS

COMPANY SERVICES PROVIDED AT NO ADDITIONAL COST

¶3.14 Employees are not taxed on the receipt of services usually sold by their employer to customers where the employer does not incur additional costs in providing them to the employees. Examples are free or low-cost flights provided by an airline to its employees; free or discount lodging for employees of a hotel; and telephone service provided to employees of telephone companies. These tax-free fringes also may be provided to the employee's spouse and dependent children; retired employees, including employees retired on disability; and widows or widowers of deceased or retired employees. Tax-free treatment also applies to free or discount flights provided to parents of airline employees. Benefits provided by another company under a reciprocal arrangement, such as standby tickets on another airline, may also qualify as tax free.

The employer must have excess service capacity to provide the service and not forego potential revenue from regular customers. For example, airline employees who receive free reserved seating on company planes must pay tax on the benefit because the airline is foregoing potential revenue by reserving seating that could otherwise be sold.

Highly compensated employees. Highly compensated employees can receive tax-free company services *only if* the same benefits are available to other employees on a nondiscriminatory basis. Highly compensated employees in 1992 include employees owning more than a 5% interest; employees earning more than $93,518, employees earning over $62,345 if in the top-paid 20%; and officers earning more than $56,110. The $56,110, $93,518, and $62,345 amounts are subject to annual inflation adjustments.

Line of business limitations. If a company has two lines of business, such as an airline and a hotel, an employee of the airline may not receive tax-free benefits provided by the hotel. However, there are exceptions. An employee who provides services to both business lines may receive benefits from both business lines. Benefits from more than one line in existence before 1984 may also be available under a special election made by the company for 1985 and later years. Your employer should notify you of this tax benefit.

DISCOUNTS ON COMPANY PRODUCTS OR SERVICES

¶3.15 The value of discounts on company products is a tax-free benefit if the discount does not exceed the employer's gross profit percentage. For example, if a company's profit percentage is 40%, the maximum tax-free employee discount for merchandise is 40% of the regular selling price. If you received a 50% discount, then 10% of the price charged customers would be taxable income. The employer has a choice of methods for figuring profit percentage.

Discounts on services that are not tax free under ¶3.14 for no-additional-cost services qualify for an exclusion, limited to 20% of the selling price charged customers. Discounts above 20% are taxable. An insurance policy is treated as a service. Thus, insurance company employees are not taxed on a discount of up to 20% of the policy's price.

Some company products do not qualify for the exclusion. Discounts on real estate and investment property such as securities, commodities, currency, or bullion are taxable. Interest-free or low-interest loans given by banks or other financial institutions to employees are not excludable. The loan is subject to tax under the rules of ¶4.31.

The line of business limitation discussed at ¶3.14 for no-additional-cost services also applies to qualified employee discounts. Thus, if a company operates an airline and a hotel, employees who work for the airline may generally not receive tax-free hotel room discounts. However, if a special election was made by the company, employees may receive tax-free benefits from any line of business in existence before 1984.

Highly compensated employees are subject to the nondiscrimination rules discussed at ¶3.14 for no-additional-cost services.

EXAMPLE The airline that you work for gives you a free round-trip ticket with a confirmed seat to California. The benefit is not tax free under the rule for no-additional-cost services (¶3.14), but a 20% tax-free discount is allowed. If customers are charged $300 for comparable tickets, $60 is a tax-free benefit (20% of $300) and $240 is taxable.

4

DIVIDEND AND INTEREST INCOME

Dividends and interest paid to you in 1992 are reported to the IRS on Forms 1099.

You will receive copies of:

- Forms 1099-DIV, for dividends
- Forms 1099-INT, for interest
- Forms 1099-OID, for original issue discount

Report the amounts shown on the Forms 1099 on your tax return. The IRS uses the Forms 1099 to check the income you report. If you fail to report income reported on Forms 1099, you will receive a statement asking for an explanation and a bill for the tax deficiency. If you receive a Form 1099, which you believe is incorrect, contact the payer for a corrected form.

Do not attach your copies of Forms 1099 to your return. Keep them with a copy of your tax return.

REPORTING DIVIDEND INCOME

¶4.1 Dividends paid out of current or accumulated earnings of a corporation are subject to tax. Most dividends fall into this class, except for stock dividends and stock rights on common stock which are generally not taxed; see ¶4.6.

Dividends that are paid to you during 1992 are reported to the IRS by the company

47

on Form 1099-DIV. The IRS uses this information as a check on your reporting of dividends. You receive a copy of Form 1099-DIV. You do not have to attach it to your tax return.

Publicly held corporations generally inform stockholders of the tax consequences of stock dividends and other distributions. Keep such letters with your tax records. You may also want to consult investment publications such as Moody's or Standard & Poor's annual dividend record books for details of dividend distributions and their tax treatment.

Do You Have To Use Form 1040?

You must use Form 1040 if you received any capital gain distributions or nontaxable distributions. If you received only ordinary dividends, you may use either Form 1040 or Form 1040A. Form 1040EZ may not be used to report dividend income.

For further details on dividend reporting, *see* the chart below, "Key to Dividend Reporting."

Key to Dividend Reporting

Type of Dividend Payment—

How and Where to Report—

Cash dividends

Dividends paid out of a corporation's earnings and profits are taxable. The corporation will report taxable dividends to you on Form 1099-DIV (or equivalent statement).

On Form 1040, report dividends on Line 9; Schedule B must be filed where total dividends exceed $400.

If you file Form 1040A, report dividends on Line 9, and if total dividends exceed $400, complete Part II of Schedule 1. Dividends may not be reported on Form 1040EZ.

Stock dividends and stock splits

If you own common stock and receive additional shares of the same company as a dividend, the dividend is generally not taxed. A dividend is taxed where you had the option to receive cash instead of stock, or if the stock is of another corporation. Preferred shareholders are generally taxed on stock dividends. Taxable stock dividends are discussed at ¶4.7 and ¶4.8. Your corporation will determine whether stock dividends are taxable, and report the taxable amount on Form 1099-DIV.

If you receive additional shares as part of a stock split, the new shares are not taxable; although you own more shares, your ownership percentage has not changed.

Return of capital distributions

A distribution that is not paid out of earnings is a nontaxable return of capital; that is, a partial payback of your investment. The company will report the distribution on Form 1099-DIV as a nontaxable distribution. You must reduce the cost basis of your stock by the nontaxable distribution. If your basis is reduced to zero by return of capital distributions, any further distributions are taxable as capital gains, which you report on Schedule D.

You must use Form 1040 if you received any return of capital distributions; Form 1040A may not be used. If your total dividends, including nontaxable returns of capital, are $400 or less, you do not report the nontaxable distribution on your return unless your basis has been reduced to zero. In that case, further distributions are taxable and are reported on Schedule D.

If your total dividends exceed $400, list the nontaxable distribution on Line 5 of Schedule B, along with your other dividends. Then, on Line 8, you subtract the nontaxable distribution from the total.

Money market fund dividends

Cash dividends paid by a money market mutual fund are reported on Form 1099-DIV. Report them on Line 9 of Form 1040, and include them on Schedule B if your total dividends exceed $400. On Form 1040A, report the dividend on Line 9, and fill out Part II of Schedule 1 if total dividends exceed $400.

Do not confuse money market funds managed by mutual funds with bank money market accounts. Bank money market accounts pay interest reported on Form 1099-INT, not dividends.

Dividends on accounts in credit unions, cooperative banks, savings and loan associations, mutual savings banks, and building and loan associations

Distributions from these financial institutions are called "dividends" but are actually interest and are reported to you on Form 1099-INT.

Mutual fund dividends

Mutual funds may pay several kinds of dividends. On Form 1099-DIV, the fund will report total distributions in Box 1a. This total includes: (1) fully taxable ordinary dividends that are also reported in Box 1b of Form 1099-DIV; (2) capital gain distributions that are also reported in Box 1c of Form 1099-DIV; and (3) nontaxable distributions that are also listed in Box 1d. Form 1099-DIV for 1992 will include dividends declared before the end of the year, even if not actually paid to you until January 1993. How to report these dividends on your return is detailed in ¶4.3.

Life insurance policy dividends

Dividends on individual life insurance policies are actually a refund of your premiums and are not taxed unless they exceed the total premiums paid.

Nominee distribution—joint accounts

If you receive dividends on stock held as a nominee for someone else, or you receive a Form 1099-DIV that includes dividends belonging to another person, such as a joint owner of the account, you are considered to be a "nominee recipient." If the other owner is someone other than your spouse, you should file a separate Form 1099-DIV showing you as the payer and the other owner as the recipient of the allocable income. Give the owner a copy of Form 1099-DIV by February 1, 1993, so the dividends can be reported on his or her 1992 return. File the Form 1099-DIV, together with a Form 1096 ("Transmittal of Information Return"), with the IRS by March 1, 1993.

On your Schedule B, you list on Line 5 the total amount reported to you on Form 1099-DIV. Several lines above Line 6, subtract the nominee distribution (the amount allocable to the other owner) from the total dividends. Thus, the nominee distribution is not included in the taxable dividends shown on Line 6, Schedule B.

DIVIDENDS FROM A PARTNERSHIP, S CORPORATION, ESTATE, OR TRUST

¶4.2 You report dividend income you receive as a member of a partnership, stockholder in an S corporation or as a beneficiary of an estate or trust. The fiduciary of the estate or trust should advise you of the dividend income to be reported on your return.

A distribution from a partnership or S corporation is reported as a dividend only if it is portfolio income derived from non-business activities. Your allowable share of the dividend will be shown on the Schedule K-1 you receive from the partnership or S corporation.

HOW MUTUAL FUND DIVIDENDS ARE TAXED

¶4.3 Mutual funds (open-ended regulated investment companies) pay their shareholders several kinds of dividends, as listed below. Whether the dividend is received by you or reinvested by the fund, you must report it on your return. The fund will send you Form 1099-DIV (or a similar written form), giving you a breakdown of the type of dividends paid during the taxable year. See the Filing Pointer on page 50 for where to report mutual fund dividends on your return.

Rules for figuring gain or loss when you sell mutual fund shares are at ¶30.4

Keep Track of Reinvested Dividends

If you participate in a dividend reinvestment plan instead of taking the dividends in cash, keep a record of the dividends and of the shares purchased with the reinvestment. The reinvested dividends are considered your cost basis for the acquired shares. Keep a record of your reinvestment to figure your cost when you sell all or some of your shares; *see* ¶30.4 for calculating gain on the sale of mutual fund shares.

Tax treatment of dividends shown on Form 1099-DIV. The Form 1099-DIV from your mutual fund may include several types of dividends. The gross amount shown in Box 1a must be reported on your return. The Box 1a total includes ordinary dividends from Box 1b, capital gain dividends from Box 1c, nontaxable distributions from Box 1d, and in the case of a nonpublicly offered fund, your share of fund expenses from Box 1e. Dividends that your *reinvested* are included in Box 1a.

Dividends from a fund's foreign investments are included in the appropriate boxes of Form 1099-DIV, and the fund will indicate in Boxes 3 and 4 any foreign tax paid, which you may claim as a tax credit or deduction.

Form 1099-DIV for 1992 will include a dividend received in January 1993 so long as it was declared in October, November, or December of 1992.

Here is a closer look at the types of dividends reported on Form 1099-DIV:

Ordinary dividends. In Box 1b of Form 1099-DIV, the mutual fund reports your share of the fund's earnings from investments, such as interest income from bonds or dividends from corporate stock.

Also reported in Box 1b are short-term capital gain dividends representing your share of the fund's short-term profits on its own sales of securities.

Capital gain distributions. You report capital gain dividends shown in Box 1c of Form 1099-DIV as long-term capital gain regardless of how long you have held your mutual fund shares. Capital gain distributions represent your share of the fund's long-term profits on sales of securities from its own portfolio. *See* the Filing Pointer on the next page for where to report capital gain distributions on your return.

If you own shares in a municipal bond fund, capital gain distributions from the fund are taxable as long-term capital gain. Only the exempt-interest dividends paid by a municipal bond fund avoid tax.

A few mutual funds retain their long-term capital gains and pay capital gains tax on those amounts. Even though not actually received by you, you include as a capital gain dividend on your return the amount of the undistributed capital gain allocated to you by the fund. If the mutual fund paid a tax on the undistributed capital gain, you are entitled to a credit. To claim the credit, review Form 2439 sent to you by your company which lists your share of undistributed capital gain and the amount of tax paid on it. Enter your share of the tax the company paid on this gain on Line 59 of Form 1040, and check the box for Form 2439. Attach Copy B of Form 2439 to your return to support your tax credit. Increase the basis of your stock by the excess of the undistributed capital gain over the amount of tax paid by the mutual fund, as reported on Form 2439.

A loss on the sale of mutual fund shares held for six months or less is treated as a long-term capital loss to the extent of any capital gain dividend received before the sale. This restriction does not apply to dispositions under periodic redemption plans. For example, assume that in June 1992 you bought mutual fund shares for $1,000. In August, you received a capital gain distribution of $50, and you sold the shares for $850 in September. Instead of reporting a $150 short-term capital loss ($1,000 – $850 proceeds), you must report a long-term capital loss of $50, the amount of the capital gain distribution; the remaining $100 of the loss is a short-term capital loss.

Capital Gain From Tax-Exempt Bond Funds

Income you receive from a tax-exempt municipal bond fund is generally tax free, but capital gain distributions are taxable. Exempt-interest dividends will not be shown on Form 1099-DIV. Capital gain dividends are shown on Form 1099-DIV and must be reported on your return.

When you sell your shares in a tax-exempt bond fund, or exchange the fund shares for other shares in a different fund, you make a taxable sale on which you realize capital gain or loss.

Nontaxable distributions in Box 1d. In Box 1d, the mutual fund designates amounts representing return of capital as nontaxable distributions. They reduce the cost basis of the mutual fund shares. A return of capital is not taxed unless the distribution (when added to other such distributions received in the past) exceeds your investment in the fund.

Exempt-interest dividends are also nontaxable. They do not reduce your basis in the mutual fund shares. Exempt-interest dividends are not included by the fund on Form 1099-DIV; they are separately reported. You must report them on Form 1040 with other tax-exempt interest, although they are not subject to tax.

Fund Expenses in Box 1e. If you own shares in a *publicly offered* mutual fund, you do not have to pay 1992 tax on your share of the fund expenses. There should be no entry in Box 1e of Form 1099-DIV.

However, expenses of a *nonpublicly offered* fund are included in Box 1e of Form 1099-DIV and must be reported as a taxable dividend, even though the amount has not actually been distributed to you. An offsetting deduction may be claimed on Schedule A as a miscellaneous itemized deduction, subject to the 2% floor; *see* ¶19.24.

For purposes of figuring gain or loss when you redeem or exchange shares, load charges (sales fees) paid after October 3, 1989, on the purchase of the shares may not be treated as part of your cost if you held the shares for 90 days or less and then reinvested the sales proceeds at a reduced load charge; *see* ¶30.4.

Dividends from foreign investments. The dividends are taxable, but you may be able to claim a foreign tax credit (on Form 1116) or a deduction on Schedule A for your share of the fund's foreign taxes.

In Box 3 of Form 1099-DIV, the fund will report your share of the foreign taxes paid, and in Box 4, the name of the foreign country. The fund should give you instructions for claiming the foreign tax credit or deduction; also *see* ¶36.14.

Where to Report

If all of your mutual fund dividends are ordinary dividends, you may report them on either Form 1040A or Form 1040. On Form 1040A, report the amount on Line 9, and if you have more than $400 in total dividends, complete Part II of Schedule 1.

You must file Form 1040 if you receive capital gain or nontaxable distributions. If you file Form 1040 and have more than $400 of dividends from all sources, report the total mutual fund dividends from Box 1a of Form 1099-DIV on Line 5 of Schedule B.

On Line 7 of Schedule B, capital gain distributions are subtracted from the Line 6 total. The capital gain distributions are then entered as long-term capital gain on Line 14 of Schedule D, or on Line 14 of Form 1040 if you do not need to use Schedule D for other transactions. However, even if you do not need Schedule D for other transactions, you should use Schedule D to report 1992 mutual fund capital gain distributions if your taxable income exceeds: $86,500 if married filing jointly or a qualifying widow(er); $51,900 if single; $74,150 if head of household, or $43,250 if married filing separately. In such a case, using Schedule D allows you to take advantage of the 28% maximum tax on long-term capital gains; *see* ¶5.1.

On Line 8 of Schedule B, subtract any nontaxable distributions from the total shown on Line 6. However, if your basis has been reduced to zero by nontaxable distributions, report additional nontaxable distributions on Schedule D.

If you do not have to fill out Schedule B, capital gain dividends are entered on Line 14 of Schedule D, but if you have no other capital gains or losses, you do not have to file Schedule D; report the capital gain dividend on Line 14 of Form 1040 unless filing Schedule D allows you to benefit from the 28% maximum tax on long-term gains. Nontaxable distributions do not have to be reported unless your basis has been reduced to zero; in that case, report additional distributions on Schedule D.

REAL ESTATE INVESTMENT TRUST DIVIDENDS

¶4.4   Dividends from a real estate investment trust are shown on Form 1099-DIV. Ordinary dividends are fully taxable. Dividends designated by the trust as capital gain dividends are reported as long-term capital gains regardless of how long you have held your trust shares. A loss on the sale of REIT shares held for six months or less is treated as a long-term capital loss to the extent of any capital gain dividend received before the sale. However, this long-term loss rule does not apply to sales under periodic redemption plans.

TAXABLE DIVIDENDS OF EARNINGS AND PROFITS

¶4.5   You pay tax on dividends only when the corporation distributing the dividends has earnings and profits. Publicly held corporations will tell you whether their distributions are taxable. If you hold stock in a close corporation, you may have to determine the tax status of its distribution. You need to know earnings and profits at two different periods:

1. Current earnings and profits as of the *end of the current taxable year.* A dividend is considered to have been made from earnings most recently accumulated.
2. Accumulated earnings and profits as of the *beginning of the current year.* However, when current earnings and profits are large enough to meet the dividend, you do not have to make this computation. It is only when the dividends *exceed* current earnings (or there are no current earnings) that you match accumulated earnings against the dividend. The tax term "accumulated earnings and profits" is similar in meaning to the accounting term "retained earnings." Both stand for the net profits of the company after deducting distributions to stockholders. However, "tax" earnings may differ from "retained earnings" for the following reason: Surplus accounts, the additions to which are not deductible for income tax purposes, are ordinarily included as tax earnings.

EXAMPLES 1. During 1992, Corporation A paid dividends of $25,000. At the beginning of 1992 it had accumulated earnings of $50,000. It lost $25,000 during 1992. You are fully taxed on your dividend income in 1992 because the corporation's net accumulated surplus exceeds its dividends.

2. At the end of 1991, Corporation B had a deficit of $200,000. Earnings for 1992 were $100,000. In 1992, it paid stockholders $25,000. The dividends are taxed; earnings exceeded the dividends.

STOCK DIVIDENDS ON COMMON STOCK

¶4.6   If you own common stock in a company and receive additional shares of the same company as a dividend, the dividend is generally not taxable; *see* ¶5.18 and ¶5.19 for the method of computing cost basis of stock dividends and rights and sales of such stock.

Exceptions to tax-free rule. A stock dividend on common stock is taxable when (1) you may elect to take either stock or cash; (2) there are different classes of common stock, one class receiving cash dividends and another class receiving stock; or (3) the dividend is of convertible preferred stock; *see* ¶4.8 for further details of taxable stock dividends.

Stock Splits Are Not Taxed

The receipt of stock under a split-up is not taxable. Stock splits resemble the receipt of stock dividends, but they are not dividends. They do not represent a distribution of surplus as in the case of stock dividends. The purpose of a split-up is generally to reduce the value of individual shares in order to increase their marketability. The basis of the old holding is divided among the new shares in order to find the basis for the new shares; *see* ¶5.18.

Fractional shares. If a stock dividend is declared and you are only entitled to a fractional share, you may be given cash instead. To save the trouble and expense of issuing fractional shares or scrip, many companies directly issue cash in lieu of fractional shares or they set up a plan, with shareholder approval, for the fractional shares to be sold and the cash proceeds distributed to the shareholders. Your company should tell you how to report the cash payment. According to the IRS, you are generally treated as receiving a tax-free dividend of fractional shares, followed by a taxable redemption of the shares by the company. You report on Schedule D capital gain or loss equal to the excess of the cash over the basis of the fractional share; long- or short-term treatment depends on the holding period of the original stock. In certain cases, a cash distribution may be taxed as an ordinary dividend and not as a sale reported on Schedule D; your company should tell you if this is the case.

Stock rights. The rules that apply to stock dividends also apply to distributions of stock rights. If you, as a common stockholder, receive rights to subscribe to additional common stock, the receipt of the rights is not taxable provided the terms of the distribution do not fall within the taxable distribution rules of ¶4.8.

DIVIDENDS PAID IN PROPERTY

¶4.7 A dividend may be paid in property such as securities of another corporation or merchandise. You report as income the fair market value of the property. A dividend paid in property is sometimes called a dividend in kind.

EXAMPLE You receive one share of X corporation stock as a dividend from the G company of which you are a stockholder. You received the X stock when it had a market value of $25; you report $25, the value of the property received.

Corporate benefits. On an audit, the IRS may charge that a benefit given to a shareholder-employee is a taxable dividend.

TAXABLE STOCK DIVIDENDS

¶4.8 The most frequent type of stock dividend is not taxable: the receipt by a common stockholder of a common stock dividend; *see* ¶4.6.

Dividend Reinvestment in Company Stock

Your company may allow you to take either cash dividends or automatically reinvest the dividends in company stock. If you elect the stock plan, and pay fair market value for the stock, the full cash dividend is taxable.

If the plan lets you buy the stock at a discount price, the amount of the taxable dividend is the fair market value of the stock on the dividend payment date, plus any service fee charged for the acquisition. The basis of the stock is also fair market value at the dividend payment date. The service charge may be claimed as an itemized deduction subject to the 2% adjusted gross income floor; see ¶19.24. If at the same time you also have the option to buy additional stock at a discount and you exercise the option, you have additional dividend income for the difference between the fair market value of the optional shares and the amount you paid for the shares.

Taxable stock dividends. The following stock dividends are taxable:

Stock dividends paid to holders of preferred stock. However, no taxable income is realized where the conversion ratio of convertible preferred stock is increased only to take account of a stock dividend or split involving the stock into which the convertible stock is convertible.

Stock dividend elected by a shareholder of common stock who had the choice of taking stock, property, or cash. A distribution of stock that was immediately redeemable for cash at the stockholder's option was treated as a taxable dividend.

Stock dividend paid in a distribution where some shareholders receive property or cash and other shareholders' proportionate

---

☐ CORRECTED (if checked)

PAYER'S name, street address, city, state, and ZIP code	1a Gross dividends and other distributions on stock (Total of 1b, 1c, 1d, and 1e) $ 1,384	OMB No. 1545-0110	**Dividends and Distributions**
Mutual Fund XYZ 1702 Central Lane City, State 01X1X	1b Ordinary dividends $ 1,262	19**92**	

PAYER'S Federal identification number 00-1236789	RECIPIENT'S identification number 01X-X0-1XX1	1c Capital gain distributions $ 122	2 Federal income tax withheld $	**Copy B For Recipient**
RECIPIENT'S name Joshua West		1d Nontaxable distributions $	3 Foreign tax paid $	This is important tax information and is being furnished to the Internal Revenue Service. If you are required to file a return, a negligence penalty or other sanction may be imposed on you if this dividend income is taxable and the IRS determines that it has not been reported.
Street address (including apt. no.) 9 Circle Road		1e Investment expenses $	4 Foreign country or U.S. possession	
City, state, and ZIP code City, State 01X1X		**Liquidation Distributions**		
Account number (optional)		5 Cash $	6 Noncash (Fair market value) $	

Form **1099-DIV**   (keep for your records)   Department of the Treasury - Internal Revenue Service interests in the assets, or earnings and profits of the corporation are increased.

Distributions of preferred stock to some common shareholders and common stock to other common shareholders.

Distributions of convertible preferred stock to holders of common stock, unless it can be shown that the distribution will not result in the creation of disproportionate stock interests.

Constructive stock dividends. You may not actually receive a stock dividend, but under certain circumstances, the IRS may treat you as having received a taxable distribution. This may happen when a company increases the ratio of convertible preferred stock.

WHO REPORTS THE DIVIDENDS

¶4.9 **Stock held by broker in street name.** If your broker holds stock for you in a street name, dividends earned on this stock are received by the broker and credited to your account. You report all dividends credited to your account in 1992. The broker is required to file an information return on Form 1099 (or similar form) showing all such dividends.

If your statement shows only a gross amount of dividends, check with your broker if any of the dividends represented nontaxable returns of capital.

Dividends on stock sold or bought between ex-dividend date and record date. Record date is the date set by a company on which you must be listed as a stockholder on its records to receive the dividend. However, in the case of publicly traded stock, an ex-dividend date, which usually precedes the record date by several days, is fixed by the exchange to determine who is entitled to the dividend.

If you buy stock before the ex-dividend date, the dividend belongs to you and is reported by you. If you buy on or after the ex-dividend date, the dividend belongs to the seller.

If you sell stock before the ex-dividend date, you do not have a right to the dividend. If you sell on or after the ex-dividend date, you receive the dividend and report it as income.

The dividend declaration date and date of payment do not determine who receives the dividend.

Stock sold short. For a discussion of how to treat a payment to a broker for dividends paid on stock sold short; see ¶5.20.

Nominees. If you receive dividends on stock held as a nominee for another person, other than your spouse, give that owner a Form 1099-DIV and file a copy of that return with the IRS, along with a Form 1096 ("Transmittal of U.S. Information Return"). The actual owner then reports the income. List the nominee dividends on Schedule B of Form 1040 (or Schedule 1, Form 1040A) along with your other dividends, and then subtract the nominee dividends from the total. Follow the same procedure if you receive a Form 1099-DIV for an account owned jointly with someone other than your spouse. Give the other owner a Form 1099-DIV, and file a copy with the IRS, along with a Form 1096. The other owner then reports his or her share of the joint income. On your return, you list the total dividends shown on Forms 1099-DIV and avoid tax by subtracting from the total the nominee dividends reported to the other owner.

EXAMPLE You receive Form 1099-DIV showing dividends of $960 including a $200 nominee distribution. You prepare a Form 1099-DIV for the actual owner showing the $200 distribution, and file a copy of the form with the IRS, plus Form 1096. On your own Schedule B, report the nominee distribution along with your other dividends and then subtract it from the total.

Dividend Income	Amount
Mutual Fund	$310
Computer Inc.	450
Utility Inc.	200
Subtotal	$960
Less: Nominee Distribution	(200)
Net dividends	$760

YEAR DIVIDENDS ARE REPORTED

¶4.10 Dividends are generally reported on the tax return for the year in which the dividend is unqualifiedly credited to your account or when you receive the dividend check. However, a dividend declared in December by a mutual fund (¶4.3) is taxable in the year it is declared, if it is paid before February 1 of the following year.

EXAMPLES 1. A corporation declares a dividend payable on December 20, 1992. It follows a practice of paying dividends by checks that are mailed so that stockholders do not receive them until January 1993. You report this dividend on your 1993 return.

2. On December 31, 1992, a dividend is declared by a mutual fund. You receive it in January 1993. The dividend is taxable in 1992, when it is declared, and not 1993 when it is received.

3. On December 31, 1992, a dividend is credited to a stockholder's account. The dividend is taxable in 1992, as the crediting is considered constructive receipt in 1992, even though the dividend is not paid until 1993 or a later year.

Dividends received from a corporation in a year after the one in which they were declared, when you held the stock on the record date, are taxed in the year they are received.

EXAMPLE You own stock in a corporation. In April 1991, the corporation declared a dividend. But it provided that the dividend will be paid when it gets the cash. It finally pays the dividend in September 1992; the dividend is taxable in 1992.

Back dividends on preferred stock accumulated before you bought the stock but paid after you acquired it are taxed in the year you receive them.

DISTRIBUTION NOT OUT OF EARNINGS: RETURN OF CAPITAL

¶4.11 A return of capital or "nontaxable distribution" reduces the cost basis of the stock. If the cost basis is reduced to zero, further returns of capital are taxed as capital gains on Schedule D, or on Line 14 of Form 1040 if you do not need Schedule D to report other transactions. Whether the gain is short- or long-term depends on the length of time you have held the stock. The company paying the dividend will usually inform you of the tax treatment of the payment.

Life insurance dividends. Dividends on insurance policies are not true dividends. They are returns of premiums you previously paid. They reduce the cost of the policy and are not subject to tax until they exceed the net premiums paid for the contract. Interest paid or credited on dividends left with the insurance company is taxable. Dividends on VA insurance are tax free. Where insurance premiums were deducted as a business expense in prior years, receipts of insurance dividends are either included in income or taken as a reduction of the insurance expense deduction of the current year. Dividends on capital stock of an insurance company are taxable dividends.

Key to Interest Income Rules

Item—	Pointer—
Form 1099-INT	Forms 1099-INT, sent by payers of interest income, simplify the reporting of interest income. The forms give you the amount of interest to enter on your tax return. Although they are generally correct, you should check for mistakes and notify payers of any error and request a form marked "corrected." If tax was withheld (¶26.12), claim this tax as a payment on your tax return. The IRS will check interest reported on your return against the Forms 1099-INT sent by banks and other payers.
Deposits in a savings account	Interest credited to your savings account for 1992 is taxable even though you do not present your passbook to have the interest entered. Dividends on deposits or accounts in the following institutions are reported as interest income: mutual savings banks; cooperative banks; domestic building and loan associations; and domestic and federal savings and loan associations.
Savings certificates, deferred interest, or bonus plan	The interest element on certificates of deposit and similar plans of more than one year is treated as original issue discount (OID) and is taxable on an annual basis. The bank notifies you of the taxable OID amount on Form 1099-OID. If you discontinue a savings plan before maturity, you may have a loss deduction for forfeited interest, which is listed on Form 1099-INT or Form 1099-OID; see ¶4.16. Tax on interest can be deferred on a savings certificate with a term of one year or less. Interest is taxable in the year it is available for withdrawal without substantial penalty. Where you invest in a six-month certificate before July 1, the entire amount of interest is paid six months later and is taxable in the year of payment. However, when you invest in a six-month certificate after June 30, only interest actually paid or made available for withdrawal without substantial penalty is taxable in the year of issuance. The balance is taxable in the year of maturity. You can defer interest to the following year by investing in a six-month certificate after June 30, provided the payment of interest is specifically deferred to the year of maturity by the terms of the certificate. Similarly, interest may be deferred to the following year by investing in longer term certificates of up to one year, provided that the crediting of interest is specifically deferred until the year of maturity.
U.S. Savings Bonds—Series E, EE	The increase in redemption value of these Savings Bonds is interest income. You do not have to report the annual increase in value until the year in which you cash the bond or the year in which the bond finally matures, whichever is earlier; see ¶4.28.
U.S. Savings Bonds—Series H, HH	Semi-annual interest on these bonds is taxable when received.
U.S. Treasury bills	If your T-bill matured in 1992, report as interest the difference between the amount received at redemption and your cost. If in 1992 you sold a bill before maturity, you may have a capital loss, or a gain that is partly interest income and partly capital gain; see ¶4.27.
Zero Coupon Bonds	The interest element is treated as original issue discount (OID) and is taxable annually. You receive a Form 1099-OID reporting the taxable amount.
Interest on funds invested abroad	Interest must be reported in U.S. dollars. If foreign tax has been paid, you may be entitled to a deduction or credit; see ¶36.14. See also ¶36.12 for blocked currency reporting rules.
Bearer or coupon bonds	Interest coupons due and payable in 1992 are taxable on your 1992 return regardless of when they were presented for collection. For example, a coupon due January 1992 and presented for payment in 1991 is taxable in 1992. Similarly, a coupon due December 1992 but presented for payment in 1993 is taxable in 1992.
Corporate obligations in registered form	You report interest when received or made available to you. See ¶4.15 on how to treat interest when you buy or sell bonds between interest dates.
Interest on state and local government obligations	Although you may receive a Form 1099-INT for interest on state or municipal bonds, you do not pay federal tax on the interest. You are required to list the tax-exempt interest on your tax return, although it is not taxable. The interest may be subject to state income tax.
Borrowing to meet minimum deposit requirements for savings certificates	Interest expenses are deductible as itemized investment interest deductions. Report the full amount of interest income listed on Form 1099-INT, even if you do not take interest deductions.
Insurance proceeds	You report interest paid on insurance proceeds left with an insurance company or included in installment payments (under optional modes of payment). Exception: A surviving spouse of an insured person who died before October 23, 1986, is not taxed on up to $1,000 a year of interest included in installment payments.
Interest on prepaid premium	Taxable interest is reported by insurance company on Form 1099-INT.
Interest on tax refunds	Interest on tax refunds is fully taxable.
Bank gifts	The value of gifts is taxable. To attract new deposits, banks and thrifts may offer cash, televisions, toasters, and the like as inducements. The gifts are taxable as interest and reported on Form 1099-INT.
Interest on unwithdrawn life insurance dividends	If you can withdraw the interest annually, you report the interest in the year it is credited to your account. However, if under the terms of the insurance policy, the interest can be withdrawn only on the anniversary date of the policy (or some other specified date), then you report the interest in the year in which the anniversary date of the policy (or some other specified date) falls. Interest on GI insurance dividends on deposit with the VA is not taxable; see ¶35.2.

REPORTING INTEREST INCOME

REPORTING INTEREST ON YOUR TAX RETURN

¶4.12 You must report all taxable interest. If you earn over $400 of taxable interest, you list the payers of interest on Schedule B if you file Form 1040, or on Part I of Schedule I if you file Form 1040A. Form 1040EZ may not be used if your taxable interest exceeds $400. You must also list tax-exempt interest on your return although it is not taxable.

You must also list interest that has been shown on Forms 1099 in your name although it may not be taxable to you. For example, you may have received interest as a nominee or as accrued interest on bonds bought between interest dates. In these cases, list the amounts reported on Form 1099 along with your other interest income on Schedule B if you file Form 1040, or Schedule I if you file Form 1040A. On a separate line, label the amount as "Nominee distribution," or "Accrued interest," and subtract it from the total interest shown. Accrued interest is discussed at ¶4.15 and in the chart on page 55. Nominee distributions are discussed further in the chart on page 55.

If you received interest on a frozen account (¶4.13), include the interest from Form 1099 on Schedule B if you file Form 1040, or on Schedule I if you use Form 1040A. On a separate line, write "Frozen deposits" and subtract the amount from the total interest reported.

You do not have to list the payers of interest if your interest receipts are $400 or less, unless you have to reduce the interest shown on Form 1099 by nontaxable amounts such as accrued interest, nominee distributions, or frozen deposit interest.

INTEREST ON FROZEN ACCOUNTS NOT TAXED

¶4.13 If you have funds in a bankrupt or insolvent financial institution that "freezes" your account by limiting withdrawals, you do not pay tax on interest allocable to the "frozen" deposits. The interest is taxable when withdrawals are permitted. Officers and owners of at least a 1% interest in the financial institution, or their relatives, may not take advantage of this rule and must still report interest on frozen deposits.

If you report interest on Schedule B of Form 1040 or on Schedule I of Form 1040A, report the full amount shown on Form 1099-INT, even if the interest is on a "frozen" deposit. Then, on a separate line, subtract the amount allocable to the frozen deposit from the total interest shown on the Schedule; label the subtraction "Frozen Deposits." Thus the interest on the frozen deposit is not included on the line of your return showing taxable interest.

Lost deposits. If you lose funds because of a financial institution's bankruptcy or insolvency, and you can reasonably estimate such a loss, you may deduct the loss as a nonbusiness bad debt, as a casualty loss, or as a miscellaneous itemized deduction; *see* ¶18.4.

Refund opportunity. If you reported interest on a frozen deposit on a tax return for 1989-1991, you may file a refund claim for the tax paid on the interest; *see* Chapter 38.

INTEREST INCOME ON DEBTS OWED YOU

¶4.14 You report interest earned on money which you loan to another person. If you are on the cash basis, you report interest in the year you actually receive it or when it is considered received under the "constructive receipt rule." If you are on the accrual basis, you report interest when it is earned, whether or not you have received it.

See ¶4.31 for minimum interest rates required for loans and ¶4.18 when OID rules apply.

Where partial payment is being made on a debt, or when a debt is being compromised, the parties may agree in advance which part of the payment covers interest and principal. If a payment is not identified as either principal or interest, the payment is first applied against interest due and reported as interest income to the extent of the interest due.

Interest income is not realized when a debtor gives you a new note for an old note where the new note includes the interest due on the old note.

If you give away a debtor's note, you report as income the collectible interest due at the date of the gift. To avoid tax on the interest, the note must be transferred before interest becomes due.

REPORTING INTEREST ON BONDS BOUGHT OR SOLD

¶4.15 Where you buy or sell bonds between interest dates, interest is included in the price of the bonds. The purchaser does not report as income the interest that accrued before he or she owned the bond. The seller reports the accrued interest. The purchaser reduces the basis of the bond by the accrued interest reported by the seller. The examples on the next page illustrate these rules.

EXAMPLES 1. *Purchase.* On April 30, you buy for $5,250 a $5000 corporate bond bearing interest at 8% per year, payable January 1 and July 1. The purchase price of the bond included accrued interest of $133 for the period January 1—April 30.

Interest received on 7/1	$200
Less: Accrued interest	133
Taxable interest	$ 67

Form 1099 sent to you includes the $133 of accrued interest. On Schedule B of Form 1040, you report the total interest of $200 received on July 1 and then on a separate line subtract the accrued interest of $133. Write "Accrued Interest" on the line where you show the subtraction.

Your basis for the bond is $5,117 ($5,250 − $133) for purposes of figuring gain or loss on a later sale of the bond.

2. *Sale.* On April 30, you sell for $5,250 a $5,000 8% bond with interest payable January 1 and July 1. The sales price included interest of $133 accrued from January 1—April 30. Your cost for the bond was $5,000. On your return, you report interest of $133 and capital gain of $117.

You receive	$5,250
Less: Accrued interest	133
Sales proceeds	$5,117
Less: Your cost	5,000
Capital gain	$ 117

Redemptions, bankruptcy, reorganizations. On a redemption, interest received in excess of the amount due at that time is not treated as interest income.

EXAMPLE You hold a $5,000 9% bond with interest payable January 1 and July 1. The company can call the bonds for redemption on any interest date. In May, the company announces it will redeem the bonds on July 1. But you may present the bond for redemption beginning with June 1 and it will be redeemed with interest to July 1. On June 1 you present the bond and receive $5,225—$5,000 principal, $187.50 interest to June 1, and $37.50 extra interest to July 1. The $37.50 is treated as a capital gain, not interest income. The $187.50 is interest.

Taxable interest may continue on bonds after the issuer becomes bankrupt, if a guarantor continues to pay the interest when due. The loss on the bonds will occur only when they mature and are not redeemed or when they are sold below your cost. In the meantime, the interest received from the guarantor is taxed.

Bondholders exchanging their bonds for stock, securities, or other property in a tax-free reorganization, including a reorganization in bankruptcy, have interest income to the extent the property received is attributable to accrued but unpaid interest. *See* Internal Revenue Code Section 354 for further details.

Bonds selling at a flat price. When you buy bonds with defaulted interest at a "flat" price, a later payment of the defaulted interest is not taxed. It is a tax-free return of capital that reduces your cost of the bond. This rule applies only to interest in default at the time the bond is purchased. Interest that accrues after the date of your purchase is taxed as ordinary income.

Who Reports Interest Income

If interest is—	It is reported by—
Joint account interest	The person whose Social Security number is reported to the bank (or other payer) on Form W-9 when the account is opened. If the other owner is not your spouse, and you receive a Form 1099-INT for the interest, you should report all the income on your return and also file a nominee Form 1099-INT with the other owner to indicate the other owner's share of the interest. These rules are discussed in the next item. Do not file a nominee form if you contributed all the funds and named a joint owner so that he or she may automatically inherit the account. You report all the interest.
Nominee distribution	If you receive a Form 1099-INT that includes interest belonging to someone other than you or your spouse, file a nominee Form 1099-INT with the IRS to indicate that person's income, and give a copy to that person. Complete a Form 1099-INT on which you are listed as the payer and the other person is listed as the recipient. Give the Form 1099-INT to the other owner by February 1, 1993. File Form 1099-INT plus Form 1096 ("Transmittal of Information Return") with the IRS by March 1, 1993. On your own Form 1040 or Form 1040A, you list the nominee interest, along with the other interest reported to you on Forms 1099-INT. Then, subtract the nominee interest from the total. For example, assume that your Social Security number is listed on a bank account owned jointly with your sister. You each invested 50% of the account principal and have agreed to share the interest income. You receive a Form 1099-INT for 1992 reporting total interest of $1,500 on the account. By February 1, 1993, prepare and give to your sister another Form 1099-INT which identifies you as the payer and she as the recipient of her share, or $750 interest. Send a copy of the Form 1099-INT and a Form 1096 to the IRS no later than March 1, 1993. Your sister will report the $750 interest on her return. On your Form 1040, report the full $1,500 interest on Line 1 of Schedule B, along with your other interest income. Above Line 2, subtract the $750 belonging to your sister to avoid being taxed on that amount; label the subtraction "Nominee Distribution."
Accrued interest on a bond bought between interest payment dates	Interest accrued between interest dates is part of the purchase price of the bond. This amount is taxable to the seller as explained at ¶4.15. If you received a Form 1099-INT that includes accrued interest on a bond, include the interest on Line 1 of Schedule B, and then on a separate line above Line 2 subtract the accrued interest from the Line 1 total.
Custodian account of a minor (Uniform Gifts to Minors Act)	The interest is taxable to the child. For a child under age 14, net investment income exceeding $1,200 is subject to tax at the parent's top tax rate; see Chapter 24.

FORFEITURE OF INTEREST
ON PREMATURE WITHDRAWALS

¶4.16 Banks usually impose an interest penalty if you withdraw funds from a savings certificate before the specified maturity date. You may lose interest if you prematurely withdraw funds in order to switch to higher paying investments, or if you need the funds for personal use. In some cases, the penalty may exceed the interest earned so that principal is also forfeited to make up the difference.

If you are penalized, you must still report the full amount of interest credited to your account. However, on Form 1040, you may deduct the full amount of the penalty-forfeited principal as well as interest. The deductible amount is shown in Box 2 of Form 1099-INT sent to you. You may claim the deduction, even if you do not itemize deductions. On Form 1040, enter the deduction in the section "Adjustments to Income" on Line 28, marked "Penalty on early withdrawal of savings."

Loss on redemption before maturity of a savings certificate. If you redeem a long-term (more than one year) savings certificate for a price less than the stated redemption price at maturity, you are allowed a loss deduction for the amount of original issue discount (OID) reported as income but not received. The amount of the loss is the excess of: (1) the OID reported as income for the period you held the certificate; over (2) the excess of the amount received upon the redemption over the issue price.

Do not include in the computation any amount based on a fixed rate of simple or compound interest that is actually payable or is treated as constructively received at fixed periodic intervals of one year or less. The basis of the obligation is reduced by the amount of the deductible loss.

EXAMPLE In 1989, you pay $4,000 for a $5,000 face amount four-year savings certificate that matures December 31, 1993. The original issue discount is $1,000, of which $250 is reported each year. In 1992, when you redeem the certificate, you receive $4,660. In 1989, 1990, and 1991, you reported $250 of original issue discount for a total of $750. At redemption, the $660 you received in excess of your cost ($4,660 − $4,000) is $90 less than the original issue discount of $750 which was reported as income. The $90 difference is a deductible loss claimed on Line 28 of Form 1040.

PREMIUMS AND DISCOUNTS ON BONDS

AMORTIZATION OF BOND PREMIUM

¶4.17 Bond premium is the extra amount paid for a bond in excess of its principal or face amount when the value of the bond has increased due to falling interest rates. Investors may elect to amortize the premium on a *taxable* bond by deducting it over the life of the bond. Amortizing the premium annually is usually advantageous because it gives a current deduction against ordinary income. Basis of the bond is reduced by the amortized premium.

You may not claim a deduction for a premium paid on a *tax-exempt* bond; however, you must still decrease your basis by the premium.

Dealers in bonds may not deduct amortization but must include the premium as part of cost.

If you do not elect to amortize the premium on a taxable bond, you will realize a capital loss when the bond is redeemed at par or you sell it for less than you paid for it. For example, if you bought a $1,000 corporate bond several years ago for $1,300 and did not amortize the $300 premium, you will realize a $300 capital loss when the bond is redeemed at par: $1,000 proceeds less $1,300 cost basis ($1,000 face value plus $300 premium).

Amortization method. The amount of allocable premium for the year is based on a constant interest method if the bond was issued after September 27, 1985, and on a straight-line method for earlier bonds. Pending the release of IRS guidelines, you should consult a tax professional for making the constant interest allocation.

How to Deduct Amortized Premium

If you paid a premium on a taxable bond during 1992, you offset interest income on the bond by the amortizable premium. You must file Form 1040 and show the reduction on Schedule B. Report the full interest from the bond on Line 1 of Schedule B, along with the rest of your interest income. On a separate line, subtract the premium from a subtotal of the other interest. Label the subtraction "ABP Adjustment."

This interest offset rule applies to all taxable bonds acquired at a premium after 1987; *see* the next column for bonds acquired before 1988.

Bonds acquired after October 22, 1986, but before 1988. It is generally advisable to elect to reduce interest income by the allocated premium as just discussed in the Filing Pointer for bonds acquired after 1987. If you do not make the election, you must treat the premium as investment interest subject to the deduction limits discussed at ¶15.9.

Bonds acquired before October 23, 1986. The allocable premium is fully deductible on Schedule A as a miscellaneous deduction; it is not subject to the 2% adjusted gross income limit.

Effect of amortization election on other bonds you acquire. The election to amortize does not have to be made in the year you acquire the bond. If you elect to amortize premium for one bond, you must also amortize premium on all similar bonds owned by you at the beginning of the tax year, and also to all similar bonds acquired thereafter. An election to amortize may not be revoked without IRS permission. If you file your return without claiming the deduction, you may not change your mind and make the election for that year by filing an amended return or refund claim. If an election is made after the first year, the premium allocable to earlier years is included in your cost basis for the bond and will result in capital loss when the bond is redeemed at par or sold for less than basis.

Amortized Premium Reduces Basis

You reduce the cost basis of the bond by the amount of the premium taken as a deduction.

If you hold the bond to maturity, the entire premium is amortized and you have neither gain nor loss on redemption of the bond. If in 1992 you sell the bond at a gain (selling price exceeds your basis for the bond), you realize long-term capital gain if you held the bond long term. A sale of the bond for less than its adjusted basis gives a capital loss.

Callable bonds. On fully taxable bonds, amortization is based either on the maturity or earlier call date, depending on which date gives a smaller yearly deduction. This rule applies regardless of the issue date of the bond. If the bond is called before maturity, you may deduct as an ordinary loss the unamortized bond premium in the year the bond is redeemed.

Convertible bonds. If you paid a premium for a convertible bond, the premium allocated to the conversion feature may not be amortized.

Tax-exempt bonds. You may not take a deduction for the amortization of a premium paid on a tax-exempt bond. When you dispose of the bond, you amortize the premium for the period you held the bond and reduce the basis of the bond by the amortized amount.

If the bond has call dates, the IRS may require the premium to be amortized to the earliest call date.

Acquisition premium paid on bonds with original issue discount. If you paid more than the original issue price plus accumulated OID from the date of issue, that excess, called *acquisition premium,* reduces the amount of OID that you have to include in income; see ¶4.18.

DISCOUNT ON BONDS

¶**4.18** There are two types of bond discounts: original issue discount and market discount.

Market discount. Market discount arises when the price of a bond declines because its interest rate is less than the current interest rate. For example, a bond originally issued at its face amount of $1,000 declines in value to $900 because the interest payable on the bond is less than the current interest rate. The difference of $100 is called market discount. The tax treatment of market discount is explained in ¶4.20.

Original issue discount (OID). OID arises when a bond is issued for a price less than its face or principal amount. OID is the difference between the principal amount and the issue price. For publicly offered obligations, the issue price is the initial offering price to the public at which a substantial amount of such obligations were sold. All obligations that pay no interest before maturity, such as zero coupon bonds, are considered to be issued at a discount. For example, a bond with a face amount of $1,000 is issued at an offering price of $900. The $100 difference is OID.

Generally, part of the OID must be reported as interest income each year you hold the bond. This is also true for certificates of deposit, time deposits, and similar savings arrangements with a term of more than one year, provided payment of interest is deferred until maturity. OID is reported to you by the issuer (or by your broker if you bought the obligation on a secondary market) on Form 1099-OID; see ¶4.19 for reporting OID.

No OID if bought at premium. If you pay more than face amount for a bond originally issued at a discount, you do not report OID as ordinary income. When you dispose of a bond bought at a premium, the difference between the sale or redemption price and your basis is a capital gain or loss; see ¶4.17. However, this rule does not apply if you pay more than the original issue price plus accumulated OID. Your excess payment, called the *acquisition premium,* reduces the amount of OID you must report as income. The rules for computing the reduction to OID depend on when the bond was purchased. For bonds purchased after July 18, 1984, OID is reduced by a fraction, the numerator of which is the acquisition premium; the denominator is the OID remaining after your purchase date to the maturity date. See IRS Publication 1212 for making the computation.

Exceptions to OID. OID rules do not apply to: (1) obligations with a term of one year or less held by cash basis taxpayers, *see* ¶4.21; (2) tax-exempt obligations; (3) U.S. Savings Bonds; (4) an obligation issued by an individual before March 2, 1984; and (5) loans of $10,000 or less from individuals.

You may disregard OID that is less than one-fourth of one percent (.0025) of the principal amount multiplied by the number of full years from the rate of original issue to maturity. On most long-term bonds, the OID will exceed this amount and must be reported.

EXAMPLES 1. A 10-year bond with face amount of $1,000 is issued at $980. One-fourth of one percent of $1,000 times 10 is $25. As the $20 OID is less than $25, it may be ignored for tax purposes.

2. Same facts as in Example 1 except that the bond is issued at $950. As OID of $50 is more than the $25, OID must be reported under the rules explained at ¶4.19.

HOW TO REPORT ORIGINAL ISSUE DISCOUNT (OID) ON OBLIGATIONS

¶**4.19** The issuer of the bond (or your broker) will make the OID computation and report to you in Box 1 of Form 1099-OID the *total* OID on the obligation for the calendar year. However, in some cases, the amount shown in Box 1 of Form 1099-OID may have to be reduced to avoid reporting too much income. The amount shown in Box 1 is figured on the assumption that you purchased the obligation at original issue and *also* that you owned it for every day in the year that it was outstanding. Therefore, you should report the amount shown in Box 1 if you bought the obligation at original issue and held it for all of 1992, or for the part of 1992 that it was outstanding. However, the amount shown in Box 1 may be incorrect income for your holding period, and you may reduce the taxable amount. This may happen if you bought the obligation after its original issue, or at original issue but did not hold it for the entire period it was outstanding in 1992. IRS Publication 1212 explains how to figure the lower amount of OID to be reported.

If you did not receive a Form 1099-OID, contact the issuer or check IRS Publication 1212 for OID amounts.

Stripped bonds or coupon. The amount shown in Box 1 of Form 1099-OID will not be correct for a stripped bond or coupon; *see* ¶4.22.

Where to report OID

If you are reporting the full amount of OID from Box 1 of Form 1099-OID, as previously explained, include the amount as interest on your Form 1040, 1040A, or 1040EZ. However, if you are reporting *less* OID than the amount shown in Box 1 of Form 1099-OID, you must file Form 1040 and fill out Schedule B. Include the full amount shown in Box 1 of Form 1099-OID on Line 1 of Schedule B, along with other interest income. Make a subtotal of the Line 1 amounts and subtract from it the OID you are not required to report. Write "OID Adjustment" on the line where you show the subtraction.

Your basis for the obligation is increased by the taxable OID for purposes of figuring gain on a sale or redemption; see ¶4.23.

Periodic interest reported on Form 1099-OID. If in addition to OID there is regular interest payable on the bond, such interest will be reported in Box 2 of Form 1099-OID. Report the full amount as interest income if you held the bond for the entire year. If you acquired the bond or disposed of it during the year, *see* ¶4.15 for figuring the interest allocable to your ownership period.

REPORTING INCOME ON MARKET DISCOUNT BONDS

¶4.20   Market discount arises where the price of a bond declines below its face amount because it carries an interest rate that is below the current rate of interest. The treatment of market discount generally depends on whether the bonds were issued before July 19, 1984, or on or after that date.

Bonds issued before July 19, 1984. Gain attributable to the market discount on the sale of the bond *issued* before July 19, 1984, is generally treated as capital gain. However, you may have ordinary income if you borrow money to purchase or carry a market discount bond acquired after July 18, 1984. Under a restrictive rule discussed below, the interest deduction on the loan is restricted. In the year the bond is sold, you may claim an interest deduction for any interest expense that could not be deducted in prior years under the restrictive rule. Gain on the disposition is ordinary income to the extent of the deferred interest you may deduct in the year of disposition; the balance is capital gain.

EXAMPLE   You paid $910 for a bond that had been originally issued in 1983 at its face amount of $1,000. The difference of $90 is market discount. In 1992, you sell the bond for $980. The $70 profit is long-term capital gain.

Bonds issued after July 18, 1984. Generally, market discount is taken into account when a bond is sold, but an election may be made to report the discount annually as interest income. Market discount on bonds *acquired* after October 22, 1986, may have to be included in current income where the issuer of the bond pays you part of the bond principal; *see* the next column.

On a sale of a bond *issued* after July 18, 1984, gain is taxed as ordinary interest income to the extent of the market discount accrued to the date of sale. The daily accrual is figured by dividing market discount by the number of days in the period from the date you bought the bond until the date of maturity. This method of computing the daily accrual is called the *ratable accrual method.* If you hold the bond until maturity, the discount is reported as interest income in the year of redemption.

EXAMPLE   Market discount on a bond issued after July 18, 1984, is $200, and there are 1,000 days between the date of your purchase and maturity date. The daily accrual rate is 20 cents. You hold the bond for 600 days before selling it for a price exceeding what you paid for the bond. Under the ratable accrual method, up to $120 of your profit is market discount taxable as interest income (600 × 0.20).

Optional Accrual Method

Instead of using the ratable accrual method to compute accrual of market discount, you may elect to figure the accrued discount for any bond under the constant interest method. If you make the election, you may not change it. The constant interest method initially provides a smaller accrual of market discount than the ratable method, but it is more complicated to figure. The complex constant interest method, which is based on the actual economic accrual of interest, is explained in IRS Publication 1212. If the bond was purchased with borrowed funds, making the election reduces the deferral of interest deductions that is otherwise required; the deferral is discussed at the end of this section.

Exceptions to interest income rules. The following bonds are not subject to the interest income rules for market discount bonds: (1) bonds acquired after July 18, 1984, that were issued on or before that date; (2) bonds with a maturity date of up to one year from date of issuance; (3) tax-exempt obligations; (4) installment obligations; and (5) U.S. Savings Bonds. Furthermore, you may treat as zero any market discount that is less than one-fourth of one percent of the redemption price multiplied by the number of full years after you acquire the bond to maturity. Such minimal discount will not affect capital gain on a sale.

Reporting Discount Annually

Rather than report market discount in the year you sell the bond, you may elect, in the year you acquire the bond, to report market discount currently as interest income. You may use either the ratable accrual method, as in the following example, or the constant interest rate method explained in IRS Publication 1212. Your election to report currently applies to all market discount bonds issued after July 18, 1984, that you later acquire. You may not revoke the election without IRS consent. If the election is made, the interest deduction deferral rule discussed at the end of this section does not apply. Furthermore, the election could provide a tax advantage if you sell the bond at a profit and you can benefit from the 28% maximum capital gains rate; *see* ¶5.1.

EXAMPLE   In 1992 you buy at a $200 discount a bond that was issued after July 18, 1984. There are 1,000 days between the date of your purchase and the maturity date, so that daily accrual is 20 cents. You elect to report the market discount currently using the ratable accrual method. If you held the bond for 112 days in 1992, on your 1992 return you report $22 as interest income (112 × $0.20).

Partial principal payments are taxable. If you acquired a market discount bond after October 22, 1986, and the issuer of the bond makes a partial payment of the principal (face amount), you must include the payment as ordinary interest income to the extent it does not exceed the accrued market discount on the bond. *See* IRS Publication 550 for options on determining accrued market discount. A taxable partial principal payment reduces the amount of remaining accrued market discount when figuring your tax on a later sale or receipt of another partial principal payment.

Market discount on a bond originally issued at a discount. A bond issued at original issue discount may later be acquired at a market discount because of an increase in interest rates. If you acquire at market discount an OID bond issued after July 18, 1984, the market discount is the excess of: (1) the issue price of the bond plus the total original issue discount includable in the gross income of all prior holders of the bond over (2) what you paid for the bond.

Exchanging market discount bond in corporate reorganizations. If you hold a market discount bond and exchange it for another bond as part of a merger or other reorganization, the new bond is subject to the market discount rules when you sell it. However, under an exception, market discount rules will not apply to the new bond if the old market discount bond was issued before July 19, 1984, and the terms and interest rates of both bonds are identical.

Deferral of interest deduction limited if you borrow to buy market discount bonds after July 18, 1984. If you took such a loan, deductible interest expense is generally limited to the excess of the interest expense over the interest income earned on the bond for the year (including OID income, if any) *less* any market discount allocated to the days you held the bond during the year. The limitation on the interest deduction applies to bonds you acquire after July 18, 1984, regardless of the issue date of the bond. The allocation of market discount is based on either the ratable accrual method or constant interest method.

You can avoid this interest deduction limitation if you elect to report the market discount annually as interest income, as discussed in the Filing Pointer on page 58.

EXAMPLE In 1992, you borrowed to buy a market discount bond. During 1992, your interest expense is $1,000. Income from the bond is $900 and ratable market discount allocated to the annual holding period is $75. Thus, only $25 is deductible investment interest ($1,000 − $975), subject to the limitations on investment interest; *see* ¶15.9.

When to Claim Deferred Interest

In the year the market discount bond is disposed of, you may deduct any interest expense disallowed in prior years because of the limitation. However, you may choose to deduct disallowed interest in a year before the year of disposition if you have net interest income from the bond. Net interest income is interest income for the year less the interest expense incurred during the year to purchase or carry the bond. This election lets you deduct any disallowed interest expense to the extent it does not exceed the net interest income of that year. The balance of the disallowed interest expense is deductible in the year of disposition.

DISCOUNT ON SHORT-TERM OBLIGATIONS

¶**4.21** Short-term obligations (maturity of a year or less) may be purchased at a discount from face value. If you are on the *cash basis,* you report the discount as interest income when the obligation is paid. The interest is reported on Form 1099-INT.

EXAMPLE In May 1991, you paid $920 for a short-term note with a face amount of $1,000. In January 1992, you receive payment of $1,000 on the note. On your 1992 tax return, you report $80 as interest.

Discount must be currently reported by dealers and accrual basis taxpayers. Discount allocable to the current year must be reported as income by accrual basis taxpayers, dealers who sell short-term obligation in the course of business, banks, regulated investment companies, common trust funds, certain pass-through entities, and for obligations identified as part of a hedging transaction. Current reporting also applies to persons who separate or strip interest coupons from a bond and then retain the stripped bond or stripped coupon; the accrual rule applies to the retained obligation.

For short-term *governmental* obligations (other than tax-exempts), the acquisition discount is accrued in daily installments under the ratable method, unless an election is made to use the constant interest method, as discussed in ¶4.20.

For short-term *nongovernmental* obligations, OID is generally taken into account instead of acquisition discount; but an election may be made to report the accrued acquisition discount. *See* IRS Publication 550 for details.

Interest deduction limitation for cash basis investors. A cash basis investor who borrows funds to buy a short-term discount obligation may not fully deduct interest on the loan unless an election is made to report the accrued acquisition discount as income. If the election is not made, a complicated formula limits deductible interest to the excess of the interest expense for the year over the taxable interest from the bond during the year less (1) the portion of the discount allocated to the days you held the bond during the year, and

(2) the portion of interest not taxable for the year under your method of accounting. Any interest expense disallowed under this limitation is deductible in the year in which the obligation is disposed.

The interest deduction limitation does *not* apply if you elect to include in income the accruable discount as explained in ¶4.20. The election applies to all short-term obligations acquired during the year and also in all later years.

Gain or loss on disposition of short-term obligations. If you have a gain on the sale or exchange of a discounted short-term governmental obligation (other than tax-exempt local obligations), the gain is ordinary income to the extent of the ratable share of the acquisition discount received when you bought the obligation. Follow the computation shown in ¶4.27 for Treasury bills to figure this ordinary income portion. Any gain over this ordinary income portion is capital gain; a loss would be a capital loss.

Gain on short-term nongovernmental obligations is treated as ordinary income up to the ratable share of OID. The formula for figuring this ordinary income portion is similar to that shown in ¶4.27 for short-term governmental obligations, except that the denominator of the fraction is days from original issue to maturity, rather than days from acquisition. Gain above the computed ordinary income amount is capital gain (*see* Chapter 5). For more information, *see* IRS Publication 550.

STRIPPED COUPON BONDS

¶**4.22** Brokers holding coupon bonds may separate or strip the coupons from the bonds and sell the bonds or coupons to investors. Examples include zero-coupon instruments sold by brokerage houses that are backed by U.S. Treasury bonds (such as CATS, TIGRS).

The U.S. Treasury also offers its version of zero coupon instruments, with the name STRIPS, which are available from brokers and banks.

If you buy a stripped bond or coupon, the spread between the lower cost of the bond or coupon and its face amount is treated as original issue discount (OID). This means that you annually report a part of the spread as interest income. For a stripped bond, the amount of the original issue discount is the difference between the stated redemption price of the bond at maturity and the cost of the bond. For a stripped coupon, the amount of the discount is the difference between the amount payable on the due date of the coupon and the cost of the coupon. See ¶4.19 for reporting OID.

If you strip a coupon bond, interest accrual and allocation rules prevent you from creating a tax loss on a sale of the bond or coupons. You are required to report interest accrued up to the date of the sale and also add the amount to the basis of the bond. If you acquired the obligation after October 22, 1986, you must also include in income any market discount that accrued before the date you sold the stripped bond or coupons. The method of accrual depends on the date you bought the obligation; *see* IRS Publication 1212. The accrued market discount is also added to the basis of the bond. You then allocate this basis between the bond and the coupons. The allocation is based on the relative fair market values of the bond and coupons at the date of sale. Gain or loss on the sale is the difference between the sales price of the stripped item (bond or coupons) and its allocated basis. Furthermore, the original issue discount rules apply to the stripped item which you keep (bond or coupon). Original issue discount for this purpose is the difference between the basis allocated to the retained item and the redemption price of the bond (if retained) or the amount payable on the coupons (if retained). You must annually report a ratable portion of the discount.

Recomputing Form 1099-OID Amount

Do not report the amount shown in Box 1 of Form 1099-OID for a stripped bond or coupon as income; that amount must be recomputed under complicated rules described in IRS Publication 1212. Ask your broker for information on making the computation.

SALE OR RETIREMENT OF BONDS AND NOTES

¶4.23 Gain or loss on the sale, redemption, or retirement of debt obligations issued by a government or corporation is generally capital gain or loss. If the bond was issued before 1955, there is capital gain or loss only if the obligation was issued with interest coupons or in registered form on or before March 1, 1954.

Corporate bonds with OID issued after 1954 and before May 28, 1969, and government bonds with OID issued before July 2, 1982. If the bonds were originally issued at a discount (OID), you report the OID element as ordinary income when the bonds are sold or redeemed; any gain exceeding OID is reported as capital gain. A loss is a capital loss. IRS Publication 1212 has examples for figuring the amount taxable as ordinary income. The ordinary income amount should be reported as interest income and also added to basis on Schedule D.

Corporate bonds with OID issued after May 27, 1969, and government bonds with OID issued after July 1, 1982. The ratable amount of OID is reported annually as interest income and added to basis; *see* ¶4.19. If the bonds are sold or redeemed before maturity, you realize capital gain for the amount over the adjusted basis of the bond, provided there was no intention to call the bond before maturity. If there was an intention to call the obligation before maturity, the part of the entire OID that has not yet been included in your income is taxable as ordinary income; the balance is capital gain.

Market discount on bonds issued after July 18, 1984, is taxable under the rules explained at ¶4.20.

Tax-exempts. See ¶4.26 for discount on tax-exempt bonds.

Obligations issued by individuals. On retirement of an obligation issued by an individual debtor, capital gain treatment does not apply. Capital gain treatment, however, may apply if you sell the obligation to a third party and the obligation is a capital asset; *see* Chapter 5. A note acquired by you in your business for service rendered or for the sale of merchandise is not a capital asset.

EXAMPLE You bought for $6,000 a second trust note of $10,000 from an individual. You receive payments of principal totaling $4,000. Thus, 60% ($6,000/$10,000) of the $4,000, or $2,400, is treated as a return on your investment; the balance is treated as discount or interest income. You sell the note for $3,800. To determine your profit or loss, you reduce your cost by $2,400 ($4,000 × 60%). Your capital gain is $200.

Selling price of note		$3,800
Less: Cost of note	$6,000	
Return on investment	2,400	
Discount		3,600
Capital gain		$ 200

TAX-FREE INTEREST ON STATE AND LOCAL GOVERNMENT BONDS AND OBLIGATIONS

STATE AND CITY INTEREST GENERALLY TAX EXEMPT

¶4.24 Generally, you pay no tax on interest on bonds or notes of states, cities, counties, the District of Columbia, or a possession of the United States. This includes bonds or notes of port authorities, toll road commissions, utility services activities, community redevelopment agencies, and similar bodies created for public purposes. Bonds issued after June 30, 1983, must be in registered form for the interest to be tax exempt. Interest on federally guaranteed obligations is generally taxable, but see exceptions at ¶4.25.

Check with the issuer of the bond to verify the tax-exempt status of the interest.

Private activity bonds. Interest on so-called private activity bonds is generally taxable (*see* ¶4.25), but there are certain exceptions. For example, interest on the following bonds is tax exempt even if the bond may technically be in the category of private activity bonds; qualified student loan bonds; exempt facility bonds: qualified small issue bonds; qualified mortgage bonds and veterans' mortgage bonds; qualified redevelopment bonds; and qualified 501(c)(3) bonds issued by charitable organizations and hospitals.

However, while interest on such bonds is not subject to regular tax, interest that you receive on such bonds issued after August 7, 1986, is considered a tax preference that may be subject to alternative minimum tax; *see* ¶23.3.

Check with the issuer for the tax status of a private activity bond.

Reporting tax-exempt interest on your return. On your 1992 return, you must list the amount of tax-exempt interest received during the year although it is not taxable. On Form 1040, you list the tax-exempt interest on Line 8b. On Form 1040A, you list the amount on Line 8b. On Form 1040EZ, you write "TEI" and then the amount of tax-exempt interest to the right of the last word on Line 2, but do not include it in the taxable interest shown on Line 2.

Reporting on Schedule B or Schedule 1

If you received a Form 1099-INT showing tax-exempt interest and you are filing Schedule B of Form 1040, you must list the tax-exempt amount along with taxable interest in that schedule. Then, on a separate line above Line 2 make a subtotal of the total interest and from that subtotal subtract the tax-exempt interest; label the subtracted amount as "Tax Exempt Interest." *See* the sample Schedule B on page 67.

If you file Schedule 1 of Form 1040A, use the same method of listing and then subtracting the tax-exempt interest.

TAXABLE STATE AND CITY INTEREST

¶**4.25**   Interest on certain state and city obligations is taxable. These taxable obligations include federally guaranteed obligations, mortgage subsidy bonds, private activity bonds, and arbitrage bonds.

Federally guaranteed obligations. Interest on state and local obligations issued after April 14, 1983, is generally taxable if the obligation is federally guaranteed, but there are exceptions allowing tax exemptions for obligations guaranteed by the Federal Housing Administration, Veterans Administration, Student Loan Marketing Association, and other U.S. government agencies.

Mortgage subsidy bonds. Interest on bonds issued by a state or local government after April 24, 1979, may not be tax exempt if funds raised by the bonds are used for home mortgages. There are exceptions for certain qualified mortgage bonds and veterans' bonds. Check on the tax-exempt status of mortgage bonds with the issuing authority.

Private activity bonds. Generally, a private activity bond is any bond where more than 10% of the issue's proceeds are used by a private business whose property secures the issue, or if at least 5% of the proceeds (or $5 million if less) are used for loans to parties other than governmental units. Interest on such bonds is generally taxable, but there are exceptions as discussed in ¶4.24. Check on the tax status of the bonds with the issuing authority.

Arbitrage bonds. These are state and local bonds issued after October 9, 1969, used to provide funds for reinvestment in higher yielding instruments. Interest on arbitrage bonds is taxable.

TAX-EXEMPT BONDS BOUGHT AT A DISCOUNT

¶**4.26**   Original issue discount (OID) on tax-exempt obligations is not taxable, and on a sale or redemption, gain attributed to OID is tax-exempt. Gain attributed to market discount is capital gain income.

Original issue discount tax-exempt bond. This arises when a bond is issued for a price less than the face amount of the bond. The discount is considered tax-exempt interest. Thus, if you are the original buyer and hold the bond to maturity, the entire amount of the discount is tax free. If before maturity you sell a bond that was issued before September 4, 1982, and acquired before March 2, 1984, your part of the OID is tax free. On a disposition of a tax-exempt bond issued after September 3, 1982, and acquired after March 1, 1984, you must add to basis accrued OID before determining gain or loss. OID must generally be accrued using a constant interest method; *see* IRS Publication 1212.

When bonds issued after June 8, 1980, are redeemed before maturity, the portion of the original issue discount earned to the date of redemption is tax-free interest; the balance is capital gain. Bonds issued with an intention to redeem before maturity are not subject to this rule; all interest is tax exempt.

Amortization of premiums is discussed at ¶4.17.

Market discount tax-exempts. A market discount arises when a bond originally issued at not less than par is bought at below par because its market value has declined. If you sell a tax-exempt bond purchased at a market discount for a price exceeding your purchase price, the excess is capital gain. If the bond was held long term, the gain is long term. A redemption of the bond at a price exceeding your purchase price is similarly treated. The market discount rules of ¶4.20 do not apply to tax-exempts.

Stripped tax-exempt obligations. OID is not currently taxed on a stripped tax-exempt bond or stripped coupon from the bond if you bought it before June 11, 1987. However, for any stripped bond or coupon you bought or sold after October 22, 1986, OID must be accrued and added to basis for purposes of figuring gain or loss on a disposition. Furthermore, if you bought the stripped bond or coupon after June 10, 1987, part of the OID may be taxable; *see* Publication 1212 for figuring the tax-free portion.

INTEREST ON TREASURY SECURITIES

TREASURY BILLS, NOTES, AND BONDS

¶**4.27**   Interest on securities issued by the federal government is fully taxable on your federal return. However, interest on federal obligations is not subject to state or local income taxes. Interest on Treasury bills, notes, and bonds is reported on Form 1099-INT. *See* ¶30.6 and ¶30.10 for investment information on Treasury securities.

Treasury bonds and notes. Treasury notes have maturities of two to 10 years. Treasury bonds have maturities of over 10 years. You report the fixed or coupon interest as interest income in the year the coupon becomes due and payable. Treasury bonds and notes are capital assets; gain or loss on their sale, exchange, or redemption is reported as capital gain or loss on Schedule D; *see* Chapter 5. If you purchased a federal obligation below par (at a discount) after July 1, 1982; *see* ¶4.18 for the rules on reporting original issue discount. If you purchased a Treasury bond or note above par (at a premium), you may elect to amortize the premium;

see ¶4.17. If you do not elect to amortize and you hold the bond or note to maturity, you have a capital loss.

Treasury bills. These are short-term U.S. obligations issued at a discount with maturities of 3, 6, or 12 months. On a bill held to maturity, you report as interest the difference between the discounted price and the amount you receive on a redemption of the bills at maturity.

Treasury bills are capital assets and a loss on a disposition before maturity is taxed as a capital loss. If you are a cash basis taxpayer and have a gain on a sale or exchange, ordinary income is realized up to the amount of the ratable share of the discount received when you bought the obligation. This amount is treated as interest income and is figured as follows:

$$\frac{\text{Days T-bill was held}}{\substack{\text{Days from acquisition} \\ \text{to maturity}}} \times \substack{\text{T-bill's value at} \\ \text{maturity minus your} \\ \text{cost}}$$

Any gain over this amount is capital gain; *see* example on page 62.

Accrual basis taxpayers and dealers who are required to currently report the acquisition discount element on Treasury bills using either the daily ratable accrual method or the constant interest method (¶4.21) do not apply the above formula on a sale before maturity. In figuring gain or loss, the discount included as income is added to basis.

EXAMPLE You buy at original issue a six-month $10,000 Treasury bill (180-day maturity) for $9,650 on May 11, 1992. You sell it 90 days later for $9,800. Your entire gain of $150 ($9,800 − $9,650) is taxed as interest income on your 1992 return. Under the interest income formula, gain up to $175 would be treated as interest income:

$$\frac{90 \text{ days held}}{180 \text{ days from acquisition to maturity}} \times \$350 \text{ discount} = \$175$$

Interest deduction limitation. Interest incurred on loans used to buy Treasury bills is deductible by a cash basis investor only to the extent that interest expenses exceed the following: (1) the portion of the acquisition discount allocated to the days you held the bond during the year; and (2) the portion of interest not taxable for the year under your method of accounting. The deferred interest expense is deductible in the year the bill is disposed of. If an election is made to report the acquisition discount as current income under the rules in ¶4.21 for governmental obligations, the interest expense may also be deducted currently. The election applies to all future acquisitions.

Tax Deferral: T-Bill Maturing Next Year.

If you are a cash basis taxpayer, you may postpone the receipt of interest income this year by selecting a Treasury bill maturing next year. Income is not recognized until the date on which the Treasury bill is paid at maturity, unless it has been sold or otherwise disposed of earlier.

U.S. SAVINGS BONDS

Savings Bond Tables: The Supplement will contain redemption tables showing the 1992 year-end values of Series E and EE U.S. Savings Bonds.

INTEREST ON U.S. SAVINGS BONDS

¶**4.28** **Series E and EE Bonds.** These bonds may be cashed for what you paid for them plus an increase in their value over stated periods of time. See ¶30.13 for investment information on U.S. Savings Bonds.

The increase in redemption value is taxable as interest, but you do not have to report the increase in value each year on your federal return. You may defer (¶4.29) the interest income until the year in which you cash the bond or the year in which the bond finally matures, whichever is earlier. But if you want, you may report the annual increase by merely including it on your tax return. If you use the accrual method of reporting, you must include the interest each year as it accrues. Savings bond interest is *not* subject to state or local taxes.

If you initially choose to defer the reporting of interest and later want to switch to annual reporting, you may do so. You may also change from the annual reporting method to the deferral method. *See* ¶4.29 for rules on changing reporting methods.

Education funding. If you buy EE bonds which are used to pay for educational expenses upon redemption, you may be able to exclude the accumulated interest from income. See ¶33.3 for the exclusion rules.

Bonds for child. Interest on savings bonds bought in the name of a child will be taxed to the child, even if the parent paid for the bonds and is named as beneficiary. Unless an election is made to report the increases in redemption value annually, the accumulated interest will be taxable to the child in the year he or she redeems the bond, or if earlier, when the bonds finally mature. However, if the interest is reported annually by a child under age 14, or the child is under age 14 in the year bonds are redeemed, the interest may be subject to tax at their parent's top rate under the kiddie tax; *see* Chapter 24. For example, if a child under age 14 has 1992 investment income over $1,200, the excess is taxed at the parent's top tax rate on the child's 1992 return; see ¶24.3. To avoid kiddie tax, savings bond interest may be deferred, as discussed in ¶4.29.

Where the kiddie tax does not apply, making the election to report the interest annually may be advisable, such as where the child has little or no other income and the bond interest can be offset by personal deductions. For example, a dependent child is not allowed to claim a personal exemption, but he or she may claim a 1992 standard deduction of at least $600; *see* ¶13.5. If the election to report the savings bond interest currently were made for 1992, up to $600 of the interest would be offset by the standard deduction, assuming the child had no other income.

You may make an election on behalf of your child to report the savings bond interest annually if your child is unable to file his or her own return. To make the election, report the accumulated bond interest and add a statement that the interest will be reported each year. The child may change from annual reporting to the deferral method under the rules discussed in ¶4.29.

Bonds must be reissued to make gift. Assume you have bought E or EE bonds and had them registered in joint names of yourself and your daughter. The law of your state provides that jointly owned property may be transferred to a co-owner by delivery or possession. You deliver the bonds to your daughter and tell her they now belong to her alone. According to Treasury regulations, this is not a valid gift of the bonds. The bonds must be surrendered and reissued in your daughter's name.

If you do not have the bonds reissued and you die, the bonds are taxable in your estate. Ownership of the bonds is a matter of contract between the United States and the purchaser of the bonds. The bonds are nontransferable. A valid gift cannot be accomplished by manual delivery to a donee unless the bonds also are surrendered and reissued in the name of the donee in accordance with Treasury regulations.

Series HH. These bonds are issued only in exchange for E or EE bonds, or for Freedom shares. They are issued at face value and pay semiannual interest that is taxable when received.

To be exchanged for HH bonds, the E or EE bonds must have a redemption value of at least $500. If the total value is not a multiple of $500, you will receive cash for the difference. You report the cash received as interest income to the extent of the unreported interest earned on the EE bonds exchanged.

For example, if you trade EE bonds with a redemption value of $3,723.35 for HH bonds, you get $3,500 in HH bonds and cash of $223.35. Report the cash as interest income to the extent it is unreported interest on the EE bonds exchanged.

Series H. These bonds were available before 1980. They were bought at face value and pay semiannual interest that is taxable when received. Do you own Series H bonds purchased through the exchange of Series E bonds, interest on which you did not report annually? You do not have to report the interest due on the old E bonds until the H bonds are redeemed or mature, whichever occurs first. H bonds issued after January 1957 cease earning interest when they mature in 30 years. At maturity, or on a disposal before maturity, you must report as interest the accumulated interest from any exchanged E bonds.

Freedom shares. These savings notes were available between 1967 and 1970. They have maturities of 30 years. As with E bonds, owners may defer the reporting of interest until the notes mature.

DEFERRING U.S. SAVINGS BOND INTEREST

¶4.29 You do not have to make a special election on your tax return in order to defer the interest on Series E or EE savings bonds. You may simply postpone reporting the interest until the year you redeem the bond or the year in which it reaches final maturity, whichever is earlier. If you choose to defer the interest, you may decide in a later year to begin annual reporting of the increase in value. You may also switch from annual reporting to the deferral method. These options are discussed below.

Changing from deferral to annual reporting. If you have deferred reporting of annual increases in value and want to elect to report annual increases on your 1992 return, make sure you report the total of all prior and current year increases in value. But next year, report only the increases accruing then, plus increases accruing on bonds newly purchased. Suppose you do not include the annual increase on your 1992 return and later change your mind. If the due date of the return has passed, it is too late to make the election. You may not file an amended return reporting the increase in value for 1992. You have to wait until next year's return to make the election.

Changing from annual reporting to deferral. If you have been reporting annual increases in value, you may change your method and elect to defer interest reporting until the bonds mature or are redeemed. You make the election by filing Form 3115 and attaching it to your federal income tax return for the year of the change. At the top of Form 3115, write "Filed Under Rev. Proc. 89-46." You must identify the bonds for which the election is being made. You may make the election on your 1992 tax return. You must continue to use the deferred method for at least five years following the year of the change.

 Changing to Deferral Method for Children.

If your children under age 14 have been reporting the annual increases in value on their savings bonds, and they are subject to the "kiddie" tax (¶24.3), consider making the election on Form 3115 to change to the deferral method. The election would defer tax on the interest that under the kiddie tax is subject to tax at your top marginal rate.

Extended maturity periods. E bonds may be held for additional periods of maturity after their initial maturity dates. Bonds held for additional periods increase in value and may be cashed in at any time. If you chose to postpone paying tax on accumulated interest, you may continue to postpone the tax during the extended period. You would then report the entire accumulated interest at the final maturity date or in the year you redeem the bond, whichever occurs earlier; *see* the Caution below.

 When Accumulated Interest Becomes Taxable.

You may not indefinitely defer the tax on E bond interest. E bonds cease earning interest once the bonds reach their final maturity date. For example, bonds issued during 1952 cease earning interest in 1992, 40 years from the date of issuance. On your 1992 return, you must pay tax on all the accumulated interest on 1952 bonds—unless the bonds are traded for new HH bonds in multiples of $500. Exchanging E bonds for HH bonds will continue the tax deferral on E bond interest. H bonds issued in 1962 also reach final maturity in 1992. See ¶30.13 for a listing of final maturity dates.

Changing the form of registration. Changing the form of registration of an E or EE bond may result in tax. Assume you use your own funds to purchase a bond issued in your name, payable on your death to your son. Later, at your request, a new bond is issued in your son's name only. The increased value of the original bond up to the date it was redeemed and reissued in your son's name is taxed to you as interest income.

The following examples show changes in registration that do not result in an immediate tax.

EXAMPLES 1. Jones buys an E bond and has it registered in his name and in the name of his son as co-owner. Jones has the bonds reissued solely in his own name; he is not required to report the accumulated interest at that time.

2. You and your spouse each contributed an equal amount toward the purchase of a $1,000 E bond, which was issued to you as co-owners. You later have the bond reissued as two $500 bonds, one in your name and one in your spouse's name. Neither of you has to report the interest earned to the date of reissue. But if you bought the $1,000 bond entirely with your own funds, you must report half the interest earned to the date of reissue.

3. You add another person's name as co-owner to facilitate a transfer of the bond on death. The change in registration does not result in a tax.

Transfer to a spouse. Interest on U.S. Savings Bonds transferred to a spouse in a divorce or settlement may result in tax to the transferor; *see* ¶6.6.

Transfer to a trust. If you transfer U.S. Savings Bonds to a trust giving up all rights of ownership, you are taxed on the accumulated interest to date of transfer. If, however, you are considered to be the owner of the trust and the interest earned before and after the transfer is taxable to you, you may continue to defer reporting the interest.

Transfer to a charity. Tax on the accumulated E or EE bond interest is not avoided by having the bonds reissued to a philanthropy. Further, tax may not be deferred by first converting E bonds to HH bonds and then reissuing the HH bonds in the philanthropy's name. The IRS held that by having the bonds reissued in the philanthropy's name, the owner realized taxable income on the accumulated bond interest.

CO-OWNERS OF E AND EE BONDS REPORT INTEREST THIS WAY:

1. You paid for the entire bond: Either you or the co-owner may redeem it. You are taxed on all the interest, even though the co-owner cashes the bond and you receive no proceeds. If the other co-owner does cash in the bond, he or she will receive a Form 1099-INT reporting the accumulated interest. However, since that interest is taxable to you, the co-owner should give you a nominee Form 1099-INT, as explained in the rules for nominee distributions on page 55 in the chart "Who Reports Interest."

2. You paid for only part of the bond: Either of you may redeem it. You are taxed on that part of the interest which is in proportion to your share of the purchase price. This is so even though you do not receive the proceeds.

3. You paid for part of the bond, and then had it reissued in another's name. You pay tax only on the interest accrued while you held the bond. The new co-owner picks up his or her share of the interest accruing afterwards.

4. You and another person were named co-owners on a bond bought as a gift by a third party. You are taxed on 50% of the interest income; your co-owner on the remaining half.

Transfer of an E or EE bond at death. If an owner does not report E or EE bond interest annually and dies before redeeming the bond, the income tax liability on the interest accumulated during the deceased's lifetime will be paid by the survivor, unless an election is made to report the accrued interest in the decedent's final income tax return; *see* ¶1.12. If the election is made on the decedent's final return, the new owner is taxable only on interest earned after the date of death.

Estate tax. Where an estate tax has been paid on bond interest accrued during the owner's lifetime, the new bondholder may claim the estate tax as a miscellaneous itemized deduction in the year that he or she pays tax on the accumulated interest.

Form 1099-INT When Bond is Cashed

When you cash in an E or EE bond, you receive Form 1099-INT that lists as interest the difference between the amount received and the amount paid for the bond. The form may show more taxable interest than you are required to report because you have regularly reported the interest or a prior owner reported the interest. Report the full amount shown on Form 1099-INT on Schedule B if you file Form 1040, or on Part 1 of Schedule 1 if you file Form 1040A, along with your other interest income. Enter a subtotal of the total interest and then, on a separate line, reduce the subtotal by the savings bond interest that was previously reported and identify the reduction as "Previously reported U.S. Savings Bond Interest." The interest is exempt from state and local taxes.

MINIMUM INTEREST FOR LOANS AND SELLER-FINANCED DEBT

MINIMUM INTEREST RULES

¶4.30 The law requires minimum interest on loan transactions unless a specific exception covers the transaction. Where minimum interest is not charged, the law imputes interest as if the parties agreed to the charge.

The rules are complicated and have been subject to several revisions. There are different minimum interest rates and reporting rules depending on the nature of the transaction. The following discussion provides the important details for understanding the rules. For specific cases and computations, we suggest that you consult IRS regulations for details not covered in this book.

There are two broad classes of transactions:

Loans. These are generally covered by Internal Revenue Code Section 7872. Below-market or low-rate interest loans are discussed at ¶4.31.

Seller-financed sales of property. These are covered by either Internal Revenue Code Section 1274 or Section 483. Seller-financed sales are discussed at ¶4.32. If parties fail to charge the minimum required rates, the same minimum rate is imputed by law.

INTEREST-FREE OR BELOW-MARKET INTEREST LOANS

¶4.31 For many years, the IRS tried to tax interest-free or below-market interest loans. However, court decisions supported taxpayers who argued that such loans did not result in taxable income or gifts. To reverse these decisions, the IRS convinced Congress to pass a law imposing tax on interest-free or low-interest loans made by individuals and businesses. You may no longer make interest-free or low-interest loans to a relative who uses the loan for personal or investment purposes without adverse income tax consequences, unless the exception for $10,000 or $100,000 loans applies (*see* the next page).

Given the complexity of these loan rules, you and your tax advisor should carefully review regulations to the Internal Revenue Code Section 7872 when drafting a loan agreement.

How the imputed interest rules work. If interest at least equal to the applicable federal rate set by the IRS is not charged, the law generally treats a below-market interest loan as two transactions:

1. The law assumes that the lender has transferred to the borrower an amount equal to the "forgone" interest element of the loan. In the case of a loan between individuals, such as a parent and child, the parent is subject to gift tax on this element; in the case of a stockholder borrowing from a company, the element is a taxable dividend; in the case of a loan made to an employee, taxable pay.

   Note: For *gift tax* purposes (¶33.1), a term loan is treated as if the lender gave to the borrower the excess of the amount of the loan over the present value of all payments due during the loan term. Demand loans are treated as if the lender gave to the borrower annually the amount of the forgone interest.

2. The law assumes that imputed interest equal to the applicable federal rate is paid by the borrower to the lender. Whether the borrower may claim a deduction for the interest depends on the use of the funds, as discussed in Chapter 15.

A husband and wife are treated as one person for purposes of imputing interest.

No tax withholding is required on interest imputed by the rules of the section.

Charging the applicable federal rate avoids the imputed interest rules. Gift loans qualifying for the $10,000 and $100,000 exceptions are not subject to imputed interest rules. For other loans, the rules imputing income to you as the lender may be avoided by charging interest at least equal to the applicable federal rate. Applicable federal rates are set by the IRS monthly and published in the Internal Revenue Bulletin; you can also get the rates from your local IRS office. For a term loan, the applicable rate is the one in effect as of the day on which the loan is made, computed semiannually. The short-term rate applies to loans of three years or less; the mid-term rate to loans over three and up to nine years; the long-term rate applies to loans over nine years. For a demand loan, the applicable federal rate is the short-term rate in effect at the start of each semiannual period (January and July).

Different computations for different types of loans. There are two general classes of loans:

1. Gift loans, whether term or demand, and nongift demand loans.
2. Nongift term loans.

The distinction is important for figuring and reporting imputed interest. For example, in the case of nongift term loans, the imputed interest element is treated as original issue discount; *see* ¶4.19.

Gift loans and nongift loans payable on demand. As a lender, you are taxable on the "forgone interest," that is, the interest that you would have received had you charged interest at the applicable-federal rate (*see* above) over any interest actually charged. The borrower may be able to claim an interest deduction under the rules of Chapter 15.

Nongift term loans. A term loan is any loan not payable on demand. As a lender, you are taxable on any excess of the loan principal over the present value of all payments due under the loan. The excess is treated as original issue (OID) which you report annually as interest income; *see* ¶4.19.

Exceptions to imputed interest rules. Certain below-market interest loans are exempt from the imputed interest rules, or subject to earned imputed interest reporting.

The $10,000 exception. In the case of a gift loan, no interest is imputed to any day on which the aggregate outstanding amount of all loans between the parties is not over $10,000, provided the loan is not attributed to the purchase or carrying of income-producing assets.

The $10,000 exception also applies for compensation-related and corporate-shareholder loans, provided the principal purpose of the loan is not tax avoidance. Certain low-interest loans given to employees by their employers to purchase a new residence in connection with a move to a new job location are exempt from the imputed interest requirements.

In certain cases, below-market loans of up to $100,000 may be exempt from imputed interest reporting; *see* Law Alert below.

Gift Loans Up to $100,000.

An exception in the law may allow you to give another person an interest-free or low-interest loan of up to $100,000 without having interest income imputed to you. For example, if you give a child or other relative an interest-free loan to buy a home or start a business, the imputed interest rules will not apply provided (1) The total outstanding loan balance owed to you by the borrower does not exceed $100,000, and (2) The borrower's net investment income (investment income minus investment expenses) is $1,000 or less.

If the borrower's net investment income for the year exceeds $1,000, the imputed interest rules apply, but the imputed interest is limited to his or her net investment income. If on any day during the year, the outstanding loan balance owed to you by the borrower exceeds $100,000, interest will be imputed for that day under the regular rules. If a principal purpose of a loan is the avoidance of federal taxes, imputed interest is not limited to the borrower's net investment income.

EXAMPLES 1. At the beginning of 1992, you make a $45,000 interest-free loan to your son, payable on demand, which he uses for a downpayment on a home. This is the only outstanding loan between you and your son. In 1992, your son's net investment income is $650. Since the loan does not exceed $100,000, and your son's net investment income does not exceed $1,000, the imputed interest rules do not apply; you do not have to report the "foregone interest" as interest income.

For gift tax purposes, the foregone interest is a taxable gift. For example, assume that the applicable federal rate for 1992 is 9%. The taxable gift would be the foregone interest of $4,050 ($45,000 × 9%), but *see* ¶33.1 for the annual gift tax exclusion and other gift tax reporting details.

2. Same as Example 1 except that your son's net investment income is $1,500. Since net investment income exceeds $1,000, the imputed interest income rules apply, but the imputed interest is limited to the $1,500 of net investment income. Thus, although the forgone interest using the applicable federal rate is $4,050, you report only $1,500 of imputed interest income.

Loans to continuing care facilities. Senior citizens moving into a community with a continuing care facility are required to pay a fee to the facility. The fee may be treated as a "loan" subject to the imputed interest rules to the extent the fee is refundable and it exceeds specified limits. These rules are discussed in Chapter 34.

Reporting imputed interest. Imputed interest is generally treated as transferred by the lender to the borrower and retransferred by the borrower to the lender on December 31 in the calendar year of imputation and is reported under the regular accounting method of the borrower and lender.

EXAMPLE On January 1, 1992, Jones Company makes a $200,000 interest-free demand loan to Frank, an employee. The loan remains outstanding for the entire 1992 calendar year. Jones Company has a taxable year ending September 30. Frank is a calendar year taxpayer. For 1992, the imputed compensation payment and the imputed interest payment is treated as made on December 31, 1992.

With gift loans between individuals, interest computed during the borrower's taxable year is treated for both the lender and the borrower as earned on the last day of the borrower's taxable year. Treasury regulations to Section 7872 provide rules for figuring "forgone" interest. Where a demand loan is in effect for the entire calendar year, an "annual blended rate" issued by the IRS to simplify reporting may be used to compute the imputed interest. The blended rate is not available if the loan was not outstanding for the entire year or if the loan balance fluctuated; computations provided by Treasury regulations must be used.

Tax return statement requirements. Both a lender and borrower must attach statements to their income tax returns reporting the interest, how it was calculated, and the names of the parties and their tax identification numbers.

MINIMUM INTEREST ON SELLER-FINANCED SALES

¶4.32 The law requires minimum interest charges for seller-financed sales. If the minimum rate is not charged, the IRS imputes interest at the minimum applicable rate requiring both buyer and seller to treat part of the purchase price as interest even though it is not called interest in the sales contract. For most sales, charging a rate of at least 9%

Minimum Interest Rate For Seller Financing

Type—	Description—
9% safe harbor rate	If seller financing in 1992 is $3,234,900 or less, the minimum required interest is the lower of 9% compounded semiannually or the applicable federal rate (AFR). The amount of seller financing is the stated principal amount under the contract. If the seller-financed amount exceeds $3,234,900, the minimum interest rate is 100% of the AFR. For sales after 1992, the threshold will be indexed for inflation. IRS regulations allow the parties to use an interest rate lower than the AFR if it is shown that the borrower could obtain a loan on an arm's length basis at lower interest.
Seller-financed sale-leaseback transactions	Interest equal to 110% of AFR must be charged.
Sales of land between family members	To the extent that sales price does not exceed $500,000 during a calendar year, the minimum interest rate is 6%, compounded semiannually. To prevent multiple sales from being used to avoid the $500,000 limit, the $500,000 ceiling applies to all land sales between family members during the same year. To the extent that the $500,000 sales price limit is exceeded, the general 9% or 100% of AFR rules apply.

compounded semiannually satisfies the law; *see* the chart above for minimum required rates. For example, property is sold on the installment basis for $100,000 and the parties fail to charge adequate interest. Assume the IRS imputes interest of $5,000. For tax purposes, $95,000 is allocated to the sale of the property and the principal amount of the debt; the balance is imputed interest of $5,000, taxable to the seller and deductible by the buyer if allowed under the rules of Chapter 15. However, when the property is *personal-use* property, such as a residence to be used by the buyer, imputed interest rules do not apply to the buyer. Thus, the buyer may not deduct the imputed interest. His or her deduction is limited to the payment of interest stated in the contract if a deduction is allowed under the home mortgage interest rules in Chapter 15.

Two statute classes. The minimum or imputed interest rules are covered by two Internal Revenue Code statutes: Sections 1274 and 483. Under both, the same minimum interest rates apply but the timing of interest reporting is different, as discussed in the next column.

Section 483 applies to any payment due more than six months after the date of sale under a contract which calls for some or all payments more than one year after the date of sale. If the sales price cannot exceed $3,000, Section 483 does not apply. Transactions within Section 483 are sales or exchanges of: (1) principal residences; (2) any property if total payments, including interest and any other consideration to be received by the seller, cannot exceed $250,000; (3) farms if the total price is $1 million or less; and (4) sales of land between family members to the extent the aggregate sales price of all sales between the same parties in the same year is $500,000 or less.

If the selling price exceeds the respective $250,000, $1 million, or $500,000 amount listed in (2) through (4) above, the sale is subject to Section 1274 reporting rules provided some or all payments are due more than six months after the date of sale. All other transactions involving nonpublicly traded debt instruments for nonpublicly traded property are also subject to Section 1274 where payments are deferred more than six months.

Timing of interest reporting. One important practical difference between the two statutes covering minimum interest involves the timing of the reporting and deducting of interest.

Under Section 483, a seller and lender use their regular reporting method for imputed interest. For a cash-basis seller, interest is taxed when received; a cash-basis buyer deducts interest when paid if a deduction is allowable. However, if too much interest is allocated to a payment period, the excess interest is treated as prepaid interest, and the deduction is postponed to the year or years interest is earned. Section 483 also describes imputed interest as *unstated interest*.

Under Section 1274, the interest element is generally reported by both buyer and seller ratably according to the OID accrual rules,

even if they otherwise report on the cash basis. Where the seller-financing is below an annual threshold ($2,310,600 for 1992 sales), the parties can elect the cash method to report the interest regardless of the OID and accrual rules if: (1) the seller-lender is on a cash basis method and is not a dealer of the property sold; and (2) the seller and buyer jointly elect to use the cash method. The cash basis election binds any cash basis successor of the buyer or seller. If the lender transfers his interest to an accrual basis taxpayer, the election no longer applies; interest is thereafter taxed under the accrual method rules. The OID rules also do not apply to a cash-basis buyer of *personal-use* property; here, the cash-basis debtor deducts only payments of interest required by the contract, assuming a deduction is allowed under the home mortgage rules of Chapter 15.

Figuring AFR. The IRS determines the AFR rates which are published at the beginning of each month in the Internal Revenue Bulletin. There are three AFR rates depending on the length of the contract:

Short-term AFR—a term of three years or less.
Mid-term AFR—a term of over three years but not over nine years.
Long-term AFR—a term of over nine years.

The parties may choose the lowest AFR for the three-month period ending with the month in which a binding written sales contract is entered into. Thus, if the AFR for either of the prior two months is lower than the AFR for the month of contract, the lowest of the three AFRs applies.

If insufficient interest is charged, the total unstated interest is allocated ratably to payments under an OID computation.

Where the contract provides adequate interest and the amount of principal and interest payments do not exceed $250,000, the IRS will recognize the parties' allocation of interest and principal payments, even if it does not match the actual interest accruing during the period.

Assumptions of loans. The imputed interest rules of Sections 1274 and 483 do not generally apply to debt instruments assumed as part of a sale or exchange, or if the property is taken subject to the debt, provided that neither the terms of the debt instrument nor the nature of the transactions are changed.

Safe harbor for points. Under proposed regulations in cases of seller-financed residence sales, generally one-sixth of a point per year of amortization will not be counted as OID.

Important: *In planning deferred or installment sales, review Treasury regulations to the Internal Revenue Code Sections 483 and 1274 for further examples and details.*

Schedule B—Interest and Dividend Income

Attachment Sequence No. **08**

Part I Interest Income

(See pages 14 and B-1.)

Note: If you received a Form 1099-INT, Form 1099-OID, or substitute statement from a brokerage firm, list the firm's name as the payer and enter the total interest shown on that form.

If you had over $400 in taxable interest income OR you are claiming the exclusion of interest from series EE U.S. savings bonds issued after 1989, you must complete this part. List ALL interest you received. If you had over $400 in taxable interest income, you must also complete Part III. If you received, as a nominee, interest that actually belongs to another person, or you received or paid accrued interest on securities transferred between interest payment dates, see page B-1.

Interest Income		Amount
1 List name of payer—if any interest income is from seller-financed mortgages, see page B-1 and list this interest first ▶		
National Savings Bank		925
Chase Manhattan Bank		515
Municipal Bonds		350
TOTAL		1790
Less: Tax Exempt Interest	1	(350)
		1440
2 Add the amounts on line 1	2	1440
3 Excludable savings bond interest, if any, from Form 8815, line 14, Attach Form 8815 to Form 1040	3	0
4 Subtract line 3 from line 2. Enter the result here and on Form 1040, line 8a. ▶	4	1440

Part II Dividend Income

(See pages 15 and B-1.)

Note: If you received a Form 1099-DIV or substitute statement, from a brokerage firm, list the firm's name as the payer and enter the total dividends shown on that form.

If you had over $400 in gross dividends and/or other distributions on stock, you must complete this part and Part III. If you received, as a nominee, dividends that actually belong to another person, see page B-1.

Dividend Income		Amount
5 List name of payer—include on this line capital gain distributions, nontaxable distributions, etc. ▶		
Auto Company		126
Bio-chem Corp.		217
Utility Corp.	5	155
6 Add the amounts on line 5	6	498
7 Capital gain distributions. Enter here and on Schedule D* .	7	310
8 Nontaxable distributions. (See the inst. for Form 1040, line 9.)	8	
9 Add lines 7 and 8	9	310
10 Subtract line 9 from line 6. Enter the result here and on Form 1040, line 9 . ▶	10	188

If you received capital gain distributions but do not need Schedule D to report any other gains or losses, see the instructions for Form 1040, lines 13 and 14.

Part III Foreign Accounts and Foreign Trusts

(See page B-2.)

If you had over $400 of interest or dividends OR had a foreign account or were a grantor of, or a transferor to, a foreign trust, you must complete this part.

	Yes	No
11a At any time during 1992, did you have an interest in or a signature or other authority over a financial account in a foreign country, such as a bank account, securities account, or other financial account? See page B-2 for exceptions and filing requirements for Form TD F 90-22.1		✓
b If "Yes," enter the name of the foreign country ▶		
12 Were you the grantor of, or transferor to, a foreign trust that existed during 1992, whether or not you have any beneficial interest in it? If "Yes," you may have to file Form 3520, 3520-A, or 926 .		✓

5 REPORTING GAINS AND LOSSES ON PROPERTY SALES

Capital gain or loss treatment applies to sales of property held for investment or personal purposes, except for certain items excluded by law from the category of capital assets. Sales of capital assets are reported on Schedule D. On Schedule D, long-term capital gain or loss applies to sales of assets held for more than a year, and short-term capital gain or loss to sales of assets held for one year or less. Holding period rules are discussed at ¶5.5.

Special tax-savings opportunities for sales of a principal residence are explained in Chapter 29.

Net capital gains are added to your other income and subject to regular tax rates if your top rate is 15% or 28%. If your top rate is 31%, net long-term gains in excess of short-term losses are subject to a top rate of 28%; see ¶5.1. Capital losses are deductible from capital gains and up to $3,000 of ordinary income, with a carryover for the excess over $3,000; see ¶5.2.

A sample filled-in Schedule D illustrating sales of capital assets is at ¶5.4. Sales of business assets are reported on Form 4797. As discussed in ¶44.8, most assets used in a business are considered Section 1231 assets, and capital gain or loss treatment may apply depending upon the result of a netting computation made on Form 4797 for all such assets sold during the year.

Security sales are reported by your broker to the IRS on Form 1099-B and real estate transactions on Form 1099-S, of which you receive a copy or equivalent statement. The IRS compares the amounts reported on the Forms 1099 with the amounts reported on your Schedule D. If there is a difference between the sales prices entered on Schedule D and the amounts reported on the Forms 1099, you must attach a statement explaining the difference. For example, you may receive a Form 1099-B for a transaction that is not reportable as a sale, such as nontaxable return of part of your investment. On a separate statement you would explain that no gain or loss was realized.

REPORTING GAINS AND LOSSES ON PROPERTY SALES

Tax-Saving Opportunities

Transaction—	Tax Savings—
Sale of principal residence	Tax on all or part of a profit from the sale of your home may be avoided or deferred depending on your age. If you are age 55 or over, you may elect to defer tax on gain of up to $125,000; *see* ¶29.14. If you are under age 55 or are age 55 or over and do not want to elect the $125,000 exclusion, you may defer tax by buying or building another residence. Tax deferment is not elective but mandatory if the tests of ¶29.2–¶29.5 are met. If you sell at a loss, you may not deduct the loss; however, *see* ¶29.12 and ¶29.13 and read under what conditions you may claim a loss deduction for a residence which you rent out or inherit.
Installment sale. All or some payments are deferred to years after the year of sale.	Installment selling offers you the opportunity to defer tax on a profitable sale of property. If the sale qualifies as an installment sale, you do not pay all the tax in one year, but over several years; *see* ¶5.36.
Exchange of property	Exchange of investment real estate may be made without current tax consequences; *see* ¶6.1. Unrealized gain is taxed when you sell the property taken in exchange. Where property received in a tax-free exchange is held until death, the unrecognized gain escapes tax forever because basis of the property in the hands of an heir is generally the value of the property at the death of the decedent; *see* ¶5.13.
Involuntary conversion	You may realize a gain when your property is destroyed by a casualty or taken by a government authority if insurance or other compensation exceeds the adjusted basis of the property. Tax on the gain may be postponed if you elect to defer gain and invest the proceeds in replacement property, the cost of which is equal to or exceeds the net proceeds from the conversion; *see* ¶18.18.
Worthless security	You may deduct your investment in securities that have no value. See ¶5.23 if you can claim that loss for 1992.
Bad debt	You may deduct debts that have become worthless. See ¶5.47 if you may claim the loss for 1992.
Section 1244 stock	If you are organizing a corporate business, consider an issue of Section 1244 stock which allows an ordinary loss deduction if the stock becomes worthless or is sold at a loss; *see* ¶5.24.

Reporting Gain or Loss

Your gains and losses from sales and exchanges of property are not treated equally under the tax law.
The tax reporting of a sale depends generally on your purpose in holding the property.

Property held for—	Type—	Your gain is—	Your loss is—	Reported on—
Investment is a capital asset	Stocks, bonds, land; see * below for exceptions.	Capital gain. Net capital gains are subject to ordinary income tax rates. However, the tax rate applied to net long-term capital gains may not top 28%; *see* ¶5.1.	Capital loss. Capital losses are deductible only from capital gains and up to $3,000 of ordinary income.	Schedule D
Sale to customers is a non-capital asset	Inventory, merchandise, stock in trade; also see * below.	Ordinary income. Such property is excluded by law from the definition of capital assets.	Ordinary loss. Ordinary loss is not subject to the $3,000 deduction limit imposed on capital losses. However, passive loss restrictions of Chapter 10 may defer the time when certain ordinary losses are deductible.	Schedule C if self-employed; Schedule F if a farmer; Form 1065 for a business operated as a partnership; Form 1120 or 1120S for an incorporated business.
Use in your business or profession Section 1231 asset	Depreciable buildings, trucks, autos, computers, fixtures, machinery, equipment.	Capital or ordinary income. Section 1231 as explained in ¶44.8 determines whether gain is taxable as ordinary income or capital gain.	Capital or ordinary as determined by Section 1231; *see* ¶44.8.	Form 4797
Personal use is a capital asset	Home, car, jewelry, furniture, art objects, etc., but see * for exceptions.	Capital gain. Where an asset is held both for personal and business use, such as an auto, the asset is treated as two separate assets for purposes of figuring gain or loss; *see* ¶44.12.	Not deductible. Losses on personal-use assets are not deductible although profits are taxable. However, a sale of personal assets by an executor of an estate is assumed to be profit-seeking. The estate may claim a loss on the sale of a personal asset for less than its fair market value, even though the decedent could not claim the loss deduction if he or she had sold it.	If you sell your principal residence, the sale is reported on Form 2119 whether you have a gain or loss. However, a loss is not deductible. Taxable gain, if any, is figured on Form 2119. Gain not postponed or excluded on Form 2119 is then entered on Schedule D.
Use in passive activity	Rental property; equipment used in a business in which you do not materially participate.	Passive income. The income may be used to offset passive activity losses; *see* ¶10.1.	Passive loss. The loss may be used only to offset passive income. Losses in excess of passive income may be carried forward to future years; *see* ¶10.1.	Form 8582 is used to report net passive income or loss.

*Non-capital assets. The following assets also do not come within capital gain or loss rules (by law, they are not considered capital assets): copyrights, literary, musical, or artistic compositions; a letter, memorandum, or similar property held by the creator of the property or other persons who obtained the property from the creator in a tax-free exchange or as a gift; a letter or memorandum that was prepared or produced for you; or accounts or notes receivable which were acquired in the ordinary course of your business from the sale of inventory or property held primarily for sale to customers, or for services rendered as an employee.

FIGURING CAPITAL GAINS AND LOSSES

28% TAX CEILING FOR NET LONG-TERM GAIN

¶5.1 If your regular 1992 tax bracket does not exceed 28%, net long-term capital gains are fully taxable at your regular rate, the same as your short-term gains. However, if your regular tax bracket is 31%, the tax rate applied to your net long-term gains on Schedule D is 28%. The 28% rate applies to *net capital gains*, which are net long-term gains less net short-term capital losses.

Ceiling for High Earners May Top 28%

The actual rate on long-term capital gains will be higher than 28% for taxpayers subject to the 3% reduction to itemized deductions (¶13.8) and the phaseout of personal exemptions (¶1.32). *See* Chapter 28 for examples showing how these restrictions increase the capital gains rate.

Computing the 28% Ceiling on Net Capital Gains. You will save taxes by applying the 28% ceiling if your taxable income, including net capital gains (excess of long-term capital gains over short-term capital losses), *exceeds:*

$86,500 using joint return rates (including qualifying widow or widower)

$74,150 using head-of-household rates

$51,900 using single return rates

$43,250 using married filing separately rates

These amounts are the levels at which the 28% tax bracket ends and the 31% bracket begins. If your taxable income including net capital gains does *not* exceed the above amount for your filing status, you need not concern yourself with computing the 28% ceiling because your capital gains would not be subject to rates over 28% even without the ceiling.

If your taxable income including net capital gains does exceed the above amount, use the alternative method of computing your tax on page 2 of Schedule D so that net capital gain is taxed at 28%. The alternative method follows these steps:

1. Enter your taxable income. $_____
2. Enter your net capital gain (net long-term capital gain less net short-term capital loss).   _____
3. Subtract line 2 from line 1. This is taxable income without net capital gain.   _____
4. Enter $21,450 if you are single*
   $35,800 if you use joint return rates*
   $28,750 if you use head of household rates*
   $17,900 if you are married filing separately*   _____
5. Enter the greater of line 3 or line 4.   _____
6. Subtract line 5 from line 1. This is the amount of capital gain that benefits from the 28% rate.   _____
7. Figure the amount of tax on line 5 from the tax rate schedule if Line 5 is $100,000 or more; use the tax tables if less than $100,000; *see* ¶22.1.   _____
8. Multiply line 6 by 28% and enter the result   _____
9. Add lines 7 and 8. This is your total 1992 tax. $_____

*These amounts are the taxable income levels above which the 28% rate starts in the 1992 rate schedules, which are in Chapter 22.

EXAMPLE You file a 1992 joint return showing a taxable income of $95,000 including a net capital gain of $5,000. Your tax is $22,059.

1. Taxable income	$95,000
2. Net capital gain	5,000
3. Taxable income without net capital gain	90,000
4. Starting point for 28% tax rate on joint return	35,800
5. Greater of line 3 or 4	90,000
6. Line 1 minus line 5. This is net capital gain subject to ceiling	5,000
7. Tax on line 5 before adding capital gain tax	20,659
8. 28% of $5,000 on line 6	1,400
9. Add lines 7 and 8. This is the alternative tax including the 28% ceiling for net capital gain	$22,059

Without the alternative tax, the tax on $95,000 would be $22,209. The alternative tax provides a tax savings of $150 for the $5,000 of net capital gain that would otherwise be taxed at 31%. The amount of the savings is the 3% difference between the 28% ceiling and the 31% regular rate or $150 (3% of $5,000).

CAPITAL LOSSES AND CARRYOVERS

¶5.2 Capital losses are fully deductible against capital gains, and if losses exceed gains, you may deduct the excess from up to $3,000 of other income on Form 1040. Net losses over $3,000 are carried over to future years. The $3,000 limit is reduced to $1,500 for married persons filing separately. In preparing your 1992 Schedule D, remember to include any capital loss carryovers from Part V of your 1991 Schedule D.

On Page 2 of Schedule D, you compute the carryover for both long- and short-term losses, which keep their character over the carryover period. If the original loss is short term, the carryover is short term; if long term, the carryover is long term. If you have both a net short-term capital loss and a net long-term capital loss that together exceed $3,000, the short-term loss is used up first against the $3,000 limit in figuring the amount to be carried over. Unused carryovers of a deceased person may not be used by his or her estate.

A special computation may increase your carryover deduction where you have "negative" taxable income; *see* below.

Carryover if you have "negative" taxable income. Generally, a net capital loss of up to $3,000 ($1,500 if married filing separately) is claimed on Form 1040 as a deduction from gross income and there is no carryover. However, if without considering personal exemptions, you have a "negative taxable income," the loss may not provide a tax benefit because other deductions have reduced taxable income to zero. In this case, you may be allowed a capital loss carryforward for all or part of your net capital loss.

In Part V, Schedule D, you figure how much of your net loss is treated as "used up" in the current year. The balance of the loss, if any, is carried over to the next year. To make the computation, you must *combine* the following in Part V: (1) the amount on Line 35 of Form 1040, which is adjusted gross income minus the standard deduction or itemized deductions, and (2) the allowable net loss up to the $3,000 or $1,500 limit. If the combined result of (1) and (2) is zero or a negative amount, you get a carryover for the entire net loss. If the combined result of (1) and (2) is more than zero, a carryover is allowed to the extent that the net loss (as a positive number) exceeds the combined result; *see* the next example.

EXAMPLE On your 1992 return, you report adjusted gross income of $2,050, which includes a $1,500 long-term capital loss. As a single person, you claim a $3,600 standard deduction. For carryover purposes, you ignore personal exemptions. The net result of subtracting the standard deduction from adjusted gross income is "negative" $1,550 ($2,050 – $3,600). Combining this result (–$1,550) and the allowable capital loss of $1,500 gives (– $50). Since the result is a negative amount, none of the $1,500 loss is treated in Part V of Schedule D as "used up" in 1992. You are allowed a full $1,500 long-term capital loss carryover to 1993.

CAPITAL LOSSES OF MARRIED COUPLES

¶5.3 On a joint return, the capital asset transactions of both spouses are combined in one Schedule D. A carryover loss of one spouse may be applied to capital gains of the other spouse. Where both spouses incur net capi-

tal losses, only one capital loss deduction of up to $3,000 is allowed. This rule may not be avoided by filing separate returns. If you file separately, the deduction limit for each return is $1,500.

EXAMPLE You and your spouse individually incurred capital losses of $5,000 and $4,000. If you file separate returns, the maximum amount deductible from ordinary income on each return is $1,500.

Death of a spouse. The IRS holds that if a capital loss is incurred by a spouse on his or her own property and that spouse dies, the surviving spouse may not claim any unused loss carryover on a separate return.

EXAMPLE In 1989, Smith realized a substantial long-term capital loss on separately owned property, which was reported on his 1989 joint return. Part of the excess loss was carried over to the couple's 1990 joint return, and in 1991, before the carryover loss was used up, Smith died. His widow could claim the unused carryover, up to the $3,000 limit, on a joint return filed for 1991, the year of death.

However, any remaining loss carryover to 1992 or later years is lost. Although the loss was originally reported on a joint return, the widow may claim only her allocable share of the loss on her separate returns. Since the loss property was owned solely by the deceased husband, no loss is allocable to the widow's separate returns.

SCHEDULE D

¶5.4 You report many different types of transactions on Schedule D: sales of securities; worthless personal loans; sales of stock rights and warrants; sales of land held for investment and in some cases sales of personal residences. On page 72 is a sample section from Schedule D illustrating the treatment of short-term and long-term transactions. A blank proof copy of Schedule D for 1992 may be found at the back of this book; a filled-in final version and a Schedule D that you may file with the IRS will be in the Supplement.

The IRS will compare the proceeds reported on your Schedule D with the selling prices reported by securities brokers on Form 1099-B and with real estate proceeds reported on Form 1099-S. If you receive a Form 1099-B or 1099-S that is incorrect, report the proper amount and attach a statement explaining the difference between the amount you entered on Schedule D and the amount shown on the Form 1099.

The number of each transaction is keyed to the sample schedule on page 72.

1. Sale of stock (long-term gain)—You bought 100 shares of Acme Steel stock on October 1, 1981, for $5,000. On March 2, 1992, you sell the 100 shares for $6,000.

In this and other applicable examples, broker's commissions and state and local transfer taxes, if any, are added to the cost of the stock.

2. Sale of stock (short-term gain)—You bought 200 shares of Buma Rubber stock on July 20, 1992, for $400. On October 12, 1992, you sell the 200 shares for $600.

3. Sale of stock received as a gift (long-term gain)—Your father gave you a gift of 100 shares of Crown Auto stock on March 16, 1992, which he had bought on May 18, 1960, for $4,000. The fair market value of the stock at the time of the gift was $5,900. On March 20, 1992, you sell the stock for $8,000. No gift tax was due under the annual $10,000 exclusion. Your basis is your father's basis of $4,000 (¶5.13) and your holding period includes your father's holding period (¶5.8).

4. Sale of stock received as a gift (short-term loss)—Your father gave you a gift of 100 shares of Acme auto stock on March 16, 1992, which he had bought on February 15, 1961, for $4,000. The value of the stock at the time of the gift was $3,000. You sell the stock on March 27, 1992, for $2,500. Since the value of the stock at the time of the gift was less than your father's basis, your basis is the date-of-death value (¶5.13) and the holding period begins at the date of the gift (¶5.8).

5. Sale of stock received as inheritance (long-term gain)—You inherited 300 shares of Davis Textile preferred stock from your father, who died on January 4, 1990. He had bought them in 1941 for $1,500. When he died, they were selling on the exchange for $15,000, at which value they were reported for estate tax purposes. You received the stock on February 21, 1992, when they were selling at $18,000. You sold the stock for $20,000 on June 5, 1992; see ¶5.13 for basis rules.

6. Sale of stock including stock dividends—You bought 100 shares of Box Co. stock for $1,000 on June 20, 1984. Last year, you received a stock dividend of 10 shares; this year, a stock dividend of 40 shares. On March 2, 1992, you sell the 150 shares for $3,000; see ¶5.18.

7. Sale of stock dividend—You bought 100 shares of Bale Co. stock for $1,200 on January 5, 1990. You receive a tax-free dividend for 20 shares on April 19, 1990. You sell the 20 shares received as a stock dividend on June 5, 1992, for $300; see ¶5.18.

8. Sale of stock rights—You bought 100 shares of Tel. Co. stock for $5,000 on January 3, 1962. On January 3, 1992, you receive stock rights to subscribe to 10 shares at $53 a share. The stock is worth $55 a share (ex-rights). You sell the rights for $20 on February 5, 1992; see ¶5.19.

9. Worthless bond—On August 10, 1970, you bought two $1,000 bonds of Rail Co. at par. These bonds became completely worthless during 1992; see ¶5.23.

10. Worthless personal loan—You loaned $500 to a person on May 1, 1986. He was adjudged bankrupt on March 5, 1992; see ¶5.47.

The IRS requires that you explain the deduction in a statement attached to your return. The statement should show: (1) the nature of the debt; (2) the name of the debtor and his or her business or family relationship, if any, to you; (3) when the debt was due; (4)

SCHEDULE D

Part I — Short-Term Capital Gains and Losses—Assets Held One Year or Less

(a) Description of property (Example, 100 shares 7% preferred of "XYZ" Co.)	(b) Date acquired (Mo., day, yr.)	(c) Date sold (Mo., day, yr.)	(d) Sales price (see page D-2)	(e) Cost or other basis (see page D-3)	(f) LOSS If (e) is more than (d), subtract (d) from (e)	(g) GAIN If (d) is more than (e), subtract (e) from (d)
1a Stocks, Bonds, Other Securities, and Real Estate. Include Form 1099-B and 1099-S Transactions. See pages D-1 and D-3.						
(2) 200 Sh-Buma	7-20-92	10-12-92	600	400		200
(4) 100 Sh-Acme Auto	3-16-92	3-27-92	2,500	3,000	500	
(11) 100 Sh-Fast Co.	10-22-92	9-7-92	9,000	8,500		500
1b Amounts from Schedule D-1, line 1b. Attach Schedule D-1						
1c Total of All Sales Price Amounts. Add column (d) of lines 1a and 1b ▶ 1c			12,100			
1d Other Transactions.						
(10) Worthless Loan	5-1-86	3-5-92	Worthless	500	500	
(12) Call Sand. Corp.	6-4-92	Expired 8-3-92		500	500	
2 Short-term gain from sale or exchange of your home from Form 2119, line 17 or 23.				2		
3 Short-term gain from installment sales from Form 6252, line 26 or 37				3		
4 Short-term gain or (loss) from like-kind exchanges from Form 8824				4		
5 Net short-term gain or (loss) from partnerships, S corporations, and fiduciaries.				5		
6 Short-term capital loss carryover from 1991 Schedule D, line 36				6		
7 Add lines 1a, 1b, 1d, and 2 through 6, in columns (f) and (g)				7	(1,500)	700
8 Net short-term capital gain or (loss). Combine columns (f) and (g) of line 7.					8	(800)

Part II — Long-Term Capital Gains and Losses—Assets Held More than One Year

(a)	(b)	(c)	(d)	(e)	(f)	(g)
9a Stocks, Bonds, Other Securities, and Real Estate. Include Form 1099-B and 1099-S Transactions. See pages D-1 and D-3						
(1) 100 Sh-Acme Steel	10-1-81	3-2-92	6,000	5,000		1,000
(3) 100 Sh-Crown Auto	5-18-60	3-20-92	8,000	4,000		4,000
(5) 300 Sh-Davis Text	"INHERITED"	6-5-92	20,000	15,000		5,000
(6) 150 Sh-Box Co.	6-20-84	3-2-92	3,000	1,000		2,000
(7) 20 Sh-Bale Co.	1-5-90	6-5-92	300	200		100
(8) 100 Sh-Tel. Co.	1-3-62	2-5-92	20			20
9b Amounts from Schedule D-1, line 9b. Attach Schedule D-1						
9c Total of All Sales Price Amounts. Add column (d) of lines 9a and 9b ▶ 9c			37,320			
9d Other Transactions.						
(9) 2 Bond Rail Co. Worthless	8-10-70	12-31-92	Worthless	2,000	2,000	
(13) Lot-City Stake	6-14-60	3-30-92	2,000	600		1,400
10 Long-term gain from sale or exchange of your home from Form 2119, line 17 or 23				10		
11 Long-term gain from installment sales from Form 6252, line 26 or 37				11		
12 Long-term gain or (loss) from like-kind exchanges from Form 8824.				12		
13 Net long-term gain or (loss) from partnerships, S corporations, and fiduciaries				13		
14 Capital gain distributions				14		
15 Gain from Form 4797, line 8 or 10				15		
16 Long-term capital loss carryover from 1991 Schedule D, line 43				16		
17 Add lines 9a, 9b, 9d, and 10 through 16, in columns (f) and (g)				17	(2000)	13,520
18 Net long-term capital gain or (loss). Combine columns (f) and (g) of line 17					18	11,520

how you tried to collect it; and (5) how you determined it was worthless.

11. Short sale—You sold "short" 100 shares of Fast Co. on September 7, 1992, for $9,000. You covered this sale on October 22, 1992, by buying 100 shares for $8,500 and delivering them to your broker; *see* ¶5.20.

12. Call—On June 4, 1992, you bought a 60-day call on 100 shares of Sand Corp. for $500. You did not exercise it; *see* ¶5.26.

13. Sale of lot—On June 14, 1960, you bought a lot as an investment for $600. On March 30, 1992, you sell it for $2,000.

COUNTING THE HOLDING PERIOD

LONG-TERM OR SHORT-TERM HOLDING PERIOD

¶5.5 The period of time you own a capital asset before its sale or exchange determines whether gain or loss is short term or long term.

Long-Term Holding Period for 1992 Sales

Gains or losses in 1992 and in later years are long term if the property was held more than one year.

Rules for counting the holding period:

1. A holding period is figured in months and fractions of months.
2. The beginning date of a holding month is generally the day after the asset was acquired. The same numerical date of each following month starts a new holding month regardless of the number of days in the preceding month.
3. The last day of the holding period is the day on which the asset is sold.

As a rule of thumb, use the numerical date on which you acquired the asset as the numerical date ending a holding month in each following month. However, if you acquire an asset on the last day of a month, a holding month ends on the last day of a following calendar month, regardless of the number of days in each month.

EXAMPLES 1. On March 12, 1992, you buy stock. Holding months begin on March 13, April 13, May 13, June 13, and end on April 12, May 12, June 12, etc. A sale before March 13, 1993, will result in short-term gain or loss. If you sell on or after March 13, 1993, long-term treatment will apply; your holding period is more than one year.

2. You buy property on February 29, 1992. A holding month ends on March 31, April 30, etc. To realize long-term gain on the sale of this property, you must hold it at least one day longer than February 28, 1993.

3. You buy stock on November 30. A holding month ends on December 31, January 31, February 28 (or 29 in a leap year), etc.

SECURITIES TRANSACTIONS

¶5.6 Rules for counting your holding period for various securities transactions are as follows:

Stock sold on a public exchange. The holding period starts on the day after your purchase order is executed (trading date). The day your sale order is executed (trading date) is the last day of the holding period, even if delivery and payment are not made until several days after the actual sale (settlement date).

EXAMPLES 1. On June 2, you sell a stock at a profit. Your holding period ends on June 2, although proceeds are not received until June 7.

2. You sell stock at a gain on a public exchange on December 31, 1992. The gain must be reported in 1992 even though the proceeds are received in 1993. The installment sale rule does not apply; *see* ¶5.36.

Stock subscriptions. If you are bound by your subscription but the corporation is not, the holding period begins the day after the date on which the stock is issued. If both you and the company are bound, the acceptance of the subscription by the corporation is the date of acquisition, and your holding period begins the day after.

Tax-free stock rights. When you exercise rights to acquire corporate stock from the issuing corporation, your holding period for the stock begins on the day of exercise, *not* on the day after. You are deemed to exercise stock rights when you assent to the terms of the rights in the manner requested or authorized by the corporation. An option to acquire stock is not a stock right.

Stock sold from different lots. If you purchased shares of the same stock on different dates and cannot determine which shares you are selling, the shares purchased at the earliest time are considered the stock sold first; *see* also ¶5.17.

EXAMPLE You purchased 10 shares of ABC stock on May 3, 1985, 10 shares of ABC stock on May 1, 1987, and 10 shares of ABC stock on September 2, 1988. In 1992, you sell 25 shares of ABC stock, and are unable to determine when those particular shares were bought. Using the "first-in, first-out" method, 10 shares are from May 3, 1985, 10 shares from May 1, 1987, and five shares from September 2, 1988. *See also* ¶5.17.

Commodities. If you acquired a commodity futures contract, the holding period of a commodity accepted in satisfaction of the contract includes your holding period of the contract, unless you are a dealer in commodities.

Employee stock options. When an employee exercises a stock option, the holding period of the acquired stock begins on the day after the option is exercised. If an employee option plan allows the exercise of an option by giving notes, the terms of the plan should be reviewed to determine when ownership rights to the stock are transferred. The terms may affect the start of the holding period for the stock.

EXAMPLE In April 1964, Arnold exercised a stock option by giving a note. He had to pay up by June 1965, at which time he received his stock certificate. In October 1965, he sold the shares, realizing a profit of $20,000, which he reported as a long-term gain. The IRS taxed the profit as short-term gain, claiming that he owned the stock for only four months—that is, from the time he paid the note. Arnold argued that he acquired the stock when he gave the note.

The Tax Court agreed with the IRS. The plan called for cash.

Wash sales. After a wash sale, the holding period of the new stock includes the holding period of the old stock for which a loss has been disallowed; *see* ¶5.21.

Other references: Stock dividends, *see* ¶5.18; short sales, *see* ¶5.20; convertible securities, *see* ¶5.22.

REAL ESTATE TRANSACTIONS

¶**5.7** The holding period starts the day after the date of acquisition, which is the earlier of: (1) the date title passes to you; *or* (2) the date you take possession and you assume the burdens and privileges of ownership. In disputes involving the starting and closing dates of a holding period, you may refer to the state law that applies to your sale or purchase agreement. State law determines when title to property passes.

If your purchase of a new residence qualifies under the deferral rules discussed at ¶29.5, the holding period for the new home includes the holding period of the former residence. If you convert a residence to rental property and later sell the house, the holding period includes the time you held the house for personal purposes.

Year-end sale. The date of sale is the last day of your holding period even if you do not receive the sale proceeds until the following year. For example, you sell land at a gain on December 31, 1992, receiving payment in January 1993. The holding period ends on December 31, although the sale is reported in 1993 when the proceeds are received. Note that the December 31st gain transaction can be reported in 1992 by making an election to "elect out" of installment reporting; *see* ¶5.38. A sale at a loss is reported in 1992.

Holding period of a newly constructed house. When you sell a newly constructed house after its completion, you may have long-term capital gain on the underlying land and both long-term and short-term capital gain on the house. The holding periods of the land and building are figured separately. The holding period of the land begins from the date of the purchase of the land (which you may have held long term before the sale). The holding period of the building follows this peculiar rule: You get long-term capital gain for that portion of the gain allocable to the cost of the building erected in the applicable long-term period before the sale. You realize short-term capital gain on the balance.

GIFTS, INHERITANCES, AND OTHER PROPERTY

¶**5.8** *Gift property.* If, in figuring a gain or loss, your basis for the property under ¶5.13 is the same as the donor's basis, you add the donor's holding period to the period you held the property. If you sell the property at a loss using as your basis the fair market value at the date of the gift (¶5.13), your holding period begins on the date of the gift.

Inherited property. The law gives an automatic long-term holding period for inherited property, regardless of the actual length of time you held the property. On Schedule D, you report the sale in Part II for long-term gains and losses; write "INHERITED" in the column for date acquired.

Where property is purchased by the executor or trustee and distributed to you, your holding period begins the day after the date on which the property was purchased.

Partnership property. When you receive property as a distribution in kind from your partnership, the period your partnership held the property is added to your holding period. But there is no adding on of holding periods if the partnership property distributed was inventory and was sold by you within five years of distribution.

Involuntary conversions. When you have an involuntary conversion and elect to defer tax on gain, the holding period for the qualified replacement property generally includes the period you held the converted property. A new holding period begins for new property if you do not make an election to defer tax.

FIGURING YOUR PROFIT OR LOSS

	See ¶		See ¶
Calculating gain or loss	5.9	Basis of property you inherited or received as a gift	5.13
Amount realized is the total selling price	5.10	Joint tenancy basis rules for surviving tenants	5.14
Finding your cost	5.11	When to allocate cost	5.15
Unadjusted basis of your property	5.12	How to find adjusted basis	5.16

CALCULATING GAIN OR LOSS

¶**5.9** In most cases, you know if you have realized an economic profit or loss on the sale or exchange of property. You know your cost and selling price. The difference between the two is your profit or loss. The tax computation of gain or loss is similarly figured, except that the basis adjustment rules may require you to increase or decrease your cost or selling price. As a result, your gain or loss for tax purposes may differ from your initial calculation.

FIGURING GAIN OR LOSS ON SCHEDULE D

1. Amount realized or total selling price (¶5.10) $____
2. Cost or other unadjusted basis (¶5.12) $____
3. Plus: Improvements; certain legal fees (¶5.16) $____
4. Minus: depreciation, casualty losses (¶5.16) $____
5. Adjusted basis: 2 plus 3 minus 4 $____
6. Add selling expenses to 5. This is
   the total cost shown on Schedule D $____ $____
7. Gain or loss: Subtract 6 from 1. $____

EXAMPLE You sell rental property to a buyer who pays you cash of $50,000 and assumes your $35,000 mortgage. You bought the property for $55,000 and made $12,000 of permanent improvements. You deducted depreciation of $7,250. Selling expenses were $2,000. Your gain on the sale is $23,250, figured as follows:

1.	Amount realized (¶5.10)		
	Cash	$50,000	
	Assumed mortgage	35,000	
			$85,000
2.	Original cost	55,000	
3.	Plus improvements	12,000	
		$67,000	
4.	Minus depreciation	7,250	
5.	Adjusted basis	59,750	
6.	Plus selling expenses*	2,000	
7.	Total cost: Combined result of lines 2–6		61,750
8.	Gain: Subtract 7 from 1		$23,250

Selling expenses on Schedule D. When reporting a sale on Schedule D, IRS instructions require you to include *selling expenses* (Step 6) in the column for *cost,* rather than as a reduction to the sales price. The only exception is where a broker has reported *net* sale proceeds (gross proceeds less selling expenses) on Form 1099-B; you would then report the net amount as the sales price. Where a broker has reported the *gross* sales price on Form 1099-B, the IRS wants you to treat sales commissions as an addition to cost (rather than a reduction to selling price) so that it can compare the gross amount shown on Form 1099-B with the sales price reported on your return.

Using the facts in the previous example, you report the gross selling price of $85,000 in column (d) of Schedule D. In column (e), enter the adjusted basis of $59,750 plus the selling expenses of $2,000 for a total of $61,750. The final result, a gain of $23,250 ($85,000 – $61,750) is the same as if the selling price were reduced by the selling expenses.

AMOUNT REALIZED IS THE TOTAL SELLING PRICE

¶5.10 Amount realized is the tax term for the total selling price. It includes cash, the fair market value of additional property received, and any of your liabilities which the buyer agrees to pay. The buyer's note is included in the selling price at fair market value. This is generally the discounted amount that a bank or other party will pay for the note.

Sale of mortgaged property. The selling price includes the amount of the unpaid mortgage. This is true whether or not you are personally liable on the debt, and whether or not the buyer assumes the mortgage or merely takes the property subject to the mortgage. The full amount of the unpaid mortgage is included, even where the value of the property is less than the unpaid mortgage. *See also* ¶5.28 for computing amount realized on foreclosure sales.

If at the time of the sale, the buyer pays off the existing mortgage or your other liabilities, you include the payment as part of the sales proceeds.

EXAMPLES 1. You sell property subject to a mortgage of $60,000. The seller pays you cash of $30,000 and takes the property subject to the mortgage. The sales price is $90,000.

2. A partnership receives a nonrecourse mortgage of $1,851,500 from a bank to build an apartment project. Several years later, the partnership sells the project for the buyer's agreement to assume the unpaid mortgage. At the time, the value of the project is $1,400,000 and the partnership basis in the project is $1,455,740. The partnership figures a loss of $55,740, the difference between basis and the value of the pro-

ject. The IRS figures a gain of $395,760, the difference between the unpaid mortgage and basis. The partnership claims the selling price is limited to the lower fair market value and is supported by an appeals court. The Supreme Court reverses, supporting the IRS position. That the value of property is less than the amount of the mortgage has no effect on the rule requiring the unpaid mortgage to be part of the selling price. A mortgagor realizes value to the extent that his or her obligation to repay is relieved by a third party's assumption of the mortgage debt.

Amount realized for home sale deferral purposes. In figuring whether you may defer the gain when you sell your principal residence and buy a new one, the "amount realized" on the sale is the net selling price—the selling price reduced by commissions, legal fees, transfer taxes, advertising costs, and other selling expenses; *see* ¶29.5.

FINDING YOUR COST

¶5.11 In figuring gain or loss, you need to know the "unadjusted basis" of the property sold. This term refers to the original cost of your property if you purchased it. The general rules for determining your unadjusted basis are in ¶5.12. Basis for property received by gift or inheritance is in ¶5.13; rules for surviving joint tenants are in ¶5.14. Keep in mind that you have to adjust this figure for improvements to the property, depreciation, or losses. These adjustments are explained at ¶5.16.

UNADJUSTED BASIS OF YOUR PROPERTY

¶5.12 To determine your tax cost for property, first find in the following section the unadjusted basis of the property, and then increase or decrease that basis as explained at ¶5.16.

Property you bought. Unadjusted basis is your cash cost plus the value of any property you gave to the seller. If you assumed a mortgage or bought property subject to a mortgage, the amount of the mortgage is part of your unadjusted basis.

Purchase expenses are included in your cost, such as commissions, title insurance, recording fees, survey costs, and transfer taxes.

When you buy real estate, you usually reimburse the seller for property taxes he or she paid that cover the period after you took title. If you bought the property before 1954, you add such payments to basis. If you bought the property after 1953, taxes paid are not added to basis because they are immediately deductible in the year paid; *see* ¶16.6. However, if at the closing you also paid property taxes attributable to the time the seller held the property, you add such taxes to basis.

EXAMPLE You bought a building for $120,000 in cash and a purchase money mortgage of $60,000. The unadjusted basis of the building is $180,000.

Property obtained for services. If you paid for the property by providing services, the value of the property, which is taxable compensation, is also your adjusted basis.

Property received in taxable exchange. Technically, your unadjusted basis for the new property is the fair market value of the surrendered property at the time of exchange. In practice, however, the basis usually is equal to the fair market value of the property received. *See* page 76 for "tax-free" exchanges.

EXAMPLE You acquire real estate for $35,000. When the property has a fair market value of $40,000, you exchange it for machinery also worth $40,000. You have a gain of $5,000 and the basis of the machinery is $40,000.

Property received in "tax-free" exchange—within the rules explained at ¶6.1. Your basis is that of the property which you exchange, decreased by any cash received, increased by any taxed gain, or decreased by recognized loss. Gain is taxed to the extent cash is also received; *see* ¶6.3 for discussion on taxable boot.

EXAMPLES 1. You exchange investment real estate, which cost you $20,000, for other investment real estate. Both properties have a fair market value of $35,000. You pay no tax on the exchange. The unadjusted basis of the new property received in the exchange is $20,000.

2. Same facts as in Example 1 but you receive real estate worth $30,000 and cash of $5,000. On this transaction, you realize gain of $15,000 (of which $5,000 is taxed to the extent of the cash). Your basis for the new property is $20,000 figured this way:

Basis of old property	$20,000
Less: Cash received	5,000
	15,000
Plus: Gain recognized	5,000
Basis of new property	$20,000

Property received from a spouse or former spouse. As explained at ¶6.6, tax-free exchange rules apply to property transfers after July 18, 1984, to a spouse, or to a former spouse where the transfer is incident to a divorce. The spouse receiving the property takes a basis equal to that of the transferor. Certain adjustments may be required where a transfer of mortgaged property is made in trust.

If you received property before July 19, 1984, under a prenuptial agreement in exchange for your release of your dower and marital rights, your basis is the fair market value at the time you received it.

New residence purchased under tax deferral rule. If you sell your old principal residence and buy a qualifying replacement under the rules of ¶29.2—¶29.5, your basis for the new house is what you paid for it, less any gain that was not taxed on the sale of the old residence. *See also* example of basis computation at the end of ¶29.5.

Property received as a trust beneficiary. Generally, you take the same basis the trust had for the property. But if the distribution is made to settle a claim you had against the trust, your basis for the property is the amount of the settled claim.

If you received a distribution in kind for your share of trust income before June 2, 1984, the basis of the distribution is generally the value of the property to the extent allocated to distributable net income. For distributions in kind after June 1, 1984, in taxable years ending after June 1, 1984, your basis is the basis of the property in the hands of the trust. If the trust elects to treat the distribution as a taxable sale, your basis is generally fair market value.

Property accrued with proceeds from involuntary conversion. If you acquire replacement property with insurance proceeds from destroyed property, or a government payment for condemned property, basis is the cost of the new property decreased by deferred gain; *see* ¶18.23 for figuring the deferred gain. If the replacement property consists of more than one piece of property, basis is allocated to each piece in proportion to its respective cost.

EXAMPLE A building with an adjusted basis of $100,000 is destroyed by fire. The owner receives an insurance award of $200,000, realizing a gain of $100,000. He buys a building as a replacement for $150,000. Thus, $50,000 of his gain is taxable, while the remaining $50,000 is deferred. The basis of the new building is $100,000.

Cost of the new building	$150,000
Less: deferred gain	50,000
Basis	$100,000

BASIS OF PROPERTY YOU INHERITED OR RECEIVED AS A GIFT

¶5.13 Special basis rules apply to property you received as a gift or that you inherited. Gifts from a spouse are subject to the rules of ¶6.6. If you are a surviving joint tenant who received full title to property upon the death of the other joint tenant, *see* ¶5.14.

BASIS OF PROPERTY RECEIVED AS GIFT

Selling property you received as a gift after 1920. If the fair market value of the property exceeded the donor's adjusted basis (¶5.16) at the time you received the gift, your basis for figuring gain or loss when you sell it is the donor's adjusted basis plus all or part of any gift tax paid; the gift tax rule is below.

If on the date of the gift, the fair market value was *less* than the donor's adjusted basis, your basis for purposes of figuring gain is the donor's adjusted basis, and your basis for figuring loss is the fair market value.

EXAMPLE Assume that in 1985 you received a gift of stock from your father which you sold in 1992. His adjusted basis was $1,000.

The basis you use to determine gain or loss depends on whether the fair market value of the stock exceeded your father's $1,000 adjusted basis on the date of the gift. If it did, your basis is your father's $1,000 basis and you will realize a gain if your selling price exceeds $1,000, as on Line 1 below, or a loss if the selling price is below $1,000, as on Line 4.

If the value of the stock on the date of the gift was *less* than $1,000 (father's basis) then you have: a gain if you sell for more than $1,000, as on Line 5; a loss if you sell for less than the date-of-gift value, as on Line 2; or neither gain nor loss if you sell for more than the date-of-gift value, as on Line 3.

If value of the gift at receipt was—	And you sold it for—	Your basis is —	Your gain is—	Your loss is—
1. $3,000	$2,000	$1,000	$1,000	
2. 700	500	700		$200
3. 300	500	*	none	none
4. 1,500	500	1,000		500
5. 500	1,200	1,000	200	

*In Line 3 of the example, there is neither gain nor loss. To compute gain, the donor's cost is used ($1,000) as your basis. Thus, there is no gain. But there is no loss because the property was sold for more than its value at the time of gift. To compute loss, you must use market value as the basis, which in this case is lower than donor's cost.

Did the donor pay gift tax? If the donor did pay a gift tax (¶33.1) on the gift to you, your basis for the property is increased under these rules:

1. For property received after December 31, 1976, the basis is increased for the gift tax paid by an amount which bears the same ratio to the amount of tax paid as the net appreciation in the value of the gift bears to the amount of the gift. The increase may not exceed the tax paid. Net appreciation in the value of any gift is the amount by which the fair market value

of the gift exceeds the donor's adjusted basis immediately before the gift. *See* Example 2 below.

2. For property received after September 1, 1958, but before 1977, basis is increased by the gift tax paid on the property but not above the market value of the property at the time of the gift.

3. For property received before September 2, 1958, basis is increased by the gift tax paid. But this increase may not be more than the excess of the market value of the property at the time of the gift over the basis of the property in the donor's hands. Ask the donor or his advisor for these amounts.

EXAMPLES 1. In 1975, your father gave you rental property with a fair market value of $78,000. The basis of the property in his hands was $60,000. He paid a gift tax of $15,000 on the gift. The basis of the property in your hands is $75,000 ($60,000 + $15,000).

2. In 1977, your father gave you rental property with a fair market value of $78,000. His basis in the property was $60,000. He paid a gift tax of $15,000 on the gift. The basis of the property in your hands is your father's basis increased by the gift tax attributable to the appreciation. Gift tax attributable to the appreciation is:

$$\frac{\text{Appreciation}}{\text{Fair market value}} \times \text{Gift tax paid}$$

$$\frac{\$18,000}{\$78,000} \times \$15,000 = \$3,462$$

Your basis for figuring gain or loss or depreciation is $63,462 ($3,462 + $60,000 father's basis).

Gift you received before 1921. Your basis is the fair market value of the property at the time of the gift.

Depreciation on property received as a gift. If the property is depreciable (*see* Chapter 42) by you, your basis for computing depreciation deductions is the donor's adjusted basis (¶5.16), plus all or part of the gift tax paid by the donors as discussed above.

When you sell the property, you must adjust basis (¶5.16) for depreciation claimed. If accelerated depreciation is claimed and you sell at a gain, you are subject to the ordinary income recapture rules discussed at ¶44.1.

If you receive a residence as a gift and later convert it to rental property; *see* ¶29.19.

BASIS OF INHERITED PROPERTY

Value of inherited property. Your basis for inherited property is generally the value of the property on the date of the decedent's death, regardless of when you acquire the property. If decedent died after October 21, 1942, and the executor elected to use an *alternate valuation date* after the death, your basis is the alternate value at that date.

If you inherit property that you (or your spouse) gave to the deceased person within one year of his or her death, your basis is the decedent's basis immediately before death, not its fair market value.

If the inherited property is subject to a mortgage, your basis is the value of the property, and not its equity at the date of death. If the property is subject to a lease under which no income is to be received for years, the basis is the value of the property—not the equity.

You might be given the right to buy the deceased person's property under his or her will. This is not the same as inheriting that property. Your basis is what you pay—not what the property is worth on the date of the deceased's death.

If property was inherited from a decedent dying after 1976 and before November 7, 1978, and the executor elected to apply carryover basis to all estate property, your basis is figured with reference to the decedent's basis. The executor must inform you of the basis of such property.

For the survivor of joint tenancy; see ¶5.14.

Advantage of Leaving Appreciated Property to Heir

Since your basis for inherited property is the value at the decedent's death or alternate valuation date, tax is completely avoided on the appreciation in value that occurred while the decedent owned the property.

JOINT TENANCY BASIS RULES FOR SURVIVING TENANTS

¶5.14 For deaths occurring after 1981, the law provides different basis rules for joint tenancies between husbands and wives than for tenancies between persons who are not married to each other.

Survivor of spouse who died after 1981. A "qualified joint interest" rule applies to a joint tenancy with right of survivorship or tenancy by the entirety between a husband and wife. The rule for deaths occurring *after 1981* is as follows: One-half of the fair market value of the property is includable in the decedent's gross estate, or would be if an estate tax return was due. Fair market value is fixed at the date of death, or six months later if an estate tax return is filed and the optional valuation date is elected.

The surviving spouse's basis equals the one-half estate tax share, plus one-half of the original cost basis for the property. If depreciation deductions for the property were claimed before the date of death, the surviving spouse must reduce basis by his or her share (under local law) of the depreciation.

EXAMPLES 1. John and Jennifer Jones jointly own a house that cost them $50,000 in 1970. John paid $45,000 of the purchase price and Jennifer $5,000. In 1992, John dies when the house is worth $200,000. One-half or $100,000 is included in his estate although he contributed 90% of the purchase price. For income tax purposes, Jennifer's basis for the house is $125,000.

One-half of cost basis	$ 25,000
Basis for inherited portion	100,000
Jennifer's basis	$125,000

On a sale of the home for $200,000, Jennifer would realize a $75,000 long-term capital gain ($200,000–$125,000).

2. Same as Example 1 except that the home was rental property for which $20,000 of depreciation deductions had been allowed before John's death. Under local law, Jennifer had a right to 50% of the income from the property and thus, a right to 50% of the depreciation. Her basis for the property is $115,000: $125,000 as shown in Example 1, reduced by $10,000, her share of the depreciation.

Unmarried joint tenants. If you are a surviving joint tenant who owned property with someone other than your spouse, your basis for the entire property is your basis for your share before the joint owner died plus the fair market value of the decedent's interest at death (or on the alternate valuation date if the estate uses the alternate date). The decedent's interest does not have to be included on an estate tax return (for example, when the estate is too small to be taxable) for you to use the date-of-death value. If no estate tax return is required, you may not use the alternative valuation date basis.

EXAMPLE You and your sister bought a home in 1950 for $20,000. She paid $12,000, and you, $8,000. Title to the house was held by both of you as joint tenants. In 1992, when she died, the house was worth $150,000. Since she paid 60% of the cost of the house, 60% of the value at her death, $90,000, is included in an estate tax return (or would be included if an estate tax return was due). Your basis for the house is now $98,000—the $8,000 you originally paid plus the $90,000 fair market value of your sister's share at her death.

Exception for pre-1954 deaths. Where property was held in joint tenancy and one of the tenants died before January 1, 1954, no part of the interest of the surviving tenant is treated, for purposes of determining the basis of the property, as property transmitted at death. The survivor's basis is the original cost of the property.

Survivor of spouse who died before 1982. The basis rule for a surviving spouse who held property jointly (or as tenancy by the entirety) with a spouse who died before 1982 is generally the same as the rule above for unmarried joint tenants. However, special rules applied to qualified joint interests and eligible joint interests are discussed below.

EXAMPLE Husband and wife owned rental property as tenants by the entirety that they purchased for $30,000. The husband furnished two-thirds of the purchase price ($20,000) and the wife furnished one-third ($10,000). Depreciation deductions taken before the husband's death were $12,000. On the date of his death in 1979, the property had a fair market value of $60,000. Under the law of the state in which the property is located, as tenants by the entirety, each had a half interest in the property. The wife's basis in the property at the date of her husband's death is computed as follows:

Interest acquired with her own funds	$10,000
Interest acquired from husband (⅔ of $60,000)	40,000
	$50,000
Less: Depreciation of ½ interest not acquired by reason of death (½ of $12,000)	6,000
Basis at date of husband's death	$44,000

If she had not contributed any part of the purchase price, her basis at the date of her husband's death would be $54,000 ($60,000 fair market value less $6,000 depreciation).

Qualified joint interest and eligible joint interest where spouse died before 1982. Where, after 1976, a spouse dying before 1982 elected to treat realty as a "qualified joint interest" subject to gift tax, such joint property was treated as owned fifty-fifty by each spouse, and 50% of the value was included in the decedent's estate. Thus, for income tax purposes, the survivor's basis for the inherited 50% half of the property is the estate tax value; the basis for the other half is determined under the gift rules detailed in ¶5.13. Personal property is treated as a "qualified joint interest" only if it was created or deemed to have been created after 1976 by a husband and wife and was subject to gift tax.

Where death occurred before 1982 and a surviving spouse materially participated in the operation of a farm or other business, an estate may elect to treat the farm or business property as an "eligible joint interest," which means that part of the investment in the property may be attributed to the surviving spouse's services and that part is not included in the deceased spouse's estate. Where such an election was made, the survivor's basis for income tax purposes includes the estate tax value of property included in the decedent's estate.

WHEN TO ALLOCATE COST

¶5.15 Allocation of basis is generally required in these cases: when the property includes land and building; the land is to be divided into lots; securities are purchased at different times; stock splits; and in the purchase of a business.

Purchase of land and building. To figure depreciation on the building, part of the purchase price must be allocated to the building. The allocation is made according to the fair market values of the building and land. The amount allocated to land is not depreciated.

Purchase of land to be divided into lots. The purchase price of the tract is allocated to each lot, so that the gain or loss from the sale of each lot may be reported in the year of its sale. Allocation is not made ratably, that is, with an equal share to each lot or parcel. It is based on the relative value of each piece of property. Comparable sales, competent appraisals, or assessed values may be used as guides.

Securities. See ¶5.17 for methods of identifying securities bought at different dates.

See ¶5.18 for allocating basis of stock dividends and stock splits; ¶5.19 for allocating the basis of stock rights.

Purchase price of a business. See ¶44.9 for allocation rule.

HOW TO FIND ADJUSTED BASIS

¶5.16 After determining the unadjusted cost basis under the rules at ¶5.12–¶5.15, you find your "adjusted basis" in two steps:

1. Additions to basis. You add to basis the cost of all permanent improvements and additions to the property and other capital costs, such as the cost of repairing your property after a casualty (such as a fire or storm), and legal fees for defending or perfecting title, or for obtaining a reduction of an assessment levied against property to pay for local benefits.

If you sell land with unharvested crops, add the cost of producing the crops to the basis of the property sold.

2. Deductions from basis. You reduce cost for these items—

Return of capital, such as dividends on stock paid out of capital or out of a depletion reserve when the company has no available earnings or surplus; *see* ¶4.11.

Losses from casualties, including insurance awards and payments in settlement of damages to your property.

EXAMPLE Your residence, which cost $75,000, is damaged by fire. You deducted the uninsured loss of $10,000 and spent $11,000 to repair the property. Several years later, you sell the house for $90,000. To figure your profit, you increase the original cost of the house by the $11,000 of repairs and then reduce basis by the $10,000 casualty loss to get an adjusted basis of $76,000 ($75,000 + $11,000 − $10,000). Your gain on the sale is $14,000 ($90,000 − $76,000).

Depletion allowances; see ¶9.14.

Depreciation, first-year expensing deduction, ACRS deductions, amortization, and obsolescence on property used in business or for the production of income. In some years, you may have taken more or less depreciation than was allowable. If you took more depreciation than was allowable, you may have to make the following adjustments: If you have deducted more than what was allowable and you received a tax benefit from the deduction, you deduct the full amount of the depreciation. But if the excess depreciation did not give you a tax benefit, because income was eliminated by other deductions, the excess is not deducted from basis.

If you claim less than what was allowable, you must deduct from basis the allowable amount. These rules affect all tax years after 1951.

If you hold bonds bought at a premium; *see* ¶4.17. If you did not pay tax on certain cancellations of debt on your business property (¶12.9), you reduce basis for the amount forgiven.

Investment credit. Where the full investment credit was claimed in 1983 or later years, basis was reduced by one-half the credit.

SALES OF STOCKS AND BONDS

EARMARKING STOCK LOTS

¶5.17 Keep a record of all your stock transactions, especially when you buy the stock of one company at varying prices. By keeping a record of each stock lot, you may control the amount of gain or loss on a sale of a part of your holdings.

If your stock is held by your broker, the IRS considers that an adequate identification is made if you grant your broker the power to buy and sell in your name at will. The broker notifies you at the time of sale, requesting instructions on which shares should be sold. Before the settlement date (usually four business days from the time of sale), you instruct by letter which shares to deliver. He or she, in turn, signs and dates the confirmation, which is printed at the bottom of your letter of instruction, and returns the letter to you. You also are given monthly statements of the transactions and your cash position and stock on hand.

How To Identify Securities

If your securities are—	Identify them by—
Registered in your own name	The number, your name, and any other identification which they bear.
In a margin account registered in a "street" name	A specified block or security bought on a designated day at a particular price. A mere intention to sell a particular share without informing the broker is without significance.
New certificates received for old in a recapitalization	Record the new certificate with the lowest number as being in exchange for the old certificate with the lowest number. Do this until all the new certificates are matched with all the old.
Shares exchanged for shares in a reorganization	Allocate each of the new certificates to each of the old in your records. Where the exchange involves several blocks of stock and there is no specific identification, the IRS says you must average your costs.
Shares received in a split-up	Match the new certificates with the old ones surrendered. Identification of your selling securities as the "highest cost" or "lowest cost" stock is insufficient. You have to match at the time of the split-up.
Stock dividends	The lot of stock on which you received the dividend. The new stock is part of the old lot. But, if you receive one certificate for more than one lot, you may have to apply the first-in, first-out rule when you sell.
Acquired by exercise of nontaxed stock rights	The number, or other identification of the lot you receive by exercising the rights. Each lot you so acquire is considered a separate lot received on the date of subscription.

EXAMPLE Over a three-year period, you bought the following shares of Acme Steel stock: In 1987, 100 shares at $77 per share; in 1988, 200 shares at $84 per share; in 1989, 100 shares at $105 per share. When the stock is selling at $90, you plan to sell 100 shares. You may use the cost of your 1989 lot and get a $1,500 loss if, for example, you want to offset some gains or other income you have already earned this year. Or you may get capital gains of varying amounts by either selling the 1987 lot or part of the 1988 lot. You must clearly identify the lot you want to sell. Say you want a loss and sell the 1989 lot. Unless you identify it as the lot sold, the IRS will hold that you sold the 1987 lot under the "first-in, first-out" rule. This rule assumes that, when you have a number of identical items that you bought at different times, your sale of any of them is automatically the sale of the first you bought. So the cost of your first purchase is what you match against your selling price to find your gain or loss. Here is what to do to counteract the first-in, first-out rule: If the stock certificates are registered in your name, show that you delivered the 1989 stock certificates. *See* Chapter 30 for averaging cost on the sale of mutual fund shares.

SALE OF STOCK RECEIVED AS DIVIDEND OR IN A STOCK SPLIT

¶5.18 A sale of stock originally received as a dividend is treated as any other sale of stock. The holding period of a taxable stock dividend begins on the day after the date of distribution. The holding period of a tax-free stock dividend or stock received in a split starts from the time you acquired the original stock.

EXAMPLE You bought 100 shares of X Co. stock on December 3, 1990. On August 13, 1992, you receive 10 shares of X Co. stock as a tax-free stock dividend. On December 10, 1992, you sell the 10 shares at a profit. You report the sale as long-term capital gain because the holding period of the 10 shares goes back to your original purchase date of December 3, 1990, not August 13, 1992.

Basis of tax-free dividend in the same class of stock. Assume you receive a common stock dividend on common stock. You divide the original cost by the total number of old shares and new shares to find the new basis per share.

EXAMPLE You bought 100 shares of common stock for $1,000, so that each share has a basis of $10. You receive 100 shares of common as a tax-free stock dividend. The basis of your 200 shares remains $1,000. The new cost basis of each share is now $5 ($1,000 ÷ 200 shares). You sell 50 shares for $560. Your profit is $310 ($560 − $250).

Basis of tax-free dividend in a different class of stock. Assume you receive preferred stock dividends on common stock. You divide the basis of the old shares over the two classes in the ratio of their values at the time the stock dividend was distributed.

EXAMPLE You bought 100 shares of common stock for $1,000. You receive a tax-free dividend of 10 shares of preferred stock. On the date of distribution, the market value of the common stock is $9 a share; the preferred stock, $30. That makes the market value of your common stock $900 and your preferred stock $300. So you allocate 75% ($900 ÷ $1,200) of your $1,000 original cost, or $750, to your common stock and 25% ($300 ÷ $1,200) of your cost to the preferred stock.

Basis of taxable stock dividend. The basis of a taxable stock dividend is its fair market value at the time of the distribution. Its holding period begins on the date of distribution. The basis of the old stock remains unchanged.

EXAMPLE You bought 1,000 shares of stock for $10,000. The company gives you a choice of a cash dividend or stock (one share for every hundred held). You elect the stock. On the date of the distribution, its market value was $15 a share. The basis of the new stock is $150 (10 × $15). The basis of the old stock remains $10,000.

The tax treatment of the receipt of stock as a dividend and in a split is discussed at ¶4.6.

Basis of public utility stock received under dividend reinvestment plan. For several years before 1986, an exclusion was allowed for stock dividends received from public utility companies if the dividends were reinvested in stock. If you claimed the exclusion, the stock takes a zero basis. If you sell the stock, the entire sales proceeds of the stock are reported as long-term capital gain.

SALE, EXERCISE, OR EXPIRATION OF STOCK RIGHTS

¶5.19 The tax consequences of the receipt of stock rights is discussed at ¶4.6. The following is an explanation of how to treat the sale, exercise, or expiration of nontaxable stock rights. The basis of taxable rights is their fair market value at the time of distribution.

Expiration of nontaxable distributed stock rights. When you allow nontaxable rights to expire, you do not have a deductible loss; you have no basis in the rights.

Sale of nontaxable distributed stock rights. If you sell stock rights distributed on your stock, you treat the sale as the sale of a capital asset. The holding period begins from the date you acquired the original stock on which the rights were distributed.

Purchased rights. If you buy stock rights, your holding period starts the day after the date of the purchase. Your basis for the rights is the price paid; this basis is used in computing your capital gain or loss on the sale.

If you allow purchased rights to expire without sale or exercise, you realize a capital loss. The rights are treated as having been sold on the day of expiration. When purchased rights become worthless during the year prior to the year they lapse, you have a capital loss which is treated as having occurred on the last day of the year in which they became worthless.

Exercise of stock rights. You realize no taxable income on the exercise of stock rights. Capital gain or loss on the new stock is recognized when you later sell the stock. The holding period of the new stock begins on the date you exercised the rights. Your basis for the new stock is the subscription price you paid plus your basis for the rights exercised.

Figuring the basis of nontaxable stock rights. Whether rights received by you as a stockholder have a basis depends on their fair market value when distributed. If the market value of rights is less than 15% of the market value of your old stock, the basis of your rights is zero, unless you elect to allocate the basis between the rights and your original stock. You make the election on your tax return for the year the rights are received by attaching to your return a statement that your are electing to divide basis. Keep a copy of the election and the return.

If the market value of the rights is 15% or more of the market value of your old stock, you must divide the basis of the stock between the old stock and the rights, according to their respective values on the date of distribution.

EXAMPLE You own 100 shares of M Co. that cost $10 a share. On September 15, there is a distribution of stock rights allowing for the purchase of one additional share of common for each 10 rights held at a price of $13 a share. The common stock is now worth $15 (ex-rights). The rights have a market value of 20¢ each. This is less than 15% of the market value of the stock. You can either: (1) choose not to spread the tax cost of the stock between the old stock and the rights, or (2) elect to spread the tax cost as follows:

Cost of your old stock, 100 shares at $10, or $1,000.
Fair market value of old stock, 100 shares at $15, or $1,500.
Market value of 100 rights at 20¢, or $20.
Market value of both old stock and rights, $1,520.

Apportionment of old stock:
$$\frac{\$1,500}{\$1,520} \times 1,000 = 986.84$$

Your new basis of old stock is $986.84 for 100 shares, or $9.87 a share. The tax cost of the rights is then calculated:
$$\frac{\$20}{\$1,520} \times 1,000 = \$13.16$$

Basis of the rights is $13.16 for 100 rights.
When you exercise your rights and 10 shares are bought, your basis for the new stock is $130 plus the cost of the rights of $13.16, or $143.16.
If the option of allocation is not exercised, the rights have a basis of zero and the basis of the new stock is $130. The basis of the old stock remains $1,000.

No basis adjustment is required for stock rights that become worthless during the year of issue.

EXAMPLE A corporation issued nontaxable stock rights to its common shareholders. The rights were worth more than 15% of the fair market value of the common stock. Shortly after issue, the stock market values fell and the price of common stock fell below the subscription offer. As the rights were valueless, the company decided to refund subscriptions to shareholders who exercised the option and paid the subscription price. Although the stock rights were originally 15% or more of value of stock, the IRS held that the stockholders receiving the refunds did not have to allocate basis. The allocation is not necessary as the subscription price was returned in the same taxable year in which the rights were issued.

HOW TO TREAT SHORT SALES

¶5.20 You sell short when you sell borrowed securities. You usually borrow the securities from your broker. When you sell short, you may: (1) own the identical securities but do not want to sell them just now; or (2) *not* own the securities. A short sale of securities you already own is called a short sale "against the box." You *close* the short sale when you deliver to the broker the identical securities you have been holding or identical securities you have bought after the short sale.

Investment Goal of Short Sales

Some objectives of selling short: You may want to profit from a declining market in the hope you can buy the replacement stock at lower prices, freeze paper profits in an uncertain market, or postpone gain to another year.

EXAMPLES 1. In December 1992, you want to freeze your profit in Z stock, but you want to report the sale in 1993. You sell Z short on December 18, 1992. On January 4, 1993, you close the short sale by delivering your Z stock. The short sale is reported as gain on your 1993 return. You report a short sale in the year in which you close the short sale.

2. You sell short 100 shares of Steel Co. for $5,000. You borrowed the stock from your broker. The market declines. Thirteen months later, you buy 100 shares of Steel Co. stock for $3,000, which you deliver to your broker to close the short sale. Your profit of $2,000 is taxed as short-term capital gain. Your profit would be short term regardless of how long you kept the sale open; *see* Rule 1 below.

Tax consequences of short sales. When analyzing short-sale transactions, ask yourself these two questions:

1. When you sold short, did you or your spouse hold short-term securities substantially identical to the securities sold short? (Substantially identical securities are described at ¶5.21.)
2. After the short sale, did you or your spouse acquire substantially identical securities on or before the date of the closing of the short sale?

If you answered "yes" to either or both of these questions, apply the following two rules:

Rule 1. Gain realized on the closing of the short sale are short term. The gain is short term regardless of the period of time you have held the securities as of the closing date of the short sale.

Rule 2. The beginning date of the holding period of substantially identical stock is suspended. The holding period of substantially identical securities owned or bought under the facts of questions (1) or (2) above does not begin until the date of the closing of the short sale (or the date of the sale, gift, or other disposition of the securities, whichever date occurs first). But note this rule applies only to the number of securities that do not exceed the quantity sold short.

EXAMPLES 1. *Short-term gain on closing short sale (Rule 1 above)*

Oct. 2, 1991: You buy 100 shares of Steel Co. at $10 a share.
Mar. 2, 1992: You sell "short against the box" 100 shares of Steel Co. at $16 a share.
Oct. 2, 1992: You close the short sale by delivering the stock bought on Oct. 2, 1991.
Result:
You have a short-term gain of $600. On the date of the short sale (March 2), you held 100 shares of Steel Co. stock short term, as they were not held for more than one year. That more than a year elapsed between the purchase and closing date is immaterial.

2. *Holding period suspended (Rule 2 above)*

Oct. 2, 1991: You buy 100 shares of Steel Co. at $10 a share.
Mar. 2, 1992: You sell "short against the box" 100 shares of Steel Co. at $16 a share.
Oct. 2, 1992: You close the short sale with 100 shares you buy today at $18.
Oct. 5, 1992: You sell at $18 a share the lot bought on Oct. 2, 1991.

Result:
(a) You have a short-term loss of $200 on the closing of the short sale:

Sales Price	$1,600
Cost	1,800
Loss	($ 200)

(b) You have a short-term gain of $800 on the sale of the Oct. 2 lot ($1,800 − $1,000). Gain is short term although you held the lot for more than one year. The Oct. 2 lot was substantially identical stock held short term at the time of the short sale on Mar. 2. Under the special holding period rule, the holding period of the Oct. 2 lot did not begin until the closing of the short sale on Oct. 2, 1992.

The effect of the holding period rule is to give the same tax result that would have been realized if you had sold the Oct. 2, 1991, lot on Mar. 2, instead of making a short sale on that date. On Mar. 2, a sale would have given you a short-term gain of $600.

A put as a short sale. The acquisition of a *put* (an option to sell) is treated as a short sale if you hold substantially identical securities short term at the time you buy the put. The exercise or failure to exercise the put is treated as the closing of the short sale. However, the short-sale rules do not apply if on the same day you buy a put and stock which is identified as covered by the put. If you do not exercise the put which is identified with the stock, add its cost to the basis of the stock.

Losses on Short Sales

A loss on a short sale is not deductible until shares closing the short sale are delivered to the broker. You may not realize a short-term loss on the closing of a short sale if you held substantially identical securities long term on the date of the short sale. The loss is long term. This rule prevents you from creating short-term losses when you held the covering stock long term. Loss deductions on short sales may be disallowed under the wash-sale rules of ¶5.21.

Expenses of short sales. Before you buy stock to close out a short sale, you pay the broker for dividends paid on stock you have sold short. If you itemize deductions, you may treat your payment as investment interest (¶15.9), provided the short sale is held open at least 46 days, or more than a year in the case of extraordinary dividends. If the 46-day test (or one year) is not met, the payment is generally not deductible and is added to basis; in counting the short-sale period, do not count any period during which you have an option to buy or are obligated to buy substantially identical securities, or are protected from the risk of loss from the short sale by a substantially similar position.

Under an exception to the 46-day test, if you receive compensation from the lender of the stock for the use of collateral and you report the compensation as ordinary income, your payment for dividends is deductible to the extent of the compensation; only the excess of your payment over the compensation is disallowed. This exception does not apply to payments with respect to extraordinary dividends. An extraordinary dividend is generally a dividend that exceeds in value 10% of the adjusted basis of the stock or 5% in the case of a preferred stock. For purposes of this test, dividends on stock received within an 85-day period are aggregated; a one-year aggregation period applies if dividends exceed 20% of the adjusted basis in the stock.

Arbitrage transactions. Special holding period rules apply to short sales involved in identified arbitrage transactions in convertible securities and stock into which the securities are convertible. These rules can be found in Treasury regulations to Internal Revenue Code Section 1233.

LOSSES FROM WASH SALES

¶5.21

The objective of the wash-sale rule is to disallow a loss deduction where you recover your market position in a security within a short period of time after the sale. Under the wash-sale rule, your loss deduction is barred if within 30 days of the sale you buy *substantially identical* stock or securities, or a "put" or "call" option on such securities. The wash-sale period is 61 days—running from 30 days before to 30 days after the date of sale. The end of a taxable year during this 61-day period does not affect the wash-sale rule. The loss is still denied. If you sell at a loss and your spouse buys substantially identical stock, the loss is also barred.

The wash-sale rule does not apply to gains or to acquisitions by gift, inheritance, or tax-free exchange.

The wash-sale rule applies to investors and traders. It does not apply to dealers.

Loss on sale of part of a stock lot bought less than 30 days ago. A loss on the sale is deductible; the wash-sale disallowance rule does not apply.

EXAMPLE

You buy 200 shares of stock. Within 30 days, you sell 100 shares at a loss. The loss is not disallowed by the wash-sale rule. The wash-sale rule does not apply to a loss sustained in a bona fide sale made to reduce your market position. It does apply when you sustain a loss for tax purposes with the intent of recovering your position in the security within a few days. Thus, if after selling the 100 shares, you repurchase 100 shares of the same stock within 30 days after the sale, the loss is disallowed.

Oral sale-repurchase agreement. The wash-sale rule applies to an oral sale-repurchase agreement between business associates.

Defining "substantially identical." What is substantially identical stock or securities? Buying and selling General Motors stock is dealing in an identical security. Selling General Motors and buying Chrysler stock is not dealing in an identical security.

Bonds of the same obligor are substantially identical if they carry the same rate of interest; that they have different issue dates and interest payment dates will not remove them from the wash-sale provisions. Different maturity dates will have no effect, unless the difference is economically significant. Where there is a long-time span between the purchase date and the maturity date, a difference of several years between maturity dates may be considered insignificant. A difference of three years between maturity dates was held to be insignificant where the maturity dates of the bonds, measured from the time of purchase, were 45 and 48 years away. There was no significant difference where the maturity dates differed by less than one year, and the remaining life, measured from the time of purchase, was more than 15 years.

The wash-sale rules do not apply if you buy bonds of the same company with substantially different interest rates; buy bonds of a different company; or buy substantially identical bonds outside of the wash-sale period.

Warrants. A warrant falls within the wash-sale rule if it is an option to buy substantially identical stock. Consequently, a loss on the sale of common stocks of a corporation is disallowed when warrants for the common stock of the same corporation are bought within the period 30 days before or after the sale. But if the timing is reversed—that is, you sell warrants at a loss and simultaneously buy common stock of the same corporation—the wash-sale rules may or may not apply depending on whether the warrants are substantially identical to the purchase stock. This is determined by comparing the relative values of the stock and warrants. The wash-sale rule will apply only if the relative values and price changes are so similar that the warrants become fully convertible securities.

Basis Adjusted for New Stock

Although the loss deduction is barred if the wash-sale rule applies, the economic loss is not forfeited for tax purposes. The loss might be realized at a later date when the repurchased stock is sold, because after the disallowance of the loss, the cost basis of the new lot is fixed as the basis of the old lot and adjusted (up or down) for the difference between the selling price of the old stock and purchase price of the new stock; *see* the following examples.

EXAMPLES

1. You bought common stock of Appliance Co. for $10,000 in 1980. On June 29, 1992, you sold the stock for $8,000, incurring a $2,000 loss. A week later, you repurchased the same number of shares of Appliance stock for $9,000. Your loss of $2,000 on the sale is disallowed because of the wash-sale rule. The basis of the new lot becomes $11,000. The basis of the old shares ($10,000) is increased by $1,000, which is the excess of the purchase price of the new shares ($9,000) over the selling price of the old shares ($8,000).

2. Assume the same facts as in Example 1 except that you repurchase the stock for $7,000. The basis of the new lot is $9,000. The basis of the old shares ($10,000) is decreased by $1,000, which is the excess of the selling price of the old shares ($8,000) over the purchase price of the new shares ($7,000).

3. Assume that in February 1993 you sell the stock acquired in Example 1 above for $9,000 and do not run afoul of the wash-sale rule. On the sale, you realize a loss of $2,000 ($11,000 − $9,000).

Repurchasing fewer shares. The number of shares of stock reacquired in a wash sale may be less than the amount sold. Then only a proportionate part of the loss is disallowed.

EXAMPLE

You bought 100 shares of stock A for $10,000. On December 17, 1992, you sell the lot for $8,000, incurring a loss of $2,000. On January 4, 1993, you repurchase 75 shares of stock A for $6,000. Three-quarters ($75/100$) of your loss is disallowed, or $1,500 (¾ of $2,000). You deduct the remaining loss of $500 on your return for 1993. The basis of the new shares is $7,500.

Holding period of new stock. After a wash sale, the holding period of the new stock includes the holding period of the old lots. If you sold more than one old lot in wash sales, you add the holding periods of all the old lots to the holding period of the new lot. You do this even if your holding periods overlapped as you purchased another lot before you sold the first. You do not count the periods between the sale and purchase when you have no stock.

Losses on short sales. Losses incurred on short sales are subject to the wash-sale rules. A loss on the closing of a short sale is denied if you sell the stock or enter into a second short sale within the period beginning 30 days before and ending 30 days after the closing of the short sale.

Tax Advantage of Wash-Sale Rule

Sometimes the wash-sale rule can work to your advantage. Assume that during December, you are negotiating a sale that will bring you a large capital gain. You want to offset a part of that gain by selling certain securities at a loss. You are unsure just when the gain transaction will go through. It may be on the last day of the year. Then it may be too late to sell the loss securities before the end of the year.

You can do this: Sell the loss securities during the last week of December. If the profitable deal goes through before the end of the year, you need not do anything further. If it does not, buy back the loss securities early in January. The December sale will be a wash sale and the loss disallowed. When the profitable sale occurs next year, you can sell the loss securities again. This time the loss will be allowed and will offset the gain.

CONVERTIBLE STOCKS AND BONDS

¶5.22

You realize no gain or loss when you convert a bond into stock, or preferred stock into common stock of the same corporation, if the conversion privilege was allowed by the bond or preferred stock certificate.

Holding period. Stock acquired through the conversion of bonds or preferred stock takes the same holding period as the securities exchanged. However, where the new stock is acquired partly for cash and partly by tax-free exchange, each new share of stock has a split holding period. The portion of each new share allocable to the ownership of the converted bonds (or preferred stock) includes the holding period of the bonds (or preferred stock). The portion of the new stock allocable to the cash purchase takes a holding period beginning with the day after acquisition of the stock.

Basis. Securities acquired through the conversion of bonds or preferred stock into common take the same basis as the securities exchanged. Where there is a partial cash payment, the basis of the portion of the stock attributable to the cash is the amount of cash paid.

EXAMPLES 1. On January 2, you paid $100 for the debenture of A Co. Your holding period for the debenture begins on January 3; *see* ¶5.6. The debenture provides that the holder may receive one share of A Co. common stock upon surrender of one debenture and the payment of $50. On October 19, you convert the debenture to stock on payment of $50. For tax purposes, you realize no gain or loss upon the conversion regardless of whether the fair market value of the stock is more or less than $150 on the date of the conversion. The basis and holding period for the stock is as follows: $100 for the portion attributed to the ownership of the debenture with the holding period beginning January 3; and $50 attributed to the cash payment with the holding period for this portion beginning October 20.

2. Same as above example, but you acquired the debenture on January 2 through the exercise of rights on that date, since the holding period for the debenture includes the date of exercise of the rights; *see* ¶5.19, the portion of the stock allocable to the debenture takes a holding period beginning on January 3.

If you paid a premium for a convertible bond, you may not amortize the amount of the premium attributable to the conversion feature.

WORTHLESS SECURITIES

¶5.23

You may deduct as a capital loss on Schedule D the cost basis of securities that have become worthless in 1992. Capital loss treatment applies unless ordinary loss treatment is available under ¶5.24. A loss of worthless securities is deductible only in the year the securities become *completely worthless*. The loss may not be deducted in any other year. You may not claim a loss for partially worthless stock.

To support a deduction for 1992 you must show:

1. The stock had some value in 1991. That is, you must be ready to show that the stock did not become worthless in a year prior to 1992. If you learn that the stock did become worthless in a prior year, file an amended return for that year; *see* the Refund Deadline Alert in the next column.
2. The stock became totally worthless in 1992. You must be able to present facts fixing the time of loss during this year. For example, the company went bankrupt, stopped doing business, and is insolvent. Despite evidence of worthlessness, such as insolvency, the stock may be considered to have some

value if the company continues to do business, or there are plans to reorganize the company. No deduction may be claimed for a partially worthless corporate bond.

If you are making payments on a negotiable note you used to buy the stock that became worthless and you are on the cash basis method, your payments are deductible losses in the years the payments are made, rather than in the year the stock became worthless.

If the security is a bond, note, certificate, or other evidence of a debt incurred by a corporation, the loss is deducted as a capital loss, provided the obligation is in registered form or has attached interest coupons. A loss on a worthless corporate obligation is always deemed to have been sustained on the last day of the year, regardless of when the company failed during the year.

If the obligation is not issued with interest coupons or in registered form, or if it is issued by an individual, the loss is treated as a bad debt. If you received the obligation in a business transaction, the loss is fully deductible. You may also make a claim for a partially worthless business bad debt. If it is a nonbusiness debt, the loss is a capital loss and no claim may be made for partial worthlessness; *see* ¶5.47.

When To Deduct Worthless Stock

If a company is in financial trouble but you are not sure whether its condition is hopeless, it is advisable to claim the deduction in 1992 to protect your claim. This advice was given by a court: "The taxpayer is at times in a very difficult position in determining in what year to claim a loss. The only safe practice, we think, is to claim a loss for the earliest year when it may possibly be allowed and to renew the claim in subsequent years if there is a reasonable chance of its being applicable for those years."

Sometimes you can avoid the problem of proving worthlessness. If there is still a market for the security, you can sell. For example, the company is on the verge of bankruptcy, but in 1992, there is some doubt about the complete worthlessness of its securities. You might sell the securities for whatever you can get for them and claim the loss on the sale. However, if the security became worthless in a prior year, say in 1991, a sale in 1992 will not give you a deduction in 1992.

Long-term or short-term loss. A sale is presumed to have occurred at the end of the year, regardless of when worthlessness actually occurred during the year.

EXAMPLE You bought 100 shares of Z Co. stock on June 1, 1960. On March 16, 1992, the stock is considered wholly worthless. The loss is deemed to have been incurred on December 31, 1992. The loss is deducted as a long-term capital loss; the holding period is from June 1, 1960, to December 31, 1992.

Refund Deadline for Worthless Stock

You have seven years from the due date of your return to claim a refund based on a deduction of a bad debt or worthless security.

For example, if you have held securities that you learn became worthless in 1985, you still have until April 15, 1993, to file for a refund of 1985 taxes by claiming a deduction for the worthless securities on an amended return (Form 1040X) for 1985.

Ordinary loss on Small Business Investment Company stock. On Form 4797, investors may take ordinary loss deductions for losses on the worthlessness or sale of SBIC stock. The loss may also be treated as a business loss for net operating loss purposes. However, a loss realized on a short sale of SBIC stock is deductible as a capital loss. A Small Business Investment Company is a company authorized to provide small businesses with equity capital. Do not confuse investments in these companies with investments in small business stock (Section 1244 stock) discussed at ¶5.24.

S corporation stock. If an S corporation's stock becomes worthless during the taxable year, the basis in the stock is adjusted for the stockholder's share of corporate items of income, loss, and deductions before a deduction for worthlessness is claimed.

Bank deposit loss. If you lose funds in a bank that becomes insolvent, you may claim the loss as a nonbusiness bad debt (¶5.47), a casualty loss (¶18.4), or in some cases, an investment expense (¶19.24).

SECTION 1244 SMALL BUSINESS STOCK

¶**5.24** Shareholders of qualifying "small" corporations may claim within limits an ordinary loss, rather than a capital loss, on the sale or worthlessness of Section 1244 stock. An ordinary loss up to $50,000, or $100,000 on a joint return, may be claimed in Part II of Form 4797. On a joint return, the $100,000 limit applies even if only one spouse has a Section 1244 loss. Losses in excess of these limits are deductible as capital losses. Gains on Section 1244 stock are reported as capital gain on Schedule D.

An ordinary loss may be claimed only by the original owner of the stock. If a partnership sells Section 1244 stock at a loss, an ordinary loss deduction may be claimed by individuals who were partners when the stock was issued. If a partnership distributes the Section 1244 stock to the partners, the partners may not claim an ordinary loss on their disposition of the stock.

To qualify as Section 1244 stock:

1. The corporation's equity may not exceed $1,000,000 at the time the stock is issued, including amounts received for the stock to be issued. Thus, if the corporation already has $600,000 equity from stock previously issued, it may not issue more than $400,000 worth of additional stock.

    Preferred stock issued after July 18, 1984, may qualify for Section 1244 loss treatment, as well as common stock.
2. The stock must be issued for money or property (other than stock and securities).
3. The corporation for the five years preceding your loss must generally have derived more than half of its gross receipts from business operations and not from passive income such as rents, royalties, dividends, interest, annuities, or gains from the sales or exchanges of stock or securities. The five-year requirement is waived if the corporation's deductions (other than for dividends received or net operating losses) exceed gross income. If the corporation has not been in existence for the five years before your loss, then generally the period for which the corporation has been in existence is examined for the gross receipts test.

CORPORATE LIQUIDATION

¶**5.25** Liquidation of a corporation and distribution of its assets for your stock is generally subject to capital gain or loss treatment. For example, on a corporate liquidation, you receive property worth $10,000 from the corporation. Assume the basis of your shares, which you have held long term, is $6,000. You have realized a long-term gain of $4,000.

If you incur legal expenses in pressing payment of a claim, you treat the fee as a capital expense, according to the IRS. The Tax Court and an appeals court hold that the fee is deductible as an expense incurred to earn income; the deduction is subject to the 2% adjusted gross income (AGI) floor discussed at ¶19.1.

If you recover a judgment against the liquidator of a corporation for misuse of corporate funds, the judgment is considered part of the amount you received on liquidation and gives you capital gain, not ordinary income.

If you paid a corporate debt after liquidation, the payment reduces the gain realized on the corporate liquidation in the earlier year; thus, in effect, it is a capital loss.

If the corporation distributes liquidating payments over a period of years, gain is not reported until the distributions exceed the adjusted basis of your stock.

CALLS OR OPTION TRANSACTIONS ON OPTION EXCHANGES

¶**5.26** Option exchanges, such as the Chicago Board of Option Exchange (CBOE) and the American Stock Exchange (Amex) market, provide a market for standardized options on a specific number of listed stocks, eliminating any relationship between option seller and buyer. Details and risks of these options are fully discussed in Chapter 30. The following paragraphs give the tax consequences of call options transacted by investors on option exchanges.

Buyers of options. If you buy an option, the treatment of your investment in the option depends on what you do with it.

1. If you sell it, you realize short-term or long-term capital gain or loss, depending upon how long you held the option.
2. If you allow the option to expire without exercise, you incur a short-term or long-term capital loss, depending on the holding period of the option. The expiration date is treated as the date the option is disposed of.
3. If you exercise the option and buy the stock, you add the cost of the option to the basis of the stock.

Grantors of options. If you write an option through the exchange, you do not treat the premium received for writing the option as income at the time of receipt. You do not realize profit or loss until the option transaction is closed. This may occur when the option expires or is exercised or when you "buy in" on the exchange an option similar to the one you gave to end your obligation to deliver the stock. Here are the rules for these events:

1. If the option is not exercised, you report the premium as short-term capital gain in the year the option expires.
2. If the option is exercised, you add the premium to the sales proceeds of the stock to determine gain or loss on the sale of the stock. Gain or loss is short term or long term depending upon the holding period of the stock.
3. If you "buy in" an equivalent option in a closing transaction, you realize profit or loss for the difference between the premium of the option you sold and the cost of the closing option. The profit or loss is treated as short-term capital gain or loss. However, a loss on a covered call that has a stated price below the stock price may be long-term capital loss if, at the time of the loss, long-term gain would be realized on the sale of the stock. Furthermore, the holding period of such stock is suspended during the period in which the option is open. Finally, year-end losses from covered call options are not deductible, unless the stock is held uncovered for more than 30 days following the date on which the option is closed.

Index options. Nonequity options and dealer equity options, which include options based on regulated stock indexes and interest rate futures, are taxed like regulated futures contracts. This means that they are reported annually under the marked-to-market accounting system. You treat all such options held at the end of the year as if they were disposed of at year end for a price equal to fair market value. Any gain or loss is arbitrarily taxed as if it were 60% long term and 40% short term. It is advisable to ask your broker whether the specific options which you hold come within this special rule.

STRADDLE LOSSES AND DEDUCTION RESTRICTIONS

¶5.27 Straddles are tax shelter devices to spot losses in one year and gains in another year and to convert ordinary income into capital gain. These maneuvers are now effectively barred by tax accounting rules that generally match losses against unrealized gains in offsetting positions. Straddle rules apply to commodities and actively traded stock and to stock options used in straddle positions. Straddle positions include any stock that is part of a straddle in which at least one of the offsetting positions is: (1) an option tied to the stock or to substantially identical stock or securities; or (2) a position in substantially similar or related property other than stock. For example, there is a straddle of stock and substantially similar or related property if offsetting positions of stock and convertible debentures of the same corporation are held and price movements of the two positions are related.

Straddle rules apply also to stock of a corporation formed or used to take positions in personal property that offset positions taken by any shareholder. True *hedging* transactions are not subject to the straddle tax rules.

Also, a call option is not treated as part of a straddle position if it is considered a *qualified covered call option.* A qualified covered call option is an option that a stockholder, who is not a dealer, grants on stock traded on a national securities exchange. Furthermore, the option must be granted more than 30 days before its expiration date and must not be "deep-in-the-money." A covered call option will not qualify if gain on the sale of the stock to be purchased by the option is reported in a year after the year in which the option is closed, or if the stock is not held for more than 30 days after the date on which the option is closed. In such a case, the option is subject to the straddle loss deferral rules. The same loss deferment rule applies where the stock is sold at a loss, and gain on the related option held less than 30 days is reported in the next year.

Loss on a qualified covered call option with a strike price less than its applicable stock price is treated as long-term capital loss if loss realized on the sale of the stock would be long term. The holding period for stock subject to the option does not include any period during which the taxpayer is the grantor of the option.

A "deep-in-the-money option" is an option with a strike or exercise price that is below the lowest qualified benchmark. The technical rules for determining these values are not discussed in this book.

Tax rules for straddles. The following is an overview of the subject, and if you have transacted straddles, we suggest that you consult with an experienced tax practitioner.

Realized straddle losses are deductible at the close of a taxable year only if they exceed unrealized gains in an offsetting position. Thus, an investor may not deduct losses incurred in 1992 to the extent that he or she has an unrealized gain position in the open end of the straddle. Form 6781 is used for straddle reporting.

Straddle positions of related persons (such as spouse or child) or controlled flow-through entities (such as a partnership or an S corporation) are considered in determining whether offsetting positions are held.

Realized losses that are not deductible at the end of the year are carried forward and become deductible when there is no unrealized appreciation in an offsetting position bought before the disposition of the loss position. This loss deferral rule may be avoided by identifying straddles before the close of the day of acquisition or at an earlier time that the IRS may set. Gain or loss in identified positions is generally netted; that is, a loss is recognized when the offsetting gain position has been closed.

If you are in a straddle arrangement, you must disclose all positions of unrealized gains at the close of a tax year or you may be subject to a negligence penalty unless failure to disclose is due to a reasonable cause.

The loss deferral rule does *not* apply to positions in a regulated futures contract or other Section 1256 contract subject to the marked-to-market system explained below.

The loss deferral rule also does not apply to businesses that must hedge in order to protect their supplies of inventory or financial capital. Hedging transactions are subject to ordinary income or loss treatment. Hedging transactions entered into by syndicates do not qualify for the exception and are subject to the loss deferral rule if more than 35% of losses for a taxable year are allocable to limited partners or entrepreneurs. Furthermore, hedging losses of limited partners or limited entrepreneurs are generally limited to their taxable income from the business in which the hedging transaction was entered into.

Marked-to-market rules for gain or loss on regulated futures contracts and other Section 1256 contracts. Gain or loss on regulated futures contracts is reported annually under the marked-to-market accounting system of regulated commodity exchanges. To settle margin requirements, regulated exchanges determine a party's account for futures contracts on a daily basis. Each regulated futures contract is treated as if sold at fair market value on the last day of the taxable year. Any capital gain or loss is arbitrarily allocated: 40% is short term and 60% is long term. Use Form 6781 to figure gains and losses on Section 1256 contracts that are open at the end of the year or that were closed out during the year. These amounts are then transferred from Form 6781 to Schedule D.

Under the law, a regulated futures contract is considered a Section 1256 contract. Other Section 1256 contracts subject to the marked-to-market rules are foreign currency contracts, dealer equity options, and non-equity options.

The marked-to-market rules do not apply to true hedging transactions executed in the normal course of business to reduce risks and which result in ordinary income or loss. Syndicates may generally not take advantage of this hedging exception if more than 35% of their losses during a taxable year are allocable to limited partners or entrepreneurs. Furthermore, the ability of limited partners or entrepreneurs to deduct losses from hedging transactions is generally limited to taxable income from the business to which the hedging transaction relates.

Mixed straddle contracts. If you have a mixed straddle in which at least one but not all of the positions is a Section 1256 contract, the marked-to-market rules generally apply but you may elect to avoid this treatment and apply the regular straddle tax rules. The election, made on Form 6781, is irrevocable unless the IRS allows a revocation. Furthermore, the IRS allows an election to offset gains and losses from positions that are part of mixed straddles if you separately identify each mixed straddle or establish mixed straddle accounts for a class of activities for which gain and loss will be recognized and offset on a periodic basis.

Carryback election

If for 1992 you have a net loss on Section 1256 contracts, the loss may be carried back for three years under special rules. You must file an amended return (Form 1040X) and an amended Form 6781 for the prior year. Follow the instructions to Form 6781.

Contract cancellations. Investors buying forward contracts for currency or securities may not realize ordinary loss by cancelling the unprofitable contract of the hedge transaction. Loss realized on a cancellation of the contract is treated as a capital loss.

Cash and carry transactions. You may not deduct carrying costs for any period during which the commodity or stock or option is part of a balanced position. The costs must be capitalized and added to basis. The rule does not apply to hedging straddles. Capitalized items are reduced by dividends on stock included in a straddle, market discounts, and acquisition discounts. These reductions, however, are limited to so much of the dividends and discounts as is included in income.

FORECLOSURES, VOLUNTARY CONVEYANCES, ABANDONMENTS, AND LEASE CANCELLATIONS

FORECLOSURES AND VOLUNTARY CONVEYANCES TO CREDITORS

¶**5.28** If you are unable to meet payments on a debt secured by property, the creditor may foreclose on the property. A foreclosure sale or a voluntary conveyance of the property to the creditor is treated as a sale of the property. If you are personally liable on the debt, and if the value of the property is less than the cancelled debt, you also generally realize ordinary income on the debt cancellation.

Form 1099-A Notifies IRS

If your mortgaged property is foreclosed or repossessed, and the bank or other lender reacquires it, you will receive from the lender Form 1099-A. Form 1099-A will also be sent if a lender knows that you have abandoned the property. The Form 1099-A indicates foreclosure proceeds, the amount of your debt, and whether you were personally liable. The IRS may compare its copy of Form 1099-A with your return to check if you have reported income from the foreclosure or abandonment.

Figuring gain or loss. Gain or loss is the difference between your adjusted basis in the property and the amount realized. Determining amount realized depends on your liability for the debt. If you are *not* personally liable on the debt, the amount realized includes the full amount of the cancelled debt, regardless of the value of the property.

If you *are* personally liable, the amount realized includes the portion of the cancelled debt that equals the fair market value of the property. If the fair market value of the property is *less* than the debt, the foreclosure or voluntary conveyance back to the creditor is treated as two separate transactions:

1. A sale of property. Gain or loss is the difference between adjusted basis and the amount realized, including the cancelled debt up to the fair market value of the property.

2. The receipt of income upon the cancellation of the debt for less than the face amount of the debt. However, this income may not be taxable, if you come within the exclusion rules of ¶12.9, such as being insolvent at the time of the foreclosure.

EXAMPLES 1. Jones could not meet the mortgage payments on a condominium which cost him $85,000. He had paid cash of $20,000 and taken a mortgage loan of $65,000 on which he was personally liable. When the remaining balance of the loan was $62,000, he defaulted, and the bank accepted his voluntary conveyance of the unit, cancelling the loan. Similar units at the time were selling for $60,000. On the transaction, Jones incurred a loss of $25,000: the difference between his adjusted basis of $85,000 and the fair market value of the unit of $60,000. The loss is not deductible because the unit was held for personal purposes. Jones also recognizes income on the cancellation of the loan because the amount of the debt exceeded the fair market value of the unit by $2,000. This amount is taxable, unless Jones can show he was insolvent at the time of the transfer to the bank; *see* ¶12.9.

2. Brown invested in a vacant lot. He put down cash of $10,000 and assumed a mortgage of $20,000. When he could not make payments on the mortgage, the bank foreclosed. The net proceeds from the foreclosure sale were $32,000. Brown received $12,000 and realized a capital gain of $2,000 (difference between his adjusted basis of $30,000 and the amount realized of $32,000). There is no income from cancellation of indebtedness because the debt was less than the value of the property.

3. Jane bought a car on time for personal use. The cost of the car was $15,000. She put down cash of $2,000 and financed the $13,000 balance with a credit company. She stopped making payments when the balance of the loan was $10,000 and the value of the car was $9,000. The credit company repossessed the car. The tax consequences of the repossession depend on the nature of Jane's liability on the loan. If she was personally liable, she realized a nondeductible loss on the car of $6,000 ($15,000 basis less $9,000 current value). In addition, on the cancellation of the debt, she realized income of $1,000, the excess of the cancelled debt ($10,000) over the value of the repossessed property ($9,000). This amount is taxable, unless she can show she is insolvent; see ¶12.9.

If Jane was not personally liable, her nondeductible loss on the repossession is $5,000: the difference between her basis of $15,000 and the amount of the debt of $10,000. There is no ordinary income from cancellation of indebtedness.

Reporting a Foreclosure or Voluntary Conveyance

You report a foreclosure sale or voluntary conveyance to a creditor on Schedule D if the property was held for personal or investment purposes. However, if a gain or loss was realized on a foreclosure (or voluntary reconveyance) of your principal residence, the "sale" is reported on Form 2119.

Foreclosures and reconveyances of business assets are reported on Form 4797.

If income from cancellation of indebtness is realized and it is not excludable under the rules of ¶12.9, you report the taxable amount on Line 22, Form 1040.

ABANDONMENTS

¶5.29 On an abandonment of business or investment property, you may claim an ordinary loss for the property's adjusted basis (when abandoned) on Form 4797. However, if the abandoned property is later foreclosed or repossessed, you may realize a gain or loss under the rules of ¶5.28 for foreclosures or voluntary conveyances to creditors. For example, if an abandonment loss for mortgaged property is claimed in 1992 but in 1993 the property is foreclosed upon by the lender, all or part of the cancelled debt will be treated as an amount realized by you on a sale in 1993. The amount realized depends on whether you were personally liable and the value of the property. If personally liable, you may also realize ordinary income from cancellation of the debt; see ¶5.28.

Abandoning a partnership interest. With the collapse of real estate markets, partnerships are holding realty subject to mortgage debt that exceeds the current value of the property. Some investors in partnerships have claimed that they could abandon their partnership interests and thus claim an abandonment loss. In one case, an investor in a partnership holding land in Houston, Texas, argued that he abandoned his partnership interest by making an abandonment declaration at a meeting of partners, and also declaring that he would make no further payments. He offered his interest to the others, who refused his offer. The IRS held that he failed to prove abandonment of his partnership interest or that the partnership abandoned the land. The Tax Court sided with the IRS, emphasizing his failure to show that the partnership abandoned the land. However, the appeals court for the Fifth Circuit reversed and allowed the abandonment loss. It held that the emphasis should be on the partner's actions, not the actions of the partnership. Although neither state law nor the IRS regulations described how a partnership interest is to be abandoned, the appeals court held that the partner's acts and declaration were sufficient to effect an abandonment of his partnership interest. The appeals court also held that the loss on the partnership interest could have been sustained on the basis of the worthlessness of his interest. The partnership was insolvent beyond hope of rehabilitation: (1) the partnership's only asset was land with a fair market value less than the mortgage debt; (2) the partnership had no source of income; and (3) the partners refused to contribute more funds to keep the partnership afloat.

In a subsequent case, the Tax Court held that a doctor had abandoned a movie production partnership interest when he refused to advance any more money or to participate in the venture because he disapproved of the content of the film being produced and feared it might jeopardize his position at a hospital operated by a religious organization. Also, the limited partners had voted to dissolve.

Note: If, after the year the abandoned loss is claimed, the partnership's mortgaged holdings are foreclosed upon or reconveyed to the lender, each partner's share of the cancelled debt may be treated as an amount realized on a sale, or as ordinary cancellation of debt income; see ¶5.28.

CANCELLATION OF A LEASE

¶5.30 Payments received by the tenant on the cancellation of a business lease held long term are treated as proceeds received in a Section 1231 transaction; see ¶44.8. Payments received by the tenant on cancellation of a lease on a personal residence or apartment are treated as proceeds of a capital asset transaction. Gain is long-term capital gain if the lease was held long term; losses are not deductible.

Payments received by a landlord from a tenant for cancelling a lease or modifying lease terms are reported as rental income when received; see ¶9.1.

Cancellation of a distributor's agreement is treated as a sale, if you made a substantial capital investment in the distributorship. For example, you own facilities for storage, transporting, processing, or dealing with the physical product covered by the franchise. If you have an office mainly for clerical work, or where you handle just a small part of the goods covered by the franchise, the cancellation is not treated as a sale. Your gain or loss is ordinary income or loss. If the cancellation is treated as a sale, the sale is treated under Section 1231; see ¶44.8.

OPTIONS, EASEMENTS, RESTRICTIVE COVENANTS, FRANCHISES, PATENTS, AND COPYRIGHTS

SALE OF AN OPTION

¶5.31 The tax treatment of the sale of an option depends on the tax classification of the property to which the option relates.

If the option is for the purchase of property that would be a capital asset in your hands, profit on the sale of the option is capital gain. A loss is a capital loss if the property subject to the option was investment property; if the property was personal property, the loss is not deductible. Whether the gain or loss is long term or short term depends on your holding period.

EXAMPLES 1. You pay $500 for an option to purchase a house. After holding the option for five months, you sell the option for $750. Your profit of $250 is short-term capital gain.

2. The same facts as in Example 1 above, except that you sell the option for $300. The loss is not deductible because the option is related to a sale of a personal residence.

If the option is for a "Section 1231 asset" (¶44.8), gain or loss on the sale of the option is combined with other Section 1231 asset transactions to determine if there is capital gain or ordinary loss.

If the option relates to an ordinary income asset in your hands, then gain or loss would be ordinary income or loss.

If you fail to exercise an option and allow it to lapse, the option is considered to have been sold on the expiration date. Gain or loss is computed according to the rules explained above.

The party granting the option realizes ordinary income on its expiration, regardless of the nature of the underlying property. If the option is exercised, the option payment is added to the selling price of the property when figuring gain or loss.

Note: The treatment of options traded on a public exchange is discussed at ¶5.26.

GRANTING OF AN EASEMENT

¶5.32 Granting an easement presents a practical problem of determining whether all or part of the basis of the property is allocable to the easement proceeds. This requires an opinion of whether the easement affects the entire property or just a part of the property. There is no hard and fast rule to determine whether an easement affects all or part of the property. The issue is factual. For example, an easement for electric lines will generally affect only the area over which the lines are suspended and for which the right of way is granted. In such a case, an allocation may be required; *see* Example 1 below. If the entire property is affected, no allocation is required and the proceeds reduce the basis of the property. If only part of the property is affected, then the proceeds are applied to the cost allocated to the area affected by the easement. If the proceeds exceed the amount allocated to basis, a gain is realized. Capital gain treatment generally applies to grants of easements. The granting of a perpetual easement which requires you to give up all or substantially all of a beneficial use of the area affected by the easement is treated as a sale. The contribution to a government body of a scenic easement in perpetuity is a charitable contribution, not a sale.

In reviewing an easement, the IRS will generally try to find grounds for making an allocation, especially where the allocation will result in a taxable gain. In opposition, a property owner will generally argue that the easement affects the entire property or that it is impossible to make an allocation because of the nature of the easement or the particular nature of the property. If he or she can sustain an argument, the proceeds for granting the easement reduce the basis of the entire property.

EXAMPLES 1. The owner of a 600-acre farm was paid $5,000 by a power company for the right to put up poles and power lines. The right of way covered 20 acres along one boundary which the owner continued to farm. The cost basis of the farm was $60,000 or $100 an acre. The IRS ruled that he had to allocate the basis. At $100 an acre, the allocated basis for the 20 acres was $2,000. Thus, a gain of $3,000 was realized ($5,000 − $2,000).

2. The owner of a tract of unimproved land gave a state highway department a perpetual easement affecting only part of the land. He wanted to treat the payment as reduction of the basis of the entire tract and so report no gain. The IRS ruled that he had to allocate basis to the portion affected by the road.

3. The owner of farmland gave a transmission company a 50-foot right of way for an underground pipeline that did not interfere with farming. During construction, the right of way was 150 feet. The owner received payments for damages covering loss of rental income during construction and for the 50-foot permanent right of way. The IRS ruled that the damage payment was taxable as ordinary income; the payment for the right of way was a taxable gain to the extent that it exceeded the basis allocated to the acreage within the 50-foot strip.

Condemnation. If you realize a gain on a grant of an easement under a condemnation or threat of condemnation, you may defer tax by investing in replacement property; *see* ¶18.18.

RELEASE OF RESTRICTIVE COVENANT

¶5.33 A payment received for a release of a restrictive covenant is treated as a capital gain if the release involves property held for investment.

EXAMPLE You sell several acres of land held for investment to a construction company subject to a covenant that restricts construction to residential dwellings. Later, the company wants to erect structures other than individual homes and pays you for the release of the restrictive covenant in the deed. You realize capital gain on receipt of the payment. The restrictive covenant is a property interest and a capital asset in your hands.

FRANCHISES

¶5.34 A transfer of a franchise, trademark, or trade name is not a sale or exchange of a capital asset if the grantor retains a significant power, right, or interest in it, such as the right to:

Disapprove further assignment of all or part of the franchise;
Set quality standards for products, services, equipment, or facilities;
Require that only his or her products or services be sold or advertised;
Require that substantially all supplies or equipment be purchased from him or her; and
To receive payments contingent on use of the franchise if such payments are a substantial element of the agreement.

In addition, if the grantor has an operational control over the franchise, payment may be treated as ordinary income. Operational control includes the right to: receive periodic reports; approve business methods; prevent removal of equipment from the territory; and withdraw the franchise if the territory is not developed.

To receive capital gain treatment on the sale of a franchise, the grantor must avoid the retention of any of the specified powers of operational control and, in addition, must meet the general tests for capital gains, such as not being a dealer in franchises.

SALES OF PATENTS AND COPYRIGHTS

¶5.35 A special law allows long-term capital gain on sales of patents by inventors and their backers, even if the patent property has not been held long term. The invention can be transferred even before an application for the patent is made. The imputed interest rules *do not* apply; *see* ¶5.42 and ¶4.32. The sale can be in the form of an outright sale, exclusive license, assignment, or royalty agreement.

Capital Gain Rules for an Inventor

You must transfer all *substantial rights* to the patent to a party who is not your employer and not any of the following related persons to qualify for long-term capital gain treatment:

1. Member of your immediate family, such as your husband or wife, ancestors, and lineal descendant, but not brothers and sisters.

2. A corporation of which 25% or more in value of the outstanding stock is owned, directly or indirectly, by or for you. Stock owned by your brother or sister is not considered indirectly owned by you.

3. A partnership in which you own, directly or indirectly, an interest of 25% or more.

4. Certain beneficiaries, trusts, and grantors.

The following are *not* considered substantial rights and may be retained: right to prohibit sublicensing or subassignment of rights; the retention of a security interest such as a lien; and the reservation of rights providing for forfeiture for nonperformance.

Certain retained rights bar capital gain treatment. The retention of rights that limit the period of duration of the patent to a period less than the remaining life of the patent will bar capital gain treatment. Capital gain is also not allowed where the patent license limits use to a particular industry. For example, an inventor restricted production of his patented clutch to marine use only. The clutch could have been used in other industries. An appeals court agreed with the IRS that the inventor retained a substantial right.

IRS regulations also bar capital gain treatment where the license is restricted to a geographic area and the inventor keeps the right to exploit the patent elsewhere. The Tax Court holds that the retention of geographic rights is considered substantial unless proven otherwise, thereby barring capital gain treatment.

If you are a financial backer, you must buy all of the substantial rights to the patent before the invention is put into operation. You will not get capital gain under the special rules if, at the time you bought your interest, you were the employer of the inventor or one of the related parties listed above.

If you cannot meet the special rules, such as where you bought the patent after it was put into operation, you may be able to get capital gain if your interest meets the general capital gain tests: You hold the patent as a capital asset or as a "Section 1231" asset (¶44.8), and you dispose of it in a transaction that is considered a sale or exchange after a long-term holding period. However, one court has said you may not get capital gain unless you do meet the special rules, regardless of whether you meet the general capital gain tests.

Copyrights. If you are the creator of the property covered by the copyright, you may not get capital gain on its sale, because it is not a capital asset in your hands. This rule applies to literary, musical, and artistic compositions, letters, and memoranda, as well as to theatrical productions, radio programs, and newspaper cartoon strips. Ordinary income treatment also applies if you obtained the copyright from its creator by gift or in a tax-free exchange. Report the sale on Form 4797. If a copyright is purchased, however, it may later be sold for capital gain treatment. In such a case, capital gain treatment applies to amounts received for granting the exclusive use or right to exploit the copyrighted work throughout the life of the copyright. This is true whether the payment is measured by a fixed amount or a percentage of the receipts from the sale, performance, exhibition, or publication of the copyrighted work, or by the number of copies sold, performances given, or exhibitions held.

REPORTING AN INSTALLMENT SALE

TAX ADVANTAGE OF INSTALLMENT SALES

¶5.36 If you sell property at a gain in 1992 and you will receive one or more payments in a later year or years, you may use the installment method to defer tax unless the property is publicly-traded securities or you are a dealer of the property sold. If you report the sale as an installment sale on Form 6252, your profit is taxed as installments are received. You may elect *not* to use the installment method if you want to report the entire profit in the year of sale; *see* Example 1 in the next column and ¶5.38. Losses may not be deferred under the installment method.

How the installment method works. For each year you receive installment payments, report your gain on Form 6252. Installment income from the sale of a capital asset is then transferred to Schedule D. If your gain in the year of sale is long-term capital gain, gain in later years is also long term; short-term treatment in the year of sale applies also to later years. Interest payments you receive on the deferred sale are reported with your other interest income on Schedule B of Form 1040.

Installment income from the sale of business or rental property is figured on Form 6252 and then entered on Form 4797. If you make an installment sale of depreciable property, any depreciation recapture (¶44.1) is reported as income in the year of disposition. The recapture amount is first figured on Form 4797 and then entered on Form 6252. On Form 6252, recaptured income is added to basis of the property for purposes of figuring the gross profit ratio for the balance of gain to be reported, if any, over the installment period; *see also* ¶44.7.

Installment sales of business or rental property for over $150,000

may be subject to a special tax if deferred payments exceed $5 million; *see* ¶5.46.

EXAMPLES 1. In 1992, you sell real estate for $50,000, receiving $10,000 in 1992, 1993, and 1994; and $20,000 in 1995, plus interest of 9% compounded semiannually. You realized a profit of $25,000, giving you a profit percentage of 50%. When the buyer pays the notes, you report the following:

In	payment of:	You report income of:
1992	$10,000	$5,000
1993	10,000	5,000
1994	10,000	5,000
1995	20,000	10,000
Total	$50,000	$25,000

In 1992, you file Form 6252 to figure your profit. You report only $5,000 as profit on Schedule D (or Form 4797 if applicable). If you do not want to use the installment method, you make an election by reporting the entire gain of $25,000 on Schedule D or Form 4797. Schedule D provides a special box to check if you *elect out* of the installment method and you are valuing the buyer's note at less than fair market value. Report the interest payments on Schedule B.

2. On December 21, 1992, you sell a building for $50,000, realizing a profit of $25,000. You take a note payable in January 1993. You report the gain in 1993. Receiving a lump-sum payment in a taxable year after the year of sale is considered an installment sale.

Year-end sales of publicly traded stock or securities. You have no choice about when to report the gain from a sale of publicly traded stock or securities made at the end of 1992. Any gain must be reported in 1992, even if the proceeds are not received until early 1993. The sale is not considered an installment sale.

Farm property. A farmer may use the installment method to report gain from the sale of property that does not have to be inventoried under his method of accounting. This is true, even though such property is held for regular sale.

Dealer sales. Generally, dealers must report gain in the year of sale for personal property regularly sold on an installment plan, or real estate held for resale to customers. However, the installment method may be used by dealers of certain time shares (generally timeshares of up to six weeks per year) and residential lots, but only if an election is made to pay interest on the tax deferred by using the installment method. *See* the instructions to Schedule C of Form 1040.

FIGURING THE TAXABLE PART OF INSTALLMENT PAYMENTS

¶**5.37** On the installment method, a portion of each payment other than interest represents part of your gain and is taxable. This taxable amount is based on the gross profit percentage or ratio, which is figured by dividing gross profit by contract price. By following the line-by-line instructions to Form 6252, you get the gross profit percentage or ratio. What you include in the selling price, contract price, and gross profit is explained in the following paragraphs.

Interest of at least 9% compounded semiannually must generally be charged on a deferred payment sale. Otherwise, the IRS treats part of the sale price as interest; *see* ¶4.32.

EXAMPLE On December 9, 1992, you sell real estate for $100,000. The property had an adjusted basis of $56,000. Selling expenses are $4,000. You are to receive installment payments of $25,000 in 1992, 1993, 1994, and 1995, plus interest at 9%, compounded semiannually. The gross profit ratio is determined as follows:

Selling price (contract price)	$100,000
Less: Adjusted basis and selling expenses	60,000
Gross profit	$ 40,000

$$\frac{\text{Gross profit}}{\text{Contract price}} = \frac{\$40,000}{\$100,000} = 40\%$$

In 1992, you report a profit of $10,000 (40% of $25,000) on Form 6252. Similarly, in each of the following three years, a profit of $10,000 is reported so that by the end of four years, the entire $40,000 profit will have been reported.

Selling price. Include cash, fair market value of property received from the buyer, the buyer's notes (at face value), and any outstanding mortgage on the property that the buyer assumes or takes subject to. If, under the contract of sale, the buyer pays off an existing mortgage or assumes liability for any other liens on the property, such as taxes you owe, or pays the sales commissions, such payments are also included in the selling price.

Interest is not included in the selling price.

Notes of a third party given to you by the buyer are valued at fair market value.

Contract price. If there is no outstanding mortgage on the property, the contract price is the same as the selling price. If there is a mortgage, the selling price is reduced by the amount of the mortgage, unless the mortgage exceeds your installment sale basis, which is your adjusted basis for the property (¶5.16), plus selling expenses, plus depreciation recapture income (¶44.1) if any. If the mortgage exceeds the installment sale basis, reduce the contract price only by the amount of the mortgage equal to the installment sale basis. Do this whether or not the buyer assumes the mortgage, but *see* below for wraparound mortgages. By reducing contract

price only by the mortgage that is equal to your installment sale basis, you are in effect including as part of the contract price the excess of the mortgage over the installment sale basis. As a result, the contract price will be the same as your gross profit, you will have a gross profit percentage of 100% and all of your installment payments will be taxable; *see* the Johnson example at the top of page 91.

Wraparound mortgage. The IRS has generally agreed to follow a Tax Court decision holding that in a "wraparound" mortgage transaction, where title does not pass to the buyer in the year of sale and the seller continues to make direct payments on the original mortgage, the seller does not have to reduce the *selling price* by the amount of that original direct-payment mortgage when computing the *contract price*. Thus, the contract price is the same as the selling price. The Tax Court decision had invalidated the IRS wraparound mortgage regulations that required a reduction to the contract price.

EXAMPLE Able sells real property worth $2 million, encumbered by a mortgage of $900,000. His installment sale basis (adjusted basis plus selling costs) is $700,000. The buyer pays $200,000 cash and gives an interest-bearing wraparound mortgage note for $1.8 million. Able remains obligated to pay off the $900,000 mortgage. The gross profit ratio is 65% ($1,300,000 gross profit ÷ $2,000,000 contract price). In the year of sale, Able is treated as receiving only the $200,000 cash and is taxed on 65% of $200,000, or $130,000.

Gross profit and gross profit percentage. Gross profit is the selling price less your installment sale basis, which equals your adjusted basis for the property (¶5.16), plus selling expenses, such as brokers' commissions and legal fees. Depreciation recapture income, if any (¶44.1), also increases installment sale basis.

Divide the gross profit by the contract price to get the gross profit percentage. Each year, you multiply this percentage by your payments to determine the taxable amount under the installment method.

If you change the selling price during the period payments are outstanding, the gross profit percentage is refigured on the basis of the new selling price. The adjusted profit ratio is then applied to payments received after the adjustment.

EXAMPLE Jones sold real estate in 1989 for $100,000. His basis, including selling expenses, was $40,000, so his gross profit was $60,000. The buyer agreed to pay, starting in 1990, five annual installments of $20,000 plus 10% interest. As the gross profit percentage was 60% ($60,000 ÷ $100,000), Jones reported profit of $12,000 (60% of $20,000) on the installments received in 1990 and 1991.

In 1992, the parties renegotiated the sales price, reducing it from $100,000 to $85,000, and reducing payments for 1992, 1993, and 1994 to $15,000. Jones' original profit of $60,000 is reduced to $45,000. Of the $45,000 profit, $24,000 was reported in 1990 and 1991. To get the revised profit percentage, Jones must divide the $21,000 of profit not yet received by the remaining sales price of $45,000 ($85,000 less $40,000 installments in 1990 and 1991). The revised profit percentage is 46.67% ($21,000 ÷ $45,000). In 1992, 1993, and 1994, Jones reports profit of $7,000 on each $15,000 installment (46.67% of $15,000).

Payments received. Payments include cash, the fair market value of property, and payments on the buyer's notes. Payments do not include receipt of the buyer's notes or other evidence of indebtedness, unless payable on demand or readily tradable. "Readily tradable" means registered bonds, bonds with coupons attached, debentures, and other evidences of indebtedness of the buyer that are readily tradable in an established securities market. This rule is directed mainly at corporate acquisitions. A third-party guarantee (including a standby letter of credit) is not treated as a payment received on an installment obligation.

If the buyer has assumed or taken subject to a mortgage that exceeds your installment sale basis (adjusted basis plus selling expenses plus depreciation recapture if any) you include as a payment in the year of the sale the excess of mortgage over the installment basis; *see* the example below.

EXAMPLE Johnson sells a building for $160,000, subject to a mortgage of $60,000. Installments plus interest are to be paid over five years. His adjusted basis in the building was $30,000 and his selling expenses were $10,000, so his installment sale basis is $40,000 and his gross profit is $120,000 ($160,000 − $40,000). The contract price is also $120,000, the selling price of $160,000 less $40,000, the part of the mortgage that did not exceed the installment sale basis.

The $20,000 difference between the $60,000 mortgage and the installment sale basis of $40,000 is part of the contract price and is also treated as a payment received in the year of sale. Since the mortgage exceeds Johnson's installment sale basis, he is treated as having recovered his entire basis in the year of sale, and all installment payments will be taxable, as his gross profit ratio is 100%: gross profit of $120,000 ÷ contract price of $120,000. In the year of sale, Johnson must report as taxable gain 100% of the installment payment received, plus the $20,000 difference between the mortgage and his installment sale basis.

Pledging installment obligation as security. If, as security for a loan, you pledge an installment obligation from a sale of property of more than $150,000 (excluding farm or personal-use property), the net loan proceeds must be treated as a payment on the installment obligation. The net loan proceeds are treated as received on the later of the date the loan is secured or the date you receive the loan proceeds. These pledging rules do not apply if the debt refinances a debt that was outstanding on December 17, 1987, and secured by the installment obligation until the refinancing. If the refinancing exceeds the loan principal owed immediately before the refinancing, the excess is treated as a payment on the installment obligation. *See* the Form 6252 instructions.

Sale of depreciable property. For the effect of recapture; *see* ¶5.36 and ¶44.7.

Recapture of first-year expensing deduction. The entire recaptured amount under ¶44.3 is reported in the year of sale, even though you report the sale on the installment basis. An installment sale does not defer the reporting of the recaptured deduction. You also add the recaptured amount to the basis of the sold asset to compute the amount of the remaining gain to be reported on each installment. *See* the instructions to Form 6252.

ELECTING NOT TO REPORT ON THE INSTALLMENT METHOD

¶5.38 If any sale proceeds are to be received after the year of sale, you must file Form 6252 and use the installment method unless you "elect out" by making a timely election to report the entire gain in the year of sale. If you want to report the entire gain in the year of sale, include it on Schedule D or Form 4797 by the due date for filing your return (plus extensions) for the year of sale. Do not use Form 6252. After the due date (plus extensions), a change from the installment method to full reporting in the year of sale may be made *only* with IRS consent. The IRS will give consent only in rare cases where it finds "good cause." The IRS may give consent if your tax preparer erroneously reported on the installment method and you

promptly ask IRS permission to change to reporting of the entire gain. A change in the tax law is not considered "good cause" by the IRS. For example, sellers who before 1986, reported on the installment basis on the assumption that their payments would be taxed at favorable capital gain rates, wanted to amend their returns and report the entire gain in the year of sale after the 1986 Tax Act repealed the capital gain exclusion. The IRS would not allow the change.

"Electing Out" of Installment Reporting

When you have losses to offset your gain in the year of sale, installment sale reporting may not be advantageous. In such a case, you may want to report the full gain in the year of sale so the gain may be offset by the losses. However, there is a risk. If the losses are later disallowed by an IRS audit, you may not be given a second chance to use the installment method to spread the gain over the payment period.

For example, a seller "elected out" in a year in which he planned to deduct a net operating loss carryforward from an installment sale gain. In a later year, the IRS substantially reduced the loss. The seller then asked the IRS to allow him to revoke the "election out" so he could use the installment method. The IRS refused, claiming that the seller asked for the revocation to avoid tax. The installment sale would defer gain to a later year, which is a tax avoidance purpose.

Switching from full reporting to installment method. If you *do* report the entire gain in the year of sale, you may change to the installment method on an amended return only with the consent of the IRS. In a private ruling, the IRS refused to allow a seller to use the installment method after inadvertently including the entire gain from the sale on his return. Although reporting of the entire gain was a mistake, this was treated as an election not to use the installment method. The IRS refused permission to revoke the election on the grounds that a second chance to apply the installment method would be tax avoidance. However, in other private rulings, permission to revoke was granted where the seller's accountant erroneously reported the entire gain.

RESTRICTION ON INSTALLMENT SALES TO RELATIVES

¶5.39 The installment sale method is not allowed where you sell depreciable property to a controlled business, or to a trust in which you or your spouse are beneficiaries.

Further, if you sell property to a relative on the installment basis, and the relative later resells the property, you could lose the benefit of installment reporting. The restrictions on sales to relatives are primarily aimed at the following types of transactions:

1. A buyer insists on paying cash, but the seller who wants the tax deferment advantage of installment reporting arranges an installment sale with a family member who then resells the property for cash to the buyer. If the family member's resale is within two years of the original sale, the original seller is taxed on that sale under the two-year rule discussed below.
2. Securities traded on the exchange cannot be sold on the exchange on the installment basis. To get installment basis reporting, an investor would sell to a related party on the installment basis, and the related party would then sell the securities on the exchange. However, the restrictive rule requires the original investor to report tax on the related party's later sale on the exchange.

EXAMPLE In 1992, Jones sells stock to his son for $25,000, realizing a profit of $10,000. The son agrees to pay in five annual installments of $5,000 starting in 1993. Later in 1992, the son sells the stock to a third party for $26,000. Jones Sr. reports his profit of $10,000 in 1992, even though he received no payment that year. Payments received by Jones Sr. from his son after 1992 are tax free because he reported the entire profit in 1992.

Two-year rule for property other than marketable securities. If you make an installment sale to a related party of property other than marketable securities, you are taxed on a second sale by the related party only if it occurs within two years of the initial installment sale and before all payments from the first installment sale are made. Related parties include a spouse, child, grandchild, parent, grandparent, brother or sister, controlled corporation (50% or more direct or indirect ownership), any S corporation in which you own stock or partnership in which you are a partner, a trust in which you are a beneficiary, or a grantor trust of which you are treated as the owner. You are treated as owning stock held by your spouse, brothers, sisters, children, grandchildren, parents and grandparents.

You must report as additional installment sale income: (1) the proceeds from the related party's sale or the contract price from the initial installment sale whichever is less; minus (2) installment payments received from the related party as of the end of the year. The computation is made in Part III, of Form 6252.

The two-year period is extended during any period in which the buyer's risk is lessened by a put on the property, an option by another person to acquire the property, or a short sale or other transactions lessening the risk of loss.

The two-year cutoff does not apply to the sale of marketable securities. For such marketable securities, you can be taxed on any related party's sale occurring before you receive all the payments under the initial installment sale.

Marketable securities are:

1. Securities listed on the New York Stock Exchange, the American Stock Exchange, or any city or regional exchange in which quotations appear on a daily basis, including foreign securities listed on a recognized foreign, national, or regional exchange;
2. securities regularly traded in the national or regional over-the-counter market, for which published quotations are available;
3. securities locally traded for which quotations can readily be obtained from established brokerage firms;
4. units in a common trust fund; and
5. mutual fund shares for which redemption prices are published.

Exceptions to two-year rule. There are exceptions to this related party rule. Second dispositions resulting from an involuntary conversion of the property will not be subject to the related party rule so long as the first disposition occurred before the threat or imminence of conversion. Similarly, transfers after the death of the person making the first disposition or the death of the person acquiring the property in first disposition are not treated as second dispositions. Also, a sale or exchange of stock to the issuing corporation is not treated as a first disposition. Finally, you may avoid tax on a related party's second sale by satisfying the IRS that neither the initial nor the second sale were made for tax avoidance purposes.

Where you transfer property to a related party, the IRS has two years from the date you notify it that there has been a second disposition to assess a deficiency with respect to your transfer.

Sales of depreciable property to related party. Installment reporting is not allowed for sales of depreciable property made to a controlled corporation or partnership (50% control by seller) and between such controlled corporations and partnerships. In figuring control of a corporation, you are considered to own stock held by your spouse, children, grandchildren, brothers or sisters, parents, and grandparents. Installment reporting is also disallowed on a sale to a trust in which you or a spouse is a beneficiary unless your interest is considered a remote contingent interest whose actuarial value is 5% or less of the trust property's value. On these related party sales, the entire gain is reported in the year of sale, unless the seller convinces the IRS that the transfer was not motivated by tax avoidance purposes.

On a sale of depreciable property to a related party, if the amount of payments are contingent (for example, payments are tied to profits), the seller must make a special calculation. He or she must treat as received in the year of sale all noncontingent payments plus the fair market value of the contingent payments if such value may be reasonably ascertained. If the fair market value of the contingent payments may not be reasonably calculated, the seller recovers basis ratably. The purchaser's basis for the acquired property includes only amounts that the seller has included in income under the basis recovery rule. Thus, the purchaser's basis is increased annually as the seller recovers basis.

CONTINGENT PAYMENT SALES

¶5.40 Where the final selling price or payment period of an installment sale is not fixed at the end of the taxable year of sale, you are considered to have transacted a "contingent payment sale." Special rules apply where a maximum selling price may be figured under the terms of the agreement or there is no fixed price but there is a fixed payment period, or there is neither a fixed price nor a fixed payment period.

Stated maximum selling price. Under IRS regulations, a stated maximum selling price may be determined by assuming that all of the contingencies contemplated by the agreement are met. When the maximum amount is later reduced, the gross profit ratio is recomputed.

EXAMPLE Smith sells stock in Acme Co. for a down payment of $100,000 plus an amount equal to 5% of the net profits of Acme for the next nine years. The contract provides that the maximum amount payable, including the $100,000 down payment but exclusive of interest, is $2,000,000. Smith's basis for the stock is $200,000; $2,000,000 is the selling price and contract price. Gross profit is $1,800,000. The gross profit ratio is 90% ($1,800,000 ÷ $2,000,000). Thus, $90,000 of the first payment is reportable as gain, $10,000 as a recovery of basis.

Fixed period. When a stated maximum selling price is not determinable but the maximum payment period is fixed, basis—including selling expenses—is allocated equally to the taxable years in which payment may be under the agreement. If, in any year, no payment is received or the amount of payment received is less than the basis allocated to that taxable year, no loss is allowed unless the taxable year is the final payment year or the agreement has become worthless. When no loss is allowed in a year, the basis allocated to the taxable year is carried forward to the next succeeding taxable year.

EXAMPLE Brown sells property for 10% of the property's gross rents over a five-year period. Brown's basis is $5,000,000. The sales price is indefinite and the maximum selling price is not fixed under the terms of the contract; basis is recovered ratably over the five-year period.

Year	Payment	Basis recovered	Gain
1992	$1,300,000	$1,000,000	$300,000
1993	1,500,000	1,000,000	500,000
1994	1,400,000	1,000,000	400,000
1995	1,800,000	1,000,000	800,000
1996	2,100,000	1,000,000	1,100,000

No stated maximum selling price or fixed period. If the agreement fails to specify a maximum selling price and payment period, the IRS may view the agreement as a rent or royalty income agreement. However, if the arrangement qualifies as a sale, basis (including selling expenses) is recovered in equal annual increments over a 15-year period commencing with the date of sale. If in any taxable year, no payment is received or the amount of payment received (exclusive of interest) is less than basis allocated to the year, no loss is allowed unless the agreement has become worthless. Excess basis not recovered in one year is reallocated in level amounts over the balance of the 15-year term. Any basis not recovered at the end of the 15th year is carried forward to the next succeeding year, and to the extent unrecovered, carried forward from year to year until basis has been recovered or the agreement is determined to be worthless. The rule requiring initial level allocation of basis over 15 years may not apply if you prove to the IRS that a 15-year general rule will substantially and inappropriately defer recovery of basis.

In some cases, basis recovery under an income forecast type of method may also be allowed.

An installment sale with payments to be made in foreign currency or fungible payment units (such as bushels of wheat) is a contingent payment sale, but basis is allocated as if payment was fixed in U.S. dollars.

EXAMPLE In 1991, Jones sells property for 10,000 English pounds. In 1992, 2,500 pounds are payable. In 1993, the balance of 7,500 pounds is payable. Basis in the property is $2,000. In 1992, 25% of the basis or $500 (25% of $2,000) is allocated to the first payment. In 1993, $1,500 (75% of $2,000) is allocated to the second payment.

USING ESCROW AND OTHER SECURITY ARRANGEMENTS

¶5.41 You sell property and the sales proceeds are placed in escrow pending the possible occurrence of an event such as the approval of title or your performance of certain contractual conditions. The IRS may argue that installment reporting is not allowed unless there are escrow restrictions preventing immediate payment.

EXAMPLE Anderson sold stock and mining property for almost $5 million. He agreed to place $500,000 in escrow to protect the buyer against his possible breaches of warranty and to provide security for certain liabilities. The escrow agreement called for Anderson to direct the investments of the escrow fund and receive income from the fund in excess of $500,000.

The IRS claimed that in the year of sale Anderson was taxable on the $500,000 held in escrow on the grounds that Anderson's control of the fund rendered the fund taxable immediately. Anderson argued he was only taxable as the funds were released to him, and the Tax Court agreed. The fund was not under his unqualified control. He might never get the fund if the liabilities materialize. Although Anderson had a free hand with investment of the money, he still lacked ultimate ownership.

Tax on Escrow Fund

The escrow agreement may authorize you to receive the income it produces or it may even authorize you to control the manner in which the fund is to be invested. As in the previous example, these facts do not make the fund taxable to you before the year you actually have it, assuming the escrow restricts immediate payment to you in order to protect the buyer. You are, of course, taxable on the income earned by the fund when you receive the income.

If the terms of the escrow involve no genuine conditions that prevent you from demanding immediate payment, there will be immediate tax.

EXAMPLE Rhodes sold a tract to a buyer who was willing to pay at once the entire purchase price of $157,000. But Rhodes wanted to report the sale on the installment basis over a period of years. The buyer refused to execute a purchase money mortgage on the property to allow the installment sale election (required under prior law) because he wanted clear and unencumbered title to the tract. As a solution, Rhodes asked the buyer to turn over the purchase price to a bank, as escrow agent, which would pay the sum over a five-year period.

The escrow arrangement failed to support an installment sale. Rhodes was fully taxable on the entire price in the year of the sale. The buyer's payment was unconditional and irrevocable. The escrow arrangement involved no genuine conditions that could defeat Rhodes's right to payment, as the buyer could not revoke, alter, or end the arrangement.

Substitution of an escrow account for unpaid notes or deed of trust disqualifies installment reporting.

EXAMPLE In January, an investor sold real estate for $100,000. He received $10,000 as a down payment and six notes, each for $15,000, secured by a deed of trust on the property. The notes, together with interest, were due annually over the next six years. In July, the buyer deposited the remainder of the purchase price with an escrow agent and got the seller to cancel the deed of trust.

The agreement provides that the escrow agent will pay off the buyer's notes as they fall due. The buyer remains liable for the installment payments. The escrow deposit is irrevocable, and the payment schedule may not be accelerated by any party under any circumstances. According to the IRS, the sale, which initially qualified as an installment sale, is disqualified by the escrow account.

Installment Reporting on Escrow Allowable

If an escrow arrangement imposes a substantial restriction, the IRS may allow installment reporting. An example of a substantial restriction: Payment of the escrow is tied to the condition that the seller refrain from entering a competing business for a period of five years. If, at any time during the escrow period, he engaged in a competing business, he forfeits all rights to the amount then held in escrow.

MINIMUM INTEREST ON DEFERRED PAYMENT SALES

¶5.42 The tax law requires a minimum amount of interest to be charged on deferred payment sales. The rules for imputing interest are discussed at ¶4.32. Imputed interest is included in the taxable income of the seller. Imputed interest is deductible by the buyer if the property is business or investment property, but not if it is used substantially all the time for personal purposes.

TRANSFER OF INSTALLMENT NOTES

¶5.43 A sale, a gift, or other transfer or cancellation of mortgage notes or other obligation received in an installment sale has tax consequences. If you sell or exchange the notes at other than face value, gain or loss results to the extent of the difference between the basis of the notes and the amount realized. Gain or loss is long term if the original sale was entitled to long-term capital gain treatment. This is true even if the notes were held short term. If the original sale resulted in short-term gain or ordinary income, the sale of the notes gives short-term gain or ordinary income, regardless of the holding period of the notes.

The basis of an installment note or obligation is the face value of the note less the income that would be reported if the obligation were paid in full.

EXAMPLE You sell a lot for $20,000 which cost you $10,000. In the year of the sale, you received $5,000 in cash and the purchaser's notes for the remainder of the selling price, or $15,000. A year later, before the buyer makes a payment on the notes, you sell them for $13,000 cash:

Selling price of property	$20,000
Cost of property	10,000
Total profit	$10,000
(Percentage of profit, or proportion of each payment returnable as income, is 50%)	
Unpaid balance of notes	$15,000
Amount of income reportable if notes were paid in full (50% of $15,000)	7,500
Adjusted basis of the notes	$ 7,500

Your profit on the sale is $5,500 ($13,000 − $7,500). It is capital gain if the sale of the lot was taxable as capital gain.

Suppose you make an installment sale of your real estate, taking back a land contract. Later a mortgage is substituted for the unpaid balance of the land contract. The IRS has ruled that the substitution is not the same as a disposition of the unpaid installment obligations. There is no tax on the substitution.

If the installment obligations are disposed of other than by sale or exchange, gain or loss is the difference between the basis of the obligations and their fair market value at the time of the disposition. If an installment obligation is canceled or otherwise becomes unenforceable, it is subject to the same rule for determining gain or loss.

A gift of installment obligations to a person or charitable organization is treated as a taxable disposition. Gain or loss is the difference between the basis of the obligations and their fair market value at the time of the gift. If the notes are donated to a qualified charity, you may claim a contribution deduction for the fair market value of the obligations at the time of the gift.

Not all dispositions of installment obligations result in recognition of gain or loss. A transfer of installment obligations to your spouse or a transfer to a former spouse that is incident to a divorce is treated as a tax-free exchange under the rules of ¶6.6 unless the transfer is in trust. A transfer of installment obligations at death is not taxed. As the notes are paid, the estate or beneficiaries report income in the same proportion as the decedent would have, had he lived. A transfer of installment obligations to a revocable trust is also not taxed.

REPOSSESSION OF PERSONAL PROPERTY SOLD ON INSTALLMENT

¶5.44 When the buyer defaults and you repossess personal property, either through a voluntary surrender or a foreclosure, you may realize gain or loss. The method of calculating gain or loss is similar to the method used for disposition of installment notes; see ¶5.43. Gain or loss is the difference between the fair market value of the repossessed property and your basis for the installment obligations satisfied by the repossession. This rule is followed whether or not title has been kept by you or transferred to the buyer. The amount realized is reduced by costs incurred during the repossession. The basis of the obligation is face value less unreported profit.

If the property repossessed is bid in at a lawful public auction or judicial sale, the fair market value of the property is presumed to be the purchase or bid price, in the absence of proof to the contrary.

Gain or loss in the repossession is reported in the year of the repossession.

EXAMPLE In December 1991, you sell furniture for $1,500—$300 down and $100 a month plus 9% interest beginning January 1992. You reported the installment sale on your 1991 tax return. The buyer defaulted after making three monthly payments. You foreclosed and repossessed the property; the fair market value was $1,400. The legal costs of foreclosure were $100. The gain on the repossession in 1992 is computed as follows:

Fair market value of property repossessed		$1,400
Basis of the buyer's notes at time of repossession:		
Selling price	$1,500	
Less: Payments made	600	
Face value of notes at repossession	$ 900	
Less: Unrealized profit (assume gross profit percentage of 33⅓ x $900)	300	
	$ 600	600
Gain on repossession		$ 800
Less: Repossession costs		100
Taxable gain on repossession		$ 700

Repossession gain or loss keeps the same character as the gain or loss realized on the original sale. If the sale originally resulted in a capital gain, the repossession gain is also a capital gain.

Your basis in the repossessed property is its fair market value at the time of repossession.

Real property. Repossessions of real property are at ¶31.7.

BOOT IN LIKE-KIND EXCHANGE PAYABLE IN INSTALLMENTS

¶5.45 An exchange of like-kind property is generally tax free unless boot, such as cash or notes, is received; see ¶6.3. The boot is taxable, and if payable in installments, the following rules apply. Contract price is reduced by like-kind property received. Gross profit is reduced by gain not recognized. "Payment" does not include like-kind property.

EXAMPLE In 1992, property with an installment sale basis of $400,000 is exchanged for like-kind property worth $200,000, plus installment obligations of $800,000, of which $100,000 is payable in 1993, plus interest. The balance of $700,000 plus interest will be paid in 1994. The contract price is $800,000 ($1 million selling price *less* $200,000 like-kind property received). The gross profit is $600,000 ($1 million *less* $400,000 installment sale basis). The gross profit ratio is 75% (gross profit of $600,00 ÷ contract price of $800,000). Like-kind property is not treated as a payment received in the year of sale, so no gain is reported in 1992. In 1993, gain of $75,000 will have to be reported (75% gross profit ratio x $100,000 payment), and in 1994 there will be a gain of $525,000 (75% of $700,000 payment).

The same treatment applies to certain tax-free reorganizations that are not treated as dividends, to exchanges of certain insurance policies, exchanges of the stock of the same corporation, and exchanges of United States obligations.

"INTEREST" TAX ON SALES OVER $150,000 PLUS $5 MILLION DEBT

¶**5.46** If deferred payments from installment sales of over $150,000 exceed $5 million, an interest charge is imposed on the tax deferred amount. The special tax applies to sales of business or rental personal property as well as real estate for over $150,000.

Farm property and personal-use property, such as a residence, are exempt from the tax.

How to report interest tax. The interest charge is an additional tax. The method of computing the interest tax is complicated; the rules are in Internal Revenue Code Section 453A. In general, you compute the ratio of the face amount of outstanding installment obligations in excess of $5 million to the face amount of all outstanding installment obligations. This ratio is multiplied by the year-end unrecognized gain on the obligation, the top tax rate (Chapter 22) and also by the IRS interest rate for the last month of the year.

The interest tax is reported on Line 53 of Form 1040, the line for total tax. The tax is considered personal interest, and is not deductible; *see* Chapter 15.

Pledge rule for property sales over $150,000. If as security for a debt you pledge an installment obligation received on a sale of property exceeding $150,000 (other than farm property or personal-use property), the net proceeds of the secured debt are treated as a payment on the installment obligations, as discussed at ¶5.37.

Dealer sale of timeshares and residential lots. The above interest tax and pledging rules do not apply to installment obligations from the sale of certain timeshare rights (generally timeshares of up to six weeks per year) or residential lots. However, under a separate rule, the seller must pay interest on tax deferred under the installment method.

BAD DEBT DEDUCTIONS

	See ¶		*See* ¶
Tax consequences of bad debts	5.47	Loans by stockholders	5.49
Four rules to prove bad debt deduction	5.48	Family bad debts	5.50

TAX CONSEQUENCES OF BAD DEBTS

¶**5.47** When you lend money or sell on credit and your debtor does not repay, you may deduct your loss. The type of deduction depends on whether the debt was incurred in a business or personal transaction. This distinction is important because business bad debts receive favored tax treatment.

Business bad debt is fully deductible from gross income on Schedule C if you are self employed, or on Schedule F if your business is farming. In addition, you may deduct partially worthless business debts. You must use the specific charge-off method for deducting business bad debts. If you use the accrual method for reporting income for services, you may be able to account for bad debts by not having to accrue income that you do not expect to collect; *see* IRS Publication 334 for details.

Examples of business debt transactions:
—You sell merchandise on credit and later the buyer becomes insolvent and does not pay.
—You are in the business of making loans and a loan goes bad.
—You sell your business, but retain some accounts receivable. Later, some of these become worthless.
—You liquidate your business and are unable to collect its outstanding accounts.
—You operate as a promoter of corporations.
—You finance your lessees, customers, or suppliers to help your business.
—You lend money to protect your professional and business reputation.
—You lend money to insure delivery of merchandise from a supplier.
—You make a loan to your employer to keep your job.

 Accounts and Notes Receivable.

You may claim a bad debt deduction for accounts and notes receivable on unpaid goods or services only if you have included the amount due as gross income. Thus, if a client or customer fails to pay a bill for services rendered, you do not have a deductible bad debt where you have not reported the amount as income.

Nonbusiness bad debt is deducted as a short-term capital loss on Schedule D. This is a limited deduction. In 1992, you deduct it from capital gains, if any, and $3,000 of other income. Any excess is deductible as a capital loss carryover in 1993 and later years; *see* ¶5.2. You may not deduct partially worthless nonbusiness bad debts. The debt must be totally worthless.

Examples of nonbusiness bad debts:
—You enter into a deal for profit which is not connected with your business; for example, debts arising from investments are non-business bad debts.
—You make casual personal advances with a reasonable hope of recovery and are not in the business of making loans.
—You are assigned a debt that arose in the assignor's business. The fact that he or she could have deducted it as a business bad debt, does not make it your business debt. A business debt must arise in your business.
—You pay liens filed against your property by mechanics or suppliers who have not been paid by your builder or contractor. Your payment is considered a deductible bad debt when there is no possibility of recovering reimbursement from the contractor, and a judgment obtained against him is uncollectible.
—You lose a deposit on a house when the contractor becomes insolvent.

—You had an uninsured savings account in a savings association which went into default; *see* ¶18.4.

—You are held secondarily liable on a mortgage debt assumed but not paid by a buyer of your home. Your payment to the bank or other holder of the mortgage is deductible as a bad debt if you cannot collect it from the buyer of the home.

FOUR RULES TO PROVE BAD DEBT DEDUCTION

¶5.48 To determine whether you have a bad debt deduction in 1992, read the four rules explained below. Pay close attention to the fourth rule which requires proof that the debt became worthless in the year the deduction is claimed. Your belief that your debt is bad, or the mere refusal of the debtor to pay, is not sufficient evidence. There must be an event, such as the debtor's bankruptcy, to fix the debt as worthless.

Rule 1. You must have a valid debt. You have no loss if your right to repayment is not fixed or depends upon some event which may not happen. Thus, advances to a corporation already insolvent are not valid debts. Nor are advances that are to be repaid only if the corporation has a profit. Voluntary payment of another's debt is also nondeductible. If usurious interest was charged on a worthless debt, and under state law the debt was void or voidable, the debt is not deductible as a bad debt. However, where the lender was in the business of lending money, a court allowed him to deduct the unpaid amounts as business losses.

Rule 2. A debtor-creditor relationship must exist at the time the debt arose. You have a loss if there was a promise to repay at the time the debt was created and you had the right to enforce it. If the advance was a gift and you did not expect to be repaid, you may not take a deduction. Loans to members of your family, to a controlled corporation, or to a trust may be treated as gifts or contributions to capital.

Rule 3. The funds providing the loan or credit were previously reported as income or part of your capital. If you are on the cash basis, you may not deduct unpaid salary, rent, or fees. On the cash basis, you do not include these items in income until you are paid.

Rule 4. You must show that the debt became worthless during 1992. To prove the debt became worthless in 1992, you must show:

First, that the debt had some value at the end of the previous year (1991), and that there was a reasonable hope and expectation of recovering something on the debt. Your personal belief unsupported by other facts is not enough: For example, would a businessman have placed some value on the debt on December 31, 1991?

Second, that an identifiable event occurred in 1992—such as a bankruptcy proceeding—that caused you to conclude the debt was worthless. In the case of a business debt which has become partially worthless, you need evidence that the debt has declined in value. Additionally, reasonable collection steps must have been undertaken. That you cancel a debt does not make it worthless. You must still show that the debt was worthless when you canceled it. You do not have to go to court to try to collect the debt if you can show that a court judgment would be uncollectible.

Third, that there is no hope the debt may have some value in a later year. You are not required to prove that there is no possibility of ever receiving some payment on your debt. You are not expected to be an extreme optimist.

Debt Worthless Before Due

You do not have to wait until the debt is due in order to deduct a bad debt. Claim the deduction for the year that you can prove worthlessness occurred.

Effect of statute of limitations. A debt is not deductible merely because a statute of limitations has run against the debt. Although the debtor has a legal defense against your demand for payment, he or she may still recognize the obligation to pay. A debt is deductible *only* in the year it becomes worthless. This event—for example, the debtor's insolvency—may have occurred even before the statute became effective.

What if your debtor recognized his or her moral obligation to pay in spite of the expiration of the statute of limitations, but dies before paying? Your claim would be defeated if the executor raises the statute of limitations. You then have a bad debt deduction in the year you made the claim against the estate.

Guarantor or endorsement losses as bad debts. If you guarantee a loan and must pay it off after the principal debtor defaults, your payment is deductible as a business bad debt if you had a business reason for the guarantee. For example, to protect a business relationship with a major client, you guarantee the client's loan. Your payment on the guarantee qualifies as a business bad debt. If as a result of your payment, you have a legal right to recover the amount from the client (right of subrogation or similar right), you may not claim a bad debt deduction unless that right is partially or totally worthless.

A loss on a guarantee may be a nonbusiness bad debt if you made the guarantee to protect an investment, such as where you are a main shareholder of a corporation, and guarantee a bank loan to the company. No deduction is allowed if you guaranteed the loan as a favor to a relative or friend.

Bank deposit losses; see ¶18.4.

LOANS BY STOCKHOLDERS

¶5.49 It is a common practice for stockholders to make loans to their corporations or to guarantee loans made by banks or other lenders. If the corporation fails and the stockholder is not repaid or has to make good on the guarantee, he or she is generally left with a nonbusiness bad debt unless he or she can prove that a business loan was made. To prove a business loan, the stockholder usually has to show *one* of these facts:

1. He or she is in the business of making loans and the loan was made in that capacity; or he or she is in the business of promoting corporations for a fee or for profits on their sale.
2. He or she made the loan to safeguard the business.
3. He or she wanted to protect his or her job with the company.

Loan to Protect Job

COURT DECISION The Supreme Court has ruled that a stockholder who claims to have made a loan to protect his or her job must show that protection of the job was the *primary and dominant* motive of the loan in order to get a business bad debt; *see* Example 1 on the next page.

EXAMPLES 1. To determine an executive's motive for making a loan, the Supreme Court reviewed his salary, outside income, investment in the company, and the size of his loan. His pay was $12,000 ($7,000 after tax); his outside income, $30,000. He had a $38,900 investment in the company and loaned it $165,000. On the basis of these figures, the Court concluded he could not have advanced $165,000 to protect an after-tax salary of $7,000. He was protecting his investment, not his job, and only a nonbusiness bad debt could be claimed.

2. The Tax Court followed the same approach to determine the motive for a stockholder-employee's guarantee of company loans which went bad. His salary was $12,000 ($11,000 after tax); he had little outside income. His stock investment in the company was $22,100, and he guaranteed $13,000 of corporate debt. He claimed he hoped that his salary would increase to $20,000 if the company was successful. If it was not, he would lose his job. The Court accepted his explanation and allowed a business bad debt deduction. An advance of $13,000 to protect an after-tax salary of $11,000 was not unreasonable, particularly since he expected pay increases. Also, his stock investment in the corporation was modest in relation to his salary.

Loan to key employees. A loan by a stockholder to key employees was held to be a business bad debt in the following case.

EXAMPLE Carter, the president and majority owner of two corporations, loaned money to two key employees to buy stock in the corporations. He wanted to guarantee their future participation in the company. Both corporations went bankrupt, and the employees defaulted on the loans. Carter deducted both loans as business bad debts, contending he was protecting his job.

The IRS argued he had a nonbusiness bad debt; he was merely protecting his investment as a stockholder. The Tax Court disagreed. He made the loans to encourage the future of a business which would provide him salary income rather than dividends or appreciation on his stock.

When liquidation proceeds are insufficient to repay a stockholder for his loan and redeem his stock, the proceeds are first applied to the loan and then to the stock.

FAMILY BAD DEBTS

¶5.50 The IRS views loans to relatives, especially to children and parents, as gifts, so that it is rather difficult to deduct family bad debts.

Overcoming IRS' Gift Presumption

To overcome the presumption of a gift when you advance money to a relative, take the same steps you would in making a business loan. Take a note, set a definite payment date, and require interest and collateral. If the relative fails to pay, make an attempt to collect. Failure to enforce collection of a family debt is viewed by the courts as evidence of a gift, despite the taking of notes and the receipt of interest.

Husband's default on child support—a basis for wife's deductible bad debt? A wife who supports her children when her husband defaults on court-ordered support payments may consider claiming her expenses as a nonbusiness bad debt deduction, arguing that her position is similar to a guarantor who pays a creditor when the principal debtor defaults. The IRS does not agree to the grounds of such a claim and will disallow the deduction; its position is supported by the Tax Court. However, the federal appeals court for the Ninth Circuit left open the possibility that such a claim may have merit if a wife can show: (1) What she spent on the children; and (2) that her husband's obligation to support was worthless in the year the deduction is claimed. The Tax Court has subsequently reiterated its position that defaulted child support payments are not a basis for a bad debt deduction.

6

TAX-FREE EXCHANGES OF PROPERTY

You may exchange property without incurring a tax in the year of exchange if you meet the rules of this chapter. Gain may be taxed upon a later disposition of the property because the basis of the property received in the exchange is usually the same as the basis of the property surrendered in the exchange. Thus, if you exchange property with a tax basis of $10,000 for property worth $50,000, the basis of the property received in exchange is fixed at $10,000, even though its fair market value is $50,000. The gain of $40,000 ($50,000 – $10,000) is technically called "unrecognized gain." If you later sell the property for $50,000, you realize taxable gain of $40,000 ($50,000 – $10,000).

Where property received in a tax-free exchange is held until death, the unrecognized gain escapes tax forever because basis of the property in the hands of an heir is generally the value of the property at the date of death.

If the exchange involves the transfer of boot, such as cash or other property, gain on the exchange is taxable to the extent of the value of boot.

You may not exchange tax-free U.S. real estate for foreign real estate.

Tax-free exchanges between related parties may become taxable if either party disposes of the exchanged property within a two-year period.

TRADES OF LIKE-KIND PROPERTY

¶**6.1** You do not pay tax on gain realized on the "like-kind" exchange of business or investment property. For tax-free treatment, you must trade property held for business use or investment for like-kind business or investment property. If a loss is incurred on a like-kind exchange, the loss is not deductible. Although gain on a qualifying exchange is not immediately taxed, it may be taxable in a later year when you sell the property because your basis for the new property is generally the same as the basis for the property you traded; basis is discussed at ¶5.12.

If you make a qualifying like-kind exchange with certain related parties, tax-free exchange may be lost unless both of you keep the exchanged properties for at least two years; see ¶6.5.

The term *like kind* refers to the nature or character of the property; that is, whether real estate is traded for real estate. It does not refer to grade or quality; that is, whether the properties traded are new or used. In the case of real estate, land may be traded for a building, farm land for city lots, a leasehold interest of 30 years or more for an outright ownership in realty. Trades of personal property are discussed at ¶6.2.

EXAMPLES 1. Jones, a real estate investor, purchased a parcel for investment in 1944 for $5,000. In 1982, he exchanged it for another parcel, Parcel B, which had a fair market value of $50,000. The gain of $45,000 was not taxed in 1982.

2. Same facts as above, except that in 1992 Jones sells Parcel B for $50,000. His taxable gain is $45,000. The "tax-free" rules have the effect of deferring tax on appreciation. Tax is finally imposed when the exchanged item is sold.

3. Same facts as in 1 above, but the value of Parcel B was $3,000. Jones may not deduct the loss. The basis of the parcel is $5,000. If Jones sells Parcel B in 1992 for $3,000, he may deduct a loss of $2,000.

Reporting an exchange. You must file Form 8824 to report the details of an exchange of like-kind property. You also must report the exchange on Schedule D (investment property) or Form 4797 (business property), even if there is no gain or loss.

See ¶6.5 for reporting an exchange with a related party.

Property not within the tax-free trade rules:
Property used for personal purposes (except for exchanges of personal residences; *see* Chapter 29).
Foreign real estate.
Property held for sale.
Inventory or stock-in-trade.
Securities; *see* ¶6.2 for exception.
Notes.
Partnership interest; *see* below.
See also ¶31.4 for tax-free exchanges of realty and ¶11.8 for tax-free exchanges of insurance policies.

Exchange of partnership interests. Exchanges of partnership interests in different partnerships are not within the tax-free exchange rules. Under IRS regulations, tax-free exchange treatment is denied regardless of whether the interests are in the same or different partnerships.

If you have made an election to exclude a partnership interest from the application of partnership rules, your interest is treated as interest in each partnership asset, not as an interest in the partnership.

Real estate in foreign countries. You may not exchange tax-free U.S. real estate for foreign real estate. This rule applies to exchanges made after July 10, 1989, except transfers made under a binding contract in effect on and after that date. However, in the case of an involuntary conversion, a tax-free reinvestment may be made in foreign real estate.

PERSONAL PROPERTY HELD FOR BUSINESS OR INVESTMENT

¶**6.2** An exchange of depreciable tangible personal property held for productive business or investment use may qualify for tax-free treatment if it meets either the general like-kind test of ¶6.1 or a more specific "like-class" test created by IRS regulations. The assumption of liabilities is treated as "boot;" *see* ¶6.3. Where each party assumes a liability of the other party, the respective liabilities are offset against each other to figure boot, if any.

Under the like-class test, there are two types of "like" classes: (1) General Asset Classes; and (2) Product Classes. The like-class test is satisfied if the exchanged properties are both within the same General Asset Class or the same Product Class. A specific asset may be classified within only one class. Thus, if an asset is within an Asset Class, it may not be within a Product Class. The Asset Class or Product Class is determined as of the date of the exchange. This limitation may disqualify an exchange when exchanged assets do not fit within the same Asset Class and are not allowed to qualify within the Product Class; *see* Example 2 in the next column.

Note: The regulations creating the "like-class" test, and the rules for multiple exchanges in this section apply to exchanges occurring on or after April 11, 1991.

General Asset Classes. There are 13 classes of depreciable tangible business property. Here are some of the asset classifications: Office furniture, fixtures, and equipment (class 00.11); information systems: computers and peripheral equipment (class 00.12); data handling equipment, except computers (class 00.13); airplanes and helicopters, except for airplanes used to carry passengers or freight (class 00.21); automobiles and taxis (class 00.22); light trucks (class 00.241); heavy trucks (class 00.242); and over-the-road tractor units (class 00.26).

For example, trades of trucks in class 00.241 would be of like-class.

Product Classes. Under a coding system of the Standard Industrial Classification Manual (SIC), tangible depreciable assets are assigned a 4-digit product-class number. For example, a grader is exchanged for a scraper. Neither item is within a General Asset Class, but both are in the same Product Class as SIC Code 3533. They are, therefore, of a like class.

EXAMPLES 1. Jones exchanges a personal computer used in his business for a printer. Both assets are productively used in business and are in the same General Asset Class of 00.12; the exchange meets the like-class test.

2. Smith exchanges an airplane (asset class 00.21) used in her business for a heavy truck (asset class 00.242). The exchanged properties are not of a like class. Furthermore, since each property is within a specific General Asset Class, the Product Class test may not be applied to qualify the exchange. Smith must report any gain realized on the exchange because the properties also do not meet the general like-kind test.

Intangible personal property and goodwill. Exchanges of intangible personal property (such as a patent or copyright) or nondepreciable personal property must meet the general like-kind test to qualify for tax-free treatment; the like-class tests do not apply. However, regulations close the door for qualifying exchanges of goodwill in an exchange of going businesses. According to the regulations, goodwill or going concern value of one business can never be of a like kind to goodwill or going concern value of another business.

EXAMPLES 1. Smith exchanges a copyright on a novel for a copyright on a different novel. The properties exchanged are of a like kind.

2. Jones exchanges a copyright on a novel for a copyright on a song. The properties exchanged are not of a like kind.

Exchanges of multiple properties. Generally, exchanges of assets are considered on a one-to-one basis. Regulations provide an exception for exchanges of multiple properties, such as on an exchange of businesses. Transferred assets are separated into exchange groups. An exchange group consists of all properties transferred and received in the exchange which are of a like kind or like class. All properties within the same General Asset Class or same Product Class are in the same exchange group. For example, automobiles and computers are exchanged for other automobiles and computers; two exchange groups are set up—one for the automobiles and the other for the computers. If the aggregate fair market values of the properties transferred and received in each exchange group are not equal, the regulations provide calculations for setting up a residual group for purposes of calculating taxable gain, if any.

All liabilities of which a taxpayer is relieved in the exchange are offset against all liabilities assumed by the taxpayer in the exchange, regardless of whether the liabilities are recourse, nonrecourse, or are secured by the specific property transferred or received. If excess liabilities are assumed by the taxpayer as part of the exchange, regulations provide rules for allocating the excess among the properties.

RECEIPT OF CASH AND OTHER PROPERTY—"BOOT"

¶**6.3** If, in addition to property, you receive cash or other property, gain is taxable up to the amount of the cash or other property. The additional cash or other property is called "boot." If a loss was incurred on the exchange, the receipt of boot does not permit you to deduct the loss.

Adjustments to basis for unrecognized gain or loss are discussed at ¶5.12.

If you transfer mortgaged property, the amount of the mortgage is part of your boot. If both you and the other party transfer and receive mortgaged property, the party giving up the larger debt treats the excess as taxable boot. The party giving up the smaller debt does not have boot; *see also* ¶31.4.

EXAMPLE You own an apartment house with a fair market value of $220,000, subject to an $80,000 mortgage. Your adjusted basis is $100,000. You exchange the building for Smith's apartment building, which has a value of $250,000, subject to a $150,000 mortgage. You also receive $40,000 in cash. You realize a gain of $120,000 on the exchange, but only $40,000 is taxable.

What you received:

Value of building received	$250,000
Cash received	40,000
Mortgage on building traded	80,000
Total amount realized	$370,000

Less:

Adjusted basis of building traded	$100,000	
Mortgage on building received	150,000	
		$250,000
Gain realized ($370,000 −$250,000)		$120,000

Of the $120,000 gain, you are taxed only on $40,000, the amount of the cash boot received. Although you are relieved of an $80,000 mortgage, this does not result in taxable boot because it is less than the $150,000 mortgage to which the property received is subject.

Smith will have taxable boot of $30,000, the excess of the $150,000 mortgage transferred over the total of the $80,000 mortgage assumed *and* the $40,000 cash paid to you.

TIME LIMITS FOR DEFERRED EXCHANGES

¶6.4 Assume you own property which has appreciated in value. You want to sell it and reinvest the proceeds in other property, but you would like to avoid having to pay tax on the appreciation. You can avoid the tax if you are able to arrange an exchange for similar property.

The problem is that it is difficult to find a buyer who has property you want in exchange. Before 1984, an investor could agree to exchange property with a financially secure buyer who would buy replacement property and then transfer it to complete the exchange. The parties could employ a professional intermediary to handle the details of finding and purchasing the replacement property, transferring the properties, and setting up security arrangements. The time delay in arranging these steps did not jeopardize tax-free treatment for the exchanges.

However, under the 1984 Tax Reform Act, the time for closing the exchange was restricted, and the IRS has released extensive regulations applying the restrictions and imposing tests for using intermediaries and setting up security arrangements without running afoul of constructive receipt rules that could trigger an immediate tax. The IRS regulations apply to transfers after June 9, 1991.

Time limits for completing exchanges. You generally have up to 180 days to complete an exchange, but the deadline may end sooner. Specifically, property will *not* be treated as like-kind property if received (1) more than 180 days after the date you transferred the property you are relinquishing; or (2) the due date of your return (including extensions) for the year in which you made the transfer, *whichever is earlier.* Furthermore, the property to be received must be identified within 45 days after the date on which you transferred property.

If the transaction involves more than one property, the 45-day identification period and the 180-day exchange period are determined by the earliest date on which any property is transferred. When the identification or exchange period ends on a Saturday, Sunday, or legal holiday, the deadline is not advanced to the next business day (as it is when the deadline for filing a tax return is on a weekend or holiday).

 Strict Time Limits

No extensions of time are allowed if the 45-day or 180-day statutory deadlines cannot be met. If extra time is needed for finding suitable replacement property, it is advisable to delay the date of your property transfer because the transfer date starts the 45-day identification period.

How to identify property. You must identify replacement property in a written document signed by you and either hand delivered, mailed, telecopied, or otherwise sent before the end of the 45-day identification period to a person involved in the exchange other than yourself or a related party. The identification may also be made in a written agreement. The property must be unambiguously described by a legal description or street address.

You may identify more than one property as replacement property. However, the maximum number of replacement properties that you may identify without regard to the fair market value is three properties. You may identify any number of properties provided the aggregate fair market value at the end of the 45-day identification period does not exceed 200% of the aggregate fair market value of all the relinquished properties as of the date you transferred them. If, as of the end of the identification period, you have identified more than the allowable number of properties, you are generally treated as if no replacement property has been identified.

Receipt of security. In a deferred exchange, you want financial security for the buyer's performance and compensation for delay in receiving property. To avoid immediate tax, you must not arrange a security arrangement that gives you an unrestricted right to funds before the deal is closed.

EXAMPLE You and Jones agree to enter a deferred exchange under the following terms and conditions. On May 18, 1992, you transfer to Jones real estate which has been held for investment; it is unencumbered and has a fair market value of $100,000. On or before July 2, 1992 (the end of the identification period), you must identify like-kind replacement property. On or before November 14, 1992 (the end of the exchange period), Jones is required to buy the property and transfer it to you. At any time after May 18, 1992 and before Jones has purchased the replacement property, you have the right, upon notice, to demand that he pay you $100,000 instead of acquiring and transferring the replacement property. However, you identify replacement property, and Jones purchases and transfers it to you. According to the regulations, you have an unrestricted right to demand the payment of $100,000 as of May 18, 1992. You are therefore in constructive receipt of $100,000 on that date. Thus, the transaction is treated as a taxable sale, and the transfer of the real property does not qualify as a tax-free exchange. You are treated as if you received the $100,000 for the sale of your property and then purchased replacement property.

Safe harbor tests for security arrangements. If one of the following safe harbors applies to your security arrangement, you are not taxed as if a sale were made.

The first two "safe harbors" cover transfers dealing directly with the buyer. The third allows the use of professional intermediaries who, for a fee, arrange the details of the exchange. The fourth allows you to earn interest on an escrow account. The safe harbors generally prohibit you from receiving money or other non-like-kind property before replacement property is received. The terms of the agreement govern whether your right to the funds are limited as required by the safe harbor rules; possible state law complications are disregarded.

1. The transferee may give you a mortgage, deed of trust, or other security interest in property (other than cash or a cash equivalent), or a third party guarantee. A standby letter of credit may be given if you are not allowed to draw on such standby letter except upon a default of the transferee's obligation to transfer like-kind replacement property.

2. The transferee may put cash or a cash equivalent in a qualified escrow account or a qualified trust. The escrow holder or trustee must not be related to you. Your rights to receive, pledge, borrow, or otherwise obtain the cash must be limited. For example, you may obtain the cash after all of the replacement property to which you are entitled is received. After you identify replacement property, you may obtain the cash after the later of (1) the end of the identification period; or (2) the occurrence of a contingency beyond your control that you have specified in writing. You may receive the funds after the end of the identification period if within that period you do not identify replacement property. In other cases, there can be no right to the funds until the exchange period ends.

3. You may use a *qualified intermediary* if your right to receive money or other property is limited (as discussed in safe harbor rule 2 above). A qualified intermediary is an unrelated party who, for a fee, acts to facilitate a deferred exchange by entering into an agreement with you for the exchange of properties pursuant to which the intermediary acquires your property from you, acquires the replacement property, and transfers the replacement property to you. The acquisitions may be on the intermediary's own behalf or as the agent of any party to the transaction.

   The transfer of property that is facilitated by the use of a qualified intermediary may occur through a "direct deed" of legal title by the current owner of the property to you. The transferee of your property does *not* have to receive title to the property you want and then transfer it to you.

   There are restrictions on who may act as an intermediary. You may not employ any person as an intermediary who is your employee or is related to you or has generally acted as your professional adviser such as an attorney, accountant, investment broker, real estate agent, or banker in a two-year period preceding the exchange. Related parties include family members and controlled businesses or trusts (*see* ¶33.10), except that for purposes of control, a 10% interest is sufficient under the intermediary rule. The performance of routine financial, escrow, trust, or title insurance services by a financial institution or title company within the two-year period is not taken into account. State laws which may be interpreted as fixing an agency relationship between the transferor and transferee or fixing the transferor's right to security funds are ignored.

   In a simultaneous exchange, the intermediary is not considered the transferor's agent.

4. You are permitted to receive interest or a "growth factor" on escrowed funds if your right to receive the amount is limited as discussed under safe harbor rule 2.

Payment of acquisition and closing costs. The use of funds from a security account to pay specific acquisition and closing costs such as commissions, prorated taxes, and recording and transfer fees will not result in constructive receipt of the remaining funds.

EXCHANGES BETWEEN RELATED PARTIES

¶6.5 Tax-free treatment of like-kind exchanges between related persons may be lost, if either party disposes of property received in the exchange within two years after the date of the last transfer that was part of the exchange. Any gain not recognized on the original exchange is taxable as of the date of the later disposition of the original like-kind property by either party within the two-year period. If a loss was not recognized, the loss becomes deductible if allowed under the rules of ¶33.10. This two-year rule does not apply to transfers made under a written binding contract in effect on and after July 10, 1989 or to the exceptions listed below.

Indirect dispositions of the property within the two-year period, such as transfer of stock of a corporation or interests in a partnership that owns the property, may also be treated as taxable dispositions.

Related parties. Related persons falling within the two-year rule include your children, grandchildren, parent, brother, or sister, controlled corporations or partnerships (more than 50% ownership), and a trust in which you are a beneficiary. A transfer to a spouse is not subject to the two-year rule unless he or she is a nonresident alien.

Plan to avoid two-year rule. If you set up a prearranged plan under which you first transfer property to an unrelated party who within two years makes an exchange with a party related to you, the related party will not qualify for tax-free treatment on that exchange.

Exceptions. No tax will be incurred on a disposition made because of death; in an involuntary conversion provided the original exchange occurred before the threat of the conversion; or if you can prove that neither the exchange nor the later disposition was for a tax avoidance purpose.

Filing Form 8824

The IRS requires related parties who exchange property to file Form 8824 for the year of the exchange and also for the two years following the exchange. If either party disposes of the property received in the original exchange in any of these years, the deferred gain must be reported in the year of disposition as if the property had been sold.

PROPERTY TRANSFERS BETWEEN SPOUSES AND EX-SPOUSES

¶6.6 Tax-free exchange rules apply to all transfers between spouses after July 18, 1984, other than transfers to a nonresident alien spouse, certain trust transfers of mortgaged property and transfers of U.S. Savings Bonds; these exceptions are discussed on the next page. The tax-free exchange rules apply to transfers during marriage as well as to property settlements incident to divorce. A transfer is "incident to a divorce" if it occurs either within one year after the date the marriage ceases or, if later, is related to the cessation of the marriage such as a transfer authorized by a divorce decree. Under temporary regulations, any transfer pursuant to a divorce or separation agreement occurring within six years of the end of the marriage is considered "incident to a divorce." Later transfers qualify only if a transfer within the six-year period was hampered by legal or business disputes such as a fight over the property value.

Recipient Spouse Bears Tax Consequences

Under the tax-free exchange rules, there is no taxable gain or deductible loss on the transfer of property, even if cash is received for the property or the other spouse (or former spouse) assumes liabilities or gives up marital rights as part of a property settlement. The spouse who receives property may incur tax on a later sale because his or her basis in the property is the same as the transferor-spouse's basis; *see* the examples.

Nonresident alien. The tax-free exchange rule does not apply to transfers to a nonresident alien spouse or former spouse. A transfer before June 22, 1988, to a former spouse who was a nonresident alien was subject to the tax-free exchange rule if the transfer was "incident to a divorce."

Recipient gets carryover basis. The transferee-spouse's basis for the property is the same as the transferor-spouse's basis. Thus, the transferee bears the tax consequences of a later sale and should consider the potential tax on the appreciation in negotiating a marital settlement. In a marital settlement, he or she can lessen the tax burden by negotiating for assets that have little or no unrealized appreciation.

Transfers to Third Parties

A transfer to a third party on behalf of a spouse or former spouse qualifies for tax-free exchange treatment where the transfer is required by a divorce or separation instrument, or if you have your spouse's or former spouse's written request or consent for the transfer. The transfer is treated as if made to your spouse or former spouse, who then retransfers the property to the third party. A written request or consent must specifically state that the tax-free exchange rules of Code Section 1041 are intended, and you must receive it before filing the tax return for the year of the transfer.

EXAMPLES

1. In a property settlement accompanying a divorce, a husband plans to transfer to his wife stock worth $250,000 that cost him $50,000. In deciding whether to agree to the transfer, the wife should be aware that her basis for the stock will be $50,000; if she sells the stock, she will have to pay tax on the $200,000 gain. This tax cost should be accounted for in arriving at the settlement.

2. Basis of the property in the hands of the transferee-spouse is not increased even if cash is paid as part of the transfer. For example, a husband received a house originally owned by the wife as part of a marital settlement. Her basis for the house was $32,200. He paid her $18,000 cash as part of the settlement and when he later sold the house for $64,000, he argued that his basis for purposes of computing profit was $50,200—the wife's $32,200 basis plus his $18,000 cash payment. The IRS refused to consider the cash payment as part of basis, and the Tax Court agreed that the carry-over basis rule applies.

Transfers of U.S. Savings Bonds. The IRS has ruled that the tax-free exchange rules do not apply to transfers of U.S. Savings Bonds. For example, if a husband has deferred the reporting of interest on E or EE bonds and transfers the bonds to his ex-wife as part of a divorce settlement, the deferred interest is taxed to him on the transfer. The wife's basis for the bonds is the husband's basis plus the income he realizes on the transfer. When she redeems the bonds, she will be taxed on the interest accrued from the date of the transfer to the redemption date.

Payment for release of community property interest in retirement pay. The Tax Court allowed tax-free treatment for a payment made to a wife for releasing her community property claim to her husband's military retirement pay. The IRS had argued that the tax-free exchange rules discussed in this section did not apply to the release of rights to retirement pay that would otherwise be subject to ordinary income tax. The Tax Court disagreed, holding that the tax-free exchange rule applies whether the transfer is for relinquishment of marital rights, cash, or other property.

Transfers in trust. The tax-free exchange rules generally apply to transfers in trust for the benefit of a spouse or a former spouse if incident to a divorce. However, if the trust property is mortgaged, the transferor spouse must report a taxable gain to the extent that liabilities assumed by the transferee spouse plus the liabilities to which the property is subject (even if not assumed) exceed the transferor's adjusted basis for the property. If the transferor realizes a taxable gain under this rule, the transferee's basis for the property is increased by the gain. The rule taxing transfers of mortgaged property applies to transfers in trust after July 18, 1984.

Trust Transfer of Leveraged Property

You will not be able to avoid gain on heavily mortgaged property transferred to a trust for your spouse or to a former spouse under a divorce decree. The excess of the liabilities on the property over your adjusted basis is taxable gain.

Sole proprietorship sale to spouse. Tax-free exchange rules may apply to a sale of business property by a sole proprietor to a spouse. The buyer spouse assumes a carry-over basis even if fair market value is paid. The transferor is not required to recapture previously claimed depreciation deductions or investment credits. However, the transferee is subject to the recapture rules on a premature disposition of the property or if the property ceases to be used for business purposes.

Agreements existing on July 18, 1984. The tax-free rules generally apply to transfers made after July 18, 1984. Transfers made under agreements in effect before July 19, 1984, are subject to the tax-free rule only if both spouses make an election to have the tax-free rule apply. The election must be made on a signed statement attached to the first tax return filed by the transferor-spouse for the year in which the first transfer occurs. The transferor must also attach the statement to returns for later years in which a transfer is made under the election.

TAX-FREE EXCHANGES OF STOCK

¶6.7 Gain on the exchange of common stock for other common stock (or preferred for other preferred) of the same company is not taxable. Similarly, loss realized on such an exchange is not deductible. The exchange may take place between the stockholder and the company or between two stockholders.

An exchange of preferred stock for common, or common for preferred, in the same company, is generally not tax free, unless the exchange is part of a tax-free recapitalization. In such exchanges, the company should inform you of the tax consequences.

Convertible securities. Conversion of securities under a conversion privilege is tax free under the rules discussed at ¶5.22 .

JOINT OWNERSHIP INTERESTS

¶6.8 The change to a tenancy in common from a joint tenancy is tax free. You may convert a joint tenancy in corporate stock to a tenancy in common without income tax consequences. The transfer is tax free even though survivorship rights are eliminated. Similarly, a partition and issuance of separate certificates in the names of each joint tenant is also tax free.

A joint tenancy and a tenancy in common differ in this respect. On the death of a joint tenant, ownership passes to the surviving joint tenant or tenants. But on the death of a tenant holding property in common, ownership passes to his or her heirs, not to the other tenant or tenants with whom the property was held.

A tenancy by the entirety is a form of joint ownership recognized in some states and can be only between a husband and wife.

Dividing properties held in common. A division of properties held as tenants in common may qualify as tax-free exchanges.

For example, three men owned three pieces of real estate as tenants in common. Each man wanted to be the sole owner of one of the pieces of property. They disentangled themselves by exchanging interests in a three-way exchange. No money or property other than the three pieces of real estate changed hands, and none of the men assumed any liability of the others. The transactions qualified as tax-free exchanges and no gain or loss was recognized.

Receipt of boot. Exchanges of jointly owned property are tax free as long as no "boot," such as cash or other property, passes between the parties; *see* ¶6.3.

SETTING UP CLOSELY HELD CORPORATIONS

¶6.9 Tax-free exchange rules facilitate the organization of a corporation. When you transfer property to a corporation that you control solely in exchange for corporate stock, no gain or loss is recognized on the transfer. For control, you alone or together with other transferors (such as partners, where a partnership is being incorporated) must own at least 80% of the combined voting power of the corporation and 80% of all other classes of stock immediately after the transfer to the corporation. If you receive securities in addition to stock, the securities are treated as taxable "boot."

The corporation takes your basis in the property, and your basis in the stock received in the exchange is the same as your basis in the property. Thus, gain not recognized on the organization of the corporation may be taxed when you sell your stock, or the corporation disposes of the property.

EXAMPLE You transfer a building worth $100,000, which cost you $20,000, to your newly organized corporation in exchange for all of its outstanding stock. You realize an $80,000 gain ($100,000 − $20,000) which is not recognized. Your basis in the stock is $20,000; the corporation's basis in the building is $20,000. The following year, you sell all your stock to a third party for $100,000. The $80,000 gain is now recognized.

Transfer of liabilities. When assets subject to liabilities are transferred to the corporation, the liability assumed by the corporation is not treated as a taxable "boot," but your stock basis is reduced by the amount of liability. The transfer of liabilities may be taxable when the transfer is part of a tax avoidance scheme, or the liabilities exceed the basis of the property transferred to the corporation.

CAUTION — Consider Taxable Transfer

Before making a property transfer to a closely-held corporation, consult an accountant or an attorney on the tax consequences. It may not be to your advantage to fall within the tax-free exchange rules. This is so when you have property with potential losses or you wish the corporation to take a stepped-up basis for property.

EXCHANGES OF COINS AND BULLION

¶6.10 An exchange of "gold for gold" coins or "silver for silver" coins may qualify as a tax-free exchange of like-kind investment property. An exchange is tax free if both coins represent the same type of underlying investment. An exchange of bullion-type coins for bullion-type coins is a tax-free like-kind exchange. For example, the exchange of Mexican pesos for Austrian coronas has been held to be a tax-free exchange as both are bullion-type coins.

However, an exchange of silver bullion for gold bullion is not tax free. Silver and gold bullion represent different types of property. Silver is an industrial commodity, whereas gold is primarily an investment in itself. Similarly, an exchange of U.S. gold collector's coins for South African Krugerrands is taxable. Krugerrands are bullion-type coins whose value is determined solely by metal content, whereas the U.S. gold coins are numismatic coins whose value depends on age, condition, number minted, and artistic merit, as well as metal content. Although both coins appear to be similar because of gold content, each represents a different type of investment.

7

RETIREMENT AND ANNUITY INCOME

Retirement planning may be the final frontier for achieving substantial tax shelter benefits. For employees, coverage in a qualified employer retirement plan is a valuable fringe benefit, as employer contributions are tax free within specified limits. Certain plans allow you to make tax-free contributions of salary under a salary reduction arrangement. An advantage of all qualified retirement plans is that earnings accumulate tax free until withdrawal.

Along with tax savings opportunities come technical restrictions and pitfalls. Law changes in recent years have complicated the rules for reporting retirement income. This chapter discusses tax treatment of annuities and employer plan distributions, including how to avoid tax penalties such as for premature or excessive distributions.

 In 1993, retirement plan distributions eligible for rollover are subject to a mandatory 20% withholding tax if you do not instruct your employer to make a direct trustee-to-trustee transfer of the distribution to an IRA or another qualified employer plan.

When this book went to press, Congress was also considering other retirement rule changes, including the repeal of special averaging for individuals who were not age 50 before 1986 (¶7.4) and the $5,000 death benefit exclusion (¶7.28).

See the Tax Legislation Guide at the front of this book and the Supplement for further details.

RETIREMENT DISTRIBUTIONS ON FORM 1099-R

¶7.1 Payments from pensions, annuities, IRAs, insurance contracts, profit-sharing and other employer plans are reported to you and the IRS on Form 1099-R. All retirement distributions are shown on Form 1099-R, except for Social Security and equivalent Railroad Retirement benefits, which are shown respectively on Form SSA-1099 and RRB-1099, and distributions from nonqualified plans, which are reported on Form W-2. Form 1099-R does not have to be attached to your return unless income tax has been withheld.

A guide to the entries on Form 1099-R is shown on page 106.

Roundup of Tax-Favored Retirement Plans

Type—	General Tax Considerations—	Tax Treatment of 1992 Distributions—
Company qualified plan	A company qualified pension or profit-sharing plan offers these benefits: (1) You do not realize current income on your employer's contributions to the plan on your behalf. (2) Income earned on funds contributed to your account compounds tax free. (3) Your employer may allow you to make voluntary contributions. Although these contributions may not be deducted, income earned on the voluntary contributions is not taxed until withdrawn.	If you receive a lump sum, tax on employer contributions may be reduced by a special averaging rule; *see* ¶7.4. If you receive a lump-sum distribution in company securities, unrealized appreciation on those securities is not taxed until you finally sell the stock; *see* ¶7.10. Distributions before age 59½ are generally subject to penalties, but there are exceptions; *see* ¶7.14. Furthermore, a penalty may also apply for distributions exceeding specified ceilings; *see* ¶7.15. Rather than pay an immediate tax, you may elect to roll over a lump-sum payment to an IRA account; *see* ¶7.8. If you decide to collect your retirement benefits over a period of years; *see* ¶7.25.
Keogh or self-employed plans	You may set up a self-employed retirement plan called a Keogh plan if you earn self-employment income through your performance of personal services. You may deduct contributions up to limits discussed in Chapter 41; income earned on assets held by the plan are not taxed. You must include employees under rules explained in Chapter 41.	As a self-employed person, you generally may not withdraw funds until age 59½ unless you are disabled. Premature withdrawals are subject to a 10% penalty. Qualified distributions to self-employed persons or to beneficiaries at death may qualify for favored lump-sum treatment under the rules of ¶7.2. Employees of Keogh plans follow rules of ¶7.2 applied to qualified plans.
IRA	Anyone who has earned income may contribute to an IRA, but the contribution is deductible only if income and coverage requirements are met. Your status as a participant in an employer retirement plan and your income determines whether you may claim a full $2,000 IRA deduction, a partial deduction, or no deduction at all. *See* Chapter 8 for these deduction limitations. Where deductible contributions are allowed, IRAs offer: (1) deductions of up to $2,000 for single persons, $4,000 for working couples, and $2,250 on a joint return where only one spouse works; and (2) income earned on IRA accounts is not taxed until the funds are withdrawn. This tax-free build-up of earnings also applies where you make nondeductible IRA contributions under the rules of Chapter 8.	You may not withdraw funds without penalty unless you are age 59½ or disabled or receive IRA distributions in the form of a life-annuity. Premature withdrawals are subject to a 10% penalty. If you delay withdrawals, you must begin to take money out of the account at age 70½, *see* ¶8.14. Distributions are fully taxable as ordinary income; *see* ¶8.8. Special averaging is not allowed. Distributions exceeding $150,000 are subject to a penalty for "excess" distributions; *see* ¶7.15.
SEP	A simplified employee pension plan set up by your employer allows the employer to contribute to an IRA more than you can under regular IRA rules. You do not have to include in 1992 income any employer contributions for your account. If your employer qualifies, you may be allowed to make elective deferrals of salary to the plan, but not more than $8,728; *see also* ¶8.11.	Withdrawals are taxable under rules explained above for IRAs.
Deferred salary or 401(k) plans	If your company has a profit-sharing or stock bonus plan, the tax law allows the company to add a cash or deferred pay plan which can operate in one of two ways: (1) Your employer contributes an amount for your benefit to your trust account. You are not taxed on your employer's contribution. (2) You agree to take a salary reduction or to forgo a salary increase. The reduction is placed in a trust account for your benefit. The reduction is treated as your employer's contribution. In 1992, the maximum salary reduction is $8,728. Income earned on the trust account accumulates tax free until it is withdrawn.	Withdrawals are penalized unless you have reached age 59½, become disabled, or meet other exceptions listed at ¶7.14. At the time of withdrawal, the tax on lump-sum proceeds may be computed under rules of ¶7.2.

GUIDE TO BOX DATA ON FORM 1099-R

Box 1. The total amount received from the payor is shown here. If income tax was withheld, the amount shown is the amount *before* withholdings.

If you file Form 1040, report the Box 1 total on Line 16a if the payment is from an IRA, or on Line 17a if from a pension or an annuity. However, if the amount is a qualifying lump-sum distribution for which you are claiming averaging, use Form 4972; *see* ¶7.4.

If you file Form 1040A, report the Box 1 total on Line 10a if from an IRA, or on Line 11a if from a pension or an annuity.

If the distribution exceeds $150,000, you could be subject to a 15% penalty for excess distributions; *see* ¶7.14 for exceptions.

If you are receiving the distribution as a beneficiary, you may be entitled to a $5,000 death benefit exclusion; *see* ¶7.28.

If an exchange of insurance contracts was made, the value of the contract will be shown in Box 1, but if the exchange qualified as tax free, a zero taxable amount will be shown in Box 2a and Code 6 will be entered in Box 7.

Boxes 2a and 2b. The taxable portion of distributions from employer plans and insurance contracts may be shown in Box 2a. The taxable portion does not include your after-tax contributions to an employer plan, or insurance premium payments.

If the payor cannot figure the taxable portion, the first box in 2b should be checked. You will then have to figure the taxable amount yourself. A payment from a pension or an annuity is only partially taxed if you contributed to the cost and you did not recover your entire cost investment before 1992. *See* ¶7.22 (commercial annuity) or ¶7.25 (employee annuity) for details on computing the taxable portion if you have an unrecovered investment.

The payer of an IRA distribution will probably not compute the taxable portion, and in this case, the total distribution from Box 1 will be entered as the taxable portion in Box 2a. This amount is fully taxable unless you have made nondeductible contributions, as discussed in ¶8.8.

If the payment is from an employer plan and the "total distribution" box has been checked in 2b, *see* ¶7.2 for possible rollover and special averaging options. The taxable amount in Box 2a should *not* include net unrealized appreciation in any employer securities included in the lump-sum or the value of an annuity contract included in the distribution.

Box 3. If the payment is a lump-sum distribution, and you participated in the plan before 1974, the amount shown here may be treated as capital gain; *see* ¶7.5.

Box 4. Any federal income tax withheld is shown here. Do not forget to include it on Line 54 of Form 1040 or Line 28a of Form 1040A. Attach Copy B of Form 1099-R to your return.

Box 5. If you made after-tax contributions to your employer's plan, or paid premiums for a commercial annuity or insurance contract, your contribution is shown here, *less* any such contributions previously distributed. IRA or SEP contributions (*see* Chapter 8) are not shown here.

Box 6. If you received a qualifying lump-sum distribution that includes securities of your employer's company, the net unrealized appreciation is shown here. Unless you elect to pay tax on it currently, this amount is not taxed until you sell the securities; *see* ¶7.10.

Box 7. In Box 7, the payor will indicate if the distribution is from an IRA or SEP and enter codes that are used by the IRS to check if you have reported the distribution correctly, including any penalties. For example, if you are under age 59½ and the employer knows that you qualify for an exception to the 10% premature withdrawal penalty (¶7.14), such as the exception for separation of service after age 55, your employer will enter Code 2 in Box 7. Code 3 will be used if the disability exception applies. Code 4 is the exception for distributions at death. If Code 1 is entered, this indicates that as far as the payor knows, no penalty exception applies. However, although Code 1 is entered, you may not be subject to a penalty, as where you made a tax-free rollover; *see* ¶7.14.

If you are at least age 59½ , Code 7 should be entered.

If you contribute to a 401(k) plan and are a highly compensated employee, your employer may have to make a corrective distribution to you of contributions (and allocable income) that exceed allowable nondiscrimination ceilings. In this case, the employer will enter Code 8 if the corrective distribution is taxable in 1992, Code P if taxable in 1991, or Code D if taxable in 1990.

If a lump-sum distribution qualifies for special averaging, Code A will be entered; *see* ¶7.4 for averaging rules.

Box 8. If the value of an annuity contract was included as part of a lump sum you received, the value of the contract is shown here. For purposes of computing averaging on Form 4972, this amount is added to the ordinary income portion of the distribution; *see* ¶7.4.

Box 9. If you are receiving payment as a beneficiary, this is your share of the distribution.

Boxes 10–13. The payor may make entries in these boxes to show state or local income tax withholdings.

PAYER'S name, street address, city, state, and ZIP code		1 Gross distribution $ 174,384	OMB No. 1545-0119	Distributions From Pensions, Annuities, Retirement or Profit-Sharing Plans, IRAs, Insurance Contracts, etc.

☐ CORRECTED (if checked)

PAYER'S name, street address, city, state, and ZIP code
National Computer, Inc.
100 Cambridge Avenue
City, State xx1x1

1 Gross distribution $ 174,384
2a Taxable amount $ 174,384
OMB No. 1545-0119 — 1992

2b Taxable amount not determined ☐   Total distribution ☑

PAYER'S Federal identification number	RECIPIENT'S identification number	3 Amount in Box 2a eligible for capital gain election $ 7,241	4 Federal income tax withheld $
01-X1X0X1X	XXX-1X-X10X		

RECIPIENT'S name
Anthony Armbrister

5 Employee contributions or insurance premiums $

6 Net unrealized appreciation in employer's securities $ 16,480

Street address (including apt. no.)
120 Fillmore Drive

7 Distribution code   7A   IRA/SEP ☐   8 Other $ %

City, state, and ZIP code
City, State, 1xxxx

9 Your percentage of total distribution   100 %

Copy B
Report this income on your Federal tax return. If this form shows Federal income tax withheld in Box 4, attach this copy to your return.

This information is being furnished to the Internal Revenue Service.

Account number (optional)

10 State income tax withheld $
11 State/Payer's state number   State

12 Local income tax withheld $
13 Name of locality   City

Form **1099-R**   Department of the Treasury - Internal Revenue Service

DISTRIBUTIONS FROM QUALIFIED RETIREMENT PLANS

LUMP-SUM DISTRIBUTIONS

¶7.2 If you receive a qualified lump-sum distribution from a company retirement plan or Keogh plan, you may be able to benefit from the following favorable tax elections:

Tax-free rollover to an IRA or another qualified company plan; see ¶7.8.

Special averaging if you were at least age 50 before January 1, 1986; see ¶7.4.

Capital gain treatment for gains realized before 1974 and special averaging (for those age 50 before January 1, 1986) on the taxable balance of the distribution; see ¶7.5.

You may be eligible for tax-free rollover but not averaging because of additional averaging conditions discussed under "lump-sum tests." If you receive a lump-sum distribution and you qualify for both rollover and averaging; see ¶7.3. If you do not meet the age-50 test and are therefore barred from averaging (¶7.4), a lump-sum distribution will be subject to tax at regular rates unless it is rolled over to an IRA or other qualified plan.

Distributions from an IRA or redemptions of retirement bonds do not qualify for special averaging or capital gain treatment.

Important: If you are married, you must generally obtain your spouse's consent to elect a lump-sum distribution; see ¶7.11.

Possible Penalties

You may be subject to a 10% penalty for a lump-sum distribution received before age 59½ that is not rolled over; see ¶7.14 for details and exceptions. Furthermore, lump-sum distributions exceeding $750,000 may be subject to a separate 15% penalty for excess distributions, as explained at ¶7.15.

Lump-sum tests. To qualify as a lump-sum distribution eligible for tax-free rollover (¶7.8), all of the following three tests must be met. For special averaging (¶7.4), the same three tests must be met, and in addition, you must have been born before 1936 and participated in the plan for at least five years before the year of the distribution.

1. Payment must be from a qualified pension, profit-sharing, or stock bonus plan. A qualified plan is one approved by the IRS. A civil service retirement system that has a trust fund may be treated as a qualified plan. Ask your retirement plan administrator whether the plan qualifies. If your employer has more than one plan of the *same* kind (several pension plans, or several profit-sharing plans, for example) you must receive payment from all of such plans to get lump-sum treatment.
2. If you are an *employee* under age 59½ , the payment must be made because you quit, retired, were laid off, or fired (*see*

¶7.6). After you reach age 59½, the distribution may be made for any reason.

If you are *self-employed*, a Keogh plan distribution qualifies only if made after reaching age 59½, or because you became totally and permanently disabled before age 59½.

3. Within one of your taxable years (usually a calendar year), you must receive the balance of what is due you under the plan. A distribution of only part of your account is not a lump-sum distribution. If your employer's plan uses more than one trust, you must receive a distribution of all that is due you from each of the trusts.

Under the one-year test, a series of payments received during one of your tax years can qualify as a lump-sum distribution. For example, you retired on October 15, 1992, and start receiving monthly annuity payments under your company's plan on November 2, 1992. On February 4, 1993, you take the balance to your credit in lieu of any future annuity payments. The payments do *not* qualify as a lump sum; you did not receive them within one taxable year. However, if you had taken the balance of your account on or before December 31, 1992, all the payments would have qualified.

Lump-sum treatment is not lost if you receive a qualifying lump-sum distribution after separation-from-service, and in the next year, you receive a payment that is attributable to your last year of work; the later payment is not part of the "balance" that must be received within one of your tax years.

For purposes of special averaging, (¶7.4), accumulated deductible contributions you voluntarily made after 1981 and before 1987 are not considered part of your account balance and do not qualify for averaging.

Termination of plan allows rollover. Even if the above lump-sum tests are not met, a total distribution of your account received within one of your tax years is eligible for tax-free rollover (¶7.8) if made because of the termination of the employer's plan or the complete discontinuation of contributions to a profit-sharing or stock bonus plan.

Beneficiaries. A surviving spouse who receives a lump-sum distribution upon the death of an employee may make a tax-free rollover to an IRA. Beneficiaries other than surviving spouses may not make a tax-free rollover; see ¶7.8.

If the deceased employee was born before 1936, any beneficiary (not just a surviving spouse) may elect special averaging or capital gain treatment for a 1992 lump-sum distribution of the account; see ¶7.7.

Court ordered lump-sum distribution to a spouse or former spouse. A distribution received by a spouse or former spouse of an employee under a qualified domestic relations order (QDRO) may be eligible for tax-free rollover, or in some cases, special averaging treatment; see ¶7.12.

SHOULD YOU CLAIM AVERAGING OR MAKE A ROLLOVER?

¶7.3 If you cannot claim averaging, you may avoid current tax by rolling over the lump-sum distribution. To avoid withholding tax on a 1993 distribution, you must have your employer directly transfer the distribution to an IRA or qualified plan of another employer. If *you* receive the distribution, a 20% tax will be withheld. If you later decide to make a rollover, you have 60 days from the time of receiving the distribution to do so. However, to avoid tax on the entire distribution, you will have to include in the rollover an amount equal to the withheld tax. In 1992, distributions were not subject to mandatory withholding tax. Withholding is discussed further at ¶26.11.

If you can average, you should determine whether paying tax currently using the averaging method will be more favorable to you than making a tax-free rollover. If you receive more than one lump sum during the year, you must make the same choice for all of them; you may not roll over one distribution and claim averaging for another.

If you need the lump-sum payout immediately or may need it within a few years, pay tax now using special averaging. However, a distribution before age 59½ will be subject to a 10% penalty in addition to regular tax unless an exception at ¶7.14 is available.

If you qualify for special averaging but do not plan to use the funds until retirement, estimate whether you will build a larger retirement fund by rolling over the distribution and letting earnings accumulate tax free, or by using special averaging and investing the funds to give you the greatest after-tax return. This is not an easy projection. You must consider the number of years to retirement, your expected tax bracket at retirement, and the estimated yield you can earn on your funds. Generally speaking, a younger person who is not planning to retire for many years may get a greater after-tax return by making a rollover and investing at peak rates, and then taking withdrawals over his or her life expectancy at retirement. However, if you make the rollover to an IRA and later decide to withdraw funds before age 59½, you will be subject to a penalty unless you are disabled or you receive payments over your life expectancy; *see* ¶8.12.

Finally, keep in mind the tax rule that allows you to elect averaging *only once*. If you receive a lump-sum distribution that qualifies for averaging but you plan to continue working, a later lump-sum distribution will not qualify for averaging if you elect averaging for the current distribution. If you make a rollover to an IRA and later join a company with a retirement plan that accepts rollovers, you may transfer the funds to the company plan and averaging could apply when you receive a qualifying lump sum from that plan.

If you make a rollover to an IRA, you cannot change your mind and cancel the IRA account in order to apply special averaging. The rollover election is irrevocable, according to the IRS.

Possibility of a Repeal of Averaging

It is possible that any projection of future use of averaging may be frustrated by a repeal of the averaging provision. When this book went to press, Congress was considering legislation to repeal the right to use averaging for those born after 1935. *See* the Supplement for developments.

Disqualification of retirement plan. If you receive a lump-sum distribution from a plan which loses its exempt status, the IRS may argue that the distribution does not qualify for lump-sum treatment. Under the IRS position, you may not roll over the distribution to an IRA or elect special averaging. The Tax Court holds that if the plan qualified when contributions were made, an allocable portion of the distribution is a qualified lump sum. However, the majority of appeals courts that have reviewed Tax Court decisions on this issue have supported the IRS position.

TEN-YEAR OR FIVE-YEAR AVERAGING ON FORM 4972

¶7.4 If you were born on or before December 31, 1935, and if you were a participant in the plan for five or more years before the 1992 taxable year, you may elect averaging on Form 4972 for a 1992 lump-sum distribution meeting the three tests at ¶7.2. There are two averaging methods: (1) a ten-year averaging method based on 1986 tax rates, or (2) a five-year averaging method based on current 1992 tax rates.

If you were born on or after January 1, 1936, you are not allowed to claim averaging until you receive a lump-sum distribution after age 59½. For example, assume that in 1993, at age 47, you change jobs and receive a lump-sum distribution from the plan of your old employer. You may not claim either ten-year averaging or five-year averaging for the 1993 distribution. The distribution will be taxed at regular 1993 rates unless a tax-free rollover is made under the rules of ¶7.8. If you continue to work and receive a qualifying lump-sum distribution after reaching age 59½, you will be able to make a one-time election of five-year averaging (but not ten-year), *assuming Congress does not repeal averaging.*

Averaging on 1992 returns. If you meet the age 50 test and were a participant in the plan for five years before 1992, follow IRS instructions to Form 4972 for applying either the ten-year averaging or the five-year averaging methods to a qualifying lump-sum distribution received during 1992. If you received more than one qualified lump sum in 1992, you may elect averaging for one of the distributions only if you elect averaging for all of them.

The amount eligible for averaging is the taxable portion of the distribution shown in Box 2a of Form 1099-R. You may also elect to add to the Box 2a amount any net unrealized appreciation in employer securities (shown in Box 6) included in the lump sum. If the distribution includes capital gain (Box 3 of Form 1099-R) and you want to apply the special 20% capital gain rate (*see* ¶7.5), you should subtract the capital gain in Box 3 from the taxable amount in Box 2a and apply averaging to the balance of ordinary income.

What is the difference between five-year and ten-year averaging? The five-year averaging tax is based upon the 1992 tax rate schedule for single persons, even if you use joint return or head of household rates for your other income. The ten-year averaging tax is based on the 1986 rates for single persons. Tables for applying the five-year and ten-year methods are included in the instructions to Form 4972. Whichever averaging method you use, the tax computed on Form 4972 is reported on Form 1040, Line 39, as an additional tax. It is completely separate from the tax computed on your other income reported on Form 1040.

Ten-year averaging will provide a lower tax in most cases, except for extremely large distributions. For 1992 lump sums, ten-year averaging gives a lower tax if the adjusted total taxable amount shown on Form 4972 is less than $395,293. The adjusted total taxable amount is the ordinary income portion of the distribution, decreased by any death benefit exclusion claimed by a beneficiary, and increased by the actuarial value of any annuity contract included in the lump sum. The actuarial value of an annuity contract is not taxable when you receive it, but you must add it to the ordinary income portion of the lump sum before computing averaging.

If the adjusted total taxable amount *exceeds* $395,292, five-year averaging provides a lower tax than ten-year averaging in 1992.

Once in a Lifetime Election

You are allowed to elect averaging only once after 1986. If you were born before January 1, 1936, and elect averaging for a 1992 distribution after separating from service (¶7.6), you will not be able to claim averaging again if you join another company and receive a lump-sum distribution from the new employer. On the other hand, if you do not claim averaging for a qualifying 1992 lump-sum distribution because you expect to receive another distribution in the future from a new employer, you risk the possibility that Congress will repeal the right to use the averaging method.

If before 1987, you elected ten-year averaging and were under age 59½, you may elect averaging for a 1992 distribution. However, if you were over age 59½ when you made the pre-1987 election, you are barred from electing averaging again.

Community property. Only the spouse who has earned the lump sum may use averaging. Community property laws are disregarded for this purpose. If a couple files separate returns and one spouse elects averaging, the other spouse is not taxed on the amount subject to the computation.

Form 4972—Worksheet

EXAMPLE A husband in a community property state receives a lump-sum distribution of which the ordinary income portion is $10,000. He and his wife file separate returns. If averaging is not elected, $5,000, or one-half, is taxable in the husband's return and the other $5,000 in his wife's return. However, if he elects the averaging method, only he reports the $10,000 on Form 4972.

Pre-1974 capital gain portion of distribution. If a portion of your 1992 lump-sum distribution is attributable to plan participation before 1974 (¶7.5), you may elect to treat it as capital gain if you were born before 1936. The capital gain portion may be treated as ordinary income eligible for averaging, or you may elect to have the capital gain part taxed at a flat 20% rate, with the ordinary income portion of the distribution subject to the averaging computation; *see* also ¶7.5.

If you were *not* at least age 50 on January 1, 1986, you may not treat any portion of it as capital gain. You may not apply the flat 20% rate to the pre-1974 portion of the lump-sum distribution; or include any part of it as capital gain on your 1992 Schedule D.

Part IV	Complete this part to choose the 10-year averaging method. (See instructions.)			
1	Ordinary income part from Form 1099-R, Box 2a minus Box 3. If you did not make the Schedule D election or complete Part II, enter the taxable amount from Box 2a of Form 1099-R. (See instructions.)	1	167,143	
2	Death benefit exclusion. (See instructions.)	2	0	
3	Total taxable amount—Subtract line 2 from line 1	3	167,143	
4	Current actuarial value of annuity, if applicable (from Form 1099-R, Box 8)	4	0	
5	Adjusted total taxable amount—Add lines 3 and 4. If this amount is $70,000 or more, skip lines 6 through 9, and enter this amount on line 10	5	167,143	
6	Multiply line 5 by 50% (.50), but **do not** enter more than $10,000	6		
7	Subtract $20,000 from line 5. If line 5 is $20,000 or less, enter -0-	7		
8	Multiply line 7 by 20% (.20)	8		
9	Minimum distribution allowance—Subtract line 8 from line 6	9		
10	Subtract line 9 from line 5	10	167,143	
11	Federal estate tax attributable to lump-sum distribution. Do not deduct on Form 1040 or Form 1041 the amount attributable to the ordinary income entered on line 1. (See instructions.)	11	0	
12	Subtract line 11 from line 10	12	167,143	
13	Multiply line 12 by 10% (.10)	13	16,714	30
14	Tax on amount on line 13. See instructions for Tax Rate Schedule	14	2,851	29
15	Multiply line 14 by ten (10). If no entry on line 4, skip lines 16 through 21. Enter this amount on line 22	15	28,512	90
16	Divide line 4 by line 5 and enter the result as a decimal. (See instructions.)	16		
17	Multiply line 9 by the decimal amount on line 16	17		
18	Subtract line 17 from line 4	18		
19	Multiply line 18 by 10% (.10)	19		
20	Tax on amount on line 19. See instructions for Tax Rate Schedule	20		
21	Multiply line 20 by ten (10)	21		
22	Subtract line 21 from line 15. (Multiple recipients, see instructions.)	22	28,512	90
23	Tax on lump-sum distribution—Add Part II, line 2, and Part IV, line 22. Enter on Form 1040, line 39, or Form 1041, Schedule G, line 1b ▶	23	28,512	90

CAPITAL GAIN TREATMENT
FOR PRE-1974 PARTICIPATION

¶7.5 The portion of a lump-sum distribution attributable to pre-1974 participation is eligible for capital gain treatment if you were born before 1936.

On Form 1099-R, the company paying the lump-sum distribution shows the capital gain portion in Box 3. The ordinary income portion is Box 2a (taxable amount) minus Box 3. If you are an employee, capital gain treatment is available to the extent allowed by the following rules, even if you do not elect averaging. If you are self-employed, capital gain treatment is allowed only if averaging is elected for the ordinary income (post-1973) portion.

Age 50 or over on January 1, 1986. You may elect to treat the pre-1974 portion as capital gain subject to a flat rate of 20% on Form 4972. If you meet the five-year plan participation test (¶7.4), the tax on the balance of the distribution may be figured under the averaging method. The 20% rate for the capital gain portion is fixed by law, and applies regardless of the tax rate imposed on your other capital gains. Alternatively, you may elect to treat the capital gain portion as ordinary income eligible for averaging, provided the five-year participation test has been met.

You may not elect to report any portion of the pre-1974 portion of a 1992 lump-sum distribution as long-term capital gain on Schedule D.

Under the one-time election rule, if you elect to apply the averaging and/or 20% capital gain rule for a 1992 distribution, you may not elect averaging or capital gain treatment for any later distribution.

Capital gain treatment not allowed for individuals below age 50 before January 1, 1986. After 1991, no part of a lump-sum distribution qualifies as capital gain if you were not age 50 before 1986. An election to claim capital gain treatment on Schedule D was phased out between 1987 and 1991. If you made such an election, you will not be allowed to claim five-year averaging for a lump-sum distribution received after age 59½.

SEPARATION-FROM-SERVICE TEST
FOR EMPLOYEES UNDER AGE 59½

¶7.6 Employees who have not reached the age of 59½ must be "separated from service" for a distribution to qualify as a lump-sum distribution; see ¶7.2. The separation-from-service test requires that you have retired, resigned, or have been discharged. However, even though you are separated from service, you may elect averaging (¶7.4) only if you have reached age 50 before January 1, 1986, and have been a plan participant more than five years before the year of the distribution. If you were not age 50 or over before January 1, 1986, or were a plan participant less than five years, a lump-sum distribution received upon separation from service before age 59½ may be rolled over tax free under the rules of ¶7.8, but averaging may not be claimed.

The IRS has held that a retiring employee who enters into a part-time consulting arrangement with the same firm may be considered to be separated from service, and thus, lump-sum distribution treatment is available. If a plan is terminated but you continue on the job, distributions are not entitled to special averaging treatment if you have not reached age 59½, but a rollover is allowed; see ¶7.2. Under the law, you do not have to be separated from service after you reach age 59½. However, in rulings, the IRS has held that if you receive a lump-sum distribution from a pension plan (not a profit-sharing plan) after age 59½ but continue to work for the company, you also must reach the normal retirement age as fixed in the company plan to get lump-sum treatment unless the plan was terminated.

Reorganizations or mergers. The separation-from-service test generally prevents averaging when a qualified plan is terminated following a reorganization or merger of a company. According to the IRS, an employee under age 59½ who remains with a successor corporation and who receives a lump-sum distribution following reorganization or liquidation is not separated from service. However, a lump sum paid on account of termination of a plan may be rolled over tax free to an IRA; see ¶7.8.

If there is a significant change in job responsibilities following a merger or reorganization, the IRS or Tax Court may hold that an employee was separated from service. The Tax Court has held that an executive working for a successor firm was "separated-from-service" on evidence of substantial changes in staff, duties, and company business. Finally, the IRS, in a private letter ruling, eased its position and allowed 20 employees of a merged company lump-sum tax benefits. They were given new jobs or took on additional responsibilities. The manager of engineering and maintenance of the old company became responsible for energy conservation and security; the former personnel manager was rehired as the purchasing and planning manager. Furthermore, the new company reduced salaries and employee benefits and eliminated the former profit-sharing plan. Given these changes in job positions and pay benefits, employees were considered "separated from service."

Partnership plans. Lump-sums paid on the termination of a plan when a partnership dissolves do not qualify for special averaging when the employees continue to work for the successor partnership. Similarly, an employee of a partnership, who becomes a partner and has to quit the firm's employee profit-sharing plan, may not treat a distribution as a lump sum. He or she is still serving the firm.

LUMP-SUM PAYMENTS RECEIVED
BY BENEFICIARY

¶7.7 A beneficiary of a deceased employee may elect averaging or capital gain treatment for a qualifying lump sum distribution (¶7.2) received because of the employee's death, provided the employee was born before 1936. If the payment qualifies, Form 4972 is used to compute tax under the ten-year or five-year averaging method, or to make the 20% capital gain election. Follow the Form 4972 instructions to claim the up-to-$5,000 death benefit exclusion (¶7.28). Any federal estate tax attributable to the distribution reduces the taxable amount on Form 4972. Any election made as a beneficiary does not affect your right to elect lump-sum treatment to a distribution from your own plan.

A beneficiary may elect averaging, even though the deceased employee was in the plan for less than five years. Furthermore, the age of the beneficiary is irrelevant. So long as the deceased employee was at least age 50 before January 1, 1986, the beneficiary may elect five-year or ten-year averaging, or the 20% capital gain method.

A lump sum paid because of an employee's death may qualify for capital gain and averaging treatment, although the employee received annuity payments before death.

An estate or trust receiving a lump-sum payment may also apply the lump-sum rules.

A qualifying beneficiary may elect averaging or capital gain treatment only once for distributions received as the beneficiary of a deceased employee.

Payment received by a second beneficiary (after the death of the first beneficiary) is not entitled to lump-sum treatment or the death benefit exclusion.

Beneficiaries of self-employed individuals who receive a qualifying lump-sum distribution from a Keogh plan apply the same rules as beneficiaries of deceased employees, as just discussed.

EXAMPLES 1. Gunnison's father was covered by a company benefit plan. The father died, as did Gunnison's mother, before benefits were fully paid out. Gunnison received a substantial lump sum. He argued that he collected on account of his father's death. The IRS disagreed. The Tax Court and an appeals court sided with the IRS. Gunnison was entitled to the payment following his mother's death, not his father's death. For special lump-sum treatment, the payout must arise solely on account of the death of the covered employee.

2. Robert's employer announced the termination of its pension plan. Before benefits were distributed, Robert died. His widow received a lump-sum distribution as his beneficiary. After subtracting the amount attributable to Robert's contributions, she excluded $5,000 as a death benefit and treated the balance as a lump-sum distribution. The IRS claimed she received the distribution on the termination of the plan, not because of Robert's death. The Tax Court agreed. Distribution was made to her under the termination provision, not the provisions for withdrawal due to separation-from-service or death. She could not take a death benefit exclusion, and the entire distribution (less Robert's contributions) could not be treated as a lump-sum distribution.

Lump Sums to Multiple Beneficiaries

A lump-sum distribution to two or more individuals may qualify for averaging and capital gain treatment. Each beneficiary may separately elect the averaging method for the ordinary income portion, even though other beneficiaries do not so elect. Follow the Form 4972 instructions for multiple recipients.

Distribution to trust or estate. If a qualifying lump sum is paid to a trust or an estate, the employee, or if deceased, his or her personal representative, may elect averaging.

TAX-FREE ROLLOVER

¶7.8 Total and partial distributions paid in 1992 from an employer plan are not subject to tax if they were rolled over within 60 days of receipt to an IRA or qualified plan of a new employer. The 1992 tests for total and partial distributions are explained in the next column and on page 112. These tests do not apply to distributions after 1992. In 1993 and later years, *all* distributions may be rolled over *except for* periodic payments received for life or over a period of at least 10 years, or any minimum required distribution under ¶7.13. However, to avoid the 20% mandatory withholding tax after 1992, *your employer must directly transfer* the rollover funds to an IRA or to the plan of your new employer; *see* ¶26.11.

On your return, you report a total rollover only for information purposes. For example, if you rolled over a 1992 lump-sum distribution to an IRA, report the distribution on Line 17a of Form 1040 or Line 11a of Form 1040A, but enter zero as the taxable amount on Line 17b or Line 11b. If you roll over only part of the distribution, the amount of the lump sum *not* rolled over is entered as the taxable amount.

The rollover amount may *not* include your voluntary after-tax contributions to the qualified plan; they are tax free to you when you receive them. The rollover *may* include salary deferral contributions that were excludable from income when made, such as qualifying deferrals to a 401(k) plan. The rollover may also include accumulated deductible employee contributions (and allocable income) made after 1981 and before 1987.

You may not claim a deduction for your rollover to an IRA.

Total distributions in 1992 eligible for tax-free rollover. A 1992 lump-sum distribution was considered a total distribution eligible for tax-free rollover if it met these three tests:

1. The distribution was all that was due you under the plan. If the employer plan used more than one trust, you must have received a distribution of all that was due you from each trust.
2. The payment or payments were all made within your 1992 tax year.
3. If you are an employee, the distribution was made because you separated from service, or reached age 59½. If you are self-employed, the distribution must have been made because you reached age 59½, or became totally disabled.

Even if the 1992 distribution did not meet these tests, you could roll over a "total distribution" received because of a termination of the plan, or a complete discontinuation of profit-sharing or stock basis plan contributions; a series of payments, all of which were received within your 1992 tax year, qualifies. A total distribution also includes a payment of accumulated deductible employee contributions you make after 1981 and before 1987.

A rollover is allowed regardless of how long you were in the plan; the five-year participation rule for averaging does not apply to rollovers.

Figuring the 60-day period for rollovers. A rollover must be completed by the 60th day following the day on which you receive the distribution. The IRS held in a private letter ruling that if in one year you receive several payments, constituting a lump-sum distribution from an employer plan, the 60-day period starts from the date of the last payment. For example, you retired in July 1991 and received a partial distribution from your company plan. You were told that you would receive the balance by December 1991. Provided all payments are received before the end of 1991, the payments received in July and December are considered a lump-sum distribution eligible for rollover. You have 60 days from the date of the final December payment to complete the rollover.

Extension of 60-day rollover period for frozen deposits. If you receive a qualifying distribution from a retirement plan and deposit the funds in a financial institution which becomes bankrupt or insolvent, you may be prevented from withdrawing the funds in time to complete a rollover within 60 days. If this happens, the 60-day period is extended while your account is "frozen." The 60-day rollover period does not include days on which your account is frozen. Further, you have a minimum of 10 days after the release of the funds to complete the rollover.

Beneficiaries. A surviving spouse may roll over to an IRA a lump-sum distribution paid on the death of a spouse or upon termination of a qualified retirement plan. The distribution may not be rolled over to a qualified plan of the surviving spouse's current employer; *see* ¶26.11 for withholding rules.

A beneficiary other than a surviving spouse may not make a rollover; distributions must begin under the payout rules discussed in ¶7.13, unless special averaging is elected; *see* ¶7.4.

Multiple rollover accounts allowed. You may wish to diversify a distribution in different investments. There is no limit on the number of rollover accounts you may have. A lump-sum distribution may roll over to several IRAs or retirement annuities.

IRA Rollover Election Is Irrevocable

A rollover to an IRA is irrevocable, according to the IRS. At the time of the rollover, you must elect in writing to irrevocably treat the contribution as a rollover. You may not later change your mind in order to claim averaging. Before making a rollover, figure what the current tax would be on the lump-sum distribution under the special averaging method. Compare it with an estimate of tax payable on a later distribution of the rolled-over account.

Consider further that if you make a rollover to an IRA and not to a new employer's qualified plan, you lose the right to apply the special averaging method to the sum, unless the IRA is used as a conduit between two company plans, as discussed below. Special averaging applies only to a lump-sum distribution from a qualified plan. It does not apply to a withdrawal from an IRA account. If you are under the age of 59½ also consider that a rollover to an IRA locks in your funds. If you withdraw funds from the IRA, you may be subject to a penalty; see ¶8.8. Other points to consider in deciding whether to make a rollover are discussed at ¶7.3.

Partial rollovers of lump sum allowed. You do not have to roll over the entire lump-sum distribution; you may make a partial rollover. While the amount rolled over is not taxed, the part *not* rolled over is taxable and you may not apply capital gain treatment or special averaging to the distribution; see ¶26.11 for withholding rules.

Rollover of 1992 partial distributions. If a 1992 distribution equaled at least 50% of your plan account balance, and it was not one of a series of periodic payments, it could be rolled over tax free to an IRA within 60 days. The distribution had to be paid upon your separation from service or upon disability. A self-employed person who separated from service could also make a rollover.

Under the 50% test, disregard amounts credited to you under other kinds of qualified plans maintained by the same employer.

A surviving spouse of a deceased employee could elect to roll over a qualifying partial distribution.

If you rolled over a partial distribution, a later distribution of your entire account balance will not qualify for special averaging or capital gain treatment.

IRA Conduit Between Employer Plans

An IRA may be used as a conduit between two company plans. The funds in the IRA may be transferred to another qualified plan of a company which employs you, provided the plan of your new employer accepts rollovers. A qualifying lump-sum distribution from the new employer plan may be eligible for special averaging; see ¶7.4. The IRA must consist of only the assets (or proceeds from the sale of such assets) distributed from the first qualified plan and income earned on the account. You may not contribute to the account set up as a conduit. You may set up another IRA to which you make annual contributions. In such a case, you will have two accounts; one consisting of the assets (or proceeds from assets' sale) of the plan of your prior employer and the other of your own contributions.

EXAMPLE You leave your employer and receive a lump-sum distribution of $5,000 from his qualified plan to which you did not contribute. You place the amount in an IRA. Four years later, you start work for another company that has a qualified plan. The new plan permits you to transfer the assets of the IRA to the plan. You must make the transfer within 60 days after closing the account.

Distribution includes life insurance policy. Your employer's retirement plan may invest in a limited amount of life insurance which is then distributed to you as part of a lump-sum retirement distribution. You may be able to roll over the life insurance contract to the qualified plan of your new employer but not to an IRA. The law bars investment of IRA funds in life insurance contracts.

Rollover of annuities from tax-exempt groups and schools. If you participate in a tax-sheltered annuity program described in ¶7.20, you may roll over a qualifying distribution to an IRA.

Rollover of distribution received under divorce or support proceeding. In a qualified domestic relations order (QDRO) meeting special tax law tests, a state court may give you the right to receive all or part of your spouse's or former spouse's retirement benefits. The payments you receive are generally taxable, but you may be able to elect special averaging (¶7.12), or make a tax-free rollover of a distribution to an IRA. To make a rollover, the distribution must be your entire share in the plan and be received within one of your taxable years. If property as well as cash is received, you may roll over only the same property you received from the plan. If only part of the distribution is rolled over, the balance is taxed in the year of receipt; see ¶26.11 for withholding rules. You are not subject to the 10% penalty for premature distributions even if under age 59½. In figuring your tax, you are allowed a pro-rated share of your former spouse's cost investment, if any. You may not elect averaging or capital gain treatment for the portion not rolled over.

ROLLOVER OF PROCEEDS FROM SALE OF PROPERTY

¶7.9 A lump-sum distribution from a qualified plan may include property, such as stock. If you plan to roll over the distribution, you may find that a bank does not want to take the property. If you sell the property, you may roll over the sale proceeds to an IRA as long as the sale and rollover occur within 60 days of receipt of the distribution. If you roll over all of the proceeds, neither gain nor loss is recognized. The proceeds are treated as part of the distribution. If you make a partial rollover of sale proceeds, you must report as capital gain the portion of the gain that is allocable to the retained sale proceeds.

If you receive cash and property, and you sell the property but only make a partial rollover, you must designate how much of the rolled-over cash is from the employer distribution and how much from the sale proceeds. The designation must be made by the time for filing your return (plus any extensions) and is irrevocable. If you do not make a timely designation, the IRS will allocate the rollover between cash and sales proceeds on a ratable basis; the allocation will determine tax on the retained amount.

If you made after-tax contributions to the plan, you may not roll over the portion of the distribution equal to your contributions.

SECURITIES DISTRIBUTION

¶7.10 When a plan distributes securities of your company, the value of the securities may or may not be subject to tax at the time of the distribution. The amount reported as income depends on the value of the securities, the amount contributed by the company toward their purchase, and whether or not the distribution qualifies as a total lump-sum payment.

Lump-sum payments. If the distribution is of appreciated securities and is part of a lump-sum payment meeting the tests of ¶7.2, the net unrealized appreciation is not subject to tax at the time of distribution unless you elect to treat it as taxable. Assuming the election is not made, only the amount of the employer's contribution is subject to tax. Tax on the appreciation is delayed until the shares are later sold by you at a price exceeding cost basis. If, when distributed, the shares are valued at below the cost contribution of the employer, the fair market value of the shares is subject to tax. If you contributed to the purchase of the shares and their value is less than your contribution, you do not realize a loss deduction on the distribution. You realize a loss only when the stock is sold or becomes worthless at a later date. If a plan distributes worthless stock, you may deduct your contributions to the stock as a miscellaneous itemized deduction.

The net unrealized appreciation in employer's securities is shown in Box 6 of the Form 1099-R received from the payor. It is not included in the taxable amount in Box 2.

Election to waive tax-free treatment. You may elect to include the unrealized appreciation in employer securities as income. You might consider making this election when you want to accelerate income to the current year by taking into account the entire lump-sum distribution. The election is made on Form 4972 for the year the distribution is received.

EXAMPLES 1. *Shares valued below your cost contribution.* You contributed $500 and your employer contributed $300 to buy 10 shares of company stock having at the time a fair market value of $80 per share. When you retire, the fair market value of the stock is $40 per share, or a total of $400. You do not realize income on the distribution, and you do not have a deductible loss for the difference between your cost contribution and the lower fair market value. Your contribution to the stock is its basis. This is $50 per share. If you sell the stock for $40 per share, you have a capital loss of $10 per share. However, if you sell the stock for $60 per share, you have gain of $10 per share.

2. *Appreciated shares.* You receive 10 shares of company stock to which only the employer contributed toward their purchase. Your employer's cost was $50 a share. At the time of distribution, the shares are valued at $80 a share. Your employer's contribution of $50 a share or $500 is included as part of your taxable distribution. The appreciation of $300 is not included. The cost basis of the shares in your hands is $500 (the amount currently taxable to you). The holding period of the stock starts from the date of distribution. However, if you sell the shares for any amount exceeding $500 and up to $800, your profit is long-term gain regardless of how long you held the shares. If you sell for more than $800, the gain exceeding the original unrealized appreciation of $300 is subject to long-term capital gain treatment only if the sale is long-term from the date of distribution. Thus, if within a month of the distribution, you sold the shares for $900, $300 would be long-term gain; $100 would be short-term gain.

Other than lump-sum payments. If you receive appreciated securities in a distribution that does not meet the lump-sum tests of ¶7.2, you report as ordinary income the amount of the employer's contribution to the purchase of the shares and the appreciation allocated to the employer's cost contribution. You do not report the amount of appreciation allocated to your after-tax contribution to the purchase. However, if you make a rollover of a partial distribution to an IRA (¶7.8), you are immediately taxed on the appreciation allocated to your own contributions.

EXAMPLE A qualified plan distributes ten shares of company stock with an average cost of $100, of which the employee contributed $60 and the employer, $40. At the date of distribution, the stock had a fair market value of $180. The portion of the unrealized appreciation attributable to the employee's contribution is $48 (60% of $80); the employer's is $32 (40% of $80). The employee reports $72 as income; the employer's cost of $40 and share of appreciation which is $32. The basis of each share is $132 which includes employee

contribution of $60 and the $72 reported as taxable income. Net unrealized appreciation and cost contributions must be supplied by the company distributing the stock.

SURVIVOR ANNUITY FOR SPOUSE

¶7.11 If you have been married for at least a year, the law generally requires that payments of vested benefits be in a specific annuity form to protect your surviving spouse. All defined benefit and money purchase plans must provide benefits in the form of a qualified joint and survivor annuity unless you, with the written consent of your spouse, elect a different form of benefit. A qualified joint and survivor annuity must also be provided by profit-sharing or stock bonus plans, unless you do not elect a life annuity payment and the plan provides that your nonforfeitable benefit is payable in full upon your death to your surviving spouse, or to another beneficiary if the spouse consents or there is no surviving spouse.

Under a qualified joint and survivor annuity, you receive an annuity for your life and your surviving spouse receives an annuity for his or her life that is no less than 50% of the amount payable during your joint lives. Unless you obtain spousal consent, you must take this type of annuity; you may not take a lump-sum distribution or a single-life annuity ending when you die. A single-life annuity pays higher monthly benefits during your lifetime than the qualified joint and survivor annuity.

The law also requires that a pre-retirement survivor's annuity be paid to your surviving spouse if you die before the date vested benefits become payable. For example, under a defined contribution plan such as a profit-sharing plan, the pre-retirement annuity payments must be equal to those under a single-life annuity valued at 50% or more of your account balance. The pre-retirement annuity is automatic unless you, with your spouse's consent, agree to a different benefit.

Your plan should provide you with a written explanation of these annuity rules within a reasonable period before the annuity starting date, as well as the rules for electing to waive the joint and survivor annuity benefit and the pre-retirement survivor annuity.

 Spouse Must Consent in Writing

Your spouse must consent in writing to any waiver and the selection of a different type of distribution. A spouse's consent must be witnessed by a plan representative or notary public. An election to waive the qualified joint and survivor annuity may be made during the 90-day period ending on the annuity starting date. An election to waive the qualified pre-retirement survivor annuity may be made from the first day of the plan year in which you reach age 35 up until your date of death. A waiver is revocable during the time permitted to make the election.

Exception. These survivor annuity requirements generally do not apply to couples who have been married for less than one year as of the participant's annuity starting date or, if earlier, the date of the participant's death.

Cash out of annuity. If the present value of the qualified joint and survivor annuity is $3,500 or less, your employer may "cash out" your interest without your consent by making a lump-sum distribution of the present value of the annuity before the annuity starting date. After the annuity starting date, you and your spouse must consent to a cash out. Written consent is required for a cash out if the present value of the annuity exceeds $3,500. Similar cash-out rules apply to pre-retirement surviving annuities.

COURT-ORDERED DISTRIBUTIONS TO FORMER SPOUSE

¶7.12 To cover alimony or support obligations, a state domestic relations court can require that all or part of a plan participant's retirement benefits be paid to a spouse, former spouse, child, or other dependent. Administrators of pension, profit-sharing, or stock bonus plans are required to honor a qualified domestic relations order (QDRO) that meets specific tax law tests. For example, the QDRO generally may not alter the amount or form of benefits provided by the plan, but it may authorize payments after the participant reaches the earliest retirement age, even if he or she continues working.

If you are the spouse or former spouse of an employee and you receive a distribution pursuant to a QDRO, the distribution is generally taxable to you. However, if the distribution is your entire share of the plan benefits, as fixed by the QDRO, and you receive it within one of your tax years, you may make a tax-free rollover to an IRA; *see* ¶7.8. Furthermore, if your spouse or former spouse (the plan participant) was born before 1936, a distribution of your entire share of the benefits is eligible for special averaging, provided the distribution, if received by your spouse (or former spouse), would satisfy the lump-sum distribution tests of ¶7.2; *see* ¶7.4. Transfers from a governmental or church plan pursuant to a qualifying domestic relations order are also eligible for special averaging or rollover treatment.

Distributions to a child or other dependent. Payments from a QDRO are taxed to the plan participant, not to the dependent who actually receives them, where the recipient is not a spouse or former spouse.

WHEN RETIREMENT BENEFITS MUST BEGIN

¶7.13 The longer you can defer taking retirement distributions from your company plan or Keogh plan, the greater will be the tax-free buildup of your retirement fund. To cut off this tax deferral, the law requires distributions to begin by a specified date. Unless you reached age 70½ before 1988, you will have to begin receiving distributions in the year after you reach age 70½. This is true even if you do not retire and continue to work. If you did reach age 70½ before 1988 and you continue to work, you may be able to delay the start of distributions until after you retire, as discussed in the next column.

By the required beginning date, you must start to receive annual distributions over a period no longer than your life expectancy or the joint life expectancy of you and your designated beneficiary; you may be subject to a 50% penalty if you fail to take the minimum required distribution.

Important: The rules for determining minimum required distributions are complicated. Contact your employer's plan administrator well in advance to determine your options in selecting beneficiaries and figuring a payout schedule.

If you reach age 70½ after 1987. You have to start receiving distributions no later than April 1 of the calendar year following the calendar year in which you reach age 70½, even if you continue working. For example, if you reach age 70½ during 1992, your first distribution must be no later than April 1, 1993, even if you continue to work. For all later years, including the year after the year you reach age 70½, a distribution must be taken by the end of such year.

This required beginning date applies to distributions from all qualified corporate and Keogh plans, qualified annuity plans, and Section 457 plans of tax-exempt organizations. The rules also apply to distributions from tax-sheltered annuities (¶7.20) but only for benefits accrued after 1986; there is no mandatory beginning date for tax-sheltered annuity benefits accrued before 1987.

For those reaching age 70½ during 1988, the IRS allowed a one-year extension; their first distribution was not due until April 1, 1990.

Effect of Waiting Until April Deadline

You have until April 1 of the year after the year in which you reach 70½ to take your first distribution. However, if no distribution is taken during your 70½ year, you will have to take two distributions during the following year. For example, if you reach age 70½ in 1992, and receive your first distribution between January and April 1, 1993, you must also receive a distribution for 1993 by December 31, 1993. This could substantially increase your 1993 taxable income, and possibly subject more of your social security benefits to tax; *see* chapter 34.

Pre-1984 designations. Individuals who made a special election before 1984 to receive distributions under pre-1984 rules are not subject to the age 70½ rule or the beneficiary distribution methods discussed on page 115.

Governmental or church plans. If you are covered by a governmental plan or church plan, you do not have to begin receiving distributions until April 1 of the year following the *later* of (1) the year of retirement, or (2) the year in which you reach age 70½.

If you reached age 70½ before 1988. If you are an employee or self-employed person who reached age 70½ before January 1, 1988, and do not own more than a 5% ownership interest, you do not have to start to receive distributions until April 1 of the calendar year following the calendar year in which you retire. For example, if you reached age 70½ in 1987 or in an earlier year and do not retire until 1993, your first distribution does not have to be made until April 1, 1994, the year after the year of retirement.

You qualify to delay distributions until after retirement only if you did not own more than a 5% ownership interest during the plan year ending with or within the calendar year in which you reached age 66½ or in any later year. A more than 5% owner who reached age 70½ before 1988 was required to begin receiving distributions by April 1 of the year following the year he or she reached age 70½ even if still working.

HOW MUCH MUST YOU RECEIVE AFTER AGE 70½?

All qualified retirement plans, including Keogh plans for the self-employed, are subject to the same distribution rules. When you retire or begin distributions under the above age 70½ beginning date rule, you may spread payments over your life, over the joint lives of yourself and any designated beneficiary, or over a specific period that does not exceed your life expectancy or the joint life expectancies of yourself and any designated beneficiary. In figuring the payout schedule, your life expectancy may be recalculated annually. If payments are made over the joint life expectancies of you and your spouse, your spouse's life expectancy may also be recalculated annually. To determine your life expectancy, use Table V shown at ¶7.23. For joint life expectancies, *see* the sample table in ¶8.14.

Basing payments on the joint life expectancies of yourself and a younger beneficiary will extend the withdrawal period, but the law imposes a limit if the beneficiary is someone other than your spouse. For example, a beneficiary more than 10 years younger than you will be treated as being only 10 years younger, regardless of actual age. This requirement does not affect payments required for spouses under the qualified joint and survivor annuity rule of ¶7.11. As discussed at ¶7.11, your plan must automatically provide annuity benefits in the form of a qualified joint and survivor annuity if you are married, unless you and your spouse elect otherwise.

Minimum distributions that you are required to take under these rules may not be rolled over tax free.

PAYOUTS TO BENEFICIARIES

The distribution rules for beneficiaries depend on when the employee or self-employed plan participant dies.

If employee dies after required beginning date. Where an employee or self-employed individual dies after the required beginning date (April 1 of the year after the year in which age 70½ is reached), beneficiaries must continue to take distributions at least as rapidly as the participant did during his or her lifetime. For example, if an employee had elected to receive benefits in equal annual installments over his 20-year life expectancy, but died after 10 years, the beneficiary would have to receive equal annual installments over the remaining 10 years but could elect to accelerate payments over a shorter period.

A surviving spouse receiving an annuity under the survivor benefit rules of ¶7.11 receives payments over his or her lifetime, starting at the participant's death.

If employee dies before required beginning date. If an employee or self-employed person dies before the April 1 required beginning date, distribution rules depend on who the beneficiary is and the terms of the plan. The plan may give the beneficiary the option of (1) taking distributions annually over his or her life expectancy, or (2) completing all distributions by the end of the fifth year following the year of the employee's death. On the other hand, the plan may specify which method must be used. If the plan does not specify the method and the beneficiary does not make an election by December 31 of the year following the year of death, the life expectancy method discussed below must be used by a surviving spouse; a beneficiary other than a surviving spouse must use the five-year method.

Life expectancy method. If the beneficiary has the option of taking distributions over his or her life expectancy, the distribution starting date depends on who the beneficiary is:

A *surviving spouse* who is not receiving annuity payments under the rules of ¶7.11 may delay the start of distributions until the later of: (1) December 31 of the year in which the deceased spouse would have reached 70½, or (2) December 31 of the year after the year of death. By that later date, the surviving spouse must take the first distribution based upon his or her life expectancy.

A *non-spouse beneficiary* has until December 31 of the year following the year of the employee's death to take the first distribution under his or her life expectancy. If he or she has the option to elect this life expectancy method but fails to do so by December 31 of the year following the year of the employee's death, the five-year method must be used.

Five-year method. Under this method, all distributions must be completed by December 31 of the fifth year following the year of the employee's death.

Penalty for Insufficient Distributions

If you are still working in the year you reach age 70½, set up a payment schedule with your employer's plan administrator. Otherwise, you will be subject to a 50% penalty if you fail to take a distribution from the plan by the required beginning date or you receive a distribution that is insufficient under the required distribution methods. Unless waived by the IRS, the 50% penalty will apply to the difference between the amount you should have received and the amount you did receive. The IRS may waive the penalty if you show that the shortfall was due to reasonable error and that you are taking steps to correct it. To apply for a waiver, compute the penalty on Form 5329 and attach a letter of explanation. Individuals who made a special election before 1984 to receive distributions under pre-1984 rules will not be subject to the penalty.

PENALTY FOR DISTRIBUTIONS BEFORE AGE 59½

¶7.14 Unless you are totally disabled or one of the other exceptions listed below applies, distributions before you reach age 59½ from a qualified corporate or Keogh plan, qualified annuity plan, and tax-sheltered annuity are subject to a 10% penalty. The penalty does not apply to Section 457 plans of tax-exempt employers or state or local governments.

The penalty is 10% of the taxable distribution. If you make a tax-free rollover within 60 days of receipt (¶7.8), the distribution is not taxable and not subject to the penalty. If a partial rollover is made, the part *not* rolled over is taxable and subject to the penalty. The penalty is figured on Form 5329, which you must attach to your Form 1040.

A similar 10% penalty applies to IRA distributions before age 59½; *see* ¶8.8 for IRA penalty rules. The penalty for pre-age 59½ distributions from deferred annuities is at ¶7.22.

Exceptions to the penalty. The penalty does not apply to rollovers or distributions made on or after the date you reach age 59½. Distributions made on account of your total disability or to a beneficiary after your death are exempt from the penalty regardless of age. Furthermore, the following distributions are also exempt from the 10% penalty, even if received before age 59½. If your employee "knows" that an exception applies, this will be indicated in Box 7 of Form 1099-R on which the distribution is reported.

- Distributions upon separation from service if you are age 55 or over in the year you retire or leave the company;
- Distributions used to pay deductible medical expenses exceeding 7.5% of adjusted gross income (whether or not an itemized deduction for medical expenses is claimed);
- Distributions received after separation from service which are part of a series of substantially equal payments (at least annually) over your life expectancy, or over the joint lives of yourself and your designated beneficiary. If before age 59½ you receive a lump sum or change the distribution method so that it does not qualify for the exception and you are not totally disabled, a recapture penalty tax will apply to all amounts received before age 59½, as if the exception had never been allowed. The recapture tax also applies to payments received before age 59½ if substantially equal payments are not received for at least five years;
- Distributions paid to an alternate payee pursuant to a qualified domestic relations court order (QDRO);
- Distributions made pursuant to a designation under the 1982 Tax Act (TEFRA);
- Distributions to an employee who separated from service by

March 1, 1986, provided that accrued benefits were in pay status as of that date under a written election specifying the payout schedule.

Corrective distributions from 401(k) plans. If you are considered a highly compensated employee and excess elective deferrals or excess contributions are made on your behalf, a distribution of the excess to you is not subject to the penalty.

Filing Form 5329 for Exceptions

If your employer correctly entered a penalty exception code in Box 7 of Form 1099-R, you do not have to file Form 5329 to claim the exception. You also do not have to file Form 5329 if you made a tax-free rollover of the entire distribution. You must file Form 5329 if you qualify for an exception, other than the rollover exception, that is not indicated in Box 7 of Form 1099-R.

PENALTY FOR EXCESS DISTRIBUTIONS

¶7.15 You may be subject to a 15% penalty if you withdraw amounts from an employer retirement plan or IRA *over* the following limits—

$750,000 for lump sums qualifying for averaging; or
$150,000 for IRA distributions *plus* all other types of distributions from qualified pension, profit-sharing, or stock-bonus plans, annuity plans, or tax-sheltered annuities.

The 15% penalty is imposed on the excess amount. For example, in 1992, if you receive a $200,000 IRA distribution and the following exceptions do not apply, the penalty is $7,500 (15% × $50,000 excess).

The penalty is computed on Form 5329, which must be attached to your Form 1040. If an excess distribution is also subject to the penalty for premature withdrawals (¶7.14), the 15% excess distribution penalty is offset by the 10% premature withdrawal penalty; follow the Form 5329 instructions.

"Grandfather" election for benefit accruals as of August 1, 1986. The $150,000 and $750,000 penalty thresholds do not apply if on your 1987 or 1988 return, you made a special "grandfather" election (on Form 5329) for accrued benefits on August 1, 1986, exceeding $562,500. A lower threshold of $140,276 (IRAs and pensions) or $701,380 (lump sums) applies to 1992 distributions; the amounts are adjusted annually for inflation. The penalty applies only to 1992 distributions that exceed the *greater* of (1) the $140,276 or $701,380 threshold, or (2) the amount treated as a recovery of the "grandfathered" amount, as explained in the Form 5329 instructions.

Exceptions. The following amounts are not counted as distributions for purposes of the $150,000 or $750,000 limit and may help you avoid the penalty:

- Distributions equal to your after-tax contributions to a plan or your investment in the contract, including nondeductible IRA contributions;
- Distributions from a qualified plan which you roll over tax free to an IRA or to another qualified plan, or IRA distributions which are rolled over tax free to another IRA;
- Distributions to a former spouse pursuant to a qualified domestic relations order. The former spouse takes the distributions into account in determining whether the penalty applies;
- Distributions received by a deceased individual's beneficiary;

- Distribution of excess salary reduction deferrals; and
- Distributions of excess contributions made to satisfy nondiscrimination rules.

RESTRICTIONS ON LOANS FROM COMPANY PLANS

¶7.16 Within limits, you may receive a tax-free loan from a qualified company plan, annuity plan or government plan. The maximum loan is the lesser of 50% of your vested account balance, or $50,000, but the $50,000 limit is subject to reductions as discussed below. Loans must be repaid within five years, unless they are used for buying your principal residence.

These rules generally apply only to employees. For a self-employed person, a retirement plan loan is a prohibited transaction that usually results in penalties; *see* ¶41.9.

If your vested accrued benefit is $20,000 or less, you are not taxed if the loan, when added to other outstanding loans from all plans of the employer, is $10,000 or less. However, as a practical matter, your maximum loan may not exceed 50% of your vested account balance because of a rule that only allows up to 50% of the vested balance to be used as loan security. Loans in excess of the 50% cap are allowed only if additional collateral is provided.

If your vested accrued benefit exceeds $20,000, then the maximum tax-free loan depends on whether you borrowed from any employer plan within the one-year period ending on the day before the date of the new loan. If you did not borrow within the year, you are not taxed on a loan that does not exceed the *lesser* of $50,000 or 50% of the vested benefit.

If there were loans within the one-year period, the $50,000 limit must be further reduced. The loan, when added to the outstanding loan balance, may not exceed $50,000 *less* the excess of (1) the highest outstanding loan balance during the one-year period (ending the day before the new loan), over (2) the outstanding balance on the date of the new loan. This reduced $50,000 limit applies where it is less than 50% of the vested benefit; if 50% of the vested benefit was the smaller amount, that would be the maximum tax-free loan.

EXAMPLE Your vested plan benefit is $200,000. Assume that in January 1993 you borrow $30,000 from the plan. On November 1, 1993 , when the outstanding balance on the first loan is $20,000, you want to take another loan without incurring tax. You may borrow an additional $20,000 without incurring tax: The $50,000 limit is first reduced by the outstanding loan balance of $20,000—leaving $30,000. The reduced $30,000 limit is in turn reduced by $10,000, the excess of $30,000 (the highest loan balance within one year of the new loan) over $20,000 (the balance on November 1).

The $20,000 loan limit applies because it is less than 50% of the vested benefit of $200,000.

Repayment period. Generally, loans within the previously discussed limits must be repayable within five years to be tax free. However, if you use the loan to purchase a principal residence for yourself, the repayment period may be longer than five years; any reasonable period is allowed. This exception does not apply if the plan loan is used to improve your existing principal residence, to buy a second home, or to finance the purchase of a home or home improvements for other family members; such loans are subject to the five-year repayment rule.

Level loan amortization required. Tax-free treatment for a loan is allowed only if you are required to repay using a level amortization schedule, with payments at least quarterly. According to congressional committee reports, you may accelerate repayment, and the employer may use a variable interest rate and require full repayment if you leave the company.

Spousal consent generally required. All plans subject to the joint and survivor rules of ¶7.11 must require spousal consent in order to be able to use your account balance as security for the loan in case you default. Check with your plan administrator for consent requirements.

Interest deduction limitations. If you want to borrow from your account to buy a first or second residence, and you are not a "key" employee (¶3.2), you can obtain a full interest deduction by using the residence as collateral for the loan. Your account balance may not be used to secure the loan. Key employees are not allowed any interest deduction for plan loans.

If you use a plan loan for investment purposes and are not a key employee, and the loan is not secured by your elective deferrals (or allocable income) to a 401(k) plan, the loan account interest is deductible up to investment income; *see* ¶15.9. Interest on loans used for personal purposes is not deductible, unless your residence is the security for the loan.

Unpaid Loan Taxable If You Leave Job

If you leave your company before your loan is paid off, the company will reduce your vested account balance by the outstanding debt. For example, if your vested account balance is $100,000, and the outstanding loan is $20,000, your account balance is reduced to $80,000, which your company pays you in a lump sum. However, according to the IRS, you are treated as if you received the entire $100,000. The $20,000 loan balance is treated as taxable income from cancellation of indebtedness because it was paid off from your retirement account. If you do not roll over (¶7.8) the entire $100,000 within 60 days, you will be taxed on the portion not rolled over, and possibly be subject to the 10% penalty for pre-age 59½ withdrawals; *see* ¶7.14. To avoid tax on the $20,000, you would have to use other resources or borrow funds in order to complete a total rollover within the 60-day period. If making a rollover to a new employer's plan, it might be possible to get an immediate $20,000 loan from the new plan, which could be put right back into the plan to complete the rollover.

401(K) AND OTHER TAX-DEFERRED SAVINGS PLANS

TAX BENEFITS OF 401(K) PLANS

¶**7.17** If your company has a profit-sharing or stock-bonus plan, it has the opportunity of giving you additional tax sheltered pay. The tax law allows the company to add a cash or deferred pay plan, called a 401(k) plan, which can operate in one of two ways:

1. Your employer contributes an amount for your benefit to a trust account. You are not taxed on your employer's contribution.
2. You agree to take a salary reduction or to forgo a salary increase. The reduction is placed in a trust account for your benefit. The reduction is not considered taxable pay because it is treated as your employer's contribution. In addition, your company may match part of your contribution. For 1992, the law limits salary reduction deferrals to $8,728; *see* ¶7.18.

Making salary deferrals may be an ideal way to defer income and get a tax-free buildup of earnings. Although there is no income tax, the contribution is subject to Social Security tax.

Income earned on the trust account accumulates tax free until it is withdrawn. Withdrawals before age 59½ are restricted, as explained in ¶7.19.

A lump-sum distribution may be eligible for special averaging under the rules of ¶7.4. Lump-sum distributions exceeding $750,000 may be subject to the excess distribution penalty; *see* ¶7.15.

An employer may not require you to make elective deferrals in order to obtain any other benefits, apart from matching contributions. For example, benefits provided under health plans or other compensation plans may not be conditioned on your making salary deferrals to a 401(k) plan.

Nondiscrimination rules. The law imposes strict contribution percentage tests to prevent discrimination in favor of highly compensated employees. If these tests are violated, the employer is subject to penalties and the plan could be disqualified unless the excess contributions (plus allocable income) are distributed back to the highly compensated employees within specified time limits.

Partnership plans. Partnership plans that allow partners to vary annual contributions are treated as 401(k) plans by the IRS. Thus, elective deferrals are subject to the annual limit (¶7.18) and the special 401(k) plan nondiscrimination rules apply. However, partnerships may allow new incoming partners to make a one-time irrevocable election to contribute a specified amount or percentage of compensation to the partnership plan for the entire period they are with the partnership. Contributions pursuant to the one-time election are not treated as part of a 401(k) plan.

Partnerships had the opportunity during 1989 to avoid 401(k) plan treatment by allowing current partners to make the one-time election. Partnerships that missed the 1989 deadline face plan disqualification for plan years starting before 1992 unless they distribute to the partners, by the end of the plan year that starts in 1992, any elective deferrals in excess of the 401 (k) plan limits (plus allocable income) for the prior years. Excess contributions under nondiscrimination rules also must be distributed. Such corrective distributions will be reported as income to the partners on Form 1099-R.

LIMIT ON SALARY REDUCTION DEFERRALS

¶**7.18** The law limits the maximum tax-free salary reduction contribution you can make. For 1992, the limit is $8,728, up from $8,475 in 1991. The $8,728 limit will be further increased after 1992 by an inflation factor. Employer plans must limit elective deferrals to the annual tax-free ceiling; otherwise, the plan could be disqualified. As discussed below, certain highly compensated employees may be unable to take advantage of the maximum tax-free ceiling ($8,728 in 1992) because of restrictions imposed by nondiscrimination tests.

The $8,728 limit applies to total salary reduction deferrals made to 401(k) plans as well as to simplified employee pension plans; *see* ¶8.11. If you participate in more than one such plan, the $8,728 limit applies to the total salary reductions for all the plans. If you also contribute to a tax-sheltered annuity (¶7.20), the $8,728 cap is increased by the salary reduction contributions to the tax-sheltered annuity, up to an overall total of $9,500.

The $8,728 tax-free limit applies only to an employee's elective deferrals from pay. An employer may make matching or other additional contributions, *provided* the total contribution, including the employee's salary deferral, does not exceed the lesser of 25% of compensation or $30,000.

If you make salary deferrals to more than one plan and the total exceeds the annual limit, the excess deferrals are taxable in the year of the deferral. Furthermore, if the excess contribution (plus income earned on such excess) is not distributed to you by the first April 15 following the year of the excess deferral, it is taxed again when distributed from the plan. Excess deferrals (and earnings) distributed by the April 15 deadline are not subject to the 10% penalty for premature distributions (¶7.14) even if you are under age 59½.

Exception for one-time elections. The annual ceiling on salary deferrals does not apply if at the time you become eligible to participate in the plan you make a one-time irrevocable election to have a specified percentage of your pay contributed to the plan for as long as you are employed.

Reduced Deferral Limit For Highly Compensated Employees

To avoid discrimination problems an employer may set a lower limit for elective salary deferrals by highly compensated employees than the ceiling generally allowed ($8,728 for 1992).

If after contributions are made, the plan fails to meet the nondiscrimination tests, the excess contributions will either be returned to the highly compensated employees, or kept in the plan but recharacterized as after-tax contributions. In either case, the excess contribution is taxable. Form 1099-R will indicate the excess contribution.

WITHDRAWALS FROM 401(K) PLANS RESTRICTED

¶7.19 By law, you may not withdraw funds attributable to elective salary reduction contributions until you reach age 59½, are separated from service, become totally disabled, or show financial hardship. Under IRS rules, it is difficult to qualify for hardship withdrawals; *see* below. Lump-sum withdrawals are also allowed if the plan terminates, or the corporation sells its assets or its interest in a subsidiary and you continue to work for the buyer or the subsidiary. However, the hardship provision and age 59½ withdrawal allowance do not apply to certain "pre-ERISA" money purchase pension plans (in existence June 27, 1974).

Withdrawals before 59½. If withdrawals are allowed before age 59½, including qualifying hardship withdrawals (*see* below), you are subject to the 10% penalty for premature withdrawals unless you meet one of the exceptions listed at ¶7.14.

Loans. If you are allowed to borrow from the plan, the loan restrictions at ¶7.16 apply.

Qualifying for hardship withdrawals. IRS regulations restrict

hardship withdrawals. If you qualify under the following restrictive rules you may withdraw only your elective deferrals plus a limited amount of income. Income allocable to elective deferrals may be withdrawn only if it was credited to your account as of the end of the last plan year ending before July 1, 1989; the plan may provide an even earlier cutoff date for income. Employer matching contributions, nonelective contributions, and other plan earnings may not be included.

The IRS requires you to show an immediate and heavy financial need that cannot be met with other resources.

Financial need includes the following expenses (this list may be expanded by the IRS in rulings):

- Purchase of a principal residence for yourself (but not mortgage payments);
- Tuition and related expenses over the next 12 months for yourself, your spouse, children or other dependents;
- Medical expenses previously incurred for yourself, your spouse or dependents, or expenses to obtain medical care for such persons;
- Preventing your eviction or mortgage foreclosure; and
- Paying funeral expenses for a family member.

Even if you can show financial need, you may not make a hardship withdrawal if you have other resources to pay the expenses. You do not have to provide your employer with a detailed financial statement, but you must state to your employer that you cannot pay the expenses with: compensation, insurance, or reimbursements; liquidation of your assets without causing yourself hardship by virtue of the liquidation; stopping your contributions, including salary deferrals, to the plan; other distributions or nontaxable loans from plans of any employer; or borrowing from a commercial lender. Your spouse's assets, as well as those of your minor children, are considered to be yours unless you show that they are not available to you. For example, property held in trust for a child or under the Uniform Gifts to Minors Act is not treated as your property.

Under a special rule, you are considered to lack other resources if you have taken all available distributions from all plans of the employer, including nontaxable loans, and you suspend making any contributions to any of the employer's plans for at least 12 months after receipt of the hardship distribution. Furthermore, all of the employer's plans must provide that for the year after the year of the hardship distribution, elective contributions must be limited to the excess of the annual salary deferral limitation over the elective contributions made for the year of the hardship distribution.

ANNUITIES FOR EMPLOYEES OF TAX-EXEMPTS AND SCHOOLS

¶7.20 If you are employed by a tax-exempt religious, charitable, or educational organization, or are on the civilian staff or faculty of the Uniformed Services University of the Health Services (Department of Defense), you may be able to arrange for the purchase of nonforfeitable tax-sheltered annuities.

The purchase is generally made through a reduction of salary which is used to pay for the contract. The amount of the salary reduction used to buy the contract is not taxable if it comes within specified limits. The tax rules for computing the exclusion are complicated, as there are several limitations and exceptions.

Tax-free exclusion allowance. The tax-sheltered contribution, called the exclusion allowance, is generally 20% of your pay multiplied by the number of years of service with your employer *less* tax-free contributions made in prior years by your employer to a tax-sheltered annuity or to any qualified plan: Salary reductions count as tax-free employer contributions. Under this formula, you may not be allowed to exclude any part of the current year's salary reduction because of employer contributions in prior years. Further, even though allowed by the 20% of pay/years of service formula, the maximum tax-free salary reduction may not exceed the *lower* of 25% of your pay or $9,500. However, employees with at least 15 years of service may be able to defer up to $12,500. *See* below for details of the $9,500 limit and the exceptions.

A tax-deferred plan may be funded in mutual fund shares.

EXAMPLE A public school teacher earning $20,000 agrees to a $2,000 salary reduction to be used to purchase an annuity contract. The employer also contributes $1,800 per year to a pension trust for the teacher's account. In the first year, the entire salary reduction contribution is tax free as it is within the $3,600 exclusion allowance (20% of the reduced salary of $18,000 × one-year service). In later years, part or all of the reduction may be taxed because the exclusion allowance is reduced by prior tax-free employer contributions.

Alternative contribution ceilings. Subject to the maximum $9,500 salary reduction limit, employees of schools, hospitals, churches, health and welfare service agencies, and home health services may be able to elect tax-free contributions exceeding 25% of pay (but no more than $30,000). Such employees may elect a limitation equal to the lower of (1) the general 20% of pay exclusion allowance, (2) 25% of pay plus $4,000, or (3) $15,000. Once an election is made, it is irrevocable. Such employees also may make an irrevocable election to disregard the general 20% exclusion allowance. If the election is made, the tax-free contribution equals the contribution limit for defined contribution plans, the lesser of 25% of pay or $30,000.

Finally, in the year of separation from service, such employees may elect a tax-free contribution limit equal to the lower of (1) $30,000, or (2) the exclusion allowance, taking into account no more than 10 years of service.

A church employee whose adjusted gross income is $17,000 or less is allowed a minimum exclusion allowance equal to the lesser of $3,000 of his or her includable compensation. In addition, an election may be made permitting contributions exceeding the 25% of pay test, up to $10,000 per year; however, there is a lifetime contribution limit of $40,000.

$9,500 limit. Even if allowed by the general exclusion allowance rule, the maximum tax-free salary reduction from a tax-sheltered annuity plan cannot exceed the lower of $9,500 or 25% of pay. If you work for more than one employer, the $9,500 limit applies to all tax-sheltered annuity arrangements in which you participate. The $12,500 limit for certain employees with 15 years of service is discussed in the next column.

Your contributions are *not* considered salary reductions, and, therefore, are not subject to the $9,500 or $12,500 limit, if they are made under a one-time irrevocable election at the time you became eligible to participate in the plan.

If in addition to a tax-sheltered annuity, you make salary deferrals to a 401(k) plan or simplified employee pension plan, the $9,500 limit applies to the total deferrals; *see* ¶7.18. If you defer more than $9,500, the excess is taxable. Further, if a salary reduction deferral in excess of the $9,500 limit is made and the excess is not distributed to you by April 15 of the following year, the excess will be taxed twice—not only in the year of deferral but again in the year it is actually distributed. To avoid the double tax, a distribution of any excess deferral *plus* the income attributable to such excess should be distributed no later than April 15 of the year following the year in which the excess deferral is made. A distribution by the following April 15 is not subject to the premature withdrawal penalty (¶7.14) or the penalty for excess distributions (¶7.15). A distribution

of the excess deferral is taxed in the year for which the deferral was made; distributed income is taxed in the year received.

The $9,500 limit applies only to elective contributions from your pay under a salary-reduction arrangement. If your employer makes separate contributions, the total of elective salary reductions (not to exceed $9,500) plus the employer contributions may be up to the contribution limit for defined contribution plans, which is generally the lower of 25% of pay or $30,000.

Special catch-up election may allow $12,500 deferral. If allowed under the general 20% of pay/years of service exclusion formula, and by the 25% of pay limit, the $9,500 salary reduction ceiling is increased to $12,500 for employees of educational organizations, hospitals, churches, home health service agencies, and health and welfare service agencies who have completed 15 years of service. However, the extra $3,000 annual deferral may not be claimed indefinitely. There is a lifetime limit of $15,000 on the amount of extra deferrals (over $9,500) allowed. Furthermore, the extra deferrals may not be claimed after lifetime elective deferrals to the plan exceed $5,000 multiplied by your years of service.

Note: As the annuity contribution rules have been stated in general terms and are also subject to Treasury regulations, we suggest that you rely on the amount computed by your employer or the issuer of the contract. Also *see* IRS Publication 571 for detailed examples.

Distributions from tax-sheltered annuities. Distributions from a tax-sheltered annuity do not qualify for special averaging (¶7.4), but a tax-free rollover of a lump sum or partial distribution may be made to another tax-sheltered annuity or IRA; *see* ¶7.8 for rollover rules.

Annuity payments are taxed under the general rules for employee annuities, discussed at ¶7.25. The payments are subject to the $150,000 limit for purposes of the excess distribution penalty (¶7.15). Further, benefits accruing after 1986 are subject to the age 70½ required beginning date rules of ¶7.13 and a penalty may be imposed for failure to take minimum required distributions.

To change tax-sheltered annuity investments, you may direct the issuer of your current annuity contract to make a direct transfer of your account to a different issuer. The transfer is tax free, provided that distributions with respect to salary reduction contributions are restricted under both contracts. Generally, such distributions are allowed only when the employee reaches age 59½, separates from service, becomes disabled, suffers financial hardship, or dies.

DEFERRED PAY PLANS FOR GOVERNMENT EMPLOYEES

¶7.21 Federal government employees may make tax-free salary-reduction contributions to the Federal Thrift Savings Fund. Employees of state and local governments and of tax-exempt organizations may be able to make tax-free salary-reduction contributions to a Section 457 deferred compensation plan.

Federal employees. Federal employees may elect to defer up to 10% of their basic pay to the Federal Thrift Savings Fund, but no more than the limit on elective deferrals. The deferral limit for 1992 is $8,728, the same as for 401(k) plans; *see* ¶7.18. The limit is subject to increases for inflation. Deferrals are not taxed until distributed from the plan. The deferred amount is counted as wages for purposes of computing Social Security taxes and benefits.

Distributions from the Thrift Savings Fund are generally fully taxable. However, lump-sum distributions are eligible for special averaging under the rules of ¶7.4, or tax-free rollover treatment (¶7.8). A distribution received before the year in which you reach age 55 is subject to the 10% penalty for premature distributions unless you are disabled or qualify for the medical exception discussed at ¶7.14.

Section 457 state and local government plans. State and local governments may set up deferred compensation plans which allow employees to defer annually up to the lesser of $7,500 or 33⅓% of includable compensation (not including the deferrals). A limited "catch-up" provision allows employees in the last three years before reaching normal retirement age to defer larger amounts, provided that the full $7,500 or 33⅓% limit has not been used in prior years. The catch-up deferral, figured under IRS regulations, may not exceed $15,000. Deferred pay and income allocable to the deferrals is not taxed until the year it is distributed or made available. Distributions are fully taxable; averaging and rollover treatment may not be claimed.

The $7,500 or $15,000 limits do not apply to vacation leave, sick leave, disability pay, compensatory time, severance pay, or death benefits plans.

If an employee participates in more than one Section 457 plan, the $7,500 or $15,000 limit applies to total deferrals under all the plans. Furthermore, if an employee also participates in a tax-sheltered annuity plan, simplified employee pension (SEP), 401(k) plan, or Section 501(c)(18) plan (created before June 25, 1959, and funded solely by employee contributions), the $7,500 or 33⅓% limit, and the $15,000 catch-up limit, is reduced by tax-free deferrals to the other plan.

Distributions to employees or beneficiaries may not be made before the year the employee turns age 70½, the employee separates from service, or faces an "unforeseeable" emergency, assuming the plan allows payment in cases of emergency. Under IRS regulations, an unforeseeable emergency generally means severe financial hardship resulting from a sudden illness or accident of the employee or a dependent, or loss of property due to a casualty. If the employee can obtain funds by ceasing deferrals to the plan or by liquidating assets without causing himself severe financial hardship, payment from the plan is not allowed. The regulations specifically prohibit payments from the plan to purchase a home or pay for a child's college tuition.

See ¶7.13 for required distribution starting dates after age 70½ and minimum payout rules. Where an employee dies before receiving distributions, the account balance must be paid to non-spouse beneficiaries over a period of 15 years or less. Payments to a surviving spouse may be made over the spouse's life expectancy.

Note: Check with your employer for other details on Section 457 contributions and distribution rules.

Tax-exempt organizations eligible. Section 457 plans may also be set up by nongovernmental tax-exempt organizations other than churches.

REPORTING COMMERCIAL ANNUITIES

FIGURING THE TAXABLE PART OF YOUR ANNUITY

¶7.22 Tax treatment of a distribution depends on whether you receive it before or after the annuity starting date, and on the amount of your investment. A cash withdrawal before age 59½ from an annuity contract is generally subject to a 10% penalty but there are exceptions; the penalty is discussed at the end of this section. If your annuity is from an employer plan and it started after July 1, 1986, *see* ¶7.25.

Payments before the annuity starting date. If your commercial annuity contract was purchased after August 13, 1982, withdrawals before the annuity starting date are taxable to the extent that the cash value of the contract, immediately before the distribution, exceeds your investment in the contract. This rule also applies to withdrawals that are attributed to investments made after August 13, 1982, where the contract was purchased before August 14, 1982. Loans under the contract or pledges are treated as cash withdrawals. Withdrawals from contracts bought by a qualified retirement plan are discussed at ¶7.25.

If the contract was purchased before August 14, 1982, withdrawals before the annuity starting date are taxable only if they exceed your investment. Loans are tax free and are not treated as withdrawals subject to this rule. Where additional investments were made after August 13, 1982, cash withdrawals are first considered to be tax-free distributions of the investment before August 14, 1982. If the withdrawal exceeds this investment, the balance is fully taxable to the extent of earnings on the contract, with any excess withdrawals treated as a tax-free recovery of the investment made after August 14, 1982.

Payments on or after the annuity starting date. If the withdrawal is a regular annuity payment, that part of the annuity payment allocated to your cost investment is treated as a nontaxable return of the cost; the balance is taxable income earned on the investment. You may find the taxable part of your annuity payment by following the six steps below. If you have a variable annuity, the computation of the tax-free portion is discussed following Step 6.

Payments on or after the annuity starting date that are *not* part of the annuity, such as dividends, are generally taxable, but there are exceptions. If the contract is a life insurance or endowment contract, withdrawals of earnings are tax free to the extent of your investment, unless the contract is a modified endowment contract discussed at ¶33.9.

Payments on a complete surrender of the contract or at maturity are taxable only to the extent they exceed your investment.

TAXABLE PORTION OF ANNUITY PAYMENTS

If the payor of the contract does not provide the taxable amount in Box 2a of Form 1099-R, you can compute the taxable amount of your commercial annuity using the following steps.

If you have an employee annuity (¶7.25) that started before July 2, 1986, you also can use the following six steps to figure your taxable payment. If your employee annuity started after July 1, 1986, you may use a simplified method discussed at ¶7.25 and ¶7.26.

1. Figure your investment in the annuity contract. If you have no investment in the contract, annuity income is fully taxable; therefore, ignore Steps 2 through 6.

If your annuity is—	Your cost is—
Single premium annuity contract	The single premium paid.
Deferred annuity contract	The total premiums paid.
A gift	Your donor's cost.
An employee annuity	The total of your contributions to the plan plus your employer's contributions which you were required to report as income; see ¶7.25.
With a refund feature	What was paid for the annuity, less the value of the refund feature.

From cost, you subtract the following items:

Any premiums refunded, and rebates or dividends received on or before the annuity starting date.

Additional premiums for double indemnity or disability benefits.

Amounts received under the contract before the annuity starting date to the extent these amounts were not taxed; see below.

Value of a refund feature; see below.

Value of refund feature. Your investment in the contract is reduced by the value, if any, of the refund feature.

Your annuity has a refund feature when these three requirements are present: (1) The refund under the contract depends, even in part, on the life expectancy of at least one person; (2) the contract provides for payments to a beneficiary or the annuitant's estate after the annuitant's death; and (3) the payments to the estate or beneficiary are a refund of the amount paid for the annuity.

The value of the refund feature is figured by using a life expectancy multiple which may be found in Treasury Table III or Table VII depending on the date of your investment; the tables are in IRS Publication 939.

Where an employer paid part of the cost, the refund is figured on only the part paid by the employee.

The refund feature is considered to be *zero* if (1) for a joint and survivor annuity, both annuitants are age 74 or younger, the payments are guaranteed for less than 2½ years, and the survivor's annuity is at least 50% of the first annuitant's (retiree's) annuity; or (2) for a single-life annuity without survivor benefits, the payments are guaranteed for less than 2½ years and you are age 57 or younger if using the new (unisex) annuity tables, age 42 or younger if male and using the old annuity tables, or age 47 or younger if female and using the old annuity tables.

Also subtract from cost any tax-free recovery of your investment received *before* the annuity starting date, as previously discussed.

2. Find your expected return. This is the total of all the payments you are to receive. If the payments are to be made to you for life, your expected return is figured by multiplying the amount of the annual payment by your life expectancy as of the nearest birthday to the annuity starting date. The annuity starting date is the first day of the first period for which an annuity payment is received. For example, on January 1 you complete payment under an annuity contract providing for monthly payments starting on July 1 for the period beginning June 1. The annuity starting date is June 1. Use that date in computing your investment in the contract under Step 1 and your expected return. (Those who were collecting annuities before 1954 use January 1, 1954, as the annuity starting date.)

If payments are for life, you find your life expectancy in IRS tables included in IRS Publication 939. The table for single-life annuities is in ¶7.23. When using the table, your age is the age at the birthday nearest the annuity starting date. If you have a joint and survivor annuity and after your death the same payments are to be made to a second annuitant, the expected return is based on your joint life expectancy. Use Treasury Table II in IRS Publication 939

to get joint life expectancy if the entire investment was before July 1, 1986. Use Treasury Table VI if any investment was made after June 30, 1986. If your joint and survivor annuity provides for a different payment amount to the survivor, you must separately compute the expected return for each annuitant; this method is explained in Publication 939. Adjustments to the life expectancy multiple are required when your annuity is payable quarterly, semiannually, or annually. The required adjustment is discussed in ¶7.23.

If the payments are for a fixed number of years or for life, whichever is shorter, find your expected return by multiplying your annual payments by a life expectancy multiple found in Treasury Table IV if your entire investment was before July 1, 1986, or Table VIII if any investment was made after June 30, 1986.

If payments are for a fixed number of years (as in an endowment contract) without regard to your life expectancy, find your expected return by multiplying your annual payment by the number of years.

Note: See ¶7.23 for more information on the life expectancy tables.

3. Divide the investment in the contract (Step 1) by the expected return (Step 2). This will give you the tax-free percentage of your yearly annuity payments. The tax-free percentage remains the same for the remaining years of the annuity, even if payments increase due to a cost-of-living adjustment. A different computation of the tax-free percentage applies to variable annuities; see below.

If your annuity started before 1987, and you live longer than your projected life expectancy (shown in the IRS table), you may continue to apply the same tax-free percentage to each payment you receive. Thus, you may exclude from income more than you paid. However, if your annuity starting date is after 1986, your lifetime exclusion may not exceed your cost investment, less the value of any refund feature. Once you have recovered your cost, further payments are fully taxable.

If your annuity starting date is after July 1, 1986, and you die before recovering your investment, a deduction is allowed on your final tax return for the unrecovered cost. If a refund of the investment is made under the contract to a beneficiary, the beneficiary is allowed the deduction. The deduction is claimed as a miscellaneous itemized deduction that is *not* subject to the 2% adjusted gross income floor; see Chapter 19.

4. Find your total annuity payments for the year. For example, you received 10 monthly payments of $100 as your annuity began in March. Your total payments are $1,000, the monthly payment multiplied by 10.

5. Multiply the percentage in Step 3 by the total in Step 4. The result is the nontaxable portion (or excludable amount) of your annuity payments.

6. Subtract the amount in Step 5 from the amount in Step 4. This is the part of your annuity for the year which is subject to tax.

Note: An example of figuring the taxable and nontaxable portions for a single-life annuity is in ¶7.23.

Variable annuities. If you have a variable annuity that pays different benefits depending on cost-of-living-indexes, profits earned by the annuity fund, or similar fluctuating standards, the tax-free portion of each payment is computed by dividing your investment in the contract (Step 1) by the total number of payments you expect to receive. If the annuity is for a definite period, the total number of payments equals the number of payments to be made each year multiplied by the number of years you will receive payments. If the annuity is for life, you divide the amount you invested in the contract by a multiple obtained from the appropriate life expectancy table; *see* page 123. The result is the tax-free amount of annual annuity income.

If you receive a payment which is *less* than the nontaxable amount, you may elect when you receive the next payment to recalculate the nontaxable portion. The amount by which the prior nontaxable portion exceeded the payment you received is divided by the number of payments you expect as of the time of the next payment. The result is added to the previously calculated nontaxable portion, and the sum is the amount of each future payment to be excluded from tax. A statement must be attached to your return explaining the recomputation.

EXAMPLES 1. Your total investment of $12,000 was made before July 1, 1986. Your annuity will be paid starting January 1, 1992, in varying annual installments for your life. Your age (nearest birthday) at the January 1 starting date is 65. You use a life expectancy multiple of 15.0, the amount shown in Table 1 on page 123 for a male age 65. The amount of each payment excluded from tax is:

Investment in the contract	$12,000
Multiple (from Table 1)	15.0
Amount of each payment excluded from tax ($12,000 ÷ 15)	$ 800

If your first payment is $920, then $120 ($920 − $800) is included in your 1992 income.

2. Assume that after receiving your 1992 payment of $920 in Example 1, you receive $700 in 1993 and $1,200 in 1994. None of the 1993 payment is taxed; you exclude $800 for each annual annuity payment. Also you may elect to recompute your annual exclusion when you receive your payment in 1994. You elect to recompute your exclusion as follows:

Amount excludable in 1993	$800
Amount received in 1993	700
Difference	$100
Multiple as of 1/1/94 (*see* Table 1 at ¶ 7.23 for age 67)	13.8
Amount added to previously determined annual exclusion ($100 ÷ 13.8)	$ 7.25
Revised annual exclusion for 1994 and later years ($800 + $7.25)	$807.25
Amount taxable in 1994 ($1,200 − $807.25)	$392.75

Penalty on premature withdrawals from deferred annuities. As discussed on page 120, withdrawals before the annuity starting date may be taxable or tax free, depending on whether investments were made after August 13, 1982.

Withdrawals before age 59½ are also generally subject to a penalty of 10% of the amount includable in income. A withdrawal in 1992 from an annuity contract is penalized unless:

1. You have reached age 59½ or have become totally disabled.
2. The distribution is part of a series of substantially equal payments, made at least annually over your life expectancy or life expectancies of you and a beneficiary. If you can avoid the penalty under this exception and you change to a nonqualifying distribution method within five years or before age 59½, such as where you receive a lump sum, a recapture tax will apply to the payments received before age 59½.
3. The payment is received by a beneficiary or estate after the policyholder's death.
4. Payment is from a qualified retirement plan, tax-sheltered annuity, or IRA; in this case the penalty rules of ¶7.14 (qualified plans) or ¶8.8 (IRAs) apply.
5. Payment is allocable to investments made before August 14, 1982.

6. Payment is from an annuity contract under a qualified personal injury settlement.
7. Payment is from a single-premium annuity where the starting date is no more than one year from the date of purchase.
8. Payment is from an annuity purchased by an employer upon the termination of a qualified retirement plan and held until you separated from service.

If no exception applies, you compute the 10% penalty on Form 5329. The penalty is 5% instead of 10% if as of March 1, 1986, you were receiving payments under a specific schedule pursuant to your written election. Attach an explanation to Form 5329 if you are applying the 5% rate.

LIFE EXPECTANCY TABLES

¶7.23 IRS unisex actuarial tables must be used if you made any investment in the annuity contract *after* June 30, 1986. Generally, life expectancies are longer under the unisex tables than under the prior male-female tables. The prior male-female tables are still used if your entire investment was *before* July 1, 1986. The tables are included in IRS Publication 939. Prior tables are Tables I through IV. Unisex tables are Tables V through VIII.

You may make an irrevocable election to use the unisex tables for all payments received under the contract, even if you did not make an investment after June 30, 1986.

If you invested in the contract both before July 1, 1986, and after June 30, 1986, and you are the first person to receive annuity payments under the contract, you may make a special election to use the prior tables for the pre-July 1986 investment and the unisex tables for the post-June 1986 investment. *See* IRS Publication 939 for further information. Treasury Regulation 1.72-6(d) has examples showing how to figure the post-June 1986 and pre-July 1986 investments.

The life expectancy tables for one-person annuities are on the next page. A sample of the new unisex table for joint survivor annuities is at ¶8.14; the full table is in Publication 939.

Computing expected return of single annuitant. The payments go to one individual for life; on death, the payments stop. To find the multiple here, use Table 1 or Table V on the next page. Find your age at the nearest birthday to your annuity starting date in the proper column— "Male" or "Female." Then look opposite your age to find the proper multiple. This multiple may have to be adjusted as explained on page 123 for quarterly, semiannual, or annual payments. You then multiply this multiple by the total annuity payments you are to receive in one full year. If you have a monthly annuity, you multiply it by 12 times to get your expected return.

EXAMPLES 1. Jones was 66 years old on March 14, 1992. On April 1, he received his first monthly annuity check of $100. This covered his annuity payment for March. His annuity starting date is March 1, 1992, and his entire investment was before July 1, 1986. Looking at Table 1 under "Male" at age 66, Jones finds the multiple 14.4. (Jones does not have to adjust that multiple because the payments are monthly.) Jones multiplies the 14.4 by $1,200 ($100 a month for a year) to find his expected return of $17,280. Say the annuity cost Jones $12,960. He divides his expected return into the investment in the contract (the cost) and gets his exclusion percentage of 75%. In every year for the rest of his life, Jones receives tax free 75% of his annuity payments and is taxable on 25%. For 1991 Jones reports $225.

Amount received	$900
Amount excludable	675
Taxable portion	$225

TABLE 1: Investments Before July 1, 1986.

Male	Female	Multiples	Male	Female	Multiples	Male	Female	Multiples
6	11	65.0	41	46	33.0	76	81	9.1
7	12	64.1	42	47	32.1	77	82	8.7
8	13	63.2	43	48	31.2	78	83	8.3
9	14	62.3	44	49	30.4	79	84	7.8
10	15	61.4	45	50	29.6	80	85	7.5
11	16	60.4	46	51	28.7	81	86	7.1
12	17	59.5	47	52	27.9	82	87	6.7
13	18	58.6	48	53	27.1	83	88	6.3
14	19	57.7	49	54	26.3	84	89	6.0
15	20	56.7	50	55	25.5	85	90	5.7
16	21	55.8	51	56	24.7	86	91	5.4
17	22	54.9	52	57	24.0	87	92	5.1
18	23	53.9	53	58	23.2	88	93	4.8
19	24	53.0	54	59	22.4	89	94	4.5
20	25	52.1	55	60	21.7	90	95	4.2
21	26	51.1	56	61	21.0	91	96	4.0
22	27	50.2	57	62	20.3	92	97	3.7
23	28	49.3	58	63	19.6	93	98	3.5
24	29	48.3	59	64	18.9	94	99	3.3
25	30	47.4	60	65	18.2	95	100	3.1
26	31	46.5	61	66	17.5	96	101	2.9
27	32	45.6	62	67	16.9	97	102	2.7
28	33	44.6	63	68	16.2	98	103	2.5
29	34	43.7	64	69	15.6	99	104	2.3
30	35	42.8	65	70	15.0	100	105	2.1
31	36	41.9	66	71	14.4	101	106	1.9
32	37	41.0	67	72	13.8	102	107	1.7
33	38	40.0	68	73	13.2	103	108	1.5
34	39	39.1	69	74	12.6	104	109	1.3
35	40	38.2	70	75	12.1	105	110	1.2
36	41	37.3	71	76	11.6	106	111	1.0
37	42	36.5	72	77	11.0	107	112	0.8
38	43	35.6	73	78	10.5	108	113	0.7
39	44	34.7	74	79	10.1	109	114	0.6
40	45	33.8	75	80	9.6	110	115	0.5
						111	116	0.0

TABLE V: Investments After June 30, 1986.

Age	Multiple	Age	Multiple	Age	Multiple
5	76.6	42	40.6	79	10.0
6	75.6	43	39.6	80	9.5
7	74.7	44	38.7	81	8.9
8	73.7	45	37.7	82	8.4
9	72.7	46	36.8	83	7.9
10	71.7	47	35.9	84	7.4
11	70.7	48	34.9	85	6.9
12	69.7	49	34.0	86	6.5
13	68.8	50	33.1	87	6.1
14	67.8	51	32.2	88	5.7
15	66.8	52	31.3	89	5.3
16	65.8	53	30.4	90	5.0
17	64.8	54	29.5	91	4.7
18	63.9	55	28.6	92	4.4
19	62.9	56	27.7	93	4.1
20	61.9	57	26.8	94	3.9
21	60.9	58	25.9	95	3.7
22	59.9	59	25.0	96	3.4
23	59.0	60	24.2	97	3.2
24	58.0	61	23.3	98	3.0
25	57.0	62	22.5	99	2.8
26	56.0	63	21.6	100	2.7
27	55.1	64	20.8	101	2.5
28	54.1	65	20.0	102	2.3
29	53.1	66	19.2	103	2.1
30	52.2	67	18.4	104	1.9
31	51.2	68	17.6	105	1.8
32	50.2	69	16.8	106	1.6
33	49.3	70	16.0	107	1.4
34	48.3	71	15.3	108	1.3
35	47.3	72	14.6	109	1.1
36	46.4	73	13.9	110	1.0
37	45.4	74	13.2	111	0.9
38	44.4	75	12.5	112	0.8
39	43.5	76	11.9	113	0.7
40	42.5	77	11.2	114	0.6
41	41.5	78	10.6	115	0.5

For 1993 and later years, Jones will receive annuity payments for the full year. The amount received will be $1,200; amount excludable, $900; and taxable portion, $300.

2. Same facts as in Example 1 except there was an investment after June 30, 1986, and Table V is used. Looking at Table V under age 66, Jones finds the multiple 19.2. The same multiple applies to males and females. Multiplying the 19.2 by $1,200 gives an expected return of $23,040. Using a cost of $12,960, the exclusion percentage is 56.25% ($12,960 ÷ $23,040). For 1992, Jones reports annuity income as follows:

Amount received	$900.00
Amount excludable	506.25
Taxable portion	$393.75

For 1993 and later years in which annual payments of $1,200 are received, the amount excludable will be $675, and the taxable portion, $525.

Adjustments to the life expectancy multiple. An adjustment is required when your annuity payments are received quarterly, semi-annually, or annually.

EXAMPLE You receive quarterly annuity payments. Your first payment comes on January 15, covering the first quarter of the year. Since the period between the starting date of January 1 and the payment date of January 15 is less than one month, you adjust the life expectancy multiple according to the table below by adding 0.1. If the life expectancy multiple from the IRS table was 14.4, the adjusted multiple is 14.5.

MULTIPLE ADJUSTMENT TABLE

If the number of whole months from the annuity starting date to the first payment date is —	0–1	2	3	4	5	6	7	8	9	10	11	12
And payments under the contract are to be made:												
Annually	+0.5	+0.4	+0.3	+0.2	+0.1	0.0	0.0	−0.1	−0.2	−0.3	−0.4	−0.5
Semi-annually	+0.2	+0.1	0.0	0.0	−0.1	−0.2						

WHEN YOU CONVERT YOUR ENDOWMENT POLICY

¶7.24 When an endowment policy matures, you may elect to receive a lump sum, an annuity, an interest option, or a paid-up life insurance policy. If you elect—

A lump sum. You report the difference between your cost (premium payments less dividends) and what you receive.

An annuity before the policy matures or within 60 days after maturity. You report income in the years you receive your annuity. *See* ¶7.22 for how to report annuity income. Use as your investment in the annuity contract the cost of the endowment policy less premiums paid for other benefits such as double indemnity or disability income. If you elect the annuity option more than 60 days after maturity, you report income on the matured policy as if you received the lump sum; *see* above rule. The lump sum is treated as the cost investment in the annuity contract.

An interest option before the policy matures. You report only the interest as it is received, provided you do not have the right to withdraw the policy proceeds. If you have the right to withdraw the proceeds, you are treated as in constructive receipt; the difference between your cost and what you receive would be taxed as if you had received a lump sum.

Paid-up insurance. You report the difference between the present value of the paid-up life insurance policy and the premium paid for the endowment policy. In figuring the value of the insurance policy, you do not use its cash surrender value, but the amount you would have to pay for a similar policy with the company at the date of exchange. Your insurance company can give you this figure. The difference is taxed at ordinary income tax rates.

Tax-free exchange rules apply to the policy exchanges listed at ¶11.8.

Sales of endowment, annuity, or life insurance policies are taxable as ordinary income, not as capital gains.

The proceeds of a veteran's endowment policy paid before the death of the veteran are not taxable.

EMPLOYEE ANNUITIES

REPORTING EMPLOYEE ANNUITIES

¶7.25 Tax treatment of your employee annuity payments depends on the amount of your contributions and your annuity starting date.

Fully taxable payments. If you did not contribute to the cost of a pension or employee annuity, and you did not report as income your employer's contributions, you are fully taxed on payments after the annuity starting date. On your 1992 return, you report fully taxable payments on Line 17b of Form 1040 or Line 11b of Form 1040A.

An employee is taxed on the full value of a nonforfeitable annuity contract which the employer buys him or her if the employer does not have a qualified pension plan. Tax is imposed in the year the policy is purchased. A qualified plan is one approved by the IRS for special tax benefits.

If your annuity started before July 2, 1986, and payments within the first three years under the contract exceeded your cost investment, payments were not taxable until they exceeded your cost investment. On your 1992 return, your payments are fully taxable.

Disability pension before minimum retirement age. Disability payments received before you reach the minimum retirement age (at which you would be entitled to a regular retirement annuity) are fully taxable as wages. After minimum retirement age, payments are treated as an annuity subject to the cost recovery rules of ¶7.22 or the simplified rules of ¶7.26.

Partially taxable payments. If you and your employer both contributed to the cost of your annuity, the part of each payment allocable to your investment is recovered tax free and the balance is taxable.

On Form 1099-R, the payer of a pension or annuity may tell you how much is taxable. If not, you may make your own calculation of the tax-free amount under either (1) the six-step method of ¶7.22, using IRS life expectancy tables found in Publication 939; (2) the "simplified" method explained at ¶7.26; or (3) for a $50 fee, ask the IRS to calculate the taxable amount. You may use the simplified rule *only* if your annuity starting date was after July 1, 1986 and is for your life or the lives of you and a beneficiary. Also, you may not use the simplified method if you are age 75 or over when the annuity commenced, unless there are less than five years of guaranteed payments.

Cost and cost adjustments are explained in ¶7.27 and ¶7.28.

Changing cost recovery methods. You can switch from the regular six-step method to the simplified method or from the simplified to the regular method within the period for filing an amended return for the first year (*see* Chapter 38). For example, if your annuity starts in 1992 and you use the six-step method, and realize within the amendment period that you could get a larger tax-free return with the simplified method, you may file an amended return for 1992 and later years using the simplified method to recompute your tax-free exclusion for all the years. Similarly, if your annuity began in 1989, 1990, or 1991, and you would like to switch methods, you may do so by filing an amended return for the first year of the annuity. After recomputing the tax-free percentage of each payment under the new method, use that same percentage every year until your investment has been completely recovered.

SIMPLIFIED RULE FOR CALCULATING TAXABLE ANNUITY

¶7.26 The simplified method disregards IRS life expectancy tables under the six-step method of ¶7.22, which you may find complicated. The tax-free recovery amount under the simplified method is generally larger than under the six-step method. Computations under both methods should be made, however, to determine the more advantageous method in your particular case. If you opt for the method resulting in the larger annual cost exclusion, you will get an immediate tax benefit but will accelerate the recovery of your cost investment and thus the time when benefits will become fully taxable.

1040 **Beneficiary Should Recompute Form 1099-R Amount**

If you are receiving the annuity as a beneficiary of a deceased employee, and the employer has noted a taxable amount on Form 1099-R, the amount will be too high because the employer does not consider the $5,000 death benefit exclusion (¶7.28). You should refigure the taxable amount under the simplified method, increasing the employee's investment by the death benefit exclusion. Report the lower amount and attach a signed statement to your tax return stating that you are entitled to the $5,000 death benefit exclusion.

Where other beneficiaries are also receiving payments from the same employee's account, your share should be shown in Box 9 of the Form 1099-R you receive. If you receive payments from different employers as the beneficiary of the employee, the total exclusion you may claim is $5,000.

Figuring taxable and tax-free payments under the simplified method. Under the simplified method, a level tax-free portion is determined for each monthly payment with the following steps.

1. Figure your investment in the contract; see ¶7.27. Include premiums you paid and any after-tax contributions you made to the employer's pension plan. Beneficiaries may increase the investment by any allowable death benefit exclusion, up to $5,000; see ¶7.28.
2. Divide the investment from Step 1 by the number of monthly payments shown in the following table, using your age at the birthday preceding the annuity starting date. The result is the tax-free recovery portion of each monthly payment. The tax-free portion remains the same if a spouse or other beneficiary receives payments under a joint and survivor annuity after the employee's death.

Age at starting date	Number of monthly payments
55 and under	300
56–60	260
61–65	240
66–70	170
71 and over	120

3. Multiply the Step 2 result by the number of monthly payments received during the year; this is the total tax-free payment for the current year.
4. Subtract the Step 3 tax-free payment from the total pension received this year; this is the taxable pension you must report on Form 1040 or Form 1040A. If the payer of the annuity shows a higher taxable amount on Form 1099-R, use the amount figured here.

EXAMPLE Fred Smith, age 59, retires, and beginning January 1, 1992, he receives a single-life annuity of $1,000 per month. His investment in the plan was $30,000. To figure the tax-free portion of each payment, he divides his $30,000 investment by 260; see above table. The result, $115.38, is the tax-free portion of each monthly payment ($30,000 ÷ 260 = $115.38) and $884.62 ($1,000 − $115.38) is taxable. He reports $10,615 of his pension as taxable income

(12 x $884.62); $1,385 is tax free (12 x $115.38). The $1,385 exclusion is $185 higher than under the six-step method using Table V at ¶7.23.

After 260 monthly payments, all further payments are fully taxable. If Fred dies before the receipt of 260 payments, a deduction for the unrecovered investment is allowed on his final income tax return; the deduction is a miscellaneous itemized deduction not subject to the 2% AGI floor.

COST OF EMPLOYEE ANNUITY

¶**7.27** For purposes of figuring the tax-free recovery of your investment under the general rules of ¶7.22 or the simplified rule of ¶7.26, include the following items as your cost in an employee annuity:

Premiums paid by you or by withholdings from your pay.
Payments made by your employer and reported as additional pay. Premiums paid by an employer in a nonapproved plan for your benefit give you immediate income if you have nonforfeitable rights to the policy.
Premiums paid by your employer, which, if the amounts had been paid to you directly, would have been tax free to you because you were working abroad; see Chapter 36.
Pre-1939 contributions by a city or state to its employees' pension fund. (Before 1939, salaries to state and city employees were tax free for federal income tax purposes.)

If you are a beneficiary of a deceased employee, cost may include all or part of the death benefit exclusion; see ¶7.28.

BENEFICIARY ELIGIBLE FOR $5,000 DEATH BENEFIT EXCLUSION

¶**7.28** A pension annuity paid to you in 1992 as the beneficiary of a deceased employee may qualify for a death benefit exclusion, up to $5,000. The amount of the exclusion is added to the cost of the annuity in calculating the investment in the contract as of the annuity starting date. If you are using the simplified reporting method, do not rely on the taxable amount entered on Form 1099-R by the employer; see the filing tip at ¶7.26.

The death benefit exclusion is fixed at $5,000 per deceased employee, without regard to the number of beneficiaries or employers funding pension payments. The $5,000 exclusion must be allocated among beneficiaries in proportion to their benefits.

The $5,000 exclusion may *not* be added to the investment if the deceased had received any payment under a joint and survivor contract after reaching retirement age.

Beneficiaries of self-employed individuals who died after 1983 may claim the death benefit exclusion for distributions from a qualified pension or annuity plan.

Caution: When this book went to press, Congress was considering legislation that would repeal the exclusion for distributions after 1992; see the Supplement.

WITHDRAWALS BEFORE ANNUITY STARTING DATE

¶**7.29** You generally may not make tax-free withdrawals from your employer's plan before the annuity starting date, even if your withdrawals are less than your investment. On a withdrawal before the annuity starting date, you must pay tax on a portion of the withdrawal unless the exceptions below apply. The portion of the withdrawal allocable to your investment is recovered tax free; the portion allocable to employer contributions and income earned on the contract is taxed. To compute the tax-free recovery, multiply the withdrawal by this fraction:

$$\frac{\text{Your total investment}}{\text{Your vested account balance or accrued benefit}}$$

Your investment and vested benefit are determined as of the date of distribution.

Exceptions. More favorable investment recovery rules are allowed in the following cases:

1. *Plans in effect May 5, 1986.* If on May 5, 1986, your employer's plan allowed distributions of employee contributions before separation from service, the above pro-rata recovery rule applies only to the extent that the withdrawal exceeds the total investment in the contract on December 31, 1986. For example, assume that as of December 31, 1986, you had an account balance of $9,750, which included $4,000 of your own contributions. If the plan on May 5, 1986, allowed pre-retirement distributions of employee contributions, you may receive withdrawals up to your $4,000 investment without incurring tax. Thus, if you have not made previous withdrawals and receive a $3,000 distribution in 1992, it is not subject to tax.
2. *Separate accounts for employee contributions.* A defined contribution plan (such as a profit-sharing plan) is allowed to account for employee contributions (and earnings on the contributions) separately from employer contributions. If separate accounting is maintained, withdrawals of employee contributions from the separate account may be made tax free. A defined benefit pension plan may also maintain employee contributions (and earnings) in a separate account to which actual earnings and losses are allocated.

Note: Both of the above exceptions are complicated and you should consult your plan administrator to determine if the exceptions apply and how to make the required calculations.

CIVIL SERVICE RETIREMENT

¶7.30 If your annuity starting date was before July 2, 1986, and you used the three-year cost recovery rule, all of your 1992 payments are fully taxable. If the annuity starting date was after July 1, 1986, the general rules of ¶7.22 or the simplified rule at ¶7.26 must be used to compute the tax-free and taxable portions of each withdrawal.

If you leave federal government service before retirement or transfer to a job not under the federal retirement system and you are not entitled to an immediate annuity, you may receive a refund of your contributions (plus any interest). If the refund exceeds your contributions, the excess is taxable.

If you elected a reduced annuity in order to receive a lump-sum credit for your total contributions to the plan; *see* IRS Publication 721 for figuring the taxable portion of the lump sum.

While you worked for the federal government, contributions to the Civil Service retirement fund were withheld from your pay. These contributions represent your cost. Also, if you repaid to the retirement fund amounts that you previously had withdrawn, or paid into the fund to receive full credit for certain uncovered service, the entire amount you paid, including that designated as interest, is part

of your cost. You may not claim an interest deduction for any amount designated as interest.

The annuity statement you received when your annuity was approved shows your "total contributions" to the retirement fund (your cost) and the "monthly rate" of your annuity benefit. The monthly rate is the rate before adjustment for health benefits coverage and life insurance, if any.

A future increase in your civil service pension or your survivor's benefit is not treated as annuity income but is reported in full as miscellaneous income and is not reduced by the exclusion ratio. However, an increase effective on or before a survivor's civil service annuity commences must be taken into account in computing the expected return or in determining the aggregate amount receivable under the annuity.

A lump-sum payment for accrued annual leave received upon retirement is not part of your annuity. It is treated as a salary payment and is taxable as ordinary income.

If you made voluntary contributions to the retirement fund that you use to fund an additional monthly benefit, you report the portion of your annuity attributable to the voluntary contributions as a separate annuity, taxable under the rules at ¶7.22 or ¶7.26. If you made voluntary contributions, an information return which you receive each year will state the portion of your monthly payments attributable to your voluntary contributions. If instead of increasing your monthly benefit, you receive a refund of your voluntary contributions plus accrued interest, the interest is taxable in the year you receive it.

RETIRED MILITARY PERSONNEL ALLOWED ANNUITY ELECTION

¶7.31 If, when you retire from the military, your pay is reduced to provide an annuity for your spouse or certain child beneficiaries, you do not report that part of your retirement pay used to fund the annuity.

EXAMPLE You are eligible to receive retirement pay of $500 a month. You elect to receive $400 a month to obtain an annuity of $200 a month for your spouse on your death. You report $400 a month for tax purposes during your lifetime, rather than the $500. On your death, your spouse generally will report the full $200 a month received as income.

If you received retirement pay before 1966 and elected reduced benefits, you reported more retirement pay than you actually received. In this case, amounts attributed to the reduction in retirement pay reported in prior years offset retirement pay received in 1966 and later years.

Veteran's Benefit Deposits. If you elected to receive veteran's benefits instead of some or all of your retirement pay, you may have been required to deposit with the U.S. Treasury an amount equal to the reduction for the annuity. If so, you do not report retirement pay until it equals the amount deposited.

Beneficiaries. If all of the retired person's consideration for the contract (previously taxed reductions) has not been offset against retirement income at the time of death, the beneficiary excludes all payments under the contract until the exclusions equal the remaining consideration for the contract not previously excluded by the deceased. As soon as this amount is excluded, the beneficiary reports all later payments as income.

The $5,000 death benefit exclusion is treated as a cost investment to be added to the spouse's annuity contract if the deceased serviceman retired because of disability and dies before reaching retirement age.

8

IRAs

Setting up IRAs. There are two ways in which you may set up an IRA: (1) by making annual contributions and (2) by rolling over a distribution received from a qualified employer plan. Both types of IRA accounts provide tax-free accumulation of earnings until withdrawals are made. The rollover option also allows you to avoid immediate tax when you receive a lump-sum payment upon retirement, changing jobs, or disability; *see ¶7.8.*

Deductible contributions. Contributions to a regular IRA of up to $2,000 a year are deductible if you and your spouse do not have retirement plan coverage where you work. If you have coverage, you may claim a deduction if your adjusted gross income is below a specified phaseout range; *see ¶8.3.* If your deduction is limited or eliminated under the phaseout rule, you may make nondeductible contributions, which must be reported on Form 8606; *see ¶8.5.*

SEP. Under a special type of IRA, a simplified employee pension (SEP) set up by your employer, you may make larger tax-sheltered contributions than you may to a regular IRA; *see ¶8.11.*

IRA restrictions. Offsetting the tax advantages of IRAs are these withdrawal restrictions:

Loans other than temporary 60-day loans are prohibited (¶8.8).

Distributions before age 59¹/₂ are penalized unless you meet certain exceptions (¶8.8).

Withdrawals exceeding $150,000 may be penalized (¶8.13).

Distributions must start after you reach age 70¹/₂ (¶8.14).

Tax on distributions. IRA distributions will be reported to you and to the IRS on Form 1099-R. The distributions are fully taxable, except to the extent you have made nondeductible contributions. You must file Form 8606 to figure the tax-free portion of distributions allocable to nondeductible contributions (¶8.8).

RETIREMENT SAVINGS THROUGH IRAs

¶8.1 If you are allowed an IRA deduction for 1992 contributions, you can obtain a substantial tax savings. For example, if you are in the 28% bracket, and qualify for a full deduction, a $2,000 contribution reduces your taxes by $560 in 1992. In the 31% bracket, a $2,000 deduction reduces taxes by $620. Whether you may claim a full, partial, or no deduction is explained in ¶8.3.

All IRA contributions, whether deductible or nondeductible, accumulate tax free. That is, income earned on funds in the account is not taxed until the funds are withdrawn. When you roll over a qualifying distribution from an employer plan (¶8.9), you also get the benefit of tax-free accumulation of earnings until withdrawals begin. Tax-free interest compounding can produce the following funds for retirement:

$2,000 invested annually —	6%	With interest compounded daily 8% gives you—	10%
5 years	$11,670	$12,794	$13,633
10 years	27,398	31,879	36,109
15 years	48,642	60,349	73,164
20 years	77,318	102,820	134,252
25 years	116,030	166,176	234,962
30 years	168,275	260,688	400,993

Weigh the above benefits against these restrictions: Generally, you may not freely withdraw IRA funds until the year you reach age 59¹/₂ or become disabled. If you take money out or even borrow using the account as collateral before that time, you are subject to a penalty. In the year you reach age 70¹/₂, you may no longer make IRA contributions, and you must start to withdraw from the account. All IRA withdrawals are fully taxable except for amounts allocable to nondeductible contributions; *see ¶8.8.*

Special averaging for lump-sum distribution does not apply. Excess contributions and distributions are penalized.

Whether you should make nondeductible IRA contributions is discussed at ¶8.5.

If your IRA loses value because of poor investments, you may not deduct the loss. A loss is allowed only if you make nondeductible contributions which you have not recovered when the account is depleted; *see* ¶8.8.

CONTRIBUTIONS MUST BE BASED ON EARNINGS

¶8.2 You may make IRA contributions for 1992 of up to $2,000, provided you have wage, salary, or net self-employment earnings. If your earned income is less than $2,000, the contribution limit is 100% of your pay or net earned income if self-employed. Contributions for 1992 may be made up to April 15, 1993; this is the deadline even if you obtain a filing extension.

If you are married and both you and your spouse work, you may each contribute up to $2,000 of earnings to an IRA. If you file a joint return with your spouse and only one of you has compensation, the combined contribution for both of you is $2,250; *see* ¶8.7.

Contributions up to these limits are *fully deductible* on your 1992 return if neither you nor your spouse is an active participant in an employer or self-employed retirement plan. Deductions for active plan participants are phased out for single persons with adjusted gross income over $25,000, and married persons filing jointly with adjusted gross income over $40,000. The phaseout rules are discussed at ¶8.3.

IRA contributions must be based on payments received for rendering personal services, such as salary, wages, commissions, tips, fees, bonuses, jury fees, or net earnings from self-employment (less Keogh plan contributions on behalf of the self-employed). Compensation does *not* include:

1. Income earned abroad for which the foreign earned income exclusion is claimed;
2. Deferred compensation, pensions, or annuities; or
3. Investment income such as interest, dividends, or profits from sales of property.

EXAMPLE A trader, whose sole income was derived from stock dividends and gains in buying and selling stocks, contributed to an IRA. The IRS disallowed the deduction on the grounds that his income was not earned income.

If you live in a community property state, the fact that one-half of your spouse's income is considered your income does not entitle you to make contributions to an IRA. The contribution must be based on pay earned through your services.

Only cash contributions are deductible; contributions paid by check are considered cash for this purpose.

Self-employed may make IRA contributions. IRA contributions may be based on net self-employment earnings, after taking into account deductible Keogh or SEP retirement plan contributions (Chapter 41) and the deduction for one-half of self-employment tax liability (Chapter 46). If you have a net loss for the year, you may not make an IRA contribution unless you also have wages.

If you have more than one self-employed activity, you must aggregate profits and losses from all of your self-employed businesses to determine if you have net income on which to base an IRA contribution. For example, if one self-employed business produces a net profit of $15,000 but another a net loss of $20,000, you may not make an IRA contribution based on the net profit of $15,000. This

netting rule does not apply to salary or wage income. If you are an employee who also has an unprofitable business, you may make an IRA contribution based on your salary.

If you have a self-employed retirement plan from your business, you are considered an active participant in a retirement plan for purposes of the adjusted gross income phaseout rules discussed at ¶8.3.

Taxable alimony. A divorced spouse with little or no earnings in 1992 may treat taxable alimony as compensation, giving a basis for deductible IRA contributions. If you are divorced, you make an IRA contribution equal to 100% of taxable alimony up to $2,000. However, the deduction may be reduced or eliminated if you are an active participant in an employer plan and your adjusted gross income exceeds the $25,000 threshold for unmarried individuals; *see* ¶8.3. Taxable alimony is alimony paid under a decree of divorce or legal separation, or a written agreement incident to such a decree; *see* Chapter 37. It does not include alimony payments made under a written agreement that is not incident to such a decree.

IRA DEDUCTIONS FOR THOSE WITH RETIREMENT PLAN COVERAGE

¶8.3 On 1992 returns, IRA deductions are restricted only for individuals who are covered by an employer or self-employed retirement plan, or in the case of married couples, where either spouse is covered. If you are unmarried or file as a head of household, and you are *not* covered by an employer or self-employed retirement plan, IRA contributions up to $2,000 are fully deductible provided your earned income is $2,000 or more. If you are married and *neither* spouse is covered, IRA contributions are fully deductible up to the $4,000 or $2,250 limit (¶8.2).

If you are an employee, your 1992 Form W-2 should indicate whether you are covered for the year; if you are, the "Pension plan" box within Box 6 of Form W-2 should be checked. Generally, you are considered to be covered if you are an *active participant* in the plan for any part of the plan year ending within your taxable year. This includes active participation in a self-employed Keogh plan or SEP (Chapter 41). Active participation is explained further at ¶8.4.

If you or your spouse is an active plan participant. If you, or your spouse, is an active plan participant, you still may be allowed a full or limited deduction, but this will depend on whether your 1992 adjusted gross income (AGI) is within the phaseout range shown below for your filing status. For IRA deduction purposes, AGI is the adjusted gross income shown on Line 31 of Form 1040 or Line 14 of Form 1040A, but you must add back any foreign earned income (¶36.1) or U.S. savings bond interest (¶33.3) that you are allowed to exclude from income. The phaseout rules apply only if your AGI exceeds $25,000 if you are single or head of household, or $40,000 if married filing jointly or a qualifying widow or widower. If married filing separately, the phaseout applies to the first $10,000 of AGI.

1992 PHASEOUT RANGE FOR ACTIVE PLAN PARTICIPANTS

If you are—	Deduction phased out if AGI is—	No deduction if AGI is—
Single or head of household	$25,001–$34,999	$35,000 or more
Married filing jointly	40,001– 49,999	50,000 or more
Married filing separately	0– 9,999	10,000 or more
Qualifying widow or widower	40,001– 49,999	50,000 or more

How to figure your 1992 deduction if within the phaseout range. If you or your spouse is an active participant and your AGI is *within* the phaseout range shown on page 128, you may figure your reduced deduction using the following three steps:

Step 1. From your AGI, subtract the following amount:
$25,000 if single or head of household;
$40,000 if married filing jointly or a qualifying widow or widower;
Zero if married filing separately.
If the result is $10,000 or more, stop; you are not allowed any deduction.

Step 2. Subtract Step 1 from $10,000.

Step 3. Multiply Step 2 by 20% (0.20) if your contribution limit is $2,000. Multiply Step 2 by 22.5% (0.225) if your contribution limit is $2,250 because you contribute to a spousal IRA. This is your deductible contribution. If the result is not a multiple of $10, the allowable deduction is increased to the next highest $10; *see* Example 3 below. If the result is less than $200, a $200 deduction is allowed.

EXAMPLES (All examples assume company coverage. AGI is before IRA deductions, but includes foreign earned income and U.S. savings bond interest that is tax free.)

1. *Single or head of household.* You are single and your AGI is $26,000. Your maximum deductible IRA contribution for 1992 is $1,800.

Step 1. $1,000 ($26,000 − $25,000).
Step 2. $9,000 ($10,000 − $1,000).
Step 3. $1,800 ($9,000 × 0.20).

If you contributed $2,000 to the IRA, $200 will be treated as a nondeductible contribution.

2. *Married filing jointly.* You and your spouse have a joint adjusted gross income of $43,000. You file a joint return. You each work but only you are an active participant in an employer plan. Your spouse is also considered an active participant under the IRA rules. The maximum 1992 IRA deduction for *each of you* is $1,400.

Step 1. $3,000 ($43,000 − $40,000).
Step 2. $7,000 ($10,000 − $3,000).
Step 3. $1,400 ($7,000 × 0.20).

Note: If one spouse had compensation of less than $1,400, that spouse's contribution could not exceed such compensation.

3. *Spousal IRA.* Same facts as Example 2, but only you work and are an active participant in an employer plan. You set up a spousal IRA for your nonworking spouse. The maximum deductible contribution for both accounts is $1,580.

Step 1. $3,000 ($43,000 − $40,000).
Step 2. $7,000 ($10,000 − $3,000).
Step 3. $1,575 ($7,000 × 0.225).

Since $1,575 is not a multiple of $10, the allowable deduction is increased to the next highest $10, or $1,580. You may divide the $1,580 contribution between you and your spouse however you choose; but according to the IRS, neither of you may deduct more than $1,400, the deductible limit per spouse for a couple with a $43,000 AGI, as figured under Example 2.

4. *Married filing separately.* You are married, file a separate return for 1992, and are an active participant in an employer plan. Your adjusted gross income is $7,500. Your maximum deductible IRA contribution is $500.

Step 1. $7,500 ($7,500 − $0).
Step 2. $2,500 ($10,000 − $7,500).
Step 3. $500 ($2,500 × 0.20).

Unless you lived apart for the whole year, your spouse, whether or not covered by a retirement plan, is also subject to the $0 to $10,000 deduction phaseout range under Steps 1–3. If you live apart the whole year, you figure deductions as if you were single; *see* ¶8.7.

$200 IRA deduction floor. A special rule gives a $200 deduction if your AGI without IRA deductions falls within the last $1,000 of the phaseout range. Using the three-step formula as just discussed, your reduced deduction would be less than $200 when your AGI is over $34,000 (unmarried), over $49,000 (married filing jointly), or over $9,000 (married filing separately). However, a $200 deduction may be claimed by a single person with an AGI of over $34,000 but under $35,000; by a married person filing jointly with an AGI of over $49,000 but under $50,000; and by a married person filing separately with an AGI of over $9,000 but under $10,000.

EXAMPLE Your AGI is $34,400 in 1992 and you file as a head of household.

Step 1. $9,400 ($34,400 − $25,000).
Step 2. $600 ($10,000 − $9,400).
Step 3. $120 ($600 × 0.20).

Although $120 is the deductible IRA limit under the above computation, you may deduct contributions of up to $200.

Nondeductible contributions. Any contributions above the amount allowed under the above rules are treated as nondeductible IRA contributions. *See* ¶8.5 for further details.

Figuring your IRA deduction if you receive Social Security benefits. If you or your spouse (¶8.7) is an active participant in an employer plan and either of you receives Social Security benefits, you need to make an extra computation before you can figure whether an IRA deduction is allowed. Follow Step 1 of ¶34.3 to determine if part of your Social Security benefits would be subject to tax, assuming no IRA deduction were claimed. If none of your benefits would be taxable, follow the regular rules above for determining IRA deductions. If part of your Social Security benefits would be taxable, AGI for IRA purposes is increased by the taxable benefits. The allowable IRA deduction is then taken into account to determine the actual amount of taxable Social Security.

Proposed Liberalization of IRA Benefits

LAW ALERT

When this book went to press, Congress was considering legislation to liberalize IRA contribution and deduction benefits. The proposal would generally allow taxpayers with retirement plan coverage to deduct IRA contributions of up to $2,000, with the $2,000 limit subject to inflation adjustments. A lower limit would apply for those who make elective salary deferrals to a 401(k) plan, tax-sheltered plan, or simplified employee pension. The legislation also would create a new type of nondeductible IRA from which tax-free withdrawals could be made after five years.

See the Tax Legislation Guide at the front of this book and the Supplement for an update.

ACTIVE PARTICIPATION TESTS

¶8.4 Active participants in an employer retirement plan are subject to the adjusted gross income tests for deducting contributions as discussed at ¶8.3. Married individuals are generally treated as active participants if either spouse has plan coverage; *see* ¶8.7. An employer retirement plan means:

1. A qualified pension, profit-sharing, or stock bonus plan, including a qualified self-employed Keogh plan or simplified employee pension (SEP) plan;

2. A qualified annuity plan;

3. A tax-sheltered annuity; and

4. A plan established for its employees by the United States, by a state or political subdivision, or by any agency or instrumentality of the United States or a state or political subdivision, but *not* eligible section 457 plans.

Form W-2. If your employer checks the "Pension plan" box within Box 6 of your 1992 Form W-2, this indicates that you were an active participant in your employer's retirement plan during the year. If you want to make a contribution before you receive your Form W-2, check the following guidelines and consult your plan administrator for your status.

Type of plan. The rules for determining active participation status generally depend on the type of plan your employer has. As discussed below, the tests for defined benefit pension plans are different from the tests for defined contribution plans such as profit-sharing plans, 401(k) plans, money purchase pension plans, and stock bonus plans. Under any type of plan, if you are considered an active participant for any part of the plan year ending with or within your taxable year, you are treated as an active participant. Because of this plan year rule, you may be an active participant even if you were with the employer for only part of the year.

Under IRS guidelines, it is possible to be treated as an active participant in the year of retirement and even in the year after retirement if your employer maintains a fiscal year plan.

The IRS has held that employees continue to be active participants if an employer has "frozen" their retirement plan while amendments are being made to conform to the major law changes enacted since 1986. However, if the employer indicates in a resolution or other document that no further benefit accruals will be made for the employees, they will cease to be treated as active participants.

Defined benefit pension plans. In general, you are treated as an active participant in a defined benefit pension plan if for the plan year ending with or within your taxable year, you are eligible to participate in the plan. Under this rule, as long as you are eligible, you are treated as an active participant, even if you decline participation in the plan or you fail to make a mandatory contribution specified in the plan. Furthermore, you are treated as an active participant even if your rights to benefits are not vested.

Defined contribution plan. For a defined contribution plan, you are generally considered an active participant if "with respect to" the plan year ending with or within your taxable year (1) you make elective deferrals to the plan; (2) your employer contributes to your account; or (3) forfeitures are allocated to your account. If any of these events occur, you are treated as an active participant even if you do not have a vested right to receive benefits from your account.

EXAMPLES 1. You join a company in April 1992 that has a 401(k) plan (a type of defined contribution plan) with a plan year starting July 1 and ending the following June 30. You are not eligible to participate in the plan year ending June 30, 1992. You elect to defer 6% of your 1992 salary to the 401(k) plan for the plan year ending June 30, 1993. Although you make elective deferrals to the plan during 1992, you are *not* considered an active participant for 1992 because your contributions were made for the plan year ending in 1993. You *will* be considered an active participant in 1993, even if you decide not to defer any part of your 1993 salary to the plan.

2. Your employer has a defined benefit pension plan with a plan year starting July 1 and ending the following June 30. You are not excluded from participating. If you retired during September 1992, you are considered an active participant for 1992 because you were eligible to participate during the plan year ending during 1992. You will also be considered an active participant for 1993. Although you will retire before the end of the 1992–1993 plan year, you will still be eligible to participate

during part of that plan year, and since that plan year ends within your 1993 tax year, you will be considered an active participant for 1993.

NONDEDUCTIBLE IRA CONTRIBUTIONS

¶8.5 If you are not allowed to make any deductible contributions because of the phaseout rule (¶8.3), you may make *nondeductible* contributions of up to $2,000, or $2,250 for a spousal IRA (¶8.7), where you have compensation of at least that much. If a deduction of less than $2,000 ($2,250 for spousal IRA) is allowed under the phaseout rules, you may make a nondeductible contribution to the extent the maximum contribution limit of $2,000, $2,250, or $4,000 exceeds the deductible limit figured under ¶8.3. Thus, if you are limited to an $1,800 deduction because your adjusted gross income is within the deduction phaseout range (¶8.3), you may make a $200 nondeductible contribution. As with deductible contributions, nondeductible contributions for 1992 may be made up to the April 15, 1993 filing due date (without extensions). The advantage of making nondeductible contributions is that earnings on the account accumulate tax free until withdrawn.

Note: When this book went to press, Congress was considering legislation to create a new type of nondeductible IRA from which tax-free withdrawals could be made after five years. See the Tax Legislation Guide at the front of this book for further legislative developments.

Form 8606. You must file Form 8606 to report nondeductible IRA contributions unless you withdraw the contribution as discussed below. You also must list on Form 8606 the value of all of your IRAs as of the end of the year, including amounts based on deductible contributions. If you are married and you and your spouse both make nondeductible contributions, you must each file a separate Form 8606. A $50 penalty may be imposed for not filing Form 8606 unless there is reasonable cause. Furthermore, if you overstate the amount of designated nondeductible contributions made for any taxable year, you are subject to a $100 penalty for each such overstatement unless you can demonstrate that the overstatement was due to reasonable cause. You may file an amended return for a taxable year and change the designation of IRA contributions from deductible to nondeductible or nondeductible to deductible.

If you make contributions during the year, you may not know whether you will be allowed to claim a deduction under the phaseout rules of ¶8.3. For example, you may have employer plan coverage but might not know whether your AGI will exceed the $35,000 limit (single) or $50,000 limit (married filing jointly). You can make your contribution without knowing whether it is deductible or not and figure your deduction when you file your return. Any nondeductible amount would be reported on Form 8606. However, if you do not want to make nondeductible contributions, you may wait until after the end of the year when you can determine your AGI and active participant status; you have until the April 15 filing due date (without extensions) to make your contribution.

Withdrawing nondeductible contributions. If you make an IRA contribution for 1992 and later realize it is not deductible, you may make a tax-free withdrawal of the contribution by the April 15 filing due date (or later if you get a filing extension); instead of designating the contribution as nondeductible on Form 8606. To do this, you must also withdraw the earnings allocable to the withdrawn contribution and include the earnings as income on your 1992 return. You might want to make the withdrawal if you incorrectly determined that a contribution would be deductible and you do not want to leave nondeductible contributions in your account. However, making the withdrawal could subject you to bank penalties for premature withdrawals, or other withdrawal penalties imposed by the IRA trustee. Furthermore, if you are under age 59½ and not disabled, the 10% premature withdrawal penalty (¶8.8) applies to the withdrawn earnings.

Should you make nondeductible IRA contributions? Yes, if in your case, the accumulation of tax-free income in the account, when you withdraw the account, will give you a greater return than other types of investments. Generally a nondeductible account should be considered when you intend to leave it intact until you retire. However, if you have other IRA accounts based on deductible contributions, withdrawals from a nondeductible account may be taxable as explained in ¶8.8. This is a disadvantage as you may not treat the account as a regular savings account from which you can make tax-free withdrawals at any time.

Recordkeeping for IRA Distributions

Keep a copy of each Form 8606 filed showing nondeductible contributions and keep a separate record of deductible contributions. When you make IRA withdrawals, the portion of each withdrawal allocable to nondeductible contributions is not taxed. You may not completely avoid tax even if you withdraw an amount equal to your nondeductible contributions. The tax-free portion of the withdrawal is figured on Form 8606. The rules for figuring tax on withdrawals and a sample Form 8606 are at ¶8.8.

STARTING AN IRA

¶8.6 Banks, brokerage firms, insurance companies, and credit unions offering IRA investment plans provide all of the necessary forms for starting your IRA. You may set up one type of IRA one year and choose another form the next year. You also may split your contribution between two or more investment vehicles. For example, you are eligible to contribute $2,000. You may choose to put $1,000 into an investment retirement annuity and $1,000 into an individual retirement account with your local bank.

You do not have to file any forms with your tax return when you set up or make contributions to a deductible IRA. Form 8606 must be attached to Form 1040 or Form 1040A, if you make nondeductible IRA contributions; *see* ¶8.5. The bank or company where you set up your IRA will report your contribution to the IRS on Form 5498, and you should receive a copy.

You may set up an IRA as:

1. *An individual retirement account* with a bank, savings and loan association, federally insured credit union, or other qualified person as trustee or custodian. An individual retirement account is technically a trust or custodial account. Your contribution may be invested in vehicles such as certificates of deposit, mutual funds, and certain limited partnerships.

Self-Directed IRA

If you wish to take a more active role in managing your IRA investments, you may set up a "self-directed" IRA using an IRS model form. The model trust (Form 5305) and the model custodial account agreement (Form 5305-A) meet the requirements of an exempt individual retirement account and so do not require a ruling or determination letter approving the exemption of the account and the deductibility of contributions made to the account. If you use this method, you still have to find a bank or other institution or trustee to handle your account or investment. If you have a self-directed IRA, you may not invest in collectibles, such as art works, gems, stamps, antiques, rugs, metals, or guns. Coins are not allowed unless they are state-issued coins or U.S. minted gold and silver coins of one ounce or less. Assets used to acquire a collectible are treated as distributions and are taxed.

2. *An individual retirement annuity* by purchasing an annuity contract (including a joint and survivor contract for the benefit of you and your spouse) issued by an insurance company; no trustee or custodian is required. The contract, endorsed to meet the terms of an IRA, is all that is required. Contracts issued after November 6, 1978, must provide for flexible premiums up to $2,000 a year, so that if your compensation changes, your payment may also change. As borrowing or pledging of the contract is not allowed under an IRA, the contracts will not contain loan provisions. Endowment contracts issued after November 6, 1978, that provide life insurance protection may not be used as individual retirement annuities.

Trustee's fees and brokerage commissions. Trustee's fees paid to set up or manage an IRA are not considered IRA contributions if separately paid. They are investment expenses which may be deducted as a miscellaneous itemized deduction subject to the 2% adjusted gross income floor; *see* ¶19.1. However, broker's commissions that are paid when you make investments for your IRA are not deductible, according to the IRS. They are considered IRA contributions subject to the $2,000 contribution limit.

Contributions after the end of the taxable year. You have until April 15, 1993 (the regular filing due date for your 1992 return) to make deductible or nondeductible IRA contributions for 1992. You must make your contribution by April 15, 1993 even if you get an extension to file your return. If you are short of cash, you may borrow the funds to make the contribution without jeopardizing the deduction. If an IRA deduction entitles you to a refund, you can file your return early, claim the IRA deduction, and if you receive the refund in time, apply it towards an IRA contribution before the due date.

Broker's Restriction on IRA Transfers

Before you invest in an IRA, carefully review the terms of the agreement for restrictions. One investor, who put his IRA in a brokerage account, was not allowed by the trustee to transfer from one account to another. Furthermore, the trustee reserved some of the IRA funds to cover broker fees and other transfer costs. The investor asked the IRS if these restrictions violated the tax law. The IRS, in a private letter ruling, said there was no violation. An IRA is a contractual agreement between the IRA trustee and the participant. Although the tax laws do not place limitations on direct IRA-to-IRA transfers, the trustees of a particular account may restrict such transfers.

IRA CONTRIBUTIONS FOR MARRIED COUPLES

¶8.7 If both spouses have compensation and each is eligible to set up an IRA account, each may contribute to his or her separate IRA account up to $2,000.

Working for spouse. If you work for your spouse, you may make an IRA contribution provided you actually perform services and receive an actual payment of wages. A wife who worked as a receptionist and assistant to her husband, a veterinarian, failed to meet the second test. Her husband did not pay her a salary. Instead, he deposited all income from his business into a joint bank account held with his wife. In addition, no federal income tax was withheld from her wages. In a ruling, the IRS held that the wife could not set up her own IRA, even though she performed services; she failed to receive actual payment. Depositing business income into a joint account is neither actual nor constructive payment of the wife's salary. Furthermore, any deduction claimed for the wife's wages was disallowed.

Deductions for spouses filing jointly. If a joint return is filed and either spouse is an active participant in an employer plan, contributions are fully deductible if joint adjusted gross income (AGI) before considering IRA deductions is $40,000 or less. Limited deductions are allowed if joint AGI is between $40,000 and $50,000 under the phaseout rules explained at ¶8.3. No deduction is allowed for either spouse if joint AGI is $50,000 or more.

EXAMPLE You earn a salary of $20,000, your spouse earns $10,000, and neither of you is covered by an employer retirement plan. On a joint return, the maximum deduction is up to $4,000 ($2,000 for each of you). If only one of you works and qualifies to set up an IRA, the maximum deduction is $2,000, unless an account for a nonworking spouse is set up as discussed below.

If you both work and either of you is an active participant in an employer plan, you are still allowed the maximum $4,000 deduction provided your joint AGI on a joint return was $40,000 or less. If joint return AGI is over $40,000 but less than $50,000, you may each claim a limited deduction; *see* Example 2 at ¶8.3.

Deductions for spousal IRA. If you are working, you may make a contribution on behalf of your nonworking spouse provided you file a joint return. You may have two separate IRAs, one for you and one for your spouse, or a single IRA which has a subaccount for you and another subaccount for your spouse. A joint account is not allowed. However, each spouse may have a right of survivorship in the subaccount of the other.

Generally, the maximum contribution is $2,250 and may be allocated between spouses in any way as long as no spouse receives a contribution exceeding $2,000. However, where deductions are limited under the rules of ¶8.3, the amount of deductible contributions which may be made for either spouse may be reduced; *see* Example 3 in ¶8.3.

Generally, you may set up an account (or subaccount) for your spouse only if your spouse received no compensation for the year, including tax-exempt foreign earned income. However, there is this limited exception: You may contribute to a spousal IRA if your spouse had compensation of $250 or less; your spouse is treated as if he or she had no compensation. You may set up a spousal account regardless of the amount of your spouse's unearned income, such as interest, dividends, or Social Security benefits.

Where your spouse earns less than $250, it is advantageous to set up a spousal IRA and qualify for the $2,250 contribution limit. Otherwise, the combined limit for both of you would be less than $2,250; you could contribute $2,000 to your IRA and your spouse could contribute only up to his or her compensation.

A spouse may start withdrawing from his or her spousal account (or subaccount) without penalty on reaching age 59½ and must start withdrawing on reaching age 70½.

If you are divorced, you may not maintain a spousal account for your former spouse. If you contributed to an account on behalf of your nonworking spouse and then divorce later in the year, the contribution is an excess contribution. IRAs based on alimony are discussed at ¶8.2.

An amount distributed to one spouse may not be rolled over to an IRA account of the other spouse, except in the case of divorce; *see* ¶8.10.

If you already have an IRA for yourself and you want to make contributions on behalf of your nonworking spouse, you may do so by merely opening a new IRA for your spouse and continuing your present IRA for yourself. However, if you have an annuity or endowment contract, check with your insurance agent about any contract restrictions on reducing your premium payments. Before setting up a single IRA with subaccounts for you and your spouse, check IRS regulations covering their use.

Working Spouse Over Age 70½

If you are over age 70½ and still working, you may contribute to an IRA for a nonworking spouse who is under age 70½, but the entire contribution must be allocated to the nonworking spouse. No contribution may be made to your account for the year in which you reach age 70½, or any later year. The contribution for your nonworking spouse may not exceed $2,000.

Married persons filing separately. If you are married, live together at any time during the year, file separately, and either of you is an active participant in an employer plan, the other spouse is also considered an active participant. Both of you are subject to the $0 to $10,000 AGI deduction phaseout; *see* Example 4 in ¶8.3.

If you live apart for the whole year, you each figure IRA deductions as if single. Thus, the more favorable deduction phaseout range of $25,000 to $35,000 applies if you are covered by an employer retirement plan; *see* Example 1 in ¶8.3. If you are *not* covered, you may claim a full deduction on your separate return.

IRA DISTRIBUTIONS

¶8.8 If all of your IRA contributions were deductible, any IRA distribution you receive that you do not roll over (¶8.9) will be taxable. Not only are distributions taxable, but the timing and amount of IRA payments is subject to these restrictions:

- Distributions before age 59½ are subject to a 10% tax penalty, unless you are totally disabled or you receive annual payments under an annuity-type schedule. The annuity schedule rules are at ¶8.12.
- After you reach age 70½, you must start to receive annual distributions under a life-expectancy calculation. The required starting date is the April 1 following the end of the year in which you reach age 70½. For example, if you reach age 70½ during 1992, you must start taking IRA distributions by April 1, 1993. Failure to take the minimum required annual distribution can result in penalties. These rules are discussed in ¶8.14.
- Distributions of over $150,000 at any age are subject to a 15% penalty, as discussed at ¶8.13.

How to report IRA distributions on your return. All IRA distributions are reported to you and to the IRS on Form 1099-R. Form 1099-R must be attached to your return only if federal tax has been withheld. You can avoid withholding by instructing the payer not to withhold on Form W-4P (or a substitute form); see ¶26.11.

If you have never made nondeductible contributions, your IRA withdrawals are fully taxable and should be reported on Line 16b of Form 1040 or Line 10b of Form 1040A. If you have made deductible and nondeductible contributions, complete Form 8606 to figure the nontaxable and taxable portions as discussed on page 133. Then report the total IRA withdrawal on Line 16a of Form 1040 or Line 10a of Form 1040A and enter only the taxable portion on Line 16b or Line 10b respectively.

If you have an individual retirement annuity, your investment in the contract is treated as zero so all payments are fully taxable. Distributions from an endowment policy because of death are taxed as ordinary income to the extent allocable to retirement savings; to the extent allocable to life insurance, they are considered insurance proceeds.

Proceeds from U.S. retirement bonds (which were issued by the Treasury before May 1982) are taxable in the year the bonds are redeemed. However, you must report the full proceeds in the year you reach age 70½ even if you do not redeem the bonds.

Loan treated as distribution. If you borrow from your IRA plan or use it as security for a loan, generally you are considered to have received your entire interest. Borrowing will subject the account or the fair market value of the contract to tax at ordinary income rates as of the first day of the taxable year of the borrowing. Your IRA account loses its tax-exempt status. If you use the account or part of it as security for a loan, the pledged portion is treated as a distribution.

However, under the rollover rules, a short-term loan may be made by withdrawing IRA funds and redepositing them in an IRA within 60 days; *see* ¶8.9.

10% Penalty For Pre-Age 59½ Payouts

The 10% penalty applies to any distribution you receive before age 59½, unless you are totally disabled or annual payments are made under the annuity-type schedule methods discussed at ¶8.12. Beneficiaries receiving IRA funds following the death of the owner are exempt from the penalty. Proposals have been made in Congress to expand the exception to include withdrawals for certain first-time home buyers and unemployed individuals, and for paying medical and educational expenses. *See* the Tax Legislation Guide at the front of this book for an update.

The penalty is 10% of the taxable IRA distribution. For example, if before age 59½, you withdraw $3,000 from your IRA, you must include the $3,000 as part of your taxable income and in addition, pay a $300 penalty tax. If part of a premature distribution is tax free because it is allocable to nondeductible contributions or rolled over to another IRA (¶8.9), the 10% penalty applies only to the taxable portion of the distribution. You generally must report pre-age 59½ distributions on Form 5329, but this may not be necessary if one of the penalty exceptions apply.

Reporting pre-age 59½ distributions on Form 5329. You must report pre-age 59½ distributions on Form 5329 unless the entire amount was rolled over or the payer has indicated on Form 1099-R that another of the penalty exceptions applies. For example, if the payer correctly enters in Box 7 of your Form 1099-R Code 2 (for the annuity method exception), Code 3 (disability exception) or Code 4 (beneficiary's exception) you do not have to file Form 5329. If these codes are not shown, but an exception applies, claim the exception on Form 5329. If no exception applies, the 10% penalty is computed on Form 5329, which must be attached to your return. The penalty is then entered on Line 51 of Form 1040.

Figure tax on Form 8606 if nondeductible contributions were made. All of your IRAs are treated as one contract. All distributions during a taxable year are treated as one distribution. If you withdraw an amount from an IRA during a taxable year and you previously made both deductible and nondeductible IRA contributions, part of your withdrawal will be tax free and part will be taxable. You must file Form 8606 to figure the taxable and nontaxable portions of the distribution; *see* the sample Form 8606 on page 134. The nontaxable amount is based on the ratio of the nondeductible IRA contributions over the year-end balance of all of your IRA accounts plus the amount of the distribution; *see* the Example in the next column. This withdrawal rule will penalize you if you make nondeductible contributions and later decide to make withdrawals from the "nondeductible account." You may not claim that you are withdrawing only your tax-free contributions, even if your withdrawal is less than your nondeductible contributions. If you withdraw amounts from your nondeductible account, you will incur tax.

The payor of an IRA account, such as a bank, will report withdrawals from an IRA account to the IRS on Form 1099-R as if they are taxable. It is up to you to keep records that show the nondeductible contributions you have made. IRS instructions require you to keep copies of all Forms 8606 on which nondeductible contributions have been designated, as well as copies of (1) your tax returns for years you made nondeductible contributions; (2) Forms 5498

showing all IRA contributions and showing the value of your IRAs for each year you received a distribution; and (3) Forms 1099-R and W-2P showing IRA distributions. According to the IRS, you should keep such records until you have withdrawn all IRA funds.

Follow these steps in determining the tax-free and taxable portion of IRA withdrawals made during 1992:

Step 1. Total IRA withdrawals during 1992.
Step 2. Total nondeductible contributions to all IRAs made by the end of 1992. Tax-free withdrawals of nondeductible contributions in prior years reduce the total. If you made an IRA contribution for 1992 (including a contribution made between January 1 and April 15, 1993) that may be *partly* nondeductible because your adjusted gross income is within the deduction phaseout range shown on page 128 for active plan participants, you should include that entire contribution in the Step 2 total.
Step 3. Add Step 1 to the balance of all your IRAs at the end of 1992. If you received a distribution near the end of the year and rolled it over tax free to another IRA at the beginning of 1993 (within 60 days), add the rollover to the year-end balance.
Step 4. Divide Step 2 by Step 3. This is the tax-free percentage of your IRA withdrawal.
Step 5. Multiply the Step 4 percentage by Step 1. This amount is tax free. The balance of your IRA withdrawal is fully taxable.

EXAMPLE In 1992, you withdraw $5,000 from your IRA having made deductible IRA contributions of $8,000 and nondeductible contributions of $6,000 as follows:

Year	Deductible	Nondeductible
1985	$2,000	– 0 –
1986	2,000	– 0 –
1987	2,000	– 0 –
1988	1,000	$1,000
1989	1,000	1,000
1990	– 0 –	2,000
1991	– 0 –	2,000
	$8,000	$6,000

Assume that at the end of 1992, your total IRA account balance, including earnings, is $17,500, and that this is your first IRA withdrawal. On your 1992 return, $1,350 of the $5,000 IRA withdrawal will be tax free and $3,650 will be taxable.

Step 1.	IRA withdrawal	$5,000
Step 2.	Nondeductible contributions	6,000
Step 3.	IRA balance at end of the year ($17,500) plus Step 1	22,500
Step 4.	Tax-free percentage ($6,000 ÷ $22,500)	27%
Step 5.	Tax-free withdrawal (27% × $5,000)	1,350
	Taxable withdrawal: $5,000 − $1,350	$3,650

The total $5,000 withdrawal should be reported on Line 16a of Form 1040 or on Line 10a of Form 1040A, and the taxable $3,650 portion entered on Line 16b (Form 1040) or on Line 10b (Form 1040A).

On the sample Form 8606 worksheet (*see* page 134), the $6,000 of nondeductible contributions are shown on Line 3, the $5,000 withdrawal on Line 8. The tax-free percentage of 27% is on Line 10 and the $1,350 tax-free withdrawal on Line 11. Line 12 shows the remaining IRA basis of $4,650 ($6,000 − $1,350).

Deductible IRA loss based on unrecovered nondeductible contributions. According to the IRS, a loss may be allowed if all IRA funds have been distributed and you have not recovered your basis in nondeductible contributions.

Form 8606—Worksheet

1	Enter the total value of **ALL** your IRAs as of 12/31/92. See instructions.	**1**	*17,500*
2	Enter your IRA contributions for 1992 that you choose to be nondeductible. Include those made during 1/1/93–4/15/93 that were for 1992. See instructions.	**2**	*0*
3	Enter your total IRA basis for 1991 and prior years. See instructions.	**3**	*6,000*
4	Add lines 2 and 3. If you did not receive any IRA distributions (withdrawals) in 1992, skip lines 5 through 13 and enter this amount on line 14	**4**	*6,000*
5	Enter only those contributions included on line 2 that were made during 1/1/93–4/15/93. This amount will be the same as line 2 if all of your nondeductible contributions for 1992 were made in 1993 by 4/15/93. See instructions.	**5**	*0*
6	Subtract line 5 from line 4	**6**	*6,000*
7	Enter the amount from line 1 plus any outstanding rollovers. See instructions.	**7**	*17,500*
8	Enter the total IRA distributions received during 1992. Do not include amounts rolled over before 1/1/93. See instructions.	**8**	*5,000*
9	Add lines 7 and 8	**9**	*22,500*
10	Divide line 6 by line 9 and enter the result as a decimal (to at least two places). Do not enter more than "1.00"	**10**	*.27*
11	Multiply line 8 by line 10. This is the amount of your **nontaxable distributions for 1992**. See instructions. ▶	**11**	*1,350*
12	Subtract line 11 from line 6. This is the **basis in your IRA(s) as of 12/31/92**	**12**	*4,650*
13	Enter the amount, if any, from line 5	**13**	
14	Add lines 12 and 13. This is your **total IRA basis for 1992 and prior years** ▶	**14**	*4,650*

EXAMPLE You make nondeductible IRA contributions of $10,000 from 1987–1991. At the end of 1992, you withdraw $6,000. The year-end balance is $8,000. The tax-free portion of the withdrawal is $4,286 ($10,000 ÷ $14,000 × $6,000).

After the withdrawal, your account balance is $8,000 and your basis in the account is $5,714 ($10,000 − $4,286). If because of poor investments the value of the IRA fell to $3,000 by the end of 1993 and you withdrew the entire $3,000 balance, you could claim a $2,714 loss ($5,714 basis − $3,000 distribution).

TAX-FREE ROLLOVERS TO IRAs

¶8.9 You may make a tax-free rollover of funds from one IRA to another or from a qualified employer or self-employed plan to an IRA. Such transfers are treated as a distribution of the assets from your old plan to you and you will be taxed unless you make a tax-free rollover within 60 days. Rollover transfers are not deductible.

Rollover from an employer plan to an IRA. Distributions eligible for rollover in 1992 and 1993 are discussed at ¶7.8.

In 1993, it is advisable to have your employer directly transfer the funds to an IRA that you select in order to avoid 20% withholding tax (¶26.11). If you receive the funds from your employer and make the rollover yourself, you have 60 days to complete the rollover. The amount withheld must be included in the rollover or it will be subject to tax.

The IRS has strictly applied the 60-day rollover rule even where failure to meet the deadline is not the taxpayer's fault. For example, an investor wanted to transfer a lump-sum distribution from a terminated company plan to an IRA. The company plan had been invested in five different funds maintained by a mutual fund "family," and the investor merely wanted to reregister his account as an IRA while keeping the same fund investments. However, his written instructions were followed for only four of the funds because of a clerk's error. The failure to reregister the fifth account was not discovered and corrected until six months later. An unsympathetic IRS held that the amount from the fifth fund, $15,100, was a taxable distribution because it was not rolled over within the 60-day period.

In a similar case, the Tax Court allowed tax-free rollover treatment where Merrill Lynch made a bookkeeping error by failing to properly record a rollover of a lump-sum distribution of cash and stock from a company plan. The cash was deposited into the IRA within the 60-day period but the stock was not. The court held that the date of the rollover was fixed when the taxpayer signed the necessary documentation and transferred the funds to establish the IRA within the 60-day period.

Rollover from one IRA to another IRA. To avoid tax on a rollover from one IRA to another, these tests must be met: (1) The amount you receive from your old IRA must be transferred to the new plan within 60 days of your receiving it; and (2) a tax-free rollover may occur only once in a one-year period starting on the date you receive the first distribution. If a second distribution is received from the same IRA within the one-year period, the distribution is taxable and if you are under age 59½, could be subject to the 10% penalty for premature distributions; see ¶8.8.

The once-a-year roll-over rule applies separately to each of your IRAs. For example, if you have one IRA invested in a bank and another IRA in a mutual fund, you may roll over within the same one-year period a distribution from the bank and also a distribution from the mutual fund to any other IRA.

60-Day Loan From IRA

You can take advantage of the roll-over rule to borrow funds from your IRA if you need a short-term loan to pay your taxes or other expenses. As long as you redeposit the amount in an IRA within 60 days you are not taxed on the withdrawal; the redeposit is considered a tax-free rollover. You may roll over the funds to a different IRA than the one from which the withdrawal was made. A second withdrawal from the same IRA within one year would be taxable as explained above.

Deposits in insolvent financial institutions. The 60-day limit for completing a rollover is extended if the funds are "frozen" and may not be withdrawn from a bankrupt or insolvent financial institution. The 60-day period is extended while the account is frozen and you have a minimum of 10 days after the release of the funds to complete the rollover.

If a government agency takes control of an insolvent bank, you might receive an "involuntary" distribution of your IRA account from the agency. According to the IRS and Tax Court, such a payment is subject to the regular IRA distribution rules. For example, a couple received payment for their $11,000 IRA balance from the Maryland Deposit Insurance Fund after the bank in which the funds were invested became insolvent. The Tax Court held that the payment was taxable, even though the distribution was from a state insurance fund and not from the bank itself. Furthermore, since they were under age 59½, the 10% penalty for early distributions (¶8.8) was imposed, even though the distribution was involuntary. The tax and penalty could have been avoided by making a rollover of the distribution within 60 days, but this was not done.

Direct Transfers Not Restricted

A direct transfer of IRA funds from one bank to another, or a direct transfer between other IRA trustees, is not considered a rollover subject to the once-a-year restriction. For example, you set up an IRA at Bank A in January 1992. In 1993, you decide to switch your account to Bank B. Bank B provides you with transfer request forms which it forwards to Bank A to complete the transfer. The transfer from Bank A to Bank B is tax free and is not subject to the one-year restriction on rollovers because there was no payment or distribution of the funds to you.

Rollover from employer plan after age 70½. Starting with the year you reach age 70½, you may no longer make IRA contributions. However, if you are over age 70½ and you receive a distribution from your employer's plan, you may instruct your employer to make a direct transfer of the distribution to an IRA. If you receive the distribution from the employer, a 20% tax will be withheld (¶26.11). You may make a tax-free rollover within 60 days of the distribution but in the year of the rollover, you must receive a minimum distribution from the IRA; *see* ¶8.14.

Reporting Rollover of 1992 Distribution

If you rolled over a qualifying distribution from an employer plan to an IRA, report the total distribution on Line 17a of Form 1040 or Line 11a of Form 1040A. Enter zero as the taxable amount on Line 17b or Line 11b if the entire amount was rolled over. If only part of the distribution was rolled over, enter the portion *not* rolled over on Line 17b or Line 11b.

If you roll over funds from one IRA to another, the total distribution should be reported on Line 16a of Form 1040 or Line 10a of Form 1040A. If the entire distribution was rolled over, enter zero as the taxable amount on Line 16b or Line 10b. Otherwise, enter the amount *not* rolled over on Line 16b or Line 10b.

TRANSFER OF IRA TO SPOUSE AT DIVORCE OR DEATH

¶8.10 If you receive your former spouse's IRA pursuant to a divorce decree or written instrument incident to the decree, the transfer is not taxable to either of you. From the date of transfer the account is treated as your IRA. If you are legally separated, a transfer of your spouse's IRA to you is tax free if made under a decree of separate mainte-nance or written instrument incident to the decree. The transferred account is then treated as your IRA.

Surviving spouse. If you inherit your spouse's IRA upon death, you may treat the IRA as your own or begin withdrawals from the account as explained in ¶8.15. If you treat the account as your own, you may change investments by making a tax-free rollover to another IRA, or by authorizing a direct trustee-to-trustee transfer as discussed in ¶8.9.

QDRO transfer to IRA. If you receive your share of your spouse's or former spouse's benefits from an employer plan under a qualified domestic relations order (QDRO), the distribution is taxable to you unless you roll it over to an IRA. Special averaging may be available; *see* ¶7.12. Tax on the transfer may be avoided if you roll over your entire share tax free to an IRA. You must receive your entire share of the benefit within one of your tax years. If you receive property rather than cash, you must roll over the same property you receive. If you roll over only part of a qualifying QDRO distribution, you figure the tax on the retained portion by taking into account a pro-rated share of your former spouse's cost investment.

SIMPLIFIED EMPLOYEE PENSION PLANS

¶8.11 A simplified employee pension plan set up by an employer allows the employer to contribute to an employee's IRA account more money than allowable under regular IRA rules. For 1992, your employer may contribute and deduct up to 15% of your compensation or $30,000, whichever is less. Your employer's SEP contributions are excluded from your pay and are not included on Form W-2 unless they exceed the limit. If contributions exceed the limit, a 6% penalty tax may be imposed unless the excess (plus allowable income) is withdrawn by the due date of the return, plus extensions; *see* ¶8.13.

Self-employed individuals may also set up an SEP as an alternative to a Keogh plan; *see* Chapter 41.

Employees over Age 70½

An employee over age 70½ may still participate in an employer SEP plan but may not make personal IRA contributions. Minimum distributions from the plan must begin as discussed in ¶7.13.

Eligibility. An SEP must cover all employees who are at least age 21, earn over $374 in 1992 (this amount is adjusted annually for inflation), and who have worked for the employer at any time during at least three of the past five years. Union employees covered by union agreements may generally be excluded.

SEP salary reduction arrangements. Qualifying small employers may set up salary reduction SEPs which allow employees to contribute a portion of their pay to the plan instead of receiving it in cash.

Only qualifying small companies may offer such plans. Salary reductions are allowed for a year only if the employer had no more than 25 employees eligible to participate in the SEP at any time during the prior taxable year. Furthermore, at least 50% of the eligible employees must elect the salary reduction option, and the deferral percentage for highly compensated employees may not exceed 125% of the average contribution of regular employees. State or local government agencies and tax-exempt organizations may not set up salary reduction SEPs.

If salary reductions are allowed, the maximum salary reduction contribution for 1992 is $8,728; the limit is subject to future inflation adjustments. Deferrals over $8,728 are taxable, and if not timely distributed to the employee, can be taxed again when distributed from the plan.

If an employee contributes to both a SEP and a 401(k) plan, the $8,728 limit applies to the total salary reductions from both plans. If an employee makes salary reduction contributions to an SEP and also to a tax-sheltered annuity plan (¶7.20), the maximum salary reduction to the SEP is $8,728, and an additional salary reduction may be made to the tax-sheltered annuity plan up to an overall limit of $9,500. If salary reductions were made only to the tax-sheltered annuity plan, a $9,500 limit generally applies; see ¶7.20.

If an employer makes separate contributions to an SEP apart from an employee's salary reduction contributions, the total tax-free contribution is the lesser of 15% of pay or $30,000.

WITHDRAWING IRA FUNDS BEFORE AGE 59½

¶8.12 Unless you are disabled, you generally cannot receive IRA distributions before age 59½ without paying a 10% penalty (¶8.8). However, you may avoid the penalty if you are willing to receive annual distributions under one of the annuity-type methods discussed in this section. Before arranging an annuity-type schedule, consider these points: all of the payments will be taxable (unless allocable to nondeductible contributions under ¶8.8), and if you do not continue the payments for a minimum number of years, the IRS will impose the 10% penalty for all taxable payments received before age 59½, plus interest charges.

The minimum payout period is the *longer* of five years or until you reach age 59½. Thus, if you are in your 40s, you would have to continue the scheduled payments until you are age 59½. If you are in your mid-50s, the length of payout period may not present a serious problem. Payments may be limited to a five-year period, starting with the date of the first distribution, provided that the period ends after you reach age 59½. During this minimum period, the arranged annuity-type schedule may not be changed. For example, taking a lump-sum distribution of your account balance before age 59½

would trigger the retroactive penalty. After the minimum payout period, you can discontinue the payments or change the method without penalty. The minimum payout period rules do not apply to totally disabled individuals or to beneficiaries of deceased IRA owners.

If you would like to take advantage of this penalty exception, you may apply one of the following three payout methods that have been approved by the IRS in private rulings:

1. Life expectancy method. This is the easiest method to figure but provides smaller annual payments than the other methods. Figure the annual withdrawal by dividing your account balance by your life expectancy or by the joint life and last survivor expectancy of you and your beneficiary. This is the same method discussed at ¶8.14 for figuring minimum required distributions after age 70½. For example, you are age 50 in 1993 and have an IRA of $100,000 at the beginning of the year. You may take a penalty-free payment of $3,021 in 1993; $100,000 account balance ÷ 33.1 life expectancy. Individual life expectancies are shown in Table V at ¶7.23. The annual penalty-free amount will generally rise in later years, with the exact amount depending on your account balance and whether you recalculate your life expectancy under the table each year (based on your age) or you simply reduce your life expectancy by one for each year that has elapsed since the year of the first payment.

If instead of using your single life expectancy you used the joint life and last survivor expectancy of you and your beneficiary (see sample table below) the annual penalty-free amount would be smaller given the longer joint life expectancy. For example, if your beneficiary was age 45, your joint life and last survivor life expectancy would be 42 years (using ages 50 and 45), and the penalty-free withdrawal $2,381 ($100,000 account balance ÷ 42). The full IRS Table VI showing joint life and last survivor life expectancy is in IRS Publication 939 and can also be obtained from your IRA trustee.

2. Amortization method. Under this method, you amortize your IRA account balance like a mortgage, using the same life expectancy as under Method 1 (your single life expectancy or joint life and last survivor expectancy of you and your beneficiary) and a long-term interest rate that is reasonable when the payments commence. In private rulings, the IRS has approved the use of interest

Joint Life and Last Survivor Life Expectancy

AGES	45	46	47	48	49	50	51	52	53	54	55	56	57	58	59
40	46.9	46.5	46.2	45.9	45.6	45.3	45.1	44.8	44.6	44.4	44.2	44.1	43.9	43.8	43.7
41	46.3	45.9	45.5	45.2	44.9	44.6	44.3	44.1	43.9	43.6	43.4	43.3	43.1	43.0	42.8
42	45.7	45.3	44.9	44.5	44.2	43.9	43.6	43.3	43.1	42.9	42.7	42.5	42.3	42.1	42.0
43	45.1	44.7	44.3	43.9	43.6	43.2	42.9	42.6	42.4	42.1	41.9	41.7	41.5	41.3	41.2
44	44.6	44.1	43.7	43.3	42.9	42.6	42.2	41.9	41.7	41.4	41.2	40.9	40.7	40.5	40.4
45	44.1	43.6	43.2	42.7	42.3	42.0	41.6	41.3	41.0	40.7	40.4	40.2	40.0	39.7	39.6
46	43.6	43.1	42.6	42.2	41.8	41.4	41.0	40.6	40.3	40.0	39.7	39.5	39.2	39.0	38.8
47	43.2	42.6	42.1	41.7	41.2	40.8	40.4	40.0	39.7	39.3	39.0	38.7	38.5	38.2	38.0
48	42.7	42.2	41.7	41.2	40.7	40.2	39.8	39.4	39.0	38.7	38.4	38.1	37.8	37.5	37.3
49	42.3	41.8	41.2	40.7	40.2	39.7	39.3	38.8	38.4	38.1	37.7	37.4	37.1	36.8	36.6
50	42.0	41.4	40.8	40.2	39.7	39.2	38.7	38.3	37.9	37.5	37.1	36.8	36.4	36.1	35.9
51	41.6	41.0	40.4	39.8	39.3	38.7	38.2	37.8	37.3	36.9	36.5	36.1	35.8	35.5	35.2
52	41.3	40.6	40.0	39.4	38.8	38.3	37.8	37.3	36.8	36.4	35.9	35.6	35.2	34.8	34.5
53	41.0	40.3	39.7	39.0	38.4	37.9	37.3	36.8	36.3	35.8	35.4	35.0	34.6	34.2	33.9
54	40.7	40.0	39.3	38.7	38.1	37.5	36.9	36.4	35.8	35.3	34.9	34.4	34.0	33.6	33.3
55	40.4	39.7	39.0	38.4	37.7	37.1	36.5	35.9	35.4	34.9	34.4	33.9	33.5	33.1	32.7
56	40.2	39.5	38.7	38.1	37.4	36.8	36.1	35.6	35.0	34.4	33.9	33.4	33.0	32.5	32.1
57	40.0	39.2	38.5	37.8	37.1	36.4	35.8	35.2	34.6	34.0	33.5	33.0	32.5	32.0	31.6
58	39.7	39.0	38.2	37.5	36.8	36.1	35.5	34.8	34.2	33.6	33.1	32.5	32.0	31.5	31.1
59	39.6	38.8	38.0	37.3	36.6	35.9	35.2	34.5	33.9	33.3	32.7	32.1	31.6	31.1	30.6

rates based on Federal rates, such as the applicable federal rate used for figuring minimum interest on seller-financed sales (¶4.32), or the rate of interest under Pension Benefit Guaranty Corporation regulations.

Under the amortization method, the annual penalty-free withdrawal will be larger than under Method 1. For example, using an interest rate of 8% (assuming that is a reasonable rate), a 50-year-old with a $100,000 account balance may withdraw $8,679 without penalty in the first year, as opposed to $3,021 under Method 1. The payment in future years will stay the same unless life expectancy is adjusted.

3. Annuity factor method. This method is similar to the amortization method but it allows you to use insurance mortality tables (such as the UP-1984 Mortality Table) that project shorter life expectancy tables than the IRS life expectancy tables used under Methods 1 and 2. If an interest rate of 8% and the UP-1984 mortality table were used for a 50-year-old with a $100,000 account balance, the penalty-free withdrawal in the first year would be $9,002, as opposed to $3,021 under Method 1 or $8,679 under Method 2.

Note: For Methods 2 and 3, you should get the assistance of a tax professional and an actuary to help plan a series of payments than will qualify for the penalty exception.

PENALTIES FOR EXCESS DISTRIBUTIONS AND CONTRIBUTIONS

¶**8.13** You must file Form 5329 with your 1992 Form 1040 if you are liable for the penalties on excess contributions or excess distributions.

Excess distributions. As discussed at ¶7.15, an IRA distribution exceeding $150,000 may be subject to a 15% penalty. The penalty is imposed on the excess over $150,000 unless an exception to the penalty is available. For example, the penalty on a $200,000 IRA distribution would be $7,500 (15% × $50,000, excess over $150,000). If you receive an IRA distribution and make a tax-free rollover to another IRA within 60 days, the penalty does not apply. The penalty does not apply to distributions attributable to nondeductible contributions. Beneficiaries do not have to pay the penalty on distributions after the IRA owner's death.

If on your 1987 or 1988 return you made the "grandfather" election discussed at ¶7.15, the penalty threshold for 1992 is $140,276 rather than $150,000; also *see* Form 5329.

Excess contributions. If you contribute more than the allowable amount, whether deductible or nondeductible, the excess contribution may be subject to a penalty tax of 6%. The penalty tax is cumulative. That is, unless you correct the excess, you will be subject to another penalty on the excess contribution in the following year. The penalty tax is not deductible.

The 6% penalty may be avoided by withdrawing the excess contribution by the due date for your return, including extensions, plus any income earned on it. The withdrawn excess is not taxable provided no deduction was allowed for it. The withdrawn income must be reported on your return for the year of the excess contribution. If you are under age 59½ (and not disabled) when you receive the income, the 10% premature withdrawal penalty applies to the income. Similar rules apply to withdrawals of excess employer contributions to a simplified employee pension plan (¶8.11) made by the due date for your return.

If an excess contribution for 1992 is not withdrawn by the due date for your 1992 return, the 6% penalty may be avoided for 1993 by withdrawing the excess by the end of 1993. You may also avoid a penalty for 1993 by reducing your allowable 1993 IRA contribu-

tion by the 1992 excess and then including that amount in your 1993 IRA deduction. *See* IRS Publication 590 and Form 5329 for details.

If you deducted an excess contribution in an earlier year for which total contributions were $2,250 or less, you may make a tax-free withdrawal of the excess by filing an amended return to correct the excess deduction. However, the 6% penalty tax applies for each year that the excess was still in the account at the end of the year.

After the due date of your return, you may make a tax-free withdrawal of excess employer contributions to a simplified employee pension plan (¶8.11) if they are $30,000 or less. However, the 6% penalty tax applies for each year that the excess was still in the account at the end of the year.

See IRS Publication 590 for further information on correcting excess contributions made in a prior year.

MINIMUM DISTRIBUTIONS AFTER AGE 70½

¶**8.14** If you do not start receiving distributions by April 1 following the year you reach age 70½ or you receive an insufficient distribution after this date, a penalty tax of 50% applies to the difference between the amount you should have received and the amount you did receive. The penalty is reported on Form 5329, which must be attached to Form 1040.

EXAMPLE You receive $500 from your IRA plan. The minimum amount required to be paid to you was $700. You pay a penalty tax of $100 (50% of $200).

If you reached age 70½ during 1992, you must receive a minimum distribution for 1992 by April 1, 1993. You will also have to receive a minimum distribution for 1993 by December 31, 1993. Thus, if you do not take your first distribution during 1992, and wait until between January 1 and April 1, 1993, you will have to make two distributions in 1993, one by April 1 and another by December 31. This could increase your 1992 taxable income substantially. Distributions for later years must be made by December 31 of each year.

If you reach age 70½ during 1993, your first distribution must be no later than April 1, 1994. If you have an individual retirement annuity, your insurance company should gear your payments to meet minimum distribution requirements.

Penalty Waiver for Reasonable Mistakes

The IRS may waive the penalty for insufficient withdrawals if they are due to reasonable error and if steps have been taken in order to remedy the situation. You must submit evidence to account for shortfalls in withdrawals and how you are rectifying the situation. The IRS has indicated that examples of acceptable reasons for insufficient withdrawals include erroneous advice from the sponsoring organization or other pension advisors or that your own good faith efforts to apply the required withdrawal formula produced a miscalculation or misunderstanding of the formula. You should attach your letter of explanation to Form 5329. You must pay the penalty; if the IRS grants a waiver, it will refund the penalty.

Figuring Minimum IRA Distributions. Your IRA trustee should help you figure how much you must withdraw to avoid an IRS penalty. To compute the annual minimum required distribution yourself, follow these steps for *each* of your IRAs:

Joint Life and Last Survivor Life Expectancy

Ages	60	61	62	63	64	65	66	67	68	69	70	71	72	73	74	75	76	77	78	79	80
70	26.2	25.6	24.9	24.3	23.7	23.1	22.5	22.0	21.5	21.1	20.6	20.2	19.8	19.4	19.1	18.8	18.5	18.3	18.0	17.8	17.6
71	26.0	25.3	24.7	24.0	23.4	22.8	22.2	21.7	21.2	20.7	20.2	19.8	19.4	19.0	18.6	18.3	18.0	17.7	17.5	17.2	17.0
72	25.8	25.1	24.4	23.8	23.1	22.5	21.9	21.3	20.8	20.3	19.8	19.4	18.9	18.5	18.2	17.8	17.5	17.2	16.9	16.7	16.4
73	25.6	24.9	24.2	23.5	22.9	22.2	21.6	21.0	20.5	20.0	19.4	19.0	18.5	18.1	17.7	17.3	17.0	16.7	16.4	16.1	15.9
74	25.5	24.7	24.0	23.3	22.7	22.0	21.4	20.8	20.2	19.6	19.1	18.6	18.2	17.7	17.3	16.9	16.5	16.2	15.9	15.6	15.4
75	25.3	24.6	23.8	23.1	22.4	21.8	21.1	20.5	19.9	19.3	18.8	18.3	17.8	17.3	16.9	16.5	16.1	15.8	15.4	15.1	14.9
76	25.2	24.4	23.7	23.0	22.3	21.6	20.9	20.3	19.7	19.1	18.5	18.0	17.5	17.0	16.5	16.1	15.7	15.4	15.0	14.7	14.4
77	25.1	24.3	23.6	22.8	22.1	21.4	20.7	20.1	19.4	18.8	18.3	17.7	17.2	16.7	16.2	15.8	15.4	15.0	14.6	14.3	14.0
78	25.0	24.2	23.4	22.7	21.9	21.2	20.5	19.9	19.2	18.6	18.0	17.5	16.9	16.4	15.9	15.4	15.0	14.6	14.2	13.9	13.5
79	24.9	24.1	23.3	22.6	21.8	21.1	20.4	19.7	19.0	18.4	17.8	17.2	16.7	16.1	15.6	15.1	14.7	14.3	13.9	13.5	13.2
80	24.8	24.0	23.2	22.4	21.7	21.0	20.2	19.5	18.9	18.2	17.6	17.0	16.4	15.9	15.4	14.9	14.4	14.0	13.5	13.2	12.8
81	24.7	23.9	23.1	22.3	21.6	20.8	20.1	19.4	18.7	18.1	17.4	16.8	16.2	15.7	15.1	14.6	14.1	13.7	13.2	12.8	12.5
82	24.6	23.8	23.0	22.3	21.5	20.7	20.0	19.3	18.6	17.9	17.3	16.6	16.0	15.5	14.9	14.4	13.9	13.4	13.0	12.5	12.2
83	24.6	23.8	23.0	22.2	21.4	20.6	19.9	19.2	18.5	17.8	17.1	16.5	15.9	15.3	14.7	14.2	13.7	13.2	12.7	12.3	11.9
84	24.5	23.7	22.9	22.1	21.3	20.5	19.8	19.1	18.4	17.7	17.0	16.3	15.7	15.1	14.5	14.0	13.5	13.0	12.5	12.0	11.6
85	24.5	23.7	22.8	22.0	21.3	20.5	19.7	19.0	18.3	17.6	16.9	16.2	15.6	15.0	14.4	13.8	13.3	12.8	12.3	11.8	11.4

1. Find the account balance of your IRA as of the previous December 31. If you reach age 70½ during 1992, use the account balance for December 31, 1991, even if the actual distribution is not made until the first quarter of 1993 (January 1-April 1). For purposes of figuring your 1993 distribution, use the 1992 year-end balance, reduced by the first-year distribution if you took it in the first quarter of 1993.

2. Find your life expectancy. For the year you reach age 70½, use the joint life and last survivor life expectancy of you and your beneficiary. If you name more than one beneficiary, the age of the oldest beneficiary (the shortest life expectancy) is taken into account. Joint life and last survivor life expectancy is found in IRS unisex Table VI, a sample section of which is shown above. The rest of the table is in IRS Publication 939 and can also be obtained from your IRA trustee.

The joint life and last survivor life expectancy of you and your beneficiary is determined by your ages on your respective birthdays in the year in which *you* reach age 70½. For example, assume that you reach age 70½ in April 1992. You are age 71 on your birthday in October 1992. Assume your beneficiary is age 67 on his birthday in 1992. For purposes of figuring your first required IRA distribution for the year 1992 (due by April 1, 1993), your joint life and last survivor expectancy from the table is 21.7 years (using ages 71 and 67). For figuring distributions for 1993 and later years, your life expectancy and the expectancy of a spouse named as beneficiary may be recalculated. Recalculation is generally automatic, but the IRA plan may require you and your spouse to elect before distributions begin to recalculate life expectancies in future years. Recalculation generally allows you to take smaller distributions and conserve the account principal.

If your beneficiary is not your spouse, your life expectancy may be recalculated after the first year but not the beneficiary's. His or her life expectancy as of the first distribution year, which is determined under Table V shown in ¶7.23, is reduced by one for each year that has passed since the first year. Then, find the age in Table V that is closest to the beneficiary's reduced life expectancy, using the higher age where the life expectancy falls between two ages. For example, if in the first year the beneficiary's life expectancy under Table V (¶7.23) was 18.4 years, for the second year it is reduced to 17.4 years. Since 17.4 in Table V falls between ages 68 and 69, use 69 as the beneficiary's age in looking up the joint life and last survivor life expectancy for you and the beneficiary (Table VI) in the second year.

If you elect not to recalculate your life expectancy or if your spouse as beneficiary elects not to recalculate, you and your spouse also reduce your individual life expectancy as of the first year (under Table V in ¶7.23) by one year for each year that has passed under the method just described for non-spouse beneficiaries.

There are limits to naming younger beneficiaries. If your beneficiary is not your spouse, you must treat the beneficiary as being no more than 10 years younger than yourself. Thus, if you are age 71 and your beneficiary is your teenage grandchild, the grandchild is considered to be age 61 for purposes of figuring your joint life and last survivor expectancy.

3. Divide the account balance from Step 1 by the life expectancy from Step 2. This is the minimum amount you must receive. If you have more than one IRA, divide Step 1 by Step 2 for each account and *see* Step 4.

4. If you have more than one IRA, total the Step 3 amounts for all the accounts. This is how much you must receive for the year. Although you must calculate the required distribution separately for each account, you do not have to make withdrawals from each of them. The total required distribution from all accounts may be taken from any one account, or more than one account if you prefer. For example, if you have five bank IRAs you may take the entire required distribution from the bank where you have the largest balance, or from any other combination of banks. *See* Example 2 on page 139. The entire distribution is taxable unless part is allocable to nondeductible IRA contributions, as explained in ¶8.8.

Note: For further information on calculating minimum required distributions, *see* IRS proposed regulations 1.408-8 and 1.401(a)(9)-1. Also *see* the instructions to Form 5329.

EXAMPLES 1. Joe Blake reached age 70½ in March 1992. A minimum distribution for 1992 must be received by April 1, 1993. Joe's IRA balance as of December 31, 1991, was $26,300. The 1991 year-end balance is used in the computation even if the distribution for 1992 is made in the first quarter of 1993 (by the April 1 deadline). Joe's beneficiary is his wife, who is age 63 on her birthday in 1992. On his 1992 birthday, Joe is age 71.

Step 1. Account balance of $26,300.
Step 2. Joint life and last survivor expectancy from the table is 24 years, using ages 71 and 63.
Step 3. Divide Step 1 by Step 2.
$26,300 ÷ 24=$1,096. Joe must receive the $1,096 by April 1, 1993.

The second minimum distribution, due by December 31, 1993, is based upon the 1992 year-end account balance, but if the 1992 distribution was not made until early 1993 (by April 1), the account balance is reduced by that distribution. Thus, assume that Joe took the $1,096 distribution for 1992 in March 1993 and that the 1992 year-end balance is $27,500. For purposes of figuring the required distribution for 1993, an account balance of $26,404 ($27,500 − $1,096) is used. Assuming Joe and his wife recalculate their life expectancies, their joint expectancy would be 23.1 (using ages 72 and 64). Thus, the minimum required distribution for 1993, due by December 31, 1993, would be $1,143 ($26,404 ÷ 23.1).

2. Cynthia Lowell has two IRAs. She became age 70½ on January 15, 1992, and thus must receive her first distribution by April 1, 1993. The beneficiary of IRA-1 is her brother, who is age 61 on his birthday in 1992; the account balance of IRA-1 as of December 31, 1991, was $100,000. The beneficiary of IRA-2 is her husband who was age 74 on his 1992 birthday; the account balance at the end of 1991 was $10,000.

IRA-1: The minimum required distribution is $3,952.57. This is the account balance of $100,000 divided by 25.3, the joint life and last survivor expectancy using ages 71 and 61 from the table.

IRA-2: The minimum required distribution is $537.63, the account balance of $10,000 divided by 18.6, the joint life and last survivor expectancy using ages 71 and 74.

The total required distribution of $4,490.20 from both IRAs must be received by April 1, 1993. Cynthia may withdraw the money from either one or both of the IRAs.

If the withdrawal is delayed until the first quarter of 1993, the 1992 year-end balance is reduced by the withdrawal when she figures her minimum required distribution for 1993. The distribution for 1993 must be received by December 31, 1993.

INHERITED IRAs

¶8.15 When an IRA owner dies, the rules for handling the account depend on who the beneficiary is. A surviving spouse beneficiary has certain advantages not available to other beneficiaries.

Surviving spouse. If you inherit an IRA from your deceased spouse, you may elect to treat it as your own IRA. You may make IRA contributions to the account, roll over the funds to another IRA, or make rollovers into the account from other IRAs or from a qualifying employer-plan distribution; *see* ¶8.9. Distributions from the account are taxable and if received before age 59½, may be subject to the 10% penalty for early withdrawals; *see* ¶8.8.

If you do not want to treat the account as your IRA, the payout period for withdrawing funds from the account depends on when your spouse died.

If your spouse died after the required beginning date for distributions, which is April 1 of the year after the year in which he or she reached age 70½ (¶8.14), you must receive distributions from the IRA at least as rapidly as your spouse was receiving them.

If your spouse died before the required beginning date, the IRA plan will probably allow you to either (1) withdraw funds from the IRA over your life expectancy, or (2) withdraw the entire account balance by the end of the fifth year following the year of your spouse's death. Some plans do not allow a choice but specify the method.

If you elect to receive distributions over your life expectancy, you do not have to begin the distributions until the later of (1) December 31 of the year in which your spouse would have reached age 70½, or (2) December 31 of the year following the year of your spouse's death.

Beneficiaries other than surviving spouses. If you inherit an IRA from someone who was not your spouse, you may not treat it as your IRA account. Thus, you may not make contributions to the account or roll it over to another IRA.

The inherited plan may give you the option of receiving funds from the account over your life expectancy or over the five-year period following the IRA owner's death. Some plans specify which of these methods must be used. If the IRA plan gives you the choice of taking withdrawals from the account over your life expectancy, you may choose this option by beginning distributions no later than December 31 of the year following the year of the IRA owner's death. If the plan does not allow the life-expectancy option, or if you choose to use the five-year method, you must withdraw the entire account by December 31 of the fifth year following the year of the owner's death.

9 INCOME FROM RENTS AND ROYALTIES

Use Schedule E to report rental income and expenses. Also file Form 4562 to claim depreciation deductions for buildings acquired in 1992.

Use Schedule C instead of Schedule E if you provide additional services for the convenience of the tenants, such as maid service. That is, Schedule C is used to report payments received for the use and occupancy of rooms or other areas in a hotel, motel, boarding house, apartment, tourist home, or trailer court where services are provided primarily for the occupant.

If you rent an apartment or room in the same building in which you live, you report the rent income less expenses allocated to the rental property; see ¶29.18.

Rental income of a vacation home is generally taxable. However, if the rental period is for less than 15 days during the year, the rental income is not taxable and rental deductions are not allowed. The law prevents most homeowners from deducting losses (expenses in excess of income) on renting a personal vacation home or personal residence if the owner or close relatives personally use the premises during the year. Tests based on days of personal and rental use determine whether you may deduct losses as explained in ¶29.20.

Rental losses are also limited by passive activity rules of Chapter 10. If you actively manage the property, you may deduct up to $25,000 if your adjusted gross income (AGI) is $100,000 or less. The deduction is phased out if AGI is between $100,000 and $150,000. If you do not qualify for the allowance, the loss may be deducted only from other sources of rental income and passive activity income. You also must use Form 8582 to report your loss.

Use Schedule E to report royalties, but if you are a self-employed author, artist, or inventor, report royalty income and expenses on Schedule C.

RENTAL INCOME AND DEDUCTIONS

REPORTING RENTAL INCOME AND EXPENSES

¶9.1 On the cash basis, you report rent income on your tax return for the year in which you receive payment or in which you "constructively" receive it, such as where payment is credited to your bank account.

On the accrual basis, you report income on your tax return for the year in which you are entitled to receive payment. You do not report accrued income if the financial condition of the tenant makes collection doubtful. If you sue for payment, you do not report income until you win a collectible judgment.

Advance rentals. Advance rentals or bonuses are reported in the year received, whether you are on the cash or accrual basis.

Tenant's payment of landlord's expenses. The tenant's payment of your taxes, interest, insurance, mortgage amortization (even if you are not personally liable on the mortgage), repairs, or other expenses, is considered additional rental income to you. If your tenant pays your utility bills or your emergency repairs and deducts the amount from the rent payment, you must include as rental income the full rental amount, not the actual net payment. However, you can claim an offsetting deduction for expenses, such as repairs, that would have been deductible had you paid them.

Cancellation of lease. A tenant's payment for canceling a lease or modifying its terms is considered rental income when received. You may deduct expenses incurred because of the cancellation or modification and any unamortized balance of expenses paid in negotiating the lease.

Insurance. Insurance proceeds for loss of rental income because of fire or other casualty are rental income.

Security Deposits

Distinguish advance rentals, which are income, from security deposits, which are not. Security deposits are amounts deposited with you solely as security for the tenant's performance of the terms of the lease, and as such are usually not taxed, particularly where local law treats security deposits as trust funds. If the tenant breaches the lease, you are entitled to apply the sum as rent, at which time you report it as income.

Improvements by tenants. You do not realize taxable income when your tenant improves the leased premises, provided the improvements are not substitute rent payments. Furthermore, when you take possession of the improvements at the time the lease ends, you do not realize income. However, you may not depreciate the value of the improvements as the basis to you is considered zero.

Rental losses. Rental income may be offset by deductions claimed for depreciation, mortgage interest, and repair and maintenance costs. However, if these expenses exceed rental income, the resulting loss is subject to deduction limitations. Your rental activity is treated as a passive activity, even if you actively participate in operating the property. This means that generally you may not deduct rental losses from other income (such as salary, interest, and dividends). Rental losses may offset only other rental and passive activity income. However, if you perform some management role, you may be able to deduct from other income *real estate* rental losses of up to $25,000, provided your adjusted gross income does not exceed $100,000. The passive activity restrictions have the positive effect of making rental income attractive. Consider purchasing rental property if you have passive tax losses which may be used to offset the rental income.

The full details of the passive loss restrictions, which also affect tax credits, are discussed in Chapter 10.

CHECKLIST OF RENTAL DEDUCTIONS

¶9.2 The following items are deductible from rental income on Schedule E in determining your profit from this activity.

Real estate taxes. Special assessments for paving, sewer systems, or other local improvements are not deductible; they are added to the cost of the land. *See* ¶16.6 through ¶16.9 for real estate tax deductions.

Depreciation of a rental building. You may start claiming depreciation in the month the building is ready for tenants. For example, you bought a house in May 1992 and spent June and July making repairs. The house is ready to rent in August and you advertise for tenants. You begin depreciation as of August, even if a tenant does not move in until September or some later month. The month the building is ready for tenants is the month that determines the first-year depreciation write-off under the mid-month convention. *See* ¶42.13 for the monthly-based depreciation rates.

Depreciation for furniture and appliances. These are considered seven-year property under MACRS; *see* ¶42.4.

Management expenses.

Maintenance expenses: heating, repairs, lighting, water, electricity, gas, telephone, coal, and other service costs; *see* ¶9.3.

Salaries and wages paid to superintendents, janitors, elevator operators, and service and maintenance personnel.

Traveling expenses to look after the properties. If you travel "away from home" (¶20.6) to inspect or repair rental property, be prepared to show that this was the primary purpose of your trip, rather than vacationing or other personal purposes. Otherwise, the IRS may disallow deductions for round-trip travel costs.

Legal expenses for dispossessing tenants. But expenses of long-term leases are capital expenditures deductible over the term of the lease.

Interest on mortgages and other indebtedness. But expenses and fees for securing loans are nondeductible capital expenditures.

Commissions paid to collect rentals. But commissions paid to secure long-term rentals must be deducted over the life of the lease. Commissions paid to acquire the property are capitalized.

Premiums for fire, liability, and plate glass insurance. If payment is made in one year for insurance covering a period longer than one year, you amortize and deduct the premium over the life of the policy, even though you are on a cash basis.

Also deductible is a premium paid to secure a release from a mortgage in order to get a new loan.

Construction period interest and taxes. Construction period interest and taxes generally have to be capitalized and depreciated; *see* ¶16.5.

Charging below fair market rent. If you rent your property to a friend or relative for less than the fair rental value, you may deduct expenses and depreciation only to the extent of the rent income; *see* ¶29.20.

Co-tenants. One of two tenants in common may deduct only half of the maintenance expenses although he or she pays the entire bill. A tenant in common who pays all of the expenses of the common property is entitled to reimbursement from the other co-tenant. So one-half of the bill is not his or her ordinary and necessary expense. Each co-tenant owns a separate property interest in the common property which produces separate income for each. Each tenant's deductible expense is that portion of the entire expense which each separate interest bears to the whole, and no more.

Co-Tenant's Deduction for Real Estate Taxes

In a case involving real estate taxes, the Tax Court allowed a co-tenant to deduct more than her proportionate share. According to the court, the deductibility test for real estate taxes is whether the payment satisfied a personal liability or protects a beneficial interest in the property. In the case of co-tenants, nonpayment of taxes by the other co-tenants could result in the property being lost or foreclosed. To prevent this, a co-tenant who pays the tax is protecting his or her beneficial interest and, therefore, is entitled to deduct the payment of the full tax.

Costs of cancelling lease. A landlord may pay the tenant to cancel an unfavorable lease. The way the payment is treated by the landlord depends on the reason for the cancellation. If the purpose of the cancellation is to enable the landlord to construct a new building in place of the old, the cancellation payment is added to the basis of the new building. If the purpose is to sell the property, the payment is added to the cost of the property. If the landlord wants the premises for his own use, the payment is deducted over the remaining term of the old lease. If the landlord gets a new tenant to replace the old one, the cancellation payment is also generally deductible over the remaining term of the old lease.

EXAMPLE Handlery Hotels, Inc., had to pay its lessee $85,000 to terminate a lease on a building three years before the lease term expired. Handlery entered into a new 20-year lease at more favorable terms with another lessee. Handlery amortized the

$85,000 cancellation payment over the three-year unexpired term of the old lease. The IRS claimed that the payment had to be amortized over the 20-year term of the new lease, because it was part of the cost of obtaining the new lease. A federal district court agreed with the IRS, but an appeals court sided with Handlery. Since the unexpired lease term is the major factor in determining the amount of the cancellation payment, the cost of cancellation should be amortized over that unexpired term.

DISTINGUISH BETWEEN A REPAIR AND AN IMPROVEMENT

¶9.3 Maintenance and repair expenses are not treated the same as expenses for improvements and replacements. Only maintenance and incidental repair costs are deductible against rental income. Repairs that add to the value or prolong the life of the property are capital improvements. They may not be deducted currently but may be depreciated. Capital improvements to a residential rental building are depreciable over 27¹/₂ years; over 31¹/₂ years for commercial property. *See* ¶42.13 for depreciation rates.

EXAMPLE The costs of painting the outside of a building used for business purposes and the costs of papering the inside are repair costs and may be deducted. The replacement of a roof or a change in the plumbing system is a capital expenditure which may be depreciated under MACRS; *see* ¶42.13.

Repairs may not be separated from capital expenditures when part of an improvement program.

EXAMPLE Jones buys a dilapidated business building and has the building renovated and repaired. The total cost comes to about $13,000, of which $7,800 is deducted as repairs. But the repair deduction is disallowed because it is a capital expenditure. When a general improvement program is undertaken, you may not separate repairs from improvements. They become an integral part of the overall betterment and a capital investment, although they could be characterized as repairs when viewed independently.

What if the repairs and improvements are unconnected and not part of an overall improvement program? Assume you repair the floors of one story and improve another story by cutting new windows. You may probably deduct the cost of repairing the floors provided you have separate bills for the jobs. To safeguard the deduction, schedule the work at separate times so that the two jobs are not lumped together as an overall improvement program.

Normal maintenance expenses were distinguished from major improvement costs in a case involving a major hotel where improvements and maintenance were generally done at the same time. The operators of the hotel capitalized the cost of the improvements but claimed expense deductions for the cost of painting and repapering rooms. The IRS disallowed the deductions, claiming they were part of the improvement program. The operators claimed that the papering and painting were normal and usual maintenance work required to keep the hotel in first-class condition. The Tax Court disagreed and sided with the IRS. However, on appeal, the appeals court allowed the deduction. The "rehabilitation doctrine" does not apply where it can be shown that repairs are part of a normal range of ongoing maintenance. Here, the painting and papering only served to maintain the first-class status of the hotel. The fact that the work was done under a general improvement plan does not defeat the deduction. Any commercial enterprise, such as a hotel, that annually spends large sums of money on replacements and repairs must do so under a detailed plan and budget.

SALE OF A LEASE

¶9.4 Payments received by a lessee-tenant on the assignment or cancellation of a lease used in the tenants' business are subject to Section 1231 treatment; *see* ¶44.8. Payments to a tenant for canceling the lease on a personal residence are treated as proceeds from a sale of a capital asset; gain is capital gain if the lease was held long term but losses are not deductible.

Payments received by a landlord for cancellation of a lease are ordinary rent income, not capital gain.

DEDUCTING THE COST OF DEMOLISHING A BUILDING

¶9.5 When you buy improved property, the purchase price is allocated between the land and the building; only the building may be depreciated. The land may not; *see* ¶42.2. If you later demolish the building, you may not deduct the cost of the demolition or the undepreciated basis of the building as a loss in the year of demolition. Expenses or losses in connection with the demolition of any structure, including certified historic structures, are not deductible. They must be capitalized and added to the basis of the land on which the structure is located.

DEDUCTING THE COST OF A BUSINESS LEASE

¶9.6 The cost of buying a business lease is amortized over the remaining term of the lease. However, the lease term may have to include optional renewal periods. Where less than 75% of the cost of acquiring the lease is attributed to the remaining lease term on the date of acquisition, the lease term includes all renewal options and any other period for which there is a reasonable expectation of a renewal of the lease. In determining the period of the remaining lease term on the date of acquisition, options renewable by the lessee are not considered. Your annual deduction will be smaller if the renewal periods are added to the amortization term.

HOW LESSEES DEDUCT LEASEHOLD IMPROVEMENTS

¶9.7 Leasehold improvements placed in service after 1986 by a lessee are depreciated under MACRS— 27¹/₂ years for residential property or 31¹/₂ years for commercial property. You ignore the term of the lease. If the lease term is shorter than the MACRS life and you do not retain the improvements at the end of the term, the remaining undepreciated basis is considered in computing gain or loss at that time.

Pre-1987 improvements. For leasehold improvements placed in service before 1987, the cost of improvements is deductible over the *shorter* of the following periods:
(1) The useful life of the improvement if the improvement was before 1981, or the ACRS recovery period if after 1980 but before 1987, *or*
(2) The remaining term of the lease.
If (1) is the shorter period, the cost of the improvement is depreciated. If (2) is the shorter period, the cost is amortized ratably.
In determining the shorter period, you must add optional lease renewals to the remaining lease term under (2) if at the completion of the improvement, the remaining term of the original lease

(excluding unexercised renewal options) is less than 60% of the useful life (or ACRS recovery period) of the improvement. Renewals do not have to be taken into account under the 60% test if the lessee can show that it is more probable that the lease would not be renewed than that it would be renewed.

If the lessee and lessor are related, the term of the lease is treated as being equal to the remaining useful life (or recovery period) of the improvement. Related parties include spouses, children, grandchildren, parents, grandparents, brothers, sisters, and certain controlled corporations, partnerships, and trusts.

SPECIAL TAX CREDITS FOR REAL ESTATE INVESTMENTS

¶9.8 To encourage certain real estate investments, the tax law offers the following tax credits—

Low-income housing credit for buildings placed in service after 1986 and before June 30, 1992. The credit applies to newly constructed low-income housing and also to certain existing structures that are substantially rehabilitated. The amount of the credit depends on whether the building is new and whether federal subsidies are received. To claim the credit, you, as the building owner, must receive a certification from an authorized housing credit agency. The agency allocates a credit to you on Form 8609, which you use to claim the credit on Form 8586. You must attach Form 8609, Schedule A of Form 8609, and Form 8586 to your tax return.

Investors who held an interest in qualifying low-income property before October 26, 1990, were allowed an irrevocable election to increase the credit on their 1990 return by claiming 150% of the otherwise allocable credit. For fiscal year taxpayers, the election applied to the first tax year ending after October 24, 1990. If this election was made, the low-income credit for 1991 and later years is reduced on a ratable basis; *see* the instructions to Schedule A of Form 8609 for further details.

See the Tax Legislation Guide at the front of this book for the status of legislation that would extend the credit beyond June 30, 1992.

Rehabilitation credit for pre-1936 buildings or certified historic structures. On Form 3468, you may claim a 10% tax credit for rehabilitating pre-1936 buildings or a 20% credit for rehabilitating certified historic structures. For both types of rehabilitation credits, you must generally incur rehabilitation expenses of $5,000 or your adjusted basis in the building, whichever is greater.

A certified historic structure may be used for residential or nonresidential purposes. The Secretary of the Interior must certify that a planned rehabilitation is in keeping with the building's historic status designation for the credit to be available.

In one case, a developer who rehabilitated a certified historic structure and donated a conservation easement to a historic society in the same year was required to base the credit computation on the rehabilitation expenses minus the charitable deduction claimed. If the donation had been made in a later year, a portion of the original credit claimed would be subject to recapture.

The 10% credit for pre-1936 buildings applies only to nonresidential property. A substantial portion of the building's original structure must be retained after the rehabilitation. At least 75% of the external walls must be intact, with at least 50% kept as external walls. At least 75% of the existing internal structural framework must be kept in place.

For further details and credit conditions concerning the two types of rehabilitation credits, *see* Form 3468 and IRS Publications 572.

Tax credit limitations. Tax credits for low-income housing and rehabilitating historic or pre-1936 buildings may be limited by passive activity restrictions on Form 8582 (Chapter 10) and by tax liability limits for the general business credit (Chapter 40).

DEFERRED OR STEPPED-UP RENTAL AGREEMENTS

¶9.9 Cash basis lessors who are to receive more than $250,000 in total rent payments under a deferred lease agreement may have to report rent before they receive it and report imputed interest on deferred amounts. A special law (Code Section 467) requires both lessors and lessees to use the accrual basis when reporting rental income and expenses under agreements that (1) provide for initially low lease payments that substantially increase during the later period of the lease, or (2) defer rent payments until after the close of the year following the year of rental use. The calculation of imputed interest is similar to the 110% rule of ¶4.32.

The rules are intended to prevent cash basis lessors from being able to delay reporting of rental income until the year of payment, while accrual basis tenants deduct the rent as it accrues during the rental period.

The parties may follow the rent accruals provided for in the agreement. However, rents payable after the end of the rental period must be accounted for according to their present value.

Stricter accrual rules apply if: (1) the agreement does not allocate rents; (2) the lease term exceeds 75% of the recovery period for such property; or (3) the agreement is considered a disqualified leaseback. In these cases, rents are "leveled" under a constant accrual method.

The Section 467 rules do not apply if total rental payments and other considerations for use of the property are $250,000 or less. There is also an exception for agreements entered into before June 9, 1984, or to later agreements that were pursuant to a binding written contract made on or before June 8, 1984.

ROYALTY INCOME AND DEDUCTIONS

REPORTING ROYALTY INCOME

¶9.10 Royalties are payment for use of patents or copyrights or for the use and exhaustion of mineral properties. Royalties are taxable as ordinary income and are reported on Schedule E (Form 1040). Depletion deductions relating to the royalties are also reported on Schedule E. If you own an operating oil, gas, or mineral interest, or are a self-employed writer, investor, or artist, you report royalty income, expenses, and depletion on Schedule C.

EXAMPLES OF ROYALTY INCOME—

License fees received for use, manufacture, or sale of patented article.

Renting fees received from patents, copyrights, and depletable assets (such as oil wells).

Authors' royalties including advance royalties if not a loan.

Royalties for musical compositions, works of art, etc.

Proceeds of sale of part of your rights in an artistic composition or book—for example, sale of motion picture or television rights.

Royalties from oil, gas, or other similar interests; *see* ¶9.14. To have a royalty, you must retain an economic interest in the minerals deposited in the land which you have leased to the producer. You usually have a royalty when payments are based on the amount of minerals produced. However, if you are paid regardless of the minerals produced, you have a sale which is taxed as capital gain if the proceeds exceed the basis of the transferred property interest. Bonuses and advance royalties which are paid to you before the production of minerals are taxable as royalty income and are entitled to an allowance for depletion. However, bonuses and advanced royalties for gas and oil wells and geothermal deposits are not treated as gross income for purposes of calculating percentage depletion. If the lease is terminated without production and you received a bonus or advanced royalty, you report as income previously claimed depletion deductions. You increase the basis of your property by the restored depletion deductions.

Passive income. Certain working oil and gas interests are not subject to passive activity loss rules; *see* ¶10.10.

PRODUCTION COSTS OF BOOKS AND CREATIVE PROPERTIES

¶9.11 Freelance authors, artists, and photographers may deduct the costs of producing their original works in the years of the expense. You qualify for current expense deductions if you are self-employed and you *personally create* literary manuscripts, musical or dance scores, paintings, pictures, sculptures, drawings, cartoons, graphic designs, original print editions, photographs, or photographic negatives or transparencies.

If you conduct business as an owner-employee of a personal service corporation, and you are a qualifying author, artist, or photographer, the corporation may claim current deductions related to your expenses in producing books or other eligible creative works. Substantially all of the corporation's stock must be owned by you and your relatives.

Photographers and Filmmakers

Current deductions are *not allowed* for expenses relating to films, videotapes, printing, photographic plates, or similar items; however, the three-year rule discussed below may be available.

IRS three-year expensing rule. Self-employed creators of films, sound recordings, videotapes, and other property not eligible for current deductions may deduct expenses on Schedule C over a three-year period under a special IRS election. For films or videotapes, the election is available only if the item is created with minimal assistance from actors, musicians or similar support persons. Partnerships and corporations may elect the three-year rule if an employee-owner who personally produces the property (or family members of the employee-owner) owns at least 95% of the business. Under the three-year rule, 50% of your business expenses are deductible in the first year, 25% in the second year, and 25% in the third year. The election applies not only to direct production costs but also to other business operating expenses such as marketing, selling, and distributing your property, as well as depreciation deductions for equipment used in the business. *See* IRS Notice 88–62 for details.

Hobby loss restrictions. Authors and artists with expenses exceeding income may be barred by the IRS from claiming loss deductions; *see* ¶40.9.

DEDUCTING THE COST OF PATENTS OR COPYRIGHTS

¶9.12 If you create an artistic work or invention for which you get a government patent or copyright, you may depreciate your costs over the life of the patent or copyright. Basis for depreciation includes all expenses which you are required to capitalize in connection with creating the work such as the cost of drawings, experimental models, stationery, and supplies; travel expenses to obtain material for a book; fees to counsel; government charges for patent or copyright; and litigation costs in protecting or perfecting title.

If you purchased the patent or artistic creation, depreciate your cost over the remaining life of the patent or copyright.

If you inherited the patent or rights to an artistic creation, your cost is the fair market value either at the time of death of the person from whom you inherited it or the alternate valuation date if elected by the executor. You get this cost basis even if the decedent paid nothing for it. Figure your depreciation by dividing the fair market value by the number of years of remaining life.

If your patent or copyright becomes valueless, you may deduct your unrecovered cost or other basis in the year it became worthless.

INTANGIBLE DRILLING COSTS

¶9.13 Intangible drilling and development costs include wages, fuel, repairs, hauling, and supplies incident to and necessary for the preparation and drilling of wells for the production of oil or gas, and geothermal wells. For wells you are developing in the United States, you can elect to deduct the costs currently as business expenses or treat them as capital expenses subject to depreciation or depletion.

Electing current deductions. The election applies only to costs of drilling and developing items that do not have a salvage value. You must make this election by deducting the expenses on your income tax return for the first tax year in which you pay or incur the costs.

Tax shelter investors may deduct prepayments of drilling expenses only if the well is "spudded" within 90 days after the close of the taxable year in which the prepayment is made. The prepayment must also have a business purpose, not be a deposit, and not materially distort income. The investor's deduction is limited to his cash investment in the tax shelter. For purposes of this limitation, an investor's cash investment includes loans that are not secured by his shelter interest or the shelter's assets and loans that are not arranged by the organizer or promoter. If the above tests are not met, a deduction may be claimed only as actual drilling services are provided.

Recapture of intangible drilling costs for oil, gas, geothermal, or mineral property. Upon the disposition of oil, gas, geothermal, or other mineral property placed in service after 1986, ordinary income treatment applies to previously claimed deductions for intangible drilling and development costs for oil, gas, and geothermal wells, and to mineral development and exploration costs. Depletion deductions under ¶9.14 are also generally subject to this ordinary income treatment upon disposition of the property.

For oil, gas, or geothermal property placed in service before 1987, ordinary income treatment applies on the disposition of a working or operating interest to the extent that intangible drilling and development cost deductions exceeded what would have been allowed if the costs had been deducted through cost depletion. Recapture for geothermal property applies only to wells commenced after September 30, 1978.

AMT. Certain intangible drilling costs are also treated as tax preference items subject to alternative minimum tax; *see* ¶23.3.

DEPLETION DEDUCTION

¶9.14
Properties subject to depletion deductions are mines, oil and gas wells, timber, and exhaustible natural deposits.

Two methods of computing depletion are: (1) cost depletion; and (2) percentage depletion. If you are allowed to compute under either method, you must use the one that produces the larger deduction. In most cases, this will be percentage depletion. For timber, you must use cost depletion.

Cost depletion. The cost depletion of minerals is computed as follows: (1) divide the total number of units (tons, barrels) remaining in the deposit to be mined into the adjusted basis of the property; (2) multiply the unit rate found in Step 1 by the number of units for which payment is received during the taxable year if you are on the cash basis.

Adjusted basis is the original cost of the property, less depletion allowed, whether computed on the percentage or cost depletion method. It does not include nonmineral property such as mining equipment. Adjusted basis may not be less than zero.

Timber depletion is based on the cost of timber (or other basis in the owner's hands) and does not include any part of the cost of land. Depletion takes place when standing timber is cut. Depletion must be computed by the cost method, not by the percentage method. However, instead of claiming the cost depletion method, you may elect to treat the cutting of timber as a sale subject to capital gain or loss treatment. For further details, *see* IRS Publication 535.

Percentage depletion. Percentage depletion is based on a certain percentage rate applied to annual gross income derived from the resource. In determining gross income for percentage depletion, do not include any lease bonuses, advance royalties, or any other amount payable without regard to production. A deduction for percentage depletion is allowed even if the basis of the property is already fully recovered by prior depletion deductions. However, the excess of depletion deductions over the basis at the end of the year (without any regard to the current year's deduction) is an item of tax preference; *see* ¶23.3. The percentage to be applied depends upon the mineral involved; the range is from 5% up to 22%. For example, the maximum 22% depletion deduction applies to sulphur, uranium, and U.S. deposits of lead, zinc, nickel, mica, and asbestos. A 15% depletion percentage applies to U.S. deposits of gold, silver, copper, iron ore, and shale. For timber, cost depletion must be used.

Taxable income limit. For properties other than oil and gas, the percentage depletion deduction *may not exceed 50%* of taxable income from the property computed without the depletion deduction. In computing the 50% limitation, a net operating loss deduction is not deducted from gross income. A 100% taxable income limit applies to oil and gas properties; *see* ¶9.15.

Oil and gas property. Percentage depletion for oil and gas wells was repealed as of January 1, 1975, except for the following exemptions: (1) small independent producers and royalty owners; and (2) for gas well production. These oil and gas percentage depletion exemptions are discussed at ¶9.15.

OIL AND GAS PERCENTAGE DEPLETION

¶9.15
Small independent producers and royalty owners generally are allowed to deduct percentage depletion at a 15% rate for domestic oil and gas production. However, a higher rate may be allowed for qualifying "marginal" production, as discussed on the next page. The deduction is subject to a taxable income limit.

The 15% rate applies to a small producer exemption which equals the gross income from a maximum daily average of 1,000 barrels of oil or 6,000,000 cubic feet of natural gas, or a combination of both. Gross income from the property does not include advanced royalties or lease bonuses that are payable without regard to the actual production.

The depletable natural gas quantity depends on an election made annually by independent producers or royalty owners to apply part of their 1,000 barrel per day oil limitation to natural gas. The depletable quantity of natural gas is 6,000 cubic feet times the barrels of depletable oil for which an election has been made. The election is made on an original or amended return or on a claim for credit or refund. For example, if your average daily production is 1,200 barrels of oil and 6.2 million cubic feet of natural gas, your maximum depletable limit is 1,000 barrels of oil, which you may split between the oil and gas. You could claim depletion for 500 barrels of oil per day and for 3 million cubic feet of gas per day: 3 million cubic feet of gas is the equivalent of the remaining 500 barrels of oil limit (500 barrels × 6,000 cubic feet depletable gas quantity equals 3 million cubic feet of gas).

Ineligible retailers and refiners. The small producer exemption is not allowed to any producer who owns or controls a retail outlet for the sale of oil, natural gas, or petroleum products. It is also not allowed to a refiner who refines more than 50,000 barrels of oil on any one day of the taxable year; the limit is based on inputs of crude oil into the refinery process, rather than outputs. A taxpayer is not treated as a retailer where gross sales of oil and gas products are less than $5 million in any one year or if all sales of oil or natural gas products occur outside the United States, and none of the taxpayer's domestic production is exported. Bulk sales of oil or natural gas to industrial or utility customers are not to be treated as retail sales.

Figuring average daily domestic production. Average daily production is figured by dividing your aggregate production during the taxable year by the number of days in the taxable year. If you hold a partial interest in the production (including a partnership interest), production rate is found by multiplying total production of such property by your income percentage participation in such property.

The production over the entire year is averaged regardless of when production actually occurred. If average daily production for the year exceeds the 1,000 barrel or 6,000,000 cubic feet limit, the exemption must be allocated among all the properties in which you have an interest.

Taxable income limits on percentage depletion. The percentage depletion deduction for a small producer or royalty owner may not exceed (1) the *lesser* of 100% of the taxable income from the property before the depletion allowance, or (2) 65% of your taxable income from all sources computed without regard to the depletion deduction allowed under the small producer's exemption, any net operating loss carryback, and any capital loss carryback.

100% Taxable Income Limit

To encourage investments in marginally producing properties, Congress raised the deduction limit from 50% to 100% of taxable income from the property for tax years starting after 1990.

Limitations where family members or related businesses own interests. The daily exemption rate is allocated among members of the same family in proportion to their respective production of oil. Similar allocation is required where business entities are under common control. This affects interests owned by you, your spouse, and minor children; by corporations, estates, and trusts in which 50% of the beneficial interest is owned by the same or related persons; and by a corporation which is a member of the same controlled group.

Higher depletion for marginal production. For tax years starting after 1990, independent producers and royalty owners are allowed a higher depletion rate for *marginal production,* defined as oil or natural gas from "stripper well property" or property producing substantially all "heavy" oil. A stripper well property is one from which average daily production, divided by the number of all producing wells on the property, is 15 or less "barrel equivalents." A barrel equivalent is a barrel of oil or 6,000 cubic feet of natural gas.

The 15% rate is increased by 1% for each whole dollar that the "reference price" (the average annual wellhead price as estimated by the IRS) of domestic crude oil for the previous year was below $20 per barrel. For example, if the IRS determines that the reference price for a given year is $16 per barrel, the allowable depletion rate for qualifying production in the following year would be 19% (4% increase for $4 drop below the $20 floor). The maximum annual depletion rate as a result of the increase is 25%, which would be allowed only if the previous year's reference price was $10 per barrel.

The higher rate applies only up to the maximum depletable limit, which is the average daily production of up to 1,000 barrels a day of oil, or 6 million cubic feet of gas. If the taxpayer has production from "marginal properties" eligible for the higher depletion rate, as well as production from other properties subject to the 15% rate, the marginal production is taken into account first in applying the 1,000 barrel or 6 million cubic feet overall limit. However, a special elec-

tion may be made to prorate the overall limit among all production, whether marginal or nonmarginal.

22% rate for certain natural gas. The 22% depletion allowance is allowed only for the following two classes: (1) domestic natural gas sold under a fixed contract in effect on February 1, 1975; and (2) domestic "regulated natural gas" produced and sold before July 1, 1976.

Partnerships and S corporations. For partnership property, cost or percentage depletion is figured separately by each partner and not by the partnership. However, the partnership first allocates to each partner his or her share of the adjusted basis of each partnership oil or gas property. The partner's share of the adjusted basis depends on his or her interest in partnership capital or income, or is determined by the partnership agreement. A partner reduces his or her share of the adjusted basis of each property by the amount of depletion claimed each year.

The partner reports the share of royalty income and deducts depletion on Schedule E. Each interest in a partnership is reported separately.

Each stockholder of an S corporation figures the depletion allowance separately in the same way as a partner in a partnership. The S corporation allocates to each shareholder his or her basis of each oil or gas property held by the corporation.

Anti-Transfer Rule Repealed

Prior law generally barred percentage depletion deductions for the transferee when a "proven" oil or gas property was transferred after 1974. This restriction has been repealed, effective for transfers after October 11, 1990. Transferees who receive their interest after this date are allowed depletion under the regular rules.

Transferees receiving "proven" properties before October 12, 1990, are not allowed percentage depletion *unless* the transfer was made because of the death of the prior owner, a tax-free transfer to a controlled corporation, a transfer between commonly-controlled corporations, or changes in beneficiaries of a trust where the changes are due to births, adoptions, or deaths within a single family.

10

LOSS RESTRICTIONS: PASSIVE ACTIVITIES AND AT-RISK LIMITS

The objective of the passive activity law was to discourage tax shelters, but it strikes at almost every business and rental activity. If you have losses from renting property or from a business in which you do not materially participate, you generally may not deduct the loss from salary, self-employment income, interest, dividends, or retirement income. Such losses must be reported on Form 8582 and may offset only income from other passive activities. However, if you actively manage rental real estate, you may be able to deduct up to $25,000 of a rental loss. This $25,000 amount is phased out for those with adjusted gross income over $100,000.

Another tax provision designed to restrict loss deductions, the at-risk limits, prevents the deduction of losses that exceed your actual cash investment in a venture.

To determine the deductibility of a loss, you first apply the at-risk rules, and then if your loss is not limited by the at-risk rules, you apply the passive activity rules.

 When this book went to press, Congress was considering legislation which would allow real estate developers who materially participate in such activities to offset rental losses against income from their development operations.

Also, individuals with net passive activity losses of no more than $200 would be allowed to deduct them under a *de minimis* exception.

Both provisions would apply to taxable years beginning after December 31, 1991. *See* the Tax Legislation Guide at the front of this book for legislative developments.

PASSIVE ACTIVITY RESTRICTIONS

WHAT ARE THE PASSIVE ACTIVITY RULES?

¶**10.1** The passive activity law is a case of overkill: Although its major objective was to *discourage* tax shelters, it strikes at almost every business, applying onerous restrictions and paperwork requirements. In this chapter, we provide the basic rules and principles. For further references, we suggest you consult IRS Publication 925 and regulations to Code Section 469.

In approaching a passive activity problem, keep in mind that the rules have two objectives:

1. To disallow current deductions of passive losses (PALs) from nonpassive income; and
2. To convert passive income into nonpassive income in order to prevent investors from using the income to offset passive losses.

What is a passive activity? As explained in ¶10.2, passive activities include (1) rental operations; and (2) all other businesses in which you do not materially participate, although there are certain exceptions. If you have a passive activity loss, you must compute your allowable loss on Form 8582.

Quick Guide to Passive Activity Rules

Subject—	Comment—
Who is affected by the passive activity (PA) rules?	Every individual who is in business. You can be self-employed, a stockholder, or a partner. Participation tests determine whether the activity is treated as a passive activity.
Are the PA rules limited to certain business activities?	No. PA rules cover almost all types of business and investment activities, unless specific exceptions apply, such as for working interests in oil and gas.
Are losses permanently disallowed?	No. The PA rules defer deductions for personal losses until you have income from the activity, you sell out, or dispose of a "substantial part" of an activity.
What if I retire but participate in a limited way?	If you restrict your participation in your business, you may be affected by the PA rules. A material participation test for prior work may classify income as nonpassive.
Do the PA rules affect sales of property?	Yes. Sales of property used in passive activities are subject to passive income or loss treatment.
Is there a special exception to the PA rules for rental real estate?	Yes. If you actively manage rental real estate, loss deductions of up to $25,000 are allowed, provided your modified adjusted gross income is $100,000 or less. The allowance is phased out for modified adjusted gross incomes between $100,000 and $150,000.

Loss disallowance rule. The heart of the passive activity law is the loss disallowance rule: A loss from a passive activity may be deducted only from passive income, that is, income from passive activities. The loss may not be deducted from salary or self-employment earnings from a regular job or active business, interest, dividends, royalties, retirement income, or gains from the sale of stock or similar investment property. Figuring passive income or loss is discussed at ¶10.8.

Tax credits from passive activities are also limited; they may only offset tax allocable to income from passive activities. Passive activity tax credits are figured on Form 8582-CR.

Disallowed losses are suspended. Disallowed losses and credits are suspended and carried forward to the next taxable year, when they may offset passive income. Any remaining suspended loss may be deducted when you sell your interest. Even if you do not sell your entire interest, suspended losses may be deductible upon the disposition of a "substantial part" of an activity; see ¶10.13. However, a suspended credit may not be claimed until it may be used against tax liability allocable to future passive income. See ¶10.13 for the rules for claiming suspended losses upon the disposition of your interest in a passive activity.

Phase-in losses. Partial loss deductions were allowed during the phase-in period of 1987–1990 for investments made on or before October 22, 1986. A loss not allowed during the phase-in period is carried forward and may be deducted in 1992 or a later year only if you have passive income in that year which can be offset by the carryover loss. Any carryover losses that cannot be used to offset passive income will be deductible when you dispose of your interest in the passive activity; see ¶10.13.

Casualty losses. Casualty and theft losses are deductible without regard to the passive loss restrictions, unless the loss regularly occurs in the activity. For example, losses due to hurricanes, earthquakes, storms, and fires are considered nonpassive, but shoplifting losses of a retail store could still be considered passive activity deductions on the grounds that they occur regularly in that business.

Advantage of Earning Passive Income

If you have passive losses, earning passive income is advantageous because the passive losses offset the passive income. To prevent you from entering into investments or into plans to generate passive income, the IRS has restrictive rules that convert passive income to nonpassive income. For this purpose, IRS regulations apply concepts such as "significant participation" to convert passive income into nonpassive income and treat certain rentals and gains as nonpassive income. These conversion rules are discussed in ¶10.9.

TWO TYPES OF PASSIVE ACTIVITY

¶10.2

There are two classes or types of passive activity:

1. **Rental operations.** With the exception of certain rentals (¶10.5) and qualifying low-income housing (¶10.14), the ownership of rental property is treated as a passive activity, regardless of whether or not you participate in operating the property. Thus, rental losses are generally deductible only against passive income. However, by showing that you *do* manage rental real estate, you may be able to deduct up to $25,000 of your rental loss as explained at ¶10.4.

   See the Tax Legislation Guide at the front of this book for proposals to exclude rental losses of qualifying real estate developers from the category of passive activities.

   The passive loss restriction applies to rentals of apartments and commercial office space (whether long- or short-term); long-term rentals of office equipment, automobiles, and/or a vessel under a bare-boat charter or a plane under a dry lease (no pilot or captain and no fuel); and net-leased property. A property is under a net-lease if the deductions (other than rents and reimbursed amounts) are less than 15% of rental income or where the lessor is guaranteed a specific return or is guaranteed against loss of income.

   Rental activities, however, do not include short-term car rentals and rentals of hotel rooms or similar space to transients. Providing incidental services, such as a laundry room in an apartment building, is considered part of the rental activity. Real estate dealers are generally not treated as engaging in a passive activity. Incidental rentals of investment and business property are generally not treated as rental activities within the passive activity rules. See ¶10.5 for rentals that are exempt from the passive activity rules. See ¶10.14 for low-income housing investments exempt from passive loss limitations.

   Important: If in a non-rental business, you also own rental property, the rental activity generally must be treated separately from the non-rental activities; see ¶10.3.

2. **Passive investor status in all other businesses.** The IRS has seven tests to determine material participation. Some tests require only a minimum amount of work, such as 500 hours annually and in some cases just more than 100 hours. If you come within one of the tests, you are treated as a material participant, and if you are a material participant, the activity is not treated as a passive activity. The material participant tests are discussed at ¶10.6 and they apply to you whether you do business as a sole proprietor, in an S corporation, or in a part-

nership. Losses and credits passed through S corporations and partnerships are subject to the passive activity rules. Whether you materially participate in a business is determined each year. If you are a limited partner, you do not by law meet the material participation test, unless you come within certain exceptions discussed at ¶10.11.

Closely held corporations and personal service corporations. The passive activity rules apply to personal service corporations. Thus, a personal service corporation may not offset passive losses and credits against either income from non-passive sources or portfolio income; *see* ¶10.15.

Closely held corporations are subject to a less restrictive limitation: Passive losses and credits may offset active business income but not portfolio income; *see* ¶10.15.

Working oil and gas interests outside of passive activity restrictions. The passive activity rules do not apply to an investor who holds a working interest in an oil and gas property. This is true even for an investor who does not materially participate in the activity. *If your liability is limited, you are not treated as owning a working interest,* as, for example, where you are a limited partner or a stockholder in an S corporation; *see* ¶10.10 for details.

DETERMINING PASSIVE ACTIVITIES

¶10.3

If you are in more than one business or rental activity, you have to determine whether the two or more operations are to be considered one activity or as separate activities.

Determining aggregate or separate treatment is important for:

Deducting suspended losses when you dispose of one of the activities. If the activity is considered separate from the others, you may deduct a suspended loss when you dispose of it. If it is not considered separate from the others, a suspended loss is deductible upon disposition only if it is a "substantial" part of the overall activity; *see* ¶10.13.

Applying the material participation rules. If activities are separate and apart from each other, the material participation test is applied to each separately. If the activities are aggregated as one activity, material participation in one activity applies to all.

IRS PROPOSED REGULATIONS

In the spring of 1992, the IRS released new revised regulations for determining what an "activity" is for purposes of applying the passive loss restrictions. The IRS has made a complete about-face. Whereas the prior temporary regulations released in 1989 took up a hundred or so pages, the new proposals take up only a few. But more important, the complex technical definitions and tests for undertakings and integrated businesses are gone. In their place is a vague *facts and circumstances test under which you may use any reasonable method of grouping activities.*

The revised regulations are generally effective for taxable years ending after May 10, 1992. For taxable years ending on or before May 10, 1992, prior Temporary Regulation Section 1.469-4T applies. If the May 10th date falls within a taxable year, you may elect to apply the prior temporary regulation for the entire year.

Earmarking a business activity. The revised regulations allow you to use any reasonable method under the facts and circumstances of your situation to determine if several business activities should be grouped together or treated separately. To be grouped together, the IRS says that the activities should be "an appropriate economic unit" for measuring gain or loss. For making this determination, the IRS sets these general guidelines: (1) similarities and differences in types of business; (2) the extent of common control; (3) geographic location; (4) the extent of common ownership; and (5) interdependencies between the activities. Interdependency is measured by the extent that several business activities buy or sell between themselves, use the same products or services, have the same customers, employees, or use a single set of books and records.

The IRS will not require that all five factors be present in order for multiple activities to be grouped together.

Consistent treatment required. Once you treat activities separately or group them together as a single activity, the IRS generally requires you to continue the same treatment in subsequent taxable years. You can regroup activities only if the original treatment was "clearly inappropriate" or it has become clearly inappropriate in light of a "material change" in circumstances.

The IRS proposals do *not* specifically require that a formal election be made on your tax return to group or separate activities. Under the prior temporary regulations, an election had to be made on a statement attached to your tax return in order to separate business activities that would otherwise have to be aggregated.

EXAMPLE Jones has a significant interest in a bakery and a movie theater at a shopping mall in Baltimore and in a bakery and a movie theater in Philadelphia. The IRS does not explain what constitutes a significant interest. Under the proposed regulations, Jones can: (1) group the theaters and bakeries into a single activity; (2) place the two theaters into one group and the bakeries into a second group; (3) put his Baltimore businesses into one group and his Philadelphia businesses in another group; or (4) treat each business as four separate activities.

Once he chooses a grouping, he must consistently use that grouping for all future years unless a material change makes the grouping inappropriate. His decision is also subject to IRS review and if questioned, he must show the factual basis for his grouping.

IRS may regroup activities. The IRS may regroup your activities if your grouping does not reflect one or more appropriate economic units and a primary purpose of the grouping is to circumvent the passive loss rules.

EXAMPLE Five doctors operate separate medical practices and also invest in tax shelters that generate passive losses. They form a partnership to operate x-ray equipment. In exchange for the equipment contributed to the partnership, each doctor receives limited partnership interests. The partnership is managed by a general partner selected by the doctors. Partnership services are provided to the doctors in proportion to their interests in the partnership and service fees are set at a level to offset the income generated by the partnership against individual passive losses. Under these facts, the IRS will not allow the medical practices and the partnership to be treated as separate activities as this would circumvent the passive loss limitations by generating passive income from the partnership to offset the tax shelter losses. The IRS will require each doctor to treat his or her medical practice and interests in the partnership as a single activity.

Earmarking a rental activity. The prior temporary regulations for earmarking rental activities have also been scrapped. In their place, the general facts and circumstances rule previously discussed for business activities applies for determining whether several rental activities should be grouped together or treated separately.

If you conduct rental activities as well as nonrental business activities, you may *not* group a rental activity with a nonrental activity unless either the rental activity is insubstantial in relation to the business activity, or the business activity is insubstantial in relation to the rental. No guidelines are provided for determining what is "substantial" for purposes of this test. The prior rules aggregated rental and nonrental operations conducted at the same location if either operation produced more than 80% of the total gross income.

Furthermore, an activity involving the rental of realty and one involving the rental of personal property may not be treated as a single activity, unless the personal property is provided in connection with the real property.

Partnerships and S corporations. A partnership or S corporation must group its activities under the facts and circumstances test. Once a partnership or S corporation determines its activities, the partners or shareholders are bound by that decision and may not regroup them. The partners and shareholders then apply the facts and circumstances test to combine or separate the partnership or S corporation activities with their other activities.

Special rule for certain limited partners and limited entrepreneurs. A limited entrepreneur is a person with an ownership interest who does not actively participate in management. A limited entrepreneur or limited partner in films, video tapes, farming, oil and gas, or the renting of depreciable property, generally may combine each such activity only with another of such activities in the same type of business, and only if he or she is a limited entrepreneur or partner in both. Grouping of such activities with other activities in the same type of business in which he or she is *not* a limited partner or entrepreneur is allowed if the grouping is appropriate under the general facts and circumstances test.

Disposition of suspended losses upon sales of your interest. If you have suspended losses from a passive activity, you may deduct the losses when you dispose of substantially all of your entire interest in the activity. *See also* ¶10.13 for dispositions.

REAL ESTATE RENTALS GET LIMITED LOSS ALLOWANCE

¶10.4

You may take advantage of a limited break if you perform some management role in a real estate rental. You may deduct up to $25,000 of your loss to offset income from any source if your adjusted gross income is $100,000 or less. The allowance is phased out for adjusted gross incomes between $100,000 and $150,000 as discussed below. The allowance applies only to real estate rentals , not rentals of equipment or other personal property. The loss allowance is claimed on Form 8582.

A trust may not qualify for the $25,000 allowance. Thus, you cannot circumvent the $25,000 ceiling or multiply the number of $25,000 allowances simply by transferring various rental real properties to one or more trusts. However, an estate may qualify for the allowance if the decedent actively participated in the operation. The estate is treated as an active participant for two years following the death of the owner.

Allowance Based on Income

The rental loss allowance is phased out when your modified adjusted gross income is over $100,000. For every dollar of income over $100,000, the loss allowance is reduced by 50 cents. When your modified adjusted gross income reaches $150,000, the allowance is completely phased out. An explanation of modified adjusted gross income is in the next column under the heading "Phaseout of the allowance." An example of how the phaseout works follows on page 151.

If modified AGI is—	Loss Allowance is—
Up to $100,000	$25,000
110,000	20,000
120,000	15,000
130,000	10,000
140,000	5,000
150,000 or more	–0–

Married filing separately. If you file separately but at any time during the taxable year live with your spouse, no allowance at all may be claimed. If you are married but live apart from your spouse for the entire year and file a separate return, the $25,000 allowance and the adjusted gross income phaseout range are reduced by 50%. Thus, the maximum allowance on your separate return is $12,500 and this amount is phased out by 50% of AGI over $50,000. Therefore, if your AGI exceeds $75,000, no allowance is allowed.

Qualifying for the allowance. You must meet an *active-participation test.* Having an agent manage your property does not prevent you from meeting the test. You may meet the test by showing that you or your spouse participate in decisions, such as selecting tenants, setting rental terms, and reviewing expenses. You (together with your spouse) must also have at least a 10% interest in the property. By law, limited partners are not considered active participants and thus, do not qualify for the allowance unless future IRS regulations provide an exception.

In the case of an estate of a deceased taxpayer who owned an interest in a rental real estate activity in which he actively participated, the estate is deemed to actively participate for the two years following the death of the taxpayer. Trusts do not qualify for the allowance.

EXAMPLE You live in New York and own a condominium in Florida that you rent through an agent. You set the rental terms and give final approval to any rental arrangement. You also have final approval over any repairs ordered by the agent. You are considered to be an active participant and are entitled to use the $25,000 rental allowance.

Figuring the $25,000 allowance. First match income and loss from all of your rental real estate activities in which you actively participate. A net loss from these activities is then applied to net passive income (if any) from other activities to determine the $25,000 allowance. Gains from pre-1987 installment sales are passive income if the sold property was from an activity (¶10.2) that would have been considered passive had the passive activity rules been in effect before 1987. If you rent out a personal residence, rental income or loss may be exempt from the passive activity rules; *see* Exception 7 at ¶10.5.

The allowance may not be used against carryover losses from prior taxable years when you were not an active participant.

EXAMPLES 1. You have $25,000 of losses from a rental activity in which you actively participate. You also actively participate in another real estate rental activity, from which you had a $25,000 gain. There is no net loss from real estate rental activities in which you actively participate and no loss allowance is permitted.

2. You have a $90,000 salary, $15,000 income from a limited partnership, and a $26,000 loss from rental real estate in which you actively participated. Your $26,000 loss is first reduced by the $15,000 of passive income. Also, as you have actively participated in the rental real estate activity, the remaining $11,000 rental loss may be deducted from the salary income.

Phaseout of the allowance. For purposes of the allowance phaseout, *modified adjusted gross income* is adjusted gross income shown on your return but not including:

Any passive activity income or loss.
Taxable Social Security and railroad retirement payments (Chapter 34).
Deductible IRA contributions (Chapter 8).
The deduction on Form 1040 for one half of self-employment tax liability (Chapter 46).
Excluded interest on U.S. Savings Bonds used for paying tuition

in the year the bonds are redeemed. If you are allowed to exclude the interest from income for regular tax purposes (Chapter 33) the interest must still be included for purposes of the allowance phaseout.

EXAMPLE In 1992, you had $120,000 in salary, $5,000 of partnership income from a limited partnership in which you invested in 1988 and a $31,000 loss from rental real estate activities in which you actively participate. Under the allowance, you may deduct only $15,000 of the passive rental loss. You must carry over the remaining $11,000 passive rental loss to 1993. Your deduction and carryover are computed as follows:

Modified adjusted gross income	$120,000
Less amount not subject to phaseout	100,000
Amount subject to phaseout	$ 20,000
Phaseout percentage	50%
Portion of allowance phased out	$ 10,000
Maximum rental allowance offset	$ 25,000
Less amount phased out	10,000
Deductible rental loss allowance offset in 1992	$ 15,000
Passive loss from rental real estate	$ 31,000
Less passive income from partnership	5,000
Passive activity loss	$ 26,000
Less deductible rental loss allowance in 1992	15,000
Carryover loss to 1993	$ 11,000

Real estate allowance for tax credits. *On Form 8582-CR, a deduction equivalent* of up to $25,000 may allow a credit that otherwise would be disallowed. You must meet the active participation test in the year the credit arose. The $25,000 allowance is generally subject to the regular AGI phaseout rule.

In the case of the low-income housing and rehabilitation credits (¶9.8), however, you need not meet the active participant test. Furthermore, for rehabilitation and low-income housing credits, the phaseout for the $25,000 allowance starts at AGI of $200,000 ($100,000 if married filing separately and living apart the entire year); thus, the deduction equivalent is completely disallowed when AGI reaches $250,000. The phaseout is figured on Form 8582-CR. No low-income housing credit may be claimed for an investment exempted from the passive activity rules under ¶10.14.

The *deduction equivalent* of a credit is the amount which, if allowed as a deduction, would reduce your tax by an amount equal to the credit. For example, a tax credit of $1,000 for a taxpayer in the 28% bracket equals a deduction of $3,571 and would come within the $25,000 allowance provided you actively participated. In the 28% bracket, the equivalent of a $25,000 deduction is a tax credit of $7,000 ($25,000 × 28%). Thus, if you have a rehabilitation credit of $8,000 and you are in the 28% bracket, the $25,000 allowance may allow you to claim $7,000 of the credit, while $1,000 of the credit would be held in suspense.

If in one year you have both losses and tax credits, the $25,000 allowance applies first to the losses, then to tax credits from rental real estate with active participation, and finally to tax credits for rehabilitation or low-income housing.

The allowance and net operating losses. If losses are allowed by the $25,000 allowance but your nonpassive income and other income are less than the loss, the balance of the loss may be treated as a net operating loss and may be carried back and forward; *see* ¶40.17.

RENTAL ACTIVITIES SUBJECT TO PASSIVE ACTIVITY RULES

¶10.5 The passive activity rules apply to the rental of any tangible real or personal property. The agreement under which rents are paid may be under a lease, service contract, or similar arrangement.

The rules for separating or aggregating rental activities are discussed at ¶10.3.

Exceptions. If any of the following tests are met, the activity is *not* a rental activity. Where an activity is not considered a rental activity, it is subject to the material participation tests of ¶10.6. •

1. **Incidental rental of investment property, property used in a business, or property rented to an employee for the convenience of an employer.** The rental of investment property comes within this exception if the principal purpose for holding the property during the tax year is to realize gain from its appreciation, and the gross rental income from the property for the tax year is less than 2% of the lower of the unadjusted basis of the property or fair market value of the property. The rental of business property is treated as incidental if the property was predominantly used in a business during the tax year or during at least two of the five tax years that immediately precede the tax year and gross rental income from the property for the tax year is less than 2% of the lesser of the unadjusted basis of the property or fair market value of the property.

EXAMPLE You own unimproved land with a market value of $400,000 and an unadjusted basis of $300,000. You hold it for the principal purpose of realizing gain from its appreciation. To help reduce the cost of holding the land, you lease it to a rancher for grazing purposes at an annual rental of $3,500. The gross rental income of $3,500 is less than 2% of the lower of the fair market value or the unadjusted basis of the land. The rental of the land is not a rental activity.

2. **The average period of customer use of the property is seven days or less.** You figure the average for the year by dividing the aggregate number of days in all periods of customer use for the property that end during the tax year by the number of the periods of customer use. Each period during which a customer has a continuous or recurring right to use the property is treated as a separate period. This exception covers short-term rentals of autos, video cassettes, tuxedos, and hotel and motel rooms.
3. **The average period of customer use of the property is more than seven days but is 30 days or less, and you provide significant personal services.** Personal services include only services performed by individuals and does not include (a) services necessary to permit the lawful use of the property; (b) construction or repair services that extend the useful life of the property for a period substantially longer than the average period of customer use; and (c) services that are provided with long-term rentals of high-grade commercial or residential real property such as cleaning and maintenance of common areas, routine repairs, trash collection, elevator service, and security guards.
4. **Regardless of the average period of customer use, extraordinary personal services are provided so that rental is incidental.** An example is providing hospital patients room

and board, which is incidental to receiving the medical services of the hospital staff.

Note: For purposes of Exceptions 2 and 3, if more than one class of property is rented as part of the same activity, average period of customer use is figured separately for each class. The average period of customer use (as explained in Exception 2) is multiplied by the ratio of gross rental income from that class to the total rental income from the activity; *see* the Form 8582 instructions.

5. **Providing property to a partnership or S corporation which is not engaged in rentals.** If you own an interest in a partnership or S corporation and you contributed the property as an owner, the contribution of the property is not considered a rental activity. For example, if as a partner you contribute property to a partnership, your distributive share of partnership income will not be considered as income from a rental activity. However, this exception will not apply if the partnership is engaged in a rental activity.

6. **The property is generally allowed for the nonexclusive use of customers during fixed business hours** such as operating a golf course. The customers are treated as licensees, not lessees.

7. **Rental of personal residence.** Rental of a personal residence is not treated as a passive rental activity if you personally use the home for more than the greater of either (1) 14 days, or (2) 10% of the days the home is rented for a fair rental amount. With such personal use, rental deductions are limited to gross rental income under the vacation home restrictions of ¶29.20. Furthermore, mortgage interest is generally fully deductible provided the rented home is a principal or second residence; *see* ¶15.1.

MATERIAL PARTICIPATION TESTS FOR BUSINESSES

¶**10.6** Your tax position towards the following participation rules will depend on whether the particular activity produces income or loss. If you have passive activity losses from other activities, you would prefer to have a profitable business activity treated as a passive activity. That is, you would prefer not to be a material participant in that particular business activity. The reason: If the business income is passive, you could offset the income by your losses from the other passive activities. On the other hand, if the business activity operates at a loss and you did not have passive income from other sources, you would want to meet the material participation test for that business activity in order to claim immediate loss deductions. IRS strategy in reviewing your activities would be the opposite. It would attempt to prevent you from treating income from an activity as passive. For example, the IRS, by applying Tests 5 and 6 on page 153, can prevent a retired person from treating post-retirement income from a prior business or profession as passive income to offset passive losses from another activity. If you realize a loss in one passive activity, Test 4 may prevent you from generating passive income by merely reducing your participation in another activity.

Material participation results in nonpassive treatment. There are two key terms: material participation and significant participation. If you materially participate by meeting one of the seven IRS tests, your activity is not a passive activity. For example, under Test 1, work for more than 500 hours in an activity is considered material participation. Under Test 4, significant participation is work for more than 100 hours but less than 500 hours at an activity in which you do not otherwise materially participate. The IRS applies a significant participation rule to convert passive activity income into nonpassive income and to convert several significant participation

activities into material participation if the total participation in those activities exceeds 500 hours; *see* Test 4.

Any work you do in a business you own is treated as "participation." If you are married, work by your spouse in the activity during the tax year is treated, for purposes of the following tests, as participation by you. However, the following type of work is *not* treated as participation.

1. Work that is not of a type customarily done by an owner of an activity, if one of the principal reasons for the performance of the work is to avoid the passive loss rules (*see* example below).

2. Work performed by an individual in his or her capacity as an investor unless directly involved in the day-to-day management or operations of the activity. Work performed in the capacity of an investor includes studying and reviewing financial statements or reports on the operations of the activity; preparing or compiling summaries or analyses of the finances or operations of the activity for one's own use; and reviewing the finances or operations of the activity in a nonmanagerial capacity.

EXAMPLE An attorney owns an interest in a professional football team for which he performs no services. He anticipates a net loss from the football activity and to qualify as a material participant, he hires his wife to work 15 hours a week as an office receptionist for the team. Although a spouse's participation in an activity generally qualifies as participation by both spouses, the receptionist work here does not qualify as participation because (1) it is not the type of work customarily done by an owner of a football team, and (2) the attorney hired his spouse to avoid disallowance of a passive loss.

IRS tests for material participation. If you meet one of the following tests for the year in question, you are considered to have materially participated in that activity. Tests 5 and 6 prevent retired individuals from treating post-retirement income as passive income.

Test 1. You participate in the activity for more than 500 hours during the tax year.

Test 2. Your participation in the activity for the tax year constitutes substantially all of the participation in the activity of all individuals including non-owners for the year.

Test 3. You participate in the activity for more than 100 hours during the tax year, and your participation is not less than the participation of any other person including non-owners for that year.

EXAMPLE Brown and Collins are partners in a moving van business which they conduct entirely on week ends. They both work for eight hours each weekend. Although each partner does not participate for more than 500 hours, they are treated as material participants under Test 3 because they participate for more than 100 hours and no one else participates more.

Test 4. You are active in several enterprises but each activity does not in itself qualify as material participation. However, if you spend more than 100 hours in each activity and the total hours of these more-than-100-hours activities exceed 500 hours, you are treated as a material participant in each of these activities. This test is described as the significant participation test.

EXAMPLES 1. Smith is a full-time accountant with ownership interests in a restaurant and shoe store. He works 150 hours in the shoe store and 360 hours in the restaurant. Under the significant participation test, Smith is considered a material participant in both activities as the total hours of both exceeds 500 hours.

2. During 1992, you invest in five businesses. In activity (a) you work 110 hours; in activity (b), 100 hours; in activity (c), 125 hours; in activity (d), 120 hours; and in (e), 140 hours. You do not qualify under the significant participation test. Although your total hours in the five activities exceed 500, activity (b) is ignored in the total count because the hours did not exceed 100. The total of the four other activities is 495.

3. Assume that you worked one hour more for activity (b). It and all of the other activities would be considered as meeting the material participation test. The total hours are 596. Assuming that activity (a) totaled 125 hours and activity (b) remained at 100 hours or less, you would meet the test for all of the activities except for activity (b) which did not exceed 100 hours. The total of the four qualified activities is 510 hours.

Test 5. You materially participated in the activity for any five tax years during the 10 tax years preceding the tax year in question. The five tax years do not have to be consecutive. Use only Test 1 for determining material participation in years before 1987. Thus, if you are retired but meet the five-out-of-ten-year participation test, you are currently considered a material participant, with the result that net income is treated as nonpassive, rather than passive. If you retired from a personal service profession, an even stricter rule applies; *see* Test 6.

Test 6. In a personal service activity, you materially participated for any three tax years preceding the tax year in question. The three years do not have to be consecutive. Use only Test 1 for determining material participation in years before 1987. Examples of personal services within this test are the professions of health, law, engineering, architecture, accounting, actuarial science, the performing arts, consulting, or any other trade or business in which capital is not a material income producing factor.

Test 7. Under the facts and circumstances test, you participate in the activity on a regular, continuous, and substantial basis. At the time this book went to press, the IRS had not released specific guidelines for this test, but has stated that you do not come within this test if you participate less than 100 hours in the activity. Also, performing management services will not qualify here if there is a paid manager or another person in the activity who performs management services that exceed the time spent by you.

Retired farmers. Retired or disabled farmers are treated as materially participating in a farming activity if they materially participated for five of the eight years preceding their retirement or disability. A surviving spouse is also treated as materially participating in a farming activity if the real property used in the activity meets the estate tax rules for special valuation of farm property passed from a qualified decedent and the surviving spouse actively manages the farm.

Record-keeping requirements. Although you are not required to keep contemporaneous time records, it is advisable to keep a time record of your work.

Limited partners; see ¶10.11.

Participant rules for personal service and closely held corporations; see ¶10.15.

TAX CREDITS OF PASSIVE ACTIVITIES LIMITED

¶10.7 You may generally not claim a tax credit from a passive activity unless you report and pay taxes on income from a passive activity. Furthermore, the tax allocated to that income must be at least as much as the credit. If the tax credit exceeds your tax liability on income allocable to passive activities, the excess credit is not allowed. Use Form 8582-CR to figure the allowable credit. Suspended credits are not allowed when property is disposed of. The credits may be used only when passive income is earned.

EXAMPLE You have a $1,000 credit from a passive activity. You do not report income from any passive activity. You may not deduct the credit because no part of your tax is attributed to passive activity income. The credit is suspended until you have income from a passive activity and you incur tax on that income. All or part of the credit may then be claimed to offset the tax. If you dispose of your interest before using a suspended credit, the credit may no longer be claimed.

Credits for real estate activities. As discussed at ¶10.4, more favorable tax credit rules apply to real estate activities.

Basis adjustment for suspended credits. If the basis of property was reduced when tax credits were claimed, you may elect to add back a suspended credit to the basis when the property is disposed of.

EXAMPLE Jones places in service rehabilitation credit property and claims an allowable credit of $50, which also reduces basis by $50. However, under the passive loss rule, he is prevented from claiming the credit. In a later year, he disposes of his entire interest in the activity, including the property whose basis was reduced. He may elect to increase basis of the property by the amount of the original basis adjustment.

If the property is disposed of in a transaction that is not treated as a fully taxable disposition under ¶10.13, then no basis adjustment is allowed.

FIGURING PASSIVE ACTIVITY INCOME AND LOSS

¶10.8 You figure net income and losses from passive activities on Form 8582. *See* ¶10.5 (rental activities) and ¶10.6 (non-rental business) for determining whether your income or loss is subject to the passive activity rules. You have a passive activity loss for the year if total losses from all passive activities, including carryovers of prior year disallowed losses, exceed total income from all of your passive activities for the year.

In determining the income or loss of a passive activity, be aware that certain income items of a passive activity are disregarded; that is, they are not treated as passive income and thus, cannot offset deductions of that activity. As a general rule, only income that is considered business or trade income of that activity offsets expenses of the activity. For example, income from dividends and interest that are not derived in the course of the taxpayer's business may not be offset by deductions of the activity. They are considered *portfolio income*, as discussed below. Furthermore, certain income items which are technically passive income are treated by the IRS as if they are nonpassive; these re-characterization rules are in ¶10.9.

Portfolio income. Portfolio income is broadly defined as income that is not derived in the ordinary course of business of the activity.

Portfolio income includes interest, dividends, annuities, and royalties from property held for investment. However, interest income on loans and investments made in the business of lending money or received on business accounts receivable is generally not treated as portfolio income; *see* ¶10.9 for special re-characterization rule. Similarly, royalties derived from a business of licensing property is not portfolio income to the person who created the property or performed substantial services or incurred substantial costs.

Portfolio income also includes gains from the sale of properties that produce portfolio income or are held for investment.

Expenses allocable to portfolio income, including interest expenses, do not enter into the computation of passive income or loss.

Dealers. Sales income of a dealer is generally treated as business income except for the sale of property that was held by the dealer as investment property at any time before the sale of the property.

Sale of property used in activity. Gain realized on the sale of property used in the activity is treated as passive activity income if at the time of disposition the activity was passive; *see* exception at ¶10.16. Under this rule, if you transact an installment sale, the treatment of installment payments depends on your status at the time of the initial sale. If you were not a material participant, installment payments in a later year are treated as passive income, even if you become a material participant in the later years.

Installment payments from a pre-1987 installment sale are treated as passive income if the activity would have been considered passive had the passive activity rules been in effect before 1987.

Although gain on the sale of property is generally passive income if the activity is passive at the time of sale, there is an exception that could recharacterize the gain as nonpassive income if the property was formerly used in a nonpassive activity; *see* ¶10.16 for details.

Compensation for personal services is not treated as passive activity income. The term "compensation for personal services" includes only (1) earned income, including certain payments made by a partnership to a partner and representing compensation for the services of the partner; (2) amounts included in gross income involving the transfer of property in exchange for the performance of services; (3) amounts distributed under qualified plans; (4) amounts distributed under retirement, pension, and other arrangements for deferred compensation of services; and (5) Social Security benefits includable in gross income.

Passive activity gross income also does not include (1) income from patent, copyright, or literary, musical, or artistic compositions, if your personal efforts significantly contributed to the creation of the property; (2) income from a qualified low-income housing project; (3) income tax refunds; and (4) payments on a covenant not to compete.

Passive activity deductions. Deductions that offset passive income of an activity must rise in connection with the passive activity. The following items are *not* considered as passive activity deductions:

Casualty and theft losses.
Charitable deductions.
Miscellaneous itemized deductions subject to the 2% AGI floor.
Deductible income taxes.
Carryovers of net operating losses or capital losses.
Expenses clearly and directly allocable to portfolio income.
Loss on the sale of property producing portfolio income.
Loss on sale of your entire interest in a passive activity to an unrelated party. The loss is allowed in full; *see* ¶10.13.

The passive loss rules apply to other deductions that are from passive activities, including deductions for state and local property taxes incurred with respect to passive activities, whether or not such deductions are claimed as above-the-line business deductions or as itemized deductions; *see* below for interest deductions.

Interest deductions. Interest expenses attributable to passive activities are treated as passive activity deductions and are not subject to the investment interest limitations. For example, in 1992, if you have net passive loss of $100, $40 of which is of interest expense, the entire $100 is subject to limitation under the passive loss rule. No portion of the loss is subject to the investment interest limitation of ¶15.9. Similarly, income and loss from passive activities generally are not treated as investment income or loss in figuring the investment interest limitation.

Interest expenses for a vacation home elected as a qualified second residence is not treated as passive activity interest and is deductible as residential interest; *see* ¶15.1 and ¶29.20.

PASSIVE INCOME CONVERTED INTO NONPASSIVE INCOME

¶10.9

There is an advantage in treating income as passive income when you have passive losses that can offset the income. However, the law may prevent you from treating what is passive income as passive income. The conversion of passive income to nonpassive income is technically called recharacterization. This may occur when you do not materially participate in the business activity, but are sufficiently active for the IRS to consider your participation as significant. Recharacterization may also occur when you rent nondepreciable property or sell development rental property. As discussed at ¶10.16, gain on the sale of property used in a passive activity may be re-characterized as nonpassive income if the property was formerly used in a nonpassive activity.

Significant participation. The IRS compares income and losses from all of your activities in which you work more than 100 hours but less than 500 and which are not considered material participation under the law. If you show a net aggregate gain, part of your gain is treated as nonpassive income according to the computation illustrated in the following example.

EXAMPLE You invest in three business activities—A, B, and C. You do not materially participate in any of the activities during 1992 but participate in Activity A for 105 hours, in Activity B for 160 hours, and in Activity C for 125 hours. Your net passive income or loss from the three activities is:

	A	B	C	Total
PA gross income	$600	$700	$900	$2,200
PA deductions	(200)	(1,000)	(300)	(1,500)
Net passive income	$400	($300)	$600	$700

Your passive activity gross income from significant participation passive activities of $2,200 exceeds passive activity deductions of $1,500. A ratable portion of your gross income from significant participation activities with net passive income for the tax year (Activities A and C) is treated as gross income that is *not* from a passive activity. The ratable portion is figured by dividing:

1. The excess of your passive activity gross income from significant participation over passive activity deductions from such activities (here $700) by

2. The net passive income of only the significant participation passive activities having net passive income (here $1,000). The ratable portion is 70%.

Thus, $280 of gross income from Activity A ($400 × 70%) and $420 of gross income from Activity C ($600 × 70%) is treated as nonpassive gross income. This adjustment prevents $700 from being offset by passive losses from another activity.

Rental of property with an insubstantial depreciable basis. This rule prevents you from generating passive rental income with vacant land or land on which a unit is constructed that has a value substantially less than the land. If less than 30% of the basis of rental property is depreciable, and you have net passive income from rentals (taking into account carried over passive losses from prior years), the net passive income is treated as nonpassive income. Basis here is generally adjusted basis without any adjustments.

EXAMPLE A limited partnership buys vacant land for $300,000, constructs improvements on the land at a cost of $100,000, and leases the entire property. After the rental period, the partnership sells the property for $600,000, realizing a gain. The unadjusted basis of the depreciable improvements of $100,000 is only 25% of the basis of the property of $400,000. The rent and the gain allocated to the improvements is treated as nonpassive income to the extent you have net passive income for the year.

Net interest income from passive equity-financed lending. Gross income from "equity-financed lending activity" is treated as nonpassive income to the extent of the lesser of the equity-financed interest income or net passive income. An activity is an "equity-financed lending activity" for a tax year if (1) the activity involves a trade or business of lending money; and (2) the average outstanding balance of the liabilities incurred in the activity for the tax year does not exceed 80% of the average outstanding balance of the interest-bearing assets held in the activity.

Incidental rental of property by development activity. Where gains on the sale of rental property are attributable to recent development, passive income treatment may be lost if the sale comes within the following tests: (1) the rental started less than 12 months before the date of disposition; and (2) you materially participated or significantly participated in the performance of services enhancing the value of the property. The 12-month period starts at the completion of the development services that increased the property's value.

Property rented to nonpassive activity (self-rental property). You may not generate passive income by renting property to a business in which you materially participate.

Licensing of intangible property. Your share of royalty income in a partnership, S corporation, estate, or trust is treated as nonpassive income if you invested after the organization created the intangible property, performed substantial services, or incurred substantial costs in the development or marketing of it. *See* Publication 925 for further details.

WORKING INTERESTS IN OIL AND GAS WELLS

¶10.10 Working interests are generally not treated as passive activities. This is true whether you hold your interest directly or through an entity, provided your liability is not limited. As long as you have unlimited liability, you need not materially participate in the activity. A working interest is one burdened with the financial risk of developing and operating the property, such as a share in tort liability (for example, uninsured losses from a fire); some responsibility to share in additional costs; responsibility for authorizing expenses; receiving periodic reports about drilling, completion, and expected production; and the possession of voting rights and rights to continue operations if the present operator steps out.

Limited liability. If you hold a working interest through any of the following entities, the entity is considered to limit your liability and you are subject to the following passive loss rules: (1) a limited partnership interest in a partnership in which you are not a general partner; (2) stock in a corporation; or (3) an interest in any entity other than a limited partnership or corporation that, under applicable state law, limits the liability of a holder of such interest for all obligations of the entity to a determinable fixed amount.

The following forms of loss protection are disregarded and thus, are not treated as limiting your liability: protection against loss by an indemnification agreement; a stop loss agreement; insurance; or any similar arrangement or combination of agreements.

Working interests are considered on a well-by-well basis. Rights to overriding royalties or production payments, and contract rights to extract or share in oil and gas profits without liability for a share of production costs are not working interests.

PARTNERSHIP RULES

¶10.11 If you are a partner, your level of personal participation in partnership activity during the partnership year determines whether your share of income or loss is passive or nonpassive. Generally, limited partners are subject to passive activity treatment, but there are some exceptions. On Schedule K-1 of Form 1065, the partnership will identify each activity it conducts and specify the income, loss, deductions, and credits from each activity.

EXAMPLE You are a general partner of a fiscal year partnership that ends on March 31, 1992. During that fiscal year you were inactive. Since you did not materially participate, your share of partnership income or loss reported in 1992 is passive activity income or loss, even if you become active from April 1, 1992, to the end of 1992.

Not treated as passive income are payments for services and certain guaranteed payments made in liquidation of a retiring or deceased partner's interest unless attributed to unrealized receivables and goodwill at a time the partner was passive.

Gain or loss on the disposition of a partnership interest may be attributed to different trade, investment, or rental activities of the partnership. The allocation is made according to a complicated formula included in IRS regulations.

Payments to a retired partner. Gain or loss is treated as passive only to the extent that it would be treated as such at the start of the liquidation of the partner's interest.

Limited partners. A limited partner is generally not considered to be a material participant in partnership activity, and thus, treats income or loss as passive, except in these cases:

1. The limited partner participates for more than 500 hours during the tax year; *see* Test 1 in ¶10.6.
2. The limited partner materially participated in the partnership during prior years under either Test 5 or Test 6 at ¶10.6.
3. The limited partner is also a general partner at all times during the partnership tax year that ends with or within the partner's taxable year.

A limited partner is not considered to be an "active participant" and thus does not qualify for the up-to-$25,000 rental loss allowance under ¶10.4.

Publicly traded partnerships (PTP). A PTP is a partnership whose interests are traded on established securities exchanges or are readily tradable in secondary markets. Publicly traded partnerships were organized to provide passive income to investors who could use the income to offset passive activity losses incurred from other activities. To defeat this tax purpose the tax law prevents offset of PTP income against net losses from any other passive activity or other PTP. Unallowed losses from a PTP carry forward and become deductible in a tax year only when you have passive income from that PTP or dispose of your interest in that PTP. Follow the instructions on Form 8582 for reporting net PTP income or loss on Schedule E.

The above passive activity rules apply to PTPs that were publicly traded on December 17, 1987, or which, by that date, had filed a PTP regulation statement with the SEC, or an application with a state regulatory commission to restructure part of a corporation as a PTP. A PTP not meeting the December 17, 1987, test is generally taxed as a corporation; income or loss does not pass through to the partners. However, corporate treatment does not apply if 90% or more of PTP gross income is from interest, dividends, real property rents, property sales, and other passive types of income.

FORM 8582 AFFECTS OTHER TAX FORMS

¶10.12   Form 8582 is the key to determining the application of the passive loss rules. Worksheets to Form 8582 are used to enter income and expenses from passive activities. Results from the worksheets are used to prepare Form 8582, in combination with the following forms and schedules.

Schedule A. Interest expense from a passive activity is subject to the passive loss rules rather than the investment interest limitation rules.

Schedule C. The passive activity loss rules apply to self-employed persons who are not active in the business. A loss incurred by an inactive self-employed person is entered on Form 8582 to determine the amount of any loss reported on Schedule C. If an inactive self-employed person has a profit, the profit may be entered on Form 8582 to offset losses from other passive activities.

Schedule D or Form 4797. Gains or losses from the sale of assets from a passive activity, or from the sale of an *insubstantial part* of your interest in a passive activity, are reported on Schedule D or on Form 4797 (sale of business property, *see* ¶44.1). The gain is also entered on Form 8582. Losses must first be entered on Form 8582 to see how much, if any, is allowable under the passive loss restrictions before an amount can be entered as a loss on Schedule D or Form 4797. A disposition of an insubstantial part of your interest does not trigger a deduction of suspended passive losses from prior years.

When you dispose of your *entire* interest in a passive activity to a non-related party in a fully taxable transaction, your losses for the year plus prior-year suspended losses are fully deductible. The same rule applies if you dispose of part of your entire interest, provided that you are disposing of a *substantial part* of the activity and you have proof of the current-year and prior-year suspended losses allocable to the disposed-of portion. In general, you need to file Form 8582 only if you have an investment in a different passive activity and you have an overall gain from the disposed of activity, after netting the gain or loss from the disposition with the net income or loss from current year operations and any prior year suspended passive losses. *See* the instructions to Form 8582 for details.

Schedule E. If you have a net profit from rental property or other passive activity reported on Schedule E and you also have losses from other passive activities, the income reported on Schedule E is also entered on Form 8582. A net loss from rental activities generally must be entered on Form 8582 but Form 8582 is not needed if you qualify for the full $25,000 allowance (¶10.4) for rental real estate losses and meet these tests: You have—

Losses only from rental real estate activities and no suspended passive losses from prior years;

No credits related to real estate activities;

Actively participated in the real estate operation;

Total losses from the rental real estate of $25,000 or less ($12,500 or less if married filing separately and you lived apart from your spouse all year); and

Modified adjusted gross income of $100,000 or less ($50,000 or less if married filing separately and you lived apart from your spouse all year).

If you have a loss from a passive interest in a partnership, trust, or S corporation, you first determine on Form 8582 whether the loss is deductible on Schedule E.

Schedule F. A passive activity farm loss is entered on Form 8582 to determine the deductible loss. If only part of the loss is allowed, only that portion is claimed on Schedule F. A net profit from passive farm activities is also entered on Form 8582 to offset losses from other passive activities.

Other tax forms. Other forms tied to Form 8582 are Form 4797 (sale of business assets or equipment), Form 4835 (farm rental income), and Form 4952 (investment interest deductions).

See Form 8582 for further details. Also *see* IRS Publication 925 for filled-in sample forms.

SUSPENDED LOSSES ALLOWED ON DISPOSITION OF YOUR INTEREST

¶10.13   Losses and credits that may not be claimed in 1992 because of the passive activity limitations are suspended and carried forward to 1993 and later years. The carryover lasts indefinitely, until you have passive income against which to claim the losses and credits. No carryback is allowed.

What if you have suspended losses and later materially participate in the business in which the loss was realized? The losses remain as passive losses but may offset nonpassive income of that activity.

EXAMPLE In 1992, you were not a material participant in a business activity and your share of losses was $10,000, which was suspended because you had no passive income. In 1993, you become a material participant in the business and your share of income is $1,000. The $1,000 is treated as nonpassive income. However, you may use $1,000 of the suspended loss as an offset to that income.

Allocation of suspended loss. If your suspended loss is incurred from several activities, you allocate the loss among the activities using the worksheets accompanying Form 8582. The loss is allocated among the activities in proportion to the total loss. If you have net income from significant participation activities (Test 4 of ¶10.6), such activities may be treated as one single activity in making the allocation; *see* instructions to Form 8582.

Disposition of a passive interest. A fully taxable sale of your entire interest to a nonrelated person will allow you to claim suspended deductions from the activity. Worthlessness of a security in a passive activity is treated as a disposition. An abandonment also releases suspended losses.

On a disposition, the suspended losses plus any current year loss from the activity and any loss on the disposition are deducted in the following order:

1. Income from the disposed passive activity
2. Income from other passive activities
3. Nonpassive income or gain

The new IRS proposals also allow suspended losses to be triggered upon the disposition of a *substantial part* of an activity.

Partial Dispositions

The new IRS proposed regulations provide a more favorable rule for partial dispositions than did the prior temporary regulations. If you group together activities and later dispose of a "significant part" of the overall activity, suspended losses allocable to that portion of the activity are deductible in the year of disposition. Unfortunately, the IRS has not defined when a partial disposition qualifies as a "significant part." You must keep records to prove the amount of losses allocable to the disposed-of portion.

Under the prior rules, partial dispositions did not trigger suspended losses.

$3,000 capital loss limit. Capital losses on a disposition of a passive interest are also subject to the general $3,000 loss limitation of ¶5.2.

EXAMPLES 1. You have a 5% interest in a limited partnership with an adjusted basis of $42,000. You also had carried over $2,000 of passive activity losses from prior years. In 1992, you sell your interest in the partnership to an unrelated person for $50,000. You realize an $8,000 gain from the sale and may offset $2,000 of that gain with the $2,000 carryover loss. Your $6,000 net gain is computed as follows:

Sales price	$50,000
Less adjusted basis	42,000
Gain	$ 8,000
Less passive carryover loss	2,000
Net gain	$ 6,000

The $6,000 net gain is treated as income from a passive activity which you include on Form 8582 if you also have other passive activities. If this is your only passive activity, Form 8582 does not have to be filed. The gain from the sale should be entered on Schedule D or Form 4797 and the carryover loss on Schedule E.

2. Assume you sold the interest for $30,000, instead of $50,000. Your deductible loss would be $5,000, computed as follows:

Sales price	$ 30,000
Less adjusted basis	42,000
Capital loss	$ (12,000)
Less capital loss limit	3,000
Capital loss carryover	$ (9,000)
Allowable capital loss on sale	3,000
Plus prior year passive losses	2,000
Total current deductible loss	$ 5,000

The $3,000 deductible loss on the sale is claimed in 1992 on Schedule D. The $9,000 capital loss carryover is not subject to the passive activity loss limit. You treat it in the same manner as any other capital loss carryover. The prior year passive losses are claimed on Schedule E.

Gifts. When a passive activity interest is given away, you may not deduct suspended passive losses. The donee's basis in the property is increased by the suspended loss if he or she sells the property at a gain. If a loss is realized by the donee on a sale of the interest, the donee's basis may not exceed fair market value of the gift at time of the donation.

Death. On the death of an investor in a passive interest, suspended losses are deductible on the decedent's final tax return, to the extent the suspended loss exceeds the amount by which the basis of the interest in the hands of the heir is increased.

EXAMPLE An owner dies holding an interest in a passive activity with a suspended loss of $8,000. After the owner's death, the heir's stepped-up basis for the property (equal to fair market value) is $6,000 greater than the decedent's basis. On the decedent's final return, $2,000 of the loss is deductible ($8,000–$6,000).

Tax credits. If you have tax credits that were barred under the passive activity rules, they may be claimed only in future years when you have tax liability attributable to passive income. However, in the year you dispose of your interest, a special election may be available to decrease your gain by the amount of your suspended credit; *see* below.

Basis election for suspended credits. If you qualify for an investment credit (under transition rules) or a rehabilitation credit, you are required to reduce the basis of the property even if you are unable to claim the credit because of the passive activity rules. If this occurs and you later dispose of your interest in the passive activity, including the property whose basis was reduced, your gain will be increased by virtue of the basis reduction although you never benefited from the credit. To prevent this, you may reduce the taxable gain by electing to increase the pre-transfer basis of the property by the amount of the unused credit.

EXAMPLE Brown places in service rehabilitated credit property qualifying for a $50 credit, but the credit is not allowed under the passive loss rules. However, basis is still reduced by $50. In a later year, Brown makes a taxable disposition of his entire interest in the activity and in the rehabilitation property. Assuming that no part of the suspended $50 credit has been used, Brown may elect to increase his basis in the property by the unused $50 credit.

Installment sales. If the passive activity interest is sold at a profit on the installment basis, suspended losses are deducted over the installment period in the same ratio as the gain recognized each year bears to the gain remaining to be recognized as of the start of the year. For example, if in the year of sale you report 20% of your total gain under the installment method, 20% of your suspended losses are also allowed.

LOW-INCOME HOUSING EXEMPTION

¶10.14 A transitional rule applies to qualified investors in certain qualified low-income housing projects. Losses during a fixed period are not treated as passive activity losses. The period begins with the tax year in which you made an initial investment in the qualified low-income housing project and ending with whichever of the following is the earliest: (1) the sixth tax year after the tax year in which you made your initial investment; (2) the first tax year after the tax year in which you are obligated to make your last investment; or (3) the tax year preceding the first tax year for which such project ceases to be a qualified low-income housing project.

A qualified low-income housing project is generally a project constructed or acquired under a binding written contract entered into on or before August 16, 1986, and placed in service before January 1, 1989.

A qualified investment had to be made after 1983, and if the project was placed in service on or before August 16, 1986, the investor must have held an interest in the project or had a binding contract to acquire an interest on August 16, 1986. If the project was placed in service after August 16, 1986, the investor must have made the initial investment after 1983 and held an interest in the project (or had a binding contract) on December 31, 1986.

PERSONAL SERVICE AND CLOSELY HELD CORPORATIONS

¶10.15 To prevent avoidance of the passive activity rules through use of corporations, the law imposes restrictions on income and loss offsets in closely held C corporations and personal service corporations.

Personal services. Personal services are services in the fields of health, law, engineering, architecture, accounting, actuarial sciences, performing arts, or consulting.

Unless material participation tests discussed below are met, the activities of a personal service corporation or a closely held corporation are considered passive activities, subject to the restrictions on loss deductions and tax credits. For purposes of these passive activity rules, a closely held C corporation is a corporation in which more than 50% in value of whose stock is owned by five or fewer persons during the last half of the tax year. A personal service corporation is a corporation, the principal activity of which is the performance of personal services by employee-owners. An employee-owner is any employee who on any day in the tax year owns any stock in the corporation. If an individual owns any stock in a corporation which in turn owns stock in another corporation, the individual is deemed to own a proportionate part of the stock in the other corporation. Further, more than 10% of the corporation's stock by value must be owned by owner-employees for the corporation to be a personal service corporation.

Material participation. A personal service corporation or closely held corporation is treated as materially participating in an activity during a tax year *only if* either:

1. One or more stockholders are treated as materially participating in the activity and they directly or indirectly hold in the aggregate more than 50% of the value of the corporation's outstanding shares; or
2. The corporation is a closely held corporation and in the 12-month period ending on the last day of the tax year, the corporation had at least one full-time manager, three full-time manager employees, and business deductions exceeded 15% of gross income from the activity.

A stockholder is treated as materially participating or significantly participating in the activity of a corporation if he or she satisfies one of the seven tests in ¶10.6 for material participation. For purposes of applying the significant participation test (Test 4 at ¶10.6), an activity of a personal service or closely held corporation is treated as a significant participation activity for a tax year *only if*:

1. The corporation is not treated as materially participating in the activity for the tax year; and
2. One or more individuals, each of whom is treated as significantly participating in the activity directly or indirectly, hold in the aggregate more than 50% of the value of the outstanding stock of the corporation. Furthermore, in applying the seven participation tests, all activities of the corporation are treated as activities in which the individual holds an interest in determining whether the individual participates in an activity of the corporation; and the individual's participation in all activities other than activities of the corporation are disregarded in determining whether his participation in an activity of the corporation is treated as material participation under the significant participation test (Test 4 at ¶10.6).

Closely held corporation's computation of passive loss. If a closely held corporation does not qualify under the participation tests above, it may offset passive activity deductions against the total of passive activity gross income and also *net active income*. Generally, net active income is taxable income from business operations, disregarding passive activity income and expenses, and portfolio income and expenses; *see* ¶10.8. Passive activity losses cannot offset portfolio income.

If a corporation stops being closely held, its passive losses and credits from prior years are not allowable against portfolio income but continue to be allowable only against passive income and net active income.

Tax liability on net active income may be offset by passive activity credits.

SALES OF PROPERTY AND OF PASSIVE ACTIVITY INTERESTS

¶10.16

Generally, gain on the sale or disposition of property is passive or nonpassive, depending on whether your activity is passive or nonpassive in the year of sale or disposition. Thus, gain on the sale of property used in a rental activity is treated as passive income, and gain on property used in a nonrental business is passive if you did not materially participate in the business in the year of sale. However, exceptions may prevent you from generating passive income by arranging certain sales described in this section. For example, gain on sale of substantially appreciated property formerly used in a nonpassive activity may be treated as nonpassive income, even if sold by a passive activity.

Where you transact an installment sale, treatment of gain in later years depends on your status in the year of sale. For example, if you were considered a material participant in a business, all gain is treated as nonpassive income, including gain for later installments. If you were in a rental activity or were not a material participant in a nonrental business, the gain is treated as passive income, unless the exceptions in this section apply.

Current gain from a pre-1987 installment sale is passive income if the activity would have been passive, assuming the passive activity rules were in effect at the time of the sale.

Gain on appreciated property formerly used in nonpassive activity. Gain from a disposition of substantially appreciated property is treated as passive activity income if the property was used in a passive activity for either 20% of its holding period or the entire 24-month period ending on the date of the disposition. Property is substantially appreciated if fair market value exceeds 120% of its adjusted basis.

EXAMPLE In 1988, Jones buys a building for use in a business in which he materially participates until March 31, 1998. On April 1, 1999, he rents the building. On December 31, 2000, he sells the building. Gain from the sale is treated as not from a passive activity. The building was used in a passive rental activity for 21 months before disposition (April 1, 1999, through December 31, 2000). Thus, it was not used in a passive activity for the entire 24-month period ending on the date of the sale. Further, the 21-month period during which the building was used in a passive activity is less than 20% of Jones' holding period of 13 years.

Property used in more than one activity in a 12-month period preceding disposition. You are required to allocate the amount realized on the disposition and the adjusted basis of the property among the activities in which the property was used during a 12-month period preceding the disposition. For purposes of this rule, the term activity includes personal use and holding for investment. The allocation may be based on the period for which the property is used in each activity during the 12-month period. However, if during the 12-month period the value of the property does not exceed the lesser of $10,000 and 10% of the value of all property used in the activity at the time of disposition, gain may be allocated to the predominant use.

EXAMPLE Smith sells a personal computer for $8,000. During the 12-month period that ended on the date of the sale, 70% of Smith's use of the computer was in a passive activity. Immediately before the sale, the fair market value of all property used in the passive activity, including the personal computer, was $200,000.

The computer was predominantly used in the passive activity during the 12-month period ending on the date of the sale. The value of the computer, $8,000, did not exceed the lesser of $10,000 and 10% of the $200,000 value of all property used in the activity immediately before the sale. Thus, the amount realized and the adjusted basis are allocated to the passive activity.

Disposition of partnership and S corporation interests. Gain or loss from the disposition of an interest in a partnership and S corporation is generally allocated among the entity's activities in proportion to the amount that the entity would have allocated to the partner or shareholder for each of its activities if the entity had sold its interest in the activities on an "applicable valuation date."

Gain is allocated only to appreciated activities. Loss is allocated only to depreciated activities. The entity may select either the beginning of its tax year in which the holder's disposition occurs, or the date of the disposition as the applicable valuation date.

Claiming suspended loss on disposition of interest in passive activity. A fully taxable sale of your entire interest or of substantially all of your interest to a nonrelated person will allow you to claim suspended loss deductions from the activity. These rules are fully discussed in ¶10.13.

Dealer's sale of property similar to property sold in the ordinary course of business. IRS regulations set down complex tests which determine whether the result of the sale is treated as passive or nonpassive income or loss.

AT-RISK RULES

AT-RISK LIMITS

¶ **10.17** The at-risk rules prevent investors from claiming losses in excess of their actual tax investment by barring them from including nonrecourse liabilities as part of the tax basis for their interest. Almost all ventures are subject to the at-risk limits. Real estate placed in service after 1986 is subject to at-risk rules as well, but most real estate nonrecourse financing can qualify for an exception; see ¶10.18.

EXAMPLE You invest cash of $1,000 in a venture and sign a nonrecourse note for $8,000. In 1992, your share of the venture's loss is $1,200. The at-risk rules limit your deduction to $1,000, the amount of your cash investment; as you are not personally liable on the note, the amount of the liability is not included as part of your basis for loss purposes.

Losses disallowed under the at-risk rules are carried over to the following year; see ¶10.21.

Form 6198. If you have amounts that are not at risk, you must file Form 6198 to figure your deductible loss. A separate form must be filed for each activity. However, if you have an interest in a partnership or S corporation that has more than one investment in any of the following four categories, the IRS currently allows you to aggregate all of the partnership or S corporation activities within each category. For example, all partnership or S corporation films and videotapes may be treated as one activity in determining amounts at risk. The aggregation rules may be changed by the IRS; see the instructions to Form 6198.

1. Holding, producing, or distributing motion picture films or videotapes;
2. Exploring for or exploiting oil or gas properties;
3. Exploring for, or exploiting, geothermal deposits (for wells commenced on or after October 1, 1978); and
4. Farming. For this purpose, farming is defined as the cultivation of land, raising or harvesting of any agricultural or horticultural commodity—including raising, shearing, breeding, caring for, or management of animals. Forestry and timber activities are not included, but orchards bearing fruits and nuts are within the definition of farming. Certain activities carried on within the physical boundaries of the farm may not necessarily be treated as farming.

In addition to the above categories, the law treats as a single activity all leased depreciable business equipment (Section 1245 property) that is placed in service during any year by a partnership or S corporation.

Exempt from the at-risk rules are C corporations which meet active business tests and are not in the equipment leasing business or any business involving master sound recording, films, videotapes, or other artistic, literary, or musical property. For details on the active business tests, as well as a special at-risk exception for equipment leasing activities of closely-held corporations, see IRS Publication 925.

The at-risk limitation applies only to tax losses produced by expense deductions which are not disallowed by reason of another provision of the law. For example, if a prepaid interest expense is deferred under the prepaid interest limitation (¶15.13), the interest will not be included in the loss subject to the risk limitation. When the interest accrues and becomes deductible, the expense may be considered within the at-risk provision. Similarly, if a deduction is deferred because of farming syndicate rules, that deduction will enter into the computation of the tax loss subject to the risk limitation only when it becomes deductible under the farming syndicate rules.

Effect of passive loss rules. Where a loss is also subject to the at-risk rules, you apply the at-risk rules first. If the loss is deductible under the at-risk rules, the passive activity rules then apply. On Form 6198 (at risk), you figure the deductible loss allowed as at risk and then carry the loss over to Form 8582 to determine the passive activity loss.

WHAT IS AT RISK?

¶ **10.18** The following amounts are considered at risk in determining your tax position in a business or investment:

Cash;

Adjusted basis of property that you contribute; and

Borrowed funds for which you are personally liable to pay.

A special at-risk rule for real estate loans is discussed on page 160.

At-risk basis is figured as of the end of the year. Any loss allowed for a year reduces the at-risk amount as of the start of the next year. Therefore, if a loss exceeds your at-risk investment, the excess loss will not be deductible in later years unless you increase your at-risk investment; see ¶10.21.

Personal liability alone does not assure that the borrowed funds are considered at risk. The lender must have no interest in the venture other than as creditor.

EXAMPLE An investor pays a promoter of a book purchase plan $45,000 for a limited partnership interest. The promoter is the general partner. The investor pays $30,000 cash and gives a note for $15,000 on which he is personally liable. His amount at risk is $30,000; the $15,000 personal liability note is not counted because it is owed to the general partner.

Special at-risk rule for real estate financing. For real property placed in service after 1986, you may treat nonrecourse financing from unrelated commercial lenders or from government agencies as amounts at risk if the financing is secured by the real estate. Loans from the seller or promoter do not qualify. Third party nonrecourse debt from a related lender, other than the seller or a promoter, may also be treated as at risk, providing the terms of the loan are commercially reasonable and on substantially the same terms as loans involving unrelated persons.

If you acquired an interest after 1986 in a partnership or S corporation, the above at-risk rules apply to your share of real estate losses, regardless of when the partnership or S corporation placed the property in service.

Pledges of other property as security. If you pledge personally owned real estate used outside the activity to secure a nonrecourse debt and invest the proceeds in an at-risk activity, the proceeds may be considered part of your at-risk investment. The proceeds included in basis are limited by the fair market value of the property used as collateral (determined as of the date the property is pledged as security) less any prior (or superior) claims to which the collateral is subject.

Partners. A partner is treated as at risk to the extent that basis in the partnership is increased by the share of partnership income. That partnership income is then used to reduce the partnership's nonrecourse indebtedness will have no effect on a partner's amount at risk. If the partnership makes actual distributions of the income in the taxable year, the amount distributed reduces the partner's amount at risk. A buy-sell agreement, effective at a partner's death or retirement, is not considered for at-risk purposes.

EXAMPLES 1. On January 1, 1990, an investor contributes $5,000 cash to a farming venture. He also borrows $3,000 from a bank for which he is personally liable and contributes it. By the end of 1990, he pays off $750 of the loan. The venture has no income or losses in 1990. The investor's at-risk basis as of December 31, 1990, is $7,250, determined as follows:

Contributions	$5,000
Recourse financing	3,000
	$8,000
Less: Partial loan repayment	750
Amount at risk as of 12/31/90	$7,250

2. Same as Example 1, but on February 1, 1991, he borrows $10,000 on a nonrecourse basis. He pays off $1,000 on the personal liability loan and $500 on the nonrecourse loan. The venture earns $3,000 and distributes $2,000 to him. The at-risk basis as of December 31, 1991, is $7,250, determined as follows:

Amount at risk as of 1/1/91		$7,250
Plus: Income		3,000
		$10,250
Less: Repayment of personal liability loan	$1,000	
Distribution	2,000	3,000
Amount at risk as of 12/31/91		$7,250

Payment on the nonrecourse loan with funds or other nonrecourse loans from only the activity does not affect the amount at risk.

3. Same as Example 2, but on March 1, 1992, the investor contributes $2,500 and pays off the personal liability loan. The venture has losses of $10,500 for 1992. As of December 31, 1992, the investor's amount at risk is $8,500, determined as follows:

Amount at risk as of 1/1/92	$7,250
Plus: Contribution	2,500
	$9,750
Less: Payment of personal liability loan	1,250
Amount at risk as of 12/31/92	$8,500

The investor's loss deduction is limited to the amount at risk of $8,500. The $2,000 disallowed loss is carried over to 1993.

Note: The above adjustments to basis are only for at-risk purposes. Basis for depreciation and computing gain or loss on a sale is controlled by the adjusted basis rules at ¶5.16.

Activities begun before 1976. A special rule determines the amount at risk as of the first day of the first tax year after 1975. Again, you start with the amounts considered at risk. Losses incurred and deducted in taxable years before 1976 first reduce the basis allocated to amounts considered not at risk, such as nonrecourse loans. If the losses exceed the amount not at risk, the excess reduces the at-risk investment. Distributions reduce at-risk amounts. *See* the instructions to Form 6198.

AMOUNTS NOT AT RISK

¶**10.19** The following may not be treated as part of basis for at-risk purposes in determining your tax position in a business or investment:

- Liabilities for which you have no personal liability, except in the case of certain real estate financing; *see* ¶10.18.
- Liabilities for which you have personal liability, but the lender also has a capital or profit-sharing interest in the venture.
- Recourse liabilities convertible to a nonrecourse basis.

EXAMPLE An investor purchases cattle from a rancher for $10,000 cash and a $30,000 note payable to the rancher. The investor is personally liable on the note. In a separate agreement, the rancher agrees to care for the cattle for 6% of the investor's net profits from the cattle activity. The investor is considered at risk to $10,000; he may not increase the amount at risk by the $30,000 borrowed from the rancher.

Money borrowed from a relative listed at ¶33.10, who has an interest in the venture, other than as a creditor, or from a partnership in which you own more than a 10% interest.

Funds borrowed from a person whose recourse is either your interest in the activity or property used in the activity.

Amounts for which your economic loss is limited by a nonrecourse financing guarantee, stop-loss agreement, or other similar arrangement.

Investments protected by insurance or loss reimbursement agreement between you and another person. If you are personally liable on a mortgage but you separately obtain insurance to compensate you for any mortgage payments, you are at risk only to the extent of the uninsured portion of the personal liability. You may, however, include as at risk any amount of premium paid from your personal assets. Taking out casualty insurance or insurance protecting you against tort liability is not considered within the at-risk provisions, and such insurance does not affect your investment basis.

EXAMPLES 1. Some commercial feedlots in livestock feeding operations may reimburse investors against any loss sustained on sales of the livestock above a stated dollar amount per head. Under such "stop loss" orders, an investor is at risk only to the extent of the portion of his or her capital against which he or she is not entitled to reimbursement. Where a limited partnership agrees with a limited partner that, at the partner's election, his or her partnership interest will be bought at a stated minimum dollar amount (usually less than the investor's original capital contribution), the partner is considered at risk only to the extent of his or her investment exceeding the guaranteed repurchase price.

2. A promoter of TV films sold half-hour programs in a TV series to individual investors. Each investor gave a cash down payment and a note for which he or she was personally liable for the balance. Each investor's note, which was identical in face amount, terms, and maturity date, was payable out of the distribution proceeds from the film. Each investor also bought from the promoter the right to the unpaid balance on another investor's note. The promoter arranged the distribution of the films as a unit and was to apportion the sales proceeds equally among the investors. The IRS held that each investor is not at risk on the investment evidenced by the note. Upon maturity, each may receive a payment from another investor equal to the one that he or she owes.

3. A gold mine investment offered tax write-offs of four times the cash invested. For $10,000 cash, an investor buys from a foreign mining company a seven-year mineral claim lease to a gold reserve. Under the lease, he or she can develop and extract all of the gold in the reserve. At the same time, he or she agrees to spend $40,000 to develop the lease before the end of the year. To fund this commitment, the investor authorizes the promoter to sell an option for $30,000 to a third party who is to buy all the gold to be extracted. The $30,000 along with the $10,000 down payment is to be used to develop the reserve. The promoter advises the investor that he or she may claim a $40,000 deduction for certain development costs.

The IRS ruled that $30,000 is not deductible because the amount is not "risk capital." The investor gets $30,000 by selling an option that can be exercised only if gold is found. If no gold is found, he or she is under no obligation to the option holder. His or her risk position for the $30,000 is substantially the same as if he or she had borrowed from the option holder on a nonrecourse basis repayable only from his or her interest in the activity. The Tax Court struck down a similar plan on different grounds. Without deciding the question of what was at risk, the court held that the option was only a right of first refusal. Thus, $30,000 was taxable income to the investor in the year of the arranged sale.

Limited partner's potential cash call. Under the terms of a partnership agreement, limited partners may be required to make additional capital contributions under specified circumstances. Whether such a potential cash call increases the limited partner's at-risk amount has been a matter of dispute.

In one case, the IRS and Tax Court held that a limited partner was not at risk with respect to a partnership note where under the terms of the partnership agreement, he could be required to make additional capital contributions if the general partners did not pay off the note at maturity. The possibility of such a potential cash call was too uncertain; the partnership might earn profits to pay off the note and even if there were losses, the general partners might not demand additional contributions from the limited partners. However, a federal appeals court reversed, holding that the limited partner was at risk because his obligation was mandatory and "economic reality" insured that the general partners would insure their rights by requiring the additional capital contribution.

In a recent case, limited partners relied upon the earlier favorable federal appeals court decision to argue that they were at risk where they could be required by the general partners to make additional cash contributions, but only in order to cover liabilities or expenses that could not be paid out of partnership assets. So long as the partnership was solvent, the limited partners could "elect out" of the call provision. Because of this election, the Tax Court held that the limited partners' obligation was contingent, rather than unavoidable as in the earlier federal appeals court case. Thus, the cash call provision did not increase their at-risk amount.

AT-RISK INVESTMENT IN SEVERAL ACTIVITIES

¶**10.20** If you invest in several activities, each is generally treated separately when applying the at-risk limitation on Form 6198. You generally may not aggregate basis, gains, and losses from the activities for purposes of at-risk limitations. Thus, income from one activity may not be offset by losses from another; the income from one must be reported while the losses from the other may be nondeductible because of at-risk limitations.

However, you may aggregate activities that are part of a business you actively manage. Activities of a business carried on by a partnership or S corporation qualify if 65% or more of losses for the year are allocable to persons who actively participate in management.

The law allows partnerships and S corporations to treat as a single activity all depreciable equipment (Section 1245 properties) which is leased or held for lease and placed in service in any tax year.

Furthermore, as discussed at ¶10.17, you may aggregate all partnership or S corporation activities within the four categories of films and videotapes, oil and gas properties, geothermal properties, and farms.

CARRYOVER OF DISALLOWED LOSSES

¶**10.21** A loss disallowed in a current year by the at-risk limitation may be carried over and deducted in the next taxable year, provided it does not fall within the at-risk limits in that year. The loss is subject to an unlimited carryover period until there is an at-risk basis to support the deduction. This may occur when additional contributions are made to the business or when the activity has income which has not been distributed.

Gain from the disposition of property used in an at-risk activity is treated as income from the activity. In general, the reporting of gain will allow a deduction for losses disallowed in previous years to be claimed in the year of disposition.

RECAPTURE OF LOSSES WHERE AT RISK IS LESS THAN ZERO

¶**10.22** To prevent manipulation of at-risk basis after a loss is claimed, there is a special recapture rule. If the amount at risk in an activity is reduced to below zero because of a distribution or a change in the status of an indebtedness from recourse to nonrecourse, income may be realized to the extent of the negative at-risk amount. The taxable amount may not exceed the amount of losses previously deducted.

The recaptured amount is not treated as income from the activity for purposes of determining whether current or suspended losses are allowable.

The recaptured amount is treated as a deduction allocable to that activity in the following year.

11

GIFTS, INCOME FROM TRUSTS AND ESTATES, AND LIFE INSURANCE

- Gifts and inheritances are not taxed. However, income received from inherited property is taxable. You also may receive a gift in the form of trust income. The trust income is taxable as explained in this chapter.
- Life insurance proceeds received on the death of a person are usually tax free, although interest earned on the proceeds received as installments is generally taxed.

Tax accounting for trust or estate income is complicated. As a beneficiary, you are not required to understand the rules governing the taxing of trusts and estates. That is the trustee's or executor's responsibility. The fiduciary should inform you of your share of taxable income and its source on Schedule K-1 of Form 1041. The fiduciary should also tell you whether the distribution is out of current income or accumulated income.

GIFTS, INHERITANCES, AND TRUST AND ESTATE INCOME

GIFTS AND INHERITANCES

¶**11.1** Gifts and inheritances you receive are not taxable. Income earned from gift or inherited property after you receive it is taxable.

Describing a payment as a gift or inheritance will not necessarily shield it from tax if it is, in fact, a payment for services. Treatment of gifts to employees is covered at ¶2.4.

EXAMPLES 1. An employee is promised by his employer that he will be remembered in his will if he continues to work for him. The employer dies but fails to mention the employee in his will. The employee sues the estate, which settles his claim. The settlement is taxable.

2. A nephew left his uncle a bequest of $200,000. In another clause of the will, the uncle was appointed executor, and the bequest of the $200,000 was described as being made in lieu of all commissions to which he would otherwise be entitled as executor. The bequest is considered tax-free income. It was not conditioned upon the uncle performing as executor. If the will had made the bequest contingent upon the uncle acting as executor, the $200,000 would have been taxed.

3. An attorney performed services for a friend without expectation of pay. The friend died and in his will left the attorney a bequest in appreciation for his services. The payment was considered a tax-free bequest. The amount was not bargained for.

4. A lawyer agreed to handle a client's legal affairs without charge; she promised to leave him securities. Twenty years later, under her will, he inherited the securities. The IRS taxed the bequest as pay. Both he and the client expected that he would be paid for legal services. If she meant to make a bequest from their agreement, she should have said so in her will.

A sale of an expected inheritance from a living person is taxable as ordinary income.

Campaign contributions. Campaign contributions are not taxable income to a political candidate if the funds are used for political campaign expenses or some similar purposes. Detailed records of receipts and disbursements are advisable to avoid tax on the political funds. Also nontaxable are contributions which are intended for the candidate's unrestricted personal use and qualify as gifts.

HOW BENEFICIARIES REPORT ESTATE OR TRUST INCOME

¶**11.2** Trust or estate income is treated as if you had received the income directly from the original source instead of from the estate or trust. This means capital gain remains capital gain, ordinary income is fully taxed, and tax-exempt income remains tax free. Tax preference items of a trust or estate are apportioned between the estate or trust and beneficiaries, according to allocation of income; *see* ¶23.3.

You report your share of trust or estate income as shown on the Schedule K-1 (Form 1041) sent to you by the trustee. Dividends and interest from the trust are reported on Schedule B of Form 1040; capital gains on Schedule D. Income or loss from real estate or business activities shown on Schedule K-1 are reported by you on Schedule E, subject to the passive activity restrictions discussed in Chapter 10.

Reporting rule for revocable grantor trusts. A grantor who sets up a revocable trust or keeps certain powers over trust income or corpus must report all of the trust income, deductions, and credits. This rule applies if a grantor retains a reversionary interest in the trust that is valued at more than 5% of the trust (valued at time trust is set up); *see* ¶33.6. If a grantor is also a trustee of a revocable trust and all the trust assets are in the United States, filing Form 1041 is not necessary. The grantor simply reports the trust income, deductions, and credits on Form 1040. This reporting rule is optional for revocable trusts created before 1981. Grantors of such trusts who want to report trust income on their own returns without having to file Form 1041 must first file a final Form 1041 for the current tax year with a notation on the form alerting the IRS that in later years they will report trust income on their own returns; *see* the instructions to Form 1041.

DISTRIBUTIONS OF ACCUMULATED TRUST INCOME

¶**11.3** Where you are the beneficiary of an accumulation trust, the trust accumulates income on which it pays tax. When the trust distributes income to you, the trustee tells you what part of the distribution is attributable to accumulations of prior income. The tax on an accumulation distribution is figured on Form 4970. Distributions of current income are reported according to the rules of ¶11.2. If you receive a distribution of accumulated income from a trust, contact the trustee or an experienced tax practitioner for advice in computing your tax on the accumulation.

Distributions of accumulated income are subject to tax, provided the accumulation exceeds the distributable net income of the trust for the year. However, under the throwback rule, only that portion of the accumulation distribution that would have been included in the beneficiary's income had it been distributed when earned is currently taxed. Thus, tax-exempt interest is never taxed. Income accumulated prior to the beneficiary's reaching the age of 21 and the years before a beneficiary was born are not subject to the throwback rule unless distributions are made under a multiple trust rule explained in the instructions to Form 4970.

Although a beneficiary pays a tax in the year of receiving the accumulation distribution, tax is computed as if the accumulated income were actually distributed in the years in which it was earned. For the year of the accumulation distribution, the beneficiary pays tax on the sum of: (1) a tax on taxable income exclusive of the accumulation distribution; (2) a tax on the accumulation distribution computed using a short-cut method that takes into account taxable income in three of the five years preceding the year of distribution; and (3) an interest charge in the case of a foreign trust.

In preparing your return, the tax on your regular taxable income is computed on Form 1040; the tax on the distribution is computed on Form 4970 and added to the tax on Form 1040.

Where a trust has already been subject to estate tax or the generation-skipping transfer tax, the partial tax on a distribution is reduced by the estate or generation-skipping tax attributable to the accumulated income. The reduction is limited by a special statutory formula for determining the pre-death portions. The reduction is only for estate tax from a decedent dying after 1979 or for generation-skipping transfer taxes after June 11, 1976.

Where the beneficiary receives an accumulation distribution from more than two trusts for the same year, tax for the distributions from the third trust is computed under the method described above, except that no credit is given for any taxes previously paid by the trust with respect to the accumulation distribution. A *de minimis* rule provides that accumulation distributions are not subject to the multiple trust rule unless the distribution equals or exceeds $1,000.

Sale of capital gain property by trust within two years of transfer. Capital gain is not subject to the throwback rules. However, if the trust sells appreciated property within two years of receiving it by gift or bargain sale, gain is taxed at the same rate that the grantor would have paid if the grantor sold the property. This rule for taxing gain does not apply if following the grantor's death the trust sells in the two-year period.

Trust for the benefit of a spouse. Where a spouse creates a trust for the benefit of the other spouse, income of the trust is taxed to the spouse who created the trust as income is earned. Trust transfers before October 10, 1969, are not subject to this rule.

DEDUCTIONS FOR INCOME SUBJECT TO ESTATE TAX

¶**11.4** If you receive income which was earned by, but not paid to, a decedent before death, you are said to have "income in respect of a decedent." You report the income, and if an estate has paid a federal estate tax on the income, you may deduct part of the estate tax allocated to the income. No deduction is allowed for state death taxes. Ask the executor of the estate for data in computing the deduction.

EXAMPLE When your uncle died, he was owed a fee of $1,000. He also had not collected accrued bond interest of $500. You, as the sole heir, will collect both items and pay income tax on them. These items are called income in respect of a decedent. Assume that an estate tax of $390 was paid on the $1,500. You collect the $1,000, which you report on your income tax return. You may deduct $260, computed as follows:

$$\frac{\$1,000}{\$1,500} \times \$390, \text{ or } \$260$$

When you collect the $500, you will deduct the balance, or $130 ($390 − $260).

The deduction is generally claimed as a miscellaneous itemized deduction that is *not* subject to the 2% AGI floor; *see* Chapter 19. However, if you receive long-term capital gain income, such as an installment payment on a sale transacted before a decedent's death, the estate tax attributed to the capital gain item is not claimed as a miscellaneous deduction. The deduction is treated as if it were an expense of sale and thus, reduces the amount of gain. This rule applies to capital gain received because of a decedent who died after November 6, 1978.

Lump-sum distributions from qualified retirement plans. When a beneficiary receiving a lump-sum distribution because of an employee's death reports the distribution using the special averaging method (Chapter 7), the taxable amount of the distribution must be reduced by the estate taxes attributable to the distribution. *See* the instructions for Form 4972 when calculating the tax under averaging.

LIFE INSURANCE AND OTHER INSURANCE PROCEEDS

HOW LIFE INSURANCE PROCEEDS ARE TAXED TO A BENEFICIARY

¶11.5 Life insurance proceeds received upon the death of the insured are generally tax free. However, insurance proceeds may be subject to estate tax so that the beneficiary actually receives a reduced amount; *see* ¶39.2. Interest paid on proceeds left with the insurer is taxable except in this case: A surviving spouse who elects to receive installments rather than a lump sum does not pay tax on the first $1,000 of interest received each year if the decedent died before October 23, 1986. Read the following checklist to find how your insurance receipts are taxed—

A lump-sum payment of the full face value of a life insurance policy: The proceeds are generally tax free. The tax-free exclusion also covers death benefits payments under endowment contracts, worker's compensation insurance contracts, employers' group insurance plans, or accident and health insurance contracts. The exclusion does not apply to a policy combined with a nonrefund life annuity contract where a single premium equal to the face value of the insurance is paid.

Insurance proceeds may be taxable where the policy was transferred for valuable consideration. Exceptions to this rule are made for transfers among partners and corporations and their stockholders and officers.

Installment payments spread over your life under a policy that could have been paid in a lump sum: Part of each installment attributed to interest may be taxed. Divide the face amount of the policy by the number of years the installments are to be paid. The result is the amount which is received tax free each year.

If you are the surviving spouse of an insured who died before October 23, 1986, up to $1,000 of interest paid with the annual installment is also tax free. You are still treated as a spouse if separated from the insured at the date of his or her death, but not if divorced. (If you receive payments under a policy with a "family income rider," *see* ¶11.6). The $1,000 interest exclusion is not allowed where the insured died after October 22, 1986.

EXAMPLE Alice is the wife and beneficiary under her husband John's life insurance policy of $100,000. He died September 30, 1986. She elected to take installment payments for the rest of her life. Alice's life expectancy is 20 years. Then $5,000 ($100,000 ÷ 20) is the principal amount spread to each year. The first $6,000 received each year ($5,000 principal plus $1,000 of the spouse's special interest exclusion) is exempt from tax. If Alice lives more than 20 years, she may continue to treat up to $6,000 of annual payments as tax-free receipts.

If the policy guarantees payments to a secondary beneficiary if you should die before receiving a specified number of payments, the tax-free amount is reduced by the present value of the secondary beneficiary's interest in the policy. The insurance company can give you this figure.

Installment payments for a fixed number of years under a policy which could have been paid in a lump sum. Divide the full face amount of the policy by the number of years you are to receive the installments. The result is the amount which is received tax free each year.

EXAMPLE Same facts as in the example in the previous column, but Alice elects to take installment payments for 10 years. Then $10,000 ($100,000 ÷ 10) is the principal amount received tax free. So, up to $11,000 per year may be received tax free by Alice, $10,000 of principal sum plus up to $1,000 of interest, under the surviving spouse's interest exclusion.

Installment payments when there is no lump-sum option in the policy: You must find the discounted value of the policy at the date of the insured's death and use that as the principal amount. The insurance company can give you that figure. After you find the discounted value, you divide it (as above) by the number of years you are to receive installments. The result is the amount that is tax free. The remainder is taxed.

EXAMPLE The insured died in 1992. Under an insurance policy, the surviving wife is entitled to $5,000 a year for life. Her life expectancy is 20 years. There is no lump sum stated in the policy. Say the discounted value of the wife's rights is $60,000. The principal amount spread to each year for the wife is $3,000 ($60,000 ÷ 20). Subtracting $3,000 from each annual $5,000 payment gives her taxable income of $2,000.

Payments to you along with other beneficiaries under the same policy, by lump-sum or varying installments.

EXAMPLE Under one life insurance policy of an insured man who died in 1992, a surviving wife, daughter, and nephew are all beneficiaries. The wife is entitled to a lump sum of $60,000. The daughter and nephew are each entitled to a lump sum of $35,000. Under the installment options, the wife chooses to receive $5,000 a year for the rest of her life. (She has a 20-year life expectancy.) The daughter and the nephew each choose a yearly payment of $5,000 for 10 years. This is how each yearly installment is taxed:

WIFE: The principal amount spread to each year is $3,000. Subtracting $3,000 from the yearly $5,000 payment gives the wife taxable income of $2,000.

DAUGHTER AND NEPHEW: Both are taxed the same way. The principal amount spread to each of the 10 years is $3,500. Subtracting this $3,500 from the yearly $5,000 installment gives the daughter and the nephew taxable income of $1,500 each.

Interest only option. When proceeds are left on deposit under the "interest only" option, the interest is fully taxed; the lump sum is not taxed. A surviving spouse of an insured who died before October 23, 1986, may not exclude $1,000 interest under the "interest only" option. However, if the surviving spouse later elects to receive proceeds from the policy in installments, the interest exclusion applies from the time of the election.

Universal life policy. A universal life policy allows a policyholder to apply premium payments to cash value instead of to death benefits. Death benefits may be tax free if the policies meet certain technical tests. These tests must be determined by the insurance company. Therefore, you must check with the company paying the proceeds whether the payments qualify as tax-free life insurance payments.

Other names applied to universal life may be "flexible premium" or "adjustable life premium" policies.

A POLICY WITH A FAMILY INCOME RIDER

¶**11.6** Payments received under a family income rider are taxed under a special rule. A family income rider provides additional term insurance coverage for a fixed number of years from the date of the basic policy. Under the terms of a rider, if the insured dies at any time during the term period, the beneficiary receives monthly payments during the balance of the term period, and then at the end of the term period, receives the lump-sum proceeds of the basic policy. If the insured dies after the end of the term period, the beneficiary receives only the lump sum from the basic policy.

When the insured dies during the term period, part of each monthly payment received during the term period includes interest on the lump-sum proceeds of the basic policy (which is held by the company until the end of the term period). That interest is fully taxed. The balance of the monthly payment consists of an installment (principal plus interest) of the proceeds from the term insurance purchased under the family income rider. You may exclude from this balance: (1) a prorated portion of the present value of the lump sum under the basic policy; and (2) an additional amount of up to $1,000 attributable to interest if you are a surviving spouse of an insured who died before October 23, 1986. The lump sum under the basic policy is tax free when you eventually receive it.

The rules here also apply to an integrated family income policy and to family maintenance policies, whether integrated or with an attached rider.

In figuring your taxable portions, ask the insurance company for its interest rate and the present value of term payments.

HOW OTHER INSURANCE PROCEEDS ARE TAXED

¶**11.7** Dividends paid by the insurance company as reduction of premiums (taken in cash, left as interest with the company, or used to accelerate the maturity of the policy) are not taxable. They serve to reduce the cost basis of your policy, thus increasing gain sometimes computed upon maturity of some policies. However, interest on such "dividends" is generally taxable, although the interest on GI insurance dividends left on deposit with the VA is tax free.

Matured endowment policies. You generally report as income the difference between the proceeds received and your investment; see ¶7.24. The payment on an endowment contract because of the insured's death is treated as the payment of tax-free life insurance proceeds provided the policy meets certain technical definitions not discussed in this book.

Sale of an endowment contract before maturity. Taxed as ordinary income; see ¶7.22.

Surrender of policy for cash. Taxed as ordinary income (not capital gain) if the cash received exceeds the premiums paid, less dividends received. If you take, instead, a paid-up policy, you may avoid tax; see ¶11.8. You get no deduction if there is a loss on the surrender of a policy.

Collection of proceeds on policy purchased by or assigned to you on the life of someone else. Where a policy is transferred for valuable consideration, only the amount paid and the premiums paid after the transfer are tax free when collected; the balance is taxed. There is no tax on life insurance proceeds paid under contracts which have been transferred to a partner or to a corporation in which the insured was a shareholder or officer.

TAX-FREE EXCHANGES OF INSURANCE POLICIES

¶**11.8** These exchanges of insurance policies are considered tax free—

Life insurance policy for another life insurance policy, endowment policy, or an annuity contract.
Endowment policy for another endowment policy that provides for regular payments beginning no later than the date payments would have started under the old policy, or in exchange for an annuity contract.
Annuity contract for another annuity contract with identical annuitants.

These exchanges are not tax free—

Endowment policy for a life insurance policy, or for another endowment policy that provides for payments beginning at a date later than payments would have started under the old policy.
Annuity contract for a life insurance or endowment policy.
Transfers of life insurance contracts where the insured is not the same person in both contracts. The IRS held that a company could not make a tax-free exchange of a key executive policy where the company could change insured executives as they leave or join the firm.

Financially troubled insurer. If your annuity contract or insurance policy is with an insurance company that is in a rehabilitation, conservatorship, insolvency, or a similar state proceeding, you may surrender the policy and make a tax-free reinvestment of the proceeds in a new policy with a different insurance company. The transfer must be completed within 60 days. If a government agency does not allow you to withdraw your entire balance from the troubled insurance company, you must assign all rights to any future distributions to the issuer of the new contract or policy. Full details are in IRS Revenue Procedure 92-44.

12 PRIZES, SCHOLARSHIPS, DAMAGES, REFUNDS, AND OTHER INCOME

Almost everything that you earn, win, or even find must be reported as taxable income. You must report lottery and gambling winnings, prizes, and certain refunds of state and local taxes. However, the law allows several exceptions, such as the tax-free receipt of insurance proceeds, certain scholarship awards, and gifts and inheritances. Insurance, gifts, and inheritances are discussed in Chapter 11.

Whether Social Security benefits are taxable is discussed in Chapter 34.

Jury duty pay is taxable, but if you have to turn it over to your employer in return for getting your regular salary, you may claim an offsetting deduction, even if you do not itemize deductions. Claim the deduction on Line 30 of Form 1040.

PRIZES AND GAMBLING WINNINGS

PRIZES AND AWARDS

¶**12.1** Prizes and awards are taxable income except for an award or prize that meets *all* these four tests:

1. It is for outstanding educational activities, literary, or civic achievement.
2. You were selected without any action on your part.
3. You do not have to perform services.
4. You assign the prize or award to a government unit or tax-exempt charitable organization. You must make the assignment before you use or benefit from the award. You may *not* claim a charitable deduction for the assignment. The IRS has a model form for making the donation.

Value of prize taxed at fair market value. A prize of merchandise is taxable at fair market value. For example, where a prize of first-class steamship tickets was exchanged for tourist-class tickets for a winner's family, the taxable value of the prize was the price of the tourist tickets. What is the taxable fair market value of an automobile won as a prize? In one case, the Tax Court held that the taxable value was what the recipient could realize on an immediate resale of the car.

Employee achievement awards. The above restrictions on tax-free treatment do not apply to awards from employers for length of service or safety achievement. The rules for such employee awards are at ¶3.9 and ¶20.28.

SWEEPSTAKE AND LOTTERY WINNINGS

¶**12.2** Sweepstake, lottery, and raffle winnings are taxable as "other income" on Line 22 of Form 1040. The cost of tickets is deductible only to the extent you report winnings, and only if you itemize deductions. The deduction is claimed on Schedule A as a miscellaneous deduction that is *not* subject to the 2% adjusted gross income (AGI) floor (Chapter 19). For example, if you buy state lottery tickets and win a 1992 drawing, you may deduct the cost of your losing tickets in 1992 up to the amount of your winnings.

When a minor wins a state lottery and the prize is held by his parents as custodians under the Uniform Gifts to Minors Act, the prize is taxed to the minor in the year the prize is won.

Splitting Sweepstake Winnings

To split income, potential sweepstake winnings may be divided among family members or others before the prize is won. You might buy the sweepstakes or lottery ticket in your name and the names of others. The prize is shared and each portion separately taxed. However, the IRS has not allowed income splitting after the prize is won. In one case, a couple who bought a winning lottery ticket that under state law was payable to only one person proved they shared the ticket before the draw by having their attorneys draw up a joint ownership agreement.

Installment payments. If winnings are payable in installments, you pay tax only as installments are received. This is true, even if the payer is required by state law to buy a surety bond as security for future installments. That the payments are secured does not make them immediately taxable where you have no choice in the way payments are made. If you have the chance to elect a lump-sum payment but instead choose installments, you are in "constructive receipt," and are thus taxable on the entire amount in the year the prize is awarded.

GAMBLING WINNINGS AND LOSSES

¶12.3 Gambling winnings are taxable. Losses from gambling are deductible only up to the gains from gambling. You may not deduct a net gambling loss even though a particular state says gambling is legal. Nor does it matter that your business is gambling. You may not deduct the loss.

If you are not a professional gambler, gambling income is included on Form 1040 as "other income" on Line 22. Gambling losses (not exceeding the amount of the gains) are deductible as "miscellaneous deductions" on Schedule A. The losses are *not* subject to the 2% AGI floor (Chapter 19). According to the IRS, professional gamblers who bet only for their own account are not in a business and must deduct losses (up to gains) as itemized deductions. However, the Supreme Court has held that full-time gamblers may deduct losses as business expenses even if they place wagers only for themselves. According to the Supreme Court, in order to be considered engaged in a business, a gambler must prove that he or she bets full time to earn a livelihood and not merely as a hobby.

To prove your losses in the event your return is questioned, you must retain evidence of losses.

SCHOLARSHIPS, FELLOWSHIPS, AND GRANTS

SCHOLARSHIP RULES FOR AWARDS AFTER AUGUST 16, 1986

¶12.4 Tax-free treatment for scholarships and fellowships granted after August 16, 1986 is allowed only for degree candidates who use the grant for certain types of expenses discussed in the next column.

More favorable rules applied to grants made before August 17, 1986. For example, under the prior law rules, degree candidates could exclude from income amounts used for room and board and travel allowances as well as tuition and related expenses. Payments for teaching or research were generally tax free if the services were required of all degree candidates and the "primary" purpose of the teaching or research was to further your training rather than to compensate you for the services. For non-degree candidates with grants made before August 17, 1986, the law allowed an annual tax-free exclusion equal to $300 for each month payments were received, up to 36 months during their lifetime, provided the payments were not intended as pay for services. In addition to the $300 monthly exclusion, allowances covering incidental expenses for travel, research, and equipment were tax free. The rules for grants before August 17, 1986, were covered in detail in prior editions of *Your Income Tax.*

What is tax free? Scholarships and fellowships granted after August 16, 1986 are tax free only for degree candidates and only to the extent the grant pays for tuition and course-related fees, books, supplies, and equipment. Amounts for room, board, and incidental expenses are taxable. Furthermore, no tax-free exclusion is allowed for grants or tuition reductions that pay for teaching or other services required as a condition of receiving the grant. Similarly, no tax-free exclusion is allowed for federal grants where the recipient agrees to future work with the federal government. Thus, if you are a graduate student and receive a stipend for teaching, those payments are taxable and will be reported by the school on Form W-2.

Degree test. Scholarships given to students attending a primary or secondary school, or to those pursuing a degree at a college or university meet the degree test. Also qualifying are full-time or part-time scholarships for study at an educational institution that (1) provides an educational program acceptable for full credit towards a higher degree or offers a program of training to prepare students for gainful employment in a recognized occupation; and (2) is authorized under federal or state law to provide such a program and is accredited by a nationally recognized accreditation agency.

TUITION PLANS FOR COLLEGE EMPLOYEES

¶12.5 The law allows an exclusion for free or partially free tuition for undergraduate studies provided to a faculty member or other school employee. The tuition reduction may be for education at his or her own school or at another similar school. However, such tuition benefits may be taxable to highly compensated employees if the tuition plan discriminates in their favor. Tax-free tuition benefits may be provided to the employee's spouse, dependent child, a former employee who retired or left on disability, a widow or widower of an individual who died while employed by the school, or a widow or widower of a retired or disabled employee.

If both parents have died and one of the parents qualified for tax-free tuition benefits, the fact that the child is a dependent of another person does not affect tax-free treatment of tuition benefits if the child is under age 25; if age 25 or over, tuition reductions are taxed even if both parents are deceased.

Teaching and Research Assistants

If you must teach, do research, or provide other services to obtain a tuition reduction for undergraduate studies, the tuition reduction is considered taxable pay. No exclusion is available.

If you are a graduate student who teaches or does research, a tuition reduction from the school is tax free if it is in addition to regular pay for the services. If the tuition reduction is your compensation, it is taxable.

HOW FULBRIGHT AWARDS ARE TAXED

¶12.6 Fulbright awards for teaching, lecturing, or research are generally taxable under the rules for awards made to non-degree candidates after August 16, 1986; *see* ¶12.4. However, provided you are not a U.S. government employee, you may be able to claim the foreign earned income exclusion to avoid tax on the grant (Chapter 36). If you do not qualify for the exclusion and if your overseas stay is temporary and you intend to return to your regular teaching position in the United States, you may deduct the cost of your travel, meals, and lodgings overseas.

TAX REFUNDS, DEBT CANCELLATIONS, AND COURT AWARDS

REFUNDS OF STATE AND LOCAL TAXES DEDUCTED IN PRIOR YEAR

¶12.7 You generally report as income a refund of a state or local tax which you deducted in a prior year.

EXAMPLE On your 1991 return, you deducted as an itemized deduction a state income tax of $8,500. In 1992, $500 of the tax was refunded. You report on Line 10 of Form 1040 the $500 as income for 1992.

Effect of standard deduction. If you claimed the standard deduction in the prior year and you receive a refund of state taxes, the refund is not reported as taxable income because you did not claim the tax as a deduction. Even when you claimed itemized deductions, the standard deduction you might have claimed may reduce the amount of income to be reported on the refund. The refund is taxable only to the extent that your itemized deductions exceeded the standard deduction you could have claimed in the prior year. If, in addition to the tax refund, you received recoveries of other itemized deductions, the same computation applies to determine the taxable portion of the total recovery; *see* ¶12.8.

To help you figure the taxable portion of 1991 itemized deductions recovered in 1992, 1991 standard deduction amounts are shown on page 169.

EXAMPLE In 1991, you filed as a single person. Your only itemized deduction was a state income tax payment of $3,900. This exceeded the $3,400 standard deduction you could have claimed. In 1992, you received a state tax refund of $800 for 1991. You report only $500 of the refund as 1992 income. The $500 difference between the $3,900 of itemized deductions claimed and the $3,400 standard deduction is the maximum taxable recovery. If the refund were $500 or less, the entire refund would be taxable.

If you had a *negative* taxable income in the prior year, the taxable recovery figured under the above rule is reduced by the negative amount. If in the previous example you had a negative taxable income of $100 in 1991, only $400 of the 1992 state tax refund would be taxable instead of $500.

Refund of state tax paid in installments over two tax years. If you pay estimated state or local income taxes, your last tax installment may be in the year you receive a refund. In this case, you allocate the refund between the two years according to the following example.

EXAMPLE Your estimated state income tax for 1991 was $4,000 which you paid in four equal installments. You made your fourth payment in January 1992. No state income tax was withheld during 1991. In 1992, you received a tax refund of $400. You claimed itemized deductions each year on your federal return. You allocate the $400 refund between 1991 and 1992. As you paid 75%

1991 Standard Deduction For Figuring Recoveries of 1991 Itemized Deductions

If You Were—	1991 Standard Deduction Was—
Married filing jointly	$5,700
Single	3,400
Head of household	5,000
Married filing separately	2,850
Qualifying widow or widower	5,700
Single age 65 or over	4,250
Single and blind	4,250
Single age 65 or over and also blind	5,100
Married filing jointly with:	
One spouse age 65 or over	6,350
Both spouses age 65 or over	7,000
One spouse blind under age 65	6,350
Both spouses blind under age 65	7,000
One spouse age 65 or over and also blind	7,000
One spouse age 65 or over and other spouse blind and under age 65	7,000
One spouse age 65 or over and also blind; other spouse blind and under age 65	7,650
Both spouses age 65 or over and also blind	8,300
Qualifying widow or widower age 65 or over	6,350
Qualifying widow or widower and blind	6,350
Qualifying widow or widower age 65 or over and also blind	7,000
Head of household age 65 or over	5,850
Head of household and blind	5,850
Head of household age 65 or over and also blind	6,700
Married filing separately age 65 or over	3,500
Married filing separately and blind	3,500
Married filing separately age 65 or over and also blind	4,150

($3,000/$4,000) of the estimated tax in 1991, 75% of the $400 refund or $300 is allocated to 1991. On your 1992 return, you include $300 as income on Line 10, Form 1040. You also attach a statement explaining that the amount on Line 10 is less than the $400 refund shown on the Form 1099-G received from the state because of the allocation required by the estimated tax payment in 1992.

When you figure your 1992 deduction for state income taxes, you reduce the $1,000 paid in January by $100. Your 1992 deduction for state income taxes will include the January net amount of $900 plus any estimated taxes paid in 1992 for 1992, any state income tax withheld during 1992, and any 1991 tax paid with your state income tax return filed in 1992.

Note: If the $300 refund allocated to 1991 is more than the excess of your 1991 itemized deductions over the 1991 standard deduction you could have claimed, you only have to report that excess as 1992 income, as explained on page 168. Also *see* ¶12.8 for reducing the taxable amount if you had a negative taxable income, or if you recovered a bad debt or other non-itemized deduction.

OTHER RECOVERED DEDUCTIONS

¶**12.8** The income rule applied to refunds of state income tax in ¶12.7 applies also to the recovery of other items for which you claimed a tax deduction such as a reimbursement of a deducted medical expense (¶17.5), a reimbursed casualty loss (¶18.1), a return of donated property which was claimed as a charitable deduction, and a payment of debt previously claimed as a bad debt.

EXAMPLE In 1991, you filed a joint return and claimed itemized deductions of $7,700, which exceeded your standard deduction of $5,700. In 1992, you received the following recoveries for amounts deducted in 1991:

Medical expenses	$200
State income tax refund	400
Interest expense	325
Total	$925

The total recovery of $925 is taxable. It is less than the excess of $2,000 of your itemized deductions over the allowable standard deduction ($7,700 − 5,700). You report the state and local income tax refund of $400 on Line 10, Form 1040, and the balance of $525, on Line 22, Form 1040.

If the total recovery had been $2,500 instead of $925, only $2,000 would be taxable (the excess of $7,700 over $5,700).

Negative taxable income. If your taxable income was a negative amount in the year in which the recovered item was deducted, you reduce the recovery includable in income by the negative amount. For example, if the taxable recovery is $2,000 but you had a negative taxable income of $500, only $1,500 is taxable.

Itemized and non-itemized deduction recoveries in one year. If you recover both itemized deductions and non-itemized deductions taken in the same year, follow this order:

1. Figure your non-itemized recovery;
2. Add the non-itemized recovery to taxable income; and
3. Figure your itemized recoveries based on the increased taxable income.

In figuring the recovery of a non-itemized deduction, such as a bad debt, the limitation effect of the standard deduction is ignored.

Tax credit in prior year. If you recover an item deducted in a prior year in which tax credits exceeded your tax, you refigure the prior year tax to determine if the recovery is taxable. Add the amount of the recovery to taxable income of the prior year and figure the tax on the increased taxable income. If your tax credit exceeds the recomputed tax, do not include the recovery in income. If the tax credit is less than the recomputed tax, include the recovery in income to the extent the recovery reduced your tax in the prior year.

Alternative minimum tax in the prior year. If you were subject to the alternative minimum tax (AMT) in the year the recovered deduction was claimed, recompute your regular and AMT tax for the prior year based on the taxable income you reported plus the recovered amount. If inclusion of the recovery does not change your total tax, you do not include the recovery in income. If your total tax increases by any amount, you include the recovery in income to the extent the deduction reduced your tax in the prior year.

Recovery of itemized deductions claimed before 1987. If you recover an amount that was deducted before 1987, the recovery is taxable up to the amount of excess itemized deductions for the year. Excess itemized deductions are itemized deductions over the zero bracket amount that applied to your filing status for that year.

Recovery of previously deducted items used to figure carryover. A deductible expense may not reduce your tax because you have an overall loss. If in a later year the expense is repaid or the obligation giving rise to the expense is canceled, the deduction of that expense will be treated as having produced a tax reduction if it increased a carryover that has not expired by the beginning of the taxable year in which the forgiveness occurs. For example, you are on the accrual basis and deducted, but did not pay, rent in 1991. The rent obligation is forgiven in 1992. The 1991 rent deduction is treated as having produced a reduction in tax, even if it resulted in no tax savings in 1991 if it figured in the calculation of a net operating loss that has not expired or been used by the beginning of 1992, the year of forgiveness. The same rule applies to other carryovers such as the investment credit carryover.

CANCELLATION OF DEBTS YOU OWE

¶12.9 If your creditor cancels or reduces part of a debt you owe, or the canceled debt secures property you held, you may realize taxable income. For example, a prepayment of a home mortgage at a discount is taxable. The income is reported on Line 22, Form 1040.

The tax treatment of a foreclosure sale or voluntary conveyance to a creditor is discussed at ¶5.28.

EXAMPLE A bank allows a homeowner to prepay a low-interest mortgage of $20,000 for $18,000. The discount of $2,000 is taxable as ordinary income.

You are not taxed if you can prove that your creditor intended a gift or you meet the following exceptions.

Cancellation of student loans. A canceled student loan is taxable income with this exception: If a loan by a government agency or a qualified hospital organization is canceled because you worked for a period of time in certain geographical areas (such as practice medicine in rural areas) or because you worked for certain employers (such as an inner city school), then the canceled amount is not taxable.

COURT DECISION — Gambler Not Taxed on Canceled Debt

In one case, a gambler argued that he did not owe tax when an Atlantic City casino settled a $3.4 million debt for $500,000. He claimed that he qualified for the price adjustment exception on the grounds that the settlement was a reduction in the price of the gambling chips he had used. The Tax Court agreed with the IRS that the gambler had not purchased tangible property subject to the price adjustment exception.

However, the federal appeals court for the Third Circuit (New Jersey, Pennsylvania and Delaware) held that he did not have cancellation of debt income. The debt was not enforceable under New Jersey law because the casino did not comply with state regulations on issuance of credit. Furthermore, the gambling chips were not "property" securing the debt; they had no economic value outside of the casino.

Debts discharged in bankruptcy. A discharge of a debt in a Title 11 bankruptcy case is not taxable, but is used to reduce specified "tax attributes" on Form 982 in this order:

1. Net operating losses and carryovers—dollar for dollar of debt discharge;
2. Carryovers of investment tax credit, WIN credit, jobs credit, research credit, low-income housing credit, and credit for alcohol used as a fuel—33⅓ cents for each dollar of debt cancellation;
3. Capital losses and carryovers—dollar for dollar;
4. Basis of depreciable and nondepreciable assets—dollar for dollar (but not below the amount of your total undischarged liabilities); and
5. Foreign tax credit carryovers—33⅓ cents for each dollar of debt cancellation.

After these reductions, any remaining balance of the debt discharge is disregarded. On Form 982, you may make a special election to first reduce the basis of any depreciable assets before reducing other tax attributes in the order shown in the previous column. Realty held for sale to customers may be treated as depreciable assets for purposes of the election. The election allows you to preserve your current deductions, such as a net operating loss carryover or capital loss carryover, for use in the following year. The election also will have the effect of reducing your depreciation deductions for years following the year of debt cancellation. If you later sell the depreciable property at a gain, the part of the gain attributable to the basis reduction will be taxable as ordinary income under the depreciation rules of ¶44.1; *see* Sample Form 982 on page 172.

Separate bankruptcy estate. If you are an individual debtor who files for bankruptcy under Chapters 7 or 11 of the Bankruptcy Code, a separate "estate" is created consisting of property that belonged to you before the filing date. This bankruptcy estate is a new taxable entity, completely separate from you as a taxpayer. The estate is represented by a trustee who manages the estate for the benefit of any creditors. The estate earns its own income and incurs expenses. The trustee reports the estate's income or loss on a separate return (Form 1041). The creation of a separate bankruptcy estate also gives you a "fresh start;" with certain exceptions, wages you earn and property you acquire after the bankruptcy case has begun belong to you and do not become part of the bankruptcy estate.

A separate estate is not created for an individual who files for bankruptcy under Chapter 12.

In a Title 11 case, the tax attribute reductions are made to the attributes in the bankruptcy estate. Reductions are not made to attributes of an individual debtor that come into existence after the bankruptcy case begins or that are treated as exempt property under bankruptcy rules. Basis reduction does apply to property transferred by the bankruptcy estate to the individual.

Debts discharged while you are insolvent. If your debt is canceled outside of bankruptcy while you are insolvent, the cancellation does not result in taxable income to the extent of the insolvency. Insolvency means that liabilities exceed the fair market value of your assets immediately before the discharge of the debt. The discharged debt is not taxed to the extent of your insolvency and is applied to the reduction of tax attributes on Form 982 in the same manner as a bankrupt individual. If the canceled debt exceeds the insolvency, any remaining balance is treated as if it were a debt cancellation of a solvent person and thus, it is taxable unless it is a qualifying farming debt as discussed on page 171.

Partnership debts. When a partnership's debt is discharged because of bankruptcy, insolvency, or if its qualified farm debt is cancelled, the discharged amount is allocated among the partners. Bankruptcy or insolvency is tested not at the partnership level, but separately for each partner. Thus, a bankrupt or insolvent partner applies the allocated amount to reduce the specified tax attributes as previously discussed. A solvent partner may not take advantage of the rules applied to insolvent or bankrupt partners, even if the partnership is insolvent or bankrupt.

Purchase price adjustment for solvent debtors. If you buy property on credit and the seller reduces or cancels the debt arising out of the purchase, the reduction is generally treated as a purchase price adjustment (reducing your basis in the property). Since the reduction is not treated as a debt cancellation, you do not realize taxable income on the price adjustment. This favorable price adjustment rule applies only if you are solvent and not in bankruptcy, you have not transferred the property to a third party, and the seller has not transferred the debt to a third party such as with the sale of your installment contract to a collection company.

Farmers. A solvent farmer may avoid tax from a discharge of indebtedness by an unrelated lender including any federal, state, or local government agency, if the debt was incurred in farming or is a farm business debt secured by farmland or farm equipment used in the farming business. You are eligible for this relief only if 50% or more of your total gross receipts for the preceding three taxable years was derived from farming. The excluded amount first reduces tax attributes such as net operating loss carryovers and business tax credits. The excluded amount then reduces the farmer's basis in all property other than farmland, and then the basis in land used in the farming business.

Effect of basis reduction on later disposition of property. A reduction of basis is treated as a depreciation deduction so that a profitable sale of the property at a later date may be subject to the rules of recapture of depreciation; see ¶44.1.

RECEIPTS IN COURT ACTIONS FOR DAMAGES

¶12.10

Damages for personal injuries are tax free. You do not report damages received from suits for physical injuries or nonphysical personal injuries, including slander, or libel of personal reputation. In employer discrimination cases, there have been conflicting court decisions, but the trend has been to allow tax-free treatment; see discrimination cases in the next column.

Taxable damages. According to the IRS and Tax Court, you report as taxable income damages collected for loss of profits. See the next column for discrimination and defamation rulings. Damages received for patent or copyright infringement or breach of contract are considered to be for loss of profits and thus, taxable. Courts reason that payments for loss of profits are taxable because the profits themselves would have been taxable if realized.

Evidence of Tax-Free Damages

When a payment compensates for loss of profits and good will or capital, make sure to have evidence for allocating the award between profits and good will or capital assets. Otherwise, the entire amount may be taxed as a recovery of profits. Be certain that your complaint is drawn so that it clearly demands a recovery both for loss of profits and injury to property. Seek to have any lump-sum award divided between the two in any judgment. If your action is settled, make sure the settlement agreement specifically earmarks the nature of the payments. To support a claim that good will was damaged, have evidence of the specific customers lost.

When damages compensate for the loss of property, you have taxable gain if the damages exceed adjusted basis of the property. A deductible loss will generally be allowed when the recovery is less than adjusted basis. The nature of the gain or loss takes on the same character (that is, capital gain or loss or ordinary income gain or loss) as the property lost.

Payments compensating for an anticipated invasion of the right of privacy are taxable in the absence of proof that actual damage has been suffered.

Punitive damages. Punitive damages that compensate for physical injury are tax free. Under a specific law, punitive damages are taxable in cases begun after July 10, 1989, that do not involve physical injury or sickness, such as defamation or discrimination cases.

According to the IRS, punitive damages received in cases begun before July 11, 1989, are taxable but some courts have disagreed. In a defamation case, the Tax Court treated both punitive and compensatory damages as tax-free damages for personal injury because defamation was a personal injury under state law (Maryland). However, on appeal, the Fourth Circuit agreed with the IRS that the punitive damages were a taxable "windfall" intended to punish the wrongdoer and not compensation for injuries.

Discrimination cases. Employees who win discrimination cases against their employer or former employer may get an award based upon (1) back pay for having been undercompensated due to discrimination, (2) future income lost due to discrimination, (3) liquidated damages authorized by statute against an employer that has committed discrimination to compensate the employee for certain difficult-to-measure injuries suffered in addition to lost compensation, (4) compensatory damages, such as those for mental pain and suffering, personal embarrassment, injury to reputation, humiliation and other such damages authorized by statute, and (5) punitive damages imposed to penalize the employer for having committed discrimination.

In federal discrimination cases, the type of damages awarded depends on the federal statute under which the claim is brought. The Fair Labor Standards, Equal Pay and Age Discrimination Acts provide for the recovery of liquidated damages under certain circumstances as well as compensatory damages. Title VII of the 1964 Civil Rights Act, which makes it unlawful to discriminate on the basis of sex, race, religion or national origin, only provides for the recovery of back pay for suits brought before November 21, 1991. For cases brought on or after November 21, 1991, the 1991 Civil Rights Act expands the damages allowed under Title VII to include compensatory damages for future pecuniary losses and nonpecuniary losses, such as pain and suffering, as well as punitive damages.

Sex discrimination. The Supreme Court has held that back pay damages are taxable if received in a Title VII case filed before November 21, 1991, the effective date for broader remedies provided by the 1991 Civil Rights Act. The Court did not specifically decide whether damages received in cases brought after November 21, 1991, qualify for tax-free treatment, but tax-free treatment was implied. As of the time this book went to press, the IRS had not announced its position towards the Supreme Court decision.

Age discrimination. The IRS treats age discrimination awards under the Federal Age Discrimination in Employment Act as fully taxable. However, the Tax Court and the Ninth, Third, and Sixth Circuit Courts of Appeal hold that since discrimination is a personal injury, all of the damages received are tax free, even if they compensate for lost wages.

Defamation. The IRS holds that where a libelous statement damages both personal and business reputation, damages compensating for personal injury are tax free; damages for business reputation are taxable. If the award does not specify the character of the damages the IRS may tax all of the payments as a replacement of lost earnings due to injury to business reputation. The Tax Court and an appeals court disagree with the IRS approach. According to these courts, if state law treats defamation as a personal injury, the award is tax free, even if business reputation has been damaged.

Legal fees. The rules for deducting legal fees closely follow the rules in this section. If the damages are tax free, you may not deduct your litigation costs. If your damages are fully taxed, you deduct all of your litigation costs. If your damages are only partially taxed, then you deduct only that portion of your litigation costs attributed to the taxed damages.

When your attorney receives payment of taxable damages and then turns over the money after deducting his or her fee, you are taxed in the year you receive your share.

Legal fees that are deductible as miscellaneous expenses are subject to the 2% adjusted gross income floor; *see* Chapter 19.

Employment contracts. A settlement of an employment contract is generally taxable, unless a part of the settlement is allocated to a personal injury claim.

EXAMPLE A corporate executive refused to leave when he was fired. The company sued, and the incident was widely reported in newspapers. The executive threatened a countersuit. He settled for a year's salary of $60,000 plus $45,000 for personal embarrassment. He argued that $45,000 was a tax-free payment for personal injuries. The Tax Court agreed. His "embarrassment" was part of a personal injury claim.

Form **982** (Rev. April 1992) Department of the Treasury Internal Revenue Service	**Reduction of Tax Attributes Due to Discharge of Indebtedness (and Section 1082 Basis Adjustment)** ▶ Attach this form to your income tax return.	OMB No. 1545-0046 Expires: 1-31-95 Attachment Sequence No. **94**

Name shown on return	Identifying number

Part I **General Information**

1 Amount excluded is due to (check applicable box(es)) (see instructions):

a Discharge of indebtedness in a title 11 case . . . . ☐

b Discharge of indebtedness to the extent insolvent (not in a title 11 case) . . . . ☐

c Discharge of "qualified farm indebtedness" (See instructions for line 1c before completing Part II.) . . . . . . ☐

2 Total amount of discharged indebtedness excluded from gross income . . . . | **2** |

3 Do you elect to treat all real property described in section 1221(1), relating to property held for sale to customers in the ordinary course of a trade or business, as if it were depreciable property? . . . . . . ☐ Yes ☐ No

Part II **Reduction of Tax Attributes**

Note: *You must attach a description of the transactions resulting in the reduction in basis under section 1017.*

Enter amount excluded from gross income:

4 That you elect under section 108(b)(5) to apply first to reduce the basis (under section 1017) of depreciable property. . . . . | **4** |

5 Applied to reduce any net operating loss which occurred in the tax year of the discharge or carried over to the tax year of the discharge. . . . . | **5** |

6 Applied to reduce certain credit carryovers comprising the general business credit to or from the tax year of the discharge . . . . | **6** |

7 Applied to reduce any net capital loss for the tax year of the discharge including any capital loss carryovers to the tax year of discharge . . . . | **7** |

8 Applied to reduce the basis of nondepreciable and depreciable property if not reduced on line 4. *DO NOT use in the case of discharge of qualified farm indebtedness* . . . . | **8** |

9 For discharge of qualified farm indebtedness, applied to reduce the basis of depreciable property used or held for use in a trade or business, or for the production of income, if not reduced on line 4 | **9** |

10 For discharge of qualified farm indebtedness, applied to reduce the basis of land used or held for use in a trade or business of farming . . . . | **10** |

11 For discharge of qualified farm indebtedness, applied to reduce the basis of other property used or held for use in a trade or business, or for the production of income . . . . | **11** |

12 Applied to reduce any foreign tax credit carryover to or from the tax year of the discharge . . | **12** |

Part III **Consent of Corporation to Adjustment of Basis of its Property Under Section 1082(a)(2) of the Internal Revenue Code**

The corporation named above has excluded under section 1081(b) of the Internal Revenue Code $ .... from its gross income for the tax year beginning .... , and ending .... Under that section the corporation consents to have the basis of its property adjusted in accordance with the regulations prescribed under section 1082(a)(2) of the Internal Revenue Code in effect at the time of filing its income tax return for that year. The corporation is organized under the laws of ....

(State of incorporation)

Note: *You must attach a description of the transactions resulting in the nonrecognition of gain under section 1081.*

Signature

Under penalties of perjury, I declare that I have examined this form, including accompanying schedules and statements, and to the best of my knowledge and belief, it is true, correct, and complete.

....
(Signature—if individual taxpayer)   (Date)

....
(Signature of officer—if corporate taxpayer)   (Title)   (Date)

PART III

CLAIMING DEDUCTIONS

In this part, you will learn how to reduce your tax liability by claiming the standard deduction or itemized deductions. Pay special attention to—

- The standard deduction. Although the standard deduction may provide an automatic tax reduction, read the chapters on itemized deductions to see that you have not overlooked itemized deductions for charitable donations, interest expenses, state and local taxes, medical expenses, casualty and theft losses, and miscellaneous expenses for job costs and investment expenses.

- The 3% reduction of certain itemized deductions if your adjusted gross income (line 32 of Form 1040) exceeds $105,250 (or $52,625 if you are married and file separate returns).

Deductions for expenses incurred in your business are discussed in Part VI. Rental expense deductions are discussed in Chapter 9. If you rent out part of your home, or a home that you use personally, see Chapter 29.

13 CLAIMING THE STANDARD DEDUCTION OR ITEMIZED DEDUCTIONS

Claim the standard deduction only if it exceeds your allowable itemized deductions for mortgage interest, property taxes, medical costs, charitable donations, casualty losses, and miscellaneous deductions for job costs and investment expenses. Generally, a single person may claim a 1992 standard deduction of $3,600; a head of household, $5,250; a married couple filing jointly, or a qualifying widow(er), $6,000; and a married couple filing separately, $3,000. Larger standard deductions are allowed to those who are age 65 or over or blind, and lower standard deductions are allowed to dependents with only investment income.

Before deciding whether to itemize or claim the standard deduction, read Chapters 14 through 21 to see that you have not overlooked any itemized deductions. To itemize, you must file Form 1040 and report your deductions on Schedule A.

INCREASED STANDARD DEDUCTION

¶13.1 To reflect a rise in inflation, the standard deduction for 1992 has been increased. On your 1992 return, you are allowed a standard deduction, which may be claimed regardless of your actual expenses. The basic standard deduction amount for 1992 is:

$6,000 if you are married filing a joint return or are a qualifying widow(er);
$5,250 if filing as a head of household;
$3,600 if single; and
$3,000 if married filing separately.

A married person filing separately must itemize deductions and may not claim any standard deduction if the other spouse itemizes on a separate return; see ¶13.3.

Elderly or blind. For taxpayers age 65 or over, or taxpayers of any age who are blind, larger standard deduction amounts are allowed; see ¶13.4.

Dependents. Individuals who may be claimed as a dependent by another taxpayer are generally limited to a $600 standard deduction, unless they have earned income; see ¶13.5.

Dual-status alien. You are generally not entitled to any standard deduction if for part of the year you are a nonresident and part of the year a resident alien. However, a standard deduction may be claimed on a joint return if your spouse is a U.S. citizen or resident and you elect to be taxed on your worldwide income; see ¶1.8.

Claiming the standard deduction. The standard deduction is not integrated into the tax rate schedules or tax tables. On your return, you deduct the standard deduction from adjusted gross income, assuming you do not claim itemized deductions on Schedule A of Form 1040.

EXAMPLE You are age 25 and single. You have wage income of $35,000 and interest income of $2,000. You are not covered by a company plan and have contributed $2,000 to an IRA. You have decided to claim the standard deduction because your itemized deductions are less than $3,600.

Gross income		
Salary	$35,000	
Interest income	2,000	$37,000
Deduction from gross income:		
IRA (¶8.3)		2,000
Adjusted gross income		$35,000
Less: standard deduction		3,600
		$31,400
Less: Exemption		2,300
Taxable income		$29,100

What You Should Know About Itemized Deductions and the Standard Deduction

Item—	Explanation—	Limitations and examples—
Standard deduction	The law gives a standard deduction which is fixed by law according to your filing status and age. The standard deduction in 1992 is: $6,000 if you are married filing jointly or a qualifying widow or widower. $3,600 if you are single. $5,250 if you are a head of household. $3,000 if you are married filing separately. If you are age 65 or over or blind, your standard deduction is substantially larger; see ¶13.4.	Married persons filing separately may not use the standard deduction if their spouse itemizes deductions. The standard deduction may not be claimed by a nonresident or dual-status alien—or on a return filed for a short taxable year caused by a change in accounting period. A lower standard deduction of $600 is allowed to dependents with only unearned income; see ¶13.5.
Itemized deductions	You get greater tax savings by claiming itemized deductions which exceed the standard deduction for your filing status. Itemized deductions include charitable contributions, interest expenses, local and state taxes, medical and dental costs, casualty and theft losses, job and investment expenses, and educational costs.	There is no dollar limit on the amount of itemized deductions. But individual itemized deductions are subject to limitations and some taxpayers are subject to a 3% reduction as explained below. **EXAMPLE** You are single and may claim the standard deduction of $3,600. However, your itemized deductions are $5,000. You claim $5,000 on Schedule A of Form 1040.
3% reduction	If your adjusted gross income (AGI) exceeds $105,250, itemized deductions *other than* medical expenses, casualty and theft losses, gambling losses, and investment interest expenses, are reduced by 3% of the excess AGI over $105,250. The total reduction may not exceed 80% of your deductions. If you are married filing separately, the reduction applies if your AGI exceeds $52,625; see ¶13.8.	**EXAMPLE** Your joint adjusted gross income (AGI) is $150,000. Your itemized deductions, such as mortgage interest, state income taxes, and job expenses, are $20,000. The AGI excess over $105,250 is $44,750. Therefore itemized deductions are reduced by $1,343 (3% of $44,750) to $18,657 ($20,000 − 1,343).
Charitable contributions	You may deduct donations to religious, charitable, educational, and other philanthropic organizations that have been approved to receive deductible contributions; see ¶14.15.	The contribution deduction is generally limited to 50% of adjusted gross income. Lower ceilings apply to property donations and contributions to foundations. The deductible amount is included in 3% reduction explained above.
Interest expenses	You may deduct interest on qualified home mortgages, points, home equity loans, and interest on loans to carry investments.	Interest on investment loans is deductible only up to extent of net investment income. Interest on personal and consumer loans is not deductible. Interest on home mortgages that do not meet tests of ¶15.1 is not deductible. Interest on home mortgages and points are included in 3% reduction explained above.
Taxes	You may deduct payments of state, local, and foreign real property and income taxes, as well as state and local personal property taxes. You claim your deduction on the tax return of the year in which you paid the taxes, unless you report on the accrual basis; see ¶16.6.	No dollar limitation. The deductible amount is included in 3% reduction explained above.
Medical expenses	You may deduct payments of medical expenses for yourself and dependents. A checklist of over one hundred deductible medical items is at ¶17.2. Deductible drug costs are limited to drugs prescribed by a physician.	Only expenses in excess of 7.5% of adjusted gross income are deductible.
Casualty and theft losses	You may deduct personal property losses caused by storms, fires, and other natural events and as the result of theft.	Each individual casualty loss must exceed $100 and the total of all losses during the year must exceed 10% of adjusted gross income; see ¶18.11.
Job expenses	You may deduct unreimbursed costs of union dues, job educational courses, work clothes, entertainment, travel, and looking for a new job.	Included as miscellaneous expenses of which only the excess over 2% of adjusted gross income is deductible; see ¶19.1. The 2% floor does not apply to performing artists (¶19.4), handicapped employees (¶19.4), or job related moving expenses (¶21.5). The deductible amount is included in 3% reduction explained above.
Investment expenses	You may deduct investment expenses and other expenses of producing and collecting income, expenses of maintaining income-producing property, expenses of tax return preparation, refunds, and audits.	Included as miscellaneous expenses of which only the excess over 2% of adjusted gross income is deductible; see ¶19.1.

WHEN TO ITEMIZE

¶13.2 Claim the standard deduction only if it exceeds your allowable itemized deductions for charitable donations, certain local taxes, interest, allowable casualty loss, miscellaneous expenses, and medical expenses. If your deductions exceed your standard deduction, you elect to itemize by claiming the deductions on Schedule A of Form 1040.

EXAMPLE You are single and your adjusted gross income is $35,000. Your itemized deductions total $5,200. As the $3,600 standard deduction is less than your itemized deductions, you claim itemized deductions of $5,200 on Schedule A.

Changing an election. If you filed your return using the standard deduction and want to change to itemized deductions, or you itemized and want to change to the standard deduction, you may do so within the three-year period allowed for amending your return. If you are married and filing separately, each of you must consent to and make the same change; you both must either itemize or claim the standard deduction.

HUSBANDS AND WIVES FILING SEPARATE RETURNS

¶13.3 If you file separate returns, you and your spouse must first decide whether you will claim itemized deductions or limit yourselves to a standard deduction of $3,000 each. You must make the same election. That is, if one spouse has itemized deductions exceeding $3,000 and elects to itemize, the other spouse must also itemize, even if his or her itemized deductions are less than $3,000.

On a separate return, each spouse may deduct only those itemized expenses for which he or she is liable. This is true even if one spouse pays expenses for the other. For example, if property is owned by the wife, then the interest and taxes imposed on the property are her deductions, not her husband's. If he pays them, neither one may deduct them on separate returns. The husband may not because they were not his liability. The wife may not because she did not pay them. This is true also of casualty or theft losses.

Claiming itemized deductions when you are living apart from your spouse. When a husband and wife are divorced or legally separated under a decree of divorce or separate maintenance, they are free to compute their tax as they see fit, without reference to the return of the other spouse. They are treated as single. If one spouse has itemized deductions, that spouse may elect to claim them, and the other spouse is not required to itemize. The standard deduction is not limited to $3,000. Head of household tax rates may be available under the rules of ¶1.10.

If a husband and wife are separated but do not have a decree of divorce or separate maintenance, both must either itemize or claim the standard deduction of $3,000. There is an exception if you are married and live apart from your spouse and meet the following conditions:

Your spouse was not a member of your household during the last six months of 1992;

You maintained as your home a household which was, for more than half of 1992, the principal place of abode for your child, adopted child, foster child, or stepchild.

You are entitled to claim the child as a dependent (¶1.18) or the child's other parent has the right to the exemption under the rules of ¶1.28.

You provide over half the cost of supporting the household.

If you satisfy these conditions and file a separate return, you generally may file your return as a head of household; however, a foster child must live with you for the entire year (except for temporary absences) to qualify you for head of household status. You may elect to itemize without regard to whether your spouse itemizes or not. If you elect not to itemize, your 1992 standard deduction as a head of household is $5,250 if you are under age 65 and not blind.

STANDARD DEDUCTION RAISED FOR ELDERLY AND BLIND

¶13.4 A larger standard deduction is provided for persons who are age 65 or over or who are blind. The larger deduction for blindness is allowed regardless of age.

Age and blindness are determined as of December 31, 1992. However, if your 65th birthday is January 1, 1993, you may claim the standard deduction for those age 65 or over on your 1992 return.

Your total standard deduction consists of two parts: (1) The basic standard deduction shown in ¶13.1 for your filing status; plus (2) an extra standard deduction for being age 65 or older, or blind. The amount of the extra deduction is $900 if filing as single or head of household; $700 if married filing jointly or separately, or qualifying widow(er). The chart below lists the total standard deduction, including the extra amount.

If you are married filing separately, you may claim the standard deduction shown below only if your spouse also claims the standard deduction on his or her return.

Check applicable boxes

	65 or older	Blind
Yourself	❑	❑
Your spouse if claiming spouse as exemption (¶1.19)	❑	❑
Total checks	———	

If you are—	Number of checks are—	Standard deduction is—
Single	1	$4,500
	2	5,400
Married filing jointly or qualified widow or widower (¶1.6)	1	6,700
	2	7,400
	3	8,100
	4	8,800
Married filing separately	1	3,700
	2	4,400
	3	5,100
	4	5,800
Head of household (¶1.10)	1	6,150
	2	7,050

STANDARD DEDUCTION FOR DEPENDENTS

¶13.5 The following restrictive rules apply only to dependents who may be claimed as an exemption by another person. If you earn gross income of $2,300 or more, you *may not* be claimed as a dependent unless you are a dependent child under age 19 or a full-time student under age 24; *see* ¶1.23. If you are *not* a dependent because of the $2,300 income test, your standard deduction is shown in ¶13.1 or in ¶13.4. If you *may be* claimed as a dependent, your standard deduction is figured under the rules below. You *may* elect to itemize deductions if these exceed the allowable standard deduction. If your spouse itemizes on a separate return, you must itemize (¶13.3).

Dependent under age 65 and not blind. Your standard deduction is the greater of $600 or earned income, but no more than the basic standard deduction shown in ¶13.1 for your filing status. For example, if you are claimed as a dependent by your parents and you have only investment income, your standard deduction is $600 no matter how high your investment income is. If you have wages over $600, your deduction equals the wages, up to the regular standard deduction for nondependents; see Example 1.

Dependents age 65 or older or blind. Your standard deduction is figured in two steps:

1. The greater of $600 or earned income up to the basic standard deduction amount shown in ¶13.1; *plus*
2. $700 if you are married or a qualifying widow or widower, or $900 if single or head of household. If you are age 65 or older and you are also blind, add $1,400 if married or a qualifying widow or widower, or $1,800 if single or head of household.

See Example 2 below and use the worksheets following the examples for computing your 1992 standard deduction.

EXAMPLES 1. You claim your son, age 15, as a dependent on your 1992 return. He has interest income of $600 and wages of $150. His standard deduction is $600 (the greater of $600 or earned income of $150). If his wages were $3,700, the standard deduction would be limited to $3,600, the maximum for a single dependent who is under age 65 and not blind.

2. You claim as a dependent your widowed mother who is over age 65. She has interest income of $800 and wages of $1,200. Her standard deduction is $2,100: $1,200 (the greater of $600 or her earned income of $1,200), plus $900, the additional amount for her age. Furthermore, she does not have to file a tax return reporting her income unless it is needed for a refund of withholding taxes.

STANDARD DEDUCTION FOR DEPENDENTS WITH EARNED INCOME OF $600 OR LESS

If your filing status is—	*Standard deduction is—*
Single or head of household	
Under age 65 and not blind	$ 600
Age 65 or older or blind	$1,500
Age 65 or older and blind	$2,400
Married, or qualifying widow(er)	
Under age 65 and not blind	$ 600
Age 65 or older or blind	$1,300
Age 65 or older and blind	$2,000

STANDARD DEDUCTION FOR DEPENDENTS WHO ARE UNDER AGE 65 AND NOT BLIND WITH EARNED INCOME EXCEEDING $600

1. Enter your earned income.* $_____
2. Enter $3,600 if you are single,
   $5,250 if head of household,
   $6,000 if qualifying widow(er) or
   married filing jointly, or $3,000
   if married filing separately. $_____
3. Enter the smaller of line 1 or 2.
   This is your standard deduction. $_____

STANDARD DEDUCTION FOR DEPENDENTS WHO ARE AGE 65 OR OLDER OR BLIND WITH EARNED INCOME EXCEEDING $600

1. Enter your earned income.* $_____
2. Enter:
   $3,600 if you are single,
   $5,250 if head of household,
   $6,000 if qualifying widow(er) or
   married filing jointly, or $3,000
   if married filing separately.
3. Enter the smaller of 1 or 2 $_____
4. Enter: $_____
   $900 if you are single or head
   of household and are either age 65
   or older or blind.
   $700 if you are married
   filing jointly or separately,
   or a qualifying widow(er) and
   are either age 65 or older or blind.
   If both age 65 or older and blind,
   the $900 or $700 amounts are doubled
   to $1,800 and $1,400.
5. Add lines 3 and 4. This is the dependent's standard deduction. $_____

*Include pay for services and taxable scholarships. However, if your gross income (earned and unearned) is $2,300 or more, you may not be claimed as a dependent unless you are under age 19 or a full-time student under age 24; *see* ¶1.23.

ALTERNATE USE OF STANDARD DEDUCTION

¶13.6 If you find your itemized deductions are equal to or slightly less than the amount of the standard deduction, you may reduce taxes by alternating use of the standard deduction and itemized deductions. Depending on the amount of your expenses, you may:

Prepay deductible expenses so that your itemized deductions exceed the standard deduction. In the next year, you will have less itemized deductions and will claim the standard deduction, or

Postpone payment of expenses to next year and claim the standard deduction this year. Next year, you will itemize.

In both instances, the total amount of deductions over the two years will be greater than the amount of standard deductions claimed in both years.

EXAMPLE In 1992, you are single and you estimate that your itemized deductions will be $3,100. You could choose to take the larger standard deduction of $3,600. But towards the end of 1992, you can prepay a state income tax of $800 to raise your itemized deductions to $3,900. Without increasing your expenditures over a two-year period by making the prepayment, you have increased your deductions by $300. In 1992, you deduct itemized deductions of $3,900, and in 1993, you claim a standard deduction of at least $3,600. (It may be higher if increased for inflation.) You might follow this practice every other year. Take as many itemized deductions as possible in one year; in the next year, claim the standard deduction.

Deductible items that you may prepay include the following: charitable donations, business dues or subscription fees for one year, and state and local taxes. You may get a deduction only in the year payment is due for interest, rent, and insurance premiums.

ADJUSTED GROSS INCOME

¶13.7

Adjusted gross income is a technical term used in the tax law. It is the amount used in figuring the 7.5% floor for the medical expense deductions, the 10% floor for personal casualty and theft losses, the 2% floor for miscellaneous itemized deductions, the charitable contribution percentage limitations, and the 3% reduction of itemized deductions (¶13.8) for certain taxpayers. If you follow the instructions and order of the tax return, you will arrive at adjusted gross income without having to know or understand the following steps. But if you are planning the tax consequences of a transaction in advance of preparing your return, this is how to figure adjusted gross income.

Adjusted gross income is the difference between gross income in Step 1 and deductions listed in Step 2.

Step 1. Figure gross income. This is all income received by you from any source, such as wages, salary, tips, gross business income, income from sales and exchanges, interest and dividends, rents, royalties, annuities, pensions, etc. But gross income does not include such items as tax-free interest from state or local bonds, tax-free parsonage allowance, tax-free insurance proceeds, gifts and inheritances, Social Security benefits which are not subject to tax under the rules of ¶34.3, tax-free scholarship grants, tax-free board and lodging allowance, other tax-free fringe benefits, and the first $5,000 of death benefits.

Step 2. Deduct from gross income only the following items:

Trade or business expenses.
Capital loss deduction up to $3,000.
Net operating losses.
Expenses to produce rent and royalty income.
Depreciation and depletion deductions of life tenants and income beneficiaries of property.
Contributions to a Keogh plan for yourself.
Deduction for 50% of self-employed tax liability.
Deductible contributions to IRAs.
Alimony payments.
Health insurance deduction for self-employed.
Forfeit penalties because of premature withdrawals.
Repayment of supplemental unemployment benefits required because of receipt of trade readjustment allowances.
Reforestation expenses.
Certain expenses of performing artists.
Jury duty pay turned over to your employer.
Required repayments of supplemental unemployment compensation benefits.

Step 3. The difference between Steps 1 and 2 is adjusted gross income.

3% ITEMIZED DEDUCTION REDUCTION

¶13.8

If your 1992 adjusted gross income (AGI) exceeds $105,250 ($52,625 if married filing separately) 3% of the excess reduces the amount of itemized deductions *other than*—

- Medical and dental expenses,
- Investment interest,
- Casualty losses,
- Theft losses, and
- Gambling losses

WORKSHEET FOR 3% REDUCTION

1.	Enter your adjusted gross income	$_____
2.	Enter $105,250 ($52,625 if married filing separately)	_____
3.	Subtract line 2 from line 1	_____
4.	Enter total itemized deductions	_____
5.	Enter the amount included on line 4 for allowable medical and dental expenses, investment interest, casualty or theft losses, and gambling losses	_____
*6.	Subtract line 5 from line 4	_____
7.	Multiply the amount on line 6 by .80	_____
8.	Multiply the amount on line 3 by .03	_____
9.	Enter the smaller of line 7 or line 8	_____
10.	Subtract line 9 from line 4. This is the net amount of itemized deductions you may claim.	$_____

If the amount on line 6 is zero, the reduction does not apply.

EXAMPLE   You are single and your adjusted gross income on Form 1040, Line 32, is $187,000. Your itemized deductions total $31,000:

Medical expense deduction	$ 1,000
State and local taxes	18,000
Charitable donation	6,000
Miscellaneous expenses	1,000
Mortgage interest	5,000
Total	$31,000

The medical expense deduction is the only deduction not subject to the 3% reduction.

WORKSHEET FOR 3% REDUCTION

1.	Adjusted gross income	$187,000
2.	Less threshold	105,250
3.	Excess	81,750
4.	Itemized deductions	31,000
5.	Less medical expenses (not subject to the 3% reduction)	1,000
6.	Itemized deductions subject to the 3% reduction	30,000
7.	80% of line 6	24,000
8.	3% of line 3	2,453
9.	Smaller of (7) or (8)	2,453
10.	Net itemized deductions allowable on Schedule A (Line 4 less line 9)	$28,547

SAMPLE REDUCTION AMOUNT

If $105,250 floor applies and AGI is—	Reduction is—
115,250	300
125,250	600
135,250	900
155,250	1,500
205,250	3,000
305,250	6,000
405,250	9,000
505,250	12,000
605,250	15,000
805,250	21,000
1,005,250	27,000

14 CHARITABLE CONTRIBUTION DEDUCTIONS

By making deductible donations, you can help your favorite philanthropy and at the same time receive a tax benefit. Donations to organizations qualified to receive deductible contributions give you a tax reduction if you itemize deductions. For example, if you are in the 28% tax bracket, a donation of $1,000 reduces your taxes by $280. By donating appreciated securities and real estate held long term, you can increase the amount of your tax savings. If you do volunteer work for a qualified charity, you may deduct your unreimbursed expenses.

Be aware that if you claim donations of property valued at more than $500, you must attach Form 8283 to Form 1040. If the value claimed exceeds $5,000, you also may have to obtain a written appraisal.

There are deduction ceilings depending on the type of donation and the nature of the charity. The ceiling for cash donations made to public philanthropies is 50% of adjusted gross income; for gifts of capital gain property, 30% of adjusted gross income. For other ceilings see ¶14.17.

If your adjusted gross income exceeds $105,250, ($52,625 if married filing separately), your charitable contribution deduction is subject to the 3% reduction of itemized deductions explained in ¶13.8.

DEDUCTIBLE CONTRIBUTIONS

¶14.1

Charitable contributions are deductible only as itemized deductions on Schedule A of Form 1040. The deduction is subject to the 3% reduction of total itemized deductions explained at ¶13.8 if your adjusted gross income exceeds $105,250 ($52,625 if married filing separately).

You may deduct donations to religious, charitable, educational, and other philanthropic organizations which have been approved by the IRS to receive deductible contributions; see ¶14.15. If you are unsure of the tax status of a philanthropy, ask the organization about its status, or check the IRS list of tax-exempt organizations (IRS Publication 78). Donations to the federal, state, and local government are also deductible.

Timing Your Contributions

You deduct donations on the tax return filed for the year in which you paid them in cash or property. A contribution by check is deductible in the year you give the check, even if it is cashed in the following year. A check mailed and dated on the last day of 1992 is deductible in 1992. A postdated check with a 1993 date is not deductible until 1993. A pledge or a note is not deductible until paid. Donations made through a credit card are deductible in the year the charge is made. Donations made through a pay-by-phone bank account are not deductible until the payment date shown on the bank statement. Keep a record of canceled checks or receipts from charities.

Delivering securities. If you are planning to donate appreciated securities near the end of the year, make sure that you consider these delivery rules in timing the donation. If you unconditionally deliver or mail a properly endorsed stock certificate to the donee or its agent, the gift is considered completed on the date of delivery or mailing, provided it is received in the ordinary course of the mails. If you deliver the certificate to your bank or broker as your agent, or to the issuing corporation or its agent, your gift is not complete until the stock is transferred to the donee's name on the corporation's books. This transfer may take several weeks, so if possible, make the delivery at least three weeks before the end of the year to assure a current deduction.

Debts. You may assign to a charity a debt payable to you. A deductible contribution may be claimed in the year your debtor pays the charity.

Limits on deduction. In general, the amount of your charitable deduction is limited to 50% of adjusted gross income. A 30% ceiling applies to deductions for donations of certain types of appreciated property; *see* ¶14.17. Where donations in one year exceed these percentage limits, a five-year carryover of the excess may be allowed; *see* ¶14.18.

A deduction may also be limited under the 3% reduction rule discussed at ¶13.8.

DEDUCTIBLE DUES

¶14.2

Dues paid to a qualified tax-exempt organization are deductible to the extent that you receive no benefits or privileges from the organization for the dues, such as monthly bulletins or journals, use of a library, or the right to attend luncheons and lectures. The organization should tell you how much of your dues are deductible.

If dues are paid to a social club with the understanding that a specified part goes to a named charity, you may claim a charitable deduction for dues earmarked for the charity. If the treasurer of your club is actually the agent of the charity, you take the deduction in the year you give him or her the money. If the treasurer is merely your agent, you may take the deduction only in the year the money is turned over to the charity.

BENEFIT TICKETS AND TOKEN GIFTS

¶14.3

Tickets to theater events, tours, concerts, and other entertainments are often sold by charitable organizations at prices higher than the regular admission charge. The difference between the regular admission and the higher amount you pay is deductible as a charitable contribution. If you decline to accept the ticket or return it to the charity for resale, your deduction is the price you paid.

If the benefit ticket price is the same or less than the regular admission price, you have no deduction unless you refuse to accept the ticket or you return the ticket to the charity for resale.

EXAMPLE A couple claimed a full deduction for regular-price tickets to a high-school fund-raising event that they did not attend. They argued that they were entitled to the deduction because they received no benefit from their ticket purchase. The IRS disallowed the deduction and the Tax Court agreed, holding that a donor receives a benefit by merely having the right to attend the event. To claim a deduction for the price of the tickets the couple should have returned them to the charity.

If you purchase season tickets to a charity-sponsored series of programs and your average cost per program equals or is less than the cost for individual performances, your deduction for a returned ticket depends upon how long you held the tickets. Generally, you may deduct only your cost. However, if you have held the ticket for more than a year, you may deduct the fair market value, the price the charity will charge on resale of the ticket.

You may not deduct the cost of raffle tickets, bingo games, or other types of lotteries organized by charities.

Donation for right to buy athletic stadium tickets. If you contribute to a public or nonprofit college or university scholarship program and receive the right to buy preferential seating at the school's football stadium or other sports arena, you may deduct 80% of the contribution to the scholarship program. The cost of any tickets you buy is not deductible. The deduction is allowed only if you receive the right to buy tickets rather than tickets themselves. For example, if in exchange for a substantial donation you receive a lifetime season ticket, no deduction is allowed.

Receipt of token gifts. Popular fund-raising campaigns, such as those for museums, zoos, and public TV, offer token items such as tote bags, tee shirts, and other items carrying the organization's logo. You are allowed a full deduction for your contribution if the item is considered to be of insubstantial value under IRS guidelines.

The charity must tell you how much of your contribution is deductible in the solicitation that offers the token item. If the items are insubstantial in value, the charity should tell you that your payment is fully deductible.

Program guides and newsletters. Newsletters or program guides that are not of commercial quality are treated as if having no fair market value or cost if their primary purpose is to inform members about the organization's activities, and they are not available to non-members by paid subscription or through newsstand sales. Generally, publications with paid articles and advertising are treated as commercial-quality publications for which the organization must figure value to determine if a full deduction is allowed under the "insubstantial value" test. Professional journals, whether or not articles are written for compensation and have advertising, will generally be treated as commercial-quality publications.

UNREIMBURSED EXPENSES OF VOLUNTEER WORKERS

¶14.4

If you work without pay for an organization listed at ¶14.15, you may deduct as charitable contributions your unreimbursed travel expenses, including commutation expenses to and from its place of operations, and meals and lodging on a trip away from home for the organization. To qualify for the deduction, the expenses must be incurred for a domestic organization which authorizes your travel.

You may not deduct the value of your donated services.

You may deduct either the actual operating costs of your car in volunteer work, or a flat mileage rate of 12¢ a mile allowed by the IRS. Parking fees and tolls are deductible under both methods.

EXAMPLE You are a volunteer worker for a philanthropy. In the course of your volunteer work, you drove the car approximately 1,000 miles. You may claim a contribution deduction of $120, plus tolls and parking.

The 12¢ a mile deduction rate is not mandatory. If your out-of-pocket expenses are greater, you may deduct your actual costs of operating the automobile exclusively for charitable work, such as the cost of gas and oil, in addition to tolls and parking fees.

Also deductible as charitable contributions are:

Uniform costs required in serving the organization.

Cost of telephone calls, and cost of materials and supplies you furnished (stamps, stationery).

Convention expenses of official delegates to conventions of church, charitable, veteran, or other similar organizations. Members who are not delegates get no such deduction; however, they may deduct expenses paid for the benefit of their organization at the convention.

Expenses incurred by volunteers in operating their equipment. No deduction, however, is allowed for the rental value of such equipment, depreciation, or premiums paid on liability or property damage insurance.

The IRS does not allow a deduction for "babysitting" expenses of charity volunteer workers. Although incurred to make the volunteer work possible, babysitting costs are a nondeductible personal expense. Furthermore, the expense is not a dependent care cost; it is not related to a paying job.

Travel expenses of charity research trips. To claim a charitable deduction for travel expenses of a research project for a charitable organization, you must show the trip had no significant element of personal pleasure, recreation, or vacation.

EXAMPLES 1. Jones sails from one Caribbean island to another and spends eight hours a day counting whales and other forms of marine life as part of a project sponsored by a charitable organization. According to the IRS, he may not claim a charitable deduction for the costs of the trip.

2. Smith works on an archeological excavation sponsored by a charitable organization for several hours each morning, with the rest of the day free for recreation and sightseeing. According to the IRS, she may not deduct the cost of the trip.

This restrictive rule does not apply to volunteers who travel to transact business for an organization.

EXAMPLE A member of a chapter of a local charitable organization travels to New York City and spends the entire day at the required regional meeting. According to the IRS, he or she may deduct his or her expenses as a charitable donation, even if he or she attends a theater in the evening.

SUPPORT OF A STUDENT IN YOUR HOME

¶**14.5** A limited charitable deduction is allowed for support of an elementary or high school student in your home under an educational program arranged by a charitable organization. If the student is not a relative or your dependent, you may deduct as a charitable contribution your support payments up to $50 for each month the student stays in your home. For this purpose, 15 days or more of a calendar month is considered a full month. You may not deduct any payments received from the charitable organization in reimbursement for the student's maintenance.

To support the deduction, be prepared to show a written agreement between you and the organization relating to the support arrangement. Keep records of amounts spent for such items as food, clothing, medical and dental care, tuition, books, and recreation in order to substantiate your deduction. No deduction is allowed for depreciation on your house.

PROPERTY DONATIONS

WHAT KIND OF PROPERTY ARE YOU DONATING?

¶**14.6** The tax law does not treat all donations of appreciated property the same. Whether the full amount of the fair market value of the property is deductible depends on the type of property donated, your holding period, the nature of the philanthropy, and the use to which the property is put by the philanthropy. For property donations over $500, you must attach an appraisal summary to your return; *see* ¶14.12.

Intangible personal property (such as securities) and real estate held long-term. Fair market value is deductible where you have held such property for more than one year and you give it to a publicly supported charity or to a private foundation that qualifies for the deduction ceiling of 30% of adjusted gross income as discussed at ¶14.17. A five-year carryover for the excess is allowed; *see* ¶14.18. If the donation exceeds the 30% ceiling, you may consider a special election which allows you to apply the 50% ceiling; *see* ¶14.19.

You may figure the reduced cost of such a donation of appreciated property by following these two steps.

1. Figure the tax reduction resulting from the deduction of the fair market value of the property. For example, you donate appreciated stock which is selling at $1,000. Your capital gains are subject to the 28% ceiling. The deduction for the donation reduces your taxes by $280.

2. Estimate how much tax you would have paid on a sale of the stock. Assume you would have to pay tax of $200 on a sale of the stock at $1,000. The total tax savings from your donation is $480 ($280 + $200). The cost of your contribution is $520 ($1,000 – $480).

The IRS ruled that you may not claim a deduction on donated stock if you retain the voting rights, even though the charity has the right to receive dividends and sell the stock. The right to vote is considered a substantial interest and is crucial in protecting a stockholder's financial interest.

Long-Term Securities or Realty

There is generally a tax advantage to donating securities or realty held long-term. You may claim a deduction for the fair market value of the property and also avoid tax on the appreciation in value of the property. The amount of tax you avoid further reduces the cost of your donation; however, these advantages may be lost if you are subject to the alternative minimum tax (AMT). If you plan to donate appreciated property, first check whether you may be subject to AMT. If you are, the appreciation element on the donation may be subject to AMT. If so, postpone the donation until you incur regular tax. AMT is discussed at ¶23.3.

If planning a year-end donation of securities, keep in mind that the gift is generally not considered complete until the properly endorsed securities are mailed or delivered to the charity or its agent; *see* ¶14.1.

Property held one year or less and other ordinary income property. This is property which, if sold by you at its fair market value, would not result in long-term capital gain. The deduction for donations of this kind of property is restricted to your cost for the property. Examples of ordinary income property include: stock and other capital assets held by you for one year or less, inventory items donated by business, farm crops, Section 306 stock (preferred stock received as a tax-free stock dividend, usually in a closely-held corporation), and works of art, books, letters, and memoranda donated by the person who prepared or created them. *See* ¶14.9 for art objects.

EXAMPLES 1. You hold short-term stock which cost you $1,000. It is now worth $1,500. If you donate it to a philanthropy, your deduction would be limited to $1,000. You would get no tax benefit for the appreciation of $500. On the other hand, if the stock were held long-term, you could claim a deduction for the full market value of the stock on its donation.

2. A former Congressman claimed a charitable deduction for the donation of his papers. His deduction was disallowed. His papers were ordinary income property, and since his cost basis in the papers was zero, he could claim no deduction.

Tangible personal property held long-term. Items such as furniture, books, equipment, fixtures (severed from realty), jewelry, and art objects are tangible personal property. When held long-term (more than one year), deductions for donations of this type of asset may be subject to restrictions which will limit your deduction to cost basis. If the philanthropy to which you donate the property does *not* put it to a use that is related to its charitable function, you have to reduce the deduction by the amount of long-term capital gain that would have been realized if the property had been sold at fair market value. If the charity must sell your gift to obtain cash for its exempt purposes, your deduction is also reduced by the long-term gain element. Where a donation of property is subject to this reduction as a *nonrelated* gift, the reduced gift is then subject to the 50% annual deduction ceiling of ¶14.17.

If the gift is *related* to the organization's charitable purposes, you may deduct the property's fair market value subject to the 30% ceiling (¶14.17), or you may elect to deduct up to 50% of adjusted gross income by reducing the deduction by the long-term gain element; *see* ¶14.19.

AMT Break for Certain 1992 Donations

A tax break applies to charitable contributions made before July 1, 1992, of appreciated long-term tangible personal property, such as works of art, sculptures, and manuscripts that are used by a charity for purposes related to the charity's tax-exempt functions. The appreciation on the donated property that is deductible for regular tax purposes is not treated as a preference item for 1992 alternative minimum tax (ATM) purposes.

When this book went to press, Congress was considering legislation to extend the AMT break beyond June 30, 1992 and to allow it not only for tangible personal property, but for all types of appreciated property. *See* the Supplement for an update.

Donating capital gain property to private nonoperating foundations. Generally, you may *not* deduct the full fair market value of gifts of capital gain property to private nonoperating foundations that are subject to the 20% deduction ceiling discussed at ¶14.17. (Capital gain property is property which, if sold by you at fair market value, would result in long-term capital gain.) The deduction must be reduced by the long-term gain that would have been realized if the

property had been sold at fair market value. However, if you donate appreciated corporate stock, you may deduct the full value without reduction, provided there is a readily available market quotation on an established securities market on the date of contribution. If you or family members contribute more than 10% of any corporation's stock, the full deduction may be claimed only for the first 10%.

Donating Mortgaged Property

A donation of mortgaged property may be taxable. Before you give mortgaged property to a charity, have an attorney review the transaction. You may deduct the excess of fair market value over the amount of the outstanding mortgage. However, you may realize a taxable gain. The IRS and Tax Court treat the transferred mortgage debt as cash received in a part-gift, part-sale subject to the bargain-sale rules discussed at ¶14.8. You will realize a taxable gain if the transferred mortgage exceeds the portion of basis allocated to the sale part of the transaction. This is true even if the charity does not assume the mortgage.

EXAMPLE You donate to a college land held long-term which is worth $250,000 and subject to a $100,000 mortgage. Your basis for the land is $150,000. As a charitable contribution, you may deduct $150,000 ($250,000–$100,000). You also are considered to have made a bargain sale for $100,000 on which you realized $40,000 long-term capital gain.

   40% of the transaction is treated as a bargain sale.

$$\frac{\$100,000 \text{ (amount of mortgage)}}{\$250,000 \text{ (fair market value)}} = 40\%$$

Basis allocated to sale: 40% of $150,000 or $60,000

Amount realized	$100,000
Allocated basis	60,000
Gain	$ 40,000

Figuring value. When donating securities listed on a public exchange, fair market value is readily ascertainable from newspaper listings of stock prices. It is the average of the high and low sales price on the date of the donation.

To value other property, such as real estate or works of art, you will need the services of an experienced appraiser. Fees paid to an appraiser are not deductible as a contribution, but rather as a miscellaneous itemized deduction.

Substantiating Your Deduction

Save records to support the market value and cost of donated property. Get a receipt or letter from the charitable organization acknowledging and describing the gift. Lack of substantiation may disqualify an otherwise valid deduction. If the total claimed value of your property donations exceeds $500, you must report the donation on Form 8283, which you attach to Schedule A, Form 1040. *See also* ¶14.12 for when you need an appraisal of the value of the property.

U.S. Saving Bonds. You may not donate U.S. Saving Bonds, such as EE bonds, because you may not transfer them. They are non-negotiable. You must first cash the bonds and then give the proceeds to the charity, or surrender the bonds and have new ones registered in the donee's name. When you do this, you have to report the accrued interest on your tax return. Of course, you will get a charitable deduction for the cash gift.

Gift of installment obligations. You may deduct your donation of installment notes to a qualified philanthropy. However, if you received them on your sale of property which you reported on the installment basis, you may realize gain or loss on the gift of the notes; *see* ¶5.43. The amount of the contribution is the fair market value of the obligation, not the face amount of the notes.

PROPERTY THAT HAS DECLINED BELOW COST

¶14.7 Unless the charity needs the property for its own use, you should not donate business or investment property whose value has declined below your cost. You may not claim a deductible loss when you make a gift. When the property is held for investment or business purposes, you may get the loss deduction by first selling the property and then a charitable deduction by donating the cash proceeds of the sale.

EXAMPLE You own securities which cost $20,000 several years ago but which have declined in value to $5,000. A donation of these securities gives a charitable contribution of $5,000. But selling the securities for $5,000 to make a cash donation provides a long-term capital loss of $15,000.

If property is a personal asset (clothing, automobile) you may not deduct a loss on the sale. It makes no difference whether you sell and donate the sales proceeds or donate the property.

Used clothing or furniture. If you donate used clothing, furniture, or household appliances, deduct their fair market value, which is usually much less than your original cost. For your records, get a statement from the donee organization acknowledging the gift and describing the property. Also keep a record of your original cost. If the claimed value of your donation exceeds $500, you must complete Form 8283; *see* ¶14.12.

BARGAIN SALES OF APPRECIATED PROPERTY

¶14.8 A sale of appreciated property to a philanthropy for less than fair market value allows you to claim a charitable deduction while receiving proceeds from the sale. However, you must pay a tax on part of the gain attributed to the sale. That is, the transaction is broken down into two parts: the sale and the gift.

To compute gain on the sale, you allocate the adjusted basis of the property between the sale and the gift.

1. Find the percentage of the sales proceeds over fair market value of the property. If the property is mortgaged, include the outstanding debt as sale proceeds.
2. Apply the percentage to the adjusted basis of the property.
3. Deduct the resulting basis of Step 2 from the sales proceeds to find the gain.

You may deduct the donated appreciation if full market value would be deductible on a straight donation (no sale) under the rules of ¶14.6. Thus, the donated appreciation is deductible if the property is securities or real estate held long-term, or long-term tangible personal property related to the charity's exempt function; *see* Example 1 in the next column. However, if a deduction for the property (assuming no sale) would be reduced to cost basis under ¶14.6, your charitable deduction on the sale is also reduced; *see* Example 2 in the next column. This reduction affects sales of capital gain property

held short term; ordinary income property; tangible personal property not related to the charity's exempt function; depreciable personal property subject to recapture; and sales of capital gain property to private nonoperating foundations.

EXAMPLES 1. You sell to a university for $12,000 stock held long-term. The adjusted basis of the stock is $12,000, and the fair market value, $20,000. On the sale, you have recouped your investment and donated the appreciation of $8,000, but at the same time, you have realized taxable gain of $4,800 computed as follows: The percentage of basis applied to the sale is 60% ($12,000 sale proceeds ÷ $20,000 fair market value). Thus, 60% of the $12,000 basis, or $7,200, is allocated to the sale. Gain on the sale equals the $12,000 sale proceeds less the $7,200 allocated basis, or $4,800.

2. You sell to your church stock held short-term for your basis of $4,000. The stock is worth $10,000. Using the allocation method in Example 1, 40% of your basis ($4,000 proceeds ÷ $10,000 fair market value) or $1,600 is allocated to the sale. Thus, you have a short-term capital gain of $2,400 ($4,000 sales proceeds − $1,600 allocated basis). Furthermore, your deductible charitable contribution is also $2,400, equal to the 60% of basis allocated to the gift (60% of $4,000 = $2,400).

Basis allocation applies even if a deduction is barred by the annual ceiling. The basis allocation rules for determining gain on a bargain sale apply even if the annual deduction ceilings (¶14.17) bar a deduction in the year of the donation and in the five-year carryover period.

EXAMPLE The Hodgdons contributed real estate valued at $3.9 million but subject to mortgage debt of $2.6 million. The IRS treated the mortgage debt as sales proceeds and figured gain based on the difference between the debt and the portion of basis allocated to the sale element. The Hodgdons claimed that the basis allocation rule, which increased the amount of their gain, should not apply. Earlier in the year, they had made another donation that used up their charitable deduction ceiling for that year as well as for the following five-year carryover period. The Tax Court held that the basis allocation rule applied because a charitable deduction was "allowable," even if the contribution did not actually result in a deduction in the carryover period.

ART OBJECTS

¶14.9 You may claim a charitable deduction for a painting or other art object donated to a charity. The amount of the deduction depends on (1) whether you are the artist; (2) if you are not the artist, how long you owned it; and (3) the type of organization receiving the gift.

If you are the artist, your deduction is limited to cost regardless of how long you held the art work or to what use the charity puts it. In the case of a painting, the deduction would be the lower of either the cost for canvas and paints, or the fair market value.

If you owned the art work short-term, your deduction is limited to cost, under the rules applying to donations of ordinary income property at ¶14.6.

If you owned the art work long-term, your deduction depends on how the charity uses the property; *see* the following Planner Pointer on page 184.

Appraisals. Be prepared to support your deduction with detailed proof of cost, the date of acquisition, and how value was appraised. The appraisal fee is treated as a "miscellaneous" itemized deduction subject to the 2% adjusted gross income floor; *see* Chapter 19. *See also* ¶14.12 for appraisal requirements.

The IRS has its own art advisory panel to assess whether the fair market value of art works is reasonable.

Deduction Determined by Charity's Use

If you held the art object long-term, your deduction depends upon how the charity uses it. If the charity uses it for its exempt purposes, you may deduct the fair market value. However, if the charity uses it for unrelated purposes, your deduction is reduced by 100% of the appreciation. A donation of art work to a general fund-raising agency would be reduced because the agency would have no direct use for it. It would have to sell the art work and use the cash for its exempt purposes.

If you are allowed a deduction for fair market value on a donation made before July 1, 1992, the appreciation is exempt from alternative minimum tax; see ¶23.3. Congress may extend this break beyond June 30, 1992; see the Supplement.

EXAMPLES 1. You give your college a painting which you have owned for many years. Its cost was $100 but it is now worth $1,000. The school displays the painting in its library for study by students. This use is related to the school's educational purposes. Your donation is deductible at fair market value. If, however, the school proposed to sell the painting and use the proceeds for general education purposes, its use would not be considered related. Your deduction would be reduced by the $900 appreciation to $100. That the school sells the painting does not necessarily reduce the donation if you show that, when you made the gift, it was reasonable to anticipate that your gift would not be put to such unrelated use.

2. You donate to the Community Fund a collection of first edition books held for many years and worth $5,000. Your cost is $1,000. Since the charity is a general fund-raising organization, its use of your gift is not related. Your deduction would be $1,000 ($5,000 less $4,000).

3. You contribute to a charity antique furnishings you owned for years. The antiques cost you $500 and are now worth $5,000. The charity uses the furnishings in its office in the course of carrying on its functions. This is a related use. Your contribution deduction is $5,000.

A sale by the charity of an insubstantial part of a collection does not result in a reduction of the contribution deduction.

Donating a partial interest in an art collection. You may deduct the value of a donated partial interest in an art collection, such as where you give a museum the right to exhibit the works for a specific period during the year. The deduction is allowed even if the museum does not take possession of the art works, provided it has the right to take possession.

INTERESTS IN REAL ESTATE

¶14.10 No deduction is allowable for the fair rental value of property you allow a charity to use without charge even in direct furtherance of its charitable functions as, for example, a thrift shop.

If you donate an undivided fractional part of your entire interest, a deduction will be allowed for the fair market value of the proportionate interest donated.

A donation of an option is not deductible until the year the option to buy the property is exercised.

Remainder interest in a home or farm. You may claim a charitable deduction for a gift of the remainder value of a residence or farm donated to a charity, even though you reserve the use of the property for yourself and your spouse for a term of years or life. Remainder gifts generally must be made in trust. However, where a residence or farm is donated, the remainder interest must be conveyed outright, not in trust. A remainder interest in a vacation home or in a "hobby" farm is also deductible. There is no requirement that the home be your principal residence or that the farm be profit making.

Contribution of real property for conservation purposes. A deduction may be claimed for the contribution of certain partial interests in real property to government agencies or publicly supported charities for exclusively conservational purposes. Deductible contributions include: (1) your entire interest in real property other than retained rights to subsurface oil, gas, or other minerals; (2) a remainder interest; or (3) an easement, restrictive covenant, or similar property restriction granted in perpetuity. The contribution must be in perpetuity and further at least one of the following "conservation purposes"—preservation of land areas for outdoor recreation, education, or scenic enjoyment; preservation of historically important land areas or structures; or the protection of plant, fish, and wildlife habitats or similar natural ecosystems.

To obtain the deduction, there must be legally enforceable restrictions that prevent you from using your retained interest in the property in a way contrary to the intended conservation purpose. The donee organization must be prohibited from transferring the contributed interest except to other organizations that will hold the property for exclusively conservational purposes. If you retain an interest in subsurface oil, gas, or minerals, surface mining must generally be specifically prohibited. However, there is a limited exception where the mineral rights and surface interests have been separately owned since June 12, 1976. A deduction will be allowed if the probability of surface mining is so remote as to be considered negligible. The exception does not apply if you are related to the owner of the surface interest or if you received the mineral interest (directly or indirectly) from the surface owner.

Donating Vacation Home Use Not Advisable

To raise funds, a charitable organization may ask contributors who own vacation homes to donate use of the property which the charity then auctions off to the public. Be warned that if you offer your home in this way you will not only be denied a charitable deduction for your generosity, but you may jeopardize your deduction for rental expenses. A deduction is not allowed for giving a charity the free use of your property. See the following example.

EXAMPLE To help a charity raise money, one owner allowed the charity to auction off a week's stay in his vacation home, and the highest bidder paid the charity a fair rental. The IRS ruled that not only was the owner's donation not deductible, but the one week stay by the bidder was considered personal use by the owner for purposes of figuring deductions for rental expenses. True, if the owner had directly rented the property to the bidder, the bidder's payment of a fair rental value would have been counted as a rental day and not a personal use day. However, the donation for charitable use is not a business rental, and the bidder's rental payment to the charity is not considered a payment to the owner.

Furthermore, the bidder's use of the home pushed the owner over the personal use ceiling, which in turn prevented him from deducting a rental loss. A rental loss may not be claimed if personal use of a home exceeds the greater of 14 days or 10% of the number of days the home is rented at fair rental value (¶29.20). Here, the owner personally used the home for 14 days and rented the home for 80 days. The rental expenses exceeded rental income. If the bidder's use of the home was not considered his personal use, the owner could have deducted the loss because his personal use did not exceed the 14 day limit (which was more than 10% of the 80 rental days). However, by adding the bidder's seven days of use to the owner's 14 days, the resulting 21 days of personal use exceeded the 14 day ceiling.

LIFE INSURANCE

¶14.11
You may deduct the value of a life insurance policy if the charity is irrevocably named as beneficiary and you make both a legal assignment and a complete delivery of the policy. Do not reserve the right to change the beneficiary.

The amount of your deduction generally depends on the type of policy donated. Your insurance company can furnish you with the information necessary to calculate your deduction. In addition, you may deduct premiums you pay after you assign the policy.

Deducting premium payments on donated policy. If you assign a life insurance policy to a charity and continue to pay the premiums, you generally may deduct the premiums. However, in states where charities do not have an "insurable interest" in the donor's life, the IRS may challenge income tax and gift tax deductions for the premium payments. The IRS took this position in a 1991 private ruling interpreting New York law. In response, New York amended its insurance code to allow individuals to buy a life insurance policy and immediately transfer it to a charity. The IRS then revoked the earlier ruling but it did not announce a change in its position. Thus, the IRS may challenge premium deductions of donors in other states where a charity's insurable interest is not clearly provided by state law.

FORM 8283 AND WRITTEN APPRAISAL REQUIREMENTS

¶14.12
Attach Form 8283 to your Form 1040 if the total value of your claimed donations of property for 1992 exceed $500. The IRS may disallow your deduction if you fail to attach Form 8283.

In addition to Form 8283, you are required to have written appraisals for annual property donations exceeding $5,000. The appraiser must complete Part III in Section B of Form 8283. However, you do not need a written appraisal for publicly traded securities and nonpublicly traded stock of $10,000 or less. Keep the appraisal for your record unless you donate art valued at $20,000 or more. In that case, you must attach a complete copy of the appraisal to Form 8283. Furthermore, you may be asked by the IRS to submit a color photograph (8" × 10") or a slide of the art (4" × 5").

If you need an appraisal, get one from an unrelated professional no earlier than 60 days before your gift, and you must receive it by the due date (including extensions) of your return on which you claim the deduction.

For property donations exceeding $5,000, the donee organization must acknowledge the receipt of the property on Part IV, Section B of Form 8283.

You may be penalized for overvaluing the property on your return if the overvaluation is 200% or more and the resulting tax underpayment exceeds $5,000. The penalty is 20% of the tax due because of the overvaluation or 40% if the overvaluation is 400% or more of the correct value. Even if you have such an overvaluation, you can avoid the penalty by showing that the claimed value was based on an appraisal of a qualified appraiser, and that you made a good faith, independent investigation of the value.

A professional appraiser who knowingly overvalues charitable contribution property is subject to a $1,000 penalty.

Appraisal fees. A fee paid to an appraiser is not considered a charitable deduction but is deductible as a "miscellaneous" expense subject to the 2% adjusted gross income floor; *see* Chapter 19.

Charity reports transfers within two years. If the charity sells or otherwise disposes of the appraised property within two years after your gift, it must notify the IRS on Form 8282 and send you a copy. The IRS could compare the selling price received by the charity with the value you claimed on Form 8283. Reporting is not required by the charity if on Form 8283, you indicated that the appraised value of the item was not more than $500. Similar items such as a collection of books by the same author, stereo components, or place settings of silverware may be treated as one item. Reporting is also not required for donated property that the organization uses or distributes without consideration, if this use furthers the organization's exempt function or purpose.

BUSINESS OR FARM INVENTORY

¶14.13
Business owners and accrual basis farmers generally may not deduct more than cost for donations of inventory. If a charitable deduction is claimed, costs incurred in a year prior to the donation must be removed from inventory and excluded from the cost of goods sold when figuring business gross income. No contribution deduction is allowed for a gift of merchandise which was produced or acquired in the year donated. Instead, the cost is deducted as a business expense or added to the cost of goods sold. A business expense deduction is not subject to the percentage limitation applied to donations.

A cash basis farmer may not claim a charitable deduction for a donation of inventory products. This is because the fair market value of the donated property must be reduced under the ordinary income rule to zero; *see* ¶14.6.

DONATIONS THROUGH TRUSTS

¶14.14
Outright gifts are not the only way to make deductible gifts to charities. You may transfer property to a charitable income trust or a charitable remainder trust to provide funds for charity.

A charitable income trust involves your transfer of property to a trust directed to pay income to a charity you name, for the term of the trust, and then to return the property to you or to someone else.

A charitable remainder trust is one which provides income for you or another beneficiary for life, after which the property passes to a charity.

Trust arrangements require the services of an experienced attorney who will draft the trust in appropriate form and advise you of the tax consequences.

Deductions for gifts of income interests in trust. Current law is designed to prevent a donor from claiming an immediate deduction for the present value of trust income payable to a charity for a term of years. In limited situations, you may claim a deduction if either: (1) You give away all of your interests in the property. For example, you put your property in trust, giving an income interest for 20 years to a church and the remainder to a college. A deduction is allowed for the value of the property. Or, (2) You create a unitrust or annuity trust, and are taxed on the income. A unitrust for this purpose provides that a fixed percentage of trust assets is payable to the charitable income beneficiary each year. An annuity trust provides for payment of a guaranteed dollar amount to the charitable income beneficiary each year. A deduction is allowed for the present value of the unitrust or annuity trust interest.

Because income remains taxable to the grantor alternative 2 will probably not be chosen, unless the income of the trust is from tax-exempt securities. If such a trust is created, a tax may be due if the donor dies before the trust ends or is no longer the taxable owner of trust income. The law provides for a recapture of a proportion of the tax deduction, even where the income was tax exempt.

Charitable remainder trusts. A charitable deduction is allowable for transfers of property to charitable remainder trusts only if the trust meets these requirements: The income payable for a noncharitable income beneficiary's life or a term of up to 20 years must be guaranteed under a unitrust or annuity trust. If a donor gives all of his or her interests in the property to the charities, the annuity or unitrust requirements need not be satisfied. The value of the charitable deduction allowable for a gift in trust is determined by IRS tables.

Life income plans. A philanthropy may offer a life income plan (pooled income fund) to which you transfer property or money in return for a guaranteed income for life. After your death, the philanthropy has full control over the property. If you enter such a plan, ask the philanthropy for the amount of the deduction that you may claim for the value of your gift.

LIMITATIONS PLACED ON DONATIONS

ORGANIZATIONS QUALIFIED FOR DEDUCTIBLE DONATIONS

¶14.15 The following types of organizations may qualify to receive deductible contributions:

1. The United States, a possession or political subdivision, a state, city, or town. The gift must be for public purposes. The gift may be directed to a government unit, or it may be to a government agency such as a state university, a fire department, a civil defense group, or a committee to raise funds to develop land into a public park. Donations may be made to the Social Security system (Federal Old Age and Survivors Insurance Trust Fund). Donations may be made to the federal government to help reduce the national debt; checks should be made payable to "Bureau of the Public Debt."
2. A domestic nonprofit organization, trust, community chest, fund, or foundation operated exclusively for one of the following purposes—
   Religious. Payments for pew rents, assessments, and dues to churches and synagogues are deductible.
   Charitable. In this class are organizations such as Boy Scouts, Girl Scouts, American Red Cross, Community Funds, Cancer Societies, CARE, Salvation Army, Y.M.C.A., and Y.W.C.A.
   Scientific, literary, and educational. Included in this group are hospitals, research organizations, colleges, universities, and other schools that do not maintain racially discriminatory policies; and leagues or associations set up for education or to combat crime, improve public morals, and aid public welfare.
   Prevention of cruelty to children or animals.
   Fostering amateur sports competition. However, the organization's activities may not provide athletic facilities or equipment.
3. Domestic nonprofit veteran organizations or auxiliary units.
4. A domestic fraternal group operating under the lodge system, only if contributions are to be used exclusively for religious, charitable, scientific, literary, or educational purposes; or for the prevention of cruelty to children or animals.
5. Nonprofit cemetery and burial companies, where the voluntary contribution benefits the whole cemetery, not your plot.
6. Legal services corporation established under the Legal Services Corporation Act which provides legal assistance to financially needy people in noncriminal proceedings.

Foreign Charities

You may deduct donations to domestic organizations that distribute funds to charities in foreign countries, as long as the American organization controls the distribution of the funds overseas. An outright contribution to a foreign charitable organization may not be deducted. Some exceptions to this ban are provided by international treaties. A limited exception applies to contributions to certain Canadian organizations if you have income from Canadian sources. For details, write IRS, Foreign Operations District, Washington, D.C. 20225.

NONDEDUCTIBLE DONATIONS

¶14.16 The following types of contributions to philanthropic or other types of organizations are not deductible:

1. Payments to political campaign committees or political action committees. Also, payments to an organization that devotes a substantial part of its activities to lobbying, trying to influence legislation, or carrying on propaganda or whose lobbying activities exceed certain limits set by the law, causing the organization to lose its tax-exempt status. The IRS has disallowed contributions to a civic group opposing saloons, nightclubs, and gambling places, although the group also aided libraries, churches, and other public programs.
2. Gifts to needy or worthy individuals, scholarships for specific students, or gifts to organizations to benefit only certain groups. However, the IRS in private rulings has allowed deductions for scholarship funds which are limited to members of a particular religion, so long as that religion is open to all on a racially nondiscriminatory basis, and to scholarship funds open only to male students.
3. Gifts to organizations such as—
   Fraternal groups—except when they set up special organizations exclusively devoted to charitable, educational, or other approved purposes.
   Professional groups such as those organized by accountants, lawyers, and physicians—except when they are specially created for exclusive charitable, educational, or other philanthropic purposes. The IRS will disallow unrestricted gifts made to state bar associations, although such organizations may have some public purposes. Some courts have allowed deductions for donations to bar associations on the ground that their activities benefit the general public. However, an

appeals court disallowed deductible donations to a bar association that rates candidates for judicial office.

Clubs for social purposes—fraternities and sororities are generally in this class. Unless an organization is exclusively operated for a charitable, religious, or other approved purpose, you may not deduct your contribution, even though your funds are used for a charitable or religious purpose.

4. Donations to civic leagues, communist or communist-front organizations, chambers of commerce, business leagues, or labor unions.
5. Contributions to a hospital or school operated for profit.
6. Purchase price of church building bond. To claim a deduction, you must donate the bond to the church. The amount of the deduction is the fair market value of the bond when you make the donation. Interest on the bond is income each year, under the original issue discount rules of ¶4.19, where no interest will be paid until the bond matures.
7. Donations of blood to the Red Cross or other blood banks.
8. Contributions to foreign charitable organizations or directly to foreign governments. Thus, a contribution to the State of Israel was disallowed. Similarly, contributions to international charitable organizations are nondeductible; but *see* ¶14.15.

Donation of services. You may not deduct the value of volunteer work you perform for charities. But *see* ¶14.4 for the deductions allowed for unreimbursed expenses incurred during such work.

Donations Which Provide You With Goods or Services

You may not deduct tuition payments to a parochial or other church-sponsored school for the education of your children. Payments exceeding the usual tuition charge are deductible. Similarly, fees paid to a tax-exempt rest home in which you live, or to a hospital for the care of a particular patient are not deductible if any benefit is received from the contribution. A gift to a retirement home, over and above monthly fees, is not deductible if the size or type of your quarters depends on the gift.

Members of the Church of Scientology may not deduct payments for "auditing" and "training" because religious instruction is received in exchange.

Token gifts and benefit tickets are discussed at ¶14.3.

Free use of property. You may not deduct the rental value of property you allow a charity to use without charge. That is, if you allow a charity rent-free use of an office in your building, you may not deduct the fair rental value. You also have no deduction when you lend money to a charity without charging interest.

To raise money for a charity, supporters of the organization may donate rental time for their vacation home, to be auctioned off to the public. No deduction is allowed for donating the rental time; *see* ¶14.10.

Parents' support of children serving as Mormon missionaries. Support payments made by parents directly to their children who serve as missionaries are not deductible because the church does not control the funds.

CEILING ON CHARITABLE DEDUCTIONS

¶**14.17** Depending on the type of contribution and the organization to which the donation is made, the annual deductible ceiling is either 20%, 30%, or 50% of your adjusted gross income (¶13.7), figured

without regard to any net operating loss carryback. The total deduction for the year cannot exceed 50% of adjusted gross income. A five-year carryover is allowed for contributions exceeding the applicable limit; *see* ¶14.18.

For most individuals, the 50% limit will apply, except where they contribute appreciated securities or other intangible personal property and real estate held long-term. Such contributions are subject to the 30% ceiling if made to organizations qualifying for the 50% ceiling. A 20% limit generally applies to contributions of capital gain property to organizations that do not qualify for the 50% ceiling, such as nonoperating, private foundations and charities that do not receive substantial support from the general public. However, for contributions of cash and ordinary income property to such organizations, a 30% ceiling applies. A 30% ceiling also applies to gifts, such as gifts in trust, which are considered to be "for the use of," rather than directly "to" a qualified charity.

A husband and wife filing a joint return figure the ceiling on their total joint adjusted gross income.

The 50% ceiling. Contributions of cash, ordinary income property, and capital gain property held short-term are subject to the 50% ceiling if made to the following types of charitable organizations:

Churches, synagogues, and other religious organizations.

Schools, colleges, and other educational organizations that normally have regular faculties and student bodies in attendance.

Hospitals and medical research organizations.

Foundations for state colleges.

Publicly supported organizations that receive a substantial part of their financial support from the general public or a government unit. Libraries, museums, drama, opera, ballet and orchestral societies, community funds, the American Red Cross, Heart Fund, and other groups providing research and aid in treatment of disease are generally in this category.

Private operating foundations.

Private nonoperating foundations that distribute their contributions annually to qualified charities within 2½ months after the end of their taxable year.

Private foundations that pool donations and allow donors to designate the charities to receive their gifts, if the foundation pays out all income within 2½ months after the end of the tax year.

Donations made merely *for the use* of an organization do not qualify for the 50% ceiling. This restriction affects certain trust dispositions.

The 30% limit for certain capital gain property. The 30% limit generally applies to donations of appreciated intangible personal property (like securities) and real estate held long-term where the gift is to a publicly supported charity or a foundation that qualifies for the 50% ceiling; *see* list above.

This 30% limit also applies to donations of appreciated tangible personal property held long-term (like a boat, furnishings, and art work) where the charitable organization's use of your gift is directly related to its charitable purposes. However, the 50% ceiling applies to gifts of tangible personal property held long-term where the organization's use of the gift is not directly related to its charitable purposes and the deduction is reduced for appreciation; *see* ¶14.6. The 50% ceiling may also apply to appreciated intangible personal property under an election providing for a percentage reduction explained in ¶14.19.

The 30% limit for gifts to nonoperating private foundations and certain other organizations. Gifts of cash or ordinary income property are subject to a 30% limit if made to nonoperating private foundations and other charities that are not in the above list of organizations qualifying for the 50% ceiling. For example, a gift of cash or ordinary income property to a veteran's organization, fraternal society, or nonprofit cemetery is subject to the 30% ceiling. Trust distributions for the use of an organization are subject to this 30% ceiling.

Such gifts are deductible only to the extent of the *lower* of: (1) 30% of your adjusted gross income; or (2) 50% of your adjusted gross income *less* donations to publicly supported charities or foundations qualifying for the 50% ceiling, including donations of capital gain property which are subject to the 30% ceiling.

The 20% limit for capital gain property. Gifts of capital gain property to private nonoperating foundations and other organizations not eligible for the 50% ceiling are deductible only to the extent of the *lower* of: (1) 20% of your adjusted gross income; or (2) 30% of adjusted gross income *less* donations of capital gain property which qualify for the 30% ceiling (contributed to organizations qualifying for the 50% ceiling).

Contributions not deductible due to the 20% limitation may be carried over for five years; *see* ¶14.18.

Applying the percentage ceilings. To figure your deduction follow this order in applying the various income limitations, with the total deduction not to exceed 50% of adjusted gross income.

1. Gifts qualifying for the 50% ceiling.
2. Gifts of cash and ordinary income property to nonoperating private foundations and other organizations that qualify for the 30% ceiling.
3. Gifts of capital gain property to organizations qualifying for the 50% ceiling that are subject to the 30% of income deduction limit.
4. Gifts of capital gain property to nonoperating private foundations and other organizations not qualifying under the 50% ceiling.

EXAMPLES 1. Jones contributes to a church $22,000 in cash and land held long term valued at $35,000. Her adjusted gross income is $100,000, so the total deduction for the year may not exceed $50,000 under the 50% overall limit. Since the $22,000 cash contribution subject to the 50% ceiling is considered first, the deduction for the land (subject to the 30% ceiling) is limited to $28,000, the difference between the $50,000 overall limit and the $22,000 cash gift. Jones may carryover the unused $7,000 donation attributable to the land.

2. Smith has an adjusted gross income of $100,000. He makes charitable contributions of $40,000 in 30% capital gain property to a college and $30,000 in cash to a nonoperating private foundation subject to the 30% ceiling. The 30% limitation for cash gifts to nonoperating private foundations is applied before the 30% limitation applicable to gifts of capital gain property to public charities. The deduction for the cash gift is reduced to $10,000 (50% of $100,000 adjusted gross income, or $50,000, *minus* $40,000 gift to college). The amount of the contribution of 30% capital gain property is limited to $30,000 (30% of $100,000). Accordingly, Smith's charitable contribution deduction is $40,000 ($10,000 + $30,000). Smith is allowed to carry over $10,000 ($40,000 − $30,000) from his contributions of 30% capital gain property. He is also allowed to carry over the nondeductible $20,000 cash donation ($30,000 − $10,000).

FIVE-YEAR CARRYOVER FOR EXCESS DONATIONS

¶14.18 If you make donations that are not deductible because they exceed the 50%, 30%, or 20% of adjusted gross income ceilings discussed in ¶14.17, you may carryover the excess over the next five years. In each carryover year, the original percentage ceiling

applies. For example, where contributions of appreciated long-term intangible personal property or real estate (or tangible personal property put to a related use by the charity) exceed the 30% ceiling for capital gain property (¶14.17), the excess remains subject to the 30% ceiling in the carryover years.

In any carryover year, you must first figure your deduction for contributions in the current year under the applicable 50%, 30%, or 20% ceilings. For each category of property carried over, the carryover contributions are deductible only after the deduction for current year donations is figured. The total deduction in the carryover year, for both current year and carryover contributions, cannot exceed 50% of adjusted gross income for the carryover year.

 Project Your Income

When planning substantial donations that may exceed the annual ceiling, make a projection of your income for at least five years. Although the carryover period of five years will probably absorb most excess donations, it is possible that the excess may be so large that it will not be completely absorbed during the year of the contribution and the five-year carryover period. It is also possible that your income may drop in the future so that you cannot adequately take advantage of the excess.

EXAMPLE In 1992, you contribute to a university stock held long-term with a fair market value of $19,000. The contribution is subject to the 30% ceiling for capital gain property (¶14.17). You also have a $2,000 carryover from 1991 for a cash gift to your church which in 1992 remains subject to the 50% ceiling. Your 1992 adjusted gross income is $40,000. Under the 30% ceiling, the deduction for the contribution of stock is limited to $12,000 (30% of $40,000 adjusted gross income). Since the overall deduction limit is $20,000 (50% of $40,000 adjusted gross income), the $2,000 carryover from 1991 is fully deductible. The total deduction on your 1992 return is $14,000 ($12,000 plus $2,000 carryover). You carry over to 1993 the $7,000 balance from the gift of stock that could not be deducted in 1992 because of the 30% ceiling.

ELECTION TO REDUCE PROPERTY GIFT APPRECIATION

¶14.19 Although the 30% ceiling generally applies to long-term intangible property (such as securities) and real estate, you may elect the 50% ceiling, provided you reduce the deduction by 100% of the appreciation on all donations during the year of long-term intangible property and real estate and tangible personal property related in use to the organization's charitable function. In most cases, this election will be made only where the amount of appreciation is negligible. Where there is substantial appreciation, the increase in the deduction may not make up or exceed the required 100% reduction. If the election is made in a year in which there are carryovers of capital gain property subject to the 30% ceiling, the carryovers are subject to reduction; *see* IRS Publication 526.

The election is made by attaching a statement to your original return or amended return filed by the original due date. Even where no formal electing statement is made, claiming a deduction without the appreciation in order to come within the 50% ceiling is treated as an election. A formal or "informal" election is not revocable unless a material mistake is shown. A revocation based on a reconsideration of tax consequences is not considered sufficient grounds.

15

ITEMIZED DEDUCTION FOR INTEREST EXPENSES

On Schedule A, three types of interest charges are allowed as itemized deductions:

- Home mortgage interest,
- Points, and
- Investment interest

These deductions are also subject to limitations: (1) Home mortgage interest and points are subject to the 3% reduction of itemized deductions if your adjusted gross income exceeds $105,250 ($52,625 for married persons filing separate returns). (2) Investment interest is deductible only up to the amount of net investment income but is not included in the 3% reduction computation. The 3% reduction rule is discussed at ¶13.8.

Interest on personal loans (such as loans to buy autos and other personal items and credit card finance charges) is no longer deductible.

Interest on loans for business purposes is fully deductible on Schedule C.

Interest on loans related to rental property is fully deductible from rental income on Schedule E. Whether interest is a business or a personal expense depends upon the use made of the money borrowed, not on the kind of property used to secure the loan.

Passive activity interest. Interest on loans used to finance an investment in a passive activity is subject to the limitations of Chapter 10. However, if you rent out a second home that qualifies as a second residence, the portion of mortgage interest allocable to rental use is deductible as qualified mortgage interest and is not treated as a passive activity expense.

HOME MORTGAGE INTEREST

¶15.1 Qualifying mortgage interest on up to two residences is generally deductible but is subject to the 3% reduction for itemized deductions on Schedule A if your adjusted gross income exceeds $105,250 ($52,625 if married filing separately); *see* ¶13.8.

The law distinguishes between mortgages incurred before October 14, 1987, and mortgages incurred on or after that date. If all of your mortgages were incurred *before* October 14, 1987, the law is straightforward; you may fully deduct all interest on debt secured by a principal residence and by one other residence. This is true for loans used to acquire a residence as well as home equity loans made before October 14, 1987. The amount of the mortgage may not exceed the fair market value of the house as of October 13, 1987. Fair market value is presumed to be at least equal to the purchase price of the house plus improvement costs.

As for loans *after* October 13, 1987, interest deductions may be available for debt of up to $1,100,000 on two residences. The actual amount in your case depends on the amount of the mortgage debt and how you use the mortgage proceeds. As explained in the following paragraphs, the law distinguishes between (1) debt to buy, construct, and/or improve a residence; and (2) home equity debt secured by a residence where the loan proceeds are used for nonresidential purposes.

Qualified residence interest on loans taken out after October 13, 1987. The tax law calls fully deductible home mortgage interest qualified residence interest. It is interest paid or accrued during a taxable year for either *acquisition debt* or *home equity debt* that is secured by a principal residence or a second home.

In general, you may deduct interest on up to $1 million of acquisition debt, plus an additional $100,000 of home equity debt on loans *secured* by your main home or a second home. For the loan to be "secured," it must be recorded or satisfy similar requirements under state law.

Acquisition debt is further discussed at ¶15.2.

Home-equity debt is discussed at ¶15.3.

Two residence limit. The rules for deducting qualifying acquisition debt or home equity debt apply to loans secured by your principal residence and one other residence. A residence may be a condominium or cooperative unit, houseboat, mobile home, or house trailer that has sleeping, cooking, and toilet facilities. If you own more than two houses, you decide which residence shall be considered your second residence. Interest debt secured by the designated second residence is deductible under the rules for acquisition debt (¶15.2) or home equity debt (¶15.3).

A residence that is rented out for any part of the year may be designated as a second residence only if it is used for personal non-rental purposes for the greater of 14 days or 10% of the rental days. In counting rental days, you must include days that the home is held out for rental or listed for resale. In counting days of personal use, use by close relatives generally qualifies as your personal use; *see* ¶29.20.

Mortgage Fees Not Deductible

You may not deduct expenses incurred in obtaining a mortgage such as commissions, abstract fees, or recording fees. These fees become part of the cost basis of your home; when you sell, they reduce your taxable gain.

Interest on qualified home mortgage certificates. Under special state and local programs, you may obtain "mortgage credit certificates" to finance the purchase of a principal residence or to borrow funds for certain home improvements. Generally, a qualifying principal residence may not cost more than 90% of the average area purchase price; 110% in certain targeted areas. A tax credit for interest paid on the mortgage may be claimed. The credit is computed on Form 8396 and claimed on Line 44 of Form 1040. The credit equals the interest paid multiplied by the certificate rate set by the governmental authority but the maximum annual credit is $2,000. Interest not qualifying for the credit is deductible as home mortgage interest.

EXAMPLE   You pay $5,000 interest for a mortgage issued under a qualifying mortgage credit certificate. Under its terms, you are allowed a tax credit of $750. You may claim the balance of your mortgage interest or $4,250 ($5,000 − $750) as an itemized deduction. If the allowable credit exceeds tax liability, a three-year carryover is allowed.

If you buy a home using a qualifying mortgage certificate and sell that home within nine years, you must recapture part of the tax credit on Form 8828.

When this book went to press, Congress was considering extending the qualified home mortgage program beyond June 30, 1992. See the Supplement for legislative developments.

HOME ACQUISITION LOANS

¶**15.2**   Acquisition debt is debt secured by a principal or second residence and incurred in acquiring, constructing, or substantially improving that same residence. Qualifying acquisition debt made after October 13, 1987, may not exceed $1,000,000, $500,000 for married persons filing separate returns. If your mortgages taken after October 13, 1987, exceed the $1,000,000 (or $500,000) limit, you must use IRS worksheets included in Publication 936 to figure the amount of your deductible interest.

Although interest on a pre-October 14, 1987, debt is generally fully deductible regardless of the size of the loan, refinancing a pre-October 14, 1987, debt for more than the existing balance subjects the excess to the $1 million ceiling, as discussed below.

Generally, a debt qualifies as being incurred in buying, constructing, or improving a residence if you satisfy IRS tracing rules (¶15.11) that prove the use of the loan proceeds for such residential purposes. Even if you cannot prove under the tracing rules that a loan was used to buy a residence, a loan will be treated by the IRS as incurred for buying a house to the extent you can show acquisition expenses within 90 days before, or 90 days after, incurring the loan. Special construction loan and improvement loan rules are discussed in ¶15.4 and ¶15.5.

If you incurred substantial pre-October 14, 1987, loans and later purchase a new home, your deduction for the mortgage for the new home may be limited. The $1 million limit for acquisition debt after October 13, 1987, is reduced by the amount of outstanding pre-October 14, 1987, debt.

Interest on a mortgage to buy or build a home other than your principal residence or qualifying second home is treated as nondeductible personal interest. If a nonqualifying home is rented out, the part of the mortgage interest that is allocable to the rental activity is treated as passive activity interest subject to the limitations of Chapter 10; the interest allocable to your personal use is nondeductible personal interest.

A married couple filing jointly may designate as a second residence a home owned or used by either spouse.

If a married couple files separately, each spouse may generally deduct interest on debt secured by one residence. However, both spouses may agree in writing to allow one of them to deduct the interest on a principal residence plus a designated second residence.

Cooperatives. In the case of housing cooperatives, debt secured by stock as a tenant-stockholder is treated as secured by a residence. The cooperative should provide you with the proper amount of your deductible interest. If the stock cannot be used to secure the debt because of restrictions under local law or the cooperative agreement, the debt is still considered to be secured by the stock if the loan was used to buy the stock. For further details on allocation rules, *see* IRS Publication 936.

Refinancing pre-October 14, 1987, mortgage debt. If you refinance pre-October 14, 1987, debt, the refinanced amount remains pre-October 14 debt and is not subject to the $1 million ceiling to the extent it does not exceed the outstanding principal immediately before refinancing. This rule applies only until the end of the original loan term. In the case of acquisition debt such as a "balloon" note that is not amortized over its term, interest on any otherwise qualified refinancing will be fully deductible for the term of the first refinancing of such acquisition debt, but not for more than 30 years after that first refinancing.

If you refinance a pre-October 14, 1987, mortgage debt for more than the existing balance, only the part of the new mortgage equal to the amount you owed on the mortgage at the time you refinanced is treated as a pre-October 14, 1987, debt. The part of the new mortgage that exceeds the balance of the existing mortgage is a mortgage subject to the $1 million acquisition debt limit or $100,000 home equity debt ceiling.

Line-of-credit mortgages. If you had a line-of-credit mortgage on your home on October 13, 1987, and you borrowed additional amounts on this line of credit after that date, the additional borrowed amounts are treated as a mortgage taken out after October 13, 1987.

Mixed-use mortgages. If you took out a new mortgage after October 13, 1987 (including borrowing additional amounts on a line-of-credit mortgage you had on October 13, 1987), or you refinanced for more than the balance of the outstanding mortgage, you have a mixed-use mortgage if the loan is used partly to buy, build, or improve a qualifying home and partly for other purposes. The mortgage proceeds used to buy, build, or improve the home are subject to the $1,000,000 ceiling, and the rest of the proceeds are subject to the $100,000 ceiling. Where the limits are exceeded, refer to IRS Publication 936 and its worksheets for determining the amount of your deductible interest.

EXAMPLE In 1986, you took out a mortgage on your home for $200,000. In March 1992, when the home had a fair market value of $400,000 and you owed $195,000 on the mortgage, you took out a home equity loan for $120,000. In 1992, you used $90,000 of the home equity loan proceeds for home improvements and $30,000 for other purposes. You may deduct all of the interest on both mortgages. The first mortgage qualifies because it was taken out on or before October 13, 1987. The new loan qualifies under both ceiling limitations. The $90,000 used for home improvements plus the first mortgage of $195,000 totaled less than $1 million. The $30,000 balance is within the $100,000 home equity debt ceiling.

HOME EQUITY DEBT

¶15.3 For interest deduction purposes, home equity debt is any debt secured by a first or second residence that does not exceed the fair market value of the residence less the amount of acquisition debt on the residence. The total home equity debt may not exceed $100,000 ($50,000 if a separate return is filed by a married person). Interest on a qualifying home equity loan is deductible regardless of the way you spend the loan proceeds, unless it is used to buy tax-exempts. If you have a principal residence and a second home, the total home equity loan limit for both houses is $100,000 (or $50,000 for a married person filing separately).

EXAMPLES 1. You bought your house in 1985 for $200,000 subject to a mortgage of $150,000. In 1993, the mortgage principal is $120,000 and you plan to make a home equity loan. The fair market value of the house is $210,000. Interest on a home equity loan of up to $90,000 is fully deductible. A home equity loan may not exceed the difference between the fair market value of the house ($210,000) and the current acquisition debt ($120,000). If the value of the house exceeded $220,000, up to $100,000 could have been borrowed as a qualifying home equity loan.

2. The fair market value of your house is $200,000 and the current mortgage is $160,000. You can make a home equity loan of only up to $40,000 ($200,000 − $160,000).

A loan may qualify partially as acquisition debt and partially as home equity debt where part of it is used to refinance an existing acquisition debt. The refinanced amount is still considered acquisition debt. Debt in excess of the refinanced amount is home equity debt subject to the $100,000 ceiling.

Home Equity Loan to Pay Consumer Debts

You can use a home equity line-of-credit mortgage to pay off existing consumer debts and finance future consumer expenses for which an interest deduction is no longer allowed. However, although interest on a home equity loan is fully deductible if within the $100,000 limit, the interest is not allowed for purposes of alternative minimum tax, unless used to improve your first or second home; see ¶23.2.

HOME CONSTRUCTION LOANS

¶15.4 Interest on a home construction loan may be fully deductible from the time construction begins for a period of up to 24 months while construction takes place. Within the 24-month period, the loan is considered acquisition debt subject to the $1 million ceiling (¶15.2), provided that the home is a principal residence or second home when it is actually ready for occupancy. Furthermore, the loan proceeds must be directly traceable to home construction expenses, including the purchase of a lot, and the loan must be secured by the lot to be treated as acquisition debt. According to the IRS, if construction begins before a loan is incurred, the loan is treated as acquisition debt to the extent of construction expenses within the 24-month period *before* the loan. In determining when a loan is "incurred" for purposes of this 24-month rule, you can treat the date of a written loan application as the date the loan was "incurred," provided you receive the loan within 30 days after loan approval.

Interest incurred on the loan before construction begins is treated as nondeductible personal interest (*see* Example 1 below). If construction lasts more than 24 months, interest after the 24-month period also is treated as nondeductible personal interest.

Interest on loans made within 90 days *after* construction is completed may qualify for a full deduction. The loan is treated as acquisition debt to the extent of construction expenses within the last 24 months before the residence was completed, plus expenses through the date of the loan (*see* Example 2 below). For purposes of the 90-day rule, the loan proceeds generally are treated as received on the loan closing date. However, a debt may be considered "incurred" on the date a written loan application is made, provided the loan proceeds are actually received within 30 days after loan approval. If a loan application is made within the 90-day period and it is rejected, and a new application with another lender is made within a reasonable time after the rejection, a loan from the second lender will be considered timely even if more than 90 days have passed since the end of construction.

EXAMPLES 1. On January 15, 1992, you borrow $100,000 to buy a residential lot. The loan is secured by the lot. You begin construction of a principal residence on January 1, 1993, and use $250,000 of your own funds for construction expenses. The residence is completed December 31, 1994.

The interest paid in 1992 is nondeductible personal interest. It was paid before the 24-month qualifying construction period which started January 1, 1993, and ended December 30, 1994.

Interest paid in 1993 and 1994 is fully deductible as the $100,000 loan is treated as acquisition debt for the 24-month construction period.

2. Same facts as Example 1, but on March 15, 1995, you take out a $300,000 mortgage on the completed house to raise funds. You use $100,000 of the loan proceeds to pay off the $100,000 loan on the lot and keep the balance.

All of the interest on the $300,000 loan is fully deductible because the loan qualifies as acquisition debt; $100,000 of the debt is treated as acquisition debt used for construction, since it was used to refinance the original 1992 debt to purchase the lot. The $200,000 balance is also treated as a construction loan under the 90-day rule. It was borrowed within 90 days after the residence was completed, and it reimbursed construction expenses of at least $200,000 incurred within 24 months before the completion date.

3. On January 15, 1992, you purchased a residential lot and began building a home on the lot using $45,000 of your personal funds. The home was completed on October 31, 1992. On November 28, 1992, you received a loan of $36,000 that was secured by the home. The debt may be treated as taken out to build the home as it was taken out no later than 90 days after the home was completed, and expenditures of at least $36,000 were made within the period of 24 months before the home was completed.

HOME IMPROVEMENT LOANS

¶15.5 Loans used for substantial home improvements are treated as acquisition debt subject to the $1 million ceiling for loans after October 13, 1987; *see* ¶15.2. Include only the cost of home improvements that must be added to the basis of the property because they add to the value of the home or prolong useful life. Repair costs are not considered.

EXAMPLE Your current acquisition mortgage is $100,000. You borrow $20,000 to build a new room. Your qualifying acquisition debt is now $120,000.

If substantial improvements to a home are begun but not completed before a loan is incurred, the loan will be treated as acquisition debt (assuming the debt is secured by the home) to the extent of improvement expenses made within 24 months before the loan. If the loan is incurred within 90 days after an improvement is completed, the loan is treated as acquisition debt (assuming the debt is secured by the home) to the extent of improvement expenses made within the period starting 24 months before completion of the improvement, and ending on the date of the loan.

MORTGAGE PAYMENT RULES

¶15.6 Payments to the bank or lending institution holding your mortgage may include interest, principal payments, taxes, and fire insurance premiums. Deduct only the payments of interest and taxes. You may not deduct the payments of mortgage principal and insurance premiums.

Interest Reported to IRS

Banks and other lending institutions report mortgage interest payments of $600 or more to the IRS on Form 1098. You should receive a copy of Form 1098 or a similar statement by February 1, 1993, showing your mortgage payments in 1992. Points (¶15.7) paid on the purchase of a principal home are included on Form 1098.

In the year you sell your home, check your settlement papers for interest charged up to the date of sale; this amount is deductible.

Mortgage credit. If you qualify for the special tax credit for interest on qualified home mortgage certificates, you only deduct interest in excess of the allowable credit; *see* ¶15.1.

Jointly owned property. When mortgaged property is jointly owned, a joint owner who pays the entire interest charge may deduct the amount of the entire payment.

Prepayment penalty. A penalty for prepayment of a mortgage is deductible as interest.

Mortgage assistance payments. You may not deduct interest paid on your behalf under Section 235 of the National Housing Act.

Delinquency charges for late payments are not deductible interest. The Tax Court agreed with the IRS that delinquency charges were not interest charges where there was proof that they were imposed by a bank to compensate it for lost earnings and expenses of trying to collect payment, and to discourage unlikely payments by imposing a penalty.

Joint Liability on Mortgage

If you do not personally receive a Form 1098 but a person (other than your spouse with whom you file a joint return) who is also liable for and paid interest on the mortgage received a Form 1098, you deduct your share of the interest and attach a statement to your Schedule A, showing the name and address of the person who received the form. If you are the payer of record on a mortgage on which there are other borrowers entitled to a deduction for the interest shown on the Form 1098 you received, provide them with information on their share of the deductible amount.

Graduated payment mortgages. Monthly payments are initially smaller than under the standard mortgage on the same amount of principal, but payments increase each year over the first five- or 10-year period and continue at the increased monthly amount for the balance of the mortgage term. As a cash basis taxpayer, you deduct the amount of interest actually paid even though, during the early years of the mortgage, payments are less than the interest owed on the loan. The unpaid interest is added to the loan principal, and future interest is figured on the increased unpaid mortgage loan balance. The bank, in a year-end statement, will identify the amount of interest actually paid. (An accrual basis taxpayer may deduct the accrued interest each year.)

Reverse mortgage loan. Homeowners who own their homes outright may in certain states cash in on their equity by taking a "reverse mortgage loan." Typically, 80% of the value of the house is paid by a bank to a homeowner in a lump sum or in installments. Principal is due when the home is sold or when the homeowner dies; interest is added to the loan and is payable when the principal is paid. The IRS has ruled that an interest deduction may be claimed by a cash basis homeowner only when the interest is paid, not when the interest is added to the outstanding loan balance.

Shared appreciation mortgage. Under a shared appreciation mortgage (SAM) for a personal residence, the lender agrees to charge a lower rate of interest than the prevailing market rate. In return, the homeowner promises to pay a percentage of the appreciation on the property at a later date to make up the difference. For example, you agree to pay interest of 12% plus 40% of the appreciation in the value of the property within 10 years or earlier if you sell the house or pay off the mortgage. If, at the end of 10 years, the residence is not sold or the loan repaid, you may refinance at the prevailing rate the outstanding balance plus the interest based on appreciation. If you refinance with the same lender, you may not claim an immediate deduction for the extra interest. The execution of a note is not considered payment. The amount covering the extra interest is deducted ratably over the period of the new loan. If you refinance with another lender and use the funds to pay off the old loan plus the extra interest, the extra interest is deductible in the year of payment, subject to the limits of ¶15.2.

Redeemable ground rents. These are deductible as mortgage interest if: (1) the land you lease is for a term exceeding 15 years (including renewal periods) and is freely assignable; (2) you have a present or future right to end the lease and buy the entire interest; and (3) the lessor's interest in the land is primarily a security interest. Payments to end the lease and buy the lessor's interest are not deductible ground rents.

"POINTS"

¶**15.7** Lenders charge "points" in addition to the stated interest rate. The points increase the lender's up-front fees, but in return, borrowers generally are charged a lower interest rate over the loan term. Points are either treated as a type of prepaid interest (¶15.13), or as a nondeductible service fee, depending on what the charge covers. Points are treated as interest if your payment is solely for your use of the money and is not for specific services performed by the lender which are separately charged. Whether a payment is called "points" or a "loan origination fee" does not affect its deductibility if it is actually a charge for the use of money. The purpose of the charge—that is, for the use of the money or the services rendered—will be controlling. If the points qualify as interest, they are deductible over the term of the loan unless they are paid on the purchase or improvement of your principal residence as discussed below.

Points do *not* include fees for services such as appraisal fees, preparation of a mortgage note or deed of trust, settlement fees, notary fees, abstract fees, commissions, and recording fees.

If you are *selling* property and you assume the buyer's liability for points, do not deduct the payment as interest but include it as a selling expense that reduces the amount realized on the sale.

Deduction for points on purchase or improvement of principal residence. Points are generally treated as prepaid interest (¶15.13) that must be deducted over the period of the loan. However, there is an exception for points you pay on a loan to buy or improve your principal residence. The points on such loans are deductible in the year paid if these tests are met: (1) the loan is secured by your principal residence; (2) the charging of points is an established business practice in the geographic area in which the loan is made; (3) the points charged do not exceed the points generally charged in the area; (4) you pay the points directly to the lender; and (5) the amount of points is specifically earmarked on the loan closing statement, either as "points," loan origination fees, or "loan discount."

Points withheld from the loan principal are immediately deductible provided that the fees you pay at the closing, such as attorney fees, abstract fees, and appraisal fees, are at least equal to the amount of points withheld. If this test is met, you are treated as having paid the points directly to the lender.

Points on second home. If you pay points on a mortgage secured by a second home or a vacation home, the points are not fully deductible in the year of payment; you must claim the deduction ratably over the loan term.

Points Reported to the IRS

Points you paid in 1992 on the purchase of your principal residence will be reported to the IRS by the lender on Form 1098 if they meet the above five tests for full deductibility. This will serve as an IRS check on the deduction you claim for points on Line 9a of Schedule A. Points paid on an improvement loan for your principal residence are deductible on Line 10 of Schedule A if they meet the tests but they are not shown on Form 1098. If your adjusted gross income exceeds $105,250 ($52,625 if married filing separately), points are subject to the 3% reduction of itemized deductions, discussed at ¶13.8.

Points paid on refinancing. The IRS does not allow a current deduction for points on a refinanced mortgage. According to the IRS, the points must be deducted ratably over the loan period, unless part of the new loan is used for home improvements. Thus, if you pay points of $2,400 when refinancing a 20-year loan on your principal residence, the IRS allows you to deduct only $10 a month, $120 each full year. The points are not currently deductible because they are incurred for repaying the existing mortgage debt, not buying a home or financing home improvements.

A federal appeals court has rejected the IRS allocation rule where points are paid on a long-term mortgage which replaces a short-term loan; *see* the Court Decision Tax Alert below.

If part of a refinancing is used for home improvements to a principal residence, the IRS allows a deduction for an allocable portion of the points.

EXAMPLE When interest rates are 8%, Mr. Smith refinances his 14% home mortgage which has principal of $80,000 outstanding. The new loan is for $100,000, of which $80,000 is used to pay off the old $80,000 balance and the $20,000 balance for home improvements. Assume that at the closing of the new loan, Smith pays points of $2,000, from his separate funds. In the year of payment he may deduct $400 allocable to the 20% of the loan used for home improvements. The balance of the points, or $1,600, is deducted over the period of the new loan.

Current Deduction for Points on Refinancing

Huntsman replaced a three-year loan used to purchase his principal residence with a 30-year mortgage. He deducted $4,400 of points paid on the new mortgage. The IRS and the Tax Court held that the points had to be deducted over the 30-year loan term.

However, the Federal Appeals Court for the Eighth Circuit disagreed and allowed a full deduction in the year the points were paid. It held that the first temporary loan was merely an integrated step in obtaining permanent financing. Since the new financing could be considered directly related to the purchase of the principal residence, the points paid on such purchase were immediately deductible.

The IRS has announced that in areas outside of the Eighth Circuit, it will continue to disallow full deductions in the year of payment for points paid on refinancings. The Eighth Circuit includes only these states: Minnesota, Iowa, North and South Dakota, Nebraska, Missouri, and Arkansas. In these states, the IRS will not challenge deductions for points on refinancing agreements similar to Huntman's which replace short-term financing with long-term permanent financing.

In a subsequent case, the Tax Court held that the Huntsman exception does not apply where a borrower refinances a long-term mortgage to take advantage of lower interest rates; the points must be deducted over the term of the new mortgage.

COOPERATIVE AND CONDOMINIUM APARTMENTS

¶**15.8** **Cooperative apartments.** If you are a tenant-stockholder of a cooperative apartment, you may deduct your portion of:

Interest paid by the cooperative on its debts, provided you do not pay interest on more than two residences; *see* ¶15.1. This includes your pro rata share of the permanent financing expenses (points) of the cooperative on its mortgage covering the housing project.

Taxes paid by the cooperative. However, if the cooperative does not own the land and building but merely leases them and is required to pay real estate taxes under the terms of the lease, you may not deduct your share of the tax payment.

In some localities, such as New York City, rent control rules allow tenants of a building converted to cooperatives to remain in their apartments even if they do not buy into the co-op. A holdover tenant may prevent some co-op purchasers from occupying an apartment. The IRS ruled that the fact that a holdover tenant stays in the apartment will not bar the owner from deducting his share of the co-op's interest and taxes.

Condominiums

If you own an apartment in a condominium, you have a direct ownership interest in the property and are treated, for tax purposes, just as any other property owner. You may deduct your payments of real estate taxes and mortgage interest. You may also deduct taxes and interest paid on the mortgage debt of the project allocable to your share of the property. The deduction of interest from condominium ownership is also subject to the two residences limit of ¶15.1. If you use your condominium for business or professional use, or for the production of income, or if you rent it to others, you may deduct expenses of maintenance and repairs and claim depreciation deductions subject to rules of ¶29.20.

INVESTMENT INTEREST DEDUCTIONS

INVESTMENT INTEREST LIMITATIONS

¶**15.9** Interest paid on margin accounts and debts to buy or carry other investments is deductible up to the amount of net investment income on Schedule A. Investment interest in excess of net investment income may be carried forward and deducted from next year's net investment income.

You compute the deduction for investment interest on Form 4952, which must be attached to Form 1040. The deduction is *not* subject to the 3% reduction of itemized deductions if your adjusted gross income exceeds $105,250 ($52,625 if married filing separately); *see* ¶13.8.

What is investment interest? It is all interest paid or accrued on debts incurred or continued to buy or carry investment property, such as interest on securities in a margin account. However, interest on loans to buy tax-exempt securities is not deductible; *see* ¶15.10.

Investment interest does not include any qualified residence interest (¶15.1), construction period interest that is capitalized (¶16.5), or interest related to a passive activity.

Investment property includes property producing portfolio income (interest, dividends, or royalties not realized in the ordinary course of business) under the passive activity rules of Chapter 10, and property in activities that are not treated as passive activities, even if you do not materially participate, such as working interests in oil and gas wells.

Passive activity interest is not investment interest. Interest expenses incurred in a passive activity such as rental real estate, or a limited partnership or S corporation in which you do not materially participate, are taken into account on Form 8582 when figuring net passive income or loss. This includes interest incurred on loans used to finance your investment in a passive activity. Do not treat passive activity interest as investment interest on Form 4952.

However, interest expenses allocable to *portfolio* income (nonbusiness activity interest, dividends, royalties) from a limited partnership or S corporation are investment interest and not passive interest. The investment interest will be listed separately on Schedule K-1 received from the partnership or corporation.

Interest on loans to buy market discount bonds and Treasury bills. Limits apply to the deduction for interest on loans used to buy or carry market discount bonds (¶4.20) and Treasury bills (¶4.27) acquired after July 18, 1984.

Interest on debts to purchase or carry straddles is not deductible unless the straddle is a hedging transaction; *see* ¶5.27.

Computing the deduction. The first step in computing deductible investment interest is figuring net investment income.

Net investment income is the excess of investment income over investment expenses. Investment income is generally gross income from property held for investment, including any net gain attributable to disposition of property held for investment.

Income or expenses considered in figuring profit or loss of a passive activity is not considered investment income or expenses. Property subject to a net lease is not treated as investment property as it is within the passive activity rules.

Investment expenses are expenses, other than interest, directly connected with the production of investment income. However, for purposes of determining net investment income, only those investment expenses (other than interest) allowable after figuring the 2% floor for miscellaneous itemized deductions (¶19.24) are taken into account. The 2% floor will bar a deduction for some of the miscellaneous itemized deductions. For purposes of this net investment income computation, assume that miscellaneous itemized deductions other than investment expenses are disallowed first.

After determining net investment income, you may figure your allowable 1992 deduction. Investment interest is deductible up to net investment income.

Carryover to 1993. The disallowed amount may be carried forward to 1993 and is deductible in 1993 to the extent that when added to 1993 investment interest expenses it does not exceed net investment income.

EXAMPLE For 1992, Jones has $10,000 of investment income from interest and dividends. He has investment expenses, other than interest, of $3,200, after taking into account the 2% floor on miscellaneous itemized deductions. His investment interest expense from securities margin account loans is $8,000. Jones also has income of $2,000 from a passive partnership investment.

Jones' net investment income is $6,800: $10,000 of investment income less $3,200 of non-interest investment expenses. The passive activity income from the partnership is not included in investment income.

Jones may deduct $6,800 for investment interest for 1992: $6,800 is the amount of net investment income. The disallowed interest of $1,200 that exceeds 1992 net investment income is carried forward to 1993.

Claiming the Deduction on Form 4952

The deduction figured on Form 4952 is generally entered on Line 11 of Schedule A as investment interest. However, if the interest is attributable to royalties, you may have to enter the interest on Schedule E; follow the Form 4952 instructions. Furthermore, there is an additional complication if you have investment interest for an activity for which you are not "at risk" (Chapter 10). After figuring the investment interest deduction on Form 4952, you must enter the portion of the interest that is attributable to the at-risk activity on Form 6198. The amount carried over to Form 6198 is subtracted from the investment interest deduction claimed on Schedule A; follow the instructions to Forms 4952 and 6198.

DEBTS TO CARRY TAX-EXEMPT OBLIGATIONS

¶**15.10** When you borrow money in order to buy or carry tax-exempt bonds, you may not deduct any interest paid on your loan. Application of this disallowance rule is clear where there is actual evidence that loan proceeds were used to buy tax-exempts or that tax-exempts were used as collateral. But sometimes the relationship between a loan and the purchase of tax-exempts is less obvious, as where you hold tax-exempts and borrow to carry other securities or investments. IRS guidelines explain when a direct relationship between the debt and an investment in tax-exempts will be inferred so that no interest deduction is allowed. The IRS will *not* infer a direct relationship between a debt and an investment in tax-exempts in these cases:

1. The investment in tax-exempts is not substantial. That is, it is not more than 2% of the adjusted basis of the investment portfolio and any assets held in an actively conducted business.
2. The debt is incurred for a personal purpose. For example, an investor may take out a home mortgage instead of selling his tax-exempts and using the proceeds to finance the home purchase. Interest on the mortgage is deductible under the rules of ¶15.1.
3. The debt is incurred in connection with the active conduct of a business and does not exceed business needs. But, if a person reasonably could have foreseen when he or she purchased the tax-exempts that he or she would have to borrow to meet ordinary and recurrent business needs, the interest expenses are not deductible.

The guidelines infer a direct relationship between the debt and an investment in tax-exempts in this type of case: An investor in tax-exempts has outstanding debts not directly related to personal expenses or to his or her business. The interest will be disallowed even if the debt appears to have been incurred to purchase other portfolio investments. Portfolio investments include transactions entered into for profit, including investments in real estate, which are not connected with the active conduct of a business.

EXAMPLE An investor owning $360,000 in tax-exempt bonds purchased real estate in a joint venture, giving a purchase money mortgage and cash for the price. He deducted interest on the mortgage. The IRS disallowed the deduction, claiming the debt was incurred to carry tax-exempts. A court allowed the deduction. A mortgage is the customary manner of financing such a purchase. Furthermore, since the purchase was part of a joint venture, the other parties' desires in the manner of financing had to be considered.

Mutual funds. If you receive tax-exempt interest dividends from a mutual fund during the year, you may deduct interest on a loan used to buy or carry the mutual fund shares only to the extent it can be allocated to taxable dividends you also receive.

EARMARKING USE OF LOAN PROCEEDS

¶**15.11** The IRS has set down complex recordkeeping and allocation rules for claiming interest deductions on loans used for business or investment purposes, or for passive activities. The rules deal primarily with the use of loan proceeds for more than one purpose and the commingling of loan proceeds in an account with unborrowed funds. The thrust of the rules is to base deductibility of interest on the *use* of the borrowed funds. The allocation rules do not affect mortgage interest deductions on loans secured by a qualifying first or second home; *see* ¶15.1.

To safeguard your investment and business interest deductions, you must earmark and keep a record of your loans. You should avoid using loan proceeds to fund different types of expenditures. Keep separate accounts for business, personal, and investment borrowing. For example, if you borrow for investment purposes, keep the proceeds of the loan in a separate account and use the proceeds only for investment purposes. Do not use the funds to pay for personal expenses. Furthermore, do not deposit loan proceeds in an account funded with unborrowed money, unless you intend to use the proceeds within 30 days of the deposit. By following these directions, you can pinpoint your use of the proceeds to a specific expenditure, such as for investment, personal, or business purposes, and the interest on the loan may be treated as incurred for that purpose. The 30-day rule is discussed below.

The IRS treats undisbursed loan proceeds deposited in an account as investment property, even though the account does not bear interest. When proceeds are disbursed from the account, the use of the proceeds determines how interest is treated.

EXAMPLES 1. On January 1, you borrow $10,000 and deposit the proceeds in a non-interest-bearing checking account. No other amounts are deposited in the account during the year and no part of the loan is repaid during the year. On April 1, you invest $2,000 of the proceeds in a real estate venture. On September 1, you use $4,000 to buy furniture.

From January 1 through March 31, interest on the entire undisbursed $10,000 is treated as investment interest. From April 1 through August 31, interest on $2,000 of the debt is treated as passive activity interest, and interest on $8,000 of the debt is treated as investment interest. From September 1 through December 31, interest on $4,000 of the debt is treated as personal interest; interest on $2,000 is treated as passive activity interest; and interest on $4,000 is treated as investment interest.

2. On September 1, you borrow money for business purposes and deposit it in a checking account. On October 15, you disburse the proceeds for business purposes. Interest incurred on the loan before the disbursement of the funds is treated as investment interest expense. Interest starting on October 15 is treated as business interest. However, you may elect to treat the starting date for business interest as of the first of the month in which the disbursement was made—that is, October 1—provided all other disbursements from the account during the same month are similarly treated.

30-day disbursement rule. If you deposit borrowed funds in an account with unborrowed funds, a special 30-day rule allows you to treat payments from the account as made from the loan proceeds. Where you make more than one disbursement from such an account, you may treat any expenses paid within 30 days before or after deposit of the loan proceeds as if made from the loan proceeds. Thus, you may allocate interest on the loan to that disbursement, even if earlier payments from the account have been made; *see* Example 1 below. If you make the disbursement after 30 days, the IRS requires you to allocate interest on the loan to the first disbursement; *see* Example 2 below. Furthermore, if an account includes only loan proceeds and interest earned on the proceeds, disbursements may be allocated first to the interest income and then to the loan proceeds.

EXAMPLES 1. On September 1, you borrow $5,000 to invest in stock and deposit the proceeds in your regular checking account. On September 10, you buy a TV and stereo for $2,500 and on September 11 invest $5,000 in stock, using funds from the account. As the stock investment was made within 30 days of depositing the loan proceeds in the account, interest on the entire loan is treated as incurred for investment purposes.

2. Same facts as in Example 1, but the TV and stereo were bought on October 1 and the stock on October 31. As the stock investment was not made within 30 days, the IRS requires you to treat the purchase of the TV and the stereo for $2,500 as the first purchase made with the loan proceeds of $5,000. Thus, only 10% of the loan interest allocated to the stereo purchase is deductible as personal interest.

Allocation period. Interest is allocated to an expenditure for the period *beginning* on the date the loan proceeds are used or treated as used, and ending on the earlier of the date the debt is repaid or reallocated.

Accrued interest is treated as a debt until it is paid, and any interest accruing on unpaid interest is allocated in the same manner as the unpaid interest is allocated. Compound interest accruing on such debt, other than compound interest accruing on interest that accrued before the beginning of the year, may be allocated between the original expenditure and any new expenditure from the same account on a straight-line basis. That is done by allocating an equal amount of such interest expense to each day during the taxable year. In addition, you may treat a year as *twelve 30-day months* for purposes of allocating interest on a straight-line basis.

Payments from checking account. A disbursement from a checking account is treated as made at the time the check is written on the account, provided the check is delivered or mailed to the payee within a reasonable period after the writing of the check. You may treat checks written on the same day as written in any order. A check is presumed to be written on the date appearing on the check and to be delivered or mailed to the payee within a reasonable period thereafter. However, the presumption may not apply if the check does not clear within a reasonable period after the date appearing on the check.

Debt-financed property. You must reallocate interest if you convert debt-financed property to a different use; for example, when you convert a business auto to personal use.

EXAMPLE You buy a business auto on time. Interest paid on the auto is business interest. Assume during the year you convert the auto to personal use. Interest paid after the conversion is personal interest.

Order of repayment. If you used loan proceeds for several different types of disbursements, a repayment of the debt is treated as repaid in the following order:

1. Repayment of personal debt.
2. Repayment of investment debt and passive activity debt other than Step 3 below.
3. Repayment of debt in real estate activity in which you actively participate.
4. Repayment of former passive activity debt.
5. Repayment of business debt.

Payments made on the same day may be treated as made in any order.

EXAMPLE On July 12, Smith borrows $100,000 and immediately deposits the proceeds in an account. He uses the proceeds as follows:

August 31	$40,000 for passive activity
October 5	$20,000 for rental activity
December 24	$40,000 for personal use

On January 19 of the following year, Smith repays $90,000. Of the repayment, $40,000 is allocated as a repayment of the personal expenditure, $40,000 of the passive activity, and $10,000 of the rental activity. The outstanding $10,000 is treated as debt incurred in a rental activity.

TIMING OF INTEREST DEDUCTION

YEAR TO CLAIM AN INTEREST DEDUCTION

¶15.12 As a cash basis taxpayer, you deduct interest in the year of payment except for prepayments of interest; *see* ¶15.13. Giving a promissory note is not considered payment. Increasing the amount of a loan by interest owed, as with insurance loans, is also not considered payment and will not support a deduction. If a person pays your interest obligation with the understanding you will repay him or her, you take the deduction in the year the interest is paid, not when you repay him or her. An accrual basis taxpayer generally deducts interest in the year the interest accrues; *see* ¶40.2.

Using Borrowed Funds to Pay Interest

To get an interest deduction you must pay the interest; you may not claim a deduction by having the creditor add the interest to the debt. If you do not have funds to pay the interest, you may borrow money to pay the interest. Borrow the funds from a different creditor. The IRS disallows deductions where a debtor borrows from the same creditor to make interest payments on an earlier loan; the second loan is considered merely a device for getting an interest expense deduction without actually making payments. Courts tend to side with the IRS.

Here is how a cash basis taxpayer treats interest in the following situations:

On a life insurance loan, where proceeds are used for a deductible (nonpersonal) purpose, you claim a deduction in the year in which the interest is paid. You may not claim a deduction when the insurance company adds the interest to your debt. You may not deduct your payment of interest on an insurance loan after you assign the policy.

On a margin account with a broker, interest is deductible in the year in which it is paid or your account is credited after the interest has been charged. But an interest charge to your account is not payment if you do not pay it in cash or the broker has not collected dividends, interest, or security sales proceeds which may be applied against the interest due. Interest on margin accounts is subject to investment interest limitations.

For partial payment of a loan used for a deductible (nonpersonal) purpose, interest is deductible in the year the payment is credited against interest due. When a loan has no provision for allocating payments between principal and income, the law presumes that a partial payment is applied first to interest and then to principal, unless you agree otherwise. Where the payment is in full settlement of the debt, the payment is applied first to principal, unless you agree otherwise. Where there is an involuntary payment, such as that following a foreclosure sale of collateral, sales proceeds are applied first to principal, unless you agree to the contrary. *See* also ¶15.11 for the effect of payments on the allocation of debt proceeds.

EXAMPLES 1. Assume you owe $1,000 on a note, plus interest of $120. If you should pay $800 on account, the law presumes that $120 of the $800 represents a payment of interest.

2. Same as above, but the payment is accepted in full settlement of the debt. The law presumes that the $800 represents a payment of principal for which no deduction is allowed.

Note renewed. You may not deduct interest by merely giving a new note. You claim a deduction in the year the renewed note is paid. The giving of a new note or increasing the amount due is not payment. The same is true when past due interest is deducted from the proceeds of a new loan. This is not deemed payment of the interest.

PREPAID INTEREST

¶15.13 If you prepay interest on a loan used for *investment* or *business* purposes you may not deduct interest allocable to any period falling in a later taxable year. The prepaid interest must be deducted over the period of the loan, whether you are a cash basis or accrual basis taxpayer.

Points paid on the purchase of a *principal residence* are generally fully deductible in the year paid; *see* ¶15.7.

Treatment of interest included in a level payment schedule. Where payments of principal and interest are equal, a large amount of interest allocated to the payments made in early years of a loan will generally not be considered prepaid interest. However, if the loan calls for a variable interest rate, the IRS may treat interest payments as consisting partly of interest, computed under an average level effective rate, and partly of prepaid interest allocable to later years of the loan. An interest rate which varies with the "prime rate" does not necessarily indicate a prepaid interest element.

When you borrow money for a deductible purpose and give a note to the lender, the amount of your loan proceeds may be less than the face value of the note. The difference between the proceeds and the face amount is interest discount. For loans that do not fall within the OID rules of ¶4.18, such as loans of a year or less, interest is deductible in the year of payment if you are on the cash basis. If you use the accrual basis, the interest is deductible as it accrues.

EXAMPLE In February 1991, you borrow $1,000 for an investment and receive $900 in return for your $1,000 note. You repay the full loan in January 1992. You are on the cash basis. You do not deduct the interest of $100 when the note is given. The $100 interest is deductible when the loan is paid in 1992. If the loan proceeds were used for personal purposes, none of the interest is deductible in 1992.

For loans that fall within OID rules, your lender should provide a statement showing the interest element and the tax treatment of the interest.

16

DEDUCTIONS FOR TAXES

If you itemize deductions on Schedule A, you may deduct your 1992 payments of state, local, and foreign income taxes and real property taxes, as well as state and local personal property taxes. State and local sales taxes are not deductible.

To increase your deduction for state and local taxes, consider making a year-end prepayment of estimated tax liability. You also may be able to increase withholdings from your pay to increase your deduction.

If you pay transfer taxes on the sale of securities or investment real estate, the taxes are not deductible. However, they increase your cost basis when figuring your profit or loss.

Taxes paid in operating a business are generally deductible, except for sales taxes, which are added to the cost of the property.

Taxes claimed as itemized deductions are subject to the 3% reduction of itemized deductions if your adjusted gross exceeds $105,250 or $52,625 if married filing separately; see ¶13.8.

DEDUCTIBLE TAXES

¶16.1
You may deduct as itemized deductions on Schedule A your 1992 payments of:

- State, local, and foreign income taxes.
- State, local, and foreign real property taxes.
- State and local personal property taxes.

In figuring deductible state or local income taxes, include the amount of state or local income tax withheld from your 1992 pay and any estimated tax you paid in 1992 to state or local authorities. Also, do not forget to include tax that you paid in 1992 when you filed your 1991 state and local tax returns.

Taxes incurred in your business are generally deductible on Schedule C; see ¶16.11.

If your 1992 adjusted gross income exceeds $105,250, or $52,625 if married filing separately, your deduction for taxes is subject to the 3% reduction computation explained at ¶13.8.

CHECKLIST OF DEDUCTIBLE AND NONDEDUCTIBLE TAXES

¶16.2
You may deduct as itemized deductions your payments of state, local, and foreign real property and income taxes, as well as state and local personal property taxes. Sales taxes on personal property are not deductible as itemized deductions. Transfer taxes paid on the sale of securities or investment real estate are not deductible, but you may increase your cost basis by the transfer tax in figuring profit or loss on Schedule D.

Claim the deduction for deductible taxes on the tax return for the year in which you paid the taxes, unless you report on the accrual basis; see ¶16.8.

Type of tax—	Deductible as itemized deduction—
Admission	No
Alcoholic beverage	No
Assessments for local benefits	No
Automobile license fees not qualifying as personal property tax	No
Cigarette	No
Customs duties	No
Driver's license	No
Estate—federal or state (but see ¶11.4)	No
Excise—federal or state, for example, on telephone service	No
Gasoline—federal	No
Gasoline and other motor fuel—state and local	No
Gift taxes—federal and state	No
Income—federal (including alternative minimum tax)	No
Income—state, local, or foreign	Yes
Inheritance tax	No
Mortgage tax	No
Personal property—state or local	Yes
Poll	No
Real estate (state, local, or foreign)	Yes
Regulatory license fees—(dog licenses, parking meter fees, hunting and fishing licenses)	No
Sales and use tax on personal property	No
Social Security	No
Tolls	No
Transfer taxes on securities and real estate	No

Gasoline taxes. State and local taxes on gasoline used for personal purposes are not deductible. If you travel for business, the taxes are deductible as part of your gasoline expenses.

DEDUCTING STATE INCOME TAXES

¶16.3 You may deduct on your 1992 return state and local income taxes withheld from your pay and estimated state and local taxes paid in 1992. Also deduct the balance of your 1991 state and local taxes you paid during 1992. If you pay in 1993 additional state income tax on your 1992 income, you deduct the payment on your 1993 tax return.

State income taxes may be claimed only as itemized deductions, even if attributed solely to business income. That is, state income taxes may not be deducted as business expenses from gross income.

To increase your itemized deductions on your 1992 return, consider prepaying state income taxes before the end of 1992. The prepayment is deductible provided the state tax authority accepts prepayments and state law recognizes them as tax payments. The IRS has ruled, however, that prepayments are not deductible if you do not reasonably believe that you owe additional state tax. Do not make prepayments if you may be subject to alternative minimum tax; see Chapter 23.

If you report on the accrual basis and you contest a tax liability, claim the deduction in the year of payment.

You may deduct on your federal return state and local income taxes allocable to interest income that is exempt from federal tax but not state and local income tax. However, state and local taxes allocated to other federal exempt income are not deductible. For example, state income tax allocated to a cost-of-living allowance exempt from federal income tax is not deductible as a state tax.

Mandatory employee contributions to the following state disability or unemployment insurance funds are deductible as state income

taxes: California Unemployment Insurance Code; New Jersey Nonoccupational Disability Benefit Fund; New York Nonoccupational Disability Benefit Fund; Rhode Island Temporary Disability Benefit Fund; West Virginia Unemployment Compensation Trust Fund; and the Alabama State Unemployment Fund.

However, employee contributions to a private or voluntary disability plan in California, New Jersey, or New York have been held by the IRS to be nondeductible.

Mandatory employee contributions to a state unemployment fund are deductible.

Note: A refund of state income taxes claimed as an itemized deduction may have to be reported as income; see ¶12.7.

TAXES AND CARRYING CHARGES— CAPITALIZE OR DEDUCT

¶16.4 For certain property, you may elect to capitalize certain deductible taxes and other deductible carrying charges, such as interest, by adding these amounts to the basis of the property. This may be to your advantage if you do not need the immediate deduction because you have little or no income to offset, or because you do not have itemized deductions or expect a greater tax benefit by adding the taxes to the basis.

Manufacturers, builders, and buyers for resale generally *must* capitalize carrying charges under uniform capitalization rules; see ¶40.2.

An election to capitalize applies not only to taxes but also to interest and other deductible carrying charges incurred during your ownership of the property. The election is limited to:

Unimproved and nonproductive real property.

Real property being improved or developed. You may elect to capitalize costs up to the time the development or construction work has been completed. These costs include interest on loans to furnish funds for development; Social Security taxes on pay to your employees; and taxes on the materials used and other expenses incurred in the development. See ¶16.5 for mandatory amortization of certain construction period interest and taxes.

Personal property, such as machinery, up to the time of its installation or actual use (whichever is later).

EXAMPLES 1. Jones, in 1991 and 1992, paid taxes and interest on a mortgage on vacant and nonproductive property. In 1992, he operates the property as a parking lot. Jones may capitalize the taxes and mortgage interest paid in 1991, but not the tax and interest in 1992.

2. Smith began construction of an office building in April 1992. In 1992, he paid $6,000 in employer Social Security taxes. On his 1992 return, he elected to capitalize these taxes. He must continue to capitalize them until the building is finished.

Making the election. Attach to your return a statement of expenses you elect to capitalize; IRS permission is not required. The election must apply to all similar expenses for the same project. An election for unimproved and unproductive real property applies only for the year for which it is made. An election for real property under development or machinery may not be revoked.

CONSTRUCTION PERIOD INTEREST AND TAXES

¶16.5 Construction period interest and real estate taxes incurred after 1986 on business or investment real estate are not currently deductible but *must* be capitalized. The costs are recovered through depreciation; over 27.5 years for residential buildings and 31.5 years for nonresidential buildings. However, interest on debt to finance real property for resale is not subject to these capitalization rules. Where substantial construction occurred before March 1, 1986, costs are capitalized and amortized under prior law rules. For further details, *see* IRS Publication 535 and IRS Notice 88-99.

Costs incurred *before* 1987 were generally amortized over a 10-year period. The pre-1987 rules are not discussed in this book.

DEDUCTING REAL ESTATE TAXES

¶16.6 You may deduct payments of real estate tax on your property if you claim itemized deductions on Schedule A. Real estate taxes included in a mortgage payment to a bank are not deductible until paid to the taxing authority. The monthly mortgage payment to a bank generally includes amounts allocated to real estate taxes, which the bank pays to the taxing authority on their due date. You may not deduct the amounts allocated to the taxes in the year paid to the bank, unless the bank has paid them to the tax authority. Typically, banks will furnish you with a year-end statement of disbursements to taxing authorities, indicating dates of payment.

Cooperative apartments. Tenant-stockholders of a cooperative housing corporation may deduct their share of the real estate taxes paid by the corporation. However, no deduction is allowed if the corporation does not own the land and building but merely leases them and pays taxes under the lease agreement.

Assessments by homeowner's association not deductible as taxes. Assessments paid to a local homeowner's association for the purpose of maintaining the common areas of the residential project and for promoting the recreation, health, and safety of the residents are not deductible as real property taxes.

Assessments for government services. If property is used solely as your residence, you may not deduct charges for municipal water bills (even if described as a "tax"), sewer assessments, assessments for sanitation service, or title registration fees. A permit fee to build or improve a personal residence is added to the cost basis of the house.

Assessments for local benefits are deductible if they cover maintenance or repairs of streets, sidewalks, or water or sewer systems, or interest costs on such maintenance. However, assessments for construction of streets, sidewalks, or other local improvements that tend to increase the value of your property are not deductible as real estate taxes. You add such assessments to your cost basis for the property.

If you are billed a single amount, you may deduct the portion allocable to assessments for maintenance or repairs. The burden is on you to support the allocation.

TENANTS' PAYMENT OF TAXES

¶16.7 You generally may not deduct a portion of your rent as property taxes. This is so even where state or local law identifies a portion of the rent as being tied to tax increases.

EXAMPLE A municipal rent control ordinance allowed landlords to charge real property tax increases to the tenants as a monthly "tax surcharge." The ordinance stated that the surcharge was not to be considered rent for purposes of computing cost-of-living rental increases. The IRS ruled that the tenant may not deduct the "tax surcharge" as a property tax. The tax is imposed on the landlord, not on the tenant. The city ordinance, which permitted the landlord to pass on the tax increases to a tenant, did not shift liability for the property taxes from the landlord to the tenant. For federal tax purposes, the surcharge is merely an additional rental payment by the tenant. Similarly, "rates tax" or "renters' tax" imposed on tenants was ruled to be nondeductible because the tax is imposed on the person using the property rather than the property itself.

Tenants have been allowed a deduction for property taxes in the following areas: In Hawaii, tenants with leases of 15 years or more may deduct the portion of the rent representing taxes. In California, tenants who have their names placed on the tax rolls and who pay the taxes directly to the taxing authority may claim a deduction.

In New York, liability for tax is placed directly on the tenant and the landlord is a collecting agent for paying over the tax to the taxing authorities; the landlord also remains liable for the tax. The IRS ruled that it will not permit tenants to deduct a portion of rent as a payment of taxes.

ALLOCATING TAXES WHEN YOU SELL OR BUY REALTY

¶16.8 When property is sold, the buyer and seller apportion the real estate taxes imposed on the property during the "real property year." A "real property year" is the period which a real estate tax covers. This allocation is provided for you in a settlement statement at the time of closing. If you want to figure your own allocations, your local tax authority can give you the "real property year" of the taxes you plan to apportion. With this information, you then make the following allocation. If *you* are the:

Seller, you deduct that portion of the tax covering the beginning of the real property year through the day before the sale.

Buyer, you deduct the part of the tax covering the date of the sale through the end of the real property year.

EXAMPLE The real property year in East County starts April 1 and ends March 31. On July 2, 1992, you sell realty located in East County to Jones. Assume the real estate tax for the real property year ending March 31, 1993, is $1,000. You deduct $252 (92/365 of $1,000, since there are 92 days in the period beginning April 1 and ending July 1, 1992). Jones deducts $748 (273/365 of $1,000, since there are 273 days in the period beginning July 2, 1992, and ending March 31, 1993).

The above allocation is mandatory whether or not your contract provides for an allocation. However, you do not allocate taxes of a real property year when:

Property is sold before the real property year. This rule prevents the seller from deducting any part of the tax for that year, even though it became a personal liability or lien while he or she owned the property. The buyer gets the deduction because the tax covers the property year the buyer owns the property.

Property is sold after the real property year. This rule prevents the buyer from deducting the tax even though it becomes a personal liability or lien after he or she takes possession of the property. The seller gets the deduction because the tax covers the property year the seller owns the property.

The allocation is limited to a tax covering a property year during which both the seller and the buyer own the property.

When to deduct allocated taxes. After you have made the allocation based on the "real property year," you then must fix the year in which you deduct your share of the allocated tax. Here you consider your method of reporting your income—cash or accrual basis—and the date on which either you or the other party became liable for the tax or paid the tax. If neither you nor the other party is liable for the tax under local law, then the party who holds the property at the time the tax became a lien on the property is considered liable. Check the following rules to determine when you deduct the apportioned tax:

Seller on the cash basis—If the buyer is liable for the tax under local law, the seller may deduct his or her share of the allocated tax either in the year of the sale or a later year when the tax is actually paid.

If the seller is liable for the tax under local law, and the tax is not payable until after the date of sale, the seller may deduct the tax either in the year of sale or in the year he or she pays the tax.

Buyer on the cash basis—If the seller is liable for the tax under local law, the buyer may deduct the tax either in the year of sale or when the tax is actually paid.

If the buyer is liable for the tax, he or she deducts the tax in the year the tax is paid.

Seller on the accrual basis—The seller accrues his or her share of the tax on the date of the sale, unless taxes have been accrued ratably over the years. If this is so, the last accrual is the date of the sale.

Buyer on the accrual basis—If the seller is liable for the tax, the buyer accrues his or her share of the tax on the date of the sale, unless taxes are accrued ratably. If taxes are accrued ratably, the accrual begins with the date of sale. If the buyer is liable for the tax, he or she deducts the tax in the return for the year the tax accrues unless an election is made to accrue ratably from the date of sale.

Seller's deduction in excess of the allocated amount is taxed as income. If, in the year before the sale, the seller deducts an amount for taxes in excess of the allocated amount, the excess must be reported as income in the year of the sale. This may happen when the seller is on the cash basis and pays the tax in the year before the sale.

EXAMPLE A real property tax is due and payable on November 30 for the following calendar year. On November 30, 1991, Jones, who uses the cash basis and reports on a calendar year, pays the 1992 tax. On June 30, 1992, he sells the real property. Under the apportionment rule, Jones is allowed to deduct only 180/366 (January 1—June 29, 1992) of the tax for the 1992 real property tax year. But he has already deducted the full amount in the 1991 return. Therefore, he reports as income that part of the tax deduction he was not entitled to under the apportionment.

Buyer may not deduct payment of seller's back taxes. The back taxes paid are added to the cost of the newly purchased property. The amount realized by the seller is increased by the buyer's payment of back taxes.

Seller's payment upon buyer's failure to pay. If a buyer is obligated to pay taxes under a land contract but fails to pay, the owner who pays the tax may deduct the payment if the tax is assessed to him or her.

Buyer of foreclosed property. If you buy realty at a tax sale and you do not receive immediate title to the property under state law until after a redemption period, you may not be able to deduct payment of realty taxes for several years.

WHO MAY DEDUCT REAL PROPERTY TAXES

¶16.9 A person who pays a property tax must have an ownership interest in the property to deduct the payment. The following table summarizes who may deduct payments of real property taxes.

If the tax is paid by—	Then it is deductible by—
You, for your spouse	Neither, if your spouse has title to the property, and you each file a separate return. This is true even if the mortgage requires you to pay the taxes. The tax is deductible on a joint return.
You, as owner of a condominium	You deduct real estate tax paid on your separate unit. You also deduct your share of the tax paid on the common property.
A life tenant	A court allowed the deduction to a widow required to pay the taxes under a will for the privilege of occupying the house during her life.
A tenant	The tenant of a business lease may deduct the payment of tax as additional rent, not tax. The tenant of a personal residence may not deduct the payment as either a tax or rent expense, unless placed on the real estate assessment rolls, so the tax is assessed directly against him or her; see ¶16.7.
You, as a local benefit tax to maintain, repair, or meet interest costs arising from local benefits	You deduct only that part of the tax which you can show is for maintenance, repair, or interest. If you cannot make the allocation, no deduction is allowed. If the benefit increases the value of the property, you add the nondeductible assessment to the basis of the property.
Your cooperative apartment or corporation	You deduct your share of real estate tax paid on the property; see ¶15.8. But if the organization leases the land and building and pays the tax under the terms of the lease, you may not deduct your share.
One whose property was foreclosed for failure to pay taxes	You may not deduct the taxes paid out of the proceeds of the foreclosure sale if your interest in the property ended with the foreclosure.
Tenant by the entirety or joint tenant	The tenant who is jointly and severally liable and who pays the tax. If real property is owned by husband and wife as tenants by the entirety or joint tenants, either spouse may deduct the taxes paid on a separate return or a joint return. When property is owned as a tenancy in common, under an IRS rule, a tenant may deduct only his or her share of the tax, even if the entire tax was paid. However, in one case the Tax Court allowed a deduction for the full amount; see ¶9.2.
A mortgagee	No deduction. If paid before the foreclosure, it is added to the loan. If paid after the foreclosure, it is added to the cost of property.

AUTOMOBILE LICENSE FEES

¶16.10
You may not deduct an auto license fee based on weight, model, year, or horsepower. But you may deduct a fee based on the value of the car if these three tests are met: (1) the fee is an *ad valorem* tax, based on a percentage of value of the property; (2) it is imposed on an annual basis, even though it is collected more or less frequently; and (3) it is imposed on personal property. This third test is met even though the tax is imposed on the exercise of a privilege of registering a car or for using a car on the road.

If the tax is based partly on value and partly on weight or other tests, the tax attributed to the value is deductible. For example, assume a registration fee based on 1% of value, plus 40¢ per hundred-weight. The part of the tax equal to 1% of value qualifies as an *ad valorem* tax and is deductible as a personal property tax.

The majority of state motor vehicle registration fees are not *ad valorem* taxes and do not qualify for the deduction. Various states and localities impose *ad valorem* or personal property taxes on motor vehicles that may qualify for the deduction. If you pay fees or taxes on your auto in these states, we suggest you contact a state or local authority to verify the amount of tax qualifying: Arizona, California, Colorado, Georgia, Indiana, Iowa, Maine, Massachusetts, Minnesota, Mississippi, Montana, Nebraska, Nevada, New Hampshire, Oklahoma, Washington, and Wyoming.

TAXES DEDUCTIBLE AS BUSINESS EXPENSES

¶16.11
That a tax is not deductible as an itemized deduction does not mean you may not deduct it elsewhere on your return. For example, you may generally deduct property taxes incurred as a cost of doing business on Schedule C. Here are some other examples:

If you pay excise taxes on merchandise you sell in your business, you deduct the tax as a business expense.

If you pay Social Security taxes (FICA) on your employees' wages, you deduct the tax as a business expense on Schedule C.

If you pay sales tax on business property, you add the tax to the cost of the property for depreciation purposes. If the tax is paid on nondepreciable property, the tax is included in the currently deductible cost.

If you pay sales tax on a deductible business meal, the tax is deductible as part of the meal costs, subject to the 80% cost limit discussed at ¶20.27.

50% self-employment tax deduction. One-half of the self-employment tax figured on Schedule SE is deductible from gross income on Line 25 of Form 1040, rather than on Schedule C; *see* ¶46.3.

Note: If you are not a material participant in the business, your Schedule C expenses are subject to passive activity limitations; *see* Chapter 10.

FOREIGN TAXES

¶16.12
You may deduct your payment of foreign real property taxes and income and excess profits taxes as itemized deductions. Where you pay foreign income or excess profits tax, you have an election of either claiming the tax as a deduction or a credit. Claiming the credit may provide a larger tax savings; *see* ¶36.14.

17 MEDICAL AND DENTAL EXPENSE DEDUCTIONS

Despite the high cost of medical care, tax relief is limited. Medical expenses are deductible only if you itemize and only if you have expenses exceeding 7.5% of your adjusted gross income. Expenses up to 7.5% of AGI are not allowed.

Carefully review the list of deductible expenses in this chapter so that you do not overlook any deductible expense that you have paid. Include doctors' fees, health care premiums, prescription medicines, travel costs for obtaining medical care, and eligible home improvements.

If you are married, both you and your spouse work, and one of you has substantial medical expenses, filing separate returns may result in a lower overall tax.

Deductible medical expenses are *not* subject to the 3% reduction of itemized deductions that applies if adjusted gross income exceeds $105,250 ($52,625 if married filing separately).

LIMITATIONS ON MEDICAL EXPENSE DEDUCTIONS

¶ **17.1** Medical costs, including the cost of health insurance, are high. However, the tax law provides only a limited opportunity to deduct medical costs for you, your spouse, and your dependents. It sets down these conditions:

1. You must itemize deductions on Schedule A of Form 1040.
2. You may deduct only unreimbursed medical expenses that exceed 7.5% of your adjusted gross income. For example, if your adjusted gross income is $40,000, medical expenses of up to $3,000 are *not* deductible ($40,000 × 7.5%); only expenses over $3,000 may be claimed.

Should spouses file separately? If you are married and both you and your spouse have separate incomes, and one of you has substantial medical expenses, consider filing separate returns. This way the 7.5% floor will apply separately to your individual incomes, not to the higher joint income. To make sure which option to take—filing jointly or separately—compute your tax on both types of returns and choose the one giving the lower overall tax; *see* ¶1.2.

Filing separately in community property states. If you and your spouse file separately and live in a community property state, any medical expenses paid out of community funds are treated as paid 50% by each of you. Medical expenses paid out of separate funds of one spouse can be deducted only by that spouse.

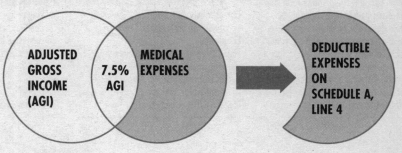

203

DEDUCTIBLE MEDICAL EXPENSES

PROFESSIONAL SERVICES

Chiropodist
Chiropractor (lic.)
Christian Science practitioner
Dermatologist
Dentist
Gynecologist
Neurologist
Obstetrician
Ophthalmologist
Optician
Optometrist
Orthopedist
Osteopath (lic.)
Pediatrician
Physician
Physiotherapist
Plastic surgeon; but see ¶17.3
Podiatrist
Practical or other nonprofessional nurse for medical services only; not for care of a healthy person or a small child who is not ill. Costs for medical care of elderly person, unable to get about, or person subject to spells, are deductible; see ¶17.12.
Psychiatrist
Psychoanalyst
Psychologist
Registered nurse
Surgeon
Payments to an unlicensed practitioner are deductible if the type and quality of his services are not illegal

DENTAL SERVICES

Artificial teeth
Cleaning teeth
Dental X-rays
Extracting teeth
Filling teeth
Gum treatment
Oral surgery
Straightening teeth

EQUIPMENT AND SUPPLIES

Abdominal supports

Air conditioner where necessary for relief from an allergy or for relieving difficulty in breathing; see ¶17.13.
Ambulance hire
Arches
Artificial eyes, limb
Autoette (auto device for handicapped person), but not if used to travel to job or business
Back supports
Braces
Contact lenses
Cost of installing stair-seat elevator for person with heart condition; see ¶17.13.
Crutches
Elastic hosiery
Eyeglasses
Fluoridation unit in home
Hearing aids
Heating devices
Invalid chair
Iron lung
Orthopedic shoes; excess cost over cost of regular shoes
Oxygen or oxygen equipment to relieve breathing problems caused by a medical condition
Reclining chair if prescribed by doctor
Repair of special telephone equipment for the deaf
Sacroiliac belt
Special mattress and plywood bed boards for relief of arthritis or spine
Splints
Truss
Wheelchair
Wig advised by doctor as essential to mental health of person who lost all hair from disease

MEDICAL TREATMENTS

Abortion
Acupuncture
Blood transfusion
Childbirth delivery
Diathermy
Electric shock treatments
Hearing services
Hydrotherapy (water treatments)

Injections
Insulin treatments
Navajo healing ceremonies ("sings")
Nursing
Organ transplant
Prenatal and postnatal treatments
Psychotherapy
Sterilization
Radium therapy
Ultra-violet ray treatments
Vasectomy
Whirlpool baths
X-ray treatments

MEDICINES AND DRUGS

Cost of prescriptions only

LABORATORY EXAMINATIONS AND TESTS

Blood tests
Cardiographs
Metabolism tests
Spinal fluid tests
Sputum tests
Stool examination
Urine analyses
X-ray examinations

HOSPITAL SERVICES

Anesthetist
Hospital bills
Oxygen mask, tent
Use of operating room
Vaccines
X-ray technician

PREMIUMS FOR MEDICAL CARE POLICIES

See ¶17.6 for how to deduct for:

Blue Cross and Blue Shield
Contact lens replacements
Federal voluntary Medicare (Part B) and Federal Medicare (Part A) by persons not covered by Social Security
Health insurance covering hospital, surgical, and other medical expenses
Membership in medical service cooperative

MISCELLANEOUS

Alcoholic inpatient care costs
Asylum; see ¶17.11.
Birth control pills or other birth control items prescribed by your doctor
Braille books—excess cost of braille works over cost of regular editions
Childbirth classes for expectant mother
Clarinet lessons advised by dentist for treatment of tooth defects
Convalescent home—for medical treatment only; see ¶17.11.
Drug treatment center—inpatient care costs
Fees paid to health institute where the exercises, rubdowns, etc., taken there are prescribed by a physician as treatments necessary to alleviate a physical or mental defect or illness
Kidney donor's or possible kidney donor's expenses
Lead-based paint removal to prevent a child who has had lead poisoning from eating the paint. The cost of repainting the scraped area is not deductible.
Legal fees for guardianship of mentally ill spouse where commitment was necessary for medical treatment
Life time care—advance payments made either monthly or as a lump sum under an agreement with a retirement home; see ¶17.11.
Nurse's board and wages, including Social Security taxes paid on wages
Remedial reading for child suffering from dyslexia
Sanitarium and similar institutions; see ¶17.11.
School—payments to a special school for a mentally or physically impaired person if the main reason for using the school is its resources for relieving the disability; see ¶17.10.
"Seeing-eye" dog and its maintenance
Special school costs for physically and mentally handicapped children; see ¶17.10.
Telephone-teletype costs and television adapter for closed caption service for deaf person
Wages of guide for a blind person

NONDEDUCTIBLE MEDICAL EXPENSES

Antiseptic diaper service
Athletic club expenses
Babysitting fees to enable you to make doctor's visits
Boarding school fees paid for healthy child while parent is recuperating from illness
Bottled water bought to avoid drinking fluoridated city water
Cost of divorce recommended by a psychiatrist
Cost of hotel room suggested for sex therapy
Cost of moving away from airport noise by person suffering a nervous breakdown
Cost of trips prescribed by a doctor for a "change of environment" to boost an

ailing person's morale
Dance lessons advised by a doctor as physical and mental therapy or for the alleviation of varicose veins or arthritis
Divorced spouse's medical bills; but see ¶17.7 to deduct them as alimony
Domestic help; but see ¶17.12 if nursing duties are performed
Ear piercing
Funeral, cremation, burial, cemetery plot, monument, or mausoleum
Health programs offered by resort hotels, health clubs, and gyms
Illegal operations and drugs

Marriage counseling fees
Maternity clothes
Premiums on policies guaranteeing you a specified amount of money each week in the event of hospitalization
Scientology fees
Smoking program to improve your general health is not deductible even if suggested by a doctor.
Special food or beverage substitutes; but see ¶17.2
Tattooing
Toothpaste
Transportation costs of a disabled person to

and from work
Travel costs to favorable climate when you can live there permanently
Travel costs to look for a new place to live—on a doctor's advice
Tuition and travel expenses to send a problem child to a particular school for a beneficial change in environment; see ¶17.10.
Weight loss program to improve general health

ALLOWABLE MEDICAL CARE COSTS

¶17.2 A deductible medical expense is any cost of diagnosis, cure, mitigation, treatment, or prevention of disease or any treatment that affects a part or function of the body. *See* the checklist on page 204.

However, expenses that are solely for cosmetic reasons are generally not deductible; nor are expenses incurred to benefit your general health deductible even if recommended by a physician; *see* ¶17.3.

Medicine and drugs. To be deductible, medicines and drugs must be obtainable solely through a prescription by a doctor. You may not deduct the cost of over-the-counter medicines and drugs, such as aspirin and other cold remedies, even if you have a doctor's prescription. The cost of insulin is deductible.

Special foods. According to the IRS, the cost of special food or beverages is not a deductible medical expense if the food or beverages are taken as substitutes for those normally consumed.

EXAMPLE To alleviate an ulcer, your doctor puts you on a special diet. According to the IRS, the cost of your food and beverages is not deductible. The special diet replaces the food you normally eat.

The Tax Court has set its own standard for deducting the extra cost of special foods as medical costs. The test is to show a medical need for taking the special food and the extra cost of the health food over ordinary food. Only the extra cost is deductible.

EXAMPLES 1. Von Kalb suffered from hypoglycemia and her physician prescribed a special high protein diet, which required her to consume twice as much protein as an average person and exclude all processed foods and carbohydrates. She spent $3,483 for food, and deducted 30%, or $1,045, as the extra costs of her high protein diet. The IRS disallowed the deduction, claiming that the protein supplements were a substitute for foods normally consumed. The Tax Court disagreed. The high protein food did not substitute for her usual diet but helped alleviate her hypoglycemia. Thus, she may deduct its additional expense.

2. The Bechers suffered from allergies and were advised by a physician to eat organically grown food to avoid the chemicals in commercial food. The Bechers claimed a medical expense deduction of $2,255, the extra cost of buying organic food.

The IRS disallowed the deduction and the Tax Court agreed. They did not present evidence that their allergies could be cured by limiting their diet to organic food. That the food was beneficial to their general health and was prescribed by a doctor is not sufficient for a deduction.

Childbirth classes. The IRS has ruled that a mother-to-be may deduct the cost of classes instructing her in Lamaze breathing and relaxation techniques, stages of labor, and delivery procedures. If her husband or other childbirth "coach" also attends the classes, the portion of the fee allocable to him or her is not deductible. Furthermore, no deduction is allowed for classes on early pregnancy, fetal development, or caring for newborns.

NONDEDUCTIBLE MEDICAL EXPENSES

¶17.3 The most common nondeductible medical expense is the cost of over-the-counter medicines and drugs, such as aspirin and other cold remedies. A deduction for over-the-counter medicines is disallowed even if you have a doctor's prescription. Also *see* the checklist on page 204.

Starting in 1991, the cost of cosmetic surgery, such as face lift operations and hair transplants, is generally not deductible but there are exceptions; see Law Alert below.

Deductible Cosmetic Surgery

LAW ALERT A medical deduction is allowed for cosmetic surgery only if the surgery is for a disfigurement related to congenital abnormality, disfiguring disease, or injury from an accident.

Exercise, stop-smoking, and weight-reduction programs. If you incur costs for such programs to improve your *general* health, the costs are not deductible even if your doctor has recommended them. However, if your doctor has recommended a program as treatment for a *specific* condition, the IRS has indicated that the cost would be deductible.

INCOME FLOOR APPLIED TO MEDICAL EXPENSE DEDUCTION

¶17.4 A wide range of expenses, such as those listed on page 207, qualify as deductible medical expenses. However, you may not be able to claim the deduction because of a percentage floor. You may deduct only expenses exceeding 7.5% of your adjusted gross income. Adjusted gross income is explained at ¶13.7. For 1992, adjusted gross income is shown on Line 32 of Form 1040.

Married persons filing joint returns figure the 7.5% limit on combined adjusted gross income.

On your 1992 return, you may deduct expenses paid in 1992 for yourself, your spouse, or dependents; *see* ¶17.7. If you borrow to pay medical or dental expenses, you claim the deduction in the year you use the loan proceeds to pay the bill, not in the later year when you repay the loan. If you pay for medical or dental expenses by credit card, the deduction is allowed in the year of the charge.

You may not deduct the payment of expenses you are not legally obliged to pay until 1993 or some later year. You may not deduct medical expenses for which you have been reimbursed by insurance or other awards (¶17.5). Furthermore, reimbursement of medical expenses deducted in prior tax years may be taxable income (¶12.8).

EXAMPLE Your adjusted gross income is $20,000. Your unreimbursed medical expenses were $1,000 for medical care, $210 for prescribed drugs and medicines, and $625 for medical insurance premiums. You deduct medical expenses of $335 figured this way:

Unreimbursed medical care	$1,000
Premiums	625
Drugs	210
Total	$1,835
Less: 7.5% of adjusted gross income (7.5% of $20,000)	1,500
Medical expense deduction	$ 335

REIMBURSEMENTS

¶17.5 Insurance or other reimbursements of your medical costs reduce your medical deductions. Reimbursements for loss of earnings or damages for personal injuries and mental suffering do not.

A reimbursement first reduces the medical expense for which it is paid. The excess is then applied to your other deductible medical costs.

EXAMPLE Premiums paid for medical insurance totaled $800. You paid doctor and hospital bills totaling $700 and purchased prescribed drugs costing $150. Group hospitalization insurance reimbursed $300 for doctors and hospital bills and $25 for medicines and drugs. Your adjusted gross income is $8,000. Your deduction is computed as follows:

Prescribed drugs	$150
Medical care expenses	700
Premiums	800
Total	$1,650
Less reimbursement	325
	$1,325
Less: 7.5% of $8000	600
Medical expense deduction	$ 725

Personal injury settlements or awards. Generally, a cash settlement recovered in a personal injury suit does not reduce your medical expense deduction. The settlement is not treated as reimbursement of your medical bills. But when part of the settlement is specifically earmarked by a court or by law for payment of hospital bills, the medical expense deduction is reduced.

If you receive a settlement for a personal injury that is partly allocable to future medical expenses, you reduce medical expenses for these injuries by the allocated amount until it is used up.

Fake claims. Medical reimbursements for fake injury claims are treated as taxable income.

EXAMPLE Dodge, with the aid of a "friendly" doctor, arranged to be hospitalized for alleged back injuries and realized over $200,000 from HIP policies. The IRS charged that the insurance proceeds were taxable income. Dodge argued they were tax-free reimbursements of medical costs.

The Tax Court sided with the IRS. The tax-free rules cover the payment of legitimate medical costs. Here there were no legitimate medical costs of actual injuries. Dodge took out the policies in a scam arrangement with the doctor.

Reimbursements in excess of your medical expenses. If you paid the entire premium of the policy, the excess payment is not taxed. If you and your employer each contributed to the policy, you generally have to include in income that part of the excess reimbursement which is attributable to employer premium contributions not included in your gross income.

However, you do not have to report any excess reimbursements that are tax-free payments for permanent disfigurement or loss of bodily functions, as discussed in ¶3.1.

If your employer paid the total cost of the policy and the contributions were not taxed to you, you report as income all of your excess reimbursement, unless it covers payment for permanent injury or disfigurement.

EXAMPLES 1. Smith pays premiums of $240 and $120 for two personal health insurance policies. His total medical expenses are $900. He receives $700 from one insurance company and $500 from the other. The excess reimbursement of $300 ($1,200 – $900) is not taxable.

2. Jones' employer paid premiums of $1,800 for two employee health insurance policies covering medical expenses. Jones' medical expenses in one year are $900. He receives $1,200 from the two companies. The entire $300 excess is taxable.

3. Brown's employer paid a premium of $1,000 for a group health policy covering Brown, and Brown himself paid $300 for a personal health policy. His medical expenses are $900. He receives reimbursements of $1,200, $700 under his employer's policy, and $500 under his own policy. Brown's reimbursements exceed expenses by $300, but the

How Your Medical Expense Deduction is Reduced by the 7.5% Limit

If your adjusted gross income is	\$200	\$300	\$400	\$500	\$600	\$700	\$800	\$900	\$1,000	\$1,500	\$2,000
					Your medical expenses are						
					You may deduct						
$ 2,000	50	150	250	350	450	550	650	750	850	1,350	1,850
3,000	0	75	175	275	375	475	575	675	775	1,275	1,775
4,000	0	0	100	200	300	400	500	600	700	1,200	1,700
5,000	0	0	25	125	225	325	425	525	625	1,125	1,625
6,000	0	0	0	50	150	250	350	450	550	1,050	1,550
7,000	0	0	0	0	75	175	275	375	475	975	1,475
8,000	0	0	0	0	0	100	200	300	400	900	1,400
9,000	0	0	0	0	0	25	125	225	325	825	1,325
10,000	0	0	0	0	0	0	50	150	250	750	1,250
11,000	0	0	0	0	0	0	0	75	175	675	1,175
12,000	0	0	0	0	0	0	0	0	100	600	1,100
13,000	0	0	0	0	0	0	0	0	25	525	1,025
14,000	0	0	0	0	0	0	0	0	0	450	950
15,000	0	0	0	0	0	0	0	0	0	375	875
18,000	0	0	0	0	0	0	0	0	0	150	650
20,000	0	0	0	0	0	0	0	0	0	0	500
25,000	0	0	0	0	0	0	0	0	0	0	125
30,000	0	0	0	0	0	0	0	0	0	0	0
40,000	0	0	0	0	0	0	0	0	0	0	0
50,000	0	0	0	0	0	0	0	0	0	0	0

taxable portion attributed to his employer's premium contribution is $175, computed this way:

Reimbursement allocated to Brown's policy, $500/$1,200 × $900	$375
Reimbursement allocated to employer's policy, $700/$1,200 × $900	$525
Taxable excess allocated to employer's policy ($700 – $525)	$175

4. Green's employer paid $1,200 for a health insurance policy but contributed only $450 and deducted $750 from Green's wages. Green also paid $300 for a personal health insurance policy. His medical expenses are $900. He recovered $700 from the employer's policy and $500 from his personal policy. The excess attributable to the employer's policy is $175 (computed as in Example 3 above). However, the taxable portion is only $65.63. Both Green and his employer contributed to the cost of the employer's policy and a further allocation is necessary:

Green's contribution	$ 750
Employer's contribution	450
Total cost of policy	$1,200
Ratio of employer's contribution to annual cost of policy (450/1,200 or 37.50%)	
Taxable portion—37.50% of excess reimbursement of $175	$65.63

Reimbursement in a later year may be taxed. If you took a medical expense deduction in one year and are reimbursed for all or part of the expense in a later year, the reimbursement may be taxed in the year received. The reimbursement is generally taxable income to the extent the deduction reduced your tax in the prior year. For further details for figuring taxable income on a recovery of a prior deduction, see ¶12.8.

EXAMPLES

1. In 1991, you had adjusted gross income of $12,000. You claimed itemized deductions which exceeded your allowable standard deduction by $1,000; on your Schedule A, you listed medical expenses of $1,300. You deducted $700 computed as follows:

Medical expenses	$1,300
Less: 7.5% of $12,000	900
Allowable deduction	$ 400

In 1992 you collect $300 from insurance, reimbursing part of your 1991 medical expenses. If you had collected that amount in 1991, your medical expense deduction would have been $100. The entire reimbursement of $300 is subject to tax in 1992. It is the amount by which the 1991 deduction of $400 exceeds the deduction of $100 that would have been allowed if the reimbursement had been received in 1991.

2. Same facts as in Example 1 above, but you did not deduct medical expenses in 1991 because you did not itemize deductions. The reimbursement in 1992 is not taxable.

PREMIUMS OF MEDICAL CARE POLICIES

¶17.6 You may deduct as medical expenses premiums paid for medical care policies covering yourself, your spouse, or dependents. There is no separate deduction for health insurance premiums. All qualifying premiums are treated as medical expenses subject to the overall 7.5% limit. Premiums are deductible for policies such as Blue Cross, Blue Shield, and Federal Voluntary Medicare insurance (Medicare Part B). Payment for coverage under Medicare (Part A)

is deductible by those over age 65 who are not covered by Social Security. Deductions may be claimed for membership payments in associations furnishing cooperative or free-choice medical services, group hospitalization, or clinical care policies, including HMOs (health maintenance organizations) and medical care premiums paid to colleges as part of a tuition bill, if the amount is separately stated in the bill.

Deduct premiums for health insurance providing reimbursements for hospital, surgical, drug costs, and other medical expenses. Also deductible are premiums paid for contact lens replacement and premiums on policies providing solely for indemnity for hospital and surgical expenses.

Premiums paid before you reach age 65 for medical care insurance for protection after you reach age 65 are deductible in the year paid if they are payable on a level payment basis under the contract (1) for a period of 10 years or more; or (2) until the year you reach age 65 (but in no case for a period of less than five years).

Nondeductible premiums. You may *not* deduct premiums for a policy guaranteeing you a specified amount each week (not to exceed a specified number of weeks) in the event you are hospitalized. Also, no deduction may be claimed for premiums paid for a policy which compensates you for loss of earnings while ill or injured, or for loss of life, limb, or sight. If your policy covers both medical care and loss of income or loss of life, limb, or sight, no part of the premium is deductible unless (1) the contract or separate statement from the insurance company states what part of the premium is allocated to medical care; and (2) the premium allocated to medical care is reasonable.

You may not deduct part of car insurance premiums for medical insurance coverage for persons injured by or in your car.

Self-Employed Deduction

On your 1992 Form 1040, you may deduct 25% of health insurance premiums paid before July 1, 1992 for coverage for yourself, spouse, and dependents. *See* the Supplement for an update on legislation that would extend the deduction to premiums paid after June 30, 1992. The deduction is claimed on Line 26 of Form 1040.

You also qualify for the 25% deduction if you received wages in 1992 from an S corporation in which you were a more than 2% shareholder. The 25% deduction may not be claimed if you are covered as an employee under another employer's plan, or if you are covered under your spouse's employer's plan. The deduction may not exceed net earned income from the business under which the health plan is established. The remaining 75% of the premiums is deductible as a medical expense on Schedule A subject to the 7.5% income floor.

EXPENSES OF YOUR SPOUSE AND DEPENDENTS

¶17.7 You may deduct as medical expenses your payments of medical bills for your spouse if you were married *either* at the time the expenses were incurred or at the time the bills were paid. That is, you may deduct your payment of your spouse's medical bills even though you are divorced or widowed, if, at the time the expenses were incurred, you were married. Furthermore, if your spouse incurred medical expenses before you married and you pay the bills after you marry, you may deduct the expense.

Expenses of Children and Other Dependents

You may deduct your payment of medical bills for your children or other dependents, subject to the 7.5% floor of ¶17.4. The person must be an individual you could have claimed as a dependent (¶1.18) except for the fact that he or she earned more than $2,300 or filed a joint return. You must be able to prove you: (1) paid the medical expenses; and (2) contributed more than half the support. See ¶1.18 for a list of persons you may claim as dependents. The relationship or member of household test must be satisfied either at the time the expense was incurred or at the time you paid it.

EXAMPLES 1. Your spouse has doctor bills covering an operation performed in 1991, before you were married. You married in 1992. You pay those bills in 1992. You may claim a medical expense deduction for your payment.

2. In October 1991, your spouse had dental work done. In February 1992 you are divorced; in April 1992, you pay your former spouse's dental bills. You may deduct the payment on your 1992 tax return.

3. In 1992, you pay medical expenses for your spouse who died in 1992. You remarry in 1992. On a joint return which you file with your new spouse in 1992, you may deduct your payment of your deceased spouse's medical expenses.

4. You contribute more than half of your married son's support, including a payment of a medical expense of $800. Because he filed a joint return with his wife, you may not claim him as a dependent. But you still may deduct your payment of the $800 medical expense. You contributed more than half of his support.

5. Your mother underwent an operation in November 1991. You paid for the operation in February 1992. You may deduct the cost of the operation in 1992 if you furnished more than one-half of your mother's support in either 1991 or 1992.

Divorced and separated parents. You may be able to deduct your payment of your child's medical costs, even though your ex-spouse is entitled to claim the child as a dependent. For purposes of the medical deduction, the child is considered to be the dependent of *both* parents if (1) they are divorced or legally separated under a court agreement, separated under a written agreement, or married but living apart during the last six months of 1992; (2) the child was in the custody of one or both parents for more than half of 1992; and (3) more than half of the child's 1992 support was provided by both parents.

A child may not deduct medical expenses paid with his parent's welfare payments.

EXAMPLE A son is the legal guardian of his mother who is mentally incompetent. As guardian, he received his mother's state welfare and Social Security benefits which he deposited in his personal bank account and used to pay part of his mother's medical expenses. On his tax return, he claimed a deduction for the total medical expenses paid on behalf of his mother. The court held that he could deduct only medical expenses in excess of the amounts received as welfare and Social Security payments. The benefits, to the extent used for medical expenses, represented the mother's payments in her own behalf.

Adopted children. You may deduct medical expenses of an adopted child if you may claim the child as a dependent either when the medical services are rendered or when you pay the expenses. An adopted child may be claimed as a dependent when a court has approved the adoption. In the absence of a court decree, the child is your dependent if he or she was placed in your home by an authorized agency and was a member of your household the rest of the year; see ¶1.20. If he or she has not been placed in your custody by an authorized agency, you have to show that the child lived in your home for the entire year.

If you reimburse an adoption agency for medical expenses it paid under an agreement with you, you are considered to have paid the expenses. But reimbursement of expenses incurred and paid before adoption negotiations does not qualify them as your medical expenses and you may not deduct them.

You may not deduct medical expenses for services rendered to the natural mother of the child you adopt.

Multiple support agreements. You may be able to deduct your payment of a relative's medical expenses although you do not contribute more than one-half of his or her support. You must meet the tests for a multiple support agreement; *see* ¶1.27. If your relative has a gross income of $2,300 or more, you may still deduct your payment of medical expenses provided the other tests for multiple support are met.

You may deduct only the amount you actually pay for the relative's medical expenses. If you are reimbursed by others who signed the multiple support agreement, you must reduce your deduction by the amount of reimbursement.

EXAMPLE You and your brother and sister share equally in the support of your mother. Part of your mother's support includes medical expenses. Should the three of you share in the payment of the bills or should only one of you pay them? The answer: Payment should be made by the person who may claim her as a dependent under a multiple support agreement. Only that person may deduct the payment. If you are going to claim her as an exemption, you should pay the bill. You may deduct the payment although you did not contribute more than half of her support. If your brother and sister reimburse you for part of the bill, you must reduce your medical deduction by the amount of the reimbursement. Neither your brother nor your sister may deduct this share. Thus, a deduction is lost for these amounts.

DECEDENT'S MEDICAL EXPENSES

¶17.8 The executor or administrator of a decedent's estate may pay the decedent's medical expenses out of the estate. Where the expenses are paid within one year of death, they may be treated as paid when incurred and claimed as income tax deductions. Thus, a claim for refund or an amended return may be filed for an earlier year when the expenses were incurred but not paid until after death by the executor.

EXAMPLE Jones incurred medical expenses of $500 in 1991 and $300 in 1992. He died June 1, 1992, without having paid these expenses. He had already filed his 1991 return before the due date. In August 1992, his executor pays the $800 in medical expenses. He may file an amended return for 1991 and claim a medical expense deduction for the $500 and get a refund for the increased deductions. He may claim the remaining $300 as a medical expense deduction on Jones' final return.

A decedent's medical expenses claimed as an income tax deduction may not again be claimed as an estate tax deduction. If the expenses may be claimed as an estate tax deduction but are claimed as an income tax deduction, the executor must file a statement with the decedent's income tax return that the expenses have not been deducted on the estate tax return and the estate waives its right to deduct them for estate tax purposes.

If medical expenses are claimed as an income tax deduction, the portion of the expenses that are below the 7.5% floor and, therefore, not deductible, may not be deducted on the estate tax return. Although the expenses were not actually deducted, the IRS considers them to be part of the overall income tax deduction.

TRAVEL COSTS MAY BE MEDICAL DEDUCTIONS

¶17.9 You may deduct the cost of travel to a place where you receive medical treatment or which is prescribed as a place that will help relieve a specific chronic ailment. Trips to and from a doctor's office are the most common type of deductible travel expense.

The amount of the deduction is limited to the cost of transportation, such as the cost of operating a car or fares for public transportation. If you use your automobile, you may deduct a flat rate of 9¢ a mile and, in addition, you may deduct parking fees and tolls. If, however, auto expenses exceed this standard mileage rate, you may deduct your actual out-of-pocket costs for gas, oil, repairs, tolls, and parking fees. Do not include depreciation, general maintenance, or car insurance.

EXAMPLE You drive your car to a doctor's office for treatment. You made 40 such round trips of 25 miles each. As the total mileage is 1,000 miles, you claim $90 (1,000 × 9¢) as medical expenses. If you incurred tolls or parking fees during the trips, you add these expenses to the deduction.

Important: The 9¢ rate was effective when this edition went to press. Any change in the rate is listed in the Supplement.

Lodging expenses. Your lodging expenses while away from home are not deductible as medical expenses unless the trip is primarily to receive treatment from a doctor in a licensed hospital, hospital-related out-patient facility, or a facility equivalent to a hospital. Food expenses are not deductible.

EXAMPLE Polyak spent the winter in Florida on the advice of her doctor to alleviate a chronic heart and lung condition. While in Florida, she stayed in a rented trailer that cost $1,426. She saw a physician for treatment of an infection and to renew medications. She deducted the trailer costs as a medical deduction, which the IRS and Tax Court disallowed. Although her Florida trip was primarily for mitigating her condition, she did not travel to receive medical care from a physician in a licensed hospital or related out-patient facility. The medical care was routine and incidental to her travel to Florida. Her deduction for transportation costs to Florida was not contested by the IRS, which conceded that the trip was primarily for and essential to her health.

The deduction for lodging while receiving treatment at a licensed hospital, outpatient clinic, or hospital-equivalent facility is limited to $50 per night per person. For example, the limit is $100 if a parent travels with a sick child. The IRS ruled that the $50 allowance could be claimed by a parent for a six-week hotel stay while her eight-year-old daughter was treated in a nearby hospital for serious injuries received in an automobile accident. The mother's presence was necessary so that she could sign release forms.

DEDUCTIBLE TRANSPORTATION COSTS—

Examples of travel costs which have been allowed as medical deductions by rulings or court decisions are:

Nurse's fare if nurse is required on trip.

Parent's fare if parent is needed to accompany child who requires medical care.

Parent's fare to visit his child at an institution where the visits are prescribed by a doctor.

Trip to visit specialist in another city.

Airplane fare to a distant city in which a patient used to live to have a checkup by a family doctor living there. That he could have received the same examination in the city in which he presently lived did not bar his deduction.

Trip to escape a climate that is bad for a specific condition. For example, the cost of a trip from a northern state to Florida during the winter on the advice of a doctor to relieve a chronic heart condition is deductible. The cost of a trip made by a person recovering from a throat operation was ruled deductible.

Travel to an Alcoholics Anonymous club meeting if membership in the group has been advised by a doctor.

Disabled veteran's commuting expenses where a doctor prescribed work and driving as therapy.

Wife's trip to provide nursing care for an ailing husband in a distant city. The trip was ordered by her husband's doctor as a necessity.

Driving prescribed as therapy.

Travel costs of kidney transplant donor or prospective donor.

NONDEDUCTIBLE TRANSPORTATION COSTS—

Trip for the general improvement of your health.

Traveling to areas of favorable climates during the year for general health reasons, rather than living permanently in a locality suitable for your health.

Meals while on a trip for medical treatment—even if cost of transportation is a valid medical cost. However, a court has allowed the deduction of the extra cost of specially prepared food.

Trip to get "spiritual" rather than medical aid. For example, cost of trip to the Shrine of Our Lady of Lourdes is not deductible.

Moving a family to a climate more suitable to an ill mother's condition. Only the mother's travel costs are deductible.

Moving household furnishings to area advised by physician.

Operating an auto or special vehicle to go to work because of disabled condition. The cost of wheelchair, autoette or special auto devices for handicapped persons is deductible.

Convalescence cruise advised by a doctor for a patient recovering from pneumonia.

Loss on sale of car bought for medical travel.

Medical seminar cruise taken by patient whose condition was reviewed by physicians taking the cruise.

SCHOOLING FOR THE MENTALLY OR PHYSICALLY HANDICAPPED

¶17.10 You may deduct as medical expenses the costs of sending a mentally or physically handicapped person to a special school or institution to overcome or alleviate his or her handicap. Such costs may cover:

Teaching of braille or lip reading.

Training, caring for, supervising, and treating a mentally retarded person.

Cost of meals and lodgings, if boarding is required at the school.

Costs of regular education courses also taught at the school, provided they are incidental to the special courses and services furnished by the school.

The parent of a child with psychological problems may deduct only that part of a private school fee directly related to psychological aid given to the child.

The fact that a particular school or camp is recommended for an emotionally disturbed child by a psychiatrist will not qualify the tuition as a deduction if the school or camp has no special program geared to the child's specific personal problem. However, you may deduct the costs of maintaining a mentally retarded person in a home specially selected to meet the standards set by his psychiatrist to aid him in his adjustment from life in a mental hospital to community living.

Payment for future medical care expenses is deductible if immediate payment is required by contract.

EXAMPLES 1. An emotionally disturbed child was sent to a private school maintaining a staff of three psychologists. His father deducted the school fee of $6,270 as a medical expense. The IRS disallowed the amount, claiming that the child, who was neither mentally retarded nor handicapped, was sent to school primarily for an education. The Tax Court allowed the father to deduct $3,000 covering the psychological treatment.

2. A retarded boy had been excluded from several schools for the mentally handicapped because he needed close attention. The director of a military academy had extensive experience in training young boys. Although it was not the usual practice of the academy to enroll mentally handicapped children, the director accepted the boy on a day-to-day basis as a personal challenge. The Tax Court held that the cost of both tuition and transportation to bring the boy to and from the school were deductible medical expenses. The primary purpose of the training given the boy was not ordinary education but remedial training designed to overcome his handicap. But note that in other cases, a deduction for tuition of a military school to which a child was sent in order to remove him from a tense family environment, and the cost of a blind boy's attendance at a regular private school which made a special effort to accommodate his braille equipment, were disallowed.

SENIOR CITIZEN CARE FACILITIES

¶17.11 A payment for meals and lodging to a nursing home, convalescent home, home for the aged, or sanitarium is a deductible medical expense if the patient is confined for medical treatment.

If you cannot prove that the patient entered the home for medical care (which would permit a deduction for meals and lodging in addition to medical costs), you may nevertheless deduct that part of the cost covering actual medical and nursing care.

In an unusual case, a court allowed a medical expense deduction for apartment rent of an aged parent.

EXAMPLE A doctor recommended to Ungar that his 90-year-old mother, convalescing from a brain hemorrhage, could receive better care at less expense in accommodations away from a hospital. A two-room apartment was rented, hospital equipment installed, and nurses engaged for seven months. The rent totaled $1,400. Ungar's sister, who worked in her husband's shoe store, nursed her mother for six weeks. Ungar paid the wages of a clerk who was hired to substitute for his sister in the store. Ungar deducted both the rent and wages as medical expenses. The IRS disallowed them; a Tax Court reversed the IRS' decision. The apartment rent was no less a medical expense than the cost of a hospital room. As for the clerk's wages, they too were deductible medical costs. The clerk was hired specifically to allow the daughter to nurse her mother, thereby avoiding the larger, though more direct, medical expense of hiring a nurse.

Establishing medical purpose. The following facts are helpful in establishing the full deductibility of payments to a nursing home, convalescent home, home for the aged, or sanitarium:

The patient entered the institution on the direction or suggestion of a doctor.

Attendance or treatment at the institution had a direct therapeutic effect on the condition suffered by the patient.

The attendance at the institution was for a specific ailment rather than for a "general" health condition. Simply showing that the patient suffers from an ailment is not sufficient proof that he or she is in the home for treatment.

Payment for future lifetime care. Generally, no deduction is allowed for prepayment of medical expenses for services to be performed in a later taxable year. However, this disallowance rule does not apply where there is a current obligation to pay.

EXAMPLES 1. A 78-year-old man entered into an agreement with a retirement home. For a lump-sum payment, the home agreed to provide lifetime care, including medical care, medicine, and hospitalization. The lifetime care fee was calculated without regard to fees received from other patients and was not insurance. The home allocated 30% of the lump-sum payment to medical expenses based on its prior experience. The IRS holds that this part of the payment is deductible in the year paid. It holds that the legal obligation to pay the medical expenses was incurred at the time the lump-sum payment was made, even though medical services would not be performed until a future time, if at all. Should any portion of the lump-sum payment be refunded, that part attributable to the deducted amount must be reported as income; see ¶12.8.

2. Parents contracted with an institution to care for their handicapped child after their death. The contract provided for payments as follows: 20% on signing, 10% within 12 months, 10% within 24 months, and the balance when the child enters. Payment of specified amounts at specified intervals was a condition imposed by the institution for its agreement to accept the child for lifetime care. Since the obligation to pay was incurred at the time payments were made, they are deductible as medical expenses, although the medical services were not to be performed until a future time, if at all.

3. A couple entered a retirement home which would provide them with accommodations, meals, and medical care for life. They agreed to pay a founder's fee of $40,000 and a monthly fee of $800. If they leave the home, they may get a refund of a portion of the founder's fee. Fifteen percent of the monthly fee and 10% of the founder's fee will be used for medical care and 5% of the founder's fee will be used for construction of a health facility. On the basis of these figures, the couple may deduct as medical costs 10% of the founder's fee and 15% of the monthly fee. However, the portion of the founder's fee for the possible health facility does not qualify as a medical expense. Finally, any refund of the founder's fee received in a later year may be income to the extent medical deductions were previously claimed for the fees.

4. An entrance fee to a retirement community gave new residents not only the right to live in the development but also the right to 30 days of free care at a nearby convalescent home in the first year, with additional free days in later years of residency. The community allocated 7% of the $20,000 entrance fee, or $1,400, to the convalescent care. Smith deducted the $1,400 as a medical expense, which the IRS disallowed. It claimed that the amount could not be deducted in the year of payment because most of the promised free services would not be received until future years. The Tax Court disagreed and allowed the deduction because the obligation to pay was incurred when the residency agreement was signed.

NURSES' WAGES

¶17.12 The costs of a nurse attending an ill person are deductible. Costs include any Social Security (FICA) tax paid by you. You may deduct the expenses of a nurse who is not registered or licensed so long as he or she provides you with medical services. Medical services include giving medications, changing dressings, and bathing and grooming the patient. If the nurse also performs domestic services, deduct only that part of the pay attributable to medical aid to the patient.

The cost of an attendant's meals is included in your medical expenses. Divide total food costs among the household members to determine the attendant's share.

Costs eligible for tax credit. If, in order to work, you pay a nurse to look after a physically or mentally disabled dependent, you may be able to claim a credit for all or part of the nurse's wages as a dependent care expense. You may not, however, claim both a credit and a medical expense deduction. First, you claim the nurse's wages as a dependent care cost. If not all of the wages are allowed as care costs because of the expense limits (Chapter 25), the remaining balance is deductible as a medical expense.

The salary of a clerk hired specifically to relieve a wife from her husband's store in order to care for her ill mother was allowed as a medical expense; *see* the example in ¶17.11.

EXAMPLES 1. Dodge's wife was arthritic. His doctor advised that he have someone take care of her to prevent her from falling. He moved her to his daughter's home and paid the daughter to care for her mother. He deducted the payments to his daughter. The IRS disallowed the deduction, claiming that the daughter was not a trained nurse. The Tax Court allowed that part of the deduction specifically attributed to nursing aid. Whether a medical service has been rendered depends on the nature of the services rendered, not on the qualifications or title of the person who renders them. Here, the daughter's services, following the doctor's advice, qualify as medical care.

2. A husband hires a domestic to care for his home so that his wife can get a complete rest as prescribed by her doctor. He may deduct only that part of the domestic's salary directly attributed to nursing aid given to the wife. No deduction is allowed for the cost of the domestic services in the home; *see* Chapter 25.

3. An attendant hired by a quadriplegic performs household duties, in addition to caring for his medical and personal needs. The quadriplegic pays him wages and also provides food and lodging. According to the IRS, a medical expense deduction is allowable only for that portion of the wages attributable to medical and personal care. The wages are apportioned on the basis of time spent performing nursing-type services and time spent performing household duties. The same allocation is used to determine the portion of the cost of the attendant's meals which are deductible as a medical expense. However, the attendant's lodging is not deductible as a medical expense, unless the quadriplegic shows additional expenditures directly attributable to lodging the attendant such as paying increased rent for an apartment with another bedroom for the attendant.

HOME IMPROVEMENTS AS MEDICAL EXPENSES

¶**17.13** A disease or ailment may require the construction of special equipment or facilities in a home: A heart patient may need an elevator to carry him or her upstairs; a polio patient, a pool; and an asthmatic patient, an air cleaning system.

You may deduct the full cost of minor equipment installed for a medical reason if it does not increase the value of your property, as for example, the cost of a detachable window air conditioner. Where equipment increases the value of your property, you may generally take a medical deduction only to the extent that the cost of the equipment exceeds the increase in the value of the property. This increased-value test does *not* apply to certain structural changes to a residence made by a handicapped person; *see* page 212. Of course, if the equipment does not increase the value of the property, its entire cost is deductible, even though it is permanently fixed to the property.

EXAMPLE Gerard's daughter suffered from cystic fibrosis. While there is no known cure for the disease, doctors attempt to prolong life by preventing pulmonary infection. One approach is to maintain a constant temperature and high humidity. A doctor recommended that Gerard install a central air-conditioning unit in his home for his daughter. It cost $1,300 and increased the value of his home by $800. The $500 balance was a deductible medical expense.

CAUTION ## Deducting Cost of Swimming Pool

If swimming is prescribed as physical therapy, the cost of constructing a home swimming pool may be partly deductible as a medical expense but only to the extent the cost exceeds the increase in value to the house. However, the IRS is likely to question any deduction because of the possibility that the pool may be used for recreation. If you can show that the pool is specially equipped to alleviate your condition and is not generally suited for recreation, the IRS will allow the deduction unless the expense is considered to be "lavish or extravagant." For example, the IRS allowed a deduction for a pool constructed by an osteoarthritis patient. His physician prescribed swimming several times a day as treatment. He built an indoor lap pool with specially designed stairs and a hydrotherapy device. Given these features, the IRS concluded that the pool was specially designed to provide medical treatment.

In one case the IRS tried to limit the cost of a luxury indoor pool built for therapeutic reasons to the least expensive construction. The Tax Court rejected the IRS position, holding that a medical expense is not to be limited to the cheapest form of treatment; on appeal, the IRS position was adopted.

If, instead of building a pool, you buy a home with a pool, can you deduct the part of the purchase price allocated to the pool? The Tax Court said no. The purchase price of the house includes the fair market value of the pool. Therefore, there is no extra cost above the increase in the home's value which would support a medical expense deduction.

The operating costs of an indoor pool were allowed by the Tax Court as a deduction to an emphysema sufferer.

EXAMPLE Cherry was advised by his doctor to swim to relieve his severe emphysema and bronchitis. He could not swim at local health spas; they did not open early enough or stay open late enough to allow him to swim before or after work. His home was too small for a pool. He bought a lot and built a new house with an indoor pool. He used the pool several times a day, and swimming improved his condition; if he did not swim, his symptoms returned. Cherry deducted pool operating costs of $4,000 for fuel, electricity, insurance, and repairs. The IRS disallowed the deductions claiming that the pool was used for personal recreation. Besides, it did not have special medical equipment. The Tax Court allowed the deduction. Cherry built the pool to swim in order to exercise his lungs. That there was no special equipment is irrelevant; Cherry did not need special ramps, railings, a shallow floor, or whirlpool. Finally, his family rarely used the pool.

A deduction is barred where the primary purpose of the improvement is for personal convenience rather than medical necessity.

EXAMPLE Haines broke his leg in a skiing accident and underwent various forms of physical therapy, including swimming. To aid his recovery, his physician recommended that he install a swimming pool at his home. The Tax Court agreed with the IRS that the cost of the pool was not deductible. Although swimming was beneficial to his condition, he needed special therapy only for a limited period of time, and he could have gotten it at less cost at a nearby public pool. Finally, because of weather conditions, the pool could not be used for about half of the year.

Cost of maintaining and operating improvement. The expense of maintaining and operating equipment installed for medical reasons may be claimed as a medical expense, even if the cost of the equipment and its installation is not deductible under the rules in this section.

Handicapped Persons

The increased-value test does not apply to a handicapped person who makes structural changes to a residence such as adding ramps, modifying doorways and stairways, installing railings and support bars, and altering cabinets, outlets, fixtures, and warning systems. Such improvements are treated for medical deduction purposes as not increasing the value of the house. Lifts, but not elevators, also are in this category. The full cost of such improvements is added to other deductible expenses and the total is deductible to the extent that it exceeds the 7.5% floor.

COSTS DEDUCTIBLE AS BUSINESS EXPENSES

¶17.14 The following examples illustrate cases in which expenses are deductible as business expenses rather than as medical expenses. Claiming a business deduction is preferable because the deduction is not subject to the 7.5% adjusted gross income floor.

Costs of a checkup required by your employer are business expenses and are not subject to the 7.5% floor.

EXAMPLE An airline pilot is required by his company to take a semi-annual physical exam at his own expense. If he fails to produce a resultant certificate of good health, he is subject to discharge. The cost of such checkups certifying physical fitness for a job is an ordinary and necessary business expense. If the doctor prescribes a treatment or further examinations to maintain the pilot's physical condition, the cost of these subsequent treatments or examinations may be deducted only as medical expenses, even though they are needed to maintain the physical standards required by the job. Thus, a professional singer who consults a throat specialist may not deduct the fee as a business expense. The fee is a medical expense subject to the 7.5% floor.

The Tax Court allowed the costs of psychoanalysis by a licensed social worker working as a therapist to be deducted as an education cost.

Handicapped persons. Some expenses incurred by a physically handicapped person due to his or her handicap may be deductible as a business expense rather than as a medical expense. A business expense deduction may be allowed if the expense is necessary for you to satisfactorily perform your job and is not required or used, except incidentally, for personal purposes.

If you are self-employed, claim the deduction on Schedule C.

If you are an employee, the expenses are listed on Form 2106 and if not reimbursed, entered on Schedule A. The expenses are a fully deductible miscellaneous itemized deduction; the 2% AGI floor does *not* apply.

EXAMPLES 1. A blind person requires a reader to help him perform his job. The costs of the reader's services are deductible as an itemized business deduction.

2. A professor is paralyzed from the waist down and confined to a wheelchair. When he attends out-of-town professional meetings, he has his wife, a friend, or a colleague accompany him to help him with baggage, stairs, narrow doors, and to sit with him on airplanes when airlines will not allow wheelchair passengers without an attendant. While he does not pay them a salary, he does pay their travel costs. He may deduct these costs as business expenses. They are incurred solely because of his occupation.

3. An attorney uses prostheses due to bilateral amputation of his legs and takes medication several times a day for other ailments. On business trips, his wife or a neighbor accompanies him to help him travel and receive medication. He may deduct the out-of-town expenses paid for his neighbor only as a medical expense. The neighbor's services are not business expenses as he regularly uses them for personal purposes. When his wife accompanies him, he may deduct her transportation costs as a medical expense; her food and lodging are nondeductible ordinary living expenses.

18 CASUALTY AND THEFT LOSSES AND INVOLUNTARY CONVERSION GAINS

The tax treatment of an unreimbursed casualty or theft loss depends on the purpose for which you held the damaged, destroyed or stolen property. A loss of property held for—

- *Personal purposes* is deducted as an itemized deduction on Schedule A (Line 17). Each loss to personal-use property must be reduced by $100; *see* ¶18.11. The loss also is subject to the 10% adjusted gross income floor (¶18.11) and the sudden events tests of ¶18.5. Personal residences, cars, jewelry, and clothing are examples of property held for personal use.

  The itemized deduction claimed for personal use property is not subject to the 3% reduction computation (¶13.8).

- *Income-producing purposes,* such as negotiable securities, is deducted on Schedule A (Line 20). The loss deduction is subject to the 2% AGI floor. It is not subject to the $100 and 10% adjusted gross income floors, or the sudden event test.

  The 3% reduction does apply to a loss deduction for income-producing property claimed on Line 20 of Schedule A.

- *Business or rental purposes* is claimed as a loss on Form 4797. It is not subject to any floor or the sudden event test.

Use Form 4684 to determine the tax treatment of a casualty or theft. It has been designed to direct you to the proper method of treating the casualty or theft, and to the schedule for reporting your loss, or gain if compensation for your loss exceeded the basis of the property. If you suffer more than one casualty or theft in 1992, use separate Forms 4684 to figure the loss for each event.

If you have realized a gain, you may defer tax by replacing or repairing the property; *see* ¶18.18.

Appraisal fees and other incidental costs, such as taking photos to establish the amount of the loss, are claimed as a miscellaneous itemized deduction on Line 20 of Schedule A.

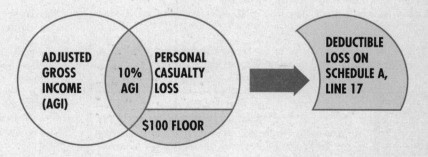

WHEN TO DEDUCT A CASUALTY OR THEFT LOSS

¶18.1 Generally, you deduct a casualty loss in the year the casualty occurs, regardless of when you repair or replace damaged or destroyed property. But say a casualty occurs in one year and you do not discover the damage until a later year, or you know damage has been inflicted, but you do not know the full extent of the loss because you expect reimbursement in a later year. Here is what to do:

If you reasonably expect reimbursement in a later year. You should deduct in the year the casualty occurred only that part of your loss (after applying the personal property floors of ¶18.11) for which you do not expect reimbursement. For example, if you expect a full insurance recovery next year for a 1992 loss, you would take no deduction in 1992.

If you do not expect any reimbursement and deduct a loss in 1992, but you receive insurance or other reimbursement in 1993, the reimbursement is taxable in 1993 to the extent that the 1992 deduction gave you a tax benefit by reducing your 1992 taxable income; *see* ¶12.8. You may not amend your 1992 tax return.

EXAMPLE In 1969, Hurricane Camille destroyed oceanfront real estate owned jointly by two brothers. The buildings were insured under two policies which included wind damage but not losses resulting from floods, tidal waves, or water. The insurers, claiming the tidal wave had caused the destruction, denied their claim. The brothers consulted an attorney about the possibility of suit against the insurance companies, but there seemed little likelihood of recovery, so they deducted their shares of the casualty loss in 1969. However, in January 1970, the adjusters of both companies changed their decisions, reimbursing the brothers for more than two-thirds of their loss. One of the brothers filed an amended 1969 tax return, reducing the previously reported casualty loss.

The IRS claimed that the insurance recovery is taxable in the year of receipt, 1970, to the extent that the prior deduction reduced 1969 income. The brother claimed that he made an error in claiming the deduction in 1969 because he had a reasonable prospect of reimbursement. Therefore, he was not entitled to the deduction; his amended return reducing the deduction by the reimbursement was proper.

The Tax Court disagreed. Tax liability is based on facts as they exist at the end of each year. A recovery in a later tax year does not prove that a reasonable prospect of recovery existed in the earlier year. Amendments to previously filed tax returns may be made only to correct mathematical errors or miscalculations, not to rearrange facts and readjust income for two years.

If your reimbursement is less than you expected. Assume you took no loss deduction in 1992 because you expected to recover your entire loss in 1993—but the insurance company refuses to pay your claim. When do you deduct your loss? You deduct your loss in the year you find that you have no reasonable prospect of recovery. For example, you sue the company in 1993, with a reasonable prospect of winning your claim. However, in 1994, a court rules against you. You deduct your loss in 1994, subject to the personal property floors of ¶18.11.

If you, as lessee, are liable to the lessor for damage to property, you may deduct the loss in the year you pay the lessor.

Loss Discovered in Later Year

If you do not discover the loss until a later year, IRS regulations do not specifically allow a deduction for the loss in the year it is discovered, but court decisions have. In one case, an unseasonable blizzard damaged a windbreak planted to protect a house, buildings, and livestock. The damage to the evergreens did not become apparent until the next year, when about half of the trees died and the others were of little value. The court held that the loss occurred in the later year. In another case, hurricane damage did not become apparent for two years. The Tax Court allowed the deduction in the later year. Where drought damage occurs; *see* ¶18.5

If your loss is in a federal disaster area. If your property is damaged in an area eligible for federal disaster assistance, you have a choice of years for which the loss may be claimed; *see* ¶18.2.

If reimbursements exceed your adjusted basis for the property. Receiving reimbursements in excess of adjusted basis results in a gain that you must report on your return unless you acquire qualifying replacement property and elect to defer the gain; *see* ¶18.18.

If a loss deduction was claimed in a prior year, you must report the reimbursement as income to the extent the prior deduction reduced your taxable income in the year claimed; *see* ¶12.8.

DISASTER LOSSES

¶18.2

If you suffer a loss to property from a disaster in an area declared by the President as warranting federal assistance, you may deduct the loss either on the return for the year of the loss or on the return of the prior tax year. The amount of the loss is figured under the rules of ¶18.12.

You may elect to claim the deduction on a tax return for the previous year any time on or before the *later* of (1) the due date (without extensions) of the return for the year of the disaster; or (2) the due date considering any extension for filing the return for the prior tax year. You make an election in a signed statement attached to your return (original or amended) or refund claim. List the date of the disaster and where the property was located (city, town, county, and state). To amend a filed return for the prior year, use Form 1040X.

EXAMPLES 1. *1992 disaster losses claimed on 1991 return.* You generally have until April 15, 1993, to amend a 1991 tax return to claim a disaster loss occurring during 1992.

2. *1993 disaster losses claimed on 1992 return.* You generally have until April 15, 1994, to amend a 1992 tax return to claim a disaster loss occurring during 1993.

Should You Claim Loss in Prior Year?

Consider making the election if the deduction on the return of the prior year gives a greater tax reduction than if claimed on the return for the year in which the loss occurred or you want a refund of all or part of the tax paid for the prior year.

Revoking your decision. After making your election of which year to claim the disaster loss, you have 90 days in which to revoke it. After the 90-day period, the election becomes irrevocable. However, where an early election is made, you have until the due date for filing your return for the year of the disaster to change your election.

Your revocation of an election is not effective unless you repay any credit or refund resulting from the election within the revocation period. A revocation made before you receive a refund will not be effective unless you repay the refund within 30 days after you receive it.

Homeowners forced to relocate. If you were forced to relocate or demolish your home in a disaster area, you may be able to claim the loss even though the damage, such as from erosion, does not meet the sudden test of ¶18.5. For example, after a severe storm, there is danger to a group of homes from nearby mudslides. State officials order homeowners to evacuate and relocate their homes. Under prior law, a deduction could be barred if there was no actual physical damage to the home. A current law allows disaster loss treatment if these tests are met: (1) the President has determined that the area warrants federal disaster relief; (2) within 120 days of the President's order, you are ordered by the state or local government to demolish or relocate your residence; and (3) the home was rendered unsafe by the erosion or other disaster. The law applies to vacation homes and rental properties, as well as to principal residences.

The loss is treated as a disaster loss so that you may elect to deduct the loss either in the year the demolition or relocation order is made or in the prior taxable year.

Fiscal year. If you are on a fiscal year, an election may be made for disaster losses occurring after the close of a fiscal year on the return for that year. For example, if your fiscal year ends June 30, and you suffer a disaster loss anytime between July 1, 1992, and June 30, 1993, you may elect to deduct it on your return for the fiscal year ending June 30, 1992.

Disaster relief grants and loans. Cancellation of part of a disaster loan under the Disaster Relief Act is treated as a reimbursement that reduces your loss; *see* ¶18.12. Grants to disaster victims under the Disaster Relief Act are not taxable, but the grant is considered a reimbursement reducing your deductible loss.

WHO MAY CLAIM THE LOSS DEDUCTION

¶**18.3** The casualty and theft loss deduction may be claimed only by the owner of the property. For example, a husband filing a separate return may not deduct the loss of jewelry belonging to his wife; only she may deduct it on her separate return.

On jointly owned property, the loss is divided among the owners. If you and your spouse own the property jointly, you deduct the entire loss on a joint return. If you file separately, each owner deducts his or her share of the loss on each separate return.

If you have a legal life estate in the property, the loss is apportioned between yourself and those who will get the property after your death. The apportionment may be based on actuarial tables that consider your life expectancy.

You may claim a casualty loss deduction for the loss or destruction of property used by your dependent if you own the property. You may not claim a loss deduction for the destruction of property belonging to your child who has reached majority, even though your child is still your dependent.

Lessee. A person leasing property may be allowed to deduct payments to a lessor that compensates for a casualty loss. A tenant was allowed to deduct as a casualty loss payment of a judgment obtained by the landlord for fire damage to the rented premises which had to be returned in the same condition as at the start of the lease. However, the Tax Court does not allow a deduction for the cost of repairing a rented car, as the lessee has no basis in the car.

Damage to nearby property. The casualty must have caused damage to your property. Damage to a nearby area which lowered the value of your property does not give you a loss deduction.

EXAMPLE You buy or lease a lot on which to build a cottage. Along with your purchase or lease, you have the privilege of using a nearby lake. The lake is later destroyed by a storm and the value of your property drops. You may not deduct the loss. The lake is not your property. You had only a privilege to use it, and this is not an ownership right which supports a casualty loss deduction.

BANK DEPOSIT LOSSES

¶**18.4** If a bank in which you deposit funds fails and your loss is not covered by insurance, generally you may claim your loss either as a bad debt deduction or casualty loss. Furthermore, if none of the deposits were federally insured, an investment loss may be claimed.

Bad debt. You may claim a bad debt deduction for a loss of a bank deposit in the year there is no reasonable prospect of recovery from the insolvent or bankrupt bank. You claim the loss as a short-term capital loss on Schedule D unless the deposit was made in your business. A nonbusiness bad debt deduction is deductible from capital gains. If you do not have capital gains or the bad debt loss exceeds capital gains, only $3,000 of the loss may offset other income. The remaining loss is carried over. A lost deposit of business funds is claimed as a business bad debt; *see* ¶5.47.

Casualty loss. You may elect to take a casualty loss deduction for the year in which the loss can be reasonably estimated. The loss is subject to the 10% AGI floor for casualty losses. Once the casualty loss election is made, it is irrevocable and will apply to all other losses on deposits in the same financial institution.

The casualty loss election may allow you to claim the loss in an earlier year because you do not have to wait until the year there is no prospect of recovery as required in the case of bad debts. The casualty loss election may also be advisable if other casualty losses may absorb all or part of the 10% AGI floor.

The casualty loss election is *not* allowed to stockholders of the bank with more than a 1% interest, officers of the bank, or their relatives.

Investment loss. If *none* of your deposits were federally insured and you reasonably estimate that you will not recover the funds, up to $20,000 ($10,000 if married filing separately) may be claimed on Schedule A as an investment loss subject to the 2% adjusted gross income floor for miscellaneous itemized deductions. The $20,000 limit (or $10,000) applies to total losses from any one financial institution, regardless of how many accounts you have. A separate $20,000 deduction limit applies to each financial institution. The $20,000 (or $10,000) limit is reduced by any insurance proceeds authorized by *state law* that you reasonably expect to receive. If your other miscellaneous deductions exceed 2% of adjusted gross income, claiming investment loss treatment may be preferable to treating the loss as a casualty subject to the 10% floor or a bad debt subject to the $3,000 limit. If you claimed a bad debt deduction for a lost deposit in a prior year and you qualify for the investment loss, you may file an amended return to claim the investment loss if the statute of limitations has not passed.

Reasonable estimate of casualty or investment loss. Generally, the trustees of the troubled bank will provide depositors with an estimate of the expected recovery and loss. In the year of that determination, you may claim the estimated loss deduction. If you deduct an estimated loss that is less than you are entitled to, you may claim the additional loss in the year of the final determination as a bad debt. If you deduct more than the actual loss, the excess loss must be reported as income in the year of the final determination. Failure to claim the loss in the year in which the loss can first be reasonably estimated does not bar a deduction in a later year.

For any particular year, only one election may be made for losses in the same bank. If you elect the up to $20,000 investment loss for losses in one bank and your loss exceeds the limit, the balance may not be claimed as a casualty deduction. Similarly, if you elect casualty loss treatment, the amount that is not deductible because of the $100 and 10% of the adjusted gross income floors is not deductible under the $20,000 investment loss rule.

SUDDEN EVENT TEST FOR PERSONAL PROPERTY LOSSES

¶18.5 A loss of personal-use property must result from a sudden and destructive force. Chance or a natural phenomenon must be present. Examples include earthquakes, hurricanes, tornadoes, floods, severe storms, landslides, and fires. Loss due to vandalism during riots or civil disorders also is treated as a casualty loss. Damage to your car from an accident is generally deductible; *see* ¶18.7. Courts have allowed deductions for other types of accidents; *see* Example 2 below. The requirement of suddenness is designed to bar deductions for damage caused by a natural action such as erosion, corrosion, and termite infestation occurring over a period of time.

EXAMPLES 1. A homeowner claimed a loss for water damage to wallpaper and plaster. The water entered through the frames of a window. The loss was disallowed. He gave no evidence that the damage came from a sudden or destructive force such as a storm. The damage might have been caused by progressive deterioration.

2. Unaware that his wife had reached back into their automobile, Mr. White slammed the door on her hand. The impact loosened a large diamond in the ring she wore. In pain, she shook her hand vigorously and the diamond flew out of its loosened setting to the leaf-covered gravel driveway. It was never found. In disallowing White's deduction, the IRS contended that a casualty loss requires a cataclysmic event. The Tax Court disagreed and allowed the deduction. Whenever an accidental force is exerted against property, and its owner is powerless to prevent the damage because of the suddenness, the resulting damage is a deductible casualty loss. The IRS has agreed to accept the decision.

3. A boat, which was in a poor state of repair, was equipped with a pump that automatically began operating when the water in the hull rose above a certain level. One day, the dockside power source failed, and the boat sank at its mooring within four hours. The IRS claimed that no deductible type of casualty occurred because the leakage was a chronic problem. The Tax Court allowed the deduction. The sinking was not a direct result of the boat's leaking hull, but of the failure of the on-board water pump.

Is Drought Damage Deductible?

The IRS does not generally allow deductions for drought damage. An agent may argue that the loss resulted from progressive deterioration which does not fit the legal definition of a personal casualty loss. Courts have allowed deductions for severe drought where the damages occur in the same year as the drought. If the damage becomes noticeable a year later, a court will view this as evidence of progressive deterioration which does not qualify as a deductible casualty. Where there are drought conditions, inspect your property for damage before the end of the year and claim a deduction for the damage in that year to negate an IRS argument that damage was caused by progressive deterioration.

Damage to surrounding property. Loss due to buyer resistance because of damage to surrounding property is generally not deductible. However, in the following case a deduction was allowed by a federal district court and appeals court.

EXAMPLE Floods damaged 12 homes which were razed by local authorities for safety reasons. Although Finkbohner's home suffered only minor damage, he claimed that the removal of the neighboring homes decreased the attractiveness of the neighborhood and made it more susceptible to crime. He estimated that the value of his home fell from $120,000 to $95,000 and claimed a casualty loss for the $25,000 difference.

The IRS disallowed the loss on the grounds that it was not based on actual physical damage. It allowed a deduction only for the cost of repairs, about $1,200. A federal district court jury allowed a $12,500 casualty loss after being instructed by the trial judge that permanent buyer resistance after the flood damage to the neighborhood is basis for a loss deduction. An appeals court upheld the loss because permanent buyer resistance affected the value of the home. The court distinguished Finkbohner's case from that of a homeowner who, after a flood and mud slide, was barred from deducting a loss based on fears of future floods. In that situation, the owner was trying to claim a loss that could only be deducted, if and when a future disaster occurred, by the future owner. Here, the buyer resistance confronting Finkbohner was not based on expected future casualties, but on changes to their neighborhood that already occurred.

Termites. Termite damage is generally nondeductible since it often results from long periods of termite infestation. Proving a *sudden* action in the sense of fixing the approximate moment of the termite invasion is difficult. Some courts have allowed a deduction, but the IRS will disallow deductions for termite damage under any conditions based on a study that found that serious termite damage results only after an infestation of three to eight years. Examples of other nondeductible casualty losses are at ¶18.9.

Damage to trees. Destruction of trees by southern pine beetles over a period of 5–10 days was held by the IRS to be a casualty. One court decided similarly where destruction occurred over a 30-day period. For figuring the deduction for tree and shrub damage; *see* ¶18.6.

Foreseeable events and preventable accidents. The IRS may try to disallow a deduction by claiming that the loss was foreseeable and therefore not a deductible casualty loss.

EXAMPLES 1. Heyn owned a hillside lot on which he contracted for the building of a home. A soil test showed a high proportion of fine-grain dense sandstone, which is unstable. His construction contract called for appropriate shoring up and support. But, because of the contractor's negligence, a landslide occurred. The IRS disallowed the loss on the grounds that it was not due to a "casualty" because the danger was known before Heyn undertook the project and because of the negligence involved. The court disagreed. The contractor's negligence is not a factor in determining whether there was a casualty. For example, an automobile collision is considered a casualty, even if caused by negligent driving. Foreseeability is not a factor. A weather report may warn property owners to take protective steps against an approaching hurricane, but losses caused by the hurricane are deductible. The IRS has agreed to accept the decision.

2. Mrs. Carpenter placed her dirty ring in a glass of ammonia beside the sink. Not knowing the contents of the glass, her husband emptied it into the sink and started the automatic garbage disposal, crushing the ring. The court allowed a full deduction for the loss which it said resulted from a destructive force. That Mr. Carpenter was negligent has no bearing on whether the event was a casualty.

3. At Christmas time in 1982, Hananel left his 1974 Plymouth Valiant in Chicago in an area in which the city was towing away cars to make room for construction work. When he returned a week later, he found that his car was missing and reported it stolen. A month later, he learned that the city pound had towed the car away and then crushed it because its ownership could not be determined. He claimed a casualty loss for the car. The IRS disallowed the deduction, claiming that the towing and crushing was not an unforeseeable event, and thus did not qualify as a casualty.

The Tax Court agreed that Hananel could have foreseen that leaving the car on the street subjected it to being towed. He was negligent. However, the penalty for this is a towing charge. He could not have foreseen its destruction. Therefore, the destruction occurred from an unusual and unexpected event, and he was allowed to claim a casualty loss deduction.

4. Destruction of a lawn through the careless use of weed killer has been held to be a casualty.

Preventive measures not deductible. The cost of preventive measures, such as burglar alarms or smoke detectors, or the cost of boarding up property against a storm, is not deductible.

COURT DECISION — Deduction Despite Faulty Construction

A plumber stepped on a pipe which was improperly installed two years before. Resulting underground flooding caused damage of over $20,000. The IRS argued that this was caused by a construction fault and did not qualify as a casualty loss. The Tax Court disagreed. The plumber caused the damage. Improper construction was only an element in the causative chain.

DAMAGE TO TREES AND SHRUBS

¶18.6

Not all damage to trees and shrubs qualifies as a casualty loss. The damage must be occasioned by a sudden event; *see* ¶18.5. Destruction of trees over a period of 5–10 days by southern pine beetles is deductible. One court allowed a deduction for similar destruction over a 30-day period. However, damage by Dutch Elm disease or lethal yellowing disease has been held to be gradual destruction not qualifying as a casualty loss. The Tax Court has allowed a deduction for the cost of removing infested trees.

If shrubbery and trees on *personal-use* property are damaged by a sudden casualty, you figure the loss on the value of the entire property before and after the casualty. You treat the buildings, land, and shrubs as one complete unit; *see* Example 2 below.

In fixing the loss on *business or income-producing property,* however, shrubs and trees are valued separately from the building; *see* Example 1 below.

EXAMPLES

1. Smith bought an office building for $90,000. The purchase price was allocated between the land ($18,000) and the building ($72,000). Smith planted trees and ornamental shrubs on the grounds surrounding the building at a cost of $1,200. When the building had been depreciated to $66,000, a hurricane caused extensive property damage. The fair market value of the land and building immediately before the hurricane was $18,000 and $70,000; immediately afterwards, $18,000 and $52,000. The fair market value of the trees and shrubs immediately before the casualty was $2,000 and immediately afterwards, $400. Insurance of $5,000 is received to cover damage to the building. The deduction for the building is $13,000, computed as follows:

Value of building immediately before casualty	$70,000
Less: Value immediately after casualty	52,000
Value of property actually destroyed	$18,000
Less: Insurance received	5,000
Deduction allowed	$13,000

The deduction for the trees and shrubs is $1,200:

Value immediately before casualty	$ 2,000
Less: Value of trees after casualty	400
Value of property actually destroyed	$ 1,600*

*However, the loss cannot exceed the adjusted basis of property, $1,200.

2. Same facts as in Example 1, except that Smith purchases a personal residence instead of an office building. Smith's adjusted gross income is $25,000, and this is his only loss. No allocation of the purchase price is necessary for the land and house because the property is not depreciable. Likewise, no individual evaluation of the fair market values of the land, house, trees, and shrubs is necessary. The amount of the deduction for the land, house, trees, and shrubs is $12,000, computed as follows:

Value of property immediately before casualty		$90,000
Less: Value of property immediately after casualty		70,400
Value of property actually destroyed		$19,600
Less: Insurance received	$5,000	
10% and $100 floors	2,600	7,600
Deduction allowed		$12,000

DEDUCTING DAMAGE TO YOUR CAR

¶18.7

Damage to your car in an accident may be a deductible casualty loss unless caused by your willful negligence, such as drunken driving.

You may not deduct legal fees and costs of a court action for damages or money paid for damages to another's property because of your negligence while driving for commuting or other personal purposes. But if at the time of the accident you were using your car on business, you may deduct as a business loss a payment of damages to the other party's car. For purposes of a business loss deduction, driving between two locations of the same business is considered business driving but driving between locations of two separate businesses is considered personal driving. Therefore, the payment of damages arising from an accident while driving between two separate businesses is not deductible.

A court has allowed deductions for damage resulting from a child pressing the starter button of a car and from flying stones while driving over a temporary road. In a private letter ruling, the IRS disallowed a loss for damage to a race car by an amateur racer on the ground that in races, crashes are not an unusual event and so do not constitute a casualty.

If the deduction is questioned, be prepared to show the amount, if any, of your insurance recovery. A deduction is allowed only for uninsured losses. Not only must the loss be proved, but also that it was not compensated by insurance.

Towing costs are not included as part of the casualty loss.

A parent may not claim a casualty loss deduction for damage to a car registered in a child's name, although the parent provided funds for the purchase of the car.

Expenses of personal injuries arising from a car accident are not a deductible casualty loss.

Automobile used partly for business. When you use an automobile partly for personal use and partly for business, your loss is computed as though two separate pieces of property were damaged—one business and the other personal. The $100 and 10% floors reduce only the loss on the part used for personal purposes.

THEFT LOSSES

¶18.8

The taking of property must be illegal under state law to support a theft loss deduction. That property is missing is not sufficient evidence to sustain a theft deduction. It may have been lost or misplaced. So, if all you can prove is that an article is missing or lost, your deduction may be disallowed. Sometimes, of course, the facts surrounding the disappearance of an article indicate that it is reasonable to assume that a theft took place. A deduction has been allowed for the theft of trees.

You deduct a theft loss in the year you discover the property was stolen. If you have a reasonable chance of being reimbursed for your loss, you may not take a deduction until the year in which you learn there is no reasonable prospect of recovery.

A legal fee paid to recover stolen property has been held to be deductible as part of the theft loss.

To figure the amount of a theft loss deduction; *see* ¶18.12.

Proving a Theft

Get statements from witnesses who saw the theft or police records documenting a break-in to your house or car. A newspaper account of the crime might also help.

When you suspect a theft, make a report to the police. Even though your reporting does not prove that a theft was committed, it may be inferred from your failure to report that you were not sure that your property was stolen. But a theft loss was allowed where the loss of a ring was not reported to the police or an attempt made to demand its return from the suspect, a domestic. The owner feared being charged with false arrest.

Fraud by building contractors. A deduction was allowed when a building contractor ran away with a payment he received to build a residence. The would-be homeowner was allowed a theft loss deduction for the difference between the money he advanced to the contractor and the value of the partially completed house. In another case, a theft deduction was allowed for payments to subcontractors. The main contractor had fraudulently claimed that he had paid them before he went bankrupt.

Embezzlement losses are deductible as theft losses in the year the theft is discovered. However, if you report on a cash basis, you may not take a deduction for the embezzlement of income you have not reported. For example, an agent embezzled royalties of $46,000 due an author. The author's theft deduction was disallowed. The author had not previously reported the royalties as income; therefore, she could not get the deduction.

Fraudulent sales offers. Worthless stock purchases made on the representation of false and fraudulent sales offers are deductible as theft losses in the year there is no reasonable prospect of recovery. However, the illegal sale of unregistered stock does not support a theft loss deduction.

Kidnapping ransom. Payment of ransom to a kidnapper is generally a deductible theft loss. However, the expense of trying to find an abducted child is not a theft loss.

Fortune tellers. The Tax Court allowed a theft loss deduction in New York where fortune telling is by law a theft-related offense. The law assumes that telling fortunes or promising to control occult forces is a form of fraud. An exception is made for fortune telling at shows for the purpose of entertaining or amusement. That a person voluntarily asks for advice does not bar the deduction. According to the court, a gullible person who gives money to fortune tellers in the belief that he or she will be helped is still defrauded or swindled. Theft is a broad term and includes theft by swindling, false pretenses, and any other form of guile. In this case, the taxpayer, who was suffering from mental depression, had become attached to two fortune tellers whom he claimed took him for over $19,000.

Riot losses. Losses caused by fire, theft, and vandalism occurring during riots and civil disorders are deductible. When a reception is canceled because of a curfew, no loss deduction is allowed for perishable food that is discarded.

To support your claim of a riot loss, keep evidence of the damage suffered and the cost of repairs. Photographs taken prior to repairs or replacement, lists of damaged or missing property, and police reports would help to establish and uphold your loss deduction.

Foreign government confiscations. The IRS and courts have disallowed deductions for confiscations of personal property by foreign governments.

If Stolen Property Is Recovered

If you claim a theft loss and in a later year the property is returned to you, you must refigure your loss deduction. If the refigured deduction is lower than what you claimed, the difference must be reported as income in the year of the recovery. To recalculate the loss, follow the steps in ¶18.12 for figuring deductible losses, but in Step 1, compute the loss in fair market value from the time the property was stolen until you recovered it. The lower of this loss in value, if any, and your adjusted basis for the property, is then reduced by insurance reimbursements and the personal floors (¶18.11) to get the recalculated loss.

NONDEDUCTIBLE LOSSES

¶18.9

Certain losses, though casualties for you, may not be deducted if they are not due to theft, fire, or from some other sudden natural phenomenon. The following losses have been held not to be deductible:

Termite damage; *see* ¶18.5.
Carpet beetle damage.
Dry rot damage.
Damages for personal injuries or property damage to others caused by your negligence.
Legal expenses in defending a suit for your negligent operation of your personal automobile.
Legal expenses to recover personal property wrongfully seized by the police.
Expenses of moving to and rental of temporary quarters.
Loss of personal property while in storage or in transit.
Loss of passenger's luggage put aboard a ship. The passenger missed the boat and the luggage could not be traced.
Accidental loss of a ring from your finger.
Injuries resulting from tripping over a wire.
Loss by husband of joint property taken by his wife when she left him.
Loss of a valuable dog which strayed and was not found.
Damages to a crop caused by plant diseases, insects, or fungi.
Damage to property from drought in an area where a dry spell is normal and usual.
Damage to property caused by excavations on adjoining property.
Damages from rust or corroding of understructure of house.
Moth damage.
Dry well.
Losses occasioned by water pockets, erosion, inundation at still water levels, and other natural phenomena. (There was no sudden destruction.)
Amount paid to a public library for damages to a book you borrowed.
Death of a saddle horse after eating a silk hat.
A watch or spectacles dropped on the ground.
Sudden drop in the value of securities.
Loss in earnings of a lawyer resulting from his illness.
Loss of contingent interest in property due to the unexpected death of a child.
Improper police seizure of private liquor stock.
Chinaware broken by a family pet.
Temporary fluctuation in value.
Loss of tree from Dutch Elm disease and lethal yellowing disease.
Loss of trees after horse ate bark.
Damage to property from local government construction project.
Fire purposely set by owner.

Note. But some of the above items may be allowed to persons in business.

FIGURING YOUR DEDUCTIBLE CASUALTY OR THEFT LOSS

PROVING A CASUALTY LOSS

¶18.10 If your return is audited, you will have to prove that the casualty occurred and the amount of the loss. The time to collect your evidence is as soon after the casualty as possible. The Key to Proving a Casualty Loss below indicates the information that you will need when computing your loss under the steps explained in ¶18.12.

FLOORS FOR PERSONAL-USE PROPERTY LOSSES

¶18.11 Casualty and theft losses to personal-use property are subject to "floors" that will reduce, and in some cases eliminate, your deduction. For each casualty or theft in 1992, a $100 reduction applies after the loss is computed under the steps of ¶18.12. In addition, personal casualty and theft losses (after the $100 reduction) are deductible only to the extent they exceed 10% of your adjusted gross income.

Congress may increase the $100 floor for years after 1992; see the Supplement.

The $100 floor. The $100 floor reduces casualty and theft losses of property used for personal purposes; *see* step 4 of ¶18.12. It does not apply to losses of business property or property held for the production of income such as securities. If property used both in business and personal activities is damaged, the $100 offset applies only to the loss allocated to personal use.

For each casualty or theft during the year, a separate $100 reduction applies. For example, you are involved in five different casualties during the year. There will be a $100 offset applied to each of the five losses. But when two or more items of property are destroyed in one event, only one $100 offset is applied to the total loss. For example, a storm damages your residence and also your car parked in the driveway. You figure the loss on the residence and car separately, but only one $100 offset applies to the total loss.

The $100 floor is applied after taking into account insurance proceeds received and insurance you expect to receive in a later year. For example, in 1992, you incur a casualty loss of $290, on which you expect a reimbursement of $250. Thus, your unreimbursed loss in 1992 is $40, but you may not deduct the amount as it does not exceed $100. Now assume that in 1993, you learn that you cannot recover the expected reimbursement of $250. In figuring a casualty loss deduction in 1993, you reduce the $250 by $60; $40 of the $100 limitation had applied to part of the same casualty loss in 1992.

The $100 floor applies separately to the loss of each individual whose property has been damaged by a single casualty, even where the damaged property is owned by two or more individuals.

EXAMPLES 1. Two sisters own and occupy a house which is damaged in a storm. Each sister applies the $100 floor to figure her separate deduction.

2. Your house is partially damaged by a fire which also damages the personal property of a house guest. You are subject to one $100 floor and the house guest is subject to a separate $100 floor.

Spouses. Where a husband and wife file a joint return, only one $100 floor applies, whether the property is owned jointly or separately. If separate returns are filed, each spouse must reduce his or her half of the loss on jointly owned property by $100. If the property is owned by one spouse, only that spouse can claim a casualty loss on a separate return.

10% AGI floor. The 10% adjusted gross income (AGI) floor applies to the total of all losses occurring during the taxable year to personal-use property. The first example on page 220 illustrates the application of the $100 floor to each separate casualty event and the 10% AGI floor to the total losses.

Key to Proving a Casualty Loss

To prove—	You need this information—
That a casualty actually occurred	With a well-known casualty, like regional floods, you will have no difficulty proving the casualty occurred, but you must prove it affected your property. Photographs of the area, before and after, and newspaper stories placing the damage in your neighborhood are helpful. If only your property is damaged, there may be a newspaper item on it. Some papers list all the fire alarms answered the previous day. Police, fire, and other municipal departments may have reports on the casualty.
The cost of repairing the property	Cost of repairs is allowed as a measure of loss of repairing the value if it is not excessive and the repair merely restored your property to its condition immediately before the casualty. Save canceled checks, bills, receipts, and vouchers for expenses of clearing debris and restoring the property to its condition before the casualty.
The value immediately before and after the casualty	Appraisals by a competent expert are important. Get them in writing—in the form of an affidavit, deposition, estimate, appraisal, etc. The expert—an appraiser, engineer, architect—should be qualified to judge local values. Any records of offers to buy your property, either before or after the casualty, are helpful. Automobile "blue books" may be used as guides in fixing the value of a car. But an amount offered for your car as a trade-in on a new car is not usually an acceptable measure of value.
Cost of your property—the deductible loss cannot be more than that	A deed, contract, bill of sale, or other document probably shows your original cost. Bills, receipts, and canceled checks show the cost of improvements. One court refused to allow a deduction because an owner failed to prove the original cost of a destroyed house and its value before the fire. In another case, estimates were allowed where a fire destroyed records of cost. A court held that the homeowner could not be expected to prove cost by documents lost in the fire that destroyed her property. She made inventories after the fire and again at a later date. Her reliance on memory to establish cost, even though inflated, was no bar to the deduction. The court estimated the market value based on her inventories. If you acquired the property by gift or inheritance, you must establish an adjusted basis in the property from records of the donor or the executor of the estate; *see* ¶5.13 and ¶5.14.

EXAMPLE In January 1992, you have an uninsured jewelry theft loss of $1,000, and in July 1992 uninsured damage of $3,000 to your personal car. Your adjusted gross income is $25,000. Your deduction is $1,300 figured as follows:

Theft loss	$1,000	
Less	100	$900
Car damage	$3,000	
Less	100	2,900
Total loss		$3,800
Less 10% of $25,000		2,500
Deductible loss		$1,300

FIGURING YOUR LOSS ON FORM 4684

¶18.12

The deductible loss is usually the difference between the fair market value of the property before and after the casualty or theft *less* (1) reimbursements received for the loss; and (2) $100 if the property was used for personal purposes. However, the deductible loss may not exceed your adjusted basis (¶5.16) for the property, which for many items will be your cost. If your adjusted basis is less than the loss in value, your deduction is limited to basis, regardless of the reduction in the value of your property. After figuring all allowable casualty and theft losses for personal use property, the total is deductible only to the extent it exceeds the 10% adjusted gross income floor (¶18.11). Follow the five-step method below for figuring the deductible amount.

Steps for calculating your deductible loss. The following five steps reflect the procedure on Form 4684 for computing a casualty or theft loss. Form 4684 is used to report casualties or thefts of personal-use property, business property, or income-producing property. However, if your loss is to business inventory, you do not have to use Form 4684, but may take the loss into account when figuring the cost of goods sold; *see* Inventory losses on page 222.

To figure your deductible loss, follow these five steps:

1. Compute the loss in fair market value of the property. This is the difference between the fair market value immediately before and immediately after the casualty. You will need written appraisals to support your claim for loss of value. You may not claim sentimental or aesthetic values or a fluctuation in property values caused by a casualty; you must deal with cost or market values of what has been lost. If the value of your property has been lowered because of damage to a nearby area, you do not have a deductible loss since your own property has not been damaged. No deduction may be claimed for estimated decline in value based on buyer resistance in an area subject to landslides.

   For household items, the Tax Court has allowed losses to be based on cost less depreciation, rather than on the decrease in fair market value; *see* the example on page 222.
2. Compute your adjusted basis for the property. This is usually the cost of the property plus the cost of improvements, less previous casualty loss deductions and depreciation if the property is used in business or for income-producing purposes. Unadjusted basis of property acquired other than by purchase is explained at ¶5.12. Adjusted basis is explained at ¶5.16.
3. Take the lower amount of Step 1 or 2. The lower amount, reduced by the adjustments in Step 4, is your casualty loss, with one exception: Where property used for business or income-producing purposes is totally destroyed, and before the casualty its market value is less than its adjusted basis, the measure of the loss is the adjusted basis, *less* any salvage value.

Indirect expenses, such as for personal injury, temporary lights, fuel, moving, or rentals for temporary living quarters, are not deductible as casualty losses.
4. Reduce the loss in Step 3 by the insurance proceeds or other compensation for the loss; *see* ¶18.15. If the property was used for personal purposes, also reduce the loss by $100; *see* ¶18.11.
5. If the property was used for personal purposes, the loss is allowed only if it exceeds 10% of your adjusted gross income. If you have more than one personal casualty or theft, reduce the total combined loss by 10% of adjusted gross income; only the excess is deductible; *see* ¶18.11.

EXAMPLES 1. Your home which cost $76,000 in 1986 was damaged by a fire. The value of the house before the disaster was $167,500, afterwards $162,500. The furniture cost $5,000 in 1987. Its value before the fire was set at $2,000. It was totally destroyed. The insurance company reimbursed you $2,000 for your house damage and $500 for your furnishings. This was the only casualty for the year. Your adjusted gross income is $28,000. You figure your loss for the furniture separately from the loss on the house but apply only one $100 reduction (¶18.11) because the damage was from a single casualty.

1. Decrease in fair market value		
Value of house before fire		$167,500
Value of house after fire		162,500
Decrease in value		$ 5,000
2. Adjusted basis		$76,000
3. Loss sustained (lower of 1 or 2)		$ 5,000
Less: Insurance		2,000
Loss on house		$ 3,000
4. Loss on furnishings (decreased value)*		$ 2,000
Less: Insurance		500
Loss on furnishings		$ 1,500
5. Total loss ($3,000 and $1,500)		$ 4,500
Less: $100 floor		100
Casualty loss (subject to 10% floor)		$ 4,400

After applying the 10% adjusted gross income floor, you may deduct $1,600 on Schedule A ($4,400 – $2,800 or 10% of $28,000).

See the sample Form 4684 on page 221 for how this loss is reported.

* The loss for the furnishings on Line 4 is $2,000, the decrease in fair market value, as this is lower than the $5,000 basis.

2. Depreciable business property with a fair market value of $1,500 and an adjusted basis of $2,000 is totally destroyed. Because the property was used in your business, your loss is measured by your adjusted basis of $2,000 which is larger than the $1,500 loss in fair market value. Disregard the $100 floor applied to casualty losses on personal property. If the property was used for personal purposes, the loss would have been limited to the $1,500 loss in market value less $100, leaving a loss of $1,400 subject to the 10% adjusted gross income floor.

Reporting on Form 4684

If you are claiming a loss for personal-use property, use Section A on page 1 of Form 4684. If you suffered more than one casualty or theft during the year, use a separate Form 4684 for each one. The total deductible casualty or theft loss from Section A of Form 4684 is then entered on Schedule A of Form 1040.

If you are claiming a loss for property used in your business or income-producing activity, use Section B on page 2 of Form 4684. Losses from income-producing property are generally entered on Schedule A as a miscellaneous itemized deduction subject to the 2% floor. Losses from business property are generally netted against gains and the result entered on Form 4797; follow the instructions to Form 4684.

Form 4684—Worksheet

Name(s) shown on tax return	Identifying number
John Bennett	XX0-X0-11X0

Note: *Use Section A for casualties and thefts of personal use property and Section B for business and income-producing property.*

SECTION A.—Personal Use Property *(Casualties and thefts of property **not** used in a trade or business or for income-producing purposes)*

1 Description of properties (show kind, location, and date acquired for each):

Property **A** Residence 2-8-86
Property **B** Furniture 3-15-87
Property **C** ....
Property **D** ....

		Properties (use a separate column for each property lost or damaged from one casualty or theft)			
		A	**B**	**C**	**D**
2	Cost or other basis of each property	76,000	5,000		
3	Insurance or other reimbursement (whether or not you submitted a claim). See instructions	2,000	500		
	Note: *If line 2 is **more** than line 3, skip line 4.*				
4	Gain from casualty or theft. If line 3 is **more than** line 2, enter the difference here and skip lines 5 through 9 for that column. (If line 3 includes an amount that you did not receive, see instructions.)				
5	Fair market value **before** casualty or theft	167,500	2,000		
6	Fair market value **after** casualty or theft	162,500	0		
7	Subtract line 6 from line 5	5,000	2,000		
8	Enter the **smaller** of line 2 or line 7	5,000	2,000		
9	Subtract line 3 from line 8 (If zero or less, enter -0-.)	3,000	1,500		

10	Casualty or theft loss. Add the amounts on line 9. Enter the total	**10**	4,500
11	Enter the amount from line 10 or $100, whichever is **smaller**	**11**	100
12	Subtract line 11 from line 10	**12**	4,400
	Caution: *Use only one Form 4684 for lines 13 through 18.*		
13	Add the amounts on line 12 of all Forms 4684, Section A	**13**	4,400
14	Combine the amounts from line 4 of all Forms 4684, Section A	**14**	-0-
15	• If line 14 is **more than** line 13, enter the difference here and on Schedule D. Do not complete the rest of this section (see instructions). • If line 14 is **less than** line 13, enter -0- here and continue with the form. • If line 14 is **equal to** line 13, enter -0- here. Do not complete the rest of this section.	**15**	-0-
16	If line 14 is **less than** line 13, enter the difference	**16**	4,400
17	Enter 10% of your adjusted gross income (Form 1040, line 32). Estates and trusts, see instructions	**17**	2,800
18	Subtract line 17 from line 16. If zero or less, enter -0-. Also enter result on Schedule A (Form 1040), line 17. Estates and trusts, enter on the "Other deductions" line of your tax return	**18**	1,600

Inventory losses. A casualty or theft loss of inventory is automatically reflected on Schedule C in the cost of goods sold, which includes the lost items as part of your opening inventory. Any insurance or other reimbursement received for the loss must be included as sales income.

You may separately claim the inventory loss as a casualty or theft loss on Form 4684 instead of automatically claiming it as part of the cost of goods sold. If you do this, you must eliminate the items from inventory by lowering either opening inventory or purchases when figuring the cost of goods sold.

Cost less depreciation method for household items. The Tax Court has allowed casualty loss deductions based on cost less depreciation, rather than on the difference in fair market value immediately before and after the casualty.

EXAMPLE The fair market rule applied to household items generally limits your deduction to the going price for secondhand furnishings. But one homeowner whose furniture was destroyed by fire claimed that the fair market value should be original cost less depreciation. He based his figures on an inventory prepared by certified public adjusters describing each item, its cost and age. The deduction figured this way came to approximately $27,500 ($55,000 cost, less $13,000 depreciation, a $14,400 insurance recovery, and the $100 floor).

The IRS estimated that the furniture was worth $15,304 before the fire and limited the deduction to $804 after setting off the insurance and the $100 floor. The Tax Court disagreed. The householder's method of valuing his furniture is consistent with methods used by insurance adjusters who have an interest in keeping values low. He is not limited to the amount his property would bring if "hawked off by a secondhand dealer or at a forced sale." However, in another case, the court refused to allow the cost less depreciation formula where the homeowner's inventory list was based on memory.

Keep Records of Deductible Losses

If your property is damaged, you must reduce the basis of the damaged property by the casualty loss deduction and compensation received for the loss (*see* ¶5.16). When you later sell the property, gain or loss is the difference between the selling price and the reduced basis.

PROPERTY USED FOR PERSONAL AND BUSINESS PURPOSES

¶18.13 For property held partly for personal use and partly for business or income-producing purposes, a casualty or theft loss deduction is computed as if two separate pieces of property were damaged, destroyed, or stolen. Follow the steps of ¶18.12 for figuring the allowable loss, but apply the $100 and 10% of adjusted gross income floors only to the personal part of the loss.

EXAMPLE A building with two apartments, one used by the owner as his home and the other rented to a tenant, is damaged by a fire. The fair market value of the building before the fire was $169,000 and after the fire, $136,000. Its cost basis was $120,000. Depreciation taken before the fire was $14,000. The insurance company paid $20,000. The owner has adjusted gross income of $40,000. This is his only loss this year. He has a business casualty loss of $6,500 and a deductible personal casualty loss of $2,400.

	Business	Personal
1. Decrease in value of building:		
Value before fire ($169,000)	$84,500	$84,500
Value after fire ($136,000)	68,000	68,000
Decrease in value	$16,500	$16,500
2. Adjusted basis of building:	$60,000	$60,000
Less: Depreciation	14,000	
Adjusted basis	$46,000	$60,000
3. Loss sustained (lower of 1 or 2)	$16,500	$16,500
4. Less: Insurance (total $20,000)	$10,000	$10,000
5. Loss	$ 6,500	$ 6,500
Less: $100 floor and 10% of adjusted gross income	——	4,100
Deductible casualty loss	$ 6,500	$ 2,400

REPAIRS MAY BE "MEASURE OF LOSS"

¶18.14 The cost of repairs may be treated as evidence of the loss of value (step 1 of ¶18.12), if the amount is not excessive and the repairs do nothing more than restore the property to its condition before the casualty. An estimate for repairs will not suffice; only actual repairs may be used as a measure of loss. However, where you are not relying on repairs as a measure of loss but rather are using appraisals of value of the property before and after the casualty, repairs may be considered in arriving at a post-casualty value even though no actual repairs are made.

Deduction Not Limited to Repairs

A casualty loss deduction is not limited to repair expense where the decline in market value is greater, according to a federal appeals court; *see* the next example.

EXAMPLE Connor claimed that the market value of his house dropped $93,000 after it was extensively damaged by fire. His cash outlay ($52,000) in repairing the house was reimbursed by insurance. Connor claimed a casualty loss deduction of approximately $40,000, the uncompensated drop in market value. The IRS disallowed the deduction. The house was restored to pre-casualty condition. The cost of the repairs is a realistic measure of the loss, and, as the expense was fully compensated by insurance, Connor suffered no loss. A federal appeals court disagreed. It found that the house dropped $70,000 in market value, of which $20,000 was uncompensated by insurance. The deduction is measured by the uncompensated difference in value before and after the casualty. It is not limited to the cost of repairs, even where the repair expense is less than the difference in fair market values. Had the repairs cost more than this difference, the IRS would not have allowed Connor a larger deduction.

INSURANCE REIMBURSEMENTS

¶18.15 You reduce the amount of your loss (¶18.12) by insurance proceeds, voluntary payments received from your employer for damage to your property, and cash or property received from the Red Cross. Also reduce your loss by reimbursements you expect to receive in a later year; *see* ¶18.1. However, cash gifts from friends and relatives to help defray the cost of repairs do not reduce the loss where there are no conditions on the use of the gift. Also, gifts of food, clothing, medical supplies, and other forms of subsistence do not reduce the loss deduction nor are they taxable income.

Cancellation of part of a disaster loan under the Disaster Relief Act is treated as a partial reimbursement of the loss and reduces the amount of the loss. Payments from an urban renewal agency to acquire your damaged property under the Federal Relocation Act of 1970 are considered reimbursements reducing the loss.

Insurance payments for the cost of added living expenses because of damage to a home do not reduce a casualty loss. The payments are treated separate and apart from payments for property damage. Payments for extra living costs are generally not taxable; see ¶18.16.

Failure to Make an Insurance Claim

If you are insured for your full loss and do not file a claim because you do not want to risk cancellation of liability coverage, you may not claim a deduction. If you do not file an insurance claim but your loss exceeds the coverage, the noncovered loss is deductible. For example, if you have a $500 deductible on your automobile insurance policy, a loss of up to $500 for car damage would be allowed, subject to the $100 and 10% of adjusted gross income floors.

Passive activity property loss reimbursements. A reimbursement of a casualty or theft loss deduction is *not* considered passive activity income if the original loss was not treated as a passive deduction; see ¶10.1. The reimbursement may be taxed under the rule of ¶12.8.

EXCESS LIVING COSTS PAID BY INSURANCE ARE NOT TAXABLE

¶18.16
Your insurance contract may reimburse you for excess living costs when a casualty or a threat of casualty forces you to vacate your house. The payment is tax free if these tests are met:

1. Your principal residence is damaged or destroyed by fire, storm, or other casualty or you are denied use of it by a governmental order because of the occurrence or threat of the casualty.
2. You are paid under an insurance contract for living expenses resulting from the loss of occupancy or use of the residence.

The tax-free amount includes only *excess* living costs paid by the insurance company. The excess is the difference between (1) the actual living expenses incurred during the time you could not use or occupy your house, and (2) the normal living expenses which you would have incurred for yourself and members of your household during the period. Living expenses during the period may include the cost of renting suitable housing and extraordinary expenses for transportation, food, utilities, and miscellaneous services. The expenses must be incurred for items and services (such as laundry) needed to maintain you in the same standard of living that you enjoyed before the loss and must be covered by the policy.

Where a lump-sum settlement does not identify the amount covering living expenses, an allocation is required to determine the tax-free portion. In the case of uncontested claims, the tax-free portion is that part of the settlement which bears the same ratio to total recovery as increased living expense bears to total loss and expense.

If your claim is contested, you must show the amount reasonably allocable to increased living expenses consistent with the terms of the insurance contract, but not in excess of coverage limitations specified in the contract.

The exclusion from income does not cover insurance reimbursements for loss of rental income or for loss of or damage to real or personal property; such reimbursements for property damage reduce your casualty loss; see ¶18.15.

If your home is used for both residential and business purposes, the exclusion does not apply to insurance proceeds and expenses attributable to the nonresidential portion of the house. There is no exclusion for insurance recovered for expenses resulting from governmental condemnation or order unrelated to a casualty or threat of casualty.

The insurance reimbursement may cover part of your normal living expenses as well as the excess expenses due to the casualty. The part covering normal expenses is income; it does not reduce your casualty loss.

EXAMPLES 1. On March 1, your home was damaged by fire. While it was being repaired, you and your spouse lived at a motel and ate meals at restaurants. Costs are $1,200 at the motel, $1,000 for meals, and $75 for laundry services. You make the required March payment of $790 on your home mortgage. Your customary $40 commuting expense is $20 less for the month because the motel is closer to your work. Your usual commuting expense is therefore treated as not being incurred to the extent of the $20 decrease. Furthermore, you do not incur your customary $700 food expense for meals at home, $75 for utilities, and $60 for laundry at home. Your insurance company pays you $1,700 for expenses. The tax-free exclusion for insurance payments is limited to $1,420, computed in the third column. You must report as income $280 ($1,700 − $1,420).

	Expenses from casualty	Expenses not incurred	Increase (Decrease)
Housing	$1,200		$1,200
Utilities		$75	(75)
Meals	1,000	700	300
Transportation		20	(20)
Laundry	75	60	15
Total	$2,275	$855	$1,420

2. Same facts as Example 1 except that you rented the residence for $400 per month and the risk of loss was on the landlord. You did not pay the March rent. The excludable amount is $1,020 ($1,420 less $400 normal rent not incurred). You would have to report as income the excess of the insurance received over the $1,020 exclusion.

DO YOUR CASUALTY LOSSES EXCEED YOUR INCOME?

¶18.17
If your casualty or theft losses exceed your income, you pay no tax in 1992. You may also carry the excess loss back to 1989 and file a refund claim for that year. Any remaining loss may be carried back to 1990 and 1991 and carried forward to 1993 through 2007, or you may just carry your loss forward 15 years until it is used up. The excess casualty loss is carried back or forward as a net operating loss. See ¶40.17 for net operating loss rules.

Note that the $100 and 10% of adjusted gross income floors for personal casualty losses apply only in the year of loss; you do not again reduce your loss in the carryback or carryover years.

GAINS FROM INVOLUNTARY CONVERSIONS

DEFER GAINS BY REPLACING PROPERTY

¶18.18 If your property is destroyed, damaged, stolen, or taken by a government authority, this is considered to be an *involuntary conversion* for tax purposes. If upon an involuntary conversion you receive insurance or other compensation that exceeds the adjusted basis of the property, you realize a taxable gain. However, you may elect to postpone tax on the gain if you invest the proceeds in replacement property, the cost of which is equal to or exceeds the net proceeds from the conversion. Reinvestment requirements are discussed at ¶18.21–¶18.23. The replacement period for personal-use property is two years; for business and investment property it is two or three years depending on the type of involuntary conversion; *see* ¶18.21.

Principal residence. If your principal residence is destroyed or condemned, you may apply the deferral rule for involuntary conversions or the home deferral rule of ¶29.5.

INVOLUNTARY CONVERSIONS QUALIFYING FOR TAX DEFERRAL

¶18.19 For purposes of an election to defer tax on gains, "involuntary conversion" is more broadly defined than casualty loss. You have an involuntary conversion when your property is:

Damaged or destroyed by some outside force.

Stolen.

Seized, requisitioned, or condemned by a governmental authority. If you voluntarily sell land made useless to you by the condemnation of your adjacent land, the sale may also qualify as a conversion. Condemnation of property as unfit for human habitation does not qualify. Condemnation, as used by the tax law, refers to the taking of private property for public use, not to the condemnation of property for noncompliance with housing and health regulations. Similarly a tax sale to pay delinquent taxes is not an involuntary conversion.

Sold under a threat of seizure, condemnation, or requisition. The threat must be made by an authority qualified to take property for public use. A sale following a threat of condemnation made by a government employee is a conversion if you reasonably believe he or she speaks with authority and could and would carry out the threat to have your property condemned. If you learn of the plan of an imminent condemnation from a newspaper or the radio, the IRS requires you to confirm the report from a government official before you act on the news.

Farmers. Farmers also have involuntary conversions when:

Land is sold within an irrigation project to meet the acreage limitations of the federal reclamation laws;
Cattle are destroyed by disease or sold because of disease; *or*
Draft, breeding, or dairy livestock is sold because of drought. The election to treat the sale as a conversion is limited to livestock sold over the number which would have been sold but for the drought. In some cases, livestock may be replaced with other farm property where there has been soil or other environmental contamination.

Should you elect to postpone gain? An election gives an immediate advantage: Tax on gain is postponed and the funds that would have been spent for the payment of tax may be used for other investments.

As a condition of deferring tax, the basis of the replacement property is usually fixed at the same cost basis as the converted property. As long as the value of the replacement property does not decline, tax on the gain is finally incurred when the property is sold.

Consider whether postponement of gain at the expense of a reduced basis for property is advisable, compared to the tax consequences of reporting the gain in the year it is realized.

 EXAMPLE Assume a rental building is destroyed by fire and a proper replacement is made. Assume that gain on the receipt of the fire proceeds is taxable as capital gain. An election is generally not advisable if you have capital losses to offset the gain. However, even if you have no capital losses, you may still decide not to make the election and pay tax in order to fix, for purposes of depreciation, the basis of the new property at its purchase price, if the future depreciation deductions will offset income taxable at a higher rate than the current tax. If there is little or no difference between the two rates so that a net after tax benefit from the depreciation would not arise, an election might be made solely to postpone the payment of tax.

HOW TO ELECT TO DEFER TAX

¶18.20 To defer tax on your gain, do not report the gain as income for the year it is realized. Attach to your return a statement giving details of the transaction, including computation of the gain and your intention to buy a replacement if you have not yet done so. *See* ¶18.21 for replacement periods and IRS notification requirements.

If your property is condemned and you are given similar property, no election is necessary. Postponement of tax on the gain is required. For example, the city condemns a store building and gives you another store building, the value of which exceeds the cost basis of the old one; gain is not taxed.

Partnerships. The election to defer gain must be made at the partnership level. Individual partners may not make separate elections unless the partnership has terminated, with all partnership affairs wound up. Dissolution under state law is not a termination for tax purposes.

⬣ CAUTION **Nullifying Deferral Election on Amended Return**

If you elect to defer tax on a gain, intending to buy replacement property, but you later decide not to make a replacement within the time limit, you must file an amended return for the year of the gain and pay the tax that you had elected to defer. You also must file an amended return and report the gain not eligible for deferral if you invest in property that does not qualify as a replacement, or which costs less than the amount realized from the involuntary conversion.

However, if you elect to defer and make a timely qualifying replacement, you may not change your mind and pay tax on the gain in order to obtain a higher basis (¶18.19) for the replacement property. The Tax Court has agreed with the IRS that the election to defer is irrevocable once a qualified replacement is made within the time limits. Similarly, once you report to the IRS (¶18.21) that a qualified replacement has been made, you may not substitute other replacement property, even if the replacement period has not yet expired.

TIME PERIOD FOR BUYING REPLACEMENT PROPERTY

¶18.21

To defer tax, you generally must buy property similar or related in use (*see* ¶18.22) to the converted property within a fixed time period. There are two replacement periods:

1. A two-year period for destroyed, damaged, or stolen property, and for condemned personal-use property.
2. A three-year period for condemned investment or business real estate property, excluding inventory.

The two-year period for damaged, destroyed, and stolen property starts on the date the property was destroyed, damaged, or stolen, and *ends* two years after the end of the year in which you realize a gain. For condemnations, the two-year (personal-use property) or three-year (investment or non-inventory business property) replacement property *starts* on the earlier of (1) the date you receive notification of the condemnation threat, or (2) the date you dispose of the condemned property. The period ends two or three years after the end of the year in which gain on the condemnation is realized.

EXAMPLES 1. On January 10, 1992, a parcel of investment real estate is condemned; the parcel cost $15,000. On February 26, 1992, you receive a check for $23,500 from the state. You may defer the tax on the gain of $8,500 if you invest at least $23,500 in other real estate not later than December 31, 1995.

2. Business property was contaminated by dangerous chemicals, and after the Environmental Protection Agency ordered businesses and residents to relocate, the property was sold to the local government under a threat of condemnation. The owner was paid the full pre-contamination fair market value for the property. The owner wanted to defer gain under the three-year replacement rule for condemnations. However, the IRS said that part of the gain was deferrable under the two-year rule, and part under the three-year rule. There were two conversions: (1) the contamination, subject to the two-year replacement rule; and (2) the later condemnation, subject to the three-year rule.

To determine the amount eligible for deferral for each period, an allocation must be made between the proceeds allocable to the destruction of the property and the proceeds allocable to the condemnation.

According to the IRS, the burden for making the allocation between the two conversions rests with the owner. The government's payments are allocable to the condemnation and therefore, eligible for the three-year replacement rule, only to the extent of the post-contamination value. Practically speaking, it may be advisable to make the replacement within the two-year period, as it may be difficult to show the contaminated land had any value after the contamination.

Advance payment of award. Gain is realized in the year compensation for the converted property exceeds the basis of the converted property. An advance payment of an award which exceeds the adjusted basis of the property starts the running of the replacement period.

An award is treated as received in the year that it is made available to you without restrictions, even if you contest the amount.

Replacement before actual condemnation. You may make a replacement after a threat of condemnation. If you buy property before the actual threat, it will not qualify as a replacement even though you still own it at the time of the actual condemnation.

Extension of Time to Replace

A contract to buy replacement property within the time limits is not considered a qualified replacement. If you cannot replace property within the time required, ask your local District Director for additional time. Apply for an extension before the end of the period. If you apply for an extension within a reasonable time after the statutory period has run out, you must have a reasonable cause for the delay in asking for the extension.

Replacement by an estate. A person whose property was involuntarily converted may die before he or she makes a replacement. According to the IRS, his or her estate may not reinvest the proceeds within the allowed time and postpone tax on the gain. The Tax Court rejects the IRS position and has allowed tax deferral where the replacement was made by the deceased owner's estate. However, the Tax Court agreed with the IRS that a surviving spouse's investment in land did not defer tax on gain realized by her deceased husband on an involuntary conversion of his land. She had received his property as survivor of joint tenancy and could not, in making the investment, be considered as acting for his estate.

Giving IRS notice of replacement. If you have not bought replacement property by the time you file your return for the year of the involuntary conversion but you intend to do so, attach a statement to your return describing the conversion and the computation of gain, and state that you intend to make a timely replacement. Then, on the return for the year of replacement, attach a statement giving the details of your replacement property. This notice starts the running of the period of limitations for any tax on the gain. Failure to give notice keeps the period open. Similarly, a failure to give notice of an intention not to replace also keeps the period open. When you do not buy replacement property after making an election to postpone tax on the gain, file an amended return for the year in which gain was realized and pay the tax (if any) on the gain.

Assume you have a gain from an involuntary conversion and do not expect to reinvest the proceeds. You report the gain and pay the tax. In a later year, but within the prescribed time limits, you buy similar property. You may make an election to defer tax on the gain and file a claim for tax refund.

TYPES OF QUALIFYING REPLACEMENT PROPERTY

¶18.22

Although exact duplication is not required, the replacement generally must be *similar or related in use* to the property that was involuntarily converted. Where *real property* held for productive use in a business or for investment is converted through a condemnation or threat of condemnation, the replacement test is more liberal. A replacement merely has to be of a *like kind* to the converted property. Under the *like-kind* test, the replacement of improved property by unimproved qualifies; *see* ¶6.1. Under the *related-use* test, the replacement of unimproved land for improved land does not qualify. Under the *related use* test, a replacement generally must be closely related in function to the destroyed property. For example, a condemned personal residence must be replaced with another personal residence. The replacement of a house rented to a tenant with a house used as a personal residence does not qualify for tax deferral; the new house is not being used for the same purpose as the condemned one. This functional test, however, is not strictly applied to conversions of rental property. Here, the role of the owner toward the properties, rather than the functional use of the buildings, is reviewed. If an owner held both properties as investments and offered similar services and took similar business risks in both, the replacement may qualify.

You may own several parcels of property, one of which is condemned. You may want to use the condemnation award to make improvements on the other land such as drainage and grading. The IRS generally will not accept the improvements as a qualified replacement. However, an appeals court has rejected the IRS approach in one case.

If it is not feasible to reinvest the proceeds from the conversion of livestock because of soil contamination or other environmental contamination, then other property (including real property) used for farming purposes is treated as similar or related and qualifies as replacement property.

Buying controlling interest in a corporation. The replacement test may be satisfied by purchasing a controlling interest (80%) in a corporation owning property that is similar or related in service to the converted property.

COST OF REPLACEMENT PROPERTY DETERMINES POSTPONED GAIN

¶18.23
To fully defer tax, the cost of the replacement property must be equal to or exceed the *net proceeds* from the conversion. If replacement cost is less than the adjusted basis of the converted property, you report the entire gain. If replacement cost is less than the amount realized on the conversion but more than the basis of the converted property, the difference between the amount realized and the cost of the replacement is reported as gain. You may elect to postpone tax on the balance of the gain reinvested; *see* Example 2.

EXAMPLES 1. The cost basis of a four-family apartment house is $175,000. It is condemned to make way for a thruway. The net award from the state is $200,000. Your gain is $25,000. If you buy a similar apartment house for $175,000 or less, you report the entire $25,000 gain.

2. Using the same figures as in Example 1, except that you buy an apartment house for $185,000. Of the gain of $25,000, you report $15,000 as taxable gain ($200,000 − $185,000). You may elect to postpone the tax on the balance of the gain, or $10,000.

3. Using the same figures as in Example 1, but you buy an apartment house for $200,000. You may elect to postpone tax on the entire gain because you have invested all of the award in replacement property.

Condemnation award. The award received from a state authority may be reduced by expenses of getting the award such as legal, engineering, and appraisal fees. The treatment of special assessments and severance damages received when part of your property is condemned is explained at ¶18.24. Payments made directly by the authority to your mortgagee may not be deducted from the gross award.

Do not include as part of the award interest paid on the award for delay in its payment; you report the interest as interest income. The IRS may treat as interest part of an award paid late, even though the award does not make any allocation for interest.

Relocation payments are not considered part of the condemnation award and are not treated as taxable income to the extent that they are spent for purposes of relocation; they increase basis of the newly acquired property.

Distinguish between insurance proceeds compensating you for loss of profits because of business interruption and those compensating you for the loss of property. Business interruption proceeds are fully taxed as ordinary income and may not be treated as proceeds of an involuntary conversion.

A single standard fire insurance policy may cover several assets. Assume a fire occurs, and in a settlement the proceeds are allocated to each destroyed item according to its fair market value before the fire. In comparing the allocated proceeds to the tax basis of each item, you find that on some items, you have realized a gain; that is, the proceeds exceed basis. On the other items, you have a loss; the proceeds are less than basis. According to the IRS, you may elect to defer tax on the gain items by buying replacement property. You do not treat the proceeds paid under the single policy as a unit, but as separate payments made for each covered item.

SPECIAL ASSESSMENTS AND SEVERANCE DAMAGES

¶18.24
When only part of a property parcel is condemned for a public improvement, the condemning authority may:

1. Levy a special assessment against the remaining property, claiming that it is benefited by the improvement. The authority usually deducts the assessment from the condemnation award.

2. Award severance damages for damages suffered by the remaining property because of the condemnation.

Special assessments reduce the amount of the gross condemnation award. If they exceed the award, the excess is added to the basis of the property. An assessment levied after the award is made may not be deducted from the award.

EXAMPLE Two acres of a 10-acre tract are condemned for a new highway. The adjusted basis of the land is $30,000 or $3,000 per acre. The condemnation award is $10,000; the special assessment against the remaining eight acres is $2,500. The net gain on the condemnation is $1,500:

Condemnation award		$10,000
Less:		
Basis of two condemned acres	$6,000	
Special assessment	2,500	8,500
Net gain		$ 1,500

When both the condemnation award and severance damages are received, the condemnation is treated as two separate involuntary conversions: (1) A conversion of the condemned land. Here, the condemnation award is applied against the basis of the condemned land to determine gain or loss on its conversion. And, (2) a conversion of part of the remaining land in the sense that its utility has been reduced by condemnation, for which severance damages are paid.

Net severance damages reduce the basis of the retained property. Net severance damages are the total severance damages, reduced by expenses in obtaining the damages and by any special assessment withheld from the condemnation award. If the damages exceed basis, gain is realized. Tax may be deferred on the gain through the purchase of replacement property under the "similar or related in use test" at ¶18.22, such as adjacent land or restoration of the property to its original condition.

Allocating the proceeds between the condemnation award and severance damages will either reduce the gain or increase the loss realized on the condemned land. The IRS will allow such a division only when the condemnation authority specifically identifies part of the award as severance damage in the contract or in an itemized statement or closing sheet. The Tax Court, however, has allowed an allocation in the absence of earmarking where the state considered severance damages, and the value of the condemned land was small in comparison to the damages suffered by the remaining property. To avoid a dispute with the IRS, make sure the authority makes this breakdown. Without such identification, the IRS will treat the entire proceeds as consideration for the condemned property.

REPORTING GAINS FROM CASUALTIES, THEFTS, AND CONDEMNATIONS

¶**18.25** If an involuntary conversion was the result of a *theft* or *casualty,* you have to prepare Form 4684. To report net gains,

Form 4684 will direct you to either Form 1040, Schedule D, or Form 4797, depending on the type of property involved. Generally, use of Form 4797 reflects the netting requirements for involuntary conversions of business, rental, or royalty property under Section 1231; *see* ¶44.8.

If the conversion occurred because of a *condemnation,* you use Form 4797 and/or Schedule D depending on the purpose you held the property and the holding period:

Condemnation sales of personal-use property are reported in Schedule D: if held for less than a year, in Part I; if more than a year, in Part II. Losses on the sale of personal-use property are not deductible.

Condemnation sales of business or investment property held for more than a year are reported in Part I, Form 4797. Investment property held for less than a year is reported in Part I, Schedule D; business and rental property held for less than a year in Part II, Form 4797.

19 DEDUCTING MISCELLANEOUS EXPENSES

Deductible miscellaneous expenses cover a wide and varied range of items such as employee travel and entertainment expenses, work clothes expenses, union and employee professional dues, investment expenses, legal expenses, tax preparation expenses, and educational expenses. They also share this common limitation: a 2% adjusted gross income floor. If your expenses do not exceed this floor, you may not deduct them. If the expenses exceed the floor, you may deduct only the excess on Schedule A, as explained in ¶19.1. A few job-related deductions, such as moving expenses and impairment-related work expenses, are not subject to the 2% AGI floor.

In addition to the 2% AGI floor, employees who incur unreimbursed meal and entertainment costs face this further restriction. Only 80% of meal and entertainment costs are deductible.

Miscellaneous deductions, except for gambling losses, are subject to the 3% reduction to itemized deductions (¶13.8) if your adjusted gross income exceeds $105,250 ($52,625 if you are married and file separate returns).

2% AGI FLOOR REDUCES MISCELLANEOUS DEDUCTIONS

¶**19.1** A floor of 2% of adjusted gross income (AGI) applies to the total of most miscellaneous deductions claimed on Schedule A of Form 1040. Adjusted gross income is the amount on Line 32 of Form 1040; also *see* ¶13.7. The purpose of the floor is to reduce or eliminate such deductions. Only expenses above the floor are deductible.

If your AGI exceeds $105,250, or $52,625 if married filing separately, deductible miscellaneous expenses (after applying the 2% floor) are then subject to a further reduction under the 3% reduction computation discussed at ¶13.8.

Miscellaneous expenses subject to the 2% AGI floor:

Unreimbursed travel, meals, and entertainment expenses of employees, ¶20.1 and ¶20.32

Reimbursed job expenses or expense allowances under nonaccountable plans, ¶20.33

Union dues, ¶19.5
Professional and business association dues, ¶19.5
Work clothes expenses, ¶19.6
Cost of looking for a new job, ¶19.7
Job agency fees, ¶19.7
Tax advice and preparation fees, ¶19.25
Appraisal fees related to casualty losses and charitable property contributions, ¶19.25
Investment expenses, such as IRA custodial fees, safe deposit rentals, and fees to investment counselors, ¶19.24
Employee home office expenses, ¶19.13
Legal fees, ¶19.26
Education costs, ¶19.15

Miscellaneous expenses not subject to 2% AGI floor:
Moving expenses to a new job location, Chapter 21
Impairment-related work expenses for handicapped employees, ¶19.4
Gambling losses up to gambling income, ¶12.3
Estate tax attributable to income in respect of a decedent, ¶11.4
The deduction for repayment of amounts held under a claim of right, ¶2.9
Amortizable bond premium on bonds purchased before October 23, 1986, ¶4.17
Unrecovered investments in pension on deceased retiree's final return, ¶7.22

EXAMPLE 1. You pay union dues of $280, work clothes costs of $300, and $150 for the preparation of your tax return. Your adjusted gross income (AGI) is $25,000. Your miscellaneous deduction on Schedule A after applying the 2% floor is $230:

Union dues	**$280**
Work clothes	**300**
Tax preparation	**150**
	$730
Less: 2% of $25,000	**500**
Deductible amount	**$230**

2. Your adjusted gross income (AGI) is $90,000. You pay the following deductible miscellaneous expenses:

Professional dues	**$100**
Investment counsel fee	**300**
Safe deposit box	**50**
Tax preparation fee	**500**
Unreimbursed travel expenses	**800**
	$1,750

The 2% floor of $1,800 (2% × $90,000) applied to your expenses prevents you from claiming any of the above expenses.

HOW THE 2% AGI FLOOR LIMITS DEDUCTIONS

¶19.2 The table on this page shows the effect of the 2% AGI floor on miscellaneous deductible expenses. For example, a taxpayer with an AGI of $40,000 and miscellaneous deductions of $3,000 can deduct only $2,200. A higher bracket taxpayer is subject to even larger reductions and also may be subject to the 3% reduction to itemized deductions discussed at ¶13.8.

How the 2% Floor Reduces Deductions

If your adjusted gross income (AGI) is—	Miscellaneous expenses must exceed this amount for a deduction—
$ 2,000	$ 40
5,000	100
10,000	200
15,000	300
20,000	400
25,000	500
30,000	600
35,000	700
40,000	800
50,000	1,000
60,000	1,200
70,000	1,400
90,000	1,800
100,000	2,000
200,000	4,000

CHECKLIST OF JOB EXPENSES SUBJECT TO THE 2% AGI FLOOR

¶19.3 The following expenses that are job related—ranging from professional dues and subscriptions to employment agency fees—are subject to the 2% AGI floor.

Generally, you must file Form 2106 to claim job-related expenses that were not reimbursed by your employer. You enter your expenses and any reimbursements on Form 2106, and the allowable amount is then transferred to Line 19 of Schedule A (unreimbursed employee expenses) where it is subject to the 2% floor along with other miscellaneous deductions (¶19.1).

You may enter your unreimbursed expenses directly on Line 19 of Schedule A without having to complete Form 2106 if you are not claiming any job-related travel, local transportation, meal or entertainment expenses and you received no employer reimbursement at all for any of your other job costs (such as education expenses, union dues or uniforms).

Agency fees for job, ¶19.7
Airfares, ¶20.5
Auto club membership, ¶43.2
Auto expenses, ¶43.1
Books used on the job, ¶19.5
Business machines, ¶5.12
Car insurance premiums, ¶43.2
Christmas gifts, ¶20.28
Cleaning costs, ¶19.6
Commerce association dues, ¶19.5
Commuting costs, ¶20.2
Computers, ¶19.9
Convention trips, ¶20.13, 20.15
Correspondence course, ¶19.16
Depreciation, ¶42.1
Dues, ¶19.5
Educational expenses, ¶19.15–¶19.23

Employment agency fees, ¶19.7
Entertainment expenses, ¶20.16–¶20.28
Equipment, ¶19.9–¶19.11
Fidelity bond costs, ¶19.24
Foreign travel cost, ¶20.15
Furniture, ¶19.13, 21.5
Garage rent, ¶43.2
Gasoline, ¶43.2
Gasoline taxes, ¶43.2
Gifts, ¶19.28
Helmets, safety, ¶19.6
Home office expenses, ¶19.13
Hotel cost, ¶20.5
House-hunting costs, ¶21.5
Instruments, ¶19.11
Labor union dues, ¶19.5
Laundry, ¶19.6
Legal expenses, ¶19.26
Local transportation, ¶20.1

Lodging, ¶20.5
Magazines, ¶19.5
Malpractice liability premi-
　ums, ¶40.5
Meals, ¶20.3, 20.4
Medical examinations,
　¶17.13
Membership dues and fees,
　¶19.5
Motel charges, ¶20.5
Moving expenses, ¶21.5
Parking fees, ¶43.2
Passport fees for business
　travel, ¶20.12
Pay turned over to employer,
　¶2.9
Periodicals, ¶19.5
Protective clothing, ¶19.6
Rail fares, ¶20.5

Reimbursed expenses,
　¶20.33–20.37
Safety shoes, ¶19.6
Secretarial convention,
　¶20.13
Subscriptions, ¶19.5
Taxi fares, ¶20.5
Telegrams, ¶19.14
Telephone calls, ¶19.14
Toll charges, ¶43.2
Tools, ¶19.11
Trade association dues, ¶19.5
Transportation and travel
　expenses, ¶20.1
Tuition, ¶19.15
Typewriter, ¶19.10
Uniforms, ¶19.6
Union dues, ¶19.5
Work clothes and uniforms,
　¶19.6

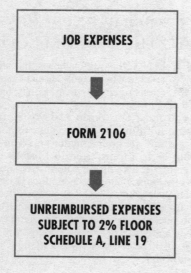

Life Insurance Agents and Food Deliverers

Statutory employees, such as full-time life insurance salespersons and food delivery persons, may deduct expenses on Schedule C and so avoid the 2% AGI floor; see ¶40.5 for further details.

JOB EXPENSES NOT SUBJECT TO THE 2% FLOOR

¶19.4 *Impairment-related work expenses.* Unreimbursed impairment-related work expenses shown on Form 2106 are deductible as miscellaneous deductions on Line 25 of Schedule A and are *not* subject to the 2% AGI floor.

To get the deduction, you have to show:

1. You are handicapped. A handicapped person must have a physical or mental disability which results in a functional limitation to employment or which substantially limits one or more major life activities. Generally, showing blindness or deafness will meet this test, but other disabilities that impair your ability to walk, speak, breathe, or perform manual tasks also may qualify if they limit the ability to work.
2. You incur the expenses in order to work. The expenses must be ordinary and necessary to allow you to work. Attendant care services at a place of employment which are necessary for you to work are also deductible.

Expenses of performing artists. A performing artist may deduct job expenses from gross income whether or not itemized deductions are claimed, if he or she has:

1. Two or more employers in the performing professions during 1992 with at least $200 of earnings from each employer;
2. Expenses from acting or other services in the performing arts that exceed 10% of gross income from such work; and
3. Adjusted gross income (before deducting these expenses) that does not exceed $16,000.

If a performing artist is married, a joint return must be filed to claim the deduction, unless the couple lives apart the whole year. If each spouse is a performing artist, the $16,000 adjusted income test applies to the couple's combined income, but each spouse must separately meet the two-employer test and 10% expense test to claim the deduction from gross income.

If you meet these tests, you report the expenses on Form 2106 and enter the total as a "write-in amount" on Line 30 of Form 1040, instead of on Schedule A. If you do not meet the tests, your expenses are deducted on Schedule A and are subject to the 2% AGI floor.

Moving expenses. Moving expenses to a new job location are not subject to the 2% floor; see Chapter 21.

DUES AND SUBSCRIPTIONS

¶19.5 You may deduct as miscellaneous itemized deductions, subject to the 2% AGI floor on Schedule A, dues paid to a—

Professional society if you are a salaried lawyer, accountant, teacher, physician, or other professional.
Trade association if it is conducted for the purpose of furthering the business interests of its members.
Stock exchange if you are a securities dealer.
Community "booster" club conducted to attract tourists and settlers to the locality where the members do business.
Chamber of Commerce if it is conducted to advance the business interests of its members.

Union costs. Union members may deduct as "miscellaneous" itemized deductions, union dues, and initiation fees. Similarly, non-union employees may deduct monthly service charges to a union. An assessment paid for unemployment benefits is deductible if payment is required as a condition of remaining in the union and holding a union job. Voluntary payments to an union unemployment benefit or strike fund are not deductible.

No deduction is allowed for mandatory contributions to a union pension fund applied toward the purchase of a retirement annuity; the contributions are treated as the cost of the annuity. Furthermore, to the extent that an assessment covers sick, accident, or death benefits payable to you or your family, it is not deductible. Similarly, an assessment for a construction fund to build union recreation centers was disallowed by the Tax Court, even though the payment was required for keeping the job.

Campaign costs for running for union office are not deductible.

Subscriptions. Subject to the 2% AGI floor, you may claim as miscellaneous itemized deductions unreimbursed payments for job-related subscriptions to professional journals and trade magazines.

UNIFORMS AND WORK CLOTHES

¶19.6 The cost of uniforms and other apparel, including their cleaning, laundering, and repair, is deductible *only* if the clothes are:

1. Required to keep your job; *and*
2. Not suitable for wear when not working.

The deduction is subject to the 2% AGI floor.

CAUTION | Special Work Clothes

Courts have held that the cost of special work clothes that protect you from injury is deductible even if you are not required to wear them to keep your job. However, you may not deduct the cost of special clothing, such as aprons and overalls, which protect your regular street clothing. Nor may you deduct the cost of ordinary clothes used as work clothes on the grounds that:

- They get harder use than customary garments receive.
- They are soiled after a day's work and cannot be worn socially.
- They were purchased for your convenience to save wear and tear on your better clothes. For example, a sanitation inspector, a machinist's helper, a carpenter, and a telephone repairman were not allowed to deduct the cost of their work clothes.

Deductions allowed. Deductions for costs of uniforms and work clothes have been allowed to—

Airline pilot
Bakery salesperson—for a uniform with a company label
Baseball player
Bus driver
Cement finisher's gloves, overshoes, and rubber boots
Civilian faculty members of a military school
Commercial fisherman's protective clothing, such as oil clothes, gloves, and boots
Dairy worker's rubber boots, white shirts, trousers, and cap worn only while inside the dairy
Entertainer's theatrical clothing used solely for performances
Factory foreman's white coat bearing the word "foreman" and the name of the company

Factory worker's safety shoes
Firefighter
Hospital attendant's work clothes; he came in contact with patients having contagious diseases
Jockey
Letter carrier
Meat cutter's special white shoes
Musician's formal wear
Paint machine operator's high top shoes and long leather gloves
Plumber's special shoes and gloves
Police officer
Railroad conductor
Railroad fireman's boots, leather gloves, raincoat, caps, and work gloves

EXAMPLES 1. A painter may not deduct the cost of work clothing consisting of a white cap, a white shirt, white bib overalls, and standard work shoes. The clothing is not distinctive in character as a uniform would be. That his union requires him to wear such clothing does not make it a deductible expense.

2. A tennis pro who taught at private clubs was not allowed to deduct the cost of tennis outfits or shoes required for his job. He did not wear them outside of work and argued that he replaced the shoes every few weeks to reduce the chances of injury. However, the Tax Court upheld the IRS' disallowance of his deductions because the clothes and shoes are suitable for everyday wear; warm-up suits and tennis clothes have become fashionable and are frequently worn as casual wear. Furthermore, there was no evidence that his tennis shoes reduced chances of injury.

Your claim of a work clothes deduction is helped if your employer requires you to wear a uniform. Uniform costs of reservists and servicemen are discussed at ¶35.8.

Employer allowance. An allowance paid by your employer for work clothes or a uniform is not reported as income, unless you do not substantiate the expenses to your employer. If you do substantiate, the expenses exceeding the reimbursement are reported on Form 2106, and the deduction is subject to the 2% AGI floor; *see* ¶20.33.

High-fashion work clothes. That your job requires you to wear expensive clothing is not a basis for deducting the cost of the clothes if the clothing is suitable for wear off the job.

1040 | Cleaning and Laundering

If you are allowed to deduct the cost of work clothes and uniforms, you also may deduct the cost of cleaning and laundering them. Also, courts have allowed the cost of cleaning and laundering in situations where:

- The clothes could only be worn one day at a time because they became too dirty.
- Dirty clothes were a hazard; they became baggy and might get caught in machinery.
- Clothes were only worn at work and a place for changing clothes was provided by the employer.
- A meat cutter had to wear clean work clothes at all times.

EXPENSES OF LOOKING FOR A NEW JOB

¶19.7 You may deduct expenses of looking for a new job in the *same line of work*, whether or not a new job is found. The deduction is subject to the 2% AGI floor. If you are unemployed when seeking a new job, and the period of unemployment has been substantial, the IRS may disallow the deduction.

EXAMPLE The IRS disallowed the driving expenses of an unemployed secretary on the ground that she was not currently employed. The Tax Court disagreed and held that for purposes of deducting job hunting expenses, she could still be considered in the business of being a secretary. She had worked as an administrative secretary with Toyota in San Francisco. The firm relocated, resulting in a 100-mile-per-day commute. She quit her job at the end of January, 1984. From February to November 1984, she drove her Cadillac El Dorado over 4,600 miles looking for a new job. The Tax Court allowed her a depreciation deduction of $2,880 and $981 for car operating costs.

Expenses of seeking your first job are not deductible, even if a job is obtained. Also, expenses of looking for a job in a different line of work are not deductible, even if you get the job.

The IRS may also dispute the deduction of search expenses of a previously employed professional who forms a partnership.

EXAMPLE A CPA working for a firm decided to go out on his own. After a period of investigation, he formed a partnership with another CPA. The IRS disallowed his deduction of search expenses claiming his expenses were incurred in a new business. As an employee he was in a different business than that of a self-employed practitioner. Thus, the expenses should be capitalized as a cost of setting up or organizing the partnership. The Tax Court disagreed, allowing the deduction. The travel expenses were incurred to seek work as a CPA, whether as a self-employed or employed CPA.

Travel expenses. If you travel to find a new job in the same line of work, such as an interview in a distant city, you may deduct travel expenses, including living costs. If, during the trip, you also do personal visiting, you may deduct the transportation expenses if the trip was primarily related to your job search. Time spent on personal activity is compared with time spent looking for a job to determine the primary purpose of the trip. If the transportation expenses to and from the destination are not deductible, you may still deduct the expenses of seeking a new job while you are away.

Are you between jobs? If you are between jobs and you continue to see and entertain your former customers, the IRS holds that you may not deduct the cost of entertainment and other business expenses during this period on the grounds that you are not in business and earning income. However, the Tax Court in the following case allowed the deduction.

EXAMPLE Haft was a successful jewelry salesman earning as much as $60,000 a year. In the fall of one year, he left his employer and started to look for a new connection. During the following year, he continued to maintain contacts with his former customers by entertaining buyers and their representatives. He deducted the expenses of entertaining and other business costs. The IRS disallowed the deduction, claiming he was not in business. The court disagreed. His lack of business income was temporary and during a period of transition which lasted a reasonable time.

Employment Agency Fee

If your new employer pays the fee under an agreement with an agency, you may disregard the payment for tax purposes. However, if you pay the fee and deduct it as a job search expense and in a later year you are reimbursed by your employer, you must report the reimbursement as taxable income to the extent you received a tax benefit from the earlier deduction; see ¶12.8.

A company interested in your services may invite you to a job interview and agree to pay all of the expenses of the trip to its office, even if you are not hired. The company payment is tax free to the extent it does not exceed your actual expenses.

UNUSUAL JOB EXPENSES

¶**19.8** The following are not typical deductible expenses. However, courts have allowed deductions in the following cases.

Shoe shine expenses of a pilot.

EXAMPLE Company rules required a commercial airline pilot to look neat, keep his hair cut, and wear conservative black shoes, properly shined. The pilot deducted as a business expense $100 for his haircuts and $25 for his shoe shines. The IRS disallowed the deductions, but the Tax Court allowed the cost of the shoe shines. The shoes were of a military type which he wore only with his pilot's uniform. The cost of keeping up a uniform is deductible. The haircuts were merely nondeductible personal expenses.

Cost of lobbying for better working conditions.

Depreciation on furnishings bought by executive for his company office.

EXAMPLE Following a quarrel with an interior decorator, a sales manager bought his own office furniture when his

firm moved to new quarters. Rather than complain or ask for reimbursement, he footed the bill and deducted depreciation. The IRS disallowed the deduction, claiming the expense was that of his company. The Tax Court allowed the deduction. The manager's action was unusual, but prudent. He did not want to cause difficulties, and at the same time had to maintain his image as a successful manager. His expenses for furniture were appropriate and helpful.

Salesman's cost of operating a private plane.

EXAMPLE Sherman flew his own plane to visit clients in six southern states and deducted $18,000 as operating costs of the plane. The IRS disallowed the deduction, claiming there was no business reason for the plane. He could have taken commercial flights or used a company car to reach his clients. Furthermore, his company did not reimburse him for the private airplane costs, although it would cover costs of his car and commercial air travel. Finally, the amount of airplane expenses was unreasonable compared to his salary of $25,000. Sherman convinced the Tax Court that use of a private airplane was the only reasonable way he could cover his six-state sales area. He showed that most of his clients were not near commercial airports. Although the airplane costs were large in relation to his salary, they were still reasonable and, therefore, deductible.

Executive's purchase of blazers for sales force.

EXAMPLE Jetty, the president of an oil equipment manufacturing firm, thought that he could generate goodwill for the company if employees who attended industrial trade shows wore a blazer and vest set in the company colors. He personally paid and deducted $6,725 for 27 blazers and vests. The IRS disallowed the deduction on the grounds that it was a company expense and that Jetty should have sought reimbursement from the company.

The Tax Court allowed the deduction. Paying for the clothes was a legitimate business expense for Jetty since he depended on bonuses for a large portion of his pay, and as company president, he had responsibility for seeing to it that there were profits to share in. Furthermore, the outlay was not the type of expense covered by the company's manual on expense reimbursements.

Repayment of layoff benefits to restore pension credit.

EXAMPLE When he was laid off, an employee received a lump-sum payment from his company based on his salary and years of service. When he was rehired a year later, he repaid the lump sum in order to restore his pension credits and other benefit rights. The IRS ruled that he may deduct the repayment as a condition of being rehired; the repayment was required to restore employee benefits.

Teaching costs. The IRS does not allow teachers a deduction for school supplies. Some courts have been lenient and have allowed teachers to deduct out-of-pocket expenses. In one case, however, a teacher could not convince a court that his deduction for the cost of paper, pens, glue, and other supplies was a business expense. He could not support his claim that the school did not supply enough equipment.

Politician's expenses. Elected officials may incur out-of-pocket expenses in excess of the allowances received from the government. They may deduct as miscellaneous deductions their payment of office expenses such as salaries, office rent, and supplies. Part-time officials may claim the deduction. The expenses are deductible even if they exceed the official's income.

EQUIPMENT USED FOR YOUR JOB

COMPUTERS AND CELLULAR PHONES

¶19.9 Computers (and peripherals) and cellular phones are treated as "listed property" subject to depreciation restrictions: To get a first-year expensing deduction (¶42.3) or to claim any type of depreciation, the computer or cellular phone must be used for the convenience of your employer and also be required as a condition of your job. The IRS strictly interprets these requirements.

Computer. Merely getting a letter from your employer stating that a computer is needed for your position does not by itself satisfy the deduction tests. Even where the employer encourages use of a personal computer that is used for basic job requirements, the IRS requires proof that you need your own computer to do your job because your employer does not provide one, or because your employer's computer is not adequate for your job. In the following examples, the IRS disallowed depreciation writeoffs.

EXAMPLES 1. An electric company offers to help pay for its engineers' personal computers where they will improve productivity. Qualifying engineers receive extra pay *and must* buy a computer meeting company specifications, take approved computer courses, and agree to restrictions on resale of the computer. An engineer buys a computer, uses it 95% of the time for writing business memos and reports, and studying business flow charts. He does not use the computer for entertainment.

The IRS held that although the engineer's computer was work related and benefited his employer, buying a computer was not required for his job; it was not "inextricably related" to proper job performance. Furthermore, his participation in the employer's computer program was optional, not mandatory.

2. A professor of nursing, trying to keep her temporary position, buys a personal computer, needing a word processor for independent research papers and to document her qualifications for research grants. The research and external grant support were implied university requirements for faculty appointments. She did not have access to university word-processing equipment during regular work hours; and because of her classroom responsibilities, her research and grant development work had to be done on her own time. To help her pursue outside grants, the university bought her a "modem" that allowed a phone hook-up with its computer at night. Her computer was used 100% for research and grant work.

As in Example 1, the IRS held that use of the computer was not "inextricably related" to proper job performance. Furthermore, there was no evidence that employees who did not use computers were professionally disadvantaged.

3. The IRS held that an insurance agent could not deduct depreciation for a portable computer he used to help develop insurance plans for clients. The insurance company encouraged its agents to buy the computer because office computers were not generally accessible. According to the IRS, it is not enough that the agent's productivity increased or that he used the computer solely for business. Purchasing the computer was optional, not a mandatory job requirement. Employees who did not purchase computers were not professionally disadvantaged.

Cellular phones. The IRS has not yet released specific guidelines or rulings covering deduction requirements for cellular phones. In general, the "convenience of the employer" and "job condition" tests apply.

Claiming a deduction. If you can meet the "convenience of the employer" and "job condition" tests for a computer or cellular phone, and the unit is used *more* than 50% of the time for your job, you may write off up to $10,000 of the cost under the first-year expensing rules; *see* ¶42.3, or regular five-year MACRS deprecia-

tion rates may be used; *see* ¶42.10. If used 50% or less for business, you may not use first-year expensing or regular MACRS but you may claim straight-line depreciation.

First-year expensing or straight-line depreciation is claimed on Form 4562 and then entered on Form 2106 along with other job-related costs. The deduction from Form 2106 is subject to the 2% AGI floor for miscellaneous deductions on Schedule A; *see* ¶19.1. If business use in a later year is 50% or less, *see* ¶42.10 for recapture rules.

You need to keep records documenting your percentage of business use for a computer or cellular phone.

Tax Court Allows Computer Deduction

COURT DECISION The Tax Court allowed a deduction to a working couple who used the same home computer given these facts. The husband, a professor, used it to store historical data; the wife, a state transportation planner, to do extensive number crunching. What apparently won the decision for the couple was evidence that (1) the husband did not have access to a computer at the university, and (2) the state office in which the wife worked did not have funds to buy a computer. The court held that the use of the computer was necessary for them to properly do their jobs, and as the purchase of a computer spared their employers from having to provide them with computers, the purchase was for the employers' convenience.

CALCULATORS, COPIERS, FAX MACHINES, AND TYPEWRITERS

¶19.10 The listed property requirements applied to computers and cellular phones (¶19.9) do not apply to calculators, copiers, adding machines, fax machines, and typewriters. This means that the restrictive convenience of the employer and job condition rules do not apply. However, to depreciate the cost of such equipment, you should be ready to prove that you need the equipment for your job, and keep a record of the time it is used for business. To claim first-year expensing (¶42.3), rather than regular depreciation, you must use the equipment *more* than 50% of the time for business.

SMALL TOOLS

¶19.11 If you furnished your own small tools used on your job, you may deduct their cost if they are expected to last for a year or less. The deduction is subject to the 2% AGI floor. The cost of tools with a useful life of more than a year must be recovered through depreciation or first-year expensing; *see* ¶42.3. Be prepared to substantiate your deduction with receipts showing the cost and type of tools purchased, and the business necessity for them.

AUTOMOBILE USED FOR WORK

¶19.12 If you buy a car that you use for work, you generally may claim the IRS mileage allowance or deduct actual unreimbursed expenses on Form 2106. If you claim actual expenses, you are allowed to deduct depreciation only if use of the car is required for the job and for the convenience of the employer. For a car bought in 1992, the maximum depreciation deduction is $2,760, reduced by the percentage of personal use.

The IRS standard mileage allowance is discussed at ¶43.1.
Depreciation rules, including annual deduction limits, are at ¶43.3.

EMPLOYEE HOME OFFICE EXPENSES

HOME OFFICE DEDUCTIONS RESTRICTED

¶19.13 The law severely limits employees from claiming deductions for home office expenses by setting conditions most employees cannot meet. To deduct office expenses, the office must be exclusively used on a regular basis as your principal place of business or as a place in which patients, clients, or customers meet or deal with you in the normal course of your profession or business. As an employee, it is only in rare situations that your home office is your principal place of business or a place for meeting patients, clients, or customers.

However, proposed IRS regulations recognize that if an outside salesman has no office space except at home and spends a substantial amount of time on paperwork at home, the office may qualify as a principal place of business. The IRS does not extend this break to other employees.

Courts have disagreed with the IRS on this issue and allowed deductions where no other office was available or an employer-provided office was inadequate. For example, the Tax Court allowed home office deductions to an anesthesiologist who had no office space at any of the hospitals where he worked and who did all of his billings and other office work at home. An appeals court upheld the Tax Court and the IRS appealed to the Supreme Court. At the time this book went to press, the Supreme Court had not yet decided the conflict between the IRS and the courts. *See* the Supplement for an update.

Exclusive use means that the space used as an office must *not* be used for personal purposes such as a family den. Furthermore, you must show that the office is used for the convenience of your employer. Finally, even if you meet these rules the amount of your deduction may be limited; deductible expenses may not exceed gross income derived from the office.

EXAMPLE A married couple both teach in an elementary school. Neither can use the school facilities after 5 P.M. and so are required to work at home, preparing lessons, constructing charts and learning materials, and reading educational literature. They do this in a room exclusively used for this purpose. The IRS rules that no home office deduction is available because the room is not their principal place of business.

Office in separate structure. If you maintain an office in a separate structure located on the same lot as your home, such as a garage, studio, or barn, and the structure is used exclusively and regularly for work required by your employer, your unreimbursed expenses are deductible as a miscellaneous itemized deduction subject to the 2% AGI floor.

Rentals to employer. Home office deductions may *not* be claimed by employees who rent home office space to their employer.

Investors. Home office deductions may *not* be claimed by investors who use a home office to review investments and make investment decisions unless the activity constitutes a business; *see* ¶19.24.

Deductible expenses. As a practical matter, qualifying for the home office deduction only determines whether you can deduct the allocable business part of your insurance, maintenance, utilities or rent costs, and depreciation (if you own your home or apartment). Real estate taxes and mortgage interest are fully deductible on Schedule A regardless of your use of the home. The other expenses, such as maintenance, depreciation, or rent, must be allocated to your home office use. The allocated portion is then entered as a miscellaneous expense on Line 19 of Schedule A, subject to the 2% AGI floor. You also may have to list these allocated expenses on Form 2106 if they are reimbursed by your employer or you need Form 2106 to claim other job expenses such as travel costs. The allocated home office expenditures may not exceed income from your employment.

You may allocate expenses to the home office by dividing the number of square feet of space used as an office into the total number of square feet in the home. Apply the resulting percentage to the total expenses. If the rooms in your home are approximately the same size, you can divide total rooms in the house by the room used as an office.

EXAMPLE One room out of a five-room apartment is used for an office; ⅕ or 20% of deductible home expenses are allocated to the use of the office.

To support your deduction, keep records to show how you allocated the expenses, in addition to canceled checks, receipts, and other evidence of the expenses paid.

You need physical evidence of an office. A bare minimum is a desk, chair, and filing cabinet.

Retain business mail directed to your home.

Keep a record of business phone calls you make, particularly charges for long-distance telephone calls, and a diary of business visitors, including those who come to your home for entertainment.

Self-employed persons. The home office provisions as they apply to a self-employed person are explained at ¶40.11.

TELEPHONE COSTS

¶19.14 For business calls made outside of your employer's office or at home, keep a record or diary of business calls to support your deduction. To avoid the problem of allocating the costs of a single home phone for both business and personal use, consider installing a separate home phone for business use only. For long-distance business calls, you might ask the phone company to transfer the charges to your office phone.

Deduction barred for basic charge of first phone line. You may not claim as a deductible home office expense any part of the standard monthly charge for the first telephone line into your home. This disallowance rule only applies to the first telephone line. If you have more than one telephone line and use additional lines in a home office, costs for these lines remain deductible, subject to the restrictions at ¶19.13.

The restriction does *not* affect deductibility of long-distance calls, phone rentals, or optional services such as call waiting, call forwarding, three-way calling, or extra directory listings.

DEDUCTIBLE EDUCATION COSTS

RULES FOR DEDUCTING EDUCATION COSTS

¶19.15 You can improve your job or professional skills by attending continuing education or refresher classes, advanced academic courses, or vocational training, and get an itemized deduction for the cost. The deduction is subject to the 2% adjusted gross income floor for miscellaneous deductions; *see* ¶19.1.

To deduct education costs, you must show that the following conditions are met:

1. You are employed or self-employed;
2. You already meet the minimum requirements of your job, business, or profession; and
3. The course maintains or improves your job skills, or you are required by your employer or by law to take the course to keep your present salary or position.

The details of these requirements are explained at ¶19.16.

That courses lead to a degree will not bar a deduction provided the above three tests are met. If the courses lead to a change of position or promotion within the same occupation, a deduction for their cost will be allowed if your new duties involve the same general type of work.

Nondeductible courses. The cost of courses preparing you for a new profession or for meeting the minimum requirements for your job are not deductible, even if you take them to improve your skills or to meet your employer's requirements. This rule prevents the deduction of law school costs; *see* ¶19.17. Furthermore, the cost of a bar review course or CPA review course is not deductible because it leads to a new profession as an attorney or CPA.

If courses lead to qualification for a new business or profession, no deduction is allowed even if you keep your current position.

DEDUCTION TESTS FOR EDUCATION COSTS

¶19.16 You must meet an employment test to deduct educational expenses. Educational costs are not deductible if you are unemployed or inactive in a business or profession. The cost of "brush-up" courses taken in anticipation of resuming work are also not deductible. However, in one case, a court allowed an unemployed teacher to deduct the cost of tuition, fees, and books where the IRS conceded that the teacher, although unemployed, remained in the teaching profession while attending college classes.

You are not considered unemployed when you take courses during a vacation or temporary leave of absence; *see* ¶19.21.

EXAMPLE A substitute teacher left his job to go to Norway for doctoral studies in linguistics and anthropology. The IRS disallowed his deduction for the cost of travel, room, board, and books, claiming that he abandoned teaching before he went abroad. Also, the studies abroad fitted him for a new career. The Tax Court disagreed. He did not abandon his teaching profession as evidenced by these facts: He applied for work at an American school in Oslo and was available for substitute teaching, although he only taught one day. He also made arrangements to teach on his return. Furthermore, his studies were appropriate and helpful to his career as a teacher of language and social studies.

If you are practicing your profession, the cost of courses leading to a specialty within that profession are deductible.

EXAMPLE A practicing dentist returned to school full time to study orthodontics while continuing his practice on a part-time basis. When he finished his training, he limited his work to orthodontics. The IRS ruled he may deduct the cost of his studies. His post-graduate schooling improved his professional skills as a dentist. It did not qualify him for a new profession.

Minimum standards. You may not deduct the cost of courses taken to meet the minimum requirements of your job. The minimum requirements of a position are based on a review of your employer's standards, the laws and regulations of the state you live in, and the standards of your profession or business. That you are presently employed does not in itself prove that you have met the minimum standards for your job.

If minimum standards change after you enter a job or profession, you are required to meet only the standards that existed when you entered.

The minimum standards for teachers are discussed at ¶19.19.

Maintaining or improving job skills. To be deductible, the education must maintain or improve your current job skills. That you are established in your position and that persons in similar positions usually pursue such education indicates that the courses are taken to maintain and improve job skills. However, the IRS may not allow a deduction for a general education course that is a prerequisite for a job-related course.

If, as a consequence of taking a job-related course, you receive a substantial advancement and the IRS questions the deduction of the course costs, be prepared to prove that you took the course primarily to maintain or improve skills of your existing job. However, if the course leads to qualification for a new profession, the IRS will disallow a deduction even if the course also improves current job skills. For example, a deduction is not allowed for the cost of law school or medical school courses if they prepare you for a new profession; see ¶19.17 and ¶19.18.

Are MBA Courses Deductible?

The cost of MBA courses is deductible if the courses enhance the skills required in your current position, are not a minimum job requirement, and do not qualify you for a new business. The IRS may question in a particular case whether there has been a change of business, particularly where taking the courses leads to a promotion. For a deduction, the courses must be related to your existing job responsibilities. The Tax Court has allowed deductions for MBA expenses where individuals with some managerial or administrative experience took the courses to improve job skills.

If your employer requires a master's degree as a minimum entrance requirement for your position, the cost of the courses is not deductible.

In one case, a college graduate who took a summer job before starting MBA courses was not allowed a deduction because he had not yet established himself in a business or employment; the summer position was just a temporary stage between schooling.

If your employer reimburses you for MBA courses that qualify for a deduction, the reimbursement is a tax-free working condition fringe benefit; see ¶3.5.

Employer's requirement. If, to retain your present job or rate of pay, your employer requires you to obtain further education, you may deduct the cost of the courses. The fact that you also qualified for a raise in pay or a substantial advancement in your position after completing the courses should not bar the deduction.

The employer's requirement must be for a bona fide business reason, not merely to benefit you. Only the minimum courses necessary for the retention of your job or rate of pay is considered by the IRS as taken to meet your employer's requirement. You must show any courses beyond your employer's minimum requirements were taken to maintain or improve your job skills.

LAW SCHOOL COSTS

¶ **19.17** The IRS does not allow deductions for law school courses because they qualify you for a new profession. Courts support the IRS position. A deduction is not allowed even if you do not intend to practice law. For example, teachers who took law school courses have been disallowed deductions although they intended to continue teaching.

Bar review courses. The costs of bar review courses and the bar exam are not deductible, even where you are seeking admission to the bar of a second state.

An attorney who practices law in one state may not deduct the later costs of getting a degree necessary to the practice of law in another state.

Additional legal education. An attorney may deduct the cost of a master's degree program (LL.M.). You must practice as an attorney before the expenses of further legal education are deductible.

EXAMPLE   The Tax Court allowed a lawyer to deduct educational expenses to obtain an LL.M. degree where he worked for a law firm as a beginning lawyer during the summer between graduating from law school and starting work on the LL.M. degree. He was admitted to the state bar before he graduated from law school, and the work he did during the summer was normally assigned to beginning lawyers rather than to law students.

In another case, the IRS and Tax Court did not allow a deduction to a law school graduate who took LL.M. courses before passing the state bar or working as an attorney.

COURSES TAKEN BY DOCTORS AND NURSES

¶ **19.18** The IRS allows general practitioners to deduct the cost of short refresher courses, even though the courses relate to specialized fields. These courses maintain or improve skills and do not qualify the doctor for a new profession.

A practicing psychiatrist may deduct the cost of attending an accredited psychoanalytic institute to qualify to practice psychoanalysis. A social worker has also been allowed a deduction for the cost of psychoanalysis. In one case, a psychiatrist was allowed by the Tax Court to deduct the cost of personal therapy sessions conducted through telephone conversations and tape cassettes. The court was convinced that the therapy improved his job skills by eliminating psychological blind spots that prevented him from understanding his patient's problems.

A licensed practical nurse may not deduct the costs of a college program which qualifies him or her as a "physician's assistant," which is a new business. Physician's assistants and practical nurses are subject to different registration and certification requirements under state law, and, more important, the physician's assistant may perform duties, such as physical examinations and minor surgery, which go beyond practical nursing duties.

COURSES TAKEN BY TEACHERS

¶ **19.19** You must meet the minimum level of education for your present position as set down by law or regulations before you may deduct the cost of courses. The educational requirements are those that existed when you were hired. If your employer set no tests fixing a minimum educational level, you meet the minimum requirements when you become a member of the faculty. Whether you are a faculty member depends on the custom of your employer. You are ordinarily considered a faculty member if: (1) you have tenure, or your service is counted toward tenure; (2) the institution is contributing toward a retirement plan based on your employment (other than Social Security or similar program); or (3) you have a vote in faculty affairs.

Employed teacher taking courses for teaching certificate. That you are already employed as a teacher, with all the responsibilities of a teacher, may not establish that you have met the minimum educational requirements. A school system which requires a bachelor's degree before granting a permanent teaching certificate may grant temporary or provisional certificates after a person has completed a number of college credits. Renewal of the provisional certificate may be conditioned on the teacher's continuing education for a bachelor's degree. In this case, the IRS will disallow a deduction for the educational costs. The minimum requirements are not met until the teacher has the degree. Current Tax Court decisions follow the IRS position, although in the past the court took a contrary view.

Teacher's Job Change

Elementary and secondary school teachers may deduct the cost of courses taken to make any of the following job changes: (1) elementary to secondary school classroom teacher; (2) classroom teacher in one subject (such as mathematics) to classroom teacher in another subject (such as art); (3) classroom teacher to guidance counselor; or (4) classroom teacher to principal.

The IRS held that a "discussion leader" in a college adult education program could not deduct the costs of a master's degree program that led to certification as a high school guidance counselor because this was a new business. The Tax Court disagreed, holding that the responsibilities of discussion leader are similar to the responsibilities of a school counselor. The court distinguished an earlier decision in which a classroom paraprofessional assistant was not allowed to deduct education costs that qualified her as a classroom teacher. The court considered this as a change in professions. A paraprofessional does not have the same control and responsibilities for classroom work as a classroom teacher.

PROFESSOR'S RESEARCH EXPENSES

¶ **19.20** Research costs incurred by a college professor are deductible under this condition: He or she is appointed to lecture and teach with the understanding that research in the field will be carried on with the goal of incorporating the findings in teaching and writing. If this test is met, the IRS is satisfied that the research is an express requirement of the teaching position and that research expenses are deductible job expenses.

Deductible research costs include traveling expenses and stenographic and other costs of preparing a manuscript. If income is later realized from the research in the form of lecture or royalty fees, the previously deducted research costs may not again be deducted in determining the income realized from the research.

Expenses of a research project undertaken for a scholarly publication are not deductible if the research is not linked to an income-producing activity or job requirement.

LEAVE OF ABSENCE TO TAKE COURSES

¶19.21 The IRS will allow a deduction for full-time graduate courses taken by a teacher during a leave of absence if these conditions are met: (1) the absence must not be for more than one year; and (2) upon completion of the education courses, the same type of employment must be resumed, although you may take a job with a new employer. You may also have to show that you had more than a vague intention to go back to your employment, for example, that you were actually negotiating for a new teaching position and that, in fact, you did obtain a position soon after finishing the graduate courses.

The IRS also has applied the one-year test to those who leave jobs to pursue MBA degrees.

Favorable Tax Court Decisions

The Tax Court considers the IRS "one-year" rule too narrow and inflexible and has allowed educational cost deductions to (1) a school principal who resigned his position to take courses over a three-year period; (2) a manager who quit his job to take a two-year MBA course; and (3) a Texas professor who took a two-year leave of absence to study in Hawaii. In one case, the IRS did not object to a teacher's two-year absence from his job. If the cost of the courses is deductible, living expenses are also deductible; see ¶19.22.

HOW TO DEDUCT EDUCATION COSTS

¶19.22 If your courses meet the requirements explained in ¶19.16, you may deduct the following education costs, subject to the 2% AGI floor on Schedule A.

1. Tuition, textbooks, fees, equipment, and other aids required by the courses.
2. Certain transportation costs described in the next column.
3. Travel to and from a school away from home.
4. Living expenses (80% of meals and lodging) while at the school away from home. The IRS will not disallow traveling expenses to attend a school away from home or in a foreign country merely because you could have taken the course in a local school. But it may disallow your board and lodging expenses at the school if your stay lasts longer than a year.

Local transportation expenses. If your courses qualify for a deduction, you may deduct transportation costs of going from your job directly to school. According to the IRS, the return trip from school is also deductible if you are going to school on a *temporary* basis. If you take a one-time course or a course that lasts a few days or weeks, the IRS considers this temporary and you are allowed a deduction for your transportation to and from school. The IRS position is illustrated in the following examples.

EXAMPLES 1. You regularly work in Camden, New Jersey, and every night for three weeks you drive from home to attend a refresher course. The course is considered temporary. You may deduct the round-trip transportation costs between home and school. The deduction is allowed regardless of how far you travel.

If you went directly from your job to the school, you may deduct transportation from work to school, and from school to home.

2. On six consecutive Saturdays, you drive from home to attend a qualifying course. This is considered a temporary course. You are allowed a deduction for round-trip transportation between home and school, even though you are traveling on a non-work day.

3. After work, you attend classes twice a week for one year. The IRS does not consider the course to be temporary. You may deduct the cost of going directly from work to school, but the costs of going between home and school are nondeductible.

Travel and living expenses away from home. "Away from home" as explained at ¶20.6 has a special tax meaning. You are not away from home unless you are away overnight.

Expenses of sightseeing, social visiting, and entertaining while taking the courses are not deductible. If your main purpose in going to the vicinity of the school is to take a vacation or for other personal reasons, you may deduct only the cost of the courses and your living expenses while attending school. You may not deduct the rest of your travel costs.

To determine the purpose of your trip, an IRS agent will pay close attention to the amount of time devoted to personal activities relative to the time devoted to the courses.

Where to claim educational expenses on your return. The way you deduct educational expenses depends on your occupational status. If you are:

An employee—You generally report your unreimbursed educational expenses on Form 2106. However, you do not need Form 2106 and may report your educational expenses directly on Schedule A as unreimbursed employee expenses if: (1) you are not claiming job expenses for travel, transportation, meals, or entertainment; and (2) you received no reimbursements for education expenses or any other job-related costs. If your expenses were partially reimbursed, you must use Form 2106.

Employer reimbursements, including expense allowances, are not reported as income on your Form W-2 if you substantiate the expenses to your employer and return amounts in excess of the substantiated expenses. If these substantiation tests are not met, the expenses are reported as income on your Form W-2, and you must claim them on Form 2106 (or Schedule A if Form 2106 is not needed) as if they were unreimbursed. If your employer pays the tuition directly to the educational institution, you are not required to report the payment in any way on your return.

Unreimbursed costs, such as travel, tuition, books, fees, and 80% of meals from Form 2106, are deductible only if you claim itemized deductions. They are claimed as miscellaneous itemized deductions and are subject to the 2% AGI floor when included with other miscellaneous deductions on Schedule A.

Teacher on sabbatical—Where a school system has a policy of paying teachers full salary during sabbatical leaves, a teacher on sabbatical may be required to pay a fixed percentage of salary into a fund to pay substitute teachers. A teacher reports the full amount of the salary paid during the sabbatical but may claim payments to the fund as miscellaneous itemized deductions subject to the 2% AGI floor.

A self-employed business owner or professional— You deduct all of your education costs on Schedule C. You also attach a statement to your return explaining your deduction and the relationship of the education to your position.

A veteran receiving educational benefits from the V.A.— The V.A. payments are tax free, whether they cover educational or living expenses. The portion of the reimbursement covering educational costs reduces your deductible expenses. If you use only part of the V.A. payment for qualifying courses, reduce your deduction by the part of the V.A. reimbursement covering the qualifying courses. The portion of the reimbursement, if any, that covers living expenses does not affect your deduction.

TRIPS TAKEN FOR EDUCATIONAL PURPOSES

¶19.23 No deduction is allowed for costs of travel claimed as a form of education. For example, no deduction will be allowed to a French teacher traveling to France to maintain general familiarity with the French language and culture, or to a social studies teacher traveling to learn about or photograph people and customs.

A deduction may still be allowed for travel that qualifies as a business expense, for example, if a teacher must travel abroad to do research that cannot be done elsewhere.

INVESTMENT, LEGAL, AND TAX ADVICE EXPENSES

CHECKLIST OF DEDUCTIBLE INVESTMENT EXPENSES

¶19.24 The following are investment expenses that are deductible as miscellaneous expenses on Schedule A subject to the 2% adjusted gross income (AGI) floor. In addition, the 3% reduction for total itemized deductions applies if your adjusted gross income exceeds $105,250, or $52,625 if married filing separately; *see* ¶13.8.

Accounting fees for keeping records of investment income.
Bank deposit loss if not federally insured; *see* ¶18.4.
Casualty or theft losses of income-producing property such as stock certificates, but not rental or royalty property; the deduction is figured on Form 4684 and entered on Schedule A.
Fees for collecting interest and dividends. Also deductible are fees paid to a bank that acts as dividend agent in an automatic dividend reinvestment plan of a publicly-owned corporation. Costs of collecting tax-exempt interest are not deductible; expenses deducted on an estate tax return are also not deductible. Fees paid to a broker to acquire securities are not deductible but are added to the cost of the securities. Commissions and fees paid by an investor on the sale of securities reduce the selling price; a dealer, however, may deduct selling commissions as business expenses.
Fees to set up or administer an IRA. The fees must be billed and paid separately from the regular IRA contribution.
Guardian fees or fees of committee for a ward or minor incurred in producing or collecting income belonging to the ward or minor or in managing income-producing property of the ward or minor.
Investment management or counsel fees. However, fees allocated to advice dealing with tax-exempt obligations are not deductible.
Legal costs; *see* ¶19.26.
Premiums and expenses on indemnity bonds for the replacement of missing securities. If part of the expenses are refunded in the year the expenses are paid, only the excess expense is deductible. A refund in a later year is taxable income to the extent the expenses were deducted and reduced your tax; *see* ¶12.8.
Proxy fight expenses where the dispute involves legitimate corporate policy issues, not a frivolous desire to gain membership on the board.
Safe deposit box rental fee or home safe to hold your securities, unless used to hold personal effects or tax-exempt securities.
Salary of a secretary, bookkeeper, or other employee hired to keep track of your investment income.
Subscriptions to investment services.

Travel costs of trip away from home (¶20.6) to look after investments, or to confer with your attorney, accountant, trustee, or investment counsel about the production of income. If you have investment property in a resort area, keep proof that the trip was taken primarily to check your investment property, not to vacation. Nondeductible travel is discussed below.

Managing investment property. Expenses incurred in managing property held for income are deductible, even if the property does not currently produce income. Similarly, expenses incurred to avoid further losses or to reduce anticipated losses on such property are deductible.

Rental or royalty expenses. Expenses of earning royalty or rental income are deducted directly from royalty or rental income, rather than as itemized deductions subject to the 2% AGI floor.

EXAMPLE You pay deductible investment management fees of $1,500; a tax preparation fee of $500; and a safe deposit box fee of $40. Your other miscellaneous expense deductions subject to the 2% floor are $500 for unreimbursed job expenses. Your adjusted gross income is $80,000. Your deduction after applying the 2% AGI floor is $940.

Investment management fees	$1,500
Tax preparation fee	500
Safe deposit box fee	40
Other miscellaneous expenses	500
	$2,540
Less 2% of $80,000	1,600
Total deductible	$ 940

Nondeductible travel costs. Investors may not deduct the costs of these types of trips:
Trips to investigate prospective rental property.
Trips to attend a convention, seminar, or similar meeting that deals with investment, financial planning, or the production or collection of income. Convention costs are deductible only in the case of a business activity; *see* ¶20.13.
Trips to attend stockholder meetings. However, in a private letter ruling, one stockholder was allowed a deduction. He owned substantial stockholdings which had lost value because his corporation had been issuing stock to the public at prices below book value. He went to the annual shareholders' meeting to present a resolution requesting management to stop the practice; the resolution passed. Under such circumstances, the IRS held that the trip was directly related to his stockholdings and allowed him the deduction. The IRS distinguished his case from a ruling which bars most stockholders from deducting the cost of travel to an annual meeting. Here the stockholder's purpose in getting the resolution passed was more closely related to his investment

activities than if he had attended the meeting, as most stockholders do, to pick up data for future investment moves.

Home office of an investor. An investor may not deduct the costs of an office at home unless investing constitutes a business. For example, you get no deduction for use of a home office in your residence where you read financial periodicals and reports, and clip bond coupons. These activities are not considered a business.

EXAMPLE In his home office, Moller spent 40 hours a week managing four stock portfolios worth over $13 million. However, an appeals court held he could not deduct home office expenses despite the time spent there managing his investment. To deduct home office expenses, Moller had to show he was a trader. A trader is in a business; an investor is not. A trader buys and sells frequently to catch daily market swings. An investor buys securities for capital appreciation and income without regard to daily market developments. Here, Moller was an investor. He was primarily interested in the long-term growth potential of stock. He did not earn his income from the short-term stock turnovers. He had no significant trading profits.

Hobby expenses. For the limitations on deducting hobby expenses, *see* ¶40.9.

COSTS OF TAX RETURN PREPARATION AND AUDITS

¶19.25 You may deduct your payment of fees charged for the services listed below, subject to the 2% AGI floor and the 3% reduction if AGI exceeds $105,250 ($52,625 if married filing separately); *see* ¶13.8.

- The preparation of your tax return or refund claim involving any tax;
- Preparing and obtaining a private IRS ruling, including IRS filing fees; *and*
- Representing you before any examination, trial, or other type of hearing involving any tax.

The term "any tax" covers not only income taxes but also gift, property, estate, or any other tax, whether the taxing authority be federal, state, or municipal.

Tax practitioner's fees. Deductible fees for services of tax practitioners are claimed on Schedule A as miscellaneous itemized deductions on the tax return for the year in which the fee was paid. For example, if in March 1992, you pay an accountant to prepare your 1991 return, the fee is deductible on your 1992 return.

You deduct fees related to preparing Schedule C or F (and related business Schedules) on the Schedule C or F, thereby avoiding the 2% floor on Schedule A. If you report rental or royalty income or loss on Schedule E, you deduct the allocated tax preparation fee on Schedule E.

Allocate Fees For Tax Advice

There have been disputes over the deductibility of fees charged for general tax advice unconnected to the preparation of a return or a tax controversy. A deduction for fees charged for general tax advice not within these areas may be disallowed, unless the fee can be related to the production of business or investment income or the management of income-producing property. The following case distinguished between advice covering tax liabilities and advice concerning the tax consequences of a possible future transaction. According to the court, no deduction was allowed for that part of the fee covering the future transaction.

EXAMPLE Stockholders of a closely held corporation negotiated with a publicly held company for a tax-free exchange of their stock. An accounting firm asked the IRS for a ruling to determine whether the exchange would be taxable or tax free. The accounting fee was $8,602. Of this, $7,602 was for the ruling and $1,000 was for fixing the basis of the new stock. The stockholders deducted the full fee, which the IRS disallowed because the fee was not charged for the preparation of a tax return nor for representation at a contest of a tax liability.

The Tax Court disagreed in part. The fee paid for the ruling is deductible; it was connected with determining the extent of the stockholders' liability, if any, in the proposed exchange. But a deduction cannot be allowed for the $1,000 charged to determine the basis of the new stock. This was computed for the stockholders' information, not for determining tax liability. The disallowed fee could be added to the cost basis of the stock.

An accountant's fee for arranging the purchase of real estate was deductible where the purchase was part of a plan to cut taxes.

EXAMPLE Collins paid an accountant $4,511 for tax advice to reduce his tax on a sweepstake winning. He was advised to buy an apartment house under a contract obligation to make a large prepayment of interest (which was deductible under prior law). The accountant helped prepare contracts, escrow agreements, and other documents to implement the plan. Collins' deduction of his accountant's fee as a business expense was disallowed. The IRS held that the fee was a capital expense in acquiring the property. The Tax Court disagreed. The accountant was hired to minimize Collins' income tax through the purchase of the building and the terms of the purchase. Therefore, his fee was deductible.

Deducting the Cost of This Book

The purchase of *Your Income Tax* in 1992 is deductible as an itemized deduction on your 1992 return. The cost, when included with other miscellaneous deductions, is subject to the 2% AGI floor.

Personal checking account fees. These are nondeductible, even though the checks are used for tax records. Similarly, the per check fee on an interest-bearing NOW account is nondeductible. However, fees charged on a bank money-market account may be deductible if check writing is severely limited and writing excess checks forfeits the status of the account as a money-market account.

DEDUCTING LEGAL COSTS

¶19.26 A legal expense is generally deductible if the dispute or issue arose in the course of your business or employment or involves income-producing property. Legal expenses for personal matters are generally not deductible. If you are self-employed, your deduction for legal fees arising from a business-related dispute is claimed on Schedule C. Legal expenses related to your job as an employee or to investment activities are claimed as miscellaneous itemized deductions subject to the 2% AGI floor. The IRS may disallow the deduction on the grounds that the legal dispute does not directly arise from the business or income activity. Thus, for example, the cost of contesting suspension of a driver's license for drunken driving is not deductible despite a business need for the license; the suspension arose out of a personal rather than a business-related activity. A deduction may also be disallowed where the dispute involves title to property. Furthermore, the deductibility of a legal expense may depend on whether the damages received are taxable.

For the deductibility of legal fees in organizing a new business; *see* ¶40.10.

Employment suits. The following cases illustrate when legal costs for employment-related matters may be deductible.

EXAMPLES　1. Waldheim, a corporate officer, director, and stockholder, incurred legal fees in a suit to prevent his discharge. His legal costs were deductible.

2. An Army officer was allowed to deduct the cost of successfully contesting a court martial based on charges of misrepresentations in official statements and reports. He would have lost his position had he been convicted.

3. Tellier, a securities dealer, was convicted of mail fraud and securities fraud. He was allowed to deduct legal fees as business expenses related to his securities business. That he was found guilty of the criminal charge does not affect the deductibility of the expense. The deduction of legal expenses is not disallowed on public policy grounds since a defendant has a constitutional right to an attorney.

4. In an alimony action, Gilmore was successful in preventing his wife from securing stock and taking control of corporations from which he earned practically all his income. He was not allowed to deduct his legal costs. The dispute did not arise from an income-producing activity; the fact that an adverse determination of the dispute might affect his income did not make the legal expenses deductible.

5. A doctor who attempted to bribe a judge to suspend his sentence for tax evasion was convicted of the bribe attempt and lost his license to practice medicine. He could not deduct his defense costs. His practice of medicine did not give rise to his need for an attorney. The fact that the conviction affected his ability to earn income was merely a consequence of personal litigation.

6. Siket, a police officer, was not allowed to deduct expenses of successfully defending a criminal charge of assault while off duty. The origin of the claim was personal, even though a conviction might have been detrimental to his position as a police officer. The arrest did not occur within the performance of his duties; he was off duty and in a different municipality at the time of the arrest.

The legal costs of defending against disbarment are deductible.

Lawyer's Bill Should Be Itemized

Your lawyer should bill you separately or itemize fees for services connected with deductible items (collection of taxable alimony or separate maintenance payments; or preparation of tax returns, tax audits, and tax litigation) and nondeductible capital items (expenses incurred in purchase of property or dispute over title).

Libel suits. The IRS holds that compensatory damages received for injury to personal reputation are tax free; damages received for injury to business reputation are taxable; *see* ¶12.10. Thus, legal expenses allocable to an award or settlement for injury to personal reputation are not deductible. If the libel action is for damage to business reputation, legal expenses are deductible as business expenses.

The Tax Court and an appeals court hold that if the libel is considered a "personal" injury under state law, damages allocable to the libel claim are tax free, even if the libel results in lost business income. Thus, under this approach, legal fees related to the libel award would not be deductible.

Will contests and wrongful death actions. Legal costs of a will contest are generally not deductible because an inheritance is not taxable income. Similarly, legal fees incurred to collect a wrongful death award (which is tax-free income) are not deductible.

EXAMPLE　Parker, an heir who was left out of his grandmother's estate, sued to recover his inheritance. In a settlement, he received his share of his grandmother's property plus income earned on that property. The allocable portion of legal fees attributed to the income, which was taxable, was deductible; the balance of the fees was not deductible.

Tax Advice and Tax Return Preparation

You may deduct legal fees paid in 1992 for preparing your tax return or refund claim, or for representing you in a trial, examination, or hearing involving any tax; *see* ¶19.25. Legal fees incurred in defending against a tax imposed by a foreign country are also deductible. However, legal fees incurred in reducing an assessment on property to pay for local benefits are not deductible; the fees are capital expenses which are added to basis.

A deductible legal fee, when included with other miscellaneous deductions, is subject to the 2% AGI floor.

Title issues or disputes. Legal costs related to the acquisition of property or to the determination of title to property, whether such property is business or personal, are nondeductible capital expenditures. They are added to the basis of the property. For example, litigation costs to fix the value of shares of dissident shareholders are not deductible because they are related to the purchase of the stock and are part of the cost of acquisition.

Legal fees incurred to acquire title to stock were also held to be nondeductible.

Where a dispute over property does not involve title, such as in a recovery of income-producing securities loaned as collateral, the Tax Court holds that legal fees are deductible.

Personal injury or marital actions. Where you recover taxable damages, you may deduct the legal fees. If the damages are not taxable, legal fees are not deductible; *see* ¶12.10. For legal expenses incurred in marital actions, *see* ¶37.8.

Collecting Social Security. If you hire an attorney to press a claim for disputed benefits, such as disability benefits, you may deduct the legal fees only to the extent that your benefits are taxable under the rules of ¶34.3. For example, if 50% of your Social Security benefits are taxable, 50% of your legal fees are treated as miscellaneous expenses subject to the 2% AGI floor.

Estate tax planning fee. Not all of an attorney's fee for estate tax planning services may be deductible. Estate tax planning usually involves tax and non-tax matters. To the extent that the services do not cover tax advice or income-producing property, the fee is not deductible. A bill allocating a fee between deductible and nondeductible services may help support a deduction claimed for the deductible portion of the fee.

Recovery of attorney's fees from government; see Chapter 47.

20

TRAVEL AND ENTERTAINMENT EXPENSE DEDUCTIONS

Unreimbursed employee travel expenses are deductible but are subject to the 2% AGI floor. If you are self-employed, the 2% floor does not apply. The types of deductible travel expenses are highlighted in the table on pages 242–243. Generally, you must be away from home to deduct travel expenses on business trips. On one-day business trips within the general area of your employment, only transportation costs may be deducted, not meals or lodging.

To support your travel expense deductions, keep records that comply with IRS rules as explained at ¶20.29. To avoid the 2% AGI floor, consider an "accountable" reimbursement arrangement of your travel expenses with your employer; see ¶20.34.

You report unreimbursed employee transportation and travel expenses on Form 2106. On the form, deductible meals are limited to 80% of cost. Entertainment costs are also subject to the 80% limit; see ¶20.16. Unreimbursed expenses from Form 2106 are entered on Schedule A where they are subject to the 2% AGI floor.

An expense allowance covering travel costs is not included as income on Form W-2 if you substantiated the expenses to your employer and returned any unsubstantiated portion of the allowance; see ¶20.34 for details.

If you are self-employed, you deduct travel costs on Schedule C. Your deduction for meals and entertainment is limited to 80% of cost on Schedule C. The 2% AGI floor does not apply.

DEDUCTION GUIDE FOR TRAVEL AND TRANSPORTATION EXPENSES

¶**20.1** The following table summarizes the rules for deducting travel expenses while "away from home" on business trips, and other deductible travel and transportation expenses; *see* ¶20.6 for when you are away from home.

Key to Deductible Travel and Transportation Expenses

Your Travel Status—	*Tax Rule*—
Trips to see customers and clients	You may deduct your transportation expenses but not the cost of personal meals on one-day business trips within the general area of your tax home.
Two job locations for one employer in the same area EXAMPLE—Your employer has two business locations in the city in which you live. You work about half of the time in each place—at one location in the morning and at the other in the afternoon.	You deduct transportation expenses from one location to the other. However, if, for personal reasons, such as the choice of a place for eating lunch, you do not go directly from one location to the other, you may deduct your transportation expenses only to the extent that they do not exceed the cost of going directly from the first location to the second. But say your employer has several locations in the same city, but you do not move from one location to another in the same day. You spend the entire day at one place. You may not deduct transportation expenses between your home and the various locations, even if you report to a different location each day.
Two different jobs in the same area EXAMPLE—You work for two different employers in the city in which you live. Most of the time you work a full work shift at your principal place of employment. Then you work a part-time shift for your second employer some distance away.	You may deduct the transportation expenses from one job to another within the same working day. But you may not claim the deduction if you return home after the first job and then after supper, go to your second job.
Permanent job in an area other than where you have your residence EXAMPLE—You live with your family in Chicago, but work in Milwaukee. During the week, you stay in a hotel in Milwaukee and eat meals in a restaurant. You return to your family in Chicago every weekend.	Milwaukee is your "home" for tax purposes; *see* ¶20.6. Thus, your expenses for traveling to Milwaukee, and your meals and lodging there are personal, nondeductible expenses.
Temporary assignment in an area other than where you have your residence EXAMPLE—You live in Kansas City where you work. You have been assigned to duty in Omaha for 60 days. Occasionally, you return to Kansas City on your days off, but most of the time you stay in Omaha.	You may deduct the necessary expenses for traveling from Kansas City to Omaha and returning to Kansas City after your temporary assignment is completed. You may also deduct expenses for meals and lodging (even for your days off) while you are in Omaha.
Weekend trip home from temporary assignment EXAMPLE—Same facts as Example above except that you return home to Kansas City during the weekend.	You are not "away from home" while you are in Kansas City on your days off and your meals and lodging while you are there are not deductible. However, you may deduct your traveling expenses (including meals and lodging, if any) en route from Omaha to Kansas City and return if they are no more than the amount it would have cost you for your meals and lodging if you had stayed in Omaha. If they are more, your deduction is limited to the amount you would have spent in Omaha. If you retain your room in Omaha while in Kansas City, your expenses of returning to Kansas City on days off are deductible only to the extent of the amount you would have spent for your meals had you stayed in Omaha.
Temporary job location away from home where there are no living accommodations EXAMPLE—You live and work in Chicago. You have been temporarily assigned to a construction job located 20 miles outside Nashville. There are no living facilities near the job site and you have to stay at a hotel in Nashville.	Under these circumstances, your necessary expenses in getting to and from your temporary job are business expenses and not commuting expenses. If you were employed at the site for an indefinite period, then the costs of commuting would be nondeductible, regardless of the distance; *see* ¶20.2.
Taxi trips between customers' locations	The cab fares are deductible; *see* ¶20.2

○━🗝 **Key to Deductible Travel and Transportation Expenses (*Continued*)**

Your Travel Status—	Tax Rule—
Seasonal jobs in different areas EXAMPLE—You live in Cincinnati where you work for eight months each year. You earn the greater share of your annual income from that job. For the remaining four months of the year, you work in Miami. When in Miami, you eat and sleep in a hotel. You have been working on both of these jobs for several years and expect to continue to do so.	You have two recurring seasonal places of employment. Cincinnati is your principal place of employment. You may deduct the costs of your traveling expenses while away from Cincinnati working at your minor place of employment in Miami, including meals and lodging in Miami.
Trailer home moved to different job sites EXAMPLE—You are a construction welder. You live in a trailer which you move from city to city where you work on construction projects. You have no other established home.	You may not deduct your expenses for meals and lodging. Each place where you locate becomes your principal place of business and, therefore, you are not "away from home."
Travel to school after work to take job-related courses	You may deduct travel costs under rules of ¶19.22.
Finding a new job in the same line of work EXAMPLE—You live in New York. You travel to Chicago for an interview for a new position.	You may deduct the cost of the trip and living expenses in Chicago; see ¶19.7.
Convention trip	You may deduct costs of travel to a business convention under the rules of ¶20.13. If you are a delegate to a charitable or veterans' convention, you may claim a charitable deduction for the travel costs; see ¶14.4.
Trip to out-of-town college for educational courses	You deduct the cost of the trip if you meet the rules at ¶19.22.
Trip for health reasons	You may deduct the cost of the trip as a medical expense if you meet the rules at ¶17.9.

COMMUTING EXPENSES

¶20.2

The cost of travel between your home and place of work is generally not deductible, even if the work location is in a remote area not serviced by public transportation. Nor can you justify the deduction by showing you need a car for faster trips to work or for emergency trips. Travel from a union hall to an assigned job is also considered commuting. If you join a car pool, you may not deduct expenses of gasoline, repairs, or other costs of driving you and your passengers to work.

According to the IRS, if you install a telephone in your car and make calls to clients or business associates while driving to your office, you are still commuting and your expenses are not deductible. Similarly, the deduction is not allowed if you drive passengers to work and discuss business. However, an IRS and Tax Court decision that barred police captains' costs of driving their specially equipped cars to and from the stationhouse, was reversed by an appeals court.

Deductible commuting expenses. The IRS allows these exceptions to its blanket ban on commuting expense deductions.

If you are on a business trip out-of-town, you may deduct taxi fares or other transportation costs from your hotel to the first business call of the day and all other transportation costs between business calls.

If you use your car to carry tools to work, a deduction is allowed where you can prove that transportation costs were incurred in addition to the ordinary, nondeductible commuting expenses. The deduction will be allowed even if you would use a car in any event to commute.

EXAMPLES

1. Jones commuted to and from work by public transportation before he had to carry tools. Public transportation cost $2 per day to commute to and from work. When he had to use the car to carry the tools, the cost of driving was $3 a day and $5 a day to rent a trailer to carry the tools. Jones may deduct only the cost of renting the trailer. The IRS does not allow a deduction for the additional $1 a day cost of operating the car. It is not considered related to the carrying of the tools. It is treated as part of the cost of commuting which is not deductible.

2. Same facts as above, but Jones does not rent a trailer. He uses the car trunk to store his tools. He may not claim a deduction because he incurs no additional cost for carrying the tools.

3. Smith uses his car regardless of the need to transport tools. He rents a trailer for $5 a day to carry tools. He may deduct $5 a day under the "additional-cost" rule.

When you commute to a temporary job location. Daily transportation expenses, whether within or outside the metropolitan area where you usually work, are deductible if you are traveling to a temporary place of business. A temporary place of business is any location where you perform services on an irregular basis or for a short-term period, generally a few days or weeks. If you are on a temporary job that lasts longer, it is important to show that the job started out as a temporary assignment and that factors beyond your control extended the time and that you looked for work closer to home.

There have been cases in which substantial commuting expenses have been allowed during a two-year period. For example, although the IRS contested the deductions, the Tax Court allowed deductions to a person who worked at a nuclear power plant 142 miles away from his home. He realistically expected the job to last less than two years and attempted to get work where he maintained his home. Similarly, the court allowed a construction electrician to deduct the daily round-trips of 140 miles to a power plant over a two-year period. The electrician showed that he could not get a permanent job where he lived and that when he started work at the power plant, he was told the job would last only three months. However, delays in construction extended his assignment over the two-year period. He also kept in touch with his union for jobs in his home area.

Regular Office at Home

COURT DECISION

If your regular office is outside your home, you may not deduct the cost of commuting to that office or from that office to your home even if you work at home at a second job.

However, in several cases, the Tax Court has allowed individuals whose home office was their principal place of business to deduct travel costs beginning with the first business call of the day; *see* the following examples.

EXAMPLES 1. Dr. St. John practiced industrial medicine; his patients were employees of his industrial clients. He was on call 24 hours a day and maintained a home office with complete records. His working day began at home where he planned his rounds by telephoning his clients and his outside office. Therefore, when he started on his rounds he was traveling on business, not commuting. The cost of these trips is deductible.

2. Mazzotta, an IRS agent, argued that he could deduct his evening commuting expenses from an IRS office to his home. He claimed that he had a second place of employment at home where he kept an office to transact business as treasurer of a credit union. Therefore, he was traveling between two places of employment. The deduction was disallowed. He would have gone home evenings even if he did not transact credit union business there.

3. Adams, a self-employed home repairman, deducted the cost of travel from his home, which served as his business headquarters, to the homes of customers where he actually did the repairs. The IRS disallowed the deduction, claiming that his principal place of business was the various job sites. The Tax Court disagreed. He contacted clients at home, listed his home phone as his place of business in newspaper advertisements, and kept tools and supplies there. Since his home was the sole fixed location of his business, the cost of travel from home to the job sites is deductible.

4. Wicker, a self-employed nurse and anesthetist, worked at a hospital as the head of the department of anesthesiology. The Tax Court allowed her deduction of driving costs from home to the hospital. The expenses were deductible because she maintained a home office as her principal place of business. Although she was the only full-time anesthetist at the hospital, she was not given hospital office space. Her only office was at home where she kept medical reference materials, patient files, billing and tax records.

5. Leitch, a Los Angeles construction inspector, deducted auto expenses incurred for travel during the day from his home to various work sites. The Tax Court allowed the deduction. It considered his home as the principal place of business. The city did not furnish him with an office nor were any of the construction sites his primary place of business. He spent more time at home performing work functions than at any of the various sites. Furthermore, his home was the only place where he could be contacted by his superiors to receive assignments or other work related information. All of his assignments were received by mail or phone. Finally, he kept his reports and diagrams in the home office.

OVERNIGHT-SLEEP TEST LIMITS DEDUCTION OF MEAL COSTS

¶20.3 The overnight-sleep rule prevents the deduction of meal costs on one-day business trips. To be deductible, meal costs must be incurred on a business trip that lasts longer than a regular working day (but not necessarily 24 hours) and requires time off to sleep (not just to eat or rest) before returning home. Taking a nap in a parked car off the road does not meet the overnight-sleep test.

EXAMPLES 1. A New Yorker flies to Washington, D.C., which is about 250 miles away, to see a client. He arrives at noon, eats lunch, and then visits the client. He flies back to New York. He may deduct the cost of the plane fare, but not the cost of the lunch. He was not away overnight nor was he required to take time out to sleep before returning home.

2. Same facts as above except he sleeps overnight in a Washington hotel. He eats breakfast there, and then sees another client and returns home to New York in the afternoon. He may deduct not only the cost of the plane fare but also the cost of the meals while on the trip and the cost of the hotel. He was away overnight.

3. A trucker's run is from Seattle to Portland and back. He leaves at about 2:00 A.M. and returns to Seattle the same day, getting in at about 6:00 P.M. While in Portland, he is released from duty for about four hours layover time to get necessary sleep before returning to Seattle. He may deduct the cost of meals because he is released at the turnaround point to obtain necessary sleep. Official release from duty is not a prerequisite to satisfying the sleep or rest test.

Several courts held that the IRS rule was unreasonable and outdated in the world of supersonic travel, and they would have allowed the New Yorker on the one-day trip to Washington, D.C., to deduct the cost of his lunch. The Supreme Court disagreed and upheld the IRS rule as a fair administrative approach.

Meal costs during overtime. Such costs are not deductible if you are not away from your place of business. Thus, for example, a resident physician could not deduct the cost of meals and sleeping quarters at the hospital during overnight or weekend duty.

IRS MEAL ALLOWANCE

¶20.4 If you find it difficult to keep records of meal costs while away from home on business trips, you may prefer to claim an IRS meal allowance. For travel within the continental U.S., the daily allowance is usually $26 per day except that in the high-cost areas listed in the chart on page 245, the allowance is $34 per day. For travel in Alaska, Hawaii, or other locations outside the continental U.S., an allowance for each locality is shown in government tables.

Employees or self-employed persons in the *transportation industry* may elect to claim a meal allowance of $30 per day for all travel within the continental U.S. instead of applying the $26 or $34 rate on a trip-by-trip basis. Also, an allowance of $34 per day may be elected for all travel outside the continental U.S.

You must keep a record of the time, place, and business purpose of the trips. As long as you have this proof, you may claim the allowance even if your actual costs are less than the allowance. Self-employed individuals may claim the allowance as well as employees who are not reimbursed for meals under an "accountable" plan; *see* ¶20.34.

Claiming the allowance. The $26/$34 allowance is allocated for the first and last day of a trip. The day is divided into four six-hour periods, starting at midnight. For each six-hour period that you are away, you are entitled to 25% of the allowance. If you start your

Locations Eligible for $34 a Day Standard Meal Allowance*

Key City	County[1]	Key City	County[1]	Key City	County[1]
California		**District of Columbia (Continued)**		**New Jersey (Continued)**	
Death Valley	Inyo	Washington, DC	Maryland counties of	Newark	Bergen, Essex,
Los Angeles	Los Angeles, Kern,		Montgomery and		Hudson, Passaic, Union
	Orange, Ventura;		Prince Georges	Ocean City/Cape May	Cape May
Edwards AFB, China	Lake Naval Center	**Florida**		Princeton/Trenton	Mercer
Oakland	Alameda, Marin, Contra	Key West	Monroe	**New Mexico**	
	Costa	Miami	Dade	Cloudcroft	Otero
Palm Springs	Riverside	West Palm Beach	Palm Beach	Santa Fe	Santa Fe
Sacramento	Sacramento	**Georgia**		**New York**	
San Diego	San Diego	Atlanta	Clayton, De Kalb,	Monticello	Sullivan
San Francisco	San Francisco		Cobb, Fulton	New York City	Bronx, Brooklyn,
San Jose	Santa Clara	**Illinois**		Manhattan, Staten	Island, Queens; Nassau,
San Luis Obispo	San Luis Obispo	Chicago	Du Page, Cook, Lake	Suffolk	
San Mateo	San Mateo	**Louisiana**		Saratoga Springs	Saratoga
Santa Barbara	Santa Barbara	New Orleans	Jefferson, St. Bernard,	White Plains	Westchester
Santa Cruz	Santa Cruz		Orleans, Plaquemines	**Ohio**	
South Lake Tahoe	El Dorado	**Maryland** (see also District of Columbia)		Cleveland	Cuyahoga
Tahoe City	Placer	Annapolis	Anne Arundel	**Pennsylvania**	
Yosemite Nat'l Park	Mariposa	Baltimore	Baltimore, Harford	Bala Cynwyd	Montgomery
Colorado		Columbia	Howard	King of Prussia/	
Aspen	Pitkin	Ocean City	Worcester	Fort Washington	Montgomery
Boulder	Boulder	**Massachusetts**		Philadelphia	Philadelphia
Denver	Denver, Adams,	Andover	Essex	Radnor/Chester	Delaware
	Arapahoe, Jefferson	Boston	Suffolk	Valley Forge	Chester
Keystone/	Summit	Lowell	Middlesex	**Rhode Island**	
Silverthorne		Martha's Vineyard/	Nantucket, Dukes	Newport	Newport
Vail	Eagle	Nantucket		**South Carolina**	
Connecticut		Quincy	Norfolk	Hilton Head	Beaufort
Hartford	Hartford, Middlesex	**Michigan**		**Texas**	
Salisbury	Litchfield	Detroit	Wayne	Dallas/Fort Worth	Dallas, Tarrant
District of Columbia		**Nevada**		Houston	Harris; LBJ Space
Washington, DC	Virginia counties of	Las Vegas	Clark; Nellis AFB	Center, Ellington AFB	
	Arlington, Loudoun,	**New Jersey**		**Virginia** (see also District of Columbia)	
	and Fairfax and	Atlantic City	Atlantic	Williamsburg	
	cities of Alexandria,	Edison	Middlesex	**Washington**	
	Falls Church, and	Freehold/	Monmouth, Fort	Seattle	King
	Fairfax	Eatontown	Monmouth		

*Any changes to this list will be in the Supplement   [1]Includes parishes, boroughs, military installations, etc.

business trip between midnight and 6 A.M., you are considered to be away for the entire day and may claim the full $26 or $34 a day allowance for the first day. If you start between 6 A.M. and noon, you claim 75% of the allowance for the first day; if you start between noon and 6 P.M., you claim 50% of the allowance for the first day; 25% if you leave between 6 P.M. and midnight.

If you are an employee and claim a deduction based on the allowance, you must reduce the deduction by 20% on Form 2106; only 80% of meal costs are deductible. Furthermore, if you are an employee, the balance, when added to your other miscellaneous deductions, is subject to 2% AGI floor on Schedule A. If you are self-employed, the deduction for meals is claimed on Schedule C where it is subject only to the 20% reduction; see ¶40.5.

Reimbursement plans. If your employer has an "accountable" reimbursement plan (¶20.34), and you are reimbursed for meals up to the $26, $30, or $34 rate, the reimbursement will not be reported as income on your Form W-2.

DEDUCTING TRAVEL EXPENSES AWAY FROM HOME

BUSINESS TRIP DEDUCTIONS

¶**20.5** The following expenses of a business trip away from home are deductible:

Plane, railroad, taxi, and other transportation fares.

Hotel and lodging expenses.

Meal costs. Only 80% of the cost of the meal is deductible. The business discussion test of ¶20.17 does not apply to meal costs on business trips provided you eat alone or with your family or personal acquaintances.

Tips, telephone, and telegraph costs.

Laundry and cleaning expenses.

Baggage charges (including insurance).

Cab fares or other costs of transportation to and from the airport or station and your hotel. Also deductible are cab fares or other transportation costs, beginning with your first business call of the day, of getting from one customer to another, or from one place of business to another.

Travel costs to find a new job are deductible; *see* ¶19.7.

Entertainment expenses incurred while traveling away from home are deductible under the rules at ¶20.16.

Cruise ship. If you travel by cruise ship on a business trip, your deductible cruise costs are limited to twice the highest federal per diem rate for travel in the United States times days in transit.

EXAMPLE You sail to Europe on business. Assume that the highest per diem federal rate is $174 and the trip lasts five days. The maximum deduction for the cost of the trip is $1,740 (2 x $174 x 5).

The double per diem rule applies without regard to the 80% limit on meal costs if meals are not separately stated in your bill. If a separate amount for meals or entertainment is included, such amount must be reduced by 20%.

The per diem limitation does not apply to cruise ship convention costs that are deductible up to $2,000 a year, if all the ports of call are in the U.S. or U.S. possessions and if the ship is registered in the United States; *see* ¶20.15. The per diem rate also does not apply if the expense comes within an exception to the 80% cost limit rule explained at ¶20.27.

Important: Recordkeeping requirements. *See* the section beginning at ¶20.29 for recordkeeping rules to support a deduction for unreimbursed travel expenses or to avoid being taxed on employer reimbursements.

WHEN ARE YOU AWAY FROM HOME?

¶**20.6** You have to meet the "away from home" test to deduct the cost of meals and lodging while traveling.

Tax Home Defined

For travel expense purposes, your *home* is your place of business, employment, or post of duty, regardless of where you maintain your family residence. This *tax home* includes the entire city or general area of your business premises or place of employment. The area of your residence may be your tax home if your job requires you to work at widely scattered locations, you have no fixed place of work, and your residence is in a location economically suited to your work.

EXAMPLES 1. Your residence is in a suburb within commuting distance of New York City where you work full time. Your personal home and tax home are the same, that is, within the metropolitan area of New York City. You are away from home when you leave this area, say for Philadelphia. Meals and lodging are deductible only if you meet the overnight-sleep test; *see* ¶20.3.

2. Your residence is in New York City, but you work in Baltimore. Your tax home is Baltimore; you may not deduct living expenses there. But you may deduct travel expenses on a temporary assignment to New York City even while living at your home there.

3. A construction worker works for a utility company on construction sites in a 12-state area. Assignments are sent from his employer's regional office; he is not required to report to the office. The IRS ruled that his residence, which is in a city in the 12-state area, is his tax home.

Are you constantly on the road? If you are, an IRS agent may disallow your travel deductions on the grounds that your tax home is wherever you work; thus, you are never "away from home." If your deduction is questioned, you may be able to show that your tax home is the area of your residence. If you meet these three tests, the IRS will treat your residence as your tax home: (1) you do some work in the vicinity of your residence, house, apartment, or room and live there while performing services in the area; (2) you have mortgage expenses or pay rent for the residence while away on the road; (3) the residence is in an area where you were raised or lived for a long time, or a member of your immediate family such as your parent or child lives in the residence, or you frequently return there.

According to the IRS, if you meet only two of these three tests, it will decide on a case-by-case basis if your residence is your tax home. If you meet less than two of the tests, the IRS will not allow a deduction; each of your work locations is treated as your tax home.

Permanent duty station of servicemen. The Supreme Court held that a member of the Armed Forces is not away from home when he or she is at a permanent duty station. This is true whether or not it is feasible or even permissible for his or her family to live with them.

FIXING A TAX HOME IF YOU WORK IN DIFFERENT LOCATIONS

¶**20.7** If you regularly work in two or more separate areas, your tax home is the area of your principal place of business or employment. You are away from home when you are away from the area of your principal place of business or employment. Therefore, you may deduct your transportation costs to and from your minor place of business and your living costs there.

Determining Your Principal Place of Business

A principal place of business or employment is determined by comparing: (1) the time ordinarily spent working in each area; (2) the degree of your business activity in each area; and (3) the amount of your income from each area.

The relative importance of each fact will vary, depending on the facts of a particular case. For example, where there are no substantial differences between incomes earned in two places of employment, your tax home is probably the area in which you spend more of your time. Where there are substantial income differences, your tax home is probably the area in which you earn more of your income.

EXAMPLES 1. Sherman lived in Worcester, Mass., where he managed a factory. He opened his own sales agency in New York. He continued to manage the factory and spent considerable time in Worcester. The larger part of his income came from the New York business. However, he was allowed to treat New York as his minor place of business and to deduct his travel expenses to New York and his living expenses there. The reason: He spent most of his time in Worcester and his income there was substantial.

2. Benson, a consulting engineer, maintained a combination residence-business office in a home he owned in New York. He also taught four days a week at a Technological Institute in West Virginia under a temporary nine-month appointment. He spent three-day weekends, holidays, and part of the summer at his New York address. At the Institute, he rented a room in the student union building. The IRS disallowed transportation expenses between New York and West Virginia and meals and lodging there as not incurred while away from home. The Tax Court disagreed.

A taxpayer may have more than one occupation in more than one city. When his occupations require him to spend a substantial amount of time in each place, he may deduct his travel expenses, including meals and lodging, at the place away from his permanent residence. That Benson's teaching salary happened to exceed his income from his private practice does not change the result.

3. For many years, Markey, a G.M. engineer, worked near and lived in Lewisburg, Ohio. He also owned rental property, farms, and a machine shop in Lewisburg and was an officer of a bank. When he retired from G.M., it rehired him as a consultant and reassigned him to Warren, Michigan, 250 miles away. He spent five days a week in Warren, returning to Lewisburg every weekend. He claimed Lewisburg as his tax home. The IRS disallowed his away-from-home deduction and allowed a deduction only for the cost of a dozen trips from Warren to Lewisburg as an expense of managing his investments. It treated Warren as Markey's tax home on the grounds that he earned $12,000 a year there while his Lewisburg investments returned less than $1,500.

The Tax Court sided with Markey. It reasoned that he considered his business and investment activities at Lewisburg more important than his job even though they generated little income. An appeals court reversed, supporting the IRS position. That Markey attached importance to his interests in Lewisburg was not relevant. Warren was his tax home because he spent more time and earned far more money there.

Professional sports players, coaches, and managers. When the only business of such persons is the professional sport, their home is the "club town." But if they are in another business in addition to their professional playing, how much time is spent and how much is earned at each place determines whether their club's home-town or the place of their off-season business is their tax home. If it is the club's home-town, they deduct travel and living expenses while away from that town—including the time they are where the second business is. (If the second place is where their families also live, they may not deduct the families' expenses there.) If the town where the other business is located is the tax home, then expenses in the club's home-town may be deducted.

TAX HOME OF MARRIED COUPLE WORKING IN DIFFERENT CITIES

¶20.8 When a husband and wife work and live in different cities during the week, one of them may seek to deduct travel expenses away from home. Such deductions have generally been disallowed, although courts have allowed some exceptions. Although for common law purposes the domicile of the husband may be the domicile of the wife, for tax purposes when each spouse works in a different city, each may have a separate tax home.

EXAMPLES 1. Robert worked in Wilmington, Delaware; his wife, Margaret, in New York City. During the weekend, she traveled to Wilmington and deducted, as travel expenses away from home, her living costs in New York and weekend travel expenses to Wilmington. She argued that because she and her husband filed a joint return, they were a single taxable unit, and the tax home of this unit was Wilmington where her husband lived. The deduction was disallowed. That a couple can file a joint return does not give them deductions that are not otherwise available to them as individuals. Margaret's tax home was New York where she worked. Therefore, her expenses there are not deductible. And, as the weekend trips to Wilmington had no relationship to her job, they, too, are not deductible.

2. Hundt and his wife worked in Washington, D.C., and lived in nearby Arlington, Va., for many years. In 1952, he became a free-lance writer and director of industrial motion pictures. He directed and did research for films in various parts of the country from New York to California. He wrote the film scripts at his Arlington home or on location. However, most of his business came from New York City, where he lived in hotels. In 1956, he spent 175 days in New York City on business and rented an apartment for $1,200 because it was cheaper than a hotel.

He deducted half the annual rent for the New York apartment, the costs of traveling between Arlington and New York, and the cost of meals in New York. The IRS disallowed the expenses, finding New York to be his tax home. The court disagreed, holding Arlington was his tax home because (1) part of his income came from his creative writing in Arlington; and (2) his travel to other parts of the country was temporary. In this case the fact that most of his income came from New York did not make New York his tax home.

DEDUCTING LIVING COSTS ON TEMPORARY ASSIGNMENT

¶20.9 A business trip or job assignment away from home may last a few days, weeks, or months. If your assignment is considered temporary, you deduct living costs away from home. If it is viewed as indefinite, you may not deduct your living costs there. An indefinite assignment shifts your tax home to the area of your work. So, if your assignment is indefinite, you may not claim for tax purposes that you are away from home, even though you keep a permanent residence elsewhere.

What is a temporary assignment? The law does not define what is meant by a temporary assignment. The IRS recognizes stays of up to two years as temporary if the tests discussed at ¶20.10 are met. It will treat an anticipated or actual employment of two years or more as indefinite regardless of circumstances. The IRS two-year test as applied to construction workers also is illustrated at ¶20.10.

Deductible costs on temporary trip. While you are on a temporary job assignment, you may deduct the cost of meals and lodging at the place of your assignment, even for your days off. If you return home, say for weekends, your living expenses at home are not deductible. You may deduct travel expenses, meals, and lodging en route between your home and your job assignment provided they do not exceed your living expenses had you stayed at the temporary job location. If you keep a hotel room at the temporary location while you return home, you may deduct your round-trip expenses for the trip home only up to the amount you would have spent for meals had you stayed at the temporary workplace.

Taking Your Family with You

If you take your family with you to a temporary job site, an IRS agent may argue that this is evidence that you considered the assignment to be indefinite. In the example below, however, such a move was not considered detrimental to a deduction of living expenses at the job location.

EXAMPLE Michaels, a cost analyst for Boeing, lived in Seattle. He traveled for Boeing, but was generally not away from home for more than five weeks. Michaels agreed to go to Los Angeles for a year to service Boeing's suppliers in that area. He rented his Seattle house and brought his family with him to Los Angeles. Ten months later, Boeing opened a permanent office in Los Angeles and asked Michaels to remain there permanently. Michaels argued that his expenses for food and lodging during the ten-month period were deductible as "away from home" expenses. The IRS contended that the Los Angeles assignment was for an indefinite period.

The Tax Court sided with Michaels. He was told that the stay was for a year only. He leased his Seattle house to a tenant for one year, planning to return to it. He regarded his work in Los Angeles as temporary until Boeing changed its plans. The one-year period justified his taking the family but did not alter the temporary nature of the assignment.

No regular job where you live. That you do not have regular employment where you live may prevent a deduction of living costs at a temporary job in another city. The IRS may disallow the deduction on the grounds that the expenses are not incurred while away from home; the temporary job site is the tax home.

CONSTRUCTION WORKER AT DIFFERENT PROJECTS

¶20.10 As explained at ¶20.9, you deduct travel expenses while away from home if your assignment at the project is considered temporary. If your employment is expected to and does last for one year or more but less than two years, you must be prepared to prove:

1. You realistically expect your employment to last less than two years and to return to the location which you claim as your tax home; *and*
2. Your residence at your claimed tax home is your regular place of abode. To prove this point, you should meet the following three IRS tests: (1) you used the residence while working in the vicinity immediately prior to the current position and you continue to look for a position there; (2) you incur living expenses for the residence; and (3) your family, spouse, and children continue to live there, *or* you use it frequently as a lodging, such as on weekends.

If you meet all three tests for your residence, and also had a realistic expectation that the assignment would last less than two years, the IRS says it will recognize that you are temporarily away from home. If you meet only two of the residence tests, you may still be able to convince the IRS of the temporary nature of the job, but if you meet only one, the IRS will rule that the stay is indefinite.

You will not be able to meet the IRS tests if you do not have an established residence. This is also true if you live in a trailer which you move from project to project and you have no other established home. Each work location becomes your principal place of business and, therefore, you are not "away from home."

EXAMPLES 1. Adams, a construction worker and union member regularly employed in Newark, N.J., takes a job in Baltimore, Md., about 200 miles away. The project is scheduled to be completed in 16 months at which time Adams plans to return to Newark. His wife and children continue to stay in the family-owned home in Newark. While in Baltimore, Adams lives in a trailer and returns most weekends to Newark to be with his family and to check on employment opportunities there. Adams satisfies the three tests that Newark is his regular place of abode. His stay is considered temporary and his living expenses in Baltimore are deductible.

2. Same facts as in Example 1 except that Adams sells his house and moves to Baltimore. His stay is not considered temporary. He did not incur duplicate living costs and his family did not remain in Newark. His living costs in Baltimore are not deductible.

DEDUCTING EXPENSES OF A BUSINESS-VACATION TRIP

BUSINESS-VACATION TRIPS WITHIN THE UNITED STATES

¶20.11 On a business trip to a resort area, you may also spend time vacationing. If the *primary purpose* of the trip is to transact business and is within the United States (50 states and District of Columbia) you may deduct all of the costs of your transportation to and from the area, lodging, and 80% of meal expenses, even if you do spend time vacationing. If the main purpose of the trip was personal, you may not deduct any part of your travel costs to and from the area. The amount of time spent on business as opposed to sightseeing or personal visits is the most important issue in determining your primary purpose. Regardless of the primary purpose of your trip, you are allowed to deduct expenses related to the business you transacted while in the area.

No deductions will be allowed if you attend a convention or

seminar where you are given videotapes to view at your own convenience and no other business-related activities or lectures occur during the convention. The trip is considered a vacation.

Primary Business Purpose

If your return is examined, proving business purpose depends on presenting evidence to convince an examining agent that the trip, despite your vacationing, was planned primarily to transact business. Keep a log or diary to substantiate business activities.

If your trip is primarily for business, and while at the business destination you extend your stay for a few days to visit relatives or take a nonbusiness sidetrip, you deduct travel expenses to and from the business destination.

EXAMPLE You work in Atlanta and make a business trip to New Orleans. You stay in New Orleans for six days and your total costs, including round-trip transportation to and from New Orleans, meals, and lodging, is $600, which you may deduct subject to the 80% limit for meals. If on your way home, you spend three days in Mobile visiting relatives and incur an additional $200 in travel costs, your deduction is limited to the $600 (less 20% of meals) you would have spent had you gone home directly from New Orleans.

BUSINESS-VACATION TRIPS OUTSIDE THE UNITED STATES

¶20.12 On a business trip abroad, you may deduct all your travel expenses, even though you take time out to vacation, provided you can prove: (1) the primary purpose of the trip was business; and (2) you did not have control over the assignment of the trip.

If the IRS determines that you were primarily on vacation, it will disallow all travel costs except for costs directly related to your business in the area such as registration fees at a foreign business convention; see ¶20.15.

Fixing the date of the trip does not mean that you had control over the assignment. IRS regulations assume that when you travel for your company under a reimbursement or allowance arrangement, you do not control the trip arrangements, provided also that you are not: (1) a managing executive of the company; (2) related to your employer; or (3) have 10% or more interest in the company. You are considered a managing executive if you are authorized without effective veto procedures to decide on the necessity of the trip. You are related to your employer if the employer is your spouse, parent, child, brother, sister, grandparent, or grandchild.

Rule for managing executives and self-employed persons. If you are a managing executive, self-employed, or related to your employer, or have a 10% or more interest, you may deduct all transportation costs if:

1. The trip outside the United States took a week or less, not counting the day you leave the U.S. but counting the day you return, *or*
2. If the trip abroad lasted more than a week, you spent less than 25% of your time, counting the days your trip began and ended, on vacation or other personal activities, *or*
3. In planning the trip you did not place a major emphasis on taking a vacation.

If the vacationing and other personal activities took up 25% or more of your time on a trip lasting more than one week, and you cannot prove that the vacation was a minor consideration in planning the trip, you must allocate travel expenses between the time spent on business and on personal affairs. The part allocated to business is deductible; the balance is not. To allocate, count the number of days spent on the trip outside the United States, including the day you leave the U.S. and the day you return. Then divide this total by the number of days on which you had business activities; include days of travel to and from a business destination.

If you vacation at, near or beyond the city in which you do business, the expense subject to allocation is the cost of travel from the place of departure to the business destination and back. For example, you travel from New York to London on business and then vacation in Paris before returning to New York. The expense subject to allocation is the cost of traveling from New York to London and back; see Example 2. However, if from London you vacationed in Dublin before returning to New York, you would allocate the round-trip fare between New York and Dublin and also deduct the

difference between that round-trip fare and the fare between New York and London; see Example 3.

EXAMPLES 1. You fly from New York to Paris to attend a business meeting for one day. You spend the next two days sightseeing and then fly back to New York. The entire trip, including two days for travel en route, took five days. The plane fare is deductible. The trip did not exceed one week.

2. You fly from Chicago to New York where you spend six days on business. You then fly to London where you conduct business for two days. You then fly to Paris for a five-day vacation after which you fly back to Chicago. You would not have made the trip except for the business that you had to transact in London. The nine days of travel outside the United States away from home, including two days for travel en route, exceeded a week, and the five days devoted to vacationing were not less than 25% of the total travel time outside the U.S. The two days spent traveling between Chicago and New York, and the six days spent in New York, are not counted in determining whether the travel outside the United States exceeded a week and whether the time devoted to personal activities was less than 25%.

Assume you are unable to prove either that you did not have substantial control over the arrangements of the trip or that an opportunity for taking a personal vacation was not a major consideration in your decision to take the trip. Thus, 5/9 (5 nonbusiness days out of 9 days outside the U.S.) of the plane fare from New York to London and from London to New York is not deductible. You may deduct 4/9 of the New York to London round-trip fare, plus lodging, 80% of meals and other allowable travel costs while in London. No deduction is allowed for any part of the costs of the trip from London to Paris.

3. Same as Example 2 except that the vacation is in Dublin, which is closer to the U.S. than London. The allocation is based on the round trip fare between New York and Dublin. Thus, 4/9 of the New York to Dublin fare is deductible and 5/9 is not deductible. Further, the IRS allows a deduction for the excess of the New York to London fare, over the New York to Dublin fare.

Weekends, holidays, and business standby days. If you have business meetings scheduled before and after a weekend or holiday, the days in between the meetings are treated as days spent on business for purposes of the 25% business test just discussed. This is true although you spend the days for sightseeing or other personal travel. A similar rule applies if you have business meetings on Friday and the next scheduled meeting is the following Tuesday; Saturday through Monday are treated as business days.

DEDUCTING EXPENSES OF BUSINESS CONVENTIONS

¶20.13 Conventions and seminars at resort areas usually combine business with pleasure. Therefore, the IRS scrutinizes deductions claimed for attending a business convention where opportunities exist for vacationing. Especially questioned are trips where you are accompanied by your spouse and other members of your family. Foreign conventions are discussed at ¶20.15.

Generally, you may not deduct expenses of attending investment conventions and seminars; see ¶19.24. You also may not deduct the costs of business conventions or seminars where you merely receive a videotape of business lectures to be viewed at your convenience and no other business-related activities occur during the event.

In claiming a deduction for convention expenses, be prepared to show that the convention was connected with your business. Cases and IRS rulings have upheld deductions for doctors, lawyers, and dentists attending professional conventions. One case allowed a deduction to a legal secretary for her costs at a secretaries' convention. If you are a delegate to a business convention, make sure you prove you attended to serve primarily your own business interests, not those of the association. However, it is not necessary for you to show that the convention dealt specifically with your job. It is sufficient that attendance at the convention may advance or benefit your position. If you fail to prove business purpose, the IRS will allocate your expenses between the time spent on your business and the time spent as a delegate. You then deduct only the expenses attributed to your business activities.

EXAMPLES 1. An attorney with a general law practice was interested in international law and relations. He was appointed a delegate to represent the American branch of the International Law Association at a convention in the former Yugoslavia. The attorney deducted the cost of the trip and convention as business expenses which the IRS and a court disallowed. He failed to prove that attending the conference on international law helped his general practice. He did not get any business referrals as a result of his attendance at the convention. Nor did he prove the chance of getting potential business from the conference.

2. An insurance agent doing business in Texas attended his company's convention in New York. One morning of the six-day convention was devoted to a business meeting and luncheon; the rest of the time was spent in sightseeing and entertainment. The company paid for the cost of the trip. The IRS added the reimbursement to the agent's pay and would not let him deduct the amount. The convention in New York served no business purpose. It was merely a method of entertaining company personnel. If there was any valid business to be transacted, the company could have called a meeting in Texas, the area of his home office.

3. A plywood company could not deduct the costs of entertaining 116 customers and employees at a New Orleans hotel during the 1981 Superbowl weekend. The company did not reserve conference rooms or make any other arrangements for organized business meetings. The IRS and two federal courts held that although business discussions may have occurred on a random basis, these were secondary to entertainment.

What expenses are deductible? If the convention trip is primarily for business, you may deduct travel costs both to and from the convention, food costs, tips, display expenses (such as sample room costs), and hotel bills. If you entertain business clients or customers, you may deduct these amounts too.

Food and beverage costs are subject to the 80% cost limitation rule as explained in ¶20.27.

Keep records of your payments identifying expenses directly connected with your business dealings at the convention and those which are part of your personal activity, such as sightseeing, social visiting, and entertaining. Recreation costs are not deductible even though a part of your overall convention costs.

EXAMPLE You attend a business convention held in a coastal resort city primarily for business reasons. During the convention period, you do some local sightseeing, social entertaining, and visiting—all unrelated to your business. You may deduct your traveling expenses to and from the resort, your living expenses at the resort, and other expenses such as business entertaining, sample displays, etc. But you may not deduct the cost of sightseeing, personal entertaining, and social visiting.

Substantiate Convention Business

Keep a copy of the convention program and a record of the business sessions you attend. If the convention provides a sign-in book, sign it. In addition, keep a record of all of your business expenses as explained in ¶20.29.

Fraternal organizations. You may not deduct expenses at conventions held by fraternal organizations, such as the American Legion, Shriners, etc. even though incidental business was carried on. However, delegates to fraternal conventions may in some instances deduct expenses as charitable contributions; *see* ¶14.4.

DEDUCTING YOUR SPOUSE'S TRAVEL EXPENSES

¶20.14 IRS agents generally disallow deductions claimed for a spouse's travel expenses. They assume that a spouse's presence is for personal reasons. A spouse's secretarial services such as typing notes of the convention may not be accepted as evidence of business purpose. In one case, a taxpayer could not claim his wife's expenses even though she was the proprietor of the business, signed business checks, and spent some time in the business. In another case, a husband could not deduct his wife's expenses at a convention even though her presence at the convention was required by his company.

When this book went to press, Congress was considering legislation that would bar a deduction for your spouse's travel costs after 1992 unless he or she is your employee; see the Supplement.

However, you may deduct the cost of your spouse's participation in the entertainment of business clients at convention or business trips if the trip or entertainment meets the tests at ¶20.22. Generally, you may deduct the cost of goodwill entertaining of associates immediately before or after convention business meetings. A convention meeting qualifies as a bona fide business meeting.

Courts have allowed the travel expenses of spouses in the following cases:

EXAMPLES 1. A court allowed the travel expenses of a wife who nursed her diabetic husband on a business trip. Facts favorable to her case were: (1) the cities visited were not cities usually associated with tourist travel; (2) her expenses were reasonable when compared to the business developed on the trip and her nursing aid; (3) a doctor advised her care; and (4) she was trained to nurse her husband's condition. But a court in another case disallowed the travel costs of a wife who attended her husband who was suffering from a heart condition.

2. A manufacturer's sales representative ran his business through a corporation. His wife occasionally helped in the office and was personally acquainted with many of his business clients whom she entertained at home and at conventions. At one meeting, she also set up large selling displays. On the basis of this evidence, the Tax Court allowed the corporation to deduct part of her salary and her expenses at the conventions. It said that her contacts and the entertainment contributed to the successful operation of the company which required the solicitation of supplies and selling to customers.

How Much to Deduct

Where your spouse accompanies you, your bills will probably show costs for both of you. These usually are less than twice the cost for a single person. To find what you may deduct where your spouse's presence is for personal not business reasons, do not divide the bill in half. Figure what it would have cost you alone for similar accommodations and transportation. Only the excess over the single person's costs is not deductible.

EXAMPLE You and your spouse travel by car to a convention. You pay $120 a day for a double room. A single room would have cost $100 a day. Your spouse's presence at the convention was for social reasons. You may deduct the total cost of operating your car to and from the convention city. You may deduct $100 a day for your room. If you traveled by plane or railroad, you would deduct only your own fare.

RESTRICTIONS ON FOREIGN CONVENTIONS AND CRUISES

¶20.15
You may not deduct expenses at a foreign convention outside the North American area, unless you can show the convention is directly related to your business and it was as reasonable for the meeting to be held outside the North American area as within it.

Apart from the United States, the North American area includes Puerto Rico, the Trust Territory of the Pacific Islands including American Samoa, U.S. Virgin Islands, Guam, Bermuda, Mexico, and Canada.

Conventions may also be held in eligible Caribbean countries that agree to exchange certain data with the U.S. and do not discriminate against conventions held in the United States. Barbados, Costa Rica, Dominica, Dominican Republic, Grenada, Honduras, Jamaica, Saint Lucia, and Trinidad and Tobago have qualified and are considered to be within the North American area.

Check with the convention operator about whether the country in which your convention is being held has qualified.

Limited cruise ship deduction. Up to $2,000 a year is allowed for attending cruise ship conventions if all the ports of call are in the U.S. or U.S. possessions and if the ship is registered in the United States. A deduction is allowed only if you attach to your return statements signed by you and by an officer of the convention sponsor that detail the daily schedule of business activities, the number of hours you attended these activities, and the total days of the trip. Do not confuse the $2,000 limitation with the per diem limitation for cruise ship costs discussed at ¶20.5. The per diem limitation does not apply to cruises that meet the tests of ¶20.15 just discussed.

MEALS AND ENTERTAINMENT EXPENSES

	See ¶
80% deduction limit	20.16
The restrictive tests for meals and entertainment	20.17
Directly related dining and entertainment	20.18
Goodwill entertainment	20.19
Home entertaining	20.20
Your personal share	20.21
Entertainment costs of spouses	20.22

	See ¶
Costs of entertainment facilities	20.23
Club dues	20.24
Recordkeeping for club use	20.25
Restrictive test exceptions	20.26
80% meal cost limitation on meals and entertainment	20.27
Business gift deductions are limited	20.28

80% DEDUCTION LIMIT

¶20.16
You may not deduct the full cost of entertainment for customers or clients at restaurants, country clubs, at home, theaters, and sporting events, even if the expenses qualify under the restrictive tests of ¶20.17. Only 80% of unreimbursed expenses is deductible and this 80% balance is reduced by the 2% AGI floor if you are an employee. Furthermore, all entertainment costs, including meals, must be backed up with records. If you do not keep adequate records, your deductions will be disallowed.

The 80% deduction limit for meals and entertainment is discussed at ¶20.27.

THE RESTRICTIVE TESTS FOR MEALS AND ENTERTAINMENT

¶20.17
You must be prepared to show that meal and entertainment costs are ordinary and necessary to your business; and also:

1. Directly related to the active conduct of your business (¶20.18), *or*
2. Directly preceding or following a substantial and bona fide business discussion on a subject associated with the active conduct of your business. This test applies to dining and entertainment in which you seek new business or to goodwill entertainment to encourage the continuation of an existing

business relationship. Under this test, you may entertain business associates in nonbusiness settings such as restaurants, theaters, sports arenas, and nightclubs, provided the entertainment directly precedes or follows the business discussion. Business associates are: established or prospective customers, clients, suppliers, employees, agents, partners, or professional advisers, whether established or prospective; *see* ¶20.19.

See ¶20.26 for expenses that are *not* subject to Tests 1 or 2.
See ¶20.27 for the 80% deduction limit.

DIRECTLY RELATED DINING AND ENTERTAINMENT

¶20.18
The directly related test limits the deduction of dining and entertainment costs at restaurants, nightclubs, on yachts, and during social events. If such dining or entertainment fails to meet the directly related tests, it may qualify under the rules discussed in ¶20.19, which require the holding of a business discussion before or after the entertainment.

The directly related test may be met in one of the three ways: (1) under the generally related test; (2) as expenses incurred in a clear business setting; or (3) as expenses incurred for services performed.

Generally related test. Under this test, you must show a business motive for the dining or entertainment and business activity during the entertainment. You must show that you had more than a general expectation of getting future income or other specific business benefit (other than goodwill). Although you do not have to prove that income or other business benefit actually resulted from the expense, such evidence will help support your claim. What type of business activity will an IRS agent look for? The agent will seek proof that a business meeting, negotiation, or discussion took place during the period of dining or entertainment. It is not necessary that more time be devoted to business than to entertainment. What if you did not talk business? You must prove that you would have done so except for reasons beyond your control.

Hunting or Fishing Trips

The IRS presumes entertainment during a hunting or fishing trip or on a yacht is not conducive to business discussion or activity. You must prove otherwise.

Clear business setting test. Expenses incurred in a clear business setting meet the directly related test provided also that you had no significant motive for incurring the expenses other than to further your business. Entertainment of people with whom you have no personal or social relationship is usually considered to have occurred in a clear business setting. For example, entertainment of business representatives and civic leaders at the opening of a new hotel or theatrical production to obtain business publicity rather than goodwill is considered to be entertainment in a clear business setting. Also, entertainment which involves a price rebate is considered to have occurred in a clear business setting, as, for example, when a hotel owner provides occasional free dinners at the hotel for a customer who patronizes the hotel.

Costs of a hospitality room displaying company products at a convention are also a directly related expense.

Entertainment occurring under the following circumstances or in the following places is generally not considered as directly related:

You are not present during the entertainment.

The distractions are substantial, as at nightclubs, sporting events, or during a social gathering such as a cocktail party.

You meet with a group which includes persons other than business associates at cocktail lounges, country clubs, golf and athletic clubs, or at vacation resorts.

Services performed test. An expense is directly related if it was directly or indirectly made for the benefit of an individual (other than an employee) either as taxable compensation for services he or she rendered or as a taxable prize or award. The amount of the expense must be reported on an information Form 1099 (unless the amount is less than $600).

EXAMPLE A manufacturer of products provides a vacation trip for retailers of his products who exceed sales quotas. The value of the vacation is a taxable prize to the retailers. The vacation cost is a directly related entertainment expense for the manufacturer.

GOODWILL ENTERTAINMENT

¶20.19   Goodwill entertaining may qualify as deductible entertainment. Dining and entertainment costs may be deductible if a substantial and *bona fide* business discussion directly preceded or followed the dining or entertainment.

A meeting at a convention is considered a *bona fide* business discussion if it is officially scheduled as part of a convention program and if (1) the expenses necessary for your attendance at the convention are ordinary and necessary business expenses, and (2) a scheduled program of business activity is the principal activity of the convention.

EXAMPLES 1. During the day, you negotiate with a group of business associates. In the evening, you entertain the group and their spouses at a theater and nightclub. The cost of the entertainment is deductible, even though arranged to promote goodwill.

2. In the evening after a business meeting at a convention, you entertain associates or prospective customers and their spouses. You may deduct the entertainment costs.

Scheduling Entertainment and Business Discussions

The business discussion generally must take place the same day as the dining or entertainment. If not, and your deduction is questioned, you must give an acceptable reason for the interval between the discussion and the dining or entertainment. IRS regulations recognize that a day may separate a business meeting and the entertainment of an out-of-town customer. He or she may come to your office to discuss business one day and you provide entertainment the next day; or you provide the entertainment on the first day and discuss business the day after.

The IRS does not estimate how long a business discussion should last. But it does warn that a meeting must involve a discussion or negotiation to obtain income or business benefits. It does not require that more time be devoted to the meeting than to the entertainment.

HOME ENTERTAINING

¶20.20   The cost of entertaining business customers or clients at home is deductible provided a business discussion occurs before, during, or after the meal. When you claim such a deduction, be ready to prove that your motive for dining with them was commercial rather than social. Have a record of the entertainment costs, names of the guests, and their business affiliations.

YOUR PERSONAL SHARE

¶20.21   If the entertaining occurred while on a business trip away from home, you deduct your own meal cost as travel expenses away from home. If the entertaining occurred within the locality of your regular place of business, whether you will be allowed a deduction for your share will depend on the agent examining your return. The IRS said in a ruling that an agent will not disallow your deduction of your own part of the meal cost unless he or she finds that you are claiming a substantial amount that includes personal living expenses. In such a case, which generally is limited to situations where personal meals are regularly claimed as part of an "abusive" pattern, the agent will follow the stricter Tax Court rule (sometimes referred to as the "Sutter" rule) and allow only that part of the meal cost that exceeds what you would usually spend on yourself when alone.

ENTERTAINMENT COSTS OF SPOUSES

¶20.22 A deduction is allowed for the spouses' share of the entertainment costs if they were present during entertainment that qualified as directly related entertainment under the general rule discussed in ¶20.18. For goodwill entertainment, the cost of entertainment of the spouses is deductible if your share and the business associate's share of the entertainment is deductible. The IRS recognizes that when an out-of-town customer is accompanied by his or her spouse, it may be impracticable to entertain the customer without the spouse. Under such circumstances, the cost of the spouse's entertainment is deductible if the customer's entertainment costs are also deductible. Furthermore, if your spouse joined the party because the customer's spouse was present, the expenses of your spouse are also deductible.

COSTS OF ENTERTAINMENT FACILITIES

¶20.23 You may not deduct the expenses of maintaining and operating facilities used to entertain. By law, entertainment facilities are not considered business assets. Examples of entertainment facilities are yachts, hunting lodges, fishing camps, swimming pools, tennis courts, automobiles, airplanes, apartments, hotel suites, or homes in a vacation area. A season box seat or pass at a sporting event or theater is not considered an entertainment facility.

The above disallowance rule applies also to depreciation, but not to such expenses as interest, taxes, and casualty losses which are deductible without having to show business purpose. Country club dues are deductible under the rules of ¶20.24.

Entertainment expenses (such as the cost of food and drinks) incurred at an entertainment facility are deductible if they meet the rules of ¶20.17 to ¶20.22.

Dues paid to a business luncheon club are not within the limitation of entertainment facility rules, as a luncheon club is not considered an entertainment facility under IRS regulations.

CLUB DUES

¶20.24 *At the time this book went to press, Congress was considering legislation to repeal the deduction for club dues. See the Supplement for an update on the legislation. If the deduction is repealed, the following rules apply to dues paid before the effective date.*

To deduct dues for a country club or any other social, athletic, or sporting club, you first have to show that you used the club more than 50% of the time during the year to further your business. (Business or personal use is figured on a day-by-day basis; *see* ¶20.25.) But this percentage of use does not give you the measure of the deduction of club dues. You must also show how much of the use of the club was for entertainment directly related (¶20.18) to the active conduct of your business. This percentage of directly related entertainment fixes the amount of your club dues deduction. This means that goodwill entertainment may be counted in determining if you may deduct any club dues at all. But the actual amount of dues to be deducted is based on entertainment directly related to your business and does not include goodwill entertainment.

In making this allocation, you include the cost of your own meals as part of the cost of directly related entertainment.

EXAMPLE Your dues at a club cost $1,000 a year, and you use the club 75% of the time for the furtherance of your business: 35% of the time for goodwill entertainment and 40% for entertainment directly related to your business. Since more than 50% of the use of the club was for business entertainment, you may partially deduct club dues. The deductible part is 40% of your club dues or $400, the part related to direct business entertainment. However, this amount is subject to the following reductions. The 80% cost limitation rule reduces the deduction to $320, which, if you are an employee, is also subject to the 2% adjusted gross income floor.

In reviewing your deduction of club dues, an IRS agent will usually consider the nature of each use, the frequency and duration of your business use as compared with your personal use, and the amount of costs incurred for business use as compared with the amount of personal costs. If your membership entitles your family to use a club, their use will also be considered in determining whether business use exceeds personal use.

Out-of-Pocket Expenses at Club

The key to deducting club dues is having records of your use of the club; *see* below. Even with records, you may find you are entitled to a small deduction of club fees or to none at all. But remember, whether or not you can take a deduction for dues, the actual cost of bona fide business entertainment at the club is deductible subject to the 80% limit of ¶20.27. That is, actual entertainment costs, for example, food and beverages, will be deductible under the rules applied to entertainment expenses without regard to the tax treatment of club dues.

RECORDKEEPING FOR CLUB USE

¶20.25 To prove you have used a club to further your business, under the more than 50% test (¶20.24), you must have records of (1) when and how the club is used; (2) the cost of the club; and (3) the number of persons entertained. If you do not have these records, the IRS will presume that the club was used for personal purposes. A club is considered to be used primarily for business during a day on which a substantial and bona fide business discussion took place even if it was used for personal or family use during the same day. Days when the club is not used are not counted. For example, if, during the year you used a country club for only 60 days, the 50% test is met if you used the club for business purposes for 31 days.

RESTRICTIVE TEST EXCEPTIONS

¶20.26 The restrictive tests of ¶20.17 do not apply to the following items. They are deductible if they are "ordinary and necessary" business expenses, and you have records to back up the deduction.

1. As an employer, you can deduct expense allowances or other reimbursements of employee expenses that you treat as compensation and from which you withhold federal tax. You are not subject to the 80% deduction limit; the employee is. A similar rule applies to meals or entertainment provided to non-employees as compensation for services that are reported to them on Form 1099-MISC.
2. As a self-employed person reimbursed by clients or customers for expenses you paid on their behalf, you must report the clients' reimbursements as income but you may claim an offsetting deduction for those reimbursed expenses. You must fully account to the client or customer for entertainment

expenses incurred on his or her behalf. In such accounting, you must keep records in a diary and receipts as required in ¶20.30. After accounting to your client for entertainment expenses, make sure you retain records of these expenses to substantiate your deduction. If the exception applies, your client is subject to the 80% limit, not you. If you do not provide the accounting, you are subject to the restrictive tests of ¶20.17 and to the 80% limit.

80% COST LIMITATION ON MEANS AND ENTERTAINMENT

¶20.27
You may not deduct the full amount of your deductible expenses for business meals and entertainment expenses, such as country club dues and tickets. Only 80% of the otherwise allowable amount for food, beverages, and entertainment is deductible.

Taxes and tips are considered part of the cost subject to the 80% limit. If your employer reimburses your expenses, the 80% limit applies to the employer.

The 80% limit applies to both employees and the self-employed. It applies to the $26, $30, or $34 IRS meal allowance deduction; *see* ¶20.4. The limit is taken into account on Form 2106 for employee expenses, and on Schedule C for self-employment expenses.

EXAMPLES **1. You pay meal and entertainment costs of $5,000. Only $4,000 ($5,000 x 80%) is considered deductible.**

2. Same facts as above, but your employer reimburses your costs after you account for the expenses. His deduction is limited to $4,000. You have no deduction.

The deductible amount for a ticket treated as an entertainment expense is restricted to face value of the ticket. Amounts in excess of face value paid to ticket agencies or scalpers are not deductible. The deductible cost of tickets is also subject to the 80% limitation.

EXAMPLE **You buy from a ticket broker five tickets to entertain clients. The face value of the tickets is $250. You paid $300 for them. The deductible amount is $200 (80% x $250).**

Exceptions to 80% cost limitation. In the following cases, you may claim a full deduction for meals and entertainment; the 80% limitation does not apply.

1. An an employer, you pay for an employee's meals and entertainment that is treated as taxable compensation to the employee and as wages for purposes of withholding of income tax.
2. As an independent contractor, you are reimbursed for expenses you incur in performing services on behalf of a client or customer after accounting to that person for the expenses. A full deduction is allowed to offset the reimbursement which you must report as income. For example, if your law firm separately accounts for meal and entertainment expenses and is reimbursed by a client, the law firm is *not* subject to the 80% limitation on these expenses. The client is subject to the 80% limitation. However, a law firm that pays the expenses for a client but does not separately account for and seek reimbursement is subject to the 80% limitation on such expenses.
3. As an employer, you incur expenses for recreational, social, or similar activities (including facilities) primarily for the benefit of employees who are not highly compensated employees. For example, the expenses of food, beverages, and entertainment for a company-wide summer party are not subject to the 80% limit.
4. As an employee, if you are reimbursed by your employer for meals and entertainment after accounting for the expenses, you generally have nothing to deduct because the reimbursement is not reported as taxable income; you have a "wash" for tax purposes (¶20.33). However, this rule does not apply if the reimbursement is for meal expenses incurred when you moved to a new job location. When figuring your moving expense deduction, you may deduct only 80% of the meal costs although you must include the entire reimbursement as income (¶21.6).
5. Expenses for meals and entertainment, including the use of facilities, made available to the general public, such as a free concert, for advertising or goodwill purposes.
6. Expenses for meals and entertainment sold to the public in your business, such as meal expenses if you run a restaurant, or the cost of providing entertainment if you run a nightclub. These expenses are fully deductible.
7. Food or beverage provided to your employees as a tax-free *de minimis* fringe benefit (¶3.8). This would include expenses of a cafeteria on your premises for employees where meal charges cover the direct operating cost of the cafeteria.
8. The price of tickets to charitable sports events (including amounts in excess of face value) provided the ticket package includes admission to the event. To qualify, a charitable sports event must: (1) be organized for the primary purpose of benefiting a tax-exempt organization; (2) contribute 100% of its net proceeds to such organization; and (3) use volunteers for substantially all work performed in carrying out the event. According to Congressional committee reports, a golf tournament that donates all its proceeds to charity is eligible to qualify under this exception, even if it offers prize money to the golfers who participate or uses paid concessionaires or security personnel. However, tickets to college or high school football or similar scholastic events generally do not qualify because they do not satisfy the requirement that substantially all work be performed by volunteers.

The cost of a charitable sports ticket may include seating, parking, and refreshments.

Allocating payment covering lodging and meals. A hotel may include meals in a room charge. In such cases, the room charge must be allocated between the meals, and entertainment and lodging. The amount allocated to meals and entertainment is subject to the 80% cost limitation. If you receive a *per diem* allowance from your employer covering both lodging and meals under an accountable reimbursement plan, you may have to allocate part of the reimbursement to meals in order to deduct expenses in excess of the reimbursement; *see* ¶20.34.

Skybox rental costs. A skybox is a private luxury seating area at a sports arena. Skybox seats are generally rented for the season or for a series of games such as the World Series. The deductible amount for a rental covering more than one game or performance may not exceed the sum of the face values of non-luxury box seat tickets for the number of seats in the box. The allowable amount is also subject to the 80% cost limitation. Separately stated charges for food or beverage charges at the box are deductible as entertainment expenses and are subject to the 80% cost rule.

EXAMPLE For two games, Jones paid $1,480 for a skybox containing 10 seats—$740 per game. The cost of 10 non-luxury box seat tickets for each game was $200 or $400 total. Jones may deduct 80% of $400 non-luxury face value or $320. If he had rented the skybox for one game, he could deduct $592 (80% of $740) for that skybox because the special limitation applies only where the rental is for more than one game or other performance.

BUSINESS GIFT DEDUCTIONS ARE LIMITED

¶**20.28** Deductions for gifts to business customers and clients are restricted. Your deduction for gifts is limited to $25 a person. You and your spouse are treated as one person in figuring this limitation even if you do not file a joint return and even if you have separate business connections with the recipient. The $25 limitation also applies to partnerships; thus a gift by the partnership to one person may not exceed $25, regardless of the number of partners.

In figuring the $25 limitation to each business associate, do not include the following items:

1. A gift of a specialty advertising item which costs $4 or less on which your name is clearly and permanently imprinted. This exception saves you the trouble of having to keep records of such items as pens, desk sets, plastic bags, and cases on which you have your name imprinted for business promotion.
2. Signs, displays, racks, or other promotional material which is used on business premises by the person to whom you gave the material.
3. Incidental costs of wrapping, insuring, mailing, or delivering the gift. However, the cost of an ornamental basket or container must be included if it has a substantial value in relation to the goods it contains.

If you made a gift to the spouse of a business associate, it is considered as made to the associate. If the spouse has an independent bona fide business connection with you, the gift is not considered as made to the associate unless it is intended for the associate's eventual use.

If you made a gift to a corporation or other business group intended for the personal use of an employee, stockholder, or other owner of the corporation, the gift generally is considered as made to that individual.

Theater or sporting event tickets given to business associates are entertainment, not gift, expenses if you accompanied them. If you do not accompany them, you may elect to treat the tickets either as gifts, which are subject to the $25 limitation, or as entertainment expenses subject to the entertainment expense rules, such as the requirement to show a business conference before or after the entertainment and the 80% cost limitations. You may change your election at any time within the period allowed for tax assessment; *see* ¶38.5.

Packaged food or drink given to a business associate is a gift if it is to be consumed at a later time.

Gifts not coming within the $25 limit are: (1) scholarships that are tax free under the rules of ¶12.4; (2) prizes and awards that are tax free under the rule of ¶12.1; (3) gifts to employees, discussed in the next column; and (4) death benefit payments coming within the

$5,000 exclusion of ¶3.3. If a death benefit exceeds $5,000 and is treated as a tax-free gift, the deduction for the excess over $5,000 is limited to $25.

Employee Bonuses

Employee bonuses should not be labeled as gifts. An IRS agent examining your records may, with this description, limit the deduction to $25 unless you can prove the excess over $25 was pay. By describing the payment as a gift, you are inviting an IRS disallowance of the excess over $25. This was the experience of an attorney who gave his secretary $200 at Christmas. The IRS disallowed $175 of his deduction. The Tax Court refused to reverse the IRS. The attorney could not prove that the payment was for services.

Awards to employees. There is an exception to the $25 gift deduction limitation for achievement awards of tangible personal property given to your employees in recognition of length of service or safety achievement. Special deduction limits apply to such achievement awards provided they are given as part of a presentation under circumstances indicating that they are not a form of disguised compensation. For example, awards will not qualify if given at the time of annual salary adjustments, or as a substitute for a prior program of cash bonuses, or if awards discriminate on behalf of highly compensated employees.

The amount of your deduction depends on whether the achievement award is considered a qualified plan award. You may deduct up to $1,600 for all qualified plan awards (safety and length of service) given to the same employee during the taxable year. If the award is not a qualified plan award, the annual deduction ceiling for each employee is $400. The $1,600 limit applies if the same employee receives some qualified plan awards and some non-qualified awards in the same year.

To be a qualified plan award, the award for length of service or safety achievement must be given under an established written plan or program that does not discriminate in favor of highly compensated employees. The average cost of all awards under the plan for the year (to all employees) must not exceed $400. In determining this $400 average cost, awards of nominal value are not to be taken into account. In case of a partnership, the deduction limitation applies to the partnership as well as to each member.

Safety and length of service. A length of service award is not subject to the above rules if it is given during the employee's first five years. Furthermore, only one length of service award every five years is considered an employee achievement award.

Safety awards granted to managers, administrators, clerical employees, or professional employees are not considered employee achievement awards. Furthermore, if during the year more than 10% of other employees (not counting managers, administrators, chemical, or professional employees) previously received safety awards, none of the later awards are subject to the employee achievement award rules.

Employee's tax. The employer's deductible amount for an employee achievement award is tax free to the employee; *see* ¶3.9.

EXAMPLE You give a qualified plan award costing $1,800 to an employee. You may deduct only $1,600. The employee is not taxed on the award up to $1,600; the $200 balance is taxable.

TRAVEL AND ENTERTAINMENT RECORDS

RECORDKEEPING REQUIREMENTS

¶20.29 Your testimony—even if accepted by an IRS agent or a judge as truthful—is not sufficient to support a deduction of travel and entertainment expenses. By law, your personal claim must be supported by other evidence such as records or witnesses. The most direct and acceptable way is to have records that meet IRS rules discussed in the following pages. Failure to have adequate records will generally result, on an examination of your return, in a disallowance of your travel and entertainment expense deductions. Only in unusual circumstances will evidence other than records provide all of the required details of proof.

If your expenses are reimbursed by your company, you must keep records to support the reimbursement arrangement with your company; *see* ¶20.33.

YOU NEED A DIARY AND, GENERALLY, RECEIPTS

¶20.30 To satisfy the IRS requirements and to substantiate your claims in the event of an audit, you need two types of records:

1. A diary, account book, or similar record to list the background and details of your travel and entertainment expenses; and

2. Receipts, itemized paid bills, or similar statements for lodging regardless of the amount and for other expenses when they exceed $25. But note these exceptions:

A receipt for transportation expenses exceeding $25 is required only when it is readily obtainable, for example, for air travel where receipts are usually provided.

A canceled check by itself is not an acceptable voucher. If you cannot produce a bill or voucher, you may have to present other evidence such as a statement in writing from witnesses to prove business purpose of the expense.

Recordkeeping rules for attorneys and other independent contractors who are reimbursed are discussed at ¶20.26.

A receipted bill or voucher must show (1) the amount of the expense; (2) the date the expense was incurred; (3) where the expense was incurred; and (4) the nature of the expense.

A hotel bill must show the name, location, date, and separate amounts for charges such as lodgings, meals, and telephone calls. A receipt for lodging is not needed if its cost is covered by a per diem allowance; *see* ¶20.35.

A restaurant bill must show the restaurant's name and location, the date and amount of the expense, and, when a charge is made for items other than meals or beverages, a description of the charge.

Diary Entries

Your diary does not have to duplicate data recorded on a receipt, provided that a notation in the diary is connected to the receipt. You are also not required to record amounts your company pays directly for any ticket or fare. Credit card charges should be recorded.

Your records must also show (1) the names of those you entertained; (2) the business purpose served by the entertainment; (3) the business relationship between you and your guests; and (4) the place of entertainment. Inattention to these details of substantiation can cost you the deduction. For example, an executive's company treasurer verified that the executive was required to incur entertainment expenses beyond reimbursed amounts. He also kept a cash diary in which he made contemporaneous notes of the amounts he spent. But he failed to note place, purpose, and business relationship. Consequently, there was no record that tied the expenses to his employment and the deduction was disallowed.

You should keep your diary and supporting records for at least three years after the due date for the return which the records support. However, you may not have to keep these records if the information from them is submitted to your company under the rules applied to reimbursed expenses and allowances described at ¶20.33.

Credit cards. Credit card charge statements for traveling and entertainment expenses meet the IRS tests, provided the business purpose of the expense is also shown. Credit card statements provide space for inserting the names of people entertained, their business relationship, the business purpose of the expense, and the portion of the expense to be allocated to business and personal purposes. These statements generally meet the IRS requirements of accounting to your employer for reimbursed expenses (¶20.35), provided a responsible company official reviews them.

EXCUSES FOR INADEQUATE RECORDS

Substantial compliance: If you have made a "good faith" effort to comply with the IRS rules, you will not be penalized if your records do not satisfy every requirement. For example, you would not automatically be denied a deduction merely because you did not keep a receipt.

Accidental destruction of records. If receipts or records are lost through circumstances beyond your control, you may substantiate deductions by reasonable reconstruction of your expenditures.

EXAMPLES 1. Bryan's 1966 records were lost by a moving company. He claimed a T&E deduction of $15,301.87. The IRS estimated his T&E and other business expenses as $8,669 on the basis of his 1971 expense records. The Tax Court affirmed the IRS's approach. True, Bryan's loss of records made his burden of proof difficult, but he had to provide a reasonable reconstruction of his records to support his claimed deduction. His testimony of what he incurred in 1966 was not sufficient. A more accurate method was the IRS's use of his 1971 records and receipts.

2. Jackson claimed the IRS lost his records. He left his records with the IRS when he was audited, and the records were never returned. The Tax Court held that to be a good excuse for not producing his records and allowed a deduction on the basis of reconstructed records. Evidence that the IRS lost them: The IRS turned up Jackson's worksheet a year after the audit interview.

3. Murray claimed he lost his records when he was evicted from his apartment for failure to pay rent for a month. The Tax Court accepted his excuse on proof that he had kept records before they were lost. The eviction was beyond his control. However, if the records had been lost during a voluntary move, the loss would not have been excused, as in Example 1 on page 256.

Exceptional circumstances: If, by reason of the "inherent nature of the situation," you are unable to keep adequate records, you may substantially comply by presenting the next best evidence. A supporting memorandum from your files and a statement from the persons entertained may be an adequate substitute. IRS regulations do not explain the meaning of "inherent nature of the situation."

REPORTING T&E EXPENSES AS SELF-EMPLOYED PERSON

¶20.31

You must keep records following the rules of ¶20.30. You may claim the meal allowance at ¶20.4 on overnight business trips. The reimbursement rules of ¶20.33 do not apply to you.

In preparing your tax return, you report your expenses on the appropriate lines of Schedule C. You do not use Form 2106. An advantage of reporting on Schedule C is that your travel and entertainment expenses (T & E) are not subject to the 2% adjusted gross income (AGI) floor. However, Schedule C does have a line for reducing meal and entertainment costs by 20%.

REPORTING T&E EXPENSES WHERE YOU ARE NOT REIMBURSED

¶20.32

If you are paid a salary with the understanding that you will pay your own expenses and you pay all of your T&E expense without reimbursement, you report all of your salary or commission income as shown on Form W-2. You report your expenses on Form 2106. Meals and entertainment are only 80% deductible. You must also keep records as required by ¶20.30 to support your deduction. The deductible amount from Form 2106 is entered on Schedule A as a miscellaneous expense subject to the 2% floor. Thus, if your total miscellaneous expenses, including the unreimbursed T&E costs, do not exceed 2% of adjusted gross income, none of the miscellaneous expenses will be deductible.

EMPLOYER REIMBURSEMENT PLANS

TAX TREATMENT OF REIMBURSEMENTS

¶20.33

Compliance rules are imposed on employees and employers for reporting reimbursed travel and entertainment expenses in order to prevent reimbursement arrangements from being used to avoid the 2% AGI floor for employee miscellaneous expenses. Plans that allow reimbursements that do *not* comply with the IRS rules are called *nonaccountable* plans. All reimbursements under a nonaccountable plan are reported as salary or wage income on Form W-2. You then deduct your expenses as miscellaneous deductions subject to the 2% AGI floor.

If a plan meets the IRS rules, the plan is called an *accountable plan* and reimbursements made by the plan are not reported on Form W-2 as taxable wages. You also do not have to deduct expenses, assuming the reimbursement equals your expenses. In other words, there is a bookkeeping "wash" in which the full amount of expenses offsets the reimbursement without being reduced by the 2% AGI floor and in the case of meal costs, by the 20% reduction.

To qualify a plan as accountable, your employer must see to it that you submit adequate proof of your expenditures, and that you return any excess advances. To reduce recordkeeping for actual costs, the company may reimburse you according to certain fixed *per diem* allowance rates; *see* ¶20.35. Your company must also determine how much of the advance or reimbursement, if any, is to be reported on your Form W-2.

EXAMPLE Your adjusted gross income is $85,000, and you incur T&E expenses of $1,600 which are reimbursed by your company. If the reimbursement arrangement does not meet the IRS rules, the $1,600 reimbursement is reported as wage income on your Form W-2. You may report the expenses on Form 2106 and claim a deduction on Schedule A as a miscellaneous expense subject to the 2% AGI floor. However, if these are your only miscellaneous expenses, you will not get the benefit of a deduction because they do not exceed 2% of $85,000 or $1,700. The $1,600 is fully taxable although spent for T&E.

If your reimbursement arrangement qualified as an accountable plan, and you made an adequate reporting to your employer, the $1,600 would not be reported as income on your Form W-2, and you would not have to be concerned with the 2% floor for miscellaneous itemized deductions. There is a bookkeeping "wash." In other words, you receive a full deduction by substantiating the expenses to your employer.

WHAT IS AN ACCOUNTABLE PLAN?

¶20.34

A reimbursement or allowance arrangement is an accountable plan if it requires you to:

Adequately account to your employer for your expenses; and
Return to your employer any excess reimbursement or allowance which you do not show was spent for ordinary and necessary business expenses.

If these terms are met and your expenses are fully reimbursed, you do not report the expenses or the reimbursement on your return.

If the reimbursement is less than your payment of expenses, you use Form 2106 and Schedule A to claim a deduction for the unreimbursed expenses. The unreimbursed expenses are subject to the 2% AGI floor on Schedule A.

What is an adequate accounting? You adequately account to your employer by submitting bills and an account book, diary, or similar record in which you entered each expense at or near the time you had it. You must account to your employer for all amounts received as advances, reimbursements, or allowances, including amounts charged on a company credit card. Your records and supporting information must meet the rules of ¶20.30. You must also pay back any reimbursements or allowances for which you do not adequately account or the nonreturned accounts will be taxable under the rules at ¶20.37 for nonaccountable plans.

The accounting requirements are eased if you are reimbursed under a *per diem* arrangement covering meals, lodging, and incidental expenses (¶20.35) or you receive a flat mileage allowance (¶20.36).

If you are entitled to reimbursement from your employer, make sure you ask for reimbursement. Failure to be reimbursed may prevent you from deducting your out-of-pocket expenses. A supervisor whose responsibility was to maintain good relations with his district and store managers entertained them and their families and also distributed gifts among them. His cost was $2,500 for which he could have been reimbursed by his company, but he made no claim. Consequently, the Tax Court disallowed it as a deduction on his return. The expense was the company's; any good will he created benefited it. But because he failed to seek reimbursement, he was not allowed to convert company expenses into his own.

Time limits for receiving advances, substantiating expenses, and returning excess payments. The general rule is that these events must occur within a reasonable time. Under an IRS "safe harbor," the following payments are considered to be within a reasonable time:

Advance payments—if given to you within 30 days before you reasonably anticipate to pay or incur expenses;

Substantiation of expenses—if provided to your employer within 60 days after the expense is paid or incurred; and

Return of excess—if done within 120 days after you pay or incur expenses.

An employer may set up a "periodic statement method" to meet IRS rules. Here, an employer gives each employee periodic statements (at least quarterly) that list the amounts paid in excess of expenses substantiated by the employee and request substantiation of the additional amounts paid, or a return of the excess, within 120 days of the date of the statement. Substantiation or return within the 120-day period satisfies the reasonable time test.

If you fail to return excess payments within a reasonable time but you meet all of the other tests applied to an accountable plan, such as providing proof, only the retained excess is taxed to you as if paid outside of an accountable plan.

Allocating reimbursements to meals and entertainment. Only 80% of meals and entertainment expenses are deductible. Therefore, if you adequately account for your expenses, and receive a flat reimbursement that is partly for meals and entertainment, and partly for other expenses, you must allocate part of the reimbursement to meals and entertainment if the employer has not provided an item-by-item breakdown. You must make this allocation if you want to deduct expenses exceeding reimbursements because on Form 2106, you must separately list meals and entertainment costs and reimbursements for meals and entertainment. The allocation is based on the percentage of which your meal costs bear to the total T&E expenses.

EXAMPLE You receive an allowance of $1,000 for travel expenses in June and have total expenses of $1,500, including $300 for meals. The percentage of your meals to total expenses is 20% (300/1,500). On Form 2106, you show 20% of the allowance or $200 as the allocable reimbursement for meals. The unreimbursed $100 balance for meals ($300-$200) must be reduced to $80 by the 20% reduction for meals. The balance of other travel expenses is $400 ($1,200 less allocated reimbursement of $800). The $480 total is transferred from Form 2106 to Schedule A, where it is deductible as a miscellaneous itemized expense subject to the 2% AGI floor.

PER DIEM TRAVEL ALLOWANCE UNDER ACCOUNTABLE PLANS

¶20.35

Instead of providing a straight reimbursement for substantiated out-of-pocket travel expenses, an employer may use a *per diem* allowance to cover meals, lodging and incidental expenses on business trips away from home. Sometimes just meals and incidental expenses are covered.

Incidental expenses covered by a *per diem* arrangement may include tips, laundry, and cleaning fees, or similar expenses, but may *not* include cab fares, telephone, or telegram costs. If the accountable plan rules are met and you are not related (*see* below) to the employer, you do not have to give your employer proof of your actual expenses if you receive a *per diem* allowance or reimbursement that is equal to or less than the federal travel rate for the particular area. For allowances covering lodging plus meals and incidental expenses within the continental U.S., an employer may use an IRS high-low rate of $93 or $147 per day, depending on the locality, instead of the federal travel rate; *see* next page.

You must submit proof of the time, place, and business purpose of the travel, and the IRS will recognize a *per diem* arrangement only if the employer's reimbursement is set to cover reasonably anticipated ordinary and necessary business expenses. If the *per diem* arrangement qualifies, you do not have to keep lodging receipts.

Tables published by the government show the federal travel rate for areas within the continental U.S. (called CONUS locations) and for areas outside the continental U.S., including Hawaii and Alaska (called OCONUS locations).

The accountable plan rule (¶20.34) that requires you to return excess amounts is satisfied if you are required to return an allowance received for days of travel that are not substantiated as to time, place, and business purpose. For example, if you are given an allowance based on an anticipated business trip of five days, but you return after three days, the plan must require you to return the allowance allocable to the last two days. You do *not* have to return any amounts received in excess of the federal travel rate for the three travel days, but if you do not return the excess, or substantiate it with actual records, it will be reported as income on your Form W-2.

Employees related to the employer. The special IRS *per diem* rules do not apply if you work for a brother, sister, spouse, parent, child, grandparent, or grandchild. They also do not apply if you are an employee-stockholder who owns more than 10% of the company's stock.

You must make an adequate accounting of actual expenses to your employer to satisfy the accountable plan requirements (¶20.34), and you must hold on to your records to prove your expenses if questioned by the IRS.

However, you may take advantage of the fixed mileage allowance test (¶20.36) as a means of substantiating automobile expenses.

Federal travel rate or IRS high-low rate for lodging, meals and incidental expenses. If a *per diem* allowance covers lodging plus meals and incidental expenses on trips within the continental U.S., your employer may base reimbursements on an IRS high-low rate as an alternative to using the federal travel rate for government employees. Your employer chooses which method to use; for a particular employee, either the high-low method or the federal travel rate method must be used for all trips within the continental U.S. during the year.

For trips from January 1, 1992 through February 29, 1992, the IRS rate for designated high-cost areas was $130, and $88 for all other areas. For trips on or after March 1, 1992, the high-cost area *per diem* rate is $147, and the rate for all other areas, $93. High-cost areas are generally major metropolitan and resort areas.

Here is a list of the areas that qualify for the $147 high-cost *per diem* rate on or after March 1, 1992. The $147 may also apply to the surrounding counties; check with your employer or ask the IRS for a copy of Publication 1542 (April 1992 edition). In 1993, the high-low rates and the high-cost areas may be changed by the IRS.

California: Death Valley, Los Angeles and San Francisco
Colorado: Aspen, Keystone/Silverthorne and Vail
District of Columbia and vicinity
Florida: Key West
Illinois: Chicago
Maryland: Columbia, and Ocean City
Massachusetts: Boston, and Martha's Vineyard/Nantucket
New Jersey: Atlantic City, Newark and Ocean City/Cape May
New York: New York City, White Plains
Pennsylvania: Philadelphia
Rhode Island: Newport
South Carolina: Hilton Head

For trips in 1992 before March 1, the $130 high-cost area rate applied to all the localities in the above list except for Keystone/Silverthorne, Colorado. In addition, the $130 rate applied to San Diego and Santa Barbara, California; Atlanta, Georgia; Annapolis, Maryland; Andover, Lowell, Quincy, and Plymouth, Massachusetts; Detroit, Michigan; and Princeton/Trenton, New Jersey.

The high-or-low-cost area rate may be used only for travel within the continental U.S.; Alaska and Hawaii are not included. For travel in Alaska, Hawaii, or other areas outside the continental U.S., *per diem* reimbursements must be based on the federal travel rate for that locality (from government OCONUS table). These rates sometimes fluctuate on a month-to-month basis.

Tax effect of per diem allowance. If your reimbursement is less than or equal to the federal travel rate or IRS high-low rate, the reimbursement is not reported on Form W-2. If your expenses do not exceed the reimbursement, you do not have to report the expenses or the reimbursement on your tax return; *see* Example 1. If your expenses exceed the reimbursement, you may deduct the excess by reporting the expenses and reimbursement on Form 2106. The net amount from Form 2106, after applying the 20% reduction for meals, is claimed on Schedule A as a miscellaneous expense subject to the 2% AGI floor; *see* Example 2.

Excess *Per Diem* Allowances

A *per diem* allowance that exceeds the federal travel rate or the IRS high-low rate will be reported as income on your Form W-2, unless you return the excess or prove to your employer that your actual expenses equal or exceed the allowance; *see* Examples 3 and 4. The excess reportable on Form W-2 is also subject to income tax and FICA tax withholding.

EXAMPLES 1. You take a three-day business trip to a locality at a time when the federal travel rate for the area is $92 per day. You account for the date, place, and business purpose of the trip. Your employer reimburses you $92 a day for lodging, meals, and incidental expenses, for a total of $276. Your actual expenses do not exceed this amount. Your employer does not report the reimbursement on your Form W-2. You do not have to report the reimbursement or deduct any expenses on your return.

2. Same facts as Example 1 except that the reimbursement is less than your actual expenses of $310 for which you have records. On Form 2106, you report the $276 reimbursement and your $310 of expenses. If a specific portion of the reimbursement has not been allocated to meals, you must make an allocation because only 80% of meal costs are deductible. The net amount from Form 2106 is deductible on Schedule A as a miscellaneous expense provided that the amount, plus other nonreimbursed job expenses and miscellaneous expenses, exceed 2% of adjusted gross income.

3. Same facts as Example 1, except that you are reimbursed at a rate of $100 per day, or $8 per day more than the federal travel rate. If you do not return the excess of $24 ($8x3 days) within a reasonable time (¶20.34), the $24 will be included as salary income in Box 10 of your Form W-2. The amount up to the federal travel rate, or $276, will be reported in Box 17 of Form W-2, but not included as income.

4. You take a two-day business trip to Los Angeles, which has been designated a "high-cost" locality by the IRS eligible for the $147 *per diem* rate. Under your employer's accountable plan, you receive an allowance of $147 per day. Your expenses do not exceed the reimbursement. The allowance will not be reported as income on your Form W-2 and you do not have to report the reimbursement or your expenses on your return.

If your employer had reimbursed you $160 for each day, only up to $147 would be treated as substantiated under the IRS rules, unless you proved that you had expenses greater than $147. Without such proof, the $26 excess reimbursement ($320 reimbursement *less* $294 at IRS rate) would be reported as income on Form W-2 and subject to withholding, unless you returned it.

Per diems **covering meals and incidental expenses only.** An employer who provides you with lodging or who pays your lodging costs directly may give you a *per diem* allowance covering only meals and incidental expenses. If you are not related to the employer and the allowance does not exceed the IRS meal allowance of $26 or $34 (in high-cost areas) per day, it is not reported as income on your Form W-2. The areas qualifying for the $34 rate are shown at ¶20.4. For meals outside the continental U.S., the $26 or $34 rate does not apply; there is a separate meals and incidental expense rate for each locality, as shown in the government OCONUS table.

For employees in the transportation industry, such as airline employees, employers may provide a $30 per day allowance for *all* trips within the continental U.S., instead of applying the $26 or $34 rate on a trip-by-trip basis. The employer may also elect to provide a $34 per day allowance for all travel outside the continental U.S.

For the first and last day of business travel, the employer generally must prorate the applicable meal allowance so that 25% of the allowance is allowed for each six hours of business travel, with the six-hour periods starting at midnight. Under this rule, an employee who began his or her trip between 6 a.m. and noon would be entitled to only 75% of the full meal allowance for that day. However, the IRS allows an employer to prorate the allowance using a normal 9 a.m.–5 p.m. business day, thereby allowing a full day's allowance for an employee who begins traveling at 9 a.m. For example, an employee who departs on a business trip at 7 p.m. and returns 9 p.m. the following day may be given an allowance equal to 1½ times the daily rate, although 1¼ times the full daily rate would be allowed under the regular proration method.

EXAMPLE On a two-day business trip to New York City, your employer directly pays for your hotel and reimburses you $40 a day for meals. The federal rate for meals in New York is $34 a day. Assume that under the proration rule, you are allowed $68 for the two days. If you do not substantiate expenses of at least $80 to your employer or return the $12 excess, your employer will report the $12 excess as taxable wages on Form W-2. Your Form W-2 will also show $68 ($34 a day × 2) as a tax-free reimbursement.

Assume you could prove that your actual meal expenses were $100. You should give that proof to your employer. None of the $80 reimbursement would be reported as income. To deduct the unreimbursed expense of $20, you would file Form 2106 and list all of your expenses and also list the tax-free reimbursement. The net amount of $20 ($100–$80) must be further reduced on Form 2106 by 20% because only 80% of meal expenses are deductible. Only $16 (80% of $20) is entered on Schedule A as a miscellaneous expense and it is subject to the 2% AGI floor.

The employer may deduct 80% of the per diem meal allowance that is not treated as income on Form W-2. If part of the allowance is reported as income on Form W-2, the employer deducts 100% of that amount as compensation paid; that portion is not subject to the 80% limit.

AUTOMOBILE MILEAGE ALLOWANCES

¶**20.36** If your employer pays you a fixed mileage allowance of up to 28 cents per mile for 1992, the amount of your automobile expenses is treated as substantiated, provided you show the time, place, and business purpose of your travel. If the allowance is in the form of an advance, it must be given within a reasonable period before the anticipated travel and you must also be required to return within a reasonable period (¶20.34) any portion of the allowance that covers mileage that you have not substantiated.

If these tests are met, the allowance will not be reported as income on Form W-2, and you will not have to report the allowance or expenses on your return; *see* Example 1. If you do not prove to your employer the time, place, and purpose of your travel the entire reimbursement is treated as paid from a nonaccountable plan and will be reported as income on Form W-2.

If you were given a 1992 mileage allowance in excess of 28 cents per mile, the excess will be included as wages on your Form W-2, unless you substantiate to the employer that your expenses were at least equal to the allowance; *see* Example 2. If your allowance was less than 28 cents per mile, you may deduct the difference as a miscellaneous itemized deduction subject to the 2% AGI floor; *see* Example 3.

Your employer may reimburse you for parking fees and tolls in addition to the mileage allowance.

EXAMPLES 1. You drive 12,000 miles for business and account to your employer for the time, place, and business purpose of each trip. Your employer reimburses you at the IRS rate of 28 cents per mile. None of the reimbursements will be reported as income on your Form W-2, and you do not have to report the reimbursements or any expenses on your return.

2. Same as Example 1 except that you were reimbursed at 30 cents per mile. The amount using the IRS rate, or $3,360 (28¢ × 12,000 miles) is $240 less than the reimbursement of $3,600 (30¢ × 12,000). If you do not provide records showing that you had expenses of at least 30 cents per mile, the $240 excess over the IRS rate will be reported as wages on your Form W-2.

3. Same as Example 1 except that you were reimbursed only 20 cents per mile. The reimbursements will not be reported as income on your Form W-2. You may deduct expenses up to the 28 cent IRS rate by reporting the expenses and reimbursements on Form 2106. The amount using the IRS rate, or $3,360 (28¢ × 12,000 miles) is $960 more than the reimbursement of $2,400 (20¢ × 12,000). The $960 may be claimed as a miscellaneous itemized deduction on Schedule A subject to the 2% AGI floor.

If you had records showing actual expenses of more than $3,360, you would claim those expenses on Form 2106 and not use the IRS fixed mileage allowance rate to figure your deduction.

Fixed and variable rate allowance (FAVR). In lieu of setting the allowance at the IRS standard mileage rate (28 cents per mile in 1992), an employer may use a fixed or variable rate allowance called a FAVR, that gives employees a cents-per-mile rate to cover gas and other operating costs, plus a flat amount to cover fixed costs such as depreciation, insurance and registration. A FAVR allowance must reflect local driving costs and allows employers to set reimbursements at a rate that more closely approximates employee expenses. If your employer sets up a qualifying FAVR under IRS guidelines, you will be required to provide records substantiating your mileage and certain car ownership information. Expenses up to the FAVR limits are deemed substantiated and will not be reported as wages on your Form W-2.

REIMBURSEMENTS UNDER NONACCOUNTABLE PLANS

¶**20.37** A nonaccountable plan is one that either does not require you to adequately account for your expenses, or allows you to keep any excess reimbursement or allowances over the expenses for which you did adequately account.

Your employer reports allowances or reimbursements for a nonaccountable plan, as part of your salary income in Box 10 of your Form W-2. The allowance is also subject to income tax and FICA tax (Social Security) withholding. To claim deductions, you must use Form 2106 and itemized your deductions on Schedule A. Your expenses are subject to the 2% AGI floor.

Important: If you adequately report expenses to your employer and return excess reimbursements, you are treated as being reimbursed under an accountable plan and generally do not have to report any reimbursement on your return; *see* ¶20.34.

21

DEDUCTING MOVING EXPENSES TO A NEW JOB LOCATION

Qualifying unreimbursed moving expenses to a new job location are deductible if you claim itemized deductions. If you do not itemize, you may *not* deduct any moving expenses. You may decide not to itemize when the standard deduction exceeds the total of your itemized deductions including the deductible moving expenses.

Moving expenses are *not* reduced by the 2% AGI floor.

Use Form 3903 to figure your deduction and attach it to Form 1040. Enter the deductible amount on Schedule A. If you move to a foreign country, figure your deduction on Form 3903F; *see* Chapter 36.

To deduct moving expenses, you must meet a 35-mile distance test explained at ¶21.1, and a time test for remaining in the area of the new job, explained at ¶21.2 and ¶21.3.

Only certain types of expenses are fully deductible, such as the cost of moving your household goods and the travel costs of you and your household members. Other expenses, such as the costs of pre-move house-hunting trips, or temporary quarters at your new job location, are deductible only within limits. These limitations are explained in ¶21.5.

THE 35-MILE DISTANCE TEST

¶21.1 The distance between your new job location and your former home must be at least 35 miles more than the distance between your old job location and your former home. For this purpose, your home may be a house, apartment, trailer, or even a houseboat, but not a seasonal residence such as a summer cottage. If you had no previous job or you return to full-time work after a long period of unemployment or part-time work, the new job location must be at least 35 miles from your former home. The 35-mile test applies to the self-employed and employees.

At the time this book went to press, Congress was considering legislation to increase the mileage test after 1992 from 35 to 55 miles. See the Supplement for an update.

Meeting the 35-Mile Test

Find the shortest of most commonly traveled routes in measuring the distances under the 35-mile test. The following worksheet may be used as an aid.

Distance between	In miles
1. Old residence and new job location	
2. Old residence and old job location	
3. Difference (must be at least 35 miles)	

The location of your new residence is not considered in applying the 35-mile test. However, if the distance between your new residence and the new job location is more than the distance between your old residence and new job location, your moving expenses may be disallowed unless you can show (1) you are required to live there as a condition of employment; or (2) an actual decrease in commuting time or expense results.

EXAMPLES 1. Your company's office is in the center of a metropolitan area. You live 18 miles from your office. You are transferred to a new office and buy a new house. To deduct moving costs, you must show that the location of the new office is at least 35 miles from your previous residence.

2. Your old job was four miles from your former residence and your new job is 40 miles from your former residence. You move to a house that is less than 35 miles from your old house. Nevertheless, you have met the 35-mile test since your new job is 36 miles further from your former home than your old job was.

If you worked for more than one employer, you find the shortest of the most commonly traveled routes from your old residence to your former principal place of employment.

Your job location is where you spend most of your working time. If you work at various locations, the job location is where you report to work. If you work for several employers on a short-term basis and get jobs through a union hall system, the union hall is considered your job location.

Moving overseas. A member of the Armed Services may deduct the cost of moving his or her family to an overseas post.

If you take a new job overseas, and qualify for the foreign earned income exclusion, moving expenses allocable to the excluded income are not deductible; *see* ¶36.7.

Alien moving to the U.S. The deduction is not limited to U.S. citizens and residents. An alien may deduct the cost of travel here to work at a full-time position.

THE 39-WEEK TEST FOR EMPLOYEES

¶21.2 In addition to meeting the 35-mile distance test, you must remain in the new locality as a full-time employee for at least 39 weeks during the 12-month period immediately following your arrival at the new job location. You do not need to have a job prior to your arrival at the new location. Your family does not have to arrive with you. The 39 weeks of work need not be consecutive or with the same employer. You may change jobs provided you remain in the same locality for 39 weeks. The 39-week test does not apply to employees who become disabled and lose their job, or who die.

If you lose your job for reasons other than your willful misconduct, the 39-week requirement is waived. Should you resign or lose your job for willful misconduct, a part-time job will not satisfy the 39-week test. The time test is not waived because you reach mandatory retirement age first, where this retirement was anticipated.

If you are temporarily absent from work through no fault of your own, due to illness, strikes, shutouts, layoffs, or natural disasters, your temporary absence is counted in the 39 weeks.

EXAMPLE You accept a position with a company 600 miles from your former position. You move to the new location. After you have worked in the new position 14 weeks, you resign and take another job with a nearby company. You may add the 14 weeks of work with the first company to 25 weeks with the second company to meet the 39-week requirement.

Job transfers. The 39-week period is also waived if you are transferred from your new job for your employer's benefit. However, it must be shown that you could have satisfied the 39-week test except for the transfer.

What if *you* initiate the transfer? The IRS held in a ruling that the 39-week test is not waived if an employee initiates the transfer, even if the employer approves. An individual was not allowed to deduct the costs of moving across the country to take a government position when within 39 weeks of taking the position, he applied for and took another government job in another area. The IRS disallowed the deduction, although the government reimbursed part of the employee's moving expenses to the new job post, thereby indicating that it considered the transfer to be in the government's interest. According to the IRS, the waiver of the 39-week test applies to transfers initiated by employers, not by employees.

Full-time status. This is determined by the customary practices of your occupation in the area. If work is seasonal, off-season weeks count as work weeks if the off-season period is less than six months and you have an employment agreement covering the off-season.

Joint returns. On a joint return, either spouse may meet the time test. But the work time of one spouse may not be added to the time of the other spouse.

EXAMPLE Smith moves from New York to a new job in Denver. After working full time for 30 weeks, he resigns from his job and cannot find another position during the rest of the 12-month period. He may not deduct his moving expenses. But assume that Mrs. Smith also finds a job in Denver at the same time as her husband and continues to work for at least 39 weeks. Since she has met the 39-week test, the moving expenses from New York to Denver paid by her husband are deductible, provided they file a joint return. However, if Mrs. Smith had worked for only nine weeks, her work period could not be added to her husband's to meet the 39-week test.

THE 78-WEEK TEST FOR THE SELF-EMPLOYED AND PARTNERS

¶21.3 In addition to meeting the 35-mile distance test, you must work full time for at least 78 weeks during the 24 months immediately following your arrival, of which at least 39 weeks occur in the first 12 months. The test is waived if death or disability prevents compliance. The full-time work requirement may prevent semi-retired hobbyists, students, or others who work only a few hours a week in self-employed trades or occupations from claiming the deduction.

You are considered to have obtained employment at a new principal place of work when you have made substantial arrangements to begin such work. You may not deduct expenses for house-hunting or temporary quarters unless you have already made substantial arrangements to begin work at the new location.

Change of employee or self-employed status. If you start work at a new location as an employee and then become self-employed before meeting the 39-week employee time test, you must meet the 78-week test. Time spent as an employee is counted along with the time spent self-employed in meeting the test.

If, during the first 12 months, you change from working as a self-employed person to working as an employee, you may qualify under the 39-week employee time test, provided you have 39 weeks of work as an *employee*. If you do not have 39 weeks as an employee in the first 12 months, you must meet the 78-week test.

Joint returns. Where you file a joint return, you deduct moving expenses if either you or your spouse can satisfy the time test based on individual work records.

CLAIMING THE DEDUCTION BEFORE MEETING THE TIME TEST

¶21.4 If the due date for filing your tax return arrives before you can satisfy the applicable time test, you may, nevertheless, deduct moving expenses. If you file your return without taking the deduction, you may file an amended return or a refund claim after meeting the time test. No matter which option you choose, any reimbursement must be reported in the year received; *see* ¶21.6.

EXAMPLE You move to a new location on November 1, 1992. At the end of the year, you have worked in your new position only nine weeks. You deduct your moving expenses on your 1992 tax return even though you did not complete the 39- or 78-week period of work. But if, after you file the 1992 return, you move from the location before completing the applicable 39-week or 78-week work period, you must report as income the amount of moving expenses deducted in 1992 on the return for the year you move from the location. As an alternative, you may file an amended 1992 return on which you eliminate the deduction and recompute your tax.

MOVING EXPENSES
YOU MAY DEDUCT

¶21.5 For 1992 returns, the law distinguishes between two types of deductible moving expenses:

1. Direct expenses of moving, which are fully deductible.
2. Indirect expenses involving the disposition of your old residence and the acquisition of a new residence. These expenses are limited by ceilings discussed below.

Direct expenses. On your 1992 return, you may deduct in full the following directly related moving expenses, except for unreimbursed meal costs which are subject to an 80% limitation:

1. Traveling costs of yourself and members of your household en route from your old to the new locality. Here, you include the costs of transportation, meals, and lodging along the direct route by conventional transportation for yourself and family; food and lodging before departure for one day after the old residence is unusable; food and lodging for the day of arrival at the new locality. If you use your own car, you may either deduct your actual costs of gas, oil, and repairs (but not depreciation) during the trip or take a deduction based on the rate of 9¢ a mile. Also add parking fees and tolls. *See* the Supplement for late-breaking rate changes, if any.

Meal costs (food and beverage) are not allowed in full; they must be reduced by 20% before they may be deducted as part of your moving expense deduction. *See* the instructions to Form 3903.

2. The actual cost of moving your personal effects and household goods. This includes the cost of packing, crating, and transporting furniture and household belongings, in-transit storage up to 30 consecutive days, insurance costs for the goods, and the cost of moving a pet or shipping an automobile to your new residence. You may also deduct expenses of moving your effects from a place other than your former home, but only up to the estimated cost of such a move from your former home. Also deduct the cost of connecting or disconnecting utilities when moving household appliances. The cost of connecting a telephone in your new home is not deductible.

In one case, a moving expense deduction was allowed for the cost of shipping a sailboat. The IRS had disallowed the deduction, claiming the sailboat was not a "personal effect." The Tax Court, however, allowed the deduction based on these facts: The couple were active sailors and frequently used the boat; they lived on the sailboat for two weeks immediately before they moved and also for nine weeks after they arrived in the new location; they kept on board personal effects such as a refrigerator, kitchen utensils, and chairs. According to the Court, the boat was so "intimately related" to their lifestyle that it should be considered a deductible personal effect.

It is not necessary for you and members of your household to travel together or at the same time to claim the deduction or the expenses incurred by each member.

Indirect expenses subject to $3,000 ceiling. An overall limit of $3,000 is applied to 1992 deductions for indirectly related moving expenses (house-hunting expenses, temporary living quarters, and costs related to the sale and purchase or lease of your residence). Of this amount, only $1,500 incurred for temporary living expenses and for pre-move house-hunting trips is deductible. These limits are increased to $6,000 and $4,500, respectively, on job-related moves outside the United States; *see* ¶36.6.

1. The cost of pre-move house-hunting trips. A maximum of $1,500 can be deducted for pre-move house-hunting and temporary living expenses in the general location of the new job. These expenses include transportation, meals, and lodging incurred by you and members of your household in traveling from your former home to the general area of your new job location and returning. Only 80% of unreimbursed meal costs are allowed.

You must obtain employment before the trip begins and the trip must be for the principal purpose of finding a place to live.

You may deduct the expenses of more than one house-hunting trip taken by you or a member of your household. Moreover, the trip need not result in your finding a residence.

2. Temporary living quarters at your new job location. This includes meals (only 80% deductible) and lodging for yourself and members of your household while waiting to move into permanent quarters, or while looking for a new residence. You may deduct expenses incurred within any 30 consecutive days after obtaining employment. You do not have to incur these expenses during the first 30 days after starting to work in order to claim the deduction. On moves outside the United States, the 30-day limit is increased to 90 days; *see* ¶36.6.

3. Expenses of selling, purchasing, or leasing a residence. Selling expenses include real estate agents' commissions, attorneys' fees, escrow fees, transfer taxes, and similar costs necessary to effect the sale or exchange of your residence. But do not deduct fix-up expenses; *see* ¶29.5.

Purchasing expenses include attorney's fees, escrow fees, appraisal fees, title costs, points or loan placement charges (which do *not* represent interest), transfer taxes, and similar expenses. Do not include real estate taxes, interest, or any part of the purchase price of your house in your moving expense deduction. A residence includes a house, apartment, cooperative or condominium unit, or similar dwelling.

Deductible leasing expenses include reasonable expenses in settling an unexpired lease on an old residence or acquiring a lease on a new residence, such as attorney's fees, real estate commissions, consideration paid to lessor to obtain a release, or other similar expenses. You may not deduct security deposits or payments of rent. However, you may deduct a security deposit for your old lease which you forfeit because certain terms of the lease are broken as a result of the move.

You may not use selling expenses which you have deducted as moving expenses to reduce the amount realized on the sale of your house for purposes of determining gain. Similarly, purchase expenses which you deduct as a moving expense are not added to the cost basis of your new residence for purposes of determining gain. However, selling or purchasing expenses which exceed the $3,000 deduction limitation discussed below may be used to reduce your gain on sale of your old house or increase your basis on your new house.

Married couples filing separate 1992 returns. Where a married couple files separate returns and each spouse paid and deducts moving expenses, the above ceiling on each return for indirect expenses is $1,500 ($750 for house-hunting and temporary quarters).

If one spouse did not incur deductible expenses, the other spouse may deduct up to $3,000 of indirect moving expenses on a separate return.

Separated spouses may each deduct up to $3,000 for indirect expenses on separate returns under these conditions: (1) They did not live together in the same residence at the new location and do not plan to within a determinable time; (2) both incurred expenses in moving to new places of work; and (3) both spouses satisfy the time and distance tests.

Under the same conditions, a separated couple filing jointly may deduct up to $6,000 for the indirect expenses of moving to new places of work (including $3,000 for house-hunting and temporary quarters). Both spouses must satisfy the time and distance tests.

Delay in Moving to New Job Location

You may delay moving to the area of a new job location. A delay of less than one year does not jeopardize a deduction for moving expenses. Furthermore, if you move to the new job area within one year, your family may stay in the old residence for a longer period. Their later moving expenses will generally be deductible, even though incurred after one year. For example, the IRS allowed a moving expense deduction to a husband who immediately moved to a new job location, although his wife and children did not join him until 30 months after he began the new job. They delayed so the children could complete their education. The IRS held that since part of the moving expenses was incurred within one year, the moving expenses incurred later were also deductible.

Nondeductible expenses. You may not deduct the cost of travel incurred for a maid, nurse, chauffeur, or similar domestic help (unless the person is also your dependent), expenses of refitting rugs and drapes, forfeited tuition, car tags or driver's license for the state you move to, losses on disposing of memberships in clubs, mortgage penalties, expenses for trips to sell your old house, or loss on the sale of the house. Furthermore, when your employer reimburses you for such costs, you realize taxable income for the amount of the reimbursement.

You may not deduct the cost of transporting furniture which you purchased en route from your old home.

YOU MUST REPORT REIMBURSEMENTS

¶21.6

Include all moving expense reimbursements received in 1992 on your return as part of your salary or wage income. Your employer will include the reimbursement in Box 10 of Form W-2.

You must report as income such items as payments made by your employer directly to a moving company. Your employer will show these payments on Form 4782. Use your copy of the form to figure reimbursements and expenses. You then deduct your actual costs to the extent they qualify as deductible moving expenses, but only if you itemize deductions. If you do not itemize, you report the reimbursements as income, even though you do not get an offsetting deduction.

Reimbursements and the payment of the expenses generally occur in the same year. If, however, you are reimbursed in a year other than the year you pay the expenses, you may elect to deduct the expenses in the year of reimbursement, provided (1) you paid the expenses in a prior year; or (2) you pay the expenses in the year following the year of reimbursement but before the due date for filing the return (including extensions) for the reimbursement year.

EXAMPLES 1. You moved and paid expenses in December 1992. Your employer reimburses you in January 1993. You may deduct your expenses on your 1993 return rather than your 1992 return.

2. In 1992, your employer gave you the cash for your move, but you moved in 1993 and paid the expenses in 1993. You may elect to deduct the expense on your 1992 return if you paid the expense before the due date of the 1992 return (including extensions). If you filed the 1992 return before deducting expenses, you may file a refund claim or an amended return.

Reimbursements by employers of deductible moving expenses are not subject to withholding tax.

Reimbursements on sale of home. To encourage or facilitate an employee's move, an employer may reimburse the employee for a loss incurred on the sale of his or her house. The IRS taxes such reimbursements as pay.

Armed Forces Transfers

A member of the Armed Forces on active duty moving pursuant to a military order and incident to a permanent change of station does not account for or report any in-kind moving and storage expense services received from the military. Cash reimbursement or allowances are taxable only if they exceed actual moving expenses. Furthermore, if the Service moves the member and his or her family to separate locations, in-kind expenses, reimbursements, and allowances are not taxable. The "distance" test and the "time" test do not apply to either spouse.

Federal payments for displacement. Payments received under the Uniform Relocation Assistance and Real Property Acquisition Policies Act of 1970 by persons displaced from their homes, farms, or businesses by federal projects are not included in income.

PART IV

PERSONAL TAX COMPUTATIONS

In this part, you will learn how to figure your tax liability. Chapter 22 explains how you find your regular tax liability. Furthermore, depending on the source of your income, you may also have to compute the following taxes:

- Alternative capital gain tax. If you have net long-term capital gain and your top regular tax bracket is 31%, you may take advantage of the alternative 28% tax applied to net long-term capital gain; *see* ¶5.1.
- Alternative minimum tax. If you have reduced your taxable income by certain deductions and tax benefits, you may be subject to the alternative minimum tax (AMT); *see* Chapter 23.
- Self-employment tax. If you are self-employed, earnings from self-employment are generally subject to a self-employment tax of 15.30%, which is effectively reduced by a special income tax deduction for half of the self-employment tax. The self-employment tax finances Social Security and Medicare benefits; *see* Chapter 46.
- Estimated tax. If you have investment and self-employment income, you generally have to pay quarterly estimated tax; *see* ¶27.1.
- "Kiddie Tax." If your child under age 14 has investment income exceeding $1,200, you must compute tax on that income as if it was your own. "Kiddie Tax" rules are discussed in Chapter 24.

22

FIGURING YOUR REGULAR TAX LIABILITY

There are three regular income tax rate brackets of 15%, 28%, and 31%. By varying the income levels at which the 28% and 31% brackets apply, the tax law gives tax-saving benefits to single persons filing as head of household and to married persons filing jointly. For example, the second bracket of 28% starts at taxable income of $35,800 for married filing jointly and qualifying widow(er); $17,900 for married filing separately; $21,450 for single; and $28,750 for head of household. The third bracket of 31% starts at $86,500 for married filing jointly and qualifying widow(er); $43,250 for married filing separately; $51,900 for single; and $74,150 for head of household. The rules determining family filing status are discussed in Chapter 1.

New tax tables will save computation time for more taxpayers. The 1992 tax tables provide the tax for those with taxable incomes of under $100,000. In prior years, use of the tax tables was limited to taxable income of less than $50,000.

	See ¶
When to Use the Tax Tables	22.1
Tax Rate Schedules	22.2

USING THE TAX RATE SCHEDULES OR TAX TABLES

WHEN TO USE THE TAX TABLES

¶22.1 If you file Form 1040EZ or Form 1040A, you use the tax tables to look up your tax liability. The tax tables are reproduced in the Tax Organizer in Part VIII of this book. If you file Form 1040, you also use the tax tables if your taxable income is *less* than $100,000; if taxable income is $100,000 or more, you use the tax rate schedules shown on the next page.

If you use the tax tables, you do not have to compute your tax mathematically. To use the tables you first figure your taxable income, then turn to your income bracket and look for the tax liability listed in the column for your filing status. Filing status (single, married filing jointly, head of household, married filing separately, and qualifying widow(er)) is discussed in Chapter 1.

You may *not* use the tax tables and *must* use the schedules if you file for a short period (less than 12 months) due to a change of accounting period.

Estates and trusts may not use the tax tables.

The amount of your tax liability may be reduced by credits; for details, *see* Chapter 25 and Chapter 40.

Figuring taxable income. By following the line-by-line steps of your tax return, you reach taxable income. If you do not claim itemized deductions, taxable income is adjusted gross income reduced by the standard deduction and exemptions.

If you do claim itemized deductions, taxable income is adjusted gross income reduced by itemized deductions and exemptions.

EXAMPLES 1. You are single and have an adjusted gross income of $25,760. You claim one personal exemption and the standard deduction.

Adjusted gross income		$25,760
Less: Standard deduction	$3,600	
Exemption	2,300	5,900
Taxable income		$19,860

Your tax liability from the tax table is $2,981. The tax is shown in the column for single persons with taxable income of at least $19,850 but less than $19,900.

2. You are married filing jointly and have adjusted gross income of $35,000, itemized deductions of $7,000, and three exemptions.

Adjusted gross income		$35,000
Less: Itemized deductions	$7,000	
Exemptions (3 X $2,300)	6,900	13,900
Taxable income		$21,100

Your tax liability from the tax table is $3,169.

TAX RATE SCHEDULES

¶22.2 You compute your 1992 tax using the tax rate schedules below if either of the following is true:

Your taxable income is $100,000 or more; *or*
You file for a short period due to a change of accounting period.

EXAMPLES 1. You file as a head of household with taxable income of $103,000. You use Schedule Z to figure your tax.

Tax on first $74,150	$17,024.50
Tax on excess $28,850 at 31%	8,943.50
Tax	$25,968.00

2. You are married and file a joint return with taxable income of $130,000. You use Schedule Y-1 to figure your tax.

Tax on first $86,500	$19,566
Tax on excess $43,500 at 31%	13,485
Tax	$33,051

Effective tax rate on income subject to exemption phaseout and itemized deduction reduction. If you are considering earning additional income that will subject you to the phaseout of personal exemptions (¶1.32) or the 3% reduction to itemized deductions (¶13.8), the effective tax rate on this marginal income will exceed the specified top rates of 31% for ordinary income and 28% for net capital gain; *see* ¶28.2.

1992 Tax Rate Schedules: Use ONLY if your taxable income is $100,000 or more. If less, use the Tax Tables in the Tax Organizer.

Schedule X—Use if your filing status is Single

If taxable income is*:

Over—	But not over—	The tax** is—	of the amount over—
$ 0	$21,450	15%	$0
21,450	51,900	$3,217.50 + 28%	21,450
51,900		11,743.50 + 31%	51,900

Schedule Y-2—Use if your filing status is Married filing separately

If taxable income is*:

Over—	But not over—	The tax** is—	of the amount over—
$ 0	$17,900	15%	$0
17,900	43,250	$2,685 + 28%	17,900
43,250		9,783 + 31%	43,250

Schedule Y-1—Use if your filing status is Married filing jointly or Qualifying widow(er)

If taxable income is*:

Over—	But not over—	The tax** is—	of the amount over—
$ 0	$35,800	15%	$0
35,800	86,500	$5,370 + 28%	35,800
86,500		19,566 + 31%	86,500

Schedule Z—Use if your filing status is Head of household

If taxable income is*:

Over—	But not over—	The tax** is—	of the amount over—
$ 0	$28,750	15%	$0
28,750	74,150	$4,312.50 + 28%	28,750
74,150		17,024.50 + 31%	74,150

* Taxable income is on Line 37, Form 1040
** Tax is entered on Line 38, Form 1040

23 ALTERNATIVE MINIMUM TAX

The alternative minimum tax (AMT) is designed to recoup tax benefits that reduce or eliminate your regular income tax. AMT is triggered if it exceeds your regular income tax or you have no tax liability after claiming certain tax deductions or credits. You may incur an AMT if you have deductions for accelerated depreciation, percentage depletion, tax shelter losses, and intangible drilling and development costs. Even when you do not have preference items, you may incur AMT if you have substantial itemized deductions that are not deductible for AMT purposes such as state and local income taxes, certain interest expenses, and miscellaneous deductions.

Use Form 6251 to figure AMT. If you are subject to AMT, you add it to the regular tax liability shown on Form 1040.

You may be able to claim a credit for a prior payment of AMT tax if you have no AMT tax liability in 1992; see ¶23.7.

Even if you do not owe AMT after completing Form 6251, you may still need to use the entries on Form 6251 to figure a limitation on certain tax credits, including the dependent care credit or credit for the elderly or disabled; see ¶23.6.

COMPUTING AMT ON FORM 6251

¶23.1 For the AMT calculation on Form 6251, start with the amount shown on Line 35 of Form 1040, which is your regular taxable income without taking into account personal exemptions. This income is then increased (sometimes decreased) by AMT adjustments (¶23.2) and by preference items (¶23.3). The total is AMT taxable income which is reduced by the AMT exemption provided it is not subject to the phaseout. *See* the "Key to AMT Rules" on page 270 for the exemption rules and for the exemption penalty on married persons filing separately with AMT taxable income exceeding $155,000.

After reducing AMT income by the allowable exemption, the balance is subject to the 24% AMT rate, and the result, less any allowable AMT foreign tax credit (¶23.6), is the "tentative minimum tax." From the "tentative minimum tax," subtract your regular tax from Form 1040, and the regular foreign tax credit, if any. The regular tax does not include self-employment tax, averaging tax on lump-sum distributions, or recapture taxes. The difference is your alternative minimum tax, which you enter on Form 1040 as a separate tax on Line 48.

EXAMPLE You are married filing jointly. Your taxable income for 1992 is $64,982 and your regular tax is $13,539. Your five personal exemptions of $11,500 are not considered for AMT purposes. Adjustments (¶23.2) for state and local taxes, mortgage interest, depreciation, and a preference item (¶23.3) for charitable contributions, are added back to figure AMT taxable income. Your AMT taxable income is $126,658, which is reduced by a $40,000 exemption. Your additional AMT liability is $7,259, figured as follows and shown on the sample worksheet on the next page.

Taxable income without personal exemptions	$76,482
Add: Taxes	13,110
Interest	11,450
Depreciation	616
Charitable deduction	25,000
AMT taxable income	126,658
Less AMT exemption	40,000
	$86,658
Multiply by AMT rate of 24%	20,798
Less regular tax	13,539
Additional tax or AMT	$ 7,259

Form 6251–Worksheet

Name(s) shown on Form 1040		Your social security number	
Michael and Jennifer Bainbridge		XIX XO IXXI	

1	Enter the amount from Form 1040, line 35. (If Form 1040, line 35 is less than zero, enter as a negative amount.)	1	76,482
2	Net operating loss deduction, if any, from Form 1040, line 22. (Enter as a positive amount.)	2	
3	Overall itemized deductions limitation (see instructions)	3	( )
4	Combine lines 1, 2, and 3	4	76,482
5	**Adjustments:** (See instructions before completing.)		
a	Standard deduction, if any, from Form 1040, line 34	5a	
b	Medical and dental expenses. (Enter the smaller of the amount from Schedule A (Form 1040), line 4 or 2½% of Form 1040, line 32.)	5b	
c	Miscellaneous itemized deductions from Schedule A (Form 1040), line 24	5c	
d	Taxes from Schedule A (Form 1040), line 8	5d	13,110
e	Refund of taxes	5e	( )
f	Certain home mortgage interest	5f	11,450
g	Investment interest expense	5g	
h	Depreciation of tangible property placed in service after 1986	5h	616
i	Circulation and research and experimental expenditures paid or incurred after 1986	5i	
j	Mining exploration and development costs paid or incurred after 1986	5j	
k	Long-term contracts entered into after 2/28/86	5k	
l	Pollution control facilities placed in service after 1986	5l	
m	Installment sales of certain property	5m	
n	Adjusted gain or loss and incentive stock options	5n	
o	Certain loss limitations	5o	
p	Tax shelter farm loss	5p	
q	Passive activity loss	5q	
r	Beneficiaries of estates and trusts	5r	
s	Combine lines 5a through 5r	5s	25,176
6	**Tax preference items:** (See instructions before completing.)		
a	Appreciated property charitable deduction	6a	25,000
b	Tax-exempt interest from private activity bonds issued after 8/7/86	6b	
c	Depletion	6c	
d	Accelerated depreciation of real property placed in service before 1987	6d	
e	Accelerated depreciation of leased personal property placed in service before 1987	6e	
f	Amortization of certified pollution control facilities placed in service before 1987	6f	
g	Intangible drilling costs	6g	
h	Add lines 6a through 6g	6h	25,000
7	Combine lines 4, 5s, and 6h	7	126,658
8	Energy preference adjustment for certain taxpayers. (Do not enter more than 40% of line 7.) See instructions	8	
9	Subtract line 8 from line 7	9	126,658
10	Alternative tax net operating loss deduction. See instructions for limitations	10	
11	**Alternative minimum taxable income.** Subtract line 10 from line 9. If married filing separately, see instructions	11	126,658
12	Enter: $40,000 ($20,000 if married filing separately; $30,000 if single or head of household)	12	40,000
13	Enter: $150,000 ($75,000 if married filing separately; $112,500 if single or head of household)	13	150,000
14	Subtract line 13 from line 11. If zero or less, enter -0- here and on line 15 and go to line 16	14	-0-
15	Multiply line 14 by 25% (.25)	15	-0-
16	**Exemption.** Subtract line 15 from line 12. If zero or less, enter -0-. If completing this form for a child under age 14, see instructions for amount to enter	16	40,000
17	Subtract line 16 from line 11. If zero or less, enter -0- here and on line 22 and skip lines 18 through 21	17	86,658
18	Multiply line 17 by 24% (.24)	18	20,798
19	Alternative minimum tax foreign tax credit. See instructions	19	
20	Tentative minimum tax. Subtract line 19 from line 18	20	20,798
21	Enter your tax from Form 1040, line 38, minus any foreign tax credit on Form 1040, line 43. If an amount is entered on line 39 of Form 1040, see instructions	21	13,539
22	**Alternative minimum tax.** Subtract line 21 from line 20. If zero or less, enter -0-. Enter this amount on Form 1040, line 48. If completing this form for a child under age 14, see instructions for amount to enter	22	7,259

Key to AMT Rules

Item—	AMT Rule—
Tax rate	24% on AMT taxable income *less* the AMT exemption.
AMT taxable income	Regular taxable income without taking into account personal exemptions, increased or decreased by adjustments and increased by preferences.
AMT exemption	$40,000 if married filing a joint return [or a qualifying widow(er)]; $30,000 if single or head of household; *or* $20,000 if married filing a separate return.
	This exemption is reduced by 25¢ for each $1 that AMT taxable income exceeds $150,000 for joint filers or a qualifying widow(er); $112,500 if you file as a single person or head of household; and $75,000 for a married person filing separately. The exemption is completely phased out at $310,000 on a joint return and $232,500 on a single or head of household return. On a married person's separate return, the exemption is eliminated if AMT taxable income is $155,000 or more.
	There is also a penalty if as a married person, you file a separate return and have AMT taxable income exceeding $155,000. You must increase AMT taxable income by 25% of the excess over $155,000, but the maximum increase is $20,000.
AMT adjustments	Itemized deductions for taxes, certain interest, and most miscellaneous deductions are not allowed.
	Personal exemptions and the standard deduction are not allowed.
	MACRS depreciation is figured under the alternative MACRS system for real estate, using 40-year straight-line recovery, and for personal property, the 150% declining balance method is used.
	Incentive stock options; *see* ¶23.2.
	Mining exploration and development costs are allowable costs amortized over 10 years.
	For long-term contracts entered into after February 28, 1986, income is figured under the percentage of completion method.
	Pollution control facilities amortization is figured under alternate MACRS.
	Alternative tax net operating loss is allowed with adjustments.
	Circulation expenditures must be amortized ratably over three years.
	Research and experimental expenditures must be amortized ratably over 10 years.
	Passive activity losses are recomputed; shelter farm losses are not allowed.
AMT preference items	Appreciation on charitable donations of long-term capital gain property that is not taxed for regular tax purposes is subject to AMT, *except* for appreciation on donations of long-term personal property to be used by the charity for tax-exempt purposes made before July 1, 1992; *see* ¶23.3.
	Tax-exempt interest from private activity bonds issued after August 7, 1986, *except* for qualifying 501(c)(3) bonds.
	Depletion—excess of depletion deduction over adjusted basis in property.*
	Intangible drilling costs—excess of deducted costs over the total of the amount allowable if costs were amortized ratably over 120 months plus 65% of net income from the property.*
	Accelerated depreciation on real property and leased personal property placed in service before 1987— excess depreciation or amortization taken over straight-line deduction.
	A special energy deduction may offset preference items for depletion and intangible drilling costs; see ¶23.4
Partnership AMT	If you are a partner, consider for AMT your distributive share of the partnership's adjustments and tax preference items. These are reported on Schedule K-1 (Form 1065). The partnership itself does not pay alternative minimum tax.
Trust or estate AMT	If you are a beneficiary of an estate or trust, consider for AMT your share of distributable net alternative minimum taxable income shown on Schedule K-1 (Form 1041). The estate or trust must pay tax on any remaining alternative minimum taxable income.
S corporation stockholder	If you are a shareholder, consider for AMT your share of the adjustments and tax preference items reported on Schedule K-1 (Form 1120S).
Children subject to "kiddie tax"	Children under age 14 who are subject to the "kiddie tax" (¶24.3) may have to compute AMT liability on Form 6251. The child's AMT exemption is generally limited to $1,000 plus his or her earned income, but legislation pending in Congress when this book went to press would increase the exemption to $1,200; *see* the Supplement. Where the child's parent is not subject to AMT because his or her AMT exemption exceeds AMT income, and the child's share of the parent's unused AMT exemption exceeds $1,000 ($1,200 if Congress changes the law), the child's AMT exemption equals that share plus earned income. By filing Form 8803, a child's AMT may be reduced or eliminated if the child's parent or sibling under age 14 had regular tax liability exceeding tentative minimum tax, if any, from Form 6251. The child's AMT cannot exceed the extra tax that the parent would pay if the child's tentative minimum tax liability, plus regular tax, was added to the parents'.

ADJUSTMENTS FOR AMT

¶23.2

The amount of your regular taxable income from Form 1040 will generally be increased by the following adjustments on Form 6251.

Itemized deductions. If you have claimed itemized deductions for state and local taxes, miscellaneous deductions subject to the 2% AGI floor, and medical expenses, you will have to add back all or part of such deductions to taxable income. Taxes directly deductible from gross income for business or rental purposes remain deductible for AMT purposes. For AMT purposes *only* the following itemized deductions are allowed:

Charitable contributions.

Medical expenses exceeding 10% of AGI. Do not confuse this limit with the 7.5% limit for regular tax purposes.

Casualty and theft losses exceeding 10% of AGI.

Unreimbursed moving expenses to a new job location.

Wagering losses.

Claim of right deduction (¶2.9).

Estate tax deductions for income in respect of a decedent.

Impairment-related work expenses.

Home mortgage interest, subject to limitations on page 271.

Investment interest to the extent of net investment income.

The 3% reduction computation for itemized deductions at ¶13.8 does not apply for AMT purposes.

Mortgage interest. Less interest may be deductible for AMT purposes than for regular tax purposes. No AMT adjustment is required for home mortgage interest paid on a debt incurred to buy, construct, or substantially rehabilitate your principal residence or qualifying second residence. The residence may be a house, apartment, cooperative apartment, condominium, houseboat, or mobile home not used on a transient basis.

Interest on a mortgage taken out after June 30, 1992, is not deductible for AMT purposes if the proceeds are used for any purpose other than to buy, build, or substantially improve your principal or second residence. Furthermore, in the case of a mortgage refinanced after June 30, 1982, interest is deductible for AMT purposes only to the extent the new debt does not exceed the amount of the old debt immediately before the refinancing. Interest on the excess is not deductible for AMT purposes.

Interest on a mortgage debt incurred before July 1, 1982, for any purpose qualifies if the mortgage is secured by the property.

Your AMT adjustment on Form 6251 is the difference between the home mortgage interest you deducted for regular tax purposes and the amount of interest allowed for alternative minimum tax.

State and local taxes. State and local taxes deducted on Schedule A must be added back to taxable income in figuring AMT. If you received in 1992 a refund of state taxes deducted in a prior year, you enter the refund on Form 6251 as a negative adjustment which reduces taxable income in arriving at AMT taxable income.

Standard deduction and exemptions. If you claimed the standard deduction instead of itemizing deductions on Form 1040, you may not claim the standard deduction as an AMT deduction. Exemptions for yourself and your dependents are also not allowed for AMT purposes. The standard deduction is added back to taxable income as an AMT adjustment. Personal exemptions are excluded from Line 1 of Form 6251 which shows taxable income from Form 1040 (without the exemptions) as the starting point for figuring AMT taxable income; thus, the exemptions do not reduce AMT taxable income.

MACRS depreciation. Less depreciation is allowed for AMT than for regular tax purposes. For property acquired after 1986 other than real estate, the AMT depreciation rate is the 150% declining balance method, switching to the straight-line method when a larger depreciation allowance results. Real property acquired after 1986 is depreciated for AMT over a 40-year period using the straight-line method. Depreciation deductions for films, videotapes, and sound recordings are not adjusted under AMT.

If for regular tax purposes, you use the regular 200% declining balance method to depreciate business equipment, the difference between the higher regular depreciation and the lower rate for AMT is an adjustment. You may avoid this adjustment by using the 150% rate for regular tax purposes. For real estate, the adjustment is the difference between the straight line depreciation claimed for regular tax purposes using the 27.5-year or 31.5-year recovery period (¶42.13) and the straight-line recovery over the AMT 40-year recovery period.

The adjustment for MACRS may result in providing more depreciation for AMT purposes where the AMT depreciation computation towards the latter part of the useful life of the property provides larger deductions than the regular MACRS deduction.

EXAMPLE In one taxable year when AMT applies, Jones has two assets acquired after 1986. The regular MACRS depreciation for asset A is $500 and for asset B, $400. When applying the AMT rules, the depreciation for asset A is $400 and for asset B, $450. AMT taxable income is increased by $50. The adjustment accounts for post-1987 MACRS property held in the year.

Asset A		
Regular depreciation	$500	
AMT depreciation	400	$100
Asset B		
Regular depreciation	$400	
AMT depreciation	450	(50)
Net adjustment to AMT taxable income		$ 50

Property placed in service before 1987, unless it qualifies under MACRS transitional rules, is subject to prior law tax preference rules. Prior law creates tax preference items when the ACRS deduction exceeds regular straight line; *see* ¶23.3. A tax preference item always increases AMT taxable income.

Basis adjustment affects AMT gain or loss. When post-1986 depreciable assets are sold, gain for AMT purposes is figured on the basis of the property as adjusted by depreciation claimed for AMT purposes. This gain or loss will be different from the gain or loss figured for regular tax purposes where regular MACRS depreciation was used. (This AMT basis rule does not apply to property placed in service before 1987 except for transitional property within the post-1986 rules).

Similarly, recalculations of basis and gain are made for prior AMT adjustments taken for circulation expenditures, research and experimental expenditures, pollution control facilities, and mining exploration and development costs.

Incentive stock options (ISO). The excess of the fair market value of the shares at the time of exercise over the option price is treated as an adjustment increasing AMT taxable income if you exercise ISO options in 1992, and the shares are freely transferable. When you sell the stock in a later year, and you are subject to AMT in that year, you may increase the basis of the stock for AMT purposes by the amount of the AMT adjustment reported in 1992.

If, in 1992, you both exercised an option and sold the stock for less than the exercise price, the AMT adjustment is limited to the amount realized on the sale less adjusted basis.

Mining exploration and development costs. The deduction allowed for regular tax purposes for mining exploration and development costs is amortized ratably over a 10-year period for AMT purposes.

If a mine is abandoned as worthless, all mining exploration and development costs that have not been written off are deductible in the year of abandonment.

Long-term contracts. The use of the completed contract method of accounting or certain other methods of accounting for long-term contracts is generally not allowable. For AMT, the percentage of completion method must be used. However, there is an exception for home construction contracts.

Amortization of certified pollution control facilities. For purposes of the alternative minimum tax, the amortization deduction for a certified pollution control facility placed in service after 1986 is determined under alternative MACRS (¶42.9).

Research and experimental expenditures. Research and experimental expenditures must be amortized over 10 years beginning with the tax year in which the expenditures were made.

Farm and passive activity losses. No loss from a tax shelter farm activity is allowed in figuring AMT income. Generally, a tax shelter farm activity is any farming syndicate or any other passive farming activity. The loss from a tax shelter farm activity is allowed in figuring alternative minimum taxable income for later years as a deduction against income from the activity or for the year you dispose of your entire interest in the activity.

Passive activity losses are generally not allowed in figuring AMT taxable income. If you had a passive loss deduction for regular tax purposes, follow the Form 6251 instructions on reducing the loss for AMT purposes by taking into account all AMT adjustment and preference items.

A disallowed loss may be reduced if you are insolvent as of the end of the tax year. You are insolvent to the extent that your liabilities exceed the fair market value of your assets.

The losses that are disallowed for regular tax purposes and AMT purposes are usually different, and therefore the carryover of disallowed losses to later years is also different. Keep records showing the separate carryover deductions.

TAX PREFERENCE ITEMS

¶23.3
The following are tax preference items that increase the amount of AMT taxable income.

Charitable contributions of appreciated property. If for regular tax purposes, you claimed a deduction for the fair market value of appreciated capital gain property held long term, the appreciation is a preference item. However, there is an exception for appreciation on donations made before July 1, 1992 of long-term tangible personal property, such as paintings or manuscripts that are used by the donee to further its tax-exempt purpose. For example, a donation of a painting to a museum that will exhibit the work qualifies for the exception.

When this book went to press, Congress was considering legislation that would extend the AMT exception beyond June 30, 1992 and also make it available to all contributions of appreciated property. See the Supplement for a legislative update.

If you elect to deduct only the adjusted basis of the property rather than fair market value for regular tax purposes, the appreciation is not treated as a preference item.

Tax-exempt interest on nonessential private activity bonds. For AMT purposes, you must include as a tax preference item the tax-exempt interest on qualified private activity bonds issued after August 7, 1986, except for qualified 501(c)(3) bonds used to benefit tax-exempt groups. Generally, private activity bonds issued after August 7, 1986, are subject to AMT, but for certain bonds meeting specific tests, the AMT rule applies to bonds issued on or after September 1, 1986. Interest paid on buying or carrying such bonds is deductible for AMT purposes.

Accelerated depreciation of property acquired before 1987. For real property placed in service before 1987, the difference between the depreciation that would have been allowable if the straight-line method had been used and accelerated depreciation claimed on real property during the taxable year is a tax preference item. The excess is computed separately for each asset depreciated through an accelerated method. For example, if you use ACRS 15-year, 18-year, or 19-year accelerated rates for regular tax purposes, figure the deduc-

tion for each such property under the straight-line method and report the excess of your regular tax deduction over the straight-line amount as a preference item.

For personal property leased to others before 1987, the preference item is the excess of the regular tax deduction over the depreciation that would have been allowed under the straight-line method, without regard to salvage value. The excess is computed separately for each asset. For five-year ACRS property, figure the straight-line amount over an eight-year period, using a half-year convention. For 10-year property, use a 15-year recovery period.

Note: See ¶23.2 for the MACRS adjustment rules for post-1986 assets.

Depletion. The difference between claimed percentage depletion and the adjusted basis of the property at the end of the year (without regard to current depletion) is a preference item. You figure the amount separately for each property for which you claim a depletion allowance. No tax preference occurs until the total depletion claimed over a period of years exceeds the cost basis of the property.

Intangible drilling costs. The preference item is the amount of excess intangible drilling costs over 65% of net income from oil and gas properties for the taxable year. Excess intangible drilling costs are those expenses in excess of the amount which could have been deducted had the expenses been capitalized and either deducted ratably over 10 years or deducted over the life of the well as cost depletion. Net income from oil and gas properties is gross income (excluding rent or royalties paid to another for use of the property) reduced by deductions other than excess intangible drilling costs. Deductions attributable to properties with no gross income are not to be taken into account. Costs incurred in drilling a nonproductive well are not counted as a tax preference.

The preference rule does not apply if you elected to capitalize intangible drilling costs. It does not apply to nonproductive wells. A nonproductive well is one which is plugged and abandoned without having produced oil and gas in commercial quantities for any substantial period of time. According to committee reports, a well which has been plugged and abandoned may have produced some relatively small amount of oil and still be considered a nonproductive well, depending on the amount of oil produced in relation to the costs of drilling. In some cases, it may not be possible to determine whether a well is, in fact, nonproductive until after the close of the taxable year. In these cases, no preference is included in the minimum tax base to any wells which are later determined to be nonproductive. If a well is proved to be nonproductive after the end of the taxable year but before the tax return for the year in question is filed, that well can be treated as nonproductive on that return. If a well is not determined to be nonproductive by the time the return for the year in question is filed, the intangible expenses related to that well are subject to the minimum tax. However, you may file an amended return and claim a credit or refund for the amount of any minimum tax paid on expenses related to that well if the well later proves to be nonproductive.

Important. If you have depletion and intangible drilling cost preferences, you may be able to claim a special deduction that offsets part of these preference items; *see* ¶23.4.

ENERGY PREFERENCE ADJUSTMENT

¶23.4
If you report preference items for intangible drilling costs or percentage depletion (¶23.3), you may be able to claim an energy preference deduction. The deduction is designed to offset part of these preference items.

The energy deduction is the total of: (1) 75% of the intangible drilling costs preference attributable to qualified exploratory costs; (2) 15% of the remaining portion of the intangible drilling cost preference; and (3) 50% of the percentage depletion preference attributable to marginal production depletion. However, the deduction may not exceed 40% of AMT income determined before claiming the energy deduction or the alternative net operating loss deduction.

Qualified exploratory costs are costs of drilling oil or gas wells in the U.S. that are completed before any other well within 1.25 miles. Also qualifying are wells that are at least 800 feet deeper than any other commercially capable well within 1.25 miles, and certain wells that are completed into new reservoirs.

Marginal production depletion is the amount by which AMT income would be reduced by disregarding the preference item for percentage depletion that is attributable to marginal production. Marginal production is oil or gas from stripper well property or properties producing substantially all heavy oil. A stripper well property is one from which the average daily production, divided by the number of producing wells, is 15 or less "barrel equivalents." Each barrel of oil and every 6,000 cubic feet of natural gas constitutes a "barrel equivalent."

The energy deduction is phased out when an IRS estimate of the price of crude oil for the prior calendar year exceeds $28. The phaseout range is set at $6 so that the deduction is reduced by this fraction: the excess of the price over $28 divided by $6. For example, if the prior year IRS reference price is $30, the deduction is reduced by 2/6 or 1/3. The deduction is completely phased out when the reference price is $34 or more.

For further details, *see* IRS publication 909.

NET OPERATING LOSSES

¶23.5 A net operating loss (NOL) claimed for regular tax purposes must be recomputed for AMT after all other AMT adjustments and preference items are taken into account. A NOL deductible for AMT purposes is generally the amount of the regular net operating loss except that in figuring the nonbusiness deduction adjustment (¶40.19), only AMT itemized deductions are taken into account. Thus, for AMT purposes, state and local taxes and certain interest that are not allowable AMT deductions do not reduce nonbusiness income in figuring the NOL adjustment.

In some cases, a net operating loss will eliminate your regular tax but not the AMT because the loss for AMT purposes is reduced by tax preference items and the amount of the NOL deduction that may be deducted from AMT taxable income may not exceed 90% of AMT taxable income before the NOL deduction and the new energy preference adjustment. Net operating losses that are disallowed because of the 90% AMT limit may be carried back 3 years or forward 15 years as under regular NOL rules (¶40.17) but the deduction in the carryback or carryover year is subject to the 90% limit. Carryovers from years beginning after 1982 and before 1987 are figured under prior law rules, subject to the 90% AMT limit.

Deferred minimum tax before 1983 because of NOL. If you had minimum tax liability in a pre-1983 year that was deferred because of a net operating loss, you must pay a minimum tax if, in 1992, you claim the net operating loss carryover deduction from that period. The tax is 15% of the net operating loss carryover deduction. You report the tax on Line 48 of Form 1040 and write in "Deferred Minimum Tax."

AMT FOREIGN TAX CREDIT AND OTHER TAX CREDITS

¶23.6 The foreign tax credit is the only credit that may be deducted from tentative AMT tax liability. It is figured in the same way as the regular foreign tax credit (¶36.15) after substituting AMT taxable income for regular taxable income.

The AMT foreign tax credit may not offset more than 90% of AMT tax determined without regard to the foreign tax credit and net operating loss deduction. Any foreign tax credit not allowed by the limit may be carried back and forward; *see* ¶36.16 and IRS Publication 909 for further details.

Other credits limited. If you have AMT adjustments or preference items, the interplay of technical rules and definitions may reduce nonrefundable credits, such as the dependent care credit and the elderly and disabled credit, even when you are *not* liable for AMT because of the AMT exemption. The amount of such nonrefundable credits is limited to the regular tax liability less the AMT tax liability. The credit limitation is figured on Form 2441 for the dependent care credit, and on Schedule R for the credit for the elderly and disabled.

Certain nonrefundable business credits may also be limited; follow the instructions to Form 3800.

EXAMPLE You have regular tax liability of $2,000 and a dependent care credit of $500. The tentative AMT tax figured on Form 6251 is $1,800. The credit may not reduce your regular tax to $1,500. On Form 2441, the credit is limited to $200 ($2,000 − $1,800). It is applied against your regular tax, reducing it to $1,800.

AMT TAX CREDIT FROM REGULAR TAX

¶23.7 You may be able to reduce your regular 1992 tax by a tax credit based on AMT taxes paid after 1986. The credit, which is computed on Form 8801, may be applied against your 1992 regular tax after deducting any credits for dependent care, the elderly or disabled, mortgage interest, foreign taxes, and general business credits. However, the credit is allowed only if your regular 1992 tax liability exceeds 1992 tentative minimum tax liability computed on Form 6251.

There are two steps in computing 1992 credit:

1. *Recomputing on Form 8801 your AMT liability for 1991.* On Form 8801, you determine how much of the prior AMT tax was based on "exclusion" items such as the standard deduction, personal exemptions, itemized deductions (such as state and local taxes) not allowed for AMT purposes, charitable donations of appreciated property, percentage depletion, and tax-exempt interest on specified private activity bonds. *No credit* is allowed to the extent your 1991 AMT was based on such "exclusion" items. A credit is allowed only to the extent 1991 AMT was based on "deferral" items such as accelerated depreciation.

The 1991 AMT from deferral items, if any, is the basic AMT tax credit potentially available for 1992, but the actual credit may be reduced or eliminated because of the tax limitation of Step 2. The potential credit for 1992 is also increased by any carryforward from your 1991 Form 8801 of a credit based on AMT from 1990, 1989, 1988, or 1987 that was not allowed in 1991 because of the Step 2 limitation.

2. *Computing tentative AMT liability for 1992 on Form 6251.* You transfer the tentative AMT to Form 8801. Your 1992 regular tax, minus tax credits, must exceed the tentative AMT on Form 6251 or no credit will be allowed for 1992.

If your 1992 tentative minimum tax exceeds your 1992 regular tax minus credits, no credit is allowed in 1992, but a carryover to 1993 is allowed.

ELECTION FOR 10-YEAR WRITE-OFF OF PREFERENCES

¶23.8 You may avoid AMT on certain expenditures by electing for regular tax purposes to deduct them ratably over a period of years. For intangible drilling costs incurred in taxable years starting after 1989, the ratable write-off period is 60 months, beginning with the month the costs are paid or incurred. The period is 10 years, beginning with the year in which the expenditure was made, for intangible drilling costs incurred in years starting before 1990, mining exploration and development costs, and research and experimental charges. A three-year write-off election is allowed for circulation expenses.

The election is made on Form 4562 on or before the due date (including extension) of the return for the year in which you want the election to be effective. Revocation of the election is allowed only with IRS consent. Partners may make separate elections.

AVOIDING AMT TAX

¶23.9 If you are within the range of the AMT tax, review periodically your income and expenses to determine whether to make certain tax elections, accelerate income and/or defer the payment of expenses.

There are elections, such as the election of alternative straight-line MACRS depreciation, that may avoid AMT adjustments. However, such elections will increase your regular tax. Similarly, adjustment treatment for mining exploration and development costs, circulation expenses, and research expenses can be avoided by elections to amortize; *see* ¶23.8. Preference treatment for donations of capital gain property may be avoided if the charitable deduction is based on the adjusted basis of the donated property. If you receive interest from private activity bonds issued after August 17, 1986, you might consider selling the bonds and reinvesting in tax-exempts paying interest not subject to preference treatment.

The following steps may also avoid or soften the impact of the AMT tax:

Defer deductible expense items to a later year in which your income will be subject to tax rates exceeding 24%. Consider deferring payment of charitable donations, home mortgage interest, and medical expenses. You will get a larger tax benefit from the deductions in the later year. In the case of unimproved real estate or realty undergoing development or machinery in its pre-installment period, consider an election to capitalize taxes and carry charges. Also, do not elect first-year expensing of business equipment.

Defer if possible the exercise of an incentive stock option to a later year when you are not subject to AMT. The bargain element of incentive stock option is an adjustment item subject to AMT. This is the difference between the option price and the fair market price of the stock on the date of exercise. If you exercise the option and it is subject to AMT, you may find yourself with an unexpected liability and short of liquid funds to meet your tax liability.

Accelerating income. If you find that you will be subject to AMT in a current year, you may want to subject additional income in that year to the 24% AMT tax rate. In such a case, consider accelerating the receipt of income to that year. If you are in business, you might ask for earlier payments from customers or clients. If you control a small corporation, you might prepay salary or pay larger bonuses. But here be careful not to run afoul of reasonable compensation rules. You might also consider paying dividends.

If you hold savings certificates with a six-month maturity in a later year, you might consider an early redemption to the current year. But here weigh the penalty cost of an early forfeiture. Similarly you might make an early sale of U.S. Treasury Bills to the current year.

If you are certain that you will be subject to AMT you may consider switching some tax-free investments into taxable investments which will give a higher after-tax return after the 24% AMT tax.

24

COMPUTING THE "KIDDIE TAX" FOR CHILDREN UNDER AGE 14

Investment income over $1,200 earned by a child under age 14 is taxed at the child's parent's top tax rate. The child's parent or legal representative generally makes this tax computation, which is nicknamed the "kiddie tax."

The kiddie tax applies only to investment income, such as interest, dividends, rents, royalties and profits on the sale of property. Income from wages and self-employment is not subject to the kiddie tax.

As the child's parent, you generally use Form 8615 to report the child's income and compute the tax which is reported on the child's personal income tax return; *see* ¶24.4. The computations on Form 8615 have no effect on the treatment of items on your own return or your tax computation. You may instead elect on Form 8814 to report the child's investment income on your own return, provided the child received only interest and dividend income. This election is generally not advisable. If you elect on Form 8814 to report the child's investment income on your own return, your adjusted gross income will increase and this could adversely affect your right to claim various deductions; *see* ¶24.5.

If you are married but file separately, the parent with the larger amount of taxable income is responsible for the kiddie tax computation. If parents are divorced, separated, unmarried, or living apart for the last six months of the year, the parent who has custody of the child for the greater part of 1992 computes the tax. If a child cannot get tax information directly from a parent, the legal representative of the child may ask the IRS for permission on Form 8615.

FILING YOUR CHILD'S RETURN

¶24.1 To discourage income splitting of investment income between parents and minor children, the tax law has complicated income reporting for parents and children by—

1. Taxing a child's investment income over $1,200 at the parent's top bracket if the child is under 14 years of age at the end of the taxable year; *see* ¶24.3.
2. Barring a dependent child from claiming a personal exemption on his or her own tax return.
3. Limiting the standard deduction to $600 for a dependent child who has only investment income; *see* ¶13.5.

Does your child have to file? For a child who can be claimed as a dependent (*see* page 19), the income filing threshold is generally $600. If your dependent child has gross income (earned and investment income) of $600 or less for 1992, he or she is not subject to tax and does not have to file a tax return.

A 1992 return must be filed for a dependent child with gross income of more than $600, but there is this exception: If a dependent child has salary or other earned income but no investment income, a return does not have to be filed unless such earned income exceeds $3,600 in 1992.

Although a dependent child may not claim a personal exemption on his or her 1992 tax return, the child is allowed to claim a $600 standard deduction. A dependent child with earned income over $600 may claim a standard deduction up to those earnings, but no more than the basic standard deduction, which is generally $3600 (*see* ¶13.1).

How to file for your child. If your child was under age 14 as of the end of 1992, and had investment income of $1,200 or less, follow the regular filing rules and use either Form 1040EZ, 1040A, or Form 1040 to report the child's income and deductions. The "kiddie" tax computation does not apply, so all of the child's income will be taxed at his or her own tax rate.

If your child's investment income exceeded $1,200, the kiddie tax computation applies; *see* ¶24.3. Form 8615 must be filed to compute the kiddie tax unless your child's only income is interest and dividends and you elect to report your child's investment earnings on your own return as discussed at ¶24.5. On Form 8615 you must provide your tax identification number and taxable income. Form 8615 is attached to the child's tax return; *see* ¶24.4.

If your child was age 14 or older as of the end of 1992, your child should file Form 1040EZ, 1040A, or 1040, depending on the type of income and deductions he or she has. The special kiddie tax rules do not apply.

Child's AMT liability. A child who has substantial tax-exempt interest, tax preferences, or tax adjustments subject to the alternative minimum tax must compute tentative AMT liability on Form 6251; see Chapter 23. However, AMT liability for a child under age 14 is reduced or eliminated on Form 8803 if that child's parent or sibling (also under age 14) has regular tax liability exceeding tentative minimum tax liability. Form 8803 allocates the proper AMT between the parent and the children. A child's AMT cannot exceed the extra tax that the parent would pay if the child's tentative minimum tax liability, plus regular tax, was added to the parent's own.

CHILDREN NOT SUBJECT TO THE "KIDDIE TAX"

¶24.2   The "kiddie tax" computation based on a parent's top tax rate applies only to children under age 14 with investment income for 1992 exceeding $1,200. The computation does *not* apply to—

A child who is 14 years old or over at the end of the taxable year.

A child who has no investment income or whose gross investment income is $1,200 or less. The kiddie tax computation applies only to investment income exceeding $1,200. Furthermore, children who itemize deductions may in some cases exempt more than $1,200 from the computation; *see* ¶24.3.

A child under age 14 if neither parent is alive at the end of the taxable year.

EXAMPLES   1. At the end of 1992, your son is age 14. He has interest income of $1,400 and salary income of $950 from his part-time job. His standard deduction is $950, the greater of earned income or $600. No personal exemption may be claimed. Assuming he has no itemized deductions, taxable income is $1,400 ($2,350 gross income — $950 standard deduction). The kiddie tax computation based on your top rate does not apply because your son is at least age 14 at the end of the year.

2. In 1992, your five-year-old daughter has interest income of $800. Taxable income of $200 is subject to tax at her own tax rate. She uses the tax tables in the Tax Organizer.

Interest income	$800
Less standard deduction	600
Taxable income	$200

The kiddie tax computation does not apply because investment income does not exceed $1,200.

CHILDREN UNDER AGE 14 SUBJECT TO THE "KIDDIE TAX"

¶24.3   The "kiddie tax" computation based on a parent's top tax rate applies to a child who—

Is under age 14 at the end of the taxable year;

Has either parent alive at the end of the taxable year; *and*

Has investment income for 1992 exceeding $1,200. For a child who has itemized deductions of more than $600 that are directly connected to the production of investment income, the $1,200 exemption is increased, as explained in the next column.

Figuring kiddie tax on child's or parent's return. The kiddie tax computation is generally made on Form 8615 which must be attached to the child's return. A sample Form 8615 is at the end of this chapter. However, if the only income of a child under age 14 is interest and dividends and other tests are met, a parent may elect on Form 8814 to include the child's investment income on his or her own tax return, instead of computing kiddie tax on Form 8615; *see* ¶24.5.

Kiddie tax on Form 8615 applies to investment income exceeding $1,200 floor. If the child files his or her own return and the "kiddie tax" is computed on Form 8615, the parent's top rate applies to *net investment income.* For purposes of this rule, net investment income equals gross investment income minus $1,200 if the child does not itemize deductions on Schedule A. Thus, for a child who does not itemize, the first $1,200 of investment income is exempt from the special computation. Investment income exceeding $1,200 is considered net investment income subject to the special computation; *see* Example 3 below.

Include as gross investment income all taxable income that is not compensation for personal services. Include interest income, unless it is tax-exempt interest, dividends, royalties, rents, and profits on the sale of property. Payments from a trust are also included to the extent of distributable net income. Most accumulation distributions received by a child from a trust are not included because of the minority exception under Code Section 665(b) for amounts accumulated before age 21. Income in custodial accounts is treated as the child's income and is subject to the "kiddie tax" computation.

Investment earnings on all of the child's property must be considered, even if the property was a gift from you or someone else, or if the property was produced from the child's wages, such as a bank account into which the wages were deposited. The wages themselves, or self-employment earnings, are not considered.

If a child does itemize deductions, and has more than $600 of deductions that are directly connected to the production of investment income, the $1,200 floor is increased. The floor is $600 plus the directly-connected deductions, as shown in Example 6 on page 277. If the directly-connected deductions are $600 or less, the regular $1,200 kiddie tax exemption applies, as in Example 5, also on page 277. Directly-connected itemized deductions are expenses paid to produce or collect income or to manage, conserve, or maintain income-producing property. Only the part of the total expenses exceeding the 2% AGI floor may be deducted. These expenses include custodian fees and service charges, service fees to collect interest and dividends, and investment counsel fees. If after you subtract the itemized deductions, your child's net investment income exceeds his or her taxable income, you apply the tax to the lower taxable income, rather than to the net investment income.

EXAMPLES   (In all the following examples, assume the child is your dependent and under age 14 as of December 31, 1992.)

1. Child has interest income of $480 and no other income. The child has no income tax liability and does not have to file a return.

Interest income	$480
Less: standard deduction	480
	—0—

2. Child has interest and dividend income of $900 and no other income. A standard deduction of $600 may be claimed. The balance of $300 is taxed at the child's regular tax bracket. Form 8615 does not have to be filed and the kiddie computation does not apply since investment income does not exceed $1,200.

3. Child has dividend income of $1,800. The child has taxable income of $1,200 of which $600 is subject to the kiddie computation based on the parent's top tax bracket on Form 8615.

Figuring taxable income:	
Dividend income	$1,800
Less: standard deduction	600
	$1,200
Income subject to tax at parent's rate:	
Investment income	$1,800
Less: $1,200	1,200
	$ 600

An example of the actual Form 8615 computation is at ¶24.4. As an alternative to computing kiddie tax on $600 on Form 8615, the parent may elect to report the child's dividend income on his or her own return; *see* ¶24.5.

4. Child has wages of $700 and $300 of interest income.

Figuring taxable income:

Total income	$1,000
Less: standard deduction (up to wages)	700
Taxable income	$ 300

The parent's tax bracket does not apply, as interest income does not exceed the $1,200 floor. Taxable income is taxed at the child's rate.

5. Child has $300 of wages and $1,750 of dividends and interest income. On Schedule A, the child claims itemized deductions of $400 related to investment income after the 2% AGI floor. The child also has $400 of other itemized deductions. Itemized deductions of $800 are claimed; they exceed the $600 standard deduction.

Figuring taxable income:

Total income	$2,050
Less: itemized deductions	800
Taxable income	$1,250

Income subject to tax at parent's rate:

Investment income	$1,750
Less: greater of (1) $1,200, or (2) $600 plus directly related expenses of $400	1,200
Net investment income subject to tax at parent's rate on Form 8615 (¶24.4); *see* ¶24.5 for parent's alternative election.	$ 550

6. Child has $700 of salary income; $3,000 of investment income; and itemized deductions of $800 (net of the 2% AGI floor) directly related to the investment income. The child also has $200 of other itemized deductions. Total itemized deductions of $1,000 are claimed as they exceed the $700 standard deduction (equal to wages).

Figuring taxable income:

Total income	$3,700
Less: itemized deductions	1,000
Taxable income	$2,700

Income subject to tax at parent's rate:

Investment income	$3,000
Less: greater of (1) $1,200, or (2) $600 plus $800 of deductions related to investment income	1,400
Net investment income subject to tax at parent's rate on Form 8615 (¶24.4); *see* ¶24.5 for parent's alternative election.	$1,600

COMPUTING "KIDDIE TAX" ON CHILD'S RETURN

¶**24.4** If your child is subject to the "kiddie tax" under ¶24.3, the tax is computed on Form 8615, which is attached to his or her return unless you make the parent's election at ¶24.5. Before your child's Form 8615 can be completed, your own taxable income must be determined. The amount to be entered on Form 8615 as the parent's taxable income depends on the parent's marital and filing status.

If the parents file a *joint return*, their joint taxable income is entered on Form 8615, along with the net investment income

(¶24.3) of all their children under age 14. If the parents file *separate returns*, the larger of the parents' separate taxable incomes is used on the child's Form 8615.

Where parents are legally separated or divorced and custody of the child is shared, Form 8615 should be completed using the taxable income of the parent who has custody for the greater part of the year. If parents are married but living apart, and the custodial parent qualifies as unmarried under Test 1 at ¶1.10, that parent's taxable income is used on Form 8615. If the custodial parent is not considered unmarried, the income of the parent with the larger taxable income is used. If the custodial parent has remarried and files a joint return with a new spouse, their joint return taxable income is used on the child's Form 8615. If the parents were never married but they live together with the child, the income of the parent with the larger taxable income is used; if the parents live apart, the income of the parent with custody for most of the year is used on Form 8615.

More than one child subject to kiddie tax. You file a separate Form 8615 for each child and on each form net investment income of all the children subject to the tax is included. The computed tax is allocated to each of your children, according to his or her share of their combined net investment income. This computation is incorporated in the steps of Form 8615 and by following the order of the form, you will make the proper allocation.

As parents, the kiddie tax computation on Form 8615 does not affect your tax liability or how you compute any limitation on deductions or credits. For example, the addition of the child's net investment income to your taxable income on Form 8615 does *not* affect the adjusted gross income floors for purposes of figuring your deduction for IRA contributions, medical expenses, and miscellaneous expenses.

Estimating the kiddie tax in case of filing delay. If you are unable to file your return by April 15th, 1993, the child's tax on Form 8615 may be based on an estimate. You may make a reasonable estimate of your taxable income on Form 8615 or may estimate the net investment income of children under age 14 if that information is not yet available. When you have the complete income details, file an amended return.

A reasonable estimate may be based on your 1991 taxable income and the 1991 investment income of the child. If a refund is due, the IRS will pay interest from April 15, or if the return was filed late, from the filing date. If additional tax is due on the amended return, interest will be charged from April 15th, but no penalty will be imposed.

EXAMPLE For 1992, Bill and Betty Brown each file Form 1040A. Bill, age 12, has dividend income of $2,000; Betty, age 10, has $1,400. Bill's taxable income after deducting a $600 standard deduction is $1,400. Betty's is $800.

Tom and Lilli Brown do not make the election (¶24.5) to report Bill's and Betty's dividends on their joint return. Forms 8615 are prepared and attached to the children's Forms 1040A, because each child is under age 14 and has more than $1,200 of investment income.

Tom and Lilli report taxable income of $52,000 on their 1992 joint return. They use the IRS tax tables to look up their tax (the tables are in the Tax Organizer, Part VIII of this book). The tax on $52,000 is $9,913. The special computation on Form 8615 does not increase their joint return tax; it determines only the amount of Bill's and Betty's tax.

As shown on page 279 on sample worksheets based on Form 8615, Bill's 1992 tax is $316 and Betty's 1992 tax is $148. If the special computation did not apply, Bill's 1992 tax would be $212 and Betty's tax would be $122. Thus, as a result of the special computation, the total tax bill for the children is increased by $130 ($464 − $334).

PARENT'S ELECTION TO REPORT CHILD'S DIVIDENDS AND INTEREST

¶24.5 Instead of filing a separate return for your child (¶24.4) whose income is subject to the "kiddie tax," you may elect on Form 8814 to compute the kiddie tax on your 1992 return if all of the following tests are met:

The child's 1992 income is only from interest and dividends (Alaska Permanent Fund dividends may be included);

The total interest and dividends are over $500 but less than $5,000 (these amounts may be increased to $600 and $6,000 respectively, under legislation being considered by Congress when this book went to press);

Estimated tax payments were not made in the child's name and Social Security number for 1992, and there was no overpayment from the child's 1991 return applied to his or her 1992 estimated tax; and

The child was not subject to 1992 backup withholding.

By making this election, and following the steps of Form 8814, you include in your income the child's interest and dividends to the extent it exceeds $1,000. You also figure an additional tax equal to the *smaller* of $75 or 15% of your child's income over $500.

Under legislation pending in Congress when this book went to press, the $1,000 floor would be increased to $1,200 for 1992 returns, and the additional tax would equal the smaller of $90 or 15% of the income over $600. If the law is not amended, making the election to report the child's income on Form 8814 will result in a higher kiddie tax than if the tax is computed on Form 8615 (¶24.4), as the Form 8615 computation does reflect the $1,200 floor. See the Supplement for an update on the legislation.

If parents are divorced, separated, unmarried, or living apart for the last six months of the year, the parent whose taxable income would be taken into account on Form 8615 (¶24.4) is the parent who may elect to report the income on his or her own return.

In figuring whether you owe alternative minimum tax (AMT), you must include as a tax preference item interest income your child receives from specified private activity bonds; *see* ¶23.3 and Form 6251 instructions.

Should you make the election? There is no advantage in making the election, except to skip the paperwork involved in preparing a return in the child's name or returns in your children's names. If you consider this an advantage, you may want to make the election. It may be preferable to take the time to prepare the child's return to keep the child's tax accounting separate from yours. Including the child's income as your own increases your AGI, which may create these disadvantages:

- Subject you to the exemption phaseout (¶1.32) and 3% reduction computation (¶13.8) for itemized deductions.
- Make it more difficult to deduct job expenses and other miscellaneous itemized deductions which are subject to a 2% AGI floor (¶19.1) and medical deductions, subject to a 7.5% AGI floor (¶17.1).
- Limit a deduction for IRA contributions under the phaseout rules (¶8.3).
- Limit your ability to claim the special $25,000 rental loss allowance under the passive activity rules (¶10.4).

Finally, if you elect to report the child's income on your own return, you may not claim any deductions that your child would have been able to claim on his or her return such as investment expenses or a penalty on premature withdrawals from a savings account. On the other hand, reporting your child's interest or dividends increases your net investment income, which may allow you to claim a larger deduction for investment interest; *see* ¶15.9. Also, your ceiling for charitable donations may be increased.

If you plan to report your child's income on your 1993 return, provide for the tax in your estimated tax payments or withholdings during 1993.

EXAMPLE Woodrow, age 10, received $2,000 of interest income in 1992. He has no other income and is not subject to backup withholding. No estimated tax payments were made in his name. His parents elect on Form 8814 to include his interest income on their 1992 tax return instead of filing a return for him. They include $1,000 of the interest ($2,000 - $1,000) on Line 22 (other income) of Form 1040. They also add $75 to their tax on Line 38 of Form 1040 and indicate that the amount is from Form 8814.

If Congress amends the law to provide an inflation adjustment, the $1,000 floor would increase to $1,200 and Woodrow's parents would include $800 (instead of $1,000) of Woodrow's interest on their Form 1040 and would add $90 (instead of $75) to their tax; *see* the Supplement for an update.

Form 8615–Worksheet

Child's name shown on return	Child's social security number
Betty Brown	X10 00 1111

A Parent's name (first, initial, and last). (Caution: See instructions on back before completing.)   **B** Parent's social security numb.

Tom Brown   XXX 11 1X11

C Parent's filing status (check one):

☐ Single, ☑ Married filing jointly, ☐ Married filing separately, ☐ Head of household, or ☐ Qualifying widow(er)

Step 1 Figure child's net investment income

1	Enter child's investment income, such as taxable interest and dividend income (see the instructions). (If this amount is $1,200 or less, stop here; do not file this form.)	1	1,400
2	If the child DID NOT itemize deductions on Schedule A (Form 1040 or Form 1040NR), enter $1,200. If the child ITEMIZED deductions, see the instructions	2	1,200
3	Subtract line 2 from line 1. (If the result is zero or less, stop here; do not complete the rest of this form but ATTACH it to the child's return.)	3	200
4	Enter child's **taxable** income (from Form 1040, line 37; Form 1040A, line 22; or Form 1040NR, line 35)	4	800
5	Compare the amounts on lines 3 and 4. Enter the **smaller** of the two amounts here ▶	5	200

Step 2 Figure tentative tax based on the tax rate of the parent listed on line A

6	Enter parent's **taxable** income (from Form 1040, line 37; Form 1040A, line 22; Form 1040EZ, line 5; or Form 1040NR, line 35). If the parent transferred property to a trust, see instructions	6	52,000
7	Enter the total, if any, of the net investment income from Forms 8615, line 5, of ALL OTHER children of the parent. (Do not include the amount from line 5 above.)	7	800
8	Add lines 5, 6, and 7	8	53,000
9	Tax on line 8 based on the **parent's** filing status (see instructions). If from Schedule D, enter amount from line 20 of that Schedule D here ▶	9	10,193
10	Enter parent's tax (from Form 1040, line 38; Form 1040A, line 23; Form 1040EZ, line 7; or Form 1040NR, line 36). If from Schedule D, enter amount from line 20 of that Schedule D here ▶	10	9,913
11	Subtract line 10 from line 9. (If line 7 is blank, enter on line 13 the amount from line 11; skip lines 12a and 12b.)	11	280
12a	Add lines 5 and 7 12a 1,000		
b	Divide line 5 by line 12a. Enter the result as a decimal (rounded to two places)	12b	×.20
13	Multiply line 11 by line 12b ▶	13	56

Step 3 Figure child's tax

	Note: If lines 4 and 5 above are the same, go to line 16.		
14	Subtract line 5 from line 4 14 600		
15	Tax on line 14 based on the **child's** filing status (see instructions). If from Schedule D, enter amount from line 20 of that Schedule D here ▶	15	92
16	Add lines 13 and 15	16	148
17	Tax on line 4 based on the **child's** filing status (see instructions). If from Schedule D, check here ▶ ☐	17	122
18	Enter the **larger** of line 16 or 17 here and on Form 1040, line 38; Form 1040A, line 23; or Form 1040NR, line 36. Be sure to check the box for "Form 8615" even if line 17 is more than line 16 ▶	18	148

Form 8615–Worksheet

Child's name shown on return	Child's social security number
Bill Brown	OXX 11 1111

A Parent's name (first, initial, and last). (Caution: See instructions on back before completing.)   **B** Parent's social security number

TOM Brown   XXX 11 1X11

C Parent's filing status (check one):

☐ Single, ☑ Married filing jointly, ☐ Married filing separately, ☐ Head of household, or ☐ Qualifying widow(er)

Step 1 Figure child's net investment income

1	Enter child's investment income, such as taxable interest and dividend income (see the instructions). (If this amount is $1,200 or less, stop here; do not file this form.)	1	2,000
2	If the child DID NOT itemize deductions on Schedule A (Form 1040 or Form 1040NR), enter $1,200. If the child ITEMIZED deductions, see the instructions	2	1,200
3	Subtract line 2 from line 1. (If the result is zero or less, stop here; do not complete the rest of this form but ATTACH it to the child's return.)	3	800
4	Enter child's **taxable** income (from Form 1040, line 37; Form 1040A, line 22; or Form 1040NR, line 35)	4	1,400
5	Compare the amounts on lines 3 and 4. Enter the **smaller** of the two amounts here ▶	5	800

Step 2 Figure tentative tax based on the tax rate of the parent listed on line A

6	Enter parent's **taxable** income (from Form 1040, line 37; Form 1040A, line 22; Form 1040EZ, line 5; or Form 1040NR, line 35). If the parent transferred property to a trust, see instructions	6	52,000
7	Enter the total, if any, of the net investment income from Forms 8615, line 5, of ALL OTHER children of the parent. (Do not include the amount from line 5 above.)	7	200
8	Add lines 5, 6, and 7	8	53,000
9	Tax on line 8 based on the **parent's** filing status (see instructions). If from Schedule D, enter amount from line 20 of that Schedule D here ▶	9	10,193
10	Enter parent's tax (from Form 1040, line 38; Form 1040A, line 23; Form 1040EZ, line 7; or Form 1040NR, line 36). If from Schedule D, enter amount from line 20 of that Schedule D here ▶	10	9,913
11	Subtract line 10 from line 9. (If line 7 is blank, enter on line 13 the amount from line 11; skip lines 12a and 12b.)	11	280
12a	Add lines 5 and 7 12a 1,000		
b	Divide line 5 by line 12a. Enter the result as a decimal (rounded to two places)	12b	×.80
13	Multiply line 11 by line 12b ▶	13	224

Step 3 Figure child's tax

	Note: If lines 4 and 5 above are the same, go to line 16.		
14	Subtract line 5 from line 4 14 600		
15	Tax on line 14 based on the **child's** filing status (see instructions). If from Schedule D, enter amount from line 20 of that Schedule D here ▶	15	92
16	Add lines 13 and 15	16	316
17	Tax on line 4 based on the **child's** filing status (see instructions). If from Schedule D, check here ▶ ☐	17	212
18	Enter the **larger** of line 16 or 17 here and on Form 1040, line 38; Form 1040A, line 23; or Form 1040NR, line 36. Be sure to check the box for "Form 8615" even if line 17 is more than line 16 ▶	18	316

25 FAMILY TAX CREDITS: DEPENDENT CARE AND EARNED INCOME (EIC) CREDITS

The dependent care and earned income credits help ease the burden of caring for dependents.

The dependent care credit is for working persons who pay care costs which allow them the freedom to work. Depending on your income, the credit is 20% to 30% of up to $2,400 of care expenses for one dependent and up to $4,800 of expenses for two or more dependents. If your adjusted gross income exceeds $28,000, the maximum credit is $480 for one dependent, and $960 for two or more dependents.

The earned income credit (EIC) is provided to low income workers who support dependents. The maximum EIC begins to phase out as earned income increases over $11,850. You look up the amount of credit in IRS tables included in the tax form instructions. The EIC is "refundable;" you will receive a refund from the IRS if the credit exceeds your tax liability.

QUALIFYING FOR CHILD OR DEPENDENT CARE CREDIT

¶**25.1** Did you hire someone to care for your children or other dependents while you work? If so, you may qualify for a tax credit for the expenses. You may claim the credit even if you work part-time. The credit is generally available to the extent you have earnings from employment. Your employer may have a plan qualifying for tax-free child care, and if you are covered, you may be unable to claim a tax credit; *see* ¶25.5.

Where to claim the credit? The credit is claimed on Form 2441 if you file Form 1040, or on Form 1040A, Schedule 2. A sample Form 2441 is on page 286. The size of the credit depends on the amount of care expenses and income. Depending on your income, the credit is 20% to 30% of up to $2,400 of care expenses for one dependent and up to $4,800 of expenses for two or more dependents. If your adjusted gross income exceeds $28,000, the maximum credit is $480 for one dependent, and $960 for two or more dependents. *See* the chart in ¶25.2.

Credit requirements. To qualify for the credit, you must:

1. Incur the care expenses in order to earn income. In the case of a married couple, this requires both spouses to work either at full- or part-time positions. An exception to the earned income rule is made for a spouse who is a full-time student or incapacitated (¶25.3). Qualifying care expenses are discussed at ¶25.5. Limits on the amount of qualifying costs are discussed at ¶25.2.
2. Maintain a household for a qualifying dependent; *see* ¶25.4.
3. File jointly if you are married, unless you are separated under the rules of ¶25.6.
4. Hire someone other than your child under age 19 or a person you can claim as a dependent; *see* ¶25.5.
5. Have qualifying expenses in excess of tax-free reimbursements received from your employer; *see* ¶25.5.

6. Report on your tax return the name, address, and taxpayer identification number (Social Security number for individuals) of the child-care provider; *see* below.

Identifying care provider on your return. You must list the name, address, and taxpayer identification number of the person you paid to care for your dependent on Form 2441 if you file Form 1040, or on Form 1040A, Schedule 2. You do not need the taxpayer identification number if a tax-exempt charity provides the dependent care services. Failure to list the correct name, address, and number may result in a disallowance of the credit. To avoid this possibility, ask the provider to fill out Form W-10 or get the identifying information from a Social Security card, driver's license, or business letterhead or invoice. If a household employee has filled out Form W-4 for you, this may act as a backup record.

Withholding tax for housekeeper. Where you employ help to care for your dependent in your home, you may be liable for FICA (Social Security) and FUTA (unemployment) taxes; *see* ¶25.7.

Employer Reimbursements Reduce Credit.

Expenses qualifying for the credit are reduced by any tax-free reimbursements under a qualified employer dependent care program. That is, the reimbursements reduce the $2,400 expense limit for one dependent, or the $4,800 expense limit for two or more qualifying dependents; *see* ¶25.5. Your employer will report reimbursements in Box 22 of your Form W-2. You figure the tax-free portion of the reimbursement, and any reduction to the credit expense base, on Form 2441 if you file Form 1040 or on Schedule 2 if you file Form 1040A.

LIMITS ON THE CARE CREDIT

¶25.2
The credit is a percentage of expenses paid for the care of a dependent to allow you to work and earn income. Qualifying expenses are discussed at ¶25.5. The credit percentage depends on your income.

Limit on expenses. In figuring the credit, you may only take into account qualifying expenses (¶25.5) up to a limit of $2,400 for one dependent, or $4,800 for two or more dependents. The $2,400 or $4,800 limit applies even if your actual expenses are much greater. Further, the $2,400 or $4,800 limit must be reduced by tax-free benefits received from an employer's dependent care plan. Finally, if your earned income is less than the $2,400 or $4,800 limit, your credit is figured on the lower income amount.

Take into account only 1992 payments for 1992 services. Your credit for 1992 must be based on payments made in 1992 for care services provided in 1992. If you paid for 1991 services in 1992, you may be able to claim an additional credit on your 1992 return, but only in the limited circumstances; *see* next column. If in 1992 you prepay for 1993 services, you must allocate your payment. Only payments attributable to 1992 services should be counted towards the $2,400 or $4,800 limit when figuring your 1992 credit.

Credit percentage. Depending on your income, a credit percentage of 20% to 30% applies to your expenses up to the $2,400 (one dependent) or $4,800 (two or more dependents) limit. The maximum credit is 30% for families with adjusted gross income of $10,000 or less. For adjusted gross income over $10,000, the 30% credit is reduced by 1% for each $2,000 of adjusted gross income or fraction of $2,000 over $10,000, but not below 20%. The 20% credit applies to adjusted gross incomes exceeding $28,000.

The dependent care credit is nonrefundable; it is limited to your tax liability. Furthermore, if you have preference items or adjustments subject to alternative minimum tax (¶23.1), the dependent care credit may be limited; follow the instructions to Form 2441.

Allowable Credit

Adjusted gross income	Credit percentage	Your maximum credit	
		One dependent	Two or more dependents
$10,000 or less	30%	$720	$1,440
10,001– 12,000	29	696	1,392
12,001– 14,000	28	672	1,344
14,001– 16,000	27	648	1,296
16,001– 18,000	26	624	1,248
18,001– 20,000	25	600	1,200
20,001– 22,000	24	576	1,152
22,001– 24,000	23	552	1,104
24,001– 26,000	22	528	1,056
26,001– 28,000	21	504	1,008
28,001 and over	20	480	960

EXAMPLES 1. You pay $6,000 to a neighbor to care for your two children while you work. Your adjusted gross income is $31,000. The credit percentage of 20% is applied to the maximum expense limit of $4,800, giving you a credit of $960.

2. Same as above except you receive a tax-free reimbursement of $2,500 from your employer's plan; *see* ¶25.5. The reimbursement reduces the $4,800 expense limit to $2,300 ($4,800 – $2,500). Your credit is $460 (20% of $2,300). If the tax-free reimbursement was $4,800 or more (it cannot exceed $5,000) no credit would be allowed.

Additional credit for 1992 payment of 1991 dependent care. Payments made in 1992 for 1991 services may be eligible for an additional credit but only if you did not use up the $2,400 or $4,800 expense limit when claiming your 1991 credit. To get the additional credit, you must claim your 1992 credit on Form 2441, not on Form 1040A, Schedule 2.

For example, the cost of day care services for your child in 1991 was $2,000, half of which you paid in 1991 and half in early 1992. On your 1991 return, a credit was based on the $1,000 of expenses paid in 1991. Since you used only $1,000 of the $2,400 expense limit in 1991, the $1,400 of "unused" expenses is carried over to 1992. On your 1992 Form 2441, you multiply $1,400 by a credit percentage based on your 1991 adjusted gross income. If your 1991 adjusted gross income was $30,000, the credit percentage is 20%. Thus, your additional 1992 credit is $280 (20% of $1,400). The $280 credit is claimed on Line 15 of Form 2441, and is in addition to the regular credit for 1992 care services. You must attach a statement to Form 2441 explaining the carryover to 1992 and the computation of the additional credit.

EARNED INCOME TEST

¶25.3
To claim the credit, you must earn wage, salary, or self-employment income figured without regard to community property laws.

Earned income rule for married couples. Generally, both spouses must work at least part-time, unless one is incapable of self-care or is a full-time student. If either you or your spouse earns less than the $2,400 or $4,800 credit base (¶25.2), the base is limited to the smaller income.

EXAMPLE John and Mary are married. John earns $4,000. Mary earns $23,500. They incur care costs of $5,000 for their two children, ages 5 and 7. Their adjusted gross income including interest earnings is $27,742; their credit percentage is 21%. The regular $4,800 credit base is limited to John's lower income of $4,000. They may claim a credit of $840 ($4,000 × 21%).

Expenses for dependent care incurred while looking for a job may be included. However, you must have earnings during the year to claim the credit.

Spouses who are students or disabled. An incapacitated spouse or a spouse who is a full-time student is considered to have earned income of $200 a month if expenses are incurred for one dependent; $400 a month for two or more such dependents.

A full-time student is one who attends school full time during each of five calendar months during the year.

EXAMPLE Same facts as in the Example above except John was a full-time student for nine months and earned no income for the year. The credit base is limited to $3,600 ($400 × 9).

No Credit if Neither Spouse Works

If both husband and wife are full-time students and neither works, they may not claim the credit for dependent care costs. While one spouse may be considered to have earned income of $200 (or $400) each month, the other spouse's earned income is zero. Care costs eligible for the credit are limited to the lesser amount of earned income, which in this case is zero.

HOUSEHOLD AND DEPENDENT TESTS

¶**25.4** You must maintain as your principal home a household for at least one of the following dependents who lives with you:

1. A dependent child *under the age of 13* for whom you are entitled to deduct a dependency exemption. If you are divorced or separated, you do not have to be entitled to the exemption if you have custody for a greater part of the year than your former spouse (the child's other parent); see ¶25.6.
2. Your spouse, if physically or mentally incapable of caring for himself or herself.
3. A dependent, regardless of age, who is physically or mentally incapable of caring for himself or herself. For example, he or she needs help to dress or to take care of personal hygiene or nutritional needs, or requires constant attention to avoid hurting himself or herself or others. Relatives who qualify, if disabled, are listed at ¶1.20. A nonrelative may qualify if he or she is a member of your household for the entire year, except for temporary absences.

That a disabled dependent has gross income of $2,300 or more, so that you may not claim an exemption, does not bar you from claiming a credit for his or her care costs.

EXAMPLE You live with your mother, who is physically incapable of caring for herself. You hire a practical nurse to care for her in the home while you are at work. Payments to the nurse qualify as care costs. However, if you placed her in a nursing home, the cost of the nursing home would not qualify as dependent care costs; but *see* ¶17.11 for possible medical expense deduction.

If your child becomes age 13 during the year. Take into account expenses incurred for his or her care prior to the 13th birthday. However, you do not prorate the $2,400 limitation. For example, if your child becomes age 13 on May 1 and you incurred $2,400 in care expenses between January 1 and April 30, the entire $2,400 qualifies for the credit.

You must pay more than half of household costs. You are considered to have maintained a household if you (or you and your spouse) provided more than half the maintenance costs in 1992. You also qualify if you paid more than half the costs during a lesser period in which you had care cost expenses. Rent, mortgage interest, property tax and insurance, utility bills, upkeep, repairs, and groceries are considered maintenance costs. Do not count costs of clothing, education, medical expenses, vacations, life insurance, mortgage principal, and capital improvements, such as replacing a boiler.

In determining costs of maintaining a household for a care period of less than a year, the annual household costs are prorated over the number of calendar months within the period care costs were incurred. A period of less than a calendar month is treated as a calendar month.

EXAMPLE The annual cost of maintaining a household is $6,600, and the period during which child care costs qualified for the deduction is from June 20 to December 31. To meet the household test, you must furnish more than $1,925 in maintaining the household from June 1 to December 31. The allocation covers seven months (June 1 to December 31).

$$7/12 \text{ of } \$6,600 = \$3,850$$
$$50\% \text{ of } \$3,850 = \$1,925$$

Household of two or more families. If two or more families share living quarters, each family is treated as a separate household.

EXAMPLE Two unrelated women, each with children, occupy common living quarters; each pays more than one-half of the household costs for her own family. Each is treated as maintaining her separate household.

EXPENSES QUALIFYING FOR THE CREDIT

¶**25.5** If you do not receive tax-free dependent care benefits from an employer's plan, you may take into account up to $2,400 of the following types of expenses when figuring the credit for one dependent; up to $4,800 for two or more dependents. If you receive employer-financed dependent care, tax-free reimbursements reduce the $2,400 or $4,800 base.

1. Costs of caring for your child under age 13, incapacitated spouse, or incapacitated dependent in your home. If you pay FICA or FUTA taxes on your housekeeper's wages (¶25.7), you may include your share of the tax (employer) as part of the wages when entering your qualifying expenses. Also include your housekeeper's share of FICA tax if you pay it. Note that these taxes may more than offset your allowable credit.
   The manner of care need not be the least expensive alternative. For example, where a grandparent resides with you and may provide adequate care for your child to enable you to work, the cost of hiring someone to care for the child is still eligible for the credit.

2. Ordinary domestic services in your home, such as laundry, cleaning, and cooking (but not payments to a gardener or chauffeur). Expenses for the dependent's food, clothing, or entertainment do not qualify. Food costs for a housekeeper who eats in your home may be added to qualifying expenses.

3. Outside-the-home care costs for a child under age 13, as in a day-care center, day camp, nursery school, or in the home of a babysitter. Outside-the-home care costs also qualify if incurred for a handicapped dependent, regardless of age, provided he or she regularly spends at least eight hours per day in your home. However, the cost of schooling in the first grade or higher does not qualify for the credit. Costs for sleep-away camp also do not qualify for the credit.

The cost of driving a dependent to or from a day-care center or similar transportation does not qualify for a child-care credit. However, the Tax Court allowed a child-care credit for supervised bus transportation; the transportation was part of the actual child care.

Payments to relatives. No credit may be claimed for payments made to relatives for whom a dependency exemption is allowable (¶1.20). Thus, if you pay your mother to care for your child and you cannot claim your mother as a dependent, such payments qualify for the credit. The same rule applies for payments to unrelated persons who live with you and qualify as your dependents (¶1.21).

No credit may be claimed for payments to your child who is under 19 years of age at the close of the tax year, whether or not you may claim the child as a dependent.

Allocating expenses when employed less than entire year. When an expense covers a period, part of which you were gainfully employed or in active search of gainful employment and part of which you were not employed or seeking employment, you must allocate expenses on a daily basis.

EXAMPLE You are employed for only two months and 10 days. Monthly care expenses are $300. Eligible care expenses amount to $700 ($300 × 2 months, plus ⅓ of $300).

Employer-financed dependent care reduces credit base. Tax-free reimbursements under an employer's dependent care program reduce the $2,400 or $4,800 credit base. For example, if you have one child and you receive a $1,500 reimbursement of child care costs from your company's plan, the amount eligible for the tax credit is reduced to $900 ($2,400–$1,500). A reimbursement of $2,400 or more would bar any credit. The $4,800 credit expense limit for two or more dependents is similarly reduced. On your Form W-2, your employer will report the amount of tax-free reimbursement; *see* ¶ 3.6.

If your employer's plan allows you to fund a reimbursement account with salary reduction contributions that are excluded from taxable pay (¶3.13), reimbursements from the account are considered employer-financed payments that reduce the $2,400 or $4,800 credit base. In deciding whether to make salary reduction contributions, you should determine whether the tax-free reduction will provide a larger tax savings than that provided by the credit. If your tax bracket is higher than 15%, taking the salary reduction is advantageous. Even if you expect to be in the 15% bracket, you should compare the estimated tax savings from the credit with the estimated savings from a salary reduction. You may find that the salary reduction provides the larger tax savings, taking into consideration not only the decrease in federal income tax, but also the Social Security tax and state and local taxes avoided by using the salary reduction. Further, by lowering your adjusted gross income, a salary reduction may enable you to claim a larger IRA deduction if you are subject to

the deduction phaseout rule (¶8.3), or a larger deduction for miscellaneous itemized deductions subject to the 2% floor (¶19.1).

Day Care Center or Nursery School

The amount you pay to a day care center or nursery school for a dependent child under age 13 is eligible for the credit, even if it covers such incidental benefits as lunch. However, tuition for a child in first grade or higher is not taken into account. If the dependent is not your child, costs for care outside the home qualify only if the dependent regularly spends at least eight hours per day in your home. Up to $2,400 a year of outside-the-home care expenses may be taken into account in figuring the credit for one dependent; up to $4,800 for two or more.

Allocation if expenses cover noncare services. If a portion of expenses is for other than dependent care or household services, only the portion allocable to dependent care or household services qualifies. No allocation is required if the nondependent care services are minimal.

EXAMPLES 1. A person accepts a full-time position and sends his 12-year-old child to boarding school. The expenses paid to the school must be allocated. The part representing care of the child qualifies; the part representing tuition does not.

2. A full-time housekeeper is hired to care for two children, ages 9 and 12. The housekeeper also drives the mother to and from work each day. The driving is no more than 30 minutes. No allocation is required because the nondependent care services of chauffeuring are minimal.

Care Costs Qualifying as Medical Expenses

Care costs, such as a nurse's wages, may also qualify as medical expenses, but you may not claim both the dependent care credit and the medical expenses deduction. If your care costs exceed the amount allowed as dependent care costs, the excess, to the extent it qualifies as a medical expense, may be added to other deductible medical costs.

EXAMPLE You pay $6,000 for care of your child in your home. The expenses also qualify as medical expenses. Assume your adjusted gross income is $17,000. Your dependent care costs are limited to $2,400 and you may claim a credit of $624 ($2,400 × 26%). The balance of $3,600 is deductible as medical expenses. If you had no other medical costs, your medical deduction would be $2,325 after deducting the 7.5% limitation on medical costs ($3,600 — $1,275 or 7.5% of $17,000).

RULES FOR SEPARATED COUPLES

¶**25.6** When you are living apart from your spouse you may claim the credit on a separate return if you meet the following tests:

1. You maintain as your home a household which is the principal place of abode of a qualifying person (¶25.4) for more than half the year;

2. You furnish over half the cost of maintaining the household for the entire year; and

3. Your spouse was not a member of the household during *the last six months* of the year.

If you satisfy these tests, you are treated as unmarried and may claim the credit on a separate return. You do not have to take your spouse's income into account or show that he or she is employed in order to claim a credit.

If you are legally divorced or separated, separated under a written agreement, or you lived apart from your spouse during the last six months of 1992, and you are the custodial parent (have custody longer than the other parent), the following favorable rule applies: You may claim the credit for care of a dependent child who is under age 13 or physically or mentally incapable of caring for himself or herself even if you waive the dependency exemption on Form 8332 or are unable to claim the exemption under a pre-1985 divorce or separation agreement. The child must be in your custody or the custody of yourself and the other parent for more than half of 1992. A noncustodial parent may not claim the credit even if he or she is allowed the exemption.

WITHHOLDING TAX FOR HOUSEHOLD EMPLOYEES

¶25.7 When you hire someone to care for a dependent in your own home, you are usually liable for employment taxes. You do not have to pay employment taxes if the household worker is the employee of an agency that assigns the position and sets the fee.

Social Security and Medicare taxes. You are liable for 1992 FICA (Social Security) taxes if you pay cash wages of $50 or more in a calendar quarter, but there is an exception for wages paid to a spouse, child, or parent; *see* next column. You report Social Security taxes quarterly on Form 942. As an employer, you pay FICA for 1992 at the rate of 7.65% of wages (up to $55,500). For example, you pay a housekeeper $125 a week ($6,500 for the year). For 1992, you must pay $497.25 in FICA as well as withhold the same amount from the housekeeper's wages. In the unlikely case that wages exceed $55,500, there is an extra Medicare tax on wages up to $130,200 of 2.9%: 1.45% tax on you as the employer and 1.45% withheld from the housekeeper. If you do not withhold the employee's share, you are liable for the full amount. If you pay the employee's share instead of deducting it from wages, you must treat your payment as additional wages when you report the employee's wages on Form W-2, but the payment is not considered wages for Social Security purposes.

Congress may change the withholding and reporting requirements for 1993. See the Supplement for a legislative update and for 1993 FICA tax changes.

Payments to your parent, child, or spouse. FICA tax does not apply to wages paid to your spouse for domestic services in your home. A similar exception applies to wages paid to your son or daughter under age 21, but note the rule that bars you from basing a dependent care credit on payments made to a child under age 19 (¶25.5). Further, FICA generally does not apply to wages paid to your father or mother for domestic work in your home unless (1) you are divorced or widowed, or your spouse is disabled; and (2) you have a child living at home who is under age 18 or is disabled.

Income taxes. Income tax withholding is not required for a household employee but if the employee requests it and you agree, you pay the withheld tax, plus Social Security taxes, on a quarterly Form 942. Withholdings are based on a Form W-4 (Withholding Allowance Certificate) filed by the employee.

An employee who qualifies for the earned income credit may receive advance payments by giving you Form W-5; *see* ¶25.11.

Federal unemployment tax. As an employer, you are also liable for FUTA (federal unemployment taxes) if you pay cash wages of $1,000 or more for household services during any calendar quarter, or if you did so in any quarter in the preceding year. You do not pay FUTA on wages paid to your spouse, your parents, or your children under age 21. Your employee is not liable for FUTA.

The FUTA rate for 1992 is 6.2% on the first $7,000 of cash wages. The tax must be deposited quarterly if the tax due exceeds $100; deposits are made using coupons from Form 8109 (Federal Tax Deposit Coupon). If tax for a quarter does not exceed $100, add it to the tax for the next quarter and make a deposit when the amount due exceeds $100. *See* the Supplement for 1993 changes.

You also report FUTA annually on Form 940, or if you qualify, on simplified Form 940-EZ. When you file, you are allowed a FUTA credit for the state unemployment taxes paid by the January 31 filing date. If you qualify for the maximum 5.4% credit, your net FUTA tax rate will be 0.8%. You may use Form 940-EZ if: (1) you paid state unemployment tax to only one state; (2) the state unemployment tax was paid by the January 31 due date for Form 940-EZ; and (3) the FUTA wages were also taxable for state unemployment tax purposes. If these tests are not met, file Form 940. The filing date is generally January 31 of the following year, but you have until February 10 if all required deposits have been timely made.

EARNED INCOME CREDIT (EIC)

1040

Basic Tests for EIC

To claim the basic EIC, you must:

- Have earned income of under $22,730, such as wages and self-employment earnings; *see* ¶25.9.
- Have a qualifying child who lived with you in your main home in the U.S. for more than 6 months in 1992; *see* ¶25.8.
- File a joint return if married.
- Use Schedule EIC whether you file Form 1040 or Form 1040A.

When this book went to press, Congress was considering legislation to revise or eliminate the supplemental credits for health insurance and newly-born children. See the Supplement for the final rules set by Congress.

QUALIFYING CHILDREN

¶25.8 You must have a qualifying child to claim the EIC credit. A qualifying child is your son, daughter, adopted child, grandchild, stepchild, or foster child who at the end of 1992 was under age 19, or under age 24 and a full-time student, or any age if permanently and totally disabled. If you do not have any qualifying children, you may not take the earned income credit.

Household requirement. To claim the earned income credit in 1992, the qualifying child must have lived with you in your main home in the U.S. for more than 6 months. A foster child must have lived with you for all of 1992. Temporary absences for school or vacation count as time lived in your home.

If you are married, you must file a joint return with your spouse to claim the credit. However, if your spouse did not live in your household for the last six months of the year, and you maintained a home for a child who lived with you for more than half of the year, you may claim the credit as a head of household; *see* ¶1.10.

Permanently and totally disabled. A person is permanently and totally disabled if:

- He or she cannot engage in any substantial gainful activity because of a physical or mental condition; and
- A physician determines that the condition has lasted or can be expected to last continuously for at least a year or can be expected to lead to death.

Married child or qualifying child of another person. You may not take the earned income credit if your child is also a qualifying child of another person who has a higher adjusted gross income in 1992 than you do.

If your child was married at the end of 1992, he or she may be a qualifying child only if the child was claimed as a dependent on Form 1040 or Form 1040A, Line 6, or you waive the exemption in favor of the child's other parent, or the other parent may claim the exemption under a pre-1985 agreement.

EARNED INCOME TESTS

¶25.9
For purposes of the credit, earned income includes wages, salary, tips, commissions, jury duty pay, union strike benefits, certain disability pensions, tax-free meals and lodging from your employer, U.S. military basic quarters and subsistence allowances, combat pay, voluntary salary deferrals, and self-employment earnings.

If your adjusted gross income (AGI) from Line 31 of Form 1040 or Line 16 of Form 1040A is $11,850 or more, the credit is based on the *larger* of earned income or AGI. No credit is allowed if either earned income or AGI is $22,370 or more.

Self-employed. If you were self-employed, your earned income for credit purposes is the net earnings shown on Schedule SE, *less* the income tax deduction for 50% of self-employment tax claimed on Line 25 of Form 1040. If your net earnings were less than $400, the net amount is your earned income for purposes of the credit. If you had a net loss, the loss is subtracted from any wages or other employee earned income.

If you are a statutory employee, the income reported on Schedule C qualifies for the credit.

For purposes of the EIC credit, earned income does *not* include: interest, dividends, Social Security and railroad benefits, welfare benefits, nondisability pensions, veteran's benefits, workers' compensation, unemployment compensation, alimony, exempt clergy income,

or taxable scholarship or fellowship grants not reported on Form W-2. Rents generally are not earned income, except where you render services to tenants or materially help in the production of farm crops grown on rented land. Income received by nonresident aliens not connected with a U.S. trade or business is not earned income.

Foreign earned income. If you work abroad and you claim the foreign earned income exclusion on Form 2555, you may not take the credit.

LOOK UP EIC IN GOVERNMENT TABLES

¶25.10
You do not have to compute the amount of your credit. Schedule EIC refers you to the IRS table in which you may look up the credit that is allowable for your income.

The tables reflect the phaseout of the credit that applies to earnings over $11,850. No credit is allowed if either earned income or adjusted gross income is $22,370 or more.

EXAMPLE Jane is divorced. Her only income is wages of $10,500. She supports her 8-year-old daughter, who lives with her for the entire year.

To find her basic credit, Jane turns to the IRS table in the instruction book accompanying her return. Her credit is $1,324. In the table, the bracket for her income appears as:

Income	Credit One Child
$7,500–$11,850	$1,324

ADVANCE PAYMENT OF EARNED INCOME CREDIT

¶25.11
If you believe you are entitled to an earned income credit, you may file a certificate, Form W-5, with your employer to have a portion of the credit added to your paycheck throughout the year.

If you receive any advance payments, you must report them on Form 1040 or Form 1040A; your employer will include the amount in Box 8 of your Form W-2. If you receive advance payments in excess of the credit you are entitled to, as figured on Schedule EIC, the excess is treated as a tax you owe when you file your return. If the credit you are entitled to from Schedule EIC exceeds the advance payments, the excess credit reduces any other tax you owe. If the credit exceeds your liability, the difference is refunded to you.

Form 2441

Name(s) shown on Form 1040	Your social security number
Andrea Byers	647 91 2583

Caution: ● If you have a child who was born in 1992 and the amount on Form 1040, line 32, is less than $22,370, see page 1 of the instructions before completing this form.

● If you paid cash wages of $50 or more in a calendar quarter to an individual for services performed in your home, you must file an employment tax return. Get **Form 942** for details.

Part I   **Persons or Organizations Who Provided the Care—You must complete this part.** (See the instructions. If you need more space, use the bottom of page 2.)

1	(a) Care provider's name	(b) Address (number, street, apt. no., city, state, and ZIP code)	(c) Identifying number (SSN or EIN)	(d) Amount paid (see instructions)
	Kelley Baker	1400 Arlen Drive City, State x11xx	O11-10-0000	6,500
	ABC Auto	see FORM W-2		

2   Add the amounts in column (d) of line 1 . . . . **2**   6,500

Next: Did you receive employer-provided dependent care benefits?
● **YES.** Complete Part III on the back now.
● **NO.** Complete Part II below.

Part II   **Credit for Child and Dependent Care Expenses**

3	Enter the number of qualifying persons cared for in 1992. See the instructions to find out who is a qualifying person. **Caution:** *To qualify, the person(s) must have shared the same home with you in 1992.* . . . . ▶		2

4   Enter the amount of **qualified** expenses you incurred and actually paid in 1992. See the instructions to find out which expenses qualify. **Caution:** *If you completed Part III on page 2, do not include on this line any excluded benefits shown on line 25* **4**   6,500

5	Enter $2,400 ($4,800 if you paid for the care of two or more qualifying persons)	5	4,800
6	If you completed Part III on page 2, enter the **excluded benefits,** if any, from line 25.	6	3,000

7   Subtract line 6 from line 5. If the result is zero or less, skip lines 8 through 13; enter -0- on line 14, and go to 15 . . . . **7**   1,800

8   Look at lines 4 and 7. Enter the **smaller** of the two amounts here **8**   1,800

9   You **must** enter your **earned income.** See the instructions for the definition of earned income   **9**   37,500
Note: *If you are not filing a joint return, go to line 11 now.*

10   If you are filing a joint return, you **must** enter your spouse's earned income. If your spouse was a student or disabled, see the instructions for the amount to enter **10**

11   ● If you are filing a joint return, look at lines 8, 9, and 10. Enter the **smallest** of the three amounts here.
● All others, look at lines 8 and 9. Enter the **smaller** of the two amounts here. **11**   1,800

12	Enter the amount from Form 1040, line 32	12	41,342		
13	Enter the decimal amount shown below that applies to the amount on line 12		13	X .20

If line 12 is:	Decimal amount is:	If line 12 is:	Decimal amount is:
Over— But not over—		Over— But not over—	
$0—10,000	.30	$20,000—22,000	.24
10,000—12,000	.29	22,000—24,000	.23
12,000—14,000	.28	24,000—26,000	.22
14,000—16,000	.27	26,000—28,000	.21
16,000—18,000	.26	28,000—No limit	.20
18,000—20,000	.25		

14   Multiply line 11 above by the decimal amount on line 13 . . . . **14**   360

15   Multiply any qualified expenses for 1991 that you paid in 1992 by the decimal amount that applies to the amount on your 1991 Form 1040, line 32, or Form 1040A, line 17. You must complete Part I and attach a statement. See the instructions **15**

16   Add lines 14 and 15. See the instructions for the amount of credit you can claim **16**   360

Part III   **Employer-Provided Dependent Care Benefits**—Complete this part only if you received employer-provided dependent care benefits.

17   Enter the total amount of employer-provided dependent care benefits you received for 1992. This amount should be shown in box 22 of your W-2 form(s). **Do not** include amounts that were reported to you as wages in box 10 of Form(s) W-2 . . . . **17**   3,000

18   Enter the amount forfeited, if any. **Caution:** *See the instructions* . . . . **18**   – 0 –

19   Subtract line 18 from line 17. . . . . **19**   3,000

20   Enter the total amount of **qualified** expenses incurred in 1992 for the care of a qualifying person. See the instructions . . . . | 20 | 9,500 |

21   Look at lines 19 and 20. Enter the **smaller** of the two amounts here | 21 | 3,000 |

22   You **must** enter your **earned income.** See the instructions for lines 9 and 10 for the definition of earned income . . . . | 22 | 37,500 |
Note: *If you are not filing a joint return, go to line 24 now.*

23   If you are filing a joint return, you **must** enter your spouse's earned income. If your spouse was a student or disabled, see the instructions for lines 9 and 10 for the amount to enter . . . . | 23 |

24   ● If you are filing a joint return, look at lines 22 and 23. Enter the **smaller** of the two amounts here. | 24 | 37,500 |
● All others, enter the amount from line 22 here.

25   **Excluded benefits.** Enter here the **smallest** of the following:
● The amount from line 21, or
● The amount from line 24, or
● $5,000 ($2,500 if married filing a separate return). **25**   3000

26   **Taxable benefits.** Subtract line 25 from line 19. Enter the result, but not less than zero. Also, include this amount in the total on Form 1040, line 7. On the dotted line next to line 7, write "DCB" . . . . **26**   –0–

Next: If you are also claiming the child and dependent care credit, fill in Form 1040 through line 40. Then, complete Part II of this form.

26

TAX WITHHOLDINGS

Withholding taxes gives the Government part of your income before you have a chance to use it. Withholding tax is imposed on salary and wage income, tip income, certain gambling winnings, pensions, and retirement distributions, but you may avoid withholding on retirement payments; *see* ¶26.11. Withholding is also imposed on interest and dividends if you do not give your taxpayer identification number to a payer of interest or dividend income.

You may increase or decrease withholdings on your wages by submitting a new Form W-4 to your employer. Withholdings may be reduced by claiming allowances based on tax deductions and credits.

Make sure that tax withholdings meet or help you meet the estimated tax rules that require withholdings plus estimated tax payments to equal 90% of your current year liability or the required percentage of the prior year's liability; *see* Chapter 27.

LAW ALERT In 1993, a 20% withholding rule is scheduled to apply to nonperiodic distributions from an employer retirement plan. You may avoid the withholding by instructing your employer to directly transfer the funds to an IRA or the plan of your new employer; *see* ¶26.11.

At the time this book went to press, legislation to repeal the 20% withholding rule was pending in Congress; *see* the Supplement.

WITHHOLDINGS SHOULD COVER ESTIMATED TAX

¶**26.1** In fixing the rate of withholding on your wages, pay attention to the 90% test for determining whether sufficient taxes have been withheld from your pay. A penalty will apply if your wage withholdings plus estimated tax payments do not equal the lesser of 90% of your current tax liability or the required percentage of the prior year's tax; *see* ¶27.5.

Taxes are withheld from payments made to you for services that you perform as an employee; *see* ¶26.2 for exceptions. By filing Form W-4, you claim exemptions for yourself, your spouse and dependents. The number of exemptions claimed will either decrease or increase the amount of withholding. You also may claim withholding allowances for itemized deductions and credits such as the credit for the elderly and totally disabled, the foreign tax credit, credit for home mortgages, the general business credit, and earned income credit (if you have not filed for an advance payment of the credit on Form W-5).

WHEN INCOME TAXES ARE WITHHELD ON WAGES

¶**26.2** The amount of income tax withheld for your wage bracket depends on your marital status and the number of exemptions you claim. Exemptions for withholding correspond to the exemptions allowed on your tax return; *see* ¶1.18. You file a withholding certificate, Form W-4, with your employer, indicating your status and exemptions. Without the certificate, your employer must withhold tax as if you are a single person with no exemptions.

If you do not expect withholdings to meet your final tax liability, ask your employer to withhold a greater amount of tax; *see* ¶26.3. On the other hand, if the withholding rate applied to your wages results in overwithholding, you may claim extra withholding allowances to reduce withholding during the year; *see* ¶26.5 and ¶26.6.

Cash payments or the cash value of benefits paid to an employee by an employer are subject to withholding, unless the payments are specifically excluded.

INCOME TAXES ARE WITHHELD ON:

Payments to employees as salaries, wages, fees, bonuses, commissions, pensions, retirement pay, vacation allowances, dismissal pay, etc. (whether paid in cash or goods). *See* ¶26.11 for withholding on pensions and annuities.

Sick pay paid by your employer. If a third party pays you sick pay on a plan funded by your employer, you may request withholding by filing Form W-4S.

Taxable group insurance coverage for amount over $50,000.

Reimbursements of expenses that do not meet qualifying rules of accountable plans discussed at ¶20.34. Also, reimbursements from accountable plans that exceed federal rates if the employee does not return the reimbursement or show that it is substantiated by proof of expenses.

Pay to members of the U.S. Armed Forces.

Prize awarded to a salesman in a contest run by his employer.

Retroactive pay and overtime under Fair Labor Standards Act.

Taxable supplemental unemployment compensation benefits.

Back pay under National Labor Relations Board order and settlements under the Civil Rights Act of 1964 for job applicants refused employment on discriminatory grounds; but *see* ¶12.10.

Payments to Canadians and Mexicans who cross borders frequently and who are not working in transportation service.

INCOME TAXES ARE NOT WITHHELD ON:

Payments to household workers. However, although income tax withholding is not required, the worker and the employer may make a voluntary withholding agreement.

Payments to agricultural workers, college domestics, ministers of the gospel (except chaplains in the Armed Forces), casual workers, nonresident aliens, public officials who receive fees directly from the public—notaries public, jurors, witnesses, precinct workers, etc.; but *see* voluntary withholding agreements, ¶26.3.

Pay for newspaper home delivery by children under age 18.

Advances for traveling expenses if the employee substantiates expenses to the employer and if the employee returns any unsubstantiated amount; *see* ¶20.34.

Value of tax-free board and lodging furnished by an employer.

Fringe benefits not subject to tax.

Substantiated reimbursements for deductible moving expenses or medical care benefits under a self-insured medical reimbursement plan.

Death benefit payments to beneficiary of employee; wages due but unpaid at employee's death and paid to estate or beneficiary.

Pay for U.S. citizen working abroad or in U.S. possessions to the extent that the pay is tax free; *see* Chapter 36 for rules.

Lump-sum settlement from employer for cancellation of employment contract.

Employer contributions to SEPs; *see* ¶8.11.

Earnings of self-employed persons as they pay their income taxes currently through estimated tax.

Form W-2. By the end of January, your employer must give you duplicate copies of Form W-2, which is a record of your pay and the withheld income and Social Security taxes. If you leave your job during the year, you may ask your employer for a Form W-2 by making a written request within 30 days of leaving the job.

INCREASING WITHHOLDING

¶26.3 For withholding tax purposes, you do not have to claim all your exemptions. This will increase the amount withheld and help reduce the final tax payment on filing your tax return. It may also relieve you of making quarterly estimated tax payments, provided the withholdings are sufficient to meet your estimated tax liability. A waiver of exemptions for withholding taxes does not prevent you from claiming the "waived" exemptions on your final tax return. The waiver is merely a bookkeeping aid to your company's payroll department. If you find that even a waiver of exemptions does not cover all of the tax you want withheld, you may ask your employer on Form W-4 to withhold additional amounts from each paycheck.

AVOIDING WITHHOLDING

¶26.4 If you had no income tax liability in 1992 and expect none for 1993, you may be exempt from income tax withholdings on your 1993 wages. However, if you can be claimed as a dependent on another person's tax return, and you have any investment income, you may claim this special exemption only if you expect total income (wages plus investments) to be no more than the minimum standard deduction for dependents, which in 1992 was $600 (¶13.5). If the $600 amount is increased due to an inflation factor, the higher amount will be on the 1993 version of Form W-4. If eligible, students working for the summer, retired persons, and other part-time workers do not have to wait for a refund of withheld taxes they do not owe.

To claim an exemption, you must file a withholding exemption certificate, Form W-4, with your employer. The form may be obtained from an IRS district office or from your employer. If you will file a joint return for 1993, do not claim an exemption on Form W-4 if the joint return will show a tax. An exemption claimed during 1993 will expire February 15, 1994.

Social Security taxes are withheld, even if you are exempt from income tax withholding.

WITHHOLDING ALLOWANCES

¶26.5 Too much may be withheld from your pay if you have tax reduction items. The overpayment will be refunded when you file your return, but you lose the use of your money during the year. By filing Form W-4 with your employer, you may avoid this and reduce withholding taxes by claiming additional withholding allowances based on (1) estimated itemized deductions; (2) IRA contribution deductions; (3) alimony deductions; (4) net losses from Schedules C, D, E, or F of Form 1040; and (5) tax credits such as the dependent care credit, credit for the elderly, earned-income credit (if you did not request advance payment on Form W-5), and general-business credit.

Working couples filing jointly figure withholding allowances on combined wage income and may allocate them between employers. On separate returns, the allowances must be figured separately.

If you work for two or more employers at the same time, you may claim withholding allowances from only one employer.

File a new Form W-4 each year for withholding allowances based on itemized deductions and credits. Furthermore, you may have to file a new form to increase your withholding if withholding allowances you had been claiming are no longer allowed; *see* ¶26.7.

A civil penalty of $500 may be imposed if, for purposes of claiming tax withholding allowances, you overstate your itemized deductions and credits or understate your wages without a reasonable basis. There is also a criminal penalty of up to $1,000 plus a jail sentence for willfully supplying false information.

Form W-4

Personal Allowances Worksheet For 1992, the value of your personal exemption(s) is reduced if your income is over $105,250 ($157,900 if married filing jointly, $131,550 if head of household, or $78,950 if married filing separately). Get Pub. 919 for details.

A Enter "1" for **yourself** if no one else can claim you as a dependent . . . . **A** _____

B Enter "1" if:
- You are single and have only one job; or
- You are married, have only one job, and your spouse does not work; or
- Your wages from a second job or your spouse's wages (or the total of both) are $1,000 or less.
B _____

C Enter "1" for your **spouse**. But, you may choose to enter -0- if you are married and have either a working spouse or more than one job (this may help you avoid having too little tax withheld) . . . . **C** _____

D Enter number of **dependents** (other than your spouse or yourself) whom you will claim on your tax return . . . . **D** _____

E Enter "1" if you will file as **head of household** on your tax return (see conditions under "Head of Household," above) . **E** _____

F Enter "1" if you have at least $1,500 of **child or dependent care expenses** for which you plan to claim a credit . . **F** _____

G Add lines A through F and enter total here. **Note:** *This amount may be different from the number of exemptions you claim on your return* ▶ **G** _____

For accuracy, do all worksheets that apply.
- If you plan to **itemize or claim adjustments to income** and want to reduce your withholding, see the Deductions and Adjustments Worksheet on page 2.
- If you are **single** and have **more than one job** and your combined earnings from all jobs exceed $29,000 OR if you are **married** and have a **working spouse or more than one job,** and the combined earnings from all jobs exceed $50,000, see the Two-Earner/Two-Job Worksheet on page 2 if you want to avoid having too little tax withheld.
- If **neither** of the above situations applies, **stop here** and enter the number from line G on line 5 of Form W-4 below.

- - - - - - - - - - - **Cut here and give the certificate to your employer. Keep the top portion for your records.** - - - - - - - - - - -

Form W-4 Department of the Treasury Internal Revenue Service

Employee's Withholding Allowance Certificate

▶ **For Privacy Act and Paperwork Reduction Act Notice, see reverse.**

OMB No. 1545-0010

1992

1 Type or print your first name and middle initial   Last name

2 Your social security number

Home address (number and street or rural route)

3 ☐ Single ☐ Married ☐ Married, but withhold at higher Single rate.
Note: *If married, but legally separated, or spouse is a nonresident alien, check the Single box.*

City or town, state, and ZIP code

4 If your last name differs from that on your social security card, check here and call 1-800-772-1213 for more information . ▶ ☐

5 Total number of allowances you are claiming (from line G above or from the Worksheets on back if they apply) **5** _____

6 Additional amount, if any, you want deducted from each paycheck . . . . **6** $ _____

7 I claim exemption from withholding and I certify that I meet **ALL** of the following conditions for exemption:
- Last year I had a right to a refund of **ALL** Federal income tax withheld because I had **NO** tax liability; **AND**
- This year I expect a refund of **ALL** Federal income tax withheld because I expect to have **NO** tax liability; **AND**
- This year if my income exceeds $600 and includes nonwage income, another person cannot claim me as a dependent.

If you meet all of the above conditions, enter the year effective and "EXEMPT" here . . . . ▶ **7** 19

8 Are you a full-time student? (**Note:** *Full-time students are not automatically exempt.*) . . . . **8** ☐ Yes ☐ No

Under penalties of perjury, I certify that I am entitled to the number of withholding allowances claimed on this certificate or entitled to claim exempt status.

Employee's signature ▶

Date ▶   , 19

9 Employer's name and address (Employer: Complete 9 and 11 only if sending to the IRS) | **10** Office code (optional) | **11** Employer identification number

SPECIAL WITHHOLDING ALLOWANCE

¶26.6 A special withholding allowance designed to eliminate overwithholding may be claimed on Form W-4 by certain employees. The withholding allowance, like an exemption, frees wage income from withholding. An unmarried person may claim this special withholding allowance, provided he or she is not working for more than one employer. If you are married, you may claim the allowance, provided you also work for only one employer and your spouse does not work, or wages from a second job or your spouse's job are $1,000 or less. This special allowance is only for withholding purposes. You may not claim it on your tax return.

WHEN TO FILE NEW FORM W-4

¶26.7 You should file a new Form W-4 any time the number of your exemptions or withholding allowances increases or decreases. For example: A child is born or adopted; you marry; you get a divorce; or your deductible expenses change.

Your employer may make the new Form W-4 effective with the next payment of wages. However, an employer may postpone the new withholding rate until the start of the first payroll period ending on or after the 30th day from the day you submit the revised form.

You must file a new Form W-4 within 10 days if the number of

allowances previously claimed by you decreases because: either you divorce or legally separate; you stop supporting a dependent; or a dependent for whom you claimed an exemption will receive more than the exemption amount for the year ($2,300 in 1992) but this income restriction does not apply to your child who is under 19 years of age or a student under age 24.

The death of a spouse or a dependent in a current year does not affect your withholding until the next year but requires the filing of a new certificate, if possible, by the first business day in December, or within 10 days if the death is in December. However, a widow or widower entitled to joint return rates in the next two years as a qualifying widow or widower with a dependent child (¶1.6) need not file a new withholding certificate.

When you file on or before December 1, your employer must reduce your withholding as of January 1 of the next year.

WHEN TIPS ARE SUBJECT TO WITHHOLDINGS

¶26.8 Tips are subject to income tax and FICA (Social Security) withholdings. If you receive cash tips amounting to $20 or more in a month, you must report the total amount of tips received during the month to your employer on Form 4070 (or a similar written report). You make the report on or before the 10th day after the end of the month in which the tips are received. (If the 10th day is a Saturday,

Sunday, or legal holiday, you must submit the report by the next business day.) For example, tips amounting to $20 or more that are received during January 1993 are reported by February 10, 1993. Your employer may require more frequent reporting.

You include cash tips paid to you in your own behalf. If you "split" or share tips with others, you include in your report only your share. You do not include tips received in the form of merchandise or your share of service charges turned over to you by your employer.

You are considered to have income from tips when you make your report to your employer. However, if you do not report your tips to your employer, you are considered to have tip income when you receive the tips. For example, if you received tips of $75 during December 1992 and reported the tips to your employer on January 6, 1993, the tips are considered paid to you in January 1993, and the $75 is included on your 1993 income tax return. On the other hand, if your tips during December 1992 totaled only $18, you are not required to report the amount to your employer. The tips are considered paid to you in 1992 and must be included in your 1992 income tax return.

Your employer withholds the Social Security and income tax due on the tips from your wages or from funds you give him or her for withholding purposes. If the taxes due cannot be collected on the tips, either from your wages or from voluntary contributions, by the 10th day after the end of the month in which tips are reported, you have to pay the tax when you file your income tax return.

Where wages are insufficient to meet all of the withholding liability, the wages are applied first to Social Security tax.

If your employer is unable to collect enough money from your wages during the year to cover the Social Security tax on the tips you reported, the uncollected amount is shown on your Form W-2 in Box 17 with code A next to it. You must report the uncollected amount on Line 53 of Form 1040 as an additional tax due; write "Uncollected Tax on Tips" and show the amount next to Line 53.

If you have *not* reported tips of $20 or more in any month, or tips are allocated to you under the special tip allocation rules discussed below, you must compute Social Security tax on that amount on Form 4137 and enter it as a tax due on Line 50 of Form 1040; attach Form 4137 to Form 1040. The unreported tips must be included as wages on Line 7 of Form 1040.

Penalty For Failure To Report

Failure to report tip income of $20 or more received during the month to your employer may subject you to a penalty of 50% of the Social Security tax due on the unreported tips, unless your failure was due to reasonable cause rather than to willful neglect.
Tips of less than $20 per month are taxable but not subject to withholding.

Tip allocation reporting by large restaurants. To help the IRS audit the reporting of tip income, restaurants employing at least 10 people must make a special report of income and allocate tips based on gross receipts. For purposes of the allocation, the law assumes tip income of at least 8%. If you voluntarily report tips equal to your allocable share of 8% of the restaurant's gross receipts, no allocation will be made to you. However, if the total tips reported by all employees is less than 8% of gross receipts and you do not report your share of the 8%, your employer must make an allocation based on the difference between the amount you reported and your share of the 8% amount. The allocated amount is shown on Form W-2. However, taxes are not withheld on the allocated amount. Taxes are withheld only on amounts actually reported by employees. An employer or majority of employees may ask the IRS to apply a tip percentage of less than 8%, but no lower than 2%.

Reporting Allocated Tips

Your employer will show allocated tips in Box 7 of your Form W-2. This amount will not be included in Box 10 wages and you must add it to income yourself by reporting it on Line 7 of Form 1040. You also must compute Social Security tax on the allocated tips on Form 4137 and enter the tax from Form 4137 on Line 50 of Form 1040. You may not use Form 1040A or Form 1040EZ.

WITHHOLDING ON GAMBLING WINNINGS

¶26.9
Your winnings from gambling may be subject to withholding. Withholding applies if your winnings *exceed:*

1. $5,000 from a state-conducted lottery;
2. $1,000 from sweepstakes and wagering pools (whether or not state-conducted) and other lotteries, including a church raffle. Wagering pools include all parimutuel betting pools and on- and off-track racing pools; and
3. $1,000 from other wagering transactions, if the proceeds are at least 300 times as large as the amount wagered such as from wagers on horse races, dog races, or jai alai.

Winnings from bingo, keno, and slot machines, however, are *not* subject to withholding.

Before 1993 the withholding rate was 20%. Congress may increase the rate for winnings after 1992; *see* the Supplement.

If your winnings exceed the $1,000 or $5,000 threshold the withholding rate applies to your gross winnings less your wagers, and not just the amounts over $1,000 or $5,000.

The IRS requires you to tell the payers of gambling winnings if you are also receiving winnings from identical wagers; winnings from identical wagers must be added together to determine if withholding is required.

If tax is withheld from your winnings, you should receive Form W-2G, which shows the total winnings and amount withheld.

If you have agreed to share your winnings with another person, give the payer a Form 5754. The payer will then prepare separate Forms W-2G for each of you.

FICA WITHHOLDINGS

¶26.10
FICA withholdings are employee contributions for Social Security and Medicare coverage. Your employer is liable for the tax if he or she fails to make proper withholdings. The amount withheld is figured on your wages and is not affected by your marital status, number of exemptions, or the fact that you may be over age 65 and are collecting Social Security. On Form W-2, Social Security withholdings are shown in Box 11; Medicare withholdings in Box 15.

Subject to FICA tax are your regular salary, commissions, bonuses, vacation pay, cash tips, group-term insurance coverage over $50,000, the first six months of sick pay, and contributions to cash or deferred (401(k)) pay plans or salary-reduction contributions to a simplified employee pension (SEP) or tax-sheltered annuity. Not subject to tax are the value of tax-free meals and lodgings under ¶3.10 and reimbursements for substantiated travel or entertainment expenses or for moving expenses.

Wages You Pay to Your Spouse or Child

Wages you pay to your spouse for working in your business are subject to FICA tax and income tax withholding. Wages you pay to your child are subject to income tax withholding but exempt from FICA if the child is under age 18. Wages you pay to your child under age 21 or to your spouse for domestic work or child care in your private home are exempt from FICA.

Excess Social Security and Railroad Retirement withholding. If you have worked for *more than one employer* during 1992, attach all Copies B of Form W-2 to your return. Check to see that the total withheld in 1992 by your employers does not exceed your liability for FICA taxes. For Social Security, the maximum 1992 liability is 6.2% on the first $55,500 of salary income. For Medicare, the maximum liability is 1.45% on salary up to $130,200. If too much was withheld, claim the excess as a payment on Line 58 of your 1992 Form 1040. On Form 1040A and Form 1040EZ, the excess is added to your total tax payments.

Employees covered by the Railroad Retirement Tax Act (RRTA) receive Form W-2 which lists total wages paid and withholdings of income and Railroad Retirement taxes. Follow tax form instructions for claiming a credit for excess withholding.

FIGURING EXCESS FICA WITHHOLDINGS

1. Total of all Boxes 11 from Forms W-2 $_____

2. Total of all Boxes 12 and 13 from Forms W-2; do not enter more than $55,500   _____

3. Multiply Line 2 by 6.2%   _____

4. Subtract Line 3 from Line 1 for excess Social Security withholdings   _____

5. Total of all Boxes 15 from Forms W-2   _____

6. Total of all Boxes 14 from Forms W-2; do not enter more than $130,200   _____

7. Multiply Line 6 by 1.45%   _____

8. Subtract Line 7 from Line 5 for excess Medicare withholdings   _____

9. Add Lines 4 and 8 for total excess to be refunded $_____

WITHHOLDING ON RETIREMENT DISTRIBUTIONS

¶26.11

Retirement distributions are subject to withholding taxes, but you may avoid withholdings. The method of avoiding withholding varies with the type of payment.

Periodic payments. If you receive periodic payments, such as an annuity, withholding is required unless you elect to avoid withholding on Form W-4P, or on a substitute form furnished by the payer. If you are a U.S. citizen or resident alien, withholding may not be avoided on pensions or other distributions paid outside the U.S. or U.S. possessions. Payment must be to your home address within the U.S. (or in a U.S. possession) to avoid withholding.

Unless you tell the payer otherwise, wage withholding tables are used to figure withholdings on periodic payments as if you were married and claiming three withholding exemptions. Withholding allowances may be claimed for estimated itemized deductions, alimony payments, and deductible IRA contributions.

You may also request the payer to withhold a specific amount of additional tax for each payment.

Nonperiodic payments in 1992. Nonperiodic payments are subject to withholding at a flat 10% rate in 1992 unless the payment is considered a total distribution or you elect to avoid withholding on Form W-4P (or substitute form). IRA distributions that are payable upon demand are considered nonperiodic and thus, subject to the 10% withholding rule.

In 1992, the flat 10% rate does not apply to lump-sum distributions from a qualified pension or profit-sharing plan, stock bonus, or annuity plan. The rate on such distributions approximates the tax that would be due under the averaging method, whether or not you are eligible to elect averaging.

Nonperiodic payments in 1993 from IRAs and commercial annuities. The withholding rules discussed above for 1992 will also apply to IRA distributions payable on demand and nonperiodic commercial annuity payments in 1993.

Nonperiodic payments from qualified employer plans in 1993. Starting in 1993, employers must withhold 20% from nonperiodic payments, such as lump-sum distributions, paid directly to employees. To avoid withholding in 1993, you must tell your employer to make a direct transfer of the funds to an IRA or to a defined contribution plan (¶8.4) of your new employer.

For state or local government tax-sheltered annuity plans (¶7.20) that were prohibited from making a trustee-to-trustee transfer as of July 1, 1992, the 20% withholding rule will not apply until the earlier of January 1, 1994, or 90 days after the day on which state law is changed to allow the direct transfer.

If you do not instruct your employer to make the direct transfer and after personally receiving the distribution, you decide to make a rollover yourself, you will confront the problems illustrated in the following example.

EXAMPLE In January 1993, John retires and is due a lump sum distribution of $100,000 from a qualified plan of his company. If he instructs his employer to transfer the amount to an IRA, there is no tax withholding and the $100,000 is transferred to the IRA.

Now assume John believes he can apply averaging to the lump sum and decides not to make a direct transfer. The plan pays him $80,000 and withholds a tax of $20,000 which John will apply to his 1993 tax liability. But say a month later, John realizes that he miscalculated the benefits of averaging and now wants to rollover his benefits to an IRA. He must make the rollover within 30 days; that is because 30 days of the 60-day rollover period have already passed; see ¶8.9. Furthermore, to avoid tax on the entire distribution, he must deposit $100,000 in the IRA, even though $20,000 tax has been withheld. If he does not have the $20,000, he must borrow the $20,000 and deposit it in the IRA. If he rolls over only $80,000, he must report $20,000 as a taxable distribution on his 1993 return.

Note: When this book went to press, legislation was being considered in Congress to repeal the 20% withholding rules. Further developments will be reported in the Supplement.

BACKUP WITHHOLDING

¶26.12

Backup withholding is designed primarily to pressure taxpayers to report interest and dividend income. You may be subject to backup withholding if you do not give your taxpayer identification number to parties paying you interest or dividend income, you give an incorrect number, or you ignore IRS notices stating that you have underreported interest or dividends. The backup withholding rate is 20%. Giving a false taxpayer identification number may result in penalties.

27 ESTIMATED TAX PAYMENTS

Income taxes are collected on a pay-as-you-go basis through withholding on wages and pensions, as well as quarterly estimated tax payments on other income. Where all or most of your income is from wages, pensions, and annuities, you will generally not have to pay estimated tax, because your estimated tax liability has been satisfied by withholding. But do not assume you are not required to pay simply because taxes have been withheld from your wages. Always check your estimated tax liability. Withholding may not cover your tax; the withholding tax rate may be below your actual tax rate when considering other income such as interest, dividends, business income, and capital gains.

Your estimated tax must also include liability for self-employment tax and alternative minimum tax (AMT).

Generally, to avoid a penalty your 1992 withholdings plus quarterly estimated tax installments must equal the lower of 90% of your 1992 liability or 100% of your 1991 liability. If your income fluctuates throughout the year, a special exception may allow you to avoid a penalty even if your payments do not meet the basic exceptions. Furthermore, the IRS might waive the penalty if you can show hardship.

WHO MUST PAY ESTIMATED TAX?

¶27.1 You have to make quarterly estimated tax payments if your estimated tax liability, after taking into account estimated withholdings, is at least $500 and the withholdings will *not* be at least 90% of the current year's tax or a percentage of the prior year's tax; *see* ¶27.2.

Make your estimated tax payment accompanied by the appropriate Form 1040-ES voucher. Failure to pay estimated tax may subject you to a penalty; *see* ¶27.5.

Farmers only have to make one installment payment, generally by January 15 of the following year. The payment for 1992 must be made by January 15, 1993, or farmers may file a final return by March 1, 1993, instead of making an estimated tax payment. To qualify under these rules, a farmer must have two-thirds of his or her 1991 or 1992 gross income from farming.

Fishermen who expect to receive at least two-thirds of their gross income from fishing pay estimated taxes as farmers do.

Residents of Puerto Rico during the entire taxable year use Form 1040-ES to make estimated tax payments. Other nonresident aliens use Form 1040-ES(NR).

The four installment dates for 1993 estimated tax are:

April 15, 1993;
June 15, 1993;
September 15, 1993; and
January 18, 1994.

If you use a fiscal year. A fiscal year is any year other than the calendar year. If you file using a fiscal year, your first estimated installment is due on or before the 15th day of the fourth month of your fiscal year. Amendments may be made on the 15th day of the sixth and ninth months of your year with the final amendment on the 15th day of the first month of your next fiscal year. Your installments are also due then.

PENALTY FOR 1992 UNDERESTIMATES

¶27.2 You are *not* subject to a penalty if your estimated tax payments for 1992, including withholdings, equal at least 90% of the tax shown on your final 1992 return (66⅔% if you are a farmer). Alternatively, if your estimated payments, including withholdings, equal at least 100% of the 1991 final tax, no penalty is imposed even though this is less than 90% of the 1992 liability. The 100% exception applies only if you filed a return for 1991 covering a full 12 months and your adjusted gross income is not within the restrictive rule discussed on page 293. These are the two basic exceptions to the penalty for underestimating. If your income fluctuates throughout the year, you may be able to avoid a penalty based on an annualized income exception; *see* ¶27.5.

If you are subject to a penalty, it will decrease any refund you are due or increase the tax owed on Form 1040 or Form 1040A.

Income restriction on 100% exception. If you made estimated tax installments in 1989, 1990, or 1991, or were charged an underpayment penalty in any of these years, and your 1992 income exceeds certain limits, you cannot use the 100% prior-year exception to avoid a 1992 penalty. This restriction applies if your 1992 adjusted gross income exceeds $75,000 ($37,500 if married filing separately) and if, after certain adjustments, your 1992 adjusted gross income also exceeds your 1991 adjusted gross income by more than $40,000 ($20,000 if married filing separately). For further details on this restriction, *see* IRS Form 2210.

The penalty is figured separately for each installment date. This means that if, after taking into account withholdings, you underpay an early installment, you may owe a penalty for that quarterly period even though you overpay later installments to make up the difference. The penalty for each period runs from the installment due date until the amount is paid or until the filing date for the final tax return, whichever is earlier. In 1992, the penalty rate was 9% for the first quarter and 8% for the second and third quarters. *See* the Supplement and Form 2210 for the last-quarter 1992 rate and the first-quarter 1993 rate.

Withholding payments are treated as if they were payments of estimated tax. In applying them, the total withholdings of the year are divided equally to each quarterly installment date unless you want to show the actual payment dates; then they are applied in the quarter they are actually withheld.

Figure the penalty for yourself on Form 2210 or let the IRS do it. You can use Form 2210 to determine any 1992 penalty. On Form 2210, the penalty is generally based on the *lower* of 90% of the 1992 tax or 100% of the 1991 tax (if your return covered 12 months). One-fourth of the lower amount is the payment required for *each* installment period. That is, the penalty for *each* 1992 installment quarter is applied to the difference between your payments for the quarter, if any, and the *lower* of (1) 22.5% of the 1992 tax, or (2) 25% of the 1991 tax (if your return covered 12 months).

However, as discussed earlier, if 100% of your 1991 tax is lower than 90% of the 1992 tax, you may not be able to use the 100% amount as the basis for the penalty computation.

There is no penalty and you do not have to file Form 2210 if the tax liability shown on your 1992 return is less than $500, after taking into account withholdings. The same rule applies if you had no tax liability for 1991, you were a U.S. citizen or resident for all of 1991, and your 1991 taxable year included 12 full months.

Even if you might be subject to a penalty, you do not have to figure it yourself on Form 2210. In fact, the IRS encourages taxpayers to let the IRS compute any penalty. The IRS will figure the amount of any penalty and bill you for the amount if you do not complete Form 2210.

However, you *must* attach Form 2210 to your return if: (1) you use the annualized income exception; (2) do not allocate wage withholdings in four equal amounts; or (3) claim a penalty waiver; *see* the next column for waiver rules.

On Form 2210, if you *underpaid* for any quarter, the amount of the underpayment reduces the payment made in the following quarter. That is, an underpayment of one quarter is carried over to succeeding quarters. If you underpay for a quarter, any payment you make after that installment date will be applied first to the earlier underpayment. Thus, even if you make the required payment for a quarter, you could still be subject to a penalty for that quarter because your payment is applied to a prior underpayment.

If you *overpaid* in any quarter, the excess carries over to the next quarter. The excess cannot be used to make up an underpayment of the prior quarter. However, these rules apply only to installment payments made with Form 1040-ES vouchers. They do not apply to withholdings, which are allocated equally over the year.

Withholdings Cover Prior Underpayment

Tax withheld from your pay may help you avoid the penalty for underpayment of estimated tax. You have a choice in allocating your withholdings over the year: (1) You may treat your entire year's withholdings as having been withheld in equal amounts for each quarter; or (2) you may allocate to each quarter the actual withholdings that were taken out of your pay for that quarter. If, toward the end of the year, you find that you have underestimated for an earlier quarter, ask your employer to withhold an extra amount which may be allocated equally over the four quarters. This way you may eliminate the underestimate for the earlier quarters.

Waiver of penalty for hardship, retirement, or disability. The IRS may waive the penalty if you can show you failed to pay the estimated tax because of casualty, disaster, or other unusual circumstances. The IRS may also waive a penalty for a 1992 underpayment if in 1992 or 1991 you retired after reaching age 62 or became disabled, and you failed to make a payment due to reasonable cause and not due to willful neglect. This rule would apply to a 1993 underpayment if you became disabled or retired (after age 62) in 1992 or 1993. To apply for the waiver, attach an explanation on Form 2210 with applicable documentation.

FINAL PAYMENT FOR 1992

¶27.3

That you paid an estimated tax for 1992 does not excuse you from filing a tax return on or before April 15, 1993. You must file a final return and pay the difference between the total of your withholding, plus your estimated tax payments and your final tax. If the tax is less than your withholdings and payments, you get a refund or credit on the 1993 estimated tax. You may also split up the amount due you. You may take part of the overpayment as a refund. The other part may be credited to your next year's estimate. You may get interest only on the part refunded.

Check your mathematics before you apply an overpayment as a credit on your next year's estimate. If you apply too much, the amount credited may not be used to offset any additional tax due that the IRS determines you owe. For example, your 1992 return shows a $500 refund due, and you apply it towards your 1993 estimated tax. However, the IRS determines that you overpaid $200, not $500. You will be billed for the additional $300 tax, plus interest due; you may not offset the extra tax with the credited amount.

ESTIMATING YOUR 1993 TAX

¶27.4

Estimate your income (including wage and salary income subject to withholding), deductions, and exemptions for 1993, and compute the tax using 1993 tax rates. Include in your estimate self-employment tax and alternative minimum tax, if any. If you receive Social Security benefits that may be taxable under the rules of ¶34.3, estimate the taxable portion as part of your projected income. Reduce the estimated tax by tax credits and withholdings from wages, pensions, and annuities. You may use the worksheet and the tax rate schedule included in the 1993 Form 1040-ES to figure your estimated tax liability. The estimated tax may be paid in full with your Form 1040-ES estimated tax voucher or in four equal installments.

If your estimated tax liability is $500 or more, you must pay the balance in installments unless withholdings from income will cover at least 90% of your estimated 1993 liability or a percentage of your 1992 liability. The required percentage of prior year liability, which was 100% before 1993, was under Congressional review when this book went to press. *See* the Supplement for the percentage finally set by Congress for 1993 estimates.

If you are due a refund when you file your 1992 return, you may credit the refund to your 1993 estimated tax by making an election on your 1992 return. The IRS will credit the refund to the April installment of 1993 estimated tax unless you attach a statement to your return instructing the IRS to apply the refund to later installments.

Members of a partnership declare their estimated taxes in their individual capacities. Each partner's estimate must include his or her share of the partnership income, whether actually paid or not.

Revising your estimate. If your original estimate changes, you may revise it and change the amount of your installment payments; *see* ¶27.6.

AVOIDING THE PENALTY FOR 1993

¶27.5 After estimating your 1993 income and tax liability (¶27.4), base your 1993 withholdings and quarterly payments on the following five penalty exceptions for underestimated taxes.

90% current-year exception. You avoid any penalty for 1993 if your estimated payments, including withholdings, equal at least 90% of the tax shown on your 1993 return and at least 22.5% of your 1993 tax ($25\% \times 90\%$) is paid by each installment date.

Prior-year exception. If you filed a 1992 return that covered 12 months, you can avoid the penalty and guesswork by figuring and paying as your 1993 estimated tax an amount based on a percentage of your 1992 tax. Before 1993, you met this exception by making estimated payments of at least 100% of the prior year's tax. However, when this book went to press, Congress was considering an increase in the percentage. *See* the Supplement for the percentage that will apply in 1993.

Annualized income exception. You may avoid the penalty on an estimated tax installment based on income which was earned in the months ending before the due date of the installment and which was *annualized* for purposes of computing the estimated tax. This exception may apply if you do not earn income evenly throughout the year, such as where you operate a seasonal business. Form 2210 and IRS Publication 505 include a worksheet for figuring the annualized income exception.

No liability in prior year. No penalty will be imposed for 1993 if you did not have a 1992 liability, your 1992 taxable year included 12 months, and you were a citizen or resident of the United States throughout 1992.

$500 exception. No penalty is imposed if your estimated tax liability, after taking into account withholdings, is less than $500.

AMENDING YOUR ESTIMATE

¶27.6 During the year, income, expense, or exemption changes may require you to amend your estimated tax. If you refigure your estimated tax, you adjust your payment schedule on the Form 1040-ES vouchers as shown in the examples in the next column.

You do not have to file the January Form 1040-ES voucher providing you file your final return and pay in full the balance of tax due by the end of the year. For 1992, you do not have to file the January 15, 1993 voucher if you file a final return and pay the balance of tax by February 1, 1993 (January 31 is a Sunday).

If taxes paid in the previous installments total more than your revised estimate, you cannot obtain a refund at that time. You must wait until you file your final return showing that a refund is due.

WHEN TO AMEND 1993 ESTIMATES

If you want to make a change—	You amend on—
After April 1 and before June 2	Voucher 2 by June 15, 1993
After June 1 and before September 2	Voucher 3 by September 15, 1993
After September 1 and before January 1	Voucher 4 by January 18, 1994

EXAMPLES 1. Smith estimates a 1993 tax of $6,000. On April 15, 1993, he pays an installment of $1,500. In June, he amends his estimate showing a tax of $3,000 instead of $6,000. He refigures the installment schedule by dividing $3,000 by 4, which gives a quarterly payment rate of $750. As he paid $1,500 in April, the $750 overpayment covers his June obligation. By September 15, he pays $750; by January 18, 1994, $750.

2. In September, Jones finds that his estimated tax liability increased from $20,000 to $25,000. He paid $5,000 as his April and June installments ($10,000 total). Under the amended schedule, he should have paid $6,250 per quarter ($25,000 ÷ 4), or $12,500 by June 15. Thus, there is a $2,500 underpayment ($12,500 − 10,000). To cover the underpayment of $2,500, which carries over to the third quarter, Jones' September installment must be at least $8,750 ($6,250 + $2,500). If less than $8,750 is paid, there will be an underpayment for the third quarter, as third quarter payments are applied first to the carried over underpayment of $2,500. The fourth quarter installment due by January 15 will be $6,250. The underpayments for the first two quarters will be subject to a penalty unless an exception at ¶27.5 applies.

TAX ESTIMATES BY HUSBAND AND WIFE

¶27.7 A married couple may pay joint or separate estimated taxes. The nature of the estimated tax does not control the kind of final return you file.

Where a joint estimated tax is paid but separate tax returns are filed, you and your spouse can decide on how to divide the estimated payments between you. Either one of you can claim the whole amount, or you can agree to divide it in any proportion. If you cannot agree, the IRS will allocate the estimated taxes proportionally according to the percentage of total tax each spouse owes.

If separate estimated taxes are paid, overpayment by one spouse is not applied against an underpayment by the other when separate final returns are filed.

A joint estimated tax may be made by a husband and wife only if they are both citizens or residents of the United States. Both must have the same taxable year. A joint estimate may not be made by a couple that is divorced or legally separated under a decree. If a joint estimate is made and the spouses are divorced or legally separated later in that year, they may divide the joint payments between them under the above rule for spouses who file separately.

Responsibility for paying estimated tax rests upon each spouse individually. Each must pay if individually required by the rules.

If a joint estimated tax is made and one spouse dies, the estate does not continue to make installment payments. The surviving spouse is required to pay the remaining installments unless he or she amends; *see* ¶1.12. Amounts paid on the joint estimate may be divided as agreed upon by the spouse and the estate of the deceased. If they do not agree, the IRS will apportion the payments according to the percentage of the total tax owed by each spouse.

PART

V

PERSONAL TAX SAVINGS PLANS

The following chapters will alert you to and tell you how to take advantage of tax-saving ideas and planning strategies.

28

TAX-SAVING IDEAS AND PLANNING

Tax planning is a year-round activity. By planning income and deduction strategies, you may be able to reduce your tax. You may defer certain income to a later year in which you expect to pay a lower tax, and accelerate deductions to a higher tax year. Tax-free investments are available and, within limits, income splitting with family members may be possible.

This chapter illustrates basic tax-planning strategies. In subsequent chapters, tax-savings plans for homeowners, families, investors, and executives are discussed.

WHEN TO DEFER INCOME AND ACCELERATE DEDUCTIONS

¶28.1 When you expect to pay less tax in a future year than in a current year, consider deferring income and accelerating deductions. There are two strategies: (1) to postpone receipt of income to a year of lower tax rates, and/or (2) to claim deductions for losses and expenses in the year you are subject to the higher tax rates. In planning to defer income and accelerate deductions, however, watch these tax rule limitations.

Postponing income. You may not defer salary income by not cashing a paycheck or not taking salary that you have earned and that you can receive without restrictions. Under certain conditions, you may contract with your employer to defer the taxable receipt of current compensation to future years. To defer pay to a future period, you must take some risk. You cannot have any control over your deferred pay account. If you are not confident of your employer's ability to pay in the future, you should not defer pay.

If you are self-employed and are on the cash basis, you can defer income by delaying your billing at the end of the year or extending the time of collection. If you own a closely-held corporation, you can time the payment of dividends and bonuses.

Accelerating deductions. In accelerating deductions, there are these limitations. You may not deduct prepaid interest and rent. Prepaid interest must be deducted over the period of the loan. Rentals must also be deducted over the rental period. However, you can generally deduct prepayments of state income tax and accelerate your payments of charitable contributions. Annual subscriptions to professional journals and business magazines can be renewed before the end of the year. If the subscription is for more than a year, you may deduct only the first-year prepayment. The cost of the later subscription must be deducted in the later year. Contributions, purchases, and business expenses charged to credit card accounts are deductible in the year of charge, even though you do not pay your charge account bill until the next year. You can also realize losses by selling property which has lost value in the year you want to incur the loss.

Making an extra donation at the end of the year also may provide an added deduction which may lower your tax. You may deduct a charitable gift made by check on the last day of the year, even if the check is not cashed until the new year begins. Charitable donations may be timed to give you the largest possible tax savings. If, toward the end of the year, you find that you need an extra deduction, you may make a deductible donation in late December. Doing so would be especially beneficial if you know that your tax bracket will be lower the following year; *see* Chapter 14 for further planning details.

Also *see* Chapter 13 for claiming the standard deduction and itemizing deductions in alternate years, and Chapter 23 for planning steps when you may be subject to alternative minimum tax.

Deferring interest income to next year. Buying six-month certificates after June 30 can defer interest reporting to the next year. As a general rule, you have to report interest credited to your savings account for 1992, even though you do not present your passbook to have the amount entered. Similarly, interest coupons due and payable in 1992 are taxable on your 1992 return, regardless of when they were presented for collection. For example, a coupon due in December 1992, but presented for payment in 1993, is taxable in 1992. However, there are opportunities to defer interest in the following ways:

1. Buy a savings certificate after June 30 with a maturity of six months or more. Interest is taxable in the next year when the certificate matures, provided that interest is specifically deferred until the following year by the terms of the certificate. Your bank may offer you the choice of when to receive the interest.
2. Buy Treasury bills which come due next year. Six-month bills bought after June 30 will mature in the next year. You can make these purchases through your bank or broker.
3. Buy Series EE bonds. These bonds may be cashed for their purchase price, plus an increase in their value over stated periods of time. The increase in redemption value is taxed as interest. You may defer the interest income until the year you cash the bond or the year the bond finally matures, whichever is earlier.

Timing sales of property. A sale is generally taxable in the year title to the property passes to the buyer. Since you can control the year title passes, you can usually defer income realized on the sale to the year in which you will pay less tax.

TAX COST OF EARNING OVER THE THRESHOLDS FOR THE EXEMPTION PHASEOUT AND ITEMIZED DEDUCTION REDUCTION

¶28.2 In figuring the tax cost of earning additional income, consider the phaseout of personal exemptions (¶1.32) or the 3% reduction to itemized deductions (¶13.8). When extra income, such as from a bonus, a free-lance assignment, or a year-end sale of stock pushes you over the *threshold* for the exemption phaseout or the 3% reduction, the marginal tax rate on the extra income will be higher than the stated maximum rate of 31% for ordinary income or 28% for net capital gains. If your adjusted gross income (AGI) is already over the threshold, additional income will also be effectively taxed at more than 28% or 31% because of the exemption phaseout or the 3% reduction. By earning over a threshold amount, your taxable income is increased not only by the earnings over the threshold but also by the amounts disallowed by the phaseout or the 3% reduction.

For the 3% itemized deduction reduction on 1992 returns, the AGI threshold is $105,250, except for married persons filing separately who are subject to a $52,625 threshold.

For the exemption phaseout, the AGI threshold is $105,250 for single persons, $131,550 for heads of household, $157,900 for married persons filing jointly and qualifying widow(er)s, and $78,950 for married persons filing separately.

Effective rate increase. The amount of the increase in the effective rate due to the exemption phaseout or 3% itemized deduction reduction can be estimated by this equation:

$$\text{Increase in effective rate} = \frac{31\% \text{ of disallowed amount}}{\text{Excess income over threshold}}$$

EXAMPLE You are single with salary and taxable dividends of $95,250. You claim three personal exemptions. You have itemized deductions totaling $20,000 for taxes, interest, and charitable contributions that are subject to the 3% reduction. At the end of 1992, you make a year-end sale of securities that gives you a $34,000 net long-term capital gain, increasing your adjusted gross income (AGI) to $129,250.

By earning $24,000 over the $105,250 threshold for the 3% reduction of itemized deductions and also over the $105,250 threshold (for single persons) for the exemption phaseout, your taxable income is increased not just by $24,000 but also by the amount of the deductions that are disallowed.

Under the 3% reduction, your taxable income is increased by the $720 of itemized deductions that are disallowed under the 3% computation (3% of $129,250 AGI − $105,250 threshold = $720).

Under the phaseout rule for personal exemptions, Table 1 on page 27 shows that for AGI of $129,250, each personal exemption claimed is reduced by 20%, from $2,300 to $1,840. The phaseout reduces your deductible exemptions from $6,900 (3 × $2,300) to $5,520 (3 × $1,840). As a result, your taxable income is increased by the $1,380 of disallowed exemptions.

Thus, the $24,000 capital gain over the $105,250 threshold increases your taxable income by $26,100: the $24,000 gain plus $2,100, the $720 of disallowed itemized deductions, and the $1,380 of phased out personal exemptions.

The $24,000 gain over the threshold will be subject to the top rate of 28% net capital gain (¶5.1) but the $2,100 of additional taxable income due to the disallowed deductions will be taxed at 31%. As a result, the effective rate on the $24,000 gain is increased by approximately 2.71% from 28% to 30.71%. The 2.71% increase is figured this way:

$$\frac{31\% \times \$2,100}{\$24,000} = 2.71\%$$

Of the extra 2.71% tax, 0.93% is attributable to the reduction of itemized deductions and 1.78% is attributable to the phaseout of personal exemptions, which is about 0.59% per exemption.

The phaseout of exemptions is costly to taxpayers who claim several exemptions. The following chart shows the approximate effective tax increases for phased-out exemptions. The percentages are based on the income range of the example above. Percentages will vary slightly for other income ranges.

Exemptions phased out—	Phaseout is— Effective rate—
1	0.59%
2	1.18
3	1.77
4	2.36
5	2.95
6	3.54
7	4.13
8	4.72
9	5.31
10	5.90

Key to Tax Planning

Objective—	Explanation—
Earning tax-free income	You can earn tax-free income by— 1. Investing in tax-exempt securities. However, before you invest, determine whether the tax-free return will exceed the after-tax return of taxed income; *see* ¶30.12. 2. Taking a position in a company that pays substantial tax-free pay fringes such as health and life insurance protection. *See* Chapter 3 for a complete discussion of tax-free fringe benefits. 3. Seeking tax-free benefits offered by scholarship arrangements; *see* ¶12.4. 4. Taking a position overseas to earn up to $70,000 of tax-free pay; *see* Chapter 36.
Deferring income	You can defer income to years when you will pay less tax through— 1. Deferred pay plans which are discussed in Chapter 32. 2. Qualified retirement plans such as through Keogh plans and IRA investments; *see* Chapter 41 and Chapter 8. 3. The year-end planning techniques explained in ¶28.1. 4. Transacting installment sales when you sell property; *see* ¶5.36. 5. Investing in U.S. Savings EE bonds; *see* ¶4.28.
Income splitting	Through income splitting you divide your income among several persons or taxpaying entities that will pay an aggregate tax lower than the tax that you would pay if you reported all of the income. Although the tax law limits income-splitting opportunities, certain business and family income planning can provide tax savings. Family income planning is discussed in Chapter 33.
Tax-free exchanges	You can defer tax on appreciated property by transacting tax-free exchanges as discussed at ¶6.1 and ¶31.4.
Buying a personal residence rather than renting	Homeowners are favored by the tax law. 1. Rather than paying rent, buy a home, condominium, or cooperative apartment. You may deduct interest and taxes. When you sell your house, you may defer tax on gain. And, if you are age 55 or over, you also may take advantage of a onetime $125,000 exclusion; *see* Chapter 29. 2. Homeowners can borrow on their home equity and fully deduct interest expenses; *see* ¶15.3.

29

TAX SAVINGS FOR HOMEOWNERS

Tax on all or a part of a profit from the sale of your home may be avoided or deferred depending on your age.

If you are age 55 or over, you may elect to avoid tax on gain of up to $125,000; see ¶29.14.

If you are under age 55 or are age 55 or over and do not want to elect to avoid tax, you may defer tax by buying or building another residence. If you do not meet the deferment tests of ¶29.2, your profit is taxed. If you held the house long term, the profit is taxable as long-term capital gain.

Where some or all of the sales proceeds will be received after the year of sale and you do not qualify for deferral or elect the exclusion, your gain must be reported on the installment basis, unless you elect to report the entire gain in the year of sale. Installment sales are reported on Form 6252; see ¶5.36.

You may not deduct the loss on the sale of a personal residence. Losses on the sale of property devoted to personal use are nondeductible. However, see ¶29.12 and ¶29.13 which explain under what conditions you may claim a loss deduction on the sale of a residence which you rent out or inherit.

If you rent out residential property and you or family members also use the residence during the year, rental expenses are subject to the special restrictions discussed at ¶29.20.

Form 1099-S. Sales and exchanges of residences are reported to the IRS on Form 1099-S by the attorney or other party responsible for closing the transaction. The IRS may check your return to verify that you have reported proceeds shown on Form 1099-S.

CHECKLIST OF DEDUCTIONS FOR HOMEOWNERS

¶29.1 Some of the costs of acquiring and maintaining your personal residence or rental property are eased by deductions, such as for mortgage interest and real estate taxes. Other expenses are not deductible but are added to basis and thus reduce your taxable gain on a profitable sale of the property; see ¶29.5.

Here is how you treat residence-related expenses for tax purposes:

Closing costs when you buy your house. Most costs incurred in acquiring or buying a home are not immediately deductible, except for payments of mortgage interest and real estate taxes you paid at closing. These are listed in the settlement statement.

The following closing costs are added to the basis of the residence: appraisal fees, attorneys' fees, your payment of back taxes or interest owed by the seller, broker commissions, installation of utilities, recording charges, title searches, abstract fees, and transfer taxes.

Keep careful records of these additions to basis. When you sell the home, they reduce your taxable gain; *see* ¶29.5. The following costs are nondeductible personal expenses which do not increase basis: fire and homeowners insurance premiums, occupancy charges before closing, and sewer and water taxes.

Closing costs incurred when you sell your home reduce the selling price; see ¶29.6.

Real estate taxes. You may deduct real estate taxes in the year paid. If you include payment for real estate taxes in your monthly mortgage payment, the portion of your payment allocated to the taxes is deductible only if the bank (or other lender) has paid them over to the taxing authority by the end of the year. The amount you can deduct is shown in the year end statement from the bank.

Assessments for local benefits. Local assessments for improvements, such as for building sewer or water lines, or new streets or sidewalks, are not deductible but are added to basis.

You may deduct local taxes if they are clearly for repairs or maintenance, rather than for construction of new improvements; *see* ¶16.6.

Improvements and repairs. Repairs are nondeductible personal expenses unless they are allocable to business or rental use of the property; *see* ¶29.18 for rental expenses. The cost of permanent improvements that add to your home's value or prolong its life are added to basis. Examples of permanent improvements to your home: installing a new roof; paving your driveway; or installing new plumbing or wiring.

Casualty losses. Unreimbursed damage to your home from a fire or storm may be deductible as an itemized deduction subject to a $100 reduction and a 10% adjusted gross income floor; *see* ¶18.11.

A deductible casualty loss reduces the basis of your home.

Mortgage interest. Interest is deductible on loans up to $1 million for buying, building, or improving your principal residence and one other home. Interest on home equity loans up to $100,000 is also deductible. The $1 million and $100,000 debt limits are cut in half for married persons filing separate returns. *See* Chapter 15 for mortgage interest details.

Points. You may deduct points paid on loans to buy or improve your principal residence in the year of the payment, provided the charges are within the normal range charged in the area under established business practice. Points on any home other than your principal residence must be deducted ratably over the term of the loan.

The IRS and Tax Court do not allow an immediate deduction for points on refinancing a home mortgage unless part of the loan proceeds are used for home improvements. For example, if you use $10,000 of a $100,000 refinancing to make improvements to your principal home, 10% of the points paid are deductible. *See* ¶15.7 for more on points.

Operating expenses of rental units. If you rent out part of your home, you may deduct on Schedule E expenses allocable to the rental; *see* ¶29.18. Deductions for vacation home rentals may be limited under the rules of ¶29.20.

Home office expenses. If you are self-employed and use a room in your home exclusively as your principal place of business, expenses allocable to the office are deductible on Schedule C; *see* ¶40.11. If you are an employee, it is extremely difficult to qualify for a home office deduction; *see* ¶19.13.

DEFERRING TAX ON GAIN

THREE TESTS FOR DEFERRING TAX ON PROFITABLE SALE

¶29.2
You defer tax on the sale of residential property in which you live, if you meet these three tests:

Principal residence test—requires that you have used your old residence as your principal residence and now use or intend to use your new residence as a principal residence; *see* ¶29.3.

Time test—requires you to buy or build your new residence and use it within two years before or after you sell the old residence; *see* ¶29.4.

Investment test—requires you to buy or build a residence at a cost at least equal to the amount you received from the sale of the old residence. If the replacement property costs less, part or all of the gain is taxed; *see* ¶29.5.

If you come within the above three tests, tax deferment is mandatory. If you later sell the new residence and meet the three tests, you may defer gain on that sale as well, but only if more than two years have passed since the first sale on which gain was deferred.

Condemnation of residence. When a residence is condemned by a government authority, a homeowner may elect to treat the condemnation as a sale rather than as an involuntary conversion. Under current law, there is no advantage in making this election, as the involuntary conversion rules allow more time to replace the residence than the rules for deferral; *see* ¶18.21.

Exchanging residences. When you exchange residences, the trade is considered to be a sale of your old house and a purchase of a new house. If you make an even exchange or pay additional cash, there is no tax on the exchange. If you receive cash in addition to the new residence you generally realize taxable gain.

EXAMPLES 1. Your old house cost $158,000. You exchange it for a new house worth $161,000. You also receive $1,000 in cash. Your gain is $4,000 ($162,000 less your $158,000 cost). As you reinvest $161,000 in the new house, taxable gain is $1,000. Cost basis of the new house is $158,000 ($161,000 price less the $3,000 nontaxable gain).

2. Your old house cost $158,000. You exchanged it for a new house worth $160,000, and paid an additional $2,000. You have no taxable gain. The cost of your new house is $160,000 (the cost of your old house, $158,000, plus the $2,000 cash).

Sale of residence held by a trust. Whether the tax deferral rules apply to a sale of a residence by a trust depends on whether or not the trust is considered the owner of the trust property. If the trust is considered the owner, the tax deferment rules do not apply as the trust cannot qualify as a person who uses the residence.

In the case of a grantor trust, where the grantor is considered the owner of the trust property for tax purposes, tax deferral is allowed on the sale of a house used as the principal residence by the grantor if the trust acquires a new home which is used by the grantor as a principal residence and if the time (¶29.4) and investment (¶29.5) tests are also met.

PRINCIPAL RESIDENCE TEST

¶29.3
Deferring tax is allowed only on a sale of your principal residence that meets the time test of ¶29.4 and the investment test of ¶29.5. You may not defer tax on the profitable sale of a second house such as a summer cottage. Nor may you defer tax on the sale of a principal residence by buying a summer home; the new home must also be a principal residence.

If you own two homes and you decide to sell your principal residence and move into the second home, the cost basis of the second house is *not* considered in figuring tax deferral unless it was bought during the replacement time period. However, remodeling and capital improvement expenses made within the replacement period may be counted.

EXAMPLE The Shaws sold their house and immediately moved into a house bought 10 years earlier. They did not report gain from the sale, claiming that the cost basis of the new residence exceeded the sales price of the old house. They treated as cost the market value of the house as of the date they began using it as a principal residence. They argued that, although they owned it for 10 years, they did not acquire it for purposes of tax deferral until they began using it as a principal residence. The IRS and Tax Court held that only reconstruction expenses paid within the replacement period could be considered costs of purchasing a new residence.

Types of Qualifying Homes

Tax deferment is not restricted to one-family houses. You may defer tax on the sale and purchase of a mobile home, trailer, houseboat, cooperative apartment (tied to stock ownership), and condominium apartment, which you use as a principal residence. For example, in a private letter ruling, the IRS allowed deferral of gain recognized on the conversion of a co-op apartment to a condominium. An investment in a retirement home community does not qualify if you do not receive equity in the property.

Tax deferment also applies to your sale of a multifamily building in which you have an apartment. You may defer tax on gain allocated to your apartment; see ¶29.10. Similarly, where you actively use part of your house for business purposes, such as in operating a farm or a store while living in an apartment in the same building, an allocation is required. If part of your home was used as an office for which no deduction was allowed, no allocation is required.

If you sell your old house to one buyer and the adjacent land to another buyer, the land sale may be treated as part of the sale of your principal residence and tax on gain is deferred if the other tests are met. However, if the tract of land is substantial, the IRS may attempt to treat the sales as separate transactions. To avoid this possibility where you want to avoid or defer tax on the sale, try to arrange for the sale of the entire property to one buyer who, in turn, may sell the part he does not want to the other buyer.

If you sell only part of a lot on which your residence stands, the gain on the sale may not be postponed by reinvesting in a similar lot or by purchasing a residence. Similarly, if you sell the lot and move your house to a new lot, you may not defer gain on the sale of the old lot. The sale is not of the personal residence.

The location of the old and new residences is not relevant. Tax deferment may apply to residences in a foreign country.

Title to both the old and new home must be in your name. If you place title to the new home in someone else's name, the new home does not qualify you for deferral. An exception exists for a married couple who files a consent form; see ¶29.8.

Delay in sale of old residence after you move. When you cannot find a buyer and must move, you may face a problem in deferring tax on a later sale of the house. If you have bought a new house, there is the possibility that the sale of the old house may not occur within the time limits of ¶29.4. If you rent a new residence and delay the purchase of a new house until the sale of the old one, you may face this problem: The IRS may charge that, at the time of the sale, you no longer considered the house as your principal residence.

Temporary Rentals

You may defer tax if you move into a new home and temporarily rent out your old home while trying to sell it; see ¶29.18.

You also may defer tax in this case: You buy a new house and rent it before selling your old house that you continue to live in. You later sell your old house and move into the new house.

EXAMPLES 1. An executive left his residence in suburban New York to live in a New York City apartment near his office; he made no efforts to sell his old home for two years until just before he purchased a new home in Virginia. The Tax Court held that he had abandoned the old home as a principal residence. He timed the sale merely to take advantage of the tax deferral. In another case, a serviceman rented his residence over a six-year period until he could sell at a profit. He had refused earlier offers which would have given him a loss. The Tax Court held that he had abandoned his home as a residence.

In later decisions, the Tax Court commented that these two cases should not be interpreted as laying down a rule of law that an intention not to return to a home is, by itself, an abandonment of the home as a principal residence. Whether a homeowner has abandoned his residence is a question of fact. The absence of an intention to return is only one fact to be considered.

2. Thomas, between 1974 and 1978, lived in four different homes. One was in Springfield, Illinois, where his publishing business was located, and the other three were in Florida. He tried to defer tax on the sale of the Springfield house. The IRS disallowed the deferral, but Thomas won his case in the Tax Court by showing that in the four years before the sale, he and his family actually lived in the Springfield home more than in any of the Florida residences. The Springfield home was never rented out, its furnishings were not removed, and it was maintained by a full-time housekeeper. Even while living in Florida, Thomas spent substantial time at the Springfield home while there on business. Other Illinois contacts supported Thomas' case. He and his wife filed Illinois tax returns as full-year residents, had only Illinois driver licenses, and contributed to and attended the church in Springfield.

TIME TEST

¶29.4 If you buy or build a new home, you must do so and *begin to use it* within two years before or after you sell your old one. The two-year period is suspended for workers abroad and members of the armed services, as discussed below. The time test is strictly applied; failure to comply will not be excused for any reason.

A contract to purchase a new home is not sufficient to satisfy the time test. A sale is considered to occur at the earlier of the passage of title or the assumption of the benefits and burdens of ownership.

When you build, you must complete construction and occupy the house within the two-year period.

EXAMPLES 1. Bayley sold his house at a profit, started construction on a new house, and elected to defer tax. The new house was not completed before the end of the required time period. A day before the end of the period, Bayley moved some of his furniture into the house but could not live there. The house had no water or sewage connections. He finally moved in two months later. The IRS taxed the gain because the house had not been timely occupied. The Tax Court agreed. Bayley had made the necessary investment but failed to meet the requirement of occupying the house.

2. The Lokans bought land to farm and build a new home. Several months later, they sold their old house at a profit. During construction,

they set up a trailer on the property. When one bedroom and a bath in the new house was completed, three children slept in the house; they, plus one other child, slept in the trailer. The house was not fully completed until three years after the sale. The IRS and the Tax Court held that the Lokans did not reside in the new house; the trailer was their principal residence.

Surviving spouse. If a married couple reports a sale on a joint return and one spouse dies before a new residence is purchased during the two-year period, the surviving spouse may defer tax on the original sale by making the purchase within the period.

Deferment for Workers Abroad

If your tax home (¶20.6) is outside the United States, the replacement period is suspended while you are abroad. The suspension applies only if your stay abroad began before the end of the replacement period and lasts until you return from abroad or until four years after the sale, whichever occurs first. Your spouse is also protected by the suspension provided that you both used the old home and new home as your principal residence.

Deferment on entering the Armed Forces. If you go on active duty for more than 90 days, the two-year replacement period is suspended while you are in the service. The suspension applies only if your service began before the end of the two-year replacement period. The suspension generally lasts until your discharge, when the balance of the two-year replacement period starts to run again. However, regardless of the length of service, the replacement period ends four years after the date of sale. Thus, even if you remain in the service, you must buy and live in your new home no more than four years after you sell your old home. If you are stationed outside the U.S. on extended duty or have to live in government quarters at a remote site after returning from a tour of duty outside the U.S., the replacement period may extend beyond the four-year period. For sales after July 18, 1984, the replacement period is suspended while you are at the foreign or remote site plus one year after the last day you were so stationed. However, the replacement period ends on the date which is eight years after the sale. If your spouse is in the armed forces and you are not, you are also protected by the suspension if you jointly owned the old home and both you and your spouse used the old home and new home as principal residences. If you divorce or separate during the suspension period, your replacement period starts to run again the day after the divorce or separation.

INVESTMENT TEST

¶29.5

To defer tax on the full amount of gain from the sale of your principal residence, you must buy another principal residence, and your investment must generally equal or exceed the net sales price of your old home.

You first have to figure your *actual gain* by subtracting *basis* for the sold house from the *amount realized* on the sale. Then, to determine how much of the actual gain may be deferred, you have to figure the *adjusted sales price* and also the *cost of the new home.* If the cost of the new home equals or exceeds the adjusted sales price, no part of the gain is taxable in the year of sale; that is, 100% of your gain is deferred. If the cost of the new house is less than the adjusted sales price, the difference is generally taxable; *see* Example 1 on page 303. The key terms *basis, amount realized, adjusted sales price,* and *cost of the new home* are explained in this section.

Amount realized. This is the selling price of your old house less selling expenses for commissions, advertising, preparing the deed,

and other legal and title services. "Points" paid by you as the seller also reduce the selling price. Transfer taxes, stamp taxes, or similar taxes are selling expenses that reduce the amount realized; do not deduct them as taxes on Schedule A. If the taxes are incurred in a job-related move and you deduct the costs as moving expenses (*see* ¶21.5 for limitations), you may not also use them to reduce the amount realized on the sale or to increase basis of the new home.

The selling price includes the amount of the mortgages on the old house, whether the buyer has assumed or bought the property subject to them. If immediately after the sale you discount notes received on a deferred payment contract, include the discounted value of the notes, not the face amounts.

Do not include amounts received for furnishings, such as rugs and furniture, sold with the house. Profit on a sale of furnishings is reported separately; a loss is not deductible.

Basis. The basis of the old house is the original cost, including legal and recording fees, transfer taxes, and other expenses paid when you bought the house, plus the cost of home improvements. You must reduce this amount by any depreciation or casualty loss deductions, or energy credits claimed in prior years, and also by any deferred gains from prior home sales.

Adjusted sales price. This is the amount realized less *fix-up costs* spent to make your old house saleable, like papering, painting, and similar repairs. To qualify as fix-up costs, the work must be done within the 90-day period ending on the day on which the contract to sell is entered into and paid for within 30 days after the sale.

If you do not buy or build a house within the rules explained in this section, you may not deduct fix-up costs from the amount realized. Nor may you deduct them separately on your tax return. Furthermore, fix-up costs do not include costs of permanent improvements spent to clinch a sale, for example, installing a new roof or furnace. Such improvements are capital expenditures added to the cost basis of the old house.

Cost of the new house. You are not required to reinvest the actual cash proceeds of the sale of your old house. You may buy the new house with a small cash payment plus a large mortgage loan. The cost of the new house includes not only cash payments but also any mortgages you assume or take subject to. Also include purchase expenses such as broker's commissions, title search, transfer taxes, and lawyer's fees. Points on the purchase of a principal residence are generally immediately deductible and not added to basis; *see* ¶15.7.

If you reinvest proceeds in two homes, you may not figure the investment in both houses. You consider only the investment in your new principal residence.

The present value of future land lease payments may not be added to the cost of your new house.

Construction costs. When you build a house, include all costs paid for construction of the house during the two years prior to the sale and two years after the sale. Costs paid after the two-year period are not included even if you have incurred liability for them before the end of the two-year period. However, these costs do become a part of the cost of the new house to figure gain or loss if you later sell it. If you inherit or receive as a gift all or part of a new home, do not count the value of that part in figuring whether you have reinvested your gain on the sale of your old residence. However, you may include costs of reconstructing an inherited house to make it habitable.

Remodeling a vacation home as a permanent residence. A couple, planning to sell their principal home and remodel their vacation home into a permanent residence, asked the IRS if the remodeling costs could be considered as a purchase of a new residence. They planned to add 35% more living space by converting storage space to living areas, putting in a new roof, installing heating and air conditioning systems, and expanding the basement. The IRS answered that the remodeling qualified because of the substantial structural alterations. Furthermore, the remodeling costs were to be paid within the qualifying replacement period discussed at ¶29.4.

The IRS warned that merely adding a tennis court, pool, or new roof would not have qualified for tax deferral. However, once the major alterations are made, all improvements, such as the construction of a pool, could be considered part of the total cost of the renovation.

Cost basis of a cooperative apartment. In addition to the cash paid for the stock in the cooperative, include your share of the cooperative's outstanding mortgage, determined as of the date you purchased the stock if these three tests are met:

1. The mortgage is properly allocated to your apartment. (The IRS will accept a mortgage allocation based on the same ratio as your stock interest bears to the total value of all the stock in the corporation.)
2. The corporation retains your stock as a pledge for payment of your annual charges such as interest and principal payments on the mortgage.
3. Your share of corporate assets will be reduced by the unpaid balance of your proportionate share of the mortgage if the corporation is liquidated.

How Much Gain Can You Defer?

Compare the adjusted sales price with the cost of the new house. If the cost of the new house is the same or greater than the adjusted sales price of the old house, then none of the actual gain is taxed. But if the cost of the new house is less than the adjusted sales price, you are taxed on the difference—but not on more than your actual gain; *see* Example 1.

Cost basis of the new home. If your gain is completely or partially deferred, basis of the new home is reduced by the non-taxed gain. *See* Example 1 below. Because of this basis reduction rule, deferred gain may eventually be taxed if you later sell the new home and do not replace it. *See* Example 2 in the next column.

EXAMPLES 1. You are under age 55. You plan to sell your house, which has a basis of $124,500. To make it more attractive to buyers, you paint the outside at a cost of $800 in April 1992. You pay for the painting when the work is finished. In May 1992, you sell the house for $175,000. Broker's commissions and other selling expenses are $11,500. In October 1992, you buy a new house for $161,000. This is how you compute the amount realized, the adjusted sales price, gain taxable on your 1992 return, and your basis in the replacement property:

Selling price	$175,000
Less: Selling expenses	11,500
Amount realized	$163,500
Less: Basis of old house	124,500
Actual gain	$ 39,000
Amount realized	$163,500
Less: Fix-up costs	800
Adjusted sales price	$162,700
Less: Cost of new house	161,000
Taxable gain	$ 1,700

Of the $39,000 gain, $1,700 is taxable in 1992; the balance, $37,300, is not taxable. The cost basis of the new house is reduced by the deferred gain, giving you a basis of $123,700 ($161,000 − $37,300).

The Form 2119 worksheet on page 304 shows how gain on the sale and basis of the new home is figured.

2. Same facts as in Example 1, except that in 1993 you sell the new house for $161,000 and move to a rental apartment. Taxable gain is $37,300:

Selling price	$161,000
Less: Cost basis	123,700
Taxed gain	$ 37,300

The exact amount of additional gain would have been taxed on the sale of your old house if you had not bought the second house. In other words, you merely deferred tax on the sale of your first house until you sold the new house without a further replacement.

Loss on repayment of foreign mortgage. If you sell a foreign residence at a gain but incur a loss in the repayment of the mortgage because of currency fluctuations, you may not offset the loss against the gain. The loss is not deductible.

REVIEWING PURCHASE AND SALES RECORDS

¶**29.6** Arrange your records into three groups: (1) records of the purchase of the old house and improvements; (2) records of the sale of your old house; and (3) records of the new purchase.

Energy conserving capital improvements do not increase your basis to the extent of an energy credit claimed. The basis of your old house is the total costs shown by these records. If you deduct a casualty loss for damage incurred to your house, the basis of the house should be reduced by the amount deducted.

Sale of old house. You should have: (1) the sales contract showing the sales price of the old house; (2) a statement showing settlement costs at the closing and allocating taxes and fire insurance; (3) the bill and record of payment of legal fees; (4) records of payment of broker's fees, if any; (5) a closing statement from the bank holding the mortgage on your old house showing final interest charges up to the date of transfer of title and prepayment penalties, if any; (6) if you incurred fix-up costs, records of when the work was done and when payment was made; and (7) a record of payments for advertising the sale of the house, if any.

You reduce the selling price of the house by payments for broker's commissions, legal fees, and advertising expenses. The allocated property taxes are deducted according to the rules at ¶16.8. Mortgage interest and any prepayment penalty are deductible as interest if you itemize deductions. You may not deduct fire insurance premium payments. The treatment of fix-up costs is explained at ¶29.5. The paying off of the principal balance of the mortgage to the bank does not enter into the tax computation.

Proving Costs of Old House

Your records here should show the purchase price of the old house plus title insurance fees, recording fees, transfer taxes, and attorney's fees. Also, bills or other records detailing capital improvements made to the house for additional rooms, equipment, landscaping, and similar capital items. In one case, an accountant forgot to keep adequate records. He bought his house for $5,000 and later sold it for $11,000. In figuring his taxable gain, he claimed he had spent $5,000 for improvements; the IRS allowed him only $2,750. A court permitted him to increase his cost by $4,000. While his proof was not adequate, he was able to show that the house was in dilapidated condition when he bought it. The court estimated that he spent at least $4,000 to make the house habitable.

Worksheet for Form 2119 (Lines on 1992 format may vary.)

Part I	**General Information**		
1a	Date your former main home was sold (month, day, year) . . . . ▶	**1a**	5 / 12 / 92
b	Face amount of any mortgage, note (e.g., second trust), or other financial instrument on which you will get periodic payments of principal or interest from this sale (see instructions) . . .	**1b**	
2	Have you bought or built a new main home?		☑ Yes ☐ No
3	Is or was any part of either main home rented out or used for business? (If "Yes," see instructions.) . .		☐ Yes ☑ No

Part II	**Gain on Sale** (Do not include amounts you deduct as moving expenses.)		
4	Selling price of home. (Do not include personal property items that you sold with your home.)	**4**	175,000
5	Expense of sale. (Include sales commissions, advertising, legal, etc.)	**5**	11,500
6	Amount realized. Subtract line 5 from line 4	**6**	163,500
7	Basis of home sold (see instructions)	**7**	124,500
8a	**Gain on sale.** Subtract line 7 from line 6	**8a**	39,000

- If line 8a is zero or less, stop here and attach this form to your return.
- If line 2 is "Yes," you **must** go to Part III or Part IV, whichever applies. Otherwise, go to line 8b.

b If you haven't replaced your home, do you plan to do so within the replacement period (see instructions)? ☐ Yes ☐ No
- If "Yes," stop here, attach this form to your return, and see **Additional Filing Requirements** in the instructions.
- If "No," you **must** go to Part III or Part IV, whichever applies.

Part III	**One-Time Exclusion of Gain for People Age 55 or Older** (If you are not taking the exclusion, go to Part IV now.)		
9a	Who was age 55 or older on date of sale?. . . . . ☐ You ☐ Your spouse		☐ Both of you
b	Did the person who was age 55 or older own and use the property as his or her main home for a total of at least 3 years (except for short absences) of the 5-year period before the sale? (If "No," go to Part IV now.)		☐ Yes ☐ No
c	**If line 9b is "Yes,"** do you elect to take the one-time exclusion? (If "No," go to Part IV now.) . . .		☐ Yes ☐ No
d	At time of sale, who owned the home? . . . . ☐ You ☐ Your spouse		☐ Both of you
e	Social security number of spouse at time of sale if you had a different spouse from the one above at time of sale. (If you were not married at time of sale, enter "None.") . . . . . ▶	**9e**	
f	**Exclusion.** Enter the **smaller** of line 8a or $125,000 ($62,500, if married filing separate return)	**9f**	

Part IV	**Adjusted Sales Price, Taxable Gain, and Adjusted Basis of New Home**		
10	Subtract line 9f from line 8a	**10**	39,000

- If line 10 is zero, stop here and attach this form to your return.
- If line 2 is "Yes," go to line 11 now.
- If you are reporting this sale on the installment method, stop here and see the line 1b instructions.
- All others, stop here and **enter the amount from line 10 on Schedule D, line 2 or line 9.**

11	Fixing-up expenses (see instructions for time limits)	**11**	800
12	**Adjusted sales price.** Subtract line 11 from line 6	**12**	162,700
13a	Date you moved into new home (month, day, year) ▶ 10 / 14 / 92 **b** Cost of new home	**13b**	161,000
14a	Add line 9f and line 13b	**14a**	161,000
b	Subtract line 14a from line 12. If the result is zero or less, enter -0-	**14b**	1,700
c	**Taxable gain.** Enter the **smaller** of line 10 or line 14b	**14c**	1,700

- If line 14c is zero, go to line 15 and attach this form to your return.
- If you are reporting this sale on the installment method, see the line 1b instructions and go to line 15.
- All others, **enter the amount from line 14c on Schedule D, line 2 or line 9,** and go to line 15.

15	Postponed gain. Subtract line 14c from line 10	**15**	37,300
16	**Adjusted basis of new home.** Subtract line 15 from line 13b	**16**	123,700

Purchase of the new residence. Here you should have (1) your contract showing the cost of the new house plus any additional improvements; and (2) the closing statement showing title insurance fees, adjustment of taxes, mortgage fees, and recording fees.

The cost basis of your new house includes the purchase price (even though all or part is covered by a mortgage), attorney's fees, mortgage fees, title insurance fees, and recording fees less the gain not taxed on the sale of your old home. Deduct taxes according to the allocation rules at ¶16.8. The payment of fire insurance premiums on the house is not deductible. The treatment of "points" is discussed at ¶15.7.

REPORTING RESIDENCE SALES ON YOUR RETURN

¶29.7 Report the details of a 1992 sale of a principal residence on Form 2119, which must be attached to Form 1040. On Form 2119, you compute gain or loss on the sale. If you bought another principal residence, you figure whether all of the gain is deferred and also the basis of the new residence on Form 2119. The exclusion for sellers age 55 or over (¶29.14) is also claimed on Form 2119. If you do not qualify for tax deferral or the exclusion, taxable gain from Form 2119 is entered on Schedule D.

If by the time you file your return you have already purchased a new home, details of the purchase are shown on Form 2119. You qualify for deferral if the cost of the new home equals or exceeds the adjusted sale price of the old home.

If you plan to buy a new home within the two-year replacement period but have not yet done so when you file your 1992 return, you indicate your intention on Form 2119; you do not have to report the gain from the sale on your 1992 return. If you later make a timely replacement that qualifies for full deferral (purchase price exceeds adjusted sales price of old home), you should notify the IRS and attach a new Form 2119 for 1992. If the purchase price of a replacement home does not at least equal the adjusted sales price of the old home, or if you do not make a timely replacement, you must file an amended return on Form 1040X to report taxable gain for 1992 and attach a new Form 2119 and Schedule D; you will also owe interest on the tax due. You may also file an amended return to claim a refund if you paid tax on a 1992 gain and later buy a new home within the two-year replacement period.

The IRS may tax you on the unreported gain from the sale of your residence during a three-year period that starts when you notify the IRS on Form 2119 of the cost of your new residence, your intention not to buy one, or your failure to acquire one before the required time limit. In the absence of notice, the IRS may assess the tax on unreported taxable gain at any time.

Federal Subsidy Recapture

If after 1990 your home was financed with the proceeds of a tax-exempt bond or a qualified mortgage credit certificate (¶15.1) and you sell or dispose of the home within nine years of the financing, you may have to recapture the federal subsidy received. Use Form 8828 to figure the amount of the recapture tax, which is reported on Form 1040 as a separate tax.

DEFERRAL FOR MARRIED AND DIVORCED COUPLES

¶29.8 If you are married and title to your new house differs from title to your old house, you and your spouse should file a consent statement to defer tax. This situation arises when you or your spouse individually held title to the old house and now you both hold title jointly to the new house, *or* title to the old house was in your joint names and now only one of you holds title to the new house. The consent, signed by both spouses, may be written on Form 2119 or an attached statement. By consenting, you both agree to divide the gain from the old house and to reduce the basis of the new home by the deferred gain. Consents are ineffective to defer tax unless the old and new houses were principal residences of both spouses.

EXAMPLES 1. John Smith holds title to his condominium apartment. Its cost basis is $70,000. He sells the apartment for an adjusted sales price of $80,000 and realizes $10,000 gain. However, within the year, he and his wife, Alice, contribute $40,000 each to buy a new house for $80,000 in their joint names. John pays no tax on the gain if he and Alice file consent statements in which they agree to allocate the basis of the new house between them. They file the consent on Form 2119 or on an attached statement in the year that gain on the sale is realized. John and Alice each have a $35,000 basis in the new house—$80,000 cost, minus $10,000 deferred gain, divided by two.

If the consent was not filed, John's entire gain of $10,000 would be taxable, since the adjusted sales price of $80,000 exceeded by more than $10,000 his $40,000 share of the cost of the new home; *see* ¶29.5.

2. Same facts as in the above example except the condominium was owned jointly by John and Alice, and the new house is bought by Alice alone and placed in her name. Tax on the gain is deferred if both sign a consent statement. The basis of the new house to Alice is $70,000. Without the consent, only Alice would qualify for deferral, since she reinvested in a new home. John, who did not reinvest, would be taxed on his half of the gain from the old house.

Surviving spouses. Consent requirements are deemed satisfied if one spouse dies after the sale of the old home and before a new home is purchased, and if the surviving spouse purchases and occupies a new principal residence within the replacement period.

Couple replacing premarriage homes with single home. If you and your spouse sell separate homes owned before marriage, tax on the gain from both sales is postponed if the combined adjusted sales prices of the two sales is reinvested in a new home within the time limit, you each contribute one-half the purchase price, and you take joint title to the new home. No consent statement is required. Report each sale on a separate Form 2119, attached to your joint return.

Separated couples. If you and your spouse agree to live apart, sell your jointly owned home, and buy and live in separate new homes, you may each be able to defer tax. You each report the sale on Form 2119 as if two separate homes were sold. For example, assume that under state law, each of you is entitled to half the proceeds. On Form 2119, you each report half of the sales price. If the cost of your new home exceeds your respective half of the old home's adjusted sales price, you defer tax on your half of the gain. The same deferral test applies to your spouse.

Divorce after reporting sale on joint return. If a married couple elects to defer tax on a joint return by indicating on Form 2119 that they plan to buy a replacement residence, and then they are divorced, the home sale deferral rules apply separately to each ex-spouse. If within two years of the sale the wife buys a new home and spends at least her share of the adjusted sales price of the old home (sales price less selling expenses less fix-up costs), she can defer her share of the tax. The same is true for her ex-husband. Each spouse who reinvests should follow the reporting rules in ¶29.7.

However, if one spouse reinvests in a new home within two years and the other does not, the IRS could assess the tax due on the non-deferred portion of the sale proceeds against either spouse. The spouse who *does* reinvest could still be held liable because both spouses are liable for any tax owed on a sale that was originally reported on a joint return. To avoid this possibility, a couple that is contemplating divorce when they sell their home might consider filing separate tax returns in the year of sale. If they file jointly, one option may be to place the sales proceeds in escrow until the replacement period ends, with each spouse's share of any tax due to come from the escrow fund before division of sale proceeds. If the proceeds are divided before a divorce agreement is finalized and one spouse will be paying alimony, a provision in the agreement could note the prospective tax liabilities on the sale of the house and allow the spouse paying alimony to reduce future alimony payments by any tax liability on the sale that is owed but not paid by the other spouse.

EXAMPLE A couple reported on their 1983 joint return a $150,000 profit on the sale of their jointly-owned home. They did not pay an immediate tax for they indicated on Form 2119 that they anticipated buying a new home within two years. The adjusted sales price of the house was $300,000. They divorced in 1984, and in 1985, the husband bought a new home for $120,000; the wife did not buy a new home within two years. Their divorce agreement provided that each spouse would be responsible for half of any tax due in the event that the taxable gain was not completely deferred. The husband wanted to amend the 1983 joint return in order to report as income the $30,000 difference between the cost of his new home ($120,000) and his half of the adjusted sales price of the old home ($150,000, half of $300,000). The IRS said that he also had to include his wife's $75,000 share of the original gain since he was jointly and severally liable with her for any tax due. He also had to pay interest on the total tax due. If the wife cannot be located, or refuses to sign the amended joint return, the husband must explain this on the amended joint return.

In this case, the husband would have to sue the wife under the divorce agreement to recover the tax payment attributable to her failure to buy a new home within two years.

MORE THAN ONE UNIT
SOLD IN TWO YEARS

¶29.9 Under current law, tax may not be deferred on a home sale if, within two years before the sale, you previously deferred tax on a profitable sale of another principal residence. However, this rule does not apply if you moved to a new job location; *see* Example 2.

When this book went to press, Congress was considering legislation that would allow deferral for more than one sale within two years even if not job related. See the Supplement for legislative developments.

EXAMPLES 1. In August 1991, you sell your house at a profit and buy a new principal residence with the sale proceeds in the same month. In July 1992, you sell the new residence at a profit and buy another principal residence in September 1992. You may not defer tax on the July 1992 sale because it was within two years of the August 1991 sale. The house purchased in September 1992 is treated as a new principal residence for purposes of postponing tax on the gain on the August 1991 sale.

2. Same facts as in Example 1, but you had to sell your house in July 1992 because of a job relocation to a new city 500 miles away from your prior area of work and residence. Your moving expenses also meet the other tests of ¶21.5. You may defer tax on the sale made in August 1991 and the sale made in July 1992. For deferring tax on the August 1991 sale, you compare the cost of the residence bought in August 1991 with the adjusted sales price of the residence sold in August 1991. To defer tax on the July 1992 sale, compare the cost of the residence bought in September 1992 with the adjusted sales price of the house sold in July 1992.

When you buy a new residence before the sale of the old house and then sell the new house, you may not defer tax on a subsequent sale of the original house, even if all sales and purchases fall within two years. To defer tax on the sale of the original house, you must own the new house at the time of the sale of the old house.

EXAMPLE You own a house which cost $100,000. In January, you buy another house for $110,000. In July, you sell the house you bought in January for $112,000. In October, you sell your original house for $120,000. You have a $20,000 taxed gain on the October sale. Even though you bought another residence within two years before the October sale, you sold that new residence before you sold the original residence. So you may not avoid tax and have a $2,000 gain on the July sale.

SALE OF HOUSE USED
PARTLY FOR BUSINESS

¶29.10 If in the year of sale, you use part of your residence for business or rental to tenants, you treat the sale as if you sold two separate pieces of property. You apportion the sales price and basis of the house between the rented portion and the residential portion. You deduct depreciation from only the rented part.

You do not pay tax on gain allocated to your personal use of the house if your reinvestment in a new residence is at least equal to the selling price of the portion of the old house allocated to your personal use. Similarly, if only part of the new property is used as your personal residence, only the cost allocated to that use is considered as reinvested for purposes of deferring tax on gain.

If you have a *loss* on the sale, a loss allocated to rental use is deductible on Form 4797. A loss on the personal part is not deductible, but must be reported to the IRS on Form 2119.

EXAMPLES 1. You sell for $97,000 a three-family house that cost you $33,000. Selling expenses (commissions and legal fees) were $7,000. You lived in one of the apartments. You rented the other two. On the rental part, you took $4,400 of straight-line depreciation. You compute your gain by allocating two-thirds of the selling price and cost to the rental part and one-third to the personal part:

		Rental	Personal
Net sales price ($97,000 − $7,000)		$60,000	$30,000
Cost ($33,000)	$22,000		
Less: Depreciation	4,400	17,600	11,000
Net gain		$42,400	$19,000

You pay tax on the gain of $42,400, which is reported on Form 4797. Only the residential portion is reported on Form 2119. You defer tax on the gain of $19,000 if you invest at least $30,000 in a new residence or you buy a new multifamily house and the cost allocated to your apartment is at least $30,000. If you are age 55 or over, you may elect under ¶29.14 to avoid tax on the personal profit even though you do not make a reinvestment.

2. Same facts as in Example 1, except the net selling price is only $30,000. Here you have a gain of $2,400 ($20,000 − $17,600) on the rental part and a loss of $1,000 on the residential part ($10,000 − $11,000). You may not offset the $1,000 loss against the gain. Each is treated as a separate transaction. The loss is not deductible because it is a personal loss.

Business office in your home. Tax treatment depends on whether or not in the year of sale, your home office use qualified for a deduction. If it did, you treat the sale as if you sold two separate properties. You allocate the sales price and basis between the space used for the office and residence. The residence portion is reported on Form 2119; the office portion on Form 4797. Gain on the office part is not deferrable. If you did not use the office for business in the year of sale or the office did not qualify for a deduction because it was *not* exclusively used as a principal place of business or place for seeing clients, patients, or customers, a full tax deferral is allowed. In figuring gain, reduce basis by depreciation claimed for the office in prior years.

SELLING YOUR HOUSE AT A LOSS

NO LOSS ALLOWED ON PERSONAL RESIDENCE

¶29.11 A loss on the sale of your principal residence is not deductible. However, you must still report the sale on Form 2119 and attach it to Form 1040. Do not claim the loss on Schedule D. If part of your principal residence was used for business in the year of sale, treat the sale as if two pieces of property were sold (¶29.10). Report the personal part on Form 2119 and the business part on Form 4797. A loss is deductible only on the business part.

See the Supplement for the status of pending legislation that would allow a loss on the sale of a principal residence to be added to the basis of another home bought within the two-year replacement period.

If you sell at a loss a second home or vacation home (not your principal residence) that was used entirely for personal purposes, the loss is reported on Schedule D, even though it is not deductible. Instead of entering the amount of the loss in column (f) of Schedule D, write "Personal Loss." If in the year of sale part of the home was rented out or used for business, allocate the sale between the personal part and the rental or business part; report the personal part on Schedule D; the rental or business part on Form 4797.

Losses allowed. A loss may be claimed if you sell a house that has been converted from personal to rental use; see ¶29.12. A loss may also be claimed on the sale of a house received as an inheritance or gift if you immediately put it up for sale or rental; *see* ¶29.13.

LOSS ON RESIDENCE CONVERTED TO RENTAL PROPERTY

¶29.12 You are not allowed to deduct a loss on the sale of your personal residence. If you convert the house from personal use to rental use you may claim a loss on a sale if the value has declined below the basis fixed for the residence as rental property.

Basis on the conversion to rental property is the *lower* of (1) your adjusted basis for the house at the time of conversion, or (2) the fair market value at the time of conversion. To deduct a loss, you have to be able to show that the conversion date basis exceeds the sales price. For example, if you paid $200,000 for your home and convert it to rental property when the value has declined to $150,000, your basis for the rental property is $150,000. If the property continues to decline in value, and you sell for $125,000, you may claim a loss of $25,000 ($150,000 – $125,000). Your loss deduction will not reflect the $50,000 loss occurring before the conversion.

Profit-making purposes. Renting a residence is a changeover from personal to profit-making purposes. If the house is merely put up for rent or has an isolated rental of several months, it may not be recognized by the IRS as being converted to rental property.

The Tax Court has approved a loss deduction where a house was rented on a 90-day lease with an option to buy. The court set down the following two tests for determining when a house is converted to rental property: (1) the rental charge returns a profit; and (2) the lease prevents you from using or reoccupying the house during the lease period. Under the Tax Court approach, you have a conversion if you have a lease that gives possession of the house to the tenant during the lease period, and if the rent, after deducting taxes, interest, insurance, repairs, depreciation, and other charges, returns you a profit.

Temporary Rental Before Sale

A rental loss may be barred on temporary rental before sale. The IRS and Tax Court held that where a principal residence was rented for several months while being offered for sale, the rental did not convert the home to rental property. Tax on a profitable sale could be deferred if a replacement home was purchased (¶29.5), but deductions for rental expenses were limited to rental income; no loss could be claimed. A federal appeals court disagreed and allowed both tax deferral and a rental loss deduction; also *see* ¶29.20.

Loss allowed on house bought for resale. A loss deduction is also allowed where you acquired the house as an investment with the intention of selling it at a profit even though you occupied it incidentally as a residence prior to sale, as in the following examples.

EXAMPLES 1. An owner bought a house with the intention of selling it. He lived in it for six years, but during that period it was for sale. He was allowed to deduct the loss on its sale by proving he lived in it to protect it from vandalism and to keep it in good condition so it would be attractive to possible buyers.

2. An architect and builder built a house and offered it for sale through an agent and advertisements. He had a home and no intention to occupy the new house. On a realtor's advice, he moved into the house to make it more saleable. Ten months later, he sold the house at a loss of $4,065 and promptly moved out. The loss was allowed on proof that his main purpose in building and occupying the house was to realize a profit by a sale; the residential use was incidental.

Stock in cooperative apartment. Normally, you get no deduction for a loss on the sale of your stock in a cooperative housing corporation. It makes no difference that you occasionally sublet your apartment. It is still not considered property used in a business. But you may get a loss deduction when there were nonstockholder tenants in the cooperative housing corporation when you bought your stock. Then, you get a partial capital loss deduction if you sell your stock or if it becomes worthless. To figure capital loss—

First find the difference between your cost and your selling price. This would ordinarily be your capital loss. Then, find the percentage of nonstockholding tenants (based on rental values) in the housing corporation when you bought your stock.

Apply this percentage to the loss you figured above. This is the capital loss you are allowed.

See ¶29.19 for when depreciation may be taken on the basis of the cooperative stock ownership.

Gain on rented residence. You have a gain on the sale of rental property if you sell for more than your adjusted basis at the time of conversion, plus subsequent capital improvements, and minus depreciation and casualty loss deductions. The sale is subject to the rules of Chapter 44 for depreciable property.

Partially Rented Home

You may deduct a loss on a home sale if you rented part and occupied part for your own purposes. A loss on a sale is allowable on the rented portion. You report the sale as if two properties were sold. The residential part is reported on Form 2119; the rental part on Form 4797.

LOSS ON RESIDENCE ACQUIRED BY GIFT OR INHERITANCE

¶29.13 You may deduct a loss on the sale of a house which was received as an inheritance or gift if you personally did not use it and you offered it for sale or rental immediately or within a few weeks after acquisition.

If you inherit a residence in which you do not intend to live, it may be advisable to put it up for rent for an ordinary loss deduction. If you merely try to sell, and you finally do so at a loss, you are limited to a capital loss.

EXAMPLES 1. A couple owned a winter vacation home in Florida. When the husband died, his wife immedi- ately put the house up for sale and never lived in it. It was sold at a loss. The IRS disallowed the capital loss deduction, claiming it was personal and nondeductible. The wife argued that her case was no different from the case of an heir inheriting and selling a home, since at the death of her husband her interest in the property was increased. The court agreed with her reasoning and allowed the capital loss deduction.

2. A widow inherited a house owned by her late husband and rented out by his estate. Shortly after getting title to the house, she sold it at a loss which she deducted as an ordinary loss. The IRS limited her to a capital loss deduction. The Tax Court agreed. She could not show any business activity. She did not negotiate the lease with the tenant who was in the house when she received title. She never arranged any maintenance or repairs for the building. Moreover, she sold the property shortly after receiving title which indicates she viewed the house as investment, not rental property.

$125,000 EXCLUSION FOR HOMESELLERS AGE 55 OR OVER

QUALIFYING FOR THE EXCLUSION

¶29.14 If you are 55 years of age or older and sell or exchange your home at a profit, you may avoid tax on profits up to $125,000 ($62,500 for married persons filing separately). To claim this exclusion, you must (1) elect to avoid tax on Form 2119; (2) be age 55 or over on the date of sale; and (3) have owned and occupied the house as your principal residence for at least three of the five years ending on the day of sale. The age, ownership and use tests are discussed below. For sales after July 26, 1978, the election may be claimed only once. An election is allowed if you excluded gain under prior law rules for sales before July 27, 1978.

Married couples are subject to special exclusion rules; *see* ¶29.15.

The election applies to cooperative apartment ownership tied to stock ownership and to condominiums. It also applies to gain realized from an involuntary conversion of your home through fire, storm or other casualty, or condemnation. Although you avoid tax on gain, you consider the gain as gross income in determining whether you are required to file a return.

The election to exclude gain does not apply where only a partial interest in the home is sold. In a private letter ruling, the IRS refused to permit an exclusion to a homeowner who sold the remainder interest in her home while retaining the right to live in it for life. However, the exclusion is allowed if a homeowner gives away a remainder interest in the house and then sells the retained life interest. The exclusion may be claimed because the life interest is the owner's entire interest in the residence.

Age test. You must be age 55 or over by the date of sale. It is not sufficient that you will be age 55 sometime during the year in which the sale occurs. A sale on the date of your 55th birthday qualifies.

If you receive an offer that you want to accept before your 55th birthday, contract to sell but do not give title or possession until you are age 55 if you want to make the election. A sale may be considered to have occurred for tax purposes when you give the buyer possession of the house, although you have not formally passed title.

The use and ownership test. You must have owned *and* occupied your home as your principal residence for at least three out of the five years ending on the date of sale. Ownership and use for 36 full months or for 1,095 days (365 × 3) during the five-year period qualifies. The three years need not be consecutive, and the periods of use and ownership may be different. Short, temporary absences for vacations are counted as periods of use, even if the house is rented while you are away.

However, if you are away from the house for a more substantial period, such as a job transfer or sabbatical lasting a year or more, the IRS will not treat that period as your use of the home.

 CAUTION **Rentals In Five-Year Period**

Rental of the house while you are away on vacation or other seasonal absences during the five-year period preceding the date of sale will not disqualify the election. Where you rent your house for longer periods and you want to avail yourself of the tax-free election, make sure that a rental during the five-year period does not exceed two years. If it does, the three-year residence test will not be met.

Disabled owners. If an illness requires an owner to move to a nursing home or similar state or city-licensed facility because of mental or physical disability, the period in the facility may be counted as "use" of the residence as long as the person owned and used the residence for at least one year during the five-year period preceding the sale.

EXAMPLES 1. You are over age 55. You bought your principal residence in 1970. On January 1, 1991, you move to another state and rent the house. On July 1, 1992, you sell it. You may elect tax-free gain. You owned and used the house as your principal residence for three out of the five years preceding the sale.

2. You are age 62 and have lived with your son and daughter-in-law since 1985. Your son owned the house until you bought it from him in January 1990. You sell it on March 31, 1992. You may not make the election in 1992. Although you used the property as your principal residence for more than three years, you did not own it for three of the five years preceding the date of the sale.

3. On January 1, 1989, a teacher, age 55, bought and moved into a house which he used as his principal residence. On February 1, 1991, he went abroad on a one-year sabbatical and, during part of the year, leased the house. On March 1, 1992, one month after his return, he sold the house. He may not make the election. He did not use the residence for the required three years. Under IRS regulations, his one-year leave is not considered a temporary absence that may be counted as part of the three-year occupancy period.

Jointly-owned residences. If you are married on the date of sale and the home is owned jointly with your spouse, only one of you must meet the age, use, and ownership tests to claim the exclusion on a joint return for the year of sale.

If a home is not jointly owned, the spouse owning the home must meet the age, ownership, and use tests. If you hold title but are under age 55, filing a joint return with a spouse over age 55 who does not have title will not qualify you for the exclusion because neither spouse meets all three tests. Similarly, a spouse under age 55 with full title may not qualify for an immediate exclusion by putting the house in joint names; you must still wait three years before selling. This is because a spouse over age 55 who has lived in the home at least three years must also have the ownership interest for at least *three* of the five years before the sale.

If you are married at the time of sale, both spouses must consent to an election of the exclusion, and an election bars either of you from claiming the exclusion again. *See* ¶29.15 for these and other election rules for married couples.

Joint ownership with someone other than spouse. A husband and wife selling a jointly owned residence are considered as one taxpayer for purposes of the exclusion limitation. But if joint owners are not married, each owner who meets the tests for age (55), use (principal residence), and holding period (three of five years), may exclude gain up to $125,000 on his or her interest in the residence. The fact that one owner meets the requirements does not qualify the other for the exclusion.

Part of Home Used for Business

Partial business use of your residence during the five-year period preceding the sale may affect the amount of the exclusion. If you used *part* of your residence for business purposes, for example as a home office, for more than two years during the five-year period preceding the sale, the exclusion does not apply to the gain allocated to that business part of the home. If business use was two years or less, business use is ignored in figuring the exclusion.

THE EXCLUSION AND MARRIED COUPLES

¶29.15

If you are married at the time of the sale and the home is jointly owned, one of you must meet all three tests for the exclusion—age, use, and ownership. If only one of you holds title, that person must meet all the tests. Regardless of who owned the home, both of you must agree to elect the exclusion. Under the one lifetime election rule, neither of you may claim the $125,000 exclusion again, as discussed below.

A married person who files a separate return may exclude up to $62,500 of profit, provided the other spouse consents to the election on Form 2119 or in an attached statement. By so consenting, the other spouse is barred from electing the exclusion for a future sale.

If you later decide to revoke the election, you also must have your spouse's consent. If you are divorced after the election but then want to revoke, you must get your former spouse's consent to the revocation. A revocation is made in a signed statement showing (1) your name and Social Security number; (2) the year in which the election was made and filed; and (3) the Internal Revenue office where you filed the election.

Election Applies To Both Spouses

Only one lifetime election is allowed to a married couple; you and your spouse do not each have a separate election to claim the exclusion. If either you or your spouse has previously elected the exclusion, neither of you may make another election. If spouses make an election during marriage and later divorce, no further elections are available to either of them or to either of their new spouses if they remarry.

Sales before marriage. What if before your marriage you and your spouse each owned and used a separate residence, and after your marriage both residences are sold? May two elections be made? No. An election may be made for a sale of either residence (but not for both residences) provided the age, ownership, and use requirements are met. To take advantage of two exclusions, the sales should take place before marriage.

EXAMPLE A woman, age 56, plans to marry at the end of 1992. She also plans to sell her home at a substantial profit. Her fiance sold his home at a profit of $100,000 in August 1990 and elected on his 1990 return to avoid tax. If she sells the house before the marriage, she may claim the exclusion on a 1992 joint return or separate return. True, only one lifetime election of the exclusion is allowed to a married couple, but for purposes of this test, marital status is determined at the time of sale. Thus, if she sells before she marries, her right to claim the election is not affected by her spouse's prior election. However, if she sells after the marriage, she may not claim the $125,000 exclusion because of her spouse's 1990 election. Once married, the right to claim the election on a sale of her home is forfeited because of her spouse's prior election, even though the spouse's home sale may have taken place prior to their marriage.

If an election is made before the marriage and the electing spouse dies, the survivor may be free to make the election as illustrated in the following example.

EXAMPLE John and Mary, both over age 55, planned to marry and to live in Mary's home. Before the wedding, John sold his residence and elected to avoid tax on the sale of his house. A few years later, John died and Mary sold her house and elected to avoid tax on the sale. The IRS allowed the election. Since John's sale was made before they married, his election did not affect her right to make an election after his death.

If John had not died and the couple had sold Mary's house, the election would not have been allowed. John's prior election would have barred Mary from making the election.

Death of spouse. A surviving spouse who inherits a residence upon the death of his or her spouse may be able to qualify for an exclusion even before three-out-of-five-year ownership and use tests are satisfied. The surviving spouse is treated as meeting the ownership and use tests and may elect the exclusion on a sale after reaching age 55, provided (1) he or she has not remarried as of the date of the sale; and (2) the deceased spouse met the ownership and use tests and had not previously elected the exclusion or consented to a former spouse's exclusion on a sale after July 26, 1978.

If you are married on the date of sale and your spouse dies after the sale but before you could make an election, your deceased spouse's personal representative (administrator or executor) must join with you in making an election. Similarly, the personal representative must join in a revocation of any election previously made by you and your deceased spouse. Joint elections and revocations are required, even though the residence was separately owned, separate tax returns are filed, or the nonowning spouse does not meet the three-year residence requirement.

In one case, the IRS permitted an election by an executor where a sale was completed after the death of the owner under an executory contract made by the owner prior to his death.

Sale by irrevocable trust. Where a residence is transferred to an irrevocable trust by a married couple, whether they can claim the exclusion on a sale by the trust depends on whether they are treated as the owners of the trust for tax purposes. The IRS in a private ruling held that if they are treated as owners under the grantor trust rules because of retained powers over the property, they may claim the exclusion if they meet the age, ownership, and use tests.

Sale by marital trust for surviving spouse. Property may be left to a marital trust for the benefit of a surviving spouse if there is concern that the survivor may be unable to manage the property. A personal residence may be put into the trust. If the surviving spouse is entitled to all the trust income and has an unlimited power to receive trust corpus upon request or appoint the property to any other person, the surviving spouse is considered the owner of the trust for tax purposes. If the trust sells the personal residence, the surviving spouse can elect to claim the $125,000 home sale exclusion, provided he or she is over age 55 on the date of sale and has (1) owned (through the trust) and used the residence as a principal residence for three of the last five years preceding the date of sale; and (2) the $125,000 exclusion was not previously elected by the surviving spouse or the deceased spouse with respect to a prior sale.

HOW TO CLAIM THE EXCLUSION

¶29.16

If you meet the tests at ¶29.14, you elect the exclusion on Form 2119 or in a signed statement which you attach to your income tax return for the year of sale. If you do not have Form 2119, write on a separate statement that you elect to exclude from income the gain realized on the sale. In addition, give the following data: (1) your name, age, Social Security number, and marital status as of the date of sale; (2) the dates you bought and sold your residence; (3) the adjusted sale price and the adjusted basis of the property on the date of sale; and (4) the length of any absences during the five years preceding the sale, apart from vacations and other seasonal absences.

If you were married at the time of sale, both you and your spouse must agree to elect the exclusion, and an election bars either of you from claiming the exclusion again; *see* ¶29.15.

Changing an exclusion decision. The tax-free exclusion is available to you only once in your lifetime. If, at the time you sell your home, you plan to invest the money in another home of sufficient cost to completely defer tax but later change your plans, you can make the election at any time before the end of the period for making a refund claim for the year in which the sale occurred. This is generally within three years from the due date of the return filed for the year of the sale. Similarly, if you make the election and then decide to revoke it, you may do so within the same three-year period.

When Election May Be Inadvisable

If you sell your principal residence at a gain which is substantially less than the maximum $125,000 exclusion, and you plan to reinvest at least all of the net proceeds from the sale in a new home, consider deferring tax rather than electing to exclude gain. You are permitted only one lifetime exclusion. For example, if you have a gain of $10,000 and elect to exclude it, you have used up your once-in-a-lifetime election; a later home sale will not be entitled to a $115,000 exclusion. If you buy a new house at a cost at least equal to the adjusted sales price of the old home, the entire gain from the sale of your old home is deferred; *see* ¶29.5. If and when you sell the new house without a further home purchase, the election to exclude gain may then be made.

COMBINING THE EXCLUSION WITH TAX DEFERRAL

¶29.17

If you sell your principal residence at a gain of over $125,000 and plan to purchase a new home, you may take advantage of the exclusion and the tax-free deferral rules. Where you qualify for the exclusion (¶29.14), your gain up to $125,000 is tax free. You may then defer all or part of the remaining gain, depending on the amount of your investment in the new home. You may defer all of the remaining gain by making an investment at least equal to the adjusted sales price of the old house (sales price less selling expenses and fix-up costs; *see* ¶29.5) less the tax-free gain. If you invest less than this amount, the difference between (1) the adjusted sales price of the old house less the tax-free gain, and (2) the new investment, is taxed, but not exceeding the remaining gain.

In determining whether you have to file a return, the tax-free gain realized from the sale of your house is counted as gross income, although not taxed.

EXAMPLE You and your spouse are both over age 55. You sell your jointly-owned home, which you have lived in since 1951. The selling price is $192,000, and you have selling expenses of $12,000. You also have fix-up costs (¶29.5) of $2,000. Basis of the house is $40,000. Your profit is $140,000 ($180,000 − $40,000). You elect to exclude $125,000 of the profit from tax. You may still defer all of the remaining profit of $15,000 of gain by investing in a new home which costs at least $53,000.

Amount realized (net selling price)	$180,000
Less: Fix-up costs	2,000
Adjusted sales price	$178,000
Less: Excluded gain	125,000
Revised adjusted sales price	$ 53,000

If you buy a new residence for $50,000, $12,000 of the remaining gain is deferred and $3,000 of the gain is taxable ($53,000 − $50,000). Basis for the new residence is reduced by the deferred gain; thus, basis here would be $38,000 ($50,000 cost less $12,000 deferred gain).

Selling on the installment method. Where you sell your home and take a purchase money mortgage, you have made an installment sale. Only a portion of each payment is taxable where you do not reinvest in a new home qualifying for deferral.

EXAMPLE Smith sold his home, which cost him $140,000, for $300,000 and elects the exclusion. The buyer is unable to get outside financing so Smith agrees to take back a purchase money mortgage of $150,000, payable over 15 years with 10% interest. Of the $160,000 profit ($300,000 − $140,000), only $35,000 is taxable; $125,000 is tax free. The $35,000 gain is reported over the 15 years in which payment on the mortgage loan is received. To determine the amount of each payment taxable as income, the gross profit ratio is applied to each payment actually received. The gross profit ratio is figured by dividing the taxable gain by the total contract price. Here, this is $35,000 divided by $300,000, which gives a profit ratio of 11.66%. Thus, in the year of sale, $17,490 (11.66% of the $150,000 down payment) is taxable. Of each annual $10,000 installment over the 15 years, $1,166 is taxable ($10,000 × 11.66%).

Worksheet for Form 2119: Combining Exclusion with Tax Deferral (Lines on 1992 format may vary.)

Part I   General Information

1a	Date your former main home was sold (month, day, year) . . . . ▶	1a	7 / 17 / 92
b	Face amount of any mortgage, note (e.g., second trust), or other financial instrument on which you will get periodic payments of principal or interest from this sale (see instructions) . . .	1b	
2	Have you bought or built a new main home?		☑ Yes ☐ No
3	Is or was any part of either main home rented out or used for business? (If "Yes," see instructions.) . .		☐ Yes ☐ No

Part II   Gain on Sale (Do not include amounts you deduct as moving expenses.)

4	Selling price of home. (Do not include personal property items that you sold with your home.)	4	192,000
5	Expense of sale. (Include sales commissions, advertising, legal, etc.)	5	12,000
6	Amount realized. Subtract line 5 from line 4	6	180,000
7	Basis of home sold (see instructions)	7	40,000
8a	Gain on sale. Subtract line 7 from line 6	8a	140,000

- If line 8a is zero or less, stop here and attach this form to your return.
- If line 2 is "Yes," you **must** go to Part III or Part IV, whichever applies. Otherwise, go to line 8b.

b	If you haven't replaced your home, do you plan to do so within the replacement period (see instructions)? ☐ Yes ☐ No

- If "Yes," stop here, attach this form to your return, and see **Additional Filing Requirements** in the instructions.
- If "No," you **must** go to Part III or Part IV, whichever applies.

Part III   One-Time Exclusion of Gain for People Age 55 or Older (If you are not taking the exclusion, go to Part IV now.)

9a	Who was age 55 or older on date of sale? . . . . ☐ You ☐ Your spouse ☑ Both of you		
b	Did the person who was age 55 or older own and use the property as his or her main home for a total of at least 3 years (except for short absences) of the 5-year period before the sale? (If "No," go to Part IV now.) ☑ Yes ☐ No		
c	**If line 9b is "Yes,"** do you elect to take the one-time exclusion? (If "No," go to Part IV now.) ☑ Yes ☐ No		
d	At time of sale, who owned the home? . . . . ☐ You ☐ Your spouse ☑ Both of you		
e	Social security number of spouse at time of sale if you had a different spouse from the one above at time of sale. (If you were not married at time of sale, enter "None.") . . . . ▶	9e	
f	**Exclusion.** Enter the **smaller** of line 8a or $125,000 ($62,500, if married filing separate return)	9f	125,000

Part IV   Adjusted Sales Price, Taxable Gain, and Adjusted Basis of New Home

10	Subtract line 9f from line 8a	10	15,000

- If line 10 is zero, stop here and attach this form to your return.
- If line 2 is "Yes," go to line 11 now.
- If you are reporting this sale on the installment method, stop here and see the line 1b instructions.
- All others, stop here and **enter the amount from line 10 on Schedule D, line 2 or line 9.**

11	Fixing-up expenses (see instructions for time limits)	11	2,000
12	Adjusted sales price. Subtract line 11 from line 6	12	178,000
13a	Date you moved into new home (month, day, year) ▶ 8 / 5 / 92 b Cost of new home	13b	50,000
14a	Add line 9f and line 13b	14a	175,000
b	Subtract line 14a from line 12. If the result is zero or less, enter -0-	14b	3,000
c	Taxable gain. Enter the **smaller** of line 10 or line 14b	14c	3,000

- If line 14c is zero, go to line 15 and attach this form to your return.
- If you are reporting this sale on the installment method, see the line 1b instructions and go to line 15.
- All others, **enter the amount from line 14c on Schedule D, line 2 or line 9,** and go to line 15.

15	Postponed gain. Subtract line 14c from line 10	15	12,000
16	**Adjusted basis of new home.** Subtract line 15 from line 13b	16	38,000

RENTING PERSONAL AND VACATION RESIDENCES

DEDUCTIONS FOR RENTING PART OF A HOME

¶29.18 If you rent out one unit in a multi-unit residence, you report rent receipts and deduct expenses allocated to the rented part of the property on Schedule E of Form 1040. Expenses allocated to rental are deductible, whether or not you itemize deductions. You deduct interest and taxes on your personal share of the property as itemized deductions if you itemize deductions.

If expenses exceed rental income on Schedule E, your loss deduction is subject to the passive loss rules of Chapter 10. The loss, if it comes within the $25,000 allowance (¶10.4), may be deducted from any type of income. If you cannot claim the allowance, the loss may be deducted only from passive activity income.

You generally must use Form 8582 to figure how much, if any, of the $25,000 allowance you may claim, and to figure whether any part of a rental loss is deductible from other rental income or income from other passive activities. However, you may not need to file Form 8582 if your only passive activity losses are losses of $25,000 or less from actively-managed rental real estate and your adjusted gross income is $100,000 or less (disregarding passive activity losses, IRA deductions, and taxable Social Security, if any). Follow the instructions to Schedule E and Form 8582.

Personal use may bar loss deductions. If you or close relatives personally use the rented portion during the year and expenses exceed income, loss deductions may be disallowed under Test 2 of ¶29.20.

EXAMPLE You bought a three-family house in 1971. You occupy one apartment as a personal residence. The house cost you $30,000 ($27,000 for the building, $3,000 for the land). It has a useful life of 30 years. Two thirds of the basis of the building is depreciable, or $18,000 (⅔ of $27,000). This is how you deduct expenses:

Building	Useful life	Depreciation
$18,000	30 years	$600

	Total	Deduct itemized deductions	Deduct in rent schedule	Not deductible
Taxes	$ 600	$200	$ 400	
Interest	390	130	260	
Repairs	300		200	$100
Depreciation	600		600	
	$1,890	$330	$1,460	$100

The taxes and interest allocated to personal use are deductible on Schedule A if you itemize deductions. Repairs allocated to your apartment are nondeductible personal expenses.

TAKING DEPRECIATION WHEN YOU RENT YOUR RESIDENCE

¶29.19 When you convert your residence to rental property, you can begin to take depreciation on the building. You figure depreciation on the *lower* of the building's:

Fair market value at the time you convert it to rental property; or
Adjusted basis. This is your original cost for the building, exclusive of land, plus permanent improvements minus casualty or theft loss deductions claimed on prior year tax returns.

You claim MACRS depreciation based on a 27½ year recovery period. The specific rate for the year of conversion to rental is shown below; you use the rate for the month in which the property is ready for tenants. For example, you move out of your home in May and make some minor repairs. You advertise the house for rent in June. Depreciation starts in June because that is when the home is ready for rental, even if you do not actually obtain a tenant until some later month. Under a mid-month convention, the house is treated as placed in service during the middle of the month. This means that one-half of a full month's depreciation is allowed for that month.

EXAMPLE In 1984, you bought a house for $125,000, of which $100,000 is allocated to the house. In June 1992 you move out of the house and rent it. At that time, the fair market value of the house exclusive of land is $150,000. The depreciable basis of the house is the lower adjusted basis of $100,000. Under MACRS, residential property has a 27½ year life or annual rate of 3.64%. In 1992, you may claim depreciation of $1,970 according to the table below for placing the house in service in June ($100,000 ¥ 1.97%).

Depreciating a rented cooperative apartment. If you rent out a co-op apartment, you may deduct your share of the cooperative corporation's total depreciation. The method for computing your share depends on whether you bought your co-op shares as part of the cooperative corporation's first offering. If you did, follow these steps. (1) Ask the co-op corporation officials for the corporation's total real estate depreciation deduction, not counting depreciation for office space that cannot be lived in by tenant-shareholders. And, (2) multiply Step 1 by the following fraction: number of your co-op shares divided by total shares outstanding. The result is your share of the co-op's depreciation, but you may not deduct more than your adjusted basis.

The computation is more complicated if you bought your co-op shares after the first offering. You must compute your depreciable basis as follows. Increase your cost for the co-op shares by your share of the co-op's total mortgage. Reduce this amount by your share of the value of the co-op's land and your share of the commercial space not available for occupancy by tenant-stockholders. Your "share" of the co-op's mortgage, land value, or commercial space is the co-op's total amount for such items multiplied by the fraction in Step 2; that is, the number of your shares divided by the total shares outstanding. After computing your depreciable basis, multiply that basis by the depreciation percentage for the month your apartment is ready for rental, as shown in the chart below.

Basis to use when you sell a rented residence. For purposes of figuring gain, you use adjusted basis at the time of the conversion, plus subsequent capital improvements, and minus depreciation and casualty loss deductions. For purposes of figuring loss, you use the *lower* of adjusted basis or fair market value at the time of the conversion, plus subsequent improvements and minus depreciation and casualty losses. You may have neither gain nor loss to report; this would happen if you figure a loss when using the above basis rule for gains, and you figure a gain when using the basis rule for losses.

Have an appraiser estimate the fair market value of the house when it is rented. The appraisal will help support your basis for depreciation or a loss deduction on a sale if your return is examined.

Depreciation on a vacant residence. If you move from your house before it is sold, you may generally not deduct depreciation on the vacant residence while it is held for sale. The IRS will not allow the deduction, and according to a Tax Court case, a deduction is possible only if you can show that you held the house, expecting to make a profit on an increase in value over and above the value of the house when you moved from it. That is, you held the house for sale on the expectation of profiting on a future increase in value after abandoning the house as a residence.

EXAMPLE In 1967, Lowry put his summer home up for sale. It was worth $50,000, but he decided not to sell the house for less than $150,000. He expected the value of his land to appreciate greatly during the next few years. He did not rent the house because he felt it would be easier to sell an empty house, and the amount of rental income would not justify the expense of equipping the house for rental. He deducted the maintenance expenses, claiming he held the property as an investment. The IRS disallowed the deduction, claiming that since he did not try to rent it, he held it for personal use.
A federal district court allowed the deduction. Lowry had sound business reasons for not renting. He intended to benefit from post-abandonment appreciation in land values. When he put the house on the market, it was worth $50,000. Six years later, he finally got his asking price of $150,000. That he immediately listed the house for sale did not negate his intention to hold the house for future appreciation.

An investor may claim depreciation on a vacant building held for resale. However, the IRS may dispute the deduction as it has withdrawn a prior acceptance of a court decision which allowed the deduction to an investor.

Rental losses. Loss deductions for depreciation and other rental expenses are limited by the passive activity rules; *see* ¶29.20 for losses on temporary rentals before sale.

LIMITS ON RENTAL EXPENSES OF VACATION AND PERSONAL HOMES

¶29.20 There are two obstacles to deducting losses of renting a vacation home or other residence that you or close relatives use for personal purposes during the year: (1) determining whether you are allowed to deduct expenses in excess of income; and (2) if you may deduct the loss, determining whether the losses are deductible from salary and portfolio investment income, or only against passive activity income.

Apply the three tests on pages 313 and 314 to determine whether you are entitled to rental deductions. In general, if you personally

Depreciation Rate: Month of Taxable Year Residence Is Ready For Rental

1	2	3	4	5	6	7	8	9	10	11	12
3.485%	3.182%	2.879%	2.576%	2.273%	1.970%	1.667%	1.364%	1.061%	0.758%	0.455%	0.152%

use the residence for the greater of 14 days during the year, or 10% of the number of fair rental days, rental deductions are limited under Tests 1 and 2. If under Test 3 you may deduct expenses in excess of income, the passive activity rules of Chapter 10 determine the type of income from which you may claim the loss. All or part of the deduction may be allowed from all types of income if you qualify for the $25,000 rental allowance; *see* Chapter 10.

Deduction Restrictions Apply to All Dwelling Units

The deduction restrictions apply to any "dwelling unit" you rent out which is also used as a residence during the year by yourself or family members. A dwelling unit may be a house, apartment, condominium, cooperative, house trailer, mini motor home, boat, or similar property, including any appurtenant structure such as a garage. The term does not include any portion of a dwelling unit that is used exclusively as a hotel, motel, inn, or similar establishment.

Test 1. You rent the home for less than 15 days during the year and personal use exceeds the 14-day or 10% rental time test. If your personal use exceeds the 14-day or 10% rental time limit of Test 2, rental periods of less than 15 days are disregarded for tax purposes. You do not have to report the rental income you receive, and the only deductions you are allowed are those you would be allowed anyway as a homeowner. That is, if you itemize deductions on Schedule A, you deduct mortgage interest, real estate taxes and casualty losses, if any. No other rental expenses are deductible. Interest is generally fully deductible if the home qualifies as a first or second home under the mortgage interest rules; *see* ¶15.1.

See the Supplement for the status of pending legislation that would repeal tax-free treatment on rentals of less than 15 days.

Test 2. You rent out the home for at least 15 days during the year and your personal use of the home exceeds the 14-day or 10% rental time limit. If your personal use of the home exceeds the greater of (1) 14 days or (2) 10% of the number of days the home is rented at a fair rental value, the personal use limit has been exceeded. In this case, the home is treated as if it were residential rather than rental property, and rental expenses are deductible on Schedule E only to the extent of rental income, following the allocation rules in ¶29.21. Expenses that are not deductible in the current year under this limitation may be carried forward and will be deductible up to rental income in the following year.

The deduction limit is irrelevant if your rental income exceeds expenses. Report the income and deduct the expenses on Schedule E.

In counting the days that the home is rented at a fair rental value, do not count days that the home is available for rental through a rental pool arrangement but not actually rented. But *see* ¶29.21 for a rule allowing rental pool participants to average actual rentals.

Personal use by relatives or co-owners may count as your personal use. In determining whether your personal use exceeds the 14-day/10% rental day limit, you must count the following as "personal use days:"

- Days you used the residence for personal purposes other than days primarily spent making repairs or getting the property ready for tenants.
- Days that a co-owner of the property uses the residence, unless the co-owner's use is under a shared-equity financing agreement discussed later in this section.
- Days on which the residence is used by your spouse, children, grandchildren, parents, brothers, sisters, or grandparents. However, if such a relative pays you a fair rental value to use

the home as a *principal* residence, their use is not considered personal use by you. If you rent a vacation home to such relatives, their use is considered personal use by you even if they pay a fair rental value amount; the exception applies only to fair rentals paid for a relative's principal residence.

- Days on which the residence is used by any person under a reciprocal arrangement that allows you to use some other dwelling during the year.
- Days on which you rent the residence to any person for less than fair market value.

An owner is not considered to have personally used a home that is used by an employee if the value of such use is tax-free lodging required as a condition of employment; *see* ¶3.10.

Renting to Close Relatives

Generally, you are not charged with a "personal use day" under the 14-day/10% rental day limit for days on which you rent your home at a fair rental value amount. However, this exception does not apply if you rent a vacation unit to your children, parents, brothers or sisters, grandchildren or grandparents. If the home is not your relative's principal residence, their use counts as your personal use even if they pay you a fair rental value.

For example, in one case, a son rented a condominium in Florida to his parents, who split their time between the Florida apartment and the home they owned in Illinois. Although the parents paid a fair rental amount for the Florida condo, the son's rental deductions were limited by the IRS and the Tax Court to interest and real estate taxes that did not exceed the rental income. The parents' rental days were attributed to the son under the 14-day/10% rental day limit since the home in Illinois, and not the Florida apartment, was their principal residence.

Shared-equity financing agreements for co-owners. Use by a co-owner is not considered personal use by you if you have a shared-equity financing agreement under which: (1) the co-owner pays you a fair rent for using the home as his or her principal residence; and (2) you and your co-owner each have undivided interests for more than 50 years in the entire home and in any appurtenant land acquired with the residence.

Any use by a co-owner which does not meet these two tests is considered personal use by you if, for any part of the day, the home is used by a co-owner or a holder of any interest in the home (other than a security interest or an interest under a lease for fair rental) for personal purposes. For this purpose, any other ownership interest existing at the time you have an interest in the home is counted, even if there are no immediate rights to possession and enjoyment of the home under such other interest. For example, you have a life estate in the home and your friend owns the remainder interest. Use by either of you is personal use.

Shared-Equity Financing Agreements

As an investor, you can help finance the purchase of a principal residence for a family member or other individual. The rental income you receive for your ownership share in the property may be offset by deductions for your share of the mortgage interest, taxes, and operating expenses you pay under the terms of the agreement, as well as depreciation deductions for your percentage share. Rental losses are subject to the passive loss restrictions of Chapter 10.

The other co-owner living in the house may claim itemized deductions for payment of his or her share of the mortgage interest and taxes.

Rental of principal residence prior to sale. You are not considered to have made any personal use of a principal residence which you rent or try to rent at a fair rental for a consecutive period of 12 months or more or for a period of less than 12 months that ends with the sale or exchange of the residence. This means that deductions are not limited by the personal use tests of Test 2 above. However, rental expense deductions for the period have been limited under "profit motive rules;" as discussed under Test 3.

3. You rent the home for 15 days or more, but the days of your personal use are less than the days fixed by the 14-day/10% test. If your personal use of the residence does *not* exceed the greater of 14 days or 10% of the fair rental value days, as discussed under Test 2, the home is treated as rental property rather than as a residence. You must still allocate expenses between personal and rental days under the methods in ¶29.21. Rental expenses in excess of rental income may be deductible, but the loss is subject to the passive activity rules of Chapter 10. *See* the instructions to Schedule E and Form 8582. Furthermore, the IRS may disallow the loss deduction if you cannot prove that you rent the residence to make a profit under the "profit motive" tests of ¶40.9.

The Tax Court has allowed loss deductions under the "profit motive" test where the owner made little personal use of the home and proved he bought the house to make a profitable resale.

The loss limitation rules also apply to trusts, estates, partnerships, and S corporations owning vacation residences.

EXAMPLES 1. *(Loss allowed)* In 1973, Clancy purchased a house and land in a coastal resort area of California. Prior to the purchase, Clancy was told by a renting agent that he could expect reasonable income and considerable appreciation from the property. Previously, he had sold similar property in the same development at a profit. After the purchase, Clancy spent $5,000 to prepare the house for rental, and gave a rental agency the exclusive right to offer the property for rent. The house was available for rent 95% of the time in 1973, and 100% of the time in 1974. However, rentals proved disappointing, totaling only $280 in 1973 and $1,244 in 1974, despite the active efforts of the agency to rent the property. However, the house did appreciate in value and was eventually sold at a profit of $14,000. In 1973 and 1974, Clancy deducted rental expenses of approximately $21,000 which the IRS disallowed. The IRS claimed that the house was not rental property used in a business. Furthermore, as Clancy knew that he could not make a profit from the rentals, he could not be considered to hold the property for the production of income.

The Tax Court agrees that the expenses are not deductible business expenses. But this does not mean that they are not deductible as expenses of income production. Although the rental income from the property was minimal, Clancy acquired and held the property expecting to make a profit on a sale. He had previously sold similar property at a profit and was told to expect considerable rental income as well as appreciation from the new house. Where an owner holds property, as Clancy did here because he believed that it may appreciate in value, such property is held for the production of income. Further evidence that Clancy held the property to make a profit: He rarely used it for personal purposes and an agent actively sought to rent it.

2. *(Loss allowed)* Nelson bought a condominium, hired a rental agent, and even advertised in the *Wall Street Journal* and *Indianapolis Star*. He also listed the unit for sale. During 1974, he was unable to rent the apartment but deducted expenses and depreciation of over $6,100, which the IRS disallowed. The IRS argued he did not buy the unit to make a profit but to tax shelter substantial income. The Tax Court disagreed. Although his efforts to rent were not successful in 1974, he was

successful in later years in renting the unit. He rarely visited the apartment other than to initially furnish it. When he went on vacation, he went abroad or to other vacation spots.

3. *(Loss disallowed)* The Lindows purchased a condominium which they rented out during the prime winter rental season. However, over an eight-year period their expenses consistently exceeded rental income. The Tax Court agreed with the IRS that expenses in excess of rental income were not deductible. Substantial, repeated losses, even after the initial years of operation, indicate that the operation was not primarily profit oriented. The rental return during the prime rental season could not return a profit. Even if the condominium was fully rented for the entire prime rental season, annual claimed expenses would exceed rent income. The couple also used the unit for several months and intended to live there on retirement. They did not consider putting the unit up for sale with an agent. Finally, that they had detailed records of income and expenses did not prove a business venture. Records, regardless of how detailed, are insufficient to permit the deduction of what are essentially personal expenses.

IRS may challenge losses claimed on temporary rental before sale. If you are unable to sell your home and must move, it may be advisable to put it up for rent. This way, you may be able to deduct maintenance expenses and depreciation on the unit even if it remains vacant. However, the IRS has disallowed loss deductions for rentals preceding a sale on the grounds that there was no "profit motive" for the rental under the rules of ¶40.9. Courts have allowed loss deductions in certain cases. Under current law, allowable losses are subject to the passive activity restrictions, but may be fully deductible against regular income if you qualify for the $25,000 rental loss allowance explained in Chapter 10.

EXAMPLES 1. The IRS and Tax Court disallowed a loss deduction for rental expenses under the "profit motive rules" (¶40.9) where a principal residence was rented for 10 months until it could be sold. According to the Tax Court, the temporary rental did not convert the residence to rental property. Since the sales effort was primary, there was no profit motive for the rental. Thus, no loss could be claimed; rental expenses were deductible only to the extent of rental income; *see* ¶40.9. The favorable side of the Tax Court position: Since the residence was not converted to rental property, the owners could defer tax on the gain from the sale by buying a new home. An appeals court reversed the Tax Court and allowed both tax deferral and a loss deduction. The rental loss was allowed since the old home was actually rented for a fair rental price. Furthermore, the owners had moved and could not return to the old home, which was rented almost continuously until sold.

2. In 1976, a couple bought a condo apartment in Pompano Beach, Florida. In 1983, they decided to move and listed the unit for either sale or rent with a local real estate broker. Sale of the unit was difficult because of the saturation of the Florida real estate market. Rental of the unit was also difficult because the condominium association's rules barred the rental of condominium units on a seasonal basis. The unit remained unrented until it was sold in 1986 for a substantial gain. In 1984, the couple deducted a $9,576 rental loss ($7,596 for maintenance expenses and $1,980 for depreciation). The IRS disallowed the deduction as not incurred in a bona fide rental activity. The Tax Court allowed the deduction. The couple made an honest and reasonable effort to rent the condominium. Lack of rental income was caused by a slack rental market and the condominium association rules prohibiting short-term rentals.

ALLOCATION OF EXPENSES TO RENTAL ACTIVITY

¶29.21

When you personally use a home on any day during the taxable year, expenses must be allocated between personal and rental use. By law, deductible expenses of renting, except for interest and taxes, are limited by this fraction:

$$\frac{\text{Days of fair rental}}{\text{Total days of rental and personal use}}$$

The number of days a vacation home is held out for rent but not actually rented are not counted as rental days.

The IRS has also used the above fraction for allocating interest and taxes to rental use, but the Tax Court and an appeals court disagree, as explained below.

Tax Court's Allocation More Favorable

COURT DECISION

The Tax Court disagrees with the IRS formula for allocating interest and taxes. According to the Tax Court, interest and taxes are allocated on a daily basis. Thus, if the house is rented for 61 days in the year, one-sixth of the deductible interest and taxes (61/365) is deducted first from rental income. This rule allows a larger amount of other expenses to be deducted from rental income; *see* Example 2 in the next column.

Order of claiming deductions if personal use exceeds the greater of 14 days or 10% of the fair rental days. If expenses allocated to rental exceed rental income and your personal use exceeds the 14-day/10% test (*see* Test 2 at ¶29.20), the allocated rental expenses are deducted in a specific order. First, gross rental income is reduced by otherwise deductible interest and taxes allocated to the rental activity. Second, the remaining income is reduced by expenses not related to the property itself such as office supplies, rent collection fees, and advertising. Next, operating expenses (other than depreciation) are deducted to the extent of remaining rental income. Finally, if there is any rental income remaining, depreciation may be deducted up to the balance of income.

The IRS method of allocating interest and taxes generally results in a lower deduction for rental operating expenses and depreciation than does the Tax Court method as seen in the following examples.

EXAMPLES 1. You rent out your vacation home for 61 days in 1992, receiving rent of $2,000. You use it yourself for 61 days. You may deduct expenses only up to the amount of this income because your personal use exceeds the 14-day or 10% rental time limit (Test 2 at ¶29.20). Your expenses are mortgage interest of $1,600, real estate taxes of $800, and maintenance and utility costs of $1,200. Depreciation (based on 100% rental use) is $1,500. Assume the vacation home is a qualifying second home (¶15.1), so that all the interest is deductible under the mortgage interest rules. Under the IRS method, one-half of all the expenses, including the interest and taxes, is deducted in this order:

Rent income		$2,000
Less: Interest	$800	
Taxes	400	1,200
		$ 800
Less: Maintenance		600
		$ 200
Less: Depreciation		$ 200

The balance of the depreciation is not deductible. It may be carried forward to the following year.

The balance of interest and taxes is deductible as itemized deductions provided you claim itemized deductions.

If the vacation home were not a qualifying second residence under ¶15.1, the interest would not be deducted with taxes from the $2,000 of rental income, but would be treated as an operating expense and deducted along with the maintenance expenses.

Under the Tax Court's method of allocating interest and taxes, only one-sixth of the interest and taxes (61/365) would be deducted from rental income, rather than one-half as under the IRS method.

2. The Boltons paid interest and property taxes totaling $3,475 on their vacation home. Maintenance expenses (not including depreciation) totaled $2,693. The Boltons stayed at the home 30 days and rented it for 91 days, receiving rents of $2,700. Because the personal use for 30 days exceeded the 14 day or 10% fair rental day limit, the Boltons could deduct rental expenses only up to the gross rental income of $2,700 reduced by interest and taxes allocable to rental. In figuring the amount of interest and taxes deductible from rents, they divided the number of rental days, or 91, by 365, the number of days in the year. This gave them an allocation of 25%. After subtracting $868 for interest and taxes (25% of $3,475) from rental income, they deducted $1,832 ($2,700 − $868) of maintenance expenses from rental income.

The IRS argued that 75% of the Boltons' interest and tax payments had to be allocated to the rental income. The IRS used an allocation base of 121 days of personal and rental use. Thus, the IRS allocated 75% (91/121) of the interest and taxes, or $2,606, to gross rental income of $2,700. This allocation allowed only $94 maintenance expenses to be deducted ($2,700 − $2,606).

The Tax Court sided with the Boltons and an appeals court agreed. The IRS method of allocating interest and taxes to rental use is bizarre. Interest and taxes are expenses that accrue ratably over the year and are deductible even if a vacation home is not rented for a single day. Thus, the allocation to rental use should be based on a ratable portion of the annual expense by dividing the number of rental days by the number of days in a year.

Interest expenses. If you personally use a rental vacation home for more than the greater of 14 days or 10% of the rental days, the residence may be treated as a qualifying second residence under the mortgage interest rules; *see* ¶15.1. The interest on a qualifying second home is generally fully deductible and is not subject to disallowance under the passive activity restrictions of Chapter 10. In figuring deductible rental expenses, the portion of the deductible mortgage interest allocable to the rental portion is deducted from rental income (along with taxes) before other expenses are considered.

Rental pool arrangements. Such arrangements have been devised to avoid the loss restriction by attempting to increase the days the home is held for a fair rental value. They have not been successful. Courts have ruled that only days on which a home is actually rented count as fair rental days, not days of availability through the rental pool.

In proposed regulations, the IRS also holds that a rental pool is not a basis for counting fair rental days. However, the proposed regulations permit rental pool participants to elect to average the actual rental use of their units. Unanimous consent is required to elect the averaging rule. If the election is made, the number of rental days for a unit is determined by multiplying the aggregate number of days that all units in the rental pool were rented at fair rental during the pool season by a fraction. The numerator of the fraction is the number of participation days of a particular unit; the denominator is the aggregate number of participation days of all units.

30

TAX SAVINGS FOR INVESTORS IN SECURITIES

There is a 28% tax rate ceiling for net long-term capital gains. Therefore, if your income tax bracket exceeds 28% (for example, you are in the top 31% tax bracket in 1992) you will pay attention to the more than one-year holding period for realizing long-term capital gains on the sale of securities. Realizing long-term capital gains will give you some tax savings. However, do not overlook the effect of realizing substantial capital gains that subject you to the exemption phaseout and/or 3% reduction of itemized deductions. As explained in ¶28.2, the 3% reduction increases the effective 28% capital gain rate by at least 0.93% and depending on the number of exemptions phased out, the effective rate will be even higher. Thus, it may be advisable to avoid realizing too much capital gain income in a year you are subject to the exemption phaseout if that income can be deferred to a year in which you will have lower income and not be subject to the phaseout.

If your tax rate bracket will not exceed 28%, so that short-term and long-term capital gains are subject to the same tax rate, you generally will not pay attention to holding periods. Your test for judging investment return will be the same for both gains and interest and dividend income, which is the net after-tax return over a given period. If the projected after-tax return on a stock held for investment will give only 5% over a two-year period, an investment which will return net after-tax income of 7% during the same period will be the preferred investment.

The $3,000 limitation on deducting capital losses from other types of income is a substantial restriction. If you have capital losses exceeding $3,000, it is advisable to realize capital gains income that can be offset by the losses.

TIMING SALES OF SECURITIES

¶30.1 Gain on the sale of securities is fully taxable at ordinary income rates, subject to the 28% ceiling for net long-term gains; *see* ¶28.2. However, you have the opportunity of controlling the taxable year in which to realize gains and losses. Gains and losses are realized only when you sell, and you can time sales to your advantage following the suggestions discussed in this chapter.

PLANNING YEAR-END SECURITIES TRANSACTIONS

¶30.2 First establish your current gain and loss position for the year. List gains and losses already realized from completed transactions. Then review the records of earlier years to find any carryover capital losses. Include nonbusiness bad debts as short-term capital losses. Then review your paper gains and losses and determine what losses might now be realized to offset actual gains or what gains might be realized to absorb your losses.

If you have already realized net capital losses exceeding $3,000, you may want to realize capital gains that will be absorbed by the excess loss. Remember, only up to $3,000 of capital losses exceeding net capital gain may be deducted from other income such as salary, interest, and dividends. Also, project your tax bracket ranges in the current and next tax year. For example, assume that you are close to the threshold for the phaseout of exemptions, and that realizing substantial gains will place you in the exemption phaseout range (¶1.32). You may want to defer gain transactions to a year in which you will be in a lower bracket or not subject to the phaseout.

December 31 deadline for 1992 gains and losses. If you want to realize gains on publicly traded securities, you have until December 31, 1992, to transact the sale. Gain is reported in 1992, although cash is not received until the settlement date in 1993. If you do not want to realize the gain in 1992, delay the trade date until 1993.

Losses are also realized as of the trade date; a loss on a sale made by December 31, 1992, is reported on your 1992 return.

Planning for losses. Realizing losses may pose a problem if you believe the security is due to increase in value sometime in the near future. Although the wash-sale rule (¶5.21) prevents you from taking the loss if you buy 30 days before or after the sale, the following possibilities are open to you.

If you believe the security will go up, but not immediately, you can sell now, realize your loss, wait 31 days, then recover your position by repurchasing before the expected rise.

You can hedge by repurchasing similar securities immediately after the sale provided they are not identical. They can be in the same industry, of the same quality, without being considered substantially identical. Check with your broker to see if you can use a loss and still maintain your position. Some brokerage firms maintain recommended "switch" lists and suggest a practice of "doubling up"—that is, buying the stock of the same company and then 31 days later selling the original shares. Doubling up has disadvantages: It requires additional funds for the purchase of the second lot, exposes you to additional risks should the stock price fall, and the new shares take a new holding period.

EXAMPLE You own 100 shares of Steel stock which cost you $10,000. In November 1992, the stock is selling at $6,000 ($60 a share×100 shares). You would like to realize the $4,000 loss but at the same time, you want to hold on to the investment. You buy 100 shares at a market price of $60 a share (total investment $6,000) and 31 days later sell your original 100 shares, realizing the loss of $4,000. You retain your investment in the new lot. In 1992, November 29 is the last day to buy new shares to allow a loss sale on December 31.

Short sale postponed taxable gain to 1993. If you do not want to realize taxable gains on a security sale in 1992, but you think that the price of your stock may decline by the time you sell in 1993, you can freeze your profit by ordering a short sale of the stock in 1992. You transact a short sale by selling shares borrowed from your broker. A short sale of securities you already own is called a short sale "against the box." You close the sale when you deliver to the broker the identical securities you have been holding or identical securities you have bought after the short sale. For example, in January 1993, you deliver your shares to the broker as a replacement for the borrowed shares you sold in 1992. By delivering the stock in 1993, the gain on the short sale is fixed in 1993. For tax purposes, a short sale is not completed until the covering stock is delivered.

PUTS AND CALLS AND INDEX OPTIONS

¶30.3 You may buy options to buy and sell stock. On the stock exchange, these options are named calls and puts. A call gives you the right to require the seller of the option to sell you stock during the option period at a fixed price, called the exercise or strike price. A put gives you the right to require the seller of the option to buy stock you own at a fixed price during the option period.

Speculate with Puts and Calls

Puts and calls allow you to speculate at the expense of a small investment—a call, for expected price rises; a put, for expected price declines. They may also be used to protect paper profits or fix the amount of your losses on securities you own.

You do not have to exercise a put or call to realize your profit. You may sell the option to realize your profit. If you exercise a call, the cost of the call is added to the cost of the stock purchased. If you exercise a put, you reduce the selling price of stock sold by the cost of the put. If you do not exercise a call or put, you realize a capital loss.

The option price depends on the value of the stock, the length of the option period, the volatility of the stock, and the demand and supply for options for the particular stock.

Puts may be treated as short sales. Be careful in using puts when you own stock covered by the put. If you have held the stock short term, the purchase of the put is a short sale. The exercise or expiration of the put will then be treated as the closing of the short sale. Short sale rules, however, do not apply (1) when you hold stock long term, and (2) when you buy a put and the related stock on the same day and identify the stock with the put; *see* ¶5.20.

Using a call as leverage. You expect a stock to appreciate in value but you do not have sufficient capital for a further investment. Instead of investing your limited amount of capital in an outright purchase, you might buy a call covering such stock. With a call, the same amount of capital allows you to speculate in many more shares than you could if you purchased stock outright. If the stock rises in value, your call also increases in value.

Exchange option trading. Option market exchanges provide market conditions for trading-in puts and call options. The overwhelming number of options transacted are calls. Financial sections of the daily newspapers provide data on the market prices and volume of the options.

Options are currently traded on the following U.S. exchanges: The American Stock Exchange (AMEX), The Chicago Board Options Exchange (CBOE), the New York Stock Exchange, (NYSE), the Pacific Stock Exchange, (PSE), and the Philadelphia Stock Exchange (PHLX). Like trading in stocks, option trading is regulated by the Securities and Exchange Commission (SEC). Furthermore, all option contracts traded on U.S. exchanges are issued, and cleared by the Options Clearing Corporation (OCC).

Trading in options is highly speculative, attracting those who hope to make profits on minimum investments. At the same time, the market has provided investors and institutions holding large portfolios with an opportunity to earn income through the sale of options based on their holdings. Thus, it takes two to play the option game: (1) the owner of shares who sells an option on his or her stock; and (2) the option buyer who generally speculates that, by buying an option for a smaller price than he or she would have to pay for the stock, a profit can be made if the price of the stock goes up. The odds generally favor the option seller.

The income tax consequences of option trading are at ¶5.26.

If you are inexperienced in the use of options, read several technical explanations of the use of options before investing. Master the technical use of options such as straddles and hedges used by professional traders, as the outright purchase of straight calls is generally too speculative. Finally, do not overlook commission costs which can cut into your profits or increase your losses.

Stock index options. Index options give you a chance to speculate on the general movement of stock. The success of the index option has tended to reduce interest in regular stock options given on individual stocks. On the other hand, index options are pegged to the price movement of the stocks that comprise the index option. Thus, with index options, you do not have to be concerned about the market fate of a particular stock. The stock group of the index option follows the general stock market movement. For example, assume that 100 stocks make up the index. The option contract represents an index multiplier of $100 times the index value of the group or basket of 100 stocks. Therefore, when a newspaper reports an index value of 170, which is also called the *strike price*, the contract is worth $17,000. However, as the option is only a right to buy or sell this particular contract, you pay an option price that is only a percentage of the contract value. The particular option price is set by the market in an open auction.

Key to Option Terms

Item	Explanation
Call option	An option contract that gives the holder the right to buy a specified number of shares of the underlying stock at the given exercise price on or before the option expiration date.
Put option	An option contract that gives the holder the right to sell a specified number of shares of the underlying stock at the given exercise price on or before the option expiration date.
Strike price/Exercise price	The stated price per share for which the underlying stock may be bought (in the case of a call) or sold (in the case of a put) by the option holder upon exercise of the option contract.
At-the-money	An option is at-the-money if the exercise price of the option is equal to the market price of the underlying security.
In-the-money	A call option is in-the-money if the exercise price is less than the market price of the underlying security. A put option is in-the-money if the exercise price is greater than the market price of the underlying security.
Out-of-the-money	A call option is out-of-the-money if the exercise price is greater than the market price of the underlying security. A put option is out-of-the-money if the strike price is less than the market price of the underlying security.
Premium	The price of the option contract determined in the competitive marketplace, which the buyer of the option pays to the option writer.
Intrinsic value	The amount by which the option is in-the-money
Time value (premium-intrinsic value)	The portion of the premium that is attributable to the amount of time remaining until the option's expiration date and to the fact that the underlying components that determine the value of the option may change during that time.
Secondary market	A market that provides for the purchase or sale of previously sold or bought options through closing transactions.
Expiration date	The expiration date is the last day on which an option may be exercised.
Writer	The seller of an option contract.

Your role is to weigh how the market will fare within the option period. Should you anticipate lower interest rates within the option period, which can be from approximately a week up to three months, you might buy an index option, betting that the stock market will advance. For example, when the index is at 165, you buy an option for $1,200 with a strike price of 170. If the stock market advances during the option period, pushing the strike price to 177, you have won your bet. At 177, you might sell your option for $7,000, thereby making a $5,800 profit.

Do not let this example encourage you to enter the index option market precipitously. If you guess wrong, you have lost your money. In the example just cited, had the index not moved above 170, you would have lost $1,200. However, unlike other investments where the risk may be unlimited, options offer buyers a known risk in that the buyer cannot lose more than the premium paid for the option; in other words, the price paid for the option.

The S&P 100 index option is offered by the Chicago Board Options Exchange. It is based on Standard & Poor's 100 list of stocks, and it also offers an index option of 500 shares. The Philadelphia Stock Exchange trades the Value Line index option that has an index basket of approximately 1700 stocks traded on several exchanges. The New York Stock Exchange and the American Stock Exchange also offer index options.

If you are interested in playing the index option market, track the market for several months until you get used to the movement of the option. Plot hypothetical purchases and see how you would have fared. You might make a bundle—but, as at roulette, you might lose your shirt in a very short time.

INVESTING IN MUTUAL FUNDS

¶30.4

A mutual fund is a professionally managed pool of individual investors' contributions, invested in a variety of securities. Different funds are designed to meet different investor objectives. Money

market mutual funds allow investors to earn a return based on swings in the short-term money market; see ¶30.7. Income mutual funds invest in stocks paying high current dividends. There are also bond funds geared to realizing income. Growth mutual funds invest in securities that are expected to appreciate over the long term.

There are different types of growth funds. Some aggressive funds invest in small, developing companies with short track records; other growth funds invest primarily in established firms. There are also sector funds that specialize in specific industries, such as utilities, gold, or high technology companies.

By doing some research, you can find a fund that matches your investment objectives and risk tolerance. Check the fund's performance over a substantial period, say five to 10 years. Keep in mind that yields fluctuate and are not guaranteed. In funds other than money markets (¶30.7), the value per share also fluctuates. Gain or loss may be realized when you redeem shares in growth or income mutual funds.

Also compare sales charges and redemption fees, if any, before you buy. No-load funds do not have a sales charge. In the financial sections of major newspapers, there are listings of mutual fund offerings that indicate whether there is a sales charge; the no-load funds have the same purchase price and redemption price for fund shares. The names of funds which charge commissions may also be available through your broker.

Timing your purchase. You may buy a tax liability if you invest in a mutual fund which has already realized significant capital gains during the year. The cost of your shares is based on the current value of its portfolio. At the end of the year, the gains realized by the fund before your investment are distributed to you as a capital gain distribution. Then you have to pay tax on the return of your own money.

You also have to pay tax on your own investment if you buy shares shortly before the fund declares a capital gain dividend. On the date the dividend is declared, called the ex-dividend date, the value of fund shares drops by the amount of the dividend distribution. If you buy just before that, the higher cost for your shares will be offset by the dividend you receive, but you will have to pay tax on the dividend. To limit your tax, you can postpone investing until the stock goes ex-dividend. By that time, your buying price is based on an asset value which has been reduced by the capital gain distribution. Before investing, you may be able to find out from the fund when dividend distributions for the year are expected; investment publications showing the dividend dates for the previous year also may be consulted.

Figuring gain or loss on sales. You need careful records to compute gain or loss on the sale of some or all of your mutual fund shares. If you exchange shares of one fund for shares of another fund within the same fund "family," the exchange is treated as a sale.

To figure gain or loss on an exchange or redemption of shares, you need to know the total cost basis of your shares; *see* the Planning Pointer in the next column. You also need to identify the basis of the particular shares you are selling when you sell only some of your shares. There are several methods of identifying which shares you are selling, which in turn determines the basis. The specific identification method allows you to select exactly which shares are being sold and is an advantage if you want to designate shares that will produce a particular gain or loss result. You may elect to average the cost basis of all of your shares under either a single-category or double-category method. Finally, a first-in, first-out method applies if you do not specifically identify the share or make an averaging election. *See* the table below for details on these identification methods.

Keeping Track of Cost Basis

Keep confirmation statements for purchases of shares as well as a record of dividends that are automatically reinvested in your account. These will show the cost basis for your shares. Your basis is increased by amounts reported to you by the fund on Form 2439, representing the difference between undistributed capital gains you were required to report as income and the tax paid by the fund on undistributed gains. Your basis is reduced by nontaxable dividends that are a return of your investment. Keep copies of Form 2439 and information returns showing nontaxable dividends.

Basis does not include load charges (sales fees) paid after October 3, 1989, on the purchase of mutual fund shares if you held the shares for 90 days or less and then exchanged them for shares in a different fund in the same family of funds at a reduced load charge; see Example 3 on page 320.

EXAMPLES

1. In 1986, you bought 100 shares of a mutual fund for $10 a share. In 1988, you bought another 200 shares for $11 a share, and in 1989, another 500 shares for $15 a share. In 1992, you sell 130 shares at $20 a share, but do not specifically identify the shares being sold. Under the IRS FIFO method, you are treated as having first sold the original 100 shares from 1986, then 30 of the shares bought in 1988. Your basis for the sold shares is $1,330:

100 shares from 1986 costing $10 each	$1,000
30 shares from 1988 costing $11 each	330
	$1,330

Key to Identifying Mutual Fund Shares When You Sell

Method—	Tax Effect—
Specific identification of shares sold	If you sell some of your shares that have been left on deposit with an agent for the fund, and you identify the specific lot of shares being sold in your sell order, you can fix profit or loss on the sale, depending on the cost of the shares selected. You should give the fund written instructions to sell shares that you bought on a particular date and at a particular price. Ask the fund for a written confirmation that acknowledges your instructions.
FIFO (First-in, first-out)	If you do not specifically identify the sold shares as just discussed, *and* you do not elect to average cost basis as discussed below, the IRS requires you to compute gain or loss as if shares were sold in the order that you acquired them. If the earliest acquired shares are treated as sold, taxable gain on a current sale will generally be higher than if the specific identification method was used; see Example 1 above.
Averaging your basis	You may elect to average the cost of shares acquired at different times and prices. The election applies to open-end mutual fund shares held by an agent, usually a bank, in an account kept for the periodic acquisition or redemption of shares in the particular fund. You still need records of your total basis, but averaging avoids the difficult task of identifying the exact shares being sold. There are two averaging methods: The single-category method and double-category method. The single-category method is easier to apply as explained below. To elect either averaging method, attach a note to your return specifying the chosen method. Once elected, you must continue to apply the same method for all sales or exchanges of shares in the "family" of funds managed by the particular fund company. You may change an averaging election only with IRS permission. You can use the average cost basis for sales of shares in one mutual fund family, and use the specific identification method for sales of shares of other fund families. If you received shares as a gift that were worth less than the donor's basis, you may elect either averaging method only if you include a statement on your return that the basis used in applying the method will be the value of the shares when you received them. This treatment also applies to gift shares you receive after the election. *Note: Congress is considering legislation that would ease recordkeeping burdens for investors opening new accounts by requiring mutual funds to report annually on Form 1099-DIV the average basis of all shares held in the account using the single category method; see the Supplement for a legislative update.*
Single-category averaging	You figure the average cost per share by dividing your total basis for all shares in the account by the number of shares. For example, if you bought 100 shares of a fund in 1990 at $20 per share and another 100 shares in 1991 at $30 per share, your average basis per share is $25 ($5,000 total cost ÷ 200 shares). If you sell 50 shares in 1992 for $35 a share, your basis for the sold shares is $1,250 (50 x $25 average basis) and your gain on the sale is $500 ($1,750 sales proceeds *less* $1,250 basis). For purposes of determining whether gain or loss is long-term or short-term capital gain, you are treated as having sold shares in the order you acquired them (first-in, first-out).
Double-category averaging	You have to separate your account shares into a long-term category for shares held more than one year, and a short-term category for shares held one year or less. You figure the average cost per share in each category by dividing the total basis for all shares in that category by the number of shares in that category. You may specify to the agent handling share transactions the category from which you are selling. If you do not so specify, the long-term shares are deemed to have been sold first. If the number of shares sold exceeds the number in the long-term class, the excess shares are charged to the short-term class.

Your taxable gain is $1,270 ($2,600 sales price less $1,330 basis). Had you specifically designated shares from the most recent lot, which cost you more, you would have reduced the taxable gain. For example, if you had given the fund written instructions to sell 130 of the 500 shares that you bought in 1989 at $15 per share, your basis on the sale under the specific identification method would be $1,950 (130 x $15) instead of $1,330. Gain would be reduced to $650 ($2,600 sales price *less* $1,950 basis).

2. An investor sold by phone part of his holdings in two mutual funds acquired over a number of years without specifying the particular shares being sold. On his return, Hall claimed a net long-term capital loss of about $2,400 using a LIFO method (last-in, first-out). However, using the FIFO method, the IRS held that he had a long-term capital gain of $163,000. In the Tax Court, Hall argued that the specific identification rule applies only to stock certificates, not noncertificate shares left on deposit with a mutual fund. The court disagreed. Without specific identification, the IRS FIFO method is reasonable. If good records are kept, an investor can select the specific shares that are being sold, but only if done at the time of sale. He or she should not be allowed to wait until the end of the year to allot specific sales to his or her overall holdings to gain a tax advantage.

What if an investor provides written instructions to a mutual fund that specific shares purchased on a specific date should be sold, but the fund does not acknowledge such specification in its written confirmation? Regulations on specific identification require such a written confirmation within a reasonable time after the sale. However, language in the Tax Court's Hall decision suggests that proof of written sale identification instructions might be acceptable whether or not the fund's written confirmation makes the same identification.

3. You pay a $200 load charge on purchasing shares for $10,000 in Fund A. Within 90 days, you exchange the Fund A shares for Fund B. Because Fund A and Fund B are in the same family of funds, the $200 load charge that would otherwise be due on the purchase of the Fund B shares is waived. For purposes of figuring your gain or loss on the exchange of Fund A shares, your basis is $10,000, not $10,200. The disallowed $200 is added to the basis of the new Fund B shares, provided those shares are held more than 90 days. If the waived load charge on Fund B shares had been $100, basis for the original Fund A shares would be increased by $100, the excess of the original $200 load charge over the amount waived on the reinvestment.

REDUCING THE TAX ON DIVIDEND INCOME

¶30.5   The tax on dividend income may be reduced by the following types of transactions:

Selling stock on which a dividend has been declared but not yet paid. During the period a dividend is declared but not paid, the price of the stock includes the value of the dividend. If you plan to sell stock in this position and figure that the tax on the dividend reflected in the selling price will be less than the tax on the dividend received, transact the sale before the stock goes ex-dividend; see ¶4.9.

Investing in companies paying tax-free dividends. Some companies pay tax-free dividends. A list of companies that do may be provided by your broker. When you receive a tax-free dividend, you do not report the dividend as income as long as the dividend does not exceed your stock basis. A tax-free dividend reduces the tax cost of your stock. Dividends in excess of basis produce capital gain; see ¶4.11.

Investing in companies paying stock dividends. On receipt of a stock dividend, you generally do not have taxable income.

TREASURY BILLS AND CDs

¶30.6   Short-term paper (maturity of one year or less) provides an opportunity for earning income on funds during periods of uncertainty in the stock and other investment markets. Funds which you do not wish to tie up long term and do not want to remain unproductive may be invested in Treasury bills, notes, or certificates of deposit. These investments offer safety and negotiability, earning current interest rates from the day of purchase to the day of redemption, either on maturity or sale.

Treasury bills. These are direct obligations of the U.S. Treasury issued to finance budgetary needs. Bills are offered for 3-month, 6-month, and 12-month maturities in minimum amounts of $10,000 and multiples of $5,000 above the minimum. Bills are sold at a discount at Treasury auctions held at the Federal Reserve Banks which serve as agents for the Treasury. They are redeemed at face value. Your return on a Treasury bill is the difference between the discount price you pay for the bill and its face value, if you hold it to maturity, or the amount you receive for it on a sale before maturity. The selling price of a Treasury bill before maturity will vary with changes of current interest rates.

You may buy Treasury bills directly without charge from any Federal Reserve Bank, which gives you a receipt indicating that a book entry of your purchase has been recorded. You also may buy or sell Treasury bills through your bank or stockbroker who will charge you for handling the transaction.

Most investors submit noncompetitive tenders (bids) for the Treasury bills they wish to buy. To submit a *competitive* tender, you must specify the price you are willing to pay for your bill, and you run the risk of bidding too low and not getting the bills you want. Noncompetitive tenders do not have to specify a price. They are filled at a price which is the average of the accepted competitive tenders for that specific auction. Check the Federal Reserve Bank or branch in your area for auction dates on Treasury bills. You may also buy or sell Treasury bills through your bank or your stockbroker who will charge you for handling the transaction.

Figuring the yield on your Treasury bill. On the day of the auction, the Treasury will figure the average price bid by those who submitted acceptable competitive tenders. The difference between this average price and the full value of the Treasury bill is the *discount* at which the bill is sold. All noncompetitive tenders are filled at this price. The Treasury pays you the difference between the purchase price and the face value.

EXAMPLE Assume the accepted average bid on three-month bills is $9,850. You gave the government $10,000. To reflect the actual purchase price of $9,850, a "discount" of $150 is paid to you.

Figuring treasury bill yield. The equivalent annual yield on your Treasury bill is figured this way:

1. Find the yield on your investment by dividing discount by purchase price.
2. Convert this yield to the annual rate by multiplying the yield by 4.0110 (365 ÷ 91 days to maturity) if the bill is for three months; by 2.0055 (365 ÷ 182 days to maturity) if the bill is for six months.

On a three-month bill your discount is $150 (cost $9,850); the equivalent annual yield is 0.0610:

$$\frac{\$150}{\$9,850} = 0.0152 \qquad 0.0152 \times 4.0110 = 0.0610 \text{ or } 6.10\% \text{ per year}$$

Financial pages of the newspapers report the previous day's auction, including the discount rate and what this amounts to as an annual percentage yield.

Cashing bills before maturity. If you decide you need funds before the maturity date of your bill, you can sell it through a commercial bank or a securities broker. The Federal Reserve Bank and the Treasury do not handle bills which have not matured.

For bills sold before maturity, current interest rates will determine the amount you receive. The market value of Treasury bills is listed daily in the financial section of newspapers.

At maturity. Redemption is automatic at maturity, unless you notify the Federal Reserve Bank that you wish to roll over matured bills into new bills. The Treasury will electronically deposit the face amount of the bill into a savings or checking account you have previously designated. If you bought your bill through a bank, the bank will credit your account on the date the bill matures. To roll over your maturing bill, you follow the same procedures as in buying a new bill and use your matured bill as payment. If you purchase bills directly from the Treasury, a payment for the difference between the price of the new bills and the face value of your matured bills will be transferred electronically to your designated account.

Certificates of deposit. Certificates of deposit (CDs) are another form of short-term investment which offers a high return with safety and negotiability.

Certificates of deposit represent money lent by investors to a bank for a specified short period of time, generally 30, 60, or 90 days, although certificates of deposit for six months to several years are also available.

Purchasing CDs. Certificates of deposit are generally purchased through your bank or broker. The rate of interest that banks will pay depends on supply and demand in the money market. The interest rate may vary with the size of your investment. For deposits of $100,000 or more, you may be able to get a "heavy duty" CD at a higher rate than offered on smaller deposits.

Before investing, check with the bank for minimum investment requirements, charges, and restrictions on withdrawals, including penalties for withdrawals before maturity.

Also *see* ¶30.8 for more on CDs.

If you have an account with a broker, you may prefer to invest in CDs through your broker. The CDs bought through a broker are federally insured up to $100,000. Brokers offer CDs from various banks throughout the U.S. and can provide at times a higher current rate offered by a bank in an area that is not directly accessible to you.

Repurchase agreements (repos). This investment offered by banks and thrifts allows you to earn high interest rates by sharing in a portion of the bank's portfolio of government securities. The bank is required to repurchase your investment from you at your request. The minimum investment is $1,000; maturities vary, on average, three months. Repos are not FDIC or FSLIC insured, and there is no interest penalty for early repurchase, as long as you hold them for a minimum of a week or more. There may be a small service charge for early repurchase.

Commercial paper. Periodically during the year, many corporations requiring large sums of money to finance short-term customer receivables offer short-term promissory notes at high rates of interest. These notes are generally referred to as commercial paper. Although much of this paper is sold in units of $100,000 or more, commercial paper in denominations of $25,000 and even less is sometimes available.

Finance companies, automobile manufacturers, and large retail stores are types of businesses which typically issue commercial paper for periods ranging from one week to 270 days.

Investments in commercial paper may not be as liquid as other short-term paper and are subject to greater risks.

Tax-exempt notes are discussed at ¶30.11.

INVESTING IN MONEY MARKET MUTUAL FUNDS

¶30.7 The investor who does not have the capital needed to invest in specific money market obligations may consider a money market mutual fund. A fund portfolio will generally include U.S. government obligations, CDs of major commercial banks, bankers acceptances, and commercial paper of prime-rated firms. Most funds have a minimum investment requirement, varying from $500 to $10,000. Money market funds charge a yearly management fee. Investors should check each fund's charges because they differ.

Yields, which change daily, are not guaranteed. Investments are not federally insured. Some state-chartered banks, however, offer money market funds insured by a state insurance fund.

Gains and losses are generally not realized in money market funds; shares are redeemed for exactly what you paid (usually $1 per share) plus accrued interest. Withdrawals may be requested by mail, wire, or telephone. Some funds offer limited checking privileges.

To compare yields, check newspaper financial sections that periodically list the yields of both taxable and tax-exempt money market mutual funds.

Tax-free money funds. These funds invest in short-term notes of state and local governments issued in anticipation of tax receipts, bond sales, and other revenues, and in "project notes" issued by local entities and backed by the federal government. The interest paid by these funds is exempt from federal tax. The yields are lower than those of taxable funds, and are attractive only if they provide greater after-tax returns than similar taxable funds. Minimum investments range from $1,000 to $50,000. These funds may offer check writing privileges.

Investors in certain states may be able to earn interest that is exempt from state and local, as well as federal, tax.

A tax-free interest return may also be available through unit-investment trusts holding tax-exempt state and municipal bonds. These trusts mature in a specified number of years or as called.

INVESTING IN SAVINGS INSTITUTIONS

¶30.8 Bank money market accounts compete with money market mutual funds. The bank money market funds guarantee for one-week or one-month periods interest rates tied to the Treasury bill rate or the average money market rate. Bank funds also offer this added attraction: They are federally insured. Bank money market accounts require certain average monthly balances and if the account falls below the minimum, the interest rate is reduced.

Investments in money market funds allow you to take advantage of volatile interest rates which are rising. Investments in CDs allow you to lock into the highest available interest rate for a fixed period of time if you are concerned with a decline of rates during that period.

Current banking regulations allow banks and savings institutions to pay what they please on certificates of deposit and do not require minimum balances on CDs with terms over 31 days.

Withdrawals within certain limits may be made from money market accounts without penalty. Premature withdrawals from CDs are penalized.

CD investments in savings institutions allow you to lock into high interest rates only for the short term, generally up to five years. If you are concerned that rates will substantially decline in the future, you may want to invest in a currently available investment that fixes a high rate over longer periods such as bonds with long-term maturities. Bond investments are discussed in ¶30.9.

As indicated in ¶30.6, stockbrokers may offer to their customers issues of CDs from various banks and may allow you to invest at a slightly higher rate than that offered by a local bank.

Deferring Interest Income

Defer interest income by buying a six-month tax-deferred certificate after June 30. Interest is taxable in the next year when the certificate matures if the terms of the certificate specifically defer the interest to maturity. Your bank may offer you the choice of when to receive the interest. You may also defer interest by buying Treasury bills which come due next year.

Savings certificates versus Treasury bills. Treasury bills require a minimum $10,000 investment while certificates keyed to the Treasury bill rate usually require much lower minimums. Treasury bill investments over the minimum must be made in multiples of $5,000; for certificates, additional investments may be made in smaller increments. There is no fee charged for the purchase of certificates, while a fee may be charged to purchase Treasury bills unless purchased directly from the Treasury or a Federal Reserve Bank. Where you do not have the minimum to invest, some institutions may lend the difference at a lower interest rate, typically 1% to 2% over the rate earned on the certificate. Treasury bills have a tax advantage over the certificates. Interest on saving certificates is subject to state and local taxes; interest on Treasury bills is exempt from state and local taxes. Furthermore, there are penalties for redeeming certificates before maturity. *See* ¶4.16 for taxation of interest and for forfeiture of interest on premature withdrawals.

Investment options vary from bank to bank. Not all banks offer the maximum rates or compound interest in the same manner. Whether interest is compounded daily or annually will affect your rate of return. Each bank also has its own policy on procedures concerning maturity of certificates. Some banks automatically renew the CD for another term at the current rate unless notified to the contrary; some banks will not renew a matured CD without express authority from you. If you fail to act, you may find your funds switched to a day-of-deposit account on maturity. Banking institutions can also change their rules after you have opened an account.

INVESTING IN CORPORATE BONDS

¶30.9

When you buy a corporate bond, you are lending money to the issuer of the bonds. You become a creditor of the issuing company. The corporation pledges to pay you interest on specified dates, generally twice a year, and to repay the principal on the date of maturity stated on the bond.

For investment purposes, a bond may be described according to the length of the period of maturity. Short-term bonds usually mature within one to five years; medium-term bonds in five to 20 years; long-term bonds in 20 or more years.

Where the interest is paid out on a regular schedule, the bond is called a "current income" bond. An accrual or discount bond is a bond on which interest is accumulated and paid as part of the specified maturity value (the bond having been issued at a price lower than the specified maturity value).

Figuring the yield of a bond. The investment value of bonds is generally expressed in rates of yield. There are four types of yield: the nominal or coupon yield; the actual yield; the current market yield; and the net yield to maturity.

The nominal or coupon yield is the fixed or contractual rate of interest stated on the bond. A bond paying 6% has a 6% nominal yield.

The actual yield is the rate of return based on the price at which the bond was purchased. If bought below par, the actual yield will exceed the nominal or coupon yield. If bought at a premium (above par), the actual yield will be less than the coupon or nominal yield. For example, if you paid $850 for a $1,000 bond paying 5% interest, the actual yield is 5.88% ($50 divided by $850).

The current market yield is the rate of return on the bond if bought at the prevailing market price. It is figured in the same manner as actual yield. For example, if the 5% bond was quoted at $750, its current yield would be 7%.

Net yield to maturity represents the rate of return on the bond if it is held to maturity, plus appreciation allocated to a discount purchase or less reductions for any premium paid on a bond selling above par. If you buy a bond below par at a market discount, your annual return is proportionately increased by a part of the discount allocated to the number of years before maturity. If the discount was $50 on a bond with a five-year maturity, then your annual income return on the bond is increased by $10 ($50 divided by 5). On the other hand, if you bought at a premium, the extra cost is a reduction against your income because you paid more than can be recovered at maturity. This cost is allocated over the remaining life of the bond. Thus, if you bought a five-year bond at $50 over par, your average annual return is reduced by $10 ($50 divided by 5).

Call privileges may reduce the investment value of the bond. A call privilege gives the issuer a chance to redeem the obligation before maturity if interest rates have declined below the rate fixed by the obligation. The existence of a call is a disadvantage to an investor; a favorable investment may be lost at a time the investor may not be able to replace it with another. To take some of the "sting" out of a call provision, the issuer may provide for the payment of a "premium" on the exercise of the call and a minimum period during which the bonds will not be called. The call premium is usually expressed as a percentage of the maturity value, for example, 105%. The amount of the premium varies with the length of the period in which the bond may be called. As the maturity date approaches, the call premium will decrease. Some bonds now carry a guarantee that they will not be called for a specified number of years such as five or 10 years.

A call privilege generally will not be exercised if the going interest rate remains about the same as, or is higher than, the interest rate of the bond. If interest rates decline below the interest rate of the bond, the bond will probably be called because the issuer can obtain the borrowed money at lower cost elsewhere.

Interest on bearer bonds issued with coupons attached is paid when a bondholder clips the coupon and deposits it for payment. A registered bond carries the name of the owner who receives his interest by mail from the issuing corporation.

Whether a bond is registered or in bearer form has no effect on its investment quality or yield. A coupon-type or bearer bond may be preferred by institutional investors because it can be transferred by hand without registration. However, this advantage must be weighed against the risks of loss through fire, theft, or casualty.

Issuing and trading bonds. New bond issues are generally placed through investment bankers who usually assist in the preparation of the issue. Often an issue may be sold directly by the issuing organization to an institutional investor. Many newly issued bonds are purchased directly from issuers or from their investment bankers by institutional investors before the bonds are offered to individual investors. Issuers prefer this type of placement as it involves less expense than a public offering. Normally, only the new issues (or part of new issues) which cannot be marketed this way are offered to private investors.

Bonds are also traded on the open market where individuals, as well as institutional buyers, may buy or sell them at competitive, market determined prices, through dealers or brokers.

Investment return on a bond is generally limited to the stated interest. You cannot expect any appreciation of principal as you can in a stock investment, unless you have bought bonds selling at a discount.

Bond sales and prices on the major exchanges are listed in the major financial dailies. Bond prices fluctuate in response to changes in interest rates and business conditions. In setting the daily price of a bond, the market weighs the current status, performance, and future prospects of the issuing corporation, as well as the interest rate and maturity period of the bond.

Quotations are based on 100 as equal to par, even though the basic unit for an actual bond may be in denominations of $1,000. A quote of 90 1/2 simply means a bond with a face value of $1,000 will cost $905 at market.

Calls under sinking fund redemption. A bond may be called in at par under the terms of a sinking fund arrangement. Not all bonds are called and those that are selected are picked by lot. Redemptions for sinking fund purposes account for only a small percentage of a single bond issue. But some issues may retain the right to use a blanket sinking fund under which they may redeem bonds paying interest at their highest rate.

Put privileges. A put privilege is the flip side of a call privilege. It permits the buyer to sell the bonds at par to the issuer after a stated number of years. This feature is valuable to investors for long-term bonds. If interest rates rise, investors are not locked into low yields.

Current interest rates affect the selling price of bonds:

1. *If current interest rates increase over the interest rate of your bond, the market value of your bond will decline.* The decline in value has nothing to do with the credit rating of the issue. It simply means that other investors will buy only at terms that will give them the current higher return. If you bought a $1,000 bond paying a rate of 6% at par, and a few months later interest rates go to 8%, another investor will not pay $1,000 for the bond for a 6% return. To match the 8% return on a dollar, the market value of the bond will drop to a level which will return 8% on the money invested, based on its actual 6% return and the period remaining before maturity. Thus, during periods of rising interest, the price of bonds issued at lower rates in prior years declines. This occurs to even top quality bonds; the highest credit rating will not protect the market value of a low-interest paying bond. When this happens there may be bond bargains available, as prices on outstanding bonds decrease.

2. *If interest rates decline below the interest rate of your bond, the value of your bond will increase;* but at the same time, the company, if it has an exercisable call option, may redeem the bond to rid itself of the high interest cost and attempt to raise funds at current lower rates. Thus, an early redemption of the bond could upset your long-range investment plans in that particular issue.

With these points in mind, you can understand why investors have shied away from long-term bonds when volatile interest rates ran into double digits. Investors preferred the high short-term rates. The effect of the investor flight from long-term issues hurt the ability of lenders to raise funds and forced them to devise new types of issues such as zero coupon bonds and floating rate bonds.

Corporate zero coupon bond. A zero coupon bond is a deep discount obligation issued by companies that have found it difficult to market traditional long-term bonds. The zero coupon bond allows them to compete during periods of high interest rates. The bonds are issued at considerably less than face value and redeemed at face at a set date. No annual interest is paid. A zero coupon bond allows an investor to lock in a return. He or she knows how much will be received at maturity and so avoids the problem of turning over investments at fluctuating short-term rates. However, zero coupon bonds may be subject to "call" provisions; an early call would upset your projected return, as discussed previously. Brokers have lists of zero coupon bonds; the prices vary with the credit rating of the companies, current market rates, maturity dates, and whether the bond is callable.

Floating rate or variable interest bonds. For investors unwilling to gamble on the future of interest rates, some bonds have been offered with floating interest rates. The rate is updated periodically, but there may be a floor and ceiling limiting the changes. The market price of the bond should remain near par since its interest rate moves with the market. Although this feature is a form of insurance for the investor, it may not be worth its added cost.

Reporting Zero Coupon Bond Discount

Zero coupon bond discount is reported annually as interest over the life of the bond, even though interest is not received. This tax cost tends to make zero coupon bonds unattractive to investors, unless the bonds can be bought for IRA and other retirement plans which defer tax on income until distributions are made.

Zero coupon bonds also may be a means of financing a child's education. A parent buys the bond for the child. The child must report the income, and if the income is not subject to the parent's marginal tax bracket under the "kiddie tax" (Chapter 22), the income subject to tax may be minimal.

The value of zero coupon bonds fluctuates sharply with interest rate changes. Consider this fact before investing in long-term zero coupon bonds. If you sell before the maturity term, at a time when interest rates rise, you may lose part of your investment.

TREASURY BONDS, NOTES, AND U.S. AGENCY OBLIGATIONS

¶30.10

The federal government offers the following obligations for investment opportunities. They are guaranteed by the federal government and are exempt from state and local taxes.

Treasury bonds and notes. Treasury bonds have maturity dates in excess of 10 years. The minimum denomination is $1,000. Interest is paid semiannually at a rate which varies with each issue. These bonds may be purchased through a commercial bank or directly from the Federal Reserve Bank.

Treasury notes are similar to Treasury bonds but have shorter maturity dates from two to 10 years. Minimum investments range from $1,000 to $5,000, depending on the issue. Interest is paid semiannually and interest varies with each issue. Notes are purchased from commercial banks or directly from the Federal Reserve Bank.

Treasury notes and bonds are issued in book-entry form only; you do not receive a certificate. Under a direct deposit system, semiannual interest and principal at maturity is electronically deposited in a bank account which you designate.

Zero coupon Treasury bonds. Certain major brokerage houses have created zero coupon Treasury bonds by stripping the coupons from Treasury bonds and selling the bonds at deep discounts. They have been promoted under such names as TIGRS, LIONS, COUGARS, and CATS as investments suitable for IRAs, retirement plan trusts, and custodian accounts for minors. The U.S. Treasury itself offers its own version of the zero coupon bond under the name STRIPS. The government does not offer STRIPS directly to individual investors, but sells them to banks and brokers who then sell them to the public. Because STRIPS have the direct backing of the U.S. government, they are considered to be the safest zeros and generally yield up to one-tenth of one percent less than TIGRS, CATS or similar brokerage firm or bank created zeros. With all zero coupon Treasury obligations, an investor can select a particular maturity date suited to his or her needs, such as the year the investor will start taking IRA distributions or the year a child will start college. For tax reporting rules, *see* ¶30.9 on corporate zero coupon bonds.

Other U.S. obligations, such as savings bonds, are discussed at ¶30.13 and Treasury bills at ¶30.16.

Certain federal agencies, like the Tennessee Valley Authority, offer their own securities. The types of securities offered vary. Such securities must be purchased through brokers or commercial banks.

Federally chartered companies, such as Government National Mortgage Association ("Ginnie Maes"), and Federal National Mortgage Association ("Fannie Maes"), authorize certain firms and institutions to issue securities based on insured mortgages. While interest on these securities is generally not exempt from state and local taxes, they offer the investor a higher yield than Treasury securities. Some of these obligations carry a U.S. government full faith and credit guarantee; some have only an implied guarantee; and some no backing from the federal government, but risk is generally considered to be negligible.

Ginnie Maes are offered in minimum denominations of $25,000. Monthly payments to security holders include not only interest, but also a return of principal. Rather than buying Ginnie Maes in the open market, you may consider investing in a fund or trust which has a portfolio of such securities. Minimum investment units typically begin at $1,000.

INVESTING IN TAX-EXEMPTS

¶30.11

Interest on state and local obligations is not subject to federal income tax. It is also exempt from the tax of the state in which the obligations are issued. In comparing the interest return of a tax-exempt with that of a taxable bond, you figure the taxable return that is equivalent to the tax-free yield of the tax-exempt. This amount depends on your tax bracket. For example, a municipal bond of $5,000 yielding 7% is the equivalent of a taxable yield of 9.7% subject to the tax rate of 28%.

You can compare the value of tax-exempt interest to taxable interest for your tax bracket by using this formula:

Tax-exempt interest return = E
Taxable interest (to be found) = T
Your tax bracket = B

$$T = \frac{E}{1 - B}$$

EXAMPLE You are deciding between a tax-exempt bond and a taxable bond. You want to find which will give you more income after taxes. You have a choice between a tax-exempt bond paying 6% and a taxable bond paying 8%. Your tax bracket is 28%.

Using this formula, you find that the tax-exempt bond is a better buy in your tax bracket as it is the equivalent of a taxable bond paying 8.3%.

$$T = \frac{0.06}{.72\,(1 - 0.28)}$$

$$T = .083 \text{ or } 8.3\%$$

The following table shows the amount a taxable bond would have to earn to equal the tax-exempt bond, according to the investor's income tax bracket.

If top income tax rate is—	*A tax-exempt yield of—					
	3%	4%	5%	6%	7%	8%
	is the equivalent of these taxable yields:					
28%	4.2	5.5	6.9	8.3	9.7	11.1
31%	4.3	5.8	7.2	8.7	10.1	11.6

*Exemption from the tax of the state issuing the bond will increase the yield.

To lock in high rates, you may have to invest in a long-term bond. However, consider these drawbacks: You may not want to tie up your capital long term. There is the possibility that a future increase in interest rates may reduce the value of your investment if you should need the principal before maturity.

Ratings of tax-exempt bonds. As in the case of commercial bonds, tax-exempt issues are rated by services such as Standard & Poor's and Moody's. In rating a bond, the services will consider the size of the issuer, the amount of its outstanding debt, its past record in paying off prior debts, whether it has competent officials and a balanced budget, its tax assessment and collection record, and whether the community is dominated by a single industry which might be subject to economic change. Generally, an issuer with a good credit rating will offer lower interest rates than one plagued with revenue deficits or similar problems. A basic test is the sufficiency of tax yields or revenues even in times of economic stress.

General obligation bonds will normally be rated higher than revenue bonds because they have the support of the taxing power of the community. Revenue bonds (backed by the revenue of the issuer) may receive high ratings once a capacity to produce earnings is shown.

Purchase and trading of tax-exempts. Tax-exempt municipals are traded over the counter and are generally handled through a firm specializing in this field or having a department for municipals. Prices quoted represent a percentage of par. For example, a par value $5,000 bond quoted at 90 is selling for $4,500 (90% of $5,000); a par value $1,000 bond quoted at 90 is selling for $900 (90% of $1,000). It may not pay to buy tax-exempts unless you intend to hold them to maturity because the additional cost of selling a small order might be as much as a year's interest.

The bid and asked prices of tax-exempt bonds are generally not quoted in the daily newspapers, although some brokerage houses which specialize in them do print such prices. As in the general bond market, an offer of unusually high interest compared with the average bond rates may be an indication that the bonds are riskier than others.

The market for tax-exempts is not as large as the market for stock. This poses a risk if you ever need ready cash and are forced to sell a tax-exempt bond at a discount. If you are concerned with liquidity, restrict your investments to major general obligation bonds of state governments and revenue bonds of major authorities.

Mutual funds. Instead of purchasing tax exempts directly, you may consider investing in municipal bond funds. The funds invest in various municipal bonds and thus, offer the safety of diversity. The value of fund shares will fluctuate with the bond markets. Also, an investment in the fund may be as small as $1,000 compared with the typical $5,000 municipal bond. Check on fees and other restrictions in municipal bond funds.

You may also invest in tax-free money market mutual funds. These provide ready liquidity and protect the value of your principal by maintaining a $1 value per share. The tax-exempt yield is generally lower than from a municipal bond fund.

Tax-exempt notes. Although generally bought by banks and large corporations, short-term tax-exempt notes may be available to individuals. The majority of the notes are offered in face amounts of $25,000 and up, but sometimes in denominations of $5,000 and $10,000. They are issued by states and municipalities to tide them over until expected revenues are received or until longer-term money can be raised through an issue of long-term bonds. Where rising interest rates have made the cost of long-term issues high, a government authority may postpone a long-term offering and try to fill the gap with short-term notes. The interest rates on tax-exempt notes may be higher than on tax-exempt bonds if the authority is willing to pay the extra interest for the short term in the expectation that a future long-term offering may be placed at lower rates.

Interest on these short-term notes is exempt from federal tax. Many of the notes are from housing authorities and issued to pay construction costs on projects for which bonds will eventually be issued. Housing notes are guaranteed by the FHA and, because of their safety, yields are lower than more speculative paper.

Tax law restrictions. Most municipal bonds issued before July 1, 1983, except for housing issues, are in the form of bearer bonds; the owners are not identified, and interest coupons are cashed as they come due. However, state and municipal bonds issued after June 30, 1983, with a maturity of more than one year, as well as obligations of the federal government and its agencies, are in registered form. Principal and interest are transferable only through an entry on the books of the issuer. The Treasury plans a system for registering obligations now held in street name.

In buying state or local bonds, check the prospectus for the issue date and tax status of the bond. The tax law treats bonds issued after August 7, 1986, as follows:

1. "Public-purpose" bonds. These include bonds issued directly by state or local governments or their agencies to meet essential government functions, such as highway construction and school financing. These bonds are generally tax exempt.
2. "Qualified private activity" bonds. These include bonds issued to finance housing and student loans. There are limits on the amount of qualifying private activity bonds an authority may issue. Interest on qualifying bonds issued after August 7, 1986 (or after August 31, 1986, for certain bonds), is tax free for regular income tax purposes, but is a preference item to be added to taxable income if you are subject to alternative minimum tax. Because of the AMT, a nongovernment purpose bond may pay slightly more interest than public-purpose bonds. These may be a good investment if you are not subject to AMT tax or if your AMT liability is not substantial. Your broker can help you identify such bonds.
3. "Taxable" municipals. These are bonds issued for nonqualifying private purposes such as building a sports stadium. They are subject to federal income tax, but may be exempt from state

and local taxes in the states in which they are issued. Generally, bonds issued after August 15, 1986, are subject to this rule.

INVESTING IN UNIT INVESTMENT TRUSTS

¶30.12 A unit investment trust is a closed-end unmanaged portfolio of bonds marketed by investment houses. Yield is fixed for the life of the trust with interest payable semiannually or more frequently. As bonds in the portfolio mature, a unit holder receives a repayment of principal. Unit trusts provide investors with the possibility of locking into high yields for the long term. However, a trust has this disadvantage: If principal is needed before the end of the trust term, an investor may sacrifice substantial amounts of principal if interest rates rise or if the general investment market is shying away from long-term investments; even where the trust may offer a current return equal to market value, its price may be depressed because there may be few investors willing to take the risk of tying up their funds in long-term investments. Despite these drawbacks, the performance of unit trusts has been rated higher than that of similar mutual funds.

Unit trusts hold varying types of debt instruments. Tax-exempt municipal bond trusts, made up of tax-exempt obligations, are generally favored by investors in the top tax brackets. Taxable unit trusts hold investments such as corporate bonds, bank certificates of deposit, and Treasury obligations. Usually, units are offered in denominations of $1,000. An investor pays a front-end sales charge, but no management fee as there is no need for management once a unit trust is closed.

Maturities of the various trusts range as follows: The short-term, tax-exempt average is three years; intermediate, six to 12 years; and long-term, 18 to 30 years. An average for corporate intermediate is six years; 25 years for long-term.

SAVINGS BOND PLANS

¶30.13 Savings Bond purchases give you an opportunity to defer tax; *see* ¶4.28. EE bonds can be purchased for one half the face value (ranging from $50 to a maximum of $10,000). If held at least five years, EE bonds earn interest at either a guaranteed minimum rate, or a semiannually-set rate tied to five-year Treasury securities, whichever is *higher*. The guaranteed minimum rate has been 6% since November 1986. Bonds held less than five years earn interest on a fixed graduated scale.

Savings bonds can be used to build up equity during a lifetime without paying taxes if the election to defer annual reporting (¶4.29) is made. Heirs may continue to defer tax on the interest until the bonds reach final maturity (*see* below). When the bonds are finally cashed, the person cashing them and reporting the income gets a deduction for the estate tax paid (if any) on the income; *see* ¶4.29. The accumulated income will be subject to federal tax but not to state or local taxes.

Funding college expenses. U.S. savings bonds can be used in an investment program for a child's college education. *See* ¶33.3 for a complete discussion, including a possible interest exclusion.

Final maturity for savings bonds. Do not neglect the final maturity date for older bonds. After the final maturity date, no further interest will accrue. For example, Series E savings bonds issued in 1952 mature in 1992 and will not earn further interest. If you have bonds that are maturing, and have deferred the reporting of interest, you may continue the deferral by exchanging the matured bonds for HH bonds. HH bonds are available in multiples of $500, and pay taxable interest semiannually. If the exchange is made, and you choose to continue the deferral, the interest on the E bonds will not be taxed until the HH bonds are cashed or reach maturity. HH bonds mature in 20 years. The exchange may be made within one year after the E bond reaches final maturity.

Bond	Issue Date	Final Maturity
Series E	May 1941-November 1965	40 years after issue
	December 1965-June 1980	30 years after issue
Series EE	January 1980 or later	30 years after issue
Savings notes (Freedom Shares)	May 1967-October 1970	30 years after issue

Timing Bond Redemptions

In the year you cash in a savings bond you could lose interest by cashing it in too soon. Interest on E and EE bonds accrues only twice a year. Bonds issued at different times have different accrual dates. If you cash your bonds before the accrual date that applies to your bond, you will lose interest. For a list of interest accrual dates, *see* below.

Interest accrual dates for Series EE bonds. Interest on EE bonds always accrues in the month of original issue, and six months later. For example, if you bought a Series EE bond in November 1982, interest accrues in November and in May. A bond cashed in during September 1993 would earn interest only through May 1993.

Interest accrual dates for Series E bonds. Interest accrues twice a year. The months of accrual depend on the issue date of the bond, as shown in the table below. If you cash a bond in between accrual months, you will earn interest only through the last preceding accrual period. For example, if interest accrues in February and August, and you cash a bond in during July, you would earn interest only through February.

ACCRUAL DATES

Issue Date—	Interest Accrues—
May 1952–January 1957	In the month that is two months after the month of original issue, and also six months later. For example, if your bond was issued in December 1955, interest accrues every February (two months after the December issue month) and every August (six months after the February accrual month).
February 1957–May 1959	In the month that is five months after the month of original issue, and also six months later. For example, if you have a bond issued in June 1958, interest accrues every November (five months after the June issue month) and every May (six months after the November accrual month).
June 1959–November 1965	In the month that is three months after the month of original issue, and also six months later. For example, if you have a bond issued in September 1964, interest accrues every December (three months after the September issue month) and every June (six months after the December accrual month).
December 1965–May 1969	In the month of original issue, and also six months later. For example, if you have a bond issued in October 1968, interest accrues every October (month of original issue) and every April (six months after the October accrual month).

ACCRUAL DATES

Issue Date—	Interest Accrues—
June 1969–November 1973	In the month that is four months after the month of original issue, and also six months later. For example, if you have a bond issued in July 1971, interest accrues every November (four months after the July issue month) and every May (six months after the November accrual month).
December 1973–June 1980	In the month of original issue, and also six months later. For example, if you have a bond issued in May 1979, interest accrues every May (month of original issue) and every November (six months after the May accrual month).

REPORTING INCOME FROM INVESTMENT CLUBS

¶30.14

Investment clubs are a method of pooling funds for stock market investments. The club may be formed by any number of persons who may manage the investments of the club under an informal or a formal agreement or charter. A majority of clubs currently operating are, for tax purposes, partnerships. Some, however, are taxable as corporations or trusts. Corporate or trust status is usually evidenced by formal incorporation or the creation of a trust. However, a group may be taxed as a corporation, even though it has not been formally incorporated, if its manner of operation gives it the characteristics of a corporation. IRS regulations provide tests for determining when a group is a corporation. If the club is considered a corporation, it reports and pays a tax on the club's earnings. You report dividend distributions made by the club to you. The overall cost of corporate tax reporting is generally more than the tax cost of partnership reporting.

If the club is a partnership, the club files a partnership return on which it reports the tax consequences of its transactions and the shares of each member. The club does not pay a tax. You and the other members pay tax on your shares of dividends, interest, capital gain, and other income earned by the club. You report your share as if you earned the income personally. For example, you report your share of the club's capital gains and losses on your Schedule D on the line provided for partnership gains and losses; you report your share of dividends and interest in the respective dividend and interest schedules of your personal tax return. You may also deduct as itemized deductions your share of the club's investment expenses, subject to the 2% AGI floor.

The following is an example of a club treated as a partnership under IRS regulations:

EXAMPLE Twenty-five persons each contribute $10 a month for the purpose of jointly investing in securities. They share investment income equally. Under the agreement, the club will operate until terminated by a three-quarter vote of the total membership and will not end upon the withdrawal or death of any member. However, under local law, each member has the power to dissolve the club at any time. Members meet monthly; buy or sell decisions must be voted on by a majority of the organization's membership present. Elected officers perform only ministerial functions such as presiding at meetings and carrying out the directions of the members. Members of the club are personally liable for all debts of, or claims against, the club. No member can transfer his or her membership. The club does not have the corporate characteristics of limited liability, free transferability of interests, continuity of life, and centralized management. Therefore, it is treated as a partnership; *see* Chapter 45.

31

TAX SAVINGS FOR INVESTORS IN REAL ESTATE

In the case of profits, the tax law provides real estate investors the following tax benefits:

- Sale of investment property may be taxed as capital gain subject to the 28% tax ceiling; *see* ¶5.1;
- Depreciation can provide a source of temporary tax-free income; *see* ¶31.1;
- Rental income can be used to offset passive losses; *see* Chapter 10;
- Tax-free exchanges make it possible to defer tax on exchanges of real estate held for investment; *see* ¶31.4;

In the case of losses, real estate transactions may be subject to these disadvantages:

- Rental losses may not be deductible from other income such as salary interest and dividends unless within the special $25,000 allowance; *see* ¶10.4;
- Compromises of mortgage liability may subject you to tax; *see* ¶31.6.

INVESTING IN REAL ESTATE VENTURES

¶31.1 The ideal real estate investment should provide a current income return and an appreciation in the value of the original investment. As an additional incentive, a real estate investment may in the early years of the investment return income subject to little or no tax. That may happen when depreciation and other expense deductions reduce taxable income without reducing the amount of cash available for distribution. This tax savings is temporary and limited by the terms and the amount of the mortgage debt on the property. Mortgage amortization payments reduce the amount of cash available to investors without an offsetting tax deduction. Thus, the amount of tax-free return depends on the extent to which depreciation deductions exceed the amortization payments.

To provide a higher return of tax-free income, at least during the early years of its operations, a venture must obtain a constant payment mortgage that provides for the payment of fixed annual amounts which are allocated to continually decreasing amounts of interest and increasing amounts of amortization payments. Consequently, in the early years, a tax-free return of income is high while the amortization payments are low, but as the amortization payments increase, nontaxable income decreases. When this tax-free return has been substantially reduced, a partnership must refinance the mortgage to reduce the amortization payments and once again increase the tax-free return.

EXAMPLES 1. A limited partnership of 100 investors owns a building that returns an annual income of $100,000 after a deduction of operating expenses, but before a depreciation deduction of $80,000. Thus, taxable income is $20,000 ($100,000 − $80,000). Assuming that there is no mortgage on the building, all of the $100,000 is available for distribution. (Since the depreciation requires no cash outlay, it does not reduce the cash available for distribution.) Each investor receives $1,000. Taxable income being $20,000, only 20% ($20,000 ÷ $100,000) of the distribution is taxable. Thus, each investor reports as income only $200 of his $1,000 distribution; $800 is tax free.

2. Same facts as in Example 1, except that the building is mortgaged, and an annual amortization payment of $40,000 is being made. Consequently, only $60,000 is available for distribution, of which $20,000 is taxable. Each investor receives $600, of which ⅓ ($20,000 ÷ $60,000) or $200 is taxed, and $400 is tax free. In other words, the $60,000 distribution is tax free to the extent that the depreciation deduction of $80,000 exceeds the amortization of $40,000—namely $40,000. If the amortization payment was increased to $50,000, only $30,000 of the distribution would be tax free ($80,000 − $50,000).

The tax-free return is based on the assumption that the building does not actually depreciate at as fast a rate as the tax depreciation rate. If the building is depreciating physically at a faster rate, the so-called tax-free return on investment does not exist. Distributions to investors (over and above current income return) that are labeled tax-free distributions are, in fact, a return of the investor's own capital.

The above advantages are available for investments made by you individually or in partnership with other associates. They are also available to investors in limited partnerships. However, before investing in a limited partnership, consider these disadvantages of limited partnerships.

1. Investors in limited partnerships are by law generally treated as receiving passive activity income or loss. Furthermore, as a limited partner, you may not take advantage of the $25,000 rental loss allowance, as you are not considered an "active participant"; *see* ¶10.4. In view of the passive activity rules, if you and others join together to buy rental property, you should not organize as a limited partnership if any losses are anticipated. Limited partnerships are advisable only if income is expected or where two or more investment activities will produce income and loss, which will offset each other.

2. Although limited partnerships are organized to prevent double taxation, which occurs in doing business as a corporation, there is a danger that the partnership may be taxed as a corporation if its operations resemble those of a corporation.

3. Partnership operations do not provide for the diversification of investments or for the free transfer of individual interests. Investors may find it difficult to sell their interests because of transferability restrictions and a lack of an open market for the sale of their interests. This liquidity problem may be overcome by buying interests sold through public exchanges. However, interests in publicly-traded master limited partnership (MLP) are subject to the passive activity restrictions and in some cases are taxed as corporations; *see* ¶10.11.

Reviewing an investment offer. Consider the following pointers in reviewing an offering.

1. If the venture is constructing a development, discount projected income which may be eroded by increasing construction costs caused by inflation, material shortages, and labor disputes. Escalating costs not accounted for in long-term construction can jeopardize the project or income prospects. Adequate cash reserves should be available for emergencies.

2. Check the market conditions. Has there been overconstruction in the area? Is the area changing socially and economically?

3. Check the fees of managers. See that they are reasonable for your area. A promoter may conceal the amount of money he is drawing from the project. He may be taking a real estate commission by having a commission paid to a company which he controls. A reliable promoter should disclose this fact and be willing to collect the commission only after the investors have recovered their capital. Also check the reasonableness of prepaid management fees and loan fees and whether or not the sale of property to the syndicate is from a corporation in which the syndicator has an interest. If there is such a sale, check its terms, price, interest rates, and whether there is any prepaid interest which may conceal a cash profit payout to the syndicator.

4. Check the experience and reliability of the manager.

Real estate investment trusts (REITS). The tax treatment of real estate investment trusts resembles that of open-end mutual funds. Distributions generally are taxed to the investors in the trust as dividend income. Distributed long-term capital gains are reported by the investors as long-term gains; *see* also ¶4.4. If the trust operates at a loss, the loss may not be passed on to the investors.

A REIT may not necessarily invest in equities. It may operate for interest return by providing loans. Before investing, check the scope of the REIT's operations and current market conditions and projections.

REMICs. A real estate mortgage investment company (REMIC) holds a fixed pool of mortgages. Investors are treated as holding a regular or residual interest. A REMIC is not a taxable entity for federal income tax purposes. It is generally treated as a partnership, with the residual interest holders as partners.

Investors with regular REMIC interests are treated as holding debt obligations. Interest income will be reported on Form 1099-INT; original issue discount (OID) on Form 1099-OID.

The net income of the REMIC, after payments to regular interest holders, is passed through to the holders of residual interests. The pass-through status of the REMIC applies regardless of whether the REMIC was formed as a corporation, partnership, or trust. Income or loss from a REMIC is reported to residual interest holders on Schedule Q of Form 1066. Residual holders report the income or loss on Schedule E.

WHEN A TENANCY IN COMMON IS A PARTNERSHIP

¶31.2 In a tenancy in common, each tenant owns an undivided share in the property. Upon the death of a co-tenant, his or her interest passes to the heirs, not to the other tenants as in a joint tenancy. Tenants in common may or may not be considered as holding the property in a partnership. The determination of whether they are partners affects whether a partnership return must be filed, whether the involuntary conversion election (¶18.20) and first-year expensing (¶42.3) must be made by the partnership or the co-tenants, and the deductibility of property taxes beyond a co-tenant's percentage of ownership (¶16.9).

IRS regulations defining partnerships note that the co-ownership of property which is merely maintained, kept in repair, and rented or leased is not a partnership. If you wish to operate the property as a partnership, you may do so by forming a partnership. Even if you do not formally set up a partnership, the IRS may treat your co-ownership as a partnership if the services or other activity in holding the property is considered a business. Collecting rents or hiring agents to collect rents is not considered a business activity. In one case, tenants were held to be partners where the property had been previously owned by a corporation in which they were stockholders. Upon liquidation, they received interests in the property equal to their former stock interests. As they continued the business of the corporation using the same assets and the same methods of operation, they were treated as being in business as a partnership.

SALES OF SUBDIVIDED LAND—DEALER OR INVESTOR?

¶31.3 An investor faces a degree of uncertainty in determining the tax treatment of sales of subdivided realty. In some situations, investor status may be preferred; in others, dealer status.

Capital gain on sale. Investor status allows capital gain treatment which may be preferred if you want to take advantage of the 28% tax rate ceiling applied to long-term capital gains (¶5.1), or if you have capital losses to offset the gains. For capital gain, the investor generally has to show that his activities did not make him a dealer but were steps in a liquidation of the investment. To convince an IRS agent or a court of investment activity, this type of evidence may present a favorable argument for capital gain treatment:

The property was bought either as an investment, to build a residence, or received as a gift or inheritance.
No substantial improvements were added to the tract.
The property was subdivided to liquidate the investment.
Sales came through unsolicited offers. There was no advertising or agents.
Sales were infrequent.
There were no previous activities as a real estate dealer.
The seller was in a business unrelated to real estate.
The property was held for a long period of time.
Sales proceeds were invested in other investment property.

Limited capital gain opportunity is also possible through Section 1237 that applies arbitrary holding period rules and contains restrictions against substantial improvements. Few investors have attempted to meet the terms of this limited tax provision.

Installment sales. The distinction between an investor and dealer is significant if land is sold on the installment basis. Investor status is preferable if you want to elect the installment basis here. Dealers may not elect installment sale treatment; *see* ¶5.36.

Interest expense deductions. The distinction between an investor in land and a dealer is also important in the case of interest expenses. Dealer status is preferable here. Interest expenses incurred by an investor are subject to investment interest deduction limitations; *see* Chapter 15. On the other hand, interest expenses of a dealer in the course of business activities are fully deductible.

EXAMPLE Morley was interested in buying farm acreage to resell at a profit. Two and a half million dollars was set as the purchase price. To swing the deal, Morley borrowed $600,000. A short time later, his attempts to resell the property failed, and he allowed the property to be foreclosed. While he held the property he incurred interest costs of over $400,000, which he deducted. The IRS held the interest was not fully deductible. It claimed the interest was investment interest subject to investment interest restrictions. That is, the debt was incurred to purchase and carry investment property. The IRS position was based on the so-called "one-bite" rule, which holds that a taxpayer who engages in only one venture may not under any circumstances be held to be in a business as to that venture. Morley argued that he bought the property not as an investment property but as business property for immediate resale. The IRS then countered that negotiations for resale were not sufficient to support an ordinary asset classification for the property. He needed a prior binding commitment from the prospective buyer at the time he bought the property.
The Tax Court sided with Morley, holding that he held the acreage as ordinary business property. The court rejected the "one-bite" rule. The fact that he had not previously sold business property does not mean that he cannot prove that he held acreage for resale. Here, he intended promptly to resell it, and the facts support his intention. Furthermore, there was no need to show prior binding commitment for resale as claimed by the IRS.

Passive activity. Income from sales of lots is not considered passive activity income. Thus, losses from sales of land may offset salary and other investment income. If you hold rental property and also sell land, make sure that your accounts distinguish between and separate each type of income. This way income and losses from land sales will not be commingled with rent income subject to the passive activity restrictions of Chapter 10.

EXCHANGING REAL ESTATE WITHOUT TAX

¶31.4 You may trade real estate held for investment for other investment real estate and incur no tax. The potential tax on the gain is postponed to the time you sell the exchanged property at a price exceeding the tax basis of the property. A tax-free exchange may also defer a potential tax due on gain from depreciation recapture and might be considered where the depreciable basis of a building has been substantially written off. Here, the building may be exchanged for other property which will give off larger tax deductions.

Fully tax-free exchanges. To transact a fully tax-free exchange, you must satisfy these conditions:

1. The property traded must be solely for property of a like kind. The words "like kind" are liberally interpreted. They refer to the nature or character of the property, not its grade, quality, or use. Some examples of "like kind" exchanges are: farm or ranch for city property; unimproved land for improved real estate; rental house for a store building; and fee in business property for 30-year or more leasehold in the same type of property; *see* Chapter 6.
2. The property exchanged must have been held for productive use in your business or for investment and traded for property to be held for productive use in business or investment. Therefore, trades of property used, or to be used, for personal purposes, such as exchanging a residence for rental property, cannot receive tax-free treatment. Special rules, however, apply when you trade your residence for another home; *see* Chapter 29.
3. The trade must generally occur within a 180-day period, and property identification must occur within 45 days of the first transfer; *see* ¶6.4 for further details of this test.

A real estate dealer cannot transact a tax-free exchange of property held for sale to customers. Also, an exchange is not tax free if the property received is held for immediate resale. You may not exchange tax-free U.S. real estate for real estate in foreign countries.

Disadvantage of tax-free exchange. Although the postponement of tax from a tax-free exchange is equivalent to an interest-free loan from the government equal to the amount you would have owed in taxes had you sold the property, this tax advantage is offset by a disadvantage in the case of an exchange of depreciable real estate. You must carry over the basis of the old property to the new property; *see* the example below.

EXAMPLE You have property with a basis of $25,000, now valued at $50,000, that you exchange for another property worth $50,000. Your basis for depreciation for the new property is $25,000.
If—instead of making an exchange—you sell the old property and use the proceeds to buy new property, the tax basis for depreciation is $50,000, giving you larger deductions than you are getting in the exchange transaction. If increased depreciation deductions are desirable, then it may pay to sell the property and purchase new property. Tax may be spread by transacting an installment sale. Project the tax consequences of a sale and an exchange and choose the one giving the greater overall tax benefits. You may find it preferable to sell the property and purchase new property on which MACRS may be claimed.

A tax-free exchange may be advantageous in the case of land which is not depreciable. It may be exchanged for a depreciable rental building. The exchange is tax free and depreciation may be claimed on the building.

A tax-free exchange is not desirable if the transaction will result in a loss, since you may not deduct a loss in a tax-free exchange. To ensure the loss deduction, first sell the property, then buy new property with the proceeds.

A nonresident alien may not defer tax on an exchange of U.S. realty, unless he or she gets realty which—if sold—is taxed in the U.S.

Tax-free exchanges between related parties are subject to tax if either party disposes of the exchanged property within a two-year period; *see* ¶6.5.

Partially tax-free exchanges. Not all property exchanges are without tax. To be completely tax-free, the exchange must be a property-for-property exchange. If the trade includes boot, such as cash or other property, gain is taxed up to the amount of the boot; *see* ¶6.3.

If you trade mortgaged property, the mortgage released is treated as boot; *see* ¶6.3. When there are mortgages on both properties, the mortgages are netted. The party giving up the larger mortgage and getting the smaller mortgage treats the excess as boot.

EXAMPLE You own a small office building with a fair market value of $70,000, and an adjusted basis of $50,000. There is a $30,000 mortgage on the building. You exchange it for Low's building valued at $55,000, having a $20,000 mortgage, and for $5,000 in cash. You compute your gain in this way:

What you received

Present value of Low's property		$55,000
Cash		5,000
Mortgage on building traded		30,000
Total received		$90,000
Less:		
Adjusted basis of building traded	$50,000	
Mortgage assumed by you	20,000	70,000
Actual gain on the exchange		$20,000

However, the actual gain of $20,000 is taxed only up to the amount of boot, $15,000.

Figuring boot

Cash received		$ 5,000
Mortgage on building traded	$30,000	
Less: Mortgage assumed on Low's property	20,000	10,000
Gain recognized up to boot		$15,000

If the amount of boot exceeds your actual gain, taxable boot is limited to the amount of your gain.

TIMING YOUR REAL PROPERTY SALES

¶31.5 Generally, a taxable transaction occurs in the year in which title or possession to property passes to the buyer. By controlling the year title and possession passes, you may select the year in which to report profit or loss. For example, you intend to sell property this year, but you estimate that reporting the sale next year will incur less in taxes. You can postpone the transfer of title and possession to next year. Alternatively, you can transact an installment sale, giving title and possession this year but delaying the receipt of all or most of the sale proceeds until next year; *see* ¶5.36.

RESTRUCTURING MORTGAGE DEBT

¶31.6 Rather than foreclosure on a mortgage, a lender (mortgagee) may be willing to restructure the mortgage debt by either cancelling all or part of the debt. As a borrower (mortgagor), do not overlook the tax consequences of the new debt arrangement. A debt cancellation or reduction is taxable unless it fits within specific exceptions, such as insolvency or bankruptcy. As discussed at ¶12.9, there is no tax if the debt is restructured by the seller of the property or where a debt is reduced by a third party lender and you are either insolvent, bankrupt, or are a qualifying farmer. These rules apply also to a restructuring of a nonrecourse debt on which you are not personally liable.

EXAMPLE In 1988, Jones borrowed $1,000,000 from Chester and signed a note payable for $1,000,000. Jones was not personally liable on the note, which was secured by an office building valued at $1,000,000 that he bought from Baker with the proceeds of Chester's loan. In 1989, when the value of the building declined to $800,000, Chester agreed to reduce the principal of the loan to $825,000. At the time, Jones held other assets valued at $100,000 and owed another person $50,000. In 1989, Jones realized income of $175,000 on the reduction of the debt, but he can avoid tax to the extent he is insolvent.

To determine Jones' insolvency, the IRS compares Jones' assets and liabilities. His assets total $900,000: the building valued at $800,000 plus other assets of $100,000. His liabilities total $1,025,000: the debt of $50,000 plus the liability on the note of $975,000, which is the $800,000 value of the building and the $175,000 discharged debt. The difference between the assets of $900,000 and liabilities of $1,025,000 is $125,000, the amount by which Jones is insolvent. As Jones is insolvent by $125,000, only $50,000 of the $175,000 discharged debt is treated as taxable income.

In the case of partnership property, tax consequences of the restructuring of a third party loan are determined at the partner level. This means that if you are a partner and are solvent (¶12.9) you may not avoid tax on the transaction, even if the partnership is insolvent.

REPOSSESSION AFTER BUYER'S DEFAULT ON MORTGAGE

¶31.7 When you, as a seller, repossess realty on the buyer's default of a debt which the realty secures, you may realize gain or loss. (If the realty was a personal residence, the loss is not deductible.) A debt is secured by real property whenever you have the right to take title or possession or both in the event the buyer defaults on his obligation under the contract.

Figuring gain on the repossession. Gain on the repossession is the excess of:

1. Payments received on the original sales contract prior to and on the repossession, including payments made by the buyer for your benefit to another party; *over*
2. The amount of taxable gain previously reported prior to the repossession.

Gain computed under these two steps may not be fully taxable. Taxable gain is limited to the amount of original profit less gain on the sale already reported as income for periods prior to the repossession and less your repossession costs.

The limitation on gain does not apply if the selling price cannot be computed at the time of sale as, for example, where the selling price is stated as a percentage of the profits to be realized from the development of the property sold.

EXAMPLE Assume you sell land for $25,000. You take a $5,000 down payment plus a $20,000 mortgage, secured by the property, from the buyer, with principal payable at the rate of $4,000 annually. The adjusted basis of the land was $20,000 and you elected to report the transaction on the installment basis. Your gross profit percentage is 20% ($5,000 profit over $25,000 selling price). In the year of sale, you include $1,000 in your income on the installment basis (20% of $5,000 down payment). The next year you reported profit of $800 (20% of $4,000 annual installment). In the third year, the buyer defaults on his payments, and you repossess the property. The amount of gain on repossession is computed as follows:

1. Compute gain.

Amount of money received ($5,000 plus $4,000)		$9,000
Less: Amount of gain taxed in prior years ($1,000 plus $800)		1,800
Gain		$7,200

2. Compute limit on taxable gain, assuming cost of repossession is $500.

Original profit		$5,000
Reduced by:		
Gain reported as income	$1,800	
Cost of repossession	500	2,300
Taxable gain on repossession		$2,700

These rules do not affect the character of the gain. Thus, if you repossess property as a dealer, the gain is subject to ordinary income rates. If you, as an investor, repossess in 1992 a tract originally held long term whose gain was reported on the installment method, the gain is capital gain.

The basis of repossessed property. It is the adjusted basis of the debt (face value of the debt less the unreported profits) secured by the property, figured as of the date of repossession, increased by (1) the taxable gain on repossession, *and* (2) the legal fees and other repossession costs you paid.

EXAMPLE Same facts as in the example above. The basis of the repossessed property is computed as follows:

1. Face value of debt ($20,000 note less $4,000 payment)		$16,000
2. Less: Unreported profit (20% of above)		3,200
3. Adjusted basis at date of repossession		$12,800
4. Plus: Gain on repossession	$2,700	
Cost of repossession	500	3,200
5. Basis of repossessed property		$16,000

If you treated the debt as having become worthless or partially worthless before repossession, you are considered to receive, upon the repossession of the property securing the debt, an amount equal to the amount of the debt treated as worthless. You report as income the amount of any prior bad debt deduction and increase the basis of the debt by an amount equal to the amount reported as income.

If your debt is not fully discharged as a result of the repossession, the basis of the undischarged debt is zero. No loss may be claimed if the obligations subsequently become worthless. This rule applies to undischarged debts on the original obligation of the purchaser, a substituted obligation of the purchaser, a deficiency judgment entered in a court of law into which the purchaser's obligation was merged, and any other obligations arising from the transaction.

The repossession rules do not apply if you repurchase the property by paying the buyer a sum in addition to the discharge of the debt, unless the repurchase and payment was provided for in the original sale contract, or the buyer has defaulted on his or her obligation, or default is imminent.

Personal residence. Special rules apply to repossessions and resales of a personal residence if: (1) at least some of the gain on the original sale was not taxed because you made an election to avoid tax (¶29.14) or to defer gain on the purchase of a new residence (¶29.2); and (2) within a year after the repossession you resell the property.

The original sale and resale is treated as one transaction. You refigure the amount realized on the sale. You combine the selling price of the resale with the selling price of the original sale. From this total, you subtract selling expenses for both sales, the part of the original installment obligation that remains unpaid at the time of repossession, and repossession costs. The net is the amount realized on the combined sale-resale. Subtracting basis in the home from the amount realized gives the gain on the combined sale-resale before taking into account the exclusion (¶29.14) or deferral (¶29.2) rules.

EXAMPLE In 1991, you, at age 60, sell a house for $250,000. You take back a purchase money mortgage of $250,000. Selling expenses were $3,000; the adjusted basis of the house was $167,000. You realized a profit of $80,000.

Amount realized	$247,000
Adjusted basis	167,000
Gain	$ 80,000

You elected to avoid tax by claiming the exclusion of ¶29.14.

In 1992, the buyer defaulted and you repossessed the house and sold it for $300,000, incurring selling expenses of $5,000 and repossession costs of $2,000. The buyer also owed you $200,000 on his installment note. You have a $48,000 taxable gain on the combined sale-resale as follows:

Selling price on resale		$300,000
Selling price on original sale		250,000
Total selling price		$550,000
Less:		
Unpaid buyer's note	$200,000	
Repossession costs	2,000	
Selling expenses ($3,000+$5,000)	8,000	210,000
Amount realized		$340,000
Less: basis		167,000
Gain on sale-resale		$173,000
Less $125,000 exclusion		125,000
Taxable gain		$48,000

FORECLOSURE ON MORTGAGES OTHER THAN PURCHASE MONEY

¶31.8

If you, as a mortgagee (lender), bid in on a foreclosure sale to pay off a mortgage that is *not a purchase money mortgage,* your actual financial loss is the difference between the unpaid mortgage debt and the value of the property. For tax purposes, however, you may realize a capital gain or loss and a bad debt loss which are reportable *in the year of the foreclosure sale.*

Your bid is treated as consisting of two distinct transactions:

1. The repayment of your loan. To determine whether this results in a bad debt, the bid price is matched against the face amount of the mortgage.
2. A taxable exchange of your mortgage note for the foreclosed property, which may result in a capital gain or loss. This is determined by matching the bid price against the fair market value of the property.

EXAMPLES 1. *Mortgagee's bid less than market value.* You hold a $40,000 mortgage on property having a fair market value of $30,000. You bid on the property at the foreclosure sale at $28,000. The expenses of the sale are $2,000, reducing the bid price to $26,000. The mortgagor is insolvent, so you have a bad debt loss of $14,000 ($40,000 − $26,000). You also have a $4,000 capital gain (the fair market value of the property of $30,000 − $26,000).

2. *Mortgagee's bid equal to market value.* Suppose your bid was $32,000, and the expenses $2,000. The difference between the net bid price of $30,000 and the mortgage of $40,000 is $10,000. As the mortgagor is insolvent, there is a bad debt loss of $10,000. Since the net bid price equals the fair market value, there is neither capital gain nor loss.

3. *Mortgagee's bid greater than market value.* Suppose you had bid $36,000 and had $2,000 in expenses. Your bad debt deduction is $6,000—the difference between the mortgage debt of $40,000 and the net bid price of $34,000. You also had a capital loss of $4,000 (difference between the net bid price of $34,000 and the fair market value of $30,000).

Where the bid price equals the mortgage debt plus unreported but accrued interest, you report the interest as income. But where the accrued interest has been reported, the unpaid amount is added to the collection expenses.

Preserve evidence of the property's fair market value. At a later date, the IRS may claim that the property was worth more than your bid and may tax you for the difference. Furthermore, be prepared to prove the worthlessness of the debt to support the bad debt deduction.

Voluntary conveyance. Instead of forcing you to foreclose, the mortgagor may voluntarily convey the property to you in consideration for your canceling the mortgage debt. Your loss is the amount by which the mortgage debt plus accrued interest exceeds the fair market value of the property. If, however, the fair market value exceeds the mortgage debt plus accrued interest, the difference is taxable gain. The gain or loss is reportable in the year you receive the property. Your basis in the property is its fair market value when you receive it.

FORECLOSURE SALE TO THIRD PARTY

¶31.9

When a third party buys the property in a foreclosure, the mortgagee receives the purchase price to apply against the mortgage debt. If it is less than the debt, the mortgagee may proceed against the mortgagor for the difference. Foreclosure expenses are treated as offsets against the foreclosure proceeds and increase the bad debt loss.

You deduct your loss as a bad debt. The law distinguishes between two types of bad debt deductions: business bad debts and non-business bad debts. A business bad debt is fully deductible. A non-business bad debt is a short-term capital loss that can be offset only against capital gains, plus a limited amount of ordinary income (¶5.47). In addition, you may deduct a partially worthless business bad debt, but you may not deduct a partially worthless non-business bad debt. Remember this distinction if you are thinking of forgiving part of the mortgage debt as a settlement. If the debt is a non-business bad debt, you will not be able to take a deduction until the entire debt proves to be worthless. But whether you are deducting a business or a non-business bad debt, your deduction will be allowed only if you show the debt to be uncollectible—for example, because a deficiency judgment is worthless or because the mortgagor is bankrupt.

EXAMPLE You hold a $30,000 note and mortgage which are in default. You foreclose, and a third party buys the property for $20,000. Foreclosure expenses amount to $2,000. The deficiency is uncollectible. Your loss of $12,000 is figured as follows:

Unpaid mortgage debt		$30,000
Foreclosure proceeds	$20,000	
Less: Expenses	2,000	
Net proceeds		18,000
Bad debt loss		$12,000

TRANSFERRING MORTGAGED REALTY

¶31.10

Mortgaging realty that has appreciated in value is one way of realizing cash on the appreciation without current tax consequences. The receipt of cash by mortgaging the property is not taxed; tax will generally be imposed only when the property is sold. However, there is a possible tax where the mortgage exceeds the adjusted basis of the property and the property is given away or transferred to a controlled corporation. Where the property is transferred to a controlled corporation, the excess is taxable gain. Furthermore, if the IRS successfully charges that the transfer is part of a tax avoidance scheme, the taxable gain may be as high as the amount of the mortgage liability.

Gifts. The IRS holds that a gift of mortgaged property results in taxable income to the donor to the extent that the mortgage liability exceeds the donor's basis.

32

TAX SAVINGS FOR EXECUTIVES

Executive pay plans have one objective—to reduce or eliminate the tax cost of earning salary income.

There are pay benefits that are not taxable such as certain fringe benefits, disability pensions, health, accident and death benefits, and certain housing costs while working abroad. Other tax saving benefits may be developed through pension and profit-sharing plans, stock options, and deferred pay plans.

The objective of deferring pay is to postpone the receipt of salary income to a time when you expect to be in a lower tax bracket.

DEFERRED PAY PLANS

¶**32.1** The major objective of a deferred pay plan is to postpone the tax on pay benefits to a year in which you will be in a lower tax bracket than that of the current year. However, a deferred pay plan is generally not advisable where a projection of future income shows that there probably will be no substantial income decline, and/or the tax bracket differentials will not be wide. An after-tax dollar in hand for current use is preferable to an expectation of a tax saving that may not materialize.

FRINGE BENEFITS

¶**32.2** Fringe benefits provided to executives by employers increase after-tax income by being either tax exempt or subject to special tax treatment. The tax consequences of fringe benefits and other pay benefits are discussed in the following sections of this book:

PENSION AND PROFIT-SHARING PLANS

¶**32.3** A company qualified pension or profit-sharing plan offers the following benefits: (1) You do not realize current income on your employer's contributions to the plan on your behalf; (2) funds contributed by both your employer and you compound tax free within the plan; (3) if you receive a lump-sum distribution, tax on employer contributions may be reduced by a special averaging rule; and, (4) if you receive a lump-sum distribution in company securities, unrealized appreciation on those securities is not taxed until you finally sell the stock.

Where you are allowed to choose the type of payout from a qualified plan, make sure that you compare the tax on receiving a lump-sum distribution with the projected tax cost of deferring payments over a period of years or rolling over the distribution to an IRA account; *see* ¶7.3.

401(k) plan. If your company has a profit-sharing or stock bonus plan, it has the opportunity of giving you additional tax-sheltered pay. The tax law allows the company to add a cash or deferred pay plan, called a 401(k) plan. For further details, *see* ¶7.17.

INSURANCE PLANS MAY BE TAX FREE

¶32.4
Company-financed insurance for employees is a common method of giving additional benefits at low or no tax cost.

Group life insurance. Group insurance plans may furnish not only life insurance protection but also accident and health benefits. Premium costs are low and tax deductible to the company while tax free to you unless you have nonforfeitable rights to permanent life insurance; or, in the case of group-term life insurance, your coverage exceeds $50,000; *see* ¶3.2. Even where your coverage exceeds $50,000, the tax incurred on your employer's premium payment is generally less than what you would pay privately for similar insurance.

It may be possible to avoid estate tax on the group policy proceeds if you assign all of your ownership rights in the policy, including the right to convert the policy, and if the beneficiary is other than your estate. Where the policy allows assignment of the conversion right, in addition to all other rights, and state law does not bar the assignment, you are considered to have made a complete assignment of the group insurance for estate tax purposes.

The IRS has ruled that where an employee assigns a group life policy and the value of the employee's interest in the policy cannot be ascertained, there is no taxable gift. This is so where the employer could simply have stopped making payments. However, there is a gift by the employee to the assignee to the extent of premiums paid by the employer. That gift is a present interest qualifying for the $10,000 annual exclusion.

Split-dollar insurance. Where you want more insurance than is provided by a group plan, your company may be able to help you get additional protection through a split-dollar insurance plan. Under this type of plan, your employer purchases permanent life insurance on your life and pays the annual premium to the extent of the yearly increases in the cash surrender value of the policy. You pay only the balance of the premium. At your death, your employer is entitled to part of the proceeds equal to the cash surrender value or any lesser amount equaling the total premiums he or she paid. You have the right to name a beneficiary to receive the remaining proceeds which, under most policies, is substantial compared with the employer's share.

You annually report as taxable income an amount equal to the one-year term cost of the declining life insurance protection to which you are entitled, less any portion of the premium provided by you. Simplified somewhat, here is how the tax would be figured in one year. Assume the share of the proceeds payable to your beneficiary (face value less cash surrender value) from a $100,000 policy is $77,535. If the term cost of $77,535 insurance provided by the employer is $567, you pay a tax on $567, less your payment of premium. So, if you paid a premium of $209, you pay tax on $358. Assume in the fourth year that you pay no premium and the amount

payable to your family is $69,625. (Under the split-dollar plan, the benefits payable to your beneficiary continuously decline; the employer's share increases annually because of the continued payment of premiums and the increase in the cash surrender value.) The term cost provided by your employer toward $69,625 is $549; you pay tax on the full $549.

Despite the tax cost, you may find the arrangement an inexpensive method of obtaining additional insurance coverage with your employer's help. For example, taking the taxable premium benefit of $549 from the above example, if you are in the 28% bracket, the cost of almost $70,000 insurance protection in that year is $153.72 ($549 × 28%).

STOCK APPRECIATION RIGHTS (SARs)

¶32.5
SARs are a form of cash bonus tied to an increase in the price of employer stock. Each SAR entitles an employee to cash equal to the excess of the fair market value of one share on the date of exercise over the value on the date of the grant of the SAR.

EXAMPLE   When a stock is worth $30 a share, you get 100 SARs exercisable within five years. Two years later when the stock price increases to $50 a share, you exercise the SAR and receive $2,000. You are taxed when you receive the cash.

 Watch SAR Expiration Date

If the rights increase in value, keep a close watch on the expiration date. Do not let them expire before exercise. If you do, not only will you lose income but you will be taxed on income you never received. According to the IRS, an employee who does not exercise the SARs is taxed as if they had been exercised immediately before they expire. The IRS claims that an employee has constructive receipt of income immediately before they expire. At that time, the amount of gain realized from the SARs is fixed because the employee can no longer benefit from future appreciation in value.

An executive may realize taxable income when he or she becomes entitled to the maximum SAR benefit allowed by the company plan. For example, in 1987, when company stock is worth $30, an executive is granted 100 SARs exercisable within five years. By exercising the SARs, the executive may receive cash equal to the appreciation up to $20 per share. If the stock appreciates to $50 per share in 1992, the executive realizes taxable income of $2,000 ($20 per share × 100) in 1992, even if he or she does not exercise the SARs. The reason is that once the stock value appreciated to $50, the maximum SAR benefit of $20 was realized.

Performance shares. The company promises to make an award of stock in the future, at no cost to you, if the company's earnings reach a set level. You are taxed on the receipt of stock (unless the stock is restricted, as discussed in ¶32.6).

STOCK OPTIONS AND RESTRICTED STOCK

¶32.6
Executives receiving qualified statutory stock options generally do not incur tax liability either at the time the option is granted or when the option is exercised, although the option spread may be subject to AMT; *see* ¶23.2. Qualified statutory options include

incentive stock options and options under an employee stock purchase plan. Receipt of a nonqualified stock option may result in an immediate tax.

Incentive stock options (ISOs). A corporation may provide its executives with incentive stock options to acquire its stock (or the stock of its parent or subsidiaries). For regular income tax purposes, ISOs are not taxed when granted or exercised. The option spread is taxable as capital gain if the stock acquired by the exercise of the option is not sold until more than one year after it was acquired and more than two years after the option was granted. If a corporation grants an executive ISOs to purchase stock valued over $100,000, the maximum ISO limit for options first exercisable in any one year is $100,000. For other restrictions on ISOs, see the terms of your company plan.

For AMT tax consequences, *see* ¶23.2.

Employee stock purchase plans. These plans allow employees to buy their company's stock, usually at a discount. The plan must be nondiscriminatory and meet tax law tests on option terms. Options granted under qualified plans are not taxed until the shares acquired are sold. If you do not sell the shares until more than two years have passed since granting of the option, and the stock is held more than one year, gain on the sale is reported as ordinary wage income to the extent the option price was less than the fair market value of the shares when the option was granted. Any excess gain is capital gain. For sales before the end of the two-year/one-year holding period, the amount reportable as ordinary wage income is the excess of the value of the shares when the option was exercised over the option price.

Nonqualified stock options. Where a nonqualified option has no ascertainable fair market value, as is generally the case, no income is realized on the receipt of the option. Income is realized when the option is exercised. If a nonqualified stock option has an ascertainable fair market value, the value of the option less any amount paid by the employee is taxable as ordinary wage income in the first year that the employee's right to the option is freely transferable or not subject to a substantial risk of forfeiture. For other details and requirements, *see* IRS regulation Section 1.83-7.

Nonqualified stock options may be granted in addition to or in place of incentive stock options. There are no restrictions on the amount of nonqualified stock options that may be granted.

When sale of stock is treated as grant of option. If company stock is purchased on the basis of the executive's promissory note and he or she is not personally liable, the company can recover only its stock in the event of default on the note. In terms of risk, the executive has given nothing and is somewhat in the same position as the optionee. If the stock value drops, he or she may walk away from the deal with no personal risk. According to IRS regulations, the deal may be viewed as an option arrangement. Application of the IRS regulation would give the executive ordinary taxable income when the stock is purchased if the value of the stock at the time of purchase exceeds the purchase price. For example, on July 1, 1986, a corporation sells 100 shares of its stock to an executive. The stock has a fair market value on that date of $25,000 and the executive executes a nonrecourse note secured by the stock in that amount, plus 8% annual interest. He or she is required by the note to make an annual payment of $5,000 of principal, plus interest, beginning the following year. In 1991, the executive pays the interest on the note but no principal. He or she also collects dividends and votes the stock. In 1992, when the stock has appreciated in value to $30,000, the executive pays off the note. Under the IRS regulation, the executive would realize ordinary income upon payment of the nonrecourse note to the extent of the difference between the amount paid ($25,000 in 1992) and the value of the stock ($30,000).

Restricted stock. Stock subject to restrictions is taxed as pay in the first year in which it is either transferable or not subject to a substantial risk of forfeiture. A risk of forfeiture exists where your rights are conditioned upon the future performance of substantial services. Generally, taxable income is the difference between the amount, if any, that you pay for the stock and its value at the time the risk of forfeiture is removed. The valuation at the time the forfeiture restrictions lapse is not reduced because of restrictions imposed on the right to sell the property. However, restrictions which will never lapse do affect valuation.

SEC restriction on insider trading is considered a substantial risk of forfeiture, so that receipt of stock subject to such restriction is a nontaxable event. However, under an SEC rule change, insiders may immediately resell stock acquired through exercise of an option granted at least six months earlier. As the stock acquired through such options is not subject to SEC restrictions, the executive is subject to immediate tax.

If the stock is subject to a restriction on transfer to comply with SEC pooling-of-interests accounting rules, the stock is considered to be subject to a substantial restriction.

Electing Immediate Tax On Restricted Stock

You may elect to be taxed on the unrestricted value of the stock at the time you receive it, less any payment you made. If you do, you are treated as an investor and later appreciation in value is not taxed as pay when your rights to the stock become vested. If you later forfeit the stock, a capital loss is allowed for your cost, minus any amount realized on the forfeiture. The election must generally be made by filing a statement with the IRS not later than 30 days after the date of the transfer of the stock.

The restricted stock rule is not restricted to compensation of employees; it may apply to any type of fee arrangement for services.

EDUCATIONAL BENEFITS FOR EMPLOYEES' CHILDREN

¶32.7 *Private foundations.* The IRS has published guidelines under which a private foundation established by an employer may make tax-free grants to children of employees. If the guidelines are satisfied, employees are not taxable on the benefits provided their children. Advance approval of the grant program must be obtained from the IRS.

IRS guidelines require:

Grant recipients must be selected by a scholarship committee which is independent of the employer and the foundation. Former employees of the employer or the foundation are not considered independent.

Eligibility for the grants may be restricted to children of employees who have been employed for a minimum of up to three years, but eligibility may not be related to the employee's position, services, or duties.

Once awarded, a grant may not be terminated if the parent leaves his job with the employer, regardless of the reason for the termination of employment. If a one-year grant is awarded or a multi-year grant is awarded subject to renewal, a child who reapplies for a later grant may not be considered ineligible because his parent no longer works for the employer.

Grant recipients must be based solely upon objective standards unrelated to the employer's business and the parent's employment such as prior academic performance, aptitude tests, recommendations from instructors, financial needs, and conclusions drawn from personal interviews.

Recipients must be free to use the grants for courses which are not of particular benefit to the employer or the foundation.

The grant program must not be used by the foundation or employer to recruit employees or induce employees to continue employment.

There must be no requirement or suggestion that the child or parent is expected to render future employment services.

The grant program must also meet a percentage test. The number of grants awarded in a given year to children of employees must not exceed (1) 25% of the number of employees' children who were eligible, applied for the grants, and were considered by the selection committee in that year; or (2) 10% of the number of employees' children who were eligible during that year, whether or not they applied. Renewals of grants are not considered in determining the number of grants awarded.

If all guidelines other than the percentage test are satisfied, the IRS will determine whether the primary purpose of the program is to educate the children. If it is, the grants will be considered tax-free scholarships or fellowships; if it is not, the grants are taxed to the parent-employee as extra compensation.

Educational benefit trusts and other plans. A medical professional corporation set up an educational benefit plan to provide the payment of college costs to the children of "key" employees. The plan defined a key employee as an employee who was salaried at over $15,000. To receive benefits, the child must have been a candidate for a degree within two years after graduating from high school. If an eligible employee quit for reasons other than death or permanent disability, his children could no longer receive benefits except for expenses actually incurred before termination. The company made annual contributions to the trust for which a bank was trustee. According to the IRS, amounts contributed to the trust are a form of pay to qualified employees, as they are contributed on the basis of employment and earnings record, rather than on the basis of competitive standards such as need, merit, or motivation. However, employees are not currently taxable. The right to have their children receive benefits is conditioned upon each employee's future performance of services. Furthermore, there is a substantial risk of forfeiture. Tax is not incurred until a child has a vested right to receive benefits; here, vesting does not occur until a child becomes a candidate for a degree at an educational institution, has actually incurred educational expenses, and his parent is employed by the company. Once the right to receive a distribution from the plan becomes vested, the parent of the child who has incurred the expenses is taxable on the amount of the distribution. The company may then claim a deduction for the amount reported as income by the employee.

The Tax Court and appeals court have upheld the IRS position in similar plans.

33 TAX SAVINGS IN FAMILY INCOME PLANNING

Each additional dollar of ordinary income you receive, such as interest, dividends, and rent, is taxed in your highest bracket. If you can deflect income to a lower tax bracket of a child or other dependent relative, he or she will pay a smaller tax on the income than you would pay. However, the tax advantages of shifting income to children under age 14 are sharply reduced by the kiddie tax; *see* Chapter 24.

To split income, you must do more than make gifts of income. You must transfer the actual property from which the income is produced. For example, you do not avoid tax on interest by instructing your savings bank to credit interest to your children's account. Unless you actually transfer the complete ownership of the account to your children, the interest income is earned on money owned by you and must be reported by you. The same holds true with dividends, rents, and other forms of income. Unless you transfer the income producing property, the income will be taxed to you.

You may not split earned income; income resulting from your services is taxed to you. You may not avoid this result by setting up trusts to receive your earned income.

GIFT TAX BASICS

¶33.1 As family income planning generally requires the transfer of property, you must consider possible gift tax liability. The gift tax rates and credit are the same as those of the estate tax listed in Chapter 39.

However, gift tax liability may be avoided by making gifts within an annual exclusion of $10,000 (or $20,000 for joint gifts). To each donee, you may give annually up to $10,000 tax free; furthermore, if your spouse joins in the gift, you may give annually tax free to each donee up to $20,000. Thus, if you (with your spouse's consent) make annual gifts to four persons, you could give away without gift tax up to $80,000 (4 ¥ $20,000 exclusion). The $10,000 (or $20,000) annual exclusion is allowed only for cash gifts or gifts of present interests in property; gifts of future interests do not qualify.

Gifts to a spouse who is a U.S. citizen are completely tax free through the marital deduction. There also is an unlimited gift tax exclusion for paying someone else's tuition or medical expenses, provided you directly pay the educational organization or care provider.

If you make an interest-free or low-interest loan to a family member, you may be subject to income and gift taxes; *see* ¶4.31.

Filing a gift tax return. A gift tax return generally must be filed on Form 709 for a gift made to someone other than your spouse if it exceeds $10,000 or is a gift of a future interest (regardless of value). A return does not have to be filed for gifts qualifying for the tuition or medical expense exclusion.

Married couples who consent to "split" gifts of up to $20,000 must report the gifts to the IRS, although no gift tax is due under the annual exclusion. If your spouse consents to split gifts with you, you may be able to use a short form, Form 709-A, rather than Form 709; *see* the form instructions.

Form 709 or Form 709-A generally must be filed by April 15th of the year following the year of the gift. If you get a filing extension for your income tax return, the extension also applies to the gift tax return. An additional extension may be granted by the IRS for gift tax returns filed on Form 709 if you show good cause; further extensions are not allowed for filing Form 709-A.

Even where Form 709 must be filed, gift tax liability computed on the form may be offset by the unified credit applied to gift taxes as well as estate taxes. You and your spouse each have a credit of $192,800 that exempts up to $600,000 of lifetime taxable gifts (exceeding the annual exclusion) from gift tax, or transfers at death from estate tax. When you report taxable gifts exceeding the annual exclusion, your unified credit offsets the gift tax liability, so that you do not actually have to pay gift tax to the IRS. The portion of the credit used to offset gift taxes reduces the credit available for estate tax purposes upon your death. *See* Chapter 39.

CUSTODIAN ACCOUNTS

¶33.2

Custodian accounts set up in a bank, mutual fund, or brokerage firm can achieve income splitting; the tax consequences discussed below generally apply to such accounts. Trust accounts which are considered revocable under state law are ineffective in splitting interest income.

Although custodian accounts may be opened anywhere in the United States, the rules governing the account may vary from state to state. The differences between the laws of the states generally do not affect federal tax consequences.

Custodian Securities Account

Purchase of securities through custodian accounts provides a practical method for making a gift of securities to a minor child, eliminating the need for a trust. The mechanics of opening a custodian account are simple. An adult opens a stock account for a minor child at a broker's office. He or she registers the securities in the name of a custodian for the benefit of the child. The custodian may be a parent, a child's guardian, grandparent, brother, sister, uncle, or aunt. In some states, the custodian may be any adult or a bank or trust company. The custodian has the right to sell securities in the account, collect sales proceeds, and investment income, and use them for the child's benefit or reinvestment. *See* below for tax treatment.

There are limitations placed on the custodian. Proceeds from the sale of an investment or income from an investment may not be used to buy additional securities on margin. While a custodian should prudently seek reasonable income and capital preservation, he or she generally is not liable for losses unless they result from bad faith, intentional wrongdoing, or gross negligence.

When the minor reaches majority age (depending on state law), property in the custodian account is turned over to him or her. No formal accounting is required. The child, now an adult, may sign a simple release freeing the custodian from any liability. But on reaching majority, the child may require a formal accounting if there are any doubts as to the propriety of the custodian's actions while acting as custodian. For this reason and also for tax record-keeping purposes, a separate bank account should be opened in which proceeds from sales of investments and investment income are deposited pending reinvestment on behalf of the child. Such an account will furnish a convenient record of sales proceeds, investment income, and reinvestment of the same.

Income tax treatment. Income from a custodian account is taxable to the child as long as it is not used by the parent who set up the account to pay for the child's support. Tax-exempt income from a custodian account is not taxable to the parent even when used for child support. Income from a custodian account in excess of $1,200 is taxed at the parent's tax rate if the child is under age 14. Computation of the kiddie tax is discussed in Chapter 24.

Gift tax treatment. When setting up a custodian account, you may have to pay a gift tax. A transfer of cash or securities to a custodian account is a gift. But you are not subject to a gift tax if you properly plan the cash contributions or purchase of securities for your children's accounts. You may make gifts up to $10,000 to one

person, which is shielded from gift tax by the annual exclusion. The exclusion applies each year to each person to whom you make a gift. If your spouse consents to join with you in the gift, you may give annually tax free up to $20,000 to each person.

If the custodian account is set up at the end of December, another tax-free transfer of $20,000 may be made in the first days of January of the following year. In this way, a total of $40,000 is shifted within the two-month period.

Even if gifts exceeding the $10,000 (or $20,000) exclusion are made, gift tax liability may be offset by the unified credit applied to gift and estate taxes; *see* Chapter 39.

Estate tax treatment. The value of a custodian account will be taxed in your estate if you die while acting as custodian of an account before your child reaches his or her majority. However, you may avoid the problem by naming someone other than yourself as custodian. If you should decide to act as custodian, taking the risk that the account will be taxed in your estate, remember no estate tax is incurred if the tax on your estate is offset by the estate tax credit; *see* Chapter 39.

If you act as custodian and decide to terminate the custodianship, care should be taken to formally close the account. Otherwise, if you die while retaining power over the account, the IRS may try to tax the account in your estate.

U.S. SAVINGS BOND TUITION PLANS

¶33.3

Because interest on Series EE bonds may be deferred (¶4.29), consider the use of EE bonds to fund part of a college savings program. You can defer the interest until final maturity (30 years) or report the interest annually. EE bonds must be held at least five years to get the maximum yield; *see* ¶30.13. The interest is not subject to state or local tax. For bonds purchased in your child's name, having your child report the interest annually may be advisable where it can be offset by the child's standard deduction or itemized deductions. To the extent interest is offset each year, the interest escapes tax; *see* ¶4.29.

If you purchase bonds issued after 1989 in your name, or in the joint names of you and your spouse, you may be able to exclude accumulated interest from federal tax if in the year you redeem the bonds you pay tuition and similar education fees. Under current law, the interest exclusion is a limited tax break hedged with restrictions, which were being reviewed by Congress when this book went to press.

Current law requires you to be age 24 or over before the month in which the bonds are purchased, and the bonds must be issued solely in your name or in the joint names of you and your spouse. You may not claim the exclusion for bonds bought in your child's name, or which you own jointly with your child. In the year the bonds are redeemed, you must pay tuition and similar educational fees for yourself, your spouse, or your dependents. Thus, grandparents may not claim the exclusion if they buy savings bonds to fund the college education of grandchildren, unless the children are dependents of the grandparents in the year the bonds are cashed. Tuition and fees must be for a college, university, or a vocational school that meets federal financial aid standards. Room and board are not eligible expenses. Finally, the exclusion is available only if your income does not exceed a phaseout range in the year the bonds are redeemed to pay education costs; see page 339 for the 1992 exclusion and income phaseout rules.

Under the proposals being considered by Congress, the phaseout rule and the age 24 restriction would be repealed, and the educational fees could be for any individual, whether or not your dependent. See the Supplement for an update on the legislation.

Excludable amount and phaseout rule for 1992 returns. The tax-free amount of interest depends on the educational expenses and your adjusted gross income (AGI) in the year of the redemption. Educational expenses must be reduced by nontaxable scholarship or fellowship grants. The exclusion is figured on Form 8815.

If the redemption amount exceeds the educational expenses, the excludable amount is based on the ratio of expenses to redemption amount. For example, if expenses are $6,000 and upon redemption you receive $8,000 consisting of $4,000 principal and $4,000 interest, the ratio is 75% ($6,000/$8,000) and thus, 75% of the interest—or $3,000 (75% × $4,000)—is potentially excludable from income, subject to the phaseout rules.

A full interest exclusion is allowed only to persons with AGI below a phaseout threshold. On 1992 returns, the full exclusion is allowed to unmarried persons with AGI below $44,150, and to married couples filing jointly with AGI below $66,200. *The savings bond interest is included in AGI for purposes of applying the phaseout.* No exclusion is allowed to married persons filing separately, regardless of income. The exclusion is phased out over an AGI range of $44,150 to $59,150 for unmarried persons, and $66,200 to $96,200 for married couples filing jointly. After 1992, these income phaseout ranges will be adjusted by an inflation factor if Congress does not repeal the phaseout rule.

EXAMPLE In 1990, you bought a $10,000 EE Bond for $5,000. In 1992, you redeem the bond for $5,632 to pay 1992 college tuition of $6,000 for your dependent child. Your 1992 joint return adjusted gross income is $69,368. By preparing Form 8815, you will figure that of the EE Bond interest of $632, $552 is tax free and $80 is taxable.

OTHER TYPES OF INVESTMENTS FOR CHILDREN

¶33.4 A minor generally lacks the ability to manage property. Yet, if you exercise control over the property you give to a child, the gift may not be recognized for purposes of shifting income. You might appoint a fiduciary for the child, but this step may be costly. Alternatively, you might select property which does not require management and which can be transferred by a minor. For example—

1. Bonds may be purchased and registered in a minor's name and coupons or the proceeds on sale or maturity of bonds may be cashed or deposited in a minor's name.

    See also ¶30.13 for U.S. Savings Bond plan tips. Zero coupon bonds are discussed at ¶30.9 and ¶30.10.
2. Insurance companies will write policies on the lives of minors and recognize their ownership of policies covering the lives of others. Depending on the age of the minor, state law, and company practice, it may be necessary to appoint a guardian for the purpose of cashing in or borrowing on insurance policies given to a minor. A gift of a life insurance policy or an annuity will usually qualify as a gift of a present interest in property for the annual gift tax exclusion.
3. Mutual fund shares, such as money market funds, may be purchased and registered in the name of a minor. The problem of management and sale for reinvestment is minimized because the investment trust itself provides continuous super-

vision. Changes in the underlying investments of the fund are made without reference to the minor. Most funds provide for automatic reinvestment of dividends in additional shares.

Tax consequences of college tuition prepayment plans are discussed at ¶33.11.

JOINT TENANTS

¶33.5 Owning property jointly with one's spouse seems a reasonable solution to a family estate problem. It is easy to arrange; have both names listed as owners. On the death of one, the surviving spouse becomes sole owner of the property. The property does not pass through the estate incurring probate and other costs. Furthermore, there is no estate tax on the property. One-half the property is included in the deceased spouse's estate, but it is not taxed because of the marital deduction.

Disadvantages of Joint Ownership

The principal objection to joint ownership is that it deprives each owner of the ability to direct the transfer of ownership of his or her interest. The owner cannot specify who is ultimately to inherit it or the time and method of inheritance. The best way to control an estate is through a program of estate planning. While joint ownership offers what seems an easy solution, it involves a fixed disposition of property. Through estate planning it is possible to provide alternatives to meet unexpected events at the lowest possible tax cost.

Jointly owned property may pass to people whom the couple would not have named as heirs. Assume a married man with no children puts nearly all of his property in his and his wife's joint names and then the couple is in an automobile accident that is fatal to the husband. His wife survives for a few weeks. Upon her death, under local law, all the property goes to her brothers and sisters. Both the husband and wife might have wanted to assure his parents of support for their lives. Perhaps the couple might have chosen to distribute the property between both families. The survivorship feature of joint ownership is rigid and cannot be changed once one or both of the joint owners die.

Joint brokerage account in a street name. Setting up a joint brokerage account in a street name is not an effective transfer for gift tax purposes. Securities are held in a "street" name—that is, the name of the broker—when you have a margin account. Even when you have a cash account, securities may be held in a street name to facilitate trading. The IRS has ruled that where you, with your separate funds, have set up a joint brokerage account for yourself and another person, and the securities are registered in the name of a broker, you have not made a gift for gift tax purposes. The gift is completed only when the other party draws on the account without any obligation to account to you. The value of the gift would be the amount of money or property withdrawn. The IRS contends in a ruling that an account in a street name is like a joint bank account set up by one person. Control over the funds has not been given up in either type of account. Income tax consequences were not covered by the ruling. However, a strong inference from the ruling is that the dividends and sales and exchanges are taxable to the party who contributed the funds to the account.

TRUSTS IN FAMILY PLANNING

¶33.6 You establish a trust by transferring legal title to property to a trustee who manages the property for one or more beneficiaries. As the one who set up the trust, you are called the grantor or settlor of the trust. The trustee may be one or more individuals or an institution such as a bank or a trust company.

You can create a trust during your lifetime or by your will. A trust created during your lifetime is called an inter vivos trust; one established in your will is a testamentary trust. An inter vivos trust can be revocable or irrevocable. An irrevocable trust does not allow for changes of heart; it requires a complete surrender of property. By conveying property irrevocably to a trust, you may relieve yourself of tax on the income from the trust principal. Furthermore, the property in trust usually is not subject to estate tax, although it may be subject to gift tax. A trust should be made irrevocable only if you are certain you will not need the trust property in a financial emergency.

Trust income. Where a child is a trust beneficiary, the child reports as taxable income distributable net trust income. If the child is under the age of 14, distributable net income is subject to the kiddie tax of ¶24.3. Income that is accumulated for the benefit of a minor child is generally not taxable and thus, not subject to the kiddie tax.

Revocable Trusts

In a revocable trust, you retain control over the property by reserving the right to revoke the trust. As such, it is considered an incomplete gift and offers no present income tax savings. Furthermore, the trust property will be included as part of your estate. But a revocable trust minimizes delay in passing property to beneficiaries if you die while the trust is in force. When you transfer property to a trust, the property is generally not subject to probate, administration expenses, delays attendant on distributions of estates, or claims of creditors. The interests of trust beneficiaries are generally more secure than those of heirs under a will because a will may be denied probate if found invalid.

Short-term trusts. Before the tax laws were changed, ten-year (Clifford) trusts were widely used to shift income to relatives in lower tax brackets. Where a trust met the 10-year exception, trust income was taxed to the beneficiary, usually a minor child. Another type of trust used for income splitting was the spousal remainder trust set up for less than 10 years. It allowed income shifting to a child beneficiary when the trust property went to the grantor's spouse after the trust period ends.

Under current law, both types of trust may no longer be used to shift income to the income beneficiary. The 10-year exemption for grantor trusts has been repealed.

Grantor trusts. The grantor of a grantor trust is taxed on the income of the trust. A trust is treated as a grantor trust where the grantor has a reversionary interest (at the time of the transfer) of more than 5% of the value of the property transferred to the trust. Under an exception, a grantor is not treated as having a reversionary interest if that interest can take effect only upon the death before age 21 of a beneficiary who is a lineal descendant of the grantor. The beneficiary must have the entire present interest in the trust or trust portion for this exception to apply.

Spousal remainder trusts. Spousal remainder trusts have been neutralized as tax-saving techniques by current law that treats the grantor as holding a reversionary interest held by his or her spouse.

This spousal attribution rule applies to a reversionary interest of a spouse who marries the grantor after the trust is created.

The current tax rules apply to trust transfers made after March 1, 1986. An exception applies to a 10-year trust created pursuant to a binding property settlement entered into before March 2, 1986, which required the taxpayer to establish a grantor trust.

Status of prior 10-year trusts. Trusts created before the effective date continue to shift income to the income beneficiary. However, tax savings are nullified for trust beneficiaries under the age of 14. Unearned income over $1,100 of a child under age 14 is taxed to the child at the top marginal rate of the parents; *see* ¶22.5.

Pre-March 2, 1986, 10-year trusts continue to shift income and provide tax savings to trust beneficiaries age 14 or over.

Tax rates for trusts and estates. The 15% rate applies to 1992 taxable income under $3,600; the 28% rate to taxable income between $3,600 and $10,900; the 31% rate applies to taxable income over $10,900.

OTHER TRANSFERS THAT MAY SAVE TAXES

¶33.7 Making a gift of appreciated property that will eventually be sold may reduce income tax. To shift the profit and the tax, the gift must be completed before the sale or before the donor has made a binding commitment to sell. By making a gift of interests in the property to several family members, it is possible to spread the tax among a number of taxpayers in the lowest tax bracket. Note: The IRS may claim that the gift was never completed if after sale the donor controls the sales proceeds or has the use of them.

Do not make a gift of property which has decreased in value if you want a deduction for the loss. Once you give the property away, the loss deduction is gone forever. Neither you nor your donee can ever take advantage of it. The better way is to first sell the property, get a loss deduction, and then make a gift of the proceeds.

Transfers of Appreciated Property

Before making a gift of appreciated property, consider the fact that the appreciation on property passed by inheritance escapes income tax; the heir takes a basis equal to estate tax value, usually fair market value at the date of death. Furthermore, appreciated property encumbered by a mortgage may result in income tax to the donor when a gift of the property is made.

Interest-free loans. The tax law discourages income splitting through interest-free loans by imposing gift and income tax on loans coming within the rules of ¶4.31.

SPLITTING BUSINESS INCOME WITH YOUR FAMILY

¶33.8 Tax on your business income may be reduced if you can shift it to members of your family. If you keep within the annual gift tax exclusion for each donee (on gifts made by husband and wife), there will be no gift tax consequences. However, the estate tax advantages of "estate freeze" techniques has been limited, making it difficult to avoid estate tax on the appreciation in capital interests transferred to children; *see* ¶39.7.

Business income may be shifted by forming a family partnership or by making your family stockholders in a corporation. An S corporation in which stockholders elect to report income may be used more freely than a partnership to split income.

A minor child will not be recognized as a partner unless he or she is competent to manage his or her own property, or control of the property is exercised by another person as fiduciary for the minor's sole benefit. Here, a trust may be set up to hold the partnership interest. The IRS may review not only the terms of the trust and the partnership agreement but also actual operation of the trust to make certain the grantor-partner has not retained any ownership rights over the interest he transferred.

Transfers of stock to a trust for a minor terminate an S election, unless the trust is a qualified trust. For this purpose, a "Subchapter S trust" may be used. Alternatively, stock may be transferred for the minor's benefit to a custodian account in which the parent may act as custodian.

In order to get the income-shifting benefits from setting up a stock custodian account, there must be a *bona fide* transfer of stock entailing a complete surrender by you of any control over the transferred stock.

With a partnership, shifting income may be more difficult, depending on whether capital is a material income-producing factor in the business. If it is, a gift or sale of a partnership interest to a family member is effective. But in a service partnership—real estate or insurance brokers, for example—a mere gift of a partnership interest to a family member will not shift partnership income unless the person actually performs services for the partnership. In one case, the Tax Court held that where substantially all of a family partnership's capital consists of borrowed funds guaranteed by family members, the family partnership interests may be disregarded on the grounds that the borrowed funds are not a material income-producing factor in the business.

In an S corporation, pass-through items must reflect the value of services rendered or capital contributed by family members of the shareholders. If a relative of an S corporation shareholder performs services for or loans money to the corporation without receiving reasonable pay or interest, the IRS may allocate income to reflect the value of the services or capital provided. The term "family" of an individual includes only spouse, ancestors, lineal descendants, and any trusts for the primary benefit of such persons.

Payment of wages to your child. Wages paid to your child are not subject to the kiddie tax of ¶24.3. You may also deduct the wages as a business expense if the payments are reasonable. Set the wages at the scale that you would pay an outsider; keep records of the child's work; withhold tax; and provide the child with a Form W-2. If the child is age 17 or under, you do not have to withhold FICA taxes on the wages. FICA taxes are due on wages paid to a child age 18 or over.

LIFE INSURANCE OFFERS TAX ADVANTAGES

¶33.9 Insurance may provide a tax-free accumulation of cash. During the time you pay premiums, the value of your contract increases at compound interest rates. The increase is not subject to income tax. In addition, when your policy is paid at death, the proceeds are not subject to income tax.

Estate tax planning. To shelter life insurance proceeds from estate tax, you must not have ownership rights. If you have an existing policy, you must assign your ownership rights such as the right to change beneficiaries, the right to surrender or cancel the policy, the right to assign it, and the right to borrow against it. An assignment must occur more than three years before death to exclude the proceeds from your estate.

Policy Owned by Beneficiary

If you are buying a new policy, you must buy the policy in another's name, such as in your spouse's name, or have your beneficiary buy the policy. For example, a daughter applies for a $1 million policy on her father's life and is the policy owner under the terms of the policy. Although the father pays the premiums, the proceeds paid at his death are not subject to estate tax because he never had ownership rights in the policy. In the past, the IRS contested this tax-free treatment, but now agrees to follow court decisions that allow it.

Assigning group-term policies. Group insurance provided by an employer may be assigned. The IRS has agreed to follow a court decision holding that the power to convert a group policy into an individual policy when you leave the company will not subject the group-term insurance proceeds to estate tax. Since the conversion privilege is exercisable only by taking an economically disadvantageous step of quitting, this right is too remote to be considered a retained ownership right in the policy. If other incidents of ownership are transferred, such as the power to name beneficiaries and fix the type of benefit payable, the transfer will remove the policy from your estate.

The substitution of a new group carrier does not jeopardize assignments under a prior carrier.

When you plan to assign a policy, review your gift tax liability on such a transfer. In the case of an assignment of a group policy, the cost of the policy is determined by actuarially apportioning the employer's total premium payment among the covered employees. This is difficult for an individual employee to do, particularly where there are many employees, so the IRS generally allows employees to value the assigned policy using the same tax tables used to determine the amount of the employee's compensation where group coverage exceeds $50,000. *See* the table at ¶3.2. Key employees may not use the table to determine gift tax liability.

EXAMPLE An employee assigns his $80,000 group-term policy to a family trust. Several months later, when he is age 54, the employer pays the annual premium on the group policy. The value of the gift equals the annual cost of the $80,000 coverage as determined under the table at ¶3.2. Under the table, the value of the gift is $460.80. Gift tax may be avoided under the annual $10,000 gift tax exclusion.

You may want to readjust your coverage to meet new family conditions. You can exchange your policies without tax; *see* ¶11.8.

Using a trust to purchase insurance. If you create a trust to carry a policy on your life by transferring income-producing property the income of which is used to pay the premiums, you are taxable on the trust income. Similarly, if your spouse creates the trust to carry the policy on your life, he or she is taxable on the trust income. This tax rule does not apply to the trust funding of life insurance covering the life of a third party other than your spouse. For example, a grandparent transfers income-producing property to a trust to pay the premiums on a policy on the life of his son. His grandchildren are named trust beneficiaries. The grandparent is not taxed on the income earned by the trust on the transferred property because the trust purchased insurance on his son's life, not his own.

Insurance trust to receive proceeds. A trust may be used to receive insurance proceeds where there is concern that the beneficiary may be unable to manage a large insurance settlement. The trustee may be a bank or a person directed to invest the proceeds and pay income to beneficiaries according to standards provided in the trust. The trustee may be given the discretion to pay out more or less as circumstances warrant. He may be directed to terminate the trust when the beneficiaries reach a certain age, or when they demonstrate their ability to manage money. There may also be investment advantages in a trust. The trust investments may yield a higher rate of return than that of an insurance company under a settlement option.

Insurance proceeds are not subject to income tax whether paid directly to named beneficiaries or to a trust.

Single-premium policies. Single-premium policies have been touted as tax-sheltered investments. Companies offer competitive current returns and tax-free appreciation on your investment fund. The name of the policy is descriptive: You make a single-premium payment—$5,000, $10,000, $50,000, or more. Part of the premium goes for life insurance coverage and part towards an investment fund.

However, tax benefits of single-premium and other cash value policies have been cut back, as discussed below.

Universal life insurance plans. Universal life insurance offers tax-free buildup of interest income at current high market rates and on death, tax-free receipt of insurance proceeds. A universal life insurance policy is made up of (1) life insurance protection, and (2) a cash reserve on which interest income accumulates without tax.

Universal life insurance differs from regular whole life in that the interest rate of universal life is pegged to current bond market rates; whole life rates are low, currently about 5%. Furthermore, a universal life policy lets you withdraw the cash reserve if you want to invest it elsewhere and to allocate how much of your premium payment is to cover insurance protection and how much is to go into the cash reserve.

The tax law sets limits on the amount of premiums that may be earmarked for the cash reserve. If these limits are violated, tax free treatment for the proceeds may be lost. For these limits, check with the company issuing the policy.

A disadvantage of universal life is that you must incur an upfront commission payment which may be 50% or more of the first premium. There may also be a fee for withdrawing the cash reserve. Therefore, before considering a universal plan, determine the possibility that the purchase of term insurance and an investment in money market funds or long-term bonds may be a better alternative to a universal life plan.

See below for restrictions on cash value policies.

Caution: restrictions on cash value modified endowment policies. Contracts entered into after June 20, 1988 may be subject to tax penalties if they are considered "modified endowment contracts." Generally, a modified endowment contract is a contract that fails to satisfy a technical "7-year-pay test."A contract fails the "7-year-pay test" if the premiums paid during the first seven contract years exceed the sum of the net level premiums that would have been paid by that time had the contract provided for paid-up future benefits after the payment of seven level annual premiums.

Amounts received under modified endowment contracts that are not received as an annuity, such as dividends, cash withdrawals, loans, and amounts received upon a partial surrender of the contract, are taxable to the extent the cash surrender value of the contract exceeds the policyholder's investment. Withdrawals that are greater than the excess of cash surrender value over the investment are a tax-free return of capital.

To prevent marketing of multiple contracts as a means of avoiding these tax limitations, all modified endowment contracts issued by the same insurer or its affiliates to the same policyholder within the same calendar year are aggregated to determine the amount includible in income.

For policies *other* than modified endowment contracts, non-annuity withdrawals continue to be tax free until they exceed the policyholder's investment. Assignments or pledges of a contract to cover burial or pre-arranged funeral expenses are not considered taxable distributions if the contractual death benefit is $25,000 or less.

Penalty for early withdrawals from cash value policy. A 10% premature withdrawal penalty applies to taxable distributions and loans unless the policyholder is over age 59½, disabled, or the distribution is one of a series of substantially equal payments over life expectancy or over joint life expectancy with a beneficiary.

LOSSES MAY BE DISALLOWED ON SALES TO RELATED PERSONS

¶33.10

A loss on a sale to certain related taxpayers may not be deductible, even though you either make the sale in good faith, the sale is involuntary (for example, a member of your family forecloses a mortgage on your property), or you sell through a public stock exchange and related persons buy the equivalent property.

EXAMPLES 1. You sell 100 shares of A Co. stock to your brother for $1,000. They cost you $5,000. You may not deduct your $4,000 loss, even though the sale was made in good faith.

2. The stock investments of a mother and son were managed by the same investment counselor. But neither the son nor mother had any right or control over each other's securities. The counselor followed separate and independent policies for each. Without the son's or his mother's prior approval, the counselor carried out the following transactions: (1) on the same day, he sold at a loss the son's stock in four companies and bought the same stock for the mother's account; and (2) he sold at a loss the son's stock in a copper company, and 28 days later bought the same stock for his mother. The losses of the first sale were disallowed, but not the losses of the copper stock sale because of the time break of 28 days. However, the court did not say how much of a minimum time break is needed to remove a sale-purchase transaction from the rule disallowing losses between related parties.

Related parties. Losses are not allowed on sales between you and your brothers or sisters (whether by the whole or half blood), parents, grandparents, children, or grandchildren. Furthermore, no loss may be claimed on a sale to your spouse; the tax-free exchange rules of ¶6.6 apply.

A loss is disallowed where the sale is made to your sister-in-law, as nominee of your brother. This sale is deemed to be between you and your brother. But you may deduct the loss on sales to your spouse's relative (for example, your brother-in-law or spouse's stepparent) even if you and your spouse file a joint return.

The Tax Court has allowed a loss on a direct sale to a son-in-law. In a private ruling, the IRS allowed a loss on a sale of a business to a son-in-law where it was shown that his wife (the seller's daughter) did not own an interest in the company. Losses have been disallowed upon withdrawal from a joint venture and from a partnership conducted by members of a family. Family members have argued that losses should be allowed where the sales were motivated by family hostility. The Tax Court ruled that family hostility may not be considered; losses between proscribed family members are disallowed in all cases.

Losses are not allowed on sales between an individual and a controlled partnership or controlled corporation (where that individual owns more than 50% in value of the outstanding stock or capital interests).

EXAMPLES 1. In calculating the stock owned, not only must the stock held in your own name be taken into account, but also that owned by your family. You also add (1) the proportionate share of any stock held by a corporation, estate, trust, or partnership in which you have an interest as a shareholder, beneficiary, or partner; and (2) any other stock owned individually by your partner.

2. You may own 30% of the stock of a company. A trust in which you have a one-half beneficial interest owns 30%. Your partner owns 10% of the stock of the same company. You are deemed the owner of 55% of the stock of that company (30%, plus one-half of 30%, plus 10%).

Losses may also be disallowed in sales between controlled companies, a trust and its creator, a trust and a beneficiary, a partnership and a corporation controlled by the same person (more than 50% ownership), or a tax-exempt organization and its founder. Check with your tax counselor whenever you plan to sell property at a loss to a buyer who may fit one of these descriptions.

Related buyer's resale at profit. Sometimes, the disallowed loss may be saved. When you sell to a related party who resells the property at a profit, he or she gets the benefit of your disallowed loss. Your purchaser's gain up to the amount of your disallowed loss is not taxed.

EXAMPLE Smith bought securities in 1960 which cost $10,000. In 1983, he sold them to his sister for $8,000. The $2,000 loss was not deductible by Smith. His sister's basis for the securities is $8,000. In 1990, she sells them for $9,000. The $1,000 gain is not taxed because it is washed out by part of the disallowed loss. If she sold securities for $11,000, then only $1,000 of the $3,000 gain would be taxed.

TAX CONSEQUENCES OF COLLEGE TUITION PREPAYMENT PLANS

¶33.11 With college costs soaring, several states have set up prepayment plans offering parents a hedge against tuition cost increases. A typical prepayment plan allows a parent to prepay tuition costs, even though the child will not start college for 10 or more years. Prepayments are made to a state trust which holds and invests the fund until the child reaches college age. The parent's prepayment covers the tuition, regardless of how much tuition has increased in the interim. A refund, less an administrative fee, is allowed if the state ends the plan, the child is not admitted or decides not to attend college, or dies. Some plans allow part of the prepayment to be used for out-of-state colleges.

The IRS has issued a ruling spelling out the tax consequences of the Michigan prepayment plan, which has been followed by several other states. The IRS imposes taxes on the parents, children, and the sponsoring states that will reduce the cost-saving benefits of the plan.

Gift tax on parent. The parent's prepayment of tuition may be subject to gift tax. Tax may not be avoided under the $10,000 annual gift tax exclusion. The $10,000 per-donee exclusion is not available to the parent because the child does not receive a current benefit from the prepayment. The benefit is delayed until the child enters college and only gifts of present interests qualify for the $10,000 exclusion. Also unavailable is a gift tax exclusion for payments of tuition that are made directly to educational organizations. Since the tuition prepayment is made to a state trust and not to a college, the exclusion does not apply.

Although the parent will be required to file a gift tax return, in most cases no tax will actually have to be paid because of the unified gift and estate tax credit; *see* Chapter 39. However, that part of the credit which is used to offset gift tax reduces the estate tax credit.

Income accumulation taxed to trust. Income accumulating on the prepaid tuition fund is not currently taxable to the parent or child, but is taxable to the state trust. The IRS rejected the state's claim that the income was earned as part of its governmental functions and, thus, is tax free. The exemption does not apply because the prepayment fund is for the benefit of the participating families and not the community at large. The IRS did not specify whether the trust would be taxed as a corporation, a complex trust, or a simple trust. The tax cost may affect how much the state will charge parents to make the prepayment.

Student taxed when tuition is paid by the trust. When the child enters college, he or she will have to pay tax on a gain element provided by the parent's deferred gift. Each year, the child will be taxed on the excess of the current tuition costs over 25% of the parent's prepayment. If the child does not enter college and a refund is made, the parent or other beneficiary of the refund will be taxed on the difference between the refund and an allocable portion of the prepayment.

A tuition prepayment plan may still be advantageous, despite the tax cost.

EXAMPLE Assume a parent makes a prepayment of $8,000 and 15 years later when the child enters college, the annual tuition charge is $18,000. The child would be taxed on $16,000 each year ($18,000 tuition − $2,000, which is 25% of the $8,000 prepayment). Assuming the applicable tax rate is 28%, he or she would pay an annual tax of $4,480 for a total of $17,920. Under the plan, there would be a cost savings of about $40,000 considering the prepayment of $8,000, taxes of $17,920, and income that might be earned over a 15-year period if the parent had invested $8,000 in tax-free bonds paying 6%.

Parent's legal obligation to provide college education. Under grantor trust rules, a parent making a tuition prepayment could be taxed on trust income if under state law there is a legal obligation to provide the children with a college education. The IRS ruling did not raise this issue.

34
TAX POINTERS FOR SENIOR CITIZENS

All or part of your Social Security benefits may be tax free, if your adjusted gross income is below the base amount of $25,000 if you are single, $32,000 if you are married and file a joint return. If your adjusted gross income exceeds the base amount, up to 50% of your Social Security benefits are taxable. The method of computing benefits subject to tax is explained at ¶34.3.

If you continue to earn wages or self-employed income, you must pay FICA taxes or self-employment tax on that income regardless of your age. Do not confuse this rule with the Social Security benefit rule that does not reduce benefits for working after you reach age 70; *see* ¶34.5.

SPECIAL RULES FOR SENIOR CITIZENS

¶34.1 The following special tax rules favor senior citizens:

- *Higher filing thresholds.* If your are age 65 or older and single, you do not have to file a return unless your gross income is at least $6,600; *see* the chart on page 2 for further details.

- *Higher standard deduction.* If you are age 65 or older, you receive an additional standard deduction allowance if you do not itemize deductions. If in 1992 you are single and age 65 or older you get an additional $900; $700 if married or qualifying widow(er); *see* ¶13.4 for a complete list of the standard deductions for senior citizens.

- *$125,000 exclusion for home sellers age 55 or over.* If you are age 55 or older and sell or exchange your home at a gain, you may avoid tax on profits up to $125,000 ($62,500 for married persons filing separately). To claim this exclusion you must (1) elect to avoid tax on Form 2119; (2) be age 55 or over on the date of sale; and (3) have owned and occupied the house as your principal residence for at least three of the five years ending on the day of the sale; *see* ¶29.14.

- *Elderly credit.* If you are age 65 or older and do not receive Social Security or Railroad Retirement benefits, you may be eligible for a tax credit; the credit is also available to persons under age 65 who are totally disabled; *see* ¶34.8. For example, if you are single, or married but only you are eligible, and receive more than $417 each month from Social Security, you may not claim the credit. If you are married and both you and your spouse are eligible for the credit and file a joint return, you may not claim the credit if you receive more than $625 each month from Social Security.

- *Social Security benefits.* If you are married and filing jointly, all of your net Social Security benefits are tax free if your income is not more than a base amount of $32,000; or $25,000 if your filing status is single, head of household, qualifying widow(er), or if you are married filing separately and did not live with your spouse at any time during 1992. Married persons who file separately and live together at any time during the year are not allowed any base amount; *see* ¶34.3 for computing taxable Social Security benefits.

SOCIAL SECURITY BENEFITS

SOCIAL SECURITY BENEFITS SUBJECT TO TAX

¶34.2 If you received or repaid Social Security benefits in 1992, you should receive Form SSA-1099 by February 1, 1993. The form will show the total of paid or repaid benefits. Amounts withheld for Medicare premiums, worker's compensation offset, or attorney's fees are itemized and included in the total benefits you received. Keep Form SSA-1099 for your records; do not attach it to your return.

The *net benefit* shown on Form SSA-1099 (benefits paid less benefits repaid) is the benefit amount used to determine taxable benefits under ¶34.3. In the sample form shown below net benefits of $8,500 shown in Box 5 is the amount used to determine whether all or part of your Social Security benefits are taxable. Box 5 equals your gross benefits shown in Box 3 minus your repayments, shown in Box 4.

Railroad Retirement benefits. The portion of your Tier 1 Railroad Retirement Benefits which is equivalent to Social Security retirement benefits is subject to the computation at ¶34.3 for determining taxable benefits. If any part of your 1992 Tier 1 benefits is equivalent to Social Security benefits, you should receive Form RRB-1099 from the government by February 1, 1993. The *net* Social Security Equivalent Benefit shown on Form RRB-1099 is the amount used to determine taxable benefits under ¶34.3. Other Tier 1 Railroad Retirement benefits, as well as Tier 2 benefits, are treated as pension income and not as Social Security benefits subject to tax.

Benefits paid on behalf of child or incompetent. If a child is entitled to Social Security benefits, such as after the death of a parent, the benefit is considered to be the child's regardless of who actually receives the payment. Whether the child's benefit is subject to tax will depend on the amount of the child's income.

Sample Form SSA-1099

1992

- PART TO YOUR SOCIAL SECURITY BENEFITS SHOWN IN BOX 5 MAY BE TAXABLE INCOME
- SEE ENCLOSED NOTICES FOR MORE INFORMATION.

Box 1. Name	Box 2. Beneficiary's Social Security Number
Lisa Green	*X10-XX-X110*

Box 3. Benefits paid in 1992	Box 4. Benefits Repaid to SSA in 1992	Box 5. Net Benefits *(Box 3 minus Box 4)* for 1992
9,200	*700*	*8,500*

DESCRIPTION OF AMOUNT IN BOX 3

Paid by check or direct deposit
Add:
Medicare premiums paid for you
Workers' compensation offset
Deductions for work or other adjustments
Paid to another family member
Attorney fees and SSI offset

Total Additions _____*0*_____

Subtract:
Amounts for other family members paid to you
Non-taxable payments

Total Subtractions _____*0*_____

Benefits for 1992 $ _____*9,200*_____

*Box 3 includes
$ _____ paid in 1992 for 1991
$ _____ paid in 1992 for 1990
$ _____ paid in 1992 for 1989
$ _____ paid in 1992 for 1988
$ _____ paid in 1992 for other taxable years

DESCRIPTION OF AMOUNT IN BOX 4

Check(s) returned to SSA

Deductions for work or other adjustments
Other repayments

Benefits Repaid to SSA in 1992 $ _____*700*_____

Box 6. Address

*1379 Main St.
City, State XXX10*

Box 7. Claim Number *(Use this number if you need to contact SSA.)*

X10-XX-X110

Workers' compensation. If you are receiving Social Security disability payments and workers' compensation for the same disability, your Social Security benefits may be reduced by the workers' compensation. For example, you are entitled to Social Security disability benefits of $5,000 a year. After receiving a $1,000 workers' compensation award, your disability benefits are reduced to $4,000. For purposes of the computation steps of ¶34.3, you treat the full $5,000 as Social Security benefits.

Repayment of benefits. If you forfeit part of your Social Security benefits because of excessive outside income, the forfeited amount reduces your benefits for purposes of the computation of taxable benefits. You make the reduction even if the forfeit relates to benefits received in a prior year. For example, your regular 1992 benefit of $5,000 is reduced by $1,000 because of earnings of the prior year. For tax purposes, your 1992 benefits are considered $4,000.

If in 1991, Social Security benefits were subject to tax, and in 1992, you repaid 1991 benefits that were taxed, the repayment will be reflected in the *net benefit* shown on Form SSA-1099. If the repayment exceeds 1992 benefits, you may claim the excess as a miscellaneous itemized deduction or as a credit, depending on the amount of the repayment; *see* ¶2.9 for details.

Taxable Social Security benefits are not considered earnings and therefore may not be the basis of an IRA contribution (¶8.2), earned income credit (¶25.8), or foreign earned income exclusion (¶36.2).

Nonresident aliens. A special rule applies to Social Security and Tier 1 Railroad Retirement benefits received by nonresident aliens. Unless provided otherwise by tax treaty, one-half of a nonresident alien's Social Security benefits will be subject to the 30% withholding tax imposed on U.S. source income that is not connected with a U.S. trade or business. *See* IRS Publication 519 for further details.

COMPUTING TAXABLE SOCIAL SECURITY BENEFITS

¶34.3

Part of your net Social Security benefits may be subject to tax if your income exceeds a base amount. The base amount is $32,000 if you file a joint return, or $25,000 if you are single, head of household, a qualifying widow(er), or married filing separately and living apart for the entire year; *see* Step 2 in the next column. Depending on the excess of income over the base amount, up to 50% of your net Social Security benefits may be taxable.

Follow these steps in figuring tax on your Social Security benefits:

Step 1. You need to know modified adjusted gross income (MAGI). MAGI equals adjusted gross income (AGI) shown on your return, *plus* any tax-exempt interest income you received in 1992; *see* tax alert below. Also, include 50% of your net Social Security benefits as shown on Form SSA-1099 or Form RRB-1099 (amount received less amount repaid, if any). If you excluded from AGI foreign-earned income (¶36.2), or income from U.S. possessions (¶36.9) or Puerto Rico (¶36.10), these must be added back to AGI. The total is your MAGI.

If you file a joint return, combine your spouse's income and net Social Security benefits with your own when figuring Step 1.

Tax-Exempt Interest

Tax-exempt interest, such as interest you receive from municipal bonds is not included in your income when figuring your regular tax. However, you must add this interest to your AGI to arrive at your MAGI, which is used to determine your taxable Social Security benefits.

If you are an active participant in an employer retirement plan and you plan to make deductible IRA contributions (¶8.3), you must make two computations of Step 1. You first determine the amount of Social Security benefits that would be subject to tax following Steps 1–3 here, assuming you did not claim any IRA deduction. In other words, for purposes of Step 1, IRA deductions are initially ignored. If, under Steps 2 and 3, part of your benefits would be subject to tax, those taxable benefits are added to adjusted gross income for purposes of determining whether you are eligible for an IRA deduction under the phaseout rules of ¶8.3. If an IRA deduction is allowed under the phaseout rules, you then figure Step 1 again by reducing AGI by the allowable IRA deduction. Then proceed to Step 2 below.

Step 2. Reduce Step 1 modified adjusted gross income by the following base amounts: $25,000 if your filing status is single, head of household, or qualifying widow(er); $32,000 if you are married filing jointly; and $25,000 if you are married filing separately and did not live with your spouse at any time during 1992. Married persons who file separately and live together at any time during the year are not allowed any base amount.

If the base amount *exceeds* the Step 1 MAGI amount, none of your benefits are taxed. If Step 1 MAGI exceeds the base amount, part of your benefits are subject to tax. Go to Step 3 to determine how much.

EXAMPLES 1. You are married and have dividend and interest income of $28,000 and tax-exempt interest of $2,000. Your net Social Security benefits are $4,000, and you file a joint return.

Adjusted gross income		$28,000
Plus: Tax-exempt interest	$2,000	
50% of net benefits	2,000	4,000
MAGI		$32,000
Less: Base amount		32,000
No excess		$ 0

None of your benefits are taxable.

2. Same as in Example 1, except your net Social Security benefits are $8,000.

Adjusted gross income		$28,000
Plus: Tax-exempt interest	$2,000	
50% of net benefits	4,000	6,000
MAGI		$34,000
Less: Base amount		32,000
Excess		$ 2,000

Part of your benefits are subject to tax under the rules of Step 3.

Step 3. The amount of benefits subject to tax is the smaller of 50% of MAGI *minus* the base amount, or 50% of net benefits. In Example 2 above, the taxable benefit is $1,000, 50% of $2,000, which is $34,000 MAGI *minus* the $32,000 base amount. This is less than 50% of net benefits, or $4,000.

ELECTION FOR LUMP-SUM SOCIAL SECURITY BENEFIT PAYMENT

¶34.4

If in 1992 you receive a lump-sum payment of benefits covering prior years, you have a choice: (1) You may treat the entire payment as a 1992 benefit taxable under the rules of ¶34.3; or (2) you may allocate the benefits over the taxable years in which they were payable. Choose the method that provides the lowest required increase to income in the current year. The payer will notify you of the years covered by the payments.

When you elect to allocate benefits to a prior year, you do not amend the return for that year. You compute the increase in income (if any) that would have resulted if the Social Security benefits had been received in that year. You then add that amount to the income of the current year.

EXAMPLE In 1991, you apply for Social Security disability benefits but the Social Security office rules that you are ineligible. You appeal and are awarded benefits. In 1992, you receive a lump-sum payment of $8,000 ($3,000 for 1991 and $5,000 for 1992). You may include the $8,000 benefit in 1992 benefits to figure if Social Security benefits are taxable, or you may elect to treat $3,000 of benefits as received in 1991 and $5,000 in 1992.

You make the allocation and figure that in 1991, $1,000 of the $3,000 would have been taxable. Then figure whether your 1992 net benefits shown on Form SSA-1099 (or RRB-1099), *minus* the $3,000 allocated to 1991, is taxable under the steps of ¶34.3. Assume that $2,500 of the net benefits would be taxable under the steps of ¶34.3.

Thus, $3,500 of benefits ($1,000 + $2,500) would be taxable in 1992 if the lump sum was allocated between 1991 and 1992. If this is less than what the taxable benefit would be if the entire $8,000 lump sum was treated as a 1992 benefit, choose the allocation method. Write "LSE" next to the line on Form 1040 or Form 1040A for Social Security benefits to indicate that you are using the allocation method.

RETIRING ON SOCIAL SECURITY BENEFITS

¶34.5 Benefits are not paid automatically. You must register at the local Social Security office three months before your 65th birthday to allow time for your application to be processed and to locate all necessary information. Even if you do not plan to retire at age 65, you must register to insure your Medicare coverage.

If you retire before age 65, you may elect reduced Social Security benefits. The reduction formula is based on the number of months before age 65 that you retire. If you retire at the earliest age, 62, the reduction is about 20%. By electing benefits at age 62, a person receives a larger total amount of benefits than the total payable starting at age 65, provided he or she does not live beyond the age of 77. After age 77, the total benefits paid to those retiring at age 65 is greater than the amount paid to those retiring at age 62.

If you do not retire at age 65, your potential Social Security benefit increases for each year you delay retirement. For those born in 1916 or earlier, the increase is 1% per year for each year of delayed retirement; for those born in 1917 through 1924, the increase is 3% per year. The increase is 3½% for those born in 1925 and 1926 and 4% for those born in 1927 or 1928.

If you are under age 70, Social Security benefits are reduced by earned income (wages and self-employment income). If you were age 65 or older but under age 70 in 1992, you could earn $10,200 without losing benefits. If you were under age 65 for the whole year, you could earn $7,440 without losing benefits. These ceilings are subject to annual inflation adjustments. Once you earn more than these ceilings, benefits are reduced. If you are age 65 or over and under age 70, you lose $1 in benefits for each $3 you earn above the earnings ceiling. A special monthly ceiling applies in the year you reach retirement age. If you are under age 65, $1 of benefits is lost for every $2 of excess earnings.

For those age 70 or over, benefits are not reduced by earnings. You can work, earn any amount, and receive full Social Security benefits.

So long as you continue to work, you pay Social Security taxes on your earnings, regardless of your age.

Regardless of your age, you may receive any amount of income from sources other than work—for example, private pensions or investments—without affecting the amount of Social Security retirement benefits. However, benefits may be taxable if your income exceeds $25,000 if single, or $32,000 if married filing separately; *see* ¶34.3.

Request an estimate of benefits and copy of earnings record. The Social Security Administration has improved its system of giving workers an estimate of retirement benefits. You can get an estimate of retirement benefits by sending for Form SSA-7004-PC. After mailing in a completed Form SSA-7004-PC, you will receive a Personal Earnings and Benefit Estimate Statement, showing your earnings history, Social Security tax payments, and an estimate of your retirement, disability and survivor's benefits.

Form SSA-7004-PC is available at your local Social Security office. You can also request the form from the Social Security Administration by calling 1-800-772-1213.

HOW TAX ON SOCIAL SECURITY REDUCES YOUR EARNINGS

¶34.6 There is an added tax cost of earning income if the earnings will subject your Social Security benefits to tax. Therefore, if your benefits are not currently exposed to tax, you have to figure *not only* the tax on the extra income *but also* the amount of Social Security benefits subjected to tax by those earnings. If the additional earnings will put you over the $25,000 or $30,000 base amount, then you will not only have to pay tax on the additional earnings but also on the Social Security benefits that will be subject to tax. As a result, the marginal tax rate on the extra income will be higher than the 28% or 31% rate; *see* Example 2 below.

EXAMPLE 1. You are over age 70 and plan to work part time. You and your spouse receive net Social Security benefits of $8,000. You file jointly. Your adjusted gross income is $25,000 and you have $3,000 in tax-exempt interest. Your MAGI after adding 50% of Social Security benefits is $32,000. At this point, no part of your Social Security benefits is taxable.

Adjusted gross income	$25,000
Plus: Tax-exempt interest	$3,000
Plus: 50% of benefits	4,000
MAGI	$32,000
Less: Base amount	32,000
No excess	$ 0

2. Same as in Example 1, except that you plan to earn up to $8,000 from a part-time job. The $8,000 will subject $4,000 of Social Security benefits to tax.

AGI plus tax-exempt interest	$28,000
Plus: Part-time earnings	8,000
	$36,000
Plus: 50% of benefits	4,000
MAGI	$40,000
Less: Base amount	32,000
Excess	$ 8,000
50% of excess taxable	$ 4,000

In this case, the $8,000 of additional earnings will increase your taxable income by $12,000. Assuming a 15% tax rate, the tax on the $12,000 is $1,800 ($12,000 x 15%); the effective tax rate on the $8,000 earnings is 22.5% ($1,800 ÷ $8,000), rather than 15%.

If you are under age 70, you must also consider that Social Security benefits may be reduced by earnings from a job or self-employment; *see* ¶34.5.

If you earn extra pay, making a deductible IRA contribution can reduce your income to avoid or reduce a tax on your Social Security benefits.

EXAMPLE Your investment income is $26,000, and your Social Security benefits are $8,000. You have part-time earnings of $4,000 and qualify for fully deductible IRA contributions because you are not an active participant in a company retirement plan; *see* ¶8.3. If you make a deductible $2,000 IRA contribution, you will avoid tax on Social Security benefits.

Investment income	$26,000
Earnings	4,000
	$30,000
Less: IRA	2,000
	$28,000
Plus: 50% of benefits	4,000
MAGI	$32,000
Less: Base amount	32,000
No excess	$ 0

If you are an active participant in a company plan and expect to make IRA contributions, *see* Step 1 of ¶34.3 for special computations you must make.

TAX CREDIT FOR THE ELDERLY AND DISABLED

CLAIMING THE CREDIT FOR ELDERLY AND DISABLED

¶34.7 The amount of the credit is 15% times the base amount after reductions. For a single person, the tax credit for the elderly may be as high as $750, for a married couple, $1,125, if there are no reductions to the "base amount." The base amount for the credit is generally $7,500, $5,000, or $3,750, as shown in ¶34.9 and ¶34.10. The base amount is reduced by nontaxable Social Security and other tax-free pensions, as well as by adjusted gross income exceeding specific limits as explained in ¶34.11.

Where To Claim The Credit

You claim the credit on Schedule R if you file Form 1040. If you file Form 1040A, claim the credit on Schedule 3. You may not claim the credit on Form 1040EZ.

The credit is not refundable. That is, it is allowed only up to your tax liability. Furthermore, the credit may be limited if you have tax adjustments or preference items subject to alternative minimum tax (¶23.3), even though you are not actually subject to AMT because of the AMT exemption. Follow the tax form instructions.

Married couples. A married couple may claim the credit only if they file a joint return. However, if a husband and wife live apart at all times during the taxable year and file separately, the credit may be claimed on a separate return.

WHO QUALIFIES?

¶34.8 You may qualify for the tax credit for 1992 if you meet one of the following conditions:

Your 65th birthday is on or before January 1, 1993; *or*
You are under age 65, permanently and totally disabled, and receiving taxable disability income at the end of 1992.

Disabled. You are considered permanently and totally disabled if you are unable to engage in any substantial gainful activity by reason of any medically determinable physical or mental impairment which can be expected to result in death or which has lasted or can

be expected to last for a continuous period of not less than 12 months.

For the first year you claim the credit, you need a physician's certification of your disability. For later years, new certifications are generally not required.

Nonresident aliens. You may not claim the credit if you are a nonresident alien at any time during 1992, unless you are married to a citizen or resident and you have elected to be treated as a resident; *see* ¶1.8.

INITIAL BASE AMOUNT FOR THOSE AGE 65 OR OVER

¶34.9 The law fixes an initial base amount for figuring the credit. This base amount is reduced by certain tax-free benefits and excess adjusted gross income; *see* ¶34.11. The credit is 15% of the base amount after reductions. You do not have to have retirement income to claim the credit.

The base amount is:

$5,000, if you are single, head of household, or qualified widow(er).
$5,000, if you file a joint return and only one spouse is eligible for the credit.
$7,500, if you file a joint return and both spouses are eligible for the credit. The credit is figured solely on this base; a separate computation is not made for each spouse.
$3,750, if you are married and file a separate return. The credit may be claimed on a separate return only if you and your spouse have lived apart at all times during the year.

INITIAL BASE AMOUNT FOR DISABLED PERSONS

¶34.10 If you are under age 65 and permanently and totally disabled, the base for figuring the credit is the lower of your 1992 disability income or the initial base amount for your filing status in ¶34.9.

348

EXAMPLE 1. You are single, under age 65, and permanently and totally disabled. You received disability income of $4,800. You figure the credit on $4,800, which is less than the base of $5,000 for single persons.

2. Same facts as in Example 1, except your disability income is $7,000. You figure the credit on the initial base of $5,000 for singles.

Joint return and both spouses qualify for the credit. If one spouse is age 65 or over and one spouse is under age 65 and receives disability income, the initial base amount is the lesser of (1) $7,500, or (2) $5,000 *plus* the disability income of the spouse under age 65. If both spouses are under age 65 and disabled, the initial base amount is the total of their disability income, not exceeding $7,500.

Disability income is taxable wages or payments in lieu of wages paid while absent from work because of permanent and total disability.

REDUCTION OF BASE AMOUNT

¶**34.11** The base amount is reduced by nontaxable pensions and "excess" adjusted gross income, as follows:

Nontaxable Social Security and pensions. The base amount is reduced by:

Social Security and Railroad Retirement benefits which are *not taxable* under rules of ¶34.3; and

Tax-free pension, annuity, or disability income paid under a law administered by the Veterans' Administration or under other federal laws.

You do *not* reduce the base amount for: military disability pensions received for active service in the Armed Forces or in the Coast and Geodetic Survey or Public Health Service; certain disability annuities paid under the Foreign Service Act of 1980; and workers' compensation benefits. However, if Social Security benefits are reduced by workers' compensation benefits, the amount of workers' compensation benefits is treated as Social Security benefits that reduce the base.

EXAMPLE You receive Social Security benefits of $6,000. If under the rules of ¶34.3, $1,500 of the benefits are taxable, only $4,500 of the benefits reduce the base.

Excess adjusted gross income. You reduce the base amount by one-half of adjusted gross income exceeding: $7,500 if you are single, head of household, or a qualified widow(er); $10,000 if you are married filing a joint return; or $5,000 if you are married and file a separate return. Applying these income floors, the credit is no longer available to a single person when adjusted gross income reaches $17,500, $20,000 on a joint return where one spouse is eligible for the credit, and $25,000 where both spouses are eligible for the credit.

EXAMPLES 1. A single person over age 65 has adjusted gross income (AGI) of $9,000 and receives Social Security benefits of $4,200 which are not taxable under ¶34.3. His credit is $7.50.

Initial base amount (¶34.9)	$5,000
Less: Social Security	4,200
	$ 800
Less: 50% of AGI over $7,500	750
Credit base	$ 50
Credit (15%)	$ 7.50

2. A married couple over age 65 files a joint return showing adjusted gross income of $12,000. They received tax-free Social Security benefits of $5,000.

Initial base amount (¶34.9)	$7,500
Less: Social Security	5,000
	$2,500
Less: 50% of AGI over $10,000	1,000
Credit base	$1,500
Credit (15%)	$ 225

CONTINUING CARE COMMUNITIES

TAX EFFECTS OF MOVING TO A CONTINUING CARE FACILITY

¶**34.12** Senior citizens who move into "continuing care" or "life care" facilities must pay large upfront entrance fees upon admittance, as well as monthly fees thereafter in return for a residence, meals, and lifetime health care, including long-term skilled nursing care, should that become necessary. The payments raise several tax issues discussed in this section and in ¶34.13.

Portion of monthly fees deductible as medical expense. Part of the monthly fees to a life-care community is allocable to health care, which you may deduct as an itemized medical expense subject to the 7.5% floor; see ¶17.4. Continuing care facilities generally send a statement to the residents, specifying what portion of their monthly service fees went towards health care.

What about the upfront payments required by life-care communi-

ties? Part may be allowable as a medical expense deduction if you can prove what part of the lump sum is allocable to future medical coverage. The IRS recognizes that a deduction may be based on a showing that the care facility historically allocates a specified percentage of the fee to future medical care. With such proof there is a current obligation to pay and the allocable medical expenses are deductible when the lump sum is paid. *See* ¶17.11 for examples of deductible allocations to future medical care.

Charitable contribution deductions. Payments made to a tax-exempt organization that operates a life-care community are generally not deductible charitable contributions because you are receiving services in exchange. If you donate amounts over and above your regular monthly fees and do not receive any extra benefit as a result, you may deduct the excess payment as a charitable contribution; *see* ¶14.16.

In one case, an individual was allowed by the Tax Court and an appeals court to claim a charitable contribution deduction for a "sponsorship gift" paid to a life-care retirement facility where she and her husband were residents. The sponsorship gift was entirely separate from her entrance fee; it was not required for admission and did not entitle her to reduced monthly payments. She did not receive any extra benefit from her gift and was not entitled to a refund of any part of it.

Home sale prior to entering a care facility. If you sell a home and move into a life-care community, you generally may not defer tax on the sale by claiming that the entrance fee is the equivalent of buying a new residence. The IRS has ruled that an investment in a retirement community is not the same as buying an actual home.

In some retirement communities, you may be able to purchase an actual condominium or co-op unit as part of the arrangement entitling you to lifetime care. In that case, tax deferral on a prior home sale would be allowed if the cost of the new unit was as much as the adjusted sales price of the old house under the rules of ¶29.5. Furthermore, sale of the new unit would qualify for the $125,000 exclusion if you have not previously claimed an exclusion and you live in the new unit for at least three of the five years before the sale; *see* ¶29.14.

IMPUTED INTEREST ON CONTINUING CARE PAYMENTS

¶34.13

You must pay a lump-sum entrance fee when you enter a continuing care community. Depending on the type of plan, a portion of the lump-sum fee may be refundable either to you if you move from the community or to your heirs upon your death.

This refund feature may result in an unexpected tax liability under the imputed interest rules. If you are granted a partial refund upon moving from the community, regardless of how long you live there, part of the refundable fee is considered a "loan" to the continuing care facility. As a result, the payment may be subject to imputed interest rules because interest on the "loan" has not been charged. If the imputed interest rules apply, you must report interest income based on prevailing federal rates; *see* ¶4.31. However, you may be able to avoid imputed interest under the special exception discussed below. Furthermore, limited refund plans which phase out the right to a refund over a period of years (generally no more than five years) are exempt from the imputed interest rules according to Congressional committee reports.

Exception. Under a special exception, the "loan" portion of the upfront payment is not subject to imputed interest unless it exceeds an annual floor.

For 1992, refundable loans of up to $114,100 are exempt from the imputed interest rules provided that (1) you or your spouse were at least age 65 during the year; and (2) the care community provides a separate living unit, meals, maintenance, routine medical care, and, if necessary, future long-term nursing care. The $114,100 exception is subject to increases for inflation.

Since only the refundable portion of the upfront payment is treated as a loan, the larger the upfront payment or refund percentage is, the greater the potential imputed interest liability is. For example, in 1992, you and your spouse paid $140,000 for a two bedroom apartment. If your guaranteed refund percentage is 75%, the imputed interest rules would not apply in 1992 because the "loan" or $105,000 (75% of $140,000) is below the $114,100 floor. However, if the refund percentage is 85%, the loan is $119,000 (85% of $140,000), and the $4,900 excess over the $114,100 floor is subject to imputed interest. Imputed interest could also result if the upfront payment was higher. For example, if the payment was $160,000 instead of $140,000 and the refund percentage 75%, the loan is $120,000 (75% of $160,000), and the $5,900 excess loan over the $114,100 floor would be subject to imputed interest.

If imputed interest applies, the care facility should give you a Form 1099 indicating the taxable amount.

35 TAX SAVINGS FOR MEMBERS OF THE ARMED FORCES

Special tax benefits are provided to Armed Forces personnel. A major tax-free benefit is the combat pay exclusion for Desert Storm participants. Under this exclusion, members of the Armed Forces, including active duty reservists, may exclude from gross income all compensation for active service received for any month in which they served in a combat zone or were hospitalized as a result of any wound, injury, or disease incurred while serving in a combat zone. Commissioned officers are limited to an exclusion of $500 per month.

Other pay benefits may be tax free, and you may be able to get filing extensions and time extensions for home residence replacements. A list of tax-free benefits may be found at ¶35.2. Filing extensions are discussed at ¶35.5.

TAXABLE ARMED FORCES PAY AND BENEFITS

¶35.1 Armed Forces personnel report as taxable pay the following items:

- Basic pay for active duty, attendance at a designated service school, back wages, drills, reserve training, and training duty.
- Special pay for aviation career incentives, diving duty, foreign duty (for serving outside the 48 contiguous states and the District of Columbia), hazardous duty, medical and dental officers, nuclear-qualified officers, and special duty assignment pay.
- Enlistment and reenlistment bonuses.
- Payments for accrued leave, and personal money allowances paid to high-ranking officers.
- Scholarships, such as the Armed Forces Health Profession Scholarship Program (AFHPSP) and similar programs, granted after August 16, 1986; and
- Student loan repayment from programs such as the General Educational Loan Repayment Program.

Community property. If you are married and domiciled in one of the following states, your military pay is subject to community property laws of that state: Arizona, California, Idaho, Louisana, Nevada, New Mexico, Texas, Washington, and Wisconsin. *See* ¶1.9 for community property reporting rules.

 Where and When to File

Mail your return to the Internal Revenue Service Center for the place you are stationed. For example, you are stationed in Arizona but have a permanent home address in Missouri; you send your return to the Service Center for Arizona. For filing extensions on entering the service; *see* ¶35.7.

State income tax withholding. A state that makes a withholding agreement with the Secretary of the Treasury may subject members of the Armed Forces regularly stationed within that state to its payroll withholding provisions. National Guard members and reservists are not considered to be members of the Armed Forces for purposes of this section.

TAX-FREE ARMED FORCES BENEFITS

¶35.2

The following benefits are *not* subject to tax:

- Combat pay; *see* ¶35.4.
- Living allowances for: BAQ (Basic Allowance for Quarters). You may deduct mortgage interest and real estate taxes on your home even if you pay these expenses with BAQ funds.
- BAS (Basic Allowance for Subsistence) living allowances.
- Housing and cost-of-living allowances abroad whether paid by the U.S. Government or by a foreign government.
- VHA (Variable Housing Allowance).
- Family allowances for educational expenses for dependents, emergencies, evacuation to a place of safety, and separation.
- Death allowances for burial services, death gratuity payments to eligible survivors (not more than $3,000) and travel of dependents to burial site.
- Moving allowances for dislocation, moving household and personal items, moving trailers or mobile homes, storage, and temporary lodging.
- Travel allowances for annual round trip for dependent students, leave between consecutive overseas tours, reassignment in a dependent-restricted status, and transportation for you or your dependents during ship overhaul or inactivation.
- Defense counseling payments.
- Mustering-out payments received before November 5, 1990.
- ROTC educational and subsistence allowances.
- Survivor and retirement protection plan premium payments.
- Uniform allowances paid to officers, and uniforms furnished to enlisted personnel.
- Medical or hospital treatment provided by the United States in government hospitals.
- Pay forfeited on order of a court martial.
- Education, training, or subsistence allowances paid under any law administered by the Veterans' Administration. However, deductible education costs must be reduced by the VA allowance.
- Adjustments in pay to compensate for losses resulting from inflated foreign currency.
- Payments to former prisoners of war from the U.S. Government in compensation for inhumane treatment suffered at the hands of an enemy government.
- Benefits under Servicemembers' Group Life Insurance.
- Dividends on GI insurance. These are a tax-free return of premiums paid.

  Interest on dividends left on deposit with the VA is not taxable. The IRS has revoked a prior ruling that subjected such interest to tax.

Disability Retirement Pay

Your disability retirement pay may be tax free if you are a former member of the Armed Forces of any country, the Foreign Service, the Coast Guard, the National Oceanic and Atmospheric Administration, or the Public Health Service. For details; *see* ¶2.13.

Tax-free treatment of disability retirement pay is retroactive to the date of the application for benefits.

DEDUCTIONS FOR ARMED FORCES PERSONNEL

¶35.3

Members of the Armed Services may deduct as miscellaneous itemized deductions subject to the 2% AGI floor (¶19.1) the following items:

- Board and lodging costs over those paid to you by the government while on temporary duty away from your home base.
- Costs of rank insignia, collar devices, gold braid, etc. The cost of altering rank insignia when promoted or demoted is also deductible.
- Contributions to a "Company" fund made according to Service regulations. But personal contributions made to stimulate interest and morale in a unit are not deductible.
- Court martial legal expenses in successfully defending against the charge of conduct unbecoming an officer.
- Dues to professional societies. But you cannot deduct dues for officers' and noncommissioned officers' clubs.
- Expense of obtaining increased retirement pay.
- Out-of-pocket moving expenses for service connected moves. The 35-mile test and the 39-week test generally required to deduct moving expense do *not* have to be met. *See* ¶21.5 for deductible expenses.
- Subscriptions to professional journals.
- Transportation, food, and lodging expenses while on official travel status. But you are taxed on mileage and *per diem* subsistence allowance.
- Travel expenses while ship or squadron is "away from home" post or base. However, you are not considered "away from home" if you are at your *permanent* duty station or you are a naval officer assigned to *permanent* duty aboard a ship; *see* also ¶20.6.
- Uniforms. The cost and cleaning of uniforms are deductible if: (1) they must be worn on duty; (2) they cannot under military regulations be worn off duty; and (3) the cost exceeds any tax-free clothing allowance.

TAX-FREE COMBAT PAY

¶35.4

If your grade is below commissioned officer and you serve in a designated combat zone during any part of a month, *all* of your qualifying military pay (*see* below) for that month is excluded from your income. You may also exclude military pay earned during any part of a month that you are hospitalized as a result of wounds, disease, or injury incurred in the combat zone. The exclusion for military pay while hospitalized does not apply to any month that begins more than two years after the end of combat activities in that combat zone. Your hospitalization does not have to be in the combat zone.

Members of the U.S. Armed Forces qualifying for the exclusion include commissioned officers and enlisted personnel in all regular and reserve units under control of the Secretaries of the Defense, Army, Navy, and Air Force. It also includes the Coast Guard. Members of the U.S. Merchant Marines or the American Red Cross are not included.

Officers. If you are a commissioned officer, you may exclude up to $500 of your military pay for each month during any part of which you served in a combat zone.

If you are a commissioned warrant officer, you are considered an enlisted person; your exclusion is *not* limited to $500 a month.

What is included as tax-free combat pay? The term combat pay is somewhat misleading as the exclusion is not restricted to pay for combat action. The following military pay is considered combat pay: (1) active duty pay earned in any month you served in a combat zone; (2) a dislocation allowance if the move begins or ends in a month you served in a combat zone; (3) a reenlistment bonus if the voluntary extension or reenlistment occurs in a month you served in a combat zone; (4) pay for accrued leave earned in any month you served in a combat zone (the Department of Defense must determine that the unused leave was earned during that period); (5) pay received for duties as a member of the Armed Forces in clubs, messes, post and station theaters, and other nonappropriated fund activities. The pay must be earned in a month you served in a combat zone; (6) awards for suggestions, inventions, or scientific achievements you are entitled to because of a submission you made in a month you served in a combat zone.

Service in the combat zone includes any periods you are absent from duty because of sickness, wounds, or leave. If, as a result of serving in a combat zone, you become a prisoner of war or missing in action, you are considered to be serving in the combat zone as long as you keep that status for military pay purposes.

Combat zone must be designated by President. A combat zone is any area the President of the United States designates by Executive Order as an area in which the U.S. Armed Forces are or have engaged in combat. An area becomes a combat zone and ceases to be a combat zone on the dates designated by the President by Executive Order.

Persian Gulf Combat Zone

The President designated the following locations (including airspace) as a combat zone beginning January 17, 1991: the total land areas of Iraq, Kuwait, Saudi Arabia, Oman, Bahrain, Qatar, and the United Arab Emirates; the Persian Gulf; the Red Sea; the Gulf of Oman; the part of the Arabian Sea that is north of 10 degrees north latitude and west of 68 degrees east longitude; and the Gulf of Aden.

Pay for services in these areas before January 1991 does not qualify for the exclusion. However, tax deadlines are extended if you were in these areas on or after August 2, 1990; see ¶35.5.

An exclusion is also available for service outside of the designated areas if it was in direct support of combat zone military operations and qualified you for special hostile fire pay. At the time this book went to press, the Persian Gulf area continued to be a combat zone; see the Supplement to this book for any later change.

Qualifying service outside combat zone. Military service outside of a combat zone is considered to be performed in a combat zone if: (1) the service is in direct support of military operations in the combat zone, and (2) the service qualifies you for special military pay for duty subject to hostile fire or imminent danger. Military pay received for this service will qualify for the combat pay exclusion if the other requirements are met.

Nonqualifying service in combat zone. The following military service does not qualify as service in a combat zone: (1) presence in a combat zone while on leave from a duty station located outside the combat zone; (2) passage over or through a combat zone during a trip between two points that are outside a combat zone; and (3) presence in a combat zone solely for your personal convenience.

Such service will not qualify you for the combat pay exclusion.

Hospitalized while serving in a combat zone. If you are hospitalized while serving in a combat zone, the wound, disease, or injury causing the hospitalization will be presumed to have been incurred while serving in the combat zone unless there is clear evidence to the contrary.

EXAMPLES 1. You are hospitalized for a specific disease after serving in a combat zone for three weeks, and the

disease for which you are hospitalized has an incubation period of two to four weeks. The disease is presumed to have been incurred while you were serving in the combat zone. On the other hand, if the incubation period of the disease is one year, the disease would not have been incurred while you were serving in the combat zone.

2. You were hospitalized for a specific disease three weeks after you left the combat zone. The incubation period of the disease is from two to four weeks. The disease is considered to have been incurred while serving in the combat zone.

Form W-2. The wages shown in Box 10 of your 1992 Form W-2 should not include combat pay. Retirement pay does not qualify as combat pay.

TAX DEADLINES EXTENDED FOR COMBAT ZONE SERVICE

¶**35.5** You are allowed an extension of at least 180 days (see below) to take care of tax matters if you are a member of the Armed Forces who served in a combat zone. The extension applies to filing tax returns, paying taxes, filing a Tax Court petition, filing refund claims, making an IRA contribution, and purchasing a new home for tax deferral (¶29.2) purposes. The time allowed for the IRS to begin an audit or take collection actions is also extended.

Support personnel. The deadline extension also applies if you are serving in a combat zone in support of the Armed Forces. This includes Red Cross personnel, accredited correspondents, and civilian personnel acting under the direction of the Armed Forces in support of those forces.

Extensions for Persian Gulf Service

You qualify for the tax deadline extension if you were in a combat zone on or after August 2, 1990. The qualifying areas are at ¶35.4.

As discussed below, the minimum extension of 180 days is further extended by the number of days you had left to file or take other action with the IRS when you entered the combat zone.

Extension is minimum of 180 days. Your deadline for taking actions with the IRS is extended for at least 180 days after the *later* of: (1) the last day you are in a combat zone (or the last day the area qualifies as a combat zone), or (2) the last day of any continuous qualified hospitalization for injury from service in the combat zone. Hospitalization may be outside the United States, or up to five years of hospitalization in the United States.

Time in a missing status (missing in action or prisoner of war) counts as time in a combat zone.

In addition to the 180 days, your deadline is also extended by the number of days you had left to file with the IRS when you entered a combat zone. If you entered the combat zone before the time to file began, the deadline is extended by the entire filing time.

Spouses of combat zone personnel. If your spouse serves in a combat zone, you are generally entitled to the same deadline extension as he or she is. However, any extra extension for your spouse's hospitalization within the United States is not available to you. Further, a spouse's extension does not apply to any year beginning more than two years after the end of combat activities.

TAX FORGIVENESS FOR COMBAT ZONE DEATHS

¶**35.6** If a member of the Armed Forces is killed in a combat zone or dies from wounds or disease incurred while in a combat zone, any income tax liability for the year of death is waived. In addition, the servicemember's estate is entitled to a refund for income tax paid while serving in a combat zone.

If a member of the Armed Forces was a resident of a community property state and his or her spouse reported half of the military pay on a separate return, the spouse may get a refund of taxes paid on his or her share of the combat zone pay.

Forgiveness benefits also apply to a member of the Armed Forces serving outside the combat zone if the service: (1) was in direct support of military operations in the zone, and (2) qualified the member for special military pay for duty subject to hostile fire or imminent danger.

Missing status. The date of death for a member of the Armed Forces who was in a missing status (missing in action or prisoner of war) is the date his or her name is removed from missing status for military pay purposes. This is true even if death actually occurred earlier.

How tax forgiveness is claimed. If the individual died in a combat zone or in a terroristic or military action, you file as the individual's representative:

1. Form 1040 if a U.S. individual income tax return (Form 1040, 1040A, or 1040EZ) has not been filed for the tax year. Form W-2, Wage and Tax Statement, must accompany the return.
2. File Form 1040X if a U.S. individual income tax return has been filed. A separate Form 1040X must be filed for each year in question.

Check with your local IRS office for the address of the IRS office to which the return is filed.

An attachment should accompany any return or claim and should include a computation of the decedent's tax liability before any amount is forgiven and the amount that is to be forgiven.

The following documents must also accompany all returns and claims for refund: (1) Form 1310, Statement of Person Claiming Refund Due a Deceased Taxpayer; and (2) a certification from the Department of Defense. Department of State certification is required if the decedent was a civilian employee of an agency other than the Department of Defense.

Tax abatement for civilian or military personnel killed in terroristic or military action. Tax liability is waived for civilian or military personnel killed in terroristic or military actions outside the U.S., even if the President has not designated the area as a combat zone. Tax liability is waived for the period beginning with the taxable year before the year in which the injuries were incurred and ending with the year of death. Refund claims for prior years must generally be filed on Form 1040X by the later of three years from the time the original return was filed or two years from the time the tax was paid. However, if death occurred in a combat zone, the filing period is extended by the time served in the combat zone, plus the period of continuous hospitalization outside the U.S., plus an additional 180 days. The individual must also be a U.S. employee both on the date of injury and date of death.

Tax abatement does not apply to a U.S. civilian or military employee who dies as a result of an accident or a training exercise. Abatement also does not apply to terroristic action within the United States. However, abatement does apply if the individual dies in the U.S. from a wound or injury incurred in a terroristic or military action outside the United States.

Determination of death for Vietnam MIAs. Under prior law, MIAs were generally presumed dead as of December 31, 1982. Under current law, the date of death of servicemen missing in action in Vietnam is the date determined by the Armed Forces. Thus, under current law, tax abatement may be available for years after 1982. Furthermore, the date of death, as determined by the Armed Forces, also applies for such rules as whether to file as a surviving spouse, and for postponing the due date for filing returns and paying taxes.

EXTENSION TO PAY YOUR TAX WHEN ENTERING THE SERVICE

¶**35.7** If you are unable to pay your tax when you enter the Armed Forces, you may get an extension until six months after your initial period of service ends. File your return by April 15, 1993, and get a form at the office of your District Director of Internal Revenue, or write a letter to the District Director (your spouse or parent may do it for you). An extension, without interest, may be given if payment involves hardship, *and* you actually apply for it.

The extension does not cover your spouse who must file a separate return and pay the tax due. But you and your spouse may file a joint return before the postponement period expires even though your spouse filed a separate return for that particular year. No interest is charged on this postponement of your tax.

Automatic extension of time to file your return. If you are on duty outside the U.S. or Puerto Rico on April 15, 1993, you get an automatic two-month extension to file your return; *see* page 4.

Interest charged on back taxes. If you owe back taxes to the IRS, and do not show hardship qualifying you for the extension discussed above, the IRS may reduce its interest rate on the deficiency to 6%. This reduced rate applies only to the period of your active duty.

TAX INFORMATION FOR RESERVISTS

¶**35.8** Transportation costs to reservist meetings generally are not deductible according to the IRS. A possible exception is where the meeting is held on your regular workday; the cost of transportation from your job to the meeting would be deductible, subject to the 2% adjusted gross income floor for miscellaneous itemized deductions.

If you travel overnight away from your tax home (¶20.6) to a meeting or camp training, you may deduct expenses for transportation, meals (80% deductible) and lodging.

If you are called for active duty away from your tax home, you may deduct travel expenses provided you keep your regular job while on active duty, return to it after you are released, and pay for those expenses at the military post. To the extent they exceed BAQ (quarters) and BAS (subsistence) allowances, the expenses are deductible only as a miscellaneous itemized deduction subject to the 2% floor; *see* ¶19.1.

Uniform Costs. The cost and upkeep of uniforms is deductible only if you are prohibited from wearing them when off duty. A deduction allowed under this test must be reduced by any uniform allowance you receive, and the unreimbursed cost is subject to the 2% floor for miscellaneous itemized deductions.

Deferring tax payments and reduction of IRS interest rate. If you owed a tax deficiency to the IRS before being called to active duty, the IRS may defer payment, without interest, if your ability to pay has been severely impaired by your call up. If you are not allowed a deferment, the IRS will reduce its interest charge to 6% on the taxes you owed before your call up.

36 HOW TO TREAT FOREIGN INCOME

There is a tax incentive for working abroad—up to $70,000 of income earned abroad may escape U.S. income taxes and you may be entitled to an exclusion or deduction for certain housing costs. In measuring the economic value of this tax savings, consider the extra cost of living abroad. In some areas, the high cost of living and currency exchange rates will erode your tax savings and may make the position economically unfeasible.

The exclusion does not apply to investment income or to any other earned income that does not meet the exclusion tests.

To claim a foreign income exclusion you must satisfy a foreign residence or physical presence test.

Employees of the U.S. Government may not claim an exclusion based on the government pay earned aboard.

CLAIMING THE FOREIGN EARNED INCOME EXCLUSION

¶**36.1** You must file a U.S. return if your gross income *exceeds* the filing threshold for your personal status, even though all or part of your foreign earned income may be tax free. The exclusion is not automatic; you must elect it. You elect the foreign earned income exclusion on Form 2555, which you attach to Form 1040. The housing cost exclusion (¶36.3) is also elected on Form 2555.

You may file a new simplified Form 2555-EZ, if your 1992 foreign wages are $70,000 or less, you do not have self-employment income, and do not claim the foreign housing exclusion, moving expenses or the foreign tax credit.

A separate exclusion is allowed for the value of meals and lodging received by employees living in qualified camps; *see* ¶36.8.

If you claim the foreign earned income exclusion of $70,000, you may not:

- Claim business deductions allocable to the excluded income;
- Make a deductible IRA contribution based on the excluded income; or
- Claim foreign taxes, paid on excluded income, as a credit or deduction.

In deciding whether to claim the exclusion, compare the overall tax (1) with the exclusion; and (2) without the exclusion but with the full foreign tax credit and allocable deductions. Choose whichever gives you the lower tax; *see* ¶36.2 and ¶36.6.

Once you elect the exclusion, that election remains in effect for all future years unless you revoke it. If you revoke the election, you cannot elect the exclusion again during the next five years without IRS consent. A revocation is made in a statement attached to your return for the year you want it to take effect. The foreign earned income exclusion and the housing cost exclusion must be revoked separately.

CAUTION

Claiming Foreign Tax Credit Revokes Prior Election

If you have been claiming the $70,000 exclusion, and decide that it would be advantageous this year to forego the exclusion and instead claim the foreign tax credit for foreign earned income, be aware that claiming the credit is treated by the IRS as a revocation of the prior exclusion election. You will not be able to claim a credit for the next five years unless the IRS allows you to reelect the exclusion.

Claiming a foreign tax credit also may revoke a prior election to claim the housing cost exclusion. Depending on the foreign earned income in the year the credit is claimed, the credit may be considered a revocation of a prior earned income exclusion election and also a prior housing cost exclusion election, or as a revocation of only one of the elections.

A good faith error in calculating foreign earned income that leads to claiming a foreign credit will not be treated as a revocation of prior elections.

QUALIFYING FOR THE FOREIGN EARNED INCOME EXCLUSION

¶36.2 You may elect the exclusion for foreign earned income only if your tax home is in a foreign country *and* you meet either the foreign residence test *or* the foreign physical presence test of 330 days. The tests are discussed at ¶36.5. Tax home is discussed at ¶20.6. If your tax home is in the U.S., you may not claim the exclusion but may claim the foreign tax credit and your living expenses while away from home if you meet the rules at ¶20.9 for temporary assignments.

U.S. government employees may not claim either the earned income exclusion or housing exclusion based on government pay.

If you are married and you and your spouse each have foreign earned income and meet the foreign residence or physical presence test, you may each claim a separate exclusion. If your permanent home is in a community property state, your earned income is not considered community property for purposes of the exclusion.

Exclusion prorated on a daily basis. If you qualify under the foreign residence or physical presence test for only part of 1992, the $70,000 exclusion limit is reduced on a daily basis.

EXAMPLES 1. You were a resident of France from February 20, 1990, until June 30, 1992, when you returned to the U.S. Since your period of foreign residency included all of 1991, thereby satisfying the foreign residence test, you may claim a prorated exclusion for 1992. As you were abroad for 182 of the 366 days in 1992, you exclude earnings up to 182/366 of the $70,000 maximum exclusion. If you earned $60,000 from January through June 1992, you would exclude $34,809 ($70,000 × 182/366).

2. You worked in France from June 1, 1991, through September 30, 1992. Your only days outside France were a 15-day vacation to the U.S. in December 1991. You do not qualify for an exclusion under the foreign residence test because you were not abroad for a full taxable year; you were not abroad for either the full year of 1991 or 1992. You *do* qualify under the physical presence test; you were physically present abroad for at least 330 full days during a 12-month period. The 12-month period giving you the largest 1992 exclusion is the 12-month period starting October 21, 1991, and ending October 20, 1992. *See* ¶36.5 for figuring the 12-month period. Since you were abroad for at least 330 full days during that 12-month period, you may claim an exclusion. In 1992, you were abroad for 294 days within the 12-month period (January 1 to October 20, 1992, is 294 days). Thus, you exclude earnings up to 294/366 of the maximum exclusion. If your earnings in France for 1992 were $80,000, your exclusion is limited to $56,230 ($70,000 × 294/366).

Foreign earnings from a prior year. Foreign income earned in a prior year but paid in 1992 does not qualify for the 1992 exclusion. However, if the income was attributable to foreign services performed in 1991, the pay is tax free provided you did not use the full 1991 exclusion of $70,000. Under an exception, payments received in 1992 for 1991 services are treated as 1992 income if the payment was within a normal payroll period of 16 days or less that included the last day of 1991. If the services were performed before 1991, no exclusion is available to shelter the pay.

Income for services performed in the U.S. does not qualify for the exclusion, even though it is paid to you while you are abroad.

Foreign tax credit. Foreign taxes paid on tax-free foreign earned income do not qualify for a credit or deduction. But if your foreign pay exceeds $70,000, you may claim a foreign tax credit or deduction for the foreign taxes allocated to taxable income. The instructions to Forms 2555 and 1116, and IRS Publication 514 provide details for making the computation.

Countries subject to travel restrictions. You may not claim the exclusion if you work in a country subject to U.S. government travel restrictions. You are not treated as a bona fide resident of, or as present in, a country subject to the travel ban. Libya, Cuba, and Iraq are within this ban. Check Form 2555 for changes to this list.

HOW TO TREAT HOUSING COSTS

¶36.3 The housing costs of employees and self-employed persons are treated differently by the tax law. Employees get a housing exclusion; self-employed persons, a deduction from *taxable* foreign earned income. If you live in a special camp provided by your employer, all housing costs are excluded; *see* ¶36.8.

Exclusion for employer-financed housing costs. If the total of your foreign wage or salary income plus the value of employer-financed housing costs in 1992 does not exceed $70,000, both parts of your pay package are tax free. Your housing costs are considered to be employer-financed as long as they are covered by salary, employer reimbursements, a housing allowance, or if they are paid directly by your employer. If wages plus employer-financed housing exceeds $70,000, a special housing exclusion will shelter part of your housing costs from tax. The housing exclusion is the difference between the employer's payment of reasonable housing expenses and a "base housing amount." The base housing amount is 16% of the salary for a U.S. government employee at the GS-14, Step 1 level as of the beginning of the year (the 1992 base amount may be found in Form 2555). If you qualify under the foreign residence or physical presence test for only part of 1992, the base housing amount is reduced on a daily basis. Follow instructions to Form 2555. The housing cost exclusion is elected on Form 2555. Employer-financed housing payments exceeding this housing cost exclusion may also escape tax if your foreign salary is below the maximum foreign earned income exclusion. That part of the foreign earned income exclusion not applied to your salary may be applied to housing costs; *see* Example 1 below.

On Form 2555, you figure the housing exclusion before the foreign earned income exclusion. The earned income exclusion is limited to the excess of foreign earned income over the housing exclusion.

EXAMPLES 1. In 1992, your salary for work abroad is $58,483 and your employer pays $12,035 for your housing. The total amount of salary and housing costs is tax free. On Form 2555, you list $70,518 (salary *plus* housing) as your foreign earned income. Assume that the housing cost exclusion is $3,650 (housing costs of $12,035 exceeding a base housing amount of $8,385). Your earned income exclusion is $66,868: $70,518 earned income *less* $3,650 housing exclusion.

2. In 1992, you earn $61,000 abroad and your employer pays $12,035 for your housing. Assume the housing exclusion is $3,650 (housing costs of $12,035 exceeding a base housing amount of $8,385). All of your salary plus the full amount of the housing costs avoids tax: the housing cost exclusion of $3,650 and an earned income exclusion of $69,385 ($73,035 foreign earned income *less* $3,650 housing exclusion).

3. Same as Example 2 above, except that you earn $65,000. Foreign earned income is $77,035 ($65,000 *plus* $12,035), but the total amount of income not subject to tax is $73,650. The total tax-free amount is made up of the housing cost exclusion of $3,650 and the maximum foreign earned income exclusion of $70,000.

Reasonable housing expenses. Include rent, utilities other than telephone costs, insurance, parking, furniture rentals, and repairs for yourself, your spouse, and dependents living with you. The following expenses do not qualify: cost of purchasing a home, furniture, or accessories; home improvements; payments of mortgage principal; domestic labor; and depreciation on a home or on improvements to leased housing. Furthermore, interest and taxes which are otherwise deductible do not qualify for the exclusion.

You may include the costs of a separate household that you maintain outside the U.S. for your spouse and dependents because living conditions at your foreign home are adverse.

Self-employed persons. On Form 2555, self-employed individuals may claim a limited deduction for housing costs exceeding the base housing amount. You may claim this deduction only to the extent it offsets taxable foreign earned income. The deduction is claimed as an "adjustment to income" on Line 30 of Form 1040 even if you do not itemize deductions.

Where you may not deduct expenses because you do not have taxable foreign earned income, expenses may be carried forward one year and deducted in the next year to the extent of taxable foreign earned income.

If you are employed and self-employed during the same year. Housing expenses above the base amount are partly excludable and partly deductible. For example, if half of your foreign earned income is from services as an employee, half of the excess housing expenses over the base amount are excludable. The remaining excess housing costs are deductible to the extent of taxable foreign earned income. Follow the instructions to Form 2555.

Countries ineligible for tax benefits. Housing expenses incurred in a country subject to a U.S. government travel restriction are not eligible for the tax benefits explained in this section. *See* Form 2555 instructions.

WHAT IS FOREIGN EARNED INCOME?

¶36.4

Earned income includes salaries, wages, commissions, professional fees, and bonuses. Earned income also includes allowances from your employer for housing or other expenses, as well as the value of housing or a car provided by the employer. It may also include business profits, royalties, and rents, provided this income is tied to the performance of services. Earned income does not include pension or annuity income, payments for nonqualified employee trusts or nonqualified annuities, dividends, interest, capital gains, gambling winnings, alimony, or the value of tax-free meals or lodging under the rules at ¶3.10. Foreign earned income does not include amounts earned in countries subject to U.S. government travel restrictions.

Foreign earned income eligible for the exclusion must be received no later than the taxable year after the year in which you perform the services. Pay is excludable in the year of receipt if you did not use the full exclusion in the year of the services.

U.S. government pay ineligible. If you are an employee of the U.S. government or its agencies, you may not exclude any part of your pay from your government employer. Courts have agreed with the IRS that workers were U.S. employees even though they were paid from sources other than Congressionally appropriated funds. If you are not an employee of the U.S. government or any of its agencies, your pay is excludable even if paid by a government source. You are not an employee of the U.S. if you work under a contract made between your employer and the government.

Under a special law, tax liability is waived for a civilian or military employee of the U.S. government killed in a military action overseas; *see* ¶35.6.

Profits from sole proprietorship or partnership. If your business consists solely of services (no capital investment), 100% of gross income is considered earned income. If services and capital are both income-producing factors, no more than 30% of your net profit may be considered earned income.

If you do not contribute any services to a business (for example, you are a "silent partner"), your share of the net profits is *not* earned income.

EXAMPLES 1. A U.S. citizen resides in England. He invests in an English partnership that sells manufactured goods outside the U.S. He performs no services for the business. His share of net profits does not qualify as earned income.

2. Same facts as Example 1, except he devotes his full time to the partnership business. Then 30% of his share of the net profits qualifies as earned income. Thus, if his share of profits is $50,000, earned income is $15,000 (30% of $50,000), assuming the value of his services is at least $15,000.

3. You and another person are consultants, operating as a partnership in Europe. Since capital is not an income-producing element, the entire gross income of the business is earned income.

The partnership agreement generally determines the tax status of partnership income in a U.S. partnership with a foreign branch. Thus, if the partnership agreement allocates foreign earnings to partners abroad, the allocation will be recognized unless it lacks substantial economic effect.

Fringe benefits. The value of fringe benefits, such as the right to use company property and facilities, is added to your compensation when figuring the amount of your earned income.

Royalties. Royalties from articles or books are earned income if you receive them for transferring all of your rights to your work, or you have contracted to write the articles or book for an amount in cash plus a royalty on sales.

Royalties from the leasing of oil and mineral lands and from patents are not earned income.

Rental income. Rental income is generally not earned income. However, if you perform personal services, for example as an owner-manager of a hotel or rooming house in a foreign country, then up to 30% of your net rents may be earned income.

Reimbursement of employee expenses. Do not include reimbursement of expenses in earned income to the extent they equal expenses which you adequately accounted for to your employer; *see* ¶20.34. If your expenses exceed reimbursements, the excess is allocated according to the rules in ¶36.6. If reimbursements exceed expenses, the excess is treated as earned income.

Straight commission salespersons or other employees who arrange with their employers, for withholding purposes, to consider a percentage of their commissions as attributable to their expenses, treat such amounts as earned income.

Reimbursed moving expenses. Employer reimbursement of moving expenses must be reported on your return in the year of receipt. However, for purposes of claiming the earned income exclusion, the reimbursement may be considered to have been earned in a different year. This is important because an exclusion is allowed only for the year income is earned. If the move is from the U.S. to a foreign country, the reimbursement is considered foreign earned income in the year of the move if you qualify under the foreign residence or physical presence test for at least 120 days during that tax year. Reimbursement of moving expenses from one foreign country to another is considered foreign earned income in the year of the move, if you qualify under the residency or physical presence test at the new location for at least 120 days during the tax year. If you do not meet one of these tests in the year of the move, the reimbursements are earned income which must be allocated between the year of the move and the following tax year.

Employer reimbursements for moves back to the U.S. are considered income from U.S. sources if you continue to work for the same employer. If you move back to the U.S. and take a job with a new employer *or* if you retire and move back to the U.S. and your old employer reimburses your moving expenses under a prior written agreement or company policy, the reimbursement is considered to be for past services in the foreign country and qualifies as foreign earned income eligible for the exclusion. The reimbursement is considered earned in the year of the move if you qualified under the residency or physical presence test for at least 120 days during the tax year. Otherwise, the reimbursement is allocated between the year of the move and the year preceding the move. *See* IRS Publication 54 for details.

MEETING THE FOREIGN RESIDENCE OR PHYSICAL PRESENCE TEST

¶36.5   To qualify for the foreign earned income exclusion, you must be either a U.S. citizen meeting the foreign residence test or a U.S. citizen or resident meeting the physical presence test in a foreign country. The following areas are not considered foreign countries: Puerto Rico, Virgin Islands, Guam, Commonwealth of the Northern Mariana Islands, American Samoa, or the Antarctic region.

If war or civil unrest prevented you from meeting the foreign residence or physical presence test, you may claim the exclusion for the period you actually were a resident or physically present abroad. Foreign locations and the time periods which qualify for the waiver of the residency and physical presence tests are listed in the instructions to Form 2555.

If, by the due date of your 1992 return (April 15, 1993), you have not yet satisfied the foreign residence or physical presence test, but you expect to meet either test after the filing date, you may either file on the due date and report your earnings or ask for a filing extension under the rules at ¶36.7.

Foreign residence test. You must be a U.S. citizen who is a bona fide resident of a foreign country for an uninterrupted period that includes one full tax year. Business or vacation trips to the U.S. or another country will not disqualify you from satisfying the foreign residence test. If you are abroad more than one year but less than two, the entire period qualifies if it includes one full tax year.

EXAMPLE You are a bona fide foreign resident from September 30, 1991, to March 25, 1993. The period includes your entire 1992 tax year. Therefore, up to $70,000 of your 1992 earnings is excludable. Your overseas earnings in 1993 will qualify for a proportionate part of the exclusion in 1993.

To prove you are a foreign resident, you must show your intention to be a resident of the foreign country. Evidence tending to con-

firm your intention to stay in a foreign country is: (1) Your family accompanies you; (2) you buy a house or rent an apartment rather than a hotel room; (3) you participate in the foreign community activities; (4) you can speak the foreign language; (5) you have a permanent foreign address; (6) you join clubs there; or (7) you open charge accounts in stores in the foreign country.

Residence does not have the same meaning as *domicile.* Your domicile is a permanent place of abode; it is the place to which you eventually plan to return wherever you go. You may have a residence in a place other than your domicile. Thus, you may go, say, to Amsterdam, and take up residence there and still intend to return to your domicile in the U.S. But your leaving your domicile does not, by itself, establish a bona fide residence in a new place. You must intend to make a new place your residence.

You will not qualify if you take inconsistent positions toward your foreign residency. That is, you will *not* be treated as a bona fide resident of a foreign country if you have earned income from sources within that country, filed a statement with the authorities of that country that you are not a resident there, and have been held not subject to the income tax of that country. However, this rule does not prevent you from qualifying under the physical presence test.

If you cannot prove that you are a resident, check to determine if your stay qualifies under the physical presence test.

Physical presence test. To qualify under this test, you must show you were on foreign soil 330 days (about 11 months) during a 12-month period. Whether you were a resident or a transient is of no importance. You have to show you were physically present in a foreign country or countries for 330 full days during any 12-consecutive-month period. The 12-month period may begin with any day. There is no requirement that it begin with your first full day abroad. It may begin before or after arrival in a foreign country and may end before or after departure from a foreign country. A *full* day is from midnight to midnight (24 consecutive hours). You must spend each of the 330 days on foreign soil. In departing from U.S. soil to go directly to the foreign country, or in returning directly to the U.S. from a foreign country, the time you spend on or over international waters does not count toward the 330-day total.

EXAMPLES 1. On August 9, you fly from New York City to Paris. You arrive there at 10 A.M. August 10. Your first full qualifying day toward the 330-day period is August 11. You may count in your 330-day period:

Time spent traveling between foreign countries.

Time spent on a vacation in foreign countries. There is no requirement that the 330 days must be spent on a job.

Time spent in a foreign country while employed by the U.S. government counts towards the 330-day test, even though pay from the government does not qualify for the earned income exclusion.

Time in foreign countries, territorial waters, or travel in the air over a foreign country. However, you will lose qualifying days if any part of such travel is on or over international waters and takes 24 hours or more, or any part of such travel is within the U.S. or its possessions.

2. You depart from Naples, Italy, by ship on June 10 at 6:00 P.M. and arrive at Haifa, Israel, at 7:00 A.M. on June 14. The trip exceeded 24 hours and passed through international waters. Therefore, you lose as qualifying days June 10, 11, 12, 13, and 14. Assuming you remain in Haifa, Israel, the next qualifying day is June 15.

Choosing the 12-month period. You qualify under the physical presence test if you were on foreign soil 330 days during any period of 12 consecutive months. Since there may be several 12-month periods during which you meet the 330-day test, you should choose the 12-month period allowing you the largest possible exclusion if you qualify under the physical presence test for only part of 1992.

EXAMPLE You worked in France from June 1, 1991, through September 30, 1992, when you left the country. During this period, you left France only for a 15-day vacation to the U.S. during December 1991. You earned $70,000 for your work in France during 1992. Your maximum 1992 exclusion is $56,421, figured as follows:

1. Start with your last full day, September 30, 1992, and count back 330 full days during which you were abroad. Not counting the vacation days, the 330th day is October 22, 1991. This is the first day of your 12-month period.

2. From October 22, 1991, count forward 12 months, to October 21, 1992, which is the last day of your 12-month period.

3. Count the number of days in 1992 which fall within the 12-month period ending October 21, 1992. Here, the number of qualifying days is 295, from January 1 through October 21, 1992.

4. The maximum 1992 exclusion is $70,000 × 295/366 or $56,421. You may exclude $56,421, the lesser of the maximum exclusion or your actual earnings of $70,000.

CLAIMING DEDUCTIONS

¶36.6 You may not deduct expenses that are allocable to the foreign earned income and housing exclusions. If you elect the earned income exclusion, you deduct expenses as follows:

Personal or non-business deductions, such as medical expenses, mortgage interest, and real estate taxes paid on a personal residence, are deductible if you itemize deductions. Business expenses attributable to earning excludable income are not deductible. Dependency exemptions are fully deductible.

EXAMPLE You were a resident of Denmark and elect to exclude your wages of $70,000 from income. You also incurred unreimbursed travel expenses of $2,000. You may not deduct the travel expenses, since the amount is attributable to the earning of tax-free income.

If your foreign earnings exceed the exclusion ceiling, you allocate expenses between taxable and tax-exempt income and deduct the amount allocated to taxable earned income.

EXAMPLE You earn $100,000 and satisfy the physical presence test. Your unreimbursed travel expenses are $5,000, after reducing meals and entertainment by 20%. If you elect the $70,000 exclusion, you may deduct 30% of the travel expenses, or $1,500, since 30% of your earnings or $30,000 are taxed. The expenses are deductible as a miscellaneous itemized deduction subject to the 2% AGI floor.

If your job expenses are reimbursed and the expenses are adequately accounted for to your employer (¶20.34), the reimbursements are not reported as income on your Form W-2. If the reimbursement is less than expenses, the excess expenses are allocated as in the example above.

You may have to allocate state income taxes paid on your income.

If either you or your spouse elects the earned income or housing exclusion, you may not claim an IRA deduction based on excluded income.

Overseas moving expenses. These expenses are generally treated as related to your foreign earnings. Thus, if you move to a foreign country and exclude your income, you may not deduct your moving expenses. If your earned income exceeds the exclusion limit, you allocate moving expenses between your tax-exempt and taxable earned income. Employer reimbursement is considered earned income in the year of receipt and is added to other earned income before taking the exclusion and making the allocation. *See* ¶36.4 for allocating reimbursements between the year of the move and the following year for purposes of claiming the exclusion. In allocating moving expenses to taxable earned income, apply the following rules for computing the moving expense deduction. (1) A deduction of up to $6,000 is allowed for the cost of temporary living arrangements at the foreign location, house hunting costs, and expenses incident to the sale of your old home and purchase of a new one at the foreign location; of this amount, up to $4,500 may be claimed for temporary living arrangements and house hunting costs. (2) You may deduct expenses for temporary living arrangements incurred within any 90 consecutive days after obtaining work abroad. (3) You may deduct in full as directly related moving expenses the cost of moving household goods and personal effects to and from storage and the cost of storing the goods or effects while your new foreign work site is your principal place of work.

If, after working in a foreign country, your employer transfers you back to the U.S. or you move back to the U.S. to take a different job, your moving expenses are deductible under the general rules of Chapter 21. If your residence and principal place of work was outside the U.S. and you retire and move back to the U.S., your moving expenses are also deductible, except that you do not have to meet the 39-week test for employees or the 78-week test for the self-employed and partners.

Survivors of workers abroad returning to U.S. If you are the spouse or dependent of a worker who died while his or her principal place of work was outside the U.S., you may deduct your moving expenses back to the U.S. For the costs to be deductible, the move must begin within six months of the worker's death. The requirements for deducting moving expenses apply, except for the 39-week test for employees or the 78-week test for the self-employed and partners.

Compulsory home leave. Foreign service officers stationed abroad must periodically return to the U.S. to re-orient themselves to American ways of life. Because the home leave is compulsory, foreign service officers may deduct their travel expenses; travel expenses of the officer's family are not deductible.

EXCLUSION NOT ESTABLISHED WHEN YOUR RETURN IS DUE

¶36.7 When your 1992 return is due, you may not have been abroad long enough to qualify for the exclusion. If you expect to qualify under either the residence or physical presence test after the due date for your 1992 return, you may either (1) ask for an extension of time for filing your return on Form 2350 until after you qualify under either rule; or (2) file your return on the due date, reporting the foreign income in the return, pay the full tax, and then file for a refund when you qualify.

If you will have tax to pay even after qualifying—for example, your earned income exceeds the exclusion—you may file for an extension to file but you will owe interest on the tax due. To avoid interest charges on the tax, you may take one of the following steps:

1. File your return on time and pay the total tax due without the application of the exclusion. When you do qualify, make sure you file a refund claim within the time limits discussed at Chapter 38; or
2. Pay the estimated tax liability when you apply for the extension to file on Form 2350. If the extension is granted, the payment is applied to the tax shown on your return when you file.

Extension of Time to File

If you are living and working abroad on April 15, 1993, you have an automatic extension to June 15, 1993. For an additional two months, file Form 4868 by June 15, 1993, and pay an estimated tax. For a longer extension, in anticipation of owing no tax on your foreign income, you may file Form 2350 either with the Internal Revenue Service, Philadelphia, Pennsylvania 19255, or with a local IRS representative. File Form 2350 before the due date for filing your 1992 return, which is June 15, 1993, if you are abroad and are on a calendar year. If you cannot get Form 2350, apply for the extension on your own stationery. State the facts you rely on to justify the extension and the earliest date you expect to be in a position to determine under which rule you will qualify. You will receive an official letter and copy granting the extension. Generally, you will be granted an extension of time for a period ending 30 days after the date you expect to qualify for the foreign earned income exclusion.

TAX-FREE MEALS AND LODGING FOR WORKERS IN CAMPS

¶36.8 If you must live in a camp provided by your employer, you may exclude from income the value of the lodging and meals furnished if the camp is (1) provided because you work in a remote area where satisfactory housing is not available; (2) located as near as practical to the worksite; and (3) a common area not open to the public normally accommodating at least 10 employees.

You also may qualify for the earned income exclusion.

VIRGIN ISLANDS, SAMOA, GUAM, NORTHERN MARIANAS

¶36.9 The Virgin Islands, Guam, American Samoa, and the Commonwealth of the Northern Mariana Islands have their own independent tax departments. Therefore, contact the particular tax authority for the proper treatment of your income and ask the IRS for the 1992 edition of Publication 570, *Tax Guide for Individuals With Income From U.S. Possessions*. If you have a mailing address overseas, write to Forms Distribution Center, P.O. Box 25866, Richmond, VA 23289, for Publication 570.

For tax information from Guam, write to Commissioner of Revenue and Taxation, Government of Guam, 855 West Marine Drive, Agana, Guam 96910. For information from the Commonwealth of the Northern Mariana Islands, write to the Division of Revenue and Taxation, Commonwealth of the Northern Mariana Islands, Central Office, Saipan, Mariana Islands 96950. For information from American Samoa, write to the Tax Division, Government of American Samoa, Pago Pago, American Samoa 96799.

For information about tax liability in the Virgin Islands, write to Virgin Islands Bureau of Internal Revenue, Lockhart's Garden, No. 1-A, Charlotte Amalie, St. Thomas, U.S. Virgin Islands 00802. Also *see* IRS Publication 570.

EARNINGS IN PUERTO RICO

¶36.10 If you are a U.S. citizen who is also a resident of Puerto Rico for the entire year, you generally report all of your income on your Puerto Rico tax return. Where you report income from U.S. sources on the Puerto Rico tax return, a credit against the Puerto Rico tax may be claimed for income taxes paid to the United States.

If you are not a resident of Puerto Rico, you report on a Puerto Rico return only income from Puerto Rican sources. Wages earned for services performed in Puerto Rico for the U.S. government or for private employers is treated as income from Puerto Rican sources.

U.S. tax returns. As a U.S. citizen, you must file a U.S. tax return reporting income from all sources. But, if you are a bona fide resident of Puerto Rico for an entire tax year, you do not report on a U.S. tax return any income from Puerto Rican sources during your residence there, except amounts received for services performed in Puerto Rico as an employee of the U.S. government. Similar rules apply if you have been a bona fide resident of Puerto Rico for at least two years before changing your residence from Puerto Rico. On a U.S. tax return, you may not deduct expenses or claim tax credits applicable to the excludable income. Personal exemptions are fully deductible.

If you are not a bona fide resident of Puerto Rico for the entire tax year, or were not a bona fide resident for two years prior to the tax year, you report on your U.S. tax return all of your Puerto Rican income, as well as all income from other sources. If you are required to report Puerto Rican income on your U.S. tax return, you may claim a credit for income tax paid to Puerto Rico. You figure the credit on Form 1116.

EXAMPLE You and your spouse are bona fide residents of Puerto Rico during the entire year of 1992. You receive $25,000 in wages as an employee of the U.S. government working in Puerto Rico, a $100 dividend from a Puerto Rican corporation that does business in Puerto Rico and a $500 dividend from a U.S. corporation that does business in the U.S. Your spouse earned $18,000 in wages from a Puerto Rican corporation for services performed in Puerto Rico. Your exempt and taxable income for U.S. federal tax purposes is as follows:

	Taxable	Exempt
Your wages	$25,000	
Your spouse's wages		$18,000
Puerto Rican corporation dividend		100
U.S. corporation dividend	500	
Totals	$25,500	$18,100

You file tax returns with both Puerto Rico and the U.S. You have gross income of $25,500 for U.S. tax purposes and $43,600 for Puerto Rican tax purposes. A tax credit may be claimed on the U.S. tax return for income taxes paid to Puerto Rico and on your Puerto Rico return for income taxes paid to the U.S on U.S. source income.

Information on Puerto Rico tax returns may be requested from Negociado de Contribución Sobre Ingresos, Apartado S 2501, San Juan, Puerto Rico 00903.

TAX TREATIES WITH FOREIGN COUNTRIES

¶36.11 Tax treaties between the United States and foreign countries modify some of the rules discussed above. The purpose of the treaties is to avoid double taxation. Consult your tax advisor about the effect of these treaties on your income. IRS Publication 54 contains a list of tax treaties.

EXCHANGE RATES AND BLOCKED CURRENCY

¶36.12 Income reported on your federal income tax return must be stated in U.S. dollars. Where you are paid in foreign currency, you report your pay in U.S. dollars on the basis of the exchange rates prevailing at the time the income is actually or constructively received. You use the rate that most closely reflects the value of the foreign currency—the official rate, the open market rate, or any other relevant rate. You may even be required to use the black market rate if that is the most accurate measure of the actual purchasing power of U.S. dollars in the foreign country. Be prepared to justify the rate you use.

Currency gains and losses. A special statute, Section 988, governs the treatment of gain or loss on currency transactions. In the case of individuals, Section 988 applies if expenses attributable to the transaction would be deductible as business expenses or expenses for the production of income.

Fulbright grants. If 70% of a Fulbright grant is paid in nonconvertible foreign currency, U.S. tax may be paid in the foreign currency. *See* IRS Publication 520 for details.

Blocked currency. A citizen or resident alien may be paid in a foreign currency that cannot be converted into American dollars and removed from the foreign country. If your income is in blocked currency, you may elect to defer the reporting of that income until (1) The currency becomes convertible into dollars. (2) You actually convert it into dollars. (3) You use it for personal expenses (for example, in the foreign country when you go there). Purchase of a business or investment in the foreign country is not the kind of use that is treated as a conversion. (4) You make a gift of it or leave it in your will. (5) You are a resident alien and you give up your U.S. residence.

If you use this method to defer the income, you may not deduct the expenses of earning it until you report it. You must continue to use this method after you choose it. You may only change with permission of the IRS.

You do not defer the reporting of capital losses incurred in a country having a blocked currency.

There may be these disadvantages in deferring income:

1. Many years' income may accumulate and all be taxed in one year.
2. You have no control over the year in which the blocked income becomes taxable. You usually cannot control the events that cause the income to become unblocked.

You choose to defer income in blocked currency by filing a tentative tax return reporting your blocked taxable income and explain that you are deferring the payment of income tax because your income is not in dollars or in property or currency which is readily convertible into dollars. You must attach to your tentative return a regular return, reporting any unblocked taxable income received during the year or taxable income which became unblocked during the year. When the currency finally becomes unblocked or convertible into a currency or property convertible to dollars, you pay tax on the earnings at the rate prevailing in the year the currency became unblocked or convertible. On the tentative return, note at the top: "Report of Deferrable Foreign Income, pursuant to Revenue Ruling 74-351." File separate returns for each country from which blocked currency is received. The election must be made by the due date for filing a return for the year in which an election is sought.

INFORMATION RETURNS ON FOREIGN CURRENCY

¶36.13 If you have a financial interest in, signature, or other authority over a foreign bank account, a foreign securities account, or any other foreign financial account, you must report this fact on Form TDF 90-22.1 (Report of Foreign Bank and Financial Accounts) if the aggregate value of the accounts at any time during the year exceeds $10,000. The form does not have to be filed if the accounts were with a U.S. military banking facility operated by a U.S. financial institution. Taxpayers filing Form 1040 must also indicate on Schedule B whether they had an interest in a foreign account during the year. Form TDF 90-22.1 is not filed with your income tax return. The form must be filed by June 30 of the year following the year in which you had this financial interest. Foreign accounts for 1992 must be reported by June 30, 1993, to the Department of the Treasury, Post Office Box 32621, Detroit, MI 48232.

Treasury regulations impose reporting and record-keeping requirements for currency transactions outside the United States. Generally, transactions involving a physical transfer of funds or monetary instruments into or outside the U.S. must be reported if the amount involved exceeds $10,000 on any one occasion; *see* Form 4790.

Financial institutions must file a Form 4789 for each deposit, withdrawal, exchange of currency, or any other currency transaction of more than $10,000.

FOREIGN TAX CREDIT

¶36.14 You must file Form 1116 to compute your credit. You may not claim a foreign tax credit or deduction for taxes paid on income not subject to U.S. tax. If all of your foreign earned income is excluded, none of the foreign taxes paid on such income may be taken as a credit or deduction on your U.S. return. If you exclude only part of your foreign pay, you determine which foreign taxes are attributable to excluded income and thus disallowed as foreign tax credits by applying the fractional computation provided in the instructions to Form 1116 and IRS Publication 514.

Choosing Credit or Deduction

If you qualify for a credit or deduction, you will generally receive a larger tax reduction by claiming a tax credit rather than a deduction. A deduction is only a partial offset against your tax, whereas a credit is deducted in full from your tax. Also, taking a deduction may bar you from carrying back an excess credit from a later year. However, a deduction may give you a larger tax saving if the foreign tax is levied at a high rate and the proportion of foreign income to U.S. income is small. Compute your tax under both methods and choose the one providing the larger tax reduction.

In one tax year, you may not elect to deduct some foreign taxes and claim others as a credit. One method must be applied to all taxes paid or accrued during the tax year. If you are a cash basis taxpayer, you may claim a credit for accrued foreign taxes, but you must consistently follow this method once elected.

The credit is the amount of foreign taxes paid or accrued, not to exceed the effective U.S. tax on foreign income multiplied by a ratio of foreign taxable income over total taxable income.

Credit disallowed. The credit may *not* be claimed if:

You are a nonresident alien. However, under certain circumstances, an alien who is a bona fide resident for an entire taxable year in Puerto Rico may claim the credit. Also a nonresident alien engaged in a U.S. trade or business may claim a credit if he or she receives income *effectively connected* to that business. You receive tax-exempt income from a U.S. possession.

No credit is allowed for taxes imposed by a country designated by the government as engaging in terroristic activities; *see* IRS Publication 514 for a list of these countries.

Taxes qualifying for the credit. The credit is allowed only for foreign income, excess profits taxes, and similar taxes in the nature of an income tax. It is not allowed for any taxes paid to foreign countries on sales, gross receipts, production, the privilege to do business, personal property, or export of capital. But it may apply to a—

Tax similar to a U.S. tax on income.

Tax paid by a domestic taxpayer in lieu of the tax upon income, which would otherwise be imposed by any foreign country or by any U.S. possession.

Tax of a foreign country imposing income tax, where for reasons growing out of the administrative difficulties of determining net income or basis within that country, the tax is measured by gross income, sales, and number of units produced.

Pension, unemployment, or disability funds of a foreign country; certain foreign social security taxes do not qualify.

Reporting foreign income on your return. You report the gross amount of your foreign income in terms of United States currency. You also attach a schedule showing how you figured the foreign income in United States currency.

EXAMPLE You earn Canadian dividends of $100 (Canadian dollars), from which $15 of Canadian taxes were withheld. When the dividends were declared, a Canadian dollar could be exchanged for $.82 of United States currency. Therefore, the dividend of $100 (in Canadian dollars) is reported on your return as $82 ($100 × .82). The tax withheld which may be taken as a credit is $12.30 ($15 × .82).

COMPUTING THE FOREIGN TAX CREDIT

¶36.15
The foreign tax credit is based on the amount of foreign taxes you paid or accrued, subject to this overall limitation figured on Form 1116:

$$\text{U.S. tax} \times \frac{\text{Taxable income from all foreign countries}}{\text{Taxable income from all sources}}$$

Separate limitation categories. The above fractional limitation must be figured separately for specific categories of foreign income. These categories are (1) passive income (such as dividends, interest, rents, royalties, and gains on certain commodity transactions; (2) foreign interest income subject to withholding at more than a 5% rate; (3) shipping and aircraft related income; (4) lump-sum retirement distributions from foreign sources subject to special averaging; (5) certain income derived in banking, insurance, or financing businesses. Taxable income for each category must be separately computed and the overall limitation fraction applied. A separate computation also must be made for all other foreign income not within these categories; this "other" income group is called general limitation income. Follow the instructions to Form 1116 and *see* IRS Publication 514 for further details.

When this book went to press, Congress was considering legislation to provide a simplified credit computation to those who have only passive foreign income; see the Supplement.

Taxable income. Income which is tax free under the foreign earned income exclusion is not taken into account when figuring taxable income. Foreign taxable income, for purposes of computing the ratio, is reduced by all expenses directly related to earning the income. Itemized deductions, such as medical expenses, that are not directly related to foreign sources are allocated to foreign income according to relative gross incomes from foreign and U.S. sources. You do not consider personal exemptions when figuring foreign or total taxable income.

The foreign tax credit may not exceed foreign taxes actually paid or accrued. Where a joint return is filed, the limitation is applied to the aggregate taxable income of both spouses.

A limited foreign tax credit may be applied against the alternative minimum tax; *see* ¶23.6.

EXAMPLE Jones, a single individual, receives taxable salary income from three countries as follows:

	Taxable income	Income taxes paid
Country A	$ 2,000	$ 100
Country B	4,000	$ 1,200
United States	4,000	
Total taxable income	$10,000	

Assume that the U.S. tax is $2,000.

	Tax credit on overall basis	Actual foreign tax	Foreign tax credit allowable
Countries A and B:	$\frac{\$6,000}{\$10,000} \times \$2,000 =$ $1,200	$1,300	$1,200
Total taxable income:			

If the income from Country A was salary and the income from Country B was passive income, separate computations of taxable income and separate credit limitations would have to be figured for each country. *See* Form 1116 and IRS Publication 514.

Capital gains. In figuring the overall limitation, taxable income from foreign countries (the numerator) includes gain from the sale of capital assets only to the extent of foreign source capital gain net income, which is the lower of net capital gain from foreign sources or net capital gain from all sources. Gain on the sale of nondepreciable personal property sold outside the country of your residence may be treated as gain from U.S. sources, unless the gain is subject to a foreign income tax at a rate of 10% or more of the gain. *See* instructions to Form 1116.

Recapture of foreign losses. If you sustain an "overall foreign loss" for any taxable year, a recapture provision treats part of foreign income realized in a later year as income from U.S. sources. By treating part of the later year's foreign income as U.S. income, the numerator of the fraction used to compute the overall limitation (*see* above) is reduced and this in turn reduces the maximum foreign tax credit that may be claimed in the later year. More specifically, the portion of foreign income in succeeding years which is treated as U.S. income equals the lower of (1) the amount of the loss, or (2) 50% (or a larger percentage, as you may choose) of taxable income from foreign sources. An "overall foreign loss" means the amount by which the gross income for the taxable year from foreign sources for that year is exceeded by the sum of allocated deductions. For this purpose, the following deductions are not subject to recapture: operating loss deductions, any uncompensated foreign expropriation, or casualty loss. Special rules apply to dispositions of property if used predominantly outside the United States in a trade or business. *See* IRS Publication 514 for recapture details.

CARRYBACK AND CARRYOVER OF EXCESS FOREIGN TAX CREDIT

¶36.16
Where the amount allowable as a credit under the overall basis is restricted, the excess may be carried back to the two preceding years and then carried forward to the five succeeding taxable years. The carryback or carryover will not be allowed in a year you have no income from foreign sources or the credit limitation already applies to taxes of that year. For further details, *see* IRS Publication 514.

37

PLANNING ALIMONY AND MARITAL SETTLEMENTS

Alimony payments that meet tax law tests are deductible if you pay them, taxable if you receive them. Payments are not deductible by the payer unless taxable to the recipient. For payments to be deductible and taxable, the rules discussed in ¶37.1–¶37.7 must be met.

You claim a deduction for deductible alimony that you pay on Line 29 of Form 1040. You deduct the payments even if you claim the standard deduction rather than itemizing deductions. You must enter the Social Security number of your ex-spouse. Otherwise, your deduction may be disallowed and you may have to pay a $50 penalty. If you pay deductible alimony to more than one ex-spouse, enter the Social Security number of one of them and provide similar information for the others on a separate statement attached to your return.

If you receive taxable alimony, report the payments on Line 11 of Form 1040. You must give your ex-spouse your Social Security number and could be subject to a $50 penalty if you fail to do so.

PLANNING ALIMONY AGREEMENTS

¶37.1 You can arrange beforehand how the costs of a divorce are to be borne. You may specifically state in the decree or agreement that the alimony is neither taxable to the payee-spouse (under IRC section 71), nor deductible by the payer-spouse (under IRC section 215). Such a statement effectively disqualifies payments that otherwise would be taxable to the payee-spouse and deductible by the payer-spouse. A copy of the agreement that contains the statement must be attached to the tax return of the payee-spouse for each year the statement is applicable.

Planning the after-tax consequences of alimony is difficult. The first problem is for a couple to be convinced that they may have a common financial interest; the second, projecting future tax consequences.

For example, assume that the husband is to make payments to the wife. If tax planning is approached from the viewpoint of each spouse separately, the tax deduction is an advantage for the husband; tax-free income is an advantage for the wife. However, both advantages cannot be achieved, and the couple must face the reality of the tax law, which allows the husband to deduct payments only if they are taxed as alimony to the wife. They must compromise and approach the setting of amounts and tax consequences by balancing their interests.

One equitable approach is to view both spouses as a single economic tax unit. If this is done and the husband will be in a higher tax bracket during the payout period than the wife, an agreement should generally provide for taxable and deductible alimony. The tax savings provided by the deduction can conserve more of the husband's assets while providing funds required by the wife. The final amount of alimony to be paid depends on the spouses' tax brackets. Where there is no favorable difference in tax brackets, there may be no advantage in tailoring an agreement for taxable and deductible alimony when viewing the positions of the two parties as a unit.

If you agree that one spouse is to pay deductible alimony and the other spouse is to report the alimony as income, these rules must be met:

1. The alimony must be paid under the decree of divorce or legal separation agreement or decree of support; *see* ¶37.2.
2. The agreement must provide for cash payments; *see* ¶37.3. There is no minimum payout period for annual alimony payments of $15,000 or less. One payment of $15,000 can qualify as deductible and taxable alimony. Technically, there is also no minimum payout period for annual alimony payments exceeding $15,000.

Key to Alimony and Marital Settlement Issues

Item—	Comments—
Alimony	The same rules determine whether alimony is deductible and taxable. For example, if a husband makes deductible alimony payments to his ex-wife, the payments are taxable to her. He may not deduct payments that are not taxable to her. If you are currently planning an alimony agreement, consider the tax consequences to both spouses. As current tax rates are limited to 15%, 28%, and a top bracket of 31%, there may be little or no savings to the couple, when considered as an economic unit, in negotiating an agreement that qualifies the payments as deductible alimony; *see* ¶37.1. *Note:* Prior tax rules that apply to pre-1985 agreements are not discussed in this chapter. If you have a problem involving a payment of alimony under a pre-1985 agreement, refer to a past issue of *Your Income Tax* or to IRS Publication 504.
Child support agreements	A payment fixed as payable for the support of your child may not qualify as deductible or taxable alimony; *see* ¶37.5.
Property settlements	Transfers of property between a couple that are incident to a divorce are treated as a tax-free exchange. There is no recognition of gain or loss. Future tax consequences should be considered by the spouse receiving appreciated property. When the property is sold, that spouse will be taxed on the appreciation. If this is so, that spouse may want to bargain for larger alimony payments or additional property to compensate for the projected future tax; *see* ¶6.6.
Alimony to nonresident alien	If you pay alimony payments to a nonresident alien, and you are a U.S. citizen or resident, you must withhold 30% (or a lower rate as set by treaty) on each payment for income tax purposes. See IRS Publications 504 and 515 for more information.
Exemptions for children	Exemptions for children of a divorced couple are governed by the rules explained at ¶1.28. Further, where a spouse is in the income range requiring the phaseout or disallowance of personal exemptions (¶1.32), there may be no advantage in providing the exemption to that spouse. The exemption should be given to the spouse who may claim a full deduction for the exemption.
Annuity or endowment policy	Funds for payments of alimony may be provided through the purchase of an annuity or endowment policy. You may not deduct payments made under the policies assigned or purchased for your spouse. For example, to meet an alimony obligation of $500 a month, you buy your spouse a commercial annuity contract. The full $500 a month received by him or her is taxable. You may not deduct these payments.
Trust to pay alimony	To meet your alimony obligations, you may transfer income-producing property to a trust that is to pay the income to your spouse. You may not deduct payments made by the trust. You are not taxable on the income earned by the trust, even though it meets your alimony obligations. This tax treatment is the equivalent of receiving a tax deduction for paying alimony. If you receive alimony from a trust, ask the trustee how to report such income. Tax treatment may depend on whether the trust was created before 1985 or after 1984. If the trust was set up after 1984, as a beneficiary you generally report trust income under the general trust reporting rules in Chapter 11. These general trust rules may not apply to certain alimony trusts created before 1985 that were subject to the prior alimony rules. Distributions from such trusts may be treated as taxable alimony regardless of whether the distributions are from income or principal. In any event, the trustee should provide you with the necessary tax information.
Retirement plans	A state court can allocate your interest in a qualified retirement plan to a former spouse in a qualified domestic relations order. The benefits are taxed to your former spouse when they are paid to her or him. Benefits paid to another beneficiary, such as a child, are taxable to you.
Remarriage's effect on pre-1985 agreement	The tax deduction allowed for alimony payments made under a pre-1985 decree or agreement hinges on the obligation to support. Once the spouse receiving alimony remarries, the obligation to support generally ends under state law. In these states, any payment after remarriage is not considered alimony and is not deductible. For example, payments to a former wife made after remarriage are considered tax-free gifts, if the former husband knows of the remarriage and that he is no longer obligated to pay. If she does not inform him of her remarriage, his payments are taxable to her but are not deductible by him.
Voluntary payments in excess of required alimony	Voluntary payments in excess of required alimony are not deductible or taxable as alimony. Amending the decrees retroactively to cover an increase does not qualify the increase as deductible and taxable alimony. The increase has to be approved by the court before the increased payments are made.

However, recapture of alimony deductions claimed in the first or second year may occur where annual payments of over $15,000 are scheduled and paid, but in the second or third year a reduced payment is made. To avoid recapture of deductions for payments exceeding $15,000, carefully plan schedules of declining payments within the rules of ¶37.7.

3. In providing for the support of children, a specific allocation to their support or the setting of certain contingencies disqualifies payments as deductible and alimony as taxable; *see* ¶37.5.

4. Divorced and legally separated parties may not live in the same household. If they live in the same household, alimony payments are not deductible or taxable. However, there are these exceptions: A spouse who makes payments while preparing to leave the common residence may deduct payments made within one month before the departure. Also, where you are separated under a written agreement, but not legally separated under a decree of divorce or separate maintenance, you may deduct alimony payments even if you both are members of the same household.

5. The payer spouse's liability to pay alimony must end on the death of the payee spouse. The alimony agreement does not have to state expressly that payments end on death if liability ends under state law; *see* ¶37.4.

Reporting Alimony

If you paid alimony in 1992 meeting the deductible tests, claim your deduction on Line 29 of Form 1040, and enter the recipient's Social Security number. If you receive qualifying alimony payments, report them on Line 11 of Form 1040.

DECREE OR AGREEMENT REQUIRED

¶37.2 Alimony, to be deductible and taxable, must be required by one of the following: (1) a decree of divorce or legal separation; (2) a written separation agreement; or (3) a decree of support. This rule applies to both pre-1985 and post-1984 decrees and agreements. Voluntary payments are not deductible.

Divorced or legally separated. The obligation to pay alimony must be imposed by the decree of divorce or separate maintenance or a written agreement incident to the divorce or separation.

Alimony paid under a Mexican divorce decree qualifies. Payments under a Mexican or state decree declared invalid by another jurisdiction do not qualify according to the IRS. Two appeals courts have rejected the IRS position.

Support payments ordered by a court in a wife's home state qualify as alimony, even though not provided for by an *ex parte* divorce decree obtained by the husband in another state. Similarly, payments qualified when a state court increased support originally ordered before the husband obtained an uncontested Mexican divorce.

Payments made under a separation approved by a Roman Catholic ecclesiastical board do not qualify.

When a decree of divorce or separate maintenance fails to mention alimony, payments qualify as long as they are made under a written agreement considered "incident to" the decree.

Payments made under an agreement *amended* after a divorce or legal separation may also qualify, if the amendment is considered "incident" to the divorce or separation. For example, the IRS agrees that a *written* amendment changing the amount of alimony payments is incident to the divorce where the legal obligation to support under the original agreement survived the divorce. However, payments under an amended agreement did not qualify where the original agreement settled all rights between the husband and wife and made no provision for future support. The legal obligation to support the wife did not survive the divorce and could not be revived by the new agreement.

Annulments. Payments made under an annulment decree qualify as deductible (and taxable) alimony.

Where a couple is separated and living apart, alimony is deductible by the payer-spouse and taxable to the payee-spouse if paid under either a written separation agreement or decree of support. A written separation agreement made before August 17, 1954 does not qualify unless materially modified after August 16, 1954.

Oral changes agreed to by the parties will not be recognized for tax purposes unless they are incorporated into the written separation agreement.

A decree of support. Any court decree or order requiring support payments qualifies, including alimony *pendente lite* (temporary alimony while the action is pending), and an interlocutory (not final) divorce decree.

In certain community property states, payments under a decree of alimony *pendente lite* which do not exceed the wife's interest in community income are neither deductible by the husband nor taxable to the wife; payments exceeding the wife's interest are taxable to her and deductible by the husband.

CASH PAYMENTS REQUIRED

¶37.3 Only payments of cash, checks, and money orders payable on demand qualify as taxable and deductible alimony.

Providing services or transferring or providing property do not qualify. For example, you may not deduct as alimony your note, the assignment of a third party note, or an annuity contract.

Your cash payment to a third party for a spouse qualifies if made under the terms of a divorce decree or separation instrument. For example, you pay the rent, mortgage, tax, medical expenses, or tuition liabilities of your former spouse. The payments qualify if made under the terms of the divorce or separation instrument. If taxable as alimony, your former spouse may deduct your payment of real estate taxes, mortgage interest, or medical expenses if he or she claims itemized deductions. You may not deduct payments to maintain property owned by you but used by your spouse. For example, you pay the mortgage expenses, real estate taxes, and insurance premiums for a house which you own and in which your former spouse lives. You may not deduct those payments as alimony even if required by a decree or agreement.

Premiums paid for term or whole life insurance on your life made under the terms of the divorce or separation instrument qualify as deductible alimony to the extent your former spouse owns the policy.

Payments to a Third Party

Cash payments to a third party may be deducted as alimony if they are under the terms of a divorce decree or separation instrument, as discussed above. You may also deduct as alimony payments made to a third party at the written request of the payee spouse. For example, your former wife asks you to make a cash donation to a charitable organization instead of paying alimony installments to her. Her request must be in writing and state that both she and you intend the payment to be treated as an alimony. You must receive the written request before you file your return for the taxable year in which the payment was made. Your former wife may deduct the payment as a charitable contribution if she claims itemized deductions.

PAYMENTS MUST STOP AT DEATH

¶37.4 Payments must stop on the death of the payee-spouse. If not, none of the payments, whether made before or after the payee's death, qualify as taxable or deductible alimony.

Under prior law, an agreement or decree had to specifically state that payments end at death. Under current law, such a statement is not necessary, if under state law the liability to pay ends on the death of the payee-spouse.

To the extent that one or more payments are to begin, increase in amount, or accelerate after the death of the payee-spouse, such payments may be treated as a substitute for the continuation of payments terminating on the death of the payee-spouse.

EXAMPLES 1. Under the terms of a divorce decree, Smith is obligated to make annual alimony payments of $30,000, terminating on the earlier of the end of six years or the death of Mrs. Smith. She also is to keep custody of their two minor children. The decree also provides that if on her death the children are still minors, Jones is to pay annually $10,000 to a trust each year. The trust income and corpus are to be used for the children until the youngest child reaches the age of majority. Under these facts, Smith's possible liability to make annual $10,000 payments to the trust is treated as a substitute for $10,000 of the $30,000 annual payments. $10,000 of each of the $30,000 annual payments does not qualify as alimony.

2. Same facts as in Example 1, but the alimony is to end on the earlier of the expiration of 15 years or the death of Mrs. Smith. Further, if Mrs. Smith dies before the end of the 15-year period, Smith will pay her estate the difference between the total amount that he would have paid had she survived less the amount actually paid. For example, if she dies at the end of the tenth year, he will pay her estate $150,000 ($450,000 – $300,000). Under these facts, his liability to make a lump-sum payment to the estate is a substitute for the full amount of each of the annual $30,000 payments. Accordingly, none of the annual $30,000 payments qualifies as alimony.

CHILD SUPPORT PAYMENTS ARE NOT ALIMONY

¶37.5 A payment is fixed as payable for the support of your child if the divorce or separation instrument specifically fixes an amount payable for support. That amount is not deductible or taxable as alimony.

Even if there is not a specific allocation to child support, a payment will be treated as payable for child support if it is to be reduced on the happening of a contingency relating to the child, such as: the child reaches a specific age or income level, or the child leaves school, marries, leaves the parents' household, or begins to work.

Alimony Reductions Tied to Child's Age

If a reduction in your payments is not specifically tied to your child's reaching majority age but the scheduled date for the reduction is within six months before or after your child reaches age 18 or 21 (or other age of majority under local law), the IRS *presumes* that the reduction is tied to the child's age. The reduction amount will be treated as child support unless you can prove that the reduction is for some other purpose. The IRS makes the same presumption if you have more than one child and your alimony payments are to be reduced at least twice and each reduction is within one year of a different child's reaching a particular age between ages 18 and 24; *see* the following example.

EXAMPLE On July 1, 1986, a couple is divorced when their children John (born July 15, 1971) and Jane (born September 23, 1973) are ages 14 and 12. Under the divorce decree, the husband is to make monthly alimony payments of $2,000. The monthly payments are to be reduced to $1,500 on January 1, 1992, and to $1,000 on January 1, 1996. On January 1, 1992, the date of the first reduction, John will be 20 years, 5 months and 17 days old. On January 1, 1996, the date of the second reduction, Jane will be 22 years, 3 months and 9 days old. As each reduction is to occur not more than one year before or after each child reaches the age of 21 years and four months, the IRS will presume that the deductions are associated with the happening of a contingency relating to the children. The two reductions total $1,000 per month and are treated as the amount fixed for the support of the children. Thus, $1,000 of the $2,000 monthly payment does not qualify as alimony. To avoid this result, the husband must prove that the reductions were not related to the support of the children.

If both alimony and child support are specified and a payment is less than the total of the two amounts, then the payment is first allocated to child support.

Tax refund diversion for delinquent child support. The IRS can give your tax refund to a state which is paying support to your child, if you fail to make support payments. For past-due support of a child in a family receiving AFDC welfare payments, the IRS has the authority to make the diversion where the delinquency is $150 or more and is overdue for at least three months. The IRS will not notify you of the diversion until it is made to the state. However, a federal court has held that a state must provide notice to all those whose refunds may be intercepted, specifying possible defenses and how to challenge the diversion before it is made; judicial review of the state's administrative decision must also be available.

For support of non-AFDC families, the IRS may divert your refund if you owe child support of $500 or more; the state agency must provide prior notice of the proposed offset and procedures for contesting it.

MINIMUM PAYMENTS AND RECAPTURE OF ALIMONY

MINIMUM PAYMENT PERIOD FOR ALIMONY

¶37.6 For agreements executed after 1986, there is no minimum payment period, but a recapture rule applies where payments fall by more than $15,000 within the first three years. *See* ¶37.7 for recapture rules.

1985 and 1986 alimony arrangements. Payments exceeding $10,000 under agreements and decrees made in 1985 and 1986 were subject to a minimum six-year payment period. Under this rule, if the agreement did not require payments exceeding $10,000 to continue for at least six years, payments over $10,000 were not treated as taxable and deductible alimony.

3RD YEAR RECAPTURE IF ALIMONY DROPS $15,000 OR MORE

¶37.7 The recapture rules are designed to prevent the so-called "front loading" of property settlement payments disguised as alimony. However, the rules apply even where no property settlement was

intended if you come within its terms. Here are the rules: For agreements executed *after 1986,* deductible payments made in the first year or second year may be recaptured (that is, reported as income) in the third year where payments within the first three years decline by more than $15,000. The three years are called "post-separation years." The first post-separation year is the first calendar year in which you pay alimony under a decree of divorce or separation agreement. The period does not begin with the year of the decree or agreement if no payments are made. Recapture does not apply to temporary support payments made before the final decree or agreement. The second and third post-separation years are the next two calendar years after the first post-separation year whether or not payments are made during those years.

Payments made in the second post-separation year are recaptured if the payments exceed the payments made in the third post-separation year by more than $15,000. Payments made in the first post-separation year are recaptured if they exceed the average payments made in the second post-separation year and the third post-separation year by more than $15,000. The examples in the next column illustrate how to make these computations.

When recapture does not apply. Recapture is not triggered if payments in both the first and second post-separation years do not exceed $15,000. Recapture also does not apply to:

Payments made under a continuing liability to pay for at least three years a fixed part of your income from a business or property or from a job or self-employed business or profession, or

Payments that end because of your death or the death of your former spouse or the remarriage of your former spouse at any time before the end of the third post-separation year.

Reporting recapture on your return. The payer-spouse reports the recaptured amount as income in the third year and the payee-spouse claims a deduction for the same amount. The payer reports the recaptured amount on Form 1040 on the line for alimony received; on the same line cross out "received" and write "recapture" along with the payee spouse's Social Security number.

The payee spouse deducts the recaptured amount on the line marked alimony paid. He or she crosses out the word "paid" and writes "recaptured," and also enters on that line the former spouse's Social Security number.

Steps of recapture:

1. Recapture for the second-year payment is computed first. This is the amount by which the second-year payment exceeds the third-year payment by more than $15,000.
2. Recapture for the first-year payment is computed next. There is recapture if the first-year payment exceeds by more than $15,000 the average payment made in the second and third years. In figuring the average payment, reduce the second-year payment by any recapture amount for the second year figured under Step 1.

EXAMPLES 1. In 1990, Jones obtains a divorce and pays deductible alimony of $50,000. His wife reports $50,000 as income. In 1991 and 1992, he makes no payments. On his 1992 return, $35,000 of the first year 1990 deduction is recaptured ($50,000 − $15,000) and reported as income by Jones. His ex-spouse deducts $35,000.

2. In 1990, Smith makes his first alimony payment of $50,000; in 1991, $20,000, and in 1992, nothing. On his 1992 return, $32,500 is recaptured as follows:

Recapture of second-year payment:		
Payment in 2nd year		$20,000
Less 3rd-year payment	$0	
Less allowance	15,000	15,000
Recapture for second year		$ 5,000

Recapture of first-year payment:		
Average calculation:		
Payment over the 2nd and 3rd years	$20,000	
Less recapture in the 2nd year	$5,000	
	$15,000	
Average ($15,000 ÷ 2)	$ 7,500	
Payment in first year		$50,000
Less Average	$ 7,500	
Less Allowance	15,000	22,500
Recapture for first year		$27,500

Total recaptured in 1992:

For second year	$5,000
For first year	$27,500
Total:	$32,500

LEGAL FEES OF MARITAL SETTLEMENTS

¶37.8 ***If you are receiving taxed alimony,*** you may deduct part of your legal fees. Ask your attorney to divide his or her fees into charges for arranging: (1) the divorce or separation; and (2) details of the alimony payments.

You may deduct the legal fees allocated to (2), but you may not deduct the fee attributed to the divorce or separation negotiation. The deduction is subject to the 2% adjusted gross income floor on miscellaneous deductions (*see* Chapter 19). If the alimony is not taxed to you, you may not deduct any part of the fee. However, part of a fee allocated to a property settlement may be added to the basis of the property.

If you are paying deductible alimony, you may not deduct legal fees paid for arranging a divorce or for resisting your spouse's demands for alimony. Furthermore, you may not deduct legal fees incurred in resisting your spouse's claims to income-producing property, the loss of which would affect your earnings. However, these rules do not bar you from deducting that part of your legal fee that is identified as being paid for tax advice. The following types of proof may support a deduction.

1. The fee is charged by a firm that limits its practice to state and federal matters and is engaged to advise on the consequences of a property settlement involving the transfer of property in exchange for other property and the release of the other spouse's marital rights in the property.

2. The fee is charged by a firm engaged in general practice which assigns tax problems, such as the tax consequences of creating an alimony trust, to its special tax department. On the bill, an allocation is made for tax advice based on time, complexity of the case, and the amount of tax involved.

3. An attorney handles the divorce for a fixed fee and also gives advice on the right to claim exemptions for the children following the divorce. The bill allocates part of the fee to the tax advice, based on time, and fees customarily charged in the locality for similar services.

You may not deduct your payment of your spouse's legal fees as a miscellaneous itemized deduction, even if the fees are only for tax advice. However, the fees may be deductible as alimony under the rules of ¶37.3 for payments to third parties.

38

FILING REFUND CLAIMS, AND AMENDED RETURNS

File a refund claim on Form 1040X if you have overpaid your tax because you failed to take allowable deductions or credits, overstated income, or want to take advantage of a retroactive change in the law. *See* the sample Form 1040X included in this chapter.

File in time. The time limits discussed at ¶38.1 must be strictly observed; otherwise, a valid refund claim will be denied because of late filing.

Before filing a refund claim for a prior year, carefully review the return of that year for accuracy. A refund claim may subject the return to an examination in which the IRS may find errors that reduce or completely eliminate the refund claim, or may even lead to the assessment of a deficiency.

Income tax overwithholding. You do not have to file a refund claim if you have overpaid your tax due to excessive withholding of taxes on your wages or salary, or if you have overestimated your estimated tax. You get a refund on these overpayments by filing your tax return and requesting a refund for these amounts. You may not recover an overpayment of estimated tax until you file your final return.

Earned income credit. If you are entitled to a refund due to the earned income credit for certain low income working families, you must file your tax return to get your refund, even though your income and filing status would not otherwise require that a return be filed. *See* Chapter 25.

File your claim with the Service Center for the area where you live as shown in the instructions to Form 1040X, unless you file for a quick refund on Form 1045.

For a refund of an overpayment of FICA taxes, *see* ¶26.10 for how to claim a refund on your tax return. If you are not required to file a tax return, you file a refund claim on Form 843.

WHEN TO FILE A REFUND CLAIM

¶38.1 You may file a refund claim within three years from the time your return was filed, or within two years from the time you paid your tax, whichever is later. A return filed before its due date is treated as having been filed on the due date.

A refund claim based on a bad debt or worthless securities may be made within seven years of the due date of the return for the year in which the debt or security became worthless.

The time for filing refund claims based on carrybacks of net operating losses or general business credits is within three years of the due date (including extensions) of the return for the year the loss or credit arose.

A refund claim based on your share of a joint return refund withheld by the IRS to pay your spouse's debts (¶38.2) may be made within six years of the date you received the IRS notice that the refund had been withheld.

If you filed an agreement giving the IRS an extended period of time in which to assess a tax against you, you are allowed an additional period in which to file a claim for refund. The claim, up to certain amounts, may be filed through the extension period and for six months afterwards.

Time Limits Must Be Observed

Failure to file a timely refund claim is fatal, regardless of its merits. Even if you expect that your claim will have to be pursued in court, you must still file a timely refund claim.

Armed Forces servicemembers and veterans. In determining the time limits within which a refund claim may be filed, you disregard intervening periods of service in a combat zone, plus periods of continuous hospitalization outside the United States as a result of combat zone injury, and the next 180 days thereafter. You may also disregard a postponement period if you were missing in action; *see* Chapter 35. Servicemembers and civilian government employees who were taxed on pay while in "missing" status also have additional time to file refund claims.

JOINT REFUND CLAIMS

¶38.2 If a joint return was filed for a year in which a refund is due, both spouses are entitled to recover jointly and both must file a joint refund claim. Where separate returns were filed, each spouse is a separate taxpayer and may not file a claim to recover a refund based on the other spouse's return, except if that spouse becomes the fiduciary when one spouse becomes incompetent or dies. If you are divorced and incur a net operating loss or credit that may be carried back to a year in which you were married, you may file a refund claim with your signature alone and the refund check will be made out only to you; *see* ¶40.17.

Refund withheld to pay spouse's debts. If you showed a refund due on a joint return filed with a spouse who owed child support or federal student loans, the IRS may have withheld payment of the refund to cover the obligations. If you are not liable for the past-due payments, and your tax payments (withholdings or estimated tax installments) exceed your income reported on the joint return, you may file Form 8379 to get back your share of the refund.

STATING THE REASONS FOR REFUND CLAIMS

¶38.3 The most important part of a refund claim is a statement of the "reasons" for the refund. A general claim simply noting an overpayment, without supporting facts and grounds, is not sufficient. If a claim is denied by the IRS, it may become the basis of a court suit. If you have not stated all the grounds, you may not be allowed to argue them in court. You must make a full claim showing all the:

Facts that support the claim. Attach all supporting documents and tax forms supporting your claim.

Grounds for the claim. If you are uncertain about the exact legal grounds, alternate and even inconsistent grounds may be given. For example: "The loss was incurred from an embezzlement; if not, from a bad debt." To protect against understating the amount of the claim, you might preface the claim with this phrase: "The following or such greater amounts, as may be legally refunded."

QUICK REFUND CLAIMS

¶38.4 Form 1045 may be used for filing refunds due to carrybacks from net operating losses, and the general business credit. Form 1045 also may be used for a quick refund based on a repayment exceeding $3,000 of income reported in an earlier year. Form 1045 must be filed within 12 months after the loss year. The IRS must act on the claim within 90 days. Payment of quick refund claims is not a final settlement of your return; the IRS may still audit and then disallow the refund claim. Note that the filing of a quick refund, if rejected, may not be the basis of a suit for refund; a regular refund claim must be filed.

Tax-shelter claims. If you file a quick refund claim on Form 1045 and the IRS determines it is likely that excessive tax-shelter benefits have been claimed, the IRS will offset the quick refund claim by a deficiency attributable to the tax-shelter items. You will receive the balance and receive a notice of the tax-shelter deficiency.

INTEREST PAID ON REFUND CLAIMS

¶38.5 If you file on or before the April 15 filing deadline, interest is not paid by the IRS on refunds made within 45 days of the due date (without regard to extensions of time). For example, you file your 1992 return on April 1, 1993, claiming an overpayment due to overwithholding on your wages. Interest does not have to be paid on refunds before May 31, which is 46 days after April 15, the day the tax was due. If the overpayment is not refunded within 45 days, interest is paid from the date the tax was overpaid up to a date determined by the IRS that can be as much as 30 days before the date of the refund check.

If you get a filing extension or otherwise file after the due date of

the return, no interest is paid if the refund is made within 45 days after the date you filed.

The IRS does not have to pay interest on overpayments resulting from net operating loss carrybacks, net capital loss carrybacks, or business credit carrybacks if a refund is paid within 45 days of the filing of the refund claim.

If a refund claim based on a loss or credit carryback is filed and subsequently a quick refund claim is filed on Form 1045 for the same refund, the 45-day period starts to run on the date Form 1045 is filed.

Interest rates applied to overpayments are as follows:

Amounts outstanding between—	Rate is—
1/1/87—9/30/87	8%
10/1/87—12/31/87	9
1/1/88—3/31/88	10
4/1/88—9/30/88	9
10/1/88—3/31/89	10
4/1/89—9/30/89	11
10/1/89—3/31/91	10
4/1/91—12/31/91	9
1/1/92—3/31/92	8
4/1/92—9/30/92	7
After 9/30/92	*See* the Supplement

REFUNDS WITHHELD BY IRS

¶38.6 The IRS may withhold all or part of your refund if you owe child support or federal debts such as student loans. If you file a joint return with a spouse who owes child support or federal debts, you may be able to obtain your share of a refund due on the joint return; *see* ¶38.2.

Tax shelter claims. The IRS may withhold refunds based on questionable tax-shelter claims. In each IRS service center, returns of tax-shelter investors are screened to determine if the tax shelter has fraudulently misrepresented tax benefits or grossly overvalued assets or services. If the tax shelter is considered to be abusive and if claimed deductions or tax credits are disallowed, refunds attributable to the tax-shelter items will not be paid. The balance of your refund claim will be paid.

A refund will also be frozen under the above rules if you file your return after receiving a pre-filing notification letter from the IRS warning you not to claim certain tax-shelter writeoffs.

The rules apply to original tax returns showing a refund due as well as to refund claims. Quick refund claims made on Form 1045 that are attributable to abusive tax-shelter items may also be offset by a deficiency; *see* ¶38.4.

AMENDED RETURNS SHOWING ADDITIONAL TAX

¶38.7 If, after filing your return, you find that you did not report some income or claimed excessive deductions, you should file an amended return on Form 1040X to limit interest charges and possible tax penalties.

If you filed early and then file an amended return by the filing due date (including any extensions) that shows additional tax due, you will not be charged interest or penalties based on the original return; the amended return is considered a substitute for the original.

You must pay the additional tax due as shown on Form 1040X. Even if you expect a refund on your original return, the IRS will not reduce the refund check to cover the additional tax. You must pay it and you will receive the original refund separately.

Use the payment voucher included in the instructions to Form 1040X to make your payment.

Form 1040X — Page 1

Form **1040X** (Rev. November 1991)

Department of the Treasury—Internal Revenue Service

Amended U.S. Individual Income Tax Return

► See separate instructions.

OMB No. 1545-0091
Expires 10-31-94

This return is for calendar year ► 19 91 , OR fiscal year ended ► _____, 19 _____

Your first name and initial: Judith — Last name: Link — Your social security number: 1X0 : 1X :0X1X

If a joint return, spouse's first name and initial — Last name — Spouse's social security number

Home address (number and street). (If you have a P.O. box, see instructions.) 817 Emory Avenue — Apt. no. — Telephone number (optional)

City, town or post office, state, and ZIP code. (If you have a foreign address, see instructions.) City, State XXXXX

For Paperwork Reduction Act Notice, see page 1 of separate instructions.

Enter name and address as shown on original return (if same as above, write "Same"). If changing from separate to joint return, enter name and addresses from original returns.

A Service center where original return was filed: City, State

B Has original return been changed or audited by the IRS? ☐ Yes ☒ No
If "No," have you been notified that it will be? ☐ Yes ☒ No
If "Yes," identify the IRS office ►

C Are you amending your return to include any item (loss, credit, deduction, other tax, benefit, or income) relating to a tax shelter required to be registered? ☐ Yes ☒ No
If "Yes," you **MUST** attach Form 8271, Investor Reporting of Tax Shelter Registration Number.

D Filing status claimed. (**Note:** *You cannot change from joint to separate returns after the due date has passed.*)
On original return ► ☐ Single ☐ Married filing joint return ☐ Married filing separate return ☐ Head of household ☐ Qualifying widow(er)
On this return ► ☐ Single ☐ Married filing joint return ☐ Married filing separate return ☐ Head of household ☐ Qualifying widow(er)

Income and Deductions (see instructions)

(Note: *Be sure to complete page 2.*)

		A. As originally reported or as adjusted (see instructions)	B. Net change—Increase or (Decrease)—explain on page 2	C. Correct amount
1	Total income	36,000	-0-	36,000
2	Adjustments to income			
3	Adjusted gross income (subtract line 2 from line 1)	36,000	-0-	36,000
4	Itemized deductions or standard deduction	3,400	1,600	5,000
5	Subtract line 4 from line 3	32,600	-0-	31,000
6	Exemptions (if changing, fill in Parts I and II on page 2)	4,300	-0-	4,300
7	Taxable income (subtract line 6 from line 5)	28,300	(1,600)	26,700
8	Tax (see instructions). (Method used in col. C _____)	5,286	(1,277)	4,009
9	Credits (see instructions)			
10	Subtract line 9 from line 8. Enter the result but not less than zero	5,286	(1,277)	4,009
11	Other taxes (such as self-employment tax, alternative minimum tax)			
12	Total tax (add lines 10 and 11)	5,286	(1,277)	4,009
13	Federal income tax withheld and excess social security, Medicare, and RRTA taxes withheld	5,534	-0-	5,534
14	Estimated tax payments			
15	Earned income credit			
16	Credits for federal tax on fuels, regulated investment company, etc.			
17	Amount paid with Form 4868, Form 2688, or Form 2350 (application for extension of time to file)		17	
18	Amount paid with original return plus additional tax paid after it was filed		18	5,534
19	Add lines 13 through 18 in column C		19	5,534

Refund or Amount You Owe

20	Overpayment, if any, as shown on original return (or as previously adjusted by the IRS)	20	248
21	Subtract line 20 from line 19 (see instructions)	21	5,286
22	**AMOUNT YOU OWE.** If line 12, col. C, is more than line 21, enter the difference and see instructions	22	
23	**REFUND** to be received. If line 12, column C, is less than line 21, enter the difference	23	1,277

Under penalties of perjury, I declare that I have filed an original return and that I have examined this amended return, including accompanying schedules and statements, and to the best of my knowledge and belief, this amended return is true, correct, and complete. Declaration of preparer (other than taxpayer) is based on all information of which the preparer has any knowledge.

Please Sign Here — Your signature: *Judith Link* — Date: 11/18/92 — Spouse's signature (If joint return, BOTH must sign) — Date

Paid Preparer's Use Only — Preparer's signature — Date — Check if self-employed ☐ — Preparer's social security no. — Firm's name (or yours if self-employed) and address — E.I. No. — ZIP code

Cat. No. 11360L

Form 1040X — Page 2

Form 1040X (Rev. 11-91) — Page 2

Part I — **Exemptions** (see Form 1040 or Form 1040A instructions)

If you are not changing your exemptions, do not complete this part.
If claiming more exemptions, complete lines 24–30 and, if applicable, line 31.
If claiming fewer exemptions, complete lines 24–29.

	A. Number originally reported	B. Net change	C. Correct number
24 Yourself and spouse. **Caution:** *If your parents (or someone else) can claim you as a dependent (even if they chose not to), you cannot claim an exemption for yourself.*	24		
25 Your dependent children who lived with you	25		
26 Your dependent children who did not live with you due to divorce or separation	26		
27 Other dependents	27		
28 Total number of exemptions (add lines 24 through 27)	28		
29 **For tax year 1991,** if the amount on page 1, line 3, is more than $75,000, see the instructions. If line 3 is $75,000 or less, multiply $2,150 by the number of exemptions claimed on line 28. **For tax year 1990,** use $2,050; for tax year 1989, use $2,000; for tax year 1988, use $1,950. Enter the result here and on page 1, line 6.	29		

30 **Dependents** (children and other) not claimed on original return:

(a) Dependent's name (first, initial, and last name)	(b) Check if under age 1 or older if a 1989 or 1990/1988 return	(c) If age 1 or older (age 2 or older if a 1989 or 1988 return) dependent's social security number	(d) Dependent's relationship to you	(e) No. of months lived in your home

No. of your children on line 30 who lived with you ▲	
No. of your children on line 30 who didn't live with you due to divorce or separation (see instructions) ▲	
No. of other dependents listed on line 30 ▲	

31 If your child listed on line 30 didn't live with you but is claimed as your dependent under a pre-1985 agreement, check here ► ☐

Part II — **Explanation of Changes to Income, Deductions, and Credits**

Enter the line number from page 1 for each item you are changing and give the reason for each change. Attach all supporting forms and schedules for items changed. Be sure to include your name and social security number on any attachments.

If the change pertains to a net operating loss carryback or a general business credit carryback, attach the schedule or form that shows the year in which the loss or credit occurred. See instructions. Also, check here ► ☐

Line 4:   When filing my original 1991 return I did not realize that I qualified for head of household status. I was unmarried at the end of 1991 and my daughter lived with me for the entire year. I was the sole provider of my daughter's support during 1991. On Line 4, I am claiming the $5,000 standard deduction allowed to a head of household for 1991.

Line 8:   The corrected 1991 tax, taken from the 1991 Tax Table, using filing status of head of household rather than single.

Part III — **Presidential Election Campaign Fund**

Checking below will not increase your tax or reduce your refund.

If you did not previously want to have $1 go to the fund but now want to, check here ► ☐
If a joint return and your spouse did not previously want to have $1 go to the fund but now wants to, check here ► ☐

39

A GUIDE TO ESTATE TAXES AND PLANNING

The federal estate tax is a transfer tax on property transferred at death. The tax applies to taxable estates over $600,000, after taking into account allowable deductions, such as deductions for charitable bequests and property passing to a surviving spouse.

Valuing your estate is not easy. By using the guidelines in this chapter, you can estimate your potential estate and if your estate might be subject to tax, begin planning a comprehensive estate plan with your attorney.

WHAT IS THE ESTATE TAX?

¶39.1 The estate you built up may not be entirely yours to give away. The federal government and, in all probability, at least one state government stand ready to claim their shares.

Do you know what will remain for your family, your favorite philanthropies, and your other beneficiaries? If you do not, you cannot intelligently estimate what you can give to each. To help you make such an estimate, we offer this general guide to federal estate taxation. It will alert you to the extent of estate tax costs, and help you plan for estate tax savings that you may discuss with your attorney.

The federal estate tax is a tax on the act of transferring property at death. It is not a tax on the right of the beneficiary to receive the property; the estate and the estate alone pays the tax, although the property passing to individual beneficiaries may be diminished by the tax.

Understand what the word *estate* means in estate tax law so that you do not underestimate the value of your taxable estate. The estate includes not only your real estate (foreign and domestic), bank deposits, securities, personal property, and other more obvious signs of wealth, but can also include insurance, your interest in trusts and jointly-held property, and certain interests you have in other estates.

TAKE INVENTORY

¶39.2 The first step in estate tax planning follows a simple business practice of taking inventory of everything you own.

Listing one's belongings takes thought, time, and a surprising amount of work with lists, records of purchases, fire and theft insurance inventories, bankbooks, brokers' statements, etc. You need to include your cash, real estate (here and abroad), securities, mortgages, rights in property, trust accounts, personal effects, collections, and art works. Life insurance is includible if (1) payable to your estate, or (2) payable to others and you have kept "incidents of ownership" such as the right to change beneficiaries, surrender or assign the policy, or pledge it for a loan.

If you own property jointly with your spouse, include only one-half the value of the property.

If you have had appraisals made of unusual or specially treasured items or collections, or property of substantial value, file such appraisals with your estate papers and enter the value on your inventory.

There are some assets that you might not ordinarily consider as part of your estate. Nevertheless, include in your inventory any trust arrangements created by you in which you have (1) a life estate (the income or other use of property for life); (2) income that is to be used to pay your legal obligations (support of a child, for example); (3) the right to change the beneficiary or his or her interest (a power of appointment); (4) the right to revoke a trust transfer or gift; and (5) a reversionary interest (possibility that the property can come back to you).

Retirement benefits. The taxable estate generally includes benefits payable at your death from any of the following retirement plans: pension plan, profit-sharing plan, Keogh plan, individual retirement account, or annuity. However, the value of an annuity from an IRA or employer plan that is payable to a beneficiary other than your estate may qualify for a full or partial exclusion if IRA distributions began before 1985 or you separated from employer service before 1985; no exclusion is allowed to the extent of your own nondeductible contributions to the plan.

A full exclusion is allowed for IRA funds if you began taking distributions from the account before 1983 under a schedule that irrevocably set the form of benefits. If IRA distributions began in 1983 or 1984 and you irrevocably elected the form of benefits before July 18, 1984, a $100,000 exclusion is allowed.

If you began receiving distributions from an employer plan before 1983 under a schedule that irrevocably set the form of benefits, a full estate tax exclusion is allowed. If you separated from service in 1983 or 1984, a $100,000 exclusion is allowed if the form of benefits is not changed before death; this is true even if distributions did not begin until after 1984.

FINDING THE VALUE OF YOUR ESTATE

¶39.3 When you have completed your inventory, assign to each asset what you consider to be its fair market value. This may be difficult to do for some assets. Resist the tendency to overvalue articles which arouse feelings of pride or sentiment and undervalue some articles of great intrinsic worth. For purposes of your initial estimate, it is better to err on the side of overvaluation.

If you have a family business, your idea of its value and that of the IRS may vary greatly. Estate plans have been upset by the higher value placed on such a business by the IRS. You can protect your estate by anticipating and solving this problem with your business associates, accountant, and legal counsel.

If your business is owned by a closely-held corporation, and there is no ready or open market in which the stock can be valued, get some factual basis for a figure that will be reported on the estate tax return. One of the ways to do this is by arranging a buy-sell agreement with a potential purchaser. This agreement must fix the value of the stock. Generally, an agreement that binds both the estate and the purchaser and restricts lifetime sales of the stock will effectively fix the value of the stock for estate tax purposes. Another way would be to make a gift of some shares to a family member and have value established in gift tax proceedings.

If a substantial part of your estate is real estate used in farming or a closely-held business, your executor may be able to elect, with the consent of heirs having an interest in the property, to value the property on the basis of its farming or business use, rather than its highest and best use. The special use valuation, however, may not reduce the gross estate by more than $750,000. But this may mean substantial tax savings. This savings may be recaptured from your heir if he or she stops using the property in farming or business within ten years of your death.

You can list ordinary personal effects at nominal value.

HOW THE ESTATE TAX IS APPLIED

¶39.4 A single unified rate schedule applies to a decedent's estate and all post-1976 lifetime gifts over the annual gift tax exclusion. Under the unified gift and estate tax rate, the overall tax on your property holdings is theoretically the same whether or not you make lifetime gifts. In actual cases, however, lifetime gifts may reduce the potential overall tax because of the annual gift tax exclusion.

If you make no taxable gifts during your life, estimating estate tax on Form 706 is fairly easy. You start with the total market value of the property in the estate. This is called the gross estate. From the gross estate you subtract certain deductions. For example, charitable bequests are deductible. An unlimited marital deduction is allowed for bequests to a surviving spouse who is a U.S. citizen. *See* ¶39.5 for noncitizen surviving spouses. The net amount after deductions is your taxable estate. The unified credit is subtracted from the tax calculated on the taxable estate. Other credits, including the state death tax credit, further reduce the tax on your estate. *See* ¶39.5 for a sample computation of estate tax.

If you make taxable gifts after 1976, estimating your estate tax is more complicated. The estate tax is cumulative. That is, the unified tax rate is applied to the sum of (1) your taxable estate at death, and (2) taxable lifetime gifts made after 1976 (other than gifts included in your estate). The tax you figure on both (1) and (2) is reduced by gift taxes payable on gifts made after 1976. The unified credit and other credits are then subtracted from the remaining amount.

Separate tax on accumulated retirement benefits. Congress has decided that individuals should not be allowed to accumulate too much in their retirement accounts. If you receive annual distributions above a specified floor, you may be subject to the 15% excess distribution penalty mentioned in ¶7.15. If you die and leave too much in your retirement accounts, a special 15% tax may be imposed. The 15% tax applies if at the date of death the value of all your interests in qualified retirement plans, IRAs, annuity plans, and tax-sheltered annuities exceed a test amount. The test amount is the present value of annual payments over an annual ceiling (currently $150,000) figured over your life expectancy immediately before death. There are exceptions and special computation rules on Schedule S of Form 706. If the 15% tax is applicable, it may *not* be offset by the unified estate tax credit or any other credit. Given the complicated formula for figuring the 15% tax, you should consult an experienced professional to help you determine how the tax could affect your overall estate tax planning.

Generation-skipping transfers. Transfers that "skip" a generation, such as a gift to a grandchild, are subject to a special tax if they exceed a lifetime exemption of $1 million per transferor. Because of other exceptions and the complexity of these rules, you should consult an experienced tax practitioner if planning "skip" transfers.

UNIFIED TAX RATES AND CREDIT

¶39.5 The unified tax credit is $192,800 for those dying after 1986. The amount of the credit is the same for gift tax and estate tax purposes. Applying it to the taxable estate, no tax applies to estates under $600,000.

These exempt amounts assume that you did not make any taxable gifts and that the taxable estate is your gross estate less allowable deductions.

The unified tax credit replaces the $60,000 estate tax exemption and $30,000 lifetime gift tax exemption allowed prior to 1977. Where part or all of the $30,000 lifetime gift tax exemption was used after September 8, 1976, and before January 1, 1977, the unified credit is reduced by 20% of the amount allowed as an exemption on those gifts. Thus, if you used the entire $30,000 exemption on a gift made after September 8, 1976, your unified credit is permanently reduced by $6,000 (20% of $30,000).

Phaseout of credit and graduated rates. The benefit of the unified credit and graduated rates is phased out for cumulative transfers (taxable gifts plus estates) above $10 million. For estates of individuals dying after 1987 and before 1993, the tentative estate tax liability figured on Form 706 is increased for estates between $10 million and $21,040,000. The increase is 5% of the excess of the estate over $10 million. Estates over $21,040,000 are taxed at a flat 55%. Taxable gifts after 1976 are added to the estate for purposes of computing the 5% adjustment.

Note: Congress may extend the above phaseout rules to estates of individuals dying after 1992; *see* the Supplement. If Congress does not act, for estates of individuals dying after 1992, the 5% adjustment will apply to estates between $10 million and $18,340,000.

YOU ARE NOW READY TO ESTIMATE THE FEDERAL ESTATE TAX

Gross estate (your estimated inventory) $ _____
Less:
1. Administration expenses (executor's commissions, attorney's fees, etc.; estimate about 5% to 10% of your estate) $ _____
2. Debts, mortgages, liens   _____
3. Funeral expenses   _____
4. Marital deduction   _____
5. Charitable deduction   _____

Total of (1), (2), (3), (4), and (5) $ _____
Your taxable estate $ _____
Plus: Post-1976 taxable gifts (over the annual exclusion) $ _____
Total taxable amount $ _____
Tentative tax on total   _____
   Less: Gift tax payable on post-1976 gifts $ _____
       Unified credit $ _____
Estate tax due $ _____

EXAMPLE Assume an unmarried person, who made no taxable gifts after 1976, dies in 1992, leaving a gross estate of $700,000. Debts, administration, and funeral expenses total $60,000. The decedent bequeaths $160,000 to charity.

Gross estate	$700,000
Less:	
Debts, administration, and funeral expenses	60,000
	$640,000
Less:	
Charitable deduction	160,000
Taxable estate	$480,000
Tentative tax $149,000	
Less: Unified credit 192,800	
Estate tax due	None

If there was an estate tax due after applying the unified credit, the tax may be reduced by the credit for state death taxes.

Nonresident alien decedents and surviving spouses. For nonresident aliens, estate tax applies only to the part of the gross estate located in the United States. The estate and gift tax rates applied to U.S. citizens and residents also apply to nonresident aliens dying after November 10, 1988. These rates are higher than the prior law rates applied to nonresident aliens. However, the unified credit is limited to $13,000, exempting the first $60,000 of the estate from

estate tax. Where required by a tax treaty, a proportionate part of the regular $192,800 unified credit is allowed, based on the percentage of the total gross estate that is situated in the U.S. Estates of certain residents of U.S. possessions are allowed a unified credit equal to the greater of $13,000, or $46,800 multiplied by the proportion of the gross estate situated in the U.S. to the total gross estate. *See* ¶39.6 for marital deduction restrictions.

Unified Gift and Estate Tax Rates

If taxable amount is:

Over—	But not over—	The tax is—	Plus %—	Of the amount over—
$ 0	$ 10,000	$ 0	18	$ 0
10,000	20,000	1,800	20	10,000
20,000	40,000	3,800	22	20,000
40,000	60,000	8,200	24	40,000
60,000	80,000	13,000	26	60,000
80,000	100,000	18,200	28	80,000
100,000	150,000	23,800	30	100,000
150,000	250,000	38,800	32	150,000
250,000	500,000	70,800	34	250,000
500,000	750,000	155,800	37	500,000
750,000	1,000,000	248,300	39	750,000
1,000,000	1,250,000	345,800	41	1,000,000
1,250,000	1,500,000	448,300	43	1,250,000
1,500,000	2,000,000	555,800	45	1,500,000
2,000,000	2,500,000	780,800	49	2,000,000
2,500,000	3,000,000	1,025,800	53	2,500,000
3,000,000		1,290,800	55*	3,000,000

*For estates of individuals dying after 1992, and gifts made after 1992, the top rate was scheduled to drop to 50% for taxable transfers over $2,500,000. However, when this book went to press, Congress was considering legislation to extend the 55% top rate to years after 1992; *see* the Supplement for an update. *See also* the phaseout rule at the top of the previous column.

REDUCING OR ELIMINATING A POTENTIAL ESTATE TAX

¶39.6 Here are general approaches to eliminating or reducing a potential estate tax: You can make direct lifetime gifts. Any appreciation on the property transferred will be removed from your estate. Furthermore, each gift, to the extent of the $10,000 annual exclusion, reduces your gross estate; *see* ¶33.1 and ¶33.2. Life insurance can be assigned to avoid estate tax, provided the assignment takes place more than three years before death; *see* ¶33.9. You can provide in your will for bequests that will qualify for the marital and charitable deductions.

The marital deduction. A married person may greatly reduce or eliminate estate tax by using the marital deduction. Property passing to a spouse is generally free from estate or gift tax because of an unlimited marital deduction.

Weigh carefully the tax consequences of leaving your spouse all of your property. For maximum tax savings, you may want to reduce your taxable estate to the exemption floor (with marital deduction property). The unified credit will then eliminate tax on that amount at the time of your death. By leaving your spouse less than the maximum deductible amount, you may also reduce the tax at the time of his or her death.

To qualify for the marital deduction, the property must generally be given to the spouse outright or by other legal arrangements that are equivalent to outright ownership in law. There is an exception in the case of income interests in charitable remainder annuity or unitrusts and certain other terminable interests (QTIPs) for which the executor makes an election.

Life insurance proceeds may qualify as marital deduction property. Name your spouse the unconditional beneficiary of the proceeds with unrestricted control over any unpaid proceeds. If your spouse is not given this control or general power of appointment, then proceeds remaining on your spouse's death must be payable to his or her estate. Otherwise, the insurance proceeds will not qualify for the marital deduction.

What should be done if you believe your spouse cannot manage property? You will not want to give complete and personal control. The law permits you to put the property in certain trust arrangements that are considered equivalent to complete ownership. Your attorney can explain how you can protect your spouse's interest and qualify the trust property for the marital deduction.

Marital deduction restrictions for noncitizen spouses. A marital deduction may be claimed by the estate of a nonresident alien for property passing to a surviving spouse who is a U.S. citizen. For estates of individuals dying after November 10, 1988, a marital deduction may not be claimed for property passing outright to a surviving spouse who is not a U.S. citizen. However, the marital deduction is allowed if the surviving spouse's interest is in a qualifying domestic trust (QDT). At least one trustee must be an individual U.S. citizen or domestic corporation with power to withhold estate tax due on distributions of trust corpus. The trust must maintain sufficient assets as required by IRS regulations. For the marital deduction to apply, the executor must make an irrevocable election on the decedent's estate tax return. On Form 706-QDT, estate tax will apply to certain distributions of trust corpus made prior to the surviving spouse's death, and to the value of the QDT property remaining at the surviving spouse's death. You should consult an experienced tax practitioner to set up a QDT trust and plan for distribution provisions.

Periodically review your estate plan. You are now aware of the costs of transferring an estate and of the amount of tax that may be levied. But no estate plan is ever really final. Economic conditions and inflation constantly change values. For this reason, your plan must be reviewed periodically as changes occur in your family and business—when a birth or death occurs; when you receive a substantial increase or decrease in income; when you enter a new business venture or resign from an old one; when you sell, retire, or bring new persons into business. A member of your family may no longer need any part of your estate, while others may need more. Estate or gift tax laws may be revised, or material changes may occur in the health or life expectancy of one of your beneficiaries.

A final word of caution: Estate tax planning is not a do-it-yourself activity. We suggest that you contact experienced counsel to help you.

ESTATE TAX FREEZE ADVISORY

¶39.7 The object of an estate tax freeze is to reduce or eliminate estate tax on the inheritance of property by fixing the value through certain property arrangements. To discourage such plans, a complicated gift and estate tax law was passed in 1990 (IRC § 2701–2704). The rules cover not only common and preferred stock holdings within the family but also partnership interests, the deferral of dividend payments on preferred stock, life and remainder interests, and buy-sell agreements in family businesses.

The estate freeze rules impose gift tax and estate tax values for property transfers subject to the law. Because of the complexity of these rules and their effect on gift and estate values, we suggest that you seek professional advice in the following situations:

As an owner of a family business, you plan to give common stock to family members while retaining preferred stock or recapitalize with common and preferred stock.

You plan to give up a voting interest or liquidating rights attached to preferred stock in a family business.

You defer payment of dividends in preferred stock in a family business.

You plan to retain an interest for life in a transfer or purchase of property.

You plan to give stock to a family member in a company in which you have a buy-sell agreement.

BUSINESS TAX PLANNING

In this part, you will learn how to report your income from a business or profession, and how to reduce your tax liability by claiming expense deductions. Pay special attention to—

- Reporting rules for income and expenses on Schedule C.
- Restrictions on deducting home office expenses. Your deduction may be limited by a restrictive income test.
- Keogh retirement plan rules if you are self-employed. Keogh plans offer tax deductions for contributions and special averaging for lump-sum distributions.
- First-year expensing and depreciation writeoffs for business assets.
- The IRS mileage allowance as an alternative to claiming operating expenses and depreciation for your business automobile.
- Partnership and S corporation reporting. Losses are generally subject to passive loss restrictions.
- Computing and paying self-employment tax on self-employment earnings from a business or profession.

40 INCOME OR LOSS FROM YOUR BUSINESS OR PROFESSION

As a self-employed person, you report income and expenses from your business or profession separately from your other income. On Schedule C, you report your business income and itemize your expenses. Any net profit is subject to self-employment tax, as well as regular tax. A net profit can also be the basis of deductible contributions to a Keogh retirement plan, as discussed in Chapter 41.

If you work out of your home, you may deduct home office expenses.

If you claim a loss on Schedule C, be prepared to show that you regularly and substantially participate in the business. Otherwise, your loss may be considered a passive loss deductible only from passive income, as discussed in Chapter 10.

If you have a business loss that exceeds your other income, you may carry back the loss to three prior years and claim a refund.

If you have self-employment income of $25,000 or less, no employees, and business expenses of $2,000 or less, you may be able to file a new simplified schedule called Schedule C-EZ; see ¶40.5.

REPORTING SELF-EMPLOYED INCOME

¶40.1 You file a separate Schedule C along with Form 1040 if you are a sole proprietor of a business or a professional in your own practice. If you are an employee with a sideline business, report the self-employment income from that business on Schedule C. Do not file Schedule C if your business is operated through a partnership or corporation.

Net business profit (or loss) figured on Schedule C is entered on Line 12, Page 1 of Form 1040. Thus, business profit (or loss) is added to (or subtracted from) nonbusiness income on Form 1040. This procedure gives you the chance to deduct your business expenses, whether or not you claim itemized deductions.

On Schedule C, you deduct all of your business expenses from your business income. Then after adding your business profit to, or subtracting a business loss from, nonbusiness income on Form 1040, you may itemize nonbusiness deductions on Schedule A, such as charitable contributions, taxes, and medical expenses—provided the total of itemized deductions exceeds the standard deduction.

You may be able to file a simplified schedule, Schedule C-EZ, if your income and expenses are below certain limits as explained in ¶40.5.

Did You Suffer a Loss?

Business persons and professionals may get a refund of taxes paid in three prior tax years, if current business losses exceed present income. If the loss is not fully eliminated by the income of the three prior years, the balance of the loss may be used to reduce the income of 15 of the following years. *See* ¶40.17 for details.

Passive loss restrictions. Pay special attention to the passive loss restrictions discussed in Chapter 10. Generally, if you do not regularly and substantially participate in a business that you wholly or partially own, losses are considered passive and are deductible only against other passive income.

Key to Reporting Business and Professional Income and Loss

Item—	Comments—
Tax return to file	If you are self-employed, prepare Schedule C to report business or professional income. If your gross receipts are $25,000 or less, your business expenses are $2,000 or less, and you have no employees, you may be able to file a simplified Schedule C-EZ; *see* ¶40.5. If you are a farmer, use Schedule F. You attach Schedule C and/or F to Form 1040. If you operate as a partnership, use Form 1065; if you operate in a corporation, use Form 1120S or Form 1120.
Method of reporting income	The cash or accrual accounting rules determine when you report income and expenses. You must use the accrual basis if you sell a product that must be inventoried. The cash and accrual basis methods are discussed at ¶40.2.
Tax reporting year	There are two general tax reporting years: calendar years which end on December 31, and fiscal years which end on the last day of any month other than December. Your taxable year must be the same for both your business and nonbusiness income. Most business income must be reported on a calendar year. If, as a self-employed person, you report your business income on a fiscal year basis, you must also report your nonbusiness income on a fiscal year basis. Use of fiscal years is restricted for partnerships and S corporations as explained in Chapter 45.
Office in home	To claim home office expenses as a self-employed person, you must use the home area exclusively and on a regular basis either as a place of business to meet or deal with patients, clients, or customers in the normal course of your business or as your principal place of business. Form 8829 must be used to compute the deduction; *see* ¶40.11.
Social Security coverage	If you have self-employed income, you may have to pay self-employment tax which goes to financing Social Security benefits; *see* Chapter 46.
Passive participation in a business	If you do not regularly, continuously, and substantially participate in the business, your business income or loss is subject to passive activity restrictions. A loss is deductible only against other passive activity income. The passive activity restrictions are discussed in detail in Chapter 10.
Self-employed Keogh plan	You may set up a retirement plan based on business or professional income. If you are self-employed, you may contribute to a self-employed retirement plan, according to the rules of Chapter 41.
Depreciation	Business assets other than real estate placed in service in 1992 are depreciable over 3, 5, 7, 10, 15, or 20 years. Automobiles and light trucks, computers, and office equipment are in the five-year class. Property in the 3-, 5-, 7-, and 10-year classes is depreciable using the double declining balance method, switching to the straight-line method so as to maximize the deduction; *see* Chapter 42 for details on depreciation. Instead of depreciating equipment, you may claim the first-year expensing deduction. You may generally deduct up to $10,000 in 1992; *see* ¶42.3.
Health insurance	If you are self-employed in 1992, you may deduct 25% of the amounts paid before July 1, 1992, for health coverage for yourself, your spouse, and dependents. The deduction may not exceed your net earnings from the business for which the health plan is established. You may not claim the deduction if you have employee coverage under another plan or coverage under your spouse's employer plan. The deduction is allowed as an adjustment to income on Line 26 of Form 1040 whether or not you claim itemized deductions. If itemized deductions are claimed, the remaining 75% of insurance costs and premium costs are deductible as a medical expense, subject to the 7.5% adjusted gross income floor; *see* ¶17.4. S corporation shareholders owning more than 2% of the stock may claim the 25% deduction subject to the same limitations. *See* the Supplement for legislation extending the deduction for premiums paid after June 30, 1992.
Net operating losses	A loss incurred in your profession or business is deducted from other income reported on Form 1040. If the 1992 loss (plus any casualty loss) exceeds income, the excess may be first carried back to 1989, 1990, 1991, and then forward 15 years to 1993 through 2007 until it is used up. A loss carried back to a prior year reduces income of that year and entitles you to a refund. A loss applied to a later year reduces income for that year. You may elect to carry forward your loss for 15 years, forgoing the three-year carryback; *see* ¶40.21.
Sideline business	You report business income of a sideline business following the rules that apply to full-time business. For example, if you are self-employed, you report business income on Schedule C or C-EZ. You may also have to pay self-employment tax on this income. You may also set up a self-employment retirement plan based on such income. If you incur losses over several years, the hobby loss rules of ¶40.9 may limit your loss deduction.

ACCOUNTING FOR BUSINESS INCOME

WHAT ACCOUNTING BASIS CAN YOU USE?

¶40.2   Your business income is reported on either the accrual or cash basis. You may figure your business income on the accrual basis, even if you report your nonbusiness income on the cash basis. If you have more than one business, you may have a different accounting method for each business.

Inventories. If you have inventories, you *must* use the accrual basis for business sales and purchases.

Cash basis. You report income items in the taxable year in which they are received; you deduct all expenses in the taxable year in which they are paid. Under the cash basis, income is also reported if it is "constructively" received. You have "constructively" received income when an amount is credited to your account, subject to your control, or set apart for you and may be drawn by you at any time. For example, in 1992 you receive a check in payment of services, but you do not cash it until 1993. You have constructively received the income in 1992, and it is taxable in 1992.

In general, you deduct expenses in the year of payment. Expenses paid by credit card are deducted in the year they are charged. Expenses paid through a "pay by phone" account with a bank are deducted in the year the bank sends the check. This date is reported by the bank on its monthly statement.

Advance payments. You may not deduct advance rent payments covering charges of a later tax year. The IRS applies a similar rule to advance payments of insurance premiums; however, an appeals court has allowed an immediate deduction.

Advantage of Cash Basis Accounting

The cash basis has this advantage over other accounting methods: You may defer reporting income by postponing the receipt of income. For example, if 1992 is a high income year or income tax rates will be lower in 1993, you might extend the date of payment of some of your customers' bills until 1993. But make certain that you avoid the constructive receipt rule. You may also postpone the payment of presently due expenses to a year in which the deduction gives you a greater tax savings.

Cash method of accounting limited. The following may not use the cash method: a regular C corporation, a partnership with a C corporation as a partner, a tax shelter, or a tax-exempt trust with unrelated business income. Exceptions: The cash method may be used by personal service corporations in the fields of medicine, law, engineering, accounting, architecture, performing arts, actuarial science, or consulting. To qualify, substantially all of the stock must be owned directly or indirectly (through partnerships, S corporations, or personal service corporations) by employees. The cash method may also be used by other businesses with average annual gross receipts of $5 million or less, and farming and timber businesses. Tax shelters may not use the cash method; the $5 million gross receipts exception is not available.

Accrual basis. You report income that has been earned, whether or not received, unless a substantial contingency affects your right to collect the income. Where you are prepaid for future services that must be completed by the end of the next tax year, you may defer the reporting of the income until you earn it. For example, if you receive full payment under a one-year contract requiring you to provide 48 music lessons and in the year of payment you give eight lessons, you report one-sixth ($8/48$) of the payment as income. The remaining five-sixths of the payment must be reported in the next year, even if you do not actually give the required number of lessons.

Economic performance test for accrual basis deductions. The treatment of expenses is subject to rigid rules. A deduction may not be claimed until economic performance has occurred. Economic performance occurs for:

Rent—as the property is used.
Services—when they are performed.
Goods—when they are delivered.
Work of subcontractor hired by the taxpayer—when the subcontractor performs services.

Taxes are generally deductible only when paid under IRS economic performance regulations. However, a deduction may be available under the exception for recurring expenses discussed below. For real estate taxes, an election may be made to accrue the taxes ratably.

You may treat *services* as performed or *goods* delivered when paid for, provided that you reasonably expect the service or goods to be provided within three and a half months after your payment.

The economic performance restrictions do not affect an employer's deduction for employee-benefit plans and vacation pay, which are covered by specific tax law provisions.

Deductions for lease expenses under deferred rental agreements are subject to the accrual rules of ¶9.9.

EXAMPLE   You are a calendar-year taxpayer using the accrual method. In December 1992, you buy office supplies. You receive the supplies and are billed for them before the end of the year but make payment in 1993. You may deduct the cost of supplies in 1992. You meet the "all events" test as liability was fixed in 1992; economic performance also occurred in 1992 with the delivery.

Even if delivery were delayed until 1993, the supplies could qualify as a recurring expense as explained below, thereby allowing a 1992 deduction.

Under an exception, a deduction may be allowed for *recurring expenses* incurred in normal business practice, even though economic performance has not yet occurred. All of these tests must be met:

1. The item meets the general "all events" test (that is, you can establish the amount of the liability) and economic performance occurs within a reasonable period after the end of the taxable year for which the expense is accrued, but not exceeding eight and one half months. However, the deduction may not be claimed if economic performance does not occur by the date the tax return for that year is filed. If economic performance occurs after the filing date, but within eight and one half months after the close of the taxable year, the deduction may be claimed on an amended return if the other tests are met.
2. The item is recurring in nature and you consistently from year to year treat such items as accrued in the year the "all events" test is satisfied.
3. Either (1) the item is not a material item, or (2) the accrual in the year the "all events" test is met results in a better matching against income than accrual in the year of economic performance. For example, where income from shipping goods is recognized in 1992 but the goods are not shipped until 1993, the shipping costs are more properly matched to income in 1992, the year of sale, than in 1993 when the goods are shipped.

Workers' compensation and tort liability do not qualify under these exceptions. Such liabilities are deductible only when paid.

Expenses owed to related cash basis taxpayers. A business expense owed to your spouse, brother, sister, parent, child, grandparent, or grandchild who reports on the cash basis may not be deducted by you until you make the payment and the relative includes it as income. The same rule applies to amounts owed to a controlled corporation (more than 50% ownership) and other related entities.

Contested liability. A deduction may be claimed only if the economic performance test is met, even though payment is made to a trust. Furthermore, if economic performance itself is the actual payment of the liability, such as for worker's compensation, payment to a trust is not treated as economic performance.

Advantage of Accrual Basis Accounting

The accrual basis has this advantage over the cash basis: It generally gives a more even and balanced financial report.

Long-term contracts. Section 460 of the Internal Revenue Code has a special percentage of completion method of accounting for long-term construction contractors.

Capitalize costs of business property you produce or buy for resale. A complicated statute (Code Section 263A) requires manufacturers and builders to capitalize certain indirect costs (such as administrative costs, interest expenses, storage fees, insurance) as well as direct production expenses, by including them in inventory costs.

Retailers and wholesalers who acquire real estate for resale also are subject to the uniform capitalization requirements. Purchasers of personal property (not real estate) for resale are exempt from the capitalization rules, unless average annual gross receipts from all businesses for the three prior tax years exceeded $10 million.

Different capitalization methods apply to resellers and manufacturers. Special exceptions apply for farm products. Inventory adjustments may be spread over four years. *See* IRS Publication 538 and, for further details, Form 3115 and Temporary Regulations 1.263A-IT.

Authors, artists, and photographers are generally exempt from the capitalization requirements; *see* ¶40.8.

Inventory. As just discussed, requirements for allocating costs to inventory are detailed in IRS Publication 538 and regulations to Code Section 263A.

Changing Your Accounting Method

Generally, you must obtain the consent of the Internal Revenue Service prior to any change in accounting method. Apply for consent by filing Form 3115 with the Commissioner of Internal Revenue, Washington, D.C. 20224, within 180 days after the beginning of the tax year in which you wish to make the change. Thus, if you report on the calendar-year basis and want to change from the cash method to the accrual method for 1993, file by June 30, 1993.

Accrual deferral of service income. If, on the basis of your experience, a percentage of billings due for your services will not be collected in that year, you do not have to report that "uncollectible" amount until the year you actually receive it.

However, if interest or a penalty is charged for a failure to make a timely payment, income is reported when the amount is billed. Furthermore, if discounts for early payments are offered, the full amount of the bill must be accrued; the discount for early payment is treated as an adjustment to income in the year payment is made.

The amount of income to be deferred is based on a percentage that considers billing and uncollectibles over the past five most recent years. The percentage is found by dividing the uncollectible amounts by the total billings during the five-year period. That percentage applied to the total billings during the tax year may be deferred. For example, if $200,000 was billed during the five-year period and $20,000 was uncollectible, the percentage is 10% and 10% of the current billings may be deferred. If you do not have a five-year experience, you use the period during which you were in business.

TAX REPORTING YEAR FOR SELF-EMPLOYED

¶40.3 Your taxable year must be the same for both your business and nonbusiness income. If you report your business income on a fiscal year basis, you must also report your nonbusiness income on a fiscal year basis.

Generally, you report the tax consequences of transactions that have occurred during a 12-month period. If the period ends on December 31, it is called a calendar year. If it ends on the last day of any month other than December, it is called a fiscal year. A reporting period, technically called a taxable year, can never be longer than 12 months unless you report on a 52 to 53 week fiscal year basis, details of which can be found in IRS Publication 538. A reporting period may be less than 12 months whenever you start or end your business in the middle of your regular taxable year, or change your taxable year.

To change from a calendar year to fiscal year reporting for self-employment income, you must ask IRS permission by filing Form 1128. Support your request with a business reason such as that the use of the fiscal year coincides with your business cycle. To use a fiscal year basis, you must keep your books and records following that fiscal year period.

Fiscal year restrictions. Restrictions on fiscal years for partnerships, personal service corporations, and S corporations are discussed in Chapter 45.

REPORTING BUSINESS CASH RECEIPTS TO THE IRS

¶**40.4** Did you receive, in the course of business, cash of more than $10,000 in one transaction or two or more related transactions? If you did, you must file an information return, Form 8300, with the IRS for each transaction. There are penalties for failure to file.

File Form 8300 with the IRS within 15 days of the transaction. Only cash payments are reported; do not report funds received by bank check or wire transfer where cash was not physically transferred. Foreign currency is considered cash. If multiple payments from a single payer (or a payer's agent) are received within a 24-hour period, the payments are aggregated, and the total must be reported if over $10,000.

The reporting requirement applies to individuals, corporations, partnerships, trusts, and estates, except for certain financial institutions that are already required to report cash transactions to the Treasury. Cash received in transactions occurring entirely outside the U.S. does not have to be reported.

The filing requirement applies to cash received for providing goods or services. Thus, an attorney, doctor, or other professional must report cash payments of over $10,000 from a client. Furthermore, cash received for setting up a trust of more than $10,000 for a client must be reported.

On an installment sale of business property, you report each payment exceeding $10,000 within 15 days of receipt. If the initial installment is $10,000 or less, you aggregate it plus all payments received within one year of the initial payment. If the total exceeds $10,000, report the total within 15 days after the receipt of the payment that raised the total to over $10,000. In addition, if—after receiving single or aggregated reportable payments—subsequent payments within one year exceed $10,000 individually or in the aggregate, you must report the payments within 15 days.

EXAMPLE On February 10, 1993, you receive an initial cash payment of $11,000. For the same transaction, you also receive cash of $4,000 on March 15, 1993; $6,000 on April 20, 1993; and $12,000 on June 15, 1993. You report the February payment by February 25, 1993. You also report the payments totaling $22,000 received from March 15, 1993, through June 15, 1993, by June 30, 1993; that is, within 15 days of the date (June 15) that the later payments, all received within a one-year period, exceeded $10,000.

Cash equivalents of $10,000 or less. Cash equivalents such as money orders, travelers' checks, cashier's checks, and bank drafts with a face value of $10,000 or less are treated as cash in sales of consumer durables, collectibles, and travel or entertainment services costing $10,000 or more. Common examples of consumer durables are autos, boats, and jewelry.

For example, if jewelry costing $12,000 is bought with $2,400 cash and traveler's checks of $9,600, the jeweler must file Form 8300 reporting the transaction. If the $2,400 were paid by personal check, the transaction would not have to be reported because personal checks are not treated as cash. Reporting exceptions are also allowed where the cash equivalent constitutes the proceeds of a bank loan, or where it is used as a down payment or promissory note payment under a payment plan used for all retail sales by the seller.

Splitting Up a Transaction

The IRS warns that the reporting requirement may not be avoided by splitting up a single transaction into separate transactions. Thus, a sale of property for $36,000 may not be broken down into four separate sales of $9,000 to avoid reporting. Similarly, an attorney who represents a client in a case must aggregate all cash payments by the client, although payments may be spread over several months. If the total exceeds $10,000, it must be reported.

Form 8300. On Form 8300, you provide the payer's home address and tax identification number to the IRS. You also must provide the payer with a copy of the form or a similar statement by January 31 of the following year.

A $50 penalty may be imposed for each failure to file a properly completed Form 8300 or provide the payer with a statement, unless reasonable cause is shown. The penalty may be reduced if a timely correction is made. For small businesses meeting a $5 million average gross receipts test, the maximum penalty for failure to file with the IRS is $100,000 per calendar year; otherwise, the maximum is $250,000. If failure to file is intentional, the penalty for each failure increases to 10% of the reportable amount, with no annual limitation; criminal penalties could also be imposed.

There is an exception to the reporting requirement for persons who act as agents if they receive cash of over $10,000 from their principal and use it within 15 days in a cash transaction, provided they identify the principal to the payee in the cash transaction.

You must keep a copy of each Form 8300 you file with the IRS for five years from the date of filing.

REPORTING INCOME AND EXPENSES ON SCHEDULE C

HOW TO FILE SCHEDULE C

¶**40.5** In this section are explanations of reporting income and expenses on Schedule C, a sample of which is on page 382. A 1992 filled-in Schedule C may be found in the Supplement.

Schedule C-EZ. This is a new simplified form designed for persons on the cash basis who did not have a net business loss and had:

- Gross receipts of $25,000 or less;
- Business expenses of $2,000 or less;
- No inventory at any time;
- Only one sole proprietorship;
- No employees;
- No home office expenses;
- No prior passive activity losses; and
- No depreciation to be reported on Form 4562.

Life insurance salespersons and other statutory employees. Full-time life insurance salespersons report income and expenses on Schedule C. Thus, expenses may be deducted in full on Schedule C rather than as a miscellaneous itemized deduction (¶19.1), subject to the 2% AGI floor on Schedule A. Schedule C is also used by (1) agent or commission drivers who deliver laundry or food or beverages other than milk; (2) individuals who do piecework at home; or (3) full-time salespersons in the food or lodging industries. Such workers are considered "statutory employees" who are subject to FICA withholding but not income tax withholding. Schedule C-EZ may be used if the tests on page 380 are met.

On Form W-2, "statutory employee" will be checked in Box 6 if you are within one of these categories. Your pay should have been subject to Social Security withholdings but not to income tax withholdings. You must check a box on Line 1, Schedule C (or C-EZ) to indicate statutory employee status. If you also have self-employment earnings, you must report the self-employment earnings and statutory employee income on separate schedules. If both types of income are earned in the same business, allocate the expenses between the two activities on the separate schedules.

Gross receipts or sales on Schedule C (Line 1): If you do not produce or sell goods but provide only services, you do not determine cost of goods sold but report only your receipts from services on Line 1. (A sample of Schedule C in the Supplement illustrates the case of a retail business selling merchandise that is required to determine the cost of goods sold using Part III of Schedule C.)

Do not report as receipts on Schedule C the following items:

Gains or losses on the sale of property used in your business or profession. These transactions are reported on Schedule D and Form 4797.

Dividends from stock held in the ordinary course of your business. These are reported as dividends from stocks held for investment.

Deductions on Schedule C: Deductible business expenses are claimed in Part II; the descriptive breakdown of items is generally self-explanatory. However, note these points:

Bad debts (Line 9): Before 1987, accrual basis taxpayers could use the reserve method of charging bad debts. Under current law, you deduct bad debts only when a specific debt becomes partially or wholly worthless. You also must report any pre-1987 balance in the bad debt reserve ratably as income over a four-year period. Rules for deducting business bad debts are at ¶5.47. Cash basis taxpayers may not claim a business bad debt for payments that have not been received or which are uncollectible, where the payments have not been reported as income.

Car and truck expenses (Line 10): In the year you place a car in service, you may choose between the IRS' mileage allowance or deducting actual expenses, plus depreciation. You also attach Form 4562 to support the deduction; see Chapter 43.

Depreciation (Line 13): Enter here the amount of your annual depreciation deduction. A complete discussion of depreciation may be found in Chapter 42. You must figure your depreciation deduction on Form 4562 for assets placed in service in 1992, or for cars, computers, or other "listed property," regardless of when placed in service.

Employee benefit programs (Line 14): Enter your cost for the following programs you provide for your employees: wage continuation; accident or health plans; self-insured medical reimbursement plans; educational assistance programs; supplemental unemployment benefits; and prepaid legal expenses. Retirement plans are reported separately on Line 19.

Insurance (Line 15): Insurance policy premiums for the protection of your business, such as accident, burglary, embezzlement, marine risks, plate glass, public liability, workers' compensation, fire, storm, or theft, and indemnity bonds upon employees, are deductible. State unemployment insurance payments are deducted here or as taxes if they are considered taxes under state law.

 ## Doctor's Malpractice Insurance

A self-employed doctor may deduct the premium costs of malpractice insurance. However, a doctor who is not self-employed but employed by someone else, say a hospital, may deduct the premium costs only as an itemized deduction. Whether malpractice premiums paid to a physician-owned carrier are deductible depends on how the carrier is organized. If there is a sufficient number of policyholders who are not economically related and none of them owns a controlling interest in the insuring company, a deduction is allowed provided the premiums are reasonable and are based on sound actuarial principles.

In one case, physicians set up a physician-owned carrier which was required by state insurance authorities to set up a surplus fund. The physicians contributed to the fund and received nontransferable certificates that were redeemable only if they retired, moved out of the state, or died. The IRS and Tax Court held the contributions to the fund were nondeductible capital expenses.

In another case, a professional corporation of anesthesiologists set up a trust to pay malpractice claims, up to specified limits. The IRS and Tax Court disallowed deductions for the trust contributions on the grounds that the PC remained potentially liable. Malpractice claims within the policy limits might exceed trust funds and the PC would be liable for the difference. Since risk of loss was not shifted to the trust, the trust was not a true insurance arrangement.

Premiums paid on an insurance policy on the life of an employee or one financially interested in a business, for the purpose of protecting you from loss in the event of the death of the insured, are not deductible.

Prepaid insurance premiums are deducted ratably over the term covered by the policy, whether you are on a cash or accrual basis. However, an appeals court allowed a cash basis taxpayer to take an immediate deduction for premiums paid on a policy covering more than a year.

Premiums for disability insurance to cover loss of earnings when out ill or injured are nondeductible personal expenses. But you may deduct premiums covering business overhead expenses.

 ## Self-Employed Health Insurance Deduction

The 25% deduction for health insurance premiums is not claimed on Schedule C but directly on Line 26 of Form 1040 as an adjustment from gross income.

Interest (Line 16): Include interest on business debts, but prepaid interest that applies to future years is not deductible.

Deductible interest on an insurance loan is limited if you borrow against a life insurance policy covering yourself as an employee or the life of any other employee, officer, or other person financially interested in your business. Interest on such a loan is deductible only if the loan is no more than $50,000 per employee or other covered person. If you own policies covering the same employees (or other persons) in more than one business, the $50,000 limit applies on an aggregate basis to all the policies. The interest deduction limit applies even if a sole proprietor borrows against a policy on his own life and uses the proceeds in his business; interest is not deductible to the extent the loan exceeds $50,000. The loan limit applies to all policies purchased after June 20, 1986, in taxable years ending after that date.

Pension and profit-sharing plans (Line 19): Keogh plan contributions made for your employees are entered here; contributions made for your account are entered directly on Line 27 of Form 1040 as an adjustment to income. In addition, you may have to file an information return by the last day of the seventh month following the end of the plan year; *see* ¶41.8.

Rent on business property (Line 20): Rent paid for the use of lofts, buildings, trucks, and other equipment is deductible. However, you may not deduct the entire amount of an advance rental in the year of its payment. This is true even if you are on the cash basis. You deduct only that portion of the payment attributed to the use of

the property in the taxable year. For example, you sign a 10-year lease calling for yearly rental payments of $2,000. You pay the first year's rent on July 1. In your tax return for the calendar year, you may deduct only $1,000 (6/12 of $2,000). However, an appeals court allowed a calendar year cash basis lessee to deduct advance rentals where the rental payments covered a period of a year or less. For example, on December 1, 1992, the lessee pays the entire rental due for the lease ending November 30, 1993. While the IRS would allow only 1/12 of the payment to be deductible in 1992, the appeals court would allow a deduction for the entire payment. The court believes this approach is within the spirit of the cash basis rule. In the case of a long-term lease where advance rental payments cover

Schedule C

Part I   Income

1	Gross receipts or sales. **Caution:** *If this income was reported to you on Form W-2 and the "Statutory employee" box on that form was checked, see page C-2 and check here* . . . . ▶ ☐	1	
2	Returns and allowance	2	
3	Subtract line 2 from line 1	3	
4	Cost of goods sold (from line 40 on page 2)	4	
5	**Gross profit.** Subtract line 4 from line 3	5	
6	Other income, including Federal and state gasoline or fuel tax credit or refund (see page C-2)	6	
7	**Gross income.** Add lines 5 and 6. . . . . ▶	7	

Part II   Expenses (Caution: Do not *enter expenses for business use of your home on lines 8-27. Instead, see line 30.*)

8	Advertising	8		21	Repairs and maintenance . .	21	
9	Bad debts from sales or services (see page C-3) . .	9		22	Supplies (not included in Part III) .	22	
				23	Taxes and licenses	23	
10	Car and truck expenses (see page C-3—also attach Form 4562)	10		24	Travel, meals, and entertainment:		
				a	Travel	24a	
11	Commissions and fees. . .	11		b	Meals and entertainment .		
12	Depletion.	12		c	Enter 20% of line 24b subject to limitations (see page C-4) . .		
13	Depreciation and section 179 expense deduction (not included in Part III) (see page C-3) . .	13					
14	Employee benefit programs (other than on line 19) . . .	14		d	Subtract line 24c from line 24b .	24d	
15	Insurance (other than health) .	15		25	Utilities	25	
16	Interest:			26	Wages (less jobs credit) . .	26	
a	Mortgage (paid to banks, etc.) .	16a		27a	Other expenses (list type and amount):		
b	Other	16b			-----------------------------------		
17	Legal and professional services .	17			-----------------------------------		
18	Office expense	18			-----------------------------------		
19	Pension and profit-sharing plans .	19			-----------------------------------		
20	Rent or lease (see page C-4):				-----------------------------------		
a	Vehicles, machinery, and equipment	20a					
b	Other business property . .	20b		27b	Total other expenses . . .	27b	

28	Total expenses before expenses for business use of home. Add lines 8 through 27b in columns . ▶	28	
29	Tentative profit (loss). Subtract line 28 from line 7	29	
30	Expenses for business use of your home. Attach **Form 8829**	30	
31	**Net profit or (loss).** Subtract line 30 from line 29. If a profit, enter here and on Form 1040, line 12. Also, enter the net profit on Schedule SE, line 2 (statutory employees, see page C-5). If a loss, you MUST go on to line 32 (fiduciaries, see page C-5)	31	

32	If you have a loss, you MUST check the box that describes your investment in this activity (see page C-5)	32a ☐ All investment is at risk.
	If you checked 32a, enter the loss on Form 1040, line 12, and Schedule SE, line 2 (statutory employees, see page C-5). If you checked 32b, you MUST attach **Form 6198.**	32b ☐ Some investment is not at risk.

no more than a year beyond the year of payment, the IRS proration rule sacrifices the simplicity of the cash basis method without a meaningful change in the timing of deductions, according to the appeals court. *See* also ¶9.9 on deferred rental agreements.

Taxes on leased property that you pay to the lessor are deductible as additional rent.

Repairs (Line 21): The cost of repairs is deductible provided they do not materially add to the value of the property or appreciably prolong its life. Expenses of replacements that arrest deterioration and appreciably increase the value of the property are capitalized and their cost recovered through depreciation.

Taxes (Line 23): Deduct real estate and personal property taxes on business assets here. Also deduct your share of Social Security taxes paid on behalf of employees and payments of Federal unemployment tax. Federal highway use tax is deductible. Federal import duties and excise and stamp taxes normally not deductible as itemized deductions are deductible as business taxes if incurred by the business. Taxes on business property, such as an *ad valorem* tax, must be deducted here; they are not to be treated as itemized deductions. However, the IRS holds that you may not deduct state income taxes on business income as a business expense. Its reasoning: Income taxes are personal taxes even when paid on business income. As such, you may deduct state income tax only as an itemized deduction.

The Tax Court supports the IRS rule on the grounds that it reflects Congressional intent toward the treatment of state income taxes in figuring taxable income. However, the Tax Court's position is inconsistent. In somewhat similar cases, it has allowed business expense deductions from gross income for interest paid on state and federal income tax deficiencies and legal fees incurred on tax audits of business income.

For purposes of computing a net operating loss, state income tax on business income is treated as a business deduction.

If you pay or accrue sales tax on the purchase of nondepreciable business property, the sales tax is a deductible business expense. If the property is depreciable, add the sales tax to the cost basis for purposes of computing depreciation deductions.

Travel, meals, and entertainment (Line 24): Travel expenses on overnight business trips while "away from home" (¶20.6) and 80% of meals and entertainment for business are deductible. Total meals and entertainment expenses are listed here and then reduced by 20%; *see* ¶20.16.

Self-employed persons may use the IRS meal allowance rates discussed at ¶20.4, instead of claiming actual expenses. *See* also ¶20.31 for record-keeping requirements for travel and entertainment expenses.

Wages (Line 26): You do not deduct your drawings. You may deduct reasonable wages paid to family members who work for you. If you have an employee who works in your office and also in your home, such as a domestic, you deduct that part of the salary allocated to the work in your office. If you take a targeted jobs credit, the credit offsets the wage deduction.

DEDUCTIONS FOR PROFESSIONALS

¶40.6 The following expenses incurred by self-employed professionals in the course of their work are generally allowed as deductions from income when figuring profit (or loss) from their professional practice on Schedule C:

Dues to professional societies.
Operating expenses and repairs of car used on professional calls.
Supplies.
Subscriptions to professional journals.

Rent for office space.
Cost of fuel, light, water, and telephone used in office.
Salaries of assistants.
Malpractice insurance; *see* ¶40.5.
Cost of books, information services, professional instruments, and equipment with a useful life of a year or less. Professional libraries are depreciable if their value decreases with time. Depreciation rules are discussed at ¶42.1.

Professionals as employees. Professionals who are not in their own practice may *not* deduct professional expenses on Schedule C. Salaried professionals may deduct professional expenses only as itemized expenses on Schedule A, subject to the 2% AGI floor; *see* ¶19.1. However, "statutory" employees may use Schedule C; *see* ¶40.5.

The cost of preparing for a profession. You may not deduct the cost of a professional education and the cost of establishing a professional reputation.

The IRS does not allow a deduction for the cost of a license to practice. However, courts have allowed an attorney to amortize the cost of a bar admission over his or her life expectancy.

The costs of courses taken to keep abreast of professional developments are usually deductible; *see* ¶19.15.

 Purchase Price of Medical Practice

If part of the purchased assets such as patients' records have a limited useful life that can be estimated, the part of the purchase price allocated to those assets may be depreciated. The IRS on an audit may disallow the deduction. However, there is court authority which has allowed the deduction. Similarly, a doctor may be able to deduct payment for the right to practice in a hospital over his or her life expectancy.

Payment of clients' expenses. An attorney may follow a practice of paying his or her clients' expenses in pending cases. He or she may not deduct the payments as the expenses are those of clients. Nor are they bad debts if reimbursement is doubtful. For a bad debt deduction, it must be shown that the claim is worthless; *see* ¶5.48.

An attorney might deduct a payment to a client reimbursing the client for a bad investment recommended by the attorney. A court upheld the deduction on the grounds that the reimbursement was required to protect the reputation of an established law practice. However, no deduction is allowed when malpractice insurance reimbursement is available but the attorney fails to make a claim.

Daily business lunches with associates have been held to lack business purpose. Courts agree with the IRS that professionals do not need to have lunch together every day to talk shop. The cost of the meals are therefore not deductible.

EXAMPLES 1. A law partnership deducted the meal costs of the staff attorneys who lunched every day at the same restaurant to discuss cases and court assignments. The deductions were disallowed as personal expenses. The Tax Court and an appeals court agreed with the IRS that daily lunches are not necessary. Co-workers generally do not need luncheons to provide social lubrication for business talk as is true with clients.

2. A physician held luncheon meetings three or four times a week with other physicians. He argued that the purpose of the luncheons was to generate referrals. A court held that such frequent luncheons became a routine personal event not tied to specific business. The cost of the meals was not deductible.

3. A medical professional corporation (PC) deducted the cost of meals taken by its physician-stockholders at a hospital cafeteria. It

argued that the doctors discussed patients and met other doctors who made referrals to them. The Tax Court agreed with the IRS that the meal costs were not deductible; doctors ate in the cafeteria for their personal convenience. Furthermore, the payments were taxed to the doctors as dividends. The court noted that the PC might have been able to claim a deduction had it treated the meal payments as taxable pay; however, the PC refused to take this position, unsuccessfully gambling that it could claim the costs as business deductions.

NONDEDUCTIBLE EXPENSE ITEMS

¶40.7 Capital expenditures may not be deducted. Generally, the cost of acquiring an asset or of prolonging its life is a capital expenditure that must be amortized over its expected life.

EXAMPLE A new roof is installed on your office building. If the roof increases the life of the building, its cost is a capital expenditure recovered by depreciation deductions. The cost of repairing a leak in the roof is a deductible operating expense. A deduction was allowed for the cost of a major roof renovation on evidence that the work was not designed to increase the value of the building but to correct the defect.

If the useful life of an item is less than a year, its cost, including sales tax on the purchase, is deductible. Otherwise, you may recover your cost only through depreciation except to the extent first-year expensing applies; *see* ¶42.3.

Expenses while you are not in business. You are not allowed to deduct business expenses incurred during the time you are not engaged in your business or profession.

EXAMPLE A lawyer continued to maintain his office while he was employed by the government. During that time he did no private law work. He only kept the office to have it ready at such time as he quit the government job and returned to practice. His costs of keeping up his office while he was working for the government were not deductible.

Payments of fines. You may not deduct the payment of a fine, even though your violation was unintentional.

Bribes and kickbacks. Bribes and kickbacks are not deductible if they are illegal under a federal or a generally enforced state law which subjects the payer to a criminal penalty or provides for the loss of license or privilege to engage in business. A kickback, even if not illegal, is not deductible by a physician or other person who has furnished items or services that are payable under the Social Security Act (including state programs). A kickback includes payments for referral of a client, patient, or customer.

In one case, the IRS, with support from the Tax Court and a federal appeals court, disallowed a deduction for legal kickbacks paid by a subcontractor. The courts held that the kickbacks were not a "necessary" business expense because the contractor had obtained nearly all of its other contracts without paying kickbacks, including contracts from the same general contractor bribed here.

HOW AUTHORS AND ARTISTS MAY WRITE OFF EXPENSES

¶40.8 Self-employed authors, artists, photographers, and other qualifying creative professionals may write off business expenses as they are

paid. They are free of the controversial law (Section 263A) that required them to amortize expenses over the period income is received. Section 263A no longer applies to freelancers who personally create literary manuscripts, musical or dance scores, paintings, pictures, sculptures, drawings, cartoons, graphic designs, original print editions, photographs, or photographic negatives or transparencies. Furthermore, expenses of a personal service corporation do not have to be amortized if they directly relate to expenses of a qualifying author, artist, or photographer who owns (or whose relatives own) substantially all of the corporation's stock.

An author or artist with expenses exceeding income may be barred by the IRS from claiming a loss; in that case, the profit-presumption rule of ¶40.9 may allow a deduction of the loss.

Current deductions are *not* allowed for expenses relating to motion picture films, videotapes, printing, photographic plates, or similar items. However, creators of films, sound recordings, videotapes, and photographs may elect to deduct expenses over a three-year period under the special IRS rule of Notice 88-62; *see* ¶9.11 and IRS Publication 538 for further details.

DEDUCTING EXPENSES OF A SIDELINE BUSINESS OR HOBBY

¶40.9 There is a one-way tax rule for hobbies: Income from a hobby is taxable; expenses are deductible only to the extent you have income, and the deduction is limited on Schedule A by the 2% AGI floor for miscellaneous itemized deductions. Hobby losses are considered nondeductible personal losses. A profitable sale of a hobby collection held long term is taxable as capital gain; losses are not deductible.

 LAW ALERT

Hobby or Sideline Business

The question of whether an activity, such as dog breeding or collecting and selling coins and stamps, is a hobby or sideline business arises when losses are incurred. As long as you show a profit, you may deduct the expenses of the activity. But when expenses exceed income and your return is examined, an agent may allow expenses only up to the amount of your income and disallow the remaining expenses that make up your loss. At this point, to claim the loss, you may be able to take advantage of a "profit presumption" discussed in this section, or you may have to prove that you are engaged in the activity to make a profit.

Allowance and disallowance of expenses. If the profit presumption discussed later does not apply and the activity is held *not* to be engaged in for profit, expenses are deductible only as itemized deductions and only up to the extent of income from the activity; a deduction for expenses exceeding the income is disallowed. A special sequence is followed in determining which expenses are deductible from income. Deducted first on Schedule A are amounts allowable without regard to whether the activity is a business engaged in for profit, such as interest, state and local taxes, as well as casualty losses. If any income remains, first deduct "business" operating expenses such as wages, utilities, advertising, repairs, and maintenance. Then deduct depreciation to the extent of remaining income. The "business" expenses and depreciation are allowed only as miscellaneous itemized deductions subject to the 2% AGI floor; *see* ¶19.1. Thus, even if the expenses offset income from the activity, the expenses will not be deductible unless your total miscellaneous expenses (including those from the activity) exceed 2% of your adjusted gross income.

Presumption of profit-seeking. For taxable years beginning before January 1, 1987, if you showed a profit in two or more years during a period of five consecutive years, the law presumed that you were in an activity for profit. For taxable years beginning after December 31, 1986, you must show a profit for three or more years in the five-year period to take advantage of the presumption. If the activity is horse breeding, training, racing, or showing, the profit presumption applies if you show profits in two of seven consecutive years. The presumption does not necessarily mean that losses will automatically be allowed; the IRS may try to rebut the presumption. You would then have to prove a profit motive by showing these types of facts: You spend considerable time in the activity; you keep businesslike records; you relied on expert advice; you expect the assets to appreciate in value; and losses are common in the start-up phase of your type of business.

Election postpones determination of profit presumption. If you have losses in the first few years of an activity and the IRS tries to disallow them as hobby losses, you have this option: You may make an election on Form 5213 to postpone the determination of whether the above profit presumption applies. The postponement is until after the end of the fourth taxable year following the first year of the activity. For example, if you enter a farming activity in 1989, you can elect to postpone the profit motive determination until after 1993. Then, if you have realized profits in at least three of the five years 1989 to 1993, the profit presumption applies. When you make the election on Form 5213, you agree to waive the statute of limitations for all activity-related items in the taxable years involved. The waiver generally gives the IRS an additional two years after the filing due date for the last year in the presumption period to issue deficiencies related to the activity.

To make the election, you must file Form 5213 within three years of the due date of the return for the year you started the activity. Thus, if you started your activity during 1992, you have until April 15, 1996, to make the election. If before the end of this three-year period you receive a deficiency notice from the IRS disallowing a loss from the activity and you have not yet made the election, you can still do so within 60 days of receiving the notice.

These election rules apply to individuals, partnerships, and S corporations. An election by a partnership or S corporation is binding on all partners or S corporation shareholders holding interests during the presumption period.

DEDUCTING EXPENSES OF LOOKING FOR A NEW BUSINESS

¶40.10 When you are planning to invest in a business, you may incur preliminary expenses for traveling to look at the property and for legal or accounting advice. Expenses incurred during a general search or preliminary investigation of a business are not deductible, including expenses related to the decision whether or not to enter a transaction. However, when you go beyond a general search and focus on acquiring a particular business, you may deduct the start-up expenses. The timing of the deduction depends on whether or not you actually go into the business.

Nonamortizable expenses. Amortizable expenses are restricted to expenses incurred in investigating the acquisition or creation of an active business, and setting up such an active business. They do not include taxes, interest, research, or experimental costs deductible under Section 174. Expenses of looking for investment property may not be amortized. For rental activities to qualify as an active business, there must be significant furnishing of services incident to the rentals. For example, the operation of an apartment com-

plex, an office building, or a shopping center would generally be considered an active business.

You may *not* amortize the expenses incurred in acquiring or selling securities or partnership interests such as securities registration expenses or underwriters' commissions. You may *not* amortize the costs of acquiring property to be held for sale or property which may be depreciated or amortized, including expenses incident to a lease and leasehold improvements.

You may not claim any deduction for start-up expenses if you do not elect to amortize. For example, if you incur expenses prior to completion of a building to be used in an active rental business, such as rental payments for leasing the land on which the building is to be constructed, you must elect to amortize the expenses or you will lose a deduction. If you do not elect to amortize, you treat expenses as follows:

Costs connected with the acquisition of capital assets are capitalized and depreciated; and

Costs related to assets with unlimited or indeterminable useful lives are recovered only on the future sale or liquidation of the business.

Amortizable Start-Up Expenses

When you go into a business, you may elect to amortize over at least a 60-month period the costs of investigating and setting up the business, such as expenses of surveying potential markets, products, labor supply, and transportation facilities; travel and other expenses incurred in lining up prospective distributors, suppliers, or customers; and salaries or fees paid to consultants and similar professional services. The business may be one you acquire from someone else or a new business you create. The amortization period starts when you actually begin or acquire a going business. The election is made by claiming the deduction on Form 4562, and by attaching a statement to the return for the tax year in which you start to claim the amortization deduction. In the statement, describe the expenses, when they were incurred, the date the business began, and the amortization period.

Organizational costs for a partnership or corporation. Costs incident to the creation of a partnership or corporation are also amortizable over a period of at least 60 months. For a partnership, qualifying expenses include legal fees for negotiating and preparing a partnership agreement, and management, consulting or accounting fees in setting up the partnership. Amortization is not allowed for syndication costs of issuing and marketing partnership interests such as brokerage and registration fees, fees of an underwriter, and costs of preparing a prospectus.

For a corporation, amortizable expenses include the cost of organizational meetings, incorporation fees, and accounting and legal fees for drafting corporate documents. Costs of selling stock or securities, such as commissions, do not qualify.

The election to amortize is made on Form 4562 for the first year the partnership or corporation is in business. A statement attached to the return must describe the expenses and the amortization period.

If the acquisition fails. Where you have gone beyond a general search and have focused on the acquisition of a particular business, but the acquisition falls through, you may deduct the expenses as a capital loss.

EXAMPLES 1. In search of a business, you place newspaper advertisements and travel to investigate various prospective ventures. You pay for audits to evaluate the potential of some of the ventures. You then decide to purchase a specific business and hire a law firm to draft necessary documents. However, you change your mind and later abandon your plan to acquire the business. According to the IRS, you may not deduct the related expenses for advertisements, travel, and audits. These are considered investigatory. You may deduct the expense of hiring the law firm.

2. Domenie left his job to invest in a business. He advertised and was contacted by a party who wished to sell. He agreed to buy, hired an attorney, transferred funds to finance the business, and worked a month with the company manager to familiarize himself with the business. Discovering misrepresentations, he refused to buy the company

and deducted over $5,000 for expenses, including travel and legal fees. The IRS disallowed the deduction as incurred in a business search. The Tax Court disagreed. Domenie thought he had found a business and acted as such in transferring funds and drawing legal papers for a takeover.

Job-hunting costs. For deducting the expenses of looking for a new job, *see* ¶19.7.

BUSINESS USE OF A HOME

EXCLUSIVE AND REGULAR USE OF A HOME OFFICE

¶40.11

You may operate your business from your home, using a room or other space as an office or area to assemble or prepare items for sale. To deduct home expenses allocated to this activity, as a self-employed person, you must be able to prove that you use the home area *exclusively* and on a *regular basis* either as:

A place of business to meet or deal with patients, clients, or customers in the normal course of your business. In one case, the Tax Court held that telephoning clients at home met this requirement, but an appeals court reversed, holding that the physical presence in the office of clients or customers is required.

Your principal place of business. Your home office will qualify as your principal place of business if you spend most of your working time there and most of your business income is attributable to your activities there. In one case, the Tax Court disallowed a deduction where a road stand was operated a mile from a home where items were prepared for sale at the stand. Although the home space was used for a business purpose, the deduction was barred because the home was not the principal place of business; the road stand was.

In another case, an appeals court allowed an owner of a laundromat to deduct the costs of a home office where there was no space in the laundromat for an office, and more time was spent in the home office than at the laundromat.

Exclusive use and regular basis tests. If you use a room, such as a den, both for business and family purposes, you must be prepared to show that a specific section of the den is used exclusively as office space. A partition or other physical separation of the office area is helpful but not required.

Under the regular basis test, expenses attributable to incidental or occasional trade or business use are not deductible, even if the room is used for no other purpose but business.

Restrictive income limit test. Even if you meet these tests, your deduction for allocable office expenses may be substantially limited or barred by a restrictive rule that limits deductions to the income from the office activity. This computation is made on Form 8829 and is illustrated in ¶40.14.

Principal Place of Business Test

CAUTION

The tests for deducting office expenses will generally not present problems where the home area is the principal place of business or professional activity. For example, you are a doctor and see most of your patients at an office set aside in your home. Problems may arise where you have a principal place of business elsewhere and use a part of your home for occasional work or administrative paperwork. If your deduction is questioned, you must prove that the area is used regularly and exclusively to receive customers, clients, or patients. Have evidence that you have actual office facilities. Furnish the room as an office—with a desk, files, and a phone used only for business calls. Also keep a record of work done and business visitors.

If you use the office only to do administrative paperwork, whether you can treat the office as your principal place of business was being decided by the Supreme Court when this edition went to press. *See* the Supplement for a discussion of the decision.

Employees using a home office. Employees who use a home office must also meet the tests in the left column. Because of the conditions of employment, most employees are unable to prove that their home office is the principal place of business. However, an appeals court has allowed home office deductions to a professor who was provided inadequate office space at his school, and to a musician whose home office was his only place to practice. Home office expenses of employees are discussed further at ¶19.13.

Multiple business use of home office. If you use a home office for more than one business, make sure that the home office tests are met for all businesses before you claim deductions. If one business use qualifies and another use does not, the IRS will disallow deductions even for the qualifying use.

Employees who use a home office for their job and for a sideline business also should be aware of this problem. Most employees are unable to show that their home office is the principal place of their work. Claiming an unallowable deduction for employee home use will jeopardize the deduction for sideline business use. This happened to Hamacher, who as a self-employed actor earned $24,600 over a two-year period from an Atlanta theatre and a few radio and television commercials. He also earned $18,000 each year as the administrator of an acting school at the theatre. For his job as administrator, Hamacher shared an office at the theatre with other employees. He had access to this office during non-business hours. He also used one of the six rooms in his apartment for an office. Because of interruptions at the theatre, he used the home office to work on the school curriculum and select plays for the theatre. In connection with his acting business, he used the home office to receive phone calls, to prepare for auditions, and rehearse for acting roles.

The IRS disallowed his deduction for both self-employment and employee purposes because Hamacher's office use as an employee did not qualify. The Tax Court agreed. A single-office space may be used for different business activities, but all of the uses must qualify for a deduction. Here, Hamacher's use of the home office as an employee did not qualify. He had suitable office space at the theatre. He was not expected or required to do work at home. As the employee use of the home office did not qualify, the Tax Court did not have to determine if the sideline business use qualified. Even if it had qualified, no allocation of expenses between the two uses would have been made. By requiring that a home office be used "exclusively" as a principal place of business or place for seeing clients, patients, or customers, the law imposes an all-or-nothing test.

Separate structure. If in your business you use a separate structure not attached to your home, such as a studio adjacent but unattached to your home, the expenses are generally deductible if you satisfy the exclusive use and regular basis tests discussed earlier. A separate structure does not have to qualify as your principal place of business or a place for meeting patients, clients, or customers. However, the income limitation discussed at ¶40.14 applies. In one case, a taxpayer argued that an office located in a separate building in his backyard was not subject to the exclusive and regular business use tests and the gross income limitation. However, the IRS and Tax Court held that it was. The office building was "appurtenant" to the home and thus part of it, based on these facts: The office building was 12 feet away from the house and within the same fenced-in residential area; it did not have a separate address; it was included in the same title and subject to the same mortgage as the house, and all taxes, utilities, and insurance were paid as a unit for both buildings.

Day care services. The exclusive use test does not apply to business use of a home to provide day care service for children and handicapped or elderly persons, provided certain state licensing requirements are met. When day care services are provided, a care provider allocates expenses by multiplying the total costs by two fractions: (1) The total square footage in the home exclusively available for day care use throughout each business day, divided by the total square footage for the home. (2) The total hours of operation divided by the total number of hours in a year (8,760).

EXAMPLE A day care operator has a full-time day care center at home. It is open from 7 a.m. to 6 p.m., five days a week, 250 days a year. Annual home expenses total $10,000 ($5,000 for interest and taxes; $4,000 for electricity, gas, water, trash collection, maintenance, and insurance; and $1,000 for depreciation). The total floor area of the home is 2,000 square feet; 1,500 square feet are used exclusively for day care purposes. The operator may deduct $2,354 of the $10,000 expenses attributable to the 1,500 square feet used for day care for 2,750 hours (11 hours per day for 250 days): 1,500/2,000 × 2,750/8,760 × $10,000 = $2,354. The full $2,354 is deductible only if net income generated from the day care facility is at least that much.

Storage space and inventory. If your home is the only location of a business selling products, expenses allocated to space regularly used for inventory storage are deductible if the space is separately identifiable and suitable for storage.

Form 8829

You must report deductible home office expenses on Form 8829. Form 8829 provides special parts: Part I for showing the space allocated to business use (¶40.13); Part II for reporting deductible expenses allocated to business use (¶40.14); Part III for figuring depreciation on the business area (¶40.12); and Part IV, for carryover of expenses not allowed in 1992 because of income limitations applied in Part II (¶40.14). A sample copy of Form 8829 is on page 389.

WHAT HOME OFFICE EXPENSES ARE DEDUCTIBLE

¶40.12 Depending on your income (¶40.14), a deduction for home business use may include real estate taxes, mortgage interest, operating expenses (such as home insurance premiums and utility costs), and depreciation allocated to the area used for business.

The deduction is figured on Form 8829 and entered on Line 30 of Schedule C.

Household expenses and repairs that do not benefit that space are not deductible. However, a pro rata share of the cost of painting the outside of a house or repairing a roof may be deductible. Costs of lawn care and landscaping are not deductible. No portion of the basic rental charge for the first telephone line in your home is deductible; *see* ¶19.14.

If you install a security system for all your home's windows and doors, the portion of your monthly maintenance fee that is allocable to the office area is a deductible operating expense. Furthermore, the business portion of your cost for the system is depreciable. Thus, if the office takes up 20% of your home (¶40.13) you may deduct, subject to the income limitation of ¶40.14, 20% of the maintenance fee and a 20% depreciation deduction.

Figuring depreciation. For depreciation purposes, the cost basis of the house is the *lower* of the fair market value of the house at the time you started to use a part of it for business, or its adjusted basis, exclusive of the land. Only that part of the cost basis allocated to the office is depreciable. Form 8829 has a special section, Part III, for making this computation.

EXAMPLE In April 1992, you start to use one room in your house to meet clients. This room is 10% of the square footage of your home. In 1980, you bought the property for $100,000, of which $90,000 was allocated to the house. The house now has a fair market value of $185,000. You compute depreciation on the cost basis of $90,000, which is lower than the value. You multiply $90,000 by 10% (business use percentage) which gives $9,000 as the depreciable basis of the business part of the house. As you started business use in the fourth month of 1992, you multiply the depreciable basis of $9,000

Nonresidential Real Property (31.5 Years—See the Law Alert on Page 405)

Use the column for the month of taxable year placed in service

Year	1	2	3	4	5	6	7	8	9	10	11	12
1	3.042%	2.778%	2.513%	2.249%	1.984%	1.720%	1.455%	1.190%	0.926%	0.661%	0.397%	0.132%
2–7	3.175	3.175	3.175	3.175	3.175	3.175	3.175	3.175	3.175	3.175	3.175	3.175

by 2.249%. This percentage is listed for the fourth month in the depreciation rate table shown on page 387. Your depreciation deduction is $202.41 (9,000 × 2.249%).

ALLOCATING EXPENSES TO BUSINESS USE

¶40.13 You may allocate to home office use qualifying expenses (¶40.12) as follows: If the rooms are not equal or approximate in size, compare the number of square feet of space used for business with the total number of square feet in the home and then apply the resulting percentage to the total deductible expenses.

If all rooms in your home are approximately the same size, you may base the allocation on a comparison of the number of rooms used as an office to the total number of rooms.

EXAMPLE A doctor rents an apartment using three rooms for his office and seven rooms for his residence. The rooms are not equal in size. The apartment has 2,000 square feet; the office space 600 square feet. He allocated 30% (600/2000) of the following expenses to his office:

	Total	Office	Residence
Rent	$ 7,200	$2,160	$5,040
Light	600	180	420
Heat	1,000	300	700
Wages of domestic	2,000	600	1,400
	$10,800	$3,240	$7,560

Thus, $3,240 is deductible as office expenses, subject to the income limitation of ¶40.14.

BUSINESS INCOME MAY LIMIT HOME OFFICE DEDUCTIONS

¶40.14 Deductions for the business portion (¶40.13) of utilities, maintenance, and insurance costs, as well as depreciation deductions, may not exceed net income derived from the office use. To make sure that deductible expenses do not exceed income, the IRS requires you to use Form 8829. If you do not realize income during the year, no deduction is allowed. For example, you are a full-time writer and use an office in your home. You do not sell any of your work this year or receive any advances or royalties. You may not claim a home office deduction for this year. *See* also ¶40.8 on rules for writers and artists.

Part II of Form 8829 limits the deduction of home office expenses to net income derived from office use. The following expenses are listed in Part II of Form 8829 for purposes of applying the income limit: Casualty losses affecting the residence, deductible mortgage interest, real estate taxes, home insurance premiums, repair and maintenance expenses for the residence, utility expenses, and depreciation. Business expenses not related to the home are deducted on the appropriate lines of Schedule C. For example, a salary paid to a secretary is deducted on Line 26 of Schedule C; the cost of depreciable equipment on Line 13 of Schedule C.

Expenses disallowed because of the income limitation may be carried forward and treated as home office expenses in a later tax year (Part IV, Form 8829). The carryover as well as the expenses of the later year are subject to the income limitation of that year. For example, tentative net profit on Line 29, Schedule C is $1,000. Rent and other expenses allocated to home office business are $2,000.

Only $1,000 of the expenses are deductible; $1,000 is carried over to 1993.

The amount of real estate taxes, mortgage interest, or casualty losses not allocated to home office use may be claimed as itemized deductions on Schedule A.

EXAMPLE Smith does sideline business consulting from a home office. His income from consulting services is $5,900. He paid $1,800 for a photocopy machine and had office telephone expenses of $300, and office supply costs of $400.

In addition, his home costs are:

Mortgage interest	$10,000
Real estate taxes	4,000
Insurance	1,200
Utilities	1,800

His office space took up 20% of the area of his home, and he figured depreciation allocated to business use was $1,200.

He deducts first-year expensing for the copier, the cost of the business phone, and supplies on Schedule C. This gives a tentative profit of $3,400 ($5,900 − 2,500) on Line 29, Schedule C.

In Part I of Form 8829, he lists the total area of the home and the area used for business, showing 20% business use.

In Part II, he enters the home costs listed above. We have taken only the relevant lines of the Form 8829 as an illustration. A sample Form 8829 is on page 389.

LINE—	COLUMN B ENTRIES—	
8. Tentative profit from Schedule C, Line 29		$3,400
10. Mortgage interest	$10,000	
11. Real estate taxes	4,000	
12. Total	$14,000	
13.&14. Business portion of Line 12		2,800
15. Remaining tentative profit		600
17. Insurance	1,200	
19. Utilities	1,800	
21. Total	3,000	
22. Business portion of Line 21		600
26. Remaining tentative profit		0

No depreciation is deductible because there is no remaining business income and excess home office expenses may not generate a loss deduction. The depreciation is carried over to 1993. Office expenses of $3,400 within the income limit are deducted on Line 30, Schedule C.

HOME OFFICE FOR SIDELINE BUSINESS

¶40.15 You may have an occupation and also run a sideline business from an office in your home. The home office expenses are deductible on Form 8829 if the office is a principal place of operating the sideline business; *see* the income limit computation at ¶40.14. Managing rental property may qualify as a business.

EXAMPLE A doctor is employed full time by a hospital. He also owns six rental properties which he personally manages. He uses one bedroom in his two-bedroom home exclusively as an office to manage the properties. The room is furnished with a desk, bookcase, filing cabinet, calculators, and answering service; furnishings and other materials for preparing rental units for tenants are stored there. He may deduct expenses allocable to the home office.

Substantiating the sideline business. In claiming home office expenses of a sideline business, it is important to be ready to prove that you are actually in business; *see* ¶40.9. The Tax Court has held

BUSINESS USE OF A HOME

¶40.15

Form 8829—Worksheet

Name of proprietor	Your social security number
Gerard Smith	X1X 01 1111

Part I — Part of Your Home Used for Business

1	Area used exclusively for business (see instructions). Include area used for inventory storage or as a day-care facility that does not meet exclusive use test	1	500 Sq. feet
2	Total area of home	2	2500 Sq. feet
3	Divide line 1 by line 2 (enter result as a decimal amount)	3	.20
	• For day-care facilities not used exclusively for business, also complete lines 4–6.		
	• All others, skip lines 4–6 and enter the amount from line 3 on line 7.		
4	Total hours facility used. Multiply days used by number of hours used per day	4	hrs.
5	Total hours available (365 days x 24 hours)	5	8,760 hrs.
6	Divide line 4 by line 5 (enter result as a decimal amount)	6	
7	Business percentage. Multiply line 6 by line 3 (enter result as a decimal amount)	7	.20

Part II — Figure Your Allowable Deduction

		(a) Direct expenses	(b) Indirect expenses		
8	Enter the amount from Schedule C, line 29			8	3,400
9	Casualty losses	9			
10	Deductible mortgage interest	10	10,000		
11	Real estate taxes	11	4,000		
12	Add lines 9, 10, and 11	12	14,000		
13	Multiply line 12, column (b) by line 7		13	2,800	
14	Add line 12, column (a) and line 13			14	2,800
15	Subtract line 14 from line 8. If zero or less, enter -0-			15	600
16	Excess mortage interest (see instructions)	16			
17	Insurance	17	1,200		
18	Repairs and maintenance	18			
19	Utilities	19	1,800		
20	Other expenses	20			
21	Add lines 16 through 20	21	3,000		
22	Multiply line 21, column (b) by line 7		22	600	
23	Carryover of operating expenses from 1991		23		
24	Add line 21 in column (a), line 22, and line 23			24	600
25	Allowable operating expenses. Enter the **smaller** of line 15 or line 24			25	600
26	Limit on excess casualty losses and depreciation. Subtract line 25 from line 15			26	0
27	Excess casualty losses (see instructions)		27		
28	Depreciation of your home from Part III below		28	1,200	
29	Carryover of excess casualty losses and depreciation from 1991		29		
30	Add lines 27 through 29			30	1,200
31	Allowable excess casualty losses and depreciation. Enter the **smaller** of line 26 or line 30			31	0
32	Add lines 14, 25, and 31			32	3,400
33	Casualty losses included on lines 14 and 31. (Carry this amount to **Form 4684**, Section B.)			33	0
34	Allowable expenses for business use of your home. Subtract line 33 from line 32. Enter here and on Schedule C, line 30 ▶			34	3,400

Part III — Depreciation of Your Home

35	Enter the **smaller** of your home's adjusted basis or its fair market value (see instructions)	35	238,975
36	Value of land included on line 35	36	50,000
37	Basis of building. Subtract line 36 from line 35	37	188,975
38	Business basis of building. Multiply line 37 by line 7	38	37,795
39	Depreciation percentage (see instructions)	39	3.175 %
40	Depreciation allowable. Multiply line 38 by the percentage on line 39. Enter here and on line 28 above	40	1,200

Part IV — Carryover of Unallowed Expenses to 1993

41	Operating expenses. Subtract line 25 from line 24. If less than zero, enter -0-	41	0
42	Excess casualty losses and depreciation. Subtract line 31 from line 30. If less than zero, enter -0-	42	1,200

that activities in seeking new tenants, supplying furnishings, and cleaning and preparing six units for tenants is sufficiently systematic and continuous to put a person in the rental real estate business. In some cases, the rental of even a single piece of real property may be a business if additional services are provided such as cleaning or maid service.

Managing your own securities portfolio. Investors managing their own securities portfolio may find it difficult to convince a court that investment management is a business activity. According to Congressional committee reports, a home office deduction should be denied to an investor who uses a home office to read financial periodicals and reports, clip bond coupons, and perform similar activities. In one case, the Claims Court allowed a deduction to Moller who spent about 40 hours a week at a home office managing a substantial stock portfolio. The Claims Court held these activities amounted to a business. However, an appeals court reversed the decision. According to the appeals court, the test is whether or not a person is a trader. A trader is in a business; an investor is not. A trader buys and sells frequently to catch daily market swings. An investor buys securities for capital appreciation and income without regard to daily market developments. Therefore, to be a trader, one's activities must be directed to short-term trading, not the long-term holding of investments. Here, Moller was an investor; he was primarily interested in the long-term growth potential of stock. He did not earn his income from the short-term turnovers of stocks. He had no significant trading profits. His interest and dividend income was 98% of his income.

DEPRECIATION OF COOPERATIVE APARTMENT USED AS OFFICE

¶40.16 If your home office meets the tests of ¶40.11, you may deduct depreciation on your stock interest in the cooperative. The basis for depreciation may be your share of the cooperative corporation's basis for the building or an amount computed from the price you paid for the stock. The method you use depends on whether you are the first or a later owner of the stock.

You are the first owner. In figuring your depreciation, you start with the basis of the building to the cooperative in which you own stock. You then take your share of depreciation according to the percentage of stock interest you own. The cooperative can provide the details needed for the computation.

If space in the building is rented to commercial tenants who do not have stock interests in the corporation, the total allowable depreciation is reduced by the amount allocated to the space used by the commercial tenants.

You are a later owner of the cooperative's stock. When you buy stock from a prior owner, your depreciable basis is determined by the price of your stock and your share of the coop's outstanding mortgage, reduced by amounts allocable to land and to commercial space. *See* ¶29.19 for further details.

FIGURING NET OPERATING LOSSES FOR REFUND OF PRIOR TAXES

NET OPERATING LOSSES FOR REFUND OF PRIOR TAXES

¶40.17 A loss incurred in your profession or unincorporated business is deducted from other income reported on Form 1040. If the 1992 loss (plus any casualty loss) exceeds income, the excess may be first carried back to 1989, 1990, 1991, and *then* forward 15 years to 1993 through 2007 until it is used up. A loss carried back to a prior year reduces income of that year and entitles you to a refund. A loss applied to a later year reduces income for that year.

You may elect to carry forward your loss for 15 years, forgoing the three-year carryback; *see* ¶40.21.

The rules below apply not only to self-employed individuals, farmers, and professionals, but also to individuals whose casualty losses exceed income, stockholders in S corporations, and partners whose partnerships have suffered losses. Each partner claims his share of the partnership loss.

Net operating losses from product liability may be carried back ten years. Product liability losses do not include liabilities under a warranty or resulting from services (e.g., legal or medical malpractice).

Carryover of loss from prior year to 1992. If you had a net operating loss in an earlier year which is being carried forward to 1992, the loss carryover is reported as a minus figure on Line 22 of Form 1040. You must attach a detailed statement showing how you

figured the carryover. The example below shows you how a 1992 loss could be carried back and forward:

EXAMPLE You have a 1992 operating loss of $650.

Year	Income	Loss	Loss carried back or forward to income
1989	$ 50		($ 50)
1990	80		(80)
1991	60		(60)
1992		($650)	
1993	20		(20)
1994	40		(40)
1995	50		(50)
1996	100		(100)
1997	100		(100)
1998	125		(125)
1999	150		(25)

Change in marital status. If you incur a net operating loss while single but are married filing jointly in a carryback or carryforward year, the loss may be used only to offset your own income on the joint return.

If the net operating loss was claimed on a joint return and in the carryback or carryforward year you are not filing jointly with that same spouse, only your allocable share of the original loss may be claimed; *see* IRS publication 536.

Passive activity limitation. Losses subject to passive activity rules of Chapter 10 are not deductible as net operating losses. However, losses of rental operations coming within the $25,000 allowance of ¶10.4 may be treated as a net operating loss if the loss exceeds passive and other income.

Restrictions on loss after accounting method change. You may realize a net operating loss for a short taxable year created by the accounting change. As a condition of allowing the accounting method change, the IRS may require you to forgo the right to a loss carryback and agree to a six-year carryforward period.

EXAMPLE **You want to change from a calendar year to a fiscal year ending April 30. Assume further that May through October is your peak selling period. Thus, you may have a net operating loss for the short taxable year January 1–April 30 because of slack business. According to the IRS, if the net operating loss is $10,000 or less, you may apply the regular net operating loss rules that allow you to carry back the loss three years and then forward 15 years. But if the net operating loss exceeds $10,000 and the short period is less than nine months, the operating loss must be deducted ratably over a six-year period starting with the first tax year after the short period.**

YOUR NET OPERATING LOSS

¶**40.18** A net operating loss is generally the excess of deductible business expenses over business income. The net operating loss may also include the following losses and deductions:

Casualty and theft losses, even if the property was used for personal purposes; *see* Chapter 18.

Expenses of moving to a new job location; *see* Chapter 21.

Deductible job expenses such as travel expenses, work clothes, costs, and union dues; *see* ¶19.3.

Your share of a partnership or S corporation operating loss.

Loss on the sale of Small Business Investment Company stock; *see* ¶5.6.

Loss incurred on Section 1244 stock; *see* ¶5.7.

An operating loss may *not* include:

Net operating loss carryback or carryover from any year.

Capital losses that exceed capital gain.

Excess of nonbusiness deductions over nonbusiness income plus nonbusiness net capital gain.

Deductions for personal exemptions.

A self-employed's contribution to a Keogh plan.

An IRA deduction.

Income from other sources may eliminate or reduce your net operating loss.

EXAMPLE **You are self-employed and incur a business loss of $10,000. Your spouse earns a salary of $10,000. When you file a joint return, your business loss will be eliminated by your spouse's salary. Similarly, if you also had salary from another position, the salary would reduce your business loss.**

FIGURING A NET OPERATING LOSS

¶**40.19** Form 1045 has a schedule for computing your net operating loss deduction. On the schedule, you start with adjusted gross income and personal deductions shown on your tax return. As these figures include items not allowed for net operating loss purposes, you follow the line by line steps of Form 1045 to eliminate them.

That is, you reduce the loss by the nonallowed items such as deductions for personal exemptions, net capital loss, and nonbusiness deductions exceeding nonbusiness income. On the schedule, the reductions are described as adjustments. The example below illustrates the steps in the schedule.

Adjustment for nonbusiness deductions. Nonbusiness expenses that exceed nonbusiness income may not be included in a net operating loss deduction. Nonbusiness deductions include deductions for IRA and Keogh plans and itemized deductions such as charitable contributions, interest expense, state taxes, and medical expenses. Do not include in this nonallowed group deductible casualty and theft losses, which for net operating loss purposes are treated as business losses. If you do not claim itemized deductions in the year of the loss, you treat the standard deduction as a nonbusiness deduction.

Nonbusiness income is income that is *not* from a trade or business—such as dividends, interest, and annuity income. The excess of nonbusiness capital gains over nonbusiness capital losses is also treated as part of nonbusiness income.

EXAMPLE **Income from dividends and interest is $6,000 and nonbusiness deductions are $6,500. The excess deduction of $500 is an adjustment that reduces your loss on Form 1045.**

Adjustment for capital losses. A net nonbusiness capital loss may not be included in a net operating loss. If nonbusiness capital losses exceed nonbusiness capital gains, the excess is an adjustment that reduces your loss on Form 1045. In figuring your loss, you may take into account business capital losses only up to the total of business capital gains plus any nonbusiness capital gains remaining after the nonbusiness deduction adjustment discussed earlier.

At risk loss limitations. The loss used to figure your net operating loss deduction is subject to the at risk rules discussed at ¶10.17. If part of your investment is in nonrecourse loans or is otherwise not at risk, you must compute your deductible loss on Form 6198, which you attach to Form 1040. The deductible loss from Form 6198 is reflected in the income and deduction figures you enter on the Form 1045 schedule to compute your net operating loss deduction.

EXAMPLE **In 1992, you have a salary of $2,000, interest of $1,000, a net business loss of $10,000 (income $50,000 and expenses of $60,000); itemized Schedule A deductions of $3,850, and a net nonbusiness capital gain of $1,000. Your net operating loss is $8,000. The following computation approximates the steps of the Form 1045 computation schedule starting from the line showing your adjusted gross income of ($6,000).**

Salary		$2,000
Interest		1,000
Capital gain income		1,000
Business loss		($10,000)
Adjusted gross income		($ 6,000)
Add: Exemption and itemized deductions		(6,000)
		($12,000)
Adjustments:		
Exemption	$2,150	
Excess nonbusiness deduction*	1,850	4,000
Net operating loss		($ 8,000)

The excess nonbusiness expenses deduction was figured as follows:

Itemized deductions		$3,850
Net capital gain income	$1,000	
Interest income	1,000	2,000
Excess		$1,850

HOW TO CLAIM YOUR NET OPERATING LOSS DEDUCTION

¶40.20 Tax year 1989 is the first year to which you may carry back your 1992 net operating loss. When you carry back the loss to 1989, you recompute your 1989 tax on Form 1045 by deducting the 1992 net operating loss. The net operating loss is deducted from the amount of your original 1989 adjusted gross income. Because of the reduction to adjusted gross income, you have to increase any 1989 medical expense and casualty loss deduction when recomputing 1989 income. You do not have to change the amount of your 1989 charitable deduction. *See* the instructions to Form 1045 and also IRS Publication 536 for details of the recomputation calculation.

After recomputing the 1989 tax on Form 1045, your refund is the difference between the tax originally paid for 1989 and the lower tax figured after deducting the net operating loss deduction.

Use Form 1045 as a "quick refund" claim. The IRS will usually allow or reject your claim within 90 days from the time you file Form 1045. Do not attach Form 1045 to your 1992 Form 1040. File Form 1045 separately, together with a copy of your return. You may file Form 1045 within 12 months after the end of your tax year. Thus, if you are a calendar year taxpayer, you have until December 31, 1993, to carry back a 1992 loss to 1989 on Form 1045. If the IRS allows the refund, it may still determine later that the refund was excessive and assess additional tax.

Although using Form 1045 is the quickest way to obtain the refund, you may instead file an amended return on Form 1040X to claim the refund. You have three years after the due date (including extensions) of your 1992 tax return to file Form 1040X. Thus, to claim a refund on Form 1040X for 1989, because of a net operating loss carried back three years from 1992, you have until April 15, 1996, to file. On Form 1040X, you must attach a statement detailing how the loss carryback was figured; the schedule from Form 1045 for computing the loss may be used.

Operating losses from more than one year. If you have more than one year net operating loss to be carried to the same taxable year, you apply the loss from the earliest year first.

EXAMPLE You had net operating losses in both 1991 and 1992 of $6,000 and $10,000, respectively. Your taxable income in 1988 was $5,000. You carried the $6,000 loss from 1991 to 1988, leaving an unused portion of $1,000 to be carried to 1989. Therefore, you have two losses to be applied against 1989 income—the unused portion of the 1991 loss, and the 1992 loss. First apply the unused portion of the 1991 loss, and then apply the 1992 loss. On Forms 1045 or 1040X, attach a detailed schedule showing the net operating loss computation for each year.

Any part of the loss that may not be deducted in 1989 is carried to 1990. See the instructions to Form 1045 and also IRS Publication 536 for details of this computation.

ELECTION TO RELINQUISH THE CARRYBACK

¶40.21 The discussion in ¶40.20 is based on the general carryback and carryforward rules. You may elect to forgo the carryback. Instead, you just carry forward losses. The carryforward period is still 15 years under the election. The election is irrevocable.

Advantage of Relinquishing the Carryback

You will generally make the election to relinquish the carryback if you expect greater tax savings by carrying the loss forward. You might also make the election if you are concerned you might be audited for earlier years if you carry back a loss for a refund. You make the election by attaching a statement to this effect to your return for the year of the loss, which must be filed by the due date plus extensions. The IRS refuses to allow a late election and received court approval for its position.

BUSINESS TAX CREDITS

GENERAL BUSINESS CREDIT

¶40.22 *The general business credit* includes the targeted jobs credit (Form 5884), alcohol fuels credit (Form 6478), research credit (Form 6765), enhanced oil recovery credit (Form 8830), low-income housing credit (Form 8586), the rehabilitation property investment credit (Form 3468), the disabled access credit (Form 8826) and business energy investment credit (Form 3468) for geothermal and solar energy property.

Extension legislation. When this book went to press, Congress was considering legislation to extend the low-income housing credit, targeted jobs credit, research credit and energy credit beyond June 30, 1992. *See* the Supplement for a legislative update.

The low-income housing credit and the rehabilitation tax credit are discussed at ¶9.8.

You compute each credit separately. If you claim only one credit, that credit is considered your *general business credit* for 1992. The credit is subject to a limitation based on tax liability which is figured on the form used to compute that particular credit. You then enter the allowable credit as your general business credit on Form 1040.

If you claim more than one credit, the credits are combined into one general business credit on Form 3800. Each credit is first computed separately and then listed on Form 3800. The combined credit is subject to a limitation based on tax liability. To figure the limit, compute alternative minimum tax (AMT) on Form 6251. The limit is your regular tax liability plus AMT (if any), minus whichever of the following is larger: either (1) tentative AMT from Form 6251; or (2) 25% of your regular income tax liability over $25,000.

If your full 1992 general business credit may not be claimed because of the tax liability limitation, you may *carry back* the excess three years, starting with the earliest year. After the carryback, any remaining credit may be *carried forward* 15 years until used up. The carrybacks and carryforwards are listed on Form 3800.

If you have business credits from a passive activity under the rules of Chapter 10, you must figure the credits on Form 8582-CR; generally, the credits are limited to tax liability from passive activities.

Disabled Access Credit

The credit is allowed on Form 8826 if your gross receipts for the preceding year were $1 million or less, and you had no more than 30 full-time employees. Qualifying for the credit are costs of removing barriers that impede access to your business property by individuals with disabilities, providing special materials or assistance to hearing or visually-impaired persons, or buying or modifying equipment for disabled persons. The credit is 50% of expenses over a $250 floor, but it may not exceed $5,000.

Other Business Tax Credits

Credit—	Pointers—
Diesel vehicle	If in 1992, you bought a diesel-powered car or truck weighing 10,000 pounds or less, you may claim a one-time credit for the diesel fuel tax. You must be the original purchaser—that is, the first purchaser for use other than resale. The credit for an auto is $102; for a truck or van, $198. The credit is claimed on Form 4136. For depreciation purposes, basis is reduced by the credit. Thus, if a new diesel-powered business car is purchased for $18,000, basis is reduced by the $102 credit to $17,898.
Federal gasoline and fuels tax	For a qualified business use, a refundable credit may be claimed for gasoline or special fuels. For example, a credit applies for fuel used in non-highway vehicles (other than motorboats), including generators, compressors, fork-lift trucks, and bulldozers. A credit may also be claimed for aviation fuel used for farming or commercial aviation. Different credit rates apply depending on the type of fuel. You must claim the credit on a timely filed income tax return, including extensions. You compute the credit on Form 4136, which you attach to Form 1040. If you do not claim the credit on your tax return, you may do so on a timely filed refund claim or amended return for that year. If the credit exceeds $1,000 during any of the first three quarters of the taxable year, you may file a refund claim on a quarterly basis. A quarterly refund claim must be filed on Form 843 on or before the last day of the quarter following the quarter for which the refund is claimed. For further explanation, *see* IRS Publication 378; farmers should *see* IRS Publication 225. If the cost of the gasoline and special fuel is deducted as a business expense, a later refund or credit claim on these items is reported as income. If you use the cash basis method of reporting, you report the credit as income in the year in which you file a tax return on which the credit is claimed. If you are on the accrual basis, you report the credit in the year the fuel is used.
Prior investment credit	*Carryovers.* You may have an investment credit carryover from a pre-1986 year. The investment credit may be carried back three years and forward 15 years. Credits carried over from earlier years are deductible following a first-in, first-out order. Furthermore, the carryover claimed in 1992 must be reduced by 35%. *See* Form 3468 for further details. *Recapture.* You must report income from credit recapture if in 1992 you dispose of property for which you claimed an investment credit in a prior year, and which you held for less than the holding period required for the credit. You figure the recapture on Form 4255 and add the recaptured amount to your regular tax on Form 1040. Recapture generally occurs when you sell the asset, or stop using it for business purposes. Recapture also applies if the percentage of business use drops below the business-use percentage in the year you placed the asset in service. There is no credit recapture on three-year recovery property if it is held at least three years. There is no recapture on other recovery property held at least five years. Special rules apply to energy property. *See* Form 4255 for recapture percentages. To the extent the investment credit did not reduce tax liability in the year claimed, but resulted in a credit carryback or carryover, any recaptured amount does not increase tax liability in the year of recapture but is used to adjust the credit carrybacks and carryovers. Property is considered disposed of whenever it is sold, exchanged, transferred, distributed, involuntarily converted, or given away. A disposition occurs when property is contributed to a partnership or a corporation, but not where the contribution is part of a mere change in the form of operating your business and you retain a substantial ownership interest. An election of S corporation status is considered a mere change in form. Generally, a lease of property is not considered to be a disposition. However, if you lease out property which you would ordinarily dispose of by sale or exchange and it appears that a purpose of the lease is to avoid the recapture of the credit, the lease may be considered a disposition. If property on which an investment credit has been taken is involuntarily converted before the end of the recovery period used in figuring the credit, the recapture rules apply.

41 RETIREMENT PLANS FOR SELF-EMPLOYED

You may set up a tax-sheltered Keogh retirement plan or simplified employee pension plan (SEP) if you are self-employed in your own business or professional practice, or you are a partner in a business. The advantages of setting up a plan flow from: (1) tax deductions allowed for contributions made to the plan (a form of forced savings); (2) tax-free accumulations of income earned on assets held by the plan; and (3) special averaging provisions for lump-sum benefits paid on retirement.

If you have employees, you must consider the cost of covering them when setting up your plan. Most self-employed persons are considered key employees and may be subject to the restrictions for top-heavy plans discussed in this chapter.

WHO MAY SET UP A KEOGH PLAN

¶41.1 You may set up a self-employed retirement plan called a Keogh plan if you earn self-employment income from personal services and have *net earnings* (gross business or professional income less allowable business deductions). Income earned abroad and excluded from federal income tax is not considered earned income for purposes of the plan. If you are an inactive owner, such as a limited partner, you do not qualify for a Keogh plan—unless you receive guaranteed payments for services which are treated as earnings from self-employment.

If you control more than one business (own more than 50% of the capital or profits interest in a partnership or the entire share of an unincorporated business), (1) you must set up pension or profit-sharing plans for all businesses under your control. These may be incorporated in one plan or remain separate. (2) Any additional plans must also conform to all regulations governing the original plan. And (3) the additional plans must make contributions in an equal ratio and provide equal benefits.

Employees Who Are Self-Employed on the Side

The above rules for controlled businesses prevent you from increasing your deductible contribution for your own benefit by contributing to more than one retirement plan. However, if you are an employee-member of a company retirement plan, you may set up a Keogh plan if you carry on a self-employed enterprise or profession on the side. For example, you are an attorney employed by a company that has a qualified pension plan in which you are a member. At the same time, you have an outside practice. You may set up a Keogh plan based on your self-employed earnings. Each plan is independent of the other. As an alternative to a Keogh plan, you may contribute to a simplified employee pension plan (SEP) as discussed in ¶41.4.

Partnership plans. An individual partner or partners, although self-employed, may not set up a Keogh plan. The plan must be established by the partnership. Partnership deductions for an individual partner's account are reported on the partner's Schedule K-1 (Form 1065) and reported by the partner on Line 27 of Form 1040.

Including employees in your plan. You must include in your plan all employees who have reached age 21 with at least one year of service. If your plan provides for full and immediate vesting of benefits, an employee may be required to complete two years of service before participating. You are not required to cover seasonal or part-time employees who work less than 1,000 hours during a 12-month period.

Your plan cannot exclude an employee because he or she has reached a certain age.

A plan may not discriminate in favor of officers or other highly compensated personnel. Benefits must be for the employees and their beneficiaries, and their plan rights may not be subject to forfeiture. A plan may not allow any of its funds to be diverted for purposes other than pension benefits. Contributions made on your behalf may not exceed the ratio of contributions made on behalf of employees.

Deadline for Setting Up Keogh Plan or SEP

You must formally set up a Keogh plan in writing on or before the end of the taxable year in which you want the plan to be effective. For example, if you want to make a contribution for 1992, your plan must be set up on or before December 31, 1992, if you report on a calendar-year basis; see ¶41.5.

If you miss the deadline for setting up a plan, you may contribute to a simplified employee pension plan (SEP) set up by the filing deadline for Form 1040, including extensions. See ¶41.4 and ¶8.11 for SEP details.

CHOOSING A KEOGH PLAN

¶41.2 There are two general types of Keogh plans: defined-benefit plans and defined-contribution plans. A defined-benefit plan provides in advance for a specific retirement benefit funded by quarterly contributions based on an IRS formula and actuarial assumptions. A defined-contribution plan does not fix a specific retirement benefit, but rather sets the amount of annual contributions so that the amount of retirement benefits depends on contributions and income earned on those contributions. If contributions are geared to profits, the plan is a profit-sharing plan. A plan that requires fixed contributions regardless of profits is a money-purchase plan.

A defined-benefit plan may prove costly if you have older employees who also must be provided with proportionate defined benefits. Furthermore, a defined-benefit plan requires you to contribute to their accounts even if you do not have profits. The maximum annual retirement benefit for basing 1992 plan year contributions may not exceed $112,221 and the $112,221 limit may have to be reduced if benefits begin before the Social Security age, currently 65. The $112,221 limit is subject to annual inflation adjustments. All plans of a controlled group of businesses are aggregated for purposes of the limitations applied to defined benefits. A defined-benefit plan or defined-contribution plan may take into account Social Security benefits for employees subject to technical nondiscrimination limitations.

Prohibited Transactions

As an owner-employee (owning more than 10% of the business), your dealings with the trust are subject to restrictions. You are generally subject to penalties if you borrow funds from the trust (¶41.9); buy property from or sell property to the trust; or charge any fees for services you render to the trust. These restrictions also apply to any member of your immediate family and any corporation in which you own more than half the voting stock, either directly or indirectly.

Setting up a trust for investing in Keoghs. If you are interested in following an aggressive investment policy for funds in your Keogh plan, you will set up a trust to receive Keogh contributions. You may name yourself or an independent trustee to oversee the plan.

If you use funds to buy nontransferrable annuity contracts from an insurance company, use of a trust is optional. Premium payments may be made directly to the insurance company. The annuity contract may pay a fixed monthly income for life or for a fixed period of years, or may be a variable annuity contract. Life insurance can be included only if it is incidental to retirement benefits.

If you are investing in savings certificates, you need not set up a trust; you may use a custodial account with the bank.

TOP-HEAVY PLAN RESTRICTIONS

¶41.3 "Top-heavy" plan rules, which apply to corporate plans favoring "key employees," may also apply to a Keogh plan of a self-employed person. The top-heavy rules apply if more than 60% of the account balances or accrued benefits are for key employees; see below for definition of key employees. Even if your Keogh plan is not currently considered top heavy, your plan may be disqualified, unless it includes provisions that would automatically take effect if the plan becomes top heavy. The major top-heavy restriction requires an accelerated vesting schedule. There is also a lower limit on benefits where a key employee participates in both a defined-contribution plan and defined-benefit plan.

Vesting. A top-heavy plan must provide either 100% vesting after three years of service or graded vesting at the rate of at least 20% after two years of service, 40% after three years of service, 60% after four years of service, 80% after five years of service, and 100% after six years of service. There may be an advantage in electing three-year vesting if you have a high turnover of employees.

The $228,860 pay limit. The first $228,860 of a self-employed person's net earnings in 1992 is considered in determining deductible contributions, whether or not the plan is top heavy. The pay limit is subject to annual inflation adjustments.

Distributions before age 59½. The 10% penalty for distributions before age 59½ (¶7.14) applies whether or not the plan is top heavy. The penalty does not apply to distributions made because you are disabled. Other exceptions to the penalty are listed at ¶7.14.

The IRS has ruled that a tax-free rollover may be made when the Keogh plan is terminated. A timely rollover will avoid the 10% penalty on premature distributions if the recipient is under age 59½.

Retirement plan bonds. If you invested Keogh plan funds in Treasury Department Retirement Plan Bonds before May 1, 1982, you may redeem them at any time, even if you are under age 59½. To avoid immediate tax, a rollover may be made within 60 days to an IRA or qualified pension or profit-sharing plan.

Who are key employees? The above top-heavy restrictions apply if more than 60% of a defined-contribution plan account balances or more than 60% of the accrued benefits of a defined-benefit plan are for key employees. Key employees are employees who at any time during the plan year or in any of the four preceding plan years own: (1) one of the 10 largest ownership interests and have compensation exceeding $30,000; (2) more than a 5% interest; or (3) more than a 1% interest and also earn compensation of more than $150,000. Officers of corporations are also considered key employees if they have compensation exceeding $56,111 (subject to annual inflation adjustments).

CHOOSING A SEP

¶41.4 Under a SEP (simplified employee pension plan), you may contribute to a special type of IRA more than is allowed under the regular IRA rules. Contributions must be based on a written allocation formula and must not discriminate in favor of yourself, other owners with more than a 5% interest, or highly compensated employees. Coverage requirements for employees are at ¶8.11.

Deductible contributions to your SEP account may not exceed 13.0435% of your net earnings (less 50% of self-employment tax liability), as discussed at ¶41.5.

The deadline for both setting up and contributing to a SEP is the due date for your return, *including extensions.* Thus, if you have not set up a Keogh plan by the end of the taxable year (¶41.1), you may still make a deductible retirement contribution for the year by contributing to a SEP by the due date of your return.

DEDUCTIBLE KEOGH OR SEP CONTRIBUTIONS

¶41.5 Before figuring the deductible contribution you can make to a profit-sharing Keogh or SEP (simplified employee pension) account for 1992, you must first figure your self-employment tax liability on Schedule SE and the 50% deduction for self-employment tax to be claimed on Line 25 of Form 1040. In computing your deductible plan contribution, your net earnings from Line 31 of Schedule C, Line 3 of Schedule C-EZ, or Line 36 of Schedule F are *reduced* by the deduction for 50% of self-employment tax.

The deductible contribution rate. As a self-employed person, you are not allowed to figure your deductible contribution by applying the contribution rate stated in your plan. The rate must be reduced, as required by law, to reflect the reduction of net earnings by the deductible contribution itself. If your plan rate is a whole number, you need not make the computation. Use Table A which provides an adjusted decimal to apply to net earnings to figure the deductible contribution.

Table A: Self-Employment Person's Rate Table

If plan rate is—	The adjusted decimal rate is—
1%	.009901
2	.019608
3	.029126
4	.038462
5	.047619
6	.056604
7	.065421
8	.074074
9	.082569
10	.090909
11	.099099
12	.107143
13	.115044
14	.122807
15*	.130435*
16	.137931
17	.145299
18	.152542
19	.159664
20	.166667
21	.173554
22	.180328
23	.186992
24	.193548
25**	.200000**

* The maximum deduction percentage for contributions to your profit-sharing Keogh or SEP account is 13.0435%. For your employees, the maximum rate is 15%.

** The maximum deduction percentage for contributions to your money-purchase plan is 20%; for employees, 25%.

Fractional rates. If the plan rate is fractional and thus not listed in Table A, figure your deductible percentage this way:

1. Write the plan rate as a decimal. For example, if the plan rate is 10.5%, write .105 as the decimal amount;
2. Add 1 to the decimal rate. For example, if the rate is .105, the result is 1.105;
3. Divide Step 1 by Step 2. This is the deductible percentage. If the plan rate is .105, the deductible percentage is .095023 (.105 ÷ 1.105).

Contribution ceiling. Your 1992 contribution may not exceed the *lesser* of:

1. $30,000, or
2. $228,860 multiplied by the plan contribution rate (left column of Table A). $228,860 is the maximum amount of compensation that may be taken into account for 1992.

Your deduction may not exceed the *lesser* of this ceiling, or the amount figured by multiplying reduced net earnings by the deduction percentage.

EXAMPLE You are a sole proprietor with no employees and have a profit-sharing plan which provides for a 15% contribution rate. Your net self-employment earnings for 1992 from Schedule C are $137,120 and you claimed a 50% deduction for self-employment taxes of $5,277 (¹/₂ of $10,554) on Line 25 of Form 1040. Your maximum deductible contribution is $17,197:

Step 1.	Net earnings reduced by 50% of self-employment tax liability ($137,120 − $5,277)	$131,843
Step 2.	Decimal rate from Table A	.130435
Step 3.	Decimal rate multiplied by reduced net earnings ($131,843 × .130435)	$17,197
Step 4.	Overall contribution limit: $228,860 multiplied by 15% plan rate, but no more than $30,000	$30,000
Step 5.	Lesser of Step 3 or Step 4. This is your maximum deductible contribution	$17,197

Money-purchase plan may supplement profit-sharing plan. A money-purchase plan requires an employer to make fixed contributions each year, without regard to profit.

As shown in Table A, the maximum deduction percentage for a money-purchase plan is 20% (25% for regular employees).

To maximize your deductible contributions, you may establish a separate money-purchase plan to supplement a profit-sharing plan. A bank or other Keogh plan trustee can help you set up separate plans and stay within the overall contribution limit of 20% of net earnings.

Contributions for your employees. The previously discussed deduction formula does not apply to contributions for employees. You continue to make contributions for your employees at the rate specified in your plan, based upon their compensation (up to the $228,860 limit as adjusted for inflation). Thus, in the above example, you would contribute 15% of your employees' pay to the plan. You deduct contributions for employees when figuring your net earnings from self-employment on Schedule C or Schedule F before figuring your own deductible contribution using the above formula.

Contributions after age 70¹/₂. You may continue to make contributions for yourself as long as you have self-employment income. At the same time, if you reached age 70¹/₂, you generally have to begin to receive minimum distributions from the plan no later than the April 1 in the year following the year you reach age 70¹/₂; *see* ¶7.13. A penalty may be imposed if the minimum distribution is not received. The minimum distribution must be based on your life expectancy. If you are married, withdrawals may be spread over the joint lives of you and your spouse. Use the IRS actuarial tables to figure life expectancy, as explained at ¶7.23.

Excess and unused contributions. Contributions to a profit-sharing plan exceeding the 13.0435% deduction ceiling (15% for your employees) may be carried over and deducted in later years subject to the ceiling for those years. However, if contributions exceed the deductible amount, you are generally subject to a 10% penalty on nondeductible contributions that are not returned by the end of your tax year. The penalty is computed on Form 5330, which must be filed with the IRS by the end of the seventh month following the end of the tax year.

If you contribute less than the allowable deduction limit for a profit-sharing plan in taxable years starting after 1986, you may not carry forward the unused limit to a later year. However, the deduction limit for years after 1986 is increased by any unused pre-1987 carryforwards, but the increased limit may not exceed 25% of net earnings (after reduction for deductible contributions).

Contributions to defined-benefit plan. Generally, you may deduct contributions needed to produce the accrued benefits provided for by the plan. This is a complicated calculation requiring actuarial computations that call for the services of a pension expert.

HOW TO CLAIM THE DEDUCTION

¶41.6 Contributions made to your Keogh or SEP account as a self-employed person are deducted from gross income to find your adjusted gross income. Your 1992 deduction is claimed on Line 27 of Form 1040. However, a deduction for a contribution made for your benefit may not be part of a net operating loss.

Contributions for your employees are entered as deductions on Schedule C (or Schedule F) for purposes of computing profit or loss from your business. Trustees' fees not provided for by contributions are deductible in addition to the maximum contribution deduction.

Deductible Keogh plan contributions may generally be made at any time up to the due date of your return, including any extension of time. However, the plan itself must be set up before the close of the taxable year for which the deduction is sought. If you miss the December 31 deadline for setting up a Keogh plan, you have at least up to April 15, 1993, to set up an SEP for 1992. If you have a filing extension, you have until the extended due date to set up an SEP and make your contribution.

HOW TO QUALIFY A PLAN

¶41.7 You may set up a Keogh plan and contribute to it without advance approval. But, since advance approval is advisable, you may, in a determination letter, ask the IRS to review your plan. Approval requirements depend on whether you set up your own administered plan or join a master plan administered by a bank, insurance company, mutual fund, or a prototype plan sponsored by a trade or professional association. If you start your own individually designed plan, you apply for a determination letter on Form 5300 whether the plan is a defined-benefit plan or defined-contribution plan. You must pay a fee to the IRS when you apply for a determination letter. File Form 8717 showing your fee, together with Form 5300.

If you join a master or prototype plan, the sponsoring organization applies to the IRS for approval of its plan. You should be given a copy of the approved plan and copies of any subsequent amendments.

To set up a SEP with a bank, broker or other financial institution, you do not need IRS approval. If you do not maintain any other qualified retirement plan and other tests are met, a model SEP may be adopted using Form 5305-SEP.

ANNUAL KEOGH PLAN RETURN

¶41.8 Relief from one burdensome IRS paperwork requirement is available if your pension or profit-sharing Keogh plan covers only yourself, or you and your spouse. You do not have to file a 1992 information return if the plan assets at the end of the 1992 plan year are $100,000 or less. If the year-end plan assets exceed $100,000, you must file Form 5500EZ with the IRS by the end of the seventh month following the end of the plan year. Thus, for a calendar year plan, the form would be due by July 31, 1993.

The $100,000 exception applies if you, or you and your spouse, are sole proprietors or sole shareholders of a corporation maintaining the plan. The exception also applies if your business is operated as a partnership and the only plan participants are the partners and their spouses. Employers who maintain two or more such plans must file a separate Form 5500EZ for each plan if the combined assets of all the plans exceed $100,000 at the end of the plan year. Also file Form 5500EZ for the final plan year regardless of the amount of plan assets.

If you cannot use Form 5500EZ, you must file Form 5500-C/R if there are fewer than 100 plan participants (Form 5500 if 100 or more participants). On Form 5500-C/R, you check a box indicating whether the form is being filed as a Form 5500-C or Form 5500-R. Form 5500-R is a shorter form that may be used for a plan year that is *not* the first plan year or final plan year, provided that you used the longer Form 5500-C for at least one of the two prior plan years. Thus, after the first year, Form 5500-R may be filed in two of every three years. Only some of the Form 5500-C/R pages are filled in by Form 5500-R filers; follow the form instructions. The form must be filed by the end of the seventh month following the end of the plan year. There are penalties for late filing, unless you show reasonable cause.

Electronic filing allowed. Forms 5500EZ and 5500-C/R may be filed electronically or on magnetic tape by qualifying tax return filers. To file electronically or on magnetic tape, the plan administrator must provide a signed declaration on Form 8453-E.

RESTRICTIONS ON LOANS

¶41.9 Keogh plan loans to an owner-employee (more than 10% ownership) are subject to prohibited transaction penalties. There are two penalties: (1) a 5% penalty, and (2) a 100% penalty.

The 5% penalty applies in the year of the loan and in later years until the loan is repaid with interest. The penalty is figured on a fair market interest factor which is explained in the instructions to Form 5330. You are required to report loans to the IRS on Form 5330 and pay the 5% penalty when you file the form. Form 5330 must be filed within seven months after the end of the taxable year; extensions may be granted by the IRS if you apply in writing before the due date.

The 100% penalty is imposed if the loan is not repaid. The penalty may be avoided by repaying the loan within 90 days after the IRS sends a deficiency notice for the 100% tax. The 90-day period may be extended by the IRS to allow a reasonable time for repayment.

Exception. An owner-employee may apply to the Department of Labor for a special exemption from the prohibited transaction penalties.

Loans treated as taxable distributions. Self-employed individuals are taxable on loans from their Keogh plan under the same rules applied to regular employees, as discussed at ¶7.16.

Loans from SEP are prohibited. Borrowing from a SEP is a prohibited transaction under the IRA rules and will result in the loss of the account's tax-exempt status. The account will be treated as if it were distributed to you on the first day of the year; *see* ¶8.8.

HOW KEOGH PLAN DISTRIBUTIONS ARE TAXED

¶41.10 Distributions from a Keogh plan generally may not be received without penalty before age 59½ unless you are disabled or meet the other exceptions listed at ¶7.14. After reaching age 70½, you generally must begin to receive distributions by the following April 1, and penalties may apply if an insufficient distribution is received; *see* ¶7.13.

Qualifying lump-sum distributions are taxable under special averaging methods, or may be rolled over tax free to an IRA or other qualified plan; *see* ¶7.2 for details. Pension distributions from a Keogh are taxed under the annuity rules of ¶7.25, but for purposes of figuring your cost investment, include only nondeductible voluntary contributions; deductible contributions made on your behalf are not part of your investment. The excess distribution penalty discussed at ¶7.15 generally applies to lump-sum distribution exceeding $750,000 and to pensions and annuity payments (plus IRAs) exceeding $150,000. Furthermore, if you receive amounts in excess of the benefits provided for you under the plan formula and you own more than a 5% interest in the employer, the excess benefit is subject to a 10% penalty. The penalty also applies if you were a more-than-5% owner at any time during the five plan years preceding the plan year that ends within the year of an excess distribution.

Other rules discussed at ¶7.1 to ¶7.16 apply to Keogh plans as well as qualified corporate plans.

After the death of a Keogh plan owner, distributions to beneficiaries may be spread over the periods discussed at ¶7.13.

SEP distributions. Distributions from a SEP are subject to the IRA rules at ¶8.8.

5500EZ—Worksheet

This return is: (i) ☐ the first return filed (ii) ☐ an amended return (iii) ☐ the final return

Use IRS label. Otherwise, please type or machine print.	**1a** Name of employer ALICE WEST	**1b** Employer identification number XIXIXOXXX
	Number, street, and room or suite no. (If a P.O. box, see instructions for line 1a.) 19 CENTER ROAD	**1c** Telephone number of employer (212) XII-IIII
	City or town, state, and ZIP code CITY, STATE XIXIX	**1d** If plan year has changed since last return, check here . ▶ ☐

2a (i) Name of plan ▶ WESTMORE FASHIONS PROFIT-SHARING PLAN

2b Date plan first became effective Month 1 Day 1 Year 80

(ii) ☐ Check if name of plan has changed since last return

2c Enter three-digit plan number ▶ 0 0 1

			Yes	No
3a Enter the date the most recent plan amendment was adopted . N/A . Month ___ Year ___				
b Enter the date of the most recent IRS determination letter . . . . . Month 3 Year 90				
c Is a determination letter request pending with IRS?				✓
4a Enter the number of other qualified pension benefit plans maintained by the employer ▶ 0				
b If you have more than one pension plan and the total assets of all plans are more than $100,000, check this box . . . . ☐				
5 Type of plan: a ☐ Defined benefit pension plan (attach Schedule B (Form 5500)) b ☐ Money purchase plan c ☑ Profit-sharing plan d ☐ Stock bonus plan e ☐ ESOP plan (attach Schedule E (Form 5500))				
6 Were there any noncash contributions made to the plan during the plan year?				✓

7 Enter the number of participants in each category listed below:

		Number
a Under age 59½ at the end of the plan year	**7a**	2
b Age 59½ or older at the end of the plan year, but under age 70½ at the beginning of the plan year	**7b**	0
c Age 70½ or older at the beginning of the plan year	**7c**	0

8a A fully insured plan with no trust and which is funded entirely by allocated insurance contracts that fully guarantee the amount of benefit payments should check the box at the right and not complete 8b through 10d . . . . ▶ ☐		
b Contributions received for this plan year	**8b**	26,000
c Net plan income other than from contributions	**8c**	6,500
d Plan distributions	**8d**	0
e Plan expenses other than distributions	**8e**	250
9a Total plan assets at the end of the year	**9a**	108,000
b Total plan liabilities at the end of the year	**9b**	0

10 During the plan year, if any of the following transactions took place between the plan and a party-in-interest (see instructions), check "Yes" and enter amount. Otherwise, check "No."

		Yes	Amount	No
a Sale, exchange, or lease of property	**10a**			✓
b Loan or extension of credit	**10b**			✓
c Acquisition or holding of employer securities	**10c**			✓
d Payment by the plan for services	**10d**			✓

		Yes	No
11a Does your business have any employees other than you and your spouse (and your partners and their spouses)? If "No," do NOT complete the rest of this question; go to question 12.			✓
b Total number of employees (including you and your spouse and your partners and their spouses) ▶ _____			
c Does this plan meet the coverage test of Code section 410(b)? See the specific instructions for line 11c.			

12 Answer these questions only if there was a benefit payment, loan, or distribution of an annuity contract made during the plan year and the plan is subject to the spousal consent requirements (see instructions).

a Was there consent of the participant's spouse to any benefit payment or loan within the 90-day period prior to such payment or loan?

b If "No," check the reason for no consent: (i) ☐ the participant was not married (ii) ☐ the benefit payment made was part of a qualified joint and survivor annuity (iii) ☐ other

c Were any annuity contracts purchased by the plan and distributed to the participants? . . . .

Under penalties of perjury and other penalties set forth in the instructions, I declare that I have examined this return, including accompanying schedules and statements, and to the best of my knowledge and belief, it is true, correct, and complete.

Signature of employer/plan sponsor ▶ *Alice West*   Date ▶ 5/31/93

42

CLAIMING DEPRECIATION DEDUCTIONS

There are two methods of claiming expense deductions for your purchases of equipment, fixtures, autos, and trucks used in your business:

- First-year expensing (Section 179 deduction) which allows you to deduct up to $10,000 in the year the equipment is first placed in service and/or,
- Regular depreciation which allows a prorated deduction over a period of years. Most business equipment is depreciable under MACRS over a six-year period. The objective of MACRS is to provide rapid depreciation and to eliminate disputes over useful life, salvage value, and depreciation methods. Useful life and depreciation methods are fixed by law; salvage value is treated as zero. If you do not want to use MACRS accelerated rates, you may elect the straight-line method. MACRS applies to new and used property.

Capital investments in buildings are subject only to depreciation using the straight-line method; residential buildings are depreciated over 27.5 years; commercial buildings over 31.5 years. Congress may extend the write-off period to 40 years for commercial buildings; see the Guide to New Legislation in the front of this book.

Specific annual rates for each class of property are provided by IRS tables.

WHAT PROPERTY MAY BE DEPRECIATED

¶42.1 Depreciation deductions may be claimed only for property used in your business or other income-producing activity.

Depreciation may not be claimed on property held for personal purposes such as a personal residence or pleasure car. If property, such as a car, is used both for business and pleasure, only the business portion may be depreciated.

Property bought for income-producing purposes, although yielding no current income, may be depreciated.

EXAMPLES 1. An anesthesiologist suspended his practice indefinitely because of malpractice premium rate increases. He continued to maintain his professional competence by taking courses and keeping up his equipment. The IRS ruled that he could not take depreciation on his equipment. Since he was no longer practicing, the depreciation did not relate to a current trade or business.

2. An electrician spent $1,325 on a trailer to carry his tools and protective clothing. Based on a useful life of three years less salvage value of $25, annual depreciation deductions came to $433. However, the IRS claimed that he could not claim depreciation during the months he was unemployed and the trailer was not used. The Tax Court disagrees. Depreciation is allowed as long as the asset is held for use in a trade or business, even though the asset is idle or its use is temporarily suspended due to business conditions.

Nondepreciable assets. Not all assets used in your business or for the production of income may be depreciable. Property having no determinable useful life (property that will never be used up or become obsolete), such as treasured art works or good will, may not be depreciated. Although land is not depreciable, the cost of landscaping business property may be depreciated if the landscaping is so closely associated with a building that the landscaping would have to be destroyed if the building were replaced. Qualifying trees and bushes are depreciable over 15 years.

While good will is not depreciable, a restrictive covenant (a covenant not to compete), if separately bargained and paid for, may be "amortized"—that is, deducted in equal amounts over the term of the covenant. If a business is purchased and its former owners agree not to compete for a specified period of time, be sure that the covenant is segregated and severable from good will, which may also have been purchased at the same time, in order to be able to amortize the cost of the covenant; *see* ¶44.10. Similarly, customer lists or records, if segregated from good will, may also be amortized. *See* the Law Alert in ¶44.9.

Property held primarily for sale to customers or property includible in inventory is not depreciable, regardless of its useful life.

Trademark and trade name costs, although capitalized, are *not* depreciated or amortized.

Residences. For depreciation of rental residences, *see* ¶29.19.

For depreciation of a sublet cooperative apartment or one used in business, *see* ¶40.16.

Farm property. Farmland is not depreciable; farm machinery and buildings are. Livestock acquired for work, breeding, or dairy purposes and not included in inventory may also be depreciated. For a detailed explanation of the highly technical rules for depreciating farm property and livestock, *see* IRS Publication 225, *Farmer's Tax Guide.*

Prior-year returns. Incorrect deductions claimed in prior years may not be corrected by an adjustment to your present depreciation deduction. If the year in which the error was made is not yet closed by the statute of limitations, you may file an amended return to adjust the depreciation deduction for that year. *See* also ¶5.16 for other adjustments of incorrect depreciation taken in prior years.

CLAIMING DEPRECIATION ON YOUR TAX RETURN

¶42.2 If you report business or professional self-employed income, use Form 4562 for assets placed in service during 1992 and enter the total deduction on Line 13, Schedule C. For claiming depreciation on "listed property" such as cars, computers, and cellular phones, you use Form 4562, regardless of the year placed in service. Listed property is explained at ¶42.10. If your only depreciation deduction is for pre-1992 assets, other than listed property, you do not need to use Form 4562; figure the deduction on your own worksheet, and enter it on Line 13, Schedule C.

If you are an employee claiming auto expenses, you use Form 2106 to claim depreciation on an automobile used for business purposes.

If you report rental income on Schedule E, use Form 4562 for buildings placed in service in 1992. For buildings placed in service before 1992, enter the depreciation deduction directly on Schedule E. If you have a rental loss on Schedule E, your deduction for depreciation and other expenses may have to be included on Form 8582 to figure net passive activity income or loss; *see* Chapter 10.

Samples of Forms 2106 and 4562 and Schedule E will be in the Supplement.

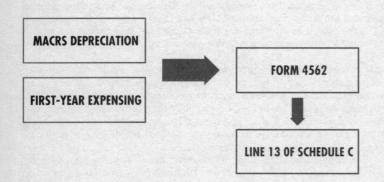

FIRST-YEAR EXPENSING DEDUCTION

¶42.3 You may elect to deduct up to $10,000 of the cost of certain business equipment in the year you place it in service. For an automobile, the maximum expensing deduction in 1992 is $2,760; *see* ¶43.4. The election is limited to tangible personal property bought for business use, such as machinery, office equipment, a computer, car, or truck acquired from non-related parties. The deduction is *not* allowed for buildings, structural components of buildings, furniture or refrigerators used in operating apartment buildings, property held for the production of income, or equipment previously used for personal purposes, such as an automobile bought for pleasure but later used for business. The portion of cost not eligible for first-year expensing may be recovered by depreciation under the regular MACRS rules. The first-year expensing deduction is technically called "the Section 179 deduction."

You elect the first-year expensing deduction on Form 4562, which you attach to your Form 1040. You may not revoke the expensing election without IRS consent.

When this book went to press, Congress was considering legislation that would increase the expensing limit to $20,000 for businesses in designated "enterprise zones." See the Tax Legislation Guide at the front of this book.

Losses and Low Income May Limit Deduction

The expensing deduction cannot exceed the net taxable income from *all* businesses which you actively conduct. Net income from active businesses is figured without regard to expensing, the deduction for 50% of self-employment liability or any net operating loss carryback or carryforward.

You may include wage or salary income as active business income. If you have a 1992 loss or net income that is less than the cost of qualifying assets, the cost over the income limit is carried forward to 1993 on Form 4562.

Partial business use. If you use the equipment for both business and personal use, business use must exceed 50% in the year the equipment is first placed into service to claim a first-year expensing deduction. The expensing deduction may be claimed for the cost allocated to business use up to the $10,000 limit; the 1992 limit for a car is $2,760 (¶43.4).

To elect first-year expensing for listed property such as a computer or car (¶42.10), business use in the first year you use it must exceed 50%. If it does, you show the amount eligible for expensing in the section for "Listed Property" on Form 4562 and then transfer the amount to the part of Form 4562 where the expensing election is claimed.

Figuring the deduction. The maximum annual deduction is $10,000 of the cost of qualifying property; $2,760 for a car (¶43.4). For business use of less than 100% (but more than 50%), the expensing deduction is limited to the business portion of the cost. As discussed on page 401, the $10,000 limit may have to be reduced because your taxable income is lower than $10,000, eligible purchases exceed $200,000, or you are married filing separately.

If you qualify for the full $10,000 limit, you do not have to claim the entire amount. If in 1992, you place in service more than one item of property, you may allocate the $10,000 deduction between the items. If you placed in service only one item of qualifying property which cost less than $10,000, your deduction is limited to that cost.

If you acquire property in a *trade-in,* the cost eligible for expensing is limited to the cash you paid. You may not include the adjusted basis of the property traded in, although your basis for the new property includes that amount.

Year-End Purchases

Equipment placed in service on the last day of the taxable year may qualify for the entire $10,000 deduction. You do not have to prorate the $10,000 limit for the amount of time you held the property.

Effect on regular depreciation. If the cost basis of the property exceeds the first-year expensing limit, you compute depreciation on the cost of the property less the amount of the first-year deduction.

EXAMPLE In 1992, you placed in service a $20,000 machine and a $1,200 lathe. You elect to deduct as a first-year expense $1,200 for the lathe and $8,800 for the machine, a total of $10,000, the maximum first-year deduction. The $1,200 deduction has completely recovered the cost of the lathe. The cost of the machine is reduced by $8,800 giving a depreciable basis of $11,200 ($20,000 – 8,800).

$10,000 limit reduced if taxable income is lower. Your expensing deduction may not exceed net income from all your active businesses; see the Caution Alert on page 400.

$10,000 limit reduced if qualifying purchases exceed $200,000. If the total cost of qualifying property placed in service during a taxable year is over $200,000, the $10,000 expensing limit is reduced dollar for dollar by the cost of qualifying property exceeding $200,000. For example, if you place in service machinery costing $206,000, the $10,000 limit is reduced by $6,000. The reduced limit of $4,000 is shown on the line labeled "Dollar limitation for tax year." If the total cost is $210,000 or more, no first-year expensing deduction is allowed.

$10,000 limit reduced if married filing separately. If you and your spouse file separate returns, the expensing limit for both of you is $10,000. Unless you agree to a different allocation, you are each allowed only a $5,000 expensing limit. The $200,000 cost threshold also applies to both of you as a unit. For example, if you place in service qualifying property costing $195,000, and your spouse places $9,000 of property in service, the total cost of $204,000 reduces the $10,000 limit by $4,000 to $6,000. The reduced limit for each of you on separate returns is $3,000.

Partners and S corporation stockholders. For property bought by a partnership or an S corporation, the $10,000 limit applies to the business, as well as the owners as individual taxpayers. For example, an individual partner's expensing deduction may not exceed $10,000, regardless of how many partnership interests he or she has. However, the partner must reduce the basis of each partnership interest by the full allocable share of each partnership's expensing deduction, even if that amount is not deductible because of the $10,000 limit.

Disqualified acquisitions from related parties. Property does not qualify for the expense election if:

1. It is acquired from a spouse, ancestor or lineal descendant, or from non-family related parties subject to the loss disallowance rule of ¶33.10. For purposes of the expensing election, a corporation is controlled by you and thus subject to the loss disallowance rule of ¶33.10 if 50% or more of the stock is owned by you, your spouse, your ancestors, or descendants.
2. The property is acquired by a member of the same controlled group (using a 50% control test).
3. The basis of the property is determined in whole or in part (a) by reference to the adjusted basis of the property of the person from whom you acquired it, or (b) under the stepped-up basis rules for inherited property.

Recapture of expensing deduction. Recapture of the first-year expensing deduction may occur on a disposition of the asset or if business use falls to 50% or less. If the business use falls to 50% or less after the year the property is placed in service but before the end of the depreciable recovery period (¶42.4, ¶42.10) you must "recapture" the benefit from the first-year expensing deduction. The amount recaptured is the excess of the expensing deduction over the amount of depreciation that would have been claimed (through the year of recapture) without expensing; see ¶42.10. Recaptured amounts are reported as ordinary income on Form 4797.

When you sell or dispose of the property, the first-year expensing deduction is treated as depreciation for purposes of the recapture rules (¶44.1) that treat gain realized as ordinary income to the extent of depreciation claimed.

MACRS CLASS LIVES

¶42.4 Depreciable assets other than buildings fall within a three-, five-, seven-, 10-, 15-, or 20-year class life. For property in the three-, five-, seven-, and 10-year classes, the depreciation method is 200% declining balance, with a switch to straight line. Instead of the 200% rate, you may elect a 150% rate; see ¶42.8. For 15- and 20-year property, the 150% declining balance method is used with a switch to straight line. The conversion to straight line is made when larger annual deductions may be claimed over the remaining life.

Straight-line recovery for buildings is discussed at ¶42.13.

Note: The actual write-off period of depreciation for an asset is one year longer than the class life because of the convention rules explained in the following sections.

MACRS does not apply to intangible property, such as patents or covenants not to compete. You must use straight-line depreciation over the estimated useful life of intangible property.

Three-year property. This class includes property with a class life of four years or less, other than cars and light-duty trucks which are in the five-year class.

This class includes: special handling devices for the manufacture of food and beverages; special tools and devices for the manufacture of rubber products; special tools for the manufacture of finished plastic products, fabricated metal products, or motor vehicles; and breeding hogs. By law, racehorses more than two years old when placed in service and other horses more than 12 years old when placed in service, are also in the three-year class.

Five-year class. This class includes property with a class life of more than four years and less than 10 years such as computers, typewriters, copiers, duplicating equipment, heavy general-purpose trucks, trailers, cargo containers, and trailer-mounted containers. Also included by law in the five-year class are cars, light-duty trucks (actual unloaded weight less than 13,000 pounds), computer-based telephone central office switching equipment, computer-related peripheral equipment, semi-conductor manufacturing equipment, and property used in research and experimentation.

Seven-year class. This class includes any property with a class life of 10 years or more but less than 16 years. This is also a catch-all category for assets with no class life that have not been assigned by law to another class. Included in the seven-year class are: office furniture and fixtures—such as desks and files—cellular phones, fax machines, refrigerators, dishwashers, and machines used to produce jewelry, musical instruments, toys and sporting goods. Single-purpose agricultural or horticultural structures placed in service in 1987 or 1988 are in the seven-year class; they are in the 10-year class if placed in service after 1988.

Ten-year property. This includes property with a class life of 16 years or more and less than 20 years, such as vessels and water transportation equipment, and assets used in petroleum refining or in the manufacture of tobacco products and certain food products.

The 10-year class includes single-purpose agricultural and horticultural structures, and trees or vines bearing fruit or nuts, if placed in service after 1988. Under a transition rule, the seven-year period will apply to single purpose agricultural or horticultural structures under construction on July 14, 1988, or acquired pursuant to a written contract binding on that date.

Fifteen-year property. This includes property with a class life of 20 years or more but less than 25 years such as municipal sewage plants and telephone distribution plants.

Twenty-year property. This class includes property with a class life of 25 years or more, such as farm buildings and municipal sewers, except that residential and nonresidential real estate is excluded; see ¶42.13.

MACRS RATES

¶42.5

The MACRS rate depends on the recovery period (¶42.4) for the property and whether the half-year or mid-quarter convention applies. The 200% declining rate for three-year property is 66.67%, for five-year property, 40%; and for seven-year property it is 28.57%. *See* ¶42.8 for the 150% rate election. These rates, when adjusted for the convention rules explained below, are applied to the adjusted basis of the property. When the double declining rate provides a lower annual deduction than the straight-line rate, the double declining rate is replaced by the straight-line rate. Under MACRS, these general rules are modified because of the *half-year* and *mid-quarter conventions*.

Under the *half-year convention,* all property acquired during the year, regardless of when acquired during the year, is treated as acquired in the middle of the year. As a result, only one-half of the full first-year depreciation is deductible and in the year after the last class life year, the balance of the depreciation is written off. Furthermore, in the year property is sold, only half of the full depreciation for that year is deductible; see ¶42.6.

The half-year convention applies unless the total cost bases of depreciable assets placed in service during the last three months of the taxable year exceed 40% of the total bases of all property placed in service during the entire year. If this 40% test is met, you must use a *mid-quarter convention* to figure your annual depreciation deduction, as explained at ¶42.7.

Buildings are depreciated using a *mid-month convention; see* ¶42.13.

EXAMPLE During June 1992, you place in service a machine costing $20,000. It is your only acquisition in 1992. The machine is in the five-year class and subject to the half-year convention. The depreciation rate for the first year is 20% (*see* the table of MACRS rates). Your 1992 depreciation deduction is $4,000 ($20,000×20%).

Summary of Deductions:

Year	Deduction
1	$4,000
2	6,400
3	3,840
4	2,304
5	2,304
6	1,152
Total	$20,000

Depreciation tables. The following table provides year-by-year rates for property in the three-, five-, and seven-year class. The rates incorporate the adjustment for the half-year or mid-quarter convention and the switch from the 200% declining rate to the straight-line method.

Use the rate shown in the table under the convention for your asset. The rate is applied to original basis, minus any first-year expensing deduction (¶42.3).

You claim the deduction from the table on Form 4562 in the section for MACRS depreciation. In column (f), enter "200DB" as the MACRS method.

MACRS DEPRECIATION RATES

Year	Half-Year Convention	Mid-Quarter Convention 1st	2nd	3rd	4th (Quarter)
		3-Year Property			
1	33.33%	58.33%	41.67%	25.00%	8.33%
2	44.45	27.78	38.89	50.00	61.11
3	14.81	12.35	14.14	16.67	20.37
4	7.41	1.54	5.30	8.33	10.19
		5-Year Property			
1	20.00%	35.00%	25.00%	15.00%	5.00%
2	32.00	26.00	30.00	34.00	38.00
3	19.20	15.60	18.00	20.40	22.80
4	11.52	11.01	11.37	12.24	13.68
5	11.52	11.01	11.37	11.30	10.94
6	5.76	1.38	4.26	7.06	9.58
		7-Year Property			
1	14.29%	25.00%	17.85%	10.71%	3.57%
2	24.49	21.43	23.47	25.51	27.55
3	17.49	15.31	16.76	18.22	19.68
4	12.49	10.93	11.97	13.02	14.06
5	8.93	8.75	8.87	9.30	10.04
6	8.92	8.74	8.87	8.85	8.73
7	8.93	8.75	8.87	8.86	8.73
8	4.46	1.09	3.33	5.53	7.64

HALF-YEAR CONVENTION FOR MACRS

¶42.6

The half-year convention treats all business equipment placed in service during a tax year as placed in service in the midpoint of that tax year. The same rule applies in the year in which the property is disposed of. The effect of this rule is as follows: A half-year of depreciation is allowed in the first year property is placed in service, regardless of when the property is placed in service during the tax year. For each of the remaining years of the recovery period, a full year of depreciation is claimed. If you hold the property for the entire recovery period, a half-year of depreciation is claimed for the year following the end of the recovery period. If you dispose of the property before the end of the recovery period, a half-year of depreciation is allowable for the year of disposition.

See the Table of MACRS Depreciation Rates in ¶42.5 for year-by-year rates under the half-year convention. Apply the rate from the table to original basis, minus any first-year expensing (¶42.3) deduction.

The example in ¶42.5 shows the year-by-year deduction computation for five-year property under the half-year convention. If you dispose of the property before the end of the recovery period shown in ¶42.5, your deduction for the year of disposition is one-half of the deduction that would be allowed for the full year using the rate shown in the table.

LAST QUARTER PLACEMENTS— MID-QUARTER CONVENTION

¶42.7

A mid-quarter convention applies if the total cost bases of business equipment placed in service during the last three months of the tax year exceed 40% of the total bases of all the property placed in service during the year. You must use a mid-quarter convention for *all* property (other than nonresidential real property and residential rental property) placed in service during the year. In applying the 40% rule, you do not count residential rental property, nonresidential realty, and assets that were placed in service and disposed of during the same year.

Under the mid-quarter convention, the first-year depreciation allowance is based on the number of quarters that the asset was in service. Property placed in service at any time during a quarter is treated as having been placed in service in the middle of the quarter. The mid-quarter convention also applies to sales and disposals of property. The disposal is treated as occurring in the midpoint of the quarter.

To figure your MACRS deduction for property subject to the mid-quarter convention, use the rate shown in the table in ¶42.5 for the quarter of the tax year the property is placed in service. In using the table, multiply the original basis, minus any first-year expensing deduction, by the applicable rate.

EXAMPLE

During August 1992, you place in service office furniture costing $1,000, and in October, a computer costing $5,000. You are on the calendar year. The total basis of all property placed in service in 1992 is $6,000. As the basis of the computer of $5,000 placed in service in the last quarter exceeds 40% of the total basis of all property placed in service during 1992, you must use the mid-quarter convention for the furniture and the computer. The office furniture which is seven-year property and the computer which is five-year property are depreciated using MACRS and a mid-quarter convention.

You first multiply the $1,000 basis of the furniture by 10.71%—the seven-year mid-quarter convention rate for the third quarter. The depreciation deduction is $107. You multiply the $5,000 basis of the computer by 5%—the five-year mid-quarter convention rate for the fourth quarter. The deduction is $250. Total depreciation is $357.

150% RATE ELECTION

¶42.8

Instead of using the 200% rate for property in the three-, five-, seven-, and 10-year classes, you may elect a 150% rate. You may prefer the 150% rate when you are subject to the alternative minimum tax (AMT). For AMT purposes, you must use the 150% rate and adjust your taxable income if the 200% rate was used for regular tax purposes; *see* ¶23.2. To avoid this double accounting, you may elect to apply the 150% rate for regular tax purposes. The 150% rate is applied over the alternative straight-line recovery period (¶42.9). Thus, the recovery period is five years for cars and computers; 10 years for furniture and fixtures. If a half-year convention applies, the first year rate for the five-year class is 15%, and 7.50% for the 10-year class; *see* the table in the next column. If you are subject to the mid-quarter convention, *see* IRS Publication 534 for the alternative minimum tax tables showing mid-quarter convention rates.

The election to use the 150% rate must be made for all property within a given class placed in service in the same year. The election is irrevocable.

Apply the rate from the table to your original basis, minus any first-year expensing deduction claimed. On Form 4562, enter "150DB" in column (f) as your depreciation method.

Half-Year Convention—150% rate

Year—	Property Class 5-year—	Property Class 10-year—
1	15.00%	7.50%
2	25.50	13.88
3	17.85	11.79
4	16.66	10.02
5	16.66	8.74
6	8.33	8.74
7		8.74
8		8.74
9		8.74
10		8.74
11		4.37

STRAIGHT-LINE DEPRECIATION

¶42.9

You may not want an accelerated rate and may prefer to write off depreciation at an even pace. There are two types of straight-line methods. You may make an irrevocable election to use the straight-line method over the regular MACRS recovery period (¶42.4). Or, you may elect straight-line recovery over the designated recovery period for the class life under the alternative depreciation system (ADS).

Half-year and quarter-year conventions apply to both straight-line methods; *see* ¶42.6 and ¶42.7. A mid-month convention applies under the straight-line rule for buildings; *see* ¶42.13.

Straight-line over regular recovery period. You make this election on Form 4562 on the line labeled "General Depreciation System." In column (f), enter "SL" as the depreciation method. To elect this method for one asset, you must also use it for all other assets in the same class that are placed in service during the year. The straight-line election is irrevocable.

Alternative straight-line depreciation system (ADS). For purposes of the alternative straight-line method, the recovery period for cars, light trucks, and computers is five years. For business furniture and fixtures, the alternative straight-line recovery period is 10 years, but as discussed above, you may instead elect to use straight-line recovery over the regular seven-year MACRS recovery period. The recovery period for personal property with no class life is 12 years. For nonresidential real and residential rental property, you may elect straight-line recovery over 40 years. *See* IRS Publication 534 for class lives.

Except for real estate, the alternative election applies to all property within the same class, placed in service during the taxable year. For real estate, the election to use the alternative depreciation method may be made on a property by property basis. The election is irrevocable.

The deduction is claimed on the line of Form 4562 labeled "Alternative Depreciation System."

Should you elect straight-line recovery? Accelerated rates of MACRS do not give any greater depreciation than your investment in an asset. They merely give you an opportunity to advance the time of taking your deduction. This may be a decided advantage where the immediate increased annual deductions will provide you with cash for working capital or for investments in other income-producing sources. That is, by taking increased deductions, you defer the payment of taxes that would be due if you claimed smaller depreciation deductions, using more conservative estimates of depreciation. The tax deferral lasts until the rapid method provides less depreciation deductions than would the more conservative method. Your ability to receive the benefits of MACRS generally is more feasible in an ongoing business.

If you are starting a new business in which you expect losses or low income at the start, MACRS may waste depreciation deductions that could be used in later years when your income increases. Therefore, before deciding to use the faster write-offs of MACRS, consider your income prospects.

Straight-line rate table. Here is a table showing straight-line rates for five-year, seven-year, and 10-year property under the half-year convention. As discussed earlier, the recovery period depends on which straight-line method is used. If you are subject to the mid-quarter convention (¶42.7), *see* Publication 534 for tables showing the rates.

Half-Year Convention—Straight-Line Rate

Property Class

Year—	5-year—	7-year—	10-year—
1	10.00%	7.14%	5.00%
2	20.00	14.29	10.00
3	20.00	14.29	10.00
4	20.00	14.28	10.00
5	20.00	14.29	10.00
6	10.00	14.28	10.00
7		14.29	10.00
8		7.14	10.00
9			10.00
10			10.00
11			5.00

AMT depreciation. For alternative minimum tax (AMT) purposes, depreciation is figured using the 150% declining rate if double declining MACRS rates were used for regular tax purposes. If straight-line depreciation was used for regular tax purposes, AMT depreciation is figured using the alternative straight-line method over the class life recovery period. Also *see* ¶42.8 and ¶23.2. For real estate placed in service after 1986, AMT depreciation is figured using the 40-year alternative straight-line method.

Mandatory straight-line depreciation. You are required to use the alternative depreciation system for automobiles (¶43.3) and computers used 50% or less for business.

Alternative MACRS depreciation should also be used for:

Figuring earnings and profits;
Tangible property which, during the taxable year, is used predominantly outside the United States;
Tax-exempt use property;
Tax-exempt bond financed property; and
Imported property covered by an executive order.

COMPUTERS AND OTHER LISTED PROPERTY

¶42.10 "Listed property" is a term applied to certain equipment that may be used for personal and business purposes. For such property, the law allows MACRS and first-year expensing deductions only if business use exceeds 50%. Deductions for listed property are claimed on Form 4562. If business use of listed property falls to 50% or less during the alternative straight-line recovery period (¶42.9), you must "recapture" first-year expensing and accelerated MACRS deductions; *see* Example 2 in the next column.

What is "listed property"? Listed property includes passenger autos weighing 6,000 pounds or less, trucks (*see* ¶43.3 for exceptions), cellular phones, computers and peripheral equipment, boats,

airplanes, and any photographic, sound, or video recording equipment that could be used for entertainment or recreational purposes. However, *exceptions* remove some items from the listed property class for many businesses. Listed property does *not* include (1) any computer or peripheral equipment used exclusively at a regular business establishment owned or leased by you, *and* (2) photographic, phonographic, communications, or video equipment used exclusively and regularly in your business or regular business establishment. A home office that meets the rules of ¶40.11 is considered a business establishment.

EXAMPLES 1. You buy a computer in 1992 and use it exclusively in your regular business office. The computer is not listed property. You may claim first-year expensing (¶42.3) or MACRS depreciation (¶42.5) for your investment on Form 4562. If business use falls to 50% or less after 1992, the only deduction subject to recapture is the first-year deduction; see ¶42.3.

2. You have no regular business establishment and use a computer bought in 1992 as a free lance consultant. The computer is listed property and you may claim MACRS and/or first-year expensing only if you use the computer more than 50% for business. If business use does not exceed 50%, you may only claim straight-line depreciation. Your deductions are claimed in the section for "Listed Property" on Form 4562.

If business use in a later year drops to 50% or less, MACRS and any first-year depreciation are subject to "recapture." In the year in which business use drops to 50% or less, you recapture the excess of (1) the MACRS and first-year expensing deductions claimed in prior years *over* (2) the deduction that would have been allowed using the straight-line alternative depreciation rates of ¶42.9. For the rest of the recovery period, you continue to use the alternative straight-line rate.

Recapture is figured on Form 4797. The recapture computation follows the steps shown in ¶43.9 for recapture of excess depreciation on an automobile.

Investor's use of computer. For an investor who uses a home computer for managing an investment portfolio, the computer is treated as listed property. Unless the computer is also used more than 50% of the time for *business*, only straight-line depreciation may be claimed. Furthermore, unless the more than 50% business-use test is met, first-year expensing may not be claimed. Business and investment uses are combined for determining the depreciable cost percentage.

EXAMPLES 1. In 1992, Jane buys a computer; she uses it 50% of the time to manage her investments and 40% in a part-time research business. The more than 50% business-use test is not met for claiming MACRS or first-year expensing deductions. She must use alternative straight-line depreciation (¶42.9); her depreciable basis is 90% of cost.

2. Assume that Jane used the computer 60% of the time for business and 30% for investment. As business use exceeds 50%, she may claim MACRS, and the allowable deductible percentage is 90% of the MACRS deduction. First-year expensing may also be elected under the rules of ¶42.3.

Leasing a computer or cellular phone. You may deduct the portion of your lease payments attributable to business use. However, if business use is 50% or less for any year, you must report as income an amount based on the fair market value of the unit, the percentage of business plus investment use, and percentages from two IRS tables shown in Publication 534.

Computer software. Software used for business or investment purposes is depreciable under the above rules for computers if the software is separately purchased and has a useful life exceeding one year. If the useful life does not exceed one year as in the case of tax preparation software, the cost is deductible as a miscellaneous item-ized deduction subject to the 2% floor; *see* ¶19.25.

ACRS RECOVERY FOR ASSETS IN SERVICE BEFORE 1987

¶42.11
Assets other than real estate placed in ser-vice after 1980 and before 1987 fell within one of the following ACRS classes—three-, five-, or 10-year property.

Three-year property. This class included automobiles, taxis, light-duty trucks (actual unloaded weight of less than 13,000 pounds), equipment used for research and experimentation, hogs used for breeding, racehorses more than two years old, and any other horse more than twelve years old when placed in service.

With the exception of certain automobiles (¶43.6), three-year property is no longer depreciable unless a straight-line recovery over 12 years was elected; *see* ¶42.12.

Five-year property. All tangible personal property had a five-year recovery period, unless specifically included in the three-year or 10-year class. Thus, most equipment and other business assets qualified for a five-year write-off, including office furniture, type-writers, computers, calculators, copiers, and single-purpose agricul-tural structures. Facilities used for storage of petroleum and its pri-mary products also fell within the five-year class.

Five-year property is no longer depreciable unless you elected straight-line recovery over a period of 12 years or 25 years; *see* ¶42.12.

Ten-year property. This is a limited category covering assets in residential mobile homes, theme and amusement parks, railroad tank cars, public utility equipment with an ADR class life of more than 18 but not more than 25 years (except research and experimen-tation equipment included in the three-year class), and public utility equipment used in coal conversions.

If 1992 is the seventh through the tenth recovery year; the deductible 1992 rate is 9%.

No deduction is allowed in the year the property is disposed of.

If a straight-line recovery over 10, 25, or 35 years was elected; *see* ¶42.12.

Real estate. *See* ¶42.14 for ACRS rates.

Pre-ACRS assets. For assets placed in service before 1981, the straight-line and declining balance methods are discussed in IRS Publication 534.

STRAIGHT-LINE RECOVERY FOR EQUIPMENT IN SERVICE BEFORE 1987

¶42.12
Straight-line deductions may still be claimed for three-year ACRS property if you elected a recovery period of 12 years, or for five-year property if a recovery period of 12 or 25 years was elected. For ten-year property, an election could have been made to elect straight-line depreciation over 10, 25, or 35 years.

If you made the straight-line election, the straight-line rate to be used on your 1992 return is as follows:

Recovery Period—	Rate—
10 years	10.000%
12 years	8.333
25 years	4.000
35 years	2.857

Because of the half-year convention, only 50% of the above per-centages was allowed in the year the property was placed in ser-vice. If the property is held for the entire elected recovery period, another half-year of depreciation is allowed for the year following the end of the recovery period. If property is disposed of prior to the end of the recovery period, no cost recovery is allowable in the year of disposition.

MACRS FOR REAL ESTATE PLACED IN SERVICE AFTER 1986

¶42.13
The recovery period for buildings placed in service after December 31, 1986, is: 27.5 years for residential rental property and 31.5 years for nonresidential real property. The method of recovery is the straight-line method using a mid-month convention; *see* below.

Possible Recovery Period Increase

When this book went to press, Congress was considering an increase in the recovery period for nonresidential real property from 31.5 years to 40 years. As proposed, this change would apply to certain buildings placed in service during 1992. For a legislative update, *see* the Supplement, which will include a 40-year rate table if the provision is enacted.

Residential rental property is a rental building or structure for which 80% or more of the gross rental income for the tax year is rental income from dwelling units. If you occupy any part of the building, the gross rental income includes the fair rental value of the part you occupy.

A dwelling unit is a house or an apartment used to provide living accommodations in a building or structure, but not a unit in a hotel, motel, inn, or other establishment where more than one-half of the units are used on a transient basis.

Mid-month convention. Under a mid-month convention, all property placed in service or disposed of during any month is treated as placed in service or disposed of on the midpoint of that month. You may determine the first-year deduction by applying the percentage from the table on page 406 to the original depreciable basis. In later years, use the same column of the table to figure your deduction.

EXAMPLE In February 1992, you buy and place in service an office building for $100,000 and land for $20,000. You use the calendar year. The table on page 406 gives a first-year depreciation rate of 2.778% for nonresidential property placed in ser-vice during February. Applying this rate, you get a deduction of $2,778. For 1993, the rate will be 3.175%, for a deduction of $3,175.

Additions or improvements to property. The depreciation deduc-tion for any additions to, or improvement of, any property is figured in the same way as the deduction for the property would be figured if the property had been placed in service at the same time as the addition or improvement.

The MACRS class for the addition or improvement is deter-mined by the MACRS class of the property to which the addition or improvement is made. The period for figuring depreciation begins on the date that the addition or improvement is placed in service, or if later, the date that the property to which the addition or improve-ment was made is placed in service.

Residential Rental Property (27.5 Years)

Use the column for the month of taxable year placed in service

Year	1	2	3	4	5	6	7	8	9	10	11	12
1	3.485%	3.182%	2.879%	2.576%	2.273%	1.970%	1.667%	1.364%	1.061%	0.758%	0.455%	0.152%
2–9	3.636	3.636	3.636	3.636	3.636	3.636	3.636	3.636	3.636	3.636	3.636	3.636

Nonresidential Real Property (31.5 Years—See the Law Alert on Page 405)

Use the column for the month of taxable year placed in service

Year	1	2	3	4	5	6	7	8	9	10	11	12
1	3.042%	2.778%	2.513%	2.249%	1.984%	1.720%	1.455%	1.190%	0.926%	0.661%	0.397%	0.132%
2–7	3.175	3.175	3.175	3.175	3.175	3.175	3.175	3.175	3.175	3.175	3.175	3.175

DEPRECIATING REAL ESTATE PLACED IN SERVICE BEFORE 1987

¶42.14

The ACRS recovery period of a building that is not low-income housing depends on the year in which the building was placed in service:

For buildings placed in service after May 8, 1985, and before 1987, the recovery period is 19 years.

For buildings placed in service after March 15, 1984, and before May 9, 1985, the recovery period is 18 years.

For buildings placed in service before March 16, 1984, and for all low-income housing, the recovery period is 15 years.

Mobile homes and theme parks are in a 10-year class and agricultural, horticultural, and petroleum storage structures are in the five-year class.

Under transitional rules, some 19-year buildings may be depreciated over 18 years, and some 18-year buildings over 15 years if placed in service before 1987. Specifically, recovery over 18 years is allowed for a building placed in service after May 8, 1985, provided that *before* May 9, 1985, (1) you began construction or had a binding contract to buy the building, and (2) you placed the building in service before the end of 1986. The 18-year period also applies if construction was begun, or a contract entered into by a person who transferred the rights to you and you placed the building in service before 1987. Recovery over 15 years is allowed for a building that you (or a prior owner who transferred the right to you) began constructing or contracted for before March 16, 1984, provided you placed it in service before the end of 1986.

Election to use straight-line depreciation. You may have elected to use the straight-line method over the regular recovery period: 19 years for 19-year property, 18 years for 18-year property, 15 years for 15-year property. Furthermore, for any building, a longer recovery period of either 35 or 45 years was available. An election of the straight-line method for real property had to be made on a property-by-property basis, by the return due date, plus extensions, for the year the property was placed in service.

Rate of recovery. The rate of recovery is listed in Treasury tables which are available in IRS Publication 534. The specific rates are adjusted according to the month in the first year in which a building or improvement is placed in service.

Substantial improvements made after 1986 to a building are depreciable under MACRS, not ACRS.

If you dispose of 15-year real property, the ACRS deduction for the year of disposition is based on the number of months in use. However, no deduction is allowed for the month of disposition.

If you dispose of 18-year or 19-year real property, the ACRS deduction for the year of disposition is based on the number of months in use; the number of months in use is determined under a mid-month convention. Under the mid-month convention, real property disposed of any time during a month is treated as disposed of in the middle of that month. You count the month of disposition as one-half of a month of use.

See ¶44.1 for recapture rules on the sale of ACRS property.

WHEN MACRS IS NOT ALLOWED

¶42.15

If you place in service personal property which you previously used or which was previously owned by a related taxpayer before 1987, you may not be able to apply MACRS rules. This anti-churning restriction is designed to discourage asset transfers between related persons to take advantage of MACRS deductions that exceed the deductions allowed before 1987 under ACRS. The anti-churning restriction does not apply to personal property if, for the first full taxable year of service, the deduction allowable under ACRS would be greater than the deduction allowable under MACRS.

The anti-churning rule also does not bar MACRS rules for real estate acquired after 1986, unless you lease back the real estate to a related party who owned it before 1987.

Special rules also apply to the transfer of property in certain tax-free corporate or partnership transactions where the property was used before 1987. If you receive property in a tax-free exchange, you may have to use the method used by the transferor in computing the ACRS deduction for that part of basis that does not exceed what was the transferor's basis in the property. To the extent that basis exceeds the transferor's, the MACRS rules may apply; for example, when you paid boot in addition to transferring property.

Where property is disposed of and reacquired, the depreciation deduction is computed as if the disposition had not occurred.

43

DEDUCTING AUTOMOBILE EXPENSES

The costs of buying and operating a car for business are deductible under rules hedged with restrictions. The top depreciation deduction for a car placed in service in 1992 may not exceed $2,760, and this limit is reduced further by the percentage of your personal use. If you do not use your car more than 50% of the time for business, depreciation must be based on the straight-line method.

To avoid accounting for actual auto expenses and depreciation, you may claim an IRS mileage allowance of 28 cents per mile. Whatever choice you make, keep a record of business trip mileage.

If you are self-employed, you deduct your automobile expenses on Schedule C or new Schedule C-EZ if eligible; see ¶40.5. Use Form 4562 to compute depreciation if you claim actual operating costs instead of the IRS mileage allowance. If you are an employee, use Form 2106 to claim unreimbursed automobile expenses, which are deductible only to the extent that together with other miscellaneous itemized deductions they exceed 2% of your adjusted gross income.

IRS AUTOMOBILE ALLOWANCE

¶43.1 If you start to use your car for business in 1992, you have a choice of either deducting the actual operating costs of your car during business trips or deducting a flat IRS allowance of 28 cents per mile for all business mileage traveled during 1992.

If you placed a business car in service before 1992 and have always used the IRS mileage allowance, you may apply the 28 cents per mile rate to your 1992 business mileage or deduct your actual operating costs plus straight-line depreciation (assuming the car is not considered fully depreciated).

The mileage rate also may apply to business trips in vans or pickup or panel trucks.

The rate may not be used to deduct the costs of an automobile used for nonbusiness income-producing activities such as looking after investment property.

The choice of the allowance must be made in the first year you place an auto in service for business travel. If you do not use the allowance in the year you first use the car for business, you may not use the allowance for that car in any other year. Thus, if you bought a car for business in 1991 and on your 1991 return you deducted actual operating costs plus depreciation, you may not use the mileage allowance on your 1992 return or in any later year.

The allowance takes the place of fixed operating costs such as gasoline (including state and local taxes), oil, repairs, license tags, insurance, and depreciation. You may not take the allowance and deduct your actual outlays for these expenses. Parking fees and tolls during business trips are allowed in addition to the mileage allowance. The IRS will not disallow a deduction based on the allowance, even though it exceeds your actual car costs.

EXAMPLE You drive your car on business trips. You keep a record of your business mileage. You traveled 20,000 miles on business. You may deduct $5,600 (20,000 × 28 cents). In addition, you spend $300 on tolls and parking. You may deduct a total of $5,900.

You may decide to use the allowance if you do not keep accurate records of operating costs. However, you must keep a record of your business trips, dates, customers or clients visited, business purpose of the trips, your total mileage during the year, and the number of miles traveled on business. An IRS agent may attempt to verify mileage by asking for repair bills near the beginning and end of the year if the bills note mileage readings.

Key to Deducting Automobile Expenses

Item—	Tax Rule—

IRS mileage allowance

You may avoid the trouble of keeping a record of actual auto expenses and calculating depreciation by electing the IRS mileage allowance of 28 cents a mile. The allowance may give you a larger deduction than your actual outlays plus depreciation. You must elect the allowance in the first year you use the car for business.

If business mileage is—	Your mileage allowance is—	If business mileage is—	Your mileage allowance is—
5,000	$1,400	16,000	$4,480
7,500	2,100	17,000	4,760
10,000	2,800	18,000	5,040
11,000	3,080	19,000	5,320
12,000	3,360	20,000	5,600
13,000	3,640	22,000	6,160
14,000	3,920	25,000	7,000
15,000	4,200	30,000	8,400

To claim the allowance, you must be ready to prove business use of the auto and keep a record of your mileage. Of course, if your actual operating costs plus depreciation exceed the allowance, claim your actual operating expenses and depreciation.

Depreciation

If you claim your actual operating expenses, such as gasoline, repairs, and insurance costs, you may also claim depreciation. There is a cap on the annual depreciation deduction. If you placed a car in service in 1992, your top deduction may not exceed $2,760. If you placed your car in service in 1991, your maximum 1992 depreciation deduction is $4,300; $2,550 if placed in service in 1990; $1,475 if in 1989, 1988 or 1987. For earlier year limits, *see* ¶43.4. These amounts are reduced if business use is not 100%. Furthermore, MACRS or ACRS depreciation is allowed only for autos used for business driving exceeding 50%. Where business driving is 50% or less, straight-line depreciation must be used. MACRS and ACRS depreciation deductions claimed in prior years may be recaptured if business use declines to 50% or less; *see* ¶43.9.

First-year expensing

If you claim actual costs, you may claim the first-year expensing deduction if it provides a larger deduction than allowed by depreciation under the MACRS rules of ¶43.5. For example, first-year expensing may give a larger deduction than depreciation if the cost of your auto is $13,800 or less, or if the mid-quarter convention applies. The first-year expensing rules are explained at ¶42.3. To claim first-year expensing, the auto must be used more than 50% for business travel. In 1992, the top deduction may not exceed $2,760. If business use is less than 100% but more than 50%, the $2,760 limit is reduced. For example, if you use the auto 80% for business, the top deduction is $2,208 ($2,760 × 80%). If you elect first-year expensing in 1992, you may not use the IRS mileage allowance in later years for travel in that car. In 1993, you may claim MACRS depreciation, applying the second-year MACRS rate to your original basis reduced by the first-year deduction claimed in 1992; *see* ¶43.5.

Auto used for business and personal driving

You may deduct only the amount allocated to business mileage. For example, total mileage is 20,000 miles in 1992 and your business mileage is 15,000 miles. You may claim only 75% of your deductible costs (15,000/20,000).

Tax return reporting

If you are an *employee*, you claim actual auto expenses or the IRS allowance on Form 2106. Form 2106 requires you to list mileage for business, commuting, and other personal trips. If your auto costs are not reimbursed by your employer, you must deduct them as miscellaneous deductions subject to the 2% AGI floor on Schedule A.

If you are *self-employed*, you deduct business costs on Schedule C and use Form 4562 to compute depreciation if you claim actual operating costs. Costs deducted on Schedule C are not limited by the 2% AGI floor.

Interest on a car loan and taxes. See ¶43.2 for when a deduction is allowed.

First-Year Election Affects Later Years

In deciding whether to elect the allowance in the first year, consider not only whether you will get a bigger first-year deduction using the allowance, or deducting actual operating costs plus depreciation, but also project your mileage, operating expenses, and depreciation expenses over the years you expect to use the car. If in the first year you elect to deduct actual costs and MACRS or elect straight-line recovery, you may not use the IRS auto allowance for *that car* in a later year. On the other hand, claiming the IRS allowance in the first year you put a car in service forfeits your privilege to use MACRS and first-year expensing. If you switch from the allowance to deducting actual expenses in later years, you may claim straight-line depreciation if the car is not considered fully depreciated.

Mileage allowance disallowed. You may not claim the allowance if:

1. You deducted actual operating costs, including MACRS or first-year expensing, or straight-line depreciation, in the first year you used the car for business.
2. You have depreciated your car using a depreciation method other than the straight-line method.
3. You use in your business two or more cars simultaneously, such as in a fleet operation.
4. You use your car for hire. That is, you use it as a taxicab, carrying passengers for a fare.
5. You lease the car.

EXAMPLES 1. In 1992, you place in service a new auto costing $15,000 and use it only for business. You travel 20,000 miles on business trips. If you claim the allowance, your deduction is $5,600 (20,000 × 28 cents). If you claim actual costs, your depreciation deduction is limited to $2,760; *see* ¶43.3. To match the IRS allowance, you need actual operating costs (gas, oil, maintenance) of at least $2,840. If these costs exceed $2,840, it is advisable to claim your actual expenses plus depreciation. Moreover, in 1993, you may deduct depreciation of up to $4,400 in addition to operating costs.

2. Same facts as Example 1, but you travel only 9,600 business miles. If you elect the allowance, you may deduct only $2,688. If you elect to deduct actual costs, your depreciation deduction of $2,760 by itself exceeds the allowance. Assume your operating costs are $1,500. Your total deduction is $4,260 and exceeds the allowance.

If you use more than one automobile in your business travel and elect the allowance, total the business mileage traveled in both cars.

EXAMPLE You use one car primarily for business and occasionally your spouse's car for business trips. During the taxable year, on business trips, you drove your car 10,000 miles; your spouse's car, 2,000 miles. Total business mileage is 12,000 miles.

Rural mail carriers allowed higher auto mileage rate. U.S. Postal Service mail carriers who use their cars to deliver and collect mail on rural routes may deduct a mileage rate equal to 150% of the basic rate. As the basic rate is 28 cents per mile, the special allowance is 42 cents per mile and applies to all rural delivery mileage.

Important: See *the Supplement for 1993 changes to the allowance rates.*

Employer reimbursements. If your employer reimburses your auto costs at a rate lower than the IRS allowance, you may use the IRS rate to deduct the excess over your employer's reimbursement; *see* Example 3 at ¶20.36.

IRS allowance includes depreciation. When you use the IRS allowance, you may not claim a separate depreciation deduction. The IRS mileage allowance includes an estimate for depreciation. However, for purposes of figuring gain or loss on a disposition, you must reduce the basis of the car according to the following rates: 7 cents per business mile for 1980—1981; 7.5 cents per mile for 1982; 8 cents per mile for 1983—1985; 9 cents per mile for 1986; 10 cents per mile for 1987; 10.5 cents per mile for 1988; 11 cents per mile for 1989, 1990, and 1991 and 11.5 cents for 1992. For years before 1990, the annual cents-per-mile reduction applies only to the first 15,000 miles of business use per year for which the IRS allowance was claimed.

Depreciation when switching from allowance to actual costs. If you use the IRS mileage allowance in the first year, you may switch to the actual cost method in a later year, but depreciation must be based on the straight-line method over the remaining estimated useful life. However, no depreciation may be claimed if basis has been reduced to zero under the annual cents-per-mile reduction rule just discussed.

AUTO EXPENSE ALLOCATIONS

¶43.2 If you do not claim the IRS mileage allowance, you may deduct car expenses on business trips such as the cost of gas and oil (including state and local taxes), repairs, parking, and tolls.

If you use your car exclusively for business, all of your operating expenses are deductible. However, if you are an employee, the deduction is limited by the 2% AGI floor; *see* ¶19.1.

Apportioning car expenses between business and personal use. For a car used for business and personal purposes, deduct only the depreciation and expenses allocated to your business use of the car. Depreciation is discussed at ¶43.3, ¶43.4, and ¶43.5.

The business portion of car expenses is determined by the percentage of mileage driven on business trips during the year.

EXAMPLE In 1992, you drove your car 15,000 miles. Of this, 12,000 miles was on business trips. The percentage of business use is 80%:

$$\frac{\text{Business mileage}}{\text{Total mileage}} = \frac{12,000}{15,000} = 80\%$$

Your actual car expenses (gas, oil, repairs, etc.) for the year were $1,000, of which $800 ($1,000 × 80%) is deductible. If you are an employee, the $800 is deductible as a miscellaneous itemized deduction subject to the 2% AGI floor; *see* ¶19.1.

Interest on car loan. Interest paid on a car loan is deductible as follows: If you are an *employee*, all of the interest, regardless of the allocation percentage, is considered personal interest and is not deductible. If you are *self-employed*, the business percentage of the interest is fully deductible on Schedule C; the personal percentage is not deductible.

Taxes on purchase. Sales tax is not deductible whether you are an employee or self-employed; the tax is added to the basis of the auto for depreciation purposes; *see* ¶43.3. State and local property taxes are deductible as itemized deductions on Schedule A if you are an employee. If self-employed, deduct the business portion of the property taxes on Schedule C; the personal percentage on Schedule A if you itemize.

Leased car. If you lease a car for business use, you deduct the rental fee plus other costs of operating the car. If the car is also used for personal driving, the rental fee must be allocated between business and personal mileage. *See* also ¶43.11 for rules requiring the reporting of extra income attributable to the lease.

AUTO DEPRECIATION RESTRICTIONS

¶43.3 The law contains restrictions that limit and, in some cases, deny depreciation deductions for a business car. Employees may be unable to claim any deduction at all under an employer convenience test. Employees meeting that test and self-employed individuals must determine if they can use MACRS rates or must use straight-line rates. Finally, regardless of which depreciation method is used, the annual deduction may not exceed a ceiling set by law. For a car placed in service in 1992, the ceiling is $2,760; *see* ¶43.4 for details on the annual ceilings.

Employer convenience test. If you are an employee and use your own car for work, you must be ready to prove that you use a car for the *convenience of your employer* who requires you to use it in your job. If you do not meet this employer-convenience test, you may not claim depreciation or first-year expensing. A letter from your employer stating you need the car for business will not meet this test.

The facts and circumstances of your use of the car may show that it is a condition of employment. For example, an inspector for a construction company uses his automobile to visit construction sites over a scattered area. The company reimburses him for his expenses. According to the IRS, the inspector's use of the car is for the convenience of the company and is a condition of the job. However, if a company car were available to the inspector, the use of his own car would not meet the condition of employment and convenience of the employer tests.

More-than-50% business-use test for claiming MACRS depreciation. An automobile is considered "listed property" as explained in ¶42.10, whether you are an employee or are self-employed. As such, you may claim MACRS for a car placed in service during 1992 only if you use it in 1992 more than 50% of the time for business. MACRS rates are discussed at ¶43.5. First-year expensing also may be claimed only if business use exceeds 50%; *see* ¶42.3.

If business use is *50% or less* in the year the auto is placed in service, first-year expensing and MACRS is barred; the auto is depreciable over a six-year period under the straight-line method. Technically, the recovery period is five years but the period is extended to six years because in the first year, a convention rule limits the deductible percentage. *See* the straight-line rate tables at ¶43.6. The straight-line method must also be used in future years, even if business use in those years exceeds 50%.

If a car is used for both business and investment purposes, only business use is considered in determining whether you meet the more than 50% business use and therefore qualify for MACRS. However, if your business use does exceed 50%, investment use is added to business use in determining your actual deduction.

EXAMPLE Brown buys an automobile for $30,000 and placed it in service in 1992. He uses it 40% for business and 20% for investment activity. Because he does not use his car more than 50% in his business, he may not claim MACRS. He figures depreciation using the straight-line method. The business use allocation rate for depreciation is 60% (40% for business use plus 20% investment use).

Trucks and other vehicles. The more-than-50% business-use test generally applies to vehicles other than automobiles such as trucks, vans, boats, motorcycles, airplanes, and buses. However, the test does not apply to taxicabs and other vehicles used substantially all of the time to transport persons or property for hire. The test also does not apply to vehicles that are exempt from record-keeping requirements under ¶43.10 such as a school bus, dump truck, farm tractor or other specialized farm vehicle, delivery truck with seating only for the driver or with a folding jump seat, flat bed truck, garbage truck, passenger bus with capacity of at least 20, refrigerated truck, combine, specialized utility repair truck, unmarked law enforcement vehicle officially authorized for use, and a moving van if personal use is limited by the employer to travel from the employee's home to a move site. A vehicle not in this list is subject to the more-than-50% test for claiming MACRS depreciation or first-year expensing. If you do not satisfy the more-than-50% test, you must apply the straight-line recovery rates shown at ¶43.6.

Do your employees use the car? In certain cases, an employer who provides a company car to employees as part of their compensation may be unable to count the employee's use as qualified business use, thereby preventing the employer from meeting the more-than-50% business test for claiming MACRS. An employer is allowed to treat the employee's use as qualified business use only if: (1) the employee is not a relative and does not own more than 5% of the business; and (2) the employer treats the fair market value of the

employee's personal use of the car as wage income and withholds tax on that amount. If such income is reported, all of the employee's use, including personal use, may be counted by an employer as qualified business use.

If an employee owning more than a 5% interest is allowed use of a company car as part of his compensation, the employer may not count that use as qualified business use, even if the personal use is reported as income. The same strict rule applies if the car is provided to a person who is related to the employer.

Recapture of MACRS Deductions

If you meet the more-than-50% test in the year the car or other vehicle is placed in service but business use falls to 50% or less in a later year, the recapture rules discussed at ¶43.9 apply.

ANNUAL CEILINGS ON DEPRECIATION

¶43.4 For cars placed in service after 1986, annual ceilings limit the amount of depreciation you may deduct. The ceilings apply both to self-employed individuals and employees. As a result of the ceilings, the actual write-off period for your car may be several years longer than the minimum recovery period of six years (¶43.5).

If the ceiling is less than the amount of depreciation figured under the regular MACRS rules, you are limited to the ceiling amount. For example, if in 1992 you bought a car for $20,000 which you used 100% for business, the regular MACRS rules would allow a deduction of $4,000 in 1992 (20% x $20,000), assuming the half-year convention applied; *see* ¶43.5. However, your 1992 depreciation deduction is limited to $2,760, the ceiling for cars placed in service duing 1992. The ceiling is reduced if you use the car for both personal and business driving as discussed on page 411.

You may not exceed the ceiling by claiming first-year expensing (¶42.3). The $2,760 limit for cars placed in service in 1992 also applies to the first-year expensing deduction. Thus, the first-year expensing deduction in 1992 may not exceed $2,760. If you claim first-year expensing of $2,760, you may not deduct any other depreciation. Claiming first-year expensing on Form 4562 (if self-employed) or Form 2106 (if an employee) may provide a larger deduction than regular MACRS depreciation where your deduction is subject to the mid-quarter convention; *see* ¶43.5.

The table below shows the year-by-year ceilings for cars placed in service between 1987 and 1992.

Annual Depreciation Ceiling for Cars Placed in Service After 1986

Ceiling In—	For Auto Placed in Service in —					
	1987	1988	1989	1990	1991	1992
1987	$2,560					
1988	4,100	$2,560				
1989	2,450	4,100	$2,660			
1990	1,475	2,450	4,200	$2,660		
1991	1,475	1,475	2,550	4,200	$2,660	
1992	1,475	1,475	1,475	2,550	4,300	2,760
1993	1,475	1,475	1,475	1,475	2,550	4,400
1994	1,475	1,475	1,475	1,475	1,575	2,650
1995 and later years	1,475	1,475	1,475	1,475	1,575	1,575

Personal driving reduces the annual ceiling. The annual ceilings are reduced if you use a car for both personal and business use. The reduced ceiling is equal to the regular ceiling multiplied by the percentage of business use. For example, in 1992, you buy a car costing $40,000. You use the car 70% for business travel. The MACRS deduction is limited to $1,932 ($2,760 × 70%). Furthermore, for purposes of figuring whether depreciation is allowed after the end of the recovery period, the basis of the car is reduced by the amount of the depreciation that would have been allowed if you had used the car 100% for business travel.

Ceilings for cars placed in service before 1987. The luxury car ceilings for cars placed in service after June 18, 1984, and before 1987, vary depending on when the car was placed in service.

For cars placed in service—	Current ceiling—
Before 6/19/84	None
After 6/18/84 and before 1985	$6,000
After 1984 and before 4/3/85	$6,200
After 4/2/85 and before 1987	$4,800

Light trucks and vans subject to the ceilings. The annual depreciation ceilings apply only to "passenger automobiles." For this purpose, a passenger automobile is generally considered to be any four-wheeled vehicle that is manufactured primarily for use on public streets, roads, and highways and that is weight-rated by the manufacturer at 6,000 pounds or less when unloaded (without passengers or cargo). However, a light truck or van that is weight-rated by the manufacturer at 6,000 pounds or less when loaded (gross vehicle weight) is treated as a passenger automobile.

The following are not considered "passenger" automobiles and thus are exempt from the annual ceilings: (1) an ambulance, hearse, or combination ambulance-hearse used directly in a business; or (2) a vehicle such as a taxicab used directly in the business of transporting persons or property for compensation or hire.

MACRS RATES FOR CARS

¶**43.5** Business autos placed in service in 1987 and later years are technically in a five-year MACRS class, but because of the half-year or mid-quarter convention and the annual deduction ceilings, the minimum depreciation period is six years.

MACRS rate. To use MACRS or first-year expensing, you must meet the more-than-50% business use test explained at ¶43.3. If you do, the MACRS rate is based on the 200% declining balance method with a switchover to straight line. The declining balance rate for a car that is five-year property is 40%. However, the full amount of the deduction is not allowed, because of the convention rules and the annual car limits discussed in this section. As explained in ¶42.5, each year the declining balance rate of 40% is applied against the declining balance of the basis of property.

As a shortcut, you may apply the half-year convention rates shown in the next column, or the mid-quarter convention rates shown on page 412, whichever applies in your case. The rates are applied against unadjusted basis, which is your cost minus any first-year expensing deduction. The deduction may not exceed the annual ceiling for auto depreciation, multiplied by the percentage of business use; *see* Example 2 on page 412.

Straight-line election for car if business use exceeds 50%. If business use of your car exceeds 50%, you may elect to write off your cost under the straight-line method instead of using the regular MACRS 200% declining balance method. The straight-line rates are shown in ¶43.6. The straight-line deduction is limited by the annual ceilings shown in ¶43.4. By electing straight-line depreciation, you avoid the recapture of excess MACRS deductions if busi-

ness use drops to 50% or less in a later year; *see* ¶43.9. If the election is made, you must also use the straight-line method for all other five-year property placed in service during the same year as the car.

Electing 150% rate. The rates shown in this section for the half-year and mid-quarter convention are based on the 200% declining balance method. You may instead elect to apply a 150% declining balance rate. The 150% rate may be advantageous when you are subject to alternative minimum tax (AMT); *see* ¶42.8.

Half-year or mid-quarter convention. Regardless of the time of year you bought the car in 1992, your deduction is limited by a convention rule. If the only business equipment bought in 1992 was the car, then the half-year convention applies, unless you bought the car in the last quarter of 1992 (October, November, or December). Under the half-year convention, the car is treated as if it were placed in service in the middle of the year and the 40% declining balance rate is reduced to 20%. Use the table on page 412 to determine your deduction under the half-year convention.

If the only business equipment bought in 1992 was a car bought in the last quarter (October, November, or December), the mid-quarter convention applies. Under the table on page 412 for mid-quarter convention rates, a 5% rate applies for fourth-quarter property, subject to the $2,760 deduction ceiling in 1992.

If you bought other business equipment in addition to the car, you must consider the total cost bases of property placed in service during the last quarter of 1992. If the total bases of such acquisitions (other than realty) exceed 40% of the total bases of all property placed in service during the year, then a mid-quarter rate applies to all property (other than realty). The mid-quarter rate for each asset then depends on the quarter the asset was placed in service. If the 40% test is not met, then the half-year convention applies to all of the property acquisitions. As shown in the mid-quarter convention table, mid-quarter rates for each year of the recovery period depend on the quarter the property is placed in service.

MACRS Deduction: Half-Year Convention

Year—	Lower of percentage below or annual ceiling*—
1	20.00%
2	32.00
3	19.20
4	11.52
5	11.52
6	5.76

*The annual ceiling for the year depends on the year the car was placed in business service. For cars placed in service in 1992, the ceiling on 1992 returns is $2,760. As the table on page 410 shows, the ceiling on 1992 returns is $4,300 if the car was placed in service in 1991; $2,550 if placed in service in 1990; and $1,475 if placed in service in 1989, 1988 or 1987.

If your car is not used 100% for business in 1992, multiply the business-use percentage by the applicable ceiling and compare the result to the deduction figured by multiplying the business-use portion of the unadjusted basis (cost minus first-year expensing) of the car by the rate in the above table. Your deduction is the lower amount; *see* Example 2 on page 412.

EXAMPLES 1. In May 1992, you place in service a car used 100% in business. The car cost $20,000. Here is the depreciation schedule assuming the car is kept for the period shown below and is used 100% for business trips:

1992	$2,760
1993	4,400
1994	2,650
1995	1,575
1996	1,575
1997	1,152
1998	1,575
1999	1,575
2000	1,575
2001	1,163

2. Assume you use the car only 60% for business. You deduct $1,656 in 1992, which is 60% of the annual limit of $2,760. Your deduction may not be based on 60% of depreciable basis; this would give a larger deduction of $2,400 ($20,000 × 60% business use × 20% first-year depreciation rate) without considering the first-year deduction limit.

MACRS Deduction: Mid-Quarter Convention*

	Placed in service in—			
Year	First Quarter	Second Quarter	Third Quarter	Fourth Quarter
1	35.00%	25.00%	15.00%	5.00%
2	26.00	30.00	34.00	38.00
3	15.60	18.00	20.40	22.80
4	11.01	11.37	12.24	13.68
5	11.01	11.37	11.30	10.94
6	1.38	4.26	7.06	9.58

*If business use is 100%, you deduct the *lower* of the annual ceiling (see table on page 410) *or* the applicable mid-quarter rate multiplied by the unadjusted basis (cost less any first-year expensing deduction). If business use is less than 100%, multiply the lower amount by the business use percentage to get the allowable deduction.

EXAMPLE In November 1992, you buy a car for $23,000 that you use 100% for business. Applying the 5% rate for the fourth quarter from the above table, your deduction is $1,150 ($23,000 × 5%). This is less than the ceiling of $2,760.

If the car had been bought in May 1992, the 25% rate for the second quarter would give a deduction of $5,750 ($23,000 × 25%). However, your deduction would be limited to the $2,760 ceiling.

Mid-Quarter Rate Limitation

If the application of the mid-quarter convention limits your deduction in the first year to less than $2,760, consider an election to claim the first-year expensing deduction at ¶42.3 if your business use percentage exceeds 50%. This may allow you to deduct up to $2,760, as in the following example.

EXAMPLE In December 1992, you place in service an auto used solely for business. It costs $25,000. Applying the fourth-quarter rate of 5% gives a depreciation deduction of only $1,250. If you elect first-year expensing, the deduction is $2,760.

Capital improvements. A capital improvement to a business auto is depreciable under MACRS in the year the improvement is made. The MACRS deductions for the improvement and auto are considered as a unit for applying the limits on the annual MACRS deduction.

Basis reduced by depreciation. The basis of a car is reduced by the full amount of depreciation that is allowable. Thus, if you use the car less than 100% for business, the unadjusted basis of the car is reduced by the depreciation that would have been allowed for 100% use. Basis is not reduced by the depreciation actually allowed.

Converting a pleasure car to business use. The basis for depreciation is the lower of the market value of the car at the time of conversion or its adjusted basis, which is your original cost plus any substantial improvements and minus any deductible casualty losses or diesel fuel tax credit claimed for the car. In most cases, the value of the car will be lower than adjusted basis, and thus the value will be your depreciable basis. For a car converted to business use in 1992, the MACRS rate is applied to basis allocated to business travel. Unless you have mileage records for the entire year, you should base your business use percentage on driving after the con-

version. For example, in April 1992, you started to use your car for business and in the last nine months of the year you drove 10,000 miles, 8,000 of which were for business. This business percentage of 80% is multiplied by the fraction 9/12 (months used for business divided by 12) to give you a business use percentage for the year of 60% (9/12 of 80%).

STRAIGHT-LINE RATE FOR BUSINESS USE OF 50% OR LESS

¶43.6 You may not use MACRS if your business use of your car is 50% or less. The following charts list mandatory straight-line recovery rates for business use of 50% or less using the half-year or mid-quarter convention. These straight-line rates are also used if you elect straight-line recovery (¶43.5) instead of the regular MACRS method. Because of the half-year convention, the straight-line recovery period is extended from five to six years.

The annual depreciation ceilings of ¶43.4 apply.

Straight-Line Year—	Half-year convention Rate—
1	10%
2	20
3	20
4	20
5	20
6	10

EXAMPLE In April 1992, you place in service an automobile which cost $15,000. You used it 40% for business. The depreciable basis is $6,000 (40% of $15,000). The depreciation deduction in 1992 is $600 (10% of $6,000) if the half-year convention applies.

If the mid-quarter convention applies (¶43.5), the depreciation deduction depends on the quarter the car was placed in service.

Straight-Line Mid-Quarter Convention*

	Placed in service in—			
Year	First Quarter	Second Quarter	Third Quarter	Fourth Quarter
1	17.50%	12.50%	7.50%	2.50%
2	20.00	20.00	20.00	20.00
3	20.00	20.00	20.00	20.00
4	20.00	20.00	20.00	20.00
5	20.00	20.00	20.00	20.00
6	2.50	7.50	12.50	17.50

* The deduction may not exceed the annual deduction ceiling; *see* ¶43.5.

EXAMPLE In 1992, you place in service a car costing $15,000 used 40% in business. Assume the mid-quarter convention applies. Depending on the applicable quarter, the deduction is listed below, figured on a basis of $6,000 ($15,000 × 40%). The first-year ceiling at 40% business use is $1,104 ($2,760 × 40%). The limit does not apply because the mid-quarter rates provide a lower deduction.

Quarter	Deduction
1	$1,050 ($6,000 × 17.5%)
2	750 ($6,000 × 12.5%)
3	450 ($6,000 × 7.5%)
4	150 ($6,000 × 2.5%)

DEPRECIATION FOR AUTOS PLACED IN SERVICE BEFORE 1987

¶43.7 If the car was placed in service before June 18, 1984, and was used 100% for business, you have fully depreciated the auto. If you used the car less than 100% for business, you may continue to take ACRS deductions if the percentage of business use (and investment use) exceeds the average business (and investment) use in the first three years. If you show such an increase, the car is treated as placed in service at the start of the taxable year in which the increased use occurs. The first-year ACRS rate is applied, but the deduction is limited by the percentage of increased business use. Basis for this new period is the lower of fair market value at the beginning of the new recovery period or the unadjusted cost basis of the car. ACRS rates: for the first year, 25%; second year, 38%; and third year, 37%.

If your car was placed in service after June 18, 1984, and if in the first three years business use was 100%, any remaining basis, which was not deductible because of the annual ceilings, may be depreciated up to the applicable ceiling until basis is written off. For example, if the car was placed in service after 1984 but before April 3, 1985, the annual deduction may be as high as $6,200 until basis is written off. If placed in service in 1985 but after April 2, 1985, or in 1986, the top deduction may be as high as $4,800. The top deduction is $6,000 if placed in service after June 18, 1984, and before 1985.

If the car was used less than 100% for business, any unrecovered basis may be deductible, but to determine unrecovered basis, original basis must be reduced by the depreciation that would have been allowed had the car been used 100% for business.

Note: Where an auto was depreciated under ACRS or alternative (straight-line) ACRS, no depreciation deduction is allowed in the year the auto is sold or traded for another auto.

TRADE-IN OF BUSINESS AUTO

¶43.8 No gain or loss is recognized on a trade-in of a business auto. Generally, the basis of the new auto is the adjusted basis of the old auto *plus* any additional payment. However, if you trade in an auto acquired after June 18, 1984, and it was not used solely for business, basis for figuring MACRS for the new auto is subject to a reduction. To find the basis of the new car, you start with the basis of the car that was traded in, add any cash paid on the trade-in and reduce the total by the excess, if any, of (1) the total depreciation that would have been allowable if the old auto had been used solely for business or investment, over (2) the total of the depreciation actually allowed.

EXAMPLES 1. You traded in a car with an adjusted basis of $5,000 for a new car and, in addition, paid $8,000 cash for the new car. Both cars are used 100% for business. The unadjusted basis of the new car is $13,000 ($5,000 adjusted basis of the old car *plus* the $8,000 cash paid).

2. In 1990, you bought a car for $20,000 and used it 80% for business in 1990 and 1991. In January 1992, you traded it in for a new car and paid an additional $11,000.

In 1990, you deducted MACRS depreciation of $2,128 (80% of $2,660 ceiling) and in 1991, $3,360 (80% of $4,200 ceiling). Your basis for purposes of figuring 1992 MACRS depreciation is $24,140, figured as follows.

Adjusted basis of old car	
Cost	$20,000
Less: depreciation	5,488
Adjusted basis of old car	$14,512
Basis of new car	
Adjusted basis of old car	$14,512
Cash paid for new car	11,000
	$25,512
Less: depreciation adjustment*	1,372
Basis of new car	$24,140

*Depreciation adjustment for partial use:	
Depreciation if 100% business use	
1990	$2,660
1991	4,200
	$6,860
Less: actual depreciation	5,488
Adjustment	$1,372

RECAPTURE OF DEDUCTIONS ON BUSINESS AUTO

¶43.9 If you use your car more than 50% for business in the year you place it in service, you may use MACRS accelerated rates; *see* ¶43.5. If business use drops to 50% or less in the second, third, fourth, fifth, or sixth year, earlier MACRS deductions must be recaptured and reported as ordinary income. In the year in which business use drops to 50% or less, you must recapture excess depreciation for all prior years. Excess depreciation is the difference between: (1) the MACRS deductions allowed in previous years, including the first-year expensing deduction, if any; and (2) the amount of depreciation that would have been allowed if you claimed straight-line depreciation based on a six-year recovery period. *See* ¶43.6 for straight-line rates.

The recapture rules do not apply if you elected straight-line recovery instead of applying accelerated MACRS rates.

Recapture is computed on Form 4797, which must be attached to Form 1040. The 50% business use test and recapture rule applies to trucks and airplanes in addition to cars, but *see* the list of exceptions for taxicabs and other specialty vehicles at ¶43.3.

Any recaptured amount increases the basis of the property. To compute depreciation for the year in which business use drops to 50% or less and for later years within the six-year straight-line recovery period, you apply the straight-line rates shown at ¶43.6.

EXAMPLE On June 25, 1989, you bought a car for $11,000 which you used exclusively for business in 1989, 1990, and 1991. During 1992, you used it 40% for business and 60% for personal purposes. In 1992, as you did not meet the more-than-50% use test, excess depreciation of $2,332 is recaptured and reported on Form 4797:

Total MACRS depreciation claimed (1989–1991)		$7,832
Total straight-line depreciation allowable:		
1989—10% of $11,000	$1,100	
1990—20% of $11,000	2,200	
1991—20% of $11,000	2,200	5,500
Excess depreciation recaptured		$2,332

Your 1992 depreciation deduction is $880 ($11,000 x 20% straight-line rate in fourth year x 40% business use).

The amount of recaptured depreciation increases the adjusted basis for purposes of computing gain or loss on a disposition of the automobile.

KEEPING RECORDS OF BUSINESS USE

¶43.10 Keep a log or diary or similar record of the business use of a car. Record the purpose of the business trips and mileage covered for business travel. In the record book, also note the odometer reading for the beginning and end of the taxable year. You need this data to prove business use. If you do not keep written records of business mileage and your return is examined, you will have to convince an IRS agent of your business mileage through oral testimony. Without written evidence, you may be unable to convince an IRS agent that you use the car for business travel or that you meet the business use tests for claiming MACRS. You may also be subject to general negligence penalties for claiming deductions that you cannot prove you incurred.

Mileage records are not required for vehicles that are unlikely to be used for personal purposes such as delivery trucks with seating only for the driver or with a folding jump seat, flat bed trucks, dump trucks, garbage trucks, passenger buses (capacity of at least 20), school buses, ambulances or hearses, tractors and other specialized farm vehicles, combines, marked police or fire vehicles, unmarked law enforcement vehicles that are officially authorized for use, and moving vans if personal use is limited by the employer to travel from an employee's home to a move site.

Furthermore, unless the IRS provides otherwise in regulations, mileage records are not required for taxicabs or other vehicles that are used substantially all of the time for transporting persons or property for hire.

Employees using company cars are not required to keep mileage records if (1) a written company policy allows them to use the car for commuting and no other personal driving other than personal errands while commuting home, or (2) a written company policy bars all personal driving except for minor stops for lunch between business travel. Control employees such as more than 1% owners, employees earning at least $100,000, directors, and officers earning at least $50,000 do not qualify for exception (1) concerning commuting use.

LEASED BUSINESS AUTOS: DEDUCTIONS AND INCOME

¶43.11 If you lease rather than purchase a car for business use, you may deduct the lease charges as a business expense deduction if you use the car exclusively for business. If you also use the car for personal driving, you may deduct only the lease payments allocated to business travel. Also keep a record of business use; *see* ¶43.10.

Added income. If in 1992 you lease for 30 days or more a car valued at over $14,000, you must treat as income an amount based on an IRS table. This income rule indirectly limits deductions of lease payments to the amounts that would be deductible as depreciation if you had bought the car outright. The income amount is reduced where you leased the car for less than the entire year or business use is less than 100%. See below for an example and a sample from the IRS table showing the 1992 income amount for a car leased in 1992.

The full table, which is in IRS Publication 917, shows income amounts for each year of the lease. For cars valued between $13,700 and $14,000, the table shows a small amount as income in future lease years although there is no income amount for 1992. Publication 917 also has tables showing income amounts for cars leased before 1992.

EXAMPLE You leased a car on January 20, 1992, for three years. The car was valued at $25,500 on the first day of the lease. Assuming you use the car 80% for business in 1992, the income amount for 1992 is $75, figured as follows: table amount of $99 × 80% business use × 94.81% (347 lease days in 1992 ÷ 366) = $75.

If you are self-employed, your deduction for lease payments is reduced by $75 on Schedule C. If you are an employee, lease payments are reduced by $75 on Form 2106.

Cars Leased in 1992

Fair market value of automobile Over—	Not over—	Income amount (before reduction)	Fair market value of automobile Over—	Not over—	Income amount (before reduction)
$14,000	$14,300	$ 3	$26,000	$27,000	$107
14,300	14,600	5	27,000	28,000	116
14,600	14,900	8	28,000	29,000	124
14,900	15,200	11	29,000	30,000	133
15,200	15,500	13	30,000	31,000	141
15,500	15,800	16	31,000	32,000	150
15,800	16,100	18	32,000	33,000	158
16,100	16,400	21	33,000	34,000	167
16,400	16,700	23	34,000	35,000	175
16,700	17,000	26	35,000	36,000	184
17,000	17,500	29	36,000	37,000	192
17,500	18,000	33	37,000	38,000	200
18,000	18,500	38	38,000	39,000	209
18,500	19,000	42	39,000	40,000	217
19,000	19,500	46	40,000	41,000	226
19,500	20,000	50	41,000	42,000	234
20,000	20,500	55	42,000	43,000	243
20,500	21,000	59	43,000	44,000	251
21,000	21,500	63	44,000	45,000	260
21,500	22,000	67	45,000	46,000	268
22,000	23,000	74	46,000	47,000	277
23,000	24,000	82	47,000	48,000	285
24,000	25,000	90	48,000	49,000	293
25,000	26,000	99	49,000	50,000	302

44 SALES OF BUSINESS PROPERTY

The tax treatment of sales of business property is cluttered with technicalities imposed by rules that attempted to reduce capital gain opportunities. Although capital gains do not currently receive favored tax treatment, other than the ceiling of 28% discussed at ¶5.1, the technical rules of Section 1231 and the recapture provisions of Sections 1245 and 1250 still apply.

If gain on the sale of depreciable property is attributable to prior depreciation deductions, the gain is taxed as ordinary income under the recapture provisions of Section 1245 and Section 1250. The treatment of losses and gains related to appreciation in value are determined by Section 1231.

You report sales of business property on Form 4797 which incorporates the computation requirements of Sections 1231, 1245, and 1250.

RECAPTURE OF DEPRECIATION ON SALE OF PROPERTY

¶44.1 On Form 4797, you report gain or loss on depreciable property. Gain realized on the sale of depreciable personal property is treated as ordinary income to the extent the gain is attributed to depreciation deductions that reduced basis. In other words, the depreciation deductions are "recaptured" as ordinary income. If gain exceeds the amount of depreciation subject to recapture, the excess may be treated as capital gain under a Section 1231 computation; see ¶44.8. Gain on the sale of real estate placed in service before 1987 may be subject to recapture as discussed in this section.

Personal property (Section 1245 property). Adjusted basis of personal property depreciable under ACRS, such as business equipment and machinery, is fixed as of the beginning of the year of disposition. However, property depreciated under MACRS is subject to the convention rules so that partial depreciation under the applicable convention is allowed in the year of sale; this year of sale depreciation reduces adjusted basis. Gain on the sale is taxed as ordinary income (Form 4797) to the extent of allowable depreciation.

Where basis was reduced by an investment credit for property placed in service after 1982, the basis reduction is treated as a depreciation deduction when figuring recapture; see Form 4797.

Gain subject to recapture for Section 1245 property is limited to the lower of (1) the amount realized less adjusted basis; or (2) recomputed basis less the adjusted basis. Recomputed basis is adjusted basis increased by depreciation deductions allowed or allowable.

Generally, the depreciation deduction taken into account for each year is the amount allowed or allowable, whichever is greater. For purposes of assigning ordinary income (but not for purposes of figuring gain or loss), the depreciation deductions taken into account for any year will be the amount "allowed" rather than the amount "allowable," if the allowed deduction is smaller and you can prove its amount.

How the Sale of Business Property Is Taxed

The following checklist summarizes how sales of assets and property used in business are taxed.

Sales of—	Tax treatment—
Merchandise, stock in trade, etc.	Profits are taxable as ordinary income; losses are fully deductible. Sales of merchandise are reported on Schedule C if you are self-employed.
Machinery, buildings, office equipment, fixtures, van, truck, and other business property subject to depreciation	If you sell at a gain, the gain is taxable as ordinary income to the extent depreciation is recaptured under ¶44.1. Any remaining gain may be treated as capital gain or ordinary income, depending on the Section 1231 computation at ¶44.8. Losses may be deductible as ordinary or capital losses under the rules of ¶44.8. Sales are reported on Form 4797. Technically, depreciable business equipment subject to recapture is described as Section 1245 assets. Depreciable livestock are also Section 1245 assets. Depreciable realty is generally described as Section 1250 assets. Recapture provisions do not apply to realty placed in service after 1986 and subject to MACRS straight-line depreciation.
Land	If used in your business, capital gain or ordinary income may be realized under the rules of Section 1231; see ¶44.8. If land owned by your business is held for investment, gain or loss is subject to capital gain treatment. Sales of capital assets are reported on Schedule D.

EXAMPLE In 1990, you placed in service equipment (five-year property) costing $10,000. In 1990 you deducted depreciation of $2,000 and in 1991 you deducted $3,200. In January 1992, you sell it for $6,000. The MACRS deduction allowed for 1992, the year of sale, is $960 (19.20% × $10,000 ÷ 2). The adjusted basis is $3,840 ($10,000 − $6,160 total depreciation). Recomputed basis is $10,000 ($3,840 + $6,160). The amount of recapture is the lower of—

1. $6,160, the recomputed basis of $10,000, less adjusted basis of $3,840; or

2. $2,160, the amount realized of $6,000, less adjusted basis of $3,840.

The lower amount of $2,160 is recaptured as ordinary income on Form 4797.

Dispositions other than sales. Exchanges of property (¶6.1), involuntary conversions (¶18.19), and corporate distributions may result in recapture of depreciation. For distributions which are not sales, exchanges, or involuntary conversions, the amount of recapture is all depreciation claimed, but not in excess of the difference between fair market value at disposition or original cost, whichever is less, and adjusted basis.

Real property. For real property placed in service after 1981 and before 1987 that was subject to ACRS, adjusted basis for computing gain or loss is the adjusted basis at the start of the year reduced by the ACRS deduction allowed for the number of months the realty is in service in the year of disposition; see ¶42.14. Realty subject to MACRS after 1986 is not subject to recapture.

Nonresidential pre-1987 ACRS recovery period building. If the prescribed accelerated method is used to recover the cost of nonresidential property, all gain on the disposition of the realty is recaptured as ordinary income to the extent of recovery allowances previously taken. Thus, nonresidential realty will be treated the same as personal property for purposes of recapture if the accelerated recovery allowance is claimed. If the straight-line method is elected, there is no recapture. All gain is capital gain subject to the netting rules of Section 1231; see ¶44.8.

If accelerated cost recovery is used for a nonresidential building and straight-line depreciation is used for a substantial improvement to that building which you are allowed to depreciate separately (¶42.14), all gain on a disposition of the entire building is treated as ordinary income to the extent of the accelerated cost recovery claimed; remaining gain is capital gain taxed under the rules for Section 1231 assets (¶44.8).

Residential pre-1987 ACRS recovery period building. Gain is ordinary income to the extent the depreciation allowed under the prescribed accelerated method exceeds the recovery that would have been allowable if the straight-line method over the ACRS recovery period had been used. If the straight-line method was elected, there is no recapture. All gain is capital gain, subject to Section 1231 netting; see ¶44.8.

Pre-1987 ACRS 15-year low-income rental housing. The same rule as for residential realty applies except that recapture is phased out at the rate of one percentage point per month for property held at least 100 months, so that there is no recapture of cost recovery deductions for property held at least 200 months (16 years, 8 months).

Pre-1981 realty; see ¶44.2.

RECAPTURE ON DEPRECIABLE REALTY IN SERVICE PRE-1981

¶44.2 Real property for recapture purposes (Section 1250) includes buildings and structural components, *except* for elevators and escalators or other tangible property used as an integral part of manufacturing, production, or extraction, or of furnishing transportation, electrical energy, water, gas, sewage disposal services, or communications. Property may initially be Section 1250 property and then, on a change of use, become Section 1245 property. Such property may not be reconverted to Section 1250 property.

EXAMPLE A company builds a parking lot for its employees. Five years later, it converts the lot into a loading area for its trucks. The parking lot, which was originally Section 1250 property, is now Section 1245 property.

General recapture pattern on Form 4797. The amount of recapture depends on the rate of depreciation claimed, the length of time you held the property, and the type of realty. Recapture applies only to rapid depreciation claimed after 1969 in *excess* of the amount allowed under the straight-line method. The amount actually recaptured will vary, depending upon whether the property is residential or nonresidential realty, low-income housing, or rehabilitation expenditures. The special rules relating to low-income housing and rehabilitation expenditures are not discussed in this book; *see* IRS Publication 544.

Depreciation claimed on realty during the years 1964 through 1969. Depreciation claimed during this period is not recaptured.

Depreciation claimed after 1969. For nonresidential realty, one hundred percent of the excess depreciation claimed after 1969 is subject to recapture, but not in excess of the actual gain. For residential realty, this percentage is reduced, depending on the holding period, for depreciation claimed from 1970 through 1975. For this period, the amount subject to recapture on residential property is reduced 1% per month for each month the property is held beyond 100 months. Only full months are counted; see table below.

Real property is considered residential realty for periods after 1975 if 85% or more of gross income is from dwelling units. For periods before 1976, the gross income test was 80% or more.

1970–1975 Percentage Reductions for Residential Realty

Held—	%	Held—	%
Up to 100 months	100	156 months (13 years)	44
108 months (9 years)	92	168 months (14 years)	32
120 months (10 years)	80	180 months (15 years)	20
132 months (11 years)	68	192 months (16 years)	8
144 months (12 years)	56	200 months (16 years, 8 months) or longer	0

Special recapture rules not discussed here apply to property under certain financial arrangements sponsored by the National Housing Act or similar state or local laws.

Special recapture rules not discussed here also apply to separate elements of improvements.

RECAPTURE OF FIRST-YEAR EXPENSING

¶44.3 On Form 4797, the first-year expensing deduction under ¶42.3 is treated as depreciation for purposes of recapture. When expensed property is sold or exchanged, gain is ordinary income to the extent of the first-year expense deduction plus ACRS or MACRS deductions, if any; see ¶44.1.

Expensing deductions are also subject to recapture if property placed in service after 1986 is not used more than 50% of the time for business in any year before the end of the recovery period. The amount recaptured is the excess of the first-year *expensing* deduction *over* the amount of depreciation that would have been claimed in prior years and in the recapture year without expensing.

Automobiles and other "listed property." If the more-than-50% business-use test for a business automobile or other "listed property" such as certain computers (see ¶42.10) is not met in a year after the auto or other "listed property" is placed in service and before the end of the recovery period, any first-year expensing deduction is subject to recapture on Form 4797; see the example at ¶43.9.

Installment sale. If you sell property on the installment basis, the first-year expensing deduction claimed for the property in a prior year is recaptured in the year of sale on Form 4797. An installment sale does not defer recapture of the first-year deduction.

LEASEHOLD IMPROVEMENTS

¶44.4 Leasehold improvements placed in service after 1986 are not subject to recapture as depreciation is determined by MACRS rules; see ¶9.7. However, a disposition of leasehold improvements placed in service before 1987 may be subject to recapture. To determine the recaptured amount, the lease period for figuring what would have

been the straight line depreciation and for figuring the additional depreciation includes all periods for which the lease may be renewed, extended, or continued under an option, exercisable by the lessee. However, the inclusion of renewal periods may not extend the lease by more than two-thirds of the period that was the basis on which the actual depreciation was allowed.

Recapture on a disposition of an acquired lease is also determined by these renewal rules.

GIFTS AND INHERITANCES OF DEPRECIABLE PROPERTY

¶44.5 Gifts and charitable donations of depreciable property may be affected by the recapture rules. On the gift of depreciable property, the ordinary income potential of the depreciation carries over into the hands of the donee. When the donee later sells the property at a profit, he or she will realize ordinary income to the extent described in ¶44.1. For purposes of the applicable percentage, the person receiving the gift includes in the holding period the period for which the donor held the property.

On the donation of depreciable property, the amount of the contribution deduction is reduced by the amount which would be taxed as ordinary income had the donor sold the equipment at its fair market value.

On the death of a decedent, the transfer of depreciable property to an heir through inheritance is not a taxable event for recapture purposes. The ordinary income potential does not carry over to the heir because his basis is usually fixed as of the date of the decedent's death.

Important: A gift of depreciable property subject to a mortgage may be taxed to the extent that the liability exceeds the basis of the property; see ¶14.6 and ¶31.10.

INVOLUNTARY CONVERSIONS AND TAX-FREE EXCHANGES

¶44.6 **Involuntary conversions.** Gain may be taxed as ordinary income in either of the following two cases: (1) You do not buy a qualified replacement; or (2) you buy a qualified replacement, but the cost of the replacement is less than the amount realized on the conversion. See ¶18.23. The amount taxable as ordinary income may not exceed the amount of gain that is normally taxed under involuntary conversion rules when the replacement cost is less than the amount realized on the conversion. Also, the amount of ordinary income is increased by the value of any nondepreciable property which is bought as a qualified replacement property, such as the purchase of 80% or more of stock in a company that owns property similar to the converted property.

Tax-free exchanges. Ordinary income generally is not realized on a tax-free exchange or trade-in (unless some gain is taxed because the exchange is accompanied by "boot" such as money). The ordinary income potential is assumed in the basis of the new property.

Distributions by a partnership to a partner. A distribution of depreciable property by a partnership to a partner does not result in ordinary income to the distributee at the time of the distribution. But the partner assumes the ordinary income potential of the depreciation deduction taken by the partnership on the property. When he or she later disposes of the property, ordinary income may be realized.

INSTALLMENT SALE OF DEPRECIABLE PROPERTY

¶44.7
If you report on an installment basis a profitable sale of depreciable property made before June 7, 1984, "recaptured" ordinary income is reported before any of the capital gain is reported. You do not allocate the profit element of each installment payment between ordinary income and capital gain. As installments are received, you report all of the ordinary income until that amount is exhausted.

For a sale after June 6, 1984, all recaptured ordinary income is fully taxable in the year of sale, without regard to the time of payment. However, this rule does not apply to installment sales made under a contract binding on March 22, 1984, and all times thereafter.

Recapture is figured on Form 4797.

PROPERTY USED IN A BUSINESS (SECTION 1231 ASSETS)

¶44.8
Form 4797 is used to report the sale or exchange of Section 1231 assets. The following properties used in a business are considered "Section 1231 assets."

Depreciable assets such as buildings, machinery, and other equipment held more than one year.

Land (including growing crops and water rights underlying farmland) held more than one year.

Timber, coal, or domestic iron ore subject to special capital gain treatment.

Leaseholds held more than one year.

An unharvested crop on farmlands, if the crop and land are sold, exchanged, or involuntarily converted at the same time and to the same person and the land has been held more than one year. Such property is not included here if you retain an option to reacquire the land.

Cattle and horses held for draft, breeding, dairy, or sporting purposes for at least 24 months.

Livestock (other than cattle and horses) held for draft, breeding, dairy, or sporting purposes for at least 12 months. Poultry is not treated as livestock for purposes of Section 1231.

Capital Gain or Ordinary Loss

Profitable sales and involuntary conversions of Section 1231 assets are generally taxed as capital gain, except for profits on equipment and real estate allocated to depreciation (¶44.1), and losses are deducted as ordinary loss. However, the exact tax result depends on the net profit and loss realized for all sales of such property made during the tax year. Under the netting rules explained below, the net result of these sales determines the tax treatment of each individual sale. In making the computation on Form 4797, you must consider also losses and gains from casualty, theft, and other involuntary conversions involving business and investment property held more than one year.

Section 1231 netting. On Form 4797, you combine all losses and gains, except gains allocated to depreciation recapture, from:

Sale of Section 1231 assets (listed above).

The involuntary conversion of Section 1231 assets and capital assets held long term for business or investment purposes. You include casualty and theft losses incurred on business or investment property held long term, whether or not insured. However,

there is an exception if losses exceed gains from casualties or thefts in one taxable year, as discussed below.

Involuntary conversions of capital assets held for personal purposes are not subject to a Section 1231 computation but are subject to a separate computation; *see* ¶18.25.

For an explanation of the ordinary income treatment of gain attributed to depreciation, *see* ¶44.1.

Result of netting. A net gain on Section 1231 assets is entered on Schedule D as a long-term capital gain unless the recapture rule discussed below for net ordinary losses applies. A net loss on Section 1231 assets is combined on Form 4797 with ordinary income from depreciation recapture (¶44.1) and with ordinary gains and losses from the sale of business property that does not qualify for Section 1231 netting.

Recapture of net ordinary losses. Net Section 1231 gain is not treated as capital gain but as ordinary income to the extent of net Section 1231 losses realized in the five most recent prior taxable years. Losses are recaptured in chronological order on Form 4797. Losses that have already been "recaptured" under this rule in prior years are not taken into account.

Installment sale. Gain realized on the installment sale of business or income-producing property held long term may be long-term gain one year and ordinary gain another year. Actual treatment in each year depends on the net result of all sales, including installment payments received in that year; also *see* ¶44.7.

EXAMPLES 1. You realize these gains and losses:

	Gain	Loss
Gain on sale of rental property held two years	$5,000	
Loss on sale of business assets held four years		$3,000
	$5,000	$3,000
Net gain treated as long-term capital gain	$2,000	

As your gain exceeded the loss, each sale is treated as a sale of a capital asset held for a long-term period. The net gain is included in Schedule D along with your other long-term gains and losses, if any. The effect of this treatment is to give you a long-term capital gain of $2,000, unless you realized a net Section 1231 loss in 1987, 1988, 1989, 1990, or 1991.

2. Assume the same facts as above, but your gain on the sale of rental property was $2,500. Since the gain does not exceed the loss and a net loss of $500 was realized, all of the transactions are treated as dispositions of noncapital assets. The net result is an ordinary loss of $500.

Losses exceed gains from casualties or thefts. You must compute the net financial result from all involuntary conversions arising from fire, storm, shipwreck, or other casualty or theft of assets used in your business and capital assets held for business or income-producing purposes and held more than one year. The purpose of the computation is to determine whether these involuntary conversions enter into the above Section 1231 computation. If the net result is a gain, all of the assets enter into the Section 1231 computation. If the net result is a loss, then these assets do not enter into the computation; the losses are deducted separately as casualty losses, and the gains reported separately as ordinary income. If you incur only losses, the losses similarly do not enter into the Section 1231 computation.

EXAMPLE You suffer an uninsured fire loss of $2,000 on equipment used in your business and gain of $1,000 on other insured investment property damaged by a storm. All of the property was held more than one year. Because loss exceeds gain, neither transaction enters into a Section 1231 computation. The gain is reported as ordinary income and the loss is deducted as an ordinary loss. The effect is a net $1,000 loss deduction. If the figures were reversed, that is, if the gain was $2,000 and the loss $1,000, both assets would enter into the Section 1231 computation. If they are the only two transactions in the year, the net effect may be a net capital gain of $1,000. If only the fire loss had occurred, the loss would be treated as a casualty loss and would not enter into the Section 1231 computation.

SALE OF A BUSINESS

¶44.9 **Proprietorship.** The sale of a sole proprietorship is not considered as the sale of a business unit but as sales of individual business assets. Each sale is reported separately on your tax return.

A purchase of a business involves the purchase of various individual business assets of the business. Under prior law, the seller would generally assign a larger portion of the sales price to capital assets such as goodwill to realize capital gain. The buyer would assign a larger part of the sale price to inventory and deductible costs items in order to get larger current deductions. To force buyers and sellers to follow the same allocation rules, current law requires both the buyer and the seller to allocate the purchase price of a business among the transferred assets using a residual method formula. Generally, under the formula, the sales price is first allocated to the assets other than goodwill and going concern value. Allocations are based on the proportion of sales price to an asset's fair market value and allocations are made in the following order: first allocate selling price to cash, demand deposits, and similar accounts; then to certificates of deposit, U.S. government securities, marketable stock or securities, and foreign currency; and finally to other assets, except goodwill and going concern value. Any balance of the selling price is allocated to goodwill. Both the buyer and seller must show the allocation on Form 8594 and attach it to their tax return for the year of the sale. For further details, *see* the instructions to Form 8594 and Temp. Reg. Sec. 1.1060—IT.

The current law applies to an "applicable asset acquisition," which is a sale of a group of assets considered a business in which the basis of assets of the business are determined by the price paid for the business. A group of assets is considered a business if their character is such that goodwill or going concern value could, under any circumstances, attach to the assets.

Capital Asset

Assets Held Long Term—	Yes	No
Customer's accounts		x
Inventory and supplies and stock in trade		x
Stocks and bonds held as investments	x	
Machinery, building, and other equipment used in your business	x*	
Land used in business	x	
Good will and nondepreciable franchises	x	
Depreciable franchises		x
Copyrights by a playwright of dramatic works		x
Literary manuscripts, etc., of a playwright		x
Assignable liquor license	x	
Noncompete contract (officer or employee)		x
Life insurance policy	x	

*See ¶44.8 for the rule governing assets used in business. It is possible to get a full deduction for a net loss on a sale or treat net gain as long-term capital gain; but gain allocated to depreciation may be taxed as ordinary income (¶44.1).

Partnership interests. A sale of a partnership interest generally gives capital gain. But you have ordinary income to the extent the sales price covers unrealized partnership receivables, appreciated inventory items, and depreciation "recapture" on assets held by the partnership.

Unrealized receivables include any partnership rights to payment for goods delivered or services rendered that have not yet been included in the partnership income under its regular accounting method. Appreciated inventory items are those whose value is more than 120% of the partnership's basis for them *and* more than 10% of the fair market value of all the partnership's property (except cash).

To compute the amount of ordinary income when you sell out, part of the basis of your partnership interest must be allocated to the interest in the receivables, inventory, and depreciation recapture items. You must attach a statement to your return showing the allocation of basis to receivables and inventory. Furthermore, you must notify the partnership within 30 days of transferring a partnership interest that includes unrealized receivables or appreciated inventory. The partnership in turn notifies the IRS. *See* Chapter 45 for these reporting rules.

If you contributed appreciated property to the partnership, you are taxed on the pre-contribution appreciation if the partnership sells the property. If the property is distributed to other partners and you contributed the property before October 4, 1989, you are not taxed. However, if the property was contributed after October 3, 1989, and within five years of your contribution, the property is distributed to other partners, you will realize gain or loss on the distribution, unless you receive like-kind property, generally within a 180-day period. *See* time limits for completing like-kind exchanges at ¶6.4. This rule also applies to a person who buys your interest. You are not taxed on a distribution to you of property that you contributed.

Poor timing of the sale of your partnership interest may be costly if the partnership reports on a fiscal year basis. In the year of sale, you may bunch more than a year of partnership income. The sale of a partnership interest closes the partnership year for the selling partner. Thus, in the year that you sell out, you must report your share of earnings up to the time of sale, in addition to the earnings from the regular partnership fiscal year. A sale of only a partial interest does not close your partnership tax year.

Amortization for Intangibles

At the time this book went to press, Congress was considering legislation to allow an amortization deduction for certain intangible assets including goodwill, covenants not to compete, franchises, trademarks, and customer lists. *See* the Supplement for an update.

COVENANTS NOT TO COMPETE AND SALE OF GOODWILL

¶44.10 Payments for the sale of business goodwill are subject to capital gain treatment. If, along with the sale of goodwill, a covenant not to compete is also given, the amount allocated to the covenant is subject to capital gain treatment if the covenant is given to protect the transferred goodwill. If the covenant is not tied to goodwill, the payments received for the covenant are taxed as ordinary income. Payments for a noncompete covenant are treated as a form of compensation—that is, compensation not to perform services.

Professionals (lawyers, accountants, engineers, consultants, etc.) have goodwill in their firm names, which when sold is treated as a sale of a capital asset. This is true even if the seller remains a member of the firm after the sale, provided goodwill is shown and the incoming partner has paid for part of it. According to the IRS, a consultant is subject to self-employment tax, even if he or she may not compete for other employers because of a covenant not to compete; *see* Chapter 46.

See the Law Alert in ¶44.9 for pending legislation that would allow an amortization deduction for amounts paid to the seller under a covenant not to compete.

SALE OF SECURITIES PURCHASED TO PROTECT BUSINESS INTERESTS

¶44.11 To protect a business interest, you may purchase securities of a company, or you may make the purchase of the securities to guarantee the supply of merchandise produced by the company. Under such circumstances, you might want to argue that your securities are not capital assets. You might take this position when you sell the securities at a loss or when they become worthless. The loss would be fully deductible as an ordinary loss rather than a capital loss. In some cases, courts allowed such treatment. However, the Supreme Court has foreclosed ordinary loss treatment by holding that capital loss treatment applies, unless the asset is specifically excluded from the definition of capital assets such as inventory.

SALE OF PROPERTY FOR BUSINESS AND PERSONAL USES

¶44.12 One sale will be reported as two separate sales for tax purposes when you sell a car or any other equipment used for business and personal purposes, or a house used partly as a residence and partly as a place of business or to produce rent income.

You allocate the sales price and the basis of the property between the business portion and the personal portion. The allocation is based on use. For example, with a car, the allocation is based on mileage used in business and personal driving.

Other references: Allocation on sale of a partly rented residence; *see* ¶29.10. Trade-in of car; *see* ¶43.8. Recapture of depreciation; *see* ¶44.1.

SHOULD YOU TRADE IN BUSINESS EQUIPMENT?

¶44.13 The purchase of new business equipment is often partially financed by trading in old equipment. For tax purposes, a trade-in may not be a good decision. If the market value of the equipment is below its adjusted basis, it may be preferable to sell the equipment to realize an immediate deductible loss. You may not deduct a loss on a trade-in. However, if you do trade, the potential deduction reflected in the cost basis of the old equipment is not forfeited. The undepreciated basis of the old property becomes part of the basis of the new property and may be depreciated. Therefore, in deciding whether to trade or sell where a loss may be realized, determine whether you will get a greater tax reduction by taking an immediate loss on a sale or by claiming larger depreciation deductions.

If the fair market value of the old equipment exceeds its adjusted basis, you have a potential gain. To defer tax on this gain, you may want to trade the equipment in for new equipment. Your decision to sell or trade will generally be based on a comparison between (1) tax imposed on an immediate sale and larger depreciation deductions taken on the cost basis of the new property, and (2) the tax consequences of a trade-in in which the tax is deferred but reduced depreciation deductions are taken on a lower cost basis of the property. In making this comparison, you will have to estimate your future income and tax rates. Also pay attention to the possibility that gain on a sale may be taxed as ordinary income under the depreciation recapture rules; *see* ¶44.1.

The tax consequences of a trade-in may not be avoided by first selling the used property to the dealer who sells you the new property. The IRS will disregard the sale made to the same dealer from whom you purchase the new equipment. The two transactions will be treated as one trade-in.

When you trade in a car used partly for business and partly for pleasure, treat the deal as if you had exchanged and received two different types of assets: a personal asset and a business asset. Allocate part of the costs of the old and new car to your business use and part to your personal use. Figure the results on each part. Trade-in rules for a business auto are discussed at ¶43.8.

45

REPORTING PARTNERSHIP, S CORPORATION, AND FARM INCOME

Income or loss from partnerships and S corporations is reported on Schedule E. However, if you have a loss and are not a material participant in the activity, you must compute your allowable loss on Form 8582; the loss is subject to the passive activity restrictions detailed in Chapter 10. Most limited partners are subject to the loss restrictions.

An S corporation election allows an incorporated business to avoid payment of corporate income taxes while providing the owners with the legal advantages of the corporate form, such as limited liability. S corporation shareholders are taxed on their share of the corporation's income, deductions, losses, and tax credits. The rules for making an S election and the tax reporting rules are explained in this chapter.

PARTNERSHIP INCOME

HOW PARTNERS REPORT PARTNERSHIP PROFIT AND LOSS

¶**45.1** A partnership files Form 1065, which informs the IRS of partnership profit or loss and each partner's share on Schedule K. The partnership pays no tax on partnership income; each partner reports his or her share of partnership net profit or loss and special deductions and credits, whether or not distributions are received from the partnership as shown on Schedule K-1. Income that is not distributed or withdrawn increases the basis of a partner's partnership interest.

Your share reported to you on Schedule K-1 (Form 1065) is generally based on your proportionate capital interest in the partnership, unless the partnership agreement provides for another allocation.

Your partnership must give you a copy of Schedule K-1 (Form 1065) which lists your share of income, loss, deduction, and credit items and where to report them on your return. For example, your share of income or loss from a business or real estate activities is reported on Schedule E and is subject to passive activity adjustments, if any. Interest and dividends are reported on Schedule B, royalties on Schedule E, and capital gains and losses on Schedule D. Your share of charitable donations is claimed on Schedule A if you itemize deductions. Tax preference items for alternative minimum tax purposes are also listed.

Health insurance premiums. A partnership that pays premiums for health insurance for partners has a choice. It may treat the premium as a reduction in distributions to the partners. Alternatively, it may deduct the premium as an expense and charge each partner's share as a guaranteed salary payment taxable to the partner. The partner reports the amount shown on Schedule K-1 as nonpassive income on Schedule E and may deduct 25% of the amount as health insurance on Line 26, Form 1040.

When this book went to press, the 25% deduction was allowed only for premiums paid before July 1, 1992, for coverage before that date. However, Congress was expected to extend the deduction to premiums paid after June 30, 1992; see the Supplement for an update on the extension legislation.

Partnership Elections

The partnership, not the individual partners, makes elections affecting the computation of partnership income such as the election to defer involuntary conversion gains, to amortize organization and start-up costs, and to choose depreciation methods, including first-year expensing. An election to claim a foreign tax credit is made by the partners.

Guaranteed salary and interest. A guaranteed salary which is fixed without regard to partnership income is reported as ordinary income. If you receive a percentage of the partnership income with a stipulated minimum payment, the guaranteed payment is the amount by which the minimum guarantee exceeds your share of the partnership income before taking into account the minimum guarantee.

Interest on capital is reported as interest income.

Self-employment tax. You pay 1992 self-employment tax on up to $130,200 of your partnership profits, including a guaranteed salary and other guaranteed payments. Limited partners do not pay self-employment tax, unless guaranteed payments are received; *see* Chapter 46.

Special allocations. Partners may agree to special allocations of gain, income, loss, deductions, or credits disproportionate to their capital contributions. The allocation should have a substantial economic effect to avoid an IRS disallowance. The IRS will not issue an advance ruling on whether an allocation has a substantial economic effect. If the allocation is rejected, a partner's share is determined by his or her partnership interest.

To have substantial economic effect, a special allocation must be reflected by adjustments to the partner's capital account; liquidation proceeds must be distributed in accordance with the partners' capital accounts, and following a liquidating distribution, the partners must be liable to the partnership to restore any deficit in their capital.

If there is a change of partnership interests during the year, items are allocated to a partner for that part of the year he or she is a member of the partnership. Thus, a partner who acquires an interest late in the year is barred from deducting partnership expenses incurred prior to his entry into the partnership. If the partners agree to give an incoming partner a disproportionate share of partnership losses for the period after he becomes a member, the allocation must meet the substantial economic effect test to avoid IRS disallowance.

See IRS regulations to Code Section 704, IRS Publication 541, and Form 1065 instructions for further details.

Reporting transfers of interest to IRS. If you transfer a partnership interest that includes an interest in partnership receivables and appreciated inventory, you must report the disposition to the partnership within 30 days, or if earlier, by January 15 of the calendar year after the year of the transfer. The partnership in turn files a report with the IRS on Form 8308. You must also attach a statement to your income tax return describing the transaction and allocating

basis to the receivables and inventory items. The IRS wants to keep track of such dispositions because partners have to pay ordinary income tax on the portion of profit attributable to the receivables and inventory.

Gains on the sale or exchange of property between a partner and partnership, or between two partnerships, are treated as ordinary income if more than 50% of the capital or profits interest is owned, directly or indirectly, by the same person or persons.

Within 30 days of your transfer, provide the partnership with a statement that includes the date of the exchange and identifies the transferee (include Social Security number if known). You can be penalized for failure to notify the partnership. You and your transferee should receive a copy of the Form 8308 which the partnership will send to the IRS along with its Form 1065.

Generally, the partnership must file a separate Form 8308 for each transfer but the IRS may allow a composite Form 8308 for the calendar year if there were at least 25 reportable transfers.

Contributions by and distributions to a partner made within a two-year period. These may be treated by the IRS as disguised sales. The partnership has the burden of proof of showing that such transactions within the two-year period are not sales. However, distributions of guaranteed payments for use of capital and cash flow distributions will not be considered sales proceeds related to a contribution of property. If a distribution is treated as sales proceeds but is less than the value of the contributed property, the balance is considered a contribution to partnership capital by the partner.

If a contribution and distribution within the two-year period is *not* treated as a sale on the partner's return, the partner must "disclose" that fact to the IRS on Form 8275 or a similar statement attached to the return.

Important: The discussion in ¶45.1—45.4 covers only the general features of partnership tax reporting. Specific partnership rules are complex and their implementation requires the services of an experienced tax practitioner. IRS Publication 541 has further information on partnership reporting.

Also see the Supplement for an update on pending legislation changes that would affect partnership reporting.

WHEN A PARTNER REPORTS INCOME OR LOSS

¶45.2

You report your share of the partnership gain or loss for the partnership year which ends in your tax reporting year. If you and the partnership are on a calendar year basis, you report your share of the 1992 partnership income on your 1992 income tax return. If the partnership is on a fiscal year ending March 31, for example, and you report on a calendar year, you report on your 1992 return your share of the partnership income for the whole fiscal year ending March 31, 1992—that is, partnership income for the fiscal year April 1, 1991, through March 31, 1992.

A partnership generally may use a fiscal year only if a business purpose supports its use. However, a newly organized partnership may elect a fiscal year that allows a deferral period to owners of no more than three months. This "Section 444" election is made on Form 8716. Form 8716 must be filed by the *earlier* of (1) the due date (without extensions) of the tax return for the elected fiscal year, which is the 15th day of the fourth month following the close of the elected year, *or* (2) the 15th day of the fifth month after the first month of the elected fiscal year. If a business purpose claim is made to support a fiscal year, a Section 444 election may be made as a "backup" in case the business purpose request is rejected by the IRS.

A calendar year partnership may not make a Section 444 election to change to a fiscal year. This is because the deferral period of the tax year that is being elected may not exceed the deferral period of the year being changed, which is zero for calendar year partnerships.

If a Section 444 election is made, a special tax payment must be computed for each fiscal year and if the computed payment exceeds $500, it must be paid to the IRS. The tax payment is figured and reported on Form 8752. The tax does not apply to the first year of a partnership's existence but Form 8752 must still be filed. In later years, a refund of prior payments is available to the extent the prior payments exceed the payment required for the current fiscal year. For example, if the required payment was $12,000 for the fiscal year July 1, 1992—June 30, 1993, and the required payment for the fiscal year starting July 1, 1993, is $10,000, a $2,000 refund may be claimed on Form 8752. Refunds of prior year payments also are available if the fiscal year election is terminated and a calendar year adopted or if the partnership liquidates.

PARTNERSHIP LOSS LIMITATIONS

¶45.3 Your share of partnership losses may not exceed the adjusted basis of your partnership interest. If the loss exceeds basis, the excess loss may not be deducted until you have partnership earnings to cover the loss or contribute capital to cover the loss. The basis of your partnership interest is generally the amount paid for the interest (either through contribution or purchase), *less* withdrawals plus accumulated taxed earnings that have not been withdrawn.

For partnership years beginning after September 18, 1988, the IRS does not allow a partner to increase basis by accrued but unpaid expenses such as interest costs and accounts payable. However, basis *is* increased by capitalized items allocable to future periods such as organization and construction period expenses.

Partners are subject to the "at risk" loss limitation rules. These rules limit the amount of loss that may be deducted to the amount each partner personally has at stake in the partnership such as contributions of property and loans for which the partner is personally liable. *See* ¶10.17 for a discussion of the "at risk" rules.

Furthermore, if the IRS determines that a tax shelter partnership is not operated to make a profit, deductions may be disallowed even where there is an "at risk" investment.

Finally, any loss not barred by these limitations may be disallowed under the passive activity rules discussed in Chapter 10.

UNIFIED TAX AUDITS OF PARTNERSHIPS

¶45.4 Tax audits of both a partnership of more than 10 partners and its partners must be at the partnership level. To challenge the partnership treatment of an item, the IRS must generally audit the partnership, not the individual partner. To avoid a personal audit of a partnership item, a partner should report partnership items as shown on the partnership return or identify any inconsistent treatment on his or her return. Otherwise, the IRS may assess a deficiency without auditing the partnership.

For a partnership level audit, the partnership names a "tax matters partner" (TMP) to receive notice of the audit. If one is not named, the IRS will treat as a TMP the general partner having the largest interest in partnership profits at the end of the taxable year involved in the audit. Notice of the audit must also be given to the other partners. All partners may participate in the partnership audit. If the IRS settles with some partners, similar settlement terms must be offered to the others.

Within 90 days after the IRS mails its final determination, the TMP may appeal to the Tax Court; individual partners have an additional 60 days to file a court petition if the TMP does not do so. An appeal may also be filed in a federal district court or the claims court if the petitioning partner first deposits with the IRS an amount equal to the tax that would be owed if the IRS determination were sustained. A Tax Court petition takes precedence over petitions filed in other courts. The first Tax Court petition filed is heard; if other partners have also filed petitions, their cases will be dismissed. If no Tax Court petitions are filed, the first petition filed in federal district court or the claims court takes precedence. Regardless of which petition takes precedence, all partners who hold an interest during the taxable year involved will be bound by the decision (unless the statute of limitations with respect to that partner has run out).

Partnerships with ten or fewer partners may elect to come within the unified audit procedures, provided all of the partners are individuals or estates.

S CORPORATION ELECTION

TAX ADVANTAGE OF S CORPORATION

¶45.5 An S corporation election allows an incorporated business to avoid paying income tax on corporate income, thus eliminating the double tax feature of corporate operations while retaining limited liability and other advantages of doing business as a corporation.

When Election Is Advisable

You will generally make an S election when your personal tax rates do not exceed the corporate tax rates, when you cannot take sufficient money out of a corporation without subjecting some or all of it to the double tax, or when a special advantage is offered by an S election. For example, in the early years of the corporation's existence, substantial losses are expected. The S election allows the pass-through of operating losses to stockholders who may have substantial income from other sources to offset these losses.

The S corporation files a return on Form 1120S, informing the IRS of corporate net earnings and losses and the stockholders' shares of income or loss items which they report on their personal tax returns. This tax reporting procedure is similar to that of partnerships.

An election is not advisable for an existing company which has an operating loss carryover. The loss may not be used by the corporation after the election and it may not be passed through to the stockholders. The loss may be revived if the election is terminated. Each year the election is in force counts as a year in figuring the carryover period, even though the loss has not been used.

Estimated tax. An S corporation must make estimated tax payments for the following taxes: tax on excess passive investment income (¶45.11); tax on built-in capital gains (¶45.8); and investment credit recapture (¶40.22). Payments are made with Form 8109 tax deposit coupons; *see* Form 1120S instructions.

Fiscal-year corporations. If the corporation reports on a fiscal year, the stockholders report their shares of corporate items on their tax returns for the year in which the corporate tax year ends.

A special election must be made to use a fiscal year; *see* ¶45.12.

Important: The following sections discuss general features of the S election, the implementation and review of which require the services of an experienced tax accountant or attorney. A detailed discussion of these issues along with the particular objectives of an election may be found in tax services dealing with corporate tax problems and in IRS Publication 589.

STOCKHOLDER REPORTING OF S CORPORATION INCOME AND LOSS

¶45.6 S corporations are subject to tax reporting rules similar to those applied to partnerships. However, shareholders who work for the corporation are treated as employees for FICA purposes. They do not pay self-employment tax on their salary income or other receipts from the corporation.

Allocation to shareholders. The following items are allocated to and pass through to the shareholders based on the proportion of stock held in the corporation:

Gains and losses from the sale and exchange of capital assets and Section 1231 property.

Interest and dividends on corporate investments and losses. Investment interest expenses subject to the rules of ¶15.9 also pass through.

Tax-exempt interest. Tax-exempt interest remains tax free in the hands of the stockholders but increases the basis of their stock. Dividends from other companies may qualify for the exclusion.

First-year expense deduction.

Charitable contributions made by the corporation.

Foreign income or loss.

Foreign taxes paid by the corporation. Each stockholder elects whether to claim these as a credit or deduction.

Tax preference items.

Recovery of bad debts and prior taxes.

If your interest changed during the year, your pro rata share must reflect the time you held the stock.

Reporting S Corporation Items

Your company must give you a copy of Schedule K-1 (Form 1120S) which lists your share of income or loss, deductions, and credits that must be reported on your return. For example, your share of business income or loss is reported on Schedule E and is subject to passive activity adjustments, if any. Interest and dividends from other corporations are reported on Schedule B, capital gains and losses on Schedule D, Section 1231 gains or losses on Form 4797, and charitable donations on Schedule A. Tax preference items for alternative minimum tax purposes are also listed. For reporting company payments of health premiums, *see* ¶45.10.

Basis limits loss deductions. Deductible losses may not exceed your basis in corporate stock and loans to the corporation. If losses exceed basis, the excess loss is carried over and becomes deductible when you invest or lend an equivalent amount of money to the corporation. This rule may allow for timing a loss deduction. In a year in which you want to deduct the loss, you may contribute capital to the corporation. If a carryover loss exists when an S election terminates, a limited loss deduction may be allowed.

Passive activity rules limit loss deductions. Losses allocated to you may be disallowed under the passive activity rules discussed at Chapter 10.

Expenses owed to related shareholders. An S corporation is

deemed to be on the cash method of accounting for purposes of deducting business expenses and interest owed to cash basis related shareholders. Therefore, expenses accruing to such stockholders are deductible only when paid to the stockholders.

EXAMPLE In 1991, a calendar-year S corporation accrues $5,000 of salary to a related employee-stockholder. It does not pay the salary until February 1992. In 1992, the $5,000 is deductible by the corporation and reported by the employee-stockholder as income.

Family Corporations

The IRS has the authority to change the amounts of items passed through to stockholders to properly reflect the value of services rendered or capital contributed by family members of one or more S corporation shareholders. If you are the member of a family of an S corporation shareholder and perform services or furnish capital to the corporation without receiving reasonable compensation, the IRS may reallocate salary or interest income to you from the other shareholders to reflect the value of your services or capital. The term "family" includes only a spouse, parents, ancestors, children, and any trusts for the benefit of such relatives.

Basis adjustments. Because of the nature of S corporation reporting, the basis of each stockholder's stock is subject to change. Basis is increased by the pass-through of income items and reduced by the pass-through of loss items and the receipt of distribution. Because income and loss items pass through to stockholders, an S corporation has no current earnings and profits. An income item will not increase basis, unless you actually report the amount on your tax return. The specific details and order of basis adjustments are listed in IRS Publication 589.

Allocating income and loss for changes in stock ownership during the year. In a year stock ownership changes, income and loss items are either allocated on a daily basis or all persons who were stockholders during the entire taxable year may elect to allocate income and loss items as if there were two short taxable years, the first year ending on the date the shareholder's interest ended. The allocation of items for each short taxable year is determined according to corporate records and work papers. The following examples illustrate how the allocation on a daily basis is made.

EXAMPLES 1. A calendar year corporation incurs a loss of $10,000. Smith and Jones each own 50% of the stock. On May 1, Smith sells all of his stock to Harris. For the year, Smith was a shareholder for 120 days, Jones for 365 days, and Harris for 245 days. The loss is allocated on a daily basis; the daily basis of the loss is $27.3973 ($10,000 divided by 365 days). The allocation is as follows:

Smith: $1,644 ($27.3973 × 120 days × 50% interest)
Jones: $5,000 ($27.3973 × 365 days × 50% interest)
Harris: $3,356 ($27.3973 × 245 days × 50% interest)

2. Same facts as in Example 1, except that on May 1, Smith sells only 50% of his stock to Harris. The allocation for Smith accounts for his 50% interest for 120 days and his 25% interest for the remainder of the year.

Smith: $3,322 ($27.3973 × 120 days × 50% *plus*
$27.3973 × 245 days × 25%)
Jones: $5,000 (as above)
Harris: $1,678 ($27.3973 × 245 days × 25%)

Stock Ownership Changes

In a year in which stock ownership changes, determine tax consequences both ways: using the daily allocation method and the method using two short periods. Choose the method providing the best overall tax benefit for the shareholders. Different tax results will occur, especially if substantial loss items were incurred in one short year and income items in the other short year. The daily allocation method will average the items between the two years. The short-period method basis will place the items in the period they were incurred.

QUALIFYING TESTS FOR AN S ELECTION

¶**45.7** The election may be made for a domestic corporation which is not a member of an affiliated group and which has—

1. No more than 35 stockholders, all of whom must agree to the election. For purposes of the stockholder test, a husband and wife (and their estates) are counted as one shareholder, regardless of how they hold the stock. However, when consenting to S corporation status, each spouse must consent separately. When spouses divorce, each spouse is treated as a separate stockholder, even though they own stock jointly.

For purposes of the stockholder test, each beneficiary of a voting trust is counted as a stockholder.

Each minor owning stock held by a custodian is counted. The minor, or his or her legal or natural guardian, must consent to the election. The same rule applies to incompetents.

Legislation being considered when this book went to press would increase the maximum number of stockholders to 50; see the Supplement for an update.

2. Stockholders who are either U.S. citizens or residents, estates, or certain trusts. You may not make the election if a non-approved trust, partnership, or another corporation owns stock in your company. The following trusts may be electing shareholders: (1) A trust all of which is treated for tax purposes as owned by an individual who is a U.S. citizen or resident. The trust may continue as a shareholder for a 60-day period following the death of the owner. If the entire corpus is includible in the deemed owner's gross estate, the trust may continue as a shareholder for a two-year period following the date of death. (2) A voting trust. (3) A testamentary trust which receives the stock under the terms of a will, but only for a 60-day period beginning on the day on which such stock is transferred to it. The creation of a bankruptcy estate by filing a petition for bankruptcy does not result in a non-qualified stockholding. And, (4) a qualified Subchapter S trust. A qualified trust is one in which all of the income is distributed currently to a beneficiary who is a U.S. citizen or resident and who has elected to have the trust qualify. There may be only one income beneficiary at any one time and a new election must be made for each successive income interest. Where the trust terminates during the life of the income beneficiary, all the assets must be distributed to that beneficiary. Trust shares that are treated as separate trusts by the tax law also qualify.

3. One class of stock. You may not make the election if your company has common and preferred stock. Differences in voting rights will not cause one class of stock to be treated as two classes. Only outstanding stock is counted in determining whether there is one class of stock. Treasury stock or unissued preferred stock of a different class does not disqualify the election.

The issuance of options and warrants to acquire its stock and convertible debentures does not disqualify the election.

Straight debt instruments bearing a reasonable interest rate are not treated as a second class of stock. Shareholder loans are treated as straight debt provided: (1) the loan is a written unconditional promise by the corporation to pay a specified sum on demand or on a set date; (2) the interest rate and payment date are not contingent on corporate profits or on the discretion of the corporation; and (3) the debt is not convertible into stock.

A corporation with an inactive subsidiary may make the election as long as the subsidiary has no gross income.

Under legislation being considered when this book went to press, an S corporation would be considered to have only one class of stock, and thus eligible for the S election, if all outstanding shares confer identical rights under state law to distributions and liquidation proceeds. Another proposal would allow an S corporation to own a subsidiary corporation, but prohibit it from being included in a consolidated return with affiliated corporations. See the Supplement for legislative developments.

FILING AN S ELECTION

¶**45.8** The corporation makes an election by filing Form 2553 with the IRS. All shareholders must sign written consents to the election in the space provided on Form 2553 or in an attached statement. If the election is made after the start of the first year for which the election is to be effective, consents must be filed by all shareholders who held interests *before* the date of election, even if they have sold their interests.

An election may be filed during the entire taxable year before the year in which the election is to be effective and before the 16th day of the third month of the taxable year to which the election applies. An election which is ineffective because of late filing is automatically effective in the following year. Even if the election is filed on time within the first two months and 15 days of the current year, the election will not take effect until the following year unless all those with shareholders' interests before the filing date consent to the election.

EXAMPLES 1. A calendar year corporation wants to elect S corporation status for 1993. It may file an election on Form 2553 any time during 1992 or on or before March 15, 1993.
If Form 2553 were filed after March 15, 1993, the election would take effect in 1994.

2. A Form 2553 filed by a calendar year corporation on March 11, 1993, does not contain the written consent of a shareholder who sold his interest in February 1993. The election will not take effect until 1994.

Note: Under legislation being considered by Congress when this book went to press, the IRS could waive a failure to make a timely election, as in Example 1, and allow a late election where there was reasonable cause for the delay. The IRS could also waive a failure to obtain proper consent, as in Example 2, if the failure was inadvertent; see the Supplement for a legislative update.

Once a valid election is made, it is effective for all following tax years, unless revoked or terminated under the rules of ¶45.9.

A valid election may not be filed before a corporation is formally incorporated. The first day of a tax year of a new corporation does not begin until one of these events occurs: It has shareholders, acquires assets, or begins doing business. However, if, under state law, corporate existence begins with filing articles of incorporation, even though the corporation has no assets and does not begin doing business until a later date, the first day of the tax year begins on the date of such filing.

Newly Organized Corporation

Usually, the first tax year of a newly organized corporation will be for a period less than 12 months. An election may be made for this short tax year as long as it is made before the 16th day of the third month of the corporation's first taxable year. If the first taxable year of a new corporation is for a period of less than two and a half months, the election may be made for that year within two and a half months from the beginning of the taxable year. The first taxable year begins when the corporation has shareholders, acquires assets, or begins doing business, whichever occurs first.

New stockholders. A new shareholder does not have to file any consent nor can he or she terminate the election. However, a majority stockholder may revoke the election; *see* ¶45.9.

Built-in-gains tax. If an S election is made by a C corporation—that is, one already in existence and subject to regular corporation tax—the S corporation may have to pay tax on the sale of appreciated property held by the company before the election. The gain must be reported by the S corporation if the property is sold or distributed within 10 years of the date of the S election. The rule applies to elections made after December 31, 1986, but not to S elections made before or on that date. Small qualifying S corporations that made an S election before 1989 may be able to avoid this built-in-gains tax if more than 50% of the stock is owned by 10 or fewer individuals, estates, or certain trusts, and the value of the corporation does not exceed $10 million. For further details, *see* Form 1120S and IRS Publication 589.

Corporations making S elections before 1987 are subject to the capital gains tax discussed at ¶45.13.

REVOCATION OR TERMINATION OF AN S ELECTION

¶45.9

An election may be revoked or may automatically terminate because the corporation no longer qualifies as an S corporation.

Revocation. Shareholders owning a majority of stock may agree to revoke the election by filing a statement of revocation. They may specify the future effective date of the revocation. If they do not fix a date, the revocation is effective on the first day of the taxable year in which the revocation is filed if filed on or before the 15th day of the third month of that year; if filed later in the year, the effective date is the first day of the following taxable year.

Termination. An election terminates when a company no longer qualifies under the rules of ¶45.7. A termination is effective as of the date the corporation no longer qualifies as an S corporation. The last day of the S corporation's short taxable year is the day before termination is effective; the day that termination is effective starts a short taxable year as a C corporation. A Form 1120S must be filed for the short S corporation year; a Form 1120 for the short C corporation year. The corporation's items of income and loss are allocated to the two short taxable years on a daily basis unless a unanimous election to have items assigned to the two short years under normal accounting rules is made by all of the persons who are shareholders in the corporation at any time during the S short taxable year and all persons who are shareholders on the first day of the C short year. For purposes of computing the corporate tax, the taxable income for the C short year must be annualized. This is true regardless of the method of allocation used for allocating income and loss items.

The pro rata allocation method may not be used if there is a sale or exchange of 50% or more of stock during the year of termination.

Choosing Allocation Method

It is important to determine tax consequences under the daily allocation method and the normal accounting method. Choose the method providing the best overall tax consequences for the shareholders reporting their allocated amounts for the short S corporation year and for the corporation reporting as a C corporation for the second short year. Different tax results will occur, especially if substantial loss items were incurred in one short year and income items in the other short year. The daily allocation basis will average these between the two years. The normal accounting allocation will place the items in the period they were incurred.

Election following termination. When the election is revoked or terminated, you may not make another election until the fifth year following the year in which the election was revoked or terminated, unless the IRS gives its consent. An exception to the five-year rule also applies to inadvertent termination (*see* below). The IRS will not consent to an election before the end of the five-year period if the termination is considered reasonably within the control of the corporation or controlling shareholders.

Inadvertent termination. If the IRS decides that the termination was inadvertent and steps are taken by the corporation to re-establish its qualified status within a reasonable time after discovering the disqualifying event, then the corporation is treated as an S corporation. The corporation and each shareholder must agree to adjustments required by the IRS.

TAX ON FRINGE BENEFITS RECEIVED BY STOCKHOLDERS

¶45.10

Owners of more than 2% of the stock will realize taxable income for receiving fringe benefit coverage such as in employee group insurance and accident and health plans.

Health Insurance Premiums

Health insurance premiums paid by an S corporation for more than 2% stockholders are treated as wages, deductible on Form 1120S by the corporation and reported to the stockholders on Form W-2.

A more than 2% shareholder who reports premiums as wages may claim the 25% health insurance deduction on Line 26, Form 1040. The 25% deduction was scheduled to expire June 30, 1992, but when this book went to press, Congress was considering legislation that would allow the deduction for premiums paid after June 30; *see* the Supplement.

PASSIVE INVESTMENT INCOME

¶45.11

A 34% tax may be imposed on an S corporation if at the end of the tax year it has accumulated earnings from taxable years prior to the election and its passive investment income exceeds 25% of gross receipts. Passive investment income includes dividends, interest, rents, royalties, and securities sale gains.

If a corporation does have accumulated earnings and passive

investment income exceeding 25% of gross receipts, a portion of the excess passive income is subject to tax. A worksheet included in the instructions to Form 1120S is used to compute the tax. The tax does not apply if the corporation has been an S corporation since the date of incorporation.

The IRS has authority to waive this tax where the corporation proves that it had determined in good faith that it did not have accumulated earnings and profits at the close of the taxable year, and the earnings and profits were distributed within a reasonable period of time after the corporation determined that it did have accumulated earnings and profits.

Caution. The S election may be terminated if for three consecutive years the company has prior accumulated earnings and passive investment income exceeding 25% of gross receipts.

FISCAL-YEAR RESTRICTIONS

¶45.12 S corporations must report on a calendar year basis unless a fiscal-year election is made. A fiscal year may be based on a business purpose. Alternatively, Code Section 444 allows a fiscal year that provides a deferral period to owners of no more than three months. On Form 2553, an electing S corporation makes a fiscal-year request based on a business purpose. If the corporation wants to make a Section 444 election, it indicates such intent on Form 2553, but the actual election is made on Form 8716. *See* the instructions to Form 2553 and Form 8716 for details on the fiscal-year election. Furthermore, if a Section 444 election is made, a special tax computation is required for each fiscal year. If the computed tax is over $500, it must be paid to the IRS on Form 8752. No tax is due for a newly formed corporation's first year of existence, but Form 8752 must be filed for that year. If payments for a prior year exceed the required payment for the current year, a refund for part of the prior payment may be obtained on Form 8752.

TAX ON CAPITAL GAINS

¶45.13 For corporations that made an S election before 1987, a special tax is imposed to prevent the use of the election for the pass-through of substantial capital gains. The tax applies if taxable income for the year exceeds $25,000 and the net capital gains exceed $25,000 and 50% of taxable income.

The tax may not apply to a corporation that has been an S corporation for the three preceding taxable years or to a new corporation that has been in existence for less than four years and has been an S corporation for that entire period. *See* instructions to Schedule D of Form 1120S for details.

The tax does not apply if the S election was made after 1986. However, such corporations are subject to the built-in gains tax discussed at ¶45.8.

AUDITS OF S CORPORATIONS AND SHAREHOLDERS

¶45.14 S corporations and shareholders are subject to audit rules similar to those for partnerships discussed in ¶45.4. These rules require the tax treatment of disputed items to be determined in a unified administrative proceeding at the corporate level rather than in separate proceedings with the individual shareholders. The IRS must give all shareholders notice of their right to participate in any corporate-level administrative proceeding.

Under an exception, corporate-level proceedings do not apply to S corporations with five shareholders or less, all of whom are individuals or estates. Husbands and wives are considered one person under this rule. S corporations with five or fewer shareholders may elect to come within the unified audit procedure by attaching a statement to the first S corporation return; the election is binding for all later years.

Legislation being considered by Congress when this book went to press would repeal the corporate-level audit rules; see the Supplement.

FARM INCOME AND LOSS

WHO IS A FARMER?

¶45.15 The term "farmer" includes all individuals, partnerships, syndicates, and corporations that cultivate, operate, or manage a farm for profit or gain, either as owners or tenants. Thus, partners in a partnership which operates a farm are considered farmers.

The term "farm" includes stock, dairy, poultry, fruit and truck farms, plantations, ranches, and all land used for farming operations. A fish farm where fish are specially fed and raised, and not just caught, is a farm. Animal breeding farms, such as mink, fox, and chinchilla farms, are also considered farms.

Farm loss deductions may also be restricted by at risk rules and passive activity rules of Chapter 10.

If your farm losses exceed your other income, *see* ¶40.17.

Important. A guide to reporting farm income and loss may be obtained at your local Internal Revenue office or from your County Farm Agent. It is called Farmer's Tax Guide (IRS Publication 225).

 Gentleman Farming

To be treated as farmers, individuals must be engaged in farming for gain or profit. Farm losses of part-time or "gentlemen" farmers may be disallowed on the grounds that the farm is not operated to make a profit but is a hobby. The hobby rules explained at ¶40.9 apply in determining the existence of a profit motive in farming operations. Favorable evidence of an intention to make a profit are: You do not use your farm just for recreation. You have tried to cut losses by switching from unsuccessful products to other types of farming. Losses are decreasing. Losses were caused by unexpected events. You have a bookkeeping system. You consult experts. You devote personal attention to the farm.

FORMS FARMERS FILE

¶45.16 Use Schedule F to report income from a farm you operate as an individual. The profit or loss computed on Schedule F is then included in Form 1040. Schedule F is also used as a basis for figuring self-employment tax on Schedule SE, which must also be filed with Form 1040. Sales of farm equipment and dairy or breeding livestock are reported on Form 4797.

If you operate through a partnership, the details of your farm operation are shown on Schedule F and Form 1065. Your share of the partnership net income or loss is included in Form 1040.

Individual farmers on a calendar year basis (ending December 31) may pay their entire 1992 estimated tax on Form 1040-ES by January 15, 1993, if at least two-thirds of 1992 estimated gross income is from farming, or if at least two-thirds of 1991 total gross income was from farming. A final return is required by April 15, 1993. However, you may file your final return by March 1, 1993, instead of making an estimated tax payment for 1992 in January 1993.

FARMERS' SOCIAL SECURITY

¶45.17 Farmers follow special rules for figuring their self-employment income and tax. If your gross income from farming is not more than $2,400, you may figure your self-employment income in either of two ways:

You may reduce your self-employment income by your allowable deductions (as any other self-employed person would do), and pay the self-employment tax on the difference; *or*

You may consider your net self-employment income from farming to be two-thirds of your gross farming income.

If your gross income from farming is more than $2,400 but your net self-employment income (figuring it in the usual manner by reducing gross income by the farm's expenses) is less than $1,733, you may treat $1,600 as your net farm self-employment income.

Self-employment tax on farm income is figured on Schedule SE. *See* also IRS Publication 225.

46

FIGURING SELF-EMPLOYMENT TAX

Self-employment tax provides funds for Social Security and Medicare benefits. In 1992, you receive a quarter of Social Security coverage, up to four quarters, for each $570 of self-employment income subject to self-employment tax.

You are liable for self-employment tax if you make a profit of $433.13 or more from operating a business or profession as a sole proprietor, in partnership with others, or as an independent contractor. It may also apply if you perform certain services; *see* table at ¶46.5. You continue to pay self-employment tax on self-employment income regardless of age and even if you receive Social Security benefits.

Self-employment tax is figured on Schedule SE, which is attached to your Form 1040.

You must include the self-employment tax when figuring your estimated tax (Chapter 27). Self-employment tax is added to your income tax liability. The two taxes are paid as one amount.

On Schedule SE, you apply the self-employment tax rates to net self-employment income reduced by a deduction built into the computation on Schedule SE. You also may deduct 50% of your self-employment tax on Line 25 of Form 1040.

The self-employment tax rate is made up of two rates: a 15.3% rate which applies to a taxable earnings base of $55,500 or less, and a 2.9% rate on a taxable earnings base exceeding $55,500 up to $130,200; *see* ¶46.3.

The tax on a taxable earnings base of $55,500 is $8,491.50 (15.3% x $55,500). For a taxable base between $55,500 and $130,200, the maximum 2.9% tax is $2,166.30. Thus, the self-employment tax on a taxable base of $130,200 or more is $10,657.80 ($8,491.50 + $2,166.30). Self-employment tax changes for 1993 are reported in the Supplement.

WHAT IS SELF-EMPLOYMENT INCOME?

¶46.1 On Schedule SE, your self-employment income is generally your net profit from your business or profession whether you participate in its activities full or part time. Net profit is generally the amount shown on Schedule C on Line 31 (or Line 3 of Schedule C-EZ) if you are a sole proprietor. If you are a partner, net earnings subject to self-employment tax are taken from Line 15a, Schedule K-1 of Form 1065. If you are a farmer, net farm profit is shown on Line 36, Schedule F.

If you have more than one self-employed operation, your net earnings from all the operations are combined. A loss in one self-employed business will reduce the income from another business. You file separate Schedules C for each operation and one Schedule SE showing the combined income (less losses if any). Also, you may not reduce your net profit by contributions to your *own* Keogh plan retirement account.

Married couples. Where you and your spouse *each* have self-employment income, each spouse must figure separate self-employment income on separate schedules. Each pays the tax on the separate self-employment income. Both schedules are attached to the joint return.

If you live in a community property state, business income is not treated as community property for self-employment tax purposes. The spouse who is actually carrying on the business is subject to self-employment tax on the earnings.

Exceptions. The following types of income or items are *not* included as self-employment income on Schedule SE:

1. Rent from real estate is not self-employment income, *unless* it is the business income of a real estate dealer or income in a business where substantial services are rendered to the occupant as in the leasing of—

Rooms in a hotel or in a boardinghouse.
Apartments, but only if extra services for the occupants' convenience, such as maid service or changing linens, are provided.
Cabins or cabanas in tourist camps where you provide maid services, linens, utensils, and swimming, boating, fishing, and other facilities, for which you do not charge separately.
Rents from the leasing of farmland in which the landlord materially participates in the actual production of the farm or in the management of production is considered self-employment income. For purposes of "material participation," the activities of a landlord's agent are not counted, only the landlord's actual participation.

Real Estate Investor

The owner of one office building who holds it for investment (rather than for sale in the ordinary course of business) is not a real estate dealer, but a real estate investor. The rent income is not self-employment income. Furnishing heat, light, water, and trash and garbage collection to tenants does not produce self-employment income.

2. Dividends and interest are not self-employment income. However, dividends earned by a dealer in securities and interest on accounts receivable are treated as self-employment income. A dealer is one who buys stock as inventory to sell to customers.

Income reported under an S election is not subject to self-employment tax.

3. Capital gains are not self-employment income. Similarly not treated as self-employment income are gains from the sale of property which is not inventory or held for sale to customers in the ordinary course of business. There is an exception for dealers in commodities and options; *see* the chart in ¶46.5.

Net operating loss deduction. A loss carryover from past years does not reduce business income for self-employment tax purposes. Similarly, the personal exemption may not be used to reduce self-employment income.

Self-employed health premiums. A self-employed person's 25% deduction for health premium costs is not taken into account in computing income for self-employment tax purposes.

Farmers. Cash or a payment-in-kind under the "Payment-In-Kind" program is considered earned income subject to self-employment tax.

Business interruption proceeds. The IRS and the Tax Court disagree over whether business interruption insurance proceeds must be reported as earnings subject to self-employment tax. The Tax Court held that insurance payments made to a grocer as compensation for lost earnings due to a fire were not subject to self-employment tax because the payment was not for actual services. The IRS refuses to follow the decision, holding that such payments represented income that would have been earned had business operations not been interrupted.

Wage offset. If in 1992, you had wages on which FICA taxes were withheld, these wages may reduce net earnings subject to self-employment tax. If you had wages of at least $130,200, you owe no self-employment tax. If you had wages of less than $130,200, you generally pay self-employment tax on the difference between your wages and earnings subject to self-employment tax. Follow the computation steps on Schedule SE, which will lead to the computation of any tax due.

PARTNERS PAY SELF-EMPLOYMENT TAX

¶46.2 A general partner includes his or her share of partnership income or loss in net earnings from self-employment, including guaranteed payments. If your personal tax year is different from the partnership's tax year, you include your share of partnership income or loss for the partnership tax year within 1992.

A limited partner is not subject to self-employment tax on his or her share of partnership income except for guaranteed payments for services performed, which are subject to the tax.

If a partner dies within the partnership's tax year, self-employment income includes his or her distributive share of the income earned by the partnership through the end of the month in which the death occurs. This is true, even though his or her heirs or estate succeeds to the partnership rights. For this purpose, partnership income for the year is considered to be earned ratably each month.

Partnership's Retirement Payments

Retirement payments you receive from your partnership are *not* subject to self-employment tax if the following conditions are met:

1. The payments are made under a qualified written plan providing for periodic payments on retirement of partners with payments to continue at least until death.

2. You rendered no services in any business conducted by the partnership during the tax year of the partnership ending within or with your tax year.

3. By the end of the partnership's tax year, your share in the partnership's capital has been paid to you in full, and there is no obligation from the other partners to you other than with respect to the retirement payments under the plan.

SELF-EMPLOYMENT TAX DEDUCTIONS

¶46.3 To put the self-employment tax at the same level as Social Security and Medicare taxes paid by employees, the law provides a .9235 adjustment on Schedule SE and a 50% deduction of self-employment tax on Line 25 of Form 1040. The .9235 adjustment reduces self-employment income subject to self-employment tax. However, if your 1992 net profit is $140,985 or more, the .9235 adjustment does not provide a benefit because even after application of the adjustment, your net earnings will equal or exceed the top tax base of $130,200.

You must have $433.13 or more of net profit from self-employment to be subject to self-employment tax (.9235 x $433.13 = $400). If your net profit is less than $433.13 before the reduction, you do not have to file Schedule SE (Form 1040) or pay the tax.

After applying the .9235 adjustment, you figure the self-employment tax by applying a 15.3% rate on the first $55,500 of net earnings, and a 2.9% rate on earnings over $55,500 but not over $130,200.

EXAMPLES 1. Your 1992 net profit from Schedule C is $51,300. On Schedule SE, you apply the .9235 adjustment to your self-employment income.

$$\begin{array}{r} \$51,300.00 \\ \times\ .9235 \\ \hline \$47,375.55 \end{array}$$

The self-employment tax rate of 15.30% is applied to $47,375.55, for a self-employment tax of $7,248.46. Your deduction for income tax purposes is $3,624.23 (50% of $7,248.46), which is entered on Line 25 of Form 1040.

2. Your 1992 net profit is $151,300. Applying the .9235 adjustment results in income of $139,725.55:

$$\begin{array}{r} \$151,300 \\ \times\ .9235 \\ \hline \$139,725.55 \end{array}$$

However, since $139,725.55 exceeds the top self-employment tax base of $130,200, the tax is figured on $130,200. Your self-employment tax is $10,657.80: $8,491.50 on the first $55,500 (15.3% × $55,500), *plus* $2,166.30 on earnings between $55,500 and $130,200 (2.9% x $74,700).

On Line 25 of Form 1040, you deduct from gross income $5,328.90 (50% of $10,657.80).

OPTIONAL METHOD IF 1992 WAS A LOW INCOME OR LOSS YEAR

¶46.4

The law provides a small increased tax base for Social Security coverage if you have a low net profit or loss.

Electing the optional method may also increase earned income for dependent care and earned income credit purposes.

The increased tax base is called the optional method. One optional method is for nonfarm self-employment and another for farm income. You may not use the optional method to report an amount less than your actual net earnings from self-employment.

Nonfarm method. You may use the non-farm optional method if you meet all the following tests.

1. Your actual net earnings from nonfarm self-employment on Line 31 of Schedule C, Line 3 of Schedule C-EZ, or Line 15a of Schedule K-1 (Form 1065) are less than $1,733 (.9235 x $1,733 = $1,600 maximum income subject to the optional method).
2. Your net earnings from nonfarm employment are less than 72.189% of the total gross income you made from nonfarm self-employment.
3. You had net earnings from self-employment of $400 or more in at least two of the following years: 1989, 1990 and 1991.
4. You have not previously used this method for more than four years. There is a five-year lifetime limit for use of the non-farm optional base. The years do not have to be consecutive.

Income of $2,400 or less. If your gross income from all nonfarm trades or businesses is $2,400 or less and you meet the above four tests, you may report two-thirds of the gross income from your non-farm business as net earnings from self-employment.

EXAMPLES 1. Brown had net earnings from self-employment of $800 in 1990 and $900 in 1991 and so meets Test 3 above. In 1992, she has gross self-employment income of $2,100 and net self-employment earnings of $1,200. As net earnings from self-employment of $1,200 are less than $1,733 (Test 1 above) and also less than 72.189% (Test 2 above) of gross income ($1,516), Brown may either figure self-employment tax on actual net earnings of $1,200 or on $1,400 (2/3 of $2,100).

2. Same facts as in Example 1 but Brown has a net loss of $700. She may elect to report $1,400 (2/3 of $2,100) as net earnings under the optional method.

3. Smith had gross income of $1,000 and net earnings of $800. He may not use the optional method because actual net earnings of $800 are not less than $722 (72.189% of gross income of $1,000).

4. Jones has gross income of $525 and net earnings of $175. Jones may not use the optional method because two-thirds of his gross income or $350 is less than the minimum income of $400 required to be subject to the tax.

Income over $2,400. If your gross income from all nonfarm businesses exceeds $2,400, and you meet the four tests, you may report $1,600 as your net earnings from nonfarm self-employment.

EXAMPLES 1. White had net earnings from self-employment in 1989 of $8,500; in 1990, $10,500; and in 1991, $9,500. His 1992 gross income is $12,000 and net earnings are $1,200. Because his net earnings of $1,200 from self-employment are less than $1,733 and also less than 72.189% of his gross income, he may report either $1,600 or $1,200 as his net earnings from self-employment.

2. Same as Example 1 but assume net earnings for 1992 are $1,800. White may not use the optional method because his actual net earnings of $1,800 from self-employment are not less than $1,733. He reports $1,800 as net earnings using the regular method.

3. Assume White has a net loss of $700 in 1992. He may use the optional method to report $1,600 of net earnings from self-employment.

Optional farm method. If you have farming income (other than as a limited partner) you may use the farm optional method to figure your net earnings from farm self-employment.

The nonfarm optional method does *not* have a two-year self-employment test (Test 3) or a requirement that actual net earnings be less than 72.189% of gross income (Test 2). There is also no limitation on the number of years you may use this method (Test 4).

If your gross income from farming is $2,400 or less, you may report two-thirds of your gross income as your net earnings from farm self-employment. If your gross income from farming exceeds $2,400 and your actual net earnings from farm self-employment are less than $1,733, you may report $1,600 as your net earnings from farm self-employment. If your gross income from farming exceeds $2,400 and your actual net earnings from farm self-employment are $1,733 or more, you may not use the optional method.

Farm income includes income from cultivating the soil or harvesting any agricultural commodities. It also includes income from the operation of livestock, dairy, poultry, bee, fish, fruit or truck farm, or plantation, ranch, nursery, range, orchard, or oyster bed, as well as income in the form of crop shares if you materially participate in production or management of production.

¶46.5 SELF-EMPLOYMENT TAX RULES FOR CERTAIN POSITIONS

If you are—	Tax Rule—
Babysitter	Where you perform services in your own home and determine the nature and manner of the services to be performed, you are considered to have self-employment income. However, where services are performed in the parent's home according to instructions by the parents, you are an employee of the parents and do not have self-employment earnings.
Clergy	An ordained minister, priest, or rabbi (other than a member of a religious order who has taken a vow of poverty) is subject to self-employment tax, unless he elects not to be covered on the grounds of conscientious or religious objection to Social Security benefits. Before 1968, a minister had to elect Social Security coverage. An application for exemption from Social Security coverage must be filed on or before the due date of a minister's income tax return for the second taxable year for which he has net earnings from his services as a clergyman of $400 or more (Form 4361). An exemption, once granted, is generally irrevocable. However, a law did allow revocation of the exemption for 1977 or 1978. An exemption will not be granted to a minister who elected coverage under prior law.

Self-Employment Tax Rules for Certain Positions *(continued)*

If you are—	Tax Rule—
Consultant	The IRS generally takes the position that income earned by a consultant is subject to self-employment tax. The IRS has also held that a retired executive hired as a consultant by his former firm received self-employment income, even though he was subject to an agreement prohibiting him from giving advice to competing companies. According to the IRS, consulting for one firm is a business; it makes no difference that he acts as a consultant only with his former company. The IRS has also imposed self-employment tax on consulting fees, although no services were performed for them. The courts have generally approved the IRS position.
Dealer in commodities and options	Registered options dealers and commodities dealers are subject to self-employment tax on net gains from trading in Section 1256 contracts, which include regulated futures contracts, foreign currency contracts, dealer equity options, and nonequity options. Self-employment tax also applies to net gains from trading property related to such contracts, like stock used to hedge options.
Director	You are taxed as a self-employed person if you are not an employee of the company. Fees for attendance at meetings are self-employment income. If the fees are not received until after the year you provide the services, you treat the fees as self-employment earnings in the year they are received.
Employee of foreign government or international organization	If you are a U.S. citizen and you work in the United States, you pay tax as a self-employed worker although you are an employee of a foreign government or its wholly-owned instrumentality, or of an international organization given privileges, exemptions, and immunities by the International Organizations Immunities Act.
Executor or guardian	As a professional fiduciary, you will always be treated as having self-employment income, regardless of the assets held by the estate. But if you serve as a nonprofessional executor or administrator for the estate of a deceased friend or relative, you will not be treated as having self-employment income unless all of the following tests are met: (1) The estate includes a business. (2) You actively participate in the operation of the business. And, (3) all or part of your fee is related to your operation of the business. The IRS applied similar business tests to deny self-employment treatment for a guardian who was appointed by a court to care for a disabled cousin. The guardian negotiated sales of the cousin's property and invested the proceeds, but these activities were not extensive enough to be considered management of a business.
Lecturer	You are not taxed as a self-employed person if you give only occasional lectures. If, however, you seek lecture engagements and get them with reasonable regularity, your lecture fees are treated as self-employment income.
Nonresident alien	You do not pay Social Security tax on your self-employment income derived from a trade, business, or profession. This is so even though you pay income tax. Your exemption from self-employment tax is not influenced by the fact that your business in the United States is carried on by an agent, employee, or partnership of which you are a member. However, if you live in Puerto Rico, the Virgin Islands, American Samoa, or Guam, you are not considered a nonresident alien and are subject to self-employment tax.
Nurse	If you are a registered nurse or licensed practical nurse who is hired directly by clients for private nursing services, you are considered self-employed. You are an employee if hired directly by a hospital or a private physician and work for a salary following a strict routine during fixed hours, or if you provide primarily domestic services in the home of a client. Where registered or licensed practical nurses are assigned nursing jobs by an agency which pays them, the IRS, in several rulings, has treated such nurses as employees of the agency. Nurses' aides, domestics, and other unlicensed individuals who classify themselves as practical nurses are treated by the IRS as employees, regardless of whether they work for a medical institution, a private physician, or a private household.
Public official or employee	You may be subject to self-employment tax if you are compensated solely by fees. However, you do not have to pay self-employment tax on your fees if your services are covered by a state Social Security coverage agreement, or you elected exemption. (The election must have been made in 1968 and is irrevocable.)
Real estate agent or door-to-door salesperson	Licensed real estate agents are considered self-employed if they have a contract specifying that they are not to be treated as employees and if substantially all of their pay is related to sales rather than number of hours worked. The same rule also applies to door-to-door salesmen with similar contracts who work on a commission basis selling products in homes or other non-retail establishments.
Retired insurance agents	Income based on a percentage of commissions received before retirement is self-employment income. The same treatment applies to income for renewal and deferred commissions for sales made prior to retirement.
Technical service contractor	Consulting engineers and computer technicians who receive assignments from technical service agencies are generally treated as employees and do not pay self-employment tax. The IRS distinguishes between (1) technicians who in three-party arrangements are assigned clients by a technical services agency, and (2) those who directly enter into contracts with clients. Employee status covers only technicians in Group 1. Technical specialists who contract directly with clients may be classified as independent contractors by showing that they have been consistently treated as independent contractors by the client, and that other workers in similar positions have also been treated as independent contractors. Thus, they may treat their income as self-employment income. Firms that are treated as employers of technical specialists are responsible for withholding and payroll taxes.
Writer	Royalties from writing books are self-employment income to a writer. Royalties on books by a professor employed by a university may also be self-employment income despite employment as a professor.

PART

VII

WHAT HAPPENS AFTER YOU FILE YOUR RETURN

In this part, you will learn how the IRS checks your return and initiates audit procedures. Pay special attention to—

- Information returns you receive from brokers, banks, corporation and government agencies reporting payments to you. The IRS matches these information returns with your tax return to determine if you have reported all your income.
- Penalties for underpaying your tax. You may be able to avoid penalties for positions taken on your tax return by making certain disclosures, obtaining authoritative support for your position, or showing reasonable cause for a tax underpayment.
- Odds of being audited. Your chances of being selected for an examination depends on your income, profession, deductions claimed and even where you live.
- Preparing for an audit. Advance preparations and knowing your rights can help support your position.
- Steps of disputing adverse IRS determinations. You can appeal within the IRS and go to court if you disagree with the IRS audit results. If you win, you may receive attorney fees and other expenses.

47 HOW TAX DATA IS PROCESSED BY THE IRS

Data from filed tax returns and information returns is recorded in computers on magnetic tape which is sent to the National Computer Center in Martinsburg, West Virginia, for posting to the master list of taxpayers arranged by account number. Failure to file returns, duplicate or multiple filings, and other discrepancies can be detected. Data from information returns is matched with the entries on individual returns.

You are required to put your Social Security number on your tax return. Your number also appears on information returns sent to the IRS reporting the wages, interest, dividends, royalties, etc. paid to you. Your number serves as a basis for posting and cross-referencing data to your account in the master IRS file.

You may incur penalties and interest charges if you fail to comply with reporting requirements or fail to pay your taxes on time.

IRS PRELIMINARY REVIEW

¶47.1 Your return is first checked for arithmetic accuracy by the IRS. If an error is found, you receive either a refund or a bill for additional taxes. Special IRS screening also spots the following types of errors:

- Incorrectly reporting income shown on Form W-2 or Form 1099.
- Incorrectly applying the adjusted gross income limitations for medical expenses, casualty and theft losses, and miscellaneous itemized deductions.
- Using an auto mileage rate for business travel exceeding the IRS rate.
- Claiming the dependent care credit by a married person filing separately; *see* ¶25.1.
- Using head of household rates without noting the name of a qualifying child who is not your dependent.

If you make errors of this type, you will probably be advised by mail of the corrections and of additional tax due, or you may be asked to provide additional information to substantiate tax deductions or credits. If you disagree with an IRS assessment of additional tax, you may request an interview or submit additional information. If you file early for 1992 and the correction is made before April 15, 1993, interest is not charged.

If your return is selected for a more thorough review, you are notified by letter. This may not happen for a year or two. How to handle an audit if your return is selected for examination is discussed in Chapter 48.

If you are due a refund on your return, the IRS follows a practice of expediting refunds to avoid interest costs. Interest is not required to be paid on refunds before May 31, which is 46 days after April 15, the day the tax was due. If the overpayment is not refunded within 45 days, interest is paid from the date the tax was overpaid up to a date determined by the IRS that can be as much as 30 days before the date of the refund check.

INFORMATION RETURNS REQUIRED BY IRS

¶47.2 The IRS matches tax returns with information returns from employers, payers of interest and dividends, brokers, and others to check whether income has been omitted from an individual's tax return. The IRS processes more than one billion information returns, primarily Forms W-2 and 1099. By matching these information returns against individual tax returns, the IRS assesses billions in additional tax and penalties.

Here is a list of items for which an information return will be sent to the IRS:

Wages. Employers report wage income on Form W-2.

Dividends. Dividend payments of $10 or more during the calendar year are reported to the IRS on Form 1099-DIV. Each payer must furnish you by February 1, 1993, a statement showing the dividend payments made in 1992. Corporations, banks, and other payers, as well as persons or firms who receive such payments for you as nominee, report annually the dividend payments totaling $10 or more per person. Dividends, for reporting purposes, include dividends paid by corporations, and "dividend equivalents" paid to you while your stock is on loan for a short sale. Nontaxable distributions paid to shareholders are reported to the IRS on Form 5452.

Interest. Interest payments of $10 or more during the calendar year are reported to the IRS on Form 1099-INT. Each payer must furnish you by February 1, 1993, a statement showing the interest payments made in 1992. Interest for reporting purposes includes interest on registered corporate bonds, debentures, notes, and certificates, as well as interest on deposits with savings banks, savings and loan associations, stockbrokers, and insurance companies. No returns are required for tax-free interest.

Original issue discount (OID). The discount on time deposits and certificates maturing in more than one year is reported to the IRS on Form 1099-OID if it is at least $10. You should receive a copy of the Form 1099-OID for 1992 by February 1, 1993.

Interest and dividend income information disclosed to Social Security and other agencies. To verify your eligibility for certain government benefits, agencies such as the Social Security Administration, state unemployment compensation agencies, and state welfare agencies may obtain from the IRS information on the interest and dividend income shown on your tax return.

Rents or royalties. Royalty payments of $10 or more are reported on intangible property, such as copyrights and interests in oil, gas, and other natural resources, on Form 1099-MISC. Rents collected by a real estate agent on behalf of the property owner of $600 or more also are reported on Form 1099-MISC.

State income tax refunds. States are required to report income tax refunds of $10 or more on Form 1099-G.

Unemployment compensation. Unemployment payments of $10 or more during the year are reported to the IRS on Form 1099-G, a copy of which will be furnished to unemployment benefit recipients.

Proceeds from real estate transactions. Real estate sales are reported on Form 1099-S to the IRS by the attorney or other party who is responsible for closing the transaction.

Proceeds from sales of securities. Brokers are required to report to the IRS on Form 1099-B gross proceeds from sales of stocks, bonds, commodities, regulated futures, and forward contracts. Commodity options are not covered by this reporting rule.

Miscellaneous income. Persons who, in the course of business, make payments totaling $600 or more in the calendar year must file Form 1099-MISC with IRS if the payments are in the form of:

1. Compensation for personal services (including salaries, wages, commissions, professional fees) from which no tax is withheld. However, no information return is required for payments to a domestic or other household employee;
2. Prizes and awards that are not for services such as winnings on TV shows (gambling winnings are reported on Form W-2G); or
3. Payments of fees to physicians by insurance companies, such as Blue Cross, or by a government agency under Medicare or Medicaid. The physician or other health care provider must receive a copy of Form 1099-MISC by February 1, 1993, for inclusion of the amount on his or her 1992 return.

Retirement plan distributions. Distributions from pension, profit-sharing and annuity plans, IRAs, or simplified employee pension plans (SEPs) are reported on Form 1099-R. Contributions to an IRA and the value of an IRA or SEP account are reported on Form 5498.

Mortgage interest. Banks, government agencies, and businesses receiving mortgage interest and points of $600 or more for any calendar year report the payment to the IRS on Form 1098. The reporting requirement applies to interest on all obligations secured by real property. The lender must provide you with a statement of the interest reported to the IRS for 1992 by February 1, 1993.

Foreclosures and abandonments of property. If a business or government agency lends you money and later forecloses on your property or knows that you have abandoned property secured by the loan, the lender must file a report with the IRS on Form 1099-A. The purpose of the reporting requirement is to help the IRS check whether you have realized income from the discharge of indebtedness or gain on foreclosure, or whether you must recapture a previously claimed investment credit. If a report to the IRS has been made, you will be sent a statement by the lender by January 31 following the year of the foreclosure or abandonment.

Tax shelters. A new tax shelter offering may be required to register with the IRS. If registration is required, the IRS assigns the tax shelter an identification number that must be furnished to investors. As an investor, you must report the registration number on Form 8271. Form 8271 must be attached to your tax return if you report any income or claim any deductions or credits from the shelter. Promoters of registered tax shelters and any other tax shelter arrangements which the IRS considers as potentially abusive must also keep a list of investors for seven years and provide the list to the IRS upon request. Furthermore, an investor who sells his interest in such a tax shelter to another investor must keep records identifying the buyer.

Cooperatives. Cooperatives must file annual information returns for patronage dividends totaling $10 or more during the calendar year. A statement showing the amount reported must be furnished to the patron by the end of January of the following year; *see* Form 1099-PATR.

Partnerships. A partnership does not pay income taxes, but must file an annual information return (Form 1065), stating all items of income and deductions. Also included in the return are the names and addresses of all partners, and the amount of each partner's distributive share. The return is filed at the close of the partnership's tax year, whether or not it coincides with that of its partners. Failure to file the return will result in a penalty assessable against the partnership. If a partner sells or exchanges a partnership interest and payment is partly attributable to the partner's share of unrealized receivables or substantially appreciated inventory, the partnership must be notified of the transaction and the partnership must then file an information return with the IRS, Form 8308. The purpose of the reporting requirement is to enable the IRS to verify the income attributable to the receivables and inventory, which is taxable as ordinary income. Statements to the transferor and transferee of the partnership interest must also be provided.

Barter transactions. The value of the trades by members of a barter club is subject to income tax. If you exchanged services or goods through a barter exchange during 1992, you should receive Form 1099-B from the exchange by February 1, 1993, showing the value received during 1992. The IRS also gets a copy of Form 1099-B.

WHEN THE IRS CAN ASSESS ADDITIONAL TAXES

¶47.3

Three-year statute. The IRS has three years after the date on which your return is filed to assess additional taxes. When you file a return before the due date, however, the three-year period starts from the due date, generally April 15.

Where the due date of a return falls on a Saturday, Sunday, or legal holiday, the due date is postponed to the next business day.

EXAMPLES 1. You filed your 1989 return on February 4, 1990. The last day on which the IRS can make an assessment on your 1989 return is April 15, 1993.

2. You file your 1992 return on May 25, 1993. The IRS has until May 25, 1996, to assess a deficiency.

IRS request for audit extension. If the IRS cannot complete an audit within three years, it may request that you sign Form 872 to extend the time for assessing the tax. However, where an individual was "scared" into signing such an agreement, it was held invalid.

EXAMPLE Robertson, a plumber, won $30,000 in a sweepstakes. An IRS agent asked him to sign an extension agreement. Robertson never had any prior dealings with the IRS, did not know his return was under examination, and was not in touch with the lawyer who prepared the return on which his sweepstakes winnings were averaged.

Robertson wanted to see his lawyer before signing Form 872, but the agent pressed hard for the signature, phoning him and his wife at home and at work twenty times in a week. The agent did not tell him the amount of additional tax that might be involved, or explain that if he refused to sign he would have an opportunity before the IRS and the courts to contest any additional tax. Instead, the agent's comments gave him the impression that his home could be confiscated if he refused to sign. Robertson signed and the IRS later increased his tax.

Robertson argued that the agreement was not valid. He signed under duress. The Tax Court agreed. He convinced the court that he really believed he could lose his house and property if he did not comply. No adequate explanation of the real consequences of refusal to sign was made, although Robertson asked. Since he signed Form 872 under duress, the IRS could not increase his tax after the three-year period.

Amended returns. If you file an amended return shortly before the three-year limitations period is about to expire and the return shows that you owe additional tax, the IRS has 60 days from the date it receives the return to assess the additional tax, even though the regular limitations period would expire before the 60-day period.

Six-year statute. When you fail to report an item of gross income which is more than 25% of the gross income reported on your return, the IRS has six years after the return is filed to assess additional taxes.

Where a false or fraudulent return is filed with intent to evade the tax, or where no return is filed, there is no limitation on when the tax may be assessed.

INTEREST ON DEFICIENCIES

¶47.4

Interest is charged on a deficiency at rates listed in the next column. For periods after 1986, the rate changes quarterly. Interest begins to accrue from the due date of the return. As of January 1, 1983, interest is compounded daily except for estimated tax penalties. IRS tables on compound interest may be found in IRS Revenue Procedure 83-7. Where a taxpayer has relied on IRS assistance in preparing a return, and taxes are owed because of a mathematical or clerical error, interest does not begin to accrue until 30 days from a formal demand by the IRS for the payment of additional taxes.

Rates on amounts outstanding are as follows:

From—	To—	Rate—
10/1/92	12/31/92	See Supplement
4/1/92	9/30/92	8%
1/1/92	3/31/92	9
4/1/91	12/31/91	10
10/1/89	3/31/91	11
4/1/89	9/30/89	12
10/1/88	3/31/89	11
4/1/88	9/30/88	10
1/1/88	3/31/88	11
10/1/87	12/31/87	10
7/1/86	9/30/87	9
1/1/86	6/30/86	10
7/1/85	12/31/85	11
1/1/85	6/30/85	13

Refunds. A lower rate is paid on refunds. For periods after 1986, the interest rate you receive on refunds is 1% less than the rate you must pay on deficiencies. Generally, no interest is paid on a refund made within 45 days of the due date of the return (including extensions). If you file after the due date, no interest is paid on a refund made within 45 days of the actual filing date.

TAX PENALTIES

¶47.5

Late payments. If you are late in paying your taxes, a nondeductible monthly penalty of 0.5% (½ of 1%) is imposed on the net amount of tax due and not paid by the due date. The maximum penalty is 25% of the tax due. The penalty is in addition to the regular interest charge. A similar penalty applies for failure to pay a tax deficiency within 10 days of the date of notice and demand for payment. The penalty does not apply if you can show that the failure to pay is due to reasonable cause and not to willful neglect. The penalty does not apply to the estimated tax.

The monthly penalty may be doubled to 1% if after repeated requests to pay and a notice of levy, you do not pay. The increased penalty applies starting in the month that begins after the earlier of the following IRS notices: (1) a notice that the IRS will levy upon your assets within 10 days unless payment is made or (2) a notice demanding immediate payment where the IRS believes collection of the tax is in jeopardy. If the tax is not paid after such a demand for immediate payment, the IRS may levy upon your assets without waiting 10 days.

Late filing. If your return is filed late without reasonable cause, the IRS may impose a penalty of 5% of the net tax due for each month the return is late, with a maximum penalty of 25%. If the return is more than 60 days late, the penalty will not be less than the smaller of $100 or 100% of the tax due.

If failure to file is fraudulent, the monthly penalty is 15% of the net tax due, with a maximum penalty of 75%.

If you are subject to penalties for both late payment and late filing, the 0.5% penalty for late payment (but not the 1% penalty) offsets the penalty for late filing.

Penalties for inaccurate returns. For returns due after 1989 (without extensions), a 20% penalty generally applies to the portion of any tax underpayment attributable to (1) negligence or disregard of IRS rules and regulations; (2) substantial understatement of tax liability; (3) overvaluation of property; or (4) undervaluation of property on a gift tax or estate tax return. These penalties may be avoided by showing good faith and reasonable cause for the underpayment; a stricter version of this exception applies to charitable contribution overvaluations as discussed later in this section.

Negligence or disregard of IRS rules or regulations. The 20% penalty applies to the portion of the underpayment attributable to negligence. Negligence is defined as failing to make a reasonable attempt to comply with the law. If you take a position on your return that is "arguable," but fairly unlikely to succeed in court, your position is considered to have a reasonable basis and is not negligent. Failure to report income shown on an information return, such as interest or dividends, is considered strong evidence of negligence, but negligence is not presumed as it was under prior law. For returns with an original due date before 1990, a 5% negligence penalty is applied to the entire underpayment where any part of it was attributable to negligence.

Too Good To Be True

If you claim a deduction, credit, or exclusion on your return that would seem to a reasonable person to be "to good to be true," under the circumstances, the IRS is likely to consider you negligent unless you show you made an attempt to verify the correctness of the position.

The 20% penalty may also apply if you take a position on a return which is contrary to IRS revenue rulings, notices, or regulations. To avoid the penalty for a position contrary to a ruling or notice, you must be ready to show that your position has a "realistic possibility" of being sustained on its merits or you must disclose your position on Form 8275. The vague "realistic possibility" test requires that a person knowledgeable in the tax law would conclude that the position had a one-in-three chance of being sustained. Positions contrary to a regulation must be disclosed on Form 8275-R. A disclosure on Form 8275 or on Form 8275-R will not be effective to avoid a penalty if the position taken was frivolous.

Substantial underpayment of tax. If you understate tax liability on a return by the greater of $5,000 or 10% of the proper tax, you may be subject to a penalty equal to 20% of the underpayment attributable to the understatement on returns due after 1989. A 25% penalty applied to returns due after October 21, 1986, and before 1990.

The penalty may be avoided if you provide the IRS with a statement of facts relating to your position on Form 8275, or on Form 8275-R in the case of a position that is contrary to a regulation. For itemized deductions and certain other expenses, providing all the information required on IRS tax forms is sufficient to constitute disclosure; see Revenue Procedure 92-23 for details.

The penalty also may be avoided if you can show that your position was supported by "substantial authority" such as statutes, court decisions, final, temporary, or proposed IRS regulations, IRS revenue rulings and procedures, and press releases or notices published by the IRS in the weekly Internal Revenue Bulletin. You may also rely on IRS private letter rulings and technical advice memoranda issued after October 31, 1976, and IRS actions on decisions and general counsel memoranda issued after March 12, 1981. However, according to the IRS, such rulings and internal IRS memoranda that are more than 10 years old should be accorded very little weight. Congressional committee reports and the tax law explanations prepared by Congress' Joint Committee on Taxation, known as the "Blue Book," may be relied on as authority for your position.

A position that is merely arguable but fairly unlikely to prevail (which satisfies the reasonable basis test for negligence) is not enough to satisfy the substantial authority test, but the likelihood of success does not have to be "more likely than not" (over 50%) for your position to have substantial authority.

However, if an understatement of tax is due to tax-shelter items, giving substantial authority for your position is not enough to avoid the penalty; you must also reasonably believe that your position was "more likely than not" correct.

Overvaluing property or basis. The 20% penalty for overvaluing property, such as where inflated charitable contribution deductions are claimed or where the basis of depreciable property is inflated, applies *only* if the claimed value or basis is 200% or more of the correct amount. Furthermore, there is no penalty unless the tax underpayment attributable to the overvaluation exceeds $5,000. The penalty rate is doubled to 40% if the overvaluation is 400% or more of the correct value. To avoid the penalty for donated property on the grounds that you had reasonable cause, the value must be based on a qualified appraisal (¶14.12), and your own good faith investigation of value.

Undervaluation on gift or estate tax return. If property is undervalued on a gift tax return or estate tax return by 50% or more, and if the tax underpayment attributed to the undervaluation exceeds $5,000, a 20% penalty applies. The penalty doubles to 40% if the undervaluation is 75% or more.

Fraud penalty. A 75% penalty applies to the portion of any tax underpayment due to fraud. If the IRS establishes that any part of an underpayment is due to fraud, the entire underpayment will be attributed to fraud, unless you prove otherwise.

Interest on penalties. A higher interest cost is imposed on individuals subject to the following penalties: failure to file a timely return, negligence or fraud, overvaluation of property, undervaluation of gift or estate tax property, *or* substantial understatement of tax liability. Interest starts to run from the due date of the return (including extensions) until the date the penalty is paid. For other penalties, interest is not imposed, unless the penalty is not paid within 10 days of the IRS' demand for payment.

Acting on wrong IRS advice. A penalty will not be imposed if you rely on erroneous advice provided in writing by IRS officials. It is necessary for you to show that you provided accurate information when asking for advice.

NOTIFY IRS OF ADDRESS CHANGES

¶47.6 If the IRS does not have your current address, payment of a refund due you may be delayed. If you owe taxes, the IRS may enforce a deficiency notice sent to the address on your most recently filed tax return, even if you never receive the IRS notice.

To avoid these problems, file Form 8822 with the IRS to provide notice of an address change. Alternatively, you may send a signed written statement to the IRS service center covering your old residence. The statement should state the new and old address, your full name, and Social Security or employer identification number.

If you and your spouse separate after filing a joint return, you should each notify the IRS of your current address.

If after you move you receive an IRS correspondence that has been forwarded by the Post Office, you may correct the address shown on the letter and mail it back to the IRS. Your correction is considered notice of an address change.

48

IRS TAX AUDITS

Because the IRS is unable to examine every return, it follows a policy of examining returns which, upon preliminary inspection, indicate the largest possible source of potential tax deficiency.

Returns are rated for audit according to a mathematical formula called the discriminant function system (DIF). Various weights are assigned to separate items on each tax return, thus permitting the ranking of returns for the greatest potential error. The method is based on data the IRS compiled from extensive audits of taxpayers under the Taxpayer Compliance Measurement Program (TCMP). The specific factors entering into the DIF formula are not disclosed by the IRS. However, its general procedure for selecting returns for audit may be found in an IRS classification handbook which is part of the Internal Revenue Manual (Part IV, Audit).

This chapter discusses what may trigger an audit and how you can handle an audit if your return is selected for examination.

ODDS OF BEING AUDITED

¶48.1 The odds are low that your return will be picked for an audit. The IRS does not have the personnel and resources to examine every return, so it selects those returns which upon preliminary inspection have a high audit potential—those that are most likely to result in a substantial tax deficiency. In recent years, less than 1% of all individual income tax returns have been examined, and the number has been decreasing. However, for 1991, there was a substantial increase in the number of returns audited for 1040A filers with total positive income under $25,000. Total returns examined for such filers increased from 185,935 in 1990 to 388,195 in 1991. Furthermore, audit percentages also increased for Schedule C filers in two categories, those with total gross receipts of under $25,000 and $100,000 and over.

Audit odds vary greatly depending on your income, type of return, and where you live. In the tables below, individual returns are classified by all income items on the return without regard to losses. Professional or business income reported on Schedule C and farm income reported on Schedule F is classified by total gross receipts, and corporate returns are classified by total assets. Overall audit percentages in the tables include correspondence examinations by IRS service centers, office examinations by tax auditors, and field examinations by revenue agents.

PERCENTAGE OF RETURNS AUDITED

Individuals (Non-business)	1991	1990
Under $25,000	.80%	.48%
$25,000 to $50,000	.64	.74
$50,000 to $100,000	1.11	1.09
$100,000 and over	5.26	4.71
Self-employed (Schedule C)		
Under $25,000	1.45	1.36
$25,000 to $100,000	1.85	1.86
$100,000 and over	3.63	3.38
Farmers (Schedule F)		
Under $100,000	1.30	1.30
$100,000 and over	3.82	2.69

Your return may command special IRS scrutiny because of your profession, type of transactions reported, or deductions claimed. The chances of being audited are greater under the following circumstances:

Your itemized deductions exceed IRS targets.

You claim tax shelter losses.

You report complex investment or business transactions without clear explanations.

You receive cash payments in your work that the IRS thinks are easy to conceal such as cash fees received by doctors or tips received by cab drivers and waiters.

Business expenses are large in relation to income.

Cash contributions to charity are large in relation to income.

You are a shareholder of a close corporation whose return has been examined.

A prior audit resulted in a tax deficiency.

An informer gives the IRS grounds to believe that you are omitting income from your return.

Itemized deductions. If your itemized deductions exceed target ranges set by the IRS, the chances of being audited increase. The IRS does not make public its audit criteria for excessive deductions, but it does release statistics showing the average amount of deductions claimed according to income. Here is a guide based on deductions claimed on 1990 returns:

Average Itemized Deductions

Adjusted Gross Income (thousands)	Interest*	Taxes	Medical and Dental	Donations
$15-20	$ 5,393	$ 1,520	$ 4,281	$ 1,142
20-25	4,314	1,806	3,812	1,249
25-30	4,662	2,069	3,306	1,129
30-40	5,011	2,477	3,137	1,213
40-50	5,667	3,015	3,612	1,315
50-75	6,595	4,049	4,002	1,665
75-100	8,847	5,888	6,003	2,112
100-200	13,323	9,359	12,087	3,442
200-500	20,831	20,075	26,295	7,367
500-1 mil	30,315	42,609	58,296	16,815
1 mil and over	67,440	140,715	68,915	80,144

* Included personal interest deduction which is no longer allowed.

CAUTION

TCMP Audit

No matter how carefully you prepare your return, your return may be selected at random for a special type of audit, a TCMP (Taxpayer Compliance Measurement Program) audit. The TCMP audit is more comprehensive than an ordinary tax examination because the IRS uses the results for setting audit guidelines for others in your tax and economic position. You can be asked to verify virtually all entries on your return. The IRS is protected from having to disclose the standards used in TCMP audits.

TYPES OF AUDITS

¶48.2 An examination may be held by correspondence, at a local IRS office, or at the taxpayer's place of business, office, or home. An examination at an IRS office is called a desk or office examination; an examination at a place of business or home is called a field examination. When you are contacted by the IRS, you should receive an explanation of the examination process.

In a correspondence audit, the IRS sends you a letter asking for additional information about an item on your return. For example, the IRS may ask you to document a claimed deduction for charitable contributions or medical expenses. If the IRS is not satisfied with your response, you may be called in for an office audit. The IRS also notifies you by letter of mathematical or clerical errors you have made on your return, or if you have failed to report income, such as interest or dividends, that are shown by payers on information returns and matched to taxpayer returns by IRS computers.

The complexity of the transactions reported on a return generally determines whether a return will be reviewed at an office or field examination.

Most audits of individual returns, except for the self-employed, are conducted at IRS offices. An office audit usually covers only a few specific issues which the IRS specifies in its notice to you. For example, the examining agent may only be interested in seeing proof for travel expense deductions or educational expenses.

Field audits generally involve business returns; they are more extensive and time-consuming than office audits and are handled by more experienced IRS agents. For self-employed individuals, most examinations are field audits at their place of business. It is advisable to have a tax professional go over the potential weak spots in your return and represent you at the examination.

PREPARING FOR THE AUDIT

¶48.3 After an office audit is scheduled, the first thing to do is look over your return. Refresh your memory. Examine the items the IRS questioned in its notice of audit, and organize your records accordingly. Also check the rest of your return and gather proof for items you are unsure of. At this point, you should take a broad view of your return to anticipate problems you may encounter. Before the actual examination begins, consider possible settlement terms. Assume that the agent will assess additional tax, but establish the range you will consider reasonable. You can always change your mind, but giving some thought beforehand to possible settlement terms will help you later when settlements are actually discussed.

You may authorize an attorney, CPA, enrolled agent, or other individual recognized to practice before the IRS to represent you at the examination, without your being there. Give your representative authorization on Form 2848.

If you attend the audit, take only the records related to the items questioned in the IRS notice. Do not volunteer extra records; if the agent sees them, it might suggest new areas for investigation.

If you are concerned that there may be a problem of negligence or fraud, see a qualified attorney before you come into contact with an IRS official. The attorney can put your actions in perspective and help protect your legal rights. Besides, what you tell an attorney is privileged information; he or she cannot divulge or be forced to divulge data you have provided, so you need not be concerned that disclosures to an attorney will jeopardize your position.

A field audit of your business return is likely to involve a comprehensive examination and requires careful preparation. Together with your tax adviser, go over your return for potential areas of weakness. For example, the agent is likely to question deductions you have claimed for business travel. If you are an incorporated professional, the corporation's deductions for expenses of company-owned cars or planes will probably be reviewed. The agent may suspect that a portion of these business deductions are actually nondeductible personal travel costs; be prepared to substantiate the business portion of your total mileage and operating expenses.

Make sure that the examination is scheduled far enough in advance for you to get ready. Do not let the IRS hurry you into an examination until you are prepared. In some localities, particularly rural areas, the IRS may give short notice in scheduling a field audit. An agent may even appear at your home or place of business and try to begin the audit immediately. Resist this pressure and reschedule the meeting at your convenience.

Under the Taxpayer Bill of Rights, the IRS is generally required to hold an office audit at the office located nearest to your home.

The IRS generally may not conduct a field audit at the site of a small business if the audit would essentially require the shutting down of the business, unless a direct visit is necessary to determine inventory or verify assets.

HANDLING THE AUDIT

¶48.4
If you have authorized someone to represent you at the examination, your representative may appear at the examination without you. If the IRS wants to question you, it must issue you an administrative summons. If you are present and questioned, you may stop the examination to consult with counsel, unless the examination is pursuant to an administrative summons.

Audits conducted at an IRS office may conclude quickly because they usually involve only a few specific issues. In some cases, the audit may take less than an hour. The key to handling the audit is advance preparation. When you arrive at the IRS office, be prepared to produce your records quickly. Records should be organized by topic so that you do not waste time leafing through pages for a receipt or other document.

If the agent decides to question an item not mentioned in the notice of audit, refuse politely but firmly to answer the questions. Tell the agent that you must first review your records. If the agent insists on pursuing the matter, another meeting will have to be scheduled. The agent might decide it is not worth the time and drop the issue.

Common sense rules of courtesy should be your guide in your contacts with the agent. Avoid personality clashes; they can only interfere with a speedy and fair resolution of the examination. However, be firm in your approach and, if the agent appears to be unreasonable in his or her approach, make it clear that—if necessary—you will go all the way to court to win your point. A vacillating approach may weaken your position in reaching a settlement.

If the IRS has scheduled a field audit, ask that the examination be held at your representative's office. If you have not retained professional help and the examination takes place on your business premises, do not allow the agent free run of the area: Provide the agent with a comfortable work area for examining your records. If possible, the workplace should be isolated so that the agent can concentrate on the examination without being distracted by office operations that might spark questions. Tell your employees not to answer questions about your business or engage in small talk with the agent. As with an office audit, help speed along the field examination by having prepared your records so that requested information can be quickly produced.

Recording the examination. You have the right to make an audio recording of any interview with an IRS official. Video recordings are not permitted. No later than 10 calendar days before the interview, give written notice to the agent conducting the interview that you will make a recording. Later requests are at the discretion of the IRS. You must pay for all recording expenses and supply the equipment. The IRS may also make a recording of the interview, upon giving notice of at least 10 calendar days. However, IRS notice is not necessary if you have already submitted a request to make a recording. You have the right to obtain a transcript, at your own expense, of any recording made by the IRS. Generally, a request for a copy must be received by the IRS agent within 30 calendar days after the recording, although later requests may be honored.

AGREEING TO AUDIT CHANGES

¶48.5
After the audit, the agent will discuss proposed changes either with you or your representative.

If you agree with the agent's proposed changes, you will be asked to sign a Form 870 which, when signed, permits an immediate assessment of a deficiency plus penalties and interest, if due. The Form 870 is called "Waiver of Restrictions on Assessment and Collection of Deficiency in Tax and Acceptance of Overassessment."

Before deciding whether to sign the Form 870, consider that, by signing, you are giving up your right of appeal to both an IRS Appellate Conference and the Tax Court. However, you may still file a refund suit in a federal district court or in the Claims Court unless you have agreed not to do so on the Form 870.

If you believe that you have done as well or better than expected regarding the proposed deficiency, you can bring the case to a close by signing the Form 870, but the agent's supervisor must also approve the assessment.

By signing the form, you limit the amount of interest charges added to the deficiency; interest stops running within 30 days after the date it is signed. A signed Form 870 does not prevent the IRS from reopening the case to assess an additional deficiency. If on review the deficiency is increased, you will receive a revised Form 870. You can refuse to sign the form. The signed first form has the effect of stopping the interest on the original deficiency. As a matter of practice, however, waivers of acceptances ordinarily result in closing of the case.

It is possible, although unlikely, that upon examining your return, the agent will determine that you are due a refund. In this situation, a signed Form 870 is merely an acknowledgment of the overassessment. You should file a protective refund claim even if you sign the Form 870 acknowledging the overassessment. Generally, the agent will process the refund, but if he or she fails to do so or the review staff puts it aside for some reason and the limitations period expires, the refund will be lost. The refund claim will protect you from such a mishap.

The payment of tax before the deficiency notice (90-day letter) is mailed is, in effect, a waiver of the restrictions on assessment and collection. If the payment satisfies your entire tax liability for that year, you cannot appeal to the Tax Court. You must sue for a refund in either the district court or court of claims.

DISPUTING THE AUDIT CHANGES

¶48.6
If you disagree with the agent and the examination takes place in an IRS office, you may ask for an immediate meeting with a supervisor to argue your side of the dispute. If an agreement is not reached at this meeting or the audit is at your office or home, the agent prepares a report of the proposed adjustments. You will receive a 30-day letter in which you are given the opportunity to request a conference. You may decide not to ask for a conference and await a formal notice of deficiency.

If your examination was conducted as an office audit or by correspondence, or the disputed amount does not exceed $2,500, you do not have to prepare a written protest for a conference. The written protest presents your reason for disagreeing with the agent's report. *See* IRS Publication 5, "Appeal Rights and Preparation of Protests for Unagreed Cases."

At the conference you may appear for yourself or be represented by an attorney or other agent, and you may bring witnesses. The conference is held in an informal manner and you are given ample opportunity to present your case.

If you cannot reach a settlement, you will receive a Notice of Deficiency, commonly called a 90-day letter. In it, you are notified that at the end of 90 days from the date it was mailed, the government will assess the additional tax.

Going to court. When you receive a 90-day letter, if you are still convinced that your position is correct, you may take your case to one of three courts. You may within 90 days file a petition with the

Tax Court; *or*, you may pay the additional tax, file a refund claim for it, and—after the refund claim is denied—sue for a refund in a federal district court or the U.S. Claims Court.

Generally, the decision to litigate should be considered by an experienced tax practitioner.

The Tax Court has a small tax case procedure for deficiencies of $10,000 or less. Such cases are handled expeditiously and informally. Cases may be heard by appointed special trial judges. A small claim case may be discontinued at any time before a decision, but the decision when made is final. No appeal may be taken.

Penalty for frivolous court action. If you bring a frivolous case to the Tax Court or unreasonably failed to discuss your position within the IRS audit procedures, the Tax Court may impose a penalty of up to $25,000. If an attorney unreasonably multiplies Tax Court proceedings, the attorney may be required to pay excess court costs or attorney fees incurred because of the resulting delay. Furthermore, if you appeal a Tax Court decision and the appeals court finds that the appeal was frivolous, you may be penalized.

RECOVERING LEGAL FEES

¶48.7 In a tax dispute, you may feel that the IRS has taken an unreasonable position that forced you to incur legal fees and other expenses to win your point. You may be able to recover all or part of your costs under the following rules in a civil tax case.

Cases begun after November 10, 1988. Generally, taxpayers who win their case in the Tax Court or other federal court after exhausting all administrative remedies within the IRS may recover up to $75 an hour for attorney fees plus related litigation expenses by proving that the IRS position was not substantially justified. An award may be based on unjustified conduct by the IRS during pre-trial administrative proceedings as well as on IRS conduct after litigation begins.

Individuals *cannot* recover legal fees if their net worth exceeds $2 million. No recovery is allowed to sole proprietors, partnerships, and corporations if net worth exceeds $7 million or they have more than 500 employees.

The $75 per hour recovery for fees of an attorney or other qualified representative may be increased if the court determines that a higher rate is justified. A higher rate may be based on the high cost of attorneys in urban areas, or the limited availability of attorneys. In one case, an award of $180 per hour was approved by a federal court because of the attorney's specialized skills and the complexity of corporate tax issues involved in the case. However, in another case, the Tax Court refused to allow fees of $150 per hour, which was the going rate for tax litigation experts in Albuquerque.

When this book went to press, Congress was considering legislation to increase the maximum recovery from $75 to $110 per hour and to adjust the limit for inflation; see the Supplement.

To recover administrative or litigation costs, you must "substantially prevail" as to the key issue in the case or the amount of tax involved. You also must show that the IRS position was not "substantially justified," which the Tax Court and other courts interpret to be a "reasonableness" standard. The reasonableness of an IRS position at the administrative stage is determined as of the earlier of two dates: (1) the date you received notice of an IRS decision from its appeals office, or (2) the date of the deficiency notice. If the IRS position as of the earlier date was not justified and you win your case in Tax Court or other federal court, the court may award the following costs incurred on or after that date: (1) administrative fees or similar charges imposed by the IRS; (2) reasonable expenses of expert witnesses; (3) the reasonable cost of any study, analysis, engineering report, test, or project that is necessary for the preparation of the

case; and (4) reasonable fees (generally not to exceed $75 per hour) paid or incurred for the services of a qualified representative in connection with the administrative action.

If your case is settled with the IRS before going to court, the IRS may settle your claim for administrative expenses. If it denies or limits your claim, you may appeal to the Tax Court under the informal "small" case procedures.

An award for litigation expenses may also include court costs and other reasonable fees based on prevailing market rates for expert witnesses and special reports, such as an engineer's report necessary to the preparation of your court case. However, the recovery for expert witnesses may not exceed the amount paid by the government to its own expert witnesses. Litigation expenses are recoverable only if you have exhausted administrative remedies within the IRS.

Suing the IRS for unauthorized collection action. If an IRS employee recklessly or intentionally disregards the law or IRS regulations when making a tax assessment or taking some other collection action, you may sue the IRS in federal district court for actual economic damages resulting from the IRS employee's misconduct plus certain costs of bringing the action. The maximum damage award is $100,000. *Under legislation being considered by Congress when this book went to press, the $100,000 maximum amount would be increased to $1 million for reckless or intentional IRS acts and the $100,000 limit would be retained for negligent acts; see the Supplement.*

Suits for damages must be based on IRS employee conduct after November 10, 1988. Before you sue, you must bring an administrative claim to the IRS for your damages. The lawsuit must be filed within two years of the date your right to sue accrued.

According to IRS regulations, actual economic damages that may be recovered are monetary losses you suffer as a direct result of the IRS' unlawful action. For example, a business may lose loyal customers and suffer an actual cash loss if the IRS' action damages the business' reputation. Other actual expenses could include the cost of renting a house or a car if the IRS puts a lien on or seizes your property, or loss of income due to the garnishment of your paycheck. Damages from the IRS for loss of reputation, inconvenience, or emotional distress are allowed only to the extent that they result in such actual monetary loss.

The IRS defines "costs of action" that you may recover as (1) fees of the clerk and marshall; (2) fees of the court reporter; (3) fees and disbursements for printing and witnesses; (4) copying fees; (5) docket fees; and (6) compensation for court-appointed experts and interpreters.

Litigation costs and administrative proceeding costs are not treated as "costs of the action." However, if the IRS denies your administrative claim for damages and you successfully sue in federal district court, you are considered a "prevailing party" and may recover attorney fees, related litigation expenses, and administrative costs before the IRS as previously discussed.

Warning: If you start a court action and the court holds that it is frivolous, you may be penalized up to $10,000.

IRS failure to release lien. A suit for damages may also be brought in federal district court against the IRS if IRS employees improperly fail to release a lien on your property. Before you sue, you must file an administrative claim for damages. The lawsuit must be filed within two years after your claim arose. You may sue for actual economic damages plus costs of the action; the types of damages that may be recovered are similar to those previously discussed for suing the IRS for unauthorized collection actions.

Cases begun after 1985 and before November 11, 1988. The rules for recovering legal costs after litigation begins are similar to the rules previously discussed for cases begun after November 10, 1988. With respect to administrative proceedings, an award may be based only on unjustified conduct by the IRS District Counsel and not on earlier administrative proceedings.

Cases begun on or after March 1, 1983, and before 1986. You may recover litigation expenses, including attorneys' fees, of up to $25,000 from the government. The $25,000 limit applies to attorneys' fees, fees of expert witnesses, cost of reports or studies necessary for your case, and court costs.

Whether the IRS has acted unreasonably during litigation is a factual issue which courts decide on a case by case basis. Court decisions have split on the issue of whether attorneys' fees may be awarded if the IRS concedes before trial. Some federal courts have allowed awards if the IRS conduct before trial was unreasonable. Other federal courts have held that if the IRS concedes before trial, no award is allowed even if the IRS acted unreasonably before trial.

The Tax Court has held that unreasonable IRS conduct during its administrative proceedings is not a basis for claiming a legal fee award. Only if the IRS acts unreasonably after a Tax Court petition is filed may an award be made. If the IRS concedes the case after a Tax Court petition is filed, the costs of preparing and filing the petition and later legal expenses are recoverable only if the IRS litigating position was unreasonable. The IRS position may be reasonable even though it eventually concedes the case. Expenses paid or incurred during pretrial administrative proceedings may not be recovered. Federal appeals courts have split on the issue of whether unreasonable IRS conduct before litigation may support an award.

TAXPAYER BILL OF RIGHTS

¶48.8

The provisions of the Taxpayer Bill of Rights are generally intended to protect taxpayers during IRS examination and tax collection procedures. The chart below lists the key provisions.

When this book went to press, Congress was considering additional Taxpayer Bill of Rights rules, such as an increase in the amount of personal property exempt from IRS levy and an expansion of the availability of Taxpayer Assistance Orders to obtain hardship relief; see the Supplement for an update.

Taxpayer Bill of Rights

Item—	Rule—
Being informed of your rights	If the IRS sends you notice of a deficiency or collection action, it must include a nontechnical statement of your rights during an audit and an explanation of IRS collection procedures and appeals procedures within the IRS and the courts.
Having a representative handle your case	To represent you at an examination, you may give a written power of attorney to a lawyer, CPA, or enrolled agent or actuary qualified to practice before the IRS. You do not have to attend the examination unless the IRS issues an administrative summons requesting your presence.
Recording your examination	As discussed at ¶48.3, you may, at your own expense, make an audio recording of an interview if you give advance notice to the IRS. The IRS may also record an interview; you must be given prior notice and an opportunity to obtain a transcript by reimbursing the IRS for the printing costs.
Getting hardship relief from IRS	If the IRS is threatening to seize your property or take some other collection measure that could cause you significant hardship, you may apply for a Taxpayer Assistance Order by filing Form 911 with the Problem Resolution Office in the IRS district where you live. While the Problem Resolution Officer or the IRS Taxpayer Ombudsman reviews your application, enforcement actions are suspended.
Relying on erroneous IRS advice	You may avoid penalties but not tax or interest if you rely on written IRS advice when preparing a return and the advice turns out to be erroneous. You must provide specific information to the IRS in writing when making a request for advice. You may no longer rely on the advice if the IRS gives you written notice that the advice is no longer the IRS position; if it takes a contrary position in regulations or in a published revenue ruling, procedure, or notice; or if the law is changed by a Supreme Court decision or tax treaty. If you have not been notified of a change in IRS position but a penalty is nevertheless assessed, file Form 843 for an abatement of the penalty and attach copies of your request for advice and the IRS, erroneous advice. Write at the top of Form 843: "Abatement of penalty or addition to tax pursuant to Section 6404(f)." If the penalty has been paid, file Form 843 as a refund claim.
Property exempt from IRS seizure	The weekly amount of wages exempt from IRS levy (seizure) is equal to your standard deduction plus allowable personal exemptions divided by 52. The amount of personal property exempt from IRS seizure under current law is $1,650 for fuel, provisions, furniture, and household effects. The exempt amount for books, tools, machinery, or equipment used in a business or profession is $1,100. A personal residence is exempt from IRS levy, unless an IRS district director or assistant district director personally authorizes it in writing or the Treasury Secretary finds that collection of the tax would be jeopardized if the residence is not seized. Before the IRS may seize property, it must give 30 days' notice. The notice must clearly describe the levy procedures, your options to avoid the levy, such as beginning installment payments for overdue tax, and steps for redeeming property if property is seized by the IRS. A bank will hold your account for 21 days after receiving notice of an IRS levy before turning over the money to the IRS. The 21-day freeze allows you time to contact the IRS. If the IRS attempts to levy your property after you have paid the underlying tax liability, the statute of limitations has expired, or if the property is exempt under bankruptcy rules, you should appeal to the IRS to release the levy. Send a written statement to the District Director of the IRS district in which the lien was filed, explaining your grounds for appeal.
Recovering attorney fees in IRS administrative proceedings	As discussed at ¶48.7, reasonable legal costs incurred during certain administrative proceedings may be recovered if you prevail in court.

PART

VIII

TAX ORGANIZER

This part is designed to help you—

- Organize your tax data, whether you plan to prepare your own tax return or have someone else prepare it. Even if you do not prepare your own tax return, you must first organize and collect your tax information for a tax professional.

- Prepare your tax return. Here you will find guides for selecting which tax forms to file and where to report income and expense deductions—plus sample copies of forms and schedules for 1992 filing. If your tax liability is under $100,000, use the Tax Tables in this part to look up your tax liability.

Note: Mail the card at the front of this book for the free Supplement of filled-in sample forms and blank forms suitable for filing with the IRS.

PREPARING YOUR RETURN

HOW TO PROCEED

We recommend that you follow these steps in preparing your return.

Step 1. Before preparing your return, collect your records. You cannot prepare your return unless you get your personal tax data in order. Even if you employ a tax professional to prepare your return, you must complete this important step. The records you need are listed on page 448.

Step 2. Review your tax returns for prior years. They will refresh your memory of how you handled prior items and remind you of deductions, carryover losses, and other items you might otherwise overlook. You may obtain copies of prior year tax returns by filing Form 4506 with the IRS and paying a fee.

Step 3. Decide whether to use Form 1040EZ, 1040A, or 1040 with the aid of the checklist on page 451.

Step 4. After you have decided which return to file, review the form to familiarize yourself with its details. You will find sample copies of the forms starting on page 453.

Step 5. Use the tax tables starting on page 477 to look up your tax liability if your taxable income is less than $100,000. If taxable income is $100,000 or more, use the tax rate schedules on page 267. After you have completed your return, put it aside and postpone checking your completed return for several hours or even a day so that you can review it with a fresh state of mind. Look in the next column for common errors that might delay a refund or result in a tax deficiency and interest costs.

Step 6. Finally, photocopy your return and keep the copy along with receipts, canceled checks, and other items to support your deductions.

CHECKING YOUR RETURN FOR POSSIBLE ERRORS.

Check your return to ensure the following *before* mailing it to the IRS:

- Your arithmetic is correct.
- Your Social Security number is recorded correctly on each form and schedule.
- You have filled in the proper boxes that state your filing status and exemption claims, and reported the Social Security number of each dependent age one or older as of the end of 1992.
- You have claimed the full standard deduction you are entitled to if you are age 65 or older, or blind.
- You have claimed the earned income credit if you have a qualifying child and your adjusted gross income is less than $22,370.
- You have used the tax table or schedule applicable to your tax status.
- You have put on the correct line the refund due you or the tax payable.
- If you owe any tax, you have included your check made out to the IRS for the correct amount due and written your Social Security number on the check.
- You have signed your return and if you file a joint return, your spouse has also signed.
- You have attached the correct copy of your Form W-2 and all appropriate forms and schedules.

APPLY FOR EXTENSION IF YOU CANNOT FILE ON TIME

If you cannot file your return on time, apply before the due date to the Internal Revenue Service office with which you file your return for an extension of time to file.

Automatic filing extension. You may get an extension without waiting for the IRS to act on your request. You receive an automatic four-month extension for your 1992 return if you file Form 4868 by April 15, 1993, and pay the full amount of tax you estimate that you owe. The extension gives you until August 16, 1993.

Abroad on April 15, 1993. You do not get an automatic two-month extension for filing and paying your tax merely by being out of the country on the filing due date. Thus, if you plan to be traveling abroad on April 15, 1993, and want to get a filing extension, you must claim the automatic four-month filing extension on Form 4868 and pay the estimated tax bill by April 15.

The only exception is for U.S. citizens or residents who live and have their main place of business outside the U.S. or Puerto Rico, or military personnel stationed outside the U.S. or Puerto Rico, on April 15, 1993. Such taxpayers still qualify for the automatic two-

month extension, until June 15. Such taxpayers may also receive an additional two-month extension by filing Form 4868 and paying the estimated taxes due by June 15.

Persian Gulf service. Military and support personnel who served in the Persian Gulf combat zone are allowed a special filing extension even if they had returned to the U.S. by April 15; see ¶35.5.

Interest and penalty for underpayment. An extension of time for filing does not extend the time for payment of tax. If on filing Form 4868, you pay less than the balance of the final tax you owe, you will be charged interest on the unpaid amount. If the tax paid with Form 4868, plus withholdings and estimated tax payments during 1992, is less than 90% of the amount due, you may also be subject to a late-payment penalty—unless you can show reasonable cause.

When you file your return within the extension period, you attach a duplicate of Form 4868 and include the balance of the unpaid tax, if any.

While the extension is automatically obtained by a proper filing on Form 4868 (including payment of tax), the IRS may terminate the extension on 10 days notice to you.

Extensions beyond August 16. Extensions beyond the automatic four-month period are allowed only if you file Form 2688 and show good cause such as illness of yourself or a family member, or lack of information returns needed to complete your return. Form 2688 must be filed before the end of the original four-month extension period. If the IRS agrees to your request, an additional two-month filing extension will be allowed, until October 15.

Getting an extension of time to pay tax. Do not allow your inability to pay the tax stop you from filing a return. Inability to pay the tax is not a reason for receiving an extension to file. By filing on time, you avoid a penalty for late filing. If you cannot pay your tax, file your return on time and pay what you can. You may apply for an extension of time to pay your tax on Form 1127.

With Form 1127, you must show that you do not have cash above necessary working capital, liquid assets, or the financial ability to get a loan to meet the tax liability. If you have other assets, such as a house, you must also show that a sale of the asset would be at a sacrifice price and cause you undue financial hardship. You attach to Form 1127 a list of receipts and disbursements for the three months before the due date and also a statement of assets and liabilities as of the end of the month preceding your application.

If the extension is allowed, you are usually given six months from the date the tax was due. An additional extension may be allowed if you are abroad. You may also be required to put up property you own as collateral. Collateral is not required if you do not own property.

Receiving an extension does not stop the running of interest on the tax.

If an extension is not allowed, you may be able to work out an installment payment schedule with the IRS.

WHERE TO SEND YOUR RETURN

Address the envelope containing your return to the Internal Revenue Service Center for the area where you live. No street address is needed. If your tax package includes a pre-printed address label and envelope, use them.

ALABAMA—Memphis, TN 37501
ALASKA—Ogden, UT 84201
ARIZONA—Ogden, UT 84201
ARKANSAS—Memphis, TN 37501
CALIFORNIA—File with the IRS Service Center at Ogden, UT 84201, if you live in the counties of Alpine, Amador, Butte, Calaveras, Colusa, Contra Costa, Del Norte, El Dorado, Glenn, Humboldt, Lake, Lassen, Marin, Mendocino, Modoc, Napa, Nevada, Placer, Plumas, Sacramento, San Joaquin, Shasta, Sierra, Siskiyou, Solano, Sonoma, Sutter, Tehama, Trinity, Yolo, and Yuba. All other California residents file at Fresno, CA 93888.
COLORADO—Ogden, UT 84201
CONNECTICUT—Andover, MA 05501
DELAWARE—Philadelphia, PA 19255
DISTRICT OF COLUMBIA—Philadelphia, PA 19255
FLORIDA—Atlanta, GA 39901
GEORGIA—Atlanta, GA 39901
HAWAII—Fresno, CA 93888
IDAHO—Ogden, UT 84201
ILLINOIS—Kansas City, MO 64999
INDIANA—Cincinnati, OH 45999
IOWA—Kansas City, MO 64999
KANSAS—Austin, TX 73301
KENTUCKY—Cincinnati, OH 45999
LOUISIANA—Memphis, TN 37501
MAINE—Andover, MA 05501
MARYLAND—Philadelphia, PA 19255
MASSACHUSETTS—Andover, MA 05501
MICHIGAN—Cincinnati, OH 45999
MINNESOTA—Kansas City, MO 64999
MISSISSIPPI—Memphis, TN 37501
MISSOURI—Kansas City, MO 64999
MONTANA—Ogden, UT 84201
NEBRASKA—Ogden, UT 84201
NEVADA—Ogden, UT 84201
NEW HAMPSHIRE—Andover, MA 05501

NEW JERSEY—Holtsville, NY 00501
NEW MEXICO—Austin, TX 73301
NEW YORK—New York City and counties of Nassau, Rockland, Suffolk, and Westchester—Holtsville, NY 00501
All Other Counties—Andover, MA 05501
NORTH CAROLINA—Memphis, TN 37501
NORTH DAKOTA—Ogden, UT 84201
OHIO—Cincinnati, OH 45999
OKLAHOMA—Austin, TX 73301
OREGON—Ogden, UT 84201
PENNSYLVANIA—Philadelphia, PA 19255
RHODE ISLAND—Andover, MA 05501
SOUTH CAROLINA—Atlanta, GA 39901
SOUTH DAKOTA—Ogden, UT 84201
TENNESSEE—Memphis, TN 37501
TEXAS—Austin, TX 73301
UTAH—Ogden, UT 84201
VERMONT—Andover, MA 05501
VIRGINIA—Philadelphia, PA 19255
WASHINGTON—Ogden, UT 84201
WEST VIRGINIA—Cincinnati, OH 45999
WISCONSIN—Kansas City, MO 64999
WYOMING—Ogden, UT 84201
FOREIGN COUNTRY: U.S. citizens and those filing Form 2555 or Form 4563, even if you have an A.P.O. or F.P.O. address—Philadelphia, PA 19255
A.P.O. or F.P.O. addresses—Philadelphia, PA 19255
PUERTO RICO (or if excluding income under Section 933)—Philadelphia, PA 19255
VIRGIN ISLANDS—Nonpermanent residents file with the IRS Center in Philadelphia, PA 19255; permanent residents file with the V.I. Bureau of Internal Revenue, Lockharts Garden No. 1A, Charlotte Amalie, St. Thomas, VI 00802
GUAM—Commissioner of Revenue and Taxation, 855 West Marine Dr., Agana, GU 96910
AMERICAN SAMOA—Philadelphia, PA 19255

GETTING YOUR REFUND FROM THE IRS

Speeding up a refund via electronic filing. If you are due a refund, filing your return electronically over telephone lines directly to an IRS computer may give you a refund in about three weeks, instead of waiting about two months after mailing your return. To file electronically, you must pay a fee to a tax preparer or filing service that has been accepted into the IRS electronic filing program. You also must file a consent on Form 8453 on which you may request direct deposit of your refund to a specific savings or checking account. Direct deposit speeds up the refund even more, to about two weeks. The advantage of obtaining a refund more quickly must be weighed against the cost. The IRS has encouraged the use of electronic filing because it reduces paperwork and return processing costs.

Call the IRS about your refund. You can call the IRS to check on the status of an expected refund. When you call the IRS' automated phone service, you must provide the Social Security number shown on the return (or the first number where you file jointly), filing status, and the amount of the refund.

The general IRS phone number is *1-800-829-4477*. However, in the following areas, you must dial a different number.

Arizona, Phoenix: 640-3933; *California*, Oakland: 839-4245; Counties of Alpine, Amador, Calaveras, Colusa, Contra Costa, Del Norte, El Dorado, Glenn, Humboldt, Lake, Lassen, Marin, Mendocino, Modoc, Napa, Nevada, Placer, Plumas, Sacramento, San Joaquin, Shasta, Sierra, Siskiyou, Solano, Sonoma, Sutter, Tehama, Trinity, Yolo, and Yuba: 1-800-829-4032; *Colorado*, Denver: 592-1118; *District of Columbia*, 628-2929; *Georgia*, Atlanta: 331-6572; *Illinois*, Chicago: 886-9614; In area code 708: 1-312-886-9614; Springfield: 789-0489; *Indiana*, Indianapolis: 631-1010; *Iowa*, Des Moines: 284-7454; *Maryland*, Baltimore: 244-7306; *Massachusetts*, Boston: 536-0789; *Michigan*, Detroit: 961-4282; *Minnesota*, St. Paul: 644-7748; *Missouri*, St. Louis: 241-4700; *Nebraska*, Omaha: 221-3324; *New York*, Manhattan: 406-4080; Bronx, Brooklyn, Queens and Staten Island: 858-4461; Buffalo: 685-5533; *Ohio*, Cincinnati: 421-0329; Cleveland: 522-3037; *Oregon*, Portland: 294-5363; *Pennsylvania*, Philadelphia: 627-1040; Pittsburgh: 261-1040; *Texas*, Dallas: 767-1792; Houston: 850-8801; *Virginia*, Richmond: 783-1569; *Washington*, Seattle: 343-7221; *Wisconsin*, Milwaukee: 273-8100.

Any late changes to these numbers will be in the Supplement.

KEEPING TAX RECORDS

Tax saving requires keeping records, which will help you to figure your income and deductions. Do not trust your memory. With bills accumulating during the year, you are bound to overlook items. But more importantly, you will have no record to present to the IRS if your return is audited.

- Make a habit of jotting down deductible items as they come along.
- Keep a calendar or diary of expenses to record deductible items.
- Keep a file of bills. This can be an ordinary folder in which you arrange your bills and receipts alphabetically. This will remind you of deductible items and provide you with supporting evidence.
- Use your checkbook stubs as a record. If you own a business, you must keep a complete set of account books for it.

IRA records. If you make nondeductible IRA contributions, keep a record of both your nondeductible and deductible contributions and also of any distributions so that when you withdraw IRA money you can figure the tax-free and taxed parts of the withdrawal. For this purpose keep copies of Form 8606 and Form 5498; *see ¶8.8.*

Passive losses. If you have losses that are suspended and carried forward to future years under the passive loss restrictions (¶10.13), keep the worksheets to Form 8582 as a record of the carry-forward losses.

Home mortgage interest. Keep your bank statements and cancelled checks. If a loan secured by a first or second home is used to make substantial home improvements, keep records of the improvement costs to support your home interest deduction (¶15.5).

How long should you keep your records? Your records should be kept for a minimum of three years after the year to which they are applicable. Some authorities advise keeping them for six years, since in some cases where income has not been reported, the IRS may go back as far as six years to question a tax return. In cases of suspected tax fraud, there is no time limitation at all.

Keep records of transactions relating to the *basis* of property for as long as they are important in figuring the basis of the original or replacement property. For example, records of the purchase of a residence or improvements must be held as long as you own the house.

As mentioned above, if you have made any nondeductible IRA contributions, records of IRA contributions and distributions must be kept until all funds have been withdrawn. Similarly, you should save mutual fund confirmations or other records that show reinvested dividends and cash purchases of shares; these are part of your cost basis that reduce taxable gain when you sell shares in the fund.

Finally, if you make taxable gifts of property (above the annual gift tax exclusion), save all records of appraisals and other valuation information concerning your gifts. The IRS could try to revalue post-1976 taxable gifts for purposes of computing estate tax liability at your death; the Tax Court has upheld IRS authority to revalue.

TAX RETURN PREPARERS

If you need a professional tax return preparer to help you prepare your return, factors to consider in choosing a preparer include the complexity of your return, the preparer's qualifications, and the comprehensiveness of the services provided.

If your return is relatively simple, you may want to avoid the expense of hiring a tax preparer and prepare the return yourself using YOUR INCOME TAX and IRS forms and instructions as a guide.

If you choose to use a professional preparer, find out what the fees are and what services are included. For example, is advance tax planning offered?

If you are entitled to a refund and willing to pay a fee to receive it faster, consider choosing a preparer who participates in the IRS' electronic filing program. The fee for electronic filing may be lower if your return is prepared by the same firm.

Another important consideration is whether the preparer is qualified to represent you at an IRS audit. An attorney or CPA may practice before the IRS.

Enrolled agents are admitted to practice before the IRS after passing an IRS examination or after completing five years of audit-level service as an IRS employee. Enrolled agents are the only tax professionals required to complete continuing education courses every year.

Tax preparers are subject to IRS regulations. Tax return preparers may be subject to penalties for understating the tax on a return or failing to keep proper records. Anyone who prepares a return or refund claim for a fee is considered a preparer under the tax law. When more than one person works on the return or claim, each schedule or entry is reviewed separately to determine the preparer of that schedule or item. A practitioner who gives advice directly relevant to a determination of the existence, characterization, or amount of an entry on a return is considered the preparer of that item.

A practitioner who prepares entries on a return that affect entries on the return of another taxpayer may be considered the preparer of the other return if the entries are directly reflected on the other return and constitute a substantial portion of that return. For example, a practitioner preparing a partnership return may be considered the preparer of a partner's return if the entries picked up from the partnership return constitute a substantial portion of the partner's individual tax return. Regulations provide tests for determining whether a part of a return is considered substantial. Under the regulations, an entry is not considered substantial if it is (1) less than $2,000, or (2) less than $100,000 and also less than 20% of adjusted gross income.

You are not a preparer if you merely type or reproduce a return or claim, or prepare a return for your employer or an officer of your employer or a fellow employee.

Preparer penalties. For tax returns prepared after 1989, a $250 penalty may be imposed if all of the following apply: (1) tax is understated on the return; (2) the preparer knew (or reasonably should have known) that the understatement was based on a taxpayer position that did not have a realistic possibility of being sustained on its merits; and (3) the taxpayer position was frivolous or, if not frivolous, was not adequately disclosed. If the preparer can show good faith and a reasonable cause for the understatement, the $250 penalty will not be imposed. If a tax understatement is willful, or due to reckless disregard of IRS rules, a $1,000 penalty may be imposed; the penalty is $750 if the $250 penalty also applies to the return.

According to the IRS, a taxpayer position has a "realistic possi-bility" of being sustained on its merits if a person knowledgeable in the tax law would conclude, after a well-informed analysis, that there is at least a one-in-three likelihood that the position will be sustained.

For purposes of the $250 or $1,000 penalty, IRS proposed regulations provide that only one person associated with a firm is considered the preparer of the return. The practitioner who signs the return is considered to be the preparer. If none of the persons considered to be preparers under IRS rules signs the return, the person with overall supervisory responsibility is treated as the preparer for penalty purposes.

However, a nonsigning preparer may be subject to a $1,000 penalty for knowingly aiding and abetting the understatement of tax liability on a return ($10,000 for corporate returns).

Preparers must satisfy the following requirements:

1. Retain a record of the name, Social Security number, and place of work of each preparer whom he or she employs. The records must be kept for three years following the close of the return period and must be made available for inspection upon request of the district director. There is a $50 penalty for each failure to keep and make available a proper record and a $50 penalty for each required item that is missing from the record. The maximum penalty for any return period is $25,000.
2. Furnish a completed copy of the return or refund claim to the taxpayer not later than when it is presented for the taxpayer's signature. There is a $50 penalty for each failure, up to a maximum of $25,000 for documents filed during any one calendar year.
3. Keep for three years and have available for inspection by the IRS a completed copy of each return or claim prepared, or a list of the names and identification numbers of taxpayers for whom returns or claims were prepared. A $50 penalty is imposed for each failure, up to a maximum of $25,000 for any return period. A preparer who sells his or her business is not relieved of the requirement of retaining those records.
4. Sign the return and include his or her identifying number or the identifying number of his or her employer. A $50 penalty is imposed for each failure, up to a maximum of $25,000 for documents filed during any calendar year. Where more than one practitioner has worked on a return, the individual with primary responsibility for overall accuracy must sign the return.

The penalty for failure to meet these four requirements may be avoided by showing reasonable cause for the failure.

Tax preparers are subject to a $500 penalty if they endorse or negotiate a refund check issued to a taxpayer whose return they have prepared. Business managers for athletes, actors, or other professionals who prepare their clients' tax returns and handle their tax refunds may also be subject to the penalty. To avoid the penalty, the manager must act only as an agent in depositing the client's refund check.

In addition to the penalties imposed, the IRS may also seek to enjoin fraudulent or deceptive practice or to enjoin a person from acting as an income tax return preparer. The IRS may seek an injunction against a preparer for "aiding and abetting" a taxpayer to underpay tax. The IRS publishes a list of enjoined preparers in its Internal Revenue Bulletin.

Note: *For additional details regarding income tax return preparers, see the Professional Edition of* YOUR INCOME TAX.

INCOME TAX FORMS

Tax Record and Return Directory

The following table lists tax records you need for specific items of income and expense and directs you to the return, schedule, and line on which to report the items. The items are listed in the order in which they appear on Forms 1040, 1040A, and 1040EZ.

Item—	Records Needed—	Reporting—
Exemptions for dependents	Records of support contribution for food, lodging, medical expenses, such as canceled checks, diary entries. Birth certificates in case age of a child is questioned. School attendance record if student status is questioned. Form 8332 allowing noncustodial parent to claim the exemption. This form must also be attached to return by noncustodial parent claiming exemption; see ¶1.28. Forms 2120 if dependent's support is shared by other persons; see ¶1.27.	Form 1040A, Line 6(c) Form 1040, Line 6(c)
Wages and salaries	Form W-2. Your employer must send your 1992 Form W-2 by February 1, 1993. Attach Copy B to your federal return. Keep Copy C for your records. If you worked for more than one employer during 1992, attach all Copy B forms to your return.	Form 1040EZ, Line 1 Form 1040A, Line 7 Form 1040, Line 7
Tip income	Form 4070 or other record showing your monthly reports of cash tips of $20 or more. Form W-2. Also see ¶26.8 for reporting FICA taxes on unreported tips.	Form 1040EZ, Line 1 Form 1040A, Line 7 Form 1040, Line 7
Interest income	Form 1099-INT Form 1099-OID Deposit slips of interest received on money you loaned to others.	Form 1040EZ, Line 2 ($400 or less) Form 1040A, Line 8(a); Schedule 1, Part I (over $400) Form 1040, Line 8(a); Schedule B, Part I (over $400)
Dividend income	Form 1099-DIV. Company statements of dividend payments, especially if stock dividends have been paid.	Form 1040A, Line 9; Schedule 1, Part II (over $400) Form 1040, Line 9; Schedule B, Part II (over $400)
Taxable refund of state and local income tax	Form 1099-G	Form 1040, Line 10
Alimony received	Deposit slips of alimony received and ex-spouse's Social Security number. Copy of divorce or separation decree or agreements.	Form 1040, Line 11 if taxable
Business income or loss	Business accounting records, deposit slips. Business checkbook, deposit slips, invoice receipts, canceled checks, bank statements. Form 1099-MISC	Form 1040, Line 12; Schedule C or C-EZ Form 8582 if passive activity rules apply; see Chapter 10.
Sale of stocks and bonds	Form 1099-B and broker confirmation statements.	Schedule D Form 1040, Line 13
Sale of personal residence	Closing papers, records of purchase, improvements; see ¶29.6.	Schedule D Form 2119 Form 1040, Line 13 if gain is reported; losses are not deductible.
Sale of real estate	Closing statement, records of cost and improvements. Records of depreciation.	Schedule 4797 Schedule D Form 1040, Line 13
IRA distributions	Form 1099-R	Form 1040A, Line 10 Form 1040, Line 16(c)
Pensions and annuities	Form 1099-R if you receive annuity payments or lump-sum distributions.	Form 1040A, Line 11 Form 1040, Line 17
Commercial annuity income	Form 1099-R	Form 1040A, Line 11 Form 1040, Line 17
Rent income	Account records, checkbook, canceled checks, and receipts.	Schedule E Form 1040, Line 18 Form 8582 if passive activity rules apply
Royalty income	Form 1099-MISC	Schedule E Form 1040, Line 18
Partnership income	Schedule K-1, Form 1065	Schedule E Form 1040, Line 18

TAX ORGANIZER

Item—	Records Needed—	Reporting—
Beneficiary of trust or estate	Schedule K-1, Form 1041	Schedule E Form 1040, Line 18
S Corporation	Schedule K-1, Form 1120S	Schedule E Form 1040, Line 18
Unemployment compensation	Form 1099-G	Form 1040A, Line 12 Form 1040, Line 20
Social Security benefits	Form SSA-1099	Form 1040A, Line 13 Form 1040, Line 21
Gambling income	Form W-2G, diary or other record showing wins and losses, losing tickets.	Form 1040, Line 22
Other income	Form 1099-MISC, records of amounts received, date received.	Form 1040, Line 22
IRA deductible contribution	Trustee's statements of contribution, copy of plan.	Form 1040A, Lines 15(a) and 15(b) Form 1040, Lines 24(a) and 24(b)
Deduction for self-employment tax	Schedule SE, Form 1040	Form 1040, Line 25
Self-employed health insurance premium	Canceled check of payment, copy of contract, insurance statement	Form 1040, Line 26
Keogh or SEP contribution for yourself	Trustee statement, copy of plan.	Form 1040, Line 27
Penalty on early withdrawal of savings	Form 1099-INT	Form 1040, Line 28
Alimony deduction	Canceled checks, copy of divorce or separation decree, written separation agreement, ex-spouse's Social Security number.	Form 1040, Line 29
Employee expenses	Diary logs, receipts, copy of accounting to employer.	Form 2106 Schedule A, Line 19
Home office expenses	Records of expenses, business use and allocation.	Form 2106 if an employee; Schedule A, Line 19 Form 8829 if self-employed; Schedule C, Line 30
Medical and dental expenses	Canceled checks, statements, prescriptions; log of travel expenses and lodging costs.	Form 1040 Schedule A, Lines 1-4
Taxes—state and local income, personal property, real estate	Form W-2 for withholding of income tax. Canceled checks. Bank statements of property taxes paid by bank (mortgages). Form 1099-DIV for foreign tax. Form 1099-INT or tax receipt for foreign tax withheld at source.	Form 1040 Schedule A, Lines 5-8
Mortgage interest	Bank statement showing interest paid. Form 1098	Form 1040 Schedule A, Line 9
Points	Copy of bank statements, canceled check.	Form 1040 Schedule A, Line 10
Cash donations	Canceled checks, receipt from charity.	Form 1040; Schedule A, Line 13
Volunteer expenses for charitable organizations	Log of travel, canceled checks show purpose.	Form 1040 Schedule A, Line 13
Property donation	Description of property, records of fair market value and cost. Receipt from organization. If in excess of $5,000, qualified appraisal report and statement from organization.	Form 1040 Schedule A, Line 14
Casualty losses	The records and steps are detailed at ¶18.11 and 18.12.	Form 1040; Schedule A, Line 17 Form 4684
Theft losses	Statements from witnesses who saw the theft or police records of a breaking into your house or car. A newspaper account of the crime might also help.	Form 1040 Form 4684 Schedule A, Line 17
Moving expenses	Canceled checks or receipts for expenses incurred, diary or log.	Form 1040; Schedule A, Line 18 Form 3903
Gambling losses	Losing tickets or receipts, diary showing daily wagers, wins, and losses.	Form 1040 Schedule A, Line 25
Union dues	Wage statements showing withholding for dues or canceled checks.	Form 1040 Schedule A, Line 19

Item—	Records Needed—	Reporting—
Unreimbursed travel and entertainment expenses	Diary log, and receipts kept according to the rules of ¶20.29.	Form 2106 Form 1040; Schedule A, Line 19
Unreimbursed auto expenses if you are employed	Statement from employer requiring use of car. Mileage log. Receipts of expenses if actual costs are claimed. Cost records of auto if depreciation is claimed.	Form 2106 Form 1040 Schedule A, Line 19
Investment expenses	Canceled checks.	Form 1040; Schedule A, Line 20
Bank deposit boxes	Bank statements.	Form 1040; Schedule A, Line 20
Tax preparation fees	Canceled checks.	Form 1040; Schedule A, Line 20
"Kiddie" tax	Child's Forms 1099-INT, 1099-DIV, and 1099-OID	Form 1040A, Line 23 Form 1040, Line 38 Form 8615 if income is reported on child's return. Form 8814 if parent elects to report child's income on Form 1040.
Child and dependent care expenses	Canceled checks for amounts paid to care for child.	Form 1040A, Line 24(a); Schedule 2 Form 1040, Line 41; Form 2441
Credit for the elderly or the disabled	Physician's statement of condition.	Form 1040A, Line 24(b); Schedule 3 Form 1040, Line 42; Schedule R
Advanced earned income credit payments	Form W-2	Form 1040A, Line 26 Form 1040, Line 52
Federal taxes withheld	Form 1099 Form W-2	Form 1040EZ, Line 6 Form 1040A, Line 28(a) Form 1040, Line 54
Estimated tax payments	Canceled checks and copy of Form 1040-ES.	Form 1040A, Line 28(b) Form 1040, Line 55
Earned income credit	Form W-2 if an employee, Schedule SE if self-employed to show earnings. Form W-5 if advanced payment of credit was received.	Form 1040A, Line 28(c); Schedule EIC Form 1040, Line 56; Schedule EIC
Foreign tax credit	Form 1099-DIV; foreign tax returns or statements.	Form 1116 Form 1040, Line 43
Prior alternative minimum tax credit	Copy of prior year's Form 6251.	Form 8801 Form 1040, Line 44

CHOOSING YOUR TAX FORM

There are three tax forms: Form 1040, Form 1040A, and Form 1040EZ. Use the simplified Form 1040EZ or Form 1040A only if you find the return will save you time and not cause you to give up tax-saving deductions or credits. To help you make your selections, fill in the following chart.

By checking the box that indicates your tax status, income, expenses, and credit items, you will be guided in choosing which form to use.

Choosing Your Tax Form

Item—	Form 1040EZ*—	Form 1040A*—	Form 1040—
Single	□**	□	□
Head of household		□	□
Married filing jointly		□	□
Married filing separately		□	□
Widow and widower		□	□
EXEMPTION for			
Relatives and dependents		□	□
Wages, salary	□***	□	□
Interest	□****	□	□
Dividends		□	□
Unemployment compensation		□	□
Self-employment income			□
Pension-annuity		□	□
IRA distributions		□	□
Rents and royalties			□
Gains and loss from property sales			□
Alimony			□
State tax refunds			□
Social Security benefits		□	□
IRA deduction		□	□
Alimony paid			□
Penalty for early withdrawal of savings			□
Deduction for Keogh plan			□
Employee business expenses			□
State and local income taxes			□
Real estate taxes			□
Home mortgage interest, investment and business interest			□
Charitable contributions			□
Medical and dental expenses			□
Casualty and theft losses			□
Moving expenses			□
Miscellaneous deductions (investment expenses, tax preparation)			□
Credit for child and dependent care		□	□
Earned income credit		□	□
Credit for elderly and totally disabled		□	□
Foreign tax credit			□
All other credits			□
Estimated tax payments and estimated tax penalty		□	□
Advance earned income credit (EIC) payments		□	□
Self-employment tax			□
Penalty tax on an IRA			□
Alternative minimum tax			□
Social Security tax on tips not reported to your employer			□
Uncollected Social Security tax on tips shown on your Form W-2			□
"Kiddie" tax on child's return		□	□
"Kiddie" tax on parent's return			□
All other taxes or penalties			□

*Total taxable income less than $50,000.
**Under age 65 and not blind on 1-1-93.
***No more than $55,500 if you worked for more than one employer.
****Up to $400.

LIST OF SUPPLEMENTAL FORMS

In addition to Form 1040 and its accompanying schedules, the IRS provides other forms for claiming tax credits, for supporting deductions and exemptions, for requests for extensions of time, etc. These forms, as well as others not listed below, may be obtained from any Internal Revenue Service office or by calling 1–800–829–3676. The use of many of these forms is optional; a statement may suffice. Supplemental forms include the following:

Form 1040X—Amended U.S. Individual Income Tax Return (page 370)

Form 1045—Quick Refund for Carryback Adjustments (¶38.4)

Form 1065, Schedule K-1—Partner's Share of Income Credits, Deductions (¶45.1)

Form 1098—Mortgage Interest Statement (¶15.6)

Form 1116—Foreign Tax Credit (¶36.14)

Form 1120S, Schedule K-1—S Corporation Shareholder's Share of Income, Credits, Deductions (¶45.6)

Form 1127—Application for Extension of Time for Payment of Tax (page 445)

Form 1128—Application for Change in Accounting Period

Form 1310—Statement of Claimant to Refund Due Deceased Taxpayer (¶1.12)

Form 2106—Statement of Employee Business Expenses (¶19.3)

Form 2119—Statement Concerning Sale or Exchange of Personal Residence (¶29.7)

Form 2120—Multiple Support Declaration (¶1.27)

Form 2210—Statement Relating to Underpayment of Estimated Tax (Chapter 27); Form 2210F (for farmers and fishermen)

Form 2350—Application for Extension of Time for Filing Tax Return (for U.S. citizens abroad who expect to receive exempt earned income) (¶36.7)

Form 2439—Notice to Shareholder of Undistributed Long-Term Capital Gains (¶4.3)

Form 2441—Credit for Dependent Care Expenses (¶25.1)

Form 2553—Election by Corporation as to Taxable Status Under Subchapter S (¶45.8)

Form 2555—Exclusion for Income Earned Abroad (for U.S. citizens abroad; file with Form 1040) (Chapter 36)

Form 2555-EZ—Foreign Earned Income Exclusion (Chapter 36).

Form 2688—Application for Extension of Time to File Tax Return (Page 445; also Form 4868 next column)

Form 2848—Power of Attorney

Form 3115—Application for Change in Accounting Method (¶40.2)

Form 3468—Computation of Investment Credit (¶9.8, ¶40.22)

Form 3800—General Business Credit (¶40.22)

Form 3903—Moving Expenses (Chapter 21)

Form 4070—Employee Tip Income Reported (¶26.8)

Form 4070A—Daily Record of Tips

Form 4136—Credit for Federal Tax on Fuels (for claiming credit for diesel vehicles, see ¶40.22)

Form 4137—Computation of Social Security Tax on Unreported Tip Income (¶26.8)

Form 4255—Tax From Recomputing a Prior Year Investment Credit (¶40.22)

Form 4506—Request for Copy of Tax Return

Form 4562—Depreciation (¶42.2)

Form 4684—Casualties and Thefts (Chapter 18)

Form 4782—Employee Moving Expense Information (¶21.5, ¶21.6)

Form 4797—Supplementary Schedule of Gains and Losses (¶44.1)

Form 4835—Farm Rental Income and Expenses

Form 4868—Application for Automatic Extension of Time to File Return (Page 444)

Form 4952—Investment Interest Deduction (¶15.9)

Form 4972—Averaging Method for Lump-Sum Distributions (¶7.4)

Form 5213—Election to Postpone Determination on Presumption that an Activity is Engaged in for Profit (¶40.9)

Form 5329—Return for Individual Retirement Savings (¶8.12)

Form 5500—Annual Return/Report of Employee Benefit Plan (100 or more participants)

Form 5500EZ—Annual Return of One-Participant Pension Benefit Plan (¶41.7)

Form 5500-C/R—Annual Return/Report of Employee Benefit Plan (fewer than 100 participants) (¶41.7)

Form 6198—Computation of Deductible Loss From At-Risk Activities (¶10.17)

Form 6251—Alternative Minimum Tax (¶23.1)

Form 6252—Computation of Installment Sale Income (¶5.36)

Form 6781—Regulated Futures Contracts and Straddles (¶5.27)

Form 8271—Investor Reporting of Tax Shelter Registration Number (¶38.6)

Form 8275—Disclosure Statement (¶47.5)

Form 8275-R—Regulation Disclosure Statement (¶47.5)

Form 8283—Noncash Charitable Contributions (¶14.12)

Form 8300—Report of Cash Payments Over $10,000 Received in a Trade or Business (¶40.4)

Form 8332—Release of Claim to Exemption for Child of Divorced or Separated Parents (¶1.28)

Form 8379—Injured Spouse Claim and Allocation (¶38.2)

Form 8396—Mortgage Interest Credit (¶15.1)

Form 8582—Passive Activity Loss Limitations (Chapter 10)

Form 8582-CR—Passive Activity Credit Limitations (¶10.7)

Form 8586—Low Income Housing Credit (¶9.8)

Form 8606—Nondeductible IRA Contributions, IRA Basis, and Nontaxable IRA Distributions (¶8.5, ¶8.8)

Form 8615—Reporting Investment Income Exceeding $1,200 of Children Under Age 14 (¶24.1)

Form 8752—Required Payment or Refund under Section 7519 (¶45.2, ¶45.12)

Form 8801—Credit For Prior Year Minimum Tax (¶23.7)

Form 8814—Parent's Election to Report Child's Interest and Dividends (¶24.5)

Form 8815—Exclusion of Interest from Series EE U.S. Savings Bonds Issued after 1989 (¶33.3)

Form 8822—Change of Address (¶47.6)

Form 8824—Like-Kind Exchanges (¶6.1)

Form 8828—Recapture of Federal Mortgage Subsidy (¶29.7)

Form 8829—Expenses for Business Use of Your Home (¶40.11)

Form 8830—Enhanced Oil Recovery Credit (¶40.22)

Form 1040A

Department of the Treasury—Internal Revenue Service

U.S. Individual Income Tax Return

1992

IRS Use Only—Do not write or staple in this space.

OMB No. 1545-0085

Label
(See page 14.)

Use the IRS label. Otherwise, please print or type.

L A B E L   H E R E

| Your first name and initial | Last name | Your social security number |
| If a joint return, spouse's first name and initial | Last name | Spouse's social security number |

Home address (number and street). If you have a P.O. box, see page 15. Apt. no.

City, town or post office, state, and ZIP code. If you have a foreign address, see page 15.

For Privacy Act and Paperwork Reduction Act Notice, see page 4.

Presidential Election Campaign Fund (See page 15.)

Do you want $1 to go to this fund? . . . .

If a joint return, does your spouse want $1 to go to this fund?

| | Yes | No |

Note: *Checking "Yes" will not change your tax or reduce your refund.*

Check the box for your filing status
(See page 15.)

Check only one box.

1 ☐ Single

2 ☐ Married filing joint return (even if only one had income)

3 ☐ Married filing separate return. Enter spouse's social security number above and full name here. ▶ _____

4 ☐ Head of household (with qualifying person). (See page 16.) If the qualifying person is a child but not your dependent, enter this child's name here. ▶ _____

5 ☐ Qualifying widow(er) with dependent child (year spouse died ▶19___). (See page 17.)

Figure your exemptions
(See page 18.)

If more than seven dependents, see page 21.

6a ☐ **Yourself.** If your parent (or someone else) can claim you as a dependent on his or her tax return, **do not** check box 6a. But be sure to check the box on line 18b on page 2.

b ☐ **Spouse**

c **Dependents:**

(1) name (first, initial, and last name)	(2) Check if under age 1	(3) If age 1 or older, dependent's social security number	(4) Dependent's relationship to you	(5) No. of months lived in your home in 1992

d If your child didn't live with you but is claimed as your dependent under a pre-1985 agreement, check here . . . . ▶ ☐

e Total number of exemptions claimed.

No. of boxes checked on 6a and 6b _____

No. of your children on 6c who:
- lived with you _____
- didn't live with you due to divorce or separation (see page 21) _____

No. of other dependents on 6c _____

Add numbers entered on lines above _____

Figure your total income

Attach Copy B of your Forms W-2 and 1099-R here.

If you didn't get a W-2, see page 22.

Attach check or money order on top of any Forms W-2 or 1099-R.

7 Wages, salaries, tips, etc. This should be shown in box 10 of your W-2 form(s). Attach Form(s) W-2. | 7

8a **Taxable** interest income (see page 24). If over $400, also complete and attach Schedule 1, Part I. | 8a

b **Tax-exempt** interest. DO NOT include on line 8a. 8b | |

9 Dividends. If over $400, also complete and attach Schedule 1, Part II. | 9

10a Total IRA distributions. 10a | 10b Taxable amount (see page 25). 10b

11a Total pensions and annuities. 11a | 11b Taxable amount (see page 25). 11b

12 Unemployment compensation (see page 29). | 12

13a Social security benefits. 13a | 13b Taxable amount (see page 29). 13b

14 Add lines 7 through 13b (far right column). This is your **total income.** ▶ 14

Figure your adjusted gross income

15a Your IRA deduction from applicable worksheet. 15a

b Spouse's IRA deduction from applicable worksheet. **Note:** *Rules for IRAs begin on page 31.* 15b

c Add lines 15a and 15b. These are your **total adjustments.** 15c

16 Subtract line 15c from line 14. This is your **adjusted gross income.** If less than $22,370, see "Earned income credit" on page 39. ▶ 16

This form is an advance proof. Use the final IRS version for filing Cat. No. 11327A

1992 Form 1040A page 1

Name(s) shown on page 1	Your social security number

Figure your standard deduction, exemption amount, and taxable income

17 Enter the amount from line 16. **17**

18a Check if: ☐ **You** were 65 or older ☐ Blind ☐ **Spouse** was 65 or older ☐ Blind } Enter number of boxes checked ▶ 18a ☐

b If your parent (or someone else) can claim you as a dependent, check here . . . . ▶ 18b ☐

c If you are married filing separately and your spouse files Form 1040 and itemizes deductions, see page 35 and check here ▶ 18c ☐

19 Enter the **standard deduction** shown below for your filing status. **But if you checked any box on line 18a or b,** go to page 35 to find your standard deduction. **If you checked box 18c, enter -0-.**

- Single—$3,600 • Head of household—$5,250
- Married filing jointly or Qualifying widow(er)—$6,000
- Married filing separately—$3,000 **19**

20 Subtract line 19 from line 17. (If line 19 is more than line 17, enter -0-.) **20**

21 Multiply $2,300 by the total number of exemptions claimed on line 6e. **21**

22 Subtract line 21 from line 20. (If line 21 is more than line 20, enter -0-.) This is your **taxable income.** ▶ **22**

Figure your tax, credits, and payments

If you want the IRS to figure your tax, see the instructions for line 22 on page 36.

23 Find the tax on the amount on line 22. Check if from: ☐ Tax Table (pages 48–53) or ☐ Form 8615 (see page 37). **23**

24a Credit for child and dependent care expenses. Complete and attach Schedule 2. **24a**

b Credit for the elder or the disabled. Complete and attach Schedule 3. **24b**

c Add lines 24a and 24b. These are your **total** credits **24c**

25 Subtract line 24c from line 23 (If line 24c is more than line 23, enter -0-.) **25**

26 Advance earned income credit payments from Form W-2. **26**

27 Add lines 25 and 26. This is your **total tax.** ▶ **27**

28a Total Federal income tax withheld. If any tax is from Form(s) 1099, check here. ▶ ☐ **28a**

b 1992 estimated tax payments and amount applied from 1991 return. **28b**

c **Earned income credit.** Complete and attach Schedule EIC. **28c**

d Add lines 28a, 28b, and 28c. These are your **total payments.** ▶ **28d**

Figure your refund or amount you owe

Attach check or money order on top of Form(s) W-2, etc., on page 1.

29 If line 28d is more than line 27, subtract line 27 from line 28d. This is the amount you **overpaid.** **29**

30 Amount of line 29 you want **refunded to you.** **30**

31 Amount of line 29 you want **applied to your 1993 estimated tax.** **31**

32 If line 27 is more than line 28d, subtract line 28d from line 27. This is the **amount you owe.** Attach check or money order for full amount payable to the "Internal Revenue Service". Write your name, address, social security number, daytime phone number, and "1992 Form 1040A" on it. **32**

33 Estimated tax penalty (see page 41). **33**

Sign your return

Keep a copy of this return for your records.

Under penalties of perjury, I declare that I have examined this return and accompanying schedules and statements, and to the best of my knowledge and belief, they are true, correct, and complete. Declaration of preparer (other than the taxpayer) is based on all information of which the preparer has any knowledge.

Your signature	Date	Your occupation
Spouse's signature. If joint return, BOTH must sign.	Date	Spouse's occupation

Paid preparer's use only

Preparer's signature ▶	Date	Check if self-employed ☐	Preparer's social security no.
Firm's name (or yours if self-employed) and address ▶		E.I. No.	
		ZIP code	

This form is an advance proof. Use the final IRS version for filing

Schedule 1
(Form 1040A)

Department of the Treasury—Internal Revenue Service

**Interest and Dividend Income
for Form 1040A Filers**

1992

OMB No. 1545-0085

Name(s) shown on Form 1040A

Your social security number

Part I Interest income (See pages 24 and 54.)	Complete this part and attach Schedule 1 to Form 1040A if:

- You had over $400 in taxable interest, or
- You are claiming the exclusion of interest from series EE U.S. savings bonds issued after 1989.

If you received, as a nominee, interest that actually belongs to another person, see page 54.

Note: *If you received a Form 1099–INT, Form 1099–OID, or substitute statement, from a brokerage firm, enter the firm's name and the total interest shown on that form.*

1	List name of payer—if any interest is from seller-financed mortgages, see page 54	Amount	
		1	
2	Add the amounts on line 1.	2	
3	Excludable savings bond interest, if any, from Form 8815, line 14. Attach Form 8815 to Form 1040A.	3	
4	Subtract line 3 from line 2. Enter the result here and on Form 1040A, line 8A.	4	

Part II

Dividend income

(See pages 24 and 55.)

Complete this part and attach Schedule 1 to Form 1040A if you had over $400 in dividends.

If you received, as a nominee, dividends that actually belong to another person, see page 55.

Note: *If you received a Form 1099–DIV, or substitute statement, from a brokerage firm, enter the firm's name and the total dividends shown on that form.*

5	List name of payer	Amount	
		5	
6	Add the amounts on line 5. Enter the total here and on Form 1040A, line 9.	6	

This form is an advance proof. Use the final IRS version for filing

455

Schedule 2
(Form 1040A)

Department of the Treasury—Internal Revenue Service
Child and Dependent Care· Expenses for Form 1040A Filers

1992

OMB No. 1545-0085

Name(s) shown on Form 1040A

Your social security number

Caution: • *If you have a child who was born in 1992 and the amount on Form 1040A, line 17, is less than $22,370, see page 55 of the instructions before completing this schedule.*

• *If you paid cash wages of $50 or more in a calendar quarter to an individual for services performed in your home, you must file an employment tax return. Get* **Form 942** *for details.*

Part I

Persons or organizations who provided the care

You MUST complete this part. (See page 57.)

	(a) Care provider's name	(b) Address (number, street, apt. no., city, state, and ZIP code)	(c) Identifying number (SSN or EIN)	(d) Amount paid (see page 57)
1				

(If you need more space, use the bottom of page 2.)

2 Add the amounts in column (d) of line 1. **2**

Next: Did you receive employer-provided dependent care benefits?
• **YES.** Complete Part III on the back now.
• **NO.** Complete Part II below.

Part II

Credit for child and dependent care expenses

3 Enter the number of qualifying persons cared for in 1992. You must have shared the same home with the qualifying person(s). See page 57 to find out who is a qualifying person. **3**

4 Enter the amount of **qualified** expenses you incurred and actually paid in 1992. See page 58 to find out which expenses qualify.
Caution: *If you completed Part III on page 2, DO NOT include on this line any excluded benefits shown on line 23.* **4**

5 Enter $2,400 ($4,800) if you paid for the care of two or more qualifying persons). **5**

6 If you completed Part III on page 2, enter the **excluded benefits,** if any, from line 23. **6**

7 Subtract line 6 from line 5. If line 6 is equal to or more than line 5, STOP HERE; you cannot claim the credit. **7**

8 Look at lines 4 and 7. Enter the **smaller** of the two amounts here. **8**

9 You **must** enter your **earned income.** See page 58 for the definition of earned income. **9**

Note: *If you are not filing a joint return, go to line 11 now.*

10 If you are filing a joint return, you **must** enter your spouse's earned income. If your spouse was a student or disabled, see page 58 for the amount to enter. **10**

11 • If you are filing a joint return, look at lines 8, 9, and 10. Enter the **smallest** of the three amounts here.
• All others, look at lines 8 and 9. Enter the **smaller** of the two amounts here. **11**

12 Enter the amount from Form 1040A, line 17. **12**

13 Enter the decimal amount shown below that applies to the amount on line 12.

If line 12 is—		Decimal amount is—	If line 12 is—		Decimal amount is—
Over	But not over		Over	But not over	
$0—10,000		.30	$20,000—22,000		.24
10,000—12,000		.29	22,000—24,000		.23
12,000—14,000		.28	24,000—26,000		.22
14,000—16,000		.27	26,000—28,000		.21
16,000—18,000		.26	28,000—No limit		.20
18,000—20,000		.25			

13 ×

14 Multiply line 11 above by the decimal amount on line 13. Enter the result here and on Form 1040A, line 24a. **14** =

For Paperwork Reduction Act Notice, see Form 1040A instructions.   Cat. No. 107491   **1992 Schedule 2 (Form 1040A)** page 1

This form is an advance proof. Use the final IRS version for filing

456

Name(s) shown on page 1	Your social security number
	⋮ ⋮

Part III	**15**	Enter the total amount of employer-provided dependent care benefits you received for 1992. This amount should be shown in box 22 of your W-2 form(s). DO NOT include amounts that were reported to you as wages in box 10 of Form(s) W-2.		**15**	
Employer-provided dependent care benefits	**16**	Enter the amount forfeited, if any. (See page 59.)		**16**	
	17	Subtract line 16 from line 15.		**17**	
Complete this part only if you received employer-provided dependent care benefits.	**18**	Enter the total amount of **qualified** expenses incurred in 1992 for the care of a qualifying person. (See page 59.)	**18**		
	19	Look at lines 17 and 18. Enter the **smaller** of the two amounts here.	**19**		
	20	You **must** enter your **earned income.** See the instructions for lines 9 and 10 for the definition of earned income.	**20**		

Note: If you are not filing a joint return, go to line 22 now.

	21	(If you are filing a joint return) you **must** enter your spouse's earned income. If your spouse was a student or disabled, see the instructions for lines 9 and 10 for the amount to enter.	**21**	
	22	● (If you are filing a joint return) look at lines 20 and 21. Enter the **smaller** of the two amounts here.		
		● (All others,) enter the amount from line 20 here.	**22**	

23   **Excluded benefits.** Enter here the **smallest** of the following:

● The amount from line 19, or

● The amount from line 22, or

● $5,000 ($2,500 if married filing a separate return).   **23**

24   **Taxable benefits.** Subtract line 23 from line 17. Enter the result. (If line 23 is more than line 17, enter -0-.) Also, include this amount in the total on Form 1040A, line 7. In the space to the left of line 7, write "DCB."   **24**

    Next: If you are also claiming the child and dependent care credit, fill in Form 1040A through line 23. Then, complete Part II of this schedule.

This form is an advance proof. Use the final IRS version for filing

Schedule 3
(Form 1040A)

Department of the Treasury—Internal Revenue Service

Credit for the Elderly or the Disabled
for Form 1040A Filers

1992

OMB No. 1545-0085

Name(s) shown on Form 1040A	Your social security number
	⋮ : ⋮

You may be able to use Schedule 3 to reduce your tax if by the end of 1992:

- You were age 65 or older, **OR**
- You were under age 65, you retired on **permanent and total** disability, and you received taxable disability income.

But you must also meet other tests. See the separate instructions for Schedule 3.

Note: *In most cases, the IRS can figure the credit for you. See page 36 of the Form 1040A instructions.*

Part I

Check the box for your filing status and age

If your filing status is:	And by the end of 1992:	Check only one box:
Single, Head of household, or Qualifying widow(er) with dependent child	**1** You were 65 or older	1 ☐
	2 You were under 65 and you retired on permanent and total disability	2 ☐
Married filing a joint return	**3** Both spouses were 65 or older	3 ☐
	4 Both spouses were under 65, but only one spouse retired on permanent and total disability	4 ☐
	5 Both spouses were under 65, and both retired on permanent and total disability	5 ☐
	6 One spouse was 65 or older, and the other spouse was under 65 and retired on permanent and total disabililty	6 ☐
	7 One spouse was 65 or older, and the other spouse was under 65 and NOT retired on permanent and total disability	7 ☐
Married filing a separate return	**8** You were 65 or older and you did not live with your spouse at any time in 1992	8 ☐
	9 You were under 65, you retired on permanent and total disability, and you did not live with your spouse at any time in 1992	9 ☐

If you checked box 1, 3, 7, or 8, skip Part II and complete Part III on the back. All others, complete Parts II and III.

Part II

Statement of permanent and total disability

Complete this part **only** if you checked box 2, 4, 5, 6, or 9 above.

IF: 1 You filed a physician's statement for this disability for 1983 or an earlier year, or you filed a statement for tax years after 1983 and your physician signed line B on the statement, **AND**

2 Due to your continued disabled condition, you were unable to engage in any substantial gainful activity in 1992, check this box . . . . ▶ ☐

- If you checked this box, you do not have to file another statement for 1992.
- If you **did not** check this box, have your physician complete the following statement:

Physician's statement (See instructions at bottom of page 2.)

I certify that _____
Name of disabled person

was permanently and totally disabled on January 1, 1976, or January 1, 1977, **OR** was permanently and totally disabled on the date he or she retired. If retired after December 31, 1976, enter the date retired ▶ _____

Physician: Sign your name on **either** line A or B below.

A The disability has lasted, or can be expected to last, continuously for at least a year . . . . . _____
Physician's signature | Date

B There is no reasonable probability that the disabled condition will ever improve . . . . . _____
Physician's signature | Date

Physician's name	Physician's address

For Paperwork Reduction Act Notice, see Form 1040A instructions.
This form is an advance proof. Use the final IRS version for filing

Cat. No. 12064K

1992 Schedule 3 (Form 1040A) page 1

Name(s) shown on page 1	Your social security number

Part III Figure your credit	**10**	**If you checked (in Part I):**	**Enter:**	
		Box 1, 2, 4, or 7	$5,000	
		Box 3, 5, or 6	$7,500	
		Box 8 or 9	$3,750	**10**

> **Caution:** *If you checked box 2, 4, 5, 6, or 9 in Part I, you **MUST** complete line 11 below. All others, skip line 11 and enter the amount from line 10 on line 12.*

11	• If you checked box 6 in Part I, add $5,000 to the taxable disability income of the spouse who was under age 65. Enter the total here.	
	• If you checked box 2, 4, or 9 in Part I, enter your taxable disability income here.	
	• If you checked box 5 in Part I, add your taxable disability income to your spouse's taxable disability income. Enter the total here.	
	TIP: For more details on what to include on line 11, see the instructions	**11**

12	• If you completed line 11 above, look at lines 10 and 11. Enter the **smaller** of the two amounts here. • All others, enter the amount from line 10 here.	**12**

13	Enter the following pensions, annuities, or disability income that you (and your spouse if filing a joint return) received in 1992 (see instructions):	
a	Nontaxable part of social security benefits, and Nontaxable part of railroad retirement benefits treated as social security.	**13a**
b	Nontaxable veterans' pensions and any other pension, annuity, or disability benefit that is excluded from income under any other provision of law.	**13b**
c	Add lines 13a and 13b. (Even though these income items are not taxable, they **must** be included here to figure your credit.) If you did not receive any of the types of nontaxable income listed on line 13a or 13b, enter -0- on line 13c.	**13c**

14	Enter the amount from Form 1040A, line 17.	**14**	

15	**If you checked (in Part I):**	**Enter:**	
	Box 1 or 2	$7,500	
	Box 3, 4, 5, 6, or 7	$10,000	
	Box 8 or 9	$5,000	**15**

16	Subtract line 15 from line 14. If line 15 is more than line 14, enter -0-.	**16**	
17	Divide line 16 above by 2.	**17**	
18	Add lines 13c and 17.		**18**
19	Subtract line 18 from line 12. If line 18 is more than line 12, stop here; you **cannot** take the credit. Otherwise, go to line 21.		**19**
20	Decimal amount used to figure the credit.		**20** × .15
21	Multiply line 19 above by the decimal amount (.15) on line 20. Enter the result here and on Form 1040A, line 24b.		**21**

Instructions for physician's statement	**Taxpayer.**—If you retired after December 31, 1976, enter the date you retired in the space provided in Part II.
	Physician.—A person is permanently and totally disabled if **both** of the following apply:
	1. He or she cannot engage in any substantial gainful activity because of a physical or mental condition, and
	2. A physician determines that the disability has lasted, or can be expected to last, continuously for at least a year or can lead to death.

This form is an advance proof. Use the final IRS version for filing

Form **1040**

Department of the Treasury—Internal Revenue Service

U.S. Individual Income Tax Return **1992**

IRS use only—Do not write or staple in this space.

For the year Jan. 1–Dec. 31, 1992, or other tax year beginning _____ , 1992, ending _____ , 19___   OMB No. 1545-0074

Label

(See instructions on page 10.)

Use the IRS label. Otherwise, please print or type.

L A B E L   H E R E

Your first name and initial Last name	Your social security number
If a joint return, spouse's first name and initial Last name	Spouse's social security number
Home address (number and street). If you have a P.O. box, see page 10. Apt. no.	**For Privacy Act and Paperwork Reduction Act Notice, see page 4.**
City, town or post office, state, and ZIP code. If you have a foreign address, see page 10.	

Presidential Election Campaign

(See page 10.)

Do you want $1 to go to this fund? . . . .   Yes ▢   No ▢

If a joint return, does your spouse want $1 to go to this fund? .   Yes ▢   No ▢

Note: *Checking "Yes" will not change your tax or reduce your refund.*

Filing Status

(See page 10.)

Check only one box.

1 ▢ Single

2 ▢ Married filing joint return (even if only one had income)

3 ▢ Married filing separate return. Enter spouse's social security no. above and full name here. ▶ _____

4 ▢ Head of household (with qualifying person). (See page 11.) If the qualifying person is a child but not your dependent, enter this child's name here ▶ _____

5 ▢ Qualifying widow(er) with dependent child (year spouse died ▶19___). (See page 11.)

Exemptions

(See page 11.)

If more than six dependents, see page 12.

6a ▢ **Yourself.** If your parent (or someone else) can claim you as a dependent on his or her tax return, **do not** check box 6a. But be sure to check the box on line 33b on page 2.

b ▢ **Spouse** . . . .

c **Dependents:**

(1) Name (first, initial, and last name)	(2) Check if under age 1	(3) If age 1 or older, dependent's social security number	(4) Dependent's relationship to you	(5) No. of months lived in your home in 1992

d If your child didn't live with you but is claimed as your dependent under a pre-1985 agreement, check here ▶ ▢

e Total number of exemptions claimed . . . .

No. of boxes checked on 6a and 6b _____

No. of your children on 6c who:

• lived with you _____

• didn't live with you due to divorce or separation (see page 13) _____

No. of other dependents on 6c _____

Add numbers entered on lines above ▶ ▢

Income

Attach Copy B of your Forms W-2, W-2G, and 1099-R here.

If you did not get a W-2, see page 9.

Attach check or money order on top of any Forms W-2, W-2G, or 1099-R.

7	Wages, salaries, tips, etc. Attach Form(s) W-2	7
8a	**Taxable** interest income. Attach Schedule B if over $400	8a
b	**Tax-exempt** interest income (see page 15). DON'T include on line 8a 8b ___	
9	Dividend income. Attach Schedule B if over $400 .	9
10	Taxable refunds, credits, or offsets of state and local income taxes from worksheet on page 15	10
11	Alimony received	11
12	Business income or (loss). Attach Schedule C (or C-EZ)	12
13	Capital gain or (loss). Attach Schedule D	13
14	Capital gain distributions not reported on line 13 (see page 16) .	14
15	Other gains or (losses). Attach Form 4797	15
16a	Total IRA distributions . 16a ___ **b** Taxable amount (see page 16)	16b
17a	Total pensions and annuities 17a ___ **b** Taxable amount (see page 16)	17b
18	Rents, royalties, partnerships, estates, trusts, etc. Attach Schedule E .	18
19	Farm income or (loss). Attach Schedule F	19
20	Unemployment compensation (see page 17)	20
21a	Social security benefits 21a ___ **b** Taxable amount (see page 17)	21b
22	Other income. List type and amount—see page 18	22
23	Add the amounts in the far right column for lines 7 through 22. This is your **total income** . ▶	23

Adjustments to Income

(See page 18.)

24a	Your IRA deduction from applicable worksheet on page 19 or 20	24a
b	Spouse's IRA deduction from applicable worksheet on page 19 or 20	24b
25	One-half of self-employment tax (see page 20)	25
26	Self-employed health insurance deduction (see page 20)	26
27	Keogh retirement plan and self-employed SEP deduction	27
28	Penalty on early withdrawal of savings	28
29	Alimony paid. Recipient's SSN ▶ _____	29
30	Add lines 24a through 29. These are your **total adjustments** . . . . ▶	30

Adjusted Gross Income

31 Subtract line 30 from line 23. This is your **adjusted gross income.** *If this amount is less than $22,370 and a child lived with you, see page EIC-1 to find out if you can claim the "Earned Income Credit" on line 56* . . . . ▶ | 31

This form is an advance proof. Use the final IRS version for filing

Form **1040** (1992)

Tax Compu-tation (See page 22.)	**32**	Amount from line 31 (adjusted gross income)	**32**
	33a	Check if: ☐ **You** were 65 or older, ☐ Blind; ☐ **Spouse** was 65 or older, ☐ Blind. Add the number of boxes checked above and enter the total here . . ▶ **33a**	
	b	If your parent (or someone else) can claim you as a dependent, check here . ▶ **33b** ☐	
	c	If you are married filing separately and your spouse itemizes deductions or you are a dual-status alien, see page 22 and check here . . . . ▶ **33c** ☐	
	34	Enter the larger of your: { **Itemized deductions** from Schedule A, line 26, **OR** **Standard deduction** shown below for your filing status. **But if you checked any box on line 33a or b,** go to page 22 to find your standard deduction. **If you checked box 33c,** your standard deduction is zero. ● Single—$3,600　　● Head of household—$5,250 ● Married filing jointly or Qualifying widow(er)—$6,000 ● Married filing separately—$3,000 }	**34**
	35	Subtract line 34 from line 32	**35**
	36	If line 32 is $78,950 or less, multiply $2,300 by the total number of exemptions claimed on line 6e. If line 32 is over $78,950, see the worksheet on page 23 for the amount to enter	**36**
If you want the IRS to figure your tax, see page 23.	**37**	**Taxable income.** Subtract line 36 from line 35. If line 36 is more than line 35, enter -0-	**37**
	38	Enter tax. Check if from **a** ☐ Tax Table, **b** ☐ Tax Rate Schedules, **c** ☐ Schedule D. or **d** ☐ Form 8615 (see page 23). Amount, if any, from Form(s) 8814 ▶ **e** ____	**38**
	39	Additional taxes (see page 23). Check if from **a** ☐ Form 4970 **b** ☐ Form 4972	**39**
	40	Add lines 38 and 39	**40**
Credits (See page 23.)	**41**	Credit for child and dependent care expenses. Attach Form 2441	**41**	
	42	Credit for the elderly or the disabled. Attach Schedule R	**42**	
	43	Foreign tax credit. Attach Form 1116	**43**	
	44	Other credits (see page 24). Check if from **a** ☐ Form 3800 **b** ☐ Form 8396 **c** ☐ Form 8801 **d** ☐ Form (specify)____	**44**	
	45	Add lines 41 through 44	**45**
	46	Subtract line 45 from line 40. If line 45 is more than line 40, enter -0-	**46**
Other Taxes	**47**	Self-employment tax. Attach Schedule SE. Also, see line 25	**47**
	48	Alternative minimum tax. Attach Form 6251	**48**
	49	Recapture taxes (see page 25). Check if from **a** ☐ Form 4255 **b** ☐ Form 8611 **c** ☐ Form 8828 . .	**49**
	50	Social security and Medicare tax on tip income not reported to employer. Attach Form 4137. . . .	**50**
	51	Tax on qualified retirement plans, including IRAs. Attach Form 5329	**51**
	52	Advance earned income credit payments from Form W-2	**52**
	53	Add lines 46 through 52. This is your **total tax** . . . . ▶	**53**
Payments Attach Forms W-2, W-2G, and 1099-R on the front.	**54**	Federal income tax withheld. If any is from Form(s) 1099, check ▶ ☐	**54**	
	55	1992 estimated tax payments and amount applied from 1991 return .	**55**	
	56	**Earned income credit.** Attach Schedule EIC	**56**	
	57	Amount paid with Form 4868 (extension request)	**57**	
	58	Excess social security, Medicare, and RRTA tax withheld (see page 26) .	**58**	
	59	Other payments (see page 26). Check if from **a** ☐ Form 2439 **b** ☐ Form 4136	**59**	
	60	Add lines 54 through 59. These are your **total payments** . . . . ▶	**60**
Refund or Amount You Owe Attach check or money order on top of Form(s) W-2, etc., on the front.	**61**	If line 60 is more than line 53, subtract line 53 from line 60. This is the amount you **OVERPAID**. ▶	**61**
	62	Amount of line 61 you want **REFUNDED TO YOU**. . . . . ▶	**62**
	63	Amount of line 61 you want **APPLIED TO YOUR 1993 ESTIMATED TAX** ▶	**63**	
	64	If line 53 is more than line 60, subtract line 60 from line 53. This is the **AMOUNT YOU OWE.** Attach check or money order for full amount payable to "Internal Revenue Service." Write your name, address, social security number, daytime phone number, and "1992 Form 1040" on it	**64**
	65	Estimated tax penalty (see page 27). Also include on line 64	**65**	

Sign Here

Keep a copy of this return for your records.

Under penalties of perjury, I declare that I have examined this return and accompanying schedules and statements, and to the best of my knowledge and belief, they are true, correct, and complete. Declaration of preparer (other than taxpayer) is based on all information of which preparer has any knowledge.

▶ Your signature	Date	Your occupation
▶ Spouse's signature. If a joint return, BOTH must sign.	Date	Spouse's occupation

Paid Preparer's Use Only

Preparer's signature ▶	Date	Check if self-employed ☐	Preparer's social security no.
Firm's name (or yours if self-employed) and address ▶		E.I. No. ZIP code	

This form is an advance proof. Use the final IRS version for filing.

SCHEDULES A&B
(Form 1040)

Department of the Treasury
Internal Revenue Service

Schedule A—Itemized Deductions
(Schedule B is on back)
▶ Attach to Form 1040. ▶ See Instructions for Schedules A and B (Form 1040).

OMB No. 1545-0074

1992

Attachment
Sequence No. **07**

Name(s) shown on Form 1040

Your social security number

Medical and Dental Expenses		Caution: *Do not include expenses reimbursed or paid by others.*		
	1	Medical and dental expenses (see page A-1)	1	
	2	Enter amount from Form 1040, line 32 . |_2_|		
	3	Multiply line 2 above by 7.5% (.075)	3	
	4	Subtract line 3 from line 1. If zero or less, enter -0- . . . . ▶	4	
Taxes You Paid	5	State and local income taxes	5	
	6	Real estate taxes	6	
(See page A-1.)	7	Other taxes. List—include personal property taxes . ▶	7	
	8	Add lines 5 through 7 . . . . ▶	8	
Interest You Paid	9a	Home mortgage interest and points reported to you on Form 1098	9a	
	b	Home mortgage interest not reported to you on Form 1098. If paid to an individual, show that person's name and address. ▶		
(See page A-2.)		--		
		--	9b	
Note: Personal interest is not deductible.	10	Points not reported to you on Form 1098. See page A-2 for special rules	10	
	11	Investment interest. If required, attach Form 4952. (See page A-3.)	11	
	12	Add lines 9a through 11 . . . . ▶	12	
Gifts to Charity		Caution: *If you made a charitable contribution and received a benefit in return, see page A-3.*		
(See page A-3.)	13	Contributions by cash or check	13	
	14	Other than by cash or check. If over $500, you **MUST** attach Form 8283	14	
	15	Carryover from prior year	15	
	16	Add lines 13 through 15 . . . . ▶	16	
Casualty and Theft Losses	17	Casualty or theft loss(es). Attach Form 4684. (See page A-4) . . . . . . ▶	17	
Moving Expenses	18	Moving expenses. Attach Form 3903 or 3903F. (See page A-4). . . . . . . ▶	18	
Job Expenses and Most Other Miscellaneous Deductions (See page A-4 for expenses to deduct here.)	19	Unreimbursed employee expenses—job travel, union dues, job education, etc. If required, you **MUST** attach Form 2106. (See page A-4.) ▶ ---------------------- ----------------------	19	
	20	Other expenses—investment, tax preparation, safe deposit box, etc. List type and amount ▶ -------------- ---------------------- ----------------------	20	
	21	Add lines 19 and 20	21	
	22	Enter amount from Form 1040, line 32 . |_22_|		
	23	Multiply line 22 above by 2% (.02)	23	
	24	Subtract line 23 from line 21. If zero or less, enter -0- . . . . ▶	24	
Other Miscellaneous Deductions	25	Other—from list on page A-5. List type and amount ▶ ------------------------------- ------------------------------- ▶	25	
Total Itemized Deductions	26	Is the amount on Form 1040, line 32, more than $105,250 (more than $52,625 if married filing separately)? • **NO.** Your deduction is not limited. Add lines 4, 8, 12, 16, 17, 18, 24, and 25. • **YES.** Your deduction may be limited. See page A-5 for the amount to enter. ▶	26	
		Caution: *Be sure to enter on Form 1040, line 34, the **LARGER** of the amount on line 26 above or your standard deduction.*		

For Paperwork Reduction Act Notice, see Form 1040 instructions.
Cat. No. 11330X
Schedule A (Form 1040) 1992

This form is an advance proof. Use the final IRS version for filing

Name(s) shown on Form 1040. Do not enter name and social security number if shown on other side. | Your social security number

Schedule B—Interest and Dividend Income

**Part I
Interest
Income**

(See
pages 14
and B-1.)

If you had over $400 in taxable interest income OR you are claiming the exclusion of interest from series EE U.S. savings bonds issued after 1989, you must complete this part. List ALL interest you received. If you had over $400 in taxable interest income, you must also complete Part III. If you received, as a nominee, interest that actually belongs to another person, or you received or paid accrued interest on securities transferred between interest payment dates, see page B-1.

Interest Income		Amount	
1	List name of payer—if any interest income is from seller-financed mortgages, see page B-1 and list this interest first ▶...............................	**1**	
2	Add the amounts on line 1	**2**	
3	Excludable savings bond interest, if any, from Form 8815, line 14, Attach Form 8815 to Form 1040	**3**	
4	Subtract line 3 from line 2. Enter the result here and on Form 1040, line 8a. ▶	**4**	

Note: If you received a Form 1099-INT, Form 1099-OID, or substitute statement from a brokerage firm, list the firm's name as the payer and enter the total interest shown on that form.

**Part II
Dividend
Income**

(See
pages 15
and B-1.)

If you had over $400 in gross dividends and/or other distributions on stock, you must complete this part and Part III. If you received, as a nominee, dividends that actually belong to another person, see page B-1.

Dividend Income		Amount	
5	List name of payer–include on this line capital gain distributions, nontaxable distributions, etc. ▶...............................	**5**	
6	Add the amounts on line 5	**6**	
7	Capital gain distributions. Enter here and on Schedule D* .	**7**		
8	Nontaxable distributions. (See the inst. for Form 1040, line 9.)	**8**		
9	Add lines 7 and 8 . . . . ▶	**9**	
10	Subtract line 9 from line 6. Enter the result here and on Form 1040, line 9 . ▶	**10**	

Note: If you received a Form 1099-DIV or substitute statement, from a brokerage firm, list the firm's name as the payer and enter the total dividends shown on that form.

If you received capital gain distributions but do not need Schedule D to report any other gains or losses, see the instructions for Form 1040, lines 13 and 14.

**Part III
Foreign
Accounts
and
Foreign
Trusts**

(See
page B-2.)

If you had over $400 of interest or dividends OR had a foreign account or were a grantor of, or a transferor to, a foreign trust, you must complete this part.

		Yes	No
11a	At any time during 1992, did you have an interest in or a signature or other authority over a financial account in a foreign country, such as a bank account, securities account, or other financial account? See page B-2 for exceptions and filing requirements for Form TD F 90-22.1		
b	If "Yes," enter the name of the foreign country ▶		
12	Were you the grantor of, or transferor to, a foreign trust that existed during 1992, whether or not you have any beneficial interest in it? If "Yes," you may have to file Form 3520, 3520-A, or 926 .		

For Paperwork Reduction Act Notice, see Form 1040 instructions.

This form is an advance proof. Use the final IRS version for filing

Schedule B (Form 1040) 1992

SCHEDULE C
(Form 1040)

Department of the Treasury
Internal Revenue Service

Profit or Loss From Business
(Sole Proprietorship)

▶ Partnerships, joint ventures, etc., must file Form 1065.

▶ Attach to Form 1040 or Form 1041. ▶ See Instructions for Schedule C (Form 1040).

OMB No. 1545-0074

1992

Attachment
Sequence No. **09**

Name of proprietor

Social security number (SSN)

A Principal business or profession, including product or service (see page C-1)

B Enter principal business code (from page 2) ▶

C Business name

D Employer ID number (Not SSN)

E Business address (including suite or room no.) ▶ ....
City, town or post office, state, and ZIP code

F Accounting method: **(1)** ☐ Cash **(2)** ☐ Accrual **(3)** ☐ Other (specify) ▶ ....

G Method(s) used to value closing inventory: **(1)** ☐ Cost **(2)** ☐ Lower of cost or market **(3)** ☐ Other (attach explanation) **(4)** ☐ Does not apply (if checked, skip line H)

	Yes	No

H Was there any change in determining quantities, costs, or valuations between opening and closing inventory? If "Yes," attach explanation

I Did you "materially participate" in the operation of this business during 1992? If "No," see page C-1 for limitations on losses

J Was this business in operation at the end of 1992?

K How many months was this business in operation during 1992? .... ▶

L If this is the first Schedule C filed for this business, check here .... ▶ ☐

Part I Income

1	Gross receipts or sales. **Caution:** If this income was reported to you on Form W-2 and the "Statutory employee" box on that form was checked, see page C-2 and check here ▶ ☐	**1**	
2	Returns and allowances	**2**	
3	Subtract line 2 from line 1	**3**	
4	Cost of goods sold (from line 40 on page 2)	**4**	
5	**Gross profit.** Subtract line 4 from line 3	**5**	
6	Other income, including Federal and state gasoline or fuel tax credit or refund (see page C-2)	**6**	
7	**Gross income.** Add lines 5 and 6. ▶	**7**	

Part II Expenses (Caution: *Do not* enter expenses for business use of your home on lines 8–27. Instead, see line 30.)

8	Advertising	**8**		**21** Repairs and maintenance	**21**	
9	Bad debts from sales or services (see page C-3)	**9**		**22** Supplies (not included in Part III)	**22**	
10	Car and truck expenses (see page C-3—also attach Form 4562)	**10**		**23** Taxes and licenses	**23**	
11	Commissions and fees	**11**		**24** Travel, meals, and entertainment:		
12	Depletion	**12**		**a** Travel	**24a**	
13	Depreciation and section 179 expense deduction (not included in Part III) (see page C-3)	**13**		**b** Meals and entertainment		
				c Enter 20% of line 24b subject to limitations (see page C-4)		
14	Employee benefit programs (other than on line 19)	**14**		**d** Subtract line 24c from line 24b	**24d**	
15	Insurance (other than health)	**15**		**25** Utilities	**25**	
16	Interest:			**26** Wages (less jobs credit)	**26**	
a	Mortgage (paid to banks, etc.)	**16a**		**27a** Other expenses (**list type and amount**):		
b	Other	**16b**		....		
17	Legal and professional services	**17**		....		
18	Office expense	**18**		....		
19	Pension and profit-sharing plans	**19**		....		
20	Rent or lease (see page C-4):			....		
a	Vehicles, machinery, and equipment	**20a**				
b	Other business property	**20b**		**27b** Total other expenses	**27b**	

28	**Total expenses** before expenses for business use of home. Add lines 8 through 27b in columns ▶	**28**	
29	Tentative profit (loss). Subtract line 28 from line 7	**29**	
30	Expenses for business use of your home. Attach **Form 8829**	**30**	
31	**Net profit or (loss).** Subtract line 30 from line 29. If a profit, enter here and on Form 1040, line 12. Also, enter the net profit on Schedule SE, line 2 (statutory employees, see page C-5). If a loss, you MUST go on to line 32 (fiduciaries, see page C-5)	**31**	

32 If you have a loss, you MUST check the box that describes your investment in this activity (see page C-5)

If you checked 32a, enter the loss on Form 1040, line 12, and Schedule SE, line 2 (statutory employees, see page C-5). If you checked 32b, you MUST attach **Form 6198**.

32a ☐ All investment is at risk.
32b ☐ Some investment is not at risk.

For Paperwork Reduction Act Notice, see Form 1040 instructions.

This form is an advance proof. Use the final IRS version for filing

Cat. No. 11334P

Schedule C (Form 1040) 1992

Part III Cost of Goods Sold. (see page C-5)

33	Inventory at beginning of year. If different from last year's closing inventory, attach explanation . .	33	
34	Purchases less cost of items withdrawn for personal use	34	
35	Cost of labor. Do not include salary paid to yourself	35	
36	Materials and supplies	36	
37	Other costs	37	
38	Add lines 33 through 37.	38	
39	Inventory at end of year.	39	
40	**Cost of goods sold.** Subtract line 39 from line 38. Enter the result here and on page 1, line 4 . .	40	

Part IV Principal Business or Professional Activity Codes

Locate the major category that best describes your activity. Within the major category, select the activity code that most closely identifies the business or profession that is the principal source of your sales or receipts. **Enter this 4-digit code on page 1, line B.** For example, real estate agent is under the major category of **"Real Estate,"** and the code is **"5520."** **Note:** *If your principal source of income is from farming activities, you should file* **Schedule F** *(Form 1040), Profit or Loss From Farming.*

Agricultural Services, Forestry, Fishing

Code
1990 Animal services, other than breeding
1933 Crop services
2113 Farm labor & management services
2246 Fishing, commercial
2238 Forestry, except logging
2212 Horticulture & landscaping
2469 Hunting & trapping
1974 Livestock breeding
0836 Logging
1958 Veterinary services, including pets

Construction

0018 Operative builders (for own account)

Building Trade Contractors, Includir Repairs
0414 Carpentering & flooring
0455 Concrete work
0273 Electrical work
0299 Masonry, dry wall, stone, & tile
0257 Painting & paper hanging
0232 Plumbing, heating, & air conditioni
0430 Roofing, siding & sheet metal
0885 Other building trade contractor (excavation, glazing, etc.)

General Contractors
0075 Highway & street construction
0059 Nonresidential building
0034 Residential building
3889 Other heavy construction (pipe laying, bridge construction, etc.)

Finance, Insurance, & Related Services

6064 Brokers & dealers of securities
6080 Commodity contracts brokers & dealers; security & commodity exchanges
6148 Credit institutions & mortgage bankers
5702 Insurance agents or brokers
5744 Insurance services (appraisal, consulting, inspection, etc.)
6130 Investment advisors & services
5777 Other financial services

Manufacturing, Including Printing & Publishing

0679 Apparel & other textile products
1115 Electric & electronic equipment
1073 Fabricated metal products
0638 Food products & beverages
0810 Furniture & fixtures
0695 Leather footwear, handbags, etc.
0836 Lumber & other wood products
1099 Machinery & machine shops
0877 Paper & allied products
1057 Primary metal industries
0851 Printing & publishing
1032 Stone, clay, & glass products
0653 Textile mill products
1883 Other manufacturing industries

Mining & Mineral Extraction

1537 Coal mining
1511 Metal mining

1552 Oil & gas
1719 Quarrying & nonmetallic mining

Real Estate

5538 Operators & lessors of buildings, including residential
5553 Operators & lessors of other real property
5520 Real estate agents & brokers
5579 Real estate property managers
5710 Subdividers & developers, except cemeteries
6155 Title abstract offices

Services: Personal, Professional, & Business Services

Amusement & Recreational Services
9670 Bowling centers
9688 Motion picture & tape distribution & allied services
9597 Motion picture & video production
9639 Motion picture theaters
8557 Physical fitness facilities
9696 Professional sports & racing, including promoters & managers
9811 Theatrical performers, musicians, agents, producers & related services
9613 Video tape rental
9837 Other amusement & recreational services

Automotive Services
8813 Automotive rental or leasing, without driver
8953 Automotive repairs, general & specialized
8839 Parking, except valet
8896 Other automotive services (wash, towing, etc.)

Business & Personal Services
7658 Accounting & bookkeeping
7716 Advertising, except direct mail
7682 Architectural services
8318 Barber shop (or barber)
8110 Beauty shop (or beautician)
8714 Child day care
7872 Computer programming, processing, data preparation & related services
7922 Computer repair, maintenance, & leasing
7286 Consulting services
7799 Consumer credit reporting & collection services
8755 Counseling (except health practitioners)
7732 Employment agencies & personnel supply
7518 Engineering services
7773 Equipment rental & leasing (except computer or automotive)
8532 Funeral services & crematories
7633 Income tax preparation
7914 Investigative & protective services
7617 Legal services (or lawyer)
7856 Mailing, reproduction, commercial art, photography, & stenographic services
7245 Management services
8771 Ministers & chaplains
8334 Photographic studios
7260 Public relations
8733 Research services

7708 Surveying services
8730 Teaching or tutoring
7880 Other business services
6882 Other personal services

Hotels & Other Lodging Places

7237 Camps and camping parks
7096 Hotels, motels, & tourist homes
7211 Rooming & boarding houses

Laundry & Cleaning Services

7450 Carpet & upholstery cleaning
7419 Coin-operated laundries & dry cleaning
7435 Full-service laundry, dry cleaning, & garment service
7476 Janitorial & related services (building, house, & window cleaning)

Medical & Health Services

9274 Chiropractors
9233 Dentist's office or clinic
9217 Doctor's (M.D.) office or clinic
9456 Medical & dental laboratories
9472 Nursing & personal care facilities
9290 Optometrists
9258 Osteopathic physicians & surgeons
9241 Podiatrists
9415 Registered & practical nurses
9431 Offices & clinics of other health practitioners (dieticians, midwives, speech pathologists, etc.)
9886 Other health services

Miscellaneous Repair, Except Computers

9019 Audio equipment & TV repair
9035 Electrical & electronic equipment repair, except audio & TV
9050 Furniture repair & reupholstery
2881 Other equipment repair

Trade, Retail—Selling Goods to Individuals & Households

3038 Catalog or mail order
3012 Selling door to door, by telephone or party plan, or from mobile unit
3053 Vending machine selling

Selling From Showroom, Store, or Other Fixed Location

Apparel & Accessories
3921 Accessory & specialty stores & furriers for women
3939 Clothing, family
3772 Clothing, men's & boys'
3913 Clothing, women's
3756 Shoe stores
3954 Other apparel & accessory stores

Automotive & Service Stations
3558 Gasoline service stations
3319 New car dealers (franchised)
3533 Tires, accessories, & parts
3335 Used car dealers
3517 Other automotive dealers (motorcycles, recreational vehicles, etc.)

Building, Hardware, & Garden Supply
4416 Building materials dealers
4457 Hardware stores
4473 Nurseries & garden supply stores
4432 Paint, glass, & wallpaper stores

Food & Beverages

0612 Bakeries selling at retail
3086 Catering services
3095 Drinking places (bars, taverns, pubs, saloons, etc.)
3079 Eating places, meals & snacks
3210 Grocery stores (general line)
3251 Liquor stores
3236 Specialized food stores (meat, produce, candy, health food, etc.)

Furniture & General Merchandise

3988 Computer & software stores
3970 Furniture stores
4317 Home furnishings stores (china, floor coverings, drapes)
4119 Household appliance stores
4333 Music & record stores
3996 TV, audio & electronic stores
3715 Variety stores
3731 Other general merchandise stores

Miscellaneous Retail Stores

4812 Boat dealers
5017 Book stores, excluding newsstands
4853 Camera & photo supply stores
3277 Drug stores
5058 Fabric & needlework stores
4655 Florists
5090 Fuel dealers (except gasoline)
4630 Gift, novelty & souvenir shops
4838 Hobby, toy, & game shops
4671 Jewelry stores
4895 Luggage & leather goods stores
5074 Mobile home dealers
4879 Optical goods stores
4697 Sporting goods & bicycle shops
5033 Stationery stores
4614 Used merchandise & antique stores (except motor vehicle parts)
5884 Other retail stores

Trade, Wholesale—Selling Goods to Other Businesses, etc.

Durable Goods, Including Machinery Equipment, Wood, Metals, etc.
2634 Agent or broker for other firms— more than 50% of gross sales on commission
2618 Selling for your own account

Nondurable Goods, Including Food, Fiber, Chemicals, etc.
2675 Agent or broker for other firms— more than 50% of gross sales on commission
2659 Selling for your own account

Transportation, Communications, Public Utilities, & Related Services

6619 Air transportation
6312 Bus & limousine transportation
6676 Communication Services
6395 Courier or package delivery
6361 Highway passenger transportation (except chartered service)
6536 Public warehousing
6114 Taxicabs
6510 Trash collection without own dump
6635 Travel agents & tour operators
6338 Trucking (except trash collection)
6692 Utilities (dumps, snow plowing, road cleaning, etc.)
6551 Water transportation
6650 Other transportation services

8888 **Unable to classify**

This form is an advance proof. Use the final IRS version for filing

Self-Employment Tax

▶ See Instructions for Schedule SE (Form 1040).

▶ Attach to Form 1040.

OMB No. 1545-0074

1992

Attachment
Sequence No. **17**

Name of person with **self-employment** income (as shown on Form 1040)	Social security number of person with **self-employment** income ▶

Who Must File Schedule SE

You must file Schedule SE if:

- Your wages (and tips) subject to social security AND Medicare tax (or railroad retirement tax) were less than $130,200; **AND**
- Your *net earnings from self-employment from other than church employee income* (line 4 of Short Schedule SE or line 4c of Long Schedule SE) were $400 or more; **OR**
- You had church employee income (as defined on page SE-1) of $108.28 or more.

Exception. If your only self-employment income was from earnings as a minister, member of a religious order, or Christian Science practitioner, AND you filed **Form 4361** and received IRS approval not to be taxed on those earnings, DO NOT file Schedule SE. Instead, write "Exempt–Form 4361" on Form 1040, line 47.

May I Use Short Schedule SE or MUST I Use Long Schedule SE?

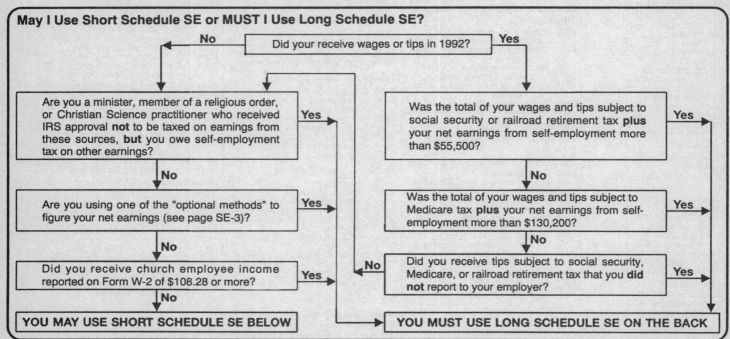

Section A—Short Schedule SE. Caution: *Read above to see if you must use Long Schedule SE on the back (Section B).*

1	Net farm profit or (loss) from Schedule F, line 36, and farm partnerships, Schedule K-1 (Form 1065), line 15a	**1**
2	Net profit or (loss) from Schedule C, line 31, Schedule C-EZ, line 3; and Schedule K-1 (Form 1065), line 15a (other than farming). See page SE-2 for other income to report	**2**
3	Combine lines 1 and 2	**3**
4	**Net earnings from self-employment.** Multiply line 3 by 92.35% (.9235). If less than $400, **do not** file this schedule; you do not owe self-employment tax . . . . ▶	**4**
5	**Self-employment tax.** If the amount on line 4 is:	
	• $55,500 or less, multiply line 4 by 15.3% (.153) and enter the result.	
	• More than $55,500 but less than $130,200, multiply the amount in excess of $55,500 by 2.9% (.029). Then, add $8,491.50 to the result and enter the total.	
	• $130,200 or more, enter $10,657.80.	
	Also, enter this amount on Form 1040, line 47	**5**
	Note: *Also, enter one-half of the amount from line 5 on Form 1040, line 25.*	

For Paperwork Reduction Act Notice, see Form 1040 instructions.

Cat. No. 11358Z

Schedule SE (Form 1040) 1992

This form is an advance proof. Use the final IRS version for filing

Name of person with **self-employment** income (as shown on Form 1040)	Social security number of person with **self-employment** income ▶	⋮ ⋮

Section B—Long Schedule SE

A If you are a minister, member of a religious order, or Christian Science practitioner AND you filed **Form 4361,** but you had $400 or more of **other** net earnings from self-employment, check here and continue with Part I . . . . . . ▶ ☐

B If your only income subject to self-employment tax is church employee income and you are **not** a minister or a member of a religious order, skip lines 1 through 4b. Enter -0- on line 4c and go to line 5a.

Part I   Self-Employment Tax

1	Net farm profit or (loss) from Schedule F, line 36, and farm partnerships, Schedule K-1 (Form 1065), line 15a. **Note:** *Skip this line if you use the farm optional method. See requirements in Part II below and on page SE-3*	**1**	
2	Net profit or (loss) from Schedule C, line 31, Schedule C-EZ, line 3; and Schedule K-1 (Form 1065), line 15a (other than farming). See page SE-2 for other income to report. **Note:** *Skip this line if you use the nonfarm optional method. See requirements in Part II below and on page SE-3*	**2**	
3	Combine lines 1 and 2	**3**	
4a	If line 3 is more than zero, multiply line 3 by 92.35% (.9235). Otherwise, enter amount from line 3	**4a**	
b	If you elected one or both of the optional methods, enter the total of lines 17 and 19 here	**4b**	
c	Combine lines 4a and 4b. If less than $400, **do not** file this schedule; you do not owe self-employment tax. **Exception.** If less than $400 and you had church employee income, enter -0- and continue. ▶	**4c**	
5a	Enter your church employee income from Form W-2. **Caution:** *See page SE-1 for definition of church employee income*	5a		
b	Mutiply line 5a by 92.35% (.9235). If less than $100, enter -0-	**5b**	
6	**Net earnings from self-employment.** Add lines 4c and 5b	**6**	
7	Maximum amount of combined wages and self-employment earnings subject to social security tax or the 6.2% portion of the 7.65% railroad retirement (tier 1) tax for 1992	**7**	55,500	00
8a	Total social security wages and tips (from Form(s) W-2) and railroad retirement (tier 1) compensation	8a		
b	Unreported tips subject to social security tax (from Form 4137, line 9)	8b		
c	Add lines 8a and 8b	**8c**	
9	Subtract line 8c from line 7. If zero or less, enter -0- here and on line 10 and go to line 12a ▶	**9**	
10	Mutiply the **smaller** of line 6 or line 9 by 12.4% (.124)	**10**	
11	Maximum amount of combined wages and self-employment earnings subject to Medicare tax or the 1.45% portion of the 7.65% railroad retirement (tier 1) tax for 1992	**11**	130,200	00
12a	Total Medicare wages and tips (from From(s) W-2) and railroad retirement (tier 1) compensation	12a		
b	Unreported tips subject to Medicare tax (from Form 4137, line 14)	12b		
c	Add lines 12a and 12b	**12c**	
13	Subtract line 12c from line 11. If zero or less, enter -0- here and on line 14 and go to line 15 .	**13**	
14	Multiply the **smaller** of line 6 or line 13 by 2.9% (.029)	**14**	
15	**Self-employment tax.** Add lines 10 and 14. Enter the result here and on Form 1040, line 47 .	**15**	

Note: *Also, enter one-half of the amount from line 15 on* **Form 1040, line 25.**

Part II   Optional Methods To Figure Net Earnings (See **Who Can File Schedule SE** and **Optional Methods** on page SE-3.)

Farm Optional Method. You may use this method **only** if **(a)** Your gross farm income[1] was not more than $2,400 **or (b)** Your gross farm income[1] was more than $2,400 and your net farm profits[2] were less than $1,733.

16	Maximum income for optional methods	**16**	1,600	00
17	Enter the **smaller** of: two-thirds (⅔) of gross farm income[1] **or** $1,600. Also include this amount on line 4b above	**17**	

Nonfarm Optional Method. You may use this method **only** if **(a)** Your net nonfarm profits[3] were less than $1,733 and also less than 72.189% of your gross nonfarm income,[4] **and (b)** You had net SE earnings of at least $400 in 2 of the prior 3 years. **Caution:** *You may use the nonfarm optional method no more than five times.*

18	Subtract line 17 from line 16	**18**	
19	Enter the **smaller** of: two-thirds (⅔) of gross nonfarm income[4] **or** the amount on line 18. Also include this amount on line 4b above	**19**	

[1]From Schedule F, line 11, and Schedule K-1 (Form 1065), line 15b.
[2]From Schedule F, line 36, and Schedule K-1 (Form 1065), line 15a.
[3]From Schedule C, line 31; Schedule C-EZ, line 3; and Schedule K-1 (Form 1065), line 15a.
[4]From Schedule C, line 7; Schedule C-EZ, line 1; and Schedule K-1 (Form 1065), line 15c.

This form is an advance proof. Use the final IRS version for filing

SCHEDULE D (Form 1040)	Capital Gains and Losses	OMB No. 1545-0074
Department of the Treasury Internal Revenue Service	(And Reconciliation of Forms 1099-B for Bartering Transactions) ► Attach to Form 1040. ► See Instructions for Schedule D (Form 1040). ► For more space to list transactions for lines 1a and 9a, get Schedule D-1 (Form 1040).	19**92** Attachment Sequence No. **12A**

Name(s) shown on Form 1040	Your social security number

Caution: *Add the following amounts reported to you for 1992 on Forms 1099-B and 1099-S (or on substitute statements):* **(a)** *proceeds from transactions involving stocks, bonds, and other securities, and* **(b)** *gross proceeds from real estate transactions not reported on another form or schedule. If this total does not equal the total of lines 1c and 9c, column (d), attach a statement explaining the difference.*

Part I — Short-Term Capital Gains and Losses—Assets Held One Year or Less

(a) Description of property (Example, 100 shares 7% preferred of "XYZ" Co.)	(b) Date acquired (Mo., day, yr.)	(c) Date sold (Mo., day, yr.)	(d) Sales price (see page D-2)	(e) Cost or other basis (see page D-3)	(f) LOSS If (e) is more than (d), subtract (d) from (e)	(g) GAIN If (d) is more than (e), subtract (e) from (d)
1a Stocks, Bonds, Other Securities, and Real Estate. Include Form 1099-B and 1099-S Transactions. See pages D-1 and D-3.						
1b Amounts from Schedule D-1, line 1b. Attach Schedule D-1				/////		
1c Total of All Sales Price Amounts. Add column (d) of lines 1a and 1b . . ►	**1c**		/////	/////	/////	/////
1d Other Transactions.						

2 Short-term gain from sale or exchange of your home from Form 2119, line 17 or 23.	**2**	/////				
3 Short-term gain from installment sales from Form 6252, line 26 or 37	**3**	/////				
4 Short-term gain or (loss) from like-kind exchanges from Form 8824	**4**					
5 Net short-term gain or (loss) from partnerships, S corporations, and fiduciaries. .	**5**					
6 Short-term capital loss carryover from 1991 Schedule D, line 36	**6**	/////				
7 Add lines 1a, 1b, 1d, and 2 through 6, in columns (f) and (g)	**7** (		)			
8 Net short-term capital gain or (loss). Combine columns (f) and (g) of line 7.		**8**				

Part II — Long-Term Capital Gains and Losses—Assets Held More than One Year

9a Stocks, Bonds, Other Securities, and Real Estate. Include Form 1099-B and 1099-S Transactions. See pages D-1 and D-3						
9b Amounts from Schedule D-1, line 9b. Attach Schedule D-1				/////		
9c Total of All Sales Price Amounts. Add column (d) of lines 9a and 9b . . ►	**9c**		/////	/////	/////	/////
9d Other Transactions.						

10 Long-term gain from sale or exchange of your home from Form 2119, line 17 or 23	**10**	/////				
11 Long-term gain from installment sales from Form 6252, line 26 or 37	**11**	/////				
12 Long-term gain or (loss) from like-kind exchanges from Form 8824	**12**					
13 Net long-term gain or (loss) from partnerships, S corporations, and fiduciaries .	**13**					
14 Capital gain distributions	**14**	/////				
15 Gain from Form 4797, line 8 or 10	**15**	/////				
16 Long-term capital loss carryover from 1991 Schedule D, line 43	**16**	/////				
17 Add lines 9a, 9b, 9d, and 10 through 16, in columns (f) and (g)	**17** (		)			
18 Net long-term capital gain or (loss). Combine columns (f) and (g) of line 17		**18**				

For Paperwork Reduction Act Notice, see Form 1040 instructions.   Cat. No. 11338H   Schedule D (Form 1040) 1992

This form is an advance proof. Use the final IRS version for filing

Name(s) shown on Form 1040. Do not enter name and social security number if shown on other side. | Your social security number

Part III   Summary of Parts I and II

19   Combine lines 8 and 18 and enter the net gain or (loss). If a gain, also enter the gain on Form 1040, line 13 . . . . | **19**

     Note: If both lines 18 and 19 are gains, see Part IV below.

20   If line 19 is a (loss), enter here and as a (loss) on Form 1040, line 13, the **smaller** of:

   a   The (loss) on line 19; **or**

   b   ($3,000) or, if married filing a separate return, ($1,500) . . . . | **20** (   )

     Note: When figuring whether line 20a or 20b is **smaller**, treat both numbers as positive.
     Complete Part V if the loss on line 19 is more than the loss on line 20 OR if Form 1040, line 37, is zero.

Part IV   Tax Computation Using Maximum Capital Gains Rate

USE THIS PART TO FIGURE YOUR TAX ONLY IF BOTH LINES 18 AND 19 ARE GAINS, AND:

You checked filing status box:	AND	Form 1040, line 37, is over:	You checked filing status box:	AND	Form 1040, line 37, is over:
1		$51,900	3		$43,250
2 or 5		$86,500	4		$74,150

21   Enter the amount from Form 1040, line 37 . . . . | **21**

22   Enter the **smaller** of line 18 or line 19 . . . . | **22**

23   Subtract line 22 from line 21 . . . . | **23**

24   Enter: $21,450 if you checked filing status box 1; $35,800 if you checked filing status box 2 or 5;
     $17,900 if you checked filing status box 3; or $28,750 if you checked filing status box 4 . . . . | **24**

25   Enter the **greater** of line 23 or line 24 . . . . | **25**

26   Subtract line 25 from line 21 . . . . | **26**

27   Figure the tax on the amount on line 25. Use the Tax Table or Tax Rate Schedules, whichever applies | **27**

28   Multiply line 26 by 28% (.28) . . . . | **28**

29   Add lines 27 and 28. Enter here and on Form 1040, line 38, and check the box for Schedule D | **29**

Part V   Capital Loss Carryovers from 1992 to 1993

30   Enter the amount from Form 1040, line 35. If a loss, enclose the amount in parentheses . . . . . | **30**

31   Enter the loss from line 20 as a positive amount . . . . | **31**

32   Combine lines 30 and 31. If zero or less, enter -0- . . . . | **32**

33   Enter the **smaller** of line 31 or line 32 . . . . | **33**

     Note: If both lines 8 and 20 are losses, go to line 34; otherwise, skip lines 34–38.

34   Enter the loss from line 8 as a positive amount . . . . | **34**

35   Enter the gain, if any, from line 18 . . . . | **35**

36   Enter the amount from line 33 . . . . | **36**

37   Add lines 35 and 36 . . . . | **37**

38   **Short-term capital loss carryover to 1993.** Subtract line 37 from line 34. If zero or less, enter -0- . | **38**

     Note: If both lines 18 and 20 are losses, go to line 39; otherwise, skip lines 39-45.

39   Enter the loss from line 18 as a positive amount . . . . | **39**

40   Enter the gain, if any, from line 8 . . . . | **40**

41   Enter the amount from line 33 . . . . . . | **41**

42   Enter the amount, if any, from line 34 . . . | **42**

43   Subtract line 42 from line 41. If zero or less, enter -0- . . . . . . | **43**

44   Add lines 40 and 43 . . . . | **44**

45   **Long-term capital loss carryover to 1993.** Subtract line 44 from line 39. If zero or less, enter -0- . | **45**

Part VI   Election Not To Use the Installment Method. Complete this part **only** if you elect out of the installment method and report a note or other obligation at less than full face value.

46   Check here if you elect out of the installment method . . . . ▶ ☐

47   Enter the face amount of the note or other obligation . . . . ▶ ....

48   Enter the percentage of valuation of the note or other obligation . . . . ▶ .... %

Part VII   Reconciliation of Forms 1099-B for Bartering Transactions.
Complete this part **only** if you received one or more Forms 1099-B or substitute statements reporting **bartering income**. | Amount of bartering income from Form 1099-B or substitute statement reported on form or schedule

49   Form 1040, line 22 . . . . | **49**

50   Schedule C, D, E, or F (specify) ▶ .... | **50**

51   Other form or schedule (identify). If nontaxable, indicate reason—attach additional sheets if necessary:
.... | **51**

52   **Total.** Add lines 49 through 51. This amount should be the same as the total bartering income on all Forms 1099-B and substitute statements received for bartering transactions . . . . | **52**

This form is an advance proof. Use the final IRS version for filing

SCHEDULE E
(Form 1040)

Department of the Treasury
Internal Revenue Service

Supplemental Income and Loss

(From rental real estate, royalties, partnerships, estates, trusts, REMICs, etc.)

▶ Attach to Form 1040 or Form 1041.
▶ See Instructions for Schedule E (Form 1040).

OMB No. 1545-0074

1992

Attachment
Sequence No. **13**

Name(s) shown on return

Your social security number

Part I   **Income or Loss From Rental Real Estate and Royalties**   **Note:** *Report income and expenses from the rental of personal property on **Schedule C or C-EZ**. Report farm rental income or loss from **Form 4835** on page 2, line 39.*

1 Show the kind and location of each **rental real estate property:**

A ....

B ....

C ....

2 For each rental real estate property listed on line 1, did you or your family use it for personal purposes for more than the greater of 14 days or 10% of the total days rented at fair rental value during the tax year? (See page E-1 of the instructions.)

	Yes	No
A		
B		
C		

Income:		Properties			Totals (Add columns A, B, and C.)
		A	B	C	
3 Rents received	3				3
4 Royalties received	4				4
Expenses:					
5 Advertising	5				
6 Auto and travel (see page E-2)	6				
7 Cleaning and maintenance	7				
8 Commissions	8				
9 Insurance	9				
10 Legal and other professional fees	10				
11 Management fees	11				
12 Mortgage interest paid to banks, etc. (see page E-2)	12				12
13 Other interest	13				
14 Repairs	14				
15 Supplies	15				
16 Taxes	16				
17 Utilities	17				
18 Other (list) ▶................	18				
19 Add lines 5 through 18	19				19
20 Depreciation expense or depletion (see page E-2)	20				20
21 Total expenses. Add lines 19 and 20	21				
22 Income or (loss) from rental real estate or royalty properties. Subtract line 21 from line 3 (rents) or line 4 (royalties). If the result is a (loss), see page E-2 to find out if you must file **Form 6198**	22				
23 Deductible rental real estate loss. **Caution:** *Your rental real estate loss on line 22 may be limited. See page E-3 to find out if you must file **Form 8582***	23	( )(	)(	)	

24 **Income.** Add rental real estate and royalty income from line 22. Enter the total income here | 24 |

25 **Losses.** Add royalty losses from line 22 and rental real estate losses from line 23. Enter the total losses here | 25 ( ) |

26 Total rental real estate and royalty income or (loss). Combine lines 24 and 25. Enter the result here. If Parts II, III, IV, and line 39 on page 2 do not apply to you, also enter this amount on Form 1040, line 18. Otherwise, include this amount in the total on line 40 on page 2 | 26 |

For Paperwork Reduction Act Notice, see Form 1040 instructions.   Cat. No. 11344L   Schedule E (Form 1040) 1992

This form is an advance proof. Use the final IRS version for filing

Name(s) shown on return. Do not enter name and social security number if shown on other side.　　　**Your social security number**

Note: *If you report amounts from farming or fishing on Schedule E, you must enter your gross income from those activities on line 41 below.*

Part II　Income or Loss From Partnerships and S Corporations

If you report a loss from an at-risk activity, you MUST check either column **(e)** or **(f)** of line 27 to describe your investment in the activity. See page E-3. If you check column **(f)**, you must attach **Form 6198.**

27	(a) Name	(b) Enter P for partnership; S for S corporation	(c) Check if foreign partnership	(d) Employer identification number	Investment At Risk?	
					(e) All is at risk	(f) Some is not at risk
A						
B						
C						
D						
E						

	Passive Income and Loss		Nonpassive Income and Loss		
	(g) Passive loss allowed (attach Form 8582 if required)	(h) Passive income from Schedule K–1	(i) Nonpassive loss from Schedule K–1	(j) Section 179 expense deduction from Form 4562	(k) Nonpassive income from Schedule K–1
A					
B					
C					
D					
E					
28a Totals					
b Totals					

29	Add columns (h) and (k) of line 28a	29	
30	Add columns (g), (i), and (j) of line 28b	30	( )
31	Total partnership and S corporation income or (loss). Combine lines 29 and 30. Enter the result here and include in the total on line 40 below	31	

Part III　Income or Loss From Estates and Trusts

32	(a) Name	(b) Employer identification number
A		
B		
C		

	Passive Income and Loss		Nonpassive Income and Loss	
	(c) Passive deduction or loss allowed (attach Form 8582 if required)	(d) Passive income from Schedule K–1	(e) Deduction or loss from Schedule K–1	(f) Other income from Schedule K–1
A				
B				
C				
33a Totals				
b Totals				

34	Add columns (d) and (f) of line 33a	34	
35	Add columns (c) and (e) of line 33b	35	( )
36	Total estate and trust income or (loss). Combine lines 34 and 35. Enter the result here and include in the total on line 40 below	36	

Part IV　Income or Loss From Real Estate Mortgage Investment Conduits (REMICs)—Residual Holder

37	(a) Name	(b) Employer identification number	(c) Excess inclusion from Schedules Q, line 2c (see page E-4)	(d) Taxable income (net loss) from Schedules Q, line 1b	(e) Income from Schedules Q, line 3b

38	Combine columns (d) and (e) only. Enter the result here and include in the total on line 40 below	38	

Part V　Summary

39	Net farm rental income or (loss) from **Form 4835.** Also, complete line 41 below	39	
40	TOTAL income or (loss). Combine lines 26, 31, 36, 38, and 39. Enter the result here and on Form 1040, line 18 . . . . ▶	40	
41	**Reconciliation of Farming and Fishing Income:** Enter your **gross** farming and fishing income reported in Parts II and III and on line 39 (see page E-4)	41	

This form is an advance proof. Use the final IRS version for filing

Schedule K-1 (Form 1065) 1992

(a) Distributive share item	(b) Amount	(c) 1040 filers enter the amount in column (b) on:

Self-employment

15a Net earnings (loss) from self-employment	15a		Sch. SE, Section A or B
b Gross farming or fishing income	15b		(See Partner's Instructions for Schedule K-1 (Form 1065).)
c Gross nonfarm income	15c		

Adjustments and Tax Preference Items

16a Depreciation adjustment on property placed in service after 1986	16a	
b Adjusted gain or loss	16b	(See Partner's Instructions for Schedule K-1 (Form 1065) and Instructions for Form 6251.)
c Depletion (other than oil and gas)	16c	
d (1) Gross income from oil, gas, and geothermal properties	d(1)	
(2) Deductions allocable to oil, gas, and geothermal properties	d(2)	
e Other adjustments and tax preference items (attach schedule)	16e	

Foreign Taxes

17a Type of income ▶		
b Name of foreign country or U.S. possession ▶		
c Total gross income from sources outside the U.S. (attach schedule)	17c	Form 1116, Part I
d Total applicable deductions and losses (attach schedule)	17d	
e Total foreign taxes (check one): ▶ ☐ Paid ☐ Accrued	17e	Form 1116, Part II
f Reduction in taxes available for credit (attach schedule)	17f	Form 1116, Part III
g Other foreign tax information (attach schedule)	17g	See Instructions for Form 1116.

Other

18a Total expenditures to which a section 59(e) election may apply	18a	See Partner's Instructions for Schedule K-1 (Form 1065).
b Type of expenditures ▶		
19 Tax exempt interest income	19	Form 1040, line 8b
20 Other tax-exempt income	20	(See Partner's Instructions for Schedule K-1 (Form 1065).)
21 Nondeductible expenses	21	
22 Recapture of low-income housing credit:		
a From section 42(j)(5) partnerships	22a	Form 8611, line 8
b Other than on line 22a	22b	

Supplemental Information

23 Supplemental information required to be reported separately to each partner (attach additional schedules if more space is needed):

This form is on advance proof. Use the final IRS version for filing

---

SCHEDULE K-1 (Form 1065)
Department of the Treasury
Internal Revenue Service

Partner's Share of Income, Credits, Deductions, Etc.
▶ See separate instructions.
For calendar year 1992 or tax year beginning ...., 1992, and ending ...., 19...

OMB No. 1545-0099

1992

Partner's identifying number ▶
Partnership's identifying number ▶

Partner's name, address, and ZIP code
Partnership's name, address, and ZIP code

A Is this partner a general partner? ☐ Yes ☐ No

B Partner's share of liabilities (see instructions):
Nonrecourse . . . . $
Qualified nonrecourse financing . . $
Other . . . . $

C What type of entity is this partner? ▶

D Is this partner a ☐ domestic or a ☐ foreign partner?

E IRS Center where partnership filed return:

F Enter partner's percentage of:

	(i) Before change or termination	(ii) End of year
Profit sharing	%	%
Loss sharing	%	%
Ownership of capital	%	%

G (1) Tax shelter registration number ▶
(2) Type of tax shelter ▶

H Check here if this partnership is a publicly traded partnership as defined in section 469(k)(2) ☐

I Check applicable boxes: (1) ☐ Final K-1 (2) ☐ Amended K-1

J Analysis of partner's capital account:

(a) Capital account at beginning of year	(b) Capital contributed during year	(c) Partner's share of lines 3, 4, and 7, Form 1065, Schedule M-2	(d) Withdrawals and distributions	(e) Capital account at end of year (combine columns (a) through (d))

(a) Distributive share item	(b) Amount	(c) 1040 filers enter the amount in column (b) on:

Income (Loss)

1 Ordinary income (loss) from trade or business activities	1	
2 Net income (loss) from rental real estate activities	2	(See Partner's Instructions for Schedule K-1 (Form 1065).)
3 Net income (loss) from other rental activities	3	
4 Portfolio income (loss):		
a Interest	4a	Sch. B, Part I, line 1
b Dividends	4b	Sch. B, Part II, line 5
c Royalties	4c	Sch. E, Part I, line 4
d Net short-term capital gain (loss)	4d	Sch. D, line 5, col. (f) or (g)
e Net long-term capital gain (loss)	4e	Sch. D, line 13, col. (f) or (g)
f Other portfolio income (loss) (attach schedule)	4f	(Enter on applicable line of your return.)
5 Guaranteed payments to partner	5	(See Partner's Instructions for Schedule K-1 (Form 1065).)
6 Net gain (loss) under section 1231 (other than due to casualty or theft)	6	
7 Other income (loss) (attach schedule)	7	

Deduc-tions

8 Charitable contributions (see instructions) (attach schedule)	8	Sch. A, line 13 or 14
9 Section 179 expense deduction	9	(See Partner's Instructions for Schedule K-1 (Form 1065).)
10 Deductions related to portfolio income (attach schedule)	10	
11 Other deductions (attach schedule)	11	

Investment Interest

12a Interest expense on investment debts	12a	Form 4952, line 1
b (1) Investment income included on lines 4a through 4f above	b(1)	(See Partner's Instructions for Schedule K-1 (Form 1065).)
(2) Investment expenses included on line 10 above	b(2)	

Credits

13a Credit for income tax withheld	13a	
b Low-income housing credit:		
(1) From section 42(j)(5) partnerships for property placed in service before 1990	b(1)	
(2) Other than on line 13b(1) for property placed in service before 1990	b(2)	
(3) From section 42(j)(5) partnerships for property placed in service after 1989	b(3)	Form 8586, line 5
(4) Other than on line 13b(3) for property placed in service after 1989	b(4)	
c Qualified rehabilitation expenditures related to rental real estate activities (see instructions)	13c	
d Credits (other than credits shown on lines 13b and 13c) related to rental real estate activities (see instructions)	13d	(See Partner's Instructions for Schedule K-1 (Form 1065).)
e Credits related to other rental activities (see instructions)	13e	
14 Other credits (see instructions)	14	

For Paperwork Reduction Act Notice, see Instructions for Form 1065.   Cat. No. 11394R   Schedule K-1 (Form 1065) 1992

This form is on advance proof. Use the final IRS version for filing

Form 2441 (1992)

Part III — **Employer-Provided Dependent Care Benefits**—Complete this part only if you received employer-provided dependent care benefits.

17 Enter the total amount of employer-provided dependent care benefits you received for 1992. This amount should be shown in box 22 of your W-2 form(s). **Do not** include amounts that were reported to you as wages in box 10 of Form(s) W-2 17

18 Enter the amount forfeited, if any. **Caution:** *See the instructions* 18

19 Subtract line 18 from line 17 19

20 Enter the total amount of **qualified** expenses incurred in 1992 for the care of a qualifying person. See the instructions 20

21 Look at lines 19 and 20. Enter the **smaller** of the two amounts here 21

22 You **must** enter your **earned income.** See the instructions for lines 9 and 10 for the definition of earned income.
Note: *If you are not filing a joint return, go to line 24 now.* 22

23 If you are filing a joint return, you **must** enter your spouse's earned income. If your spouse was a student or disabled, see the instructions for lines 9 and 10 for the amount to enter 23

24 • If you are filing a joint return, look at lines 22 and 23. Enter the **smaller** of the two amounts here.
  • **All others,** enter the amount from line 22 here. 24

25 **Excluded benefits.** Enter here the **smallest** of the following:
  • The amount from line 21, or
  • The amount from line 24, or
  • $5,000 ($2,500 if married filing a separate return). 25

26 **Taxable benefits.** Subtract line 25 from line 19. Enter the result, but not less than zero. Also, include this amount in the total on Form 1040, line 7. On the dotted line next to line 7, write "DCB" 26
Next: If you are also claiming the child and dependent care credit, fill in Form 1040 through line 40. Then, complete Part II of this form.

This form is an advance proof. Use the final IRS version for filing

---

Form **2441**	**Child and Dependent Care Expenses**	OMB No. 1545-0068 **1992**

Department of the Treasury
Internal Revenue Service
▶ Attach to Form 1040.
▶ See separate instructions.
Attachment Sequence No. **21**

Name(s) shown on Form 1040 | Your social security number

Caution: • *If you have a child who was born in 1992 and the amount on Form 1040, line 32, is less than $22,370, see page 1 of the instructions before completing this form.*
• *If you paid cash wages of $50 or more in a calendar quarter to an individual for services performed in your home, you must file an employment tax return. Get **Form 942** for details.*

Part I — **Persons or Organizations Who Provided the Care—You must complete this part.** (See the instructions.)
If you need more space, use the bottom of page 2.

1 (a) Care provider's name	(b) Address (number, street, apt. no., city, state, and ZIP code)	(c) Identifying number (SSN or EIN)	(d) Amount paid (see instructions)

2 Add the amounts in column (d) of line 1 2

Next: Did you receive employer-provided dependent care benefits?
  • **YES.** Complete Part III on the back now.
  • **NO.** Complete Part II below.

Part II — **Credit for Child and Dependent Care Expenses**

3 Enter the number of qualifying persons cared for in 1992. See the instructions to find out who is a qualifying person.
Caution: *To qualify, the person(s) **must** have shared the same home with you in 1992.* 3

4 Enter the amount of **qualified** expenses you incurred and actually paid in 1992. See the instructions to find out which expenses qualify. **Caution:** *If you completed Part III on page 2, **do not** include on this line any excluded benefits shown on line 25* 4

5 Enter $2,400 ($4,800 if you paid for the care of two or more qualifying persons) 5

6 If you completed Part III on page 2, enter the **excluded benefits,** if any, from line 25. 6

7 Subtract line 6 from line 5. If the result is zero or less, skip lines 8 through 13; enter -0- on line 14, and go to 15 7

8 Look at lines 4 and 7. Enter the **smaller** of the two amounts here 8

9 You **must** enter your **earned income.** See the instructions for the definition of earned income.
Note: *If you are not filing a joint return, go to line 11 now.* 9

10 If you are filing a joint return, you **must** enter your spouse's earned income. If your spouse was a student or disabled, see the instructions for the amount to enter 10

11 • If you are filing a joint return, look at lines 8, 9, and 10. Enter the **smallest** of the three amounts here.
  • All others, look at lines 8 and 9. Enter the **smaller** of the two amounts here. 11

12 Enter the amount from Form 1040, line 32 12

13 Enter the decimal amount shown below that applies to the amount on line 12 13

If line 12 is: Over— But not over—	Decimal amount is:	If line 12 is: Over— But not over—	Decimal amount is:
$0—10,000	.30	$20,000—22,000	.24
10,000—12,000	.29	22,000—24,000	.23
12,000—14,000	.28	24,000—26,000	.22
14,000—16,000	.27	26,000—28,000	.21
16,000—18,000	.26	28,000—No limit	.20
18,000—20,000	.25		

14 Multiply line 11 above by the decimal amount on line 13 14

15 Multiply any qualified expenses for 1991 that you paid in 1992 by the decimal amount that applies to the amount on your 1991 Form 1040, line 32, or Form 1040A, line 17. You must complete Part I and attach a statement. See the instructions 15

16 Add lines 14 and 15. See the instructions for the amount of credit you can claim 16

For Paperwork Reduction Act Notice, see separate instructions. Cat. No. 11862M Form **2441** (1992)
This form is an advance proof. Use the final IRS version for filing

Schedule R (Form 1040)

**Department of the Treasury
Internal Revenue Service**

Credit for the Elderly or the Disabled

▶ Attach to Form 1040.   ▶ See separate instructions for Schedule R.

OMB No. 1545-0074

1992

Attachment Sequence No. **16**

Name(s) shown on Form 1040 | Your social security number

You may be able to use Schedule R to reduce your tax if by the end of 1992:

• You were age 65 or older, **OR** • You were under age 65, you retired on **permanent and total disability, and you received taxable disability income.**

But you must also meet other tests. See the separate instructions for Schedule R.

Note: *In most cases, the IRS can figure the credit for you. See page 23 of the Form 1040 instructions.*

Part I   Check the Box for Your Filing Status and Age

If your filing status is:		And by the end of 1992:	Check only one box:
Single, Head of household, or Qualifying widow(er) with dependent child	1	You were 65 or older	1 ☐
	2	You were under 65 and you retired on permanent and total disability	2 ☐
Married filing a joint return	3	Both spouses were 65 or older	3 ☐
	4	Both spouses were under 65, but only one spouse retired on permanent and total disability	4 ☐
	5	Both spouses were under 65, and both retired on permanent and total disability	5 ☐
	6	One spouse was 65 or older, and the other spouse was under 65 and retired on permanent and total disability	6 ☐
	7	One spouse was 65 or older, and the other spouse was under 65 and **NOT** retired on permanent and total disability	7 ☐
Married filing a separate return	8	You were 65 or older and you did not live with your spouse at any time in 1992	8 ☐
	9	You were under 65, you retired on permanent and total disability, and you did not live with your spouse at any time in 1992	9 ☐

If you checked box 1, 3, 7, or 8, skip Part II and complete Part III on the back. All others, complete Parts II and III.

Part II   Statement of Permanent and Total Disability (Complete only if you checked box 2, 4, 5, 6, or 9 above.)

IF: 1 You filed a physician's statement for 1983 or an earlier year, or you filed a statement for tax years after 1983 and your physician signed line B on the statement, **AND**

2 Due to your continued disabled condition, you were unable to engage in any substantial gainful activity in 1992, check this box . . . . . . ▶ ☐

• If you checked this box, you do not have to file another statement for 1992.

• If you **did not** check this box, have your physician complete the following statement.

Physician's Statement (See instructions at bottom of page 2.)

I certify that _____
            Name of disabled person

was permanently and totally disabled on January 1, 1976, or January 1, 1977, **OR** was permanently and totally disabled on the date he or she retired. If retired after December 31, 1976, enter the date retired. ▶

Physician: Sign your name on **either** line A or B below.

A The disability has lasted, or can be expected to last, continuously for at least a year	Physician's signature	Date
B There is no reasonable probability that the disabled condition will ever improve	Physician's signature	Date
Physician's name	Physician's address	

For Paperwork Reduction Act Notice, see Form 1040 instructions.   Cat. No. 11359K   **Schedule R (Form 1040) 1992**

This form is an advance proof. Use the final IRS version for filing

---

Part III   Figure Your Credit

10	If you checked (in Part I):	Enter:		
	Box 1, 2, 4, or 7	$5,000		
	Box 3, 5, or 6	$7,500		
	Box 8 or 9	$3,750		10

Caution: *If you checked box 2, 4, 5, 6, or 9 in Part I, you MUST complete line 11 below. All others, skip line 11 and enter the amount from line 10 on line 12.*

11 If you checked:

• Box 6 in Part I, add $5,000 to the taxable disability income of the spouse who was under age 65. Enter the total here.

• Box 2, 4, or 9 in Part I, enter your taxable disability income here.

• Box 5 in Part I, add your taxable disability income to your spouse's taxable disability income. Enter the total here. | 11

TIP: For more details on what to include on line 11, see the instructions.

12 If you completed line 11 above, look at lines 10 and 11. Enter the smaller of the two amounts here.

• All others, enter the amount from line 10 here. | 12

13 Enter the following pensions, annuities, or disability income that you (and your spouse if filing a joint return) received in 1992 (see instructions):

a Nontaxable part of social security benefits and Nontaxable part of railroad retirement benefits treated as social security. | 13a

b Nontaxable veterans' pensions, and Any other pension, annuity, or disability benefit that is excluded from income under any other provision of law. | 13b

c Add lines 13a and 13b. (Even though these income items are not taxable, they **must** be included here to figure your credit.) If you did not receive any of the types of nontaxable income listed on line 13a or 13b, enter -0- on line 13c. | 13c

14 Enter the amount from Form 1040, line 32 | 14

15	If you checked (in Part I):	Enter:		
	Box 1 or 2	$7,500		
	Box 3, 4, 5, 6, or 7	$10,000		
	Box 8 or 9	$5,000		15

16 Subtract line 15 from line 14. If line 15 is more than line 14, enter -0- | 16

17 Divide line 16 above by 2 | 17

18 Add lines 13c and 17 | 18

19 Subtract line 18 from line 12. If line 18 is more than line 12, stop here; you **cannot** take the credit. Otherwise, go to line 21 | 19

20 Decimal amount used to figure the credit | 20   X .15

21 Multiply line 19 above by the decimal amount (.15) on line 20. Enter the result here and on Form 1040, line 42. **Caution:** *If you file Schedule C, C-EZ, D, E, or F (Form 1040), your credit may be limited. See the instructions for line 21 for the amount of credit you can claim.* | 21

Instructions for Physician's Statement

Taxpayer

If you retired after December 31, 1976, enter the date you retired in the space provided in Part II.

Physician

A person is permanently and totally disabled if both of the following apply:

1. He or she cannot engage in any substantial gainful activity because of a physical or mental condition, and

2. A physician determines that the disability has lasted, or can be expected to last, continuously for at least a year or can lead to death.

This form is an advance proof. Use the final IRS version for filing

SCHEDULE C-EZ (Form 1040)

Department of the Treasury
Internal Revenue Service

Net Profit From Business
(Sole Proprietorship)

▶ Partnerships, joint ventures, etc., must file Form 1065.

▶ Attach to Form 1040 or Form 1041.

OMB No. 1545-0074

1992

Attachment Sequence No. **09A**

Name of proprietor

Social security number (SSN)

Part I General Information

You May Use This Form If You:

- Had gross receipts from your business of $25,000 or less.
- Had business expenses of $2,000 or less.
- Use the cash method of accounting.
- Did not have an inventory at any time during the year.
- Did not have a net loss from your business.
- Had only one business as a sole proprietor.

And You:

- Had no employees during the year.
- Are not required to file Form 4562, Depreciation and Amortization. See the instructions for Schedule C, line 13, on page C-3 to find out if you must file.
- Do not deduct expenses for business use of your home.
- Do not have prior year unallowed passive activity losses from this business.

A Principal business or profession, including product or service

B Enter principal business code (from page 2) ▶

C Business name

D Employer ID number (EIN)

E Business address (including suite or room no.) Address not required if same as on Form 1040, page 1.

City, town or post office, state and ZIP code

F Was this business in operation at the end of 1992? ☐ Yes ☐ No

G How many months was this business in operation during 1992? ▲

Part II Figure Your Net Profit

1 **Gross receipts.** If more than $25,000, you **must** use Schedule C. **Caution:** *If this income was reported to you on Form W-2 and the "Statutory employee" box on that form was checked, see Statutory Employees in the instructions for Schedule C, line 1, on page C-2 and check here* .... ▶ ☐ 1

2 **Total expenses.** If more than $2,000, you **must** use Schedule C. See instructions 2

3 **Net profit.** Subtract line 2 from line 1. Enter the result here and on Form 1040, line 12, and on Schedule SE, line 2. (Statutory employees **do not** report this amount on Schedule SE, line 2.) If less than zero, you **must** use Schedule C 3

Part III Information on Your Vehicle. Complete Part III ONLY if you are claiming car and truck expenses on line 2.

4 When did you place your vehicle in service for business purposes? (month, day, year) ...... / ...... / ......

5 Of the total number of miles you drove your vehicle during 1992, enter the number of miles you used your vehicle for:

a Business .... b Commuting .... c Other

6 Do you (or your spouse) have another vehicle available for personal use? .... ☐ Yes ☐ No

7 Was your vehicle available for use during off-duty hours? .... ☐ Yes ☐ No

8a Do you have evidence to support your deduction? .... ☐ Yes ☐ No

b If "Yes," is the evidence written? .... ☐ Yes ☐ No

Instructions

Schedule C-EZ is new for 1992. You may use Schedule C-EZ instead of Schedule C if you operated a business or practiced a profession as a sole proprietorship and you have met all the requirements listed above.

Line A.—Describe the business or professional activity that provided your principal source of income reported on line 1. Give the general field or activity and the type of product or service.

Line B.—Enter on this line the four-digit code that identifies your principal business or professional activity. See page 2 for the list of codes.

Line D.—You need an employer identification number (EIN) only if you had a Keogh plan or were required to file an employment, excise, fiduciary, or alcohol, tobacco, and firearms tax return. If you don't have an EIN, leave line D blank. **Do not** enter your SSN.

Line E.— Enter your business address. Show a street address instead of a box number. Include the suite or room number, if any.

Line 1—Gross Receipts.—Enter gross receipts from your trade or business. Be sure to include any amount you received in your trade or business that is reported on Form(s) 1099-MISC. You must show all items of taxable income actually or constructively received during the year (in cash,

property, or services). Income is constructively received when it is credited to your account or set aside for you to use. Do not offset this amount by any losses.

Line 2—Total Expenses.—Enter the total amount of all deductible business expenses you actually paid during the year. Examples of these expenses include advertising, car and truck expenses, commissions, insurance, interest, legal

and professional services and fees, office expense, rent or lease expenses, repairs and maintenance, supplies, taxes, travel, 80% of business meals and entertainment, and utilities (including telephone). For details, see the instructions for Schedule C, Part II, on pages C-2 through C-5.

If you claim car and truck expense, also complete Part III.

For Paperwork Reduction Act Notice, see Form 1040 instructions.   Cat. No. 14374D   Schedule C-EZ (Form 1040) 1992

This form is an advance proof. Use the final IRS version for filing

---

Principal Business or Professional Activity Codes

Locate the major category that best describes your activity. Within the major category, select the activity code that most closely identifies the business or profession that is the principal source of your receipts. Enter this 4-digit code on page 1, line B. For example, real estate agent is under the major category of "Real Estate," and the code is "5520."

Agricultural Services, Forestry, Fishing

Code
1990 Animal services, other than breeding
1933 Crop services
2113 Farm labor & management services
2246 Fishing, commercial
2238 Forestry, except logging
2212 Horticulture & landscaping
2469 Hunting & trapping
1974 Livestock breeding
0836 Logging
1958 Veterinary services, including pets

Construction

0018 Operative builders (for own account)

Building Trade Contractors, Including Repairs
0414 Carpentering & flooring
0455 Concrete work
0273 Electrical work
0299 Masonry, dry wall, stone, & tile
0257 Painting & paper hanging
0232 Plumbing, heating, & air conditioning
0430 Roofing, siding & sheet metal
0885 Other building trade contractors (excavation, glazing, etc.)

General Contractors
0075 Highway & street construction
0059 Nonresidential building
0034 Residential building
3889 Other heavy construction (pipe laying, bridge construction, etc.)

Finance, Insurance, & Related Services

6064 Brokers & dealers of securities
6080 Commodity contracts brokers & dealers; security & commodity exchanges
6148 Credit institutions & mortgage bankers
5702 Insurance agents or brokers
5744 Insurance services (appraisal, consulting, inspection, etc.)
6130 Investment advisors & services
5777 Other financial services

Manufacturing, Including Printing & Publishing

0679 Apparel & other textile products
1115 Electric & electronic equipment
1073 Fabricated metal products
0638 Food products & beverages
0695 Leather, footwear, handbags, etc.
0836 Lumber & other wood products
1099 Machinery & machine shops
0877 Paper & allied products
0851 Printing & publishing
1032 Stone, clay, & glass products
0653 Textile mill products
1883 Other manufacturing industries

Mining & Mineral Extraction

1537 Coal mining
1511 Metal mining
1552 Oil & gas
1719 Quarrying & nonmetallic mining

Real Estate

5538 Operators & lessors of buildings, including residential
5553 Operators & lessors of other real property
5520 Real estate agents & brokers
5579 Real estate property managers
5710 Subdividers & developers, except cemeteries
6155 Title abstract offices

Services: Personal, Professional, & Business Services

Amusement & Recreational Services
9670 Bowling centers
9688 Motion picture & tape distribution & allied services
9597 Motion picture & video production
9639 Motion picture theatres
8557 Physical fitness facilities
9696 Professional sports & racing, including promoters & managers
9811 Theatrical performers, musicians, agents, producers & related services
9613 Video tape rental
9837 Other amusement & recreational services

Automotive Services
8813 Automotive rental or leasing, without driver
8953 Automotive repairs, general & specialized
8839 Parking, except valet
3996 Other automotive services (wash, towing, etc.)

Business & Personal Services
7658 Accounting & bookkeeping
7716 Advertising, except direct mail
8318 Architectural services
6312 Barber shop (or barber)
6361 Beauty shop (or beautician)
8714 Child day care
7872 Computer programming, processing, data preparation & related services
7922 Computer repair, maintenance, & leasing
7286 Consulting services
7799 Consumer credit reporting & collection services
8755 Counseling (except health practitioners)
7732 Employment agencies & personnel supply
7518 Engineering services
7773 Equipment rental & leasing (except computer or automotive)
8532 Funeral services & crematories
7617 Income tax preparation
7914 Investigative & protective services
7856 Legal services (or lawyer)
7245 Mailing, reproduction, commercial art, photography, & stenographic services
8771 Management services
8334 Ministers & chaplains
7260 Public relations
8733 Research services
7708 Surveying services
8730 Teaching or tutoring
7880 Other business services
6882 Other personal services

Hotels & Other Lodging Places
7237 Camps & camping parks
7096 Hotels, motels, & tourist homes
7211 Rooming & boarding houses

Laundry & Cleaning Services
7450 Carpet & upholster cleaning
7419 Coin-operated laundries & dry cleaning
7435 Full-service laundry, dry cleaning, & garment service
7476 Janitorial & related services (building, house, & window cleaning)

Medical & Health Services
9274 Chiropractors
9233 Dentist's office or clinic
9456 Doctor's (M.D.) office or clinic
9472 Medical & dental laboratories
9290 Nursing & personal care facilities
9258 Optometrists
9241 Osteopathic physicians & surgeons
9415 Podiatrists
9431 Registered & practical nurses
Offices & clinics of other health practitioners (dieticians, midwives, speech pathologists, etc.)
9886 Other health services

Miscellaneous Repair, Except Computers
9019 Audio equipment & TV repair
9035 Electrical & electronic equipment repair, except audio & TV
Furniture repair & reupholstery
2881 Other equipment repair

Trade, Retail—Selling Goods to Individuals & Households
3038 Catalog or mail order
3012 Selling door to door, by telephone or party plan, or from mobile unit
3053 Vending machine selling

Selling From Showroom, Store, or Other Fixed Location

Apparel & Accessories
3921 Accessory & specialty stores & furriers for women
3939 Clothing, family
3772 Clothing, men's & boys'
3913 Clothing, women's
3756 Shoe stores
3954 Other apparel & accessory stores

Automotive & Service Stations
3558 Gasoline service stations
3319 New car dealers (franchised)
3533 Tires, accessories, & parts
3335 Used car dealers
3517 Other automotive dealers (motorcycles, recreational vehicles, etc.)

Building, Hardware, & Garden Supply
4416 Building materials dealers
4457 Hardware stores
4473 Nurseries & garden supply stores
4432 Paint, glass, & wallpaper stores

Food & Beverages
0612 Bakeries selling at retail
3086 Catering services
3095 Drinking places (bars, taverns, pubs, saloons, etc.)

3079 Eating places, meals & snacks
3210 Grocery stores (general line)
3251 Liquor stores
3236 Specialized food stores (meat, produce, candy, health food, etc.)

Furniture & General Merchandise
3988 Computer & software stores
3970 Furniture stores
4317 Home furnishings stores (china, floor coverings, drapes)
4119 Household appliance stores
4333 Music & record stores
3996 TV, audio & electronic stores
3715 Variety stores
3731 Other general merchandise stores

Miscellaneous Retail Stores
4812 Boat dealers
5017 Book stores, excluding newsstands
4853 Camera & photo supply stores
4655 Drug stores
5058 Fabric & needlework stores
4655 Florists
5090 Fuel dealers (except gasoline)
4630 Gift, novelty, & souvenir shops
4838 Hobby, toy, & game shops
4671 Jewelry stores
4895 Luggage & leather goods stores
5074 Mobile home dealers
4879 Optical goods stores
4697 Sporting goods & bicycle shops
5033 Stationery stores
4614 Used merchandise & antique stores (except motor vehicle parts)
5884 Other retail stores

Trade, Wholesale—Selling Goods to Other Businesses, etc.

Durable Goods, Including Machinery Equipment, Wood, Metals, etc.
2634 Agent or broker for other firms—more than 50% of gross sales on commission
2618 Selling for your own account

Nondurable Goods, Including Food, Fiber, Chemicals, etc.
2675 Agent or broker for other firms—more than 50% of gross sales on commission
2659 Selling for your own account

Transportation, Communications, Public Utilities, & Related Services
6619 Air transportation
6312 Bus & limousine transportation
6676 Communication services
6395 Courier or package delivery
Highway passenger transportation (except chartered service)
6536 Public warehousing
6114 Taxicabs
6510 Trash collection without own dump
6635 Travel agents & tour operators
6692 Utilities (dumps, snowplowing, road cleaning, etc.)
6551 Water transportation
6650 Other transportation services

8888 Unable to classify

This form is an advance proof. Use the final IRS version for filing

Department of the Treasury—Internal Revenue Service

Form
1040EZ

Income Tax Return for
Single Filers With No Dependents **1992**

OMB No. 1545-0675

Name & address

Use the IRS label (see page 10). If you don't have one, please print.

LABEL HERE

Print your name (first, initial, last)

Home address (number and street). If you have a P.O. box, see page 10. | Apt. no.

City, town or post office, state, and ZIP code. If you have a foreign address, see page 10.

Please print your numbers like this:

9 8 7 6 5 4 3 2 1 0

Your social security number

Please see instructions on the back. Also, see the
Form 1040EZ booklet.

Presidential Election Campaign (See page 10.)
Do you want $1 to go to this fund?

Note: *Checking "Yes" will
not change your tax or
reduce your refund.* ▶

Yes No

Dollars   Cents

Report your income

**Attach
Copy B of
Form(s)
W-2 here.**
Attach tax
payment on
top of
Form(s) W-2.

Note: *You
must check
Yes or No.*

1   Total wages, salaries, and tips. This should be shown in box
    10 of your W-2 form(s). Attach your W-2 form(s).   1

2   Taxable interest income of $400 or less. If the total is more
    than $400, you cannot use Form 1040EZ.   2

3   Add lines 1 and 2. This your **adjusted gross income.**   3

4   Can your parents (or someone else) claim you on their return?
    ☐ **Yes.** Do worksheet on back; enter amount from line E here.
    ☐ **No.** Enter 5,900.00 This is the total of your standard
       deduction and personal exemption.   4

5   Subtract line 4 from line 3. If line 4 is larger than line 3,
    enter 0. This is your **taxable income.**   5

Figure your tax

6   Enter your Federal income tax withheld from box 9 of
    your W-2 form(s).   6

7   **Tax.** Look at line 5 above. Use the amount on **line 5** to
    find your tax in the tax table on pages 22-24 of the
    booklet. Then, enter the tax from the table on this line. 7

Refund or amount you owe

8   If line 6 is larger than line 7, subtract line 7 from line 6.
    This is your **refund.**   8

9   If line 7 is larger than line 6, subtract line 6 from line 7. This is the
    amount you owe. Attach your payment for full amount payable to the
    "Internal Revenue Service." Write your name, address, social security
    number, daytime phone number, and "1992 Form 1040EZ" on it.   9

Sign your return

Keep a copy
of this form
for your
records.

I have read this return. Under penalties of perjury, I declare
that to the best of my knowledge and belief, the return is true,
correct, and complete.

Your signature | Date

X | Your occupation

For IRS Use Only — Please
do not write in boxes below.

1992 Tax Table

Use if your taxable income is less than $100,000.
If $100,00 or more, use the Tax Rate Schedules.

Example: *Mr. and Mrs. Brown are filing a joint return. Their taxable income is $25,300. First, they find the $25,300–25,350 income line. Next, they find the column for married filing jointly and read down the column. The amount shown where the income line and filing status column meet is $3,799. This is the tax amount they must write on their return.*

Sample Table

At least	But less than	Single	Married filing jointly *	Married filing separately	Head of a household
			Your tax is—		
25,200	25,250	4,275	3,784	4,736	3,784
25,250	25,300	4,289	3,791	4,750	3,791
25,300	25,350	4,303	(3,799)	4,764	3,799
25,350	25,400	4,317	3,806	4,778	3,806

If taxable income is—		And you are—			
At least	But less than	Single	Married filing jointly *	Married filing separately	Head of a household
			Your tax is—		
0	5	0	0	0	0
5	15	2	2	2	2
15	25	3	3	3	3
25	50	6	6	6	6
50	75	9	9	9	9
75	100	13	13	13	13
100	125	17	17	17	17
125	150	21	21	21	21
150	175	24	24	24	24
175	200	28	28	28	28
200	225	32	32	32	32
225	250	36	36	36	36
250	275	39	39	39	39
275	300	43	43	43	43
300	325	47	47	47	47
325	350	51	51	51	51
350	375	54	54	54	54
375	400	58	58	58	58
400	425	62	62	62	62
425	450	66	66	66	66
450	475	69	69	69	69
475	500	73	73	73	73
500	525	77	77	77	77
525	550	81	81	81	81
550	575	84	84	84	84
575	600	88	88	88	88
600	625	92	92	92	92
625	650	96	96	96	96
650	675	99	99	99	99
675	700	103	103	103	103
700	725	107	107	107	107
725	750	111	111	111	111
750	775	114	114	114	114
775	800	118	118	118	118
800	825	122	122	122	122
825	850	126	126	126	126
850	875	129	129	129	129
875	900	133	133	133	133
900	925	137	137	137	137
925	950	141	141	141	141
950	975	144	144	144	144
975	1,000	148	148	148	148

1,000

At least	But less than	Single	Married filing jointly *	Married filing separately	Head of a household
1,000	1,025	152	152	152	152
1,025	1,050	156	156	156	156
1,050	1,075	159	159	159	159
1,075	1,100	163	163	163	163
1,100	1,125	167	167	167	167
1,125	1,150	171	171	171	171
1,150	1,175	174	174	174	174
1,175	1,200	178	178	178	178
1,200	1,225	182	182	182	182
1,225	1,250	186	186	186	186
1,250	1,275	189	189	189	189
1,275	1,300	193	193	193	193

At least	But less than	Single	Married filing jointly *	Married filing separately	Head of a household
			Your tax is—		
1,300	1,325	197	197	197	197
1,325	1,350	201	201	201	201
1,350	1,375	204	204	204	204
1,375	1,400	208	208	208	208
1,400	1,425	212	212	212	212
1,425	1,450	216	216	216	216
1,450	1,475	219	219	219	219
1,475	1,500	223	223	223	223
1,500	1,525	227	227	227	227
1,525	1,550	231	231	231	231
1,550	1,575	234	234	234	234
1,575	1,600	238	238	238	238
1,600	1,625	242	242	242	242
1,625	1,650	246	246	246	246
1,650	1,675	249	249	249	249
1,675	1,700	253	253	253	253
1,700	1,725	257	257	257	257
1,725	1,750	261	261	261	261
1,750	1,775	264	264	264	264
1,775	1,800	268	268	268	268
1,800	1,825	272	272	272	272
1,825	1,850	276	276	276	276
1,850	1,875	279	279	279	279
1,875	1,900	283	283	283	283
1,900	1,925	287	287	287	287
1,925	1,950	291	291	291	291
1,950	1,975	294	294	294	294
1,975	2,000	298	298	298	298

2,000

At least	But less than	Single	Married filing jointly *	Married filing separately	Head of a household
2,000	2,025	302	302	302	302
2,025	2,050	306	306	306	306
2,050	2,075	309	309	309	309
2,075	2,100	313	313	313	313
2,100	2,125	317	317	317	317
2,125	2,150	321	321	321	321
2,150	2,175	324	324	324	324
2,175	2,200	328	328	328	328
2,200	2,225	332	332	332	332
2,225	2,250	336	336	336	336
2,250	2,275	339	339	339	339
2,275	2,300	343	343	343	343
2,300	2,325	347	347	347	347
2,325	2,350	351	351	351	351
2,350	2,375	354	354	354	354
2,375	2,400	358	358	358	358
2,400	2,425	362	362	362	362
2,425	2,450	366	366	366	366
2,450	2,475	369	369	369	369
2,475	2,500	373	373	373	373
2,500	2,525	377	377	377	377
2,525	2,550	381	381	381	381
2,550	2,575	384	384	384	384
2,575	2,600	388	388	388	388
2,600	2,625	392	392	392	392
2,625	2,650	396	396	396	396
2,650	2,675	399	399	399	399
2,675	2,700	403	403	403	403

At least	But less than	Single	Married filing jointly *	Married filing separately	Head of a household
			Your tax is—		
2,700	2,725	407	407	407	407
2,725	2,750	411	411	411	411
2,750	2,775	414	414	414	414
2,775	2,800	418	418	418	418
2,800	2,825	422	422	422	422
2,825	2,850	426	426	426	426
2,850	2,875	429	429	429	429
2,875	2,900	433	433	433	433
2,900	2,925	437	437	437	437
2,925	2,950	441	441	441	441
2,950	2,975	444	444	444	444
2,975	3,000	448	448	448	448

3,000

At least	But less than	Single	Married filing jointly *	Married filing separately	Head of a household
3,000	3,050	454	454	454	454
3,050	3,100	461	461	461	461
3,100	3,150	469	469	469	469
3,150	3,200	476	476	476	476
3,200	3,250	484	484	484	484
3,250	3,300	491	491	491	491
3,300	3,350	499	499	499	499
3,350	3,400	506	506	506	506
3,400	3,450	514	514	514	514
3,450	3,500	521	521	521	521
3,500	3,550	529	529	529	529
3,550	3,600	536	536	536	536
3,600	3,650	544	544	544	544
3,650	3,700	551	551	551	551
3,700	3,750	559	559	559	559
3,750	3,800	566	566	566	566
3,800	3,850	574	574	574	574
3,850	3,900	581	581	581	581
3,900	3,950	589	589	589	589
3,950	4,000	596	596	596	596

4,000

At least	But less than	Single	Married filing jointly *	Married filing separately	Head of a household
4,000	4,050	604	604	604	604
4,050	4,100	611	611	611	611
4,100	4,150	619	619	619	619
4,150	4,200	626	626	626	626
4,200	4,250	634	634	634	634
4,250	4,300	641	641	641	641
4,300	4,350	649	649	649	649
4,350	4,400	656	656	656	656
4,400	4,450	664	664	664	664
4,450	4,500	671	671	671	671
4,500	4,550	679	679	679	679
4,550	4,600	686	686	686	686
4,600	4,650	694	694	694	694
4,650	4,700	701	701	701	701
4,700	4,750	709	709	709	709
4,750	4,800	716	716	716	716
4,800	4,850	724	724	724	724
4,850	4,900	731	731	731	731
4,900	4,950	739	739	739	739
4,950	5,000	746	746	746	746

Continued on next page

* This column must also be used by a qualifying widow(er).

If taxable income is—		And you are—				If taxable income is—		And you are—				If taxable income is—		And you are—			
At least	But less than	Single	Married filing jointly *	Married filing separately	Head of a household	At least	But less than	Single	Married filing jointly *	Married filing separately	Head of a household	At least	But less than	Single	Married filing jointly *	Married filing separately	Head of a household
		Your tax is—						Your tax is—						Your tax is—			

5,000 / **8,000** / **11,000**

At least	But less than	Single	MFJ	MFS	HoH	At least	But less than	Single	MFJ	MFS	HoH	At least	But less than	Single	MFJ	MFS	HoH
5,000	5,050	754	754	754	754	8,000	8,050	1,204	1,204	1,204	1,204	11,000	11,050	1,654	1,654	1,654	1,654
5,050	5,100	761	761	761	761	8,050	8,100	1,211	1,211	1,211	1,211	11,050	11,100	1,661	1,661	1,661	1,661
5,100	5,150	769	769	769	769	8,100	8,150	1,219	1,219	1,219	1,219	11,100	11,150	1,669	1,669	1,669	1,669
5,150	5,200	776	776	776	776	8,150	8,200	1,226	1,226	1,226	1,226	11,150	11,200	1,676	1,676	1,676	1,676
5,200	5,250	784	784	784	784	8,200	8,250	1,234	1,234	1,234	1,234	11,200	11,250	1,684	1,684	1,684	1,684
5,250	5,300	791	791	791	791	8,250	8,300	1,241	1,241	1,241	1,241	11,250	11,300	1,691	1,691	1,691	1,691
5,300	5,350	799	799	799	799	8,300	8,350	1,249	1,249	1,249	1,249	11,300	11,350	1,699	1,699	1,699	1,699
5,350	5,400	806	806	806	806	8,350	8,400	1,256	1,256	1,256	1,256	11,350	11,400	1,706	1,706	1,706	1,706
5,400	5,450	814	814	814	814	8,400	8,450	1,264	1,264	1,264	1,264	11,400	11,450	1,714	1,714	1,714	1,714
5,450	5,500	821	821	821	821	8,450	8,500	1,271	1,271	1,271	1,271	11,450	11,500	1,721	1,721	1,721	1,721
5,500	5,550	829	829	829	829	8,500	8,550	1,279	1,279	1,279	1,279	11,500	11,550	1,729	1,729	1,729	1,729
5,550	5,600	836	836	836	836	8,550	8,600	1,286	1,286	1,286	1,286	11,550	11,600	1,736	1,736	1,736	1,736
5,600	5,650	844	844	844	844	8,600	8,650	1,294	1,294	1,294	1,294	11,600	11,650	1,744	1,744	1,744	1,744
5,650	5,700	851	851	851	851	8,650	8,700	1,301	1,301	1,301	1,301	11,650	11,700	1,751	1,751	1,751	1,751
5,700	5,750	859	859	859	859	8,700	8,750	1,309	1,309	1,309	1,309	11,700	11,750	1,759	1,759	1,759	1,759
5,750	5,800	866	866	866	866	8,750	8,800	1,316	1,316	1,316	1,316	11,750	11,800	1,766	1,766	1,766	1,766
5,800	5,850	874	874	874	874	8,800	8,850	1,324	1,324	1,324	1,324	11,800	11,850	1,774	1,774	1,774	1,774
5,850	5,900	881	881	881	881	8,850	8,900	1,331	1,331	1,331	1,331	11,850	11,900	1,781	1,781	1,781	1,781
5,900	5,950	889	889	889	889	8,900	8,950	1,339	1,339	1,339	1,339	11,900	11,950	1,789	1,789	1,789	1,789
5,950	6,000	896	896	896	896	8,950	9,000	1,346	1,346	1,346	1,346	11,950	12,000	1,796	1,796	1,796	1,796

6,000 / **9,000** / **12,000**

At least	But less than	Single	MFJ	MFS	HoH	At least	But less than	Single	MFJ	MFS	HoH	At least	But less than	Single	MFJ	MFS	HoH
6,000	6,050	904	904	904	904	9,000	9,050	1,354	1,354	1,354	1,354	12,000	12,050	1,804	1,804	1,804	1,804
6,050	6,100	911	911	911	911	9,050	9,100	1,361	1,361	1,361	1,361	12,050	12,100	1,811	1,811	1,811	1,811
6,100	6,150	919	919	919	919	9,100	9,150	1,369	1,369	1,369	1,369	12,100	12,150	1,819	1,819	1,819	1,819
6,150	6,200	926	926	926	926	9,150	9,200	1,376	1,376	1,376	1,376	12,150	12,200	1,826	1,826	1,826	1,826
6,200	6,250	934	934	934	934	9,200	9,250	1,384	1,384	1,384	1,384	12,200	12,250	1,834	1,834	1,834	1,834
6,250	6,300	941	941	941	941	9,250	9,300	1,391	1,391	1,391	1,391	12,250	12,300	1,841	1,841	1,841	1,841
6,300	6,350	949	949	949	949	9,300	9,350	1,399	1,399	1,399	1,399	12,300	12,350	1,849	1,849	1,849	1,849
6,350	6,400	956	956	956	956	9,350	9,400	1,406	1,406	1,406	1,406	12,350	12,400	1,856	1,856	1,856	1,856
6,400	6,450	964	964	964	964	9,400	9,450	1,414	1,414	1,414	1,414	12,400	12,450	1,864	1,864	1,864	1,864
6,450	6,500	971	971	971	971	9,450	9,500	1,421	1,421	1,421	1,421	12,450	12,500	1,871	1,871	1,871	1,871
6,500	6,550	979	979	979	979	9,500	9,550	1,429	1,429	1,429	1,429	12,500	12,550	1,879	1,879	1,879	1,879
6,550	6,600	986	986	986	986	9,550	9,600	1,436	1,436	1,436	1,436	12,550	12,600	1,886	1,886	1,886	1,886
6,600	6,650	994	994	994	994	9,600	9,650	1,444	1,444	1,444	1,444	12,600	12,650	1,894	1,894	1,894	1,894
6,650	6,700	1,001	1,001	1,001	1,001	9,650	9,700	1,451	1,451	1,451	1,451	12,650	12,700	1,901	1,901	1,901	1,901
6,700	6,750	1,009	1,009	1,009	1,009	9,700	9,750	1,459	1,459	1,459	1,459	12,700	12,750	1,909	1,909	1,909	1,909
6,750	6,800	1,016	1,016	1,016	1,016	9,750	9,800	1,466	1,466	1,466	1,466	12,750	12,800	1,916	1,916	1,916	1,916
6,800	6,850	1,024	1,024	1,024	1,024	9,800	9,850	1,474	1,474	1,474	1,474	12,800	12,850	1,924	1,924	1,924	1,924
6,850	6,900	1,031	1,031	1,031	1,031	9,850	9,900	1,481	1,481	1,481	1,481	12,850	12,900	1,931	1,931	1,931	1,931
6,900	6,950	1,039	1,039	1,039	1,039	9,900	9,950	1,489	1,489	1,489	1,489	12,900	12,950	1,939	1,939	1,939	1,939
6,950	7,000	1,046	1,046	1,046	1,046	9,950	10,000	1,496	1,496	1,496	1,496	12,950	13,000	1,946	1,946	1,946	1,946

7,000 / **10,000** / **13,000**

At least	But less than	Single	MFJ	MFS	HoH	At least	But less than	Single	MFJ	MFS	HoH	At least	But less than	Single	MFJ	MFS	HoH
7,000	7,050	1,054	1,054	1,054	1,054	10,000	10,050	1,504	1,504	1,504	1,504	13,000	13,050	1,954	1,954	1,954	1,954
7,050	7,100	1,061	1,061	1,061	1,061	10,050	10,100	1,511	1,511	1,511	1,511	13,050	13,100	1,961	1,961	1,961	1,961
7,100	7,150	1,069	1,069	1,069	1,069	10,100	10,150	1,519	1,519	1,519	1,519	13,100	13,150	1,969	1,969	1,969	1,969
7,150	7,200	1,076	1,076	1,076	1,076	10,150	10,200	1,526	1,526	1,526	1,526	13,150	13,200	1,976	1,976	1,976	1,976
7,200	7,250	1,084	1,084	1,084	1,084	10,200	10,250	1,534	1,534	1,534	1,534	13,200	13,250	1,984	1,984	1,984	1,984
7,250	7,300	1,091	1,091	1,091	1,091	10,250	10,300	1,541	1,541	1,541	1,541	13,250	13,300	1,991	1,991	1,991	1,991
7,300	7,350	1,099	1,099	1,099	1,099	10,300	10,350	1,549	1,549	1,549	1,549	13,300	13,350	1,999	1,999	1,999	1,999
7,350	7,400	1,106	1,106	1,106	1,106	10,350	10,400	1,556	1,556	1,556	1,556	13,350	13,400	2,006	2,006	2,006	2,006
7,400	7,450	1,114	1,114	1,114	1,114	10,400	10,450	1,564	1,564	1,564	1,564	13,400	13,450	2,014	2,014	2,014	2,014
7,450	7,500	1,121	1,121	1,121	1,121	10,450	10,500	1,571	1,571	1,571	1,571	13,450	13,500	2,021	2,021	2,021	2,021
7,500	7,550	1,129	1,129	1,129	1,129	10,500	10,550	1,579	1,579	1,579	1,579	13,500	13,550	2,029	2,029	2,029	2,029
7,550	7,600	1,136	1,136	1,136	1,136	10,550	10,600	1,586	1,586	1,586	1,586	13,550	13,600	2,036	2,036	2,036	2,036
7,600	7,650	1,144	1,144	1,144	1,144	10,600	10,650	1,594	1,594	1,594	1,594	13,600	13,650	2,044	2,044	2,044	2,044
7,650	7,700	1,151	1,151	1,151	1,151	10,650	10,700	1,601	1,601	1,601	1,601	13,650	13,700	2,051	2,051	2,051	2,051
7,700	7,750	1,159	1,159	1,159	1,159	10,700	10,750	1,609	1,609	1,609	1,609	13,700	13,750	2,059	2,059	2,059	2,059
7,750	7,800	1,166	1,166	1,166	1,166	10,750	10,800	1,616	1,616	1,616	1,616	13,750	13,800	2,066	2,066	2,066	2,066
7,800	7,850	1,174	1,174	1,174	1,174	10,800	10,850	1,624	1,624	1,624	1,624	13,800	13,850	2,074	2,074	2,074	2,074
7,850	7,900	1,181	1,181	1,181	1,181	10,850	10,900	1,631	1,631	1,631	1,631	13,850	13,900	2,081	2,081	2,081	2,081
7,900	7,950	1,189	1,189	1,189	1,189	10,900	10,950	1,639	1,639	1,639	1,639	13,900	13,950	2,089	2,089	2,089	2,089
7,950	8,000	1,196	1,196	1,196	1,196	10,950	11,000	1,646	1,646	1,646	1,646	13,950	14,000	2,096	2,096	2,096	2,096

* This column must also be used by a qualifying widow(er).

Continued on next page

If taxable income is—		And you are—			
At least	But less than	Single	Married filing jointly *	Married filing separately	Head of a household
		Your tax is—			
14,000					
14,000	14,050	2,104	2,104	2,104	2,104
14,050	14,100	2,111	2,111	2,111	2,111
14,100	14,150	2,119	2,119	2,119	2,119
14,150	14,200	2,126	2,126	2,126	2,126
14,200	14,250	2,134	2,134	2,134	2,134
14,250	14,300	2,141	2,141	2,141	2,141
14,300	14,350	2,149	2,149	2,149	2,149
14,350	14,400	2,156	2,156	2,156	2,156
14,400	14,450	2,164	2,164	2,164	2,164
14,450	14,500	2,171	2,171	2,171	2,171
14,500	14,550	2,179	2,179	2,179	2,179
14,550	14,600	2,186	2,186	2,186	2,186
14,600	14,650	2,194	2,194	2,194	2,194
14,650	14,700	2,201	2,201	2,201	2,201
14,700	14,750	2,209	2,209	2,209	2,209
14,750	14,800	2,216	2,216	2,216	2,216
14,800	14,850	2,224	2,224	2,224	2,224
14,850	14,900	2,231	2,231	2,231	2,231
14,900	14,950	2,239	2,239	2,239	2,239
14,950	15,000	2,246	2,246	2,246	2,246
15,000					
15,000	15,050	2,254	2,254	2,254	2,254
15,050	15,100	2,261	2,261	2,261	2,261
15,100	15,150	2,269	2,269	2,269	2,269
15,150	15,200	2,276	2,276	2,276	2,276
15,200	15,250	2,284	2,284	2,284	2,284
15,250	15,300	2,291	2,291	2,291	2,291
15,300	15,350	2,299	2,299	2,299	2,299
15,350	15,400	2,306	2,306	2,306	2,306
15,400	15,450	2,314	2,314	2,314	2,314
15,450	15,500	2,321	2,321	2,321	2,321
15,500	15,550	2,329	2,329	2,329	2,329
15,550	15,600	2,336	2,336	2,336	2,336
15,600	15,650	2,344	2,344	2,344	2,344
15,650	15,700	2,351	2,351	2,351	2,351
15,700	15,750	2,359	2,359	2,359	2,359
15,750	15,800	2,366	2,366	2,366	2,366
15,800	15,850	2,374	2,374	2,374	2,374
15,850	15,900	2,381	2,381	2,381	2,381
15,900	15,950	2,389	2,389	2,389	2,389
15,950	16,000	2,396	2,396	2,396	2,396
16,000					
16,000	16,050	2,404	2,404	2,404	2,404
16,050	16,100	2,411	2,411	2,411	2,411
16,100	16,150	2,419	2,419	2,419	2,419
16,150	16,200	2,426	2,426	2,426	2,426
16,200	16,250	2,434	2,434	2,434	2,434
16,250	16,300	2,441	2,441	2,441	2,441
16,300	16,350	2,449	2,449	2,449	2,449
16,350	16,400	2,456	2,456	2,456	2,456
16,400	16,450	2,464	2,464	2,464	2,464
16,450	16,500	2,471	2,471	2,471	2,471
16,500	16,550	2,479	2,479	2,479	2,479
16,550	16,600	2,486	2,486	2,486	2,486
16,600	16,650	2,494	2,494	2,494	2,494
16,650	16,700	2,501	2,501	2,501	2,501
16,700	16,750	2,509	2,509	2,509	2,509
16,750	16,800	2,516	2,516	2,516	2,516
16,800	16,850	2,524	2,524	2,524	2,524
16,850	16,900	2,531	2,531	2,531	2,531
16,900	16,950	2,539	2,539	2,539	2,539
16,950	17,000	2,546	2,546	2,546	2,546

If taxable income is—		And you are—			
At least	But less than	Single	Married filing jointly *	Married filing separately	Head of a household
		Your tax is—			
17,000					
17,000	17,050	2,554	2,554	2,554	2,554
17,050	17,100	2,561	2,561	2,561	2,561
17,100	17,150	2,569	2,569	2,569	2,569
17,150	17,200	2,576	2,576	2,576	2,576
17,200	17,250	2,584	2,584	2,584	2,584
17,250	17,300	2,591	2,591	2,591	2,591
17,300	17,350	2,599	2,599	2,599	2,599
17,350	17,400	2,606	2,606	2,606	2,606
17,400	17,450	2,614	2,614	2,614	2,614
17,450	17,500	2,621	2,621	2,621	2,621
17,500	17,550	2,629	2,629	2,629	2,629
17,550	17,600	2,636	2,636	2,636	2,636
17,600	17,650	2,644	2,644	2,644	2,644
17,650	17,700	2,651	2,651	2,651	2,651
17,700	17,750	2,659	2,659	2,659	2,659
17,750	17,800	2,666	2,666	2,666	2,666
17,800	17,850	2,674	2,674	2,674	2,674
17,850	17,900	2,681	2,681	2,681	2,681
17,900	17,950	2,689	2,689	2,692	2,689
17,950	18,000	2,696	2,696	2,706	2,696
18,000					
18,000	18,050	2,704	2,704	2,720	2,704
18,050	18,100	2,711	2,711	2,734	2,711
18,100	18,150	2,719	2,719	2,748	2,719
18,150	18,200	2,726	2,726	2,762	2,726
18,200	18,250	2,734	2,734	2,776	2,734
18,250	18,300	2,741	2,741	2,790	2,741
18,300	18,350	2,749	2,749	2,804	2,749
18,350	18,400	2,756	2,756	2,818	2,756
18,400	18,450	2,764	2,764	2,832	2,764
18,450	18,500	2,771	2,771	2,846	2,771
18,500	18,550	2,779	2,779	2,860	2,779
18,550	18,600	2,786	2,786	2,874	2,786
18,600	18,650	2,794	2,794	2,888	2,794
18,650	18,700	2,801	2,801	2,902	2,801
18,700	18,750	2,809	2,809	2,916	2,809
18,750	18,800	2,816	2,816	2,930	2,816
18,800	18,850	2,824	2,824	2,944	2,824
18,850	18,900	2,831	2,831	2,958	2,831
18,900	18,950	2,839	2,839	2,972	2,839
18,950	19,000	2,846	2,846	2,986	2,846
19,000					
19,000	19,050	2,854	2,854	3,000	2,854
19,050	19,100	2,861	2,861	3,014	2,861
19,100	19,150	2,869	2,869	3,028	2,869
19,150	19,200	2,876	2,876	3,042	2,876
19,200	19,250	2,884	2,884	3,056	2,884
19,250	19,300	2,891	2,891	3,070	2,891
19,300	19,350	2,899	2,899	3,084	2,899
19,350	19,400	2,906	2,906	3,098	2,906
19,400	19,450	2,914	2,914	3,112	2,914
19,450	19,500	2,921	2,921	3,126	2,921
19,500	19,550	2,929	2,929	3,140	2,929
19,550	19,600	2,936	2,936	3,154	2,936
19,600	19,650	2,944	2,944	3,168	2,944
19,650	19,700	2,951	2,951	3,182	2,951
19,700	19,750	2,959	2,959	3,196	2,959
19,750	19,800	2,966	2,966	3,210	2,966
19,800	19,850	2,974	2,974	3,224	2,974
19,850	19,900	2,981	2,981	3,238	2,981
19,900	19,950	2,989	2,989	3,252	2,989
19,950	20,000	2,996	2,996	3,266	2,996

If taxable income is—		And you are—			
At least	But less than	Single	Married filing jointly *	Married filing separately	Head of a household
		Your tax is—			
20,000					
20,000	20,050	3,004	3,004	3,280	3,004
20,050	20,100	3,011	3,011	3,294	3,011
20,100	20,150	3,019	3,019	3,308	3,019
20,150	20,200	3,026	3,026	3,322	3,026
20,200	20,250	3,034	3,034	3,336	3,034
20,250	20,300	3,041	3,041	3,350	3,041
20,300	20,350	3,049	3,049	3,364	3,049
20,350	20,400	3,056	3,056	3,378	3,056
20,400	20,450	3,064	3,064	3,392	3,064
20,450	20,500	3,071	3,071	3,406	3,071
20,500	20,550	3,079	3,079	3,420	3,079
20,550	20,600	3,086	3,086	3,434	3,086
20,600	20,650	3,094	3,094	3,448	3,094
20,650	20,700	3,101	3,101	3,462	3,101
20,700	20,750	3,109	3,109	3,476	3,109
20,750	20,800	3,116	3,116	3,490	3,116
20,800	20,850	3,124	3,124	3,504	3,124
20,850	20,900	3,131	3,131	3,518	3,131
20,900	20,950	3,139	3,139	3,532	3,139
20,950	21,000	3,146	3,146	3,546	3,146
21,000					
21,000	21,050	3,154	3,154	3,560	3,154
21,050	21,100	3,161	3,161	3,574	3,161
21,100	21,150	3,169	3,169	3,588	3,169
21,150	21,200	3,176	3,176	3,602	3,176
21,200	21,250	3,184	3,184	3,616	3,184
21,250	21,300	3,191	3,191	3,630	3,191
21,300	21,350	3,199	3,199	3,644	3,199
21,350	21,400	3,206	3,206	3,658	3,206
21,400	21,450	3,214	3,214	3,672	3,214
21,450	21,500	3,225	3,221	3,686	3,221
21,500	21,550	3,239	3,229	3,700	3,229
21,550	21,600	3,253	3,236	3,714	3,236
21,600	21,650	3,267	3,244	3,728	3,244
21,650	21,700	3,281	3,251	3,742	3,251
21,700	21,750	3,295	3,259	3,756	3,259
21,750	21,800	3,309	3,266	3,770	3,266
21,800	21,850	3,323	3,274	3,784	3,274
21,850	21,900	3,337	3,281	3,798	3,281
21,900	21,950	3,351	3,289	3,812	3,289
21,950	22,000	3,365	3,296	3,826	3,296
22,000					
22,000	22,050	3,379	3,304	3,840	3,304
22,050	22,100	3,393	3,311	3,854	3,311
22,100	22,150	3,407	3,319	3,868	3,319
22,150	22,200	3,421	3,326	3,882	3,326
22,200	22,250	3,435	3,334	3,896	3,334
22,250	22,300	3,449	3,341	3,910	3,341
22,300	22,350	3,463	3,349	3,924	3,349
22,350	22,400	3,477	3,356	3,938	3,356
22,400	22,450	3,491	3,364	3,952	3,364
22,450	22,500	3,505	3,371	3,966	3,371
22,500	22,550	3,519	3,379	3,980	3,379
22,550	22,600	3,533	3,386	3,994	3,386
22,600	22,650	3,547	3,394	4,008	3,394
22,650	22,700	3,561	3,401	4,022	3,401
22,700	22,750	3,575	3,409	4,036	3,409
22,750	22,800	3,589	3,416	4,050	3,416
22,800	22,850	3,603	3,424	4,064	3,424
22,850	22,900	3,617	3,431	4,078	3,431
22,900	22,950	3,631	3,439	4,092	3,439
22,950	23,000	3,645	3,446	4,106	3,446

* This column must also be used by a qualifying widow(er).

Continued on next page

If taxable income is—		And you are—			
At least	But less than	Single	Married filing jointly *	Married filing separately *	Head of a household
		Your tax is—			

23,000

At least	But less than	Single	Married filing jointly	Married filing separately	Head of a household
23,000	23,050	3,659	3,454	4,120	3,454
23,050	23,100	3,673	3,461	4,134	3,461
23,100	23,150	3,687	3,469	4,148	3,469
23,150	23,200	3,701	3,476	4,162	3,476
23,200	23,250	3,715	3,484	4,176	3,484
23,250	23,300	3,729	3,491	4,190	3,491
23,300	23,350	3,743	3,499	4,204	3,499
23,350	23,400	3,757	3,506	4,218	3,506
23,400	23,450	3,771	3,514	4,232	3,514
23,450	23,500	3,785	3,521	4,246	3,521
23,500	23,550	3,799	3,529	4,260	3,529
23,550	23,600	3,813	3,536	4,274	3,536
23,600	23,650	3,827	3,544	4,288	3,544
23,650	23,700	3,841	3,551	4,302	3,551
23,700	23,750	3,855	3,559	4,316	3,559
23,750	23,800	3,869	3,566	4,330	3,566
23,800	23,850	3,883	3,574	4,344	3,574
23,850	23,900	3,897	3,581	4,358	3,581
23,900	23,950	3,911	3,589	4,372	3,589
23,950	24,000	3,925	3,596	4,386	3,596

24,000

At least	But less than	Single	Married filing jointly	Married filing separately	Head of a household
24,000	24,050	3,939	3,604	4,400	3,604
24,050	24,100	3,953	3,611	4,414	3,611
24,100	24,150	3,967	3,619	4,428	3,619
24,150	24,200	3,981	3,626	4,442	3,626
24,200	24,250	3,995	3,634	4,456	3,634
24,250	24,300	4,009	3,641	4,470	3,641
24,300	24,350	4,023	3,649	4,484	3,649
24,350	24,400	4,037	3,656	4,498	3,656
24,400	24,450	4,051	3,664	4,512	3,664
24,450	24,500	4,065	3,671	4,526	3,671
24,500	24,550	4,079	3,679	4,540	3,679
24,550	24,600	4,093	3,686	4,554	3,686
24,600	24,650	4,107	3,694	4,568	3,694
24,650	24,700	4,121	3,701	4,582	3,701
24,700	24,750	4,135	3,709	4,596	3,709
24,750	24,800	4,149	3,716	4,610	3,716
24,800	24,850	4,163	3,724	4,624	3,724
24,850	24,900	4,177	3,731	4,638	3,731
24,900	24,950	4,191	3,739	4,652	3,739
24,950	25,000	4,205	3,746	4,666	3,746

25,000

At least	But less than	Single	Married filing jointly	Married filing separately	Head of a household
25,000	25,050	4,219	3,754	4,680	3,754
25,050	25,100	4,233	3,761	4,694	3,761
25,100	25,150	4,247	3,769	4,708	3,769
25,150	25,200	4,261	3,776	4,722	3,776
25,200	25,250	4,275	3,784	4,736	3,784
25,250	25,300	4,289	3,791	4,750	3,791
25,300	25,350	4,303	3,799	4,764	3,799
25,350	25,400	4,317	3,806	4,778	3,806
25,400	25,450	4,331	3,814	4,792	3,814
25,450	25,500	4,345	3,821	4,806	3,821
25,500	25,550	4,359	3,829	4,820	3,829
25,550	25,600	4,373	3,836	4,834	3,836
25,600	25,650	4,387	3,844	4,848	3,844
25,650	25,700	4,401	3,851	4,862	3,851
25,700	25,750	4,415	3,859	4,876	3,859
25,750	25,800	4,429	3,866	4,890	3,866
25,800	25,850	4,443	3,874	4,904	3,874
25,850	25,900	4,457	3,881	4,918	3,881
25,900	25,950	4,471	3,889	4,932	3,889
25,950	26,000	4,485	3,896	4,946	3,896

26,000

At least	But less than	Single	Married filing jointly	Married filing separately	Head of a household
26,000	26,050	4,499	3,904	4,960	3,904
26,050	26,100	4,513	3,911	4,974	3,911
26,100	26,150	4,527	3,919	4,988	3,919
26,150	26,200	4,541	3,926	5,002	3,926
26,200	26,250	4,555	3,934	5,016	3,934
26,250	26,300	4,569	3,941	5,030	3,941
26,300	26,350	4,583	3,949	5,044	3,949
26,350	26,400	4,597	3,956	5,058	3,956
26,400	26,450	4,611	3,964	5,072	3,964
26,450	26,500	4,625	3,971	5,086	3,971
26,500	26,550	4,639	3,979	5,100	3,979
26,550	26,600	4,653	3,986	5,114	3,986
26,600	26,650	4,667	3,994	5,128	3,994
26,650	26,700	4,681	4,001	5,142	4,001
26,700	26,750	4,695	4,009	5,156	4,009
26,750	26,800	4,709	4,016	5,170	4,016
26,800	26,850	4,723	4,024	5,184	4,024
26,850	26,900	4,737	4,031	5,198	4,031
26,900	26,950	4,751	4,039	5,212	4,039
26,950	27,000	4,765	4,046	5,226	4,046

27,000

At least	But less than	Single	Married filing jointly	Married filing separately	Head of a household
27,000	27,050	4,779	4,054	5,240	4,054
27,050	27,100	4,793	4,061	5,254	4,061
27,100	27,150	4,807	4,069	5,268	4,069
27,150	27,200	4,821	4,076	5,282	4,076
27,200	27,250	4,835	4,084	5,296	4,084
27,250	27,300	4,849	4,091	5,310	4,091
27,300	27,350	4,863	4,099	5,324	4,099
27,350	27,400	4,877	4,106	5,338	4,106
27,400	27,450	4,891	4,114	5,352	4,114
27,450	27,500	4,905	4,121	5,366	4,121
27,500	27,550	4,919	4,129	5,380	4,129
27,550	27,600	4,933	4,136	5,394	4,136
27,600	27,650	4,947	4,144	5,408	4,144
27,650	27,700	4,961	4,151	5,422	4,151
27,700	27,750	4,975	4,159	5,436	4,159
27,750	27,800	4,989	4,166	5,450	4,166
27,800	27,850	5,003	4,174	5,464	4,174
27,850	27,900	5,017	4,181	5,478	4,181
27,900	27,950	5,031	4,189	5,492	4,189
27,950	28,000	5,045	4,196	5,506	4,196

28,000

At least	But less than	Single	Married filing jointly	Married filing separately	Head of a household
28,000	28,050	5,059	4,204	5,520	4,204
28,050	28,100	5,073	4,211	5,534	4,211
28,100	28,150	5,087	4,219	5,548	4,219
28,150	28,200	5,101	4,226	5,562	4,226
28,200	28,250	5,115	4,234	5,576	4,234
28,250	28,300	5,129	4,241	5,590	4,241
28,300	28,350	5,143	4,249	5,604	4,249
28,350	28,400	5,157	4,256	5,618	4,256
28,400	28,450	5,171	4,264	5,632	4,264
28,450	28,500	5,185	4,271	5,646	4,271
28,500	28,550	5,199	4,279	5,660	4,279
28,550	28,600	5,213	4,286	5,674	4,286
28,600	28,650	5,227	4,294	5,688	4,294
28,650	28,700	5,241	4,301	5,702	4,301
28,700	28,750	5,255	4,309	5,716	4,309
28,750	28,800	5,269	4,316	5,730	4,320
28,800	28,850	5,283	4,324	5,744	4,334
28,850	28,900	5,297	4,331	5,758	4,348
28,900	28,950	5,311	4,339	5,772	4,362
28,950	29,000	5,325	4,346	5,786	4,376

29,000

At least	But less than	Single	Married filing jointly	Married filing separately	Head of a household
29,000	29,050	5,339	4,354	5,800	4,390
29,050	29,100	5,353	4,361	5,814	4,404
29,100	29,150	5,367	4,369	5,828	4,418
29,150	29,200	5,381	4,376	5,842	4,432
29,200	29,250	5,395	4,384	5,856	4,446
29,250	29,300	5,409	4,391	5,870	4,460
29,300	29,350	5,423	4,399	5,884	4,474
29,350	29,400	5,437	4,406	5,898	4,488
29,400	29,450	5,451	4,414	5,912	4,502
29,450	29,500	5,465	4,421	5,926	4,516
29,500	29,550	5,479	4,429	5,940	4,530
29,550	29,600	5,493	4,436	5,954	4,544
29,600	29,650	5,507	4,444	5,968	4,558
29,650	29,700	5,521	4,451	5,982	4,572
29,700	29,750	5,535	4,459	5,996	4,586
29,750	29,800	5,549	4,466	6,010	4,600
29,800	29,850	5,563	4,474	6,024	4,614
29,850	29,900	5,577	4,481	6,038	4,628
29,900	29,950	5,591	4,489	6,052	4,642
29,950	30,000	5,605	4,496	6,066	4,656

30,000

At least	But less than	Single	Married filing jointly	Married filing separately	Head of a household
30,000	30,050	5,619	4,504	6,080	4,670
30,050	30,100	5,633	4,511	6,094	4,684
30,100	30,150	5,647	4,519	6,108	4,698
30,150	30,200	5,661	4,526	6,122	4,712
30,200	30,250	5,675	4,534	6,136	4,726
30,250	30,300	5,689	4,541	6,150	4,740
30,300	30,350	5,703	4,549	6,164	4,754
30,350	30,400	5,717	4,556	6,178	4,768
30,400	30,450	5,731	4,564	6,192	4,782
30,450	30,500	5,745	4,571	6,206	4,796
30,500	30,550	5,759	4,579	6,220	4,810
30,550	30,600	5,773	4,586	6,234	4,824
30,600	30,650	5,787	4,594	6,248	4,838
30,650	30,700	5,801	4,601	6,262	4,852
30,700	30,750	5,815	4,609	6,276	4,866
30,750	30,800	5,829	4,616	6,290	4,880
30,800	30,850	5,843	4,624	6,304	4,894
30,850	30,900	5,857	4,631	6,318	4,908
30,900	30,950	5,871	4,639	6,332	4,922
30,950	31,000	5,885	4,646	6,346	4,936

31,000

At least	But less than	Single	Married filing jointly	Married filing separately	Head of a household
31,000	31,050	5,899	4,654	6,360	4,950
31,050	31,100	5,913	4,661	6,374	4,964
31,100	31,150	5,927	4,669	6,388	4,978
31,150	31,200	5,941	4,676	6,402	4,992
31,200	31,250	5,955	4,684	6,416	5,006
31,250	31,300	5,969	4,691	6,430	5,020
31,300	31,350	5,983	4,699	6,444	5,034
31,350	31,400	5,997	4,706	6,458	5,048
31,400	31,450	6,011	4,714	6,472	5,062
31,450	31,500	6,025	4,721	6,486	5,076
31,500	31,550	6,039	4,729	6,500	5,090
31,550	31,600	6,053	4,736	6,514	5,104
31,600	31,650	6,067	4,744	6,528	5,118
31,650	31,700	6,081	4,751	6,542	5,132
31,700	31,750	6,095	4,759	6,556	5,146
31,750	31,800	6,109	4,766	6,570	5,160
31,800	31,850	6,123	4,774	6,584	5,174
31,850	31,900	6,137	4,781	6,598	5,188
31,900	31,950	6,151	4,789	6,612	5,202
31,950	32,000	6,165	4,796	6,626	5,216

* This column must also be used by a qualifying widow(er).

Continued on next page

If taxable income is—		And you are—			
At least	But less than	Single	Married filing jointly *	Married filing separately	Head of a household
		Your tax is—			

32,000

At least	But less than	Single	Married filing jointly	Married filing separately	Head of a household
32,000	32,050	6,179	4,804	6,640	5,230
32,050	32,100	6,193	4,811	6,654	5,244
32,100	32,150	6,207	4,819	6,668	5,258
32,150	32,200	6,221	4,826	6,682	5,272
32,200	32,250	6,235	4,834	6,696	5,286
32,250	32,300	6,249	4,841	6,710	5,300
32,300	32,350	6,263	4,849	6,724	5,314
32,350	32,400	6,277	4,856	6,738	5,328
32,400	32,450	6,291	4,864	6,752	5,342
32,450	32,500	6,305	4,871	6,766	5,356
32,500	32,550	6,319	4,879	6,780	5,370
32,550	32,600	6,333	4,886	6,794	5,384
32,600	32,650	6,347	4,894	6,808	5,398
32,650	32,700	6,361	4,901	6,822	5,412
32,700	32,750	6,375	4,909	6,836	5,426
32,750	32,800	6,389	4,916	6,850	5,440
32,800	32,850	6,403	4,924	6,864	5,454
32,850	32,900	6,417	4,931	6,878	5,468
32,900	32,950	6,431	4,939	6,892	5,482
32,950	33,000	6,445	4,946	6,906	5,496

33,000

At least	But less than	Single	Married filing jointly	Married filing separately	Head of a household
33,000	33,050	6,459	4,954	6,920	5,510
33,050	33,100	6,473	4,961	6,934	5,524
33,100	33,150	6,487	4,969	6,948	5,538
33,150	33,200	6,501	4,976	6,962	5,552
33,200	33,250	6,515	4,984	6,976	5,566
33,250	33,300	6,529	4,991	6,990	5,580
33,300	33,350	6,543	4,999	7,004	5,594
33,350	33,400	6,557	5,006	7,018	5,608
33,400	33,450	6,571	5,014	7,032	5,622
33,450	33,500	6,585	5,021	7,046	5,636
33,500	33,550	6,599	5,029	7,060	5,650
33,550	33,600	6,613	5,036	7,074	5,664
33,600	33,650	6,627	5,044	7,088	5,678
33,650	33,700	6,641	5,051	7,102	5,692
33,700	33,750	6,655	5,059	7,116	5,706
33,750	33,800	6,669	5,066	7,130	5,720
33,800	33,850	6,683	5,074	7,144	5,734
33,850	33,900	6,697	5,081	7,158	5,748
33,900	33,950	6,711	5,089	7,172	5,762
33,950	34,000	6,725	5,096	7,186	5,776

34,000

At least	But less than	Single	Married filing jointly	Married filing separately	Head of a household
34,000	34,050	6,739	5,104	7,200	5,790
34,050	34,100	6,753	5,111	7,214	5,804
34,100	34,150	6,767	5,119	7,228	5,818
34,150	34,200	6,781	5,126	7,242	5,832
34,200	34,250	6,795	5,134	7,256	5,846
34,250	34,300	6,809	5,141	7,270	5,860
34,300	34,350	6,823	5,149	7,284	5,874
34,350	34,400	6,837	5,156	7,298	5,888
34,400	34,450	6,851	5,164	7,312	5,902
34,450	34,500	6,865	5,171	7,326	5,916
34,500	34,550	6,879	5,179	7,340	5,930
34,550	34,600	6,893	5,186	7,354	5,944
34,600	34,650	6,907	5,194	7,368	5,958
34,650	34,700	6,921	5,201	7,382	5,972
34,700	34,750	6,935	5,209	7,396	5,986
34,750	34,800	6,949	5,216	7,410	6,000
34,800	34,850	6,963	5,224	7,424	6,014
34,850	34,900	6,977	5,231	7,438	6,028
34,900	34,950	6,991	5,239	7,452	6,042
34,950	35,000	7,005	5,246	7,466	6,056

35,000

At least	But less than	Single	Married filing jointly	Married filing separately	Head of a household
35,000	35,050	7,019	5,254	7,480	6,070
35,050	35,100	7,033	5,261	7,494	6,084
35,100	35,150	7,047	5,269	7,508	6,098
35,150	35,200	7,061	5,276	7,522	6,112
35,200	35,250	7,075	5,284	7,536	6,126
35,250	35,300	7,089	5,291	7,550	6,140
35,300	35,350	7,103	5,299	7,564	6,154
35,350	35,400	7,117	5,306	7,578	6,168
35,400	35,450	7,131	5,314	7,592	6,182
35,450	35,500	7,145	5,321	7,606	6,196
35,500	35,550	7,159	5,329	7,620	6,210
35,550	35,600	7,173	5,336	7,634	6,224
35,600	35,650	7,187	5,344	7,648	6,238
35,650	35,700	7,201	5,351	7,662	6,252
35,700	35,750	7,215	5,359	7,676	6,266
35,750	35,800	7,229	5,366	7,690	6,280
35,800	35,850	7,243	5,377	7,704	6,294
35,850	35,900	7,257	5,391	7,718	6,308
35,900	35,950	7,271	5,405	7,732	6,322
35,950	36,000	7,285	5,419	7,746	6,336

36,000

At least	But less than	Single	Married filing jointly	Married filing separately	Head of a household
36,000	36,050	7,299	5,433	7,760	6,350
36,050	36,100	7,313	5,447	7,774	6,364
36,100	36,150	7,327	5,461	7,788	6,378
36,150	36,200	7,341	5,475	7,802	6,392
36,200	36,250	7,355	5,489	7,816	6,406
36,250	36,300	7,369	5,503	7,830	6,420
36,300	36,350	7,383	5,517	7,844	6,434
36,350	36,400	7,397	5,531	7,858	6,448
36,400	36,450	7,411	5,545	7,872	6,462
36,450	36,500	7,425	5,559	7,886	6,476
36,500	36,550	7,439	5,573	7,900	6,490
36,550	36,600	7,453	5,587	7,914	6,504
36,600	36,650	7,467	5,601	7,928	6,518
36,650	36,700	7,481	5,615	7,942	6,532
36,700	36,750	7,495	5,629	7,956	6,546
36,750	36,800	7,509	5,643	7,970	6,560
36,800	36,850	7,523	5,657	7,984	6,574
36,850	36,900	7,537	5,671	7,998	6,588
36,900	36,950	7,551	5,685	8,012	6,602
36,950	37,000	7,565	5,699	8,026	6,616

37,000

At least	But less than	Single	Married filing jointly	Married filing separately	Head of a household
37,000	37,050	7,579	5,713	8,040	6,630
37,050	37,100	7,593	5,727	8,054	6,644
37,100	37,150	7,607	5,741	8,068	6,658
37,150	37,200	7,621	5,755	8,082	6,672
37,200	37,250	7,635	5,769	8,096	6,686
37,250	37,300	7,649	5,783	8,110	6,700
37,300	37,350	7,663	5,797	8,124	6,714
37,350	37,400	7,677	5,811	8,138	6,728
37,400	37,450	7,691	5,825	8,152	6,742
37,450	37,500	7,705	5,839	8,166	6,756
37,500	37,550	7,719	5,853	8,180	6,770
37,550	37,600	7,733	5,867	8,194	6,784
37,600	37,650	7,747	5,881	8,208	6,798
37,650	37,700	7,761	5,895	8,222	6,812
37,700	37,750	7,775	5,909	8,236	6,826
37,750	37,800	7,789	5,923	8,250	6,840
37,800	37,850	7,803	5,937	8,264	6,854
37,850	37,900	7,817	5,951	8,278	6,868
37,900	37,950	7,831	5,965	8,292	6,882
37,950	38,000	7,845	5,979	8,306	6,896

38,000

At least	But less than	Single	Married filing jointly	Married filing separately	Head of a household
38,000	38,050	7,859	5,993	8,320	6,910
38,050	38,100	7,873	6,007	8,334	6,924
38,100	38,150	7,887	6,021	8,348	6,938
38,150	38,200	7,901	6,035	8,362	6,952
38,200	38,250	7,915	6,049	8,376	6,966
38,250	38,300	7,929	6,063	8,390	6,980
38,300	38,350	7,943	6,077	8,404	6,994
38,350	38,400	7,957	6,091	8,418	7,008
38,400	38,450	7,971	6,105	8,432	7,022
38,450	38,500	7,985	6,119	8,446	7,036
38,500	38,550	7,999	6,133	8,460	7,050
38,550	38,600	8,013	6,147	8,474	7,064
38,600	38,650	8,027	6,161	8,488	7,078
38,650	38,700	8,041	6,175	8,502	7,092
38,700	38,750	8,055	6,189	8,516	7,106
38,750	38,800	8,069	6,203	8,530	7,120
38,800	38,850	8,083	6,217	8,544	7,134
38,850	38,900	8,097	6,231	8,558	7,148
38,900	38,950	8,111	6,245	8,572	7,162
38,950	39,000	8,125	6,259	8,586	7,176

39,000

At least	But less than	Single	Married filing jointly	Married filing separately	Head of a household
39,000	39,050	8,139	6,273	8,600	7,190
39,050	39,100	8,153	6,287	8,614	7,204
39,100	39,150	8,167	6,301	8,628	7,218
39,150	39,200	8,181	6,315	8,642	7,232
39,200	39,250	8,195	6,329	8,656	7,246
39,250	39,300	8,209	6,343	8,670	7,260
39,300	39,350	8,223	6,357	8,684	7,274
39,350	39,400	8,237	6,371	8,698	7,288
39,400	39,450	8,251	6,385	8,712	7,302
39,450	39,500	8,265	6,399	8,726	7,316
39,500	39,550	8,279	6,413	8,740	7,330
39,550	39,600	8,293	6,427	8,754	7,344
39,600	39,650	8,307	6,441	8,768	7,358
39,650	39,700	8,321	6,455	8,782	7,372
39,700	39,750	8,335	6,469	8,796	7,386
39,750	39,800	8,349	6,483	8,810	7,400
39,800	39,850	8,363	6,497	8,824	7,414
39,850	39,900	8,377	6,511	8,838	7,428
39,900	39,950	8,391	6,525	8,852	7,442
39,950	40,000	8,405	6,539	8,866	7,456

40,000

At least	But less than	Single	Married filing jointly	Married filing separately	Head of a household
40,000	40,050	8,419	6,553	8,880	7,470
40,050	40,100	8,433	6,567	8,894	7,484
40,100	40,150	8,447	6,581	8,908	7,498
40,150	40,200	8,461	6,595	8,922	7,512
40,200	40,250	8,475	6,609	8,936	7,526
40,250	40,300	8,489	6,623	8,950	7,540
40,300	40,350	8,503	6,637	8,964	7,554
40,350	40,400	8,517	6,651	8,978	7,568
40,400	40,450	8,531	6,665	8,992	7,582
40,450	40,500	8,545	6,679	9,006	7,596
40,500	40,550	8,559	6,693	9,020	7,610
40,550	40,600	8,573	6,707	9,034	7,624
40,600	40,650	8,587	6,721	9,048	7,638
40,650	40,700	8,601	6,735	9,062	7,652
40,700	40,750	8,615	6,749	9,076	7,666
40,750	40,800	8,629	6,763	9,090	7,680
40,800	40,850	8,643	6,777	9,104	7,694
40,850	40,900	8,657	6,791	9,118	7,708
40,900	40,950	8,671	6,805	9,132	7,722
40,950	41,000	8,685	6,819	9,146	7,736

* This column must also be used by a qualifying widow(er).

Continued on next page

41,000 / 42,000 / 43,000

If taxable income is— At least	But less than	Single	Married filing jointly *	Married filing separately	Head of a household
41,000					
41,000	41,050	8,699	6,833	9,160	7,750
41,050	41,100	8,713	6,847	9,174	7,764
41,100	41,150	8,727	6,861	9,188	7,778
41,150	41,200	8,741	6,875	9,202	7,792
41,200	41,250	8,755	6,889	9,216	7,806
41,250	41,300	8,769	6,903	9,230	7,820
41,300	41,350	8,783	6,917	9,244	7,834
41,350	41,400	8,797	6,931	9,258	7,848
41,400	41,450	8,811	6,945	9,272	7,862
41,450	41,500	8,825	6,959	9,286	7,876
41,500	41,550	8,839	6,973	9,300	7,890
41,550	41,600	8,853	6,987	9,314	7,904
41,600	41,650	8,867	7,001	9,328	7,918
41,650	41,700	8,881	7,015	9,342	7,932
41,700	41,750	8,895	7,029	9,356	7,946
41,750	41,800	8,909	7,043	9,370	7,960
41,800	41,850	8,923	7,057	9,384	7,974
41,850	41,900	8,937	7,071	9,398	7,988
41,900	41,950	8,951	7,085	9,412	8,002
41,950	42,000	8,965	7,099	9,426	8,016
42,000					
42,000	42,050	8,979	7,113	9,440	8,030
42,050	42,100	8,993	7,127	9,454	8,044
42,100	42,150	9,007	7,141	9,468	8,058
42,150	42,200	9,021	7,155	6,482	8,072
42,200	42,250	9,035	7,169	9,496	8,086
42,250	42,300	9,049	7,183	9,510	8,100
42,300	42,350	9,063	7,197	9,524	8,114
42,350	42,400	9,077	7,211	9,538	8,128
42,400	42,450	9,091	7,225	9,552	8,142
42,450	42,500	9,105	7,239	9,566	8,156
42,500	42,550	9,119	7,253	9,580	8,170
42,550	42,600	9,133	7,267	9,594	8,184
42,600	42,650	9,147	7,281	9,608	8,198
42,650	42,700	9,161	7,295	9,622	8,212
42,700	42,750	9,175	7,309	9,636	8,226
42,750	42,800	9,189	7,323	9,650	8,240
42,800	42,850	9,203	7,337	9,664	8,254
42,850	42,900	9,217	7,351	9,678	8,268
42,900	42,950	9,231	7,365	9,692	8,282
42,950	43,000	9,245	7,379	9,706	8,296
43,000					
43,000	43,050	9,259	7,393	9,720	8,310
43,050	43,100	9,273	7,407	9,734	8,324
43,100	43,150	9,287	7,421	9,748	8,338
43,150	43,200	9,301	7,435	9,762	8,352
43,200	43,250	9,315	7,449	9,776	8,366
43,250	43,300	9,329	7,463	9,791	8,380
43,300	43,350	9,343	7,477	9,806	8,394
43,350	43,400	9,357	7,491	9,822	8,408
43,400	43,450	9,371	7,505	9,837	8,422
43,450	43,500	9,385	7,519	9,853	8,436
43,500	43,550	9,399	7,533	9,868	8,450
43,550	43,600	9,413	7,547	9,884	8,464
43,600	43,650	9,427	7,561	9,899	8,478
43,650	43,700	9,441	7,575	9,915	8,492
43,700	43,750	9,455	7,589	9,930	8,506
43,750	43,800	9,469	7,603	9,946	8,520
43,800	43,850	9,483	7,617	9,961	8,534
43,850	43,900	9,497	7,631	9,977	8,548
43,900	43,950	9,511	7,645	9,992	8,562
43,950	44,000	9,525	7,659	10,008	8,576

44,000 / 45,000 / 46,000

If taxable income is— At least	But less than	Single	Married filing jointly *	Married filing separately	Head of a household
44,000					
44,000	44,050	9,539	7,673	10,023	8,590
44,050	44,100	9,553	7,687	10,039	8,604
44,100	44,150	9,567	7,701	10,054	8,618
44,150	44,200	9,581	7,715	10,070	8,632
44,200	44,250	9,595	7,729	10,085	8,646
44,250	44,300	9,609	7,743	10,101	8,660
44,300	44,350	9,623	7,757	10,116	8,674
44,350	44,400	9,637	7,771	10,132	8,688
44,400	44,450	9,651	7,785	10,147	8,702
44,450	44,500	9,665	7,799	10,163	8,716
44,500	44,550	9,679	7,813	10,178	8,730
44,550	44,600	9,693	7,827	10,194	8,744
44,600	44,650	9,707	7,841	10,209	8,758
44,650	44,700	9,721	7,855	10,225	8,772
44,700	44,750	9,735	7,869	10,240	8,786
44,750	44,800	9,749	7,883	10,256	8,800
44,800	44,850	9,763	7,897	10,271	8,814
44,850	44,900	9,777	7,911	10,287	8,828
44,900	44,950	9,791	7,925	10,302	8,842
44,950	45,000	9,805	7,939	10,318	8,856
45,000					
45,000	45,050	9,819	7,953	10,333	8,870
45,050	45,100	9,833	7,967	10,349	8,884
45,100	45,150	9,847	7,981	10,364	8,898
45,150	45,200	9,861	7,995	10,380	8,912
45,200	45,250	9,875	8,009	10,395	8,926
45,250	45,300	9,889	8,023	10,411	8,940
45,300	45,350	9,903	8,037	10,426	8,954
45,350	45,400	9,917	8,051	10,442	8,968
45,400	45,450	9,931	8,065	10,457	8,982
45,450	45,500	9,945	8,079	10,473	8,996
45,500	45,550	9,959	8,093	10,488	9,010
45,550	45,600	9,973	8,107	10,504	9,024
45,600	45,650	9,987	8,121	10,519	9,038
45,650	45,700	10,001	8,135	10,535	9,052
45,700	45,750	10,015	8,149	10,550	9,066
45,750	45,800	10,029	8,163	10,566	9,080
45,800	45,850	10,043	8,177	10,581	9,094
45,850	45,900	10,057	8,191	10,597	9,108
45,900	45,950	10,071	8,205	10,612	9,122
45,950	46,000	10,085	8,219	10,628	9,136
46,000					
46,000	46,050	10,099	8,233	10,643	9,150
46,050	46,100	10,113	8,247	10,659	9,164
46,100	46,150	10,127	8,261	10,674	9,178
46,150	46,200	10,141	8,275	10,690	9,192
46,200	46,250	10,155	8,289	10,705	9,206
46,250	46,300	10,169	8,303	10,721	9,220
46,300	46,350	10,183	8,317	10,736	9,234
46,350	46,400	10,197	8,331	10,752	9,248
46,400	46,450	10,211	8,345	10,767	9,262
46,450	46,500	10,225	8,359	10,783	9,276
46,500	46,550	10,239	8,373	10,798	9,290
46,550	46,600	10,253	8,387	10,814	9,304
46,600	46,650	10,267	8,401	10,829	9,318
46,650	46,700	10,281	8,415	10,845	9,332
46,700	46,750	10,295	8,429	10,860	9,346
46,750	46,800	10,309	8,443	10,876	9,360
46,800	46,850	10,323	8,457	10,891	9,374
46,850	46,900	10,337	8,471	10,907	9,388
46,900	46,950	10,351	8,485	10,922	9,402
46,950	47,000	10,365	8,499	10,938	9,416

47,000 / 48,000 / 49,000

If taxable income is— At least	But less than	Single	Married filing jointly *	Married filing separately	Head of a household
47,000					
47,000	47,050	10,379	8,513	10,953	9,430
47,050	47,100	10,393	8,527	10,969	9,444
47,100	47,150	10,407	8,541	10,984	9,458
47,150	47,200	10,421	8,555	11,000	9,472
47,200	47,250	10,435	8,569	11,015	9,486
47,250	47,300	10,449	8,583	11,031	9,500
47,300	47,350	10,463	8,597	11,046	9,514
47,350	47,400	10,477	8,611	11,062	9,528
47,400	47,450	10,491	8,625	11,077	9,542
47,450	47,500	10,505	8,639	11,093	9,556
47,500	47,550	10,519	8,653	11,108	9,570
47,550	47,600	10,533	8,667	11,124	9,584
47,600	47,650	10,547	8,681	11,139	9,598
47,650	47,700	10,561	8,695	11,155	9,612
47,700	47,750	10,575	8,709	11,170	9,626
47,750	47,800	10,589	8,723	11,186	9,640
47,800	47,850	10,603	8,737	11,201	9,654
47,850	47,900	10,617	8,751	11,217	9,668
47,900	47,950	10,631	8,765	11,232	9,682
47,950	48,000	10,645	8,779	11,248	9,696
48,000					
48,000	48,050	10,659	8,793	11,263	9,710
48,050	48,100	10,673	8,807	11,279	9,724
48,100	48,150	10,687	8,821	11,294	9,738
48,150	48,200	10,701	8,835	11,310	9,752
48,200	48,250	10,715	8,849	11,325	9,766
48,250	48,300	10,729	8,863	11,341	9,780
48,300	48,350	10,743	8,877	11,356	9,794
48,350	48,400	10,757	8,891	11,372	9,808
48,400	48,450	10,771	8,905	11,387	9,822
48,450	48,500	10,785	8,919	11,403	9,836
48,500	48,550	10,799	8,933	11,418	9,850
48,550	48,600	10,813	8,947	11,434	9,864
48,600	48,650	10,827	8,961	11,449	9,878
48,650	48,700	10,841	8,975	11,465	9,892
48,700	48,750	10,855	8,989	11,480	9,906
48,750	48,800	10,869	9,003	11,496	9,920
48,800	48,850	10,883	9,017	11,511	9,934
48,850	48,900	10,897	9,031	11,527	9,948
48,900	48,950	10,911	9,045	11,542	9,962
48,950	49,000	10,925	9,059	11,558	9,976
49,000					
49,000	49,050	10,939	9,073	11,573	9,990
49,050	49,100	10,953	9,087	11,589	10,004
49,100	49,150	10,967	9,101	11,604	10,018
49,150	49,200	10,981	9,115	11,620	10,032
49,200	49,250	10,995	9,129	11,635	10,046
49,250	49,300	11,009	9,143	11,651	10,060
49,300	49,350	11,023	9,157	11,666	10,074
49,350	49,400	11,037	9,171	11,682	10,088
49,400	49,450	11,051	9,185	11,697	10,102
49,450	49,500	11,065	9,199	11,713	10,116
49,500	49,550	11,079	9,213	11,728	10,130
49,550	49,600	11,093	9,227	11,744	10,144
49,600	49,650	11,107	9,241	11,759	10,158
49,650	49,700	11,121	9,255	11,775	10,172
49,700	49,750	11,135	9,269	11,790	10,186
49,750	49,800	11,149	9,283	11,806	10,200
49,800	49,850	11,163	9,297	11,821	10,214
49,850	49,900	11,177	9,311	11,837	10,228
49,900	49,950	11,191	9,325	11,852	10,242
49,950	50,000	11,205	9,339	11,868	10,256

* This column must also be used by a qualifying widow(er).

Continued on next page

If taxable income is— At least	But less than	Single	Married filing jointly *	Married filing separately	Head of a household
50,000					
50,000	50,050	11,219	9,353	11,883	10,270
50,050	50,100	11,233	9,367	11,899	10,284
50,100	50,150	11,247	9,381	11,914	10,298
50,150	50,200	11,261	9,395	11,930	10,312
50,200	50,250	11,275	9,409	11,945	10,326
50,250	50,300	11,289	9,423	11,961	10,340
50,300	50,350	11,303	9,437	11,976	10,354
50,350	50,400	11,317	9,451	11,992	10,368
50,400	50,450	11,331	9,465	12,007	10,382
50,450	50,500	11,345	9,479	12,023	10,396
50,500	50,550	11,359	9,493	12,038	10,410
50,550	50,600	11,373	9,507	12,054	10,424
50,600	50,650	11,387	9,521	12,069	10,438
50,650	50,700	11,401	9,535	12,085	10,452
50,700	50,750	11,415	9,549	12,100	10,466
50,750	50,800	11,429	9,563	12,116	10,480
50,800	50,850	11,443	9,577	12,131	10,494
50,850	50,900	11,457	9,591	12,147	10,508
50,900	50,950	11,471	9,605	12,162	10,522
50,950	51,000	11,485	9,619	12,178	10,536
51,000					
51,000	51,050	11,499	9,633	12,193	10,550
51,050	51,100	11,513	9,647	12,209	10,564
51,100	51,150	11,527	9,661	12,224	10,578
51,150	51,200	11,541	9,675	12,240	10,592
51,200	51,250	11,555	9,689	12,255	10,606
51,250	51,300	11,569	9,703	12,271	10,620
51,300	51,350	11,583	9,717	12,286	10,634
51,350	51,400	11,597	9,731	12,302	10,648
51,400	51,450	11,611	9,745	12,317	10,662
51,450	51,500	11,625	9,759	12,333	10,676
51,500	51,550	11,639	9,773	12,348	10,690
51,550	51,600	11,653	9,787	12,364	10,704
51,600	51,650	11,667	9,801	12,379	10,718
51,650	51,700	11,681	9,815	12,395	10,732
51,700	51,750	11,695	9,829	12,410	10,746
51,750	51,800	11,709	9,843	12,426	10,760
51,800	51,850	11,723	9,857	12,441	10,774
51,850	51,900	11,737	9,871	12,457	10,788
51,900	51,950	11,751	9,885	12,472	10,802
51,950	52,000	11,767	9,899	12,488	10,816
52,000					
52,000	52,050	11,782	9,913	12,503	10,830
52,050	52,100	11,798	9,927	12,519	10,844
52,100	52,150	11,813	9,941	12,534	10,858
52,150	52,200	11,829	9,955	12,550	10,872
52,200	52,250	11,844	9,969	12,565	10,886
52,250	52,300	11,860	9,983	12,581	10,900
52,300	52,350	11,875	9,997	12,596	10,914
52,350	52,400	11,891	10,011	12,612	10,928
52,400	52,450	11,906	10,025	12,627	10,942
52,450	52,500	11,922	10,039	12,643	10,956
52,500	52,550	11,937	10,053	12,658	10,970
52,550	52,600	11,953	10,067	12,674	10,984
52,600	52,650	11,968	10,081	12,689	10,998
52,650	52,700	11,984	10,095	12,705	11,012
52,700	52,750	11,999	10,109	12,720	11,026
52,750	52,800	12,015	10,123	12,736	11,040
52,800	52,850	12,030	10,137	12,751	11,054
52,850	52,900	12,046	10,151	12,767	11,068
52,900	52,950	12,061	10,165	12,782	11,082
52,950	53,000	12,077	10,179	12,798	11,096
53,000					
53,000	53,050	12,092	10,193	12,813	11,110
53,050	53,100	12,108	10,207	12,829	11,124
53,100	53,150	12,123	10,221	12,844	11,138
53,150	53,200	12,139	10,235	12,860	11,152
53,200	53,250	12,154	10,249	12,875	11,166
53,250	53,300	12,170	10,263	12,891	11,180
53,300	53,350	12,185	10,277	12,906	11,194
53,350	53,400	12,201	10,291	12,922	11,208
53,400	53,450	12,216	10,305	12,937	11,222
53,450	53,500	12,232	10,319	12,953	11,236
53,500	53,550	12,247	10,333	12,968	11,250
53,550	53,600	12,263	10,347	12,984	11,264
53,600	53,650	12,278	10,361	12,999	11,278
53,650	53,700	12,294	10,375	13,015	11,292
53,700	53,750	12,309	10,389	13,030	11,306
53,750	53,800	12,325	10,403	13,046	11,320
53,800	53,850	12,340	10,417	13,061	11,334
53,850	53,900	12,356	10,431	13,077	11,348
53,900	53,950	12,371	10,445	13,092	11,362
53,950	54,000	12,387	10,459	13,108	11,376
54,000					
54,000	54,050	12,402	10,473	13,123	11,390
54,050	54,100	12,418	10,487	13,139	11,404
54,100	54,150	12,433	10,501	13,154	11,418
54,150	54,200	12,449	10,515	13,170	11,432
54,200	54,250	12,464	10,529	13,185	11,446
54,250	54,300	12,480	10,543	13,201	11,460
54,300	54,350	12,495	10,557	13,216	11,474
54,350	54,400	12,511	10,571	13,232	11,488
54,400	54,450	12,526	10,585	13,247	11,502
54,450	54,500	12,542	10,599	13,263	11,516
54,500	54,550	12,557	10,613	13,278	11,530
54,550	54,600	12,573	10,627	13,294	11,544
54,600	54,650	12,588	10,641	13,309	11,558
54,650	54,700	12,604	10,655	13,325	11,572
54,700	54,750	12,619	10,669	13,340	11,586
54,750	54,800	12,635	10,683	13,356	11,600
54,800	54,850	12,650	10,697	13,371	11,614
54,850	54,900	12,666	10,711	13,387	11,628
54,900	54,950	12,681	10,725	13,402	11,642
54,950	55,000	12,697	10,739	13,418	11,656
55,000					
55,000	55,050	12,712	10,753	13,433	11,670
55,050	55,100	12,728	10,767	13,449	11,684
55,100	55,150	12,743	10,781	13,464	11,698
55,150	55,200	12,759	10,795	13,480	11,712
55,200	55,250	12,774	10,809	13,495	11,726
55,250	55,300	12,790	10,823	13,511	11,740
55,300	55,350	12,805	10,837	13,526	11,754
55,350	55,400	12,821	10,851	13,542	11,768
55,400	55,450	12,836	10,865	13,557	11,782
55,450	55,500	12,852	10,879	13,573	11,796
55,500	55,550	12,867	10,893	13,588	11,810
55,550	55,600	12,883	10,907	13,604	11,824
55,600	55,650	12,898	10,921	13,619	11,838
55,650	55,700	12,914	10,935	13,635	11,852
55,700	55,750	12,929	10,949	13,650	11,866
55,750	55,800	12,945	10,963	13,666	11,880
55,800	55,850	12,960	10,977	13,681	11,894
55,850	55,900	12,976	10,991	13,697	11,908
55,900	55,950	12,991	11,005	13,712	11,922
55,950	56,000	13,007	11,019	13,728	11,936
56,000					
56,000	56,050	13,022	11,033	13,743	11,950
56,050	56,100	13,038	11,047	13,759	11,964
56,100	56,150	13,053	11,061	13,774	11,978
56,150	56,200	13,069	11,075	13,790	11,992
56,200	56,250	13,084	11,089	13,805	12,006
56,250	56,300	13,100	11,103	13,821	12,020
56,300	56,350	13,115	11,117	13,836	12,034
56,350	56,400	13,131	11,131	13,852	12,048
56,400	56,450	13,146	11,145	13,867	12,062
56,450	56,500	13,162	11,159	13,883	12,076
56,500	56,550	13,177	11,173	13,898	12,090
56,550	56,600	13,193	11,187	13,914	12,104
56,600	56,650	13,208	11,201	13,929	12,118
56,650	56,700	13,224	11,215	13,945	12,132
56,700	56,750	13,239	11,229	13,960	12,146
56,750	56,800	13,255	11,243	13,976	12,160
56,800	56,850	13,270	11,257	13,991	12,174
56,850	56,900	13,286	11,271	14,007	12,188
56,900	56,950	13,301	11,285	14,022	12,202
56,950	57,000	13,317	11,299	14,038	12,216
57,000					
57,000	57,050	13,332	11,313	14,053	12,230
57,050	57,100	13,348	11,327	14,069	12,244
57,100	57,150	13,363	11,341	14,084	12,258
57,150	57,200	13,379	11,355	14,100	12,272
57,200	57,250	13,394	11,369	14,115	12,286
57,250	57,300	13,410	11,383	14,131	12,300
57,300	57,350	13,425	11,397	14,146	12,314
57,350	57,400	13,441	11,411	14,162	12,328
57,400	57,450	13,456	11,425	14,177	12,342
57,450	57,500	13,472	11,439	14,193	12,356
57,500	57,550	13,487	11,453	14,208	12,370
57,550	57,600	13,503	11,467	14,224	12,384
57,600	57,650	13,518	11,481	14,239	12,398
57,650	57,700	13,534	11,495	14,255	12,412
57,700	57,750	13,549	11,509	14,270	12,426
57,750	57,800	13,565	11,523	14,286	12,440
57,800	57,850	13,580	11,537	14,301	12,454
57,850	57,900	13,596	11,551	14,317	12,468
57,900	57,950	13,611	11,565	14,332	12,482
57,950	58,000	13,627	11,579	14,348	12,496
58,000					
58,000	58,050	13,642	11,593	14,363	12,510
58,050	58,100	13,658	11,607	14,379	12,524
58,100	58,150	13,673	11,621	14,394	12,538
58,150	58,200	13,689	11,635	14,410	12,552
58,200	58,250	13,704	11,649	14,425	12,566
58,250	58,300	13,720	11,663	14,441	12,580
58,300	58,350	13,735	11,677	14,456	12,594
58,350	58,400	13,751	11,691	14,472	12,608
58,400	58,450	13,766	11,705	14,487	12,622
58,450	58,500	13,782	11,719	14,503	12,636
58,500	58,550	13,797	11,733	14,518	12,650
58,550	58,600	13,813	11,747	14,534	12,664
58,600	58,650	13,828	11,761	14,549	12,678
58,650	58,700	13,844	11,775	14,565	12,692
58,700	58,750	13,859	11,789	14,580	12,706
58,750	58,800	13,875	11,803	14,596	12,720
58,800	58,850	13,890	11,817	14,611	12,734
58,850	58,900	13,906	11,831	14,627	12,748
58,900	58,950	13,921	11,845	14,642	12,762
58,950	59,000	13,937	11,859	14,658	12,776

* This column must also be used by a qualifying widow(er).

Continued on next page

1992 Tax Table—Continued

59,000 / 60,000 / 61,000

At least	But less than	Single	Married filing jointly *	Married filing separately	Head of a household
59,000					
59,000	59,050	13,952	11,873	14,673	12,790
59,050	59,100	13,968	11,887	14,689	12,804
59,100	59,150	13,983	11,901	14,704	12,818
59,150	59,200	13,999	11,915	14,720	12,832
59,200	59,250	14,014	11,929	14,735	12,846
59,250	59,300	14,030	11,943	14,751	12,860
59,300	59,350	14,045	11,957	14,766	12,874
59,350	59,400	14,061	11,971	14,782	12,888
59,400	59,450	14,076	11,985	14,797	12,902
59,450	59,500	14,092	11,999	14,813	12,916
59,500	59,550	14,107	12,013	14,828	12,930
59,550	59,600	14,123	12,027	14,844	12,944
59,600	59,650	14,138	12,041	14,859	12,958
59,650	59,700	14,154	12,055	14,875	12,972
59,700	59,750	14,169	12,069	14,890	12,986
59,750	59,800	14,185	12,083	14,906	13,000
59,800	59,850	14,200	12,097	14,921	13,014
59,850	59,900	14,216	12,111	14,937	13,028
59,900	59,950	14,231	12,125	14,952	13,042
59,950	60,000	14,247	12,139	14,968	13,056
60,000					
60,000	60,050	14,262	12,153	14,983	13,070
60,050	60,100	14,278	12,167	14,999	13,084
60,100	60,150	14,293	12,181	15,014	13,098
60,150	60,200	14,309	12,195	15,030	13,112
60,200	60,250	14,324	12,209	15,045	13,126
60,250	60,300	14,340	12,223	15,061	13,140
60,300	60,350	14,355	12,237	15,076	13,154
60,350	60,400	14,371	12,251	15,092	13,168
60,400	60,450	14,386	12,265	15,107	13,182
60,450	60,500	14,402	12,279	15,123	13,196
60,500	60,550	14,417	12,293	15,138	13,210
60,550	60,600	14,433	12,307	15,154	13,224
60,600	60,650	14,448	12,321	15,169	13,238
60,650	60,700	14,464	12,335	15,185	13,252
60,700	60,750	14,479	12,349	15,200	13,266
60,750	60,800	14,495	12,363	15,216	13,280
60,800	60,850	14,510	12,377	15,231	13,294
60,850	60,900	14,526	12,391	15,247	13,308
60,900	60,950	14,541	12,405	15,262	13,322
60,950	61,000	14,557	12,419	15,278	13,336
61,000					
61,000	61,050	14,572	12,433	15,293	13,350
61,050	61,100	14,588	12,447	15,309	13,364
61,100	61,150	14,603	12,461	15,324	13,378
61,150	61,200	14,619	12,475	15,340	13,392
61,200	61,250	14,634	12,489	15,355	13,406
61,250	61,300	14,650	12,503	15,371	13,420
61,300	61,350	14,665	12,517	15,386	13,434
61,350	61,400	14,681	12,531	15,402	13,448
61,400	61,450	14,696	12,545	15,417	13,462
61,450	61,500	14,712	12,559	15,433	13,476
61,500	61,550	14,727	12,573	15,448	13,490
61,550	61,600	14,743	12,587	15,464	13,504
61,600	61,650	14,758	12,601	15,479	13,518
61,650	61,700	14,774	12,615	15,495	13,532
61,700	61,750	14,789	12,629	15,510	13,546
61,750	61,800	14,805	12,643	15,526	13,560
61,800	61,850	14,820	12,657	15,541	13,574
61,850	61,900	14,836	12,671	15,557	13,588
61,900	61,950	14,851	12,685	15,572	13,602
61,950	62,000	14,867	12,699	15,588	13,616

62,000 / 63,000 / 64,000

At least	But less than	Single	Married filing jointly *	Married filing separately	Head of a household
62,000					
62,000	62,050	14,882	12,713	15,603	13,630
62,050	62,100	14,898	12,727	15,619	13,644
62,100	62,150	14,913	12,741	15,634	13,658
62,150	62,200	14,929	12,755	15,650	13,672
62,200	62,250	14,944	12,769	15,665	13,686
62,250	62,300	14,960	12,783	15,681	13,700
62,300	62,350	14,975	12,797	15,696	13,714
62,350	62,400	14,991	12,811	15,712	13,728
62,400	62,450	15,006	12,825	15,727	13,742
62,450	62,500	15,022	12,839	15,743	13,756
62,500	62,550	15,037	12,853	15,758	13,770
62,550	62,600	15,053	12,867	15,774	13,784
62,600	62,650	15,068	12,881	15,789	13,798
62,650	62,700	15,084	12,895	15,805	13,812
62,700	62,750	15,099	12,909	15,820	13,826
62,750	62,800	15,115	12,923	15,836	13,840
62,800	62,850	15,130	12,937	15,851	13,854
62,850	62,900	15,146	12,951	15,867	13,868
62,900	62,950	15,161	12,965	15,882	13,882
62,950	63,000	15,177	12,979	15,898	13,896
63,000					
63,000	63,050	15,192	12,993	15,913	13,910
63,050	63,100	15,208	13,007	15,929	13,924
63,100	63,150	15,223	13,021	15,944	13,938
63,150	63,200	15,239	13,035	15,960	13,952
63,200	63,250	15,254	13,049	15,975	13,966
63,250	63,300	15,270	13,063	15,991	13,980
63,300	63,350	15,285	13,077	16,006	13,994
63,350	63,400	15,301	13,091	16,022	14,008
63,400	63,450	15,316	13,105	16,037	14,022
63,450	63,500	15,332	13,119	16,053	14,036
63,500	63,550	15,347	13,133	16,068	14,050
63,550	63,600	15,363	13,147	16,084	14,064
63,600	63,650	15,378	13,161	16,099	14,078
63,650	63,700	15,394	13,175	16,115	14,092
63,700	63,750	15,409	13,189	16,130	14,106
63,750	63,800	15,425	13,203	16,146	14,120
63,800	63,850	15,440	13,217	16,161	14,134
63,850	63,900	15,456	13,231	16,177	14,148
63,900	63,950	15,471	13,245	16,192	14,162
63,950	64,000	15,487	13,259	16,208	14,176
64,000					
64,000	64,050	15,502	13,273	16,223	14,190
64,050	64,100	15,518	13,287	16,239	14,204
64,100	64,150	15,533	13,301	16,254	14,218
64,150	64,200	15,549	13,315	16,270	14,232
64,200	64,250	15,564	13,329	16,285	14,246
64,250	64,300	15,580	13,343	16,301	14,260
64,300	64,350	15,595	13,357	16,316	14,274
64,350	64,400	15,611	13,371	16,332	14,288
64,400	64,450	15,626	13,385	16,347	14,302
64,450	64,500	15,642	13,399	16,363	14,316
64,500	64,550	15,657	13,413	16,378	14,330
64,550	64,600	15,673	13,427	16,394	14,344
64,600	64,650	15,688	13,441	16,409	14,358
64,650	64,700	15,704	13,455	16,425	14,372
64,700	64,750	15,719	13,469	16,440	14,386
64,750	64,800	15,735	13,483	16,456	14,400
64,800	64,850	15,750	13,497	16,471	14,414
64,850	64,900	15,766	13,511	16,487	14,428
64,900	64,950	15,781	13,525	16,502	14,442
64,950	65,000	15,797	13,539	16,518	14,456

65,000 / 66,000 / 67,000

At least	But less than	Single	Married filing jointly *	Married filing separately	Head of a household
65,000					
65,000	65,050	15,812	13,553	16,533	14,470
65,050	65,100	15,828	13,567	16,549	14,484
65,100	65,150	15,843	13,581	16,564	14,498
65,150	65,200	15,859	13,595	16,580	14,512
65,200	65,250	15,874	13,609	16,595	14,526
65,250	65,300	15,890	13,623	16,611	14,540
65,300	65,350	15,905	13,637	16,626	14,554
65,350	65,400	15,921	13,651	16,642	14,568
65,400	65,450	15,936	13,665	16,657	14,582
65,450	65,500	15,952	13,679	16,673	14,596
65,500	65,550	15,967	13,693	16,688	14,610
65,550	65,600	15,983	13,707	16,704	14,624
65,600	65,650	15,998	13,721	16,719	14,638
65,650	65,700	16,014	13,735	16,735	14,652
65,700	65,750	16,029	13,749	16,750	14,666
65,750	65,800	16,045	13,763	16,766	14,680
65,800	65,850	16,060	13,777	16,781	14,694
65,850	65,900	16,076	13,791	16,797	14,708
65,900	65,950	16,091	13,805	16,812	14,722
65,950	66,000	16,107	13,819	16,828	14,736
66,000					
66,000	66,050	16,122	13,833	16,843	14,750
66,050	66,100	16,138	13,847	16,859	14,764
66,100	66,150	16,153	13,861	16,874	14,778
66,150	66,200	16,169	13,875	16,890	14,792
66,200	66,250	16,184	13,889	16,905	14,806
66,250	66,300	16,200	13,903	16,921	14,820
66,300	66,350	16,215	13,917	16,936	14,834
66,350	66,400	16,231	13,931	16,952	14,848
66,400	66,450	16,246	13,945	16,967	14,862
66,450	66,500	16,262	13,959	16,983	14,876
66,500	66,550	16,277	13,973	16,998	14,890
66,550	66,600	16,293	13,987	17,014	14,904
66,600	66,650	16,308	14,001	17,029	14,918
66,650	66,700	16,324	14,015	17,045	14,932
66,700	66,750	16,339	14,029	17,060	14,946
66,750	66,800	16,355	14,043	17,076	14,960
66,800	66,850	16,370	14,057	17,091	14,974
66,850	66,900	16,386	14,071	17,107	14,988
66,900	66,950	16,401	14,085	17,122	15,002
66,950	67,000	16,417	14,099	17,138	15,016
67,000					
67,000	67,050	16,432	14,113	17,153	15,030
67,050	67,100	16,448	14,127	17,169	15,044
67,100	67,150	16,463	14,141	17,184	15,058
67,150	67,200	16,479	14,155	17,200	15,072
67,200	67,250	16,494	14,169	17,215	15,086
67,250	67,300	16,510	14,183	17,231	15,100
67,300	67,350	16,525	14,197	17,246	15,114
67,350	67,400	16,541	14,211	17,262	15,128
67,400	67,450	16,556	14,225	17,277	15,142
67,450	67,500	16,572	14,239	17,293	15,156
67,500	67,550	16,587	14,253	17,308	15,170
67,550	67,600	16,603	14,267	17,324	15,184
67,600	67,650	16,618	14,281	17,339	15,198
67,650	67,700	16,634	14,295	17,355	15,212
67,700	67,750	16,649	14,309	17,370	15,226
67,750	67,800	16,665	14,323	17,386	15,240
67,800	67,850	16,680	14,337	17,401	15,254
67,850	67,900	16,696	14,351	17,417	15,268
67,900	67,950	16,711	14,365	17,432	15,282
67,950	68,000	16,727	14,379	17,448	15,296

* This column must also be used by a qualifying widow(er).

Continued on next page

68,000

At least	But less than	Single	Married filing jointly *	Married filing separately	Head of a household
68,000	68,050	16,742	14,393	17,463	15,310
68,050	68,100	16,758	14,407	17,479	15,324
68,100	68,150	16,773	14,421	17,494	15,338
68,150	68,200	16,789	14,435	17,510	15,352
68,200	68,250	16,804	14,449	17,525	15,366
68,250	68,300	16,820	14,463	17,541	15,380
68,300	68,350	16,835	14,477	17,556	15,394
68,350	68,400	16,851	14,491	17,572	15,408
68,400	68,450	16,866	14,505	17,587	15,422
68,450	68,500	16,882	14,519	17,603	15,436
68,500	68,550	16,897	14,533	17,618	15,450
68,550	68,600	16,913	14,547	17,634	15,464
68,600	68,650	16,928	14,561	17,649	15,478
68,650	68,700	16,944	14,575	17,665	15,492
68,700	68,750	16,959	14,589	17,680	15,506
68,750	68,800	16,975	14,603	17,696	15,520
68,800	68,850	16,990	14,617	17,711	15,534
68,850	68,900	17,006	14,631	17,727	15,548
68,900	68,950	17,021	14,645	17,742	15,562
68,950	69,000	17,037	14,659	17,758	15,576

69,000

At least	But less than	Single	Married filing jointly *	Married filing separately	Head of a household
69,000	69,050	17,052	14,673	17,773	15,590
69,050	69,100	17,068	14,687	17,789	15,604
69,100	69,150	17,083	14,701	17,804	15,618
69,150	69,200	17,099	14,715	17,820	15,632
69,200	69,250	17,114	14,729	17,835	15,646
69,250	69,300	17,130	14,743	17,851	15,660
69,300	69,350	17,145	14,757	17,866	15,674
69,350	69,400	17,161	14,771	17,882	15,688
69,400	69,450	17,176	14,785	17,897	15,702
69,450	69,500	17,192	14,799	17,913	15,716
69,500	69,550	17,207	14,813	17,928	15,730
69,550	69,600	17,223	14,827	17,944	15,744
69,600	69,650	17,238	14,841	17,959	15,758
69,650	69,700	17,254	14,855	17,975	15,772
69,700	69,750	17,269	14,869	17,990	15,786
69,750	69,800	17,285	14,883	18,006	15,800
69,800	69,850	17,300	14,897	18,021	15,814
69,850	69,900	17,316	14,911	18,037	15,828
69,900	69,950	17,331	14,925	18,052	15,842
69,950	70,000	17,347	14,939	18,068	15,856

70,000

At least	But less than	Single	Married filing jointly *	Married filing separately	Head of a household
70,000	70,050	17,362	14,953	18,083	15,870
70,050	70,100	17,378	14,967	18,099	15,884
70,100	70,150	17,393	14,981	18,114	15,898
70,150	70,200	17,409	14,995	18,130	15,912
70,200	70,250	17,424	15,009	18,145	15,926
70,250	70,300	17,440	15,023	18,161	15,940
70,300	70,350	17,455	15,037	18,176	15,954
70,350	70,400	17,471	15,051	18,192	15,968
70,400	70,450	17,486	15,065	18,207	15,982
70,450	70,500	17,502	15,079	18,223	15,996
70,500	70,550	17,517	15,093	18,238	16,010
70,550	70,600	17,533	15,107	18,254	16,024
70,600	70,650	17,548	15,121	18,269	16,038
70,650	70,700	17,564	15,135	18,285	16,052
70,700	70,750	17,579	15,149	18,300	16,066
70,750	70,800	17,595	15,163	18,316	16,080
70,800	70,850	17,610	15,177	18,331	16,094
70,850	70,900	17,626	15,191	18,347	16,108
70,900	70,950	17,641	15,205	18,362	16,122
70,950	71,000	17,657	15,219	18,378	16,136

71,000

At least	But less than	Single	Married filing jointly *	Married filing separately	Head of a household
71,000	71,050	17,672	15,233	18,393	16,150
71,050	71,100	17,688	15,247	18,409	16,164
71,100	71,150	17,703	15,261	18,424	16,178
71,150	71,200	17,719	15,275	18,440	16,192
71,200	71,250	17,734	15,289	18,455	16,206
71,250	71,300	17,750	15,303	18,471	16,220
71,300	71,350	17,765	15,317	18,486	16,234
71,350	71,400	17,781	15,331	18,502	16,248
71,400	71,450	17,796	15,345	18,517	16,262
71,450	71,500	17,812	15,359	18,533	16,276
71,500	71,550	17,827	15,373	18,548	16,290
71,550	71,600	17,843	15,387	18,564	16,304
71,600	71,650	17,858	15,401	18,579	16,318
71,650	71,700	17,874	15,415	18,595	16,332
71,700	71,750	17,889	15,429	18,610	16,346
71,750	71,800	17,905	15,443	18,626	16,360
71,800	71,850	17,920	15,457	18,641	16,374
71,850	71,900	17,936	15,471	18,657	16,388
71,900	71,950	17,951	15,485	18,672	16,402
71,950	72,000	17,967	15,499	18,688	16,416

72,000

At least	But less than	Single	Married filing jointly *	Married filing separately	Head of a household
72,000	72,050	17,982	15,513	18,703	16,430
72,050	72,100	17,998	15,527	18,719	16,444
72,100	72,150	18,013	15,541	18,734	16,458
72,150	72,200	18,029	15,555	18,750	16,472
72,200	72,250	18,044	15,569	18,765	16,486
72,250	72,300	18,060	15,583	18,781	16,500
72,300	72,350	18,075	15,597	18,796	16,514
72,350	72,400	18,091	15,611	18,812	16,528
72,400	72,450	18,106	15,625	18,827	16,542
72,450	72,500	18,122	15,639	18,843	16,556
72,500	72,550	18,137	15,653	18,858	16,570
72,550	72,600	18,153	15,667	18,874	16,584
72,600	72,650	18,168	15,681	18,889	16,598
72,650	72,700	18,184	15,695	18,905	16,612
72,700	72,750	18,199	15,709	18,920	16,626
72,750	72,800	18,215	15,723	18,936	16,640
72,800	72,850	18,230	15,737	18,951	16,654
72,850	72,900	18,246	15,751	18,967	16,668
72,900	72,950	18,261	15,765	18,982	16,682
72,950	73,000	18,277	15,779	18,998	16,696

73,000

At least	But less than	Single	Married filing jointly *	Married filing separately	Head of a household
73,000	73,050	18,292	15,793	19,013	16,710
73,050	73,100	18,308	15,807	19,029	16,724
73,100	73,150	18,323	15,821	19,044	16,738
73,150	73,200	18,339	15,835	19,060	16,752
73,200	73,250	18,354	15,849	19,075	16,766
73,250	73,300	18,370	15,863	19,091	16,780
73,300	73,350	18,385	15,877	19,106	16,794
73,350	73,400	18,401	15,891	19,122	16,808
73,400	73,450	18,416	15,905	19,137	16,822
73,450	73,500	18,432	15,919	19,153	16,836
73,500	73,550	18,447	15,933	19,168	16,850
73,550	73,600	18,463	15,947	19,184	16,864
73,600	73,650	18,478	15,961	19,199	16,878
73,650	73,700	18,494	15,975	19,215	16,892
73,700	73,750	18,509	15,989	19,230	16,906
73,750	73,800	18,525	16,003	19,246	16,920
73,800	73,850	18,540	16,017	19,261	16,934
73,850	73,900	18,556	16,031	19,277	16,948
73,900	73,950	18,571	16,045	19,292	16,962
73,950	74,000	18,587	16,059	19,308	16,976

74,000

At least	But less than	Single	Married filing jointly *	Married filing separately	Head of a household
74,000	74,050	18,602	16,073	19,323	16,990
74,050	74,100	18,618	16,087	19,339	17,004
74,100	74,150	18,633	16,101	19,354	17,018
74,150	74,200	18,649	16,115	19,370	17,032
74,200	74,250	18,664	16,129	19,385	17,048
74,250	74,300	18,680	16,143	19,401	17,063
74,300	74,350	18,695	16,157	19,416	17,079
74,350	74,400	18,711	16,171	19,432	17,094
74,400	74,450	18,726	16,185	19,447	17,110
74,450	74,500	18,742	16,199	19,463	17,125
74,500	74,550	18,757	16,213	19,478	17,141
74,550	74,600	18,773	16,227	19,494	17,156
74,600	74,650	18,788	16,241	19,509	17,172
74,650	74,700	18,804	16,255	19,525	17,187
74,700	74,750	18,819	16,269	19,540	17,203
74,750	74,800	18,835	16,283	19,556	17,218
74,800	74,850	18,850	16,297	19,571	17,234
74,850	74,900	18,866	16,311	19,587	17,249
74,900	74,950	18,881	16,325	19,602	17,265
74,950	75,000	18,897	16,339	19,618	17,280

75,000

At least	But less than	Single	Married filing jointly *	Married filing separately	Head of a household
75,000	75,050	18,912	16,353	19,633	17,296
75,050	75,100	18,928	16,367	19,649	17,311
75,100	75,150	18,943	16,381	19,664	17,327
75,150	75,200	18,959	16,395	19,680	17,342
75,200	75,250	18,974	16,409	19,695	17,358
75,250	75,300	18,990	16,423	19,711	17,373
75,300	75,350	19,005	16,437	19,726	17,389
75,350	75,400	19,021	16,451	19,742	17,404
75,400	75,450	19,036	16,465	19,757	17,420
75,450	75,500	19,052	16,479	19,773	17,435
75,500	75,550	19,067	16,493	19,788	17,451
75,550	75,600	19,083	16,507	19,804	17,466
75,600	75,650	19,098	16,521	19,819	17,482
75,650	75,700	19,114	16,535	19,835	17,497
75,700	75,750	19,129	16,549	19,850	17,513
75,750	75,800	19,145	16,563	19,866	17,528
75,800	75,850	19,160	16,577	19,881	17,544
75,850	75,900	19,176	16,591	19,897	17,559
75,900	75,950	19,191	16,605	19,912	17,575
75,950	76,000	19,207	16,619	19,928	17,590

76,000

At least	But less than	Single	Married filing jointly *	Married filing separately	Head of a household
76,000	76,050	19,222	16,633	19,943	17,606
76,050	76,100	19,238	16,647	19,959	17,621
76,100	76,150	19,253	16,661	19,974	17,637
76,150	76,200	19,269	16,675	19,990	17,652
76,200	76,250	19,284	16,689	20,005	17,668
76,250	76,300	19,300	16,703	20,021	17,683
76,300	76,350	19,315	16,717	20,036	17,699
76,350	76,400	19,331	16,731	20,052	17,714
76,400	76,450	19,346	16,745	20,067	17,730
76,450	76,500	19,362	16,759	20,083	17,745
76,500	76,550	19,377	16,773	20,098	17,761
76,550	76,600	19,393	16,787	20,114	17,776
76,600	76,650	19,408	16,801	20,129	17,792
76,650	76,700	19,424	16,815	20,145	17,807
76,700	76,750	19,439	16,829	20,160	17,823
76,750	76,800	19,455	16,843	20,176	17,838
76,800	76,850	19,470	16,857	20,191	17,854
76,850	76,900	19,486	16,871	20,207	17,869
76,900	76,950	19,501	16,885	20,222	17,885
76,950	77,000	19,517	16,899	20,238	17,900

* This column must also be used by a qualifying widow(er).

Continued on next page

If taxable income is—		And you are—			
At least	But less than	Single	Married filing jointly *	Married filing separately *	Head of a household
			Your tax is—		

77,000

At least	But less than	Single	Married filing jointly	Married filing separately	Head of a household
77,000	77,050	19,532	16,913	20,253	17,916
77,050	77,100	19,548	16,927	20,269	17,931
77,100	77,150	19,563	16,941	20,284	17,947
77,150	77,200	19,579	16,955	20,300	17,962
77,200	77,250	19,594	16,969	20,315	17,978
77,250	77,300	19,610	16,983	20,331	17,993
77,300	77,350	19,625	16,997	20,346	18,009
77,350	77,400	19,641	17,011	20,362	18,024
77,400	77,450	19,656	17,025	20,377	18,040
77,450	77,500	19,672	17,039	20,393	18,055
77,500	77,550	19,687	17,053	20,408	18,071
77,550	77,600	19,703	17,067	20,424	18,086
77,600	77,650	19,718	17,081	20,439	18,102
77,650	77,700	19,734	17,095	20,455	18,117
77,700	77,750	19,749	17,109	20,470	18,133
77,750	77,800	19,765	17,123	20,486	18,148
77,800	77,850	19,780	17,137	20,501	18,164
77,850	77,900	19,796	17,151	20,517	18,179
77,900	77,950	19,811	17,165	20,532	18,195
77,950	78,000	19,827	17,179	20,548	18,210

78,000

At least	But less than	Single	Married filing jointly	Married filing separately	Head of a household
78,000	78,050	19,842	17,193	20,563	18,226
78,050	78,100	19,858	17,207	20,579	18,241
78,100	78,150	19,873	17,221	20,594	18,257
78,150	78,200	19,889	17,235	20,610	18,272
78,200	78,250	19,904	17,249	20,625	18,288
78,250	78,300	19,920	17,263	20,641	18,303
78,300	78,350	19,935	17,277	20,656	18,319
78,350	78,400	19,951	17,291	20,672	18,334
78,400	78,450	19,966	17,305	20,687	18,350
78,450	78,500	19,982	17,319	20,703	18,365
78,500	78,550	19,997	17,333	20,718	18,381
78,550	78,600	20,013	17,347	20,734	18,396
78,600	78,650	20,028	17,361	20,749	18,412
78,650	78,700	20,044	17,375	20,765	18,427
78,700	78,750	20,059	17,389	20,780	18,443
78,750	78,800	20,075	17,403	20,796	18,458
78,800	78,850	20,090	17,417	20,811	18,474
78,850	78,900	20,106	17,431	20,827	18,489
78,900	78,950	20,121	17,445	20,842	18,505
78,950	79,000	20,137	17,459	20,858	18,520

79,000

At least	But less than	Single	Married filing jointly	Married filing separately	Head of a household
79,000	79,050	20,152	17,473	20,873	18,536
79,050	79,100	20,168	17,487	20,889	18,551
79,100	79,150	20,183	17,501	20,904	18,567
79,150	79,200	20,199	17,515	20,920	18,582
79,200	79,250	20,214	17,529	20,935	18,598
79,250	79,300	20,230	17,543	20,951	18,613
79,300	79,350	20,245	17,557	20,966	18,629
79,350	79,400	20,261	17,571	20,982	18,644
79,400	79,450	20,276	17,585	20,997	18,660
79,450	79,500	20,292	17,599	21,013	18,675
79,500	79,550	20,307	17,613	21,028	18,691
79,550	79,600	20,323	17,627	21,044	18,706
79,600	79,650	20,338	17,641	21,059	18,722
79,650	79,700	20,354	17,655	21,075	18,737
79,700	79,750	20,369	17,669	21,090	18,753
79,750	79,800	20,385	17,683	21,106	18,768
79,800	79,850	20,400	17,697	21,121	18,784
79,850	79,900	20,416	17,711	21,137	18,799
79,900	79,950	20,431	17,725	21,152	18,815
79,950	80,000	20,447	17,739	21,168	18,830

80,000

At least	But less than	Single	Married filing jointly	Married filing separately	Head of a household
80,000	80,050	20,462	17,753	21,183	18,846
80,050	80,100	20,478	17,767	21,199	18,861
80,100	80,150	20,493	17,781	21,214	18,877
80,150	80,200	20,509	17,795	21,230	18,892
80,200	80,250	20,524	17,809	21,245	18,908
80,250	80,300	20,540	17,823	21,261	18,923
80,300	80,350	20,555	17,837	21,276	18,939
80,350	80,400	20,571	17,851	21,292	18,954
80,400	80,450	20,586	17,865	21,307	18,970
80,450	80,500	20,602	17,879	21,323	18,985
80,500	80,550	20,617	17,893	21,338	19,001
80,550	80,600	20,633	17,907	21,354	19,016
80,600	80,650	20,648	17,921	21,369	19,032
80,650	80,700	20,664	17,935	21,385	19,047
80,700	80,750	20,679	17,949	21,400	19,063
80,750	80,800	20,695	17,963	21,416	19,078
80,800	80,850	20,710	17,977	21,431	19,094
80,850	80,900	20,726	17,991	21,447	19,109
80,900	80,950	20,741	18,005	21,462	19,125
80,950	81,000	20,757	18,019	21,478	19,140

81,000

At least	But less than	Single	Married filing jointly	Married filing separately	Head of a household
81,000	81,050	20,772	18,033	21,493	19,156
81,050	81,100	20,788	18,047	21,509	19,171
81,100	81,150	20,803	18,061	21,524	19,187
81,150	81,200	20,819	18,075	21,540	19,202
81,200	81,250	20,834	18,089	21,555	19,218
81,250	81,300	20,850	18,103	21,571	19,233
81,300	81,350	20,865	18,117	21,586	19,249
81,350	81,400	20,881	18,131	21,602	19,264
81,400	81,450	20,896	18,145	21,617	19,280
81,450	81,500	20,912	18,159	21,633	19,295
81,500	81,550	20,927	18,173	21,648	19,311
81,550	81,600	20,943	18,187	21,664	19,326
81,600	81,650	20,958	18,201	21,679	19,342
81,650	81,700	20,974	18,215	21,695	19,357
81,700	81,750	20,989	18,229	21,710	19,373
81,750	81,800	21,005	18,243	21,726	19,388
81,800	81,850	21,020	18,257	21,741	19,404
81,850	81,900	21,036	18,271	21,757	19,419
81,900	81,950	21,051	18,285	21,772	19,435
81,950	82,000	21,067	18,299	21,788	19,450

82,000

At least	But less than	Single	Married filing jointly	Married filing separately	Head of a household
82,000	82,050	21,082	18,313	21,803	19,466
82,050	82,100	21,098	18,327	21,819	19,481
82,100	82,150	21,113	18,341	21,834	19,497
82,150	82,200	21,129	18,355	21,850	19,512
82,200	82,250	21,144	18,369	21,865	19,528
82,250	82,300	21,160	18,383	21,881	19,543
82,300	82,350	21,175	18,397	21,896	19,559
82,350	82,400	21,191	18,411	21,912	19,574
82,400	82,450	21,206	18,425	21,927	19,590
82,450	82,500	21,222	18,439	21,943	19,605
82,500	82,550	21,237	18,453	21,958	19,621
82,550	82,600	21,253	18,467	21,974	19,636
82,600	82,650	21,268	18,481	21,989	19,652
82,650	82,700	21,284	18,495	22,005	19,667
82,700	82,750	21,299	18,509	22,020	19,683
82,750	82,800	21,315	18,523	22,036	19,698
82,800	82,850	21,330	18,537	22,051	19,714
82,850	82,900	21,346	18,551	22,067	19,729
82,900	82,950	21,361	18,565	22,082	19,745
82,950	83,000	21,377	18,579	22,098	19,760

83,000

At least	But less than	Single	Married filing jointly	Married filing separately	Head of a household
83,000	83,050	21,392	18,593	22,113	19,776
83,050	83,100	21,408	18,607	22,129	19,791
83,100	83,150	21,423	18,621	22,144	19,807
83,150	83,200	21,439	18,635	22,160	19,822
83,200	83,250	21,454	18,649	22,175	19,838
83,250	83,300	21,470	18,663	22,191	19,853
83,300	83,350	21,485	18,677	22,206	19,869
83,350	83,400	21,501	18,691	22,222	19,884
83,400	83,450	21,516	18,705	22,237	19,900
83,450	83,500	21,532	18,719	22,253	19,915
83,500	83,550	21,547	18,733	22,268	19,931
83,550	83,600	21,563	18,747	22,284	19,946
83,600	83,650	21,578	18,761	22,299	19,962
83,650	83,700	21,594	18,775	22,315	19,977
83,700	83,750	21,609	18,789	22,330	19,993
83,750	83,800	21,625	18,803	22,346	20,008
83,800	83,850	21,640	18,817	22,361	20,024
83,850	83,900	21,656	18,831	22,377	20,039
83,900	83,950	21,671	18,845	22,392	20,055
83,950	84,000	21,687	18,859	22,408	20,070

84,000

At least	But less than	Single	Married filing jointly	Married filing separately	Head of a household
84,000	84,050	21,702	18,873	22,423	20,086
84,050	84,100	21,718	18,887	22,439	20,101
84,100	84,150	21,733	18,901	22,454	20,117
84,150	84,200	21,749	18,915	22,470	20,132
84,200	84,250	21,764	18,929	22,485	20,148
84,250	84,300	21,780	18,943	22,501	20,163
84,300	84,350	21,795	18,957	22,516	20,179
84,350	84,400	21,811	18,971	22,532	20,194
84,400	84,450	21,826	18,985	22,547	20,210
84,450	84,500	21,842	18,999	22,563	20,225
84,500	84,550	21,857	19,013	22,578	20,241
84,550	84,600	21,873	19,027	22,594	20,256
84,600	84,650	21,888	19,041	22,609	20,272
84,650	84,700	21,904	19,055	22,625	20,287
84,700	84,750	21,919	19,069	22,640	20,303
84,750	84,800	21,935	19,083	22,656	20,318
84,800	84,850	21,950	19,097	22,671	20,334
84,850	84,900	21,966	19,111	22,687	20,349
84,900	84,950	21,981	19,125	22,702	20,365
84,950	85,000	21,997	19,139	22,718	20,380

85,000

At least	But less than	Single	Married filing jointly	Married filing separately	Head of a household
85,000	85,050	22,012	19,153	22,733	20,396
85,050	85,100	22,028	19,167	22,749	20,411
85,100	85,150	22,043	19,181	22,764	20,427
85,150	85,200	22,059	19,195	22,780	20,442
85,200	85,250	22,074	19,209	22,795	20,458
85,250	85,300	22,090	19,223	22,811	20,473
85,300	85,350	22,105	19,237	22,826	20,489
85,350	85,400	22,121	19,251	22,842	20,504
85,400	85,450	22,136	19,265	22,857	20,520
85,450	85,500	22,152	19,279	22,873	20,535
85,500	85,550	22,167	19,293	22,888	20,551
85,550	85,600	22,183	19,307	22,904	20,566
85,600	85,650	22,198	19,321	22,919	20,582
85,650	85,700	22,214	19,335	22,935	20,597
85,700	85,750	22,229	19,349	22,950	20,613
85,750	85,800	22,245	19,363	22,966	20,628
85,800	85,850	22,260	19,377	22,981	20,644
85,850	85,900	22,276	19,391	22,997	20,659
85,900	85,950	22,291	19,405	23,012	20,675
85,950	86,000	22,307	19,419	23,028	20,690

* This column must also be used by a qualifying widow(er).

Continued on next page

If taxable income is—		And you are—			
At least	But less than	Single	Married filing jointly *	Married filing separately	Head of a household
		Your tax is—			

86,000

At least	But less than	Single	Married filing jointly	Married filing separately	Head of a household
86,000	86,050	22,322	19,433	23,043	20,706
86,050	86,100	22,338	19,447	23,059	20,721
86,100	86,150	22,353	19,461	23,074	20,737
86,150	86,200	22,369	19,475	23,090	20,752
86,200	86,250	22,384	19,489	23,105	20,768
86,250	86,300	22,400	19,503	23,121	20,783
86,300	86,350	22,415	19,517	23,136	20,799
86,350	86,400	22,431	19,531	23,152	20,814
86,400	86,450	22,446	19,545	23,167	20,830
86,450	86,500	22,462	19,559	23,183	20,845
86,500	86,550	22,477	19,574	23,198	20,861
86,550	86,600	22,493	19,589	23,214	20,876
86,600	86,650	22,508	19,605	23,229	20,892
86,650	86,700	22,524	19,620	23,245	20,907
86,700	86,750	22,539	19,636	23,260	20,923
86,750	86,800	22,555	19,651	23,276	20,938
86,800	86,850	22,570	19,667	23,291	20,954
86,850	86,900	22,586	19,682	23,307	20,969
86,900	86,950	22,601	19,698	23,322	20,985
86,950	87,000	22,617	19,713	23,338	21,000

87,000

At least	But less than	Single	Married filing jointly	Married filing separately	Head of a household
87,000	87,050	22,632	19,729	23,353	21,016
87,050	87,100	22,648	19,744	23,369	21,031
87,100	87,150	22,663	19,760	23,384	21,047
87,150	87,200	22,679	19,775	23,400	21,062
87,200	87,250	22,694	19,791	23,415	21,078
87,250	87,300	22,710	19,806	23,431	21,093
87,300	87,350	22,725	19,822	23,446	21,109
87,350	87,400	22,741	19,837	23,462	21,124
87,400	87,450	22,756	19,853	23,477	21,140
87,450	87,500	22,772	19,868	23,493	21,155
87,500	87,550	22,787	19,884	23,508	21,171
87,550	87,600	22,803	19,899	23,524	21,186
87,600	87,650	22,818	19,915	23,539	21,202
87,650	87,700	22,834	19,930	23,555	21,217
87,700	87,750	22,849	19,946	23,570	21,233
87,750	87,800	22,865	19,961	23,586	21,248
87,800	87,850	22,880	19,977	23,601	21,264
87,850	87,900	22,896	19,992	23,617	21,279
87,900	87,950	22,911	20,008	23,632	21,295
87,950	88,000	22,927	20,023	23,648	21,310

88,000

At least	But less than	Single	Married filing jointly	Married filing separately	Head of a household
88,000	88,050	22,942	20,039	23,663	21,326
88,050	88,100	22,958	20,054	23,679	21,341
88,100	88,150	22,973	20,070	23,694	21,357
88,150	88,200	22,989	20,085	23,710	21,372
88,200	88,250	23,004	20,101	23,725	21,388
88,250	88,300	23,020	20,116	23,741	21,403
88,300	88,350	23,035	20,132	23,756	21,419
88,350	88,400	23,051	20,147	23,772	21,434
88,400	88,450	23,066	20,163	23,787	21,450
88,450	88,500	23,082	20,178	23,803	21,465
88,500	88,550	23,097	20,194	23,818	21,481
88,550	88,600	23,113	20,209	23,834	21,496
88,600	88,650	23,128	20,225	23,849	21,512
88,650	88,700	23,144	20,240	23,865	21,527
88,700	88,750	23,159	20,256	23,880	21,543
88,750	88,800	23,175	20,271	23,896	21,558
88,800	88,850	23,190	20,287	23,911	21,574
88,850	88,900	23,206	20,302	23,927	21,589
88,900	88,950	23,221	20,318	23,942	21,605
88,950	89,000	23,237	20,333	23,958	21,620

89,000

At least	But less than	Single	Married filing jointly	Married filing separately	Head of a household
89,000	89,050	23,252	20,349	23,973	21,636
89,050	89,100	23,268	20,364	23,989	21,651
89,100	89,150	23,283	20,380	24,004	21,667
89,150	89,200	23,299	20,395	24,020	21,682
89,200	89,250	23,314	20,411	24,035	21,698
89,250	89,300	23,330	20,426	24,051	21,713
89,300	89,350	23,345	20,442	24,066	21,729
89,350	89,400	23,361	20,457	24,082	21,744
89,400	89,450	23,376	20,473	24,097	21,760
89,450	89,500	23,392	20,488	24,113	21,775
89,500	89,550	23,407	20,504	24,128	21,791
89,550	89,600	23,423	20,519	24,144	21,806
89,600	89,650	23,438	20,535	24,159	21,822
89,650	89,700	23,454	20,550	24,175	21,837
89,700	89,750	23,469	20,566	24,190	21,853
89,750	89,800	23,485	20,581	24,206	21,868
89,800	89,850	23,500	20,597	24,221	21,884
89,850	89,900	23,516	20,612	24,237	21,899
89,900	89,950	23,531	20,628	24,252	21,915
89,950	90,000	23,547	20,643	24,268	21,930

90,000

At least	But less than	Single	Married filing jointly	Married filing separately	Head of a household
90,000	90,050	23,562	20,659	24,283	21,946
90,050	90,100	23,578	20,674	24,299	21,961
90,100	90,150	23,593	20,690	24,314	21,977
90,150	90,200	23,609	20,705	24,330	21,992
90,200	90,250	23,624	20,721	24,345	22,008
90,250	90,300	23,640	20,736	24,361	22,023
90,300	90,350	23,655	20,752	24,376	22,039
90,350	90,400	23,671	20,767	24,392	22,054
90,400	90,450	23,686	20,783	24,407	22,070
90,450	90,500	23,702	20,798	24,423	22,085
90,500	90,550	23,717	20,814	24,438	22,101
90,550	90,600	23,733	20,829	24,454	22,116
90,600	90,650	23,748	20,845	24,469	22,132
90,650	90,700	23,764	20,860	24,485	22,147
90,700	90,750	23,779	20,876	24,500	22,163
90,750	90,800	23,795	20,891	24,516	22,178
90,800	90,850	23,810	20,907	24,531	22,194
90,850	90,900	23,826	20,922	24,547	22,209
90,900	90,950	23,841	20,938	24,562	22,225
90,950	91,000	23,857	20,953	24,578	22,240

91,000

At least	But less than	Single	Married filing jointly	Married filing separately	Head of a household
91,000	91,050	23,872	20,969	24,593	22,256
91,050	91,100	23,888	20,984	24,609	22,271
91,100	91,150	23,903	21,000	24,624	22,287
91,150	91,200	23,919	21,015	24,640	22,302
91,200	91,250	23,934	21,031	24,655	22,318
91,250	91,300	23,950	21,046	24,671	22,333
91,300	91,350	23,965	21,062	24,686	22,349
91,350	91,400	23,981	21,077	24,702	22,364
91,400	91,450	23,996	21,093	24,717	22,380
91,450	91,500	24,012	21,108	24,733	22,395
91,500	91,550	24,027	21,124	24,748	22,411
91,550	91,600	24,043	21,139	24,764	22,426
91,600	91,650	24,058	21,155	24,779	22,442
91,650	91,700	24,074	21,170	24,795	22,457
91,700	91,750	24,089	21,186	24,810	22,473
91,750	91,800	24,105	21,201	24,826	22,488
91,800	91,850	24,120	21,217	24,841	22,504
91,850	91,900	24,136	21,232	24,857	22,519
91,900	91,950	24,151	21,248	24,872	22,535
91,950	92,000	24,167	21,263	24,888	22,550

92,000

At least	But less than	Single	Married filing jointly	Married filing separately	Head of a household
92,000	92,050	24,182	21,279	24,903	22,566
92,050	92,100	24,198	21,294	24,919	22,581
92,100	92,150	24,213	21,310	24,934	22,597
92,150	92,200	24,229	21,325	24,950	22,612
92,200	92,250	24,244	21,341	24,965	22,628
92,250	92,300	24,260	21,356	24,981	22,643
92,300	92,350	24,275	21,372	24,996	22,659
92,350	92,400	24,291	21,387	25,012	22,674
92,400	92,450	24,306	21,403	25,027	22,690
92,450	92,500	24,322	21,418	25,043	22,705
92,500	92,550	24,337	21,434	25,058	22,721
92,550	92,600	24,353	21,449	25,074	22,736
92,600	92,650	24,368	21,465	25,089	22,752
92,650	92,700	24,384	21,480	25,105	22,767
92,700	92,750	24,399	21,496	25,120	22,783
92,750	92,800	24,415	21,511	25,136	22,798
92,800	92,850	24,430	21,527	25,151	22,814
92,850	92,900	24,446	21,542	25,167	22,829
92,900	92,950	24,461	21,558	25,182	22,845
92,950	93,000	24,477	21,573	25,198	22,860

93,000

At least	But less than	Single	Married filing jointly	Married filing separately	Head of a household
93,000	93,050	24,492	21,589	25,213	22,876
93,050	93,100	24,508	21,604	25,229	22,891
93,100	93,150	24,523	21,620	25,244	22,907
93,150	93,200	24,539	21,635	25,260	22,922
93,200	93,250	24,554	21,651	25,275	22,938
93,250	93,300	24,570	21,666	25,291	22,953
93,300	93,350	24,585	21,682	25,306	22,969
93,350	93,400	24,601	21,697	25,322	22,984
93,400	93,450	24,616	21,713	25,337	23,000
93,450	93,500	24,632	21,728	25,353	23,015
93,500	93,550	24,647	21,744	25,368	23,031
93,550	93,600	24,663	21,759	25,384	23,046
93,600	93,650	24,678	21,775	25,399	23,062
93,650	93,700	24,694	21,790	25,415	23,077
93,700	93,750	24,709	21,806	25,430	23,093
93,750	93,800	24,725	21,821	25,446	23,108
93,800	93,850	24,740	21,837	25,461	23,124
93,850	93,900	24,756	21,852	25,477	23,139
93,900	93,950	24,771	21,868	25,492	23,155
93,950	94,000	24,787	21,883	25,508	23,170

94,000

At least	But less than	Single	Married filing jointly	Married filing separately	Head of a household
94,000	94,050	24,802	21,899	25,523	23,186
94,050	94,100	24,818	21,914	25,539	23,201
94,100	94,150	24,833	21,930	25,554	23,217
94,150	94,200	24,849	21,945	25,570	23,232
94,200	94,250	24,864	21,961	25,585	23,248
94,250	94,300	24,880	21,976	25,601	23,263
94,300	94,350	24,895	21,992	25,616	23,279
94,350	94,400	24,911	22,007	25,632	23,294
94,400	94,450	24,926	22,023	25,647	23,310
94,450	94,500	24,942	22,038	25,663	23,325
94,500	94,550	24,957	22,054	25,678	23,341
94,550	94,600	24,973	22,069	25,694	23,356
94,600	94,650	24,988	22,085	25,709	23,372
94,650	94,700	25,004	22,100	25,725	23,387
94,700	94,750	25,019	22,116	25,740	23,403
94,750	94,800	25,035	22,131	25,756	23,418
94,800	94,850	25,050	22,147	25,771	23,434
94,850	94,900	25,066	22,162	25,787	23,449
94,900	94,950	25,081	22,178	25,802	23,465
94,950	95,000	25,097	22,193	25,818	23,480

* This column must also be used by a qualifying widow(er).

Continued on next page

95,000

If taxable income is— At least	But less than	Single	Married filing jointly *	Married filing separately	Head of a household
95,000	95,050	25,112	22,209	25,833	23,496
95,050	95,100	25,128	22,224	25,849	23,511
95,100	95,150	25,143	22,240	25,864	23,527
95,150	95,200	25,159	22,255	25,880	23,542
95,200	95,250	25,174	22,271	25,895	23,558
95,250	95,300	25,190	22,286	25,911	23,573
95,300	95,350	25,205	22,302	25,926	23,589
95,350	95,400	25,221	22,317	25,942	23,604
95,400	95,450	25,236	22,333	25,957	23,620
95,450	95,500	25,252	22,348	25,973	23,635
95,500	95,550	25,267	22,364	25,988	23,651
95,550	95,600	25,283	22,379	26,004	23,666
95,600	95,650	25,298	22,395	26,019	23,682
95,650	95,700	25,314	22,410	26,035	23,697
95,700	95,750	25,329	22,426	26,050	23,713
95,750	95,800	25,345	22,441	26,066	23,728
95,800	95,850	25,360	22,457	26,081	23,744
95,850	95,900	25,376	22,472	26,097	23,759
95,900	95,950	25,391	22,488	26,112	23,775
95,950	96,000	25,407	22,503	26,128	23,790

96,000

If taxable income is— At least	But less than	Single	Married filing jointly *	Married filing separately	Head of a household
96,000	96,050	25,422	22,519	26,143	23,806
96,050	96,100	25,438	22,534	26,159	23,821
96,100	96,150	25,453	22,550	26,174	23,837
96,150	96,200	25,469	22,565	26,190	23,852
96,200	96,250	25,484	22,581	26,205	23,868
96,250	96,300	25,500	22,596	26,221	23,883
96,300	96,350	25,515	22,612	26,236	23,899
96,350	96,400	25,531	22,627	26,252	23,914
96,400	96,450	25,546	22,643	26,267	23,930
96,450	96,500	25,562	22,658	26,283	23,945
96,500	96,550	25,577	22,674	26,298	23,961
96,550	96,600	25,593	22,689	26,314	23,976
96,600	96,650	25,608	22,705	26,329	23,992
96,650	96,700	25,624	22,720	26,345	24,007
96,700	96,750	25,639	22,736	26,360	24,023
96,750	96,800	25,655	22,751	26,376	24,038
96,800	96,850	25,670	22,767	26,391	24,054
96,850	96,900	25,686	22,782	26,407	24,069
96,900	96,950	25,701	22,798	26,422	24,085
96,950	97,000	25,717	22,813	26,438	24,100

97,000

If taxable income is— At least	But less than	Single	Married filing jointly *	Married filing separately	Head of a household
97,000	97,050	25,732	22,829	26,453	24,116
97,050	97,100	25,748	22,844	26,469	24,131
97,100	97,150	25,763	22,860	26,484	24,147
97,150	97,200	25,779	22,875	26,500	24,162
97,200	97,250	25,794	22,891	26,515	24,178
97,250	97,300	25,810	22,906	26,531	24,193
97,300	97,350	25,825	22,922	26,546	24,209
97,350	97,400	25,841	22,937	26,562	24,224
97,400	97,450	25,856	22,953	26,577	24,240
97,450	97,500	25,872	22,968	26,593	24,255
97,500	97,550	25,887	22,984	26,608	24,271
97,550	97,600	25,903	22,999	26,624	24,286
97,600	97,650	25,918	23,015	26,639	24,302
97,650	97,700	25,934	23,030	26,655	24,317
97,700	97,750	25,949	23,046	26,670	24,333
97,750	97,800	25,965	23,061	26,686	24,348
97,800	97,850	25,980	23,077	26,701	24,364
97,850	97,900	25,996	23,092	26,717	24,379
97,900	97,950	26,011	23,108	26,732	24,395
97,950	98,000	26,027	23,123	26,748	24,410

98,000

If taxable income is— At least	But less than	Single	Married filing jointly *	Married filing separately	Head of a household
98,000	98,050	26,042	23,139	26,763	24,426
98,050	98,100	26,058	23,154	26,779	24,441
98,100	98,150	26,073	23,170	26,794	24,457
98,150	98,200	26,089	23,185	26,810	24,472
98,200	98,250	26,104	23,201	26,825	24,488
98,250	98,300	26,120	23,216	26,841	24,503
98,300	98,350	26,135	23,232	26,856	24,519
98,350	98,400	26,151	23,247	26,872	24,534
98,400	98,450	26,166	23,263	26,887	24,550
98,450	98,500	26,182	23,278	26,903	24,565
98,500	98,550	26,197	23,294	26,918	24,581
98,550	98,600	26,213	23,309	26,934	24,596
98,600	98,650	26,228	23,325	26,949	24,612
98,650	98,700	26,244	23,340	26,965	24,627
98,700	98,750	26,259	23,356	26,980	24,643
98,750	98,800	26,275	23,371	26,996	24,658
98,800	98,850	26,290	23,387	27,011	24,674
98,850	98,900	26,306	23,402	27,027	24,689
98,900	98,950	26,321	23,418	27,042	24,705
98,950	99,000	26,337	23,433	27,058	24,720

99,000

If taxable income is— At least	But less than	Single	Married filing jointly *	Married filing separately	Head of a household
99,000	99,050	26,352	23,449	27,073	24,736
99,050	99,100	26,368	23,464	27,089	24,751
99,100	99,150	26,383	23,480	27,104	24,767
99,150	99,200	26,399	23,495	27,120	24,782
99,200	99,250	26,414	23,511	27,135	24,798
99,250	99,300	26,430	23,526	27,151	24,813
99,300	99,350	26,445	23,542	27,166	24,829
99,350	99,400	26,461	23,557	27,182	24,844
99,400	99,450	26,476	23,573	27,197	24,860
99,450	99,500	26,492	23,588	27,213	24,875
99,500	99,550	26,507	23,604	27,228	24,891
99,550	99,600	26,523	23,619	27,244	24,906
99,600	99,650	26,538	23,635	27,259	24,922
99,650	99,700	26,554	23,650	27,275	24,937
99,700	99,750	26,569	23,666	27,290	24,953
99,750	99,800	26,585	23,681	27,306	24,968
99,800	99,850	26,600	23,697	27,321	24,984
99,850	99,900	26,616	23,712	27,337	24,999
99,900	99,950	26,631	23,728	27,352	25,015
99,950	100,000	26,647	23,743	27,368	25,030

100,000 or over — use tax rate schedules

* This column must also be used by a qualifying widow(er).

PART
IX

GLOSSARY AND INDEX

The following features will help you quickly find answers to your specific tax questions.

- *Treasury of Tax Terms.* This useful glossary explains technical tax terms in plain, easy to understand language.
- *Index.* The index directs you to both the exact page and section where an item you are interested in is discussed.

TREASURY OF TAX TERMS

Accelerated Cost Recovery System (ACRS). A statutory method of depreciation allowing accelerated rates for most types of property used in business and income-producing activities during the years 1981 through 1986. It has been superseded by Modified Cost Recovery System (MACRS) for assets placed in service after 1986; *see* ¶42.4.

Accelerated depreciation. Depreciation methods that allow faster write-offs than straight-line rates in the earlier periods of the useful life of an asset. For example, in the first few years of recovery, MACRS allows a 200% double declining balance write-off, twice the straight-line rate; *see* ¶42.5 and ¶42.8.

Accountable reimbursement plan. An employer reimbursement or allowance arrangement that requires you to adequately substantiate business expenses to your employer, and to return any excess reimbursement; *see* ¶20.34.

Accrual method of accounting. A business method of accounting requiring income to be reported when earned and expenses to be deducted when incurred. However, deductions generally may not be claimed until economic performance has occurred; *see* ¶40.2.

Acquisition debt. Debt used to buy, build, or construct a principal residence or second home and which generally qualifies for a full interest expense deduction; *see* ¶15.2.

Active participation. Test for determining deductibility of IRA deductions. Active participants in employer retirement plans are subject to IRA deduction phaseout rules if adjusted gross income exceeds certain thresholds; *see* ¶8.3.

Adjusted basis. A statutory term describing the cost used to determine your profit or loss from a sale or exchange of property. It is generally your original cost, increased by capital improvements, and decreased by depreciation, depletion, and other capital write-offs; *see* ¶5.16.

Adjusted Gross Income (AGI). Important tax term representing gross income *less* allowable adjustments, such as for IRA, alimony, and Keogh deductions. AGI determines whether various tax benefits are phased out, such as personal exemptions, itemized deductions, and the rental loss allowance; *see* ¶13.7.

Alimony. Payments made to a separated or divorced spouse as required by a decree or agreement. Qualifying payments are deductible by the payor and taxable to the payee; *see* Chapter 37.

Alternative minimum tax (AMT). A tax triggered if certain tax benefits reduce your regular income tax below the tax computed on Form 6251 for AMT purposes; *see* Chapter 23.

Amended return. On Form 1040X, you may file an amended return within a three-year period to correct a mistake made on an original return; *see* Chapter 38.

Amortizable bond premium. The additional amount paid over face amount of obligation which may be deducted under rules of ¶4.17.

Amortization. Writing off an investment in intangible assets over the projected life of the assets.

Amount realized. A statutory term used to figure your profit or loss on a sale or exchange. Generally, it is sales proceeds plus mortgages assumed or taken subject to, less transaction expenses, such as commissions and legal costs; *see* ¶5.10.

Amount recognized. The amount of gain reportable and subject to tax. On certain tax-free exchanges of property, gain is not recognized in the year it is realized; *see* ¶6.1.

Annualized rate. A rate for a period of less than a year computed as though for a full year.

Annuity. An annual payment of money by a company or individual to a person called the annuitant. Payment is for a fixed period or

the life of the annuitant. Tax consequences depend on the type of contract and funding; *see* ¶7.22 and ¶7.25.

Applicable federal rate. Interest rate fixed by Treasury for determining imputed interest; *see* ¶4.31 and ¶4.32.

Appreciation in value. Increase in value of property due to market conditions. When you sell appreciated property, you pay tax on the appreciation since the date of purchase. When you donate appreciated property held long term, you may generally deduct the appreciated property; *see* ¶14.6.

Assessment. The IRS action of fixing tax liability that sets in motion collection procedures, such as charging interest, imposing penalties, and if necessary, seizing property.

Asset. Anything owned that has cash or exchange value.

Assignment. The legal transfer of property, rights, or interest to another person called an assignee. You cannot avoid tax on income by assigning the income to another person.

At-risk rules. Limits loss deductions to cash investments and personal liability notes. An exception for real estate treats certain non-recourse commercial loans as amounts "at risk"; *see* ¶10.17.

Attorneys' fee awards. Taxpayers who prevail in the Tax Court or other federal court may recover up to an amount for attorneys' fees, plus other litigation expenses, by showing that the IRS position was unreasonable; *see* ¶48.7.

Audit. An IRS examination of your tax return, generally limited to a three-year period after you file; *see* ¶48.1.

Averaging. Retirees who reached age 50 by January 1, 1986, may use favorable averaging methods to compute tax on a lump-sum distribution if they participated in the plan for at least five years. Either a five-year or ten-year averaging method may be elected on Form 4972; *see* ¶7.3 and ¶7.4.

Away from home. A tax requirement for deducting travel expenses on a business trip. Sleeping arrangements are required for at least one night before returning home; *see* ¶20.3 and 20.5.

Balloon. A final payment on a loan in one lump sum.

Basis. Generally, the amount paid for property. You need to know your "basis" to figure gain or loss on a sale; *see* ¶5.12.

Boot. Generally the receipt of cash or its equivalent accompanying an exchange of property. In a tax-free exchange, boot is subject to immediate tax; *see* ¶6.3.

Calendar year. A year that ends on December 31.

Cancellation of debt. Release of a debt without consideration by a creditor. Cancellations of debt are generally taxable; *see* ¶12.9.

Capital. The excess of assets over liabilities.

Capital asset. Property subject to capital gain or loss treatment. Almost all assets you own are considered capital assets except for certain business assets or works you created; *see* page 69.

Capital expenses. Costs that are not currently deductible and that are added to the basis of property. A capital expense generally increases the value of property. When added to depreciable property, the cost is deductible over the life of the asset; *see* ¶40.7.

Capital gain or loss. The difference between amount realized and adjusted basis on the sale or exchange of capital assets. Capital gain is taxed the same as other types of income, even if it is long term. However, net long-term capital gains are subject to a tax ceiling of 28%. Capital losses are deducted first against capital gains, and then against up to $3,000 of other income; *see* ¶5.1.

Capital gain dividend. A mutual fund dividend allocated to gains realized on the sale of fund portfolio assets. You report the dividend as long-term capital gain even if you held the fund shares short term; *see* ¶4.3.

Capital loss carryover. A capital loss that is not deductible because it exceeds the annual $3,000 capital loss ceiling. A carryover loss may be deducted from capital gains of later years plus up to $3,000 of ordinary income; *see* ¶5.2.

Capitalization. Adding a cost or expense to the basis of the property; *see* ¶40.7.

Carryback. A tax technique for receiving a refund of back taxes by applying a deduction or credit from a current tax year to a prior tax year. For example, a business net operating loss may be carried back for three years; *see* ¶40.17.

Carryforward. A tax technique of applying a loss or credit from a current year to a later year. For example, a business net operating loss may be carried forward 15 years instead of being carried back for three years; *see* ¶40.17.

Cash method of accounting. Reporting income when actually or constructively received and deducting expenses when paid. Certain businesses may not use the cash method; *see* ¶40.2.

Casualty loss. Loss from an unforeseen and sudden event that is deductible, subject to a 10% income floor and $100 reduction for personal losses; *see* ¶18.11.

Charitable contributions. An itemized deduction is allowed for donations to qualifying charities. For property donations, the deductible amount depends on the type of property and donee organization, your holding period, and in some cases how it is used; *see* Chapter 14.

Child and dependent credit. A credit of up to 30% based on certain care expenses incurred to allow you to work; *see* ¶25.1.

Child support. Payments to support a minor child generally to a custodial parent under a divorce or separation decree or agreement. The payments are not deductible; *see* ¶37.5.

Clifford trust. A short-term trust in which the principal is reserved by the grantor and current income is paid to the beneficiary. The tax-saving features of such trusts have been blocked by current tax rules; *see* ¶33.6.

Community income. Income earned in community property states and treated as belonging equally to husband and wife; *see* ¶1.9.

Condemnation. The seizure of property by a public authority for a public purpose. Tax on gain realized on many conversions may be deferred; *see* ¶18.18 and ¶18.25.

Constructive receipt. A tax rule that taxes income which is not received by you but which you may draw upon; *see* ¶2.1.

Consumer interest. Interest incurred on personal debt and consumer credit. Consumer interest is no longer deductible.

Convention. Rule for determining MACRS depreciation in the year property is placed in service. Either a half-year convention or mid-quarter convention applies; *see* ¶42.5–¶42.7.

Corporation. An entity organized under state law and generally treated as a separate taxpayer unless an S election is made; *see* ¶45.5.

Credit. A tax credit directly reduces tax liability, as opposed to a deduction that reduces income subject to tax.

Declining balance method. A rapid depreciation method determined by a constant percentage based on useful life and applied to the adjusted basis of the property. For example, a 40% declining balance rate applies to business automobiles, but it must be reduced by a half-year or mid-quarter convention; *see* ¶42.5 and ¶42.8.

Deductions. Items directly reducing income. Personal deductions such as for mortgage interest, state and local taxes, and charitable contributions are allowed only if deductions are itemized on Schedule A, but deductions, such as for alimony, capital losses, business losses, and IRA and Keogh deductions are deducted from gross income even if itemized deductions are not claimed; *see* ¶13.7.

Deferred compensation. A portion of earnings withheld by an employer or put into a retirement plan for distribution to the employee at a later date. If certain legal requirements are met, the deferred amount is not taxable until actually paid, for example, after retirement; *see* ¶2.8.

Deficiency. The difference between the tax assessed by the IRS and the amount reported on your return; *see* ¶47.1.

Defined benefit plan. A retirement plan that pays fixed benefits based on actuarial projections; *see* ¶41.2.

Defined contribution plan. A retirement plan which pays benefits based on contributions to individual accounts, plus accumulated earnings. Contributions are generally based on a percentage of salary or earned income; *see* ¶41.2.

Dependency exemption. A fixed deduction allowed to every taxpayer, except those who may be claimed as a dependent by another person. Extra exemption deductions are allowed for a spouse on a joint return and for each qualifying dependent. A deduction of $2,300 is allowed for each exemption claimed on 1992 returns, but the deduction is phased out for certain high income individuals; *see* ¶1.32.

Dependent. A person supported by another person. If certain tests are met, a dependency exemption may be claimed for the dependent; *see* page 19.

Depletion. Deduction claimed for the use of mineral resources; *see* ¶9.14.

Depreciable property. A business or income-producing asset with a useful life exceeding one year; *see* ¶42.1.

Depreciation. Writing off the cost of depreciable property over a period of years, usually its class life or recovery period specified in the tax law; *see* ¶42.4.

Depreciation recapture. An amount of gain on the sale of certain depreciable property that is treated as ordinary income, rather than capital gain. Recapture is computed on Form 4797; *see* ¶44.1 and ¶44.2.

Disaster losses. Casualty losses such as from a storm, in areas declared by the President to warrant federal assistance. An election may be made to deduct the loss in the year before the loss or the year of the loss; *see* ¶18.2.

Dividend. A distribution made by a corporation to its shareholders generally of company earnings or surplus. Most dividends are taxable but exceptions are explained in Chapter 4.

Earned income. Compensation for performing personal services. You must have earned income for a deductible IRA; *see* ¶8.2.

Earned income credit. A credit to lower-income taxpayers with dependent children. For 1992, the credit is available to parents with adjusted gross income of less than $22,370; *see* Chapter 25.

Estate tax. Imposed if the value of a decedent's taxable estate, after deductions, exceeds $600,000; *see* ¶39.5.

Estimated tax. Advance payment of current tax liability based either on wage withholdings or installment payments of your estimated tax liability. To avoid penalties, you generally must pay to the IRS either 90% of your final tax liability, or 100% of the prior year's tax liability; *see* ¶27.2.

Excess distributions. Retirement payments exceeding specified limits are subject to a 15% penalty unless rolled over to an IRA or other exceptions are met; *see* ¶7.15.

Exemption. *See* **Dependency exemption.**

Fair market value. What a willing buyer would pay to a willing seller when neither is under any compulsion to buy or sell.

Fiduciary. A person or corporation such as a trustee, executor, or guardian who manages property for another person.

First-year expensing. A deduction of up to $10,000 of the cost of business equipment allowed in the year placed in service but subject to income and investment limits; *see* ¶42.3.

Fiscal year. A 12-month period ending on the last day of any month other than December. Partnerships, S corporations, and personal service corporations are limited in their choice of fiscal years and face special restrictions; *see* Chapter 45.

Flexible spending arrangements. A salary reduction plan which allows employees to pay for enhanced medical coverage or dependent care expenses on a tax-free basis; *see* ¶3.13.

Foreign earned income exclusion. Up to $70,000 of foreign earned income is exempt from tax if a foreign residence or physical presence test is met; *see* ¶36.2.

Foreign tax credit. A credit for income taxes paid to a foreign country or U.S. possession; *see* ¶36.14.

401(k) Plan. A deferred pay plan, authorized by section 401(k) of the Internal Revenue Code, under which a percentage of an employee's salary is withheld and placed in a savings account or the company's profit-sharing plan. The salary deferral is tax free within an annual limitation, which is $8,728 for 1992. Income accumulates on the deferred amount until withdrawn by the employee at age 59½ or when the employee retires or leaves the company; *see* ¶7.17.

Gift tax. Gifts in excess of a $10,000 per donee annual exclusion are subject to gift tax, but the tax may be offset by a unified gift and estate tax credit; *see* ¶33.1.

Grantor trust rules. Tax rules that tax the grantor of a trust on the trust income; *see* ¶33.6.

Gross income. The total amount of income received from all sources before exclusions and deductions.

Gross receipts. Total business receipts reported on Schedule C before deducting adjustments for returns and allowances and cost of goods sold; *see* ¶40.5.

Group-term life insurance. Employees are not taxed on up to $50,000 of group-term coverage; *see* ¶3.2.

Head of household. Generally, an unmarried person who maintains a household for dependents and is allowed to compute his or her tax based on head of household rates, which are more favorable than single person rates; *see* ¶1.10.

Hobby loss. Hobby expenses are deductible only up to income from the activity; loss deductions are not allowed; *see* ¶40.9.

Holding period. The length of time which an asset is owned and which generally determines long- or short-term capital gain treatment; *see* ¶5.5.

Home equity debt. Debt secured by a principal residence or second home to the extent of the excess of fair market value over acquisition debt. An interest deduction is generally allowed for home equity debt up to $100,000 ($50,000 married filing separately); *see* ¶15.3.

Imputed interest. Interest deemed earned on seller-financed sales or low-interest loans, where the parties' stated interest rate is below the applicable IRS federal rate; *see* ¶4.31 and ¶4.32.

Incentive stock option. Options meeting tax law tests that defer tax on the option transaction until the obtained stock is sold; *see* ¶32.6.

Income in respect of a decedent. Income earned by a person before death but taxable to estate or heir who receives it; *see* ¶1.12 and ¶11.4.

Independent contractor. One who controls his or her own work and reports as a self-employed person; *see* Chapters 40 and 46.

Individual retirement account (IRA). A retirement account to which up to $2,000 may be contributed annually, but deductions for the contribution are restricted if you are covered by a company retirement plan. Earnings accumulate tax free on IRA contributions. Restrictions and limits are discussed in Chapter 8.

Innocent spouse. A spouse who claims that he or she should not be liable on joint return because of ignorance of the other spouse's omission of income or claiming of excessive write-offs; *see* ¶1.4.

Installment sale. A sale of property that allows for tax deferment if at least one payment is received after the end of the tax year in which the sale occurs. The installment method does not apply to year-end sales of publicly-traded securities. Dealers may not use the installment method. Investors with very large installment balances could face a special tax; *see* ¶5.36.

Inter vivos or lifetime trust. A trust created during the lifetime of the person who created the trust. If irrevocable, income on the trust principal is shifted to the trust beneficiaries; *see* ¶33.6.

Investment in the contract. The total cost investment in an annuity. When annuity payments are made, the portion allocable to the cost investment is tax free; *see* ¶7.22 and ¶7.27.

Investment interest. Interest or debt used to carry investments, but not including interest expense from a passive activity. Deductions are limited to net investment income; *see* ¶15.9.

Involuntary conversion. Forced disposition of property due to condemnation, theft, or casualty. Tax on gain from involuntary conversions may be deferred if replacement property is purchased; *see* ¶18.19.

Itemized deductions. Items such as interest, state and local taxes, charitable contributions, and medical deductions that are claimed on Schedule A of Form 1040 and which reduce adjusted gross income to arrive at taxable income; *see* Chapter 13.

Joint ownership. Ownership of property by two persons. When one dies, the decedent's interest passes to the survivor; *see* ¶33.5.

Joint return. A return filed by a married couple reporting their combined income and deductions. Joint return status provides tax savings to many couples; *see* ¶1.2.

Keogh plan. Retirement plan set up by a self-employed person, providing tax deductible contributions, tax-free income accumulations until withdrawal, and favorable averaging for qualifying lump-sum distributions; *see* Chapter 41.

Kiddie tax. The tax on the investment income of a dependent child under age 14 in excess of $1,200, based on parents' marginal tax rate and computed on Form 8615; *see* ¶24.3.

Legally separated. A husband and wife who are required to live apart from each other by the terms of a decree of separate maintenance. Payments under the decree are deductible by the payor and taxable to the payee as alimony; *see* ¶37.2.

Like-kind exchange. An exchange of similar assets used in a business or held for investment on which gain may be deferred; *see* ¶6.1.

Long-term capital gain or loss. Gain or loss on the sale or exchange of a capital asset held for more than one year; *see* ¶5.5.

Lump-sum distribution. Payments within one tax year of the entire amount due to a participant in a qualified retirement plan because of retirement, separation from service, reaching age 59½, death, or in the case of a self-employed person, becoming disabled or reaching age 59½. Qualifying lump-sums may be rolled over tax free, or, in some cases, eligible for current tax under a favorable averaging method; *see* ¶7.3.

Luxury automobile limits. Ceiling placed on annual depreciation deductions for autos used for business; *see* ¶43.3.

Marital deduction. An estate tax and gift tax deduction for assets passing to a spouse. It allows estate and gift transfers completely free of tax; *see* ¶39.6.

Market discount. The difference between face value of bond and lower market price, attributable to rising interest rates. On a sale, gain on the bond is generally taxed as ordinary income to the extent of the discount; *see* ¶4.20.

GLOSSARY

Material participation tests. Rules for determining whether a person is active in a business activity for passive activity rule purposes. Unless the tests are met, passive loss limits apply; *see* ¶10.6.

Miscellaneous itemized deductions. Generally itemized deductions for job and investment expenses subject to a 2% adjusted gross income floor; *see* Chapter 19.

Modified ACRS (MACRS). Depreciation methods applied to assets placed in service after 1986. MACRS is less favorable than prior ACRS system; *see* ¶42.4.

Mortgage interest. Fully deductible interest on up to two residences if acquisition debt secured by home is $1 million or less, and home equity debt is $100,000 or less; *see* ¶15.2 and ¶15.3.

Net operating loss. Business loss which exceeds current income and which may be carried back against income of three prior years and carried forward as a deduction from future income for fifteen years until eliminated; *see* ¶40.17.

Nonrecourse financing. Debt on which a person is not personally liable. In case of nonpayment, the creditor must foreclose on property securing the debt. At risk rules generally bar losses where there is nonrecourse financing, but an exception applies to certain nonrecourse financing for real estate; *see* ¶10.17.

Nonresident alien. A person who is not a United States citizen or a permanent resident. Tax is generally limited to income from U.S. sources; *see* ¶1.14.

Ordinary and necessary. A legal requirement for deductibility of a business expense; *see* ¶40.7.

Ordinary income. Income other than capital gains.

Ordinary loss. A loss other than a capital loss.

Original issue discount (OID). The difference between the face value of a bond or its original issue price. OID is reported on an annual basis as interest income; *see* ¶4.18.

Partnership. An unincorporated business or income-producing entity organized by two or more persons. A partnership is not subject to tax but passes through to the partners all income, deductions, and credits, according to the terms of the partnership agreement; *see* Chapter 45.

Passive activity loss rules. Rules that limit the deduction of losses from passive activities to income from other passive activities. Passive activities include rental operations or businesses in which you do not materially participate; *see* ¶10. 1.

Patronage dividend. A taxable distribution made by a cooperative to its members or patrons.

Pension. Payments to employees from an employer-funded retirement plan for past services; *see* ¶7.25.

Percentage depletion. Method that applies a fixed percentage to the gross income generated by mineral property; *see* ¶9.14.

Personal exemption. An automatic exemption given to a taxpayer unless he or she may be claimed as a dependent by another taxpayer. For 1992, the exemption amount is $2,300. Exemptions are phased out for certain high income taxpayers; *see* ¶1.32.

Personal interest. Tax term for interest on personal loans and consumer purchases. Such interest is not deductible.

Placed in service. The time when a depreciable asset is ready to be used. The date fixes the beginning of depreciation period; *see* ¶42.5.

Points. Charges to the homeowner at the time of the loan. A point is equal to 1 percent. Depending on the type of loan, points may be currently deductible or amortized over the life of the loan; *see* ¶15.7.

Premature distributions. Withdrawals before age 59½ from qualified retirement plans are subject to penalties unless specific exceptions are met; *see* ¶7.14.

Principal residence. On a sale of a principal residence, you may defer tax on your profit if you buy a replacement within two years; *see* ¶29.4. On a sale of a principal residence at or after age 55, a $125,000 exclusion may be available; *see* ¶29.14.

Probate estate. Property held in a decedent's name passing by will; *see* ¶33.5 and ¶39.1.

Profit-sharing plan. A defined contribution plan under which the amount contributed to the employees' accounts is based on a percentage of the employer's profits; *see* ¶8.4 and ¶41.2.

Qualified charitable organization. A nonprofit philanthropic organization that is approved by the U.S. Treasury to receive charitable contribution deductions; *see* ¶14.1.

Qualified plan. A retirement plan that meets tax law tests and allows for tax deferment and tax-free accumulation of income until benefits are withdrawn. Pension, profit-sharing, stock bonus, employee stock ownership, and Keogh plans and IRAs may be qualified plans; *see* Chapters 7, 8, and 41.

Qualifying widow or widower. A filing status entitling the taxpayer with dependents to use joint tax rates for up to two tax years after the death of a spouse; *see* ¶1.6.

Real estate investment trust (REIT). An entity that invests primarily in real estate and mortgages and passes through income or loss to investors; *see* ¶31.1.

Real property. Land and the buildings on land. Buildings are depreciable; *see* ¶42.13 and ¶42.14.

Recognized gain or loss. The amount of gain or loss to be reported on a tax return. Gain may not be recognized on certain exchanges of property; *see* ¶6.1.

Recovery property. Tangible depreciable property placed in service after 1980 and before 1987 and depreciable under ACRS ; *see* ¶42.11 and ¶42.14.

Refundable tax credit. A credit that entitles you to a refund even if you owe no tax for the year.

Residence interest. Term for deductible mortgage interest on a principal residence and a second home; *see* ¶15.1.

Residential rental property. Real property in which 80% or more of the gross income is from dwelling units. Under MACRS, depreciation is claimed over 27.5 years under the straight-line method; *see* ¶42.13.

Return of capital. A distribution of your investment that is not subject to tax unless the distribution exceeds your investment; *see* ¶4.11.

Revocable trust. A trust that may be changed or terminated by its creator or another person. Such trusts do not provide an income tax savings to the creator; *see* ¶33.6.

Rollover. A tax-free reinvestment of a distribution from a qualified retirement plan into an IRA or other qualified plan within 60 days after receipt; *see* ¶7.3, ¶7.8 and ¶8.9.

Royalty income. Amounts received for the use of property such as mineral property, a book, a movie, or a patent; *see* ¶9.10.

Salvage value. The estimated value of an asset at the end of its useful life. Salvage value is ignored by ACRS and MACRS rules.

S corporation. A corporation that elects S status in order to receive tax treatment similar to a partnership; *see* ¶45.5.

Scholarships. Grants to degree candidates receive tax-free treatment if awarded after August 16, 1986, and used for tuition and course-related expenses, but not room and board. More favorable exclusion rules apply to awards made before August 17, 1986; *see* ¶12.4.

Section 179 deduction. First-year expensing. A deduction of up to $10,000, allowed for investments in tangible depreciable property in the year the property is placed in service; *see* ¶42.3.

Section 457 plan. Deferred compensation plan set up by state or local government, or tax-exempt organization, that allows tax-free deferrals of salary, generally up to the lesser of $7,500 or one-third of pay; *see* ¶7.21.

Section 1231 property. Depreciable property used in a trade or business and held long term. All Section 1231 gains and losses are netted; a net gain is treated as capital gain, a net loss as an ordinary loss; *see* ¶44.8.

Self-employed person. An individual who operates a business or profession as a proprietor or independent contractor and reports self-employment income on Schedule C; *see* Chapters 40 and 46.

Self-employment tax. Tax paid by self-employed persons to finance Social Security coverage. In 1992, there are two rates. A 15.3% rate applies to a taxable earnings base of $55,500 or less; and a 2.9% rate on a taxable earnings base exceeding $55,500 up to $130,200; *see* Chapter 46.

Separate return. Return filed by married person who does not file a joint return. Filing separately may save taxes where each spouse has separate deductions, but certain tax benefits require a joint return; *see* ¶1.2.

Short sale. Sale of borrowed securities made to freeze a paper profit or to gain from a declining market; *see* ¶5.20.

Short tax year. A tax year of less than 12 months. May occur with the start-up of a business or change in accounting method.

Short-term capital gain or loss. Gain or loss on the sale or exchange of a capital asset held one year or less; *see* ¶5.5.

Simplified employee plan (SEP). IRA-type plan set up by an employer, rather than the employee. Salary reduction contributions may be allowed to plans of small employers; *see* ¶8.11.

Single. The filing status of an individual who is not married on December 31 of the year for which the return is filed; *see* ¶1.1.

Standard deduction. A fixed deduction allowed to taxpayers who do not itemize deductions. The amount depends on filing status, age, and blindness; *see* ¶13.1.

Standard mileage rate. A fixed rate allowed by the IRS for business auto expenses in place of deducting actual expenses; *see* ¶43.1.

Statutory employees. Certain employees, such as full-time life insurance salespersons may report income and deductions on Schedule C rather than on Schedule A, as a miscellaneous itemized deduction; *see* ¶40.5.

Stock dividend. A corporate distribution of additional shares of its stock to its shareholders; *see* ¶4.6.

Stock option. A right to buy stock at a fixed price; *see* ¶32.6.

Straddle. Taking an offsetting investment position to reduce the risk of loss in a similar investment.

Straight-line method. A method of depreciating the cost of a depreciable asset on a pro rata basis over its useful life.

Tangible personal property. Movable property, such as desks, computers, machinery, and autos. Depreciable over a five-year or seven-year period; *see* ¶42.4.

Taxable income. Net income after claiming all deductions from gross income and adjusted gross income, such as IRA deductions, itemized deductions or the standard deduction, and personal exemptions; *see* ¶22.1.

Tax deferral. Shifting income to a later year, such as where you defer taxable interest to the following year by purchasing a T-bill or savings certificate maturing after the end of the current year; *see* Chapter 4. Investments in qualified retirement plans provide

tax deferral (*see* Chapters 7, 8, and 41). Deferral on gain from sale of your home is mandatory if you buy a qualifying replacement home within two years; *see* ¶29.4.

Tax home. The area of your principal place of business or employment. You must be away from your tax home on a business trip to deduct travel expenses; *see* ¶20.5.

Tax identification number. For an individual, his or her Social Security number; for businesses, fiduciaries, and other nonindividual taxpayers, employer identification number.

Tax preference items. Items that may subject a taxpayer to the alternative minimum tax (AMT); *see* ¶23.3.

Tax rate schedules. Used by taxpayers with taxable incomes of $100,000 or more; *see* ¶22.2.

Tax-sheltered annuity. A type of retirement annuity offered to employees of charitable organizations and educational systems, generally funded by employee salary-reduction contributions; *see* ¶7.20.

Tax table. Used by taxpayers with taxable incomes of less than $100,000 to look up their tax; *see* Tax Organizer in Part VIII.

Tax year. A period of 12 months for reporting income and expenses.

Ten-year averaging. A favorable method of computing tax on a lump-sum retirement distribution available only to those who reached age 50 by January 1, 1986; *see* ¶7.3 and ¶7.4.

Tenancy by the entireties. A joint tenancy in real property in the name of both husband and wife. On death of one tenant, survivor receives entire interest.

Tenants in common. Two or more persons who have undivided ownership rights in property. Upon death of a tenant, his or her share passes to his or her estate, rather than to the surviving tenants.

Testamentary trust. A trust established under a will; *see* ¶33.6.

Three-year recovery. A method of recovering cost in an employee annuity that is allowed only if payouts began before July 2, 1986; *see* ¶7.25.

Trust. An arrangement under which one person transfers legal ownership of assets to another person or corporation (the trustee) for the benefit of one or more third persons (beneficiaries); *see* ¶11.2 and ¶33.6.

Useful life. For property not depreciated under ACRS or MACRS, the estimate of time in which a depreciable asset will be used.

Vacation homes. The tax law limits deductions for vacation homes, broadly defined as any dwelling unit used by the owner or the owner's relatives for more than a specified period; *see* ¶29.20.

Wash sales. Sales on which losses are disallowed because you recover your market position within a 61-day period; *see* ¶5.21.

Withholding. An amount taken from income as a pre-payment of an individual's tax liability for the year. In the case of wages, the employer withholds part of every wage payment. Backup withholding from dividend or interest income is required if you do not provide the payer with a correct taxpayer identification number. Withholding on pensions and IRAs is automatic unless you elect to waive withholding; *see* Chapter 26.

INDEX

INDEX

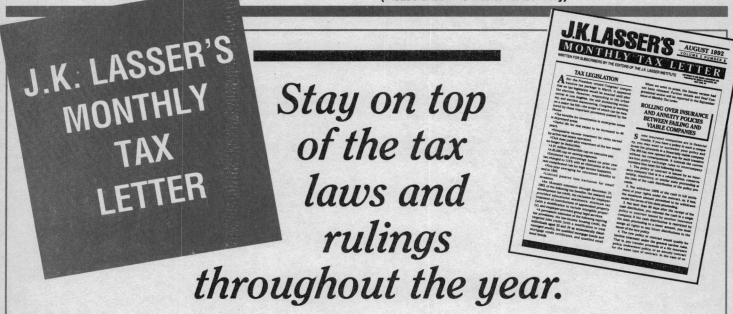

Let J.K. Lasser™ Prepare Your Return This Year!